Text Copyright © 2022 by Ste
All Rights R

Steve's Football Bible offers the best and most informative Trends and Angles information for the sophisticated football handicapper in the nation. We don't offer opinions on who is going to win games. We provide the historical facts, and you can use that to form your opinion and handicap games accordingly. We offer Pro and College football handicappers the best and most in-depth books on team trends and angles, pointspread analysis, plus each team's schedule for the upcoming season. You have everything at your fingertips with the **Pro Football Bible** or the **College Football Bible**. The **Pro Football Bible** includes the complete history of the NFL playoffs, Monday Night Football, Sunday Night Football, Thursday games and Saturday games. The **College Football Bible** includes each team's all-time records in the Polls when they were ranked and versus ranked teams. You won't find this type of information anywhere.

We also have numerous published books on College Football History and well as books on Baseball History. All of these are available on our website at: www.stevesfootballbible.com.

2022 College Football Handicapping Bible

Copyright © *(Registered) 2022 by Steve's Football Bible, LLC (All Rights Reserved)*

The 2022 College Football Trends and Angles Bible is published by Steve's Football Bible, LLC and may not be reproduced by any means without permission of the Publisher

All information in this publication is for news matter only and is not intended to be used to violate any Local, State or Federal Laws.

These books available at numerous online retailers

Steve's Football Bible also offers the Pro Football Bible, the Pro football handicapper's best friend for the 2022 football season.

Steve's Football Bible also offers the 2022 FCS College Football Bible for the FCS College Football fans.

To order Go to: www.stevesfootballbible.com

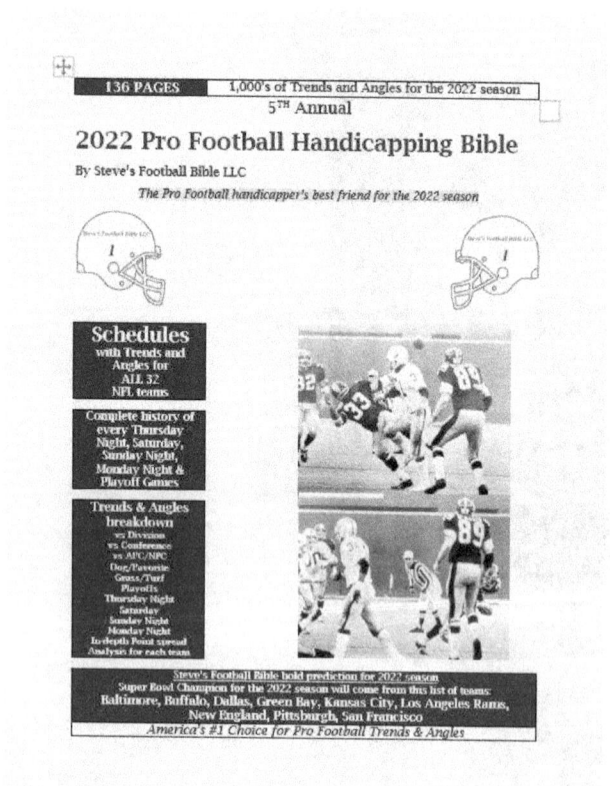

2022 Pro Football Bible $24.95   2022 FCS College Football Bible $19.95

www.stevesfootballbible.com

Books available from Steve's Football Bible LLC

Print Version $29.95 — COLLEGE FOOTBALL HISTORY "GLORIOUS GAMES OF THE PAST" — A historical look at some of college football's greatest and most memorable games — A celebration of 150 years of college football — By Steve Fulton

Print Version $34.95 — College Football History "Trophy Games" — The most complete historical look at college football's trophy games FBS, FCS, DIVISION II AND DIVISION III — A CELEBRATION OF 150 YEARS OF COLLEGE FOOTBALL — BY STEVE FULTON

Print Version $34.95 — COLLEGE FOOTBALL HISTORY "RIVALRY GAMES" — AN IN DEPTH LOOK AT SOME OF COLLEGE FOOTBALL'S BIGGEST AND MOST HISTORIC RIVALRY GAMES — FBS, FCS, DIVISION II AND DIVISION III — A CELEBRATION OF 150 YEARS OF COLLEGE FOOTBALL — BY STEVE FULTON

Print Version $24.95 — COLLEGE FOOTBALL HISTORY "MEMORABLE PLAYS" AND "MEMORABLE MOMENTS" — A LOOK AT SOME OF COLLEGE FOOTBALLS MOST MEMORABLE PLAYS AND MOMENTS — A CELEBRATION OF 150 YEARS OF COLLEGE FOOTBALL — BY STEVE FULTON

These books available at numerous online retailers

Copyright © 2022 by Steve's Football Bible, LLC

Books available from Steve's Football Bible LLC

Print Version $39.95   **Print Version $39.95**

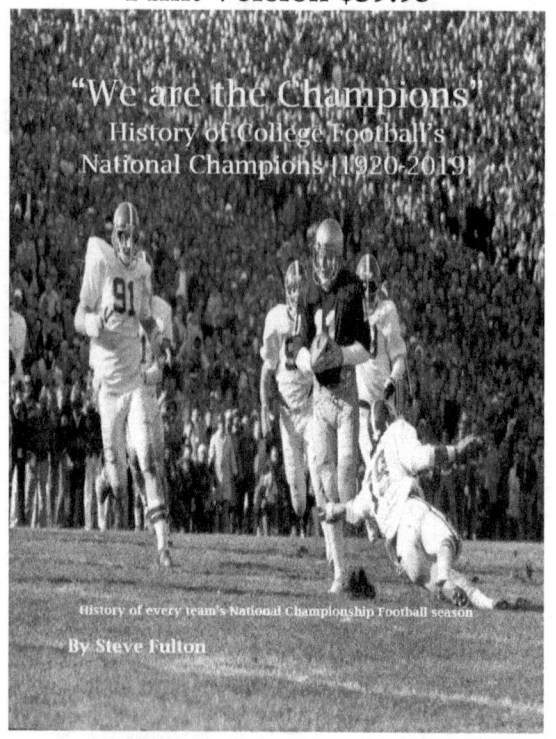

College Football Blueblood Series available at: www.stevesfootballbible.com (Blueblood)

ALABAMA    AUBURN    CLEMSON 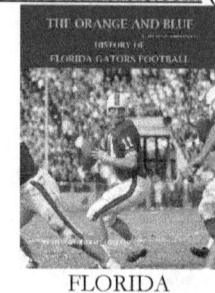   FLORIDA    FLORIDA STATE

College Football Blueblood Series available at: www.stevesfootballbible.com (Blueblood)

GEORGIA    LSU    MICHIGAN    NEBRASKA

These books are available from numerous online bookstores

Copyright © 2022 by Steve's Football Bible, LLC

TABLE OF CONTENTS

TEAM	Conference	Pages	TEAM	Conference	Pages	TEAM	Conference	Pages
Air Force	MWC	2-3	Iowa State	Big XII	92-93	Pittsburgh	ACC	182-183
Akron	MAC	4-5	James Madison	Sun Belt	94-95	Purdue	Big 10	184-185
Alabama	SEC	6-7	Kansas	Big XII	96-97	Rice	CUSA	186-187
Alabama-Birmingham	CUSA	8-9	Kansas State	Big XII	98-99	Rutgers	Big 10	188-189
Appalachian State	Sun Belt	10-11	Kentucky	SEC	100-101	San Diego State	MWC	190-191
Arizona	PAC-12	12-13	Kent State	MAC	102-103	San Jose State	MWC	192-193
Arizona State	PAC-12	14-15	Liberty	IND	104-105	South Alabama	Sun Belt	194-195
Arkansas	SEC	16-17	Louisiana-Lafayette	Sun Belt	106-107	South Carolina	SEC	196-197
Arkansas State	Sun Belt	18-19	Louisiana-Monroe	Sun Belt	108-109	Southern California	PAC-12	198-199
Army	IND	20-21	Louisiana Tech	CUSA	110-111	South Florida	AAC	200-201
Auburn	SEC	22-23	LSU	SEC	112-113	SMU	AAC	202-203
Ball State	MAC	24-25	Louisville	ACC	114-115	Southern Mississippi	Sun Belt	204-205
Baylor	Big XII	26-27	Marshall	Sun Belt	116-117	Stanford	PAC-12	206-207
Boise State	MWC	28-29	Maryland	Big 10	118-119	Syracuse	ACC	208-209
Boston College	ACC	30-31	Massachusetts	IND	120-121	TCU	Big XII	210-211
Bowling Green	MAC	32-33	Memphis	AAC	122-123	Temple	AAC	212-213
Brigham Young	IND	34-35	Miami-Fla	ACC	124-125	Tennessee	SEC	214-215
Buffalo	MAC	36-37	Miami-Ohio	MAC	126-127	Texas	Big XII	216-217
California	PAC-12	38-39	Michigan	Big 10	128-129	Texas A&M	SEC	218-219
Central Florida	AAC	40-41	Michigan State	Big 10	130-131	Texas-El Paso	CUSA	220-221
Central Michigan	MAC	42-43	Middle Tennessee	CUSA	132-133	Texas-San Antonio	CUSA	222-223
Charlotte	CUSA	44-45	Minnesota	Big 10	134-135	Texas State	Sun Belt	224-225
Cincinnati	AAC	46-47	Mississippi	SEC	136-137	Texas Tech	Big XII	226-227
Clemson	ACC	48-49	Mississippi State	SEC	138-139	Toledo	MAC	228-229
Coastal Carolina	Sun Belt	50-51	Missouri	SEC	140-141	Troy	Sun Belt	230-231
Colorado	PAC-12	52-53	Navy	AAC	142-143	Tulane	AAC	232-233
Colorado State	MWC	54-55	Nebraska	Big 10	144-145	Tulsa	AAC	234-235
Connecticut	AAC	56-57	Nevada	MWC	146-147	UCLA	PAC-12	236-237
Duke	ACC	58-59	Nevada-Las Vegas	MWC	148-149	Utah	PAC-12	238-239
East Carolina	AAC	60-61	New Mexico	MWC	150-151	Utah State	MWC	240-241
Eastern Michigan	MAC	62-63	New Mexico State	IND	152-153	Vanderbilt	SEC	242-243
Florida	SEC	64-65	North Carolina	ACC	154-155	Virginia	ACC	244-245
Florida Atlantic	CUSA	66-67	NC State	ACC	156-157	Virginia Tech	ACC	246-247
Florida International	CUSA	68-69	Northern Illinois	MAC	158-159	Wake Forest	ACC	248-249
Florida State	ACC	70-71	North Texas	CUSA	160-161	Washington	PAC-12	250-251
Fresno State	MWC	72-73	Northwestern	Big 10	162-163	Washington State	PAC-12	252-253
Georgia	SEC	74-75	Notre Dame	IND	164-165	Western Kentucky	CUSA	254-255
Georgia Southern	Sun Belt	76-77	Ohio	MAC	166-167	Western Michigan	MAC	256-257
Georgia State	Sun Belt	78-79	Ohio State	Big 10	168-169	West Virginia	Big XII	258-259
Georgia Tech	ACC	80-81	Oklahoma	Big XII	170-171	Wisconsin	Big 10	260-261
Hawaii	MWC	82-83	Oklahoma State	Big XII	172-173	Wyoming	MWC	262-263
Houston	AAC	84-85	Old Dominion	Sun Belt	174-175	Team records when ranked	.....	266-292
Illinois	Big 10	86-87	Oregon	PAC-12	176-177	Team records vs Ranked	.....	293-320
Indiana	Big 10	88-89	Oregon State	PAC-12	178-179			
Iowa	Big 10	90-91	Penn State	Big 10	180-181			

Key Word definitions

S/U - Straight Up
O/U – Over/Under

ATS – Against The Spread
s/1983 – Since 1983 {or year listed}

Copyright © 2022 by Steve's Football Bible, LLC

AIR FORCE FALCONS   MOUNTAIN WEST Mountain

2021-Air Force		Opponent	AFA	Opp	S/U	Line	ATS	Total	O/U	
9/4/2021	vs	*LAFAYETTE*	35	14	W	-40.5	L	50.5	U	
9/11/2021	@	*Navy*	23	3	W	-6.0	W	39.5	U	
9/18/2021	vs	UTAH STATE	45	49	L	-9.0	L	53.5	O	
9/25/2021	vs	*FLORIDA ATLANTIC*	31	7	W	-3.5	W	54.0	U	
10/2/2021	@	New Mexico	38	10	W	-11.5	W	45.5	O	
10/9/2021	vs	WYOMING	24	14	W	-5.5	W	46.5	U	
10/16/2021	@	Boise State	24	17	W	3.0	W	52.0	U	
10/23/2021	vs	SAN DIEGO STATE	14	20	L	-3.0	L	39.0	U	
11/6/2021	vs	*Army {@ Arlington, TX}*	14	21	L	-2.5	L	37.5	U	{OT}
11/13/2021	@	Colorado State	35	21	W	-3.5	W	45.0	O	"Ram-Falcon Trophy"
11/20/2021	@	Nevada	41	39	W	-2.0	T	54.0	O	{OT}
11/26/2021	vs	UNLV	48	14	W	-18.5	W	49.5	O	
12/28/2021	vs	**Louisville**	31	28	W	-2.0	W	55.0	O	First Responder Bowl
Coach: Troy Calhoun		Season Record >>	403	257	10-3	ATS>>	8-4-1	O/U>>	6-7	
2020-Air Force		Opponent	AFA	Opp	S/U	Line	ATS	Total	O/U	
10/3/2020	vs	*NAVY*	40	7	W	6.0	W	47.5	U	
10/24/2020	@	San Jose State	6	17	L	-7.5	L	64.5	U	
10/31/2020	vs	BOISE STATE	30	49	L	12.5	L	48.5	O	
11/21/2020	vs	NEW MEXICO	28	0	W	-8.0	W	55.5	U	
12/3/2020	@	Utah State	35	7	W	-13.5	W	52.5	U	
12/19/2020	@	*Army*	7	10	L	-2.0	L	37.5	U	
Coach: Troy Calhoun		Season Record >>	146	90	3-3	ATS>>	3-3	O/U>>	1-5	
2019-Air Force		Opponent	AFA	Opp	S/U	Line	ATS	Total	O/U	
8/31/2019	vs	*COLGATE*	48	7	W	-24.0	W	NT	---	
9/14/2019	@	*Colorado*	30	23	W	3.0	W	58.0	U	{OT}
9/21/2019	@	Boise State	19	30	L	7.0	L	55.5	U	
9/28/2019	vs	SAN JOSE STATE	41	24	W	-19.0	L	58.0	O	
10/5/2019	@	*Navy*	25	34	L	-3.0	L	46.5	O	
10/12/2019	vs	FRESNO STATE	43	24	W	-2.5	W	49.5	O	
10/19/2019	@	Hawaii	56	26	W	-3.5	W	65.5	O	"Kuter Trophy"
10/26/2019	vs	UTAH STATE	31	7	W	-3.5	W	60.0	U	
11/2/2019	vs	*ARMY*	17	13	W	-16.5	L	44.5	U	
11/9/2019	@	New Mexico	38	21	W	-10.5	W	62.0	U	
11/23/2019	@	Colorado State	44	22	W	-24.0	L	56.5	O	"Ram-Falcon Trophy"
11/30/2019	vs	WYOMING	20	6	W	-13.0	W	41.5	U	
12/27/2019	vs	**Washington State**	31	21	W	-2.5	W	71.5	U	Cheez-it Bowl
Coach: Troy Calhoun		Season Record >>	443	258	11-2	ATS>>	8-5	O/U>>	5-7	
2018-Air Force		Opponent	AFA	Opp	S/U	Line	ATS	Total	O/U	
9/1/2018	vs	*SUNY-STONY BROOK*	38	0	W	-14.5	W	NT	---	
9/8/2018	@	*Florida Atlantic*	27	33	L	7.5	W	61.5	U	
9/22/2018	@	Utah State	32	42	L	9.5	L	59.5	O	
9/29/2018	vs	NEVADA	25	28	L	-3.5	L	63.0	U	
10/6/2018	vs	*NAVY*	35	7	W	3.0	W	47.0	U	
10/13/2018	@	San Diego State	17	21	L	11.0	W	42.5	U	
10/19/2018	@	Unlv	41	35	W	-9.5	L	54.0	O	
10/27/2018	vs	BOISE STATE	38	48	L	9.5	L	57.5	O	
11/3/2018	@	*Army*	14	17	L	4.5	W	41.5	U	
11/10/2018	vs	NEW MEXICO	42	24	W	-13.0	W	55.5	O	
11/17/2018	@	Wyoming	27	35	L	2.5	L	43.0	O	
11/24/2018	vs	COLORADO STATE	27	19	W	-14.5	L	64.0	U	"Ram-Falcon Trophy"
Coach: Troy Calhoun		Season Record >>	363	309	5-7	ATS>>	6-6	O/U>>	5-6	

Wild Blue Yonder! History of Air Force Falcons Football

Available at: www.stevesfootballbible.com (Patriot Series)

Copyright © 2022 by Steve's Football Bible, LLC

AIR FORCE FALCONS — MOUNTAIN WEST Mountain

STADIUM: Falcon Stadium {46,692}   **Location:** Colorado Springs, CO   **COACH:** Troy Calhoun

DATE		Opponent	AFA	Opp	S/U	Line	ATS	Total	O/U	Trends & Angles
9/3/2022	vs	NORTHERN IOWA								17-0 S/U in 1st home game of season since 2005
9/10/2022	vs	COLORADO								0-5 S/U @ home vs Colorado since 1965
9/17/2022	@	Wyoming								0-5 ATS @ Wyoming since 2014
9/24/2022	vs	NEVADA								vs Nevada - Air Force leads series 4-2
10/1/2022	vs	NAVY								4-0 S/U & ATS @ home vs Navy since 2014
10/8/2022	@	Utah State								vs Utah State - Air Force leads series 6-4
10/15/2022	@	Unlv								Game 10-1-1 O/U vs UNLV since 2006
10/22/2022	vs	BOISE STATE								1-4 S/U @ ATS vs Boise State since 2017
11/5/2022	vs	Army {@Arlington, TX}								vs Army - Game 0-8 O/U since 2014
11/12/2022	vs	NEW MEXICO								9-0 S/U @ home vs New Mexico since 2002
11/19/2022	vs	COLORADO STATE								8-0 S/U @ home vs Colorado State since 2004
11/26/2022	@	San Diego State								0-5 S/U @ San Diego State since 2010
12/2/2022	vs									MWC Championship
	vs									BOWL GAME

Pointspread Analysis

Non-Conference
- 0-12 S/U vs Non-Conf. as 15.5-20 point Dog since 1988
- 0-10 S/U vs Non-Conf. as 10.5-15 point Dog since 1991
- 2-9 O/U vs Non-Conf. as 7.5-10 point Dog since 1984
- 3-11 O/U vs Non-Conf. as 3 point or less favorite since 1995
- 13-1 S/U vs Non-Conf. as 7.5-10 point favorite since 1989
- 2-6 ATS vs Non-Conf. as 10.5-15 point favorite since 2000
- 31-0 S/U vs Non-Conf. as 15.5 point or more favorite since 1988
- 2-9 S/U vs Colorado since 1964
- vs Colorado - Colorado leads series 12-5
- Game 1-9 O/U @ home vs Navy since 2002
- vs Navy - Game 4-19 O/U since 1999
- vs Navy - Air Force leads series 32-22
- 0-4 S/U & ATS vs Navy as 3 point or less favorite since 1993
- 5-1 S/U vs Navy as 7.5-10 point favorite since 1985
- 4-0 S/U vs Navy as 20.5-25 point favorite since 1994
- vs Army - Air Force leads series 37-19-1
- 3-0 S/U & ATS vs Army as 3 point or less Dog since 1990
- 4-1 S/U @ Army as 3.5-7 point favorite since 1992
- 5-0 S/U & ATS vs Army as 7.5-10 point favorite since 1989
- 8-1 S/U vs Army as 10.5-15 point favorite since 1985
- 6-0 S/U vs Army as 15.5-20 point favorite since 2002

Dog
- 7-2 ATS as home Dog since 2014
- 1-7 S/U on road as 20.5 point or more Dog since 1990
- 7-1 ATS on road as 20.5 or more Dog since 1990
- 0-11 S/U on road as 15.5-20 point Dog since 1988
- 2-8 S/U on road as 10.5-15 point Dog since 2000
- 5-1 ATS @ home as 7.5-10 point Dog since 2007
- 9-3 ATS on road as 7.5-10 point Dog since 1994
- 2-12 S/U on road as 3.5-7 point Dog since 2003

Favorite
- 4-10 S/U on road as 3 point or less favorite since 1988
- 3-7 O/U on road as 3 point or less favorite since 1995
- 27-5 S/U on road as 3.5-7 point favorite since 1985
- 1-5 ATS @ home as 7.5-10 point favorite since 2010
- 15-4 S/U @ home as 7.5-10 point favorite since 1989
- 10-3 O/U as 10.5-15 point favorite since 2012
- 10-0 S/U @ home as 10.5-15 point favorite since 2005
- 19-3 S/U @ home as 15.5-20 point favorite since 1984
- 7-1 S/U on road as 15.5-20 point favorite since 1985
- 34-0 S/U @ home as 20.5 point or more favorite since 1983
- 6-0 S/U as 25.5-30 point favorite since 1985
- 0-3 O/U as 25.5-30 point favorite since 2003

Conference
- vs Boise State - Boise State leads series 7-3
- vs Colorado State - Air Force leads series 38-21-1
- Game 12-2 O/U vs Colorado State since 2007
- Game 5-1 O/U vs Nevada since 2012
- vs UNLV - Air Force leads series 17-6
- vs New Mexico - Air Force leads series 24-13
- Game 7-2 O/U vs New Mexico since 2013
- vs San Diego State - Air Force leads series 20-18
- 0-9 S/U vs San Diego State since 2010
- 2-8 ATS vs San Diego State since 2009
- Game 1-7 O/U @ San Diego State since 2003
- 0-3 S/U @ Wyoming since 2014
- vs Wyoming - Air Force leads series 29-26-3
- 2-10 ATS vs Wyoming since 2009
- 3-0 ATS vs Colorado State as 7.5-10 point Dog since 2001
- 3-0 S/U vs CSU as 7.5-10 point favorite since 1988
- 0-4 ATS @ home vs Colo. State as 3.5-7 point favorite since 1992
- 5-0 S/U vs UNLV as 3.5-7 point favorite since 2002
- 5-1 O/U vs UNLV as 3.5-7 point favorite since 2000
- 4-0 S/U vs UNLV as 15.5-20 point favorite since 1998
- 3-0 S/U vs UNLV as 20.5-25 point favorite since 1997
- 4-0 S/U vs New Mexico as 15.5-20 point favorite since 1985
- 1-6 S/U vs SDSU as 3.5-7 point Dog since 1990
- 0-5 ATS vs San Diego State as 3 point or less favorite since 1991
- 0-3 S/U vs SDSU as 3.5-7 point favorite since 2003
- 0-4 ATS vs SDSU as 3.5-7 point favorite since 1997
- 0-3 S/U & ATS vs Utah State as 7.5-10 point Dog since 2013
- 3-0 O/U & ATS vs Utah State as 7.5-10 point Dog since 2013
- 1-5 ATS vs Wyoming as 10.5-15 point favorite since 1986
- 5-0 S/U vs Wyoming as 3.5-7 point favorite since 1985

Bowl Games
- 3-0 S/U & ATS in Independence Bowl

Favorite
- 11-0 S/U as 32 point or more favorite since 1988
- 3-8 ATS as 32 point or more favorite since 1988
- 4-1 O/U as 32 point or more favorite since 2010

Wyoming	15-3 ATS in 1st road game of season since 2004
NEVADA	1-5 ATS after playing Wyoming since 2014
BOISE STATE	7-0 O/U after playing UNLV since 2009
NEW MEXICO	6-1 S/U after playing Army since 2014
NEW MEXICO	1-8 ATS prior to playing Colorado State since 2012
COLO STATE	12-1 S/U in final home game of season since 2009
San Diego State	2-11-1 ATS in final road game of season since 2008

AKRON ZIPS — MAC East

2021-Akron		Opponent	Akr	Opp	S/U	Line	ATS	Total	O/U	
9/4/2021	@	Auburn	10	60	L	37.5	L	56.0	O	
9/11/2021	vs	TEMPLE	24	45	L	6.5	L	51.0	O	
9/18/2021	vs	BRYANT	35	14	W	-12.5	W	49.5	U	
9/25/2021	@	Ohio State	7	59	L	48.0	L	66.5	U	
10/2/2021	vs	OHIO	17	34	L	9.5	L	55.0	U	
10/9/2021	@	Bowling Green	35	20	W	14.0	W	46.0	O	
10/16/2021	@	Miami-Ohio	21	34	L	20.0	W	51.0	O	
10/23/2021	vs	BUFFALO	10	45	L	13.5	L	58.0	U	
11/2/2021	vs	BALL STATE	25	31	L	20.0	W	58.0	U	
11/9/2021	@	Western Michigan	40	45	L	26.0	W	62.0	O	
11/20/2021	vs	KENT STATE	0	38	L	13.5	L	72.0	U	"Wagon Wheel"
11/27/2021	@	Toledo	14	49	L	28.5	L	57.5	O	
Coach: Tom Arth		Season Record >>	238	474	2-10	ATS>>	5-7	O/U>>	6-6	

2020-Akron		Opponent	Akr	Opp	S/U	Line	ATS	Total	O/U	
11/4/2020	vs	WESTERN MICHIGAN	13	58	L	20.0	L	52.0	O	
11/10/2020	@	Ohio	10	24	L	27.0	W	58.0	U	
11/17/2020	@	Kent State	35	69	L	26.0	L	60.5	O	"Wagon Wheel"
11/28/2020	vs	MIAMI-OHIO	7	38	L	14.0	L	55.0	U	
12/5/2020	vs	BOWLING GREEN	31	3	W	-2.5	W	54.5	U	
12/12/2020	@	Buffalo	7	56	L	33.5	L	58.5	O	
Coach: Tom Arth		Season Record >>	103	248	1-5	ATS>>	2-4	O/U>>	3-3	

2019-Akron		Opponent	Akr	Opp	S/U	Line	ATS	Total	O/U	
8/31/2019	@	Illinois	3	42	L	18.0	L	60.0	U	
9/7/2019	vs	ALABAMA-BIRMINGHAM	20	31	L	8.0	L	46.5	O	
9/14/2019	@	Central Michigan	24	45	L	2.5	L	45.0	O	
9/21/2019	vs	TROY	7	35	L	18.5	L	57.0	U	
9/28/2019	@	Massachusetts	29	37	L	-9.5	L	60.5	O	
10/12/2019	vs	KENT STATE	3	26	L	14.5	L	57.5	U	"Wagon Wheel"
10/19/2019	vs	BUFFALO	0	21	L	17.5	L	48.0	U	
10/26/2019	@	Northern Illinois	0	49	L	22.5	L	41.5	O	
11/2/2019	@	Bowling Green	6	35	L	3.5	L	48.0	U	
11/12/2019	vs	EASTERN MICHIGAN	14	42	L	17.0	L	44.5	O	
11/20/2019	@	Miami-Ohio	17	20	L	28.5	W	45.0	U	
11/26/2019	vs	OHIO	3	52	L	27.5	L	52.5	O	
Coach: Tom Arth		Season Record >>	126	435	0-12	ATS>>	1-11	O/U>>	6-6	

2018-Akron		Opponent	Akr	Opp	S/U	Line	ATS	Total	O/U	
9/8/2018	vs	MORGAN STATE	41	7	W	-42.5	L	NT	---	
9/15/2018	@	Northwestern	39	34	W	21.0	W	46.5	O	
9/22/2018	@	Iowa State	13	26	L	18.5	W	47.0	U	
10/6/2018	vs	MIAMI-OHIO	17	41	L	-5.0	L	47.5	O	
10/13/2018	@	Buffalo	6	24	L	11.0	L	54.5	U	
10/20/2018	@	Kent State	24	23	W	-4.5	L	49.5	U	"Wagon Wheel"
10/27/2018	vs	CENTRAL MICHIGAN	17	10	W	-4.0	W	43.5	O	
11/1/2018	vs	NORTHERN ILLINOIS	26	36	L	6.0	L	37.0	O	
11/10/2018	@	Eastern Michigan	7	27	L	11.0	L	41.5	U	
11/17/2018	vs	BOWLING GREEN	6	21	L	-6.0	L	47.5	U	
11/23/2018	@	Ohio	28	49	L	23.5	W	56.5	O	
12/1/2018	@	South Carolina	3	28	L	28.5	W	56.5	U	
Coach: Terry Bowden		Season Record >>	227	326	4-8	ATS>>	5-7	O/U>>	4-7	

AKRON ZIPS — MAC East

STADIUM: InfoCision Stadium {30,000} **Location:** Akron, OH **COACH:** Joe Moorhead

DATE		Opponent	Akr	Opp	S/U	Line	ATS	Total	O/U	Trends & Angles
9/1/2022	vs	ST. FRANCIS-PA								1st Meeting
9/10/2022	@	Michigan State								vs Michigan State - MSU leads series 2-0
9/17/2022	@	Tennessee								vs Tennessee - Tennessee leads series 2-0
9/24/2022	@	Liberty								vs Liberty - Akron leads series 1-0
10/1/2022	vs	BOWLING GREEN								1-7 ATS @ home vs Bowling Green since 2001
10/8/2022	@	Ohio								0-8 S/U @ Ohio since 2006
10/15/2022	vs	CENTRAL MICHIGAN								1-5 S/U @ home vs Central Michigan since 2002
10/22/2022	@	Kent State								0-6 ATS vs Kent State since 2016
10/29/2022	vs	MIAMI-OHIO								1-5 S/U @ home vs Miami-Ohio since 2010
11/8/2022	vs	EASTERN MICHIGAN								5-1 S/U @ home vs Eastern Michigan since 1998
11/19/2022	@	Buffalo								1-7 ATS @ Buffalo since 2005
11/26/2022	@	Northern Illinois								0-4 S/U @ Northern Illinois since 2004
12/2/2022	vs									MAC Championship
	vs									BOWL GAME

Pointspread Analysis — Non-Conference

- 2-11 S/U vs Non-Conf. as 20.5-25 point Dog since 1989
- 1-13 S/U vs Non-Conf. as 15.5-20 point Dog since 1989
- 0-8 S/U vs Non-Conf. as 10.5-15 point Dog since 1987
- 8-3 ATS vs Non-Conf. as 7.5-10 point Dog since 1990
- 5-0 O/U vs Non-Conf. as 3.5-7 point Dog since 2008
- 1-5 ATS vs Non-Conf. as 3.5-7 point favorite since 1994

Dog
- 0-38 S/U as 25.5 point or more Dog since 1990
- 2-16 S/U on road as 20.5-25 point Dog since 1989
- 2-36 S/U as 15.5-20 point Dog since 1990
- 6-2 ATS on road as 15.5-20 point Dog since 2012
- 4-13-1 O/U as 15.5-20 point Dog since 2010
- 3-23 S/U on road as 10.5-15 point Dog since 1990
- 1-12 S/U @ home as 7.5-10 point Dog since 1997
- 8-1 ATS on road as 7.5-10 point Dog since 2001
- 1-10 S/U @ home as 3.5-7 point Dog since 2008

Favorite
- 6-0 S/U as 25.5 point or more favorite since 2000
- 9-2 S/U as 15.5-20 point favorite since 1999
- 2-9 ATS as 15.5-20 point favorite since 1999
- 0-8 O/U as 10.5-15 point favorite since 2012
- 21-4 S/U as 7.5-10 point favorite since 1989
- 2-8 S/U & ATS on road as 3 point or less favorite since 1990

- 1-20 S/U in 1st road game of season since 2000
- 0-6 S/U prior to playing Bowling Green since 2016 {1-5 ATS}
- 1-5 O/U prior to playing Bowling Green since 2016
- 1-13 S/U prior to playing Ohio since 2007
- 0-11 O/U prior to playing Ohio since 2010
- 1-9 S/U after playing Bowling Green since 2012
- 1-6 S/U prior to playing Central Michigan since 2007
- 0-6 ATS prior to playing Central Michigan since 2009
- 1-5 S/U after playing Central Michigan since 2009
- 9-3-2 ATS prior to playing Miami-Ohio since 2006
- 2-11-1 ATS after playing Kent State since 2004
- 1-6 O/U after playing Kent State since 2012
- 2-7 S/U prior to playing Eastern Michigan since 2002
- 0-5 S/U after playing Eastern Michigan since 2011
- 0-8 O/U prior to playing Northern Illinois since 2004
- 1-8 O/U after playing Buffalo since 2009
- 2-14 S/U in final road game of season since 2005

Michigan State	
Liberty	
Liberty	
B GREEN	
B GREEN	
Ohio	
Ohio	
Ohio	
Kent State	
Kent State	
MIAMI-OHIO	
MIAMI-OHIO	
MIAMI-OHIO	
Buffalo	
Buffalo	
Northern Illinois	
Northern Illinois	

Pointspread Analysis — Conference

- vs Bowling Green - BGU leads series 18-10
- 3-14 S/U vs Bowling Green as Dog since 1992
- 3-9 S/U vs Bowling Green since 2007
- 1-5 S/U @ home vs Bowling Green since 2008
- 3-10 ATS vs Bowling Green since 2006
- vs Buffalo - Akron leads series 11-10
- 0-7 S/U @ Buffalo since 2007
- 1-8 S/U vs Central Michigan since 2005
- vs Central Michigan - CMU leads series 17-10-1
- 8-1 S/U Eastern Michigan as favorite since 1993
- 0-6-1 ATS @ home vs Eastern Michigan since 1995
- Game 1-3 O/U @ home vs Eastern Michigan since 2003
- vs Eastern Michigan - Akron leads series 18-14
- vs Kent State - Akron leads series 35-27-1
- 2-18 S/U vs Miami-Ohio as Dog since 1994
- Game 4-10 O/U vs Miami-Ohio since 2006
- vs Miami-Ohio - Miami-Ohio leads series 22-8-1
- vs Northern Illinois - NIU leads series 11-4
- 0-6 S/U vs Northern Illinois since 2009
- vs Ohio - Ohio leads series 24-12-1
- 1-13 S/U vs Ohio since 2008
- 0-4 S/U & ATS vs B. Green as 3.5-7 point Dog since 2001
- 3-0 S/U vs B. Green as 7.5-10 point favorite since 1989
- 0-3 S/U vs Central Michigan as 15.5-20 point Dog since 1991
- 4-0 S/U & ATS vs C. Michigan as 3.5-7 point Dog since 1989
- 0-5 S/U vs C. Michigan as 3 point or less Dog since 1998
- 0-3 S/U vs E. Michigan as 7.5-10 point Dog since 1996
- 3-0 S/U vs E. Michigan as 7.5-10 point favorite since 1993
- 4-0 S/U vs E. Michigan as 15.5 point or more favorite since 2001
- 0-3 ATS vs E. Michigan as 15.5-20 point favorite since 2001
- 0-3 ATS @ Kent State as 3.5-7 point favorite since 2008
- 3-0 S/U vs Kent State as 7.5-10 point favorite since 1998
- 0-3 S/U vs Miami-Ohio as 15.5-20 point Dog since 1997
- 0-5 S/U vs Miami-Ohio as 10.5-15 point Dog since 1994
- 0-6 S/U vs Miami-Ohio as 7.5-10 point Dog since 1999
- 0-4 S/U & ATS vs Ohio as 3.5-7 point Dog since 2002
- 0-4 O/U vs Ohio as 3.5-7 point Dog since 2002

- 1-20 S/U vs ranked teams since 1999 {0-18 on road}

ALABAMA CRIMSON TIDE — SEC West

2021-Alabama		Opponent	Bama	Opp	S/U	Line	ATS	Total	O/U	
9/4/2021	vs	Miami	44	13	W	-19.5	W	61.5	U	
9/11/2021	vs	MERCER	48	14	W	-55.5	L	62.5	U	
9/18/2021	@	Florida	31	29	W	-14.0	L	60.0	T	
9/25/2021	vs	SOUTHERN MISS	63	14	W	-45.5	W	57.5	O	
10/2/2021	vs	MISSISSIPPI	42	21	W	-14.5	W	79.5	U	
10/9/2021	@	Texas A&M	38	41	L	-19.0	L	50.5	O	
10/16/2021	@	Mississippi State	49	9	W	-17.5	W	59.5	U	
10/23/2021	vs	TENNESSEE	52	24	W	-24.5	W	68.0	O	Third Saturday in October Rivalry
11/6/2021	vs	LSU	20	14	W	-29.0	L	66.5	U	
11/13/2021	vs	NEW MEXICO STATE	59	3	W	-50.5	W	67.5	U	
11/20/2021	vs	ARKANSAS	42	35	W	-20.5	L	58.0	O	
11/27/2021	@	Auburn	24	22	W	-20.5	L	57.0	U	"Iron Bowl"
12/4/2021	vs	Georgia	41	24	W	6.0	W	48.5	O	SEC Championship Game
12/31/2021	vs	Cincinnati	27	6	W	-12.0	W	56.5	U	Cotton Bowl (National Semifinal)
1/10/2022	vs	Georgia	18	33	L	3.0	L	53.0	U	CFB Championship Game
Coach: Nick Saban		Season Record >>	598	302	13-2	ATS>>	8-7	O/U>>	5-9-1	SEC Champions

2020-Alabama		Opponent	Bama	Opp	S/U	Line	ATS	Total	O/U	
9/26/2020	vs	MISSOURI	38	19	W	-29.0	L	55.5	O	
10/3/2020	vs	TEXAS A&M	52	24	W	-18.0	W	54.0	O	
10/10/2020	@	Mississippi	63	48	W	-24.0	L	74.0	O	
10/17/2020	vs	GEORGIA	41	24	W	-5.5	W	56.5	O	
10/24/2020	@	Tennessee	48	17	W	-22.0	W	66.5	U	Third Saturday in October Rivalry
10/31/2020	vs	MISSISSIPPI STATE	41	0	W	-29.0	W	63.5	U	
11/21/2020	vs	KENTUCKY	63	3	W	-31.0	W	57.5	O	
11/28/2020	vs	AUBURN	42	13	W	-24.5	W	65.0	U	"Iron Bowl"
12/5/2020	@	Lsu	55	17	W	-28.5	W	63.5	O	
12/12/2020	@	Arkansas	52	3	W	-29.0	W	69.0	U	
12/19/2020	vs	Florida	52	46	W	-16.5	L	74.0	O	SEC Championship
1/1/2021	vs	Notre Dame	31	14	W	-18.0	L	65.5	U	Rose Bowl {CFP Semifinal}
1/11/2021	vs	Ohio State	52	24	W	-9.5	W	75.5	O	CFB Championship Game
Coach: Nick Saban		Season Record >>	630	252	13-0	ATS>>	9-4	O/U>>	8-5	SEC Champions

2019-Alabama		Opponent	Bama	Opp	S/U	Line	ATS	Total	O/U	
8/31/2019	vs	Duke	42	3	W	-33.5	W	56.5	U	Mercedes Benz Stadium
9/7/2019	vs	NEW MEXICO STATE	62	10	W	-55.0	L	64.0	O	
9/14/2019	@	South Carolina	47	23	W	-26.0	L	59.5	O	
9/21/2019	vs	SOUTHERN MISSISSIPPI	49	7	W	-38.0	L	63.0	U	
9/28/2019	vs	MISSISSIPPI	59	31	W	-37.5	L	62.5	O	
10/12/2019	@	Texas A&M	47	28	W	-17.0	W	61.0	O	
10/19/2019	vs	TENNESSEE	35	13	W	-34.5	L	62.5	U	Third Saturday in October Rivalry
10/26/2019	vs	ARKANSAS	48	7	W	-31.5	W	56.0	U	
11/9/2019	vs	LSU	41	46	L	-4.5	L	65.0	O	
11/16/2019	@	Mississippi State	38	7	W	-19.0	W	61.5	U	
11/23/2019	vs	WESTERN CAROLINA	66	3	W	-57.5	W	NT	---	
11/30/2019	@	Auburn	45	48	L	-3.5	L	51.0	O	"Iron Bowl"
1/2/2020	vs	Michigan	35	16	W	-8.0	W	60.0	U	Citrus Bowl
Coach: Nick Saban		Season Record >>	614	242	11-2	ATS>>	7-6	O/U>>	6-6	

2018-Alabama		Opponent	Bama	Opp	S/U	Line	ATS	Total	O/U	
9/1/2018	vs	Louisville	51	14	W	-23.5	W	60.0	O	Camping World Stadium
9/8/2018	vs	ARKANSAS STATE	57	7	W	-36.5	W	63.0	O	
9/15/2018	@	Mississippi	62	7	W	-22.5	W	71.0	U	
9/22/2018	vs	TEXAS A&M	45	23	W	-23.5	L	58.5	O	
9/29/2018	vs	LOUISIANA-LAFAYETTE	56	14	W	-49.0	L	69.0	O	
10/6/2018	@	Arkansas	65	31	W	-35.0	L	58.0	O	
10/13/2018	vs	MISSOURI	39	10	W	-28.0	W	72.5	U	
10/20/2018	@	Tennessee	58	21	W	-28.5	W	57.5	O	Third Saturday in October Rivalry
11/3/2018	@	Lsu	29	0	W	-13.5	W	51.5	U	
11/10/2018	vs	MISSISSIPPI STATE	24	0	W	-21.5	W	51.0	U	
11/17/2018	vs	THE CITADEL	50	17	W	-51.0	L	NT	---	
11/24/2018	vs	AUBURN	52	21	W	-27.0	W	52.5	O	Iron Bowl
12/1/2018	vs	Georgia	35	28	W	-11.0	L	63.0	T	SEC Championship
12/29/2018	vs	Oklahoma	45	34	W	-15.0	L	80.5	U	Orange Bowl (National Semi-Final)
1/7/2019	vs	Clemson	16	44	L	-5.5	L	57.5	O	CFB Championship Game
Coach: Nick Saban		Season Record >>	684	271	14-1	ATS>>	8-7	O/U>>	8-5-1	SEC Champions

ALABAMA CRIMSON TIDE — SEC West

STADIUM: Bryant-Denny Stadium {101,821} **Location:** Tuscaloosa, AL **COACH:** Nick Saban

DATE		Opponent	Bama	Opp	S/U	Line	ATS	Total	O/U	Trends & Angles
9/3/2022	vs	*UTAH STATE*								vs Utah State - Alabama leads series 2-0
9/10/2022	@	*Texas*								vs Texas - Texas leads series 7-1-1
9/17/2022	vs	*LOUISIANA-MONROE*								vs UL-Monroe - Alabama leads series 2-1
9/24/2022	vs	VANDERBILT								10-0 S/U @ home vs Vanderbilt since 1986
10/1/2022	@	Arkansas								7-0 S/U @ Arkansas since 2008
10/8/2022	vs	TEXAS A&M								Game 1-4 O/U @ home vs Texas A&M since 1985
10/15/2022	@	Tennessee								9-1 ATS @ Tennessee since 2002
10/22/2022	vs	MISSISSIPPI STATE								30-2 S/U @ home vs Mississippi State since 1959
11/5/2022	@	Lsu								5-0 S/U @ LSU since 2012 {4-1 ATS}
11/12/2022	@	Mississippi								7-1 S/U @ Mississippi since 2005
11/19/2022	vs	*AUSTIN PEAY*								14-0 S/U prior to playing Auburn since 2008
11/26/2022	vs	AUBURN								5-0 S/U @ home vs Auburn since 2012 {4-1 ATS}
12/3/2022	vs									SEC Championship
	vs									BOWL GAME

Pointspread Analysis — Non-Conference
- 0-4 S/U & ATS vs Non-Conf. as 3 point or less favorite since 2000
- 8-2 S/U vs Non-Conf. as 3.5-7 point favorite since 2001
- 10-2 S/U vs Non-Conf. as 7.5-10 point favorite since 1998
- 9-0 S/U vs Non-Conf. as 10.5-15 point favorite since 2005
- 2-8 ATS vs Non-Conf. as 15.5-20 point favorite since 1992
- 13-1 S/U vs Non-Conf. as 20.5-25 point favorite since 1984
- 44-0 S/U vs Non-Conf. as 25.5 point or more favorite since 1986

Dog
- 1-11 S/U as 11 point or more Dog since 1996
- 8-1-1 ATS as 11 point or more Dog since 1997
- 0-4 S/U as 7.5-10 point Dog since 2003
- 4-0 S/U & ATS as 3.5-7 point Dog since 2008
- 5-13 S/U as 3 point or less Dog since 1998

Favorite
- 1-6 ATS @ home as 3.5-7 point favorite since 2002
- 12-1 S/U on road as 7.5-10 point favorite since 1985
- 10-1 S/U @ home as 7.5-10 point favorite since 1998
- 13-1 S/U on road as 10.5-15 point favorite since 1997
- 14-1 S/U @ home as 10.5-15 point favorite since 2007
- 27-2 S/U as 15.5-20 point favorite since 2002
- 15-1 S/U on road as 15.5-20 point favorite since 1988
- 12-0 S/U @ home as 15.5-20 point favorite since 2002
- 1-5 O/U @ home as 15.5-20 point favorite since 2008
- 28-2 S/U @ home as 20.5-25 point favorite since 1986
- 3-7-1 O/U @ home as 20.5-25 point favorite since 2007
- 10-0 S/U on road as 20.5-25 point favorite since 1984
- 74-0 S/U as 25.5 point or more favorite since 1986
- 7-2 ATS on road as 25.5 point or more favorite since 1992

Bowl Games
- 7-2 O/U in Bowl Games as 7.5-10 favorite since 1991
- 6-0 S/U in Bowl Game as 10.5-15 point favorite since 1953
- 9-2 ATS in Bowl Games as 3.5-7 point favorite since 1981
- 6-1 vs PAC-12 in Bowl Games since 1976
- 1-4-1 vs Texas in Bowl Games
- 20-0 S/U in 1st game of season since 2002 — UTAH STATE
- 20-0 S/U in 1st home game of season since 2002 — UTAH STATE
- 14-1 S/U in 1st road game of season since 2007 — Texas
- 17-1 S/U prior to playing Arkansas since 2004 — VANDERBILT
- 11-3 ATS prior to playing Arkansas since 2008 — VANDERBILT
- 18-0 S/U prior to playing Tennessee since 2004 — Texas A&M
- 14-0 S/U prior to playing LSU since 2007 — MISSISSIPPI STATE
- 18-1 S/U prior to playing Mississippi since 2003 — Lsu
- 14-0 S/U after playing Mississippi State since 2008 — Lsu
- 48-6 S/U on road when ranked since 2008
- 54-1 S/U @ home when ranked since 2013
- 80-8 S/U when ranked #1 since 2009
- 38-9 S/U when ranked #1 vs ranked teams since 1978

Pointspread Analysis — Conference
- 15-0 S/U vs Arkansas since 2007
- vs Arkansas - Alabama leads series 24-7
- vs Auburn - Alabama leads series 48-37-1
- Game 1-4 O/U @ LSU since 2012
- 10-1 S/U vs LSU since 2012
- Game 2-8-2 O/U vs LSU since 2011
- vs LSU - Alabama leads series 55-26-5
- vs Mississippi - Alabama leads series 57-10-2
- vs Mississippi State - Alabama leads series 86-17-3
- 14-0 S/U vs Mississippi State since 2008
- Game 2-12-1 O/U vs Mississippi State since 2007
- vs Tennessee - Alabama leads series 58-37-8
- 15-0 S/U vs Tennessee since 2007
- Game 5-1 O/U @ Tennessee since 2010
- vs Texas A&M - Alabama leads series 11-3
- 8-1 S/U vs Texas A&M since 2013
- 22-0 S/U vs Vanderbilt since 1985
- 6-1 S/U vs Arkansas as 7.5-10 point favorite since 1980
- 4-0 S/U vs Arkansas as 15.5-20 point favorite since 2005
- 5-0 S/U vs Arkansas as 25.5 point or more favorite since 2013
- 6-1 S/U vs Arkansas as 7.5-10 point favorite since 1980
- 1-3 O/U vs Auburn as 3.5-7 point favorite since 1999
- 7-1 S/U @ LSU as 3.5-7 point favorite since 1983
- 3-0 S/U vs LSU as 7.5-10 point favorite since 1991
- 3-0 S/U & ATS vs LSU as 10.5-15 point favorite since 1990
- 7-1 S/U vs Mississippi as 3.5-7 point favorite since 1989
- 7-0 S/U vs Mississippi as 10.5-15 point favorite since 1996
- 0-7 O/U vs Mississippi as 10.5-15 point favorite since 1996
- 11-2 S/U vs Miss. State as 10.5-15 point favorite since 1985
- 7-0 S/U vs Miss. State as 15.5-20 point favorite since 1983
- 7-0 S/U vs Miss. State as 20.5-25 point favorite since 1987
- 4-0 S/U vs Tennessee as 10.5-15 point favorite since 1986
- 3-0 S/U vs Tennessee as 15.5-20 point favorite since 2010
- 4-0 S/U vs Tennessee as 25.5 point or more favorite since 2011
- 4-0 ATS vs Tennessee as 25.5 point or more favorite since 2011
- 7-0 S/U vs Vanderbilt as 10.5-15 point favorite since 1983
- 8-0 S/U vs Vanderbilt as 15.5-20 point favorite since 1985
- 6-0 S/U vs Vanderbilt as 20.5-25 point favorite since 1986
- 12-0 S/U on road when ranked #2 since 1992
- 35-0 S/U when ranked #2 vs unranked teams since 1986
- 21-0 S/U @ home when ranked #3 since 1964
- 2-14 S/U vs #2 ranked teams all time {0-5 on road}
- 11-0 S/U at Neutral sites when ranked #2 since 1979
- 1-9 O/U @ home vs ranked Auburn since 1988
- 24-0 S/U @ home vs Mississippi State when ranked since 1961
- 13-0 S/U vs Arkansas when ranked since 2008
- 21-1-1 S/U @ LSU when ranked since 1965

Page | 7 *Copyright © 2022 by Steve's Football Bible, LLC*

ALABAMA-BIRMINGHAM BLAZERS   CONFERENCE USA West

2021-Alabama-Birmingham		Opponent	UAB	Opp	S/U	Line	ATS	Total	O/U	
9/1/2021	vs	JACKSONVILLE STATE	31	0	W	-15.5	W	52.5	U	
9/11/2021	@	Georgia	7	56	L	23.5	L	43.5	O	
9/18/2021	@	North Texas	40	6	W	-12.5	W	58.0	U	
9/25/2021	@	Tulane	28	21	W	2.5	W	54.5	U	
10/2/2021	vs	LIBERTY	12	36	L	-2.5	L	49.0	U	
10/9/2021	vs	FLORIDA ATLANTIC	31	14	W	-3.5	W	49.0	U	
10/16/2021	@	Southern Mississippi	34	0	W	-17.5	W	43.5	U	
10/23/2021	vs	RICE	24	30	L	-24.0	L	44.5	O	
11/6/2021	vs	LOUISIANA TECH	52	38	W	-14.0	T	48.5	O	
11/13/2021	@	Marshall	21	14	W	4.5	L	55.0	U	
11/20/2021	@	Texas-San Antonio	31	34	L	3.5	W	53.5	O	
11/27/2021	vs	TEXAS-EL PASO	42	25	W	-13.5	W	49.5	O	
12/18/2021	vs	**BYU**	31	28	W	5.5	W	54.5	O	**Independence Bowl**
Coach: Bill Clark		Season Record >>	384	302	9-4	ATS>>	9-3-1	O/U>>	6-7	

2020-Alabama-Birmingham		Opponent	UAB	Opp	S/U	Line	ATS	Total	O/U	
9/3/2020	vs	CENTRAL ARKANSAS	45	35	W	-20.0	L	49.5	O	
9/10/2020	@	Miami	14	31	L	14.5	L	54.5	U	
9/26/2020	@	South Alabama	42	10	W	-7.0	W	47.5	O	
10/3/2020	vs	TEXAS-SAN ANTONIO	21	13	W	-21.5	L	55.0	U	
10/17/2020	vs	WESTERN KENTUCKY	37	14	W	-13.5	W	44.5	O	
10/23/2020	vs	LOUISIANA	20	24	L	2.5	L	50.5	U	
10/31/2020	@	Louisiana Tech	34	37	L	-13.0	L	47.0	O	{2 OT}
12/12/2020	@	Rice	21	16	W	-7.0	L	42.0	U	
12/18/2020	@	**Marshall**	22	13	W	4.0	W	44.0	U	**C-USA CHAMPIONSHIP GAME**
Coach: Bill Clark		Season Record >>	256	193	6-3	ATS>>	3-6	O/U>>	4-5	**C-USA CHAMPIONS**

2019-Alabama-Birmingham		Opponent	UAB	Opp	S/U	Line	ATS	Total	O/U	
8/29/2019	vs	ALABAMA STATE	24	19	W	-39.0	L	NT	---	
9/7/2019	@	Akron	31	20	W	-8.0	W	46.5	O	
9/21/2019	vs	SOUTH ALABAMA	35	3	W	-12.0	W	48.0	U	
9/28/2019	@	Western Kentucky	13	20	L	-3.5	L	47.0	U	
10/5/2019	vs	RICE	35	20	W	-10.0	W	43.5	O	
10/12/2019	@	Texas-San Antonio	33	14	W	-12.5	W	47.0	T	
10/19/2019	vs	OLD DOMINION	38	14	W	-17.0	W	41.5	O	
11/2/2019	@	Tennessee	7	30	L	13.5	L	49.0	U	
11/9/2019	@	Southern Mississippi	2	37	L	7.5	L	50.0	U	
11/16/2019	vs	TEXAS-EL PASO	37	10	W	-14.5	W	42.0	O	
11/23/2019	vs	LOUISIANA TECH	20	14	W	-6.5	L	44.0	U	
11/30/2019	@	North Texas	26	21	W	-3.0	W	49.5	U	
12/7/2019	@	**Florida Atlantic**	6	49	L	8.0	L	49.0	O	**C-USA Championship Game**
12/21/2019	vs	**Appalachian State**	17	31	L	17.0	W	47.5	O	**New Orleans Bowl**
Coach: Bill Clark		Season Record >>	324	302	9-5	ATS>>	8-6	O/U>>	6-6-1	

2018-Alabama-Birmingham		Opponent	UAB	Opp	S/U	Line	ATS	Total	O/U	
8/30/2018	vs	SAVANNAH STATE	52	0	W	-38.5	W	NT	---	
9/8/2018	@	Coastal Carolina	24	47	L	-8.5	L	54.5	O	
9/15/2018	vs	TULANE	31	24	W	3.5	W	57.0	U	
9/29/2018	vs	CHARLOTTE	28	7	W	-15.5	W	52.0	U	
10/6/2018	@	Louisiana Tech	28	7	W	6.5	W	55.5	U	
10/13/2018	@	Rice	42	0	W	-16.5	W	52.0	U	
10/20/2018	vs	NORTH TEXAS	29	21	W	-1.5	W	53.5	U	
10/27/2018	@	Texas-El Paso	19	0	W	-15.0	W	49.5	U	
11/3/2018	vs	TEXAS-SAN ANTONIO	52	3	W	-21.5	W	42.0	O	
11/10/2018	vs	SOUTHERN MISSISSIPPI	26	23	W	-13.5	L	45.0	O	{OT}
11/17/2018	@	Texas A&M	20	41	L	17.0	L	46.5	O	
11/24/2018	@	Middle Tennessee	3	27	L	-3.0	L	52.0	U	
12/1/2018	@	**Middle Tennessee**	27	25	W	1.0	W	44.0	O	**C-USA Championship Game**
12/18/2018	vs	**Northern Illinois**	37	13	W	-1.0	W	41.0	O	**Boca Raton Bowl**
Coach: Bill Clark		Season Record >>	418	238	11-3	ATS>>	10-4	O/U>>	6-7	**C-USA Champions**

ALABAMA-BIRMINGHAM BLAZERS — CONFERENCE USA West

STADIUM: Legion Field {71,594} | **Location:** Birmingham, AL | **COACH:** Bill Clark

DATE		Opponent	UAB	Opp	S/U	Line	ATS	Total	O/U	Trends & Angles
9/1/2022	vs	ALABAMA A&M								vs Alabama A&M - UAB leads series 2-0
9/10/2022	@	Liberty								vs Liberty - Liberty leads series 1-0
9/17/2022	vs	GEORGIA SOUTHERN								1st Meeting
10/1/2022	@	Rice								Game 0-3 O/U @ Rice since 2010
10/8/2022	vs	MIDDLE TENNESSEE								vs Middle Tennessee - Series tied 4-4
10/15/2022	vs	CHARLOTTE								vs Charlotte - Series tied 1-1
10/21/2022	@	Western Kentucky								vs Western Kentucky - Series tied 4-4
10/29/2022	@	Florida Atlantic								vs Florida Atlantic - FAU leads series 5-3
11/5/2022	vs	TEXAS-SAN ANTONIO								4-1 S/U vs Texas-San Antonio since 2017
11/12/2022	vs	NORTH TEXAS								5-0 ATS vs North Texas since 2014
11/19/2022	@	Lsu								vs LSU - Series tied 1-1
11/26/2022	@	Louisiana Tech								vs La Tech - La Tech leads series 6-4
12/3/2022										C-USA Championship
	vs									BOWL GAME

Pointspread Analysis

Dog

- 0-30 S/U on road as 20.5 point or more Dog since 1997
- 0-12 S/U on road as 15.5-20 point Dog since 1997
- 2-21 S/U as 10.5-15 point Dog since 2003
- 2-10 ATS as 10.5-15 point Dog since 2008
- 5-1 O/U on road as 7.5-10 point Dog since 2010
- 8-0 ATS on road as 3.5-7 point Dog since 2012
- 2-7 O/U as 3.5-7 point Dog since 2017

Favorite

- 22-5 S/U as 15.5 point or more favorite since 1998
- 12-2 O/U @ home as 10.5-15 point favorite since 2003
- 11-2 S/U @ home as 3.5-7 point favorite since 2001
- 6-2 O/U @ home as 3.5-7 point favorite since 2006
- 0-9 O/U on road as 3 point or less favorite since 2001

1-16 S/U on road vs ranked teams since 1997

Pointspread Analysis

Conference

- Game 7-1 O/U vs Florida Atlantic since 2008
- vs North Texas - UAB leads series 5-1
- 4-1 S/U vs Rice since 2017
- vs Rice - Series tied 5-5
- Game 7-2 O/U vs Rice since 2005
- vs Texas-San Antonio - UAB leads series 4-2
- 4-1 S/U vs Western Kentucky since 1996

Opponent	Trend
ALABAMA A&M	7-0 S/U in 1st home game of season since 2013
Liberty	1-15 S/U in 1st road game of season since 2004
Florida Atlantic	6-0 S/U prior to playing UTSA since 2013 {5-1 ATS}
UTSA	1-7 S/U prior to playing Texas-El Paso since 2005 {2-6 ATS}
Lsu	5-1 S/U prior to playing North Texas since 1995

Print Version $24.95 Print Version $34.95  Print Version $34.95

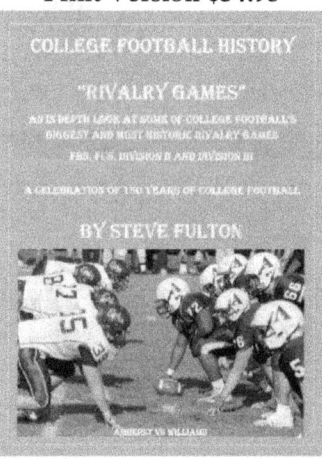

These books available at numerous online retailers

Page | 9 Copyright © 2022 by Steve's Football Bible, LLC

APPALACHIAN STATE MOUNTAINEERS SUN BELT East

2021-Appalachian State		Opponent	APP	Opp	S/U	Line	ATS	Total	O/U	
9/2/2021	vs	East Carolina {@ Charlotte}	33	19	W	-9.0	W	55.5	U	
9/11/2021	@	Miami	23	25	L	7.5	W	54.5	U	
9/18/2021	vs	ELON	44	10	W	-35.0	L	52.5	O	
9/23/2021	vs	MARSHALL	31	30	W	-7.0	L	59.0	O	
10/2/2021	@	Georgia State	45	16	W	-10.5	W	54.0	O	
10/12/2021	@	Louisiana	13	41	L	-4.0	L	57.5	U	
10/20/2021	vs	COASTAL CAROLINA	30	27	W	4.5	W	60.5	U	
10/30/2021	vs	LOUISIANA-MONROE	59	28	W	-26.5	W	57.5	O	
11/6/2021	@	Arkansas State	48	14	W	-21.5	W	67.5	O	
11/13/2021	vs	SOUTH ALABAMA	31	7	W	-21.5	W	51.5	U	
11/20/2021	@	Troy	45	7	W	-9.5	W	51.5	O	
11/27/2021	vs	GEORGIA SOUTHERN	27	3	W	-24.5	L	55.5	U	"Deeper Than Hate Rivalry"
12/4/2021	@	Louisiana	16	24	L	-2.0	L	52.0	U	SUN BELT CHAMPIONSHIP
12/18/2021	vs	Western Kentucky	38	59	L	1.0	L	69.0	O	Boca Raton Bowl
Coach: Shawn Clark		Season Record >>	483	310	10-4	ATS>>	8-6	O/U>>	6-8	

2020-Appalachian State		Opponent	APP	Opp	S/U	Line	ATS	Total	O/U	
9/12/2020	vs	CHARLOTTE	35	20	W	-17.0	L	59.0	U	
9/19/2020	@	Marshall	7	17	L	-6.0	L	59.5	U	
9/26/2020	vs	CAMPBELL	52	21	W	-32.0	L	53.0	O	
10/22/2020	vs	ARKANSAS STATE	45	17	W	-13.5	W	69.0	U	
10/31/2020	@	Louisiana-Monroe	31	13	W	-29.0	L	56.0	U	
11/7/2020	@	Texas State	38	17	W	-21.5	L	59.0	U	
11/14/2020	vs	GEORGIA STATE	17	13	W	-18.0	L	63.0	U	
11/21/2020	@	Coastal Carolina	23	34	L	3.0	L	48.0	O	
11/28/2020	vs	TROY	47	10	W	-14.0	W	50.5	O	
12/4/2020	vs	LOUISIANA	21	24	L	-3.0	L	51.0	U	
12/12/2020	@	Georgia Southern	34	26	W	-9.5	L	45.0	O	"Deeper Than Hate Rivalry"
12/21/2020	vs	North Texas	56	28	W	-22.5	W	68.0	O	Myrtle Beach Bowl
Coach: Shawn Clark		Season Record >>	406	240	9-3	ATS>>	3-9	O/U>>	5-7	

2019-Appalachian State		Opponent	APP	Opp	S/U	Line	ATS	Total	O/U	
8/31/2019	vs	EAST TENNESSEE STATE	42	7	W	-32.5	W	NT	---	
9/7/2019	vs	CHARLOTTE	56	41	W	-23.0	L	54.5	O	
9/21/2019	@	North Carolina	34	31	W	2.0	W	58.0	O	
9/28/2019	vs	COASTAL CAROLINA	56	37	W	-14.5	W	58.0	O	
10/9/2019	@	Louisiana-Lafayette	17	7	W	3.0	W	69.0	U	
10/19/2019	vs	LOUISIANA-MONROE	52	7	W	-15.5	W	65.5	U	
10/26/2019	@	South Alabama	30	3	W	-26.5	W	51.0	U	
10/31/2019	vs	GEORGIA SOUTHERN	21	24	L	-13.5	L	41.5	O	"Deeper Than Hate Rivalry"
11/9/2019	@	South Carolina	20	15	W	6.5	W	51.0	U	
11/16/2019	@	Georgia State	56	27	W	-15.0	W	61.5	O	
11/23/2019	vs	TEXAS STATE	35	13	W	-28.0	L	50.0	U	
11/30/2019	@	Troy	48	13	W	-11.0	W	64.0	U	
12/7/2019	vs	LOUISIANA-LAFAYETTE	45	38	W	-5.0	W	57.0	O	SUN BELT CHAMPIONSHIP
12/21/2019	vs	Alabama-Birmingham	31	17	W	-17.0	L	47.5	O	New Orleans Bowl
		Season Record >>	543	280	13-1	ATS>>	10-4	O/U>>	7-6	SUN BELT CHAMPIONS

2018-Appalachian State		Opponent	APP	Opp	S/U	Line	ATS	Total	O/U	
9/1/2018	@	Penn State	38	45	L	24.0	W	54.0	O	{OT}
9/8/2018	@	Charlotte	45	9	W	-14.0	W	48.5	O	
9/22/2018	vs	GARDNER-WEBB	72	7	W	-49.0	W	NT	---	
9/29/2018	vs	SOUTH ALABAMA	52	7	W	-25.0	W	56.5	O	
10/9/2018	@	Arkansas State	35	9	W	-10.5	W	58.5	U	
10/20/2018	vs	LOUISIANA-LAFAYETTE	27	17	W	-25.5	L	67.0	U	
10/25/2018	@	Georgia Southern	14	34	L	-11.0	L	47.5	O	"Deeper Than Hate Rivalry"
11/3/2018	@	Coastal Carolina	23	7	W	-13.5	W	52.0	U	
11/10/2018	@	Texas State	38	7	W	-19.0	W	45.5	U	
11/17/2018	vs	GEORGIA STATE	45	17	W	-27.5	W	54.0	O	
11/24/2018	vs	TROY	21	10	W	-11.5	L	45.5	U	
12/1/2018	vs	LOUISIANA-LAFAYETTE	30	19	W	-17.0	L	55.0	U	SUN BELT CHAMPIONSHIP
12/15/2018	vs	Middle Tennessee	45	13	W	-6.5	W	49.0	O	New Orleans Bowl
Coach: Scott Satterfield		Season Record >>	1028	481	11-2	ATS>>	9-4	O/U>>	6-6	SUN BELT CHAMPIONS

APPALACHIAN STATE MOUNTAINEERS — SUN BELT East

STADIUM: Kidd-Brewer Stadium {30,000} **Location:** Boone, NC **COACH:** Shawn Clark

DATE		Opponent	App	Opp	S/U	Line	ATS	Total	O/U	Trends & Angles
9/3/2022	vs	NORTH CAROLINA								vs North Carolina - series tied 1-1
9/10/2022	@	Texas A&M								1-10 S/U in 1st road game of season since 2011
9/17/2022	vs	TROY								4-0 S/U vs Troy since 2018
9/24/2022	vs	JAMES MADISON								6-1 S/U @ home vs JMU since 1985
10/1/2022	vs	THE CITADEL								9-1 S/U @ home vs The Citadel since 1994
10/8/2022	@	Texas State								vs Texas State - App State leads series 6-0
10/19/2022	vs	GEORGIA STATE								vs Ga State - App State leads series 8-0 {6-2 ATS}
10/29/2022	vs	ROBERT MORRIS								1st Meeting
11/3/2022	@	Coastal Carolina								vs Coastal Carolina - App State leads series 4-1
11/12/2022	@	Marshall								vs Marshall - App State leads series 15-7
11/19/2022	vs	OLD DOMINION								vs Old Dominion - App State leads series 2-0
11/26/2022	@	Georgia Southern								0-4 ATS vs Georgia Southern since 2018
12/3/2022	vs									Sun Belt Championship
	vs									BOWL GAME

Pointspread Analysis — Dog
- 1-6 S/U as 10.5 point or more Dog since 2014

Favorite
- 7-3 S/U as 3.5-7 point favorite since 2014
- 6-1 S/U as 7.5-10 point favorite since 2015
- 17-3 S/U as 10.5-15 point favorite since 2014
- 41-0 S/U as 15.5 point or more favorite since 2014

Pointspread Analysis — Conference
- vs Georgia Southern - App State leads series 20-14-1
- vs James Madison - App State leads series 12-4
- Game 0-5 O/U vs Texas State since 2016
- vs Troy - Appalachian leads series 7-3

Non-Conference
- vs The Citadel - App State leads series 29-13

10-2 S/U prior to playing the Citadel since 2002	James Madison	
5-0 S/U prior to playing Texas State since 2016	THE CITADEL	
8-0 S/U prior to playing Georgia State since 2014	Texas State	
7-1 S/U after playing The Citadel since 2006	Texas State	
10-2-1 S/U prior to playing Marshall since 1985	Coastal Carolina	
4-0 S/U after playing Coastal Carolina since 2018 {4-0 ATS}	Marshall	
23-1 S/U in final home game of season since 1998	ODU	
15-1 S/U after playing Marshall since 1983	ODU	7-3 S/U when ranked all time
11-0 S/U in final road game of season since 2011	Ga Southern	2-13 S/U vs ranked teams all time

Print Version $29.95 **Print Version $39.95**

These books available at numerous online retailers

Page | 11 Copyright © 2022 by Steve's Football Bible, LLC

ARIZONA WILDCATS   PACIFIC-12 South

2021-Arizona

Date		Opponent	AZ	Opp	S/U	Line	ATS	Total	O/U	
9/2/2021	vs	Byu {@ Las Vegas}	16	24	L	13.5	W	54.0	U	
9/11/2021	vs	SAN DIEGO STATE	14	38	L	-1.5	L	46.0	O	
9/18/2021	vs	NORTHERN ARIZONA	19	21	L	-27.0	L	54.0	U	
9/25/2021	@	Oregon	19	41	L	30.0	W	59.0	O	
10/9/2021	vs	UCLA	16	34	L	16.0	L	61.0	U	
10/16/2021	@	Colorado	0	34	L	6.0	L	47.0	U	
10/22/2021	vs	WASHINGTON	16	21	L	17.0	W	45.5	U	
10/30/2021	@	Usc	34	41	L	21.5	W	55.5	O	
11/6/2021	vs	CALIFORNIA	10	3	W	7.0	W	47.0	U	
11/13/2021	vs	UTAH	29	38	L	23.5	W	54.5	O	
11/19/2021	@	Washington State	18	44	L	14.5	L	52.0	O	
11/27/2021	@	Arizona State	15	38	L	20.0	L	52.5	O	Territorial Cup
Coach: Jedd Fisch		Season Record >>	206	377	1-11	ATS>>	6-6	O/U>>	6-6	

2020-Arizona

Date		Opponent	AZ	Opp	S/U	Line	ATS	Total	O/U	
11/14/2020	vs	USC	30	34	L	14.5	W	67.0	U	
11/21/2020	@	Washington	27	44	L	12.5	L	53.5	O	
11/28/2020	@	Ucla	10	27	L	7.5	L	70.5	U	
12/5/2020	vs	COLORADO	13	24	L	9.5	L	55.5	U	
12/11/2020	vs	ARIZONA STATE	7	70	L	8.0	L	58.0	O	Territorial Cup
Coach: Kevin Sumlin		Season Record >>	87	199	0-5	ATS>>	1-4	O/U>>	2-3	

2019-Arizona

Date		Opponent	AZ	Opp	S/U	Line	ATS	Total	O/U	
8/24/2019	@	Hawaii	38	45	L	-10.5	L	70.5	O	
9/7/2019	vs	NORTHERN ARIZONA	65	41	W	-28.0	L	NT	---	
9/14/2019	vs	TEXAS TECH	28	14	W	2.0	W	74.0	U	
9/28/2019	vs	UCLA	20	17	W	-3.0	T	68.0	U	
10/5/2019	@	Colorado	35	30	W	2.5	W	63.5	O	
10/12/2019	vs	WASHINGTON	27	51	L	6.0	L	62.0	O	
10/19/2019	@	Usc	14	41	L	10.0	L	69.0	U	
10/26/2019	@	Stanford	31	41	L	3.0	L	54.0	O	
11/2/2019	vs	OREGON STATE	38	56	L	-5.0	L	71.5	O	
11/16/2019	@	Oregon	6	34	L	27.0	L	68.5	U	
11/23/2019	vs	UTAH	7	35	L	23.5	L	56.5	U	
11/29/2019	@	Arizona State	14	24	L	12.5	W	60.5	U	Territorial Cup
Coach: Kevin Sumlin		Season Record >>	323	429	4-8	ATS>>	3-8-1	O/U>>	5-6	

2018-Arizona

Date		Opponent	AZ	Opp	S/U	Line	ATS	Total	O/U	
9/1/2018	vs	BYU	23	28	L	-11.0	L	59.0	U	
9/8/2018	@	Houston	18	45	L	3.0	L	70.0	U	
9/15/2018	vs	SOUTHERN UTAH	62	31	W	-24.5	W	NT	---	
9/22/2018	@	Oregon State	35	14	W	-4.0	W	73.5	U	
9/29/2018	vs	USC	20	24	L	3.0	L	61.5	U	
10/6/2018	vs	CALIFORNIA	24	17	W	1.0	W	57.0	U	
10/12/2018	@	Utah	10	42	L	13.5	L	52.5	U	
10/20/2018	@	Ucla	30	31	L	10.0	W	57.0	O	
10/27/2018	vs	OREGON	44	15	W	7.5	W	66.0	U	
11/2/2018	vs	COLORADO	42	34	W	-3.0	W	56.5	O	
11/17/2018	@	Washington State	28	69	L	10.5	L	63.5	O	
11/24/2018	vs	ARIZONA STATE	40	41	L	1.5	W	65.5	O	Territorial Cup
Coach: Kevin Sumlin		Season Record >>	376	391	5-7	ATS>>	7-5	O/U>>	4-7	

ARIZONA WILDCATS — PACIFIC-12 South

STADIUM: Arizona Stadium {55,675} **Location:** Tucson, AZ **COACH:** Jedd Fisch

DATE		Opponent	AZ	Opp	S/U	Line	ATS	Total	O/U	Trends & Angles
9/3/2022	@	San Diego State								vs San Diego State - Arizona leads series 10-6
9/10/2022	vs	MISSISSIPPI STATE								18-2 S/U in 1st home game of season since 2001
9/17/2022	vs	NORTH DAKOTA STATE								1st Meeting
9/24/2022	@	California								0-6 ATS @ California since 2003
10/1/2022	vs	COLORADO								vs Colorado - Colorado leads series 16-8
10/8/2022	vs	OREGON								Game 1-7 O/U vs Oregon since 2012
10/15/2022	@	Washington								0-5 S/U @ Washington since 2009
10/29/2022	vs	USC								1-9 S/U @ home vs USC since 2001
11/5/2022	@	Utah								0-5 S/U vs Utah since 2016 {1-4 ATS}
11/12/2022	@	Ucla								0-5 S/U @ Ucla since 2012
11/19/2022	vs	WASHINGTON STATE								Game 6-0 O/U vs Washington State since 2014
11/25/2022	vs	ARIZONA STATE								Game 6-0 O/U @ home vs Arizona State since 2010
12/2/2022	vs									PAC-12 Championship
	vs									BOWL GAME

Pointspread Analysis — Non-Conference
- 0-11 S/U vs Non-Conf. as 10.5 point or more Dog since 1988
- 6-1 ATS vs Non-Conf. as 7.5-10 point Dog since 1979
- 0-8 S/U vs Non-Conf. as 3.5-7 point Dog since 1995
- 0-8 O/U vs Non-Conf. as 3 point or less Dog since 1990
- 8-1 S/U vs Non-Conf. as 7.5-10 point favorite since 1996
- 9-3 S/U vs Non-Conf. as 10.5-15 point favorite since 1994
- 2-10 ATS vs Non-Conf. as 10.5-15 point favorite since 1994
- 37-1 S/U vs Non-Conf. as 15.5 point or more favorite since 1985
- 4-1 S/U vs San Diego State since 1997

Bowl Games
- 1-6 O/U in Bowl Games since 2009
- 4-0-1 O/U in Bowl Games since 2012

Dog
- 0-4 S/U as 30 point or more Dog since 1991
- 4-0 O/U as 30 point or more Dog since 1991
- 2-7 O/U as 20.5-29 point Dog since 2003
- 1-14 S/U as 20.5-29 point Dog since 1988
- 2-12 S/U on road as 15.5-20 point Dog since 1990
- 2-17 S/U on road as 10.5-15 point Dog since 1997
- 0-12 S/U as 10.5-15 point Dog since 2013
- 0-5 O/U @ home as 10.5-15 point Dog since 2005
- 3-18 S/U on road as 7.5-10 point Dog since 1984
- 9-28 S/U as 3.5-7 point Dog since 1996
- 4-11 O/U on road as 3 point or less Dog since 1999

Favorite
- 9-2-2 O/U as 3 point or less favorite since 2010
- 11-0 S/U as 7.5-10 point favorite since 2010
- 2-18 ATS @ home as 10.5-15 point favorite since 1985
- 11-1 S/U @ home as 15.5-20 point favorite since 1986
- 6-0 S/U on road as 15.5-20 point favorite since 1985
- 16-0 S/U @ home as 20.5-25 point favorite since 1985
- 23-1 S/U as 25.5 or more favorite since 1989
- 0-5 O/U prior to playing Colorado since 2017
- 1-6 S/U after playing Colorado since 2015
- 2-7 ATS after playing Colorado since 2013
- 1-11 S/U after playing Oregon since 2006
- 0-5 S/U after playing Washington since 2015
- 12-2 O/U prior to playing UCLA since 2007
- 1-5 S/U after playing Utah since 2015
- 8-2 O/U after playing Utah since 2011
- 0-6 S/U prior to playing Arizona State since 2016 {0-6 ATS}
- 0-6 S/U after playing Washington State since 2014 {1-5 ATS}

California	
OREGON	
OREGON	
Washington	
USC	
Utah	
Ucla	
Ucla	
WASH STATE	
AZ STATE	

Pointspread Analysis — Conference
- vs Arizona State - Arizona leads series 49-45-1
- 6-0 S/U vs California since 2010
- vs California - Arizona leads series 19-14-2
- 7-3 S/U vs Colorado since 2012
- Game 8-3 O/U vs Colorado since 2011
- vs Oregon - Oregon leads series 29-17
- 2-8 S/U vs UCLA since 2012 {2-7-1 ATS}
- vs Ucla - UCLA leads series 27-17-2
- 1-5 ATS @ UCLA since 2010
- 8-2 S/U vs UCLA as favorite since 1994
- 5-24 S/U vs USC as Dog since 1984
- 2-18 S/U vs USC since 2001
- vs USC - USC leads series 37-8
- 1-8 O/U @ home vs USC since 2003
- vs Utah - Utah leads series 25-19-2
- 0-5 S/U vs Washington since 2015
- vs Washington State - Arizona leads series 27-18
- 0-3 S/U & ATS vs Arizona State as 3.5-7 point favorite since 1992
- 3-0 S/U vs Arizona State as 10.5-15 point favorite since 1994
- 5-0 S/U vs California as 3.5-7 point favorite since 1984
- 0-4 ATS vs California as 7.5-10 point favorite since 1987
- 0-5 S/U vs California as 10.5-15 point favorite since 1983
- 0-4 S/U vs Oregon as 3.5-7 point Dog since 1989
- 3-0 S/U & ATS vs Oregon as 7.5-10 point favorite since 1984
- 0-5 S/U vs UCLA as 10.5-15 point Dog since 1987
- 0-5 S/U @ UCLA as 7.5-10 point Dog since 1995
- 0-4 S/U & ATS vs UCLA as 3.5-7 point Dog since 1993
- 5-0-1 O/U vs UCLA as 3 point or less Dog since 1983
- 0-4 S/U vs USC as 10.5-15 point Dog since 2008
- 0-4 S/U vs USC as 3 point or less Dog since 1984
- 0-6 S/U vs USC as 20.5 point or more Dog since 2003
- 3-0 ATS vs Washington as 3 point or less Dog since 1987
- 0-4 S/U vs Washington State as 10.5-15 point Dog since 1997
- 3-0 S/U & ATS vs Wazzu as 3 point or less favorite since 1988
- 0-4 ATS vs Washington State as 10.5-15 point favorite since 1993
- 4-0 S/U vs Wazzu as 20.5 point or more favorite since 1998

- 5-31 S/U on road vs ranked teams since 1999
- 2-20-1 S/U on road vs #3 - #9 ranked teams since 1970
- 0-7-1 S/U @ ranked UCLA all time
- 7-1 ATS vs ranked USC since 2005
- 1-9 S/U @ ranked Washington all time

ARIZONA STATE SUN DEVILS   PACIFIC-12 South

2021-Arizona State		Opponent	ASU	Opp	S/U	Line	ATS	Total	O/U	
9/4/2021	vs	SOUTHERN UTAH	41	14	W	-45.0	L	56.5	U	
9/11/2021	vs	UNLV	37	10	W	-34.5	L	56.0	U	
9/18/2021	@	Byu	17	27	L	-3.5	L	50.5	U	
9/25/2021	vs	COLORADO	35	13	W	-14.0	W	45.0	O	
10/2/2021	@	Ucla	42	23	W	3.0	W	56.5	O	
10/8/2021	vs	STANFORD	28	10	W	-13.5	W	53.5	U	
10/16/2021	@	Utah	21	35	L	-1.0	L	52.0	O	
10/30/2021	vs	WASHINGTON STATE	21	34	L	-16.5	L	55.0	T	
11/6/2021	vs	USC	31	16	W	-9.5	W	61.0	L	
11/13/2021	@	Washington	35	30	W	-6.0	L	45.5	O	
11/20/2021	@	Oregon State	10	24	L	-3.0	L	59.0	U	
11/27/2021	vs	ARIZONA	38	15	W	-20.0	W	52.5	O	Territorial Cup
12/30/2021	vs	Wisconsin	13	20	L	8.5	W	42.5	U	Las Vegas Bowl
Coach: Herm Edwards		Season Record >>	369	271	8-5	ATS>>	6-7	O/U>>	5-7-1	
2020-Arizona State		Opponent	ASU	Opp	S/U	Line	ATS	Total	O/U	
11/7/2020	@	Usc	27	28	L	11.5	W	57.5	U	
12/5/2020	vs	UCLA	18	25	L	-2.5	L	57.5	U	
12/11/2020	@	Arizona	70	7	W	8.0	W	58.0	O	Territorial Cup
12/19/2020	@	Oregon State	46	33	W	-7.5	W	54.5	O	
Coach: Herm Edwards		Season Record >>	161	93	2-2	ATS>>	3-1	O/U>>	2-2	
2019-Arizona State		Opponent	ASU	Opp	S/U	Line	ATS	Total	O/U	
8/29/2019	vs	KENT STATE	30	7	W	-24.5	L	61.0	U	
9/6/2019	vs	SACRAMENTO STATE	19	7	W	-34.5	L	NT	---	
9/14/2019	@	Michigan State	10	7	W	15.5	W	42.0	U	
9/21/2019	vs	COLORADO	31	34	L	-8.0	L	49.0	O	
9/27/2019	@	California	24	17	W	4.5	W	43.0	U	
10/12/2019	vs	WASHINGTON STATE	38	34	W	1.5	W	60.5	O	
10/19/2019	@	Utah	3	21	L	14.5	L	46.0	U	
10/26/2019	@	Ucla	32	42	L	-3.0	L	56.0	O	
11/9/2019	vs	USC	26	31	L	4.5	L	54.0	O	
11/16/2019	@	Oregon State	34	35	L	-1.5	L	56.5	O	
11/23/2019	vs	OREGON	31	28	W	13.5	W	55.0	O	
11/29/2019	vs	ARIZONA	24	14	W	-12.5	L	60.5	U	Territorial Cup
12/31/2019	vs	Florida State	20	14	W	-3.0	W	51.5	U	Sun Bowl
Coach: Herm Edwards		Season Record >>	322	291	8-5	ATS>>	5-8	O/U>>	6-6	
2018-Arizona State		Opponent	ASU	Opp	S/U	Line	ATS	Total	O/U	
9/1/2018	vs	TEXAS-SAN ANTONIO	49	7	W	-17.5	W	52.0	O	
9/8/2018	vs	MICHIGAN STATE	16	13	W	4.5	W	54.0	U	
9/15/2018	@	San Diego State	21	28	L	-5.0	L	47.5	O	
9/22/2018	@	Washington	20	27	L	18.5	W	53.0	U	
9/29/2018	vs	OREGON STATE	52	24	W	-22.0	W	64.5	O	
10/6/2018	@	Colorado	21	28	L	2.5	L	64.5	U	
10/18/2018	vs	STANFORD	13	20	L	2.5	L	57.5	U	
10/27/2018	@	Usc	38	35	W	3.0	W	52.0	O	
11/3/2018	vs	UTAH	38	20	W	7.5	W	54.0	O	
11/10/2018	vs	UCLA	31	28	W	-11.5	L	64.5	U	
11/17/2018	@	Oregon	29	31	L	3.5	W	66.0	U	
11/24/2018	@	Arizona	41	40	W	-1.5	L	65.5	O	Territorial Cup
12/15/2018	vs	Fresno State	20	31	L	6.0	L	53.5	U	Las Vegas Bowl
Coach: Herm Edwards		Season Record >>	389	332	7-6	ATS>>	7-6	O/U>>	6-7	

ARIZONA STATE SUN DEVILS PACIFIC-12 South

STADIUM: Sun Devil Stadium {53,599} **Location:** Tempe, AZ **COACH:** Herman Edwards

DATE		Opponent	ASU	Opp	S/U	Line	ATS	Total	O/U	Trends & Angles
9/3/2022	vs	NORTHERN ARIZONA								14-0-1 S/U vs Northern Arizona since 1939
9/10/2022	@	Oklahoma State								vs Oklahoma State - ASU lead series 2-1
9/17/2022	vs	EASTERN MICHIGAN								1st Meeting
9/24/2022	vs	UTAH								9-1 S/U @ home vs Utah since 1981
10/1/2022	@	Usc								2-9 S/U @ USC since 2001
10/8/2022	vs	WASHINGTON								7-0 S/U @ home vs Wash. since 2002 {7-0 ATS}
10/22/2022	@	Stanford								1-7 S/U @ Stanford since 2000 {2-6 ATS}
10/29/2022	@	Colorado								Game 0-3 O/U @ Colorado since 2014
11/5/2022	vs	UCLA								Game 0-3 O/U @ home vs UCLA since 2016
11/12/2022	@	Washington State								1-4 ATS @ Washington State since 2007
11/19/2022	vs	OREGON STATE								20-1 S/U @ home vs Oregon State since 1972
11/25/2022	@	Arizona								vs Arizona - Arizona leads series 49-45-1
12/2/2022	vs									PAC-12 Championship
	vs									BOWL GAME

Pointspread Analysis

Non-Conference
- 0-6 S/U vs Non-Conf. as 10.5-15 point Dog since 1990
- 0-6 O/U vs Non-Conf. as 7.5-10 point Dog since 1994
- 1-5 S/U vs Non-Conf. as 3.5-7 point Dog since 2008
- 7-2 S/U vs Non-Conf. as 3.5-7 point favorite since 2001
- 0-5 ATS vs Non-Conf. as 7.5-10 point favorite since 1994
- 7-0 S/U vs Non-Conf. as 15.5-20 point favorite since 1987
- 18-0 S/U vs Non-Conf. as 25.5 point or more favorite since 1985
- vs Northern Arizona - ASU leads series 22-14-4

Bowl Games
- 0-4 S/U in Holiday Bowl
- 5-1 S/U in Fiesta Bowl
- 6-3 O/U in Bowl Games since 2007
- 0-6 S/U vs ranked teams in Bowl Games since 1997

Dog
- 0-6 S/U on road as 20.5 point or more Dog since 1988
- 1-7 S/U as 20.5 point or more Dog since 1988
- 2-12 S/U as 15.5-20 point Dog since 1988
- 0-11 S/U on road as 15.5-20 point Dog since 1988
- 7-2 ATS on road as 10.5-15 point Dog since 2009
- 2-7 S/U @ home as 10.5-15 point Dog since 1990
- 5-0 ATS @ home as 10.5-15 point Dog since 2005
- 1-7 S/U & ATS on road as 7.5-10 point Dog since 2003
- 3-10 S/U as 7.5-10 point Dog since 2006
- 3-17 S/U @ home as 3.5-7 point Dog since 1984
- 2-14 S/U on road as 3.5-7 point Dog since 2001
- 11-5 O/U on road as 3.5-7 point Dog since 2001

Favorite
- 2-8 ATS as 3 point or less favorite since 2016
- 11-3 S/U on road as 3.5-7 point favorite since 1998
- 3-10 ATS as 7.5-10 point favorite since 2001
- 29-1 S/U @ home as 10.5-15 point favorite since 1985
- 14-5 ATS @ home as 10.5-15 point favorite since 1996
- 13-1 S/U @ home as 15.5-20 point favorite since 1987
- 6-0 S/U on road as 20.5-25 point favorite since 1991
- 12-2 S/U @ home as 20.5-25 point favorite since 1985
- 11-0 S/U as 25.5-30 point favorite since 1983
- 24-0 S/U as 25.5 point or more favorite since 1983
- 16-0 S/U as 30.5 point or more favorite since 1996
- 0-5 ATS as 30.5 point or more favorite since 2014

- 7-30 S/U on road vs ranked teams since 1998
- 5-0 S/U vs ranked Non-Conference teams since 2011
- 1-7 S/U @ ranked USC since 1995
- 10-2 S/U @ home when ranked since 2011
- 7-1 S/U when ranked vs Utah since 1974
- 5-0 S/U when ranked vs Washington State since 2004

Pointspread Analysis

Conference
- vs Colorado - Arizona State leads series 9-3
- 8-3 ATS vs Colorado since 2006
- 9-1 S/U vs Colorado as favorite since 2006
- vs Oregon State - Arizona State leads series 30-15-1
- 19-5-1 S/U vs Oregon State as favorite since 1983
- Game 1-7 O/U vs Stanford since 2009
- 2-6 S/U vs Stanford since 2009
- vs Stanford - Arizona State leads series 18-15
- vs UCLA - UCLA leads series 23-14-1
- Game 9-3 O/U vs UCLA since 2010
- vs Utah - Arizona State leads series 21-10
- 8-2 S/U vs Utah as favorite since 1985
- vs USC - USC leads series 24-14
- 4-21 S/U vs USC as Dog since 1985
- Game 1-5 O/U vs Washington since 2014
- 12-1-1 ATS vs Washington since 2002
- vs Washington - Arizona State leads series 21-16
- vs Washington State - ASU leads series 28-15-2
- 3-0 S/U & ATS vs Arizona as 3.5-7 point Dog since 1992
- 5-0 S/U vs Colorado as 15.5 point or more favorite since 2011
- 0-3 S/U vs Oregon State as 3.5-7 point Dog since 2003
- 6-0 S/U vs Oregon State as 10.5-15 point favorite since 1990
- 5-0 S/U vs Oregon State as 20.5 point or more favorite since 1983
- 4-0 S/U vs Stanford as 15.5 point or more favorite since 1983
- 0-4 S/U vs UCLA as 3.5-7 point Dog since 2000
- 5-1 O/U vs UCLA as 3.5-7 point Dog since 1987
- 1-5 ATS vs UCLA as 3.5-7 point favorite since 1983
- 3-0 S/U vs Utah as 10.5-15 point favorite since 1985
- 0-4 S/U vs USC as 15.5 point or more Dog since 1988
- 1-7 S/U vs USC as 10.5-15 point Dog since 1990
- 1-6 S/U vs USC as 3.5-7 point Dog since 1998
- 5-0 S/U vs Washington as 3.5-7 point favorite since 2002 {4-1 ATS}
- 3-0 ATS vs Washington as 10.5-15 point Dog since 1989
- 3-0 S/U & ATS vs Wazzu as 3 point or less favorite since 1985
- 4-0 S/U vs Wazzu as 20.5 point or more favorite since 2008
- 0-3 S/U @ Wazzu as 3 point or less Dog since 1992

N. ARIZONA	22-1 S/U in 1st home game of season since 1999
E. MICHIGAN	7-1 S/U prior to playing Utah since 2013 {7-1 ATS}
UTAH	2-8 S/U prior to playing USC since 2011 {2-8 ATS}
Usc	1-5 S/U after playing Utah since 2015 {0-5-1 ATS}
WASHINGTON	7-2 S/U prior to playing Stanford since 2007
WASHINGTON	7-2 ATS prior to playing Stanford since 2006
Colorado	6-1 ATS after playing Stanford since 2009
OREGON ST	2-11 S/U prior to playing Arizona since 2009
Arizona	12-3 ATS after playing Oregon State since 2004
Arizona	11-2 S/U after playing Oregon State since 2006

ARKANSAS RAZORBACKS — SEC WEST

2021-Arkansas		Opponent	ARK	Opp	S/U	Line	ATS	Total	O/U	
9/4/2021	vs	RICE	38	17	W	-19.5	W	50.0	O	
9/11/2021	vs	TEXAS	40	21	W	6.0	W	56.5	O	
9/18/2021	vs	GEORGIA SOUTHERN	45	10	W	-24.0	W	53.0	O	
9/25/2021	vs	Texas A&M {Arlington, TX}	20	10	W	4.0	W	47.0	U	"Southwest Classic"
10/2/2021	@	Georgia	0	37	L	16.0	L	47.0	U	
10/9/2021	@	Mississippi	51	52	L	4.5	W	66.5	O	
10/16/2021	vs	AUBURN	23	38	L	-4.5	L	54.5	O	
10/23/2021	vs	ARKANSAS-PINE BLUFF	45	3	W	-51.0	L	59.5	U	
11/6/2021	vs	MISSISSIPPI STATE	31	28	W	-4.0	L	54.0	O	
11/13/2021	@	Lsu	16	13	W	-3.0	T	59.5	U	"The Golden Boot"
11/20/2021	@	Alabama	35	42	L	20.5	W	58.0	O	
11/27/2021	vs	MISSOURI	34	17	W	-14.5	W	62.5	U	"Battle Line Trophy"
1/1/2022	vs	Penn State	24	10	W	-3.5	W	51.5	U	Outback Bowl
Coach: Sam Pittman		Season Record >>	402	298	9-4	ATS>>	8-4-1	O/U>>	7-6	

2020-Arkansas		Opponent	ARK	Opp	S/U	Line	ATS	Total	O/U	
9/26/2020	vs	GEORGIA	10	37	L	27.5	W	53.0	U	
10/3/2020	@	Mississippi State	21	14	W	17.0	W	68.5	U	
10/10/2020	@	Auburn	28	30	L	13.5	W	46.0	O	
10/17/2020	vs	MISSISSIPPI	33	20	W	1.5	W	75.0	U	
10/31/2020	@	Texas A&M	31	42	L	14.5	W	54.5	O	"Southwest Classic"
11/7/2020	vs	TENNESSEE	24	13	W	2.5	W	54.5	U	
11/14/2020	@	Florida	35	63	L	17.0	L	62.0	O	
11/21/2020	vs	LSU	24	27	L	1.5	L	65.0	O	"The Golden Boot"
12/5/2020	@	Missouri	48	50	L	2.0	T	55.5	O	"Battle Line Trophy"
12/12/2020	vs	ALABAMA	3	52	L	29.0	L	69.0	U	
Coach: Sam Pittman		Season Record >>	257	348	3-7	ATS>>	6-3-1	O/U>>	4-6	

2019-Arkansas		Opponent	ARK	Opp	S/U	Line	ATS	Total	O/U	
8/31/2019	vs	PORTLAND STATE	20	13	W	-30.0	L	NT	---	
9/7/2019	@	Mississippi	17	31	L	5.5	L	50.5	U	
9/14/2019	vs	COLORADO STATE	55	34	W	-9.5	W	64.0	O	
9/21/2019	vs	SAN JOSE STATE	24	31	L	-20.5	L	61.0	U	
9/28/2019	vs	Texas A&M	27	31	L	23.0	W	60.0	U	"Southwest Classic"
10/12/2019	@	Kentucky	20	24	L	3.0	L	52.0	U	
10/19/2019	vs	AUBURN	10	51	L	20.0	L	55.0	O	
10/26/2019	@	Alabama	7	48	L	31.5	L	56.0	U	
11/2/2019	vs	MISSISSIPPI STATE	24	54	L	7.0	L	59.0	O	
11/9/2019	vs	WESTERN KENTUCKY	19	45	L	PK	L	51.5	O	
11/23/2019	@	Lsu	20	56	L	40.0	W	68.5	O	"The Golden Boot"
11/30/2019	vs	MISSOURI	14	24	L	14.5	W	52.5	U	"Battle Line Trophy"
Coach: Chad Morris		Season Record >>	257	442	2-10	ATS>>	4-8	O/U>>	5-6	

2018-Arkansas		Opponent	ARK	Opp	S/U	Line	ATS	Total	O/U	
9/1/2018	vs	EASTERN ILLINOIS	55	20	W	-35.0	T	NT	---	
9/8/2018	@	Colorado State	27	34	L	-14.0	L	70.5	U	
9/15/2018	vs	NORTH TEXAS	17	44	L	-5.5	L	63.0	U	
9/22/2018	@	Auburn	3	34	L	29.5	L	57.5	U	
9/29/2018	vs	Texas A&M	17	24	L	20.0	W	54.0	U	"Southwest Classic"
10/6/2018	vs	ALABAMA	31	65	L	35.0	W	58.0	O	
10/13/2018	vs	MISSISSIPPI	33	37	L	6.5	W	66.5	O	War Memorial Stadium
10/20/2018	vs	TULSA	23	0	W	-7.5	W	53.0	U	
10/27/2018	vs	VANDERBILT	31	45	L	PK	L	53.0	O	
11/10/2018	vs	LSU	17	24	L	13.0	W	49.5	U	"The Golden Boot"
11/17/2018	@	Mississippi State	6	52	L	22.5	L	48.0	O	
11/24/2018	@	Missouri	0	38	L	24.0	L	59.0	U	"Battle Line Trophy"
Coach: Chad Morris		Season Record >>	260	417	2-10	ATS>>	5-6-1	O/U>>	4-7	

ARKANSAS RAZORBACKS — SEC WEST

STADIUM: Razorback Stadium {72,000} / War Memorial Stadium {54,120} **Location:** Fayetteville, AR **COACH:** Sam Pittman

DATE		Opponent	Ark	Opp	S/U	Line	ATS	Total	O/U	Trends & Angles
9/3/2022	vs	CINCINNATI								14-1 S/U in 1st home game of season since 2007
9/10/2022	vs	SOUTH CAROLINA								9-2 S/U vs South Carolina as favorite since 1995
9/17/2022	vs	MISSOURI STATE								vs Missouri State - Arkansas leads series 7-2
9/24/2022	vs	Texas A&M								1-9 S/U vs Texas A&M since 2012
10/1/2022	vs	ALABAMA								vs Alabama - Alabama leads series 25-7
10/8/2022	@	Mississippi State								3-7 S/U vs Mississippi State since 2012
10/15/2022	@	Byu								1st Meeting
10/29/2022	@	Auburn								0-6 S/U vs Auburn since 2016 {1-5 ATS}
11/5/2022	vs	LIBERTY								1st Meeting
11/12/2022	vs	LSU								Game 1-5 O/U @ home vs LSU since 2010
11/19/2022	vs	MISSISSIPPI								13-1 ATS @ home vs Ole Miss since 1994
11/25/2022	@	Missouri								0-5 S/U @ Missouri since 1906
12/3/2022	vs									SEC Championship
	vs									BOWL GAME

Pointspread Analysis — Non-Conference
- 0-6 S/U vs Non-Conf. as 15.5 point or more Dog since 1987
- 6-0 ATS vs Non-Conf. as 10.5-15 point Dog since 1991
- 15-1 S/U vs Non-conf. as 10.5-15 point favorite since 1983
- 8-0 S/U vs Non-conf. as 15.5-20 point favorite since 1985
- 13-2 S/U vs Non-Conf. as 20.5-25 point favorite since 1987
- 31-1 S/U vs Non-Conf. as 25.5 point or more favorite since 1985

Dog
- 0-14 S/U as 25.5 point or more Dog since 1996
- 0-7 S/U as 20.5-25 point Dog since 1995
- 0-3 S/U @ War Memorial as 15.5-25 point Dog since 1991
- 1-11 S/U as 15.5-20 point Dog since 2009
- 0-8 S/U @ home as 15.5-25 point Dog since 1990
- 1-16 S/U as 10.5-15 point Dog since 2008
- 0-9 S/U @ home as 10.5-15 point Dog since 2001
- 1-8 S/U @ home as 7.5-10 point Dog since 2004
- 1-9 S/U on road as 7.5-10 point Dog since 1997
- 7-0 O/U @ War Memorial as 3.5-7 point Dog since 1987
- 7-1 O/U on road as 3 point or less Dog since 2005
- 1-4 S/U & ATS @ War Memorial as 3 point or less Dog since 1992

Favorite
- 0-5 O/U @ War Memorial as 3.5-7 point favorite since 1999
- 6-1 S/U @ War Memorial as 3.5-7 point favorite since 1998
- 16-1 S/U on road as 3.5-7 point favorite since 1983
- 5-1 S/U @ War Memorial as 7.5-10 point favorite since 1984
- 8-0 ATS @ home as 10.5-15 point favorite since 2009
- 9-3 O/U @ home as 10.5-15 point favorite since 2005
- 32-2 S/U @ War Memorial as 10.5 point or more favorite since 1994
- 7-1 S/U on road as 10.5-15 point favorite since 1985
- 14-0 S/U as 15.5-20 point favorite since 1985
- 70-3 S/U as 15.5 point or more favorite since 1983
- 14-0 S/U on road as 10.5 point or more favorite since 1983
- 20-3 S/U as 20.5-25 point favorite since 1985
- 13-1 S/U as 25.5-30 point favorite since 1983
- 25-0 S/U as 30.5 point or more favorite since 1985

- 1-6 O/U prior to playing Auburn since 2015
- 0-5 O/U prior to playing LSU since 2017

Bowl Games
- 1-5 S/U in Sugar Bowl
- 1-4 S/U & ATS vs Big Ten in Bowl Games since 1999
- 1-11 O/U in Bowl Games since 2002

- 20-4 S/U @ home when ranked since 2007
- 4-23 S/U vs #1 ranked teams all time {12 straight L}
- 1-12 S/U vs #3 ranked teams all time
- 0-6 S/U vs #4 ranked teams since 1994

Pointspread Analysis — Conference
- 0-4 S/U @ Auburn since 2014
- 2-7 S/U vs Missouri since 2008
- vs Missouri - Missouri leads series 9-4
- Game 2-8 O/U vs Missouri since 2003
- 10-3 S/U @ home vs Ole Miss since 1994
- vs Mississippi - Arkansas leads series 36-28-1
- 8-1 ATS vs Mississippi since 2013
- vs Texas A&M - Arkansas leads series 42-33-3
- 4-0 ATS vs Texas A&M since 2018
- vs Auburn - Auburn leads series 19-11-1
- Game 7-1 O/U vs Auburn since 2014
- vs Mississippi State - Arkansas leads series 18-12-1
- vs LSU - LSU leads series 42-23-2
- 0-3 S/U vs South Carolina since 2012 {0-3 ATS}
- 0-14 S/U vs Alabama as 7.5 point or more Dog since 1996
- 1-6 S/U vs Auburn as 15.5 point or more Dog since 1996
- 0-5 S/U vs LSU as 15.5 point or more Dog since 1997
- 0-4 S/U vs Texas A&M as 15.5 point or more Dog since 1990
- 4-0 ATS vs Texas A&M as 15.5 point or more Dog since 1990
- 0-3 S/U vs Mississippi State as 10.5-15 point Dog since 1992
- 3-0 ATS vs Mississippi State as 10.5-15 point Dog since 1992
- 0-3 S/U vs Auburn as 7.5-10 point Dog since 2000
- 0-4 S/U vs LSU as 7.5-10 point Dog since 1996
- 0-3 S/U vs Georgia as 3.5-7 point Dog since 1987
- 3-0 ATS vs LSU as 3.5-7 point Dog since 2008
- 1-3 S/U & ATS vs Texas A&M as 3.5-7 point Dog since 1987
- 3-0 O/U vs Alabama as 3 point or less Dog since 1998
- 3-0 O/U vs Texas A&M as 3 point or less Dog since 1989
- 3-0 S/U vs LSU as 3.5-7 point favorite since 1998
- 6-1 S/U & ATS vs Ole Miss as 3.5-7 point favorite since 1985
- 3-0 S/U & ATS vs South Carolina as 3.5-7 point favorite since 2007
- 7-0 S/U vs Mississippi as 7.5-10 point favorite since 1986
- 4-0 ATS vs Mississippi as 7.5-10 point favorite since 1998
- 7-0 S/U vs Mississippi State as 10.5-15 point favorite since 1995

CINCINNATI	7-1 S/U prior to playing South Carolina since 2006
MISSOURI ST.	6-0 O/U after playing South Carolina since 2008
Byu	2-7 S/U prior to playing Auburn since 2012
LIBERTY	0-5 ATS prior to playing LSU since 2017
LSU	1-5 S/U prior to playing Ole Miss since 2016
MISSISSIPPI	0-5 S/U prior to playing Missouri since 2017
MISSISSIPPI	0-5 S/U after playing LSU since 2017
Missouri	5-1 O/U after playing Ole Miss since 2016

- 4-0 S/U @ home when ranked vs Mississippi since 1998
- 0-14 S/U vs ranked Alabama since 2005
- 0-5 S/U @ ranked Auburn since 2010 {1-4 ATS}
- 0-6 S/U vs ranked Texas A&M since 2013

ARKANSAS STATE RED WOLVES   SUN BELT West

2021-Arkansas State		Opponent	ASU	Opp	S/U	Line	ATS	Total	O/U	
9/4/2021	vs	CENTRAL ARKANSAS	40	21	W	-13.0	W	64.0	U	
9/11/2021	vs	MEMPHIS	50	55	L	5.0	T	64.5	O	"Paint Bucket Bowl"
9/18/2021	@	Washington	3	52	L	17.5	L	58.5	U	
9/25/2021	@	Tulsa	34	41	L	14.5	W	64.5	U	
10/2/2021	@	Georgia Southern	33	59	L	1.5	L	66.5	O	
10/7/2021	vs	COASTAL CAROLINA	20	52	L	20.0	L	74.5	U	
10/21/2021	vs	LOUISIANA	27	28	L	18.0	W	70.0	U	
10/30/2021	@	South Alabama	13	31	L	9.0	L	67.0	U	
11/6/2021	vs	APPALACHIAN STATE	14	48	L	21.5	L	67.5	U	
11/13/2021	@	Louisiana-Monroe	27	24	W	3.0	W	66.5	U	"Trail of Tears Classic"
11/20/2021	@	Georgia State	20	28	L	15.5	W	65.5	U	
11/27/2021	vs	TEXAS STATE	22	24	L	-2.0	L	62.0	U	
Coach: Butch Jones		Season Record >>	303	463	2-10	ATS>>	5-6-1	O/U>>	3-9	

2020-Arkansas State		Opponent	ASU	Opp	S/U	Line	ATS	Total	O/U	
9/5/2020	@	Memphis	24	37	L	18.5	W	72.5	U	"Paint Bucket Bowl"
9/12/2020	@	Kansas State	35	31	W	10.5	W	54.0	O	
10/3/2020	@	Coastal Carolina	23	52	L	-3.5	L	64.5	O	
10/10/2020	vs	CENTRAL ARKANSAS	50	27	W	-15.5	W	55.5	O	
10/15/2020	vs	GEORGIA STATE	59	52	W	-3.5	W	73.0	O	
10/24/2020	@	Appalachian State	17	45	L	13.5	L	69.0	U	
10/31/2020	vs	TROY	10	38	L	-3.5	L	70.0	U	
11/7/2020	@	Louisiana	20	27	L	14.5	W	68.5	U	
11/21/2020	@	Texas State	45	47	L	-4.5	L	69.0	O	
11/28/2020	vs	SOUTH ALABAMA	31	38	L	-7.0	L	63.5	O	
12/4/2020	vs	LOUISIANA-MONROE	48	15	W	-20.0	W	71.0	U	"Trail of Tears Classic"
Coach: Blake Anderson		Season Record >>	362	409	4-7	ATS>>	6-5	O/U>>	6-5	

2019-Arkansas State		Opponent	ASU	Opp	S/U	Line	ATS	Total	O/U	
8/31/2019	vs	SMU	30	37	L	-2.5	L	56.0	O	
9/7/2019	@	Unlv	43	17	W	PK	W	64.0	U	
9/14/2019	@	Georgia	0	55	L	32.5	L	58.0	U	
9/21/2019	vs	SOUTHERN ILLINOIS	41	28	W	-21.5	L	NT	---	
9/28/2019	@	Troy	50	43	W	7.0	W	59.5	O	
10/5/2019	@	Georgia State	38	52	L	-6.0	L	69.0	O	
10/17/2019	vs	LOUISIANA-LAFAYETTE	20	37	L	-6.0	L	68.5	U	
10/26/2019	vs	TEXAS STATE	38	14	W	-11.0	W	60.5	U	
11/2/2019	@	Louisiana-Monroe	48	41	W	1.0	W	69.5	O	"Trail of Tears Classic"
11/16/2019	vs	COASTAL CAROLINA	28	27	W	-13.5	L	60.0	U	
11/23/2019	vs	GEORGIA SOUTHERN	38	33	W	PK	W	52.5	O	
11/30/2019	@	South Alabama	30	34	L	-10.0	L	53.0	O	
12/21/2019	vs	Florida International	34	26	W	1.0	W	58.5	U	Camelia Bowl
Coach: Blake Anderson		Season Record >>	438	444	8-5	ATS>>	6-7	O/U>>	6-6	

2018-Arkansas State		Opponent	ASU	Opp	S/U	Line	ATS	Total	O/U	
9/1/2018	vs	SOUTHEAST MISSOURI	48	21	W	-31.0	L	NT	---	
9/8/2018	@	Alabama	7	57	L	36.5	L	63.0	O	-
9/15/2018	@	Tulsa	29	20	W	1.5	W	71.5	U	
9/22/2018	vs	UNLV	27	20	W	-8.0	L	66.5	U	
9/29/2018	@	Georgia Southern	21	28	L	-3.0	L	53.5	U	
10/9/2018	vs	APPALACHIAN STATE	9	35	L	10.5	L	58.5	U	
10/18/2018	vs	GEORGIA STATE	51	35	W	-13.0	W	56.5	O	
10/27/2018	@	Louisiana-Lafayette	43	47	L	-3.0	L	70.0	O	
11/3/2018	vs	SOUTH ALABAMA	38	14	W	-14.0	W	61.5	U	
11/10/2018	@	Coastal Carolina	44	16	W	-7.0	W	62.0	U	
11/17/2018	vs	LOUISIANA-MONROE	31	17	W	-8.0	W	68.0	U	"Trail of Tears Classic"
11/24/2018	@	Texas State	33	7	W	-13.0	W	48.5	U	
12/29/2018	vs	Nevada	13	16	L	PK	L	57.0	U	Arizona Bowl
Coach: Blake Anderson		Season Record >>	394	333	8-5	ATS>>	6-7	O/U>>	3-9	

ARKANSAS STATE RED WOLVES SUN BELT West

STADIUM: Liberty Bank Stadium {30,406}   **Location:** Jonesboro, AR   **COACH:** Butch Jones

DATE		Opponent	State	Opp	S/U	Line	ATS	Total	O/U	Trends & Angles
9/3/2022	vs	GRAMBLING STATE								vs Grambling - Ark State leads series 1-0
9/10/2022	@	Ohio State								2-29 S/U in 1st road game of season since 1991
9/17/2022	@	Memphis								1-11 S/U @ Memphis since 1991
9/24/2022	@	Old Dominion								1st Meeting
10/1/2022	vs	LOUISIANA-MONROE								9-0 S/U @ home vs UL-Monroe since 2003
10/8/2022	vs	JAMES MADISON								10-2 ATS after playing UL-Monroe since 2009
10/15/2022	@	Southern Mississippi								0-6 S/U vs Southern Miss since 1978
10/22/2022	@	Louisiana								1-12 S/U @ Louisiana since 1994
10/29/2022	vs	SOUTH ALABAMA								4-1 S/U @ home vs South Alabama since 2012
11/12/2022	vs	MASSACHUSETTS								1st Meeting
11/19/2022	@	Texas State								Game 1-5 O/U vs Texas State since 2016
11/26/2022	vs	TROY								0-3 ATS @ home vs Troy since 2013
12/3/2022	vs									Sun Belt Championship
	vs									BOWL GAME

Pointspread Analysis Non-Conference		Pointspread Analysis Conference
vs Memphis - HOME team 6-1 S/U since 2007		vs Louisiana - Louisiana leads series 28-21-1
0-8 S/U vs Memphis as 15.5 point or more Dog since 1991		2-6 ATS @ Louisiana since 2006
Dog		2-14 S/U vs Louisiana as Dog since 1990
0-60 S/U as 20.5 point or more Dog since 1992		12-0 S/U & ATS vs UL-Monroe since 2010
1-17 S/U on road as 15.5-20 point Dog since 1990		vs UL-Monroe - Arkansas State leads series 29-14
0-8 S/U as 15.5-20 point Dog since 2011		vs South Alabama - Arkansas State leads series 6-4
1-8 O/U as 15.5-20 point Dog since 2008		vs Southern Miss - USM leads series 9-2
4-21 S/U on road as 10.5-15 point Dog since 1993		vs Texas State - Arkansas State leads series 5-2
0-5 S/U @ home as 7.5-10 point Dog since 1995		vs Troy - Arkansas State leads series 11-8
2-7-1 O/U @ home as 3.5-7 point Dog since 2002		3-0 S/U & ATS vs UL-Monroe as 3.5-7 point Dog since 1998
Favorite		8-0 S/U vs UL-Monroe as 7.5 point or more favorite since 2003
4-12 O/U as 3 point or less favorite since 2007		3-0 S/U vs UL-Monroe as 3.5-7 point favorite since 2006
0-5 S/U & ATS as 3 point or less favorite since 2014		5-1 S/U vs Louisiana as 7.5 point or more favorite since 1999
12-4 S/U @ home as 3.5-7 point favorite since 2004		6-0 S/U vs North Texas as 7.5 point or more favorite since 2000
14-1 S/U as 7.5-10 point favorite since 2000		6-0 S/U vs Texas State as 7.5 point or more favorite since 2013
16-2 S/U as 10.5-15 point favorite since 2011 {13-5 ATS}		
10-1 S/U on road as 10.5 point or more favorite since 1999		
24-1 S/U @ home as 15.5 point or more favorite since 2007		
8-0 O/U as 20.5-25 point favorite since 2012		
9-3 S/U after playing UL-Monroe since 2009	JMU	
7-2 S/U after playing South Alabama since 2012	U MASS	1-23 S/U vs ranked teams since 1994

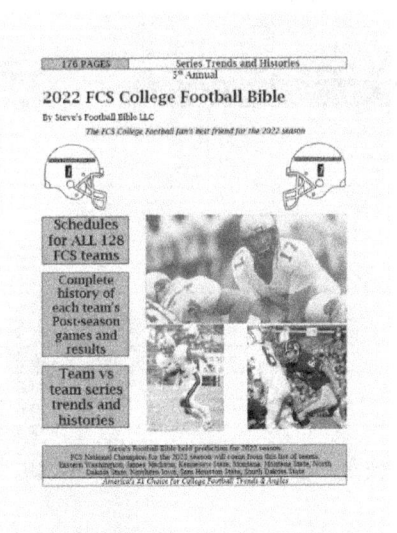

2022 FCS College Football Bible $19.95

ARMY BLACK KNIGHTS   INDEPENDENT

2021-Army		Opponent	Army	Opp	S/U	Line	ATS	Total	O/U	
9/4/2021	@	Georgia State	43	10	W	2.5	W	48.5	O	
9/11/2021	vs	WESTERN KENTUCKY	38	35	W	-6.0	L	52.0	O	
9/18/2021	vs	CONNECTICUT	52	21	W	-34.5	L	48.0	O	
9/25/2021	vs	MIAMI-OHIO	23	10	W	-8.0	W	48.5	U	
10/2/2021	@	Ball State	16	28	L	-10.5	L	47.5	U	
10/16/2021	@	Wisconsin	14	20	L	14.0	L	37.0	U	
10/23/2021	vs	WAKE FOREST	56	70	L	3.0	L	54.0	O	
11/6/2021	vs	Air Force {@ *Arlington, TX*}	21	14	W	2.5	W	37.5	U	{OT}
11/13/2021	vs	BUCKNELL	63	10	W	-50.0	W	58.5	O	
11/20/2021	vs	MASSACHUSETTS	33	17	W	-37.5	L	56.5	U	
11/27/2021	@	Liberty	31	16	W	3.0	W	52.0	U	
12/11/2021	vs	Navy	13	17	L	-7.0	L	36.0	U	"Thompson Cup"
12/22/2021	vs	**Missouri**	24	22	W	-7.0	L	54.0	U	Armed Forces Bowl
Coach: Jeff Monken		Season Record >>	427	290	9-4	ATS>>	6-7	O/U>>	6-7	
2020-Army		Opponent	Army	Opp	S/U	Line	ATS	Total	O/U	
9/5/2020	vs	MIDDLE TENNESSEE	42	0	W	-3.5	W	54.0	U	
9/12/2020	vs	LOUISIANA-MONROE	37	7	W	-22.5	W	53.5	U	
9/26/2020	@	Cincinnati	10	24	L	12.0	L	44.5	U	
10/3/2020	vs	ABILENE CHRISTIAN	55	23	W	-31.0	W	49.0	O	
10/10/2020	vs	THE CITADEL	14	9	W	-30.0	L	45.5	U	
10/17/2020	@	Texas-San Antonio	28	16	W	-7.5	W	49.0	U	
10/24/2020	vs	MERCER	49	3	W	-30.0	W	47.5	O	
11/14/2020	@	Tulane	12	38	L	3.0	L	46.5	O	
11/21/2020	vs	GEORGIA SOUTHERN	28	27	W	-3.5	L	38.5	O	
12/12/2020	vs	NAVY	15	0	W	-7.0	W	35.5	U	"Thompson Cup"
12/19/2020	vs	AIR FORCE	10	7	W	2.0	W	37.5	U	
12/26/2020	vs	**West Virginia**	21	24	L	9.0	W	41.0	O	Liberty Bowl
Coach: Jeff Monken		Season Record >>	321	178	9-3	ATS>>	8-4	O/U>>	5-7	
2019-Army		Opponent	Army	Opp	S/U	Line	ATS	Total	O/U	
8/30/2019	vs	RICE	14	7	W	-23.0	L	47.5	U	
9/7/2019	@	Michigan	21	24	L	22.0	W	47.5	U	{2 OT}
9/14/2019	@	Texas-San Antonio	31	13	W	-14.5	W	49.0	U	
9/21/2019	vs	MORGAN STATE	52	21	W	-44.0	L	NT	---	
10/5/2019	vs	TULANE	33	42	L	2.5	L	42.5	O	
10/12/2019	@	Western Kentucky	8	17	L	-5.0	L	43.5	U	
10/19/2019	@	Georgia State	21	28	L	-4.0	L	54.0	U	
10/26/2019	vs	SAN JOSE STATE	29	34	L	-9.5	L	54.0	O	
11/2/2019	@	Air Force	13	17	L	16.5	W	44.5	U	
11/9/2019	vs	MASSACHUSETTS	63	7	W	-34.5	W	61.0	O	
11/16/2019	vs	VIRGINIA MILITARY	47	6	W	NL	---	NT	---	
11/30/2019	@	Hawaii	31	52	L	2.0	L	55.0	O	
12/14/2019	vs	Navy	7	31	L	11.5	L	41.5	U	"Thompson Cup"
Coach: Jeff Monken		Season Record >>	370	299	5-8	ATS>>	4-8	O/U>>	4-7	
2018-Army		Opponent	Army	Opp	S/U	Line	ATS	Total	O/U	
8/31/2018	@	Duke	14	34	L	13.5	L	45.5	O	
9/8/2018	vs	LIBERTY	38	14	W	-7.5	W	59.5	U	
9/15/2018	vs	HAWAII	28	21	W	-7.0	T	62.0	U	
9/22/2018	@	Oklahoma	21	28	L	28.5	W	60.5	U	{OT}
9/29/2018	@	Buffalo	42	13	W	7.0	W	54.5	O	
10/13/2018	@	San Jose State	52	3	W	-17.0	W	57.5	U	
10/20/2018	vs	MIAMI-OHIO	31	30	W	-6.5	L	47.0	O	{2 OT}
10/27/2018	@	Eastern Michigan	37	22	W	-1.5	W	47.5	O	
11/3/2018	vs	AIR FORCE	17	14	W	-4.5	L	41.5	U	
11/10/2018	vs	LAFAYETTE	31	13	W	-46.0	L	NT	---	
11/17/2018	vs	COLGATE	28	14	W	-10.5	W	NT	---	
12/8/2018	vs	Navy	17	10	W	-9.0	L	38.5	U	"Thompson Cup"
12/22/2018	vs	**Houston**	70	14	W	-6.5	W	56.0	O	Armed Forces Bowl
Coach: Jeff Monken		Season Record >>	426	230	11-2	ATS>>	7-5-1	O/U>>	5-6	

Page | 20   *Copyright © 2022 by Steve's Football Bible, LLC*

ARMY BLACK KNIGHTS   INDEPENDENT

STADIUM: Blake Field @ Michie Stadium {38,000} **Location:** West Point, NY **COACH:** Jeff Monken

DATE		Opponent	Army	Opp	S/U	Line	ATS	Total	O/U	Trends & Angles
9/3/2022	@	Coastal Carolina								1st Meeting
9/10/2022	vs	TEXAS-SAN ANTONIO								vs UTSA - Army leads series 1-0
9/17/2022	vs	VILLANOVA								vs Villanova - Army leads series 18-3
10/1/2022	vs	GEORGIA STATE								vs Georgia State - GA State leads series 2-0
10/8/2022	@	Wake Forest								1-10 S/U vs Wake Forest since 1990
10/15/2022	vs	COLGATE								6-0 S/U @ home vs Colgate since 1989
10/22/2022	vs	LOUISIANA-MONROE								vs UL-Monroe - Army leads series 1-0
11/5/2022	vs	Air Force {@ Arlington, TX}								vs Air Force - Air Force leads series 37-18-1
11/12/2022	@	Troy								1st Meeting
11/19/2022	vs	CONNECTICUT								vs Connecticut - U Conn leads series 5-3
11/26/2022	@	Massachusetts								vs U Mass - Army leads series 4-0
12/10/2022	vs	Navy {@ Philadelphia}								Game 0-16 O/U vs Navy since 2006
	vs									BOWL GAME

Pointspread Analysis		Pointspread Analysis
Dog		**Non-Conference**
0-39 S/U as 20.5 point or more Dog since 1983		Game 1-4 O/U vs Wake Forest since 2013
10-3-3 ATS on road as 20.5-25 point Dog since 1983		0-3 S/U vs Wake Forest as 3.5-7 point Dog since 1994
4-33-1 S/U as 15.5-20 point Dog since 1984		vs Colgate - Army leads series 23-5-2
2-10 O/U on road as 15.5-20 point Dog since 2002		0-3 S/U & ATS vs Air Force as 3 point or less favorite since 1990
0-11 S/U @ home as 15.5-20 point Dog since 1994		0-7 S/U vs Air Force as 15.5-20 point Dog since 1999
1-18 S/U as 10.5-15 point Dog since 2006		1-7 S/U vs Air Force as 10.5-15 point Dog since 1985
4-15 ATS as 10.5-15 point Dog since 2006		0-5 S/U & ATS vs Air Force as 7.5-10 point Dog since 1989
2-11 S//U @ home as 10.5-15 point Dog since 1986		Game 3-0 O/U @ home vs Connecticut since 2003
4-13-1 O/U as 7.5-10 point Dog since 2002		vs Navy - Navy leads series 62-52-7
5-23 S/U as 7.5-10 point Dog since 1993		1-3 S/U vs Navy at East Rutherford since 1989
2-10 S/U @ home as 7.5-10 point Dog since 1993		1-3 ATS vs Navy at East Rutherford since 1989
14-1-1 ATS as 3.5-7 point Dog since 2012		vs Navy - 3-13 S/U @ Lincoln Financial since 2003
4-18 S/U on road as 3.5-7 point Dog since 1984		vs Navy - 1-13-1 O/U @ Lincoln Financial since 2004
1-11 S/U @ home as 3 point or less Dog since 2005		0-7 S/U vs Navy as 10.5-15 point Dog since 1997
2-10 ATS @ home as 3 point or less Dog since 2005		1-5 S/U vs Navy as 3.5-7 point Dog since 1999
Favorite		3-0 ATS vs Navy as 3.5-7 point Dog since 2011
10-20 ATS as road favorite since 1986		0-3 O/U vs Navy as 3.5-7 point Dog since 2011
24-2 S/U @ home as 3.5-7 point favorite since 1988		5-1 S/U vs Navy as 3 point or less favorite since 1984
1-7 S/U & ATS on road as 3.5-7 point favorite since 1997		5-1 S/U vs Navy as 3.5-7 point favorite since 1987
9-2 S/U as 7.5-10 point favorite since 1999		0-4 ATS vs Navy as 7.5-10 point favorite since 1988
5-0 S/U on road as 15.5 point or more favorite since 1985		0-4 O/U vs Navy as 7.5-10 point favorite since 1988
23-0 S/U as 20.5 point or more favorite since 1985		
Bowl Games		
5-1 S/U in Bowl Games since 2010		
8-2 ATS in Bowl Games since 1984		
7-2 O/U in Bowl Games since 1985	Massachusetts	5-24 S/U prior to playing Navy since 1992
13-1 S/U @ home when ranked since 1956	COLGATE	0-6 S/U prior to playing Wake Forest since 2012
0-49 S/U vs ranked teams since 1973	UL-MONROE	1-6 S/U after playing Colgate since 1987
0-34 S/U on road vs ranked teams since 1963	UL-MONROE	1-7 ATS after playing Colgate since 1985

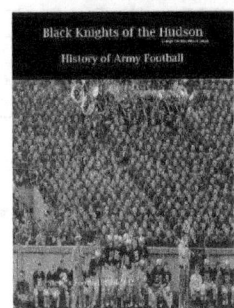

Black Knights of the Hudson – History of Army Football

Available at: www.stevesfootballbible.com (Patriot Series)

Military Police Insignia

25th Infantry Division – Tropic Lightning

AUBURN TIGERS — SEC WEST

2021-Auburn		Opponent	AUB	Opp	S/U	Line	ATS	Total	O/U	
9/4/2021	vs	AKRON	60	10	W	-37.5	W	56.0	O	
9/11/2021	vs	ALABAMA STATE	62	0	W	-49.5	W	60.0	O	
9/18/2021	@	Penn State	20	28	L	4.0	L	52.0	U	
9/25/2021	vs	GEORGIA STATE	34	24	W	-27.5	L	57.5	O	
10/2/2021	@	Lsu	24	19	W	3.0	W	56.0	U	
10/9/2021	vs	GEORGIA	10	34	L	14.5	L	45.5	U	"Deep South's Oldest Rivalry"
10/16/2021	@	Arkansas	38	23	W	4.5	W	54.5	O	
10/30/2021	vs	MISSISSIPPI	31	20	W	-3.0	W	67.5	U	
11/6/2021	@	Texas A&M	3	20	L	4.0	L	49.0	U	
11/13/2021	vs	MISSISSIPPI STATE	34	43	L	-6.0	L	51.0	O	
11/20/2021	@	South Carolina	17	21	L	-7.0	L	45.5	U	
11/27/2021	vs	ALABAMA	22	24	L	20.5	W	57.0	U	"Iron Bowl"
12/28/2021	vs	Houston	13	17	L	2.0	L	49.0	U	Birmingham Bowl
Coach: Brian Harsin		Season Record >>	368	283	6-7	ATS>>	6-7	O/U>>	5-8	

2020-Auburn		Opponent	AUB	Opp	S/U	Line	ATS	Total	O/U	
9/26/2020	vs	KENTUCKY	29	13	W	-6.5	W	48.0	U	
10/3/2020	@	Georgia	6	27	L	7.5	L	44.5	U	"Deep South's Oldest Rivalry"
10/10/2020	vs	ARKANSAS	30	28	W	-13.5	L	46.0	O	
10/17/2020	@	South Carolina	22	30	L	-3.0	L	51.5	O	
10/24/2020	@	Mississippi	35	28	W	-3.5	W	73.5	U	
10/31/2020	vs	LSU	48	11	W	PK	W	63.5	U	
11/21/2020	vs	TENNESSEE	30	17	W	-10.0	W	51.0	U	
11/28/2020	@	Alabama	13	42	L	24.5	L	65.0	U	"Iron Bowl"
12/5/2020	vs	TEXAS A&M	20	31	L	5.0	L	49.0	U	
12/12/2020	@	Mississippi State	24	10	W	-5.5	W	50.5	U	
1/1/2021	vs	Northwestern	19	35	L	3.5	L	45.0	O	Citrus Bowl
Coach: Guz Malzhan		Season Record >>	276	272	6-5	ATS>>	5-6	O/U>>	4-7	

2019-Auburn		Opponent	AUB	Opp	S/U	Line	ATS	Total	O/U	
8/31/2019	vs	Oregon	27	21	W	-3.5	W	55.5	U	AT&T Stadium
9/7/2019	vs	TULANE	24	6	W	-16.0	W	51.0	U	
9/14/2019	vs	KENT STATE	55	16	W	-36.0	W	53.5	O	
9/21/2019	@	Texas A&M	28	20	W	4.0	W	48.0	T	
9/28/2019	vs	MISSISSIPPI STATE	56	23	W	-8.0	W	46.5	O	
10/5/2019	@	Florida	14	23	L	-2.5	L	48.5	U	
10/19/2019	@	Arkansas	51	10	W	-20.0	W	55.0	O	
10/26/2019	@	Lsu	20	23	L	11.5	W	59.5	U	
11/2/2019	vs	MISSISSIPPI	20	14	W	-17.5	L	53.5	U	
11/16/2019	vs	GEORGIA	14	21	L	3.0	L	43.0	U	"Deep South's Oldest Rivalry"
11/23/2019	vs	SAMFORD	52	0	W	-45.5	W	NT	----	
11/30/2019	vs	ALABAMA	48	45	W	3.5	W	51.0	O	Iron Bowl
1/1/2020	vs	Minnesota	24	31	L	-7.0	L	53.5	O	Outback Bowl
Coach: Guz Malzhan		Season Record >>	433	253	9-4	ATS>>	9-4	O/U>>	5-6-1	

2018-Auburn		Opponent	AUB	Opp	S/U	Line	ATS	Total	O/U	
9/1/2018	vs	Washington	21	16	W	-1.5	W	50.5	U	Mercedes Benz Stadium
9/8/2018	vs	Alabama State	63	9	W	-62.5	L	NT	----	
9/15/2018	vs	LSU	21	22	L	-10.0	L	45.0	U	
9/22/2018	vs	ARKANSAS	34	3	W	-29.5	W	57.5	U	
9/29/2018	vs	SOUTHERN MISS	24	13	W	-27.0	L	50.0	U	
10/6/2018	@	Mississippi State	9	23	L	-3.0	L	45.0	U	
10/13/2018	vs	TENNESSEE	24	30	L	-14.5	L	47.0	O	
10/20/2018	@	Mississippi	31	16	W	-5.0	W	63.5	U	
11/3/2018	vs	TEXAS A&M	28	24	W	-3.5	W	47.5	O	
11/10/2018	@	Georgia	10	27	L	13.5	L	52.5	U	"Deep South's Oldest Rivalry"
11/17/2018	vs	LIBERTY	53	0	W	-28.5	W	64.5	U	
11/24/2018	@	Alabama	21	52	L	27.0	L	52.5	O	Iron Bowl
12/28/2018	vs	Purdue	63	14	W	-3.5	W	58.0	O	Music City Bowl
Coach: Guz Malzhan		Season Record >>	402	249	8-5	ATS>>	6-7	O/U>>	4-8	

- 0-6 S/U vs ranked teams in Bowl Games since 2014
- 0-5 S/U @ ranked Georgia since 2007
- 5-16 S/U on road when ranked vs ranked teams since 2007
- 43-4 S/U @ home when ranked since 2009
- 17-4 S/U @ home when ranked vs ranked teams since 2004
- 6-0 S/U @ home when ranked vs Arkansas since 2010

AUBURN TIGERS — SEC WEST

STADIUM: Jordan-Hare Stadium {87,451} **Location:** Auburn, AL **COACH:** Brian Harsin

DATE		Opponent	Aub	Opp	S/U	Line	ATS	Total	O/U	Trends & Angles
9/3/2022	vs	MERCER								vs Mercer - Auburn leads series 12-0
9/10/2022	vs	SAN JOSE STATE								vs San Jose State - Auburn leads series 2-0
9/17/2022	vs	PENN STATE								vs Penn State - Penn State leads series 2-1
9/24/2022	vs	MISSOURI								vs Missouri - Auburn leads series 2-1
10/1/2022	vs	LSU								5-1 ATS @ home vs LSU since 2010
10/8/2022	@	Georgia								0-7 S/U & ATS @ Georgia since 2007
10/15/2022	@	Mississippi								12-2 S/U @ Mississippi since 1994 {10-4 ATS}
10/29/2022	vs	ARKANSAS								vs Arkansas - Arkansas leads series 17-13-1
11/5/2022	@	Mississippi State								Game 0-8 O/U @ Mississippi State since 2006
11/12/2022	vs	TEXAS A&M								vs Texas A&M - Texas A&M leads series 7-5
11/19/2022	vs	WESTERN KENTUCKY								vs Western Kentucky - Auburn leads series 2-0
11/26/2022	@	Alabama								vs Alabama - Alabama leads series 48-37-1
12/3/2022	vs									SEC Championship
	vs									BOWL GAME

Pointspread Analysis — Non-Conference
- 0-5 S/U vs Non-Conf. as 7.5-10 point Dog since 1989
- 1-7 S/U & ATS vs Non-Conf. as 3 point or less Dog since 1996
- 6-0 S/U & ATS vs Non-Conf. as 3 point or less favorite since 2003
- 10-1 S/U vs Non-Conf. as 7.5-10 point favorite since 1983
- 0-6 ATS vs Non-Conf. as 7.5-10 point favorite since 1990
- 15-2 S/U vs Non-Conf. as 10.5-15 point favorite since 1992
- 60-0 S/U vs Non-Conf. as 15.5 point or more favorite since 1984

Bowl Games
- 4-0 S/U vs PAC-12 teams in Bowl Games
- 6-12 O/U in Bowl Games since 2001
- 5-0 S/U & ATS in Bowl Games as 3 point or less favorite since 2003

Dog
- 0-6 S/U on road as 20.5 point or more Dog since 1996
- 0-3 S/U @ home as 15.5-20 point Dog since 1999
- 1-7 O/U on road as 10.5-15 point Dog since 1992
- 0-6 S/U @ home as 7.5-10 point Dog since 1991
- 5-0-1 ATS @ home as 7.5-10 point Dog since 1992
- 0-15 S/U as 7.5-10 point Dog since 2000
- 5-1 S/U & ATS @ home as 3.5-7 point Dog since 2002
- 5-14 S/U on road as 3.5-7 point Dog since 2003
- 2-13 O/U as 3 point or less Dog since 2009

Favorite
- 13-6 S/U as 3 point or less favorite since 2002
- 1-6 O/U as 3 point or less favorite since 2015
- 10-2 S/U @ home as 3.5-7 point favorite since 2007
- 32-6-1 S/U as 7.5-10 point favorite since 1983
- 15-3-1 S/U @ home as 7.5-10 point favorite since 1983
- 12-0 S/U on road as 10.5-15 point favorite since 1983
- 24-4-1 S/U @ home as 10.5-15 point favorite since 1992
- 12-0 S/U on road as 10.5-15 point favorite since 1983
- 23-5-1 S/U @ home as 10.5-15 point favorite since 1992
- 22-0 S/U on road as 10.5 point or more favorite since 1983
- 22-2 S/U @ home as 15.5-20 point favorite since 1983
- 96-3 S/U @ home as 15.5 point or more favorite since 1983
- 7-3 ATS @ home as 25.5-30 point favorite since 1986
- 3-7 ATS as 30.5-40 point favorite since 2014
- 0-7 S/U on road vs #1 ranked teams since 1996
- 0-12 S/U vs #3 ranked teams all time
- 20-0 S/U when ranked vs Mississippi all time

Pointspread Analysis — Conference
- Game 6-2 O/U vs South Carolina since 2005
- vs Texas A&M - ROAD team 8-2 S/U since 2012 {7-2-1 ATS}
- vs Mississippi - Auburn leads series 34-10
- 9-2-1 ATS vs Mississippi since 2009
- 3-14 S/U vs Georgia since 2006 {4-13 ATS}
- Game 1-8 O/U vs Georgia since 2014
- vs Georgia - Georgia leads series 62-54-8
- Game 0-6 O/U @ Georgia since 2009
- 26-6 S/U vs Mississippi State as favorite since 1983
- vs Mississippi State - Auburn leads series 62-30-3
- Game 3-7 O/U vs Mississippi State since 2012
- vs LSU - LSU leads series 31-24-1
- Game 0-6 O/U @ home vs LSU since 2010
- Game 0-8 O/U @ Mississippi State since 2006
- 0-6 S/U vs Alabama as 20.5 point or more Dog since 2011
- 1-6 S/U & ATS vs Georgia as 3 point or less Dog since 2002
- 3-0 S/U & ATS vs Ole Miss as 3 point or less Dog since 1998
- 3-0 S/U & ATS vs Georgia as 3 point or less favorite since 1983
- 3-0 S/U vs LSU as 3 point or less favorite since 1992
- 4-0 S/U vs Alabama as 3.5-7 point favorite since 1987
- 3-0 S/U & ATS vs Georgia as 3.5-7 point favorite since 1984
- 5-1 S/U vs Mississippi State as 3.5-7 point favorite since 1993
- 6-0 S/U & ATS vs Ole Miss as 3.5-7 point favorite since 2001
- 3-0 S/U vs Arkansas as 7.5-10 point favorite since 2000
- 6-1 S/U vs Mississippi State as 10.5-15 point favorite since 1984
- 5-0 S/U vs Mississippi as 10.5-15 point favorite since 1985
- 4-1 S/U vs Arkansas as 15.5-20 point favorite since 1996
- 4-1 S/U vs Mississippi State as 15.5-20 point favorite since 1983
- 1-4 ATS vs Mississippi State as 15.5-20 point favorite since 1983
- 5-0 S/U vs Mississippi as 15.5-20 point favorite since 1995
- 3-0 S/U vs Mississippi as 20.5-25 point favorite since 1997
- 3-0 S/U & ATS vs Mississippi State as 20.5-25 point favorite since 1987

MERCER	14-1 S/U in 1st home game of season since 2006
MISSOURI	16-2 S/U prior to playing LSU since 2003
MISSOURI	1-7-1 ATS prior to playing LSU since 2012
LSU	11-1 S/U prior to playing Georgia since 2009
Georgia	8-0 O/U prior to playing Mississippi since 2013
Mississippi	3-10-1 O/U after playing Georgia since 2006
Mississippi State	8-1-1 ATS prior to Texas A&M since 2012

War Eagle! History of Auburn Tigers Football

Available at: www.stevesfootballbible.com (Blueblood Series)

BALL STATE CARDINALS   MAC WEST

2021-Ball State		Opponent	Ball	Opp	S/U	Line	ATS	Total	O/U	
9/2/2021	vs	WESTERN ILLINOIS	31	21	W	-30.5	L	58.0	U	
9/11/2021	@	Penn State	13	44	L	22.5	L	58.0	U	
9/18/2021	@	Wyoming	12	45	L	6.5	L	53.5	O	
9/25/2021	vs	TOLEDO	12	22	L	4.5	L	56.5	U	
10/2/2021	vs	ARMY	28	10	W	10.5	W	47.5	U	
10/9/2021	@	Western Michigan	45	20	W	13.0	W	57.5	O	
10/16/2021	@	Eastern Michigan	38	31	W	-1.5	W	54.5	O	
10/23/2021	vs	MIAMI-OHIO	17	24	L	-3.5	L	53.0	U	
11/2/2021	@	Akron	31	25	W	-20.0	L	58.0	U	
11/10/2021	@	Northern Illinois	29	30	L	-2.5	L	59.5	U	"Bronze Stalk Trophy"
11/17/2021	vs	CENTRAL MICHIGAN	17	37	L	2.5	L	57.0	U	
11/23/2021	vs	BUFFALO	20	3	W	-6.0	W	60.0	U	
12/25/2021	vs	Georgia State	20	51	L	6.5	L	53.0	O	Camelia Bowl
Coach: Mike Neu		Season Record >>	313	363	6-7	ATS>>	4-9	O/U>>	4-9	

2020-Ball State		Opponent	Ball	Opp	S/U	Line	ATS	Total	O/U	
11/4/2020	@	Miami-Ohio	31	38	L	-1.0	L	56.5	O	
11/11/2020	vs	EASTERN MICHIGAN	38	31	W	-8.0	L	61.5	O	
11/18/2020	vs	NOTHERN ILLINOIS	31	25	W	-14.5	L	58.5	U	"Bronze Stalk Trophy"
11/28/2020	@	Toledo	27	24	W	9.5	W	67.0	U	
12/5/2020	@	Central Michigan	45	20	W	-2.5	W	62.5	O	
12/12/2020	vs	WESTERN MICHIGAN	30	27	W	2.0	W	66.0	U	
12/18/2020	@	Buffalo	38	28	W	12.5	W	70.0	U	MAC CHAMPIONSHIP
12/31/2020	vs	San Jose State	34	13	W	7.5	W	66.0	U	Arizona Bowl
Coach: Mike Neu		Season Record >>	274	206	7-1	ATS>>	5-3	O/U>>	3-5	MAC CHAMPIONS

2019-Ball State		Opponent	Ball	Opp	S/U	Line	ATS	Total	O/U	
8/31/2019	vs	Indiana	24	34	L	18.0	W	60.5	U	Lucas Oil Stadium
9/7/2019	vs	FORDHAM	57	29	W	-29.5	L	NT	---	
9/14/2019	vs	FLORIDA ATLANTIC	31	41	L	2.5	L	64.5	O	
9/21/2019	@	NC State	23	34	L	19.5	W	58.5	U	
10/5/2019	@	Northern Illinois	27	20	W	4.0	W	54.5	U	"Bronze Stalk Trophy"
10/12/2019	@	Eastern Michigan	29	23	W	2.0	W	57.0	U	
10/19/2019	vs	TOLEDO	52	14	W	-3.0	W	58.0	O	
10/26/2019	vs	OHIO	21	34	L	-2.0	L	59.5	U	
11/5/2019	@	Western Michigan	31	35	L	6.0	W	65.0	O	
11/16/2019	vs	CENTRAL MICHIGAN	44	45	L	-1.0	L	60.0	O	
11/23/2019	@	Kent State	38	41	L	-3.5	L	67.5	O	
11/29/2019	vs	MIAMI-OHIO	41	27	W	-3.0	W	55.5	O	
Coach: Mike Neu		Season Record >>	418	377	5-7	ATS>>	7-5	O/U>>	6-5	

2018-Ball State		Opponent	Ball	Opp	S/U	Line	ATS	Total	O/U	
8/30/2018	vs	CENTRAL CONNECTICUT	42	6	W	-18.5	W	NT	---	
9/8/2018	@	Notre Dame	16	24	L	34.0	W	60.5	U	
9/15/2018	@	Indiana	10	38	L	15.0	L	60.0	U	
9/22/2018	vs	WESTERN KENTUCKY	20	28	L	-3.0	L	54.0	U	
9/29/2018	vs	KENT STATE	52	24	W	-7.0	W	61.5	O	
10/6/2018	vs	NORTHERN ILLINOIS	16	24	L	3.0	L	53.0	U	"Bronze Stalk Trophy"
10/13/2018	@	Central Michigan	24	23	W	2.5	W	54.5	U	
10/20/2018	vs	EASTERN MICHIGAN	20	42	L	3.0	L	44.0	O	
10/25/2018	@	Ohio	14	52	L	10.0	L	65.5	O	
10/31/2018	@	Toledo	13	45	L	20.0	L	63.5	U	
11/13/2018	vs	WESTERN MCIHIGAN	42	41	W	9.5	W	57.5	O	{OT}
11/20/2018	@	Miami-Ohio	21	42	L	14.5	L	55.0	O	
Coach: Mike Neu		Season Record >>	290	389	4-8	ATS>>	5-7	O/U>>	5-6	

BALL STATE CARDINALS — MAC WEST

STADIUM: Scheumann Stadium {22,500} **Location:** Muncie, IN **COACH:** Mike Neu

DATE		Opponent	Ball	Opp	S/U	Line	ATS	Total	O/U	Trends & Angles
9/1/2022	@	*Tennessee*								1-12 S/U in 1st road game of season since 2009
9/10/2022	vs	WESTERN MICHIGAN								7-2 O/U @ home vs Western Mich. since 2004
9/17/2022	vs	*MURRAY STATE*								1st Meeting
9/24/2022	@	*Georgia Southern*								1st Meeting
10/1/2022	vs	NORTHERN ILLINOIS								2-9 S/U @ home vs N. Illinois since 2000
10/8/2022	@	Central Michigan								6-0 ATS @ Central Michigan since 2010
10/15/2022	vs	*CONNECTICUT*								vs Connecticut - Ball State leads series 3-0
10/22/2022	vs	EASTERN MICHIGAN								0-4 ATS @ home vs E. Michigan since 2014
11/1/2022	@	Kent State								vs Kent State - Ball State leads series 21-8
11/8/2022	@	Toledo								7-1 ATS @ Toledo since 2006
11/15/2022	vs	OHIO								vs Ohio - Ball State leads series 15-11
11/22/2022	@	Miami-Ohio								0-3 S/U @ Miami-Ohio since 2016
12/2/2022	vs									MAC Championship
	vs									BOWL GAME

Pointspread Analysis — Non-Conference

- 0-57-1 S/U vs Non-Conference as 10.5 point or more Dog since 1989

Bowl Games
- 1-9-1 S/U in Bowl Games
- 2-7 ATS in Bowl Games since 1989

Dog
- 0-15 S/U as 30.5 point or more Dog since 1993
- 2-11 S/U as 25.5-30 point Dog since 1989
- 1-11 S/U as 20.5-25 point Dog since 1996
- 0-7 S/U @ home as 15.5-20 point Dog since 1998
- 1-33 S/U as 15.5-20 point Dog since 1991
- 10-2 ATS on road as 15.5-20 point Dog since 2009
- 1-11 O/U on road as 15.5-20 point Dog since 2009
- 5-22 S/U on road as 10.5-15 point Dog since 1994
- 8-32 S/U as 10.5-15 point Dog since 1989
- 2-7 S/U @ home as 10.5-15 point Dog since 1998
- 8-22 S/U as 7.5-10 point Dog since 1990
- 3-8 O/U as 3.5-7 point Dog since 2014
- 1-8 S/U @ home as 3.5-7 point Dog since 2005
- 2-12 S/U & ATS @ home as 3 point or less Dog since 1999

Favorite
- 9-4 S/U on road as 3 point or less favorite since 1993
- 11-1 S/U on road as 3.5-7 point favorite since 1990
- 10-1 S/U on road as 7.5-10 point favorite since 1989
- 8-0 S/U on road as 10.5-15 point favorite since 1989
- 4-0 S/U on road as 15.5-20 point favorite since 2008
- 0-4 O/U on road as 15.5-20 point favorite since 2008
- 12-0 S/U as 20.5 point or more favorite since 1993
- 1-8 ATS as 20.5 point or more favorite since 2008

- 3-11 O/U prior to playing Western Michigan since 2008
- 12-0 S/U in 1st home game of season since 2010
- 3-11 O/U prior to playing Central Michigan since 2008
- 1-6 O/U after playing Northern Illinois since 2014
- 3-10 S/U prior to playing Eastern Michigan since 2009
- 12-4 ATS after playing Eastern Michigan since 2006
- 1-5 ATS prior to playing Toledo since 2016
- 7-1 O/U prior to playing Miami-Ohio since 2006

Tennessee
W. MICHIGAN
N. ILLINOIS
Central Michigan
CONNECTICUT
Kent State
Kent State
OHIO

Pointspread Analysis — Conference

- 11-2-1 S/U vs Central Michigan as favorite since 1989
- vs Central Michigan - Ball State leads series 27-26-1
- 6-1 S/U @ Central Michigan since 2008
- vs Eastern Michigan - Ball State leads series 36-24-2
- Game 6-0 O/U @ home vs Eastern Michigan since 2010
- 12-3 S/U vs Kent State as favorite since 1989
- vs Kent State - HOME team 7-0 S/U since 2006
- vs Miami-Ohio - Miami-Ohio leads series 21-13-1
- 2-10 ATS @ home vs Northern Illinois since 1998
- 2-17 S/U vs Northern Illinois as Dog since 1997
- 1-9 ATS vs Northern Illinois since 2012
- 2-11 S/U vs Northern Illinois since 2009
- 8-1 S/U vs Ohio as favorite since 1989
- 1-5 S/U vs Ohio as Dog since 1999
- 2-6 S/U vs Toledo since 2014
- Game 0-5 O/U @ Toledo since 2012
- vs Toledo - Toledo leads series 25-21-1
- vs Western Michigan - Western Michigan leads series 26-22
- 0-3 S/U vs Central Michigan as 3.5-7 point Dog since 2004
- 4-1 S/U & ATS vs C. Michigan as 3 point or less favorite since 1996
- 4-0 S/U vs C. Michigan as 3.5-7 point favorite since 1995
- 0-4 ATS vs C. Michigan as 10 point or more favorite since 1997
- 7-1 S/U vs E. Michigan as 3.5-7 point favorite since 1990
- 10-0 S/U vs Kent State as 7.5 point or more favorite since 1989
- 1-6 S/U vs Miami-Ohio as 7.5 point or more Dog since 1997
- 4-0 S/U vs Miami-Ohio as 8 point or more favorite since 1989
- 1-11 S/U vs Northern Illinois as 7.5 point or more Dog since 1999
- 0-4 S/U vs Northern Illinois as 3 point or less Dog since 2002
- 5-0 S/U vs N. Illinois as 9 point or more favorite since 1997
- 3-0 S/U vs Ohio as 3.5-7 point favorite since 1993
- 5-0 S/U vs Ohio as 7.5 point or more favorite since 1989
- 0-9 S/U @ Toledo as 10.5 point or more Dog since 1995
- 0-8 S/U vs Toledo as 10.5 point or more Dog since 2004
- 0-3 S/U & ATS vs W. Michigan as 3 point or less Dog since 1997
- 3-0 S/U vs W. Michigan as 7.5 point or more favorite since 1996

- 3-13 S/U vs ranked teams since 2005

BAYLOR BEARS — BIG TWELVE

2021-Baylor		Opponent	BAY	Opp	S/U	Line	ATS	Total	O/U	
9/4/2021	@	Texas State	29	20	W	-13.5	L	53.0	U	
9/11/2021	vs	TEXAS SOUTHERN	66	7	W	-44.0	W	53.0	O	
9/18/2021	@	Kansas	45	7	W	-17.0	W	48.5	O	
9/25/2021	vs	IOWA STATE	31	29	W	7.0	W	46.0	O	
10/2/2021	@	Oklahoma State	14	24	L	3.5	L	48.0	U	
10/9/2021	vs	WEST VIRGINIA	45	20	W	-1.5	W	45.5	O	
10/16/2021	vs	BYU	38	24	W	-5.5	W	52.5	O	
10/30/2021	vs	TEXAS	31	24	W	-2.0	W	61.5	U	
11/6/2021	@	Tcu	28	30	L	-7.5	L	57.5	O	
11/13/2021	vs	OKLAHOMA	27	14	W	4.0	W	63.5	U	
11/20/2021	@	Kansas State	20	10	W	2.5	W	49.5	U	
11/27/2021	vs	TEXAS TECH	27	24	W	-14.0	L	52.0	U	
12/4/2021	vs	**Oklahoma State**	21	16	W	7.0	W	45.0	U	Big XII Championship
1/1/2022	vs	**Mississippi**	21	7	W	2.0	W	60.0	U	Sugar Bowl
Coach: Dave Aranda		Season Record >>	443	256	12-2	ATS>>	10-4	O/U>>	6-8	BIG XII CHAMPIONS

2020-Baylor		Opponent	BAY	Opp	S/U	Line	ATS	Total	O/U	
9/26/2020	vs	KANSAS	47	14	W	-17.5	W	62.0	U	
10/3/2020	@	West Virginia	21	27	L	-1.0	L	54.0	U	{OT}
10/24/2020	@	Texas	16	27	L	10.5	L	61.0	U	
10/31/2020	vs	TCU	23	33	L	2.5	L	47.5	O	
11/7/2020	@	Iowa State	31	38	L	14.0	W	46.5	O	
11/14/2020	@	Texas Tech	23	24	L	1.0	T	54.0	U	
11/28/2020	vs	KANSAS STATE	32	31	W	-5.5	L	44.5	O	
12/5/2020	@	Oklahoma	14	27	L	23.5	W	60.5	U	
12/12/2020	vs	OKLAHOMA STATE	3	42	L	6.0	L	49.5	U	
Coach: Dave Aranda		Season Record >>	210	263	2-7	ATS>>	3-5-1	O/U>>	3-6	

2019-Baylor		Opponent	BAY	Opp	S/U	Line	ATS	Total	O/U	
8/31/2019	vs	STEPHEN F. AUSTIN	56	17	W	-43.0	L	NT	---	
9/7/2019	vs	TEXAS-SAN ANTONIO	63	14	W	-25.0	W	58.0	O	
9/21/2019	@	Rice	21	13	W	-27.0	L	57.5	U	
9/28/2019	vs	IOWA STATE	23	21	W	2.5	W	55.5	U	
10/5/2019	@	Kansas State	31	12	W	PK	W	48.0	U	
10/12/2019	vs	TEXAS TECH	33	30	W	-10.5	L	60.0	O	{2 OT}
10/19/2019	@	Oklahoma State	45	27	W	5.5	W	68.5	O	
10/31/2019	vs	WEST VIRGINIA	17	14	W	-17.5	L	56.5	U	
11/9/2019	@	Tcu	29	23	W	-2.0	W	48.5	O	{3 OT}
11/16/2019	vs	OKLAHOMA	31	34	L	10.5	W	68.5	U	
11/23/2019	vs	TEXAS	24	10	W	-4.0	W	57.5	U	
11/30/2019	@	Kansas	61	6	W	-14.0	W	53.5	O	
12/7/2019	vs	**Oklahoma**	23	30	L	9.0	W	66.0	U	Big XII Championship
1/1/2020	vs	**Georgia**	14	26	L	3.5	L	44.0	U	Sugar Bowl
Coach: Matt Rhule		Season Record >>	471	277	11-3	ATS>>	9-5	O/U>>	5-8	

2018-Baylor		Opponent	BAY	Opp	S/U	Line	ATS	Total	O/U	
9/1/2018	vs	ABILENE CHRISTIAN	55	27	W	-40.5	L	NT	---	
9/8/2018	@	Texas-San Antonio	37	20	W	-17.0	T	55.0	O	
9/15/2018	vs	DUKE	27	40	L	-2.5	L	49.0	O	
9/22/2018	vs	KANSAS	27	6	W	-7.5	W	55.0	U	
9/29/2018	@	Oklahoma	33	66	L	21.0	L	68.0	O	
10/6/2018	vs	KANSAS STATE	37	34	W	-3.5	L	52.5	O	
10/13/2018	@	Texas	17	23	L	13.0	W	58.5	U	
10/25/2018	@	West Virginia	14	58	L	15.0	L	67.0	O	
11/3/2018	vs	OKLAHOMA STATE	35	31	W	6.5	W	68.5	U	
11/10/2018	@	Iowa State	14	28	L	17.0	W	51.0	U	
11/17/2018	vs	TCU	9	16	L	-1.0	L	50.0	U	
11/24/2018	vs	Texas Tech	35	24	W	6.5	W	63.5	U	
12/27/2018	vs	**Vanderbilt**	45	38	W	4.5	W	56.5	O	AT&T Stadium / Texas Bowl
Coach: Matt Rhule		Season Record >>	385	411	7-6	ATS>>	6-6-1	O/U>>	6-6	

BAYLOR BEARS — BIG TWELVE

STADIUM: McLane Stadium {45,140} **Location:** Waco, TX **COACH:** Dave Aranda

DATE		Opponent	Bay	Opp	S/U	Line	ATS	Total	O/U	Trends & Angles
9/3/2022	vs	SUNY-ALBANY								1st Meeting
9/10/2022	@	Byu								vs BYU - Baylor leads series 2-1
9/17/2022	vs	TEXAS STATE								vs Texas State - Baylor leads series 8-0
9/24/2022	@	Iowa State								3-8 S/U vs Iowa State as Dog since 2000
10/1/2022	vs	OKLAHOMA STATE								Game 1-6 O/U @ home vs Ok State since 2007
10/15/2022	@	West Virginia								0-5 S/U @ West Virginia since 2012
10/22/2022	vs	KANSAS								10-0 S/U @ home vs Kansas since 1989
10/29/2022	@	Texas Tech								1-10 S/U @ Texas Tech since 1992
11/5/2022	@	Oklahoma								1-14 S/U @ Oklahoma since 1974
11/12/2022	vs	KANSAS STATE								6-1 S/U @ home vs Kansas State since 2006
11/19/2022	vs	TCU								1-8 ATS @ home vs TCU since 1993
11/26/2022	@	Texas								2-13 S/U @ Texas since 1993
12/3/2022	vs									BIG XII Championship
	vs									BOWL GAME

Pointspread Analysis — Non-Conference

- 0-17 S/U vs Non-Conf. as 7.5 point or more Dog since 1989
- 7-0 S/U & ATS vs Non-Conf. as 3 point or less Dog since 1995
- 4-0 S/U vs Non-Conf. as 7.5-10 point favorite since 1995
- 13-1 S/U vs Non-Conf. as 15.5-30 point favorite since 1986
- 13-1 S/U vs Non-Conf. as 30.5 point or more favorite since 2010

Bowl Games
- 4-0 S/U & ATS in Bowl games as 3 point or less Dog since 1985
- 0-4 S/U vs Big Ten in Bowl Games
- 0-3 S/U in Cotton Bowl

Dog
- 0-21 S/U as 30.5 point or more Dog since 1996
- 6-0 ATS as 30.5 point or more Dog since 2003
- 0-18 S/U as 25.5-30 point Dog since 1997
- 10-2-1 O/U as 25.5-30 point Dog since 2002
- 1-18 S/U as 20.5-25 point Dog since 1997
- 0-43 S/U on road as 15.5 point or more Dog since 1984
- 2-25 S/U as 15.5-20 point Dog since 1984
- 2-8 ATS on road as 15.5-20 point Dog since 2000
- 3-43-1 S/U as 10.5-15 point Dog since 1983
- 12-4 ATS as 10.5-15 point Dog since 2008
- 1-14 S/U @ home as 10.5-15 point Dog since 1990
- 0-11 S/U @ home as 7.5-10 point Dog since 1997
- 2-9 ATS @ home as 7.5-10 point Dog since 1997
- 3-9 ATS as 7.5-10 point Dog since 2005
- 2-19 S/U as 7.5-10 point Dog since 1997

Favorite
- 13-4 O/U as 3 point or less favorite since 2005
- 13-2 S/U @ home as 3.5-7 point favorite since 2000
- 5-0 S/U @ home as 7.5-10 point favorite since 2001
- 27-0 S/U on road as 10.5 point or more favorite since 1984
- 14-3 S/U as 10.5-15 point favorite since 1994
- 25-2 S/U as 15.5-20 point favorite since 1984
- 9-2 S/U @ home as 20.5-25 point favorite since 1983
- 7-0 S/U @ home as 25.5-30 point favorite since 1994
- 7-1 O/U as 25.5-30 point favorite since 2013
- 15-1 S/U @ home as 30.5 point or more favorite since 2010
- 31-4 S/U @ home when ranked since 2011
- 6-0 S/U when ranked vs Texas Tech since 2011
- 2-47-1 S/U on road vs ranked teams since 1992 {11 L}
- 1-10 S/U vs #1 ranked teams since 1955
- 1-11 S/U @ ranked Oklahoma all time
- 0-18 S/U @ ranked Texas since 1953
- 5-0 S/U when ranked vs Iowa State all time
- 5-0 S/U when ranked vs Kansas all time

Pointspread Analysis — Conference

- vs Iowa State - Baylor leads series 11-9
- 8-1 S/U vs Iowa State as favorite since 1988
- 17-0 S/U vs Kansas as favorite since 1988
- 10-0 ATS vs Kansas since 2012
- 12-0 S/U vs Kansas since 2010
- vs Kansas - Baylor leads series 17-4
- Game 2-5 O/U vs Kansas since 20215
- vs Kansas State - Baylor leads series 10-9
- vs Oklahoma - Oklahoma leads series 28-4
- 1-7 S/U vs Oklahoma since 2015
- 3-21 S/U vs Oklahoma as Dog since 1984
- 8-2 ATS @ Oklahoma since 2001
- vs Oklahoma State - Oklahoma State leads series 22-19
- 4-17 S/U vs Oklahoma State as Dog since 1997
- 4-1 S/U @ home vs Oklahoma State since 2012
- Game 0-9 O/U vs Texas since 2013
- vs Texas - Texas leads series 78-28-5
- vs Tcu - TCU leads series 58-50-7
- 3-12 ATS vs TCU since 1995
- vs Texas Tech - Baylor leads series 40-38-1
- 2-18 S/U vs Texas Tech as Dog since 1988
- vs West Virginia - West Virginia leads series 6-3
- vs West Virginia - HOME team 9-1 S/U since 2012
- 1-6 S/U vs Iowa State as 7.5 point or more Dog since 2000
- 1-5 S/U vs Kansas State as 10.5 point or more Dog since 1998
- 4-0 S/U @ home vs Kansas State as 3.5-7 point favorite since 2010
- 0-3 S/U vs Kansas as 14 point or more Dog since 1999
- 0-14 S/U vs Oklahoma State as 7.5 point or more Dog since 1997
- 0-19 S/U vs Oklahoma as 7.5 point or more Dog since 1984
- 0-3 S/U vs TCU as 21 point or more Dog since 2007
- 0-13 S/U vs Texas Tech as 7.5 point or more Dog since 1998
- 1-16 S/U vs Texas as 7.5 point or more Dog since 1998
- 0-4 S/U vs West Virginia as 10.5 point or more Dog since 2012
- 7-0 S/U vs Kansas as 3.5-10 point favorite since 1998
- 3-1 S/U vs TCU as 7.5-10 point favorite since 1983
- 4-1 S/U vs TCU as 10.5-15 point favorite since 1986
- 10-0 S/U vs Kansas as 15.5 point or more favorite since 1989

OK STATE	1-7 O/U after playing Iowa State since 2014
KANSAS	8-3 S/U prior to playing Texas Tech since 2010
K STATE	0-6 O/U prior to playing TCU since 2016
Texas	1-7 O/U after playing TCU since 2013

Copyright © 2022 by Steve's Football Bible, LLC

BOISE STATE BRONCOS   MOUNTAIN WEST West

2021-Boise State		Opponent	Boise	Opp	S/U	Line	ATS	Total	O/U	
9/4/2021	@	Central Florida	31	36	L	6.0	W	67.0	T	
9/11/2021	vs	TEXAS-EL PASO	54	13	W	-15.0	W	56.5	O	
9/18/2021	vs	OKLAHOMA STATE	20	21	L	-3.5	L	57.5	U	
9/25/2021	@	Utah State	27	3	W	-9.5	W	69.5	U	
10/2/2021	vs	NEVADA	31	41	L	-3.5	L	59.0	O	
10/9/2021	@	Byu	26	17	W	6.5	W	58.0	U	
10/16/2021	vs	AIR FORCE	17	24	L	-3.0	L	52.0	U	
10/30/2021	@	Colorado State	28	19	W	-2.0	W	51.5	U	
11/6/2021	@	Fresno State	40	14	W	4.0	W	61.0	U	"Milk Can"
11/12/2021	vs	WYOMING	23	13	W	-13.5	L	48.5	U	
11/20/2021	vs	NEW MEXICO	37	0	W	-27.5	W	48.0	U	
11/27/2021	@	San Diego State	16	27	L	-3.0	L	44.0	U	
Coach: Andy Avalos		Season Record >>	350	228	7-5	ATS>>	7-5	O/U>>	2-9-1	
2020-Boise State		Opponent	Boise	Opp	S/U	Line	ATS	Total	O/U	
10/24/2020	vs	UTAH STATE	42	13	W	-17.0	W	51.0	O	
10/31/2020	@	Air Force	49	30	W	-12.5	W	48.5	O	
11/6/2020	vs	BYU	17	51	L	6.0	L	63.0	O	
11/14/2020	vs	COLORADO STATE	52	21	W	-14.0	W	62.5	O	
11/21/2020	@	Hawaii	40	32	W	-13.0	L	55.5	O	
12/12/2020	@	Wyoming	17	9	W	-9.5	L	47.0	U	
12/19/2020	vs	San Jose State	20	34	L	-6.5	L	59.5	U	MWC Championship
Coach: Brian Harsin		Season Record >>	237	190	5-2	ATS>>	3-4	O/U>>	5-2	
2019-Boise State		Opponent	Boise	Opp	S/U	Line	ATS	Total	O/U	
8/31/2019	vs	Florida State	36	31	W	6.5	W	54.5	O	
9/6/2019	vs	MARSHALL	14	7	W	-14.0	L	57.0	U	
9/14/2019	vs	PORTLAND STATE	45	10	W	-33.5	W	NT	---	
9/21/2019	vs	AIR FORCE	30	19	W	-7.0	W	55.5	U	
10/5/2019	@	Unlv	38	13	W	-24.5	W	57.5	U	
10/12/2019	vs	HAWAII	59	37	W	-12.5	W	60.0	O	
10/19/2019	@	Byu	25	28	L	-7.0	L	44.5	O	
11/2/2019	@	San Jose State	52	42	W	-16.5	L	61.0	O	
11/9/2019	vs	WYOMING	20	17	W	-16.5	L	48.0	U	
11/16/2019	vs	NEW MEXICO	42	9	W	-26.0	W	57.5	U	
11/23/2019	@	Utah State	56	21	W	-4.0	W	54.5	O	
11/30/2019	@	Colorado State	31	24	W	-13.0	L	57.0	U	
12/7/2019	vs	HAWAII	31	10	W	-14.0	W	65.0	U	MWC Championship
12/21/2019	vs	Washington	7	38	L	4.0	L	48.0	U	Las Vegas Bowl
Coach: Brian Harsin		Season Record >>	486	306	12-2	ATS>>	8-6	O/U>>	5-8	MWC CHAMPIONS
2018-Boise State		Opponent	Boise	Opp	S/U	Line	ATS	Total	O/U	
9/1/2018	@	Troy	56	20	W	-9.0	W	48.0	O	
9/8/2018	vs	CONNECTICUT	62	7	W	-34.0	W	64.0	O	
9/15/2018	@	Oklahoma State	21	44	L	-2.0	L	66.5	U	
9/29/2018	@	Wyoming	34	14	W	-10.0	W	46.0	O	
10/6/2018	vs	SAN DIEGO STATE	13	19	L	-14.0	L	51.0	U	
10/13/2018	@	Nevada	31	27	W	-14.0	L	58.0	T	
10/19/2018	vs	COLORADO STATE	56	28	W	-23.0	W	61.5	O	
10/27/2018	@	Air Force	48	38	W	-9.5	W	57.5	O	
11/3/2018	vs	BYU	21	16	W	-12.0	L	54.0	U	
11/9/2018	vs	FRESNO STATE	24	17	W	2.5	W	55.0	U	"Milk Can"
11/17/2018	@	New Mexico	45	14	W	-22.0	W	61.5	U	
11/24/2018	vs	UTAH STATE	33	24	W	-2.0	W	64.0	U	
12/1/2018	vs	FRESNO STATE	16	19	L	PK	L	51.0	U	MWC Championship
Coach: Brian Harsin		Season Record >>	460	287	10-3	ATS>>	8-5	O/U>>	5-7-1	

BOISE STATE BRONCOS — MOUNTAIN WEST West

STADIUM: Bronco Stadium {36,387} **Location:** Boise, ID **COACH:** Andy Avalos

DATE		Opponent	BSU	Opp	S/U	Line	ATS	Total	O/U	Trends & Angles
9/3/2022	@	Oregon State								vs Oregon State - Series tied 4-4
9/10/2022	@	New Mexico								5-0 S/U @ New Mexico since 2000
9/17/2022	vs	TENNESSEE-MARTIN								vs UT-Martin - Boise State leads series 1-0
9/23/2022	@	Texas-El Paso								vs Texas-El Paso - Boise State leads series 6-0
10/1/2022	vs	SAN DIEGO STATE								vs San Diego State - SDSU leads series 4-3
10/8/2022	vs	FRESNO STATE								10-1 S/U @ home vs Fresno State since 2002
10/22/2022	@	Air Force								vs Air Force - Boise State leads series 6-4
10/29/2022	vs	COLORADO STATE								vs Colorado State - Boise State leads series 11-0
11/5/2022	vs	BYU								5-1 S/U @ home vs BYU since 2004
11/12/2022	@	Nevada								7-1 S/U @ Nevada since 2002 {5-3 ATS}
11/19/2022	@	Wyoming								vs Wyoming - Boise State leads series 15-1
11/26/2022	vs	UTAH STATE								10-0 S/U @ home vs Utah St since 1998 {7-2-1 ATS}
12/3/2022	vs									MWC Championship
	vs									BOWL GAME

Pointspread Analysis — Non-Conference
- 15-2 S/U vs Non-Conf. as 3.5-10 point favorite since 1999
- 30-1 S/U vs Non-Conf. as 15.5 point or more favorite since 2001
- 7-2 S/U vs BYU as 2 point or more favorite since 2003
- vs BYU - Boise State leads series 8-4
- 5-0 S/U vs UTEP as 5.5 point or more favorite since 2000
- 0-3 S/U vs Oregon State as 3.5-7 point Dog since 2003
- 4-0 S/U vs Oregon State as 7.5 point or more favorite since 2004

Dog
- 0-5 S/U as 20.5 point or more Dog since 1996
- 4-0 ATS as 15.5-20 point Dog since 1998
- 0-4 S/U @ home as 10.5-15 point Dog since 1996
- 0-6 S/U on road as 7.5-10 point Dog since 1998
- 2-7 O/U on road as 3.5-7 point Dog since 2001
- 5-0 ATS @ home as 3 point or less Dog since 1998

Favorite
- 10-3 S/U & ATS on road as 3.5-7 point favorite since 2002
- 11-0 S/U @ home as 7.5-10 point favorite since 1999
- 27-3 S/U as 7.5-10 point favorite since 1998
- 16-3 S/U @ home as 10.5-15 point favorite since 2000
- 4-10 ATS @ home as 10.5-15 point favorite since 2009
- 26-2 S/U as 15.5-20 point favorite since 2000
- 13-0 S/U on road as 15.5-20 point favorite since 2002
- 10-1 O/U on road as 15.5-20 point favorite since 2005
- 63-0 S/U as 20.5-30 point favorite since 2000
- 3-8 ATS @ home as 30.5 point or more favorite since 2010
- 8-0 S/U on road as 30.5 point or more favorite since 2002
- 33-1 S/U as 30.5 point or more favorite since 2002

20-0 S/U in 1st home game of season since 2002	Texas-El Paso
20-3 S/U in 2nd home game of season since 1999	SAN DIEGO STATE
3-12 O/U in 2nd home game of season since 2006	SAN DIEGO STATE
16-0 S/U prior to playing Fresno State since 2001	SAN DIEGO STATE
6-0 S/U after playing San Diego State since 2011	FRESNO STATE
15-2 S/U prior to playing Nevada since 2001	BYU
11-1 S/U after playing Nevada since 2003	Wyoming
14-2 S/U prior to playing Utah State since 1999	Wyoming
22-1 S/U in final home game of season since 1999	UTAH STATE
12-3 S/U after playing Wyoming since 2002	UTAH STATE

Pointspread Analysis — Conference
- 2-5 ATS vs Fresno State since 2014
- 13-1 S/U vs Fresno State as favorite since 2002
- vs Fresno State - Boise State leads series 16-7
- Game 0-6 O/U vs Fresno State since 2014
- vs New Mexico - Boise State leads series 11-1
- 16-2 S/U vs Nevada since 1999
- vs Nevada - Boise State leads series 30-14
- 1-6 ATS vs San Diego State since 2011
- Game 12-4 O/U vs Utah State since 2002
- vs Utah State - Boise State leads series 21-5
- 17-1 S/U vs Utah State as favorite since 1998
- 18-1 S/U vs Utah State since 1998
- 1-6 ATS vs Wyoming since 2015
- 1-6 O/U vs Wyoming since 2015
- 3-0 S/U vs Air Force as 17.5 point or more favorite since 2011
- 10-0 S/U vs Colorado State as 6.5 point or more favorite since 2011
- 13-1 S/U vs Fresno State as 3 point or more favorite since 2002
- 0-4 ATS vs Fresno State as 6.5 point or more favorite since 2014
- 15-1 S/U vs Nevada as 2.5 point or more favorite since 2001
- 9-1 S/U vs New Mexico as 1.5 point or more favorite since 2000
- 0-5 ATS vs San Diego State as 6 point or more favorite since 2011

Bowl Games
- 4-1 S/U in Las Vegas Bowl
- 3-0 S/U in Fiesta Bowl

- 5-0 S/U when ranked vs Colorado State all time
- 54-4 S/U @ home when ranked all time
- 8-1 S/U when ranked vs Utah State all time {5-0 @ home}
- 5-14 S/U on road vs ranked teams since 1996
- 2-10 O/U vs ranked teams since 2014

BOSTON COLLEGE EAGLES — ACC ATLANTIC

2021-Boston College		Opponent	BC	Opp	S/U	Line	ATS	Total	O/U	
9/4/2021	vs	COLGATE	51	0	W	-43.0	W	58.0	U	
9/11/2021	vs	MASSACHUSETTS	45	28	W	-40.0	L	57.0	O	"Battle of The Bay State"
9/18/2021	@	Temple	28	3	W	-15.0	W	55.5	U	
9/25/2021	vs	MISSOURI	41	34	W	-1.0	W	58.0	O	{OT}
10/2/2021	@	Clemson	13	19	L	14.5	W	46.0	U	"O'Rourke-McFadden Trophy"
10/16/2021	vs	NC STATE	7	33	L	3.0	L	51.5	U	
10/23/2021	@	Louisville	14	28	L	4.0	L	57.5	U	
10/30/2021	@	Syracuse	6	21	L	6.5	L	51.5	U	
11/5/2021	vs	VIRGINIA TECH	17	3	W	1.0	W	51.0	U	
11/13/2021	@	Georgia Tech	41	30	W	-2.0	W	56.0	O	
11/20/2021	vs	FLORIDA STATE	23	26	L	-3.0	L	55.5	U	
11/27/2021	vs	WAKE FOREST	10	41	L	5.0	L	64.0	U	
Coach: Jeff Hafley		Season Record >>	296	266	6-6	ATS>>	6-6	O/U>>	3-9	

2020-Boston College		Opponent	BC	Opp	S/U	Line	ATS	Total	O/U	
9/19/2020	@	Duke	26	6	W	5.5	W	51.5	U	
9/26/2020	vs	TEXAS STATE	24	21	W	-20.5	L	56.5	U	
10/3/2020	vs	NORTH CAROLINA	22	26	L	14.5	W	52.5	U	
10/10/2020	vs	PITTSBURGH	31	30	W	6.0	W	42.0	O	
10/17/2020	@	Virginia Tech	14	40	L	13.5	L	61.5	U	
10/24/2020	vs	GEORGIA TECH	48	27	W	-3.5	W	57.5	O	
10/31/2020	@	Clemson	28	34	L	26.0	W	56.0	O	"O'Rourke-McFadden Trophy"
11/7/2020	@	Syracuse	16	13	W	-15.0	L	53.5	U	
11/14/2020	vs	NOTRE DAME	31	45	L	13.0	L	52.0	O	"Holy War" (Frank Leahy Memorial Bowl)
11/28/2020	vs	LOUISVILLE	34	27	W	-1.0	W	57.0	O	
12/5/2020	@	Virginia	32	43	L	6.5	L	53.0	O	
Coach: Jeff Hafley		Season Record >>	306	312	6-5	ATS>>	6-5	O/U>>	6-5	

2019-Boston College		Opponent	BC	Opp	S/U	Line	ATS	Total	O/U	
8/31/2019	vs	VIRGINIA TECH	35	28	W	4.0	W	58.0	O	
9/7/2019	vs	RICHMOND	45	13	W	-33.5	L	NT	---	
9/13/2019	vs	KANSAS	24	48	L	-19.5	L	51.0	O	
9/21/2019	@	Rutgers	30	16	W	-7.5	W	57.5	U	
9/28/2019	vs	WAKE FOREST	24	27	L	5.0	W	69.5	U	
10/12/2019	@	Louisville	39	41	L	3.5	W	61.0	O	
10/19/2019	vs	NC STATE	45	24	W	4.0	W	54.5	O	
10/26/2019	@	Clemson	7	59	L	35.0	L	59.0	O	"O'Rourke-McFadden Trophy"
11/2/2019	@	Syracuse	58	27	W	3.0	W	59.0	O	
11/9/2019	vs	FLORIDA STATE	31	38	L	-1.0	L	64.0	O	
11/23/2019	@	Notre Dame	7	40	L	21.0	L	65.5	U	"Holy War" (Frank Leahy Memorial Bowl)
11/30/2019	@	Pittsburgh	26	19	W	8.5	W	51.5	U	
1/2/2020	vs	Cincinnati	6	38	L	7.0	L	56.0	U	Birmingham Bowl
Coach: Steve Addazio		Season Record >>	377	418	6-7	ATS>>	7-6	O/U>>	7-5	

2018-Boston College		Opponent	BC	Opp	S/U	Line	ATS	Total	O/U	
9/1/2018	vs	MASSACHUSETTS	55	21	W	-20.5	W	62.5	O	"Battle of The Bay State"
9/8/2018	vs	HOLY CROSS	62	14	W	-44.0	W	NT	---	
9/13/2018	@	Wake Forest	41	34	W	-6.5	W	57.5	O	
9/22/2018	@	Purdue	13	30	L	-6.5	L	62.5	U	
9/29/2018	vs	TEMPLE	45	35	W	-11.5	L	54.0	O	
10/6/2018	@	NC State	23	28	L	6.5	W	60.5	U	
10/20/2018	vs	LOUISVILLE	38	20	W	-12.0	W	56.5	O	
10/26/2018	vs	MIAMI	27	14	W	4.0	W	49.0	U	
11/3/2018	@	Virginia Tech	31	21	W	-2.0	W	57.0	U	
11/10/2018	vs	CLEMSON	7	27	L	17.5	L	51.0	U	"O'Rourke-McFadden Trophy"
11/17/2018	@	Florida State	21	22	L	-3.0	L	48.0	U	
11/24/2018	vs	SYRACUSE	21	42	L	-6.0	L	60.5	O	
Coach: Steve Addazio		Season Record >>	384	308	7-5	ATS>>	7-5	O/U>>	5-6	

BOSTON COLLEGE EAGLES — ACC ATLANTIC

STADIUM: Alumni Stadium {44,500} **Location:** Chestnut Hill, MA **COACH:** Jeff Hafley

DATE		Opponent	BC	Opp	S/U	Line	ATS	Total	O/U	Trends & Angles
9/3/2022	vs	RUTGERS								13-0-1 S/U vs Rutgers since 1992
9/10/2022	@	Virginia Tech								8-2 ATS vs Virginia Tech since 2011
9/17/2022	vs	MAINE								6-0 S/U vs Maine since 1929
9/24/2022	@	Florida State								0-5 S/U @ Florida State since 2010
10/1/2022	vs	LOUISVILLE								Game 8-2 O/U vs Louisville since 1994
10/8/2022	vs	CLEMSON								0-11 S/U vs Clemson since 2011
10/22/2022	@	Wake Forest								3-0 S/U @ Wake Forest since 2014
10/29/2022	@	Connecticut								vs Connecticut - BC leads series 9-0-2
11/4/2022	vs	DUKE								vs Duke - ROAD team 5-0 ATS since 2006
11/12/2022	@	NC State								4-0 ATS @ NC State since 2012
11/19/2022	@	Notre Dame								0-8 S/U vs Notre Dame since 2009
11/26/2022	vs	SYRACUSE								vs Syracuse - Syracuse leads series 33-21
12/3/2022	vs									ACC Championship
	vs									BOWL GAME

Pointspread Analysis — Non-Conference

- 0-8 S/U vs Non-Conf. as 10.5-15 point Dog since 1985
- 42-2 S/U vs Non-Conf. as 15.5 point or more favorite since 1983
- 9-2 ATS vs Rutgers since 1995
- 9-0 S/U vs Rutgers as 7.5 point or more favorite since 1996
- 3-0 S/U vs Maine as 24 point or more favorite since 2012
- vs Maine - BC leads series 6-3
- 5-0 S/U vs U Conn as 7.5 point or more favorite since 2000
- vs Notre Dame - Notre Dame leads series 16-9
- Game 2-8 O/U vs Notre Dame since 2007
- 0-9 S/U vs Notre Dame as 11 point or more Dog since 1995
- 5-1 ATS vs Notre Dame as 7.0-10 point Dog since 1994
- 3-0 S/U vs Notre Dame as 3.5-7 point favorite since 2001

Bowl Games
- 1-7 S/U in Bowl Games since 2008
- 2-8 ATS in Bowl Games since 2006
- 4-1 O/U in Bowl Games since 2013
- 2-6 S/U vs ranked teams in Bowl games all time

Dog
- 0-10 S/U as 25.5 point or more Dog since 1990
- 0-14 S/U as 20.5-25 point Dog since 1991
- 0-4 S/U @ home as 20.5-25 point Dog since 1991
- 9-0 ATS on road as 15.5-20 point Dog since 1993
- 0-7 S/U @ home as 15.5-20 point Dog since 1991
- 15-3 ATS as 15.5-20 point Dog since 1987
- 2-10 O/U as 10.5-15 point Dog since 2011
- 0-11 S/U @ home as 10.5-15 point Dog since 1986
- 4-27 S/U as 10.5-15 point Dog since 1985
- 1-7 S/U @ home as 7.5-10 point Dog since 1985
- 1-9 S/U as 7.5-10 point Dog since 2009
- 4-13 O/U on road as 3.5-7 point Dog since 2007
- 3-11 S/U on road as 3.5-7 point Dog since 2012
- 9-2 S/U & ATS on road as 3 point or less Dog since 1995
- 5-1 S/U prior to playing Virginia Tech since 2015
- 7-1 S/U after playing Rutgers since 1998
- 6-1 O/U prior to playing Florida State since 2014
- 1-5 O/U prior to playing Louisville since 2016

- 13-2 S/U @ home when ranked since 2005
- 1-30 S/U vs ranked teams last 31 times
- 0-8 S/U vs #2 ranked teams all time
- 0-10 S/U vs ranked Clemson since 2011
- 1-8 S/U vs ranked Florida State all time {0-3 @ home}

Pointspread Analysis — Conference

- vs NC State - Boston College leads series 10-8
- vs Wake Forest - Boston College leads series 14-12-2
- vs Clemson - Clemson leads series 19-8-2
- Game 0-5 O/U vs Duke since 2006
- vs Florida State - Florida State leads series 14-5
- 1-10 S/U vs Florida State since 2010
- vs Louisville - Louisville leads series 8-6
- Game 1-6 O/U vs NC State since 2014
- Game 0-4 O/U @ NC State since 2012
- 4-13 S/U vs Syracuse as Dog since 1983
- vs Virginia Tech - Virginia Tech leads series 18-11
- Game 1-10 O/U vs Wake Forest since 2010
- 0-8 S/U vs Clemson as 17.5 point or more Dog since 2011
- 0-6 S/U vs Florida State as 14.5 point or more Dog since 2010
- 1-4 S/U vs Syracuse as 12 point or more Dog since 1987
- 1-9 S/U vs Virginia Tech as 13.5 point or more Dog since 1997
- 4-1 S/U & ATS vs Florida State as 4.0-9.0 point Dog since 2006
- 1-9 S/U & ATS vs Syracuse as 3.5-10 point Dog since 1983
- 2-5 S/U vs Virginia Tech as 4.0-10 point Dog since 1998
- 1-5 S/U & ATS vs Syracuse as 6 point or less favorite since 2003
- 5-1 S/U & ATS vs Wake F. as 6.5 point or less favorite since 2007
- 3-0 S/U vs NC State as 7.5 point or more favorite since 2007

Favorite
- 9-3 S/U @ home as 3 point or less favorite since 2000
- 4-12 ATS as 3.5-7 point favorite since 2009
- 18-3 S/U as 7.5-10 point favorite since 1995
- 7-1 S/U on road as 7.5-10 point favorite since 1995
- 13-0 S/U as 10.5-15 point favorite since 2005
- 20-2 S/U as 15.5-20 point favorite since 1984
- 13-0 S/U on road as 15.5 point or more favorite since 1984
- 38-0 S/U as 20.5 point or more favorite since 1983

Opponent	Trend
RUTGERS	1-10 O/U prior to playing Virginia Tech since 2010
Virginia Tech	1-10 O/U in 1st road game of season since 2011
MAINE	13-3 S/U in 2nd home game of season since 2006
Florida State	1-12 S/U in 2nd road game of season since 2009
CLEMSON	2-11 O/U prior to playing Wake Forest since 2005
Wake Forest	1-8 O/U after playing Clemson since 2013
DUKE	9-2 S/U after playing Connecticut since 1908
NC State	0-5 ATS prior to playing Notre Dame since 2012
NC State	1-7 O/U prior to playing Notre Dame since 2010
Notre Dame	3-10 O/U in final road game of season since 2009
Notre Dame	1-7 S/U prior to playing Syracuse since 2014

BOWLING GREEN FALCONS   MAC East

2021-Bowling Green		Opponent	BGU	Opp	S/U	Line	ATS	Total	O/U	
9/4/2021	@	Tennessee	6	38	L	37.0	W	60.5	U	
9/11/2021	vs	SOUTH ALABAMA	19	22	L	14.0	W	47.5	U	
9/18/2021	vs	MURRAY STATE	27	10	W	2.5	W	44.0	U	
9/25/2021	@	Minnesota	14	10	W	30.0	W	50.5	U	
10/2/2021	@	Kent State	20	27	L	17.0	W	56.5	U	"Anniversary Award"
10/9/2021	vs	AKRON	20	35	L	-14.0	L	46.0	O	
10/16/2021	@	Northern Illinois	26	34	L	9.0	W	44.5	O	
10/23/2021	vs	EASTERN MICHIGAN	24	55	L	4.5	L	49.5	O	
10/30/2021	@	Buffalo	56	44	W	13.5	W	51.5	O	
11/10/2021	vs	TOLEDO	17	49	L	10.5	L	50.0	O	"Battle of I-75 Trophy"
11/16/2021	@	Miami-Ohio	7	34	L	17.0	L	52.0	U	
11/26/2021	vs	OHIO	21	10	W	6.0	W	48.5	U	
Coach: Scott Loeffler		Season Record >>	257	368	4-8	ATS>>	8-4	O/U>>	5-7	

2020-Bowling Green		Opponent	BGU	Opp	S/U	Line	ATS	Total	O/U	
11/4/2020	@	Toledo	3	38	L	24.0	L	63.0	U	"Battle of I-75 Trophy"
11/10/2020	vs	KENT STATE	24	62	L	20.5	L	55.0	O	"Anniversary Award"
11/17/2020	vs	BUFFALO	17	42	L	31.5	W	57.5	O	
11/28/2020	@	Ohio	10	52	L	22.5	L	55.0	O	
12/5/2020	@	Akron	3	31	L	2.5	L	54.5	U	
Coach: Scott Loeffler		Season Record >>	57	225	0-5	ATS>>	1-4	O/U>>	3-2	

2019-Bowling Green		Opponent	BGU	Opp	S/U	Line	ATS	Total	O/U	
8/29/2019	vs	MORGAN STATE	46	3	W	-23.5	W	NT	---	
9/7/2019	@	Kansas State	0	52	L	24.5	L	57.5	U	
9/14/2019	vs	LOUISIANA TECH	7	35	L	12.5	L	58.5	U	
9/21/2019	@	Kent State	20	62	L	11.5	L	62.0	O	"Anniversary Award"
10/5/2019	@	Notre Dame	0	52	L	46.0	L	64.5	U	
10/12/2019	vs	TOLEDO	20	7	W	27.0	W	65.0	U	"Battle of I-75 Strophy"
10/19/2019	vs	CENTRAL MICHIGAN	20	38	L	10.5	L	54.5	O	
10/26/2019	@	Western Michigan	10	49	L	26.5	L	65.5	U	
11/2/2019	vs	AKRON	35	6	W	-3.5	W	48.0	U	
11/13/2019	@	Miami-Ohio	3	44	L	17.0	L	47.5	U	
11/19/2019	vs	OHIO	24	66	L	21.0	L	55.5	O	
11/29/2019	@	Buffalo	7	49	L	28.0	L	53.5	O	
Coach: Mike Jinks		Season Record >>	192	463	3-9	ATS>>	3-9	O/U>>	4-7	

2018-Bowling Green		Opponent	BGU	Opp	S/U	Line	ATS	Total	O/U	
9/1/2018	@	Oregon	24	58	L	34.0	T	70.0	O	
9/8/2018	vs	MARYLAND	14	45	L	13.5	L	66.0	U	
9/15/2018	vs	EASTERN KENTUCKY	42	35	W	-14.0	L	NT	---	
9/22/2018	vs	MIAMI-OHIO	23	38	L	6.5	L	54.5	O	
9/29/2018	@	Georgia Tech	17	63	L	28.5	L	65.0	O	
10/6/2018	@	Toledo	36	52	L	23.0	W	71.0	O	"Battle of I-75 Trophy"
10/13/2018	vs	WESTERN MICHIGAN	35	42	L	14.5	W	69.5	O	
10/20/2018	@	Ohio	14	49	L	16.5	L	66.5	U	
10/30/2018	vs	KENT STATE	28	35	L	PK	L	68.0	U	"Anniversary Award"
11/10/2018	@	Central Michigan	24	13	W	7.0	W	49.5	U	
11/17/2018	@	Akron	21	6	W	6.0	W	47.5	U	
11/23/2018	vs	BUFFALO	14	44	L	16.0	L	62.5	U	
Coach: Mike Jinks		Season Record >>	292	480	3-9	ATS>>	4-7-1	O/U>>	5-6	

BOWLING GREEN FALCONS   MAC East

STADIUM: Doyt-Perry Stadium {24,000} **Location:** Bowling Green, OH **COACH:** Scott Leoffler

DATE		Opponent	BG	Opp	S/U	Line	ATS	Total	O/U	Trends & Angles
9/3/2022	@	*Ucla*								0-8 S/U in 1st road game of season since 2014
9/10/2022	vs	EASTERN KENTUCKY								vs Eastern Kentucky - EKU leads series 3-2
9/17/2022	vs	MARSHALL								12-1 S/U @ home vs Marshall since 1956
9/24/2022	@	*Mississippi State*								vs Mississippi State - M State leads series 1-0
10/1/2022	@	Akron								
10/8/2022	vs	BUFFALO								Game 1-4 O/U @ home vs Buffalo since 2012
10/15/2022	vs	MIAMI-OHIO								1-7 S/U @ home vs Miami-Ohio since 1999
10/22/2022	@	Central Michigan								Game 1-6 O/U vs Central Mich. since 2003
11/2/2022	vs	WESTERN MICHIGAN								2-7 ATS @ home vs Western Mich. since 1993
11/9/2022	vs	KENT STATE								2-8 ATS @ home vs Kent State since 2001
11/15/2022	@	Toledo								1-12 S/U @ Toledo since 1996
11/22/2022	@	Ohio								8-3 ATS @ Ohio since 1999
12/2/2022	vs									MAC Championship
	vs									BOWL GAME

Pointspread Analysis — Non-Conference

- 1-33 S/U vs Non-Conf. as 15.5 point or more Dog since 1989
- 10-3 ATS vs Non-Conf. as 10.5-15 point Dog since 1994
- 9-1 S/U vs Non-Conf. as 10.5 point or more favorite since 1994
- 4-0 ATS @ home vs Marshall since 1998

Dog
- 2-10 ATS as 25.5-30 point Dog since 1997
- 2-37 S/U as 20.5 point or more Dog since 1989
- 1-19 S/U as 15.5-20 point Dog since 1989
- 1-9 S/U as 10.5-15 point Dog since 2017
- 2-7 S/U @ home as 7.5-10 point Dog since 1990
- 1-11 S/U on road as 7.5-10 point Dog since 1997
- 4-11 S/U as 3.5-7 point Dog since 2011
- 1-7 S/U @ home as 3.5-7 point Dog since 2010
- 0-6 O/U @ home as 3 point or less Dog since 2010

Favorite
- 9-1 S/U on road as 3 point or less favorite since 2008
- 3-8 ATS as 3.5-7 point favorite since 2013
- 8-2 S/U on road as 3.5-7 point favorite since 2007
- 13-0 S/U on road as 7.5-15 point favorite since 1991
- 10-3 ATS on road as 7.5-15 point favorite since 1991
- 22-3 S/U as 10.5-15 point favorite since 1991
- 1-7 ATS @ home as 15.5-20 point favorite since 1994
- 10-1 S/U @ home as 15.5-20 point favorite since 1991
- 16-3 S/U as 20.5-25 point favorite since 1993
- 15-0 S/U as 25.5 point or more favorite since 1994

Bowl Games
- 1-5 S/U & ATS in Bowl Games since 2008
- 5-0 O/U in Bowl Game since 2009

- 0-10 S/U vs teams ranked in Top Ten all time
- 0-3 S/U vs ranked teams in Bowl games all time
- 0-3 S/U vs ranked Miami-Ohio all time

- 3-11 O/U after playing Akron since 2001
- 0-7 O/U after playing Western Michigan since 2005
- 4-10 O/U after playing Kent State since 2008

Pointspread Analysis — Conference

- vs Buffalo - Bowling Green leads series 12-7
- 1-4 S/U vs Buffalo since 2017
- vs Central Michigan - Bowling Green leads series 23-19
- Game 1-3 O/U @ home vs Kent State since 2014
- vs Kent State - Bowling Green leads series 58-24-6
- 2-9 ATS @ home vs Miami-Ohio since 1994
- 2-5 O/U @ home vs Miami-Ohio since 2001
- vs Miami-Ohio - Miami-Ohio leads series 46-24-5
- 1-5 S/U vs Ohio since 2016
- Game 1-5 O/U @ Ohio since 2012
- Game 3-8 O/U vs Ohio since 2011
- vs Ohio - Bowling Green leads series 41-30-2
- vs Toledo - Toledo leads series 42-40-4
- 1-11 S/U vs Toledo since 2010
- 1-6 S/U vs Western Michigan since 2005
- 4-12 ATS vs Western Michigan since 1993
- Game 2-7 O/U vs Western Michigan since 2003
- vs Western Michigan - Bowling Green leads series 32-20-3
- 9-1 S/U vs Akron as 8 point or less favorite since 1992
- 5-2 S/U vs Akron as 11 point or more favorite since 1994
- 4-0 S/U vs Buffalo as 8.5 point or less favorite since 2012
- 0-4 O/U vs Buffalo as 8.5 point or less favorite since 2012
- 4-0 S/U vs Buffalo as 11.5 point or more favorite since 2001
- 0-3 ATS vs Buffalo as 11.5 point or more favorite since 2005
- 3-0 S/U vs C. Michigan as 16 point or more favorite since 2002
- 6-0 O/U vs Kent State as 7 point or less favorite since 2008
- 13-1 S/U vs Kent State as 11 point or more favorite since 1991
- 1-5 O/U vs Miami-Ohio as 9.5 point or less favorite since 2001
- 1-5 S/U & ATS @ home vs Miami as 9.5 pt or less favorite since 1995
- 3-0 S/U & ATS @ Ohio as 5.5 point or less favorite since 2001
- 0-7 S/U vs Ohio as 9.5 point or more Dog since 2000
- 8-0 S/U vs Ohio as 13 point or more favorite since 1992
- 6-0-1 ATS vs Ohio as 13 point or more favorite since 1993
- 1-10 S/U vs Toledo as 8.5 point or more Dog since 1990
- 0-3 S/U @ Toledo as 3 point or less Dog since 1996
- 0-5 O/U vs Toledo as 8 point or less favorite since 2007
- 0-3 S/U @ home vs W. Michigan as 8 point or less favorite since 1996
- 0-4 ATS @ home vs W. Michigan as 8 point or less favorite since 1993
- 0-3 S/U vs W. Michigan as 7.5 point or more Dog since 2001

BUFFALO
KENT STATE
Toledo

Page | 33   Copyright © 2022 by Steve's Football Bible, LLC

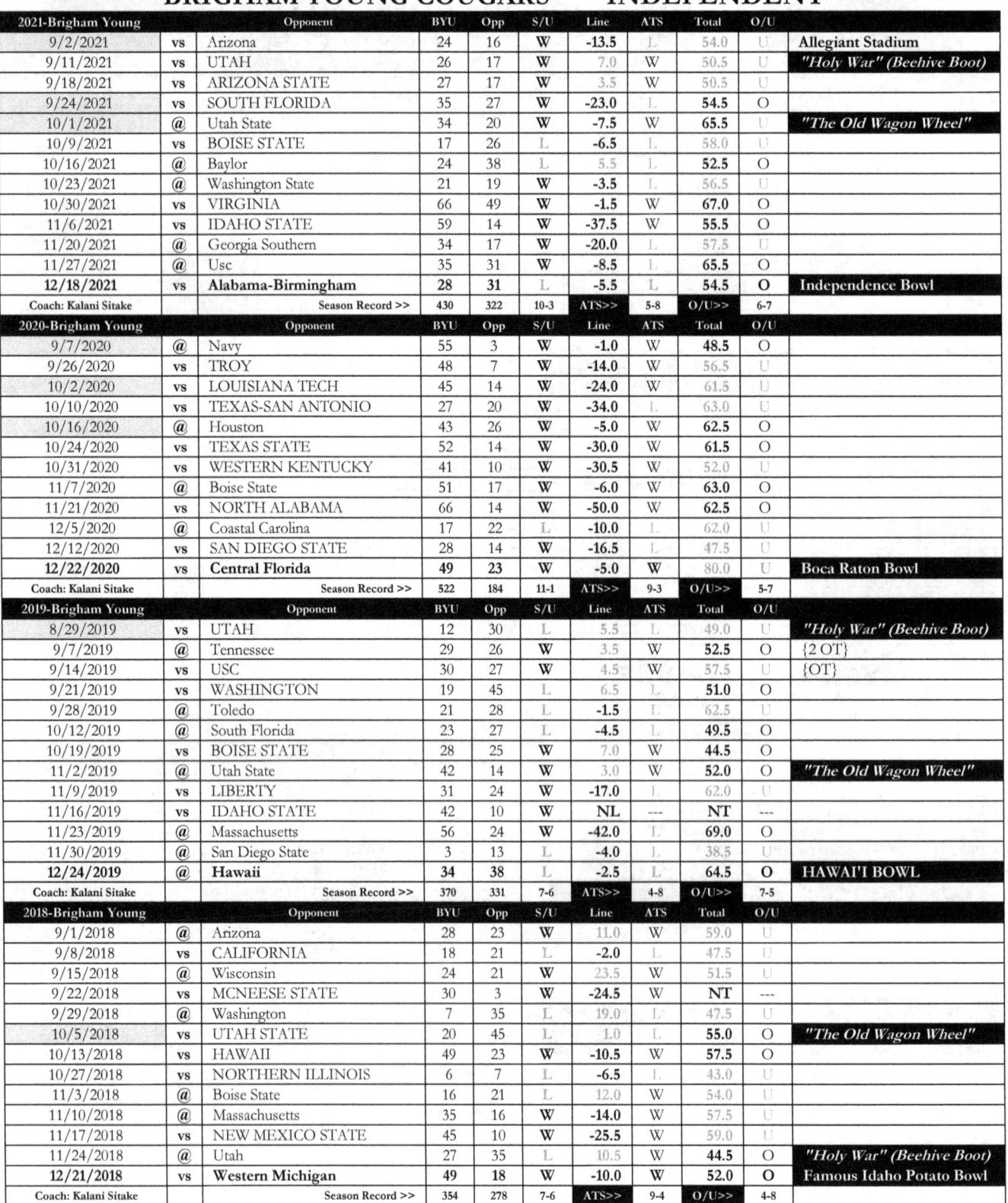

BRIGHAM YOUNG COUGARS   INDEPENDENT

2021-Brigham Young		Opponent	BYU	Opp	S/U	Line	ATS	Total	O/U	
9/2/2021	vs	Arizona	24	16	W	-13.5	L	54.0	U	Allegiant Stadium
9/11/2021	vs	UTAH	26	17	W	7.0	W	50.5	U	"Holy War" (Beehive Boot)
9/18/2021	vs	ARIZONA STATE	27	17	W	3.5	W	50.5	U	
9/24/2021	vs	SOUTH FLORIDA	35	27	W	-23.0	L	54.5	O	
10/1/2021	@	Utah State	34	20	W	-7.5	W	65.5	U	"The Old Wagon Wheel"
10/9/2021	vs	BOISE STATE	17	26	L	-6.5	L	58.0	U	
10/16/2021	@	Baylor	24	38	L	5.5	L	52.5	O	
10/23/2021	@	Washington State	21	19	W	-3.5	L	56.5	U	
10/30/2021	vs	VIRGINIA	66	49	W	-1.5	W	67.0	O	
11/6/2021	vs	IDAHO STATE	59	14	W	-37.5	W	55.5	O	
11/20/2021	@	Georgia Southern	34	17	W	-20.0	L	57.5	U	
11/27/2021	@	Usc	35	31	W	-8.5	L	65.5	O	
12/18/2021	vs	Alabama-Birmingham	28	31	L	-5.5	L	54.5	O	Independence Bowl
Coach: Kalani Sitake		Season Record >>	430	322	10-3	ATS>>	5-8	O/U>>	6-7	
2020-Brigham Young		Opponent	BYU	Opp	S/U	Line	ATS	Total	O/U	
9/7/2020	@	Navy	55	3	W	-1.0	W	48.5	O	
9/26/2020	vs	TROY	48	7	W	-14.0	W	56.5	U	
10/2/2020	vs	LOUISIANA TECH	45	14	W	-24.0	W	61.5	U	
10/10/2020	vs	TEXAS-SAN ANTONIO	27	20	W	-34.0	L	63.0	U	
10/16/2020	@	Houston	43	26	W	-5.0	W	62.5	O	
10/24/2020	vs	TEXAS STATE	52	14	W	-30.0	W	61.5	O	
10/31/2020	vs	WESTERN KENTUCKY	41	10	W	-30.5	W	52.0	U	
11/7/2020	@	Boise State	51	17	W	-6.0	W	63.0	O	
11/21/2020	vs	NORTH ALABAMA	66	14	W	-50.0	W	62.5	O	
12/5/2020	@	Coastal Carolina	17	22	L	-10.0	L	62.0	U	
12/12/2020	vs	SAN DIEGO STATE	28	14	W	-16.5	L	47.5	U	
12/22/2020	vs	Central Florida	49	23	W	-5.0	W	80.0	U	Boca Raton Bowl
Coach: Kalani Sitake		Season Record >>	522	184	11-1	ATS>>	9-3	O/U>>	5-7	
2019-Brigham Young		Opponent	BYU	Opp	S/U	Line	ATS	Total	O/U	
8/29/2019	vs	UTAH	12	30	L	5.5	L	49.0	U	"Holy War" (Beehive Boot)
9/7/2019	@	Tennessee	29	26	W	3.5	W	52.5	O	{2 OT}
9/14/2019	vs	USC	30	27	W	4.5	W	57.5	U	{OT}
9/21/2019	vs	WASHINGTON	19	45	L	6.5	L	51.0	O	
9/28/2019	@	Toledo	21	28	L	-1.5	L	62.5	U	
10/12/2019	@	South Florida	23	27	L	-4.5	L	49.5	O	
10/19/2019	vs	BOISE STATE	28	25	W	7.0	W	44.5	O	
11/2/2019	@	Utah State	42	14	W	3.0	W	52.0	O	"The Old Wagon Wheel"
11/9/2019	vs	LIBERTY	31	24	W	-17.0	L	62.0	U	
11/16/2019	vs	IDAHO STATE	42	10	W	NL	---	NT	---	
11/23/2019	@	Massachusetts	56	24	W	-42.0	L	69.0	O	
11/30/2019	@	San Diego State	3	13	L	-4.0	L	38.5	U	
12/24/2019	@	Hawaii	34	38	L	-2.5	L	64.5	O	HAWAI'I BOWL
Coach: Kalani Sitake		Season Record >>	370	331	7-6	ATS>>	4-8	O/U>>	7-5	
2018-Brigham Young		Opponent	BYU	Opp	S/U	Line	ATS	Total	O/U	
9/1/2018	@	Arizona	28	23	W	11.0	W	59.0	U	
9/8/2018	vs	CALIFORNIA	18	21	L	-2.0	L	47.5	U	
9/15/2018	@	Wisconsin	24	21	W	23.5	W	51.5	U	
9/22/2018	vs	MCNEESE STATE	30	3	W	-24.5	W	NT	---	
9/29/2018	@	Washington	7	35	L	19.0	L	47.5	U	
10/5/2018	vs	UTAH STATE	20	45	L	1.0	L	55.0	O	"The Old Wagon Wheel"
10/13/2018	vs	HAWAII	49	23	W	-10.5	W	57.5	O	
10/27/2018	vs	NORTHERN ILLINOIS	6	7	L	-6.5	L	43.0	U	
11/3/2018	@	Boise State	16	21	L	12.0	W	54.0	U	
11/10/2018	@	Massachusetts	35	16	W	-14.0	W	57.5	U	
11/17/2018	vs	NEW MEXICO STATE	45	10	W	-25.5	W	59.0	U	
11/24/2018	@	Utah	27	35	L	10.5	W	44.5	O	"Holy War" (Beehive Boot)
12/21/2018	vs	Western Michigan	49	18	W	-10.0	W	52.0	O	Famous Idaho Potato Bowl
Coach: Kalani Sitake		Season Record >>	354	278	7-6	ATS>>	9-4	O/U>>	4-8	

BRIGHAM YOUNG COUGARS — INDEPENDENT

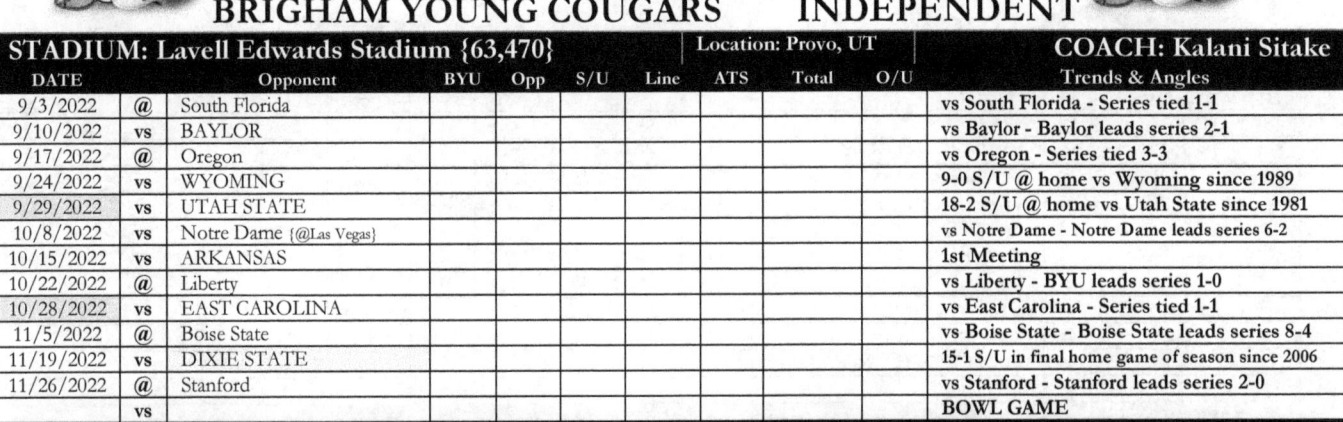

STADIUM: Lavell Edwards Stadium {63,470} **Location:** Provo, UT **COACH:** Kalani Sitake

DATE		Opponent	BYU	Opp	S/U	Line	ATS	Total	O/U	Trends & Angles
9/3/2022	@	South Florida								vs South Florida - Series tied 1-1
9/10/2022	vs	BAYLOR								vs Baylor - Baylor leads series 2-1
9/17/2022	@	Oregon								vs Oregon - Series tied 3-3
9/24/2022	vs	WYOMING								9-0 S/U @ home vs Wyoming since 1989
9/29/2022	vs	UTAH STATE								18-2 S/U @ home vs Utah State since 1981
10/8/2022	vs	Notre Dame {@Las Vegas}								vs Notre Dame - Notre Dame leads series 6-2
10/15/2022	vs	ARKANSAS								1st Meeting
10/22/2022	@	Liberty								vs Liberty - BYU leads series 1-0
10/28/2022	vs	EAST CAROLINA								vs East Carolina - Series tied 1-1
11/5/2022	@	Boise State								vs Boise State - Boise State leads series 8-4
11/19/2022	vs	DIXIE STATE								15-1 S/U in final home game of season since 2006
11/26/2022	@	Stanford								vs Stanford - Stanford leads series 2-0
	vs									BOWL GAME

Pointspread Analysis

Dog
- 1-6 S/U on road as 21 point or more Dog since 1988
- 0-6 S/U as 15.5-20 point Dog since 1992
- 3-15 S/U as 10.5-15 point Dog since 1976
- 1-10 S/U on road as 7.5-10 point Dog since 2000
- 0-5-1 O/U on road as 7.5-10 point Dog since 2005
- 2-10 O/U @ home as 3.5-7 point Dog since 2004
- 9-2 O/U on road as 3 point or less Dog since 1998

Favorite
- 7-17 O/U as 3 point or less favorite since 2002
- 5-12 ATS as 3.5-7 point favorite since 2011
- 4-11 O/U as 3.5-7 point favorite since 2013
- 13-1 S/U as 7.5-10 point favorite since 2009
- 8-1 S/U on road as 7.5-10 point favorite since 2001
- 52-4 S/U as 10.5-15 point favorite since 1986
- 21-0 S/U as 15.5-20 point favorite since 1997
- 18-0 S/U @ home as 15.5-20 point favorite since 1990
- 29-1 S/U as 20.5-25 point favorite since 1984
- 5-0 S/U on road as 20.5-25 point favorite since 1984
- 25-0 S/U as 25.5-30 point favorite since 1985
- 7-0 S/U on road as 25.5-30 point favorite since 1985
- 18-0 S/U @ home as 30.5 or more favorite since 1988
- 22-0 S/U as 30.5 point or more favorite since 1988

Bowl Games
- 0-3 S/U in Bowl Games as 10.5-15 point Dog since 1976
- 1-6 O/U in Bowl Games as 3 point or less favorite since 1985
- 1-5-1 S/U vs Big Ten in Bowl Games
- 2-9-1 S/U vs ranked teams in Bowl games since 1985

Pointspread Analysis

Non-Conference
- 23-3 S/U vs Utah State as favorite since 1985
- vs Utah State - BYU leads series 50-37-3
- Game 2-10 O/U @ home vs Utah since 1997
- 1-5 ATS @ home vs Utah since 2010
- vs Utah - Utah leads series 59-33-4
- 8-0 S/U vs Wyoming since 2004 {6-2 ATS}
- 1-7 S/U vs Boise State as 6 point or more Dog since 2003
- 3-0 ATS vs Boise State as 7.5 point or more Dog since 2004
- 0-3 O/U vs Boise State as 7.5 point or more Dog since 2004
- 1-5 S/U vs Notre Dame as 9 point or more Dog since 1992
- 0-5 S/U vs Utah as 8 point or more Dog since 2002
- 0-3 S/U vs Utah as 4 point or more favorite since 2011
- 1-9 ATS vs Utah as 3.5 or more point favorite since 1997
- 21-3 S/U vs Utah State as 4.5 point or more favorite since 1986
- 15-1 S/U @ home vs Utah State as 6.5 point or more favorite since 1986
- 0-3 S/U & ATS vs Wyoming as 3 point or less favorite since 1987
- 11-0 S/U @ home vs Wyoming as 7 point or more favorite since 1985
- 19-1 S/U vs Wyoming as 4 point or more favorite since 1985
- 0-13 S/U vs #10 - #13 ranked teams all time
- 0-7 S/U on road when ranked vs ranked teams since 1991
- 23-4 S/U @ home when ranked since 2001
- 14-1 S/U when ranked vs Utah State all time {6-0 on road}
- 9-2 ATS on road vs ranked teams since 2010
- 3-20 S/U on road vs ranked teams since 1998

Oregon	3-9 O/U in 2nd road game of season since 2010
WYOMING	8-2 S/U prior to playing Utah State since 2011
WYOMING	6-1 O/U prior to playing Utah State since 2014
UTAH STATE	5-0 S/U after playing Wyoming since 2006
E. CAROLINA	2-8 ATS prior to playing Boise State since 2004

Yea Alabama! History of the Alabama Crimson Tide
Paperback $34.95
Hardcover $36.95

Tiger Rag! History of Clemson Tigers Football
Paperback $29.95
Hardcover $34.95

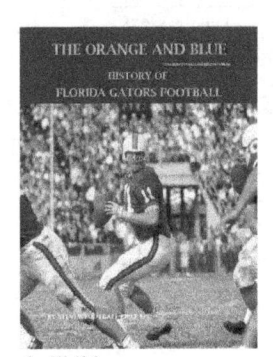

The Orange and Blue! History of the Florida Gators
Paperback $29.95
Hardcover $34.95

College Football Blueblood Series available at: www.stevesfootballbible.com

BUFFALO BULLS — MAC East

2021-Buffalo		Opponent	BUFF	Opp	S/U	Line	ATS	Total	O/U	
9/4/2021	vs	WAGNER	69	7	W	-43.5	W	55.0	O	
9/11/2021	@	Nebraska	3	28	L	13.5	L	54.5	U	
9/18/2021	vs	COASTAL CAROLINA	25	28	L	14.0	W	57.5	U	
9/25/2021	@	Old Dominion	35	34	W	-13.0	L	50.5	O	
10/2/2021	vs	WESTERN MICHIGAN	17	24	L	7.0	T	59.5	U	
10/9/2021	@	Kent State	38	48	L	7.0	L	65.5	O	
10/16/2021	vs	OHIO	27	26	W	-7.5	L	54.5	U	
10/23/2021	@	Akron	45	10	W	-13.5	W	58.0	U	
10/30/2021	vs	BOWLING GREEN	44	56	L	-13.5	L	51.5	O	
11/9/2021	@	Miami-Ohio	18	45	L	7.0	L	58.5	O	
11/17/2021	vs	NORTHERN ILLINOIS	27	33	L	2.0	L	59.0	O	{OT}
11/23/2021	@	Ball State	3	20	L	6.0	L	60.0	U	
Coach: Maurice Linguist		Season Record >>	351	359	4-8	ATS>>	3-8-1	O/U>>	6-6	
2020-Buffalo		Opponent	BUFF	Opp	S/U	Line	ATS	Total	O/U	
11/4/2020	@	Northern Illinois	49	30	W	-14.5	W	53.0	O	
11/10/2020	vs	MIAMI-OHIO	42	10	W	-7.0	W	56.0	U	
11/17/2020	@	Bowling Green	42	17	W	-31.5	L	57.5	O	
11/28/2020	vs	KENT STATE	70	41	W	-7.5	W	70.0	O	
12/12/2020	vs	AKRON	56	7	W	-33.5	W	58.5	O	
12/18/2020	vs	**BALL STATE**	28	38	L	-12.5	L	70.0	U	MAC CHAMPIONSHIP
12/25/2020	vs	**Marshall**	17	10	W	-5.0	W	53.5	U	Camelia Bowl
Coach: Lance Leipold		Season Record >>	304	153	6-1	ATS>>	5-2	O/U>>	4-3	
2019-Buffalo		Opponent	BUFF	Opp	S/U	Line	ATS	Total	O/U	
8/31/2019	vs	ROBERT MORRIS	38	10	W	-41.5	L	NT	---	
9/7/2019	@	Penn State	13	45	L	31.5	L	55.0	O	
9/14/2019	@	Liberty	17	35	L	-6.0	L	55.0	U	
9/21/2019	vs	TEMPLE	38	22	W	14.0	W	51.0	O	
9/28/2019	@	Miami-Ohio	20	34	L	-2.5	L	48.5	O	
10/5/2019	vs	OHIO	20	21	L	3.0	W	51.5	U	{OT}
10/19/2019	@	Akron	21	0	W	-17.5	W	48.0	U	
10/26/2019	vs	CENTRAL MICHIGAN	43	20	W	-2.0	W	45.5	O	
11/2/2019	@	Eastern Michigan	43	14	W	-1.5	W	49.5	O	
11/14/2019	@	Kent State	27	30	L	-6.0	L	54.5	O	
11/20/2019	vs	TOLEDO	49	30	W	-10.0	W	54.0	O	
11/29/2019	vs	BOWLING GREEN	49	7	W	-28.0	W	53.5	O	
12/20/2019	vs	**Charlotte**	31	9	W	-7.0	W	51.5	U	Bahamas Bowl
Coach: Lance Leipold		Season Record >>	409	277	8-5	ATS>>	8-5	O/U>>	8-4	
2018-Buffalo		Opponent	BUFF	Opp	S/U	Line	ATS	Total	O/U	
9/1/2018	vs	DELAWARE STATE	48	10	W	-45.0	L	NT	---	
9/8/2018	@	Temple	36	29	W	4.0	W	52.0	O	
9/15/2018	vs	EASTERN MICHIGAN	35	28	W	-3.0	W	54.0	O	
9/22/2018	@	Rutgers	42	13	W	-6.0	W	52.0	O	
9/29/2018	vs	ARMY	13	42	L	-7.0	L	54.5	O	
10/6/2018	@	Central Michigan	34	24	W	-6.5	W	52.5	O	
10/13/2018	vs	AKRON	24	6	W	-11.0	W	54.5	U	
10/20/2018	@	Toledo	31	17	W	3.0	W	62.5	U	
10/30/2018	vs	MIAMI-OHIO	51	42	W	-7.0	W	53.0	O	
11/6/2018	vs	KENT STATE	48	14	W	-17.0	W	48.0	O	
11/14/2018	@	Ohio	17	52	L	2.5	L	65.0	O	
11/23/2018	@	Bowling Green	44	14	W	-16.0	W	62.5	U	
11/30/2018	vs	**Northern Illinois**	29	30	L	-3.0	L	51.5	O	MAC CHAMPIONSHIP
12/22/2018	vs	**Troy**	32	42	L	-2.5	L	51.5	O	Dollar General Bowl
Coach: Lance Leipold		Season Record >>	484	363	10-4	ATS>>	9-5	O/U>>	10-3	

BUFFALO BULLS — MAC East

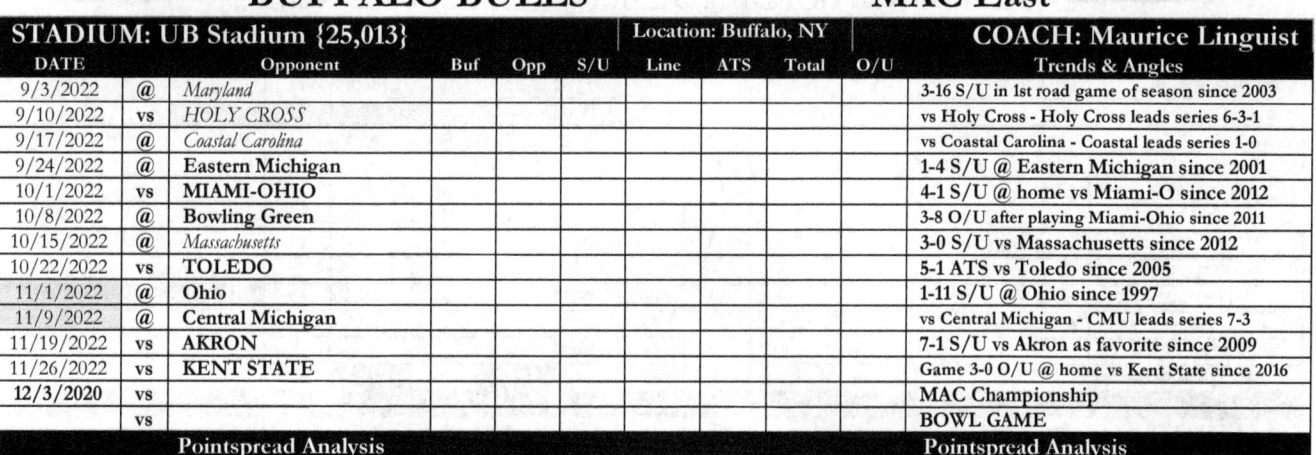

STADIUM: UB Stadium {25,013} | **Location:** Buffalo, NY | **COACH:** Maurice Linguist

DATE		Opponent	Buf	Opp	S/U	Line	ATS	Total	O/U	Trends & Angles
9/3/2022	@	Maryland								3-16 S/U in 1st road game of season since 2003
9/10/2022	vs	HOLY CROSS								vs Holy Cross - Holy Cross leads series 6-3-1
9/17/2022	@	Coastal Carolina								vs Coastal Carolina - Coastal leads series 1-0
9/24/2022	@	Eastern Michigan								1-4 S/U @ Eastern Michigan since 2001
10/1/2022	vs	MIAMI-OHIO								4-1 S/U @ home vs Miami-O since 2012
10/8/2022	@	Bowling Green								3-8 O/U after playing Miami-Ohio since 2011
10/15/2022	@	Massachusetts								3-0 S/U vs Massachusetts since 2012
10/22/2022	vs	TOLEDO								5-1 ATS vs Toledo since 2005
11/1/2022	@	Ohio								1-11 S/U @ Ohio since 1997
11/9/2022	@	Central Michigan								vs Central Michigan - CMU leads series 7-3
11/19/2022	vs	AKRON								7-1 S/U vs Akron as favorite since 2009
11/26/2022	vs	KENT STATE								Game 3-0 O/U @ home vs Kent State since 2016
12/3/2020	vs									MAC Championship
	vs									BOWL GAME

Pointspread Analysis — Non-Conference
- 0-24 S/U vs Non-conf. as 20.5 point or more Dog since 1999
- 2-18 S/U vs Non-Conf. as 10.5-20 point favorite since 2000
- vs Massachusetts - Buffalo leads series 6-5

Dog
- 0-25 S/U as 30.5 point or more Dog since 1999
- 0-11 S/U as 25-30 point Dog since 2000
- 0-10 S/U on road as 20.5-25 point Dog since 1999
- 2-10 O/U as 20.5-25 point Dog since 2003
- 0-10 S/U on road as 15.5-20 point Dog since 2001
- 0-17 S/U on road as 10.5-15 point Dog since 1999
- 1-11 S/U @ home as 7.5-10 point Dog since 2004
- 2-8 O/U as 7.5-10 point Dog since 2009
- 1-15 S/U on road as 3.5-7 point Dog since 2009

Favorite
- 14-5 S/U as 3.5-7 point favorite since 2006
- 5-0 S/U as 7.5-10 point favorite since 2011 {4-1 ATS}
- 6-2 S/U @ home as 10.5-15 point favorite since 2008
- 17-1 S/U as 15.5 point or more favorite since 2010

- 11-1 S/U in 1st home game of season since 2010 — HOLY CROSS
- 5-15 S/U in 2nd road game of season since 2002 — Coastal Carolina
- 1-6 O/U prior to playing Toledo since 2003 — Massachusetts
- 10-0 O/U after playing Bowling Green since 2009 — Massachusetts
- 2-11 S/U after playing Bowling Green since 2005 — Massachusetts
- 1-7 S/U prior to playing Central Michigan since 2004 — Ohio
- 3-8 O/U prior to playing Akron since 2009 — Central Michigan
- 3-8 S/U prior to playing Akron since 2009 — Central Michigan
- 9-2 S/U prior to playing Kent State since 2008 — AKRON

Pointspread Analysis — Conference
- 1-4 S/U vs Eastern Michigan as Dog since 2001
- vs Eastern Michigan - Eastern Michigan leads series 6-3
- vs Kent State - Buffalo leads series 14-13
- vs Miami-Ohio - Miami-Ohio leads series 15-8
- 8-1 S/U vs Miami-Ohio as favorite since 2008
- 0-13 S/U vs Miami-Ohio as Dog since 1999
- vs Ohio - HOME team 10-1 S/U since 2010
- vs Ohio - Ohio leads series 16-11
- vs Toledo - Toledo leads series 7-5
- 5-1 S/U vs Akron as 11.5 point or less favorite since 2007
- 1-6 S/U vs Ball State as 4 point or more Dog since 2000
- 1-7 S/U vs Bowling Green as 3.5 point or more Dog since 2001
- 6-1 ATS vs Bowling Green as 3.5 point or more Dog since 2005
- 0-4 O/U vs Bowling Green as 3.5 point or more Dog since 2012
- 4-0 S/U vs Bowling Green as 3.5 point or more favorite since 2017
- 1-7 S/U vs C. Michigan as 5 point or more Dog since 1999
- 0-3 S/U vs E. Michigan as 3.5-7 point Dog since 2004
- 0-14 S/U vs Miami-Ohio as 2.5 point or more Dog since 1999
- 8-1 S/U vs Miami-Ohio as 24.5 point or less favorite since 2008
- 0-9 S/U @ Ohio as 4 point or more Dog since 1999
- 0-4 S/U vs Toledo as 4.5 point or more Dog since 2003

- 1-14 S/U vs ranked teams all time

Garnet and Gold – History of Florida State Seminoles Football

Paperback $29.95
Hardcover $34.95

Wild Blue Yonder! History of Air Force Falcons Football

Paperback $29.95
Hardcover $34.95

College Football Blueblood Series available at: www.stevesfootballbible.com

College Football Patriot Series available at: www.stevesfootballbible.com

CALIFORNIA GOLDEN BEARS   PACIFIC-12 North

2021-California		Opponent	CAL	Opp	S/U	Line	ATS	Total	O/U	
9/4/2021	vs	NEVADA	17	22	L	-2.5	L	52.5	U	
9/11/2021	@	Tcu	32	34	L	12.0	W	46.0	O	
9/18/2021	vs	SACRAMENTO STATE	42	30	W	-24.0	L	50.0	O	
9/25/2021	@	Washington	24	31	L	7.5	W	47.5	O	{OT}
10/2/2021	vs	WASHINGTON STATE	6	21	L	-7.5	L	52.5	U	
10/15/2021	@	Oregon	17	24	L	13.5	W	53.5	U	
10/23/2021	vs	COLORADO	26	3	W	-8.0	W	44.0	U	
10/30/2021	vs	OREGON STATE	39	25	W	2.5	W	56.5	O	
11/6/2021	@	Arizona	3	10	L	-7.0	L	47.0	U	
11/20/2021	@	Stanford	41	11	W	-2.5	W	45.5	O	"Big Game" (Stanford Axe)
11/27/2021	@	Ucla	14	42	L	6.0	L	58.5	U	
12/4/2021	vs	USC	24	14	W	-4.5	W	57.0	U	
Coach: Justin Wilcox		Season Record >>	285	267	5-7	ATS>>	7-5	O/U>>	5-7	

2020-California		Opponent	CAL	Opp	S/U	Line	ATS	Total	O/U	
11/15/2020	@	Ucla	10	34	L	-3.0	L	58.0	U	
11/21/2020	@	Oregon State	27	31	L	-1.0	L	46.5	O	
11/28/2020	vs	STANFORD	23	24	L	2.0	W	51.0	U	"Big Game" (Stanford Axe)
12/5/2020	vs	OREGON	21	17	W	8.0	W	59.0	U	
Coach: Justin Wilcox		Season Record >>	81	106	1-3	ATS>>	2-2	O/U>>	1-3	

2019-California		Opponent	CAL	Opp	S/U	Line	ATS	Total	O/U	
8/31/2019	vs	CALIFORNIA-DAVIS	27	13	W	-14.5	L	NT	---	
9/7/2019	@	Washington	20	19	W	13.5	W	43.0	U	
9/14/2019	vs	NORTH TEXAS	23	17	W	-14.5	L	50.5	U	
9/21/2019	@	Mississippi	28	20	W	3.0	W	41.5	O	
9/28/2019	vs	ARIZONA STATE	17	24	L	-4.5	L	43.0	U	
10/5/2019	@	Oregon	7	17	L	21.5	W	46.5	U	
10/19/2019	vs	OREGON STATE	17	21	L	-11.0	L	51.0	O	
10/26/2019	@	Utah	0	35	L	21.0	L	36.5	U	
11/9/2019	vs	WASHINGTON STATE	33	20	W	8.5	W	52.0	O	
11/16/2019	vs	USC	17	41	L	4.0	L	48.5	O	
11/23/2019	@	Stanford	24	20	W	-1.0	W	41.5	O	"Big Game" (Stanford Axe)
11/30/2019	@	Ucla	28	18	W	1.0	W	51.0	U	
12/30/2019	vs	Illinois	35	20	W	-6.0	W	48.0	O	Redbox Bowl
Coach: Justin Wilcox		Season Record >>	276	285	8-5	ATS>>	7-6	O/U>>	5-7	

2018-California		Opponent	CAL	Opp	S/U	Line	ATS	Total	O/U	
9/1/2018	vs	NORTH CAROLINA	24	17	W	-7.0	T	58.0	U	
9/8/2018	@	Byu	21	18	W	2.0	W	47.5	U	
9/15/2018	vs	IDAHO STATE	45	23	W	-37.0	L	NT	---	
9/29/2018	vs	OREGON	24	42	L	2.0	L	57.5	O	
10/6/2018	@	Arizona	17	24	L	-1.0	L	57.0	U	
10/13/2018	vs	UCLA	7	37	L	-6.5	L	53.5	U	
10/20/2018	@	Oregon State	49	7	W	-8.5	W	58.5	O	
10/27/2018	vs	WASHINGTON	12	10	W	11.5	W	45.5	U	
11/3/2018	@	Washington State	13	19	L	7.0	W	51.0	U	
11/10/2018	@	Usc	15	14	W	4.0	W	45.5	U	
11/24/2018	vs	COLORADO	33	21	W	-10.5	W	44.5	O	
12/1/2018	vs	STANFORD	13	23	L	3.0	L	46.0	U	"Big Game" (Stanford Axe)
12/26/2018	vs	Tcu	7	10	L	2.5	L	38.0	U	Cheez-it Bowl
Coach: Justin Wilcox		Season Record >>	280	265	7-6	ATS>>	6-6-1	O/U>>	2-10	

- 22-6 S/U @ home when ranked since 2004
- 13-3 S/U when ranked vs Non-Conference since 2005
- 5-0 S/U when ranked @ Oregon State all time
- 0-10 O/U on road vs ranked teams since 2015
- 0-11 S/U vs #1 ranked teams all time
- 0-22-1 S/U vs #5 & #6 ranked teams all time
- 0-4 S/U & ATS @ home vs ranked Stanford since 1992
- 1-8 S/U @ home vs ranked Washington all time

CALIFORNIA GOLDEN BEARS   PACIFIC-12 North

STADIUM: Memorial Stadium {62,467} **Location:** Berkeley, CA **COACH:** Justin Wilcox

DATE		Opponent	Cal	Opp	S/U	Line	ATS	Total	O/U	Trends & Angles
9/3/2022	vs	*CALIFORNIA-DAVIS*								vs Cal-Davis - California leads series 10-0
9/10/2022	vs	*UNLV*								17-0 S/U in 2nd home game of season since 2004
9/17/2022	@	*Notre Dame*								vs Notre Dame - Notre Dame leads series 4-0
9/24/2022	vs	ARIZONA								vs Arizona - Arizona leads series 19-14-2
10/1/2022	@	Washington State								Game 1-4 O/U @ Washington State since 2010
10/15/2022	@	Colorado								0-3 ATS @ Colorado since 2011
10/22/2022	vs	WASHINGTON								1-4 S/U & ATS @ home vs Washington since 2010
10/29/2022	vs	OREGON								2-11 S/U vs Oregon since 2009
11/5/2022	@	Usc								1-8 S/U @ USC since 2002
11/12/2022	@	Oregon State								Game 4-1 O/U @ Oregon State since 2012
11/19/2022	vs	STANFORD								0-6 S/U @ home vs Stanford since 2010 {1-5 ATS}
11/26/2022	vs	UCLA								5-1 ATS @ home vs UCLA since 2008
12/2/2022	vs									PAC-12 Championship
	vs									BOWL GAME

Pointspread Analysis — Non-Conference

- 0-7 S/U vs Non-Conf. as 15.5 point or more Dog since 1987
- 0-6 S/U & ATS vs Non-Conf. as 3 point or less favorite since 2001
- 12-1 S/U vs Non-Conf. as 3.5-7 point favorite since 1997
- 9-1 O/U vs Non-conf. as 3.5-7 point favorite since 2005
- 28-0 S/U vs Non-Conf. as 15.5 point or more favorite since 1988

Dog
- 0-5 ATS as 30.5 point or more Dog since 1999
- 0-26 S/U as 20.5 point or more Dog since 1986
- 1-10 S/U @ home as 15.5-20 point Dog since 1989
- 0-10 S/U on road as 15.5-20 point Dog since 1997
- 16-1 ATS on road as 10.5-15 point Dog since 1997
- 2-10 S/U @ home as 10.5-15 point Dog since 1991
- 9-1 ATS @ home as 7.5-10 point Dog since 1987
- 2-12 S/U on road as 7.5-10 point Dog since 1989
- 4-20 S/U as 3.5-7 point Dog since 2007
- 4-0 S/U on road as 3 point or less Dog since 2000
- 4-0 ATS on road as 3 point or less Dog since 2005

Favorite
- 3-8 S/U on road as 3 point or less favorite since 2003
- 3-8 ATS on road as 3 point or less favorite since 2003
- 4-1 S/U & ATS @ home as 3 point or less favorite since 2008
- 10-1 S/U & ATS @ home as 7.5-10 point favorite since 2006
- 15-1 S/U as 7.5-10 point favorite since 2005
- 14-2 ATS as 7.5-10 point favorite since 2005
- 17-4 S/U @ home as 10.5-15 point favorite since 1987
- 16-2 S/U as 15.5-20 point favorite since 1983
- 31-0 S/U as 20.5 point or more favorite since 1988
- 12-0 O/U as 20.5 point or more favorite since 2006

Bowl Games
- 5-0 S/U in Bowl Games as 3.5-7 point favorite since 2005
- 9-3 O/U in Bowl Games since 1996
- 1-18 S/U on road vs ranked teams since 2010
- 0-8 S/U vs ranked Oregon since 2010
- 0-5 S/U @ ranked USC since 2002
- 0-7 S/U when ranked @ ranked USC since 1938
- 15-4 S/U in 1st home game of season since 2002
- 9-3 O/U in 1st home game of season since 2006
- 17-0 S/U in 2nd home game of season since 2004
- 16-4 O/U in 1st road game of season since 2001
- 2-12 S/U in 2nd road game of season since 2008
- 0-8 S/U after playing Washington State since 2012
- 0-9 S/U prior to playing Oregon since 2012
- 3-10 S/U after playing Oregon since 2007
- 2-6 S/U & ATS after playing USC since 2012
- 3-10 S/U prior to playing UCLA since 2007

CAL-DAVIS	
CAL-DAVIS	
UNLV	
Notre Dame	
Washington State	
Colorado	
WASHINGTON	
Usc	
Oregon State	
STANFORD	

Pointspread Analysis — Conference

- vs Colorado - California leads series 7-4
- Game 6-1 O/U vs Colorado since 2010
- vs Oregon - Series tied 41-41-2
- vs Oregon State - California leads series 39-35
- 2-15 S/U vs USC since 2004
- vs Usc - USC leads series 71-32-5
- Game 3-14 O/U vs USC since 2004
- 3-18-1 S/U vs Stanford as Dog since 1984
- vs Stanford - Stanford leads series 60-46-9
- 2-10 S/U vs Stanford since 2010
- 8-2 S/U @ home vs UCLA since 2000
- vs Ucla - UCLA leads series 57-34-1
- Game 0-9 O/U vs UCLA since 2013
- Game 2-10 O/U vs Washington since 2009
- 2-19 S/U vs Washington as Dog since 1983
- vs Washington - Washington leads series 53-41-4
- 5-13 S/U vs Washington State as Dog since 1983
- 11-4-1 S/U vs Washington State as favorite since 1986
- vs Washington State - California leads series 48-29-5
- 0-5 S/U vs Arizona as 10 point or less Dog since 1998
- 0-9 S/U vs Oregon as 13 point or more Dog since 2000
- 1-8 S/U vs Oregon State as Dog since 1999
- 0-3 S/U vs Oregon State as 10.5 point or more Dog since 2001
- 1-4 S/U vs Oregon State as 6.5 point or less Dog since 2000
- 0-6 S/U @ home vs Stanford as 6.5 point or less Dog since 1992
- 1-5 ATS @ home vs Stanford as 6.5 point or less Dog since 1992
- 0-6 S/U vs Stanford as 10 point or less Dog since 2010
- 4-0 S/U @ home vs Stanford as 9 point or more favorite since 2002
- 0-7 S/U vs USC as 14.5 point or more Dog since 2005
- 2-10 O/U vs USC as 9 point or less Dog since 2007
- 1-8 S/U vs USC as 7.5 point or less Dog since 2007
- 0-5 S/U @ USC as 12 point or more Dog since 2002
- 1-10 S/U vs UCLA as 10.5 point or more Dog since 1983
- 5-1 S/U @ home vs UCLA as 10 point or less Dog since 2003
- 7-0 ATS @ home vs UCLA as 10 point or less Dog since 1984
- 5-0 S/U @ home vs UCLA as 7.5 point or more favorite since 1992
- 0-5 S/U vs Washington as 10 point or less Dog since 1985
- 0-5 S/U & ATS vs Washington as 3.5-7 point favorite since 2007
- 0-4 O/U vs Washington as 3.5-7 point favorite since 2009
- 4-0 S/U vs Washington as 9 point or more favorite since 2004
- 1-4 S/U vs Wazzu as 10.5 point or more Dog since 1994
- 1-6 S/U @ Wazzu as 7.5 point or less Dog since 1983
- 1-8 S/U in final road game of season since 2012

Page | 39   Copyright © 2022 by Steve's Football Bible, LLC

CENTRAL FLORIDA GOLDEN KNIGHTS   AMERICAN

2021-Central Florida		Opponent	UCF	Opp	S/U	Line	ATS	Total	O/U	
9/4/2021	vs	BOISE STATE	36	31	W	-6.0	L	67.0	T	
9/11/2021	vs	BETHUNE-COOKMAN	63	14	W	-45.5	W	67.0	O	
9/17/2021	@	Louisville	35	42	L	-7.0	L	67.0	O	
10/2/2021	@	Navy	30	34	L	-15.0	L	53.0	O	
10/9/2021	vs	EAST CAROLINA	20	16	W	-10.0	L	65.0	U	
10/16/2021	@	Cincinnati	21	56	L	22.0	L	56.0	O	
10/22/2021	vs	MEMPHIS	24	7	W	1.5	W	63.0	U	
10/30/2021	@	Temple	49	7	W	-12.0	W	42.0	O	
11/6/2021	vs	TULANE	14	10	W	-13.5	L	57.0	U	
11/13/2021	@	Smu	28	55	L	7.0	L	61.5	O	
11/20/2021	vs	CONNECTICUT	49	17	W	-30.0	W	56.0	O	
11/26/2021	vs	SOUTH FLORIDA	17	13	W	-17.0	L	62.0	U	War on I-4 Trophy
12/23/2021	vs	Florida	29	17	W	7.0	W	56.0	U	Gasparilla Bowl
Coach: Gus Malzahn		Season Record >>	415	319	9-4	ATS>>	5-8	O/U>>	7-5-1	
2020-Central Florida		Opponent	UCF	Opp	S/U	Line	ATS	Total	O/U	
9/19/2020	@	Georgia Tech	49	21	W	-8.0	W	63.5	O	
9/24/2020	@	East Carolina	51	28	W	-27.5	L	77.0	O	
10/3/2020	vs	TULSA	26	34	L	-20.0	L	70.0	U	
10/17/2020	@	Memphis	49	50	L	-3.0	L	74.0	O	
10/24/2020	vs	TULANE	51	34	W	-21.5	W	71.0	O	
10/31/2020	@	Houston	44	21	W	-3.0	W	81.0	U	
11/14/2020	vs	TEMPLE	38	13	W	-29.0	L	71.5	U	
11/21/2020	vs	CINCINNATI	33	36	L	4.0	W	65.5	O	
11/27/2020	@	South Florida	58	46	W	-25.0	L	70.5	O	War on I-4 Trophy
12/22/2020	vs	BYU	23	49	L	5.0	L	80.0	U	Boca Raton Bowl
Coach: Josh Heupel		Season Record >>	422	332	6-4	ATS>>	4-6	O/U>>	6-4	
2019-Central Florida		Opponent	UCF	Opp	S/U	Line	ATS	Total	O/U	
8/31/2019	vs	FLORIDA A&M	62	0	W	-44.0	W	NT	---	
9/7/2019	@	Florida Atlantic	48	14	W	-13.5	W	67.5	U	
9/14/2019	vs	STANFORD	45	27	W	-9.5	W	59.0	O	
9/21/2019	@	Pittsburgh	34	35	L	-10.0	L	60.5	O	
9/28/2019	vs	CONNECTICUT	56	21	W	-42.0	L	64.5	O	
10/4/2019	@	Cincinnati	24	27	L	-3.5	L	63.5	U	
10/19/2019	vs	EAST CAROLINA	41	28	W	-34.0	L	64.5	O	
10/26/2019	@	Temple	63	21	W	-10.5	W	61.0	O	
11/2/2019	vs	HOUSTON	44	29	W	-21.0	L	72.5	O	
11/8/2019	@	Tulsa	31	34	L	-16.0	L	68.5	U	
11/23/2019	@	Tulane	34	31	W	-7.0	L	74.0	U	
11/30/2019	vs	SOUTH FLORIDA	34	7	W	-24.0	W	61.5	U	War on I-4 Trophy
12/23/2019	vs	Marshall	48	25	W	-15.5	W	59.5	O	Gasparilla Bowl
Coach: Josh Heupel		Season Record >>	564	299	10-3	ATS>>	6-7	O/U>>	7-5	
2018-Central Florida		Opponent	UCF	Opp	S/U	Line	ATS	Total	O/U	
8/30/2018	@	Connecticut	56	17	W	-24.0	W	69.0	O	
9/8/2018	vs	SOUTH CAROLINA STATE	38	0	W	-52.0	L	NT	---	
9/21/2018	vs	FLORIDA ATLANTIC	56	36	W	-14.0	W	75.0	O	
9/29/2018	vs	PITTSBURGH	45	15	W	-13.0	W	65.5	U	
10/6/2018	vs	SMU	48	20	W	-25.0	W	74.0	U	
10/13/2018	@	Memphis	31	30	W	-5.5	W	80.5	U	
10/20/2018	@	East Carolina	37	10	W	-21.5	W	65.0	U	
11/1/2018	vs	TEMPLE	52	40	W	-10.0	W	60.0	O	
11/10/2018	vs	NAVY	35	24	W	-23.5	L	68.0	U	
11/17/2018	vs	CINCINNATI	38	13	W	-6.5	W	60.5	O	
11/23/2018	@	South Florida	38	10	W	-15.5	W	69.5	U	War on I-4 Trophy
12/1/2018	vs	Memphis	56	41	W	PK	W	65.0	O	AAC Championship
1/1/2019	vs	Lsu	32	40	L	7.0	L	58.5	O	Fiesta Bowl
Coach: Josh Heupel		Season Record >>	562	296	12-1	ATS>>	9-4	O/U>>	5-7	AAC Champions

CENTRAL FLORIDA GOLDEN KNIGHTS — AMERICAN

STADIUM: Bright House Networks Stadium {44,206} **Location:** Orlando, FL **COACH:** Gus Malzahn

DATE		Opponent	UCF	Opp	S/U	Line	ATS	Total	O/U	Trends & Angles
9/1/2022	vs	SOUTH CAROLINA STATE								vs South Carolina State - UCF leads series 3-0
9/10/2022	vs	LOUISVILLE								vs Louisville - Louisville leads series 2-1
9/17/2022	@	Florida Atlantic								vs Florida Atlantic - UCF leads series 3-0
9/24/2022	vs	GEORGIA TECH								vs Georgia Tech - G TECH leads series 3-0
10/1/2022	vs	SMU								4-0 S/U @ home vs SMU since 2008
10/13/2022	vs	TEMPLE								5-0 S/U vs Temple since 2017
10/22/2022	@	East Carolina								6-0 S/U vs East Carolina since 2016
10/29/2022	vs	CINCINNATI								vs Cincinnati - Cincinnati leads series 4-3
11/5/2022	@	Memphis								6-1 S/U @ Memphis since 2006
11/12/2022	@	Tulane								vs Tulane - UCF leads series 9-2
11/19/2022	vs	NAVY								vs Navy - Central Florida leads series 2-1
11/26/2022	@	South Florida								5-0 S/U vs South Florida since 2017
12/3/2022	vs									AAC Championship
	vs									BOWL GAME

Pointspread Analysis — Non-Conference
- 0-13 S/U vs Non-Conf. as 20.5 point or more Dog since 1999
- 4-18 S/U vs Non-Conf. as 10.5-20 point Dog since 1997
- 15-0 S/U vs Non-Conf. as 25.5 point or more favorite since 1998
- 4-1 S/U vs Florida Int. as 10 point or more favorite since 2012

Dog
- 0-22 S/U as 20.5 point or more Dog since 1997
- 3-11 ATS as 20.5-25 point Dog since 2001
- 0-8 S/U @ home as 15.5 point or more Dog since 1997
- 2-35 S/U on road as 10.5 point or more Dog since 1997
- 2-8 S/U as 7.5-10 point Dog since 2002
- 15-5 ATS as 3.5-7 point Dog since 2005
- 2-7 O/U on road as 3 point or less Dog since 2003

Favorite
- 9-1 S/U @ home as 3.5-7 point favorite since 2007
- 7-3 ATS @ home as 3.5-7 point favorite since 2007
- 15-3 S/U as 7.5-10 point favorite since 2009
- 12-1 S/U on road as 10.5-15 point favorite since 1999
- 10-1 S/U @ home as 10.5-15 point favorite since 2007
- 11-1 S/U @ home as 15.5-20 point favorite since 2001
- 17-3 S/U as 15.5-20 point favorite since 1997
- 21-2 S/U as 20.5-25 point favorite since 1998
- 27-0 S/U as 25.5 point or more favorite since 1998

- 37-5 S/U when ranked all time
- 13-2 S/U on road when ranked all time
- 1-20 S/U on road vs ranked teams all time

Pointspread Analysis — Conference
- vs East Carolina - Series tied 10-10
- Game 8-3 O/U vs East Carolina since 2010
- 6-2 ATS vs Temple since 2014
- Game 7-2 OU vs Temple since 2013
- vs Temple - UCF leads series 7-2
- vs Memphis - UCF leads series 14-2
- vs SMU - UCF leads series 8-2
- vs South Florida - UCF leads series 7-6
- 0-5 S/U vs South Florida as 7.5 point or more Dog since 2005
- 0-3 S/U & ATS vs Tulsa as 3 point or less Dog since 2005
- 3-1 S/U & ATS vs Cincinnati as 6.5-15 point favorite since 2016
- 3-0 S/U & ATS @ E. Carolina as 7 point or less Dog since 2005
- 10-1 S/U vs Memphis as 2.5 point or more favorite since 2006
- 7-0 S/U vs USF as 10 point or more favorite since 2013
- 5-1 S/U vs Temple as 3.5 point or more favorite since 2013
- 8-0 S/U vs SMU as 9 point or more favorite since 2007

SC STATE	12-2 S/U in 1st home game of season since 2008
GA TECH	7-0 S/U prior to playing SMU since 2011
SMU	6-0 S/U prior to playing Temple since 2016
East Carolina	6-0 S/U prior to playing Cincinnati since 2016
East Carolina	1-5 O/U prior to playing Cincinnati since 2016
Memphis	5-0 S/U after playing Cincinnati since 2017
Tulane	6-0 S/U after playing Memphis since 2012 {6-0 ATS}
Tulane	5-1 O/U after playing Memphis since 2012
NAVY	8-2 S/U after playing Tulane since 2005

CENTRAL MICHIGAN CHIPPEWAS — MAC West

2021-Central Michigan		Opponent	CMU	Opp	S/U	Line	ATS	Total	O/U	
9/4/2021	@	Missouri	24	34	L	14.0	W	59.0	U	
9/11/2021	vs	ROBERT MORRIS	45	0	W	-37.0	W	53.0	U	
9/18/2021	@	Lsu	21	49	L	19.5	L	60.5	O	
9/25/2021	vs	FLORIDA INTERNATIONAL	31	27	W	-12.0	L	55.0	O	
10/2/2021	@	Miami-Ohio	17	28	L	-2.5	L	56.5	U	
10/9/2021	@	Ohio	30	27	W	-5.0	L	57.5	U	
10/16/2021	vs	TOLEDO	26	23	W	5.0	W	53.0	U	{OT}
10/23/2021	vs	NORTHERN ILLINOIS	38	39	L	-6.0	L	56.0	O	
11/3/2021	@	Western Michigan	42	30	W	9.0	W	64.5	O	"Victory Cannon"
11/10/2021	vs	KENT STATE	54	30	W	-2.5	W	76.5	O	
11/17/2021	@	Ball State	37	17	W	-2.5	W	57.0	U	
11/26/2021	vs	EASTERN MICHIGAN	31	10	W	-8.5	W	64.0	U	"MICHIGAN MAC TROPHY"
12/31/2021	vs	Washington State	24	21	W	5.5	W	55.5	U	Sun Bowl
Coach: Jim McElwain		Season Record >>	420	335	9-4	ATS>>	8-5	O/U>>	5-8	

2020-Central Michigan		Opponent	CMU	Opp	S/U	Line	ATS	Total	O/U	
11/4/2020	vs	OHIO	30	27	W	3.0	W	54.5	O	
11/11/2020	@	Northern Illinois	40	10	W	-6.0	W	57.0	U	
11/18/2020	vs	WESTERN MICHIGAN	44	52	L	1.0	L	59.5	O	"Victory Cannon"
11/28/2020	@	Eastern Michigan	31	23	W	-6.0	W	58.0	U	
12/5/2020	vs	BALL STATE	20	45	L	2.5	L	62.5	O	
12/12/2020	@	Toledo	23	24	L	10.0	W	55.0	U	
Coach: Jim McElwain		Season Record >>	188	181	3-3	ATS>>	4-2	O/U>>	3-3	

2019-Central Michigan		Opponent	CMU	Opp	S/U	Line	ATS	Total	O/U	
8/29/2019	vs	SUNY-ALBANY	38	21	W	-14.0	W	NT	---	
9/7/2019	@	Wisconsin	0	61	L	35.0	L	54.0	O	
9/14/2019	@	Miami	45	24	W	-2.5	W	45.0	O	
9/14/2019	vs	AKRON	12	17	L	30.5	W	48.5	U	
9/28/2019	@	Western Michigan	15	31	L	15.0	L	60.0	U	"Victory Cannon"
10/5/2019	vs	EASTERN MICHIGAN	42	16	W	3.5	W	54.0	O	
10/12/2019	vs	NEW MEXICO STATE	42	28	W	-10.5	W	56.5	O	
10/19/2019	@	Bowling Green	38	20	W	-10.5	W	54.5	O	
10/26/2019	@	Buffalo	20	43	L	2.0	L	45.5	O	
11/2/2019	vs	NORTHERN ILLINOIS	48	10	W	1.5	W	49.5	O	
11/16/2019	@	Ball State	45	44	W	1.0	W	60.0	O	
11/29/2019	vs	TOLEDO	49	7	W	-14.5	W	63.5	U	
12/7/2019	vs	Miami-Ohio	21	26	L	-5.5	L	56.5	U	MAC Championship Game
12/21/2019	vs	San Diego State	11	48	L	4.0	L	40.5	O	New Mexico Bowl
Coach: Jim McElwain		Season Record >>	426	396	8-6	ATS>>	9-5	O/U>>	9-4	

2018-Central Michigan		Opponent	CMU	Opp	S/U	Line	ATS	Total	O/U	
9/1/2018	@	Kentucky	20	35	L	17.5	W	49.0	O	
9/8/2018	vs	KANSAS	7	31	L	-3.0	L	48.0	U	
9/15/2018	@	Northern Illinois	16	24	L	14.0	W	48.0	U	
9/22/2018	vs	MAINE	17	5	W	-7.5	W	NT	---	
9/29/2018	@	Michigan State	20	31	L	28.0	W	45.0	O	
10/6/2018	vs	BUFFALO	24	34	L	6.5	L	52.5	O	
10/13/2018	vs	BALL STATE	23	24	L	-2.5	L	54.5	U	
10/20/2018	vs	WESTERN MICHIGAN	10	35	L	6.5	L	54.0	U	"Victory Cannon"
10/27/2018	@	Akron	10	17	L	4.0	L	43.5	U	
11/3/2018	@	Eastern Michigan	7	17	L	14.5	W	46.5	U	
11/10/2018	vs	BOWLING GREEN	13	24	L	-7.0	L	49.5	U	
11/23/2018	@	Toledo	13	51	L	18.5	L	57.5	O	
Coach: John Bonamego		Season Record >>	180	328	1-11	ATS>>	5-7	O/U>>	4-7	

CENTRAL MICHIGAN CHIPPEWAS — MAC West

STADIUM: Kelly-Shorts Stadium {30,255} | **Location:** Mount Pleasant, MI | **COACH:** Jim McElwain

DATE		Opponent	CMU	Opp	S/U	Line	ATS	Total	O/U	Trends & Angles
9/3/2022	@	*Oklahoma State*								vs Oklahoma State - Series tied 1-1
9/10/2022	vs	*SOUTH ALABAMA*								13-1 S/U in 1st home game of season since 2007
9/17/2022	vs	*BUCKNELL*								1st Meeting
9/24/2022	@	*Penn State*								vs Penn State - Penn State leads series 1-0
10/1/2022	@	Toledo								1-11 S/U @ Toledo as a Dog since 1996
10/8/2022	vs	BALL STATE								vs Ball State - Ball State leads series 27-26-1
10/15/2022	@	Akron								10-0 S/U after playing Ball State since 2011
10/22/2022	vs	BOWLING GREEN								vs Bowling Green - BGU leads series 23-19
11/2/2022	@	Northern Illinois								7-1 ATS vs Northern Illinois since 2014
11/9/2022	vs	BUFFALO								7-1 S/U vs Buffalo as a favorite since 1999
11/16/2022	vs	WESTERN MICHIGAN								0-4 S/U & ATS @ home vs WMU since 2012
11/25/2022	@	Eastern Michigan								Game 0-4 O/U @ E. Michigan since 2014
12/2/2022	vs									MAC Championship
	vs									Bowl Game

Pointspread Analysis

Non-Conference
- 0-26 S/U vs Non-Conf. as 20.5 point or more Dog since 1993
- 2-25 S/U vs Non-Conf. as 7.5-15 point Dog since 1989
- 3-10 S/U vs Non-Conf. as 3.5-7 point Dog since 1994
- 15-0 S/U vs Non-Conf. as 7.5 point or more favorite since 1990

Dog
- 0-9 S/U & ATS on road as 30.5 point or more Dog since 1997
- 0-8 S/U as 25.5-30 point Dog since 1996
- 6-0 ATS as 25.5-30 point Dog since 2001
- 1-16 S/U on road as 20.5-25 point Dog since 1993
- 0-7 S/U @ home as 15.5-20 point Dog since 1999
- 2-9 S/U on road as 15.5-20 point Dog since 1997
- 0-6 S/U @ home as 10.5-15 point Dog since 1997
- 2-12 S/U as 10.5-15 point Dog since 2010
- 4-25 S/U as 7.5-10 point Dog since 1989
- 2-18 S/U on road as 7.5-10 point Dog since 1989
- 5-11-1 ATS on road as Dog since 2000
- 6-2 O/U on road as 3.5-7 point Dog since 2010
- 2-7 S/U @ home as 3.5-7 point Dog since 2000
- 19-2 O/U as 3 point or less Dog since 2006
- 9-0 O/U on road as 3 point or less Dog since 2006

Favorite
- 10-1-3 ATS on road as 3 point or less favorite since 1999
- 13-1 S/U on road as 3 point or less favorite since 1999
- 2-7 O/U @ home as 3 point or less favorite since 2007
- 3-18-1 O/U as 3.5-7 point favorite since 2006
- 8-2 S/U @ home as 3.5-7 point favorite since 2005
- 7-0 S/U on road as 7.5-10 point favorite since 2001
- 12-1 S/U @ home as 7.5-10 point favorite since 1991
- 9-0 S/U on road as 10.5-15 point favorite since 1989
- 6-0-1 S/U on road as 15.5-20 point favorite since 1990
- 13-1 S/U @ home as 15.5-20 point favorite since 1989
- 9-0 S/U @ home as 30.5 point or more favorite since 1995

Bowl Games
- 0-5 S/U in Bowl Games since 2014

- 1-13 S/U vs ranked teams all time

Conference
- vs Akron - CMU leads series 17-10-1
- vs Buffalo - CMU leads series 7-3
- vs Eastern Michigan - CMU leads series 63-30-6
- Game 6-0 O/U vs Kent State since 2007
- vs Miami-Ohio - Miami leads series 16-13-1
- 1-6 O/U vs Miami-Ohio as a favorite since 2007
- 6-2 S/U vs Northern Illinois since 2014
- vs Northern Illinois - CMU leads series 31-25-1
- 10-1 S/U vs Ohio since 2005
- Game 1-5 O/U vs Ohio since 2013
- 12-0-1 S/U vs Ohio as favorite since 1991
- 5-1 ATS vs Ohio since 2013
- 4-19 S/U vs Toledo as Dog since 1993
- 6-0 S/U vs Toledo as favorite since 1992
- vs Toledo - Toledo leads series 27-20-3
- 1-6 ATS @ Toledo since 2008
- Game 5-2-1 O/U @ Toledo since 2006
- 2-10 S/U vs Toledo since 2010 {3-9 ATS}
- vs Western Michigan - WMU leads series 52-40-2
- 2-6 S/U vs Western Michigan since 2014
- 9-2 S/U vs Western Michigan as favorite since 1990
- 0-3 S/U @ home vs W. Michigan as a Dog since 2012
- 0-4 O/U @ home vs W. Michigan as a favorite since 2004
- 8-0 S/U vs Akron as 16 point or less favorite since 1998
- 1-5 S/U @ home vs Ball State as 7 point or less Dog since 1996
- 0-4 ATS @ home vs Ball State as 19 point or less favorite since 2010
- 0-5 S/U vs Bowling Green as 29 point or less Dog since 1996
- 1-4 O/U vs B. Green as 12 point or less favorite since 2006
- 5-1 S/U @ E. Michigan as 14.5 point or less favorite since 2002
- 5-1 ATS @ E. Michigan as 14.5 point or less favorite since 2002
- 4-0 O/U vs Kent State as 17 point or less favorite since 2007
- 1-4 S/U vs Miami-Ohio as 22.5 point or less Dog since 1995
- 7-0 ATS vs Northern Illinois as 14 point or less Dog since 2014

Oklahoma State	9-3 ATS in 1st road game of season since 2009
S. ALABAMA	1-5-1 O/U in 1st home game of season since 2010
Penn State	0-10 S/U in 2nd road game of season since 2011
Akron	8-1 ATS after playing Ball State since 2012
Northern Illinois	2-7 S/U prior to playing Buffalo since 1999
BUFFALO	2-8 S/U after playing Northern Illinois since 2010
W. MICHIGAN	6-1 S/U after playing Buffalo since 2004

Page | 43 — Copyright © 2022 by Steve's Football Bible, LLC

CHARLOTTE 49ERS — C-USA East

2021-Charlotte		Opponent	Char	Opp	S/U	Line	ATS	Total	O/U	
9/4/2021	vs	DUKE	31	28	W	6.5	W	60.0	U	
9/11/2021	vs	GARDNER-WEBB	38	10	W	-23.0	W	58.0	U	
9/18/2021	@	Georgia State	9	20	L	4.0	L	63.0	U	
9/24/2021	vs	MIDDLE TENNESSEE	42	39	W	-2.5	W	55.5	O	
10/2/2021	@	Illinois	14	24	L	10.0	T	53.5	U	
10/8/2021	@	Florida International	45	33	W	-3.5	W	60.5	O	
10/22/2021	vs	FLORIDA ATLANTIC	9	38	L	6.5	L	58.0	U	
10/30/2021	@	Western Kentucky	13	45	L	20.5	L	71.5	U	
11/6/2021	vs	RICE	31	24	W	-6.5	W	51.5	O	{OT}
11/13/2021	@	Louisiana Tech	32	42	L	6.5	L	58.0	O	
11/20/2021	vs	MARSHALL	29	48	L	14.5	L	62.5	O	
11/27/2021	@	Old Dominion	34	56	L	8.5	L	55.5	O	
Coach: Will Healy		Season Record >>	327	407	5-7	ATS>>	5-6-1	O/U>>	6-6	

2020-Charlotte		Opponent	Char	Opp	S/U	Line	ATS	Total	O/U	
9/12/2020	@	Appalachian State	20	35	L	17.0	W	59.0	U	
10/3/2020	@	Florida Atlantic	17	21	L	4.5	W	63.0	U	
10/10/2020	@	North Texas	49	21	W	-3.0	W	66.5	O	
10/24/2020	vs	TEXAS-EL PASO	38	28	W	-17.5	L	50.5	O	
10/31/2020	@	Duke	19	53	L	11.5	L	55.0	O	
12/6/2020	vs	WESTERN KENTUCKY	19	37	L	-3.0	L	47.0	O	
Coach: Will Healy		Season Record >>	162	195	2-4	ATS>>	3-3	O/U>>	4-2	

2019-Charlotte		Opponent	Char	Opp	S/U	Line	ATS	Total	O/U	
8/31/2019	vs	GARDNER-WEBB	49	28	W	-31.0	L	NT	---	
9/7/2019	@	Appalachian State	41	56	L	23.0	W	54.5	O	
9/14/2019	vs	MASSACHUSETTS	52	17	W	-21.0	W	66.5	O	
9/21/2019	@	Clemson	10	52	L	41.5	L	61.0	O	
9/28/2019	vs	FLORIDA ATLANTIC	27	45	L	1.0	L	64.5	O	
10/12/2019	@	Florida International	23	48	L	5.0	L	59.5	O	
10/19/2019	@	Western Kentucky	14	30	L	9.5	L	48.5	U	
10/26/2019	vs	NORTH TEXAS	39	38	W	4.0	W	64.0	O	
11/2/2019	vs	MIDDLE TENNESSEE	34	20	W	3.5	W	65.5	U	
11/9/2019	@	Texas-El Paso	28	21	W	-12.0	L	55.5	U	
11/23/2019	vs	MARSHALL	24	13	W	7.0	W	55.5	U	
11/30/2019	@	Old Dominion	38	22	W	-10.0	W	50.5	O	
12/20/2019	vs	Buffalo	9	31	L	7.0	L	51.5	U	Bahamas Bowl
Coach: Will Healy		Season Record >>	388	421	7-6	ATS>>	6-7	O/U>>	7-5	

2018-Charlotte		Opponent	Char	Opp	S/U	Line	ATS	Total	O/U	
9/1/2018	vs	FORDHAM	34	10	W	-16.5	W	NT	---	
9/8/2018	vs	APPALACHIAN STATE	9	45	L	14.0	L	48.5	O	
9/13/2018	vs	OLD DOMINION	28	25	W	1.5	W	48.0	O	
9/22/2018	@	Massachusetts	31	49	L	6.0	L	55.0	O	
9/29/2018	@	Alabama-Birmingham	7	28	L	15.5	L	52.0	U	
10/13/2018	vs	WESTERN KENTUCKY	40	14	W	9.5	W	49.0	O	
10/20/2018	@	Middle Tennessee	13	21	L	15.0	W	50.0	U	
10/27/2018	vs	SOUTHERN MISSISSIPPI	20	17	W	6.5	W	45.0	U	
11/3/2018	@	Tennessee	3	14	L	21.5	W	45.0	U	
11/10/2018	@	Marshall	13	30	L	12.0	L	41.5	O	
11/17/2018	vs	FLORIDA INTERNATIONAL	35	42	L	3.5	L	44.5	O	
11/24/2018	@	Florida Atlantic	27	24	W	17.0	W	55.0	U	
Coach: Brad Lambert		Season Record >>	260	319	5-7	ATS>>	7-5	O/U>>	6-5	

CHARLOTTE 49ERS — C-USA East

STADIUM: Jerry Richardson Stadium {15,314} | **Location:** Charlotte, NC | **COACH:** Will Healy

DATE		Opponent	Char	Opp	S/U	Line	ATS	Total	O/U	Trends & Angles
8/27/2022	@	Florida Atlantic								vs Florida Atlantic - FAU leads series 5-2
9/1/2022	vs	WILLIAM & MARY								8-1 S/U in 1st home game of season since 2013
9/10/2022	vs	MARYLAND								2-7 S/U in 2nd home game of season since 2013
9/17/2022	@	Georgia State								vs Georgia State - G State leads series 2-1
9/24/2022	@	South Carolina								1st Meeting
10/1/2022	vs	TEXAS-EL PASO								vs Texas-El Paso - Charlotte leads series 2-0
10/15/2022	@	Alabama-Birmingham								vs UAB - Series tied 1-1
10/22/2022	vs	FLORIDA INTL.								vs Florida Int - FIU leads series 5-1
10/29/2022	@	Rice								vs Rice - Rice leads series 2-1
11/5/2022	vs	WESTERN KENTUCKY								vs W Kentucky - WKU leads series 4-1
11/12/2022	@	Middle Tennessee								vs Middle Tenn - MTSU leads series 4-2
11/19/2022	vs	LOUISIANA TECH								vs Louisiana Tech - LA Tech leads series 1-0
12/3/2022	vs									C-USA Championship
	vs									BOWL GAME

Non-Conference
- 0-13 S/U vs Non-Conf. as 10.0 point or more Dog since 2015

Conference
- Game 1-6 O/U vs Florida Atlantic since 2015
- Game 4-0 O/U vs Florida International since 2017
- 4-0 ATS vs Middle Tennessee since 2017

Dog
- 0-10 S/U as 20 point or more Dog since 2015
- 0-6 S/U on road as 3.5-10 point Dog since 2017
- 0-7 S/U @ home as 10.5-20 point Dog since 2015

Favorite
- 9-0 S/U as 10 point or more favorite since 2018

Opponent	Trend
Florida Atlantic	0-6 S/U in 1st road game of season since 2016
Georgia State	0-7 S/U in 2nd road game of season since 2015
Georgia State	1-5-1 ATS in 2nd road game of season since 2015
UAB	1-5 S/U prior to playing Florida International since 2015
Rice	0-5 S/U prior to playing Western Kentucky since 2017 {1-4 ATS}
LA TECH	1-5 O/U after playing Middle Tennessee since 2015
LA TECH	1-6 S/U in final home game of season since 2015

0-3 S/U & ATS vs ranked teams all time {3-0 O/U}

Steve's Football Bible also offers the Pro Football Bible, the Pro football handicapper's best friend for the 2022 football season.

To order Go to: www.stevesfootballbible.com

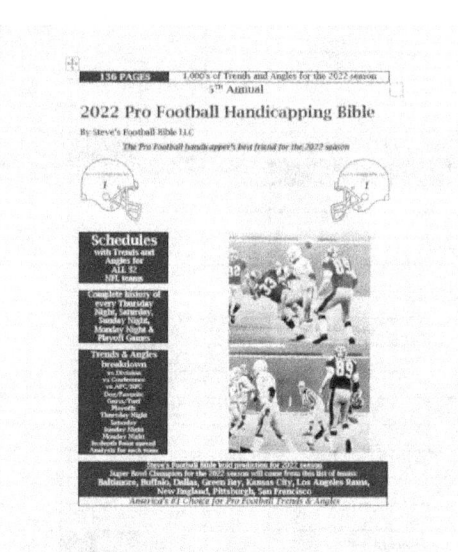

2022 Pro Football Bible $24.95

CINCINNATI BEARCATS   AMERICAN East

2021-Cincinnati		Opponent	Cincy	Opp	S/U	Line	ATS	Total	O/U	
9/4/2021	vs	MIAMI-OHIO	49	14	W	-23.5	W	48.5	O	"Victory Bell"
9/11/2021	vs	MURRAY STATE	42	7	W	-37.5	L	52.0	U	
9/18/2021	@	Indiana	38	24	W	-4.0	W	50.0	O	
10/2/2021	@	Notre Dame	24	13	W	-2.5	W	50.0	U	
10/8/2021	vs	TEMPLE	52	3	W	-30.0	W	52.5	O	
10/16/2021	vs	CENTRAL FLORIDA	56	21	W	-22.0	W	56.0	O	
10/23/2021	@	Navy	27	20	W	-29.0	L	49.0	U	
10/30/2021	@	Tulane	31	12	W	-28.0	L	61.5	U	
11/6/2021	vs	TULSA	28	20	W	-22.5	L	56.0	U	
11/12/2021	@	South Florida	38	28	W	-24.0	L	58.5	O	
11/20/2021	vs	SMU	48	14	W	-9.5	W	65.0	U	
11/26/2021	@	East Carolina	35	13	W	-15.0	W	56.5	U	
12/4/2021	vs	Houston	35	20	W	-10.5	W	52.5	O	AAC CHAMPIONSHIP
12/31/2021	vs	Alabama	6	27	L	12.0	L	56.5	U	Cotton Bowl (National Semifinal)
Coach: Luke Fickell		Season Record >>	509	236	13-1	ATS>>	8-6	O/U>>	6-8	AAC CHAMPIONS

2020-Cincinnati		Opponent	Cincy	Opp	S/U	Line	ATS	Total	O/U	
9/19/2020	vs	AUSTIN PEAY	55	20	W	NL	---	NT	---	
9/26/2020	vs	ARMY	24	10	W	-12.0	W	44.5	U	
10/3/2020	vs	SOUTH FLORIDA	28	7	W	-22.5	L	45.5	U	
10/24/2020	@	Smu	42	13	W	-1.0	W	57.5	U	
10/31/2020	vs	MEMPHIS	49	10	W	-6.5	W	56.5	O	
11/7/2020	vs	HOUSTON	38	10	W	-11.5	W	51.5	U	
11/13/2020	vs	EAST CAROLINA	55	17	W	-27.0	W	56.0	O	
11/21/2020	@	Central Florida	36	33	W	-4.0	L	65.5	O	
12/19/2020	vs	TULSA	27	24	W	-14.0	L	44.5	O	AAC CHAMPIONSHIP
1/1/2021	vs	Georgia	21	24	L	8.0	W	43.0	U	Chick-Fil-A Peach Bowl
Coach: Luke Fickell		Season Record >>	375	168	9-1	ATS>>	6-3	O/U>>	4-5	AAC CHAMPIONS

2019-Cincinnati		Opponent	Cincy	Opp	S/U	Line	ATS	Total	O/U	
8/29/2019	vs	UCLA	24	14	W	-2.5	W	55.5	U	
9/7/2019	@	Ohio State	0	42	L	14.5	L	52.5	U	
9/14/2019	vs	MIAMI-OHIO	35	13	W	-17.5	W	49.5	O	"Victory Bell"
9/28/2019	@	Marshall	52	14	W	-4.0	W	47.5	O	
10/4/2019	vs	CENTRAL FLORIDA	27	24	W	3.5	W	63.5	U	
10/12/2019	@	Houston	38	23	W	-9.5	W	50.0	O	
10/19/2019	vs	TULSA	24	13	W	-15.5	L	47.0	U	
11/2/2019	@	East Carolina	46	43	W	-24.0	L	48.5	O	
11/9/2019	vs	CONNECTICUT	48	3	W	-33.5	W	53.0	U	
11/9/2019	@	South Florida	20	17	W	-13.0	L	46.5	U	
11/23/2019	vs	TEMPLE	15	13	W	-8.5	L	45.5	U	
11/29/2019	@	Memphis	24	34	L	13.5	W	59.5	U	
12/7/2019	@	Memphis	24	29	L	8.0	W	58.0	U	AAC CHAMPIONSHIP GAME
1/2/2020	vs	Boston College	38	6	W	-7.0	W	54.0	U	Birmingham Bowl
Coach: Luke Fickell		Season Record >>	415	288	11-3	ATS>>	9-5	O/U>>	3-11	

2018-Cincinnati		Opponent	Cincy	Opp	S/U	Line	ATS	Total	O/U	
9/1/2018	@	Ucla	26	17	W	14.5	W	62.5	U	
9/8/2018	vs	MIAMI-OHIO	21	0	W	1.5	W	45.5	U	"Victory Bell"
9/15/2018	vs	ALABAMA A&M	63	7	W	-44.0	W	NT	---	
9/22/2018	vs	OHIO	34	30	W	-7.0	L	54.5	O	
9/29/2018	@	Connecticut	49	7	W	-16.5	W	62.0	U	
10/6/2018	vs	TULANE	37	21	W	-7.0	W	48.0	O	
10/20/2018	@	Temple	17	24	L	2.5	L	47.0	U	{OT}
10/27/2018	@	Smu	26	20	W	-9.5	L	49.5	L	{OT}
11/3/2018	vs	NAVY	42	0	W	-13.0	W	48.0	U	
11/10/2018	vs	SOUTH FLORIDA	35	23	W	-16.0	L	52.5	O	
11/17/2018	@	Central Florida	13	38	L	6.5	L	60.5	U	
11/23/2018	vs	EAST CAROLINA	56	6	W	-16.5	W	49.5	O	
12/31/2018	vs	Virginia Tech	35	31	W	-5.5	L	48.5	O	Military Bowl
Coach: Luke Fickell		Season Record >>	454	224	11-2	ATS>>	7-6	O/U>>	5-7	

CINCINNATI BEARCATS   AMERICAN East

STADIUM: Nippert Stadium {40,000} **Location:** Cincinnati, OH **COACH:** Luke Fickell

DATE		Opponent	Cin	Opp	S/U	Line	ATS	Total	O/U	Trends & Angles
9/3/2022	@	Arkansas								1st Meeting
9/10/2022	vs	KENNESAW STATE								20-0 S/U in 1st home game of season since 2002
9/17/2022	vs	MIAMI-OHIO								10-0 S/U @ home vs Miami-Ohio since 2004
9/24/2022	vs	INDIANA								1-5 S/U vs Indiana since 1962
10/1/2022	@	Tulsa								8-1 S/U vs Tulsa since 1993
10/8/2022	vs	SOUTH FLORIDA								0-7 ATS vs South Florida since 2015
10/22/2022	@	Smu								vs Smu - Cincinnati leads series 5-1
10/29/2022	@	Central Florida								vs Central Florida - Cincinnati leads series 4-3
11/5/2022	vs	NAVY								vs Navy - Navy leads series 3-2
11/11/2022	vs	EAST CAROLINA								10-0 ATS @ home vs East Carolina since 1991
11/19/2022	@	Temple								Game 0-4 O/U @ Temple since 2012
11/26/2022	vs	TULANE								vs Tulane - Tulane leads series 11-7
12/3/2022	vs									AAC Championship
	vs									BOWL GAME

Pointspread Analysis — Non-Conference
- 1-22 S/U vs Non-Conf. as 15.5 point or more Dog since 1984
- 2-14 S/U vs Non-Conf. as 10.5-15 point Dog since 1985
- 7-1 S/U vs Non-Conf. as 3.5-7 point favorite since 2006
- 34-1 S/U vs Non-Conf. as 10.5 point or more favorite since 1995
- vs Miami-Ohio - Series tied 59-59-7
- 15-0 S/U vs Miami-Ohio since 2006
- Game 3-8 O/U vs Miami-Ohio since 2009
- 0-3 S/U vs Miami-Ohio as 10 point or more Dog since 1991
- 5-1 S/U vs Miami-Ohio as 7 point or less Dog since 1997
- 6-0 ATS vs Miami-Ohio as 7 point or less Dog since 1997
- 12-0 S/U vs Miami-Ohio as 7 point or more favorite since 2006
- vs Indiana - Indiana leads series 9-4-1

Dog
- 1-15 S/U as 30.5 point or more Dog since 1984
- 0-7 S/U on road as 25.5-30 point Dog since 1985
- 0-10 S/U on road as 20.5-25 point Dog since 1986
- 2-8 ATS as 20.5-25 point Dog since 1987
- 2-54-1 S/U as 15.5 point or more Dog since 1984
- 0-9 S/U @ home as 10.5-15 point Dog since 1991
- 0-20 S/U as 10.5-15 Dog since 1996
- 2-10 ATS as 10.5-15 point Dog since 2004
- 0-6 S/U on road as 7.5-10 point Dog since 2003
- 0-6 S/U as 7.5-10 point Dog since 2015
- 0-7 O/U as 7.5-10 point Dog since 2015
- 2-8 S/U as 3.5-7 point Dog since 2012

Favorite
- 1-3 S/U & ATS @ home as 3 point or less favorite since 2004
- 10-3 S/U on road as 3 point or less favorite since 2009
- 9-0 S/U as 3.5-7 point favorite since 2017
- 15-2 S/U as 7.5-10 point favorite since 2008
- 21-0 S/U @ home as 10.5-15 point favorite since 1993
- 3-12 O/U as 10.5-15 point favorite since 2011
- 60-0 S/U @ home as 10.5 point or more favorite since 1992
- 11-0 S/U on road as 15.5 point or more favorite since 2007

Pointspread Analysis — Conference
- vs East Carolina - East Carolina leads series 13-12
- 4-0 S/U @ home vs East Carolina since 2003
- 9-1 S/U vs East Carolina since 2002
- 4-0 S/U vs SMU as a favorite since 2013
- Game 0-6 O/U vs SMU since 2013
- 8-1 S/U vs Tulsa since 1993
- 0-5 ATS @ South Florida since 2013
- vs South Florida - Cincinnati leads series 12-7
- vs Temple - Temple leads series 13-9-1
- Game 5-1 O/U @ home vs Temple since 2003
- 1-5 ATS vs Temple since 2015
- 0-7 S/U vs East Carolina as 7.5 point or more Dog since 1988
- 3-0 S/U & ATS vs E. Carolina as 4.5 point or less Dog since 1995
- 4-0 S/U & ATS @ home vs E. Carolina as a favorite since 1993
- 4-1 S/U & ATS vs USF as 7 point or less Dog since 2006
- 4-0 S/U @ home vs USF as 10 point or more favorite since 2012
- 7-1 S/U vs Temple as 4.5 point or more favorite since 2002
- 0-3 S/U vs Temple as 9.5 point or more Dog since 1984
- 6-0 S/U vs Tulsa as 4.5 point or more favorite since 1995

Tulsa	11-2 S/U prior to playing South Florida since 2009
Tulsa	2-9 O/U prior to playing South Florida since 2011
USF	0-5 ATS prior to playing SMU since 2014
Smu	0-8 O/U after playing South Florida since 2014
UCF	15-3 ATS in 2nd of B2B road games since 2006
UCF	6-0 S/U after playing SMU since 2013 {6-0 ATS}
NAVY	2-7 O/U prior to playing East Carolina since 2004
E. CAROLINA	7-0 S/U prior to playing Temple since 2014
Temple	8-3 ATS in final road game of season since 2011
TULANE	3-10-1 ATS in final home game of season since 2008

- 27-2 S/U @ home when ranked since 2008
- 7-0 S/U when #5 ranked all time
- 6-17 S/U vs ranked teams since 2010
- 3-32 S/U vs Top 10 ranked teams all time
- 1-18 S/U on road vs Top 10 ranked teams all time
- 0-12 S/U vs #10 - #13 ranked teams all time

Page | 47   Copyright © 2022 by Steve's Football Bible, LLC

CLEMSON TIGERS — ACC Atlantic

2021-Clemson		Opponent	CLEM	Opp	S/U	Line	ATS	Total	O/U	
9/4/2021	vs	Georgia	3	10	L	-3.0	L	57.5	U	Bank of America Stadium
9/11/2021	vs	SOUTH CAROLINA STATE	49	3	W	-50.0	L	57.0	U	
9/18/2021	vs	GEORGIA TECH	14	8	W	-27.0	L	52.5	U	
9/25/2021	@	NC State	21	27	L	-10.5	L	47.0	O	"Textile Bowl"
10/2/2021	vs	BOSTON COLLEGE	19	13	W	-14.5	L	46.0	U	"O'Rourke-McFadden Trophy"
10/15/2021	@	Syracuse	17	14	W	-13.0	L	44.0	U	
10/23/2021	@	Pittsburgh	17	27	L	3.5	L	62.5	U	
10/30/2021	vs	FLORIDA STATE	30	20	W	-9.5	W	47.5	O	
11/6/2021	@	Louisville	30	24	W	-3.5	W	46.5	O	
11/13/2021	vs	CONNECTICUT	44	7	W	-40.5	L	50.5	O	
11/20/2021	vs	WAKE FOREST	48	27	W	-3.5	W	57.0	O	
11/27/2021	@	South Carolina	30	0	W	-11.0	W	43.0	U	"The Palmetto Bowl"
12/29/2021	vs	Iowa State	20	13	W	-2.0	W	45.0	U	Cheez-it Bowl
Coach: Dabo Swinney		Season Record >>	342	193	10-3	ATS>>	5-8	O/U>>	5-8	

2020-Clemson		Opponent	CLEM	Opp	S/U	Line	ATS	Total	O/U	
9/12/2020	@	Wake Forest	37	13	W	-34.0	L	59.0	U	
9/19/2020	vs	THE CITADEL	49	0	W	-50.0	L	55.5	U	
10/3/2020	vs	VIRGINIA	41	23	W	-27.5	L	55.5	O	
10/10/2020	vs	MIAMI	42	17	W	-14.0	W	60.5	U	
10/17/2020	@	Georgia Tech	73	7	W	-27.0	W	63.5	O	
10/24/2020	vs	SYRACUSE	47	21	W	-46.5	L	64.5	O	
10/31/2020	vs	BOSTON COLLEGE	34	28	W	-26.0	L	56.0	O	"O'Rourke-McFadden Trophy"
11/7/2020	@	Notre Dame	40	47	L	-4.5	L	50.5	O	{2 OT}
11/28/2020	vs	PITTSBURGH	52	17	W	-23.5	W	58.5	O	
12/5/2020	@	Virginia Tech	45	10	W	-23.0	W	66.5	U	
12/19/2020	vs	Notre Dame	34	13	W	-11.0	W	58.0	U	ACC CHAMPIONSHIP GAME
1/1/2021	vs	Ohio State	28	49	L	-7.5	L	69.0	O	Sugar Bowl (National Semifinal)
Coach: Dabo Swinney		Season Record >>	522	245	10-2	ATS>>	5-7	O/U>>	7-5	ACC CHAMPIONS

2019-Clemson		Opponent	CLEM	Opp	S/U	Line	ATS	Total	O/U	
8/29/2019	vs	GEORGIA TECH	52	14	W	-36.5	W	61.0	O	
9/7/2019	vs	TEXAS A&M	24	10	W	-16.0	L	62.5	U	
9/14/2019	@	Syracuse	41	6	W	-28.0	W	64.5	U	
9/21/2019	vs	CHARLOTTE	52	10	W	-41.5	W	61.0	O	
9/28/2019	@	North Carolina	21	20	W	-27.5	L	60.0	U	
10/12/2019	vs	FLORIDA STATE	45	14	W	-25.5	W	60.5	U	
10/19/2019	@	Louisville	45	10	W	-25.0	W	62.0	U	
10/26/2019	vs	BOSTON COLLEGE	59	7	W	-35.0	W	59.0	O	"O'Rourke-McFadden Trophy"
11/2/2019	vs	WOFFORD	59	14	W	-48.5	L	NT	---	
11/9/2019	@	NC State	55	10	W	-35.0	W	54.0	O	"Textile Bowl"
11/16/2019	vs	WAKE FOREST	52	3	W	-34.5	W	59.0	U	
11/30/2019	@	South Carolina	38	3	W	-27.0	W	50.5	U	"The Palmetto Bowl"
12/7/2019	vs	Virginia	62	17	W	-30.0	W	57.5	O	ACC CHAMPIONSHIP GAME
12/28/2019	vs	Ohio State	29	23	W	-2.5	W	62.0	U	Fiesta Bowl (National Semi-Final)
1/13/2020	vs	Lsu	25	42	L	4.0	L	66.5	O	CFB Championship Game
Coach: Dabo Swinney		Season Record >>	659	203	14-1	ATS>>	11-4	O/U>>	6-8	ACC CHAMPIONS

2018-Clemson		Opponent	CLEM	Opp	S/U	Line	ATS	Total	O/U	NATIONAL CHAMPIONS
9/1/2018	vs	FURMAN	48	7	W	-49.0	L	NT	---	
9/8/2018	@	Texas A&M	28	26	W	-12.0	L	52.5	O	
9/15/2018	vs	GEORGIA SOUTHERN	38	7	W	-31.5	L	48.5	U	
9/22/2018	@	Georgia Tech	49	21	W	-15.5	W	56.5	O	
9/29/2018	vs	SYRACUSE	27	23	W	-24.5	L	64.5	U	
10/6/2018	@	Wake Forest	63	3	W	-20.5	W	61.0	O	
10/20/2018	vs	NC STATE	41	7	W	-18.5	W	58.0	U	"Textile Bowl"
10/27/2018	@	Florida State	59	10	W	-18.0	W	49.5	O	
11/3/2018	vs	LOUISVILLE	77	16	W	-38.0	W	61.0	O	
11/10/2018	@	Boston College	27	7	W	-17.5	W	51.0	U	"O'Rourke-McFadden Trophy"
11/17/2018	vs	DUKE	35	6	W	-28.5	W	59.5	U	
11/24/2018	vs	SOUTH CAROLINA	56	35	W	-25.5	L	58.5	O	"The Palmetto Bowl"
12/1/2018	vs	Pittsburgh	42	10	W	-27.5	W	53.0	U	ACC CHAMPIONSHIP
12/29/2018	vs	Notre Dame	30	3	W	-10.0	W	58.0	U	Cotton Bowl (National Semi-Final)
1/7/2019	vs	Alabama	44	16	W	5.5	W	57.5	O	CFB Championship Game
Coach: Dabo Swinney		Season Record >>	664	197	15-0	ATS>>	10-5	O/U>>	7-7	ACC CHAMPIONS

CLEMSON TIGERS — ACC Atlantic

STADIUM: Memorial Stadium {81,500} **Location:** Clemson, SC **COACH:** Dabo Swinney

DATE		Opponent	Clem	Opp	S/U	Line	ATS	Total	O/U	Trends & Angles
9/5/2022	@	Georgia Tech								7-0 S/U vs Georgia Tech since 2015 {5-1-1 ATS}
9/17/2022	vs	*LOUISIANA TECH*								vs Louisiana Tech - Clemson leads series 3-0
9/24/2022	@	Wake Forest								13-0 S/U vs Wake Forest since 2009
10/1/2022	vs	NC STATE								8-0 S/U @ home vs NC State since 2004
10/8/2022	vs	*FURMAN*								21-0 S/U @ home vs Furman since 1938
10/8/2022	@	Boston College								11-0 S/U vs Boston College since 2011
10/15/2022	@	Florida State								3-11 S/U @ Florida State since 1993
10/22/2022	vs	SYRACUSE								vs Syracuse - Clemson leads series 8-2
11/5/2022	@	*Notre Dame*								vs Notre Dame - Clemson leads series 4-2
11/12/2022	vs	LOUISVILLE								vs Louisville - Clemson leads series 7-0
11/19/2022	vs	MIAMI								6-1 ATS vs Miami since 2004
11/26/2022	vs	*SOUTH CAROLINA*								7-0 S/U vs South Carolina since 2014
12/3/2022	vs									ACC Championship
	vs									BOWL GAME

Pointspread Analysis — Non-Conference
- 1-5 ATS vs Non-Conf. as 7.5-10 point favorite since 2000
- 1-5 O/U vs Non-Conf. as 7.5-10 point favorite since 2000
- 9-1 S/U vs Non-Conf. as 10.5-15 point favorite since 1988
- 42-0 S/U vs Non-Conf. as 15.5 point or more favorite since 1990
- 0-5 S/U vs South Carolina as Dog since 1987
- vs South Carolina - Clemson leads series 72-41-4 (6 straight W)
- 0-4 O/U vs South Carolina as Dog since 2001
- 31-0 S/U vs Furman since 1938
- vs Furman - Clemson leads series 43-10-4

Bowl Games
- 0-3 S/U in Gator Bowl since 1996
- 0-7 O/U in Peach Bowl since 1993
- 0-3-1 O/U in Gator Bowl since 1989
- 4-0 O/U in CFB Championship Game since 2016
- 8-1 ATS in Bowl Games as 3.5-7 point Dog since 2004
- 2-6 ATS in Bowl Games as 3 point or less favorite since 1993
- 2-5 S/U in Bowl Games as 3 point or less favorite since 1996
- 4-1 S/U & ATS vs Ohio State in Bowl Games
- 3-0 S/U & ATS vs Oklahoma in Bowl Games
- 0-3 O/U vs Oklahoma in Bowl Games
- 0-3 O/U vs Kentucky in Bowl Games
- 11-1 ATS in Bowl Games since 2012
- 10-2 S/U in Bowl Game since 2012

Favorite
- 10-1 S/U as 3.5-7 point favorite since 2014
- 9-1 S/U on road as 7.5-10 point favorite since 1996
- 22-4 S/U as 7.5-10 point favorite since 1996
- 14-1-1 S/U @ home as 7.5-10 point favorite since 1989
- 26-1 S/U as 10.5-15 point favorite since 2010
- 4-10 O/U on road as 10.5-15 point favorite since 2004
- 13-0 S/U @ home as 10.5-15 point favorite since 2008
- 18-8-1 ATS as 10.5-15 point favorite since 2010
- 17-0 S/U as 15.5-20 point favorite since 2006
- 10-0 S/U on road as 15.5-20 point favorite since 1995
- 6-1 O/U on road as 15.5-20 point favorite since 2007
- 26-3 S/U as 20.5-25 point favorite since 1987
- 63-0 S/U as 25.5 point or more favorite since 1984
- 2-6 S/U vs #1 ranked teams all time
- 21-3 S/U vs ranked teams since 2015
- 25-2 S/U on road when ranked since 2015
- 40-1 S/U @ home when ranked since 2014
- 12-2 S/U when ranked #1 all time
- 22-2 S/U when ranked #2 all-time {10-0 @ home}
- 5-0 S/U & ATS vs #3 ranked teams since 2003
- 27-0 S/U when ranked vs Wake Forest since 1948 {11-0 on road}
- 12-2 S/U when ranked vs NC State since 1997 {5-0 @ home}

Pointspread Analysis — Conference
- vs Georgia Tech - Georgia Tech leads series 52-33-2
- 0-4 S/U vs Georgia Tech as a Dog since 2005
- 8-2 ATS vs Georgia Tech as a Dog since 1995
- 6-0 S/U vs Florida State since 2015
- vs Florida State - Florida State leads series 20-14
- 7-0 S/U vs Florida State as favorite since 2009
- 0-5 S/U vs Florida State as a Dog since 2008
- 1-11 S/U @ Florida State as a Dog since 1993
- Game 8-2 O/U @ Florida State since 2000
- 5-0 ATS vs Louisville since 2016
- vs NC State - Clemson leads series 59-29-1
- Game 1-6 O/U @ home vs NC State since 2006
- 15-2 S/U vs NC State since 2004
- Game 2-8 O/U vs Syracuse since 1996
- vs Wake Forest - Clemson leads series 69-17-1
- Game 3-1 O/U @ Wake Forest since 2014
- 11-0 S/U vs Boston College 5 point or more favorite since 2011
- 7-0 S/U @ home vs B.C. as 5 point or more favorite since 2009
- 0-9 S/U @ Florida State as 11 point or more Dog since 1993
- 15-2 S/U vs NC State as 3.5 point or more favorite since 2000
- 9-0 S/U @ home vs NC State as 3.5 point or more favorite since 1996
- 7-0 S/U @ Wake Forest as a 11.5 point or more favorite since 2006

Dog
- 0-5 S/U as 21 point or more Dog since 1993
- 4-0 ATS @ home as 15.5 point or more Dog since 1995
- 2-7 S/U as 10.5-15 point Dog since 1993
- 0-5 S/U on road as 7.5-10 point Dog since 1994
- 0-6 S/U as 7.5-10 point Dog since 1998
- 10-4 ATS on road as 3.5-7 point Dog since 2001

LA TECH	18-0 S/U in 1st home game of season since 2004
LA TECH	11-4-1 ATS in 1st home game of season since 2004
LA TECH	10-1 S/U after playing Georgia Tech since 2011
Wake Forest	11-0 S/U in 2nd road game of season since 2011
Wake Forest	10-0 S/U prior to playing NC State since 2011
FURMAN	10-2 S/U prior to playing Boston College since 2010
FURMAN	9-3 ATS prior to playing Boston College since 2010
Boston College	12-1 S/U prior to playing Florida State since 2008
Florida State	10-2 S/U after playing Boston College since 2010
SYRACUSE	13-3 ATS after playing Florida State since 2005
SYRACUSE	16-0 S/U after playing Florida State since 2005
MIAMI	9-0 S/U prior to playing South Carolina since 2012

COASTAL CAROLINA CHANTICLEERS   SUN BELT East

2021-Coastal Carolina		Opponent	CCU	Opp	S/U	Line	ATS	Total	O/U	
9/3/2021	vs	THE CITADEL	52	14	W	-33.5	W	55.0	O	
9/11/2021	vs	KANSAS	49	22	W	-27.0	T	51.5	O	
9/18/2021	@	Buffalo	28	25	W	-14.0	L	57.5	U	
9/25/2021	vs	MASSACHUSETTS	53	3	W	-36.0	W	66.0	U	
10/2/2021	vs	LOUISIANA-MONROE	59	6	W	-34.0	W	57.5	O	
10/7/2021	@	Arkansas State	52	20	W	-20.0	W	74.5	U	
10/20/2021	@	Appalachian State	27	30	L	-4.5	L	60.5	U	
10/28/2021	vs	TROY	35	28	W	-17.0	L	50.0	O	
11/6/2021	@	Georgia Southern	28	8	W	-16.0	W	56.5	U	
11/13/2021	vs	GEORGIA STATE	40	42	L	-12.5	L	53.0	O	
11/20/2021	vs	TEXAS STATE	35	21	W	-24.5	L	60.5	U	
11/27/2021	@	South Alabama	27	21	W	-14.5	L	55.5	U	{OT}
12/17/2021	vs	Northern Illinois	47	41	W	-12.5	L	63.5	O	Tailgreeter Cure Bowl
Coach: Joe Moglia		Season Record >>	532	281	11-2	ATS>>	5-7-1	O/U>>	6-7	
2020-Coastal Carolina		Opponent	CCU	Opp	S/U	Line	ATS	Total	O/U	
9/12/2020	@	Kansas	35	23	W	40.0	W	56.0	O	
9/19/2020	vs	CAMPBELL	43	21	W	-28.5	L	54.5	O	
10/3/2020	vs	ARKANSAS STATE	52	23	W	3.5	W	64.5	O	
10/17/2020	@	Louisiana	30	27	W	9.0	W	57.0	T	
10/24/2020	vs	GEORGIA SOUTHERN	28	14	W	-1.5	W	48.5	U	
10/31/2020	@	Georgia State	51	0	W	-4.0	W	60.5	U	
11/7/2020	vs	SOUTH ALABAMA	23	6	W	-17.0	T	57.0	U	
11/21/2020	vs	APPALACHIAN STATE	34	23	W	-3.0	W	48.0	O	
11/28/2020	@	Texas State	49	14	W	-16.5	W	59.0	O	
12/5/2020	vs	BYU	22	17	W	10.0	W	62.0	U	
12/12/2020	@	Troy	42	38	W	-11.5	L	53.0	O	
12/26/2020	vs	Liberty	34	37	L	-6.5	L	60.0	O	FBC Mortgage Cure Bowl
Coach: Joe Moglia		Season Record >>	443	243	11-1	ATS>>	8-3-1	O/U>>	7-4-1	
2019-Coastal Carolina		Opponent	CCU	Opp	S/U	Line	ATS	Total	O/U	
8/31/2019	vs	EASTERN MICHIGAN	23	30	L	4.5	L	54.0	U	
9/7/2019	@	Kansas	12	7	W	7.0	W	54.0	U	
9/14/2019	vs	NORFOLK STATE	46	7	W	-25.5	W	NT	---	
9/21/2019	@	Massachusetts	62	28	W	-17.0	W	62.0	O	
9/28/2019	@	Appalachian State	37	56	L	14.5	L	58.0	O	
10/12/2019	vs	GEORGIA STATE	21	31	L	-3.0	L	63.0	U	
10/19/2019	@	Georgia Southern	27	30	L	7.0	W	43.0	O	{2 OT}
11/2/2019	vs	TROY	36	35	W	PK	W	60.0	O	
11/7/2019	vs	LOUISIANA-LAFAYETTE	7	48	L	14.0	L	58.0	U	
11/16/2019	@	Arkansas State	27	28	L	13.5	W	60.0	U	
11/23/2019	@	Louisiana-Monroe	42	45	L	6.0	W	63.5	O	
11/30/2019	vs	TEXAS STATE	24	21	W	-7.0	L	52.0	U	
Coach: Joe Moglia		Season Record >>	364	366	5-7	ATS>>	7-5	O/U>>	5-6	
2018-Coastal Carolina		Opponent	CCU	Opp	S/U	Line	ATS	Total	O/U	
9/1/2018	@	South Carolina	15	49	L	31.0	L	55.5	O	
9/8/2018	vs	ALABAMA-BRIMINGHAM	47	24	W	8.5	W	54.5	O	
9/15/2018	vs	CAMPBELL	58	21	W	-28.5	W	NT	---	
9/22/2018	@	Louisiana-Lafayette	30	28	W	3.0	W	63.0	U	
9/29/2018	@	Troy	21	45	L	13.5	L	57.0	O	
10/13/2018	vs	LOUISIANA-MONROE	20	45	L	-6.5	L	67.5	U	
10/20/2018	@	Massachusetts	24	13	W	2.0	W	74.0	U	
10/27/2018	@	Georgia State	37	34	W	-2.5	W	60.5	O	
11/3/2018	vs	APPALACHIAN STATE	7	23	L	13.5	L	52.0	U	
11/10/2018	vs	ARKANSAS STATE	16	44	L	7.0	L	62.0	U	
11/17/2018	vs	GEORGIA SOUTHERN	17	41	L	7.5	L	53.0	O	
11/24/2018	@	South Alabama	28	31	L	-1.0	L	58.5	O	
Coach: Joe Moglia		Season Record >>	320	398	5-7	ATS>>	5-7	O/U>>	6-5	

COASTAL CAROLINA CHANTICLEERS — SUN BELT East

STADIUM: Brooks Stadium {20,000} **Location:** Conway, SC **COACH:** Joe Moglia

DATE		Opponent	CCU	Opp	S/U	Line	ATS	Total	O/U	Trends & Angles
9/3/2022	vs	ARMY								10-1 S/U in 1st home game of season since 2011
9/10/2022	vs	GARDNER-WEBB								vs Gardner-Webb - Coastal leads series 12-2
9/17/2022	vs	BUFFALO								vs Buffalo - Coastal Carolina leads series 1-0
9/22/2022	@	Georgia State								vs Georgia State - Series tied 3-3
10/1/2022	vs	GEORGIA SOUTHERN								vs Ga Southern - G. Southern leads series 5-3
10/8/2022	@	Louisiana-Monroe								vs UL-Monroe - UL-Monroe leads series 4-0
10/15/2022	vs	OLD DOMINION								vs Old Dominion - ODU leads series 1-0
10/29/2022	@	Marshall								1st Meeting
11/3/2022	vs	APPALACHIAN STATE								vs App State - Appalachian leads series 6-1
11/12/2022	vs	SOUTHERN MISS								11-2 S/U in final home game of season since 2009
11/19/2022	@	Virginia								1st Meeting
11/26/2022	@	James Madison								vs James Madison - Series tied 1-1
12/3/2022	vs									ACC Championship
	vs									BOWL GAME

Pointspread Analysis — Dog

- 1-10 S/U as 13.5 point or more Dog since 2017
- 3-8 ATS as 13.5 point or more Dog since 2017
- 7-1 O/U on road as 13.5 point or more Dog since 2017
- 5-1 S/U & ATS as 3 point or less Dog since 2017
- 1-3 O/U as 3 point or less Dog since 2017

Favorite
- 18-1 S/U as 10.5 point or more favorite since 2018

Pointspread Analysis — Conference
- vs Georgia State - ROAD team 5-0 S/U & ATS since 2017
- BUFFALO — 13-1 S/U after playing Gardner-Webb since 2003
- 15-3 S/U when ranked all time

COLLEGE FOOTBALL HISTORY
"GLORIOUS GAMES OF THE PAST"

A historical look at some of college football's greatest and most memorable games

A celebration of 150 years of college football

By Steve Fulton

This book takes a Historical look at past College Football games. Game of the Century, Memorable games, Great comebacks, great games of the 20th Century, when number 1 played number 2, when number #1 ranked teams lost to an unranked team. Everything for the College Football fan.

College Football "Glorious Games of the Past"
{8.5" x 11"} {293 pages}

{6" x 9"} {473 pages}

$29.95

These books available at numerous online retailers

COLORADO GOLDEN BUFFALOES   PACIFIC-12 South

2021-Colorado		Opponent	COL	Opp	S/U	Line	ATS	Total	O/U	
9/3/2021	vs	NORTHERN COLORADO	35	7	W	-38.0	L	56.5	U	
9/11/2021	vs	TEXAS A&M	7	10	L	17.5	W	50.0	U	
9/18/2021	vs	MINNESOTA	0	30	L	-2.0	L	49.0	U	
9/25/2021	@	Arizona State	13	35	L	14.0	L	45.0	O	
10/2/2021	vs	USC	14	37	L	9.0	L	51.5	O	
10/16/2021	vs	ARIZONA	34	0	W	-6.0	W	47.0	U	
10/23/2021	@	California	3	26	L	8.0	L	44.0	U	
10/30/2021	vs	OREGON	29	52	L	24.5	L	49.5	O	
11/6/2021	vs	OREGON STATE	37	34	W	11.5	W	55.5	O	
11/13/2021	@	Ucla	20	44	L	18.0	L	57.0	O	
11/20/2021	vs	WASHINGTON	20	17	W	6.5	W	43.0	U	
11/26/2021	@	Utah	13	28	L	24.5	W	52.5	U	"Rumble in the Rockies"
Coach: Karl Dorrell		Season Record >>	225	320	4-8	ATS>>	6-6	O/U>>	5-7	
2020-Colorado		Opponent	COL	Opp	S/U	Line	ATS	Total	O/U	
11/7/2020	vs	UCLA	48	42	W	7.0	W	56.0	O	
11/14/2020	@	Stanford	35	32	W	10.0	W	55.5	O	
11/28/2020	vs	SAN DIEGO STATE	20	10	W	-6.0	W	51.5	U	
12/5/2020	@	Arizona	24	13	W	-9.5	W	55.5	U	
12/12/2020	vs	UTAH	21	38	L	2.5	L	49.0	O	"Rumble in the Rockies"
12/19/2020	vs	**Texas**	23	55	L	9.0	L	67.0	O	Alamo Bowl
Coach: Karl Dorrell		Season Record >>	171	190	4-2	ATS>>	4-2	O/U>>	4-2	
2019-Colorado		Opponent	COL	Opp	S/U	Line	ATS	Total	O/U	
8/30/2019	vs	Colorado State	52	31	W	-13.5	W	55.5	O	"Rocky Mountain Showdown"
9/7/2019	vs	NEBRASKA	34	31	W	4.0	W	64.5	O	{OT}
9/14/2019	vs	AIR FORCE	23	30	L	-3.0	L	58.0	U	{OT}
9/21/2019	@	Arizona State	34	31	W	8.0	W	49.0	O	
10/5/2019	vs	ARIZONA	30	35	L	-2.5	L	63.5	O	
10/12/2019	@	Oregon	3	45	L	22.5	L	62.0	U	
10/19/2019	@	Washington State	10	41	L	13.0	L	68.5	L	
10/26/2019	vs	USC	31	35	L	10.5	W	64.5	O	
11/2/2019	@	Ucla	14	31	L	6.5	L	64.5	L	
11/9/2019	vs	STANFORD	16	13	W	4.0	W	56.5	U	
11/23/2019	vs	WASHINGTON	20	14	W	14.0	W	53.0	U	
11/29/2019	@	Utah	15	45	L	28.0	L	50.0	O	"Rumble in the Rockies"
Coach: Mel Tucker		Season Record >>	282	382	5-7	ATS>>	6-6	O/U>>	6-6	
2018-Colorado		Opponent	COL	Opp	S/U	Line	ATS	Total	O/U	
9/1/2018	vs	Colorado State	45	13	W	-7.0	W	66.0	U	"Rocky Mountain Showdown"
9/8/2018	@	Nebraska	33	28	W	3.0	W	63.5	U	
9/15/2018	vs	NEW HAMPSHIRE	45	14	W	-38.0	L	NT	---	
9/28/2018	vs	UCLA	38	16	W	-10.0	W	56.5	U	
10/6/2018	vs	ARIZONA STATE	28	21	W	-2.5	W	64.5	U	
10/13/2018	@	Usc	20	31	L	7.0	L	57.5	U	
10/20/2018	@	Washington	13	27	L	17.0	W	50.5	U	
10/27/2018	vs	OREGON STATE	34	41	L	-24.5	L	60.0	O	{OT}
11/3/2018	@	Arizona	34	42	L	3.0	L	56.5	O	
11/10/2018	vs	WASHINGTON STATE	7	31	L	5.5	L	59.5	U	
11/17/2018	vs	UTAH	7	30	L	7.0	L	45.5	U	"Rumble in the Rockies"
11/24/2018	@	California	21	33	L	10.5	L	44.5	O	
Coach: Mike MacIntyre		Season Record >>	325	327	5-7	ATS>>	5-7	O/U>>	3-8	

4-36 S/U vs ranked teams since 2009   1-17 S/U vs #2 ranked teams all time
1-10 S/U vs #1 ranked all time   1-8 S/U on road vs #3 ranked teams all time

COLORADO GOLDEN BUFFALOES — PACIFIC-12 South

STADIUM: Folsom Field {50,183} | **Location:** Boulder, CO | **COACH:** Karl Dorrell

DATE		Opponent	Col	Opp	S/U	Line	ATS	Total	O/U	Trends & Angles
9/2/2022	vs	TCU								1st Meeting
9/10/2022	@	Air Force								vs Air Force - Colorado leads series 12-5
9/17/2022	@	Minnesota								vs Minnesota - Colorado leads series 3-1
9/24/2022	vs	UCLA								3-0 S/U @ home vs UCLA since 2016
10/1/2022	@	Arizona								vs Arizona - Colorado leads series 16-8
10/15/2022	vs	CALIFORNIA								Game 6-1 O/U vs California since 2010
10/22/2022	@	Oregon State								vs Oregon State - Series tied 6-6
10/29/2022	vs	ARIZONA STATE								vs Arizona State - Arizona State leads series 9-3
11/5/2022	vs	OREGON								0-4 S/U @ home vs Oregon since 1987 {0-4 ATS}
11/12/2022	@	Usc								0-7 S/U @ USC since 1927
11/19/2022	@	Washington								0-4 S/U @ Washington since 1999 {1-3 ATS}
11/26/2022	vs	UTAH								2-11 S/U vs Utah since 1961
12/2/2022	vs									PAC-12 Championship
	vs									BOWL GAME

Pointspread Analysis — Non-Conference
- 0-7 S/U vs Non-Conf. as 15.5-20 point Dog since 1986
- 4-1 O/U vs Non-Conf. as 15.5-20 point Dog since 2003
- 0-6 S/U vs Non-Conf. as 7.5-10 point Dog since 1983
- 2-9 O/U vs Non-Conf. as 3 point or less favorite since 2002
- 2-11-1 ATS vs Non-Conf. as 3 point or less favorite since 1988
- 0-5 O/U vs Non-Conf. as 7.5-10 point favorite since 1996
- 10-2 S/U vs Non-Conf. as 10.5-15 point favorite since 1987
- 2-6 O/U vs Non-Conf. as 10.5-15 point favorite since 2007
- 24-1 S/U vs Non-Conf. as 15.5 point or more favorite since 1987
- 28-0 S/U as 25.5 point or more favorite since 1987
- 0-10 ATS as Non-Conf road favorite since 1988

Bowl Games
- 6-1 S/U & ATS in Bowl Games as 3.5-7 point favorite since 1993
- 0-4 S/U & ATS in Bowl Games as 3 point or less favorite since 1988

Dog
- 0-6 ATS as 30.5 point or more Dog since 2011
- 0-23 S/U as 25.5 point or more Dog since 1983
- 2-18 S/U as 20.5-25 point Dog since 1984
- 2-28 S/U as 15.5-20 point Dog since 1985
- 6-1 ATS @ home as 15.5-20 point Dog since 1986
- 3-15 S/U @ home as 10.5-15 point Dog since 1983
- 2-16 S/U on road as 10.5-15 point Dog since 2002
- 3-8 S/U on road as 7.5-10 point Dog since 1997
- 4-1 ATS @ home as 7.5-10 point Dog since 2001
- 0-11 S/U on road as 3.5-7 point Dog since 1998
- 1-10 ATS on road as 3.5-7 point Dog since 1998
- 8-18 ATS as 3.5-7 point Dog since 2007
- 5-22 S/U as 3.5-7 point Dog since 2007
- 5-11 S/U @ home as 3.5-7 point Dog since 2007
- 1-7 O/U on road as 3.5-7 point Dog since 2008
- 1-6 O/U on road as 3 point or less Dog since 2004
- 4-0 ATS after playing UCLA since 2018
- 0-5 ATS after playing Arizona since 2017
- 5-1 ATS after playing California since 2010
- 1-8 S/U prior to playing Oregon since 1986 {1-8 ATS}
- 2-7 S/U prior to playing Washington since 2000
- 2-7 S/U after playing USC since 2012
- 0-6 S/U on road when ranked vs ranked teams since 1996
- 23-5 S/U @ home when ranked since 1996
- 1-31 S/U on road vs ranked teams since 2002
- 0-7 S/U vs ranked Oregon since 2011 {1-6 ATS}
- 0-8 S/U vs ranked USC all time

Pointspread Analysis — Conference
- vs Oregon - Oregon leads series 14-9
- 1-8 S/U vs Oregon since 2002 {2-7 ATS}
- 4-1 S/U vs Oregon State as favorite since 1983
- vs Ucla - UCLA leads series 12-5
- 3-0 S/U vs UCLA as favorite since 2003
- vs Usc - USC leads series 15-0
- vs Utah - Series tied 33-33-3
- 1-5 ATS vs Utah since 2016
- 2-9 S/U vs Washington since 1999
- 3-8 ATS vs Washington since 1999
- vs Washington - Washington leads series 12-8-1
- Game 0-5 O/U vs Washington since 2016
- 0-3 S/U vs California as 10 point or more Dog since 2010
- 0-7 S/U vs Arizona State as 11 point or more Dog since 2006
- 0-3 S/U vs Arizona as 13 point or more Dog since 2012
- 0-6 S/U vs UCLA as 7.5 point or more Dog since 2012
- 4-1 ATS vs UCLA as 7.5 point or more Dog since 2013
- 0-10 S/U vs USC as 5.5 point or more Dog since 2000
- 0-7 S/U vs Utah as 7 point or more Dog since 2012
- 1-7 S/U vs Washington as 3.5 point or more Dog since 1985

Favorite
- 3-15-1 O/U as 3 point or less favorite since 2000
- 10-2 S/U on road as 7.5-10 point favorite since 1985
- 6-0 S/U @ home as 7.5-10 point favorite since 2001
- 15-1 S/U as 10.5-15 point favorite since 1999
- 2-10-1 O/U as 10.5-15 point favorite since 2004
- 26-2 S/U as 15.5-20 point favorite since 1987
- 24-3 S/U as 20.5-25 point favorite since 1985
- 8-0 S/U on road as 20.5-25 point favorite since 1986
- 27-0 S/U as 25.5 point or more favorite since 1987

Arizona	1-6 O/U prior to playing California since 2010
CALIFORNIA	5-0 O/U prior to playing Oregon State since 2014
Oregon State	1-5 O/U prior to playing Arizona State since 2015
ASU	0-7 S/U after playing Oregon State since 2013
OREGON	0-4 S/U after playing Arizona State since 2017 {0-4 ATS}
Usc	3-10 S/U after playing Oregon since 1979
Washington	0-6 O/U after playing USC since 2015
Washington	0-5 O/U prior to playing Utah since 2017
Washington	3-14 S/U in final road game of season since 2005
UTAH	1-8 S/U after playing Washington since 2000
UTAH	12-3 ATS in final home game of season since 2006

COLORADO STATE RAMS   MOUNTAIN WEST West

2021-Colorado State

Date		Opponent	CSU	Opp	S/U	Line	ATS	Total	O/U	
9/4/2021	vs	SOUTH DAKOTA STATE	23	42	L	-2.5	L	50.0	O	
9/11/2021	vs	VANDERBILT	21	24	L	-6.5	L	52.0	U	
9/18/2021	@	Toledo	22	6	W	14.5	W	58.5	U	
9/25/2021	@	Iowa	14	24	L	24.0	W	43.5	U	
10/9/2021	vs	SAN JOSE STATE	32	14	W	-3.5	W	44.0	O	
10/16/2021	@	New Mexico	36	7	W	-13.0	W	45.0	U	
10/22/2021	@	Utah State	24	26	L	-3.0	L	58.5	U	
10/30/2021	vs	BOISE STATE	19	28	L	2.0	L	51.5	U	
11/6/2021	@	Wyoming	17	31	L	-3.0	L	41.5	O	"Bronze Boot"
11/13/2021	vs	AIR FORCE	21	35	L	3.5	L	45.0	O	"Ram-Falcon Trophy"
11/20/2021	@	Hawaii	45	50	L	-3.0	L	54.0	O	
11/27/2021	vs	NEVADA	10	52	L	3.0	L	58.5	O	
Coach: Steve Addazio		Season Record >>	284	339	3-9	ATS>>	4-8	O/U>>	6-6	

2020-Colorado State

Date		Opponent	CSU	Opp	S/U	Line	ATS	Total	O/U	
10/31/2020	@	Fresno State	17	38	L	-2.5	L	57.5	U	
11/5/2020	vs	WYOMING	34	24	W	3.5	W	53.0	O	"Bronze Boot"
11/12/2020	@	Boise State	21	52	L	14.0	L	62.5	O	
12/5/2020	@	San Diego State	17	29	L	8.0	L	45.5	O	
Coach: Steve Addazio		Season Record >>	89	143	1-3	ATS>>	1-3	O/U>>	3-1	

2019-Colorado State

Date		Opponent	CSU	Opp	S/U	Line	ATS	Total	O/U	
8/30/2019	vs	Colorado	31	52	L	13.5	L	55.5	O	"Rocky Mountain Showdown"
9/7/2019	vs	WESTERN ILLINOIS	38	13	W	-13.0	W	NT	---	
9/14/2019	@	Arkansas	34	55	L	9.5	L	64.0	O	
9/21/2019	vs	TOLEDO	35	41	L	6.0	T	67.0	O	
9/28/2019	@	Utah State	24	34	L	24.0	W	69.0	U	
10/5/2019	vs	SAN DIEGO STATE	10	24	L	6.5	L	48.0	U	
10/12/2019	@	New Mexico	35	21	W	-5.0	W	66.0	U	
10/26/2019	@	Fresno State	41	31	W	13.5	W	56.5	O	
11/2/2019	vs	UNLV	37	17	W	-7.0	W	64.0	U	
11/16/2019	vs	AIR FORCE	21	38	L	10.5	L	62.0	U	"Ram-Falcon Trophy"
11/23/2019	@	Wyoming	7	17	L	4.0	L	51.0	U	"Bronze Boot"
11/30/2019	vs	BOISE STATE	24	31	L	13.0	W	57.0	U	
Coach: Mike Bobo		Season Record >>	337	374	4-8	ATS>>	6-5-1	O/U>>	4-7	

2018-Colorado State

Date		Opponent	CSU	Opp	S/U	Line	ATS	Total	O/U	
8/25/2018	vs	HAWAII	34	43	L	-17.0	L	58.0	O	
8/31/2018	vs	Colorado	13	45	L	7.0	L	66.0	U	"Rocky Mountain Showdown"
9/8/2018	vs	ARKANSAS	34	27	W	14.0	W	70.5	U	
9/15/2018	@	Florida	10	48	L	21.5	L	59.0	U	
9/22/2018	vs	ILLINOIS STATE	19	35	L	-4.5	L	NT	---	
10/6/2018	@	San Jose State	42	30	W	-3.0	W	59.5	O	
10/13/2018	vs	NEW MEXICO	20	18	W	2.5	W	69.0	U	
10/19/2018	@	Boise State	28	56	L	23.0	L	61.5	O	
10/27/2018	vs	WYOMING	21	34	L	3.0	L	47.5	O	"Bronze Boot"
11/10/2018	@	Nevada	10	49	L	14.0	L	62.0	U	
11/17/2018	vs	UTAH STATE	24	29	L	30.0	W	66.0	U	
11/24/2018	@	Air Force	19	27	L	14.0	W	64.0	U	"Ram-Falcon Trophy"
Coach: Mike Bobo		Season Record >>	274	441	3-9	ATS>>	5-7	O/U>>	4-7	

COLORADO STATE RAMS   MOUNTAIN WEST West

STADIUM: Sonny Lubick Field @ Canvas Stadium {41,000} **Location:** Fort Collins, CO **COACH:** Jay Norvell

DATE		Opponent	CSU	Opp	S/U	Line	ATS	Total	O/U	Trends & Angles
6/10/2022	vs	MIDDLE TENNESSEE								12-2 S/U in 1st home game of season since 2008
9/3/2022	@	Michigan								vs Michigan - Michigan leads series 1-0
9/17/2022	@	Washington State								vs Washington State - CSU leads series 1-0
9/24/2022	vs	SACRAMENTO STATE								vs Sacramento State - CSU leads series 1-0
10/8/2022	@	Nevada								1-4 ATS @ Nevada since 2002
10/15/2022	vs	UTAH STATE								4-1 ATS vs Utah State since 2016
10/22/2022	vs	HAWAII								6-1 S/U @ home vs Hawaii since 1989
10/29/2022	@	Boise State								vs Boise State - Boise State leads series 11-0
11/5/2022	@	San Jose State								4-0 S/U vs San Jose State since 2014
11/12/2022	vs	WYOMING								Game 4-0 O/U @ home vs Wyoming since 2014
11/19/2022	@	Air Force								0-8 S/U @ Air Force since 2004
11/26/2022	vs	NEW MEXICO								6-0 S/U @ home vs N Mex since 2008 (5-0-1 ATS)
12/3/2022	vs									MWC Championship
	vs									BOWL GAME

Pointspread Analysis — Non-Conference

- 0-15 S/U vs Non-Conf. as 20.5 point or more Dog since 1985
- 2-9 S/U vs Non-Conf. as 15.5-20 point Dog since 1986
- 7-2 ATS vs Non-Conf. as 15.5-20 point Dog since 1987
- 4-12 S/U vs Non-Conf. as 10.5-15 point Dog since 1987
- 1-11 S/U vs Non-Conf. as 3.5-7 point Dog since 1993
- 4-12-1 O/U vs Non-Conf. as 3.5-7 point Dog since 1998
- 11-1 S/U vs Non-Conf. as 15.5 point or more favorite since 1990

Bowl Games
- 0-4 S/U & ATS in Bowl Games since 2014
- 0-3 O/U in Liberty Bowl
- 3-0 O/U in New Mexico Bowl

Dog
- 0-30 S/U as 20.5 point or more Dog since 1985
- 0-8 S/U as 15.5-20 point Dog since 1995
- 1-9 S/U @ home as 10.5-15 point Dog since 2006
- 3-15 S/U as 7.5-10 point Dog since 1994
- 2-8 S/U @ home as 7.5-10 point Dog since 1988

Favorite
- 5-1 S/U on road as 3.5-7 point favorite since 2011
- 8-1 S/U on road as 7.5-10 point favorite since 1999
- 9-1 S/U on road as 10.5-15 point favorite since 1996
- 6-1 O/U on road as 10.5-15 point favorite since 1997
- 3-9 ATS on road as 10.5-15 point favorite since 1986
- 20-3 S/U as 15.5-20 point favorite since 1992
- 22-0 S/U as 20,5 point or more favorite since 1990
- 6-0 O/U as 20.5-25 point favorite since 2002

8-2 ATS in 1st home game of season since 2012	MTSU
10-2 O/U in 1st home game of season since 2007	MTSU
1-5 O/U after playing Utah State since 2015	HAWAII
6-1 O/U after playing Boise State since 2014	San Jose State
0-7 S/U prior to playing Wyoming since 2015	San Jose State
1-8 ATS prior to playing Wyoming since 2013	San Jose State
2-9 O/U prior to playing Air Force since 2010	WYOMING
6-1-1 ATS after playing San Jose State since 1996	WYOMING
0-5 S/U after playing Wyoming since 2017 {1-4 ATS}	Air Force
6-1 O/U prior to playing New Mexico since 2014	Air Force
7-3 S/U in final home game of season since 2012	NEW MEXICO
6-0 ATS on road vs ranked teams since 2012	
0-23 S/U vs ranked teams since 2004	
0-26 S/U on road vs ranked teams all time	
0-8 S/U vs #8 - #9 ranked teams all time	
0-5 S/U vs ranked Boise State all time	

Pointspread Analysis — Conference

- vs Air Force - Air Force leads series 38-21-1
- Game 11-3 O/U vs Air Force since 2007
- 7-2 S/U vs Hawaii since 1995
- Game 6-0 O/U vs Hawaii since 2012
- 5-2 ATS vs Hawaii since 1997
- vs Hawaii - Colorado State leads series 15-11
- 11-0 S/U vs New Mexico since 2010
- vs New Mexico - Colorado State leads series 43-25
- 10-0 S/U vs New Mexico as favorite since 2010
- 6-0 S/U @ New Mexico since 2011
- 10-1 S/U vs Nevada as favorite since 1997
- vs Nevada - Colorado State leads series 12-5
- 2-5 ATS vs San Jose State since 2011
- vs San Jose State - Colorado State leads series 7-4
- Game 6-1 O/U vs San Jose State since 2011
- 3-0 S/U vs San Jose State as favorite since 1997
- vs Utah State - Colorado State leads series 39-36-2
- 5-1 S/U vs Utah State as favorite since 1994
- Game 0-4 O/U vs Utah State since 2017
- 1-5 S/U & ATS vs Wyoming since 2016
- vs Wyoming - Colorado State leads series 59-49-5
- 1-8 S/U @ home vs Air Force as 3.5 point or more Dog since 1985
- 8-2 O/U vs Air Force as 3.5 point or more Dog since 2008
- 0-6 S/U @ Air Force as 6 point or more Dog since 2006
- 0-4 ATS vs Air Force as 7.5-11 point favorite since 1997
- 3-0 vs Air Force as 3.5-7 point favorite since 1994
- 0-10 S/U vs Boise State as 6.5 point or more Dog since 2011
- 7-2 S/U vs Hawaii as 30 point or less favorite since 1995
- 6-0 O/U vs Hawaii as 20.5 point or less favorite since 2012
- 7-0 S/U & ATS vs New Mexico as 7 point or less Dog since 1985
- 5-1 S/U @ New Mexico as 3.5-7 point favorite since 1994
- 4-0 S/U vs UNLV as 3.5-7 point favorite since 2000
- 0-4 S/U @ home vs Wyoming as 3 point or more Dog since 1988
- 5-2 S/U & ATS vs Wyoming as 3.5 point or less favorite since 1995
- 5-1 S/U vs Wyoming as 9 point or more favorite since 1994
- 0-5 ATS vs Wyoming as 11 point or more favorite since 1994

CONNECTICUT HUSKIES   AMERICAN East

2021-Connecticut		Opponent	Uconn	Opp	S/U	Line	ATS	Total	O/U	
8/28/2021	@	Fresno State	0	45	L	27.5	L	63.5	U	
9/2/2021	vs	HOLY CROSS	28	38	L	-3.0	L	50.0	O	
9/11/2021	vs	PURDUE	0	49	L	35.5	L	56.5	U	
9/18/2021	@	Army	21	52	L	34.5	W	48.0	O	
9/25/2021	vs	WYOMING	22	24	L	21.5	W	57.0	U	
10/2/2021	@	Vanderbilt	28	30	L	14.5	W	51.0	O	
10/9/2021	@	Massachusetts	13	27	L	-3.0	L	57.0	U	
10/16/2021	vs	YALE	21	15	W	3.5	W	46.0	U	
10/22/2021	vs	MIDDLE TENNESSEE	13	44	L	14.5	L	54.0	O	
11/13/2021	@	Clemson	7	44	L	40.5	W	50.5	O	
11/20/2021	@	Central Florida	17	49	L	30.0	L	56.0	O	
11/27/2021	vs	HOUSTON	17	45	L	32.0	W	54.0	O	
Coach: Randy Edsall		Season Record >>	187	462	1-11	ATS>>	6-6	O/U>>	7-5	
2019-Connecticut		Opponent	Uconn	Opp	S/U	Line	ATS	Total	O/U	
8/29/2019	vs	WAGNER	24	21	W	-23.0	L	NT	---	
9/7/2019	vs	ILLINOIS	23	31	L	21.5	W	59.0	U	
9/21/2019	@	Indiana	3	38	L	26.0	L	56.0	U	
9/28/2019	@	Central Florida	21	56	L	42.0	W	64.5	O	
10/5/2019	vs	SOUTH FLORIDA	22	48	L	11.0	L	48.0	O	
10/12/2019	@	Tulane	7	49	L	33.5	L	57.5	U	
10/19/2019	vs	HOUSTON	17	24	L	21.5	W	56.0	U	
10/26/2019	@	Massachusetts	56	35	W	-9.5	W	62.0	O	
11/1/2019	vs	NAVY	10	56	L	26.5	L	54.5	O	
11/9/2019	@	Cincinnati	3	48	L	33.5	L	53.0	U	
11/23/2019	vs	EAST CAROLINA	24	31	L	14.5	W	64.0	U	
11/30/2019	@	Temple	17	49	L	27.0	L	48.0	O	
Coach: Randy Edsall		Season Record >>	227	486	2-10	ATS>>	5-7	O/U>>	5-6	
2018-Connecticut		Opponent	Uconn	Opp	S/U	Line	ATS	Total	O/U	
8/30/2018	vs	CENTRAL FLORIDA	17	56	L	24.0	L	69.0	O	
9/8/2018	@	Boise State	7	62	L	34.0	L	64.0	O	
9/15/2018	vs	RHODE ISLAND	56	49	W	-9.5	L	NT	---	"Ramnapping Trophy"
9/22/2018	@	Syracuse	21	51	L	30.5	W	75.5	U	
9/29/2018	vs	CINCINNATI	7	49	L	16.5	L	62.0	U	
10/6/2018	@	Memphis	14	55	L	36.0	L	76.0	U	
10/20/2018	@	South Florida	30	38	L	33.5	W	67.5	O	
10/27/2018	vs	MASSACHUSETTS	17	22	L	3.5	L	62.5	U	
11/3/2018	@	Tulsa	14	49	L	19.0	L	60.0	O	
11/10/2018	vs	SMU	50	62	L	18.0	W	65.5	O	
11/17/2018	@	East Carolina	21	55	L	17.5	L	71.5	O	
11/24/2018	vs	TEMPLE	7	57	L	31.0	L	69.0	U	
Coach: Randy Edsall		Season Record >>	261	605	1-11	ATS>>	3-9	O/U>>	6-5	
2017-Connecticut		Opponent	Uconn	Opp	S/U	Line	ATS	Total	O/U	
8/31/2017	vs	HOLY CROSS	27	20	W	-21.5	L	59.0	U	
9/16/2017	@	Virginia	16	38	L	11.5	L	51.5	O	
9/24/2017	vs	EAST CAROLINA	38	41	L	-5.0	L	63.5	O	
9/30/2017	@	Smu	28	49	L	16.0	L	74.5	O	
10/6/2017	vs	MEMPHIS	31	70	L	16.0	L	76.0	O	
10/14/2017	@	Temple	28	24	W	10.5	W	57.5	U	
10/21/2017	vs	TULSA	20	14	W	4.0	W	76.5	U	
10/28/2017	vs	MISSOURI	12	52	L	13.0	L	75.5	U	
11/4/2017	vs	SOUTH FLORIDA	20	37	L	23.5	W	63.5	U	
11/11/2017	@	Central Florida	24	59	L	39.5	W	65.0	O	
11/18/2017	@	Boston College	16	39	L	21.0	L	51.0	O	Fenway Park
11/25/2017	@	Cincinnati	21	22	L	6.5	W	58.5	U	
Coach: Randy Edsall		Season Record >>	281	465	3-9	ATS>>	5-7	O/U>>	6-6	

CONNECTICUT HUSKIES   AMERICAN East

STADIUM: Pratt & Whitney Stadium @ Rentschler Field {38,066} | **Location:** Storrs, CT | **COACH:** Jim Mora

DATE		Opponent	Conn	Opp	S/U	Line	ATS	Total	O/U	Trends & Angles
8/27/2022	@	Utah State								vs Utah State - Utah State leads series 1-0
9/3/2022	vs	CENTRAL CONNECTICUT								vs Central Connecticut - UCONN leads series 3-0
9/10/2022	vs	SYRACUSE								vs Syracuse - U Conn leads series 6-5
9/17/2022	@	Michigan								vs Michigan - Michigan leads series 2-0
9/24/2022	@	NC State								vs NC State - NC State leads series 2-0
10/1/2022	vs	FRESNO STATE								vs Fresno State - Fresno leads series 1-0
10/8/2022	@	Florida International								1st Meeting
10/15/2022	@	Ball State								vs Ball State - Ball State leads series 3-0
10/29/2022	vs	BOSTON COLLEGE								vs Boston College - BC leads series 9-0-2
11/5/2022	vs	MASSACHUSETTS								vs Massachusetts - UMass leads series 38-35-2
11/12/2022	vs	LIBERTY								vs Liberty - UCONN leads series 1-0
11/19/2022	@	Army								vs Army - UCONN leads series 5-3
	vs									BOWL GAME

Pointspread Analysis — Dog

- 0-29 S/U as 25.5 point or more Dog since 2000
- 1-12 S/U as 20.5-25 point Dog since 2000
- 0-9 S/U @ home as 15.5 point or more Dog since 2002
- 2-20 S/U as 15.5-20 point Dog since 2000
- 7-0 O/U on road as 15.5-20 point Dog since 2007
- 0-7 S/U @ home as 10.5-15 point Dog since 2000
- 2-17 S/U as 10.5-15 point Dog since 2000
- 3-8 ATS on road as 10.5-15 point Dog since 2005
- 0-6 S/U on road as 3.5-7 point Dog since 2012
- 1-8 S/U on road as 3 point or less Dog since 2006
- 2-8 O/U on road as 3 point or less Dog since 2006

Favorite

- 1-14-1 ATS as favorite since 2013
- 0-11-1 ATS as home favorite since 2013
- 0-11 ATS as 3.5-7 point favorite since 2010
- 1-9 O/U @ home as 3.5-7 point favorite since 2004
- 12-1 O/U as 7.5-15 point favorite since 2003
- 10-1 S/U as 10.5-15 point favorite since 2000
- 17-1 S/U as 15.5 point or more favorite since 2003

Pointspread Analysis — Non-Conference

- 3-20 S/U vs Non-Conf. as 10.5 point or more Dog since 2000
- 0-7 S/U vs Non-Conf. as 3 point or less Dog since 2007
- 25-1 S/U vs Non-conf. as 7.5 point or more favorite since 2000
- 5-1 S/U vs Army as favorite since 2003
- 0-6 S/U vs Boston College as Dog since 2000
- 0-4 ATS vs Boston College as Dog since 2003

Utah State	0-8 S/U in 1st road game of season since 2013
CENTRAL CONN	0-8 ATS in 1st home game of season since 2013
SYRACUSE	1-6-2 ATS in 2nd home game of season since 2011
Michigan	0-8 S/U in 2nd road game of season since 2012
Michigan	2-6 ATS in 2nd road game of season since 2012
Michigan	2-8 S/U & ATS after playing Syracuse since 2004
BOSTON COL	2-10 S/U prior to playing Massachusetts since 1992

- 1-23 S/U on road vs ranked teams all time

Print Version $29.95   Print Version $39.95

These books available at numerous online retailers

DUKE BLUE DEVILS — ACC Coastal

2021-Duke		Opponent	Duke	Opp	S/U	Line	ATS	Total	O/U	
9/4/2021	@	Charlotte	28	31	L	-6.5	L	60.0	U	
9/10/2021	vs	NORTH CAROLINA A&T	45	17	W	-22.5	W	56.0	O	
9/18/2021	vs	NORTHWESTERN	30	23	W	2.0	W	49.5	O	
9/25/2021	vs	KANSAS	52	33	W	-16.5	W	58.5	O	
10/2/2021	@	North Carolina	7	38	L	19.5	L	74.0	U	"Victory Bell"
10/9/2021	vs	GEORGIA TECH	27	31	L	4.5	W	61.0	U	
10/16/2021	@	Virginia	0	48	L	10.5	L	69.5	U	
10/30/2021	@	Wake Forest	7	45	L	16.0	L	71.0	U	
11/6/2021	vs	PITTSBURGH	29	54	L	21.5	L	64.5	O	
11/13/2021	@	Virginia Tech	17	48	L	13.5	L	50.5	O	
11/18/2021	vs	LOUISVILLE	22	62	L	20.0	L	60.5	O	
11/27/2021	vs	MIAMI	10	47	L	20.5	L	67.0	U	
Coach: David Cutcliffe		Season Record >>	274	477	3-9	ATS>>	4-8	O/U>>	6-6	

2020-Duke		Opponent	Duke	Opp	S/U	Line	ATS	Total	O/U	
9/12/2020	@	Notre Dame	13	27	L	21.5	W	51.5	U	
9/19/2020	vs	BOSTON COLLEGE	6	26	L	-5.5	L	51.5	U	
9/26/2020	@	Virginia	20	38	L	4.5	L	45.5	O	
10/3/2020	vs	VIRGINIA TECH	31	38	L	10.5	W	54.0	O	
10/10/2020	@	Syracuse	38	24	W	-2.5	W	51.5	O	
10/17/2020	@	NC State	20	31	L	4.5	L	60.0	U	
10/31/2020	vs	CHARLOTTE	53	19	W	-11.5	W	55.0	O	
11/7/2020	vs	NORTH CAROLINA	24	56	L	11.0	L	63.0	O	"Victory Bell"
11/28/2020	@	Georgia Tech	33	56	L	-2.5	L	57.5	O	
12/5/2020	vs	MIAMI	0	48	L	14.0	L	62.5	U	
12/12/2020	@	Florida State	35	56	L	3.0	L	56.5	O	
Coach: David Cutcliffe		Season Record >>	273	419	2-9	ATS>>	4-7	O/U>>	7-4	

2019-Duke		Opponent	Duke	Opp	S/U	Line	ATS	Total	O/U	
8/31/2019	vs	Alabama	3	42	L	33.5	L	56.5	U	Mercedes Benz Stadium
9/7/2019	vs	NORTH CAROLINA A&T	45	13	W	-27.5	W	NT	---	
9/14/2019	@	Middle Tennessee	41	18	W	-6.5	W	51.0	O	
9/27/2019	@	Virginia Tech	45	10	W	2.5	W	51.5	O	
10/5/2019	vs	PITTSBURGH	30	33	L	-3.5	L	47.0	O	
10/12/2019	vs	GEORGIA TECH	41	23	W	-17.5	W	47.5	O	
10/19/2019	@	Virginia	14	48	L	3.0	L	45.0	O	
10/26/2019	@	North Carolina	17	20	L	3.0	T	53.5	U	"Victory Bell"
11/9/2019	vs	NOTRE DAME	7	38	L	7.0	L	49.5	U	
11/16/2019	vs	SYRACUSE	6	49	L	-9.0	L	49.0	O	
11/23/2019	@	Wake Forest	27	39	L	6.0	L	50.0	O	
11/30/2019	vs	MIAMI	27	17	W	9.0	W	44.0	T	
Coach: David Cutcliffe		Season Record >>	303	350	5-7	ATS>>	5-6-1	O/U>>	6-4-1	

2018-Duke		Opponent	Duke	Opp	S/U	Line	ATS	Total	O/U	
9/1/2018	vs	ARMY	34	14	W	-13.5	W	45.5	O	
9/8/2018	@	Northwestern	21	7	W	2.5	W	47.5	U	
9/15/2018	@	Baylor	40	27	W	2.5	W	49.0	O	
9/22/2018	vs	NORTH CAROLINA CENTRAL	55	13	W	-43.0	L	NT	---	
9/29/2018	vs	VIRGINIA TECH	14	31	L	-6.5	L	52.5	U	
10/13/2018	@	Georgia Tech	28	14	W	1.0	W	55.0	U	
10/20/2018	vs	VIRGINIA	14	28	L	-6.5	L	44.5	U	
10/27/2018	@	Pittsburgh	45	54	L	-3.0	L	45.5	O	
11/3/2018	@	Miami	20	12	W	8.5	W	50.5	U	
11/10/2018	vs	NORTH CAROLINA	42	35	W	-7.5	L	58.5	O	"Victory Bell"
11/17/2018	@	Clemson	6	35	L	28.5	L	59.5	U	
11/24/2018	vs	WAKE FOREST	7	59	L	-9.5	L	60.5	O	
12/27/2018	vs	Temple	56	27	W	3.5	W	56.5	O	Independence Bowl
Coach: David Cutcliffe		Season Record >>	382	356	8-5	ATS>>	6-7	O/U>>	6-6	

DUKE BLUE DEVILS — ACC Coastal

STADIUM: Wallace Wade Stadium {40,004}
Location: Durham, NC
COACH: Mike Elko

DATE		Opponent	Duke	Opp	S/U	Line	ATS	Total	O/U	Trends & Angles
9/3/2022	vs	TEMPLE								vs Temple - Duke leads series 1-0
9/10/2022	@	Northwestern								Game 0-5 O/U @ Northwestern since 2000
9/17/2022	vs	NORTH CAROLINA A&T								vs North Carolina A&T - Duke leads series 2-0
9/24/2022	@	Kansas								vs Kansas - Duke leads series 2-1
10/1/2022	vs	VIRGINIA								0-7 S/U & ATS vs Virginia since 2015
10/8/2022	@	Georgia Tech								2-11 S/U @ Georgia Tech since 1996
10/15/2022	vs	NORTH CAROLINA								vs North Carolina - UNC leads series 63-40-4
10/22/2022	@	Miami								1-6 S/U @ Miami since 2005
11/4/2022	@	Boston College								vs Boston College - BC leads series 5-3
11/12/2022	vs	VIRGINIA TECH								0-9 S/U @ home vs Virginia Tech since 1982
11/19/2022	@	Pittsburgh								0-6 S/U & ATS vs Pittsburgh since 2015
11/26/2022	vs	WAKE FOREST								1-8 S/U @ home vs Wake Forest since 2001
12/3/2022	vs									ACC Championship
	vs									BOWL GAME

Pointspread Analysis — Non-Conference

- 2-12 S/U vs Non-Conf. as 15.5 point or more Dog since 1986
- 10-3 ATS vs Non-Conf. as 10.5-15 point Dog since 1985
- 1-12-1 S/U vs Non-Conf. as 7.5-10 point Dog since 1984
- 4-13 S/U vs Non-Conf. as 3.5-7 point Dog since 1984
- 7-0 S/U & ATS vs Non-Conf. as 3 point or less Dog since 1992
- 5-1 S/U vs Non-Conf. as 3 point or less favorite since 1989
- 2-8-1 O/U vs Non-Conf. as 3.5-7 point favorite since 2005
- 7-1 S/U vs Non-Conf. as 7.5-10 point favorite since 1985
- 10-2 S/U vs Non-Conf. as 10.5-15 point favorite since 1990
- 16-0 S/U vs Non-Conf. as 15.5 point or more favorite since 1987
- 13-3 ATS vs Non-Conf. as 15.5 point or more favorite since 1987
- vs Northwestern - Duke leads series 11-10
- 0-4 S/U vs Northwestern as 9 point or less Dog since 1996
- 0-3 S/U @ home vs Northwestern as Dog since 1996
- 0-3 S/U & ATS vs Northwestern as 8 point or less favorite since 1999
- 3-0 S/U vs Northwestern as 9 point or more favorite since 1988
- 0-5 ATS vs Northwestern as favorite since 1989

Bowl Games
- 8-0 O/U in Bowl Games since 1989
- 5-0 ATS in Bowl Games since 2013

Dog
- 0-35 S/U as 25.5 point or more Dog since 1984
- 1-29 S/U as 20.5-25 point Dog since 1984
- 0-18 S/U @ home as 20.5 point or more Dog since 1987
- 2-26 S/U on road as 15.5-20 point Dog since 1983
- 0-13 S/U @ home as 15.5-20 point Dog since 1990
- 2-13 S/U @ home as 10.5-15 point Dog since 2005
- 3-16 S/U on road as 10.5-15 point Dog since 1998
- 7-26 S/U as 7.5-10 point Dog since 1996
- 2-13 S/U @ home as 7.5-10 point Dog since 1996
- 2-16 S/U @ home as 3.5-7 point Dog since 2004
- 11-4 S/U as 3 point or less Dog since 2010
- 12-3-1 ATS as 3 point or less Dog since 2010
- 13-5 O/U as 3 point or less Dog since 2002

- 3-29 S/U @ home vs ranked teams since 1996
- 2-61 S/U on road vs ranked teams since 1972
- 0-12 S/U vs #1 ranked teams all time
- 1-8 S/U vs ranked Virginia Tech all time {0-5 @ home}
- 0-6 S/U vs ranked Virginia since 1995
- 1-8 S/U @ home when ranked since 1994
- 13-1 S/U when ranked vs Wake Forest all time {6-0 on road}
- 1-6 S/U @ home vs ranked North Carolina since 1947

Pointspread Analysis — Conference

- vs Georgia Tech - Georgia Tech leads series 53-13-1
- 7-1 ATS vs Georgia Tech since 2014
- Game 2-5 O/U @ Georgia Tech since 2008
- 1-10 S/U @ Georgia Tech as Dog since 1996
- 3-15 S/U vs Miami since 1983
- vs Miami - Miami leads series 15-4
- 1-10 S/U vs Pittsburgh since 1969
- vs Pittsburgh - Pittsburgh leads series 16-9
- vs Virginia - UVA leads series 40-33
- 3-18 S/U vs Virginia Tech since 1982
- vs Virginia Tech - VPI leads series 19-10
- Game 1-4 O/U @ home vs VPI since 2011
- 0-6 S/U @ home vs Virginia Tech as Dog since 2005
- vs Wake Forest - Duke leads series 58-41-2
- 1-14 S/U vs Wake Forest as Dog since 2000
- 1-20 S/U vs Georgia Tech as 10.5 point or more Dog since 1984
- 0-10 S/U vs Miami as 12.5 point or more Dog since 1983
- 1-13 S/U vs North Carolina as 12 point or more Dog since 1983
- 0-5 ATS vs N. Carolina as 7.5 point or less favorite since 1990
- 1-16 S/U vs Virginia as 10 point or more Dog since 1990
- 3-1 S/U & ATS vs Virginia as 3 point or less Dog since 2010
- 4-0 O/U vs Virginia as 3 point or less Dog since 2010
- 1-12 S/U vs Virginia Tech as 12.5 point or more Dog since 1984
- 1-11 S/U vs Wake Forest as 6 point or more Dog since 1984
- 3-0 S/U & ATS vs Wake F. as 13 point or more favorite since 1989

Favorite
- 8-2 O/U as 3 point or less favorite since 2008
- 3-20-1 O/U as 3.5-7 point favorite since 2005
- 9-1 S/U on road as 7.5 point or more favorite since 1988
- 17-0 S/U @ home as 15.5 point or more favorite since 1987
- 15-2 ATS @ home as 15.5 point or more favorite since 1987

Northwestern	1-8 O/U in 1st road game of season since 2013
TEMPLE	9-1 S/U & ATS in 1st home game of season since 2012
NC A&T	7-0 ATS after playing Northwestern since 2008
Kansas	2-7 O/U prior to playing Virginia since 2013
VIRGINIA	1-12 S/U prior to playing Georgia Tech since 2009
VIRGINIA	3-11 O/U prior to playing Georgia Tech since 2008
Georgia Tech	0-5 S/U after playing Virginia since 2017
Georgia Tech	5-1 ATS prior to playing North Carolina since 2016
UNC	8-1 O/U prior to playing Miami since 2013
Miami	0-7 S/U after playing North Carolina since 2015 {1-6 ATS}
Boston College	0-4 ATS after playing Miami since 2015

EAST CAROLINA PIRATES — AMERICAN East

2021-East Carolina		Opponent	ECU	Opp	S/U	Line	ATS	Total	O/U	
9/2/2021	vs	Appalachian State {@ Charlotte}	19	33	L	9.0	L	55.5	U	
9/11/2021	vs	SOUTH CAROLINA	17	20	L	2.5	L	56.5	U	
9/18/2021	@	Marshall	42	38	W	10.5	W	58.5	O	
9/25/2021	vs	CHARLESTON SOUTHERN	31	28	W	-24.5	L	59.0	T	
10/2/2021	vs	TULANE	52	29	W	3.0	W	65.0	O	
10/9/2021	@	Central Florida	16	20	L	10.0	W	65.0	U	
10/23/2021	@	Houston	24	31	L	13.5	W	56.5	U	
10/30/2021	vs	SOUTH FLORIDA	29	14	W	-9.5	W	55.5	U	
11/6/2021	vs	TEMPLE	45	3	W	-15.5	W	52.0	U	
11/13/2021	@	Memphis	30	29	W	4.0	W	59.0	T	{OT}
11/20/2021	@	Navy	38	35	W	-3.5	L	46.5	O	
11/26/2021	vs	CINCINNATI	13	35	L	15.0	L	56.5	U	
Coach: Mike Houston		Season Record >>	356	315	7-5	ATS>>	7-5	O/U>>	3-8-1	

2020-East Carolina		Opponent	ECU	Opp	S/U	Line	ATS	Total	O/U	
9/26/2020	vs	CENTRAL FLORIDA	28	51	L	27.5	W	77.0	O	
10/3/2020	@	Georgia State	29	49	L	-1.5	L	70.0	O	
10/10/2020	@	South Florida	44	24	W	5.0	W	58.0	O	
10/17/2020	vs	NAVY	23	27	L	3.0	L	55.5	U	
10/30/2020	@	Tulsa	30	34	L	17.0	W	59.5	O	
11/7/2020	vs	TULANE	21	38	L	3.5	L	63.5	U	
11/13/2020	@	Cincinnati	17	55	L	27.0	L	56.0	O	
11/21/2020	@	Temple	28	3	W	-7.0	W	53.0	U	
11/28/2020	vs	SMU	52	38	W	12.5	W	72.0	O	
Coach: Mike Houston		Season Record >>	272	319	3-6	ATS>>	5-4	O/U>>	6-3	

2019-East Carolina		Opponent	ECU	Opp	S/U	Line	ATS	Total	O/U	
8/31/2019	@	NC State	6	34	L	17.5	L	51.5	U	"Victory Barrel"
9/7/2019	vs	GARDNER-WEBB	48	9	W	-31.0	W	NT	---	
9/14/2019	@	Navy	10	42	L	7.5	L	54.0	U	
9/21/2019	vs	WILLIAM & MARY	19	7	W	-14.0	L	NT	---	
9/28/2019	@	Old Dominion	24	21	W	3.0	W	46.5	U	
10/3/2019	vs	TEMPLE	17	27	L	12.5	W	46.5	U	
10/19/2019	@	Central Florida	28	41	L	34.0	W	64.5	O	
10/26/2019	vs	SOUTH FLORIDA	20	45	L	1.5	L	51.0	O	
11/2/2019	vs	CINCINNATI	43	46	L	24.0	W	48.5	O	
11/9/2019	@	Smu	51	59	L	22.5	W	74.0	O	
11/23/2019	@	Connecticut	31	24	W	-14.5	L	64.0	U	
11/30/2019	vs	TULSA	24	49	L	7.0	L	64.0	O	
Coach: Mike Houston		Season Record >>	321	404	4-8	ATS>>	6-6	O/U>>	5-5	

2018-East Carolina		Opponent	ECU	Opp	S/U	Line	ATS	Total	O/U	
9/2/2018	vs	NORTH CAROLINA A&T	23	28	L	-13.0	L	NT	---	
9/8/2018	vs	NORTH CAROLINA	41	19	W	15.5	W	59.0	O	
9/22/2018	@	South Florida	13	20	L	19.5	W	68.5	U	
9/29/2018	vs	OLD DOMINION	37	35	W	-7.0	L	60.5	O	
10/6/2018	@	Temple	6	49	L	10.5	L	52.0	O	
10/13/2018	vs	HOUSTON	20	42	L	16.0	L	69.5	U	
10/20/2018	vs	CENTRAL FLORIDA	10	37	L	21.5	L	65.0	U	
11/3/2018	vs	MEMPHIS	41	59	L	10.5	L	66.0	O	
11/10/2018	@	Tulane	18	24	L	10.5	L	54.0	U	
11/17/2018	vs	CONNECTICUT	55	21	W	-17.5	W	71.5	O	
11/23/2018	@	Cincinnati	6	56	L	16.5	L	49.5	O	
12/1/2018	@	NC State	3	58	L	26.0	L	60.5	O	"Victory Barrel"
Coach: Scottie Montgomery		Season Record >>	273	448	3-9	ATS>>	3-9	O/U>>	7-4	

EAST CAROLINA PIRATES — AMERICAN East

STADIUM: Dowdy-Ficklen Stadium {50,000} | **Location:** Greenville, NC | **COACH:** Mike Houston

DATE		Opponent	ECU	Opp	S/U	Line	ATS	Total	O/U	Trends & Angles
9/3/2022	vs	NC STATE								vs NC State - NC State leads series 18-13
9/10/2022	vs	OLD DOMINION								vs Old Dominion - ECU leads series 6-4-1
9/17/2022	vs	CAMPBELL								vs Campbell - Campbell leads series 3-1
9/24/2022	vs	NAVY								0-4 S/U & ATS @ home vs Navy since 2010
10/1/2022	@	South Florida								vs South Florida - USF leads series 9-3
10/8/2022	@	Tulane								0-5 ATS @ Tulane since 2003
10/15/2022	vs	MEMPHIS								8-1 ATS @ home vs Memphis since 1995
10/22/2022	vs	CENTRAL FLORIDA								vs Central Florida - Series tied 10-10
10/29/2022	@	Byu								vs BYU - Series tied 1-1
11/11/2022	@	Cincinnati								0-4 S/U & ATS @ Cincinnati as Dog since 1993
11/19/2022	vs	HOUSTON								vs Houston - Houston leads series 8-7
11/26/2022	@	Temple								2-6 S/U vs Temple since 2014
12/3/2022	vs									AAC Championship
	vs									BOWL GAME

Pointspread Analysis — Non-Conference
- 2-36 S/U vs Non-Conf. as 15.5 point or more Dog since 1985
- 8-1 O/U vs Non-Conf. as 3.5-7 point favorite since 2000
- 20-1-1 S/U vs Non-Conf. as 7.5 point or more favorite since 1989
- 4-0 S/U & ATS vs NC State as 6.0-10 point Dog since 1985
- 0-4 S/U & ATS vs NC State as 10.5 point or more Dog since 1997
- vs Old Dominion - East Carolina leads series 6-3-1

Bowl Games
- 2-7 S/U in Bowl Games since 2001

Dog
- 0-9 S/U as 30.5 point or more Dog since 1985
- 1-13 S/U as 25.5-30 point Dog since 1986
- 0-12 S/U on road as 20.5-25 point dog since 1985
- 1-19 S/U as 20.5-25 point Dog since 1985
- 1-17 S/U on road as 15.5-20 point Dog since 1984
- 1-16 S/U as 15.5-20 point Dog since 2003
- 5-1 ATS @ home as 15.5-20 Dog since 2003
- 7-27 S/U on road as 10.5-15 point Dog since 1984
- 2-11 S/U @ home as 10.5-15 point Dog since 1985
- 3-19 S/U on road as 7.5-10 point Dog since 1987
- 4-13 S/U & ATS @ home as 3 point or less dog since 1994

Favorite
- 2-7 S/U @ home as 3 point or less favorite since 2001
- 0-6 ATS on road as 7.5-10 point favorite since 2001
- 1-7 ATS as 7.5-10 point favorite since 2008
- 8-0 S/U @ home as 7.5-10 point favorite since 1996
- 15-3 S/U @ home as 10.5-15 point favorite since 1994
- 9-2 S/U on road as 10.5-15 point favorite since 1988
- 35-2 S/U as 15.5 point or more favorite since 1989

- 4-39 S/U on road vs ranked teams all time
- 2-26 S/U vs Top 10 ranked teams all time
- 0-5 ATS on road when ranked since 2008
- 0-4 ATS @ home when ranked since 2007

Pointspread Analysis — Conference
- vs Cincinnati - East Carolina leads series 13-12
- 17-3 ATS vs Memphis since 1994
- 12-1 S/U & ATS vs Memphis as favorite since 1991
- vs Memphis - East Carolina leads series 16-8
- Game 6-2 O/U vs Navy since 2010
- vs Navy - Navy leads series 7-2
- 1-5 S/U vs Navy since 2012 {0-6 ATS}
- 1-7 S/U vs South Florida as Dog since 2003
- Game 2-6 O/U vs Temple since 2014
- vs Temple - Temple leads series 10-9
- 0-3 S/U @ Temple as Dog since 1986
- 1-5 S/U & ATS vs Tulane as Dog since 1997
- 11-1 S/U vs Tulane as favorite since 1991 {8-0 @ home}
- Game 3-10 O/U vs Tulane since 2002
- vs Tulane - East Carolina leads series 12-6
- 8-0 S/U vs Cincinnati as 5 point or more favorite since 1988
- 0-7 S/U vs Memphis as 8 point or more Dog since 1992
- 0-3 S/U vs Houston as 11 point or more Dog since 2011
- 0-6 S/U vs UCF as 8 point or more Dog since 2010

ODU	12-2 S/U in 2nd home game of season since 2008
NAVY	5-1 O/U prior to playing South Florida since 2016
South Florida	3-17 S/U in 1st road game of season since 2002
MEMPHIS	13-1 O/U after playing Tulane since 2000
Byu	1-6 S/U after playing Central Florida since 2015
Byu	1-5 ATS prior to playing Cincinnati since 2016
HOUSTON	2-7 ATS prior to playing Temple since 1995
HOUSTON	10-2 O/U in final home game of season since 2010
Temple	3-9 ATS after playing Houston since 1998
Temple	3-9 ATS in final road game of season since 2010

EASTERN MICHIGAN EAGLES   MAC West

2021-Eastern Michigan		Opponent	ECU	Opp	S/U	Line	ATS	Total	O/U	
9/3/2021	vs	ST. FRANCIS-PA	35	15	W	-34.0	L	55.0	U	
9/11/2021	@	Wisconsin	7	34	L	26.0	L	52.0	U	
9/18/2021	@	Massachusetts	42	28	W	-22.0	L	56.5	O	
9/25/2021	vs	TEXAS STATE	59	21	W	-7.5	W	62.5	O	
10/2/2021	@	Northern Illinois	20	27	L	PK	L	63.0	U	
10/9/2021	vs	MIAMI-OHIO	13	12	W	2.5	W	58.0	U	
10/16/2021	vs	BALL STATE	31	38	L	1.5	L	54.5	O	
10/23/2021	@	Bowling Green	55	24	W	-4.5	W	49.5	O	
11/2/2021	@	Toledo	52	49	W	9.0	W	54.5	O	
11/9/2021	vs	OHIO	26	34	L	-6.0	L	62.0	U	
11/16/2021	vs	WESTERN MICHIGAN	22	21	W	5.5	W	66.0	U	
11/26/2021	@	Central Michigan	10	31	L	8.5	L	64.0	U	
12/18/2021	vs	**Liberty**	20	56	L	9.5	L	58.0	O	**Lending Tree Bowl**
Coach: Chris Creighton		Season Record >>	392	390	7-6	ATS>>	5-8	O/U>>	6-7	
2020-Eastern Michigan		Opponent	ECU	Opp	S/U	Line	ATS	Total	O/U	
11/4/2020	@	Kent State	23	27	L	4.5	W	65.5	U	
11/11/2020	@	Ball State	31	38	L	8.0	W	61.5	O	
11/18/2020	vs	TOLEDO	28	45	L	6.5	L	62.5	O	
11/28/2020	vs	CENTRAL MICHIGAN	23	31	L	6.0	L	58.0	U	
12/5/2020	@	Western Michigan	53	42	W	13.0	W	67.5	O	
12/12/2020	vs	NORTHERN ILLINOIS	41	33	W	-6.0	W	55.5	U	
Coach: Chris Creighton		Season Record >>	199	216	2-4	ATS>>	4-2	O/U>>	4-2	
2019-Eastern Michigan		Opponent	ECU	Opp	S/U	Line	ATS	Total	O/U	
8/31/2019	@	Coastal Carolina	30	23	W	-4.5	W	54.0	U	
9/7/2019	@	Kentucky	17	38	L	15.5	L	52.0	O	
9/14/2019	@	Illinois	34	31	W	7.5	W	57.0	O	
9/21/2019	vs	CENTRAL CONNECTICUT	34	29	W	NL	---	NT	---	
10/5/2019	@	Central Michigan	16	42	L	-3.5	L	54.0	O	
10/12/2019	vs	BALL STATE	23	29	L	-2.0	L	57.0	O	
10/19/2019	vs	WESTERN MICHIGAN	34	27	W	9.5	W	61.0	T	
10/26/2019	@	Toledo	34	37	L	2.5	L	53.5	O	{OT}
11/2/2019	vs	BUFFALO	14	43	L	1.5	L	49.5	O	
11/12/2019	@	Akron	42	14	W	-17.0	W	44.5	O	
11/19/2019	@	Northern Illinois	45	17	W	3.5	W	57.5	O	
11/29/2019	vs	KENT STATE	26	34	L	-3.0	L	68.5	U	
12/26/2019	vs	**Pittsburgh**	30	34	L	12.5	W	51.0	O	**Quick Lane Bowl**
Coach: Chris Creighton		Season Record >>	379	398	6-7	ATS>>	6-6	O/U>>	9-2-1	
2018-Eastern Michigan		Opponent	ECU	Opp	S/U	Line	ATS	Total	O/U	
8/31/2018	vs	MONMOUTH	51	17	W	-22.5	W	NT	---	
9/8/2018	@	Purdue	20	19	W	15.0	W	50.0	U	
9/15/2018	@	Buffalo	28	35	L	3.0	L	54.0	O	
9/22/2018	@	San Diego State	20	23	L	11.0	W	48.0	U	{OT}
9/29/2018	vs	NORTHERN ILLINOIS	23	26	L	-3.5	L	50.5	U	{3 OT}
10/6/2018	@	Western Michigan	24	27	L	4.5	W	58.5	U	
10/13/2018	vs	TOLEDO	28	26	W	2.0	W	63.0	U	
10/20/2018	@	Ball State	42	20	W	-3.0	W	44.0	O	
10/27/2018	vs	ARMY	22	37	L	1.5	L	47.5	O	
11/3/2018	vs	CENTRAL MICHIGAN	17	7	W	-14.5	L	46.5	U	
11/10/2018	vs	AKRON	27	7	W	-11.0	W	41.5	U	
11/23/2018	@	Kent State	28	20	W	-12.5	L	52.0	U	
12/15/2018	vs	**Georgia Southern**	21	23	L	3.0	W	45.5	U	**Camelia Bowl**
Coach: Chris Creighton		Season Record >>	351	287	7-6	ATS>>	8-5	O/U>>	3-9	

EASTERN MICHIGAN EAGLES   MAC West

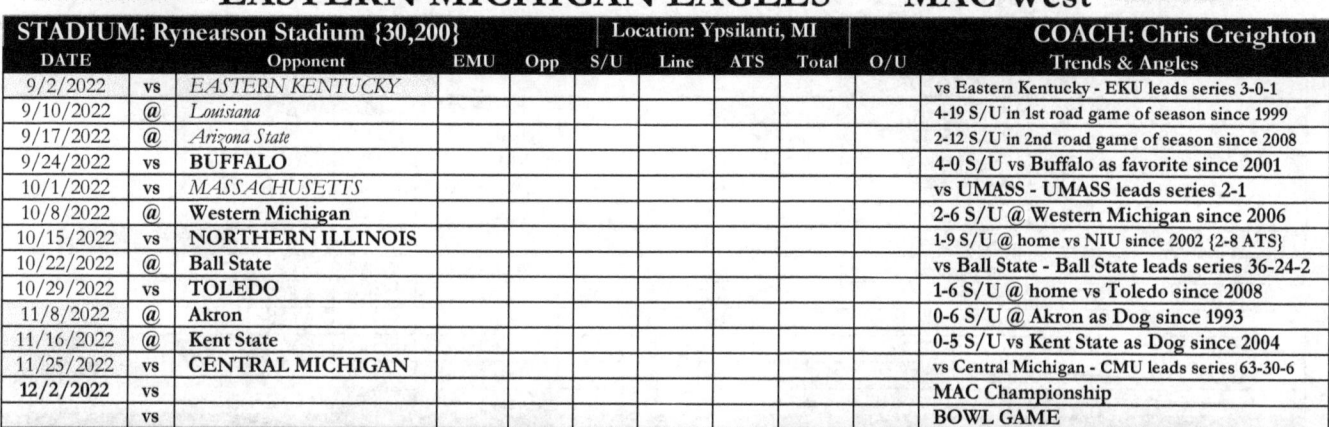

STADIUM: Rynearson Stadium {30,200}　　**Location:** Ypsilanti, MI　　**COACH:** Chris Creighton

DATE		Opponent	EMU	Opp	S/U	Line	ATS	Total	O/U	Trends & Angles
9/2/2022	vs	*EASTERN KENTUCKY*								vs Eastern Kentucky - EKU leads series 3-0-1
9/10/2022	@	*Louisiana*								4-19 S/U in 1st road game of season since 1999
9/17/2022	@	*Arizona State*								2-12 S/U in 2nd road game of season since 2008
9/24/2022	vs	BUFFALO								4-0 S/U vs Buffalo as favorite since 2001
10/1/2022	vs	*MASSACHUSETTS*								vs UMASS - UMASS leads series 2-1
10/8/2022	@	Western Michigan								2-6 S/U @ Western Michigan since 2006
10/15/2022	vs	NORTHERN ILLINOIS								1-9 S/U @ home vs NIU since 2002 {2-8 ATS}
10/22/2022	@	Ball State								vs Ball State - Ball State leads series 36-24-2
10/29/2022	vs	TOLEDO								1-6 S/U @ home vs Toledo since 2008
11/8/2022	@	Akron								0-6 S/U @ Akron as Dog since 1993
11/16/2022	@	Kent State								0-5 S/U vs Kent State as Dog since 2004
11/25/2022	vs	CENTRAL MICHIGAN								vs Central Michigan - CMU leads series 63-30-6
12/2/2022	vs									MAC Championship
	vs									BOWL GAME

Pointspread Analysis — Non-Conference
- 0-51 S/U vs Non-Conf. as 15.5 point or more Dog since 1990
- 1-14 ATS vs Non-Conf. as 20.5-25 point Dog since 1995
- 6-0 O/U vs Non-Conf. as 20.5-25 point Dog since 1995
- 2-8 S/U vs Non-Conf. as 10.5-15 point Dog since 1990
- 1-8 S/U vs Non-Conf. as 7.5-10 point Dog since 1993
- 9-1 S/U vs Non-Conf. as 7.5 point or more favorite since 1995

Dog
- 5-0 O/U as 30.5 point or more Dog since 2013
- 1-73 S/U as 20.5 point or more Dog since 1990
- 0-10 S/U @ home as 20.5 point or more Dog since 2001
- 10-1 O/U on road as 20.5-25 point Dog since 2009
- 2-13-1 ATS as 20.5-25 point Dog since 2009
- 13-3 O/U as 20.5-25 point Dog since 2009
- 0-21 S/U on road as 15.5-20 point Dog since 1991
- 7-0 ATS as 10.5-15 point Dog since 2015
- 3-12 S/U on road as 7.5-10 point Dog since 1998
- 2-12 S/U @ home as 7.5-10 point Dog since 1990
- 4-22-1 S/U @ home as 3.5-7 point Dog since 1990
- 13-4 ATS as road dog last 17 times

Favorite
- 0-6 S/U & ATS @ home as 3 point or less favorite since 2008
- 10-2 S/U as 7.5-10 point favorite since 1989
- 9-0 S/U @ home as 10.5-15 point favorite since 1989
- 22-2 S/U as 15.5 point or more favorite since 1989
- 8-0 S/U @ home as 15.5 point or more favorite since 2000
- 1-8 S/U prior to playing Buffalo since 2001
- 3-11 ATS in 2nd home game of season since 2008
- 2-13 S/U prior to playing Western Michigan
- 1-7 S/U after playing Buffalo since 2001
- 4-11 S/U prior to playing Ball State since 2007
- 4-17 S/U after playing Western Michigan since 2001
- 4-10 S/U prior to playing Toledo since 2008
- 3-11 S/U after playing Ball State since 2008
- 3-9 ATS after playing Ball State since 2010
- 1-11 S/U prior to playing Akron since 1998
- 9-3-1 ATS after playing Toledo since 2009
- 9-1 ATS prior to playing Kent State since 1996
- 3-18 S/U prior to playing Central Michigan since 2000
- 14-3 ATS in final road game of season since 2005
- 4-11 S/U after playing Akron since 1995
- 1-8 S/U after playing Kent State since 1994

Pointspread Analysis — Conference
- vs Akron - Akron leads series 19-13
- 7-0 S/U vs Akron as favorite since 1994
- vs Buffalo - Eastern Michigan leads series 6-3
- 4-0 S/U @ Kent State as favorite since 1995
- 1-5 ATS vs Kent State since 2009
- vs Kent State - Kent State leads series 19-14
- 3-18 S/U vs Northern Illinois since 2001
- 3-17 S/U vs Northern Illinois as Dog since 1998
- vs Northern Illinois - NIU leads series 34-16-2
- 3-19 S/U vs Toledo since 2000
- 2-19 S/U vs Toledo as Dog since 2000
- vs Toledo - Toledo leads series 36-13
- 5-1 ATS @ Western Michigan since 2010
- vs Western Michigan - WMU leads series 34-20-2
- 0-4 S/U vs Akron as 15.5 point or more Dog since 2001
- 0-4 S/U vs Akron as 4.0-8.5 point Dog since 1993
- 0-11 S/U vs Ball State as 2.5-5.5 point Dog since 1989
- 0-5 S/U vs C. Michigan as 18.5 point or more Dog since 1992
- 0-6 S/U vs C. Michigan as 7.0-10 point Dog since 1990
- 0-12 S/U vs N. Illinois as 16.5 point or more Dog since 2001
- 1-4 S/U & ATS vs N. Illinois as 7.5 point or less Dog since 1999
- 0-15 S/U vs Toledo as 13 point or more Dog since 1992
- 0-10 S/U vs W. Michigan as 15 point or more Dog since 1992
- 3-0 S/U & ATS @ W. Michigan as 4 point or less Dog since 1989
- 0-16 S/U vs ranked teams all time

Opponents
- Arizona State
- BUFFALO
- U MASS
- U MASS
- N. ILLINOIS
- N. ILLINOIS
- Ball State
- TOLEDO
- TOLEDO
- TOLEDO
- Akron
- Akron
- Kent State
- Kent State
- Kent State
- CENTRAL MICH

FLORIDA GATORS   SEC East

2021-Florida		Opponent	FLA	Opp	S/U	Line	ATS	Total	O/U	
9/4/2021	vs	FLORIDA ATLANTIC	35	14	W	-23.5	L	52.0	U	
9/11/2021	@	South Florida	42	20	W	-29.0	L	56.5	O	
9/18/2021	vs	ALABAMA	29	31	L	14.0	W	60.0	T	
9/25/2021	vs	TENNESSEE	38	14	W	-19.0	W	64.5	U	
10/2/2021	@	Kentucky	13	20	L	-7.5	L	56.0	U	
10/9/2021	vs	VANDERBILT	42	0	W	-39.0	W	59.5	U	
10/16/2021	@	Lsu	42	49	L	-12.5	L	61.0	O	
10/30/2021	vs	Georgia	7	34	L	14.0	L	51.0	U	"Okefenokee Oar"
11/6/2021	@	South Carolina	17	40	L	-20.5	L	52.0	O	
11/13/2021	vs	SAMFORD	70	52	W	-36.5	L	68.0	O	
11/20/2021	@	Missouri	23	24	L	-9.0	L	69.0	U	{OT}
11/27/2021	vs	FLORIDA STATE	24	21	W	-4.0	L	58.0	U	"Govenor's Cup"
12/23/2021	vs	Central Florida	17	29	L	-7.0	L	56.0	U	Gasparilla Bowl
Coach: Dan Mullen		Season Record >>	399	348	6-7	ATS>>	3-10	O/U>>	4-8-1	
2020-Florida		Opponent	FLA	Opp	S/U	Line	ATS	Total	O/U	
9/26/2020	@	Mississippi	51	35	W	-14.0	W	58.5	O	
10/3/2020	vs	SOUTH CAROLINA	38	24	W	-15.0	L	56.5	O	
10/10/2020	@	Texas A&M	38	41	L	-5.5	L	60.0	O	
10/31/2020	vs	MISSOURI	41	17	W	-13.5	W	62.5	U	
11/7/2020	vs	Georgia	44	28	W	2.5	W	51.5	O	"Okefenokee Oar"
11/14/2020	vs	ARKANSAS	63	35	W	-17.0	W	62.0	O	
11/21/2020	@	Vanderbilt	38	17	W	-31.0	L	68.0	U	
11/28/2020	vs	KENTUCKY	34	10	W	-23.5	W	60.5	U	
12/5/2020	@	Tennessee	31	19	W	-18.5	L	63.0	U	
12/12/2020	vs	LSU	34	37	L	-23.0	L	66.0	O	
12/19/2020	vs	Alabama	46	52	L	16.5	W	74.0	O	SEC Championship
12/30/2020	vs	Oklahoma	20	55	L	8.5	L	65.0	O	Cotton Bowl
Coach: Dan Mullen		Season Record >>	478	370	8-4	ATS>>	6-6	O/U>>	8-4	
2019-Florida		Opponent	FLA	Opp	S/U	Line	ATS	Total	O/U	
8/24/2019	vs	Miami	24	20	W	-7.0	L	46.0	U	"Seminole War Canoe Trophy"
9/7/2019	vs	TENNESSEE-MARTIN	45	0	W	-45.0	T	NT	---	
9/14/2019	@	Kentucky	29	21	W	-9.5	L	46.5	O	
9/21/2019	vs	TENNESSEE	34	3	W	-14.0	W	48.5	U	
9/28/2019	vs	TOWSON	38	0	W	-36.5	W	NT	---	
10/5/2019	vs	AUBURN	23	14	W	2.5	W	48.5	U	
10/12/2019	@	Lsu	28	42	L	14.0	T	55.0	O	
10/19/2019	@	South Carolina	38	27	W	-3.5	W	45.0	O	
11/2/2019	vs	Georgia	17	24	L	6.0	L	47.5	U	"Okefenokee Oar"
11/9/2019	vs	VANDERBILT	56	0	W	-27.0	W	49.5	O	
11/16/2019	@	Missouri	23	6	W	-6.5	W	51.0	U	
11/30/2019	vs	FLORIDA STATE	40	17	W	-16.5	W	55.5	O	"Governor's Cup"
12/30/2019	vs	Virginia	36	28	W	-16.5	L	55.0	O	Orange Bowl
Coach: Dan Mullen		Season Record >>	431	202	11-2	ATS>>	7-4-2	O/U>>	6-5	
2018-Florida		Opponent	FLA	Opp	S/U	Line	ATS	Total	O/U	
9/1/2018	vs	CHARLESTON SOUTHERN	53	6	W	-43.0	W	NT	---	
9/8/2018	vs	KENTUCKY	16	27	L	-13.5	L	52.5	U	
9/15/2018	vs	COLORADO STATE	48	10	W	-21.5	W	59.0	U	
9/22/2018	@	Tennessee	47	21	W	-3.5	W	45.5	O	
9/29/2018	@	Mississippi State	13	6	W	7.0	W	51.0	U	
10/6/2018	vs	LSU	27	19	W	1.5	W	44.5	O	
10/13/2018	@	Vanderbilt	37	27	W	-10.0	T	52.0	O	
10/27/2018	vs	Georgia	17	36	L	7.0	L	52.5	O	"Okefenokee Oar"
11/3/2018	vs	MISSOURI	17	38	L	-5.0	L	58.5	U	
11/10/2018	vs	SOUTH CAROLINA	35	31	W	-6.5	L	54.0	O	
11/17/2018	vs	IDAHO	63	10	W	-41.5	W	NT	---	
11/24/2018	@	Florida State	41	14	W	-4.5	W	52.0	O	"Governor's Cup"
12/29/2018	vs	Michigan	41	15	W	4.0	W	51.0	O	Chick-Fil-A Peach Bowl
Coach: Dan Mullen		Season Record >>	455	260	10-3	ATS>>	8-4-1	O/U>>	7-4	

FLORIDA GATORS — SEC East

STADIUM: Florida Field at Ben Hill Griffin Stadium {88,548} | **Location:** Gainesville, FL | **COACH:** Billy Napier

DATE		Opponent	Fla	Opp	S/U	Line	ATS	Total	O/U	Trends & Angles
9/3/2022	vs	UTAH								vs Utah - Florida leads series 1-0
9/10/2022	vs	KENTUCKY								20-1 S/U @ home vs Kentucky since 1981
9/17/2022	vs	SOUTH FLORIDA								vs South Florida - Florida leads series 2-0
9/24/2022	@	Tennessee								7-1 S/U @ Tennessee since 2006
10/1/2022	vs	EASTERN WASHINGTON								24-4 S/U after playing Tennessee since 1993
10/8/2022	vs	MISSOURI								Game 0-5 O/U vs Missouri since 2017
10/15/2022	vs	LSU								Game 4-0 O/U vs LSU since 2018
10/29/2022	vs	Georgia								vs GA - Team that wins S/U is 15-0 ATS since 2007
11/5/2022	@	Texas A&M								vs Texas A&M - Texas A&M leads series 3-2
11/12/2022	vs	SOUTH CAROLINA								15-2 S/U @ home vs South Carolina since 1935
11/19/2022	@	Vanderbilt								15-0 S/U @ Vanderbilt since 1992
11/25/2022	@	Florida State								vs Florida State - Florida leads series 36-27-2
12/3/2022	vs									SEC Championship
	vs									BOWL GAME

Pointspread Analysis — Non-Conference

- 0-7 S/U vs Non-Conf. as 10.5 point or more Dog since 1988
- 3-10 S/U & ATS vs Non-Conf. as 3.5-7 point Dog since 1984
- 17-3 S/U vs Non-Conf. as 3.5-7 point favorite since 1983
- 14-6 ATS vs Non-Conf. as 3.5-7 point favorite since 1983
- 11-2 S/U vs Non-Conf. as 10.5-15 point favorite since 1984
- 67-2-1 S/U vs Non-Conf. as 15.5 point or more favorite since 1984
- Game 3-1 O/U vs Florida State since 2017
- 0-9 S/U vs Florida State as 7.5 point or more Dog since 1987
- 2-7 ATS vs Florida State as 7.5 point or more Dog since 1987
- 0-5 O/U vs Florida State as 7.5 point or more Dog since 1993
- 4-0 S/U & ATS vs Florida State as 5.5-7.5 point Dog since 1986
- 0-6 S/U & ATS vs Florida State as 3 point or less Dog since 1998
- 13-0 S/U vs Florida State as 3.5-20 point favorite since 1983
- 11-2 ATS vs Florida State as 3.5-20 point favorite since 1983

Bowl Games

- 4-0 S/U in Orange Bowl
- 3-0 S/U vs Penn State in Bowl Games
- 7-2 S/U in Gator Bowl
- 3-0 S/U in Outback Bowl since 2006
- 4-1 O/U in Outback Bowl
- 0-3 S/U in Citrus Bowl since 2000
- 3-0 O/U in Citrus Bowl since 2000
- 1-5 S/U & ATS in Bowl Games as 3.5-7 point Dog since 1977
- 4-0 S/U & ATS in Bowl Games as 3 point or less favorite since 2000
- 7-3 S/U vs ranked teams in Bowl games since 2006
- 8-2 O/U vs ranked teams in Bowl games since 2006

Dog

- 0-6 S/U as 15.5 point or more Dog since 1988
- 2-12 S/U as 10.5-15 point Dog since 1989
- 1-7 S/U as 7.5-10 point Dog since 2007
- 1-5 S/U on road as 7.5-10 point Dog since 2007
- 1-7 S/U & ATS as 3.5-7 point Dog since 2015
- 7-1 O/U as 3.5-7 point Dog since 2015
- 4-11 O/U as 3 point or less Dog since 2010

Favorite

- 10-2 S/U on road as 3.5-7 point favorite since 2006
- 9-2 ATS on road as 3.5-7 point favorite since 2007
- 7-2 S/U on road as 7.5-10 point favorite since 2003
- 26-3 S/U @ home as 10.5-15 point favorite since 1984
- 17-2 S/U on road as 10.5-15 point favorite since 1984
- 39-5-1 S/U as 15.5-20 point favorite since 1983
- 8-0 S/U on road as 15.5-20 point favorite since 1997
- 41-7 S/U as 20.5-25 point favorite since 1987

Pointspread Analysis — Conference

- vs Georgia - Georgia leads series 54-44-2
- vs Georgia - Team that wins S/U is 14-0 ATS since 2007
- 33-2 S/U vs Kentucky since 1987
- vs Kentucky - Florida leads series 53-19
- vs LSU - Florida leads series 33-32-3
- vs Missouri - Missouri leads series 6-5
- vs South Carolina - Florida leads series 29-10-3
- Game 5-0 O/U vs South Carolina since 2017
- 0-3 S/U vs South Carolina as Dog since 2011
- 23-4 S/U vs South Carolina as favorite since 1992
- vs Tennessee - Florida leads series 31-20
- 7-1 ATS vs Tennessee as Dog since 1993
- 13-0 S/U vs Tennessee as favorite since 2005
- 16-1 S/U vs Tennessee since 2005
- 30-1 S/U vs Vanderbilt since 1989
- vs Vanderbilt - Florida leads series 43-10-2
- 12-1 S/U vs Georgia as 9.5 point or more favorite since 1990
- 25-0 S/U vs Kentucky as 14 point or more favorite since 1983
- 12-0 S/U @ Kentucky as 10 point or more favorite since 1984
- 11-2 S/U vs LSU as 10.5 point or more favorite since 1990
- 20-0 S/U vs South Carolina as 7 point or more favorite since 1992
- 14-0 S/U vs Tennessee as 4.5-16 point favorite since 1984
- 27-0 S/U vs Vanderbilt as 12 point or more favorite since 1983
- 32-0 S/U in 1st home game of season since 1990
- 14-0 S/U prior to playing Kentucky since 2008
- 17-2 S/U in 2nd home game of season since 2003
- 4-9 ATS after playing Kentucky since 2009
- 10-0 S/U prior to playing LSU since 2012 (8-1-1 ATS)
- 2-13 O/U prior to playing LSU since 2007
- 14-4 S/U after playing South Carolina since 2004
- 31-3 S/U prior to playing Florida State since 1987
- 13-0 S/U @ home when #1 ranked since 1996
- 0-7 S/U when ranked vs Alabama since 2009
- 22-2 S/U when ranked vs South Carolina all time
- 17-0 S/U @ home when ranked vs Vanderbilt since 1969
- 10-0 S/U vs #4 ranked teams since 1990 {9-0-1 ATS}
- 17-0 S/U @ home when ranked #5 all time

Favorite

- 3-12 O/U as 20.5-25 point favorite since 2009
- 9-0 S/U on road as 25.5 point or more favorite since 1995
- 76-1 S/U as 25.5 point or more favorite since 1984

Opponents noted: UTAH, UTAH, KENTUCKY, SOUTH FLA, MISSOURI, MISSOURI, Vanderbilt, Vanderbilt

FLORIDA ATLANTIC OWLS   C-USA East

2021-Florida Atlantic		Opponent	FAU	Opp	S/U	Line	ATS	Total	O/U	
9/4/2021	@	Florida	14	35	L	23.5	W	52.0	U	
9/11/2021	vs	GEORGIA SOUTHERN	38	6	W	-6.5	W	48.5	U	
9/18/2021	vs	FORDHAM	45	14	W	-30.5	W	51.5	O	
9/25/2021	@	Air Force	7	31	L	3.5	L	54.0	U	
10/2/2021	vs	FLORIDA INTERNATIONAL	58	21	W	-10.5	W	52.0	O	"Shula Bowl" (Don Shula Award)
10/9/2021	@	Alabama-Birmingham	14	31	L	3.5	L	49.0	U	
10/21/2021	@	Charlotte	38	9	W	-6.5	W	58.0	O	
10/30/2021	vs	TEXAS-EL PASO	28	25	W	-11.0	L	49.0	O	
11/6/2021	vs	MARSHALL	13	28	L	1.5	L	58.0	U	
11/13/2021	@	Old Dominion	16	30	L	-6.5	L	48.0	U	
11/20/2021	@	Western Kentucky	17	52	L	11.5	L	64.0	O	
11/27/2021	vs	MIDDLE TENNESSEE	17	27	L	-3.5	L	49.0	U	
Coach: Willie Taggert		Season Record >>	305	309	5-7	ATS>>	5-7	O/U>>	4-8	
2020-Florida Atlantic		Opponent	FAU	Opp	S/U	Line	ATS	Total	O/U	
10/3/2020	vs	CHARLOTTE	21	17	W	-4.5	L	63.0	U	
10/24/2020	@	Marshall	9	20	L	19.5	W	51.0	U	
10/31/2020	vs	TEXAS-SAN ANTONIO	24	3	W	-4.5	W	47.0	U	
11/7/2020	vs	WESTERN KENTUCKY	10	6	W	-6.5	L	37.5	U	
11/13/2020	@	Florida International	38	19	W	-9.5	W	41.5	O	"Shula Bowl" (Don Shula Award)
11/20/2020	vs	MASSACHUSETTS	24	2	W	-34.0	L	50.5	U	
12/5/2020	@	Georgia Southern	3	20	L	2.0	L	41.0	U	
12/10/2020	@	Southern Mississippi	31	45	L	-9.0	L	43.0	O	
12/23/2020	vs	Memphis	10	25	L	9.5	L	52.5	U	Montgomery Bowl
Coach: Willie Taggert		Season Record >>	780	775	5-4	ATS>>	3-6	O/U>>	2-7	
2019-Florida Atlantic		Opponent	FAU	Opp	S/U	Line	ATS	Total	O/U	
8/31/2019	@	Ohio State	21	45	L	27.5	W	65.5	O	
9/7/2019	vs	CENTRAL FLORIDA	14	48	L	13.5	L	67.5	U	
9/14/2019	@	Ball State	41	31	W	-2.5	W	64.5	O	
9/21/2019	vs	WAGNER	42	7	W	-39.0	L	NT	---	
9/28/2019	@	Charlotte	45	27	W	-1.0	W	64.5	O	
10/12/2019	vs	MIDDLE TENNESSEE	28	13	W	-12.5	W	63.5	U	
10/19/2019	vs	MARSHALL	31	36	L	-4.0	L	58.0	O	
10/26/2019	@	Old Dominion	41	3	W	-14.0	W	57.5	U	
11/2/2019	@	Western Kentucky	35	24	W	PK	W	51.0	O	
11/9/2019	vs	FLORIDA INTERNATIONAL	37	7	W	-11.0	W	59.0	U	"Shula Bowl" (Don Shula Award)
11/23/2019	@	Texas-San Antonio	40	26	W	-21.5	L	57.0	O	
11/30/2019	vs	SOUTHERN MISS	34	17	W	-9.0	W	58.5	U	
12/7/2019	vs	ALABAMA-BIRMINGHAM	49	6	W	-8.0	W	49.0	O	C-USA Championship Game
12/21/2019	vs	Smu	52	28	W	7.0	W	63.5	O	Boca Raton Bowl
Coach: Lane Kiffin		Season Record >>	510	318	11-3	ATS>>	10-4	O/U>>	8-5	C-USA Champions
2018-Florida Atlantic		Opponent	FAU	Opp	S/U	Line	ATS	Total	O/U	
9/1/2018	@	Oklahoma	14	63	L	19.0	L	68.0	O	
9/8/2018	vs	AIR FORCE	33	27	W	-7.5	L	61.5	U	
9/15/2018	vs	BETHUNE-COOKMAN	49	28	W	-40.0	L	NT	---	
9/21/2018	@	Central Florida	36	56	L	14.0	L	75.0	O	
9/29/2018	@	Middle Tennessee	24	25	L	-2.5	L	62.0	U	
10/6/2018	vs	OLD DOMINION	52	33	W	-13.0	W	63.5	O	
10/20/2018	@	Marshall	7	31	L	-2.5	L	60.0	U	
10/27/2018	vs	LOUISIANA TECH	13	21	L	-3.5	L	58.5		
11/3/2018	@	Florida International	49	14	W	1.5	W	59.5	O	"Shula Bowl" (Don Shula Award)
11/10/2018	vs	WESTERN KENTUCKY	34	15	W	-18.0	L	59.5	U	
11/17/2018	@	North Texas	38	41	L	4.0	W	63.5	O	
11/24/2018	vs	CHARLOTTE	24	27	L	-17.0	L	55.0	U	
Coach: Lane Kiffin		Season Record >>	373	381	5-7	ATS>>	3-9	O/U>>	5-6	

FLORIDA ATLANTIC OWLS   C-USA East

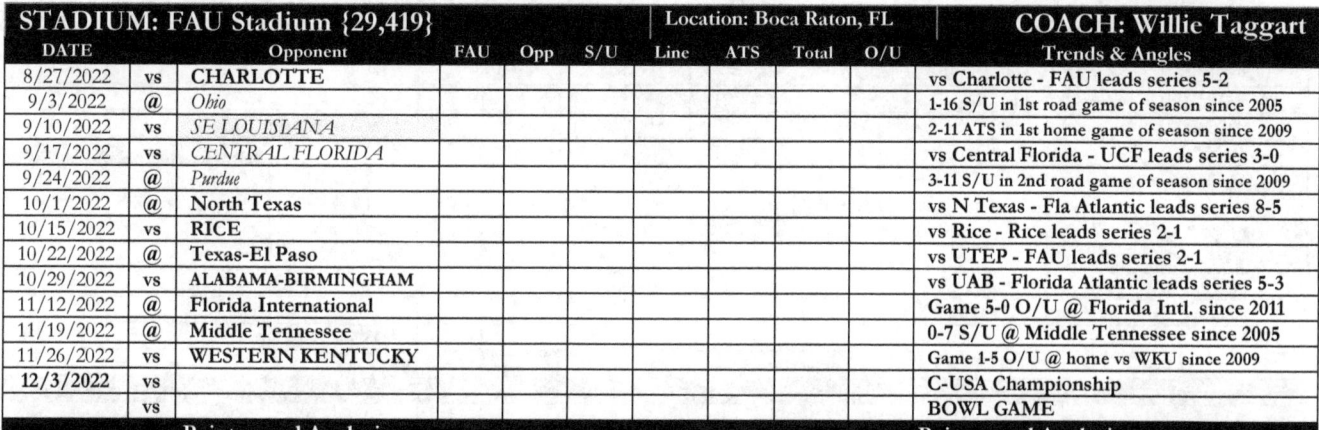

STADIUM: FAU Stadium {29,419} **Location:** Boca Raton, FL **COACH:** Willie Taggart

DATE		Opponent	FAU	Opp	S/U	Line	ATS	Total	O/U	Trends & Angles
8/27/2022	vs	CHARLOTTE								vs Charlotte - FAU leads series 5-2
9/3/2022	@	*Ohio*								1-16 S/U in 1st road game of season since 2005
9/10/2022	vs	*SE LOUISIANA*								2-11 ATS in 1st home game of season since 2009
9/17/2022	vs	*CENTRAL FLORIDA*								vs Central Florida - UCF leads series 3-0
9/24/2022	@	*Purdue*								3-11 S/U in 2nd road game of season since 2009
10/1/2022	@	North Texas								vs N Texas - Fla Atlantic leads series 8-5
10/15/2022	vs	RICE								vs Rice - Rice leads series 2-1
10/22/2022	@	Texas-El Paso								vs UTEP - FAU leads series 2-1
10/29/2022	vs	ALABAMA-BIRMINGHAM								vs UAB - Florida Atlantic leads series 5-3
11/12/2022	@	Florida International								Game 5-0 O/U @ Florida Intl. since 2011
11/19/2022	@	Middle Tennessee								0-7 S/U @ Middle Tennessee since 2005
11/26/2022	vs	WESTERN KENTUCKY								Game 1-5 O/U @ home vs WKU since 2009
12/3/2022	vs									C-USA Championship
	vs									BOWL GAME

Pointspread Analysis — Non-Conference

- 0-35 S/U vs Non-Conf. as 15.5 point or more Dog since 2004
- 1-12 ATS vs Non-Conf. as 20.5-25 point Dog since 2006

Bowl Games
- 4-0 S/U & ATS in Bowl Games

Dog
- 0-34 S/U as 20.5 point or more Dog since 2005
- 1-7 O/U as 30.5 point or more Dog since 2011
- 1-5 O/U as 25.5-30 point Dog since 2010
- 1-13 ATS as 20.5-25 point Dog since 2006
- 0-11 S/U @ home as 7.5-20 point Dog since 2004
- 0-9 S/U as 7.5-10 point Dog since 2005
- 2-13 S/U on road as 3.5-7 point Dog since 2008
- 12-4 O/U as 3.5-7 point Dog since 2012
- 7-2 ATS on road as 3.5-7 point Dog since 2012

Favorite
- 2-6 ATS on road as 3 point or less favorite since 2008
- 12-4 S/U as 3.5-7 point favorite since 2015
- 0-7 O/U as 3.5-7 point favorite since 2020
- 21-4 S/U as 7.5-15 point favorite since 2004
- 14-1 S/U as 15.5 point or more favorite since 2008
- 7-1 S/U on road as 7.5 point or more favorite since 2007

- 0-24 S/U vs ranked teams all time

Pointspread Analysis — Conference

- vs Florida International - Florida Atlantic leads series 13-5
- 5-0 S/U & ATS vs FIU since 2017
- 4-0 S/U & ATS vs FIU as 4.5 point or less Dog since 2009
- 8-2 O/U vs FIU as favorite since 2007
- vs Middle Tennessee - MTSU leads series 13-4
- 3-9 ATS vs Middle Tennessee since 2009
- 0-6 O/U vs Middle Tennessee as favorite since 2007
- 0-10 S/U vs Middle Tennessee as Dog since 2005
- 2-11 S/U vs Middle Tennessee since 2008
- Game 3-8 O/U vs North Texas since 2006
- 1-5 O/U vs North Texas as favorite since 2007
- 0-3 S/U vs North Texas as Dog since 2011
- 5-1 ATS vs North Texas as Dog since 2004
- 3-0 S/U @ Western Kentucky as favorite since 2008
- vs Western Kentucky - Florida Atlantic leads series 9-4
- 1-6 O/U vs Western Kentucky as favorite since 2008

Texas-El Paso	1-5 S/U prior to playing UAB since 2008
FIU	0-7 O/U after playing UAB since 2008
FIU	1-6 S/U prior to playing Middle Tennessee since 2014
FIU	3-8 ATS prior to playing Middle Tennessee since 2010
MTSU	0-6 ATS after playing FIU since 2016
MTSU	2-9 O/U after playing FIU since 2010
MTSU	6-1 ATS prior to playing Western Kentucky since 2015
WKU	3-15 ATS in final home game of season since 2004
WKU	2-12 S/U after playing Middle Tennessee since 2005

Print Version $24.95   Print Version $34.95    Print Version $34.95

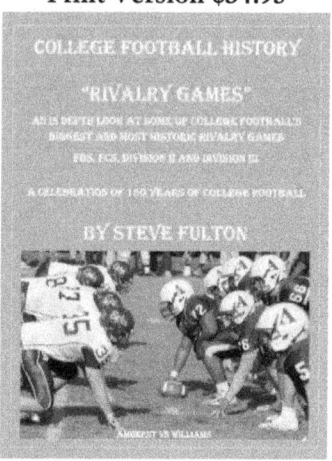

These books available at numerous online retailers

FLORIDA INTERNATIONAL   C-USA East

2021-Florida Int.		Opponent	FIU	Opp	S/U	Line	ATS	Total	O/U	
9/2/2021	vs	LONG ISLAND U.	48	10	W	-35.0	W	49.0	O	
9/11/2021	vs	TEXAS STATE	17	23	L	-2.0	L	54.5	U	{OT}
9/18/2021	@	Texas Tech	21	54	L	20.5	L	53.5	O	
9/25/2021	@	Central Michigan	27	31	L	12.0	W	55.0	O	
10/2/2021	@	Florida Atlantic	21	58	L	10.5	L	52.0	O	"Shula Bowl" (Don Shula Award)
10/8/2021	vs	CHARLOTTE	33	45	L	3.5	L	60.5	O	
10/23/2021	vs	WESTERN KENTUCKY	19	34	L	17.0	W	77.5	U	
10/30/2021	@	Marshall	0	38	L	21.5	L	64.0	U	
11/6/2021	vs	OLD DOMINION	24	47	L	3.0	L	50.0	O	
11/13/2021	@	Middle Tennessee	10	50	L	10.5	L	54.5	O	
11/20/2021	vs	NORTH TEXAS	7	49	L	10.0	L	57.0	U	
11/27/2021	@	Southern Mississippi	17	37	L	15.0	L	45.5	O	
Coach: Butch Davis		Season Record >>	244	476	1-11	ATS>>	3-9	O/U>>	8-4	

2020-Florida Int.		Opponent	FIU	Opp	S/U	Line	ATS	Total	O/U	
9/26/2020	@	Liberty	34	36	L	7.5	W	60.5	O	
10/10/2020	vs	MIDDLE TENNESSEE	28	38	L	-6.5	L	56.5	O	
10/23/2020	vs	JACKSONVILLE STATE	10	19	L	-9.5	L	55.0	U	
11/14/2020	vs	FLORIDA ATLANTIC	19	38	L	9.5	L	41.5	O	"Shula Bowl" (Don Shula Award)
11/21/2020	@	Western Kentucky	21	38	L	7.0	L	41.5	O	
Coach: Butch Davis		Season Record >>	112	169	0-5	ATS>>	1-4	O/U>>	4-1	

2019-Florida Int.		Opponent	FIU	Opp	S/U	Line	ATS	Total	O/U	
8/29/2019	@	Tulane	14	42	L	3.0	L	58.5	U	
9/7/2019	vs	WESTERN KENTUCKY	14	20	L	-9.0	L	57.0	U	
9/14/2019	vs	NEW HAMPSHIRE	30	17	W	-13.5	L	NT	---	
9/21/2019	@	Louisiana Tech	31	43	L	6.5	L	51.5	O	
10/5/2019	vs	MASSACHUSETTS	44	0	W	-28.0	W	70.0	U	
10/12/2019	vs	CHARLOTTE	48	23	W	-5.0	W	59.5	O	
10/19/2019	vs	TEXAS-EL PASO	32	17	W	-24.5	L	51.0	U	
10/26/2019	@	Middle Tennessee	17	50	L	-1.5	L	57.5	O	
11/2/2019	vs	OLD DOMINION	24	17	W	-17.0	L	47.0	U	
11/9/2019	@	Florida Atlantic	7	37	L	11.0	L	59.0	U	"Shula Bowl" (Don Shula Award)
11/23/2019	@	Miami	30	24	W	21.0	W	51.5	O	
11/30/2019	@	Marshall	27	30	L	10.0	W	49.5	O	
12/21/2019	vs	Arkansas State	26	34	L	-1.0	L	58.5	O	Camelia Bowl
Coach: Butch Davis		Season Record >>	344	354	6-7	ATS>>	4-9	O/U>>	6-6	

2018-Florida Int.		Opponent	FIU	Opp	S/U	Line	ATS	Total	O/U	
9/1/2018	vs	INDIANA	28	38	L	13.0	W	55.0	O	
9/8/2018	@	Old Dominion	28	20	W	-2.5	W	51.5	U	
9/15/2018	vs	MASSACHUSETTS	63	24	W	-3.5	W	66.5	O	
9/22/2018	@	Miami	17	31	L	25.5	W	56.5	U	
9/29/2018	vs	ARKANSAS-PINE BLUFF	55	9	W	-57.5	L	NT	---	
10/13/2018	vs	MIDDLE TENNESSEE	24	21	W	-1.5	W	60.5	U	
10/20/2018	vs	RICE	36	17	W	-23.0	L	53.5	U	
10/27/2018	@	Western Kentucky	38	17	W	-3.0	W	54.0	O	
11/3/2018	vs	FLORIDA ATLANTIC	14	49	L	-1.5	L	59.5	O	"Shula Bowl" (Don Shula Award)
11/10/2018	@	Texas-San Antonio	45	7	W	-10.5	W	47.0	O	
11/17/2018	@	Charlotte	42	35	W	-3.5	W	44.5	O	
11/24/2018	vs	MARSHALL	25	28	L	3.0	T	52.5	O	
12/21/2018	vs	Toledo	35	32	W	7.0	W	57.5	O	Bahamas Bowl
Coach: Butch Davis		Season Record >>	450	328	9-4	ATS>>	9-3-1	O/U>>	8-4	

FLORIDA INTERNATIONAL C-USA East

STADIUM: FIU Stadium **Location:** Miami, FL **COACH:** Mike MacIntyre

DATE		Opponent	FIU	Opp	S/U	Line	ATS	Total	O/U	Trends & Angles
9/1/2022	vs	BRYANT								1st Meeting
9/9/2022	@	Texas State								vs Texas State - Texas State leads series 1-0
9/24/2022	@	Western Kentucky								0-5 S/U vs W Kentucky as Dog since 2012
10/1/2022	@	New Mexico State								vs NMSU - NMSU leads series 1-0
10/8/2022	vs	CONNECTICUT								1st Meeting
10/14/2022	vs	TEXAS-SAN ANTONIO								vs UTSA - FAU leads series 2-1
10/22/2022	@	Charlotte								vs Charlotte - FIU leads series 5-1
10/29/2022	vs	LOUISIANA TECH								vs LA Tech - La Tech leads series 4-0
11/5/2022	@	North Texas								vs North Texas - FIU leads series 5-4
11/12/2022	vs	FLORIDA ATLANTIC								vs Florida Atlantic - FAU leads series 13-5
11/19/2022	@	Texas-El Paso								vs Texas-El Paso - FIU leads series 3-1
11/26/2022	vs	MIDDLE TENNESSEE								Game 7-1 O/U @ home vs MTSU since 2005
12/3/2022	vs									C-USA Championship
	vs									BOWL GAME

Pointspread Analysis

Non-Conference
- 1-21 S/U vs Non-Conf. as 20.5 point or more Dog since 2005
- 2-9 S/U vs Non-Conf. as 3.5-10 point Dog since 2004
- 10-0 S/U vs Non-Conf. as 10.5 point or more favorite since 2011

Dog
- 1-27 S/U as 20.5 point or more Dog since 2005
- 5-0 O/U as 30.5 point or more Dog since 2009
- 1-8 O/U as 25.5-30 point Dog since 2006
- 0-6 S/U @ home as 15.5-20 point Dog since 2007
- 5-1 O/U as 15.5-20 point Dog since 2014
- 2-15 S/U on road as 10.5-15 point Dog since 2004
- 2-16 S/U on road as 7.5-10 point Dog since 2004
- 0-6 S/U @ home as 7.5-10 point Dog since 2004
- 2-9 S/U on road as 3.5-7 point Dog since 2007

Favorite
- 2-5 O/U on road as 3 point or less favorite since 2011
- 6-2 S/U @ home as 3 point or less favorite since 2005
- 5-1 S/U on road as 3.5-7 point favorite since 2008
- 5-2 S/U as 7.5-10 point favorite since 2010
- 2-6 O/U as 7.5-10 point favorite since 2006
- 18-2 S/U as 10.5 point or more favorite since 2011
- 0-10 S/U vs ranked teams all time

Conference
- vs Middle Tennessee - MTSU leads series 12-5
- 4-0 S/U & ATS vs North Texas as favorite since 2008
- Game 5-2 O/U vs Western Kentucky since 2015
- vs Western Kentucky - WKU leads series 8-6
- 5-2 S/U vs Western Kentucky as favorite since 2008
- 0-5 S/U vs Florida Atlantic as 11 point or more Dog since 2004
- 0-9 S/U vs Middle Tennessee as 8 point or more Dog since 2006

Texas State	2-10 S/U prior to playing Western Kentucky since 2008
Texas State	2-10 ATS prior to playing Western Kentucky since 2005
North Texas	7-2 O/U prior to playing Florida Atlantic since 2013
UTEP	7-0 O/U after playing Florida Atlantic since 2015
LA TECH	1-5 S/U after playing Charlotte since 2015 {1-4-1 ATS}
UTEP	1-5 ATS prior to playing Middle Tennessee since 2016

2022 FCS College Football Bible $19.95

FLORIDA STATE SEMINOLES   ACC Atlantic

2021-Florida State		Opponent	FSU	Opp	S/U	Line	ATS	Total	O/U	
9/5/2021	vs	NOTRE DAME	38	41	L	7.0	W	53.5	O	{OT}
9/11/2021	vs	JACKSONVILLE STATE	17	20	L	-28.0	L	56.5	U	
9/18/2021	@	Wake Forest	14	35	L	4.5	L	62.5	U	
9/25/2021	vs	LOUISVILLE	23	31	L	-1.5	L	61.0	U	
10/2/2021	vs	SYRACUSE	33	30	W	-5.5	L	50.0	O	
10/9/2021	@	North Carolina	35	25	W	17.5	W	64.0	U	
10/23/2021	vs	MASSACHUSETTS	59	3	W	-35.0	W	59.0	O	
10/30/2021	@	Clemson	20	30	L	9.5	L	47.5	O	
11/6/2021	vs	NC STATE	14	28	L	3.0	L	55.0	U	
11/13/2021	vs	MIAMI	31	28	W	2.5	W	61.0	U	
11/20/2021	@	Boston College	26	23	W	3.0	W	55.5	U	
11/27/2021	@	Florida	21	24	L	4.0	W	58.0	U	"Govenor's Cup"
Coach: Mike Norvell		Season Record >>	331	318	5-7	ATS>>	6-6	O/U>>	4-8	
2020-Florida State		Opponent	FSU	Opp	S/U	Line	ATS	Total	O/U	
9/12/2020	vs	GEORGIA TECH	13	16	L	-13.5	L	50.0	U	
9/26/2020	@	Miami	10	52	L	10.5	L	54.0	O	
10/3/2020	vs	JACKSONVILLE STATE	41	24	W	-26.5	L	53.0	O	
10/10/2020	@	Notre Dame	26	42	L	21.0	W	54.0	O	
10/17/2020	vs	NORTH CAROLINA	31	28	W	13.5	W	65.0	U	
10/24/2020	@	Louisville	16	48	L	5.0	L	62.0	O	
11/7/2020	vs	PITTSBURGH	17	41	L	1.5	L	52.5	O	
11/14/2020	@	NC State	22	38	L	12.0	L	60.5	U	
12/12/2020	vs	DUKE	56	35	W	-3.0	W	56.5	O	
Coach: Mike Norvell		Season Record >>	232	324	3-6	ATS>>	3-6	O/U>>	6-3	
2019-Florida State		Opponent	FSU	Opp	S/U	Line	ATS	Total	O/U	
8/31/2019	vs	Boise State	31	36	L	-6.5	L	54.5	O	TIAA Bank Field
9/7/2019	vs	LOUSIAIANA-MONROE	45	44	W	-23.0	L	65.5	O	{OT}
9/14/2019	@	Virginia	24	31	L	7.0	T	54.5	O	"Jefferson-Eppes Trophy"
9/21/2019	vs	LOUISVILLE	35	24	W	-7.0	W	61.0	U	
9/28/2019	vs	NC STATE	31	13	W	-7.0	W	62.0	U	
10/12/2019	@	Clemson	14	45	L	25.5	L	60.5	U	
10/19/2019	@	Wake Forest	20	22	L	-3.0	L	69.0	U	
10/26/2019	vs	SYRACUSE	35	17	W	-12.0	W	59.5	U	
11/2/2019	vs	MIAMI	10	27	L	-3.0	L	50.5	U	
11/9/2019	@	Boston College	38	31	W	1.0	W	64.0	O	
11/16/2019	vs	ALABAMA STATE	49	12	W	-41.0	L	NT	---	
11/30/2019	@	Florida	17	40	L	16.5	L	55.5	O	"Governor's Cup"
12/31/2019	vs	Arizona State	14	20	L	3.0	L	51.5	U	Sun Bowl
Coach: Willie Taggart		Season Record >>	363	362	6-7	ATS>>	4-8-1	O/U>>	5-7	
2018-Florida State		Opponent	FSU	Opp	S/U	Line	ATS	Total	O/U	
9/3/2018	vs	VIRGINIA TECH	3	24	L	-7.5	L	54.0	U	
9/8/2018	vs	SAMFORD	36	26	W	-32.5	L	NT	---	
9/15/2018	@	Syracuse	7	30	L	-3.0	L	69.5	U	
9/22/2018	vs	NORTHERN ILLINOIS	37	19	W	-10.0	W	44.5	O	
9/29/2018	@	Louisville	28	24	W	-5.0	L	46.0	O	
10/6/2018	@	Miami	27	28	L	14.0	W	48.0	O	
10/20/2018	vs	WAKE FOREST	38	17	W	-10.5	W	57.5	U	
10/27/2018	vs	CLEMSON	10	59	L	18.0	L	49.5	O	
11/3/2018	@	NC State	28	47	L	9.0	L	52.0	O	
11/10/2018	@	Notre Dame	13	42	L	17.0	L	51.0	O	
11/17/2018	vs	BOSTON COLLEGE	22	21	W	3.0	W	48.0	U	
11/24/2018	vs	FLORIDA	14	41	L	4.5	L	52.0	O	"Governor's Cup"
Coach: Willie Taggart		Season Record >>	263	378	5-7	ATS>>	4-8	O/U>>	7-4	

Garnet and Gold – History of Florida State Seminoles Football

Paperback $29.95
Hardcover $34.95

FLORIDA STATE SEMINOLES — ACC Atlantic

STADIUM: Doak Campbell Stadium {79,560} | **Location:** Tallahassee, FL | **COACH:** Mike Norvell

DATE		Opponent	FSU	Opp	S/U	Line	ATS	Total	O/U	Trends & Angles
8/27/2022	vs	DUQUESNE								27-4 S/U in 1st home game of season since 1990
9/4/2022	vs	LSU {@ New Orleans}								vs LSU - Florida State leads series 7-2
9/24/2022	vs	BOSTON COLLEGE								vs Boston College - FSU leads series 14-5
10/1/2022	vs	WAKE FOREST								5-0 S/U @ home vs Wake Forest since 2010
10/8/2022	@	NC State								0-8 ATS @ NC State since 2006
10/15/2022	vs	CLEMSON								11-1 S/U @ home vs Clemson as favorite since 1993
10/29/2022	vs	GEORGIA TECH								0-7 ATS vs Georgia Tech since 2008
11/5/2022	@	Miami								6-2 S/U @ Miami since 2006 {6-2 ATS}
11/12/2022	@	Syracuse								5-1 S/U @ Syracuse since 1978
11/19/2022	vs	LOUISIANA								10-2 S/U prior to playing Louisville since 1986
11/19/2022	@	Louisville								Game 4-0 O/U @ Louisville since 2014
11/25/2022	vs	FLORIDA								2-16 S/U vs Florida as Dog since 1983 {4-12 ATS}
12/3/2022	vs									ACC Championship
	vs									BOWL GAME

Pointspread Analysis — Non-Conference

- 1-11 S/U vs Non-Conf. as 7.5 point or more Dog since 1980
- 4-13 S/U vs Non-Conf. as 3.5-7 point Dog since 1981
- 5-1 S/U & ATS vs Non-Conf. as 3 point or less Dog since 1991
- 8-0 S/U & ATS vs Non-Conf. as 3 point or less favorite since 1998
- 0-5 O/U vs Non-Conf. as 3 point or less favorite since 2007
- 6-2 ATS vs Non-Conf. as 3.5-7 point favorite since 2007
- 7-0 O/U vs Non-Conf. as 3.5-7 point favorite since 2008
- 20-6-1 S/U vs Non-Conf. as 3.5-7 point favorite since 1977
- 9-2 S/U vs Non-Conf. as 7.5-10 point favorite since 1987
- 20-3 S/U vs Non-Conf. as 10.5-15 point favorite since 1983
- 2-10 O/U vs Non-Conf. as 10.5-15 point favorite since 1993
- 58-1 S/U vs Non-Conf. as 15.5 point or more favorite since 1984
- vs Florida - Florida leads series 37-26-2
- 0-13 S/U vs Florida as 3.5-20 point Dog since 1983
- 2-11 ATS vs Florida as 3.5-20 point Dog since 1983
- 9-0 S/U vs Florida as 7.5 point or more favorite since 1987
- 7-2 ATS vs Florida as 7.5 point or more favorite since 1987
- 0-5 O/U vs Florida as 7.5 point or more favorite since 1993
- 6-0 S/U & ATS vs Florida as 3 point or less favorite since 1998

Dog
- 1-14 S/U on road as 10.5 point or more Dog since 1986
- 2-13 S/U as 10.5 point or more Dog since 2007
- 1-10 S/U as 7.5-10 point Dog since 1980
- 14-3 O/U as 3.5-7 point Dog since 2006
- 7-2 O/U on road as 3.5-7 point Dog since 2007

Favorite
- 7-3 S/U & ATS on road as 3 point or less favorite since 1999
- 0-6 O/U on road as 3 point or less favorite since 2008
- 2-11 AS 3 point or less favorite since 2008
- 15-4 S/U as 3.5-7 point favorite since 2013
- 7-1 S/U @ home as 7.5-10 point favorite since 2007
- 2-11 O/U @ home as 10.5-15 point favorite since 2005
- 18-2 S/U on road as 10.5-15 point favorite since 1985
- 14-1 S/U @ home as 15.5-20 point favorite since 2003
- 1-7 O/U on road as 15.5-20 point favorite since 2002
- 9-0 S/U on road as 20.5-25 point favorite since 1986
- 30-1 S/U on road as 20.5 point or more favorite since 1986
- 106-1 S/U @ home as 20.5 point or more favorite since 1984

Bowl Games
- 9-1-1 S/U vs Big Ten teams in Bowl Games
- 8-3 S/U in Bowl Games since 2008
- 11-1-1 S/U in Bowl Games as 3.5-7 point favorite since 1977
- 0-4 S/U in Bowl Games as 7.5-10 point Dog since 1980

- 25-0 S/U @ home when #1 ranked since 1993
- 0-6 S/U vs #1 ranked teams since 1999
- 18-0 S/U @ home when #3 ranked all time

Pointspread Analysis — Conference

- vs Clemson - Florida State leads series 20-14
- 0-8 S/U vs Clemson as Dog since 2009
- 6-2 O/U vs Clemson as Dog since 2009
- 5-0 S/U vs Clemson as favorite since 2008
- Game 6-2 O/U vs Louisville since 2014
- vs Louisville - Florida State leads series 16-6
- Game 2-9 O/U vs Miami since 2011
- vs Miami - Miami leads series 35-30
- 7-2 ATS vs Miami as Dog since 2005
- 5-1 S/U vs Miami as favorite since 2011
- 0-6 O/U vs Miami as favorite since 2011
- 1-5 ATS vs North Carolina as favorite since 2001
- 4-17 ATS vs NC State since 2001
- vs NC State - Florida State leads series 27-15
- 4-14 ATS vs NC State as favorite since 2001
- vs Syracuse - Florida State leads series 12-2
- 12-1 S/U vs Syracuse since 1978
- Game 5-1 O/U @ home vs Syracuse since 2005
- 7-2 S/U vs Wake Forest since 2012
- Game 0-7 O/U vs Wake Forest since 2014
- vs Wake Forest - Florida State leads series 30-8-1
- Game 1-6 O/U @ home vs Wake Forest since 2006
- 7-0 S/U vs Boston College as 9 point or more favorite since 2010
- 0-4 S/U & ATS vs B. College as 4.0-6.5 point favorite since 2006
- 13-1 S/U vs Clemson as 8 point or more favorite since 1996
- 13-1 S/U vs Georgia Tech as 7.5 point or more favorite since 1992
- 4-0 S/U vs Louisville as 24.5 point or more favorite since 1986
- 0-5 S/U vs Miami as 7 point or more Dog since 2001
- 8-0 S/U vs Miami as 9.5 point or more favorite since 1997
- 1-6 S/U & ATS vs Miami as 3.5-6 point favorite since 1988
- 9-0 S/U vs N. Carolina as 17.5 point or more favorite since 1992
- 10-0 S/U vs Syracuse as 5 point or more favorite since 1989
- 21-0 S/U vs Wake F. as 10.5 point or more favorite since 1992

BOSTON COLLEGE	27-4 S/U in 2nd home game of season since 1990
WAKE FOREST	8-2 S/U after playing Boston College since 2011
NC State	1-8-2 ATS in 1st road game of season since 2010
CLEMSON	9-1 S/U after playing NC State since 2011 (8-0-1 ATS)
GEORGIA TECH	9-3 S/U prior to playing Miami since 2008
Syracuse	17-1 S/U after playing Miami since 2003
Louisville	14-1 S/U prior to playing Florida since 2006
Louisville	3-11 O/U in final road game of season since 2007

- 2-12 ATS when ranked vs NC State since 2001
- 9-0 S/U when ranked vs Syracuse all time
- 6-0 S/U when ranked vs Miami since 2010

FRESNO STATE BULLDOGS   MOUNTAIN WEST West

2021-Fresno State

Date	H/A	Opponent	Fres	Opp	S/U	Line	ATS	Total	O/U	Notes
8/28/2021	vs	CONNECTICUT	45	0	W	-27.5	W	63.5	U	
9/4/2021	@	Oregon	24	31	L	18.0	W	62.0	U	
9/11/2021	vs	CAL POLY-SLO	63	10	W	-32.5	W	60.0	O	
9/18/2021	@	Ucla	40	37	W	11.0	W	64.5	O	
9/24/2021	vs	UNLV	38	30	W	-30.0	L	59.5	O	
10/2/2021	@	Hawaii	24	27	L	-11.5	L	63.5	U	"Golden Screwdriver Trophy"
10/16/2021	@	Wyoming	17	0	W	-3.0	W	53.5	U	
10/23/2021	vs	NEVADA	34	32	W	-3.5	L	64.0	O	
10/30/2021	@	San Diego State	30	20	W	-2.5	W	49.0	O	"Battle for the Oil Can"
11/6/2021	vs	BOISE STATE	14	40	L	-4.0	L	61.0	U	
11/13/2021	vs	NEW MEXICO	34	7	W	-24.0	W	50.5	U	
11/25/2021	@	San Jose State	40	9	W	-7.0	W	52.5	U	"Valley Rivalry"
12/18/2021	vs	Texas-El Paso	31	24	W	-13.5	L	54.5	O	New Mexico Bowl

Coach: Kalen DeBoer — Season Record >> 434-267, 10-3, ATS>> 8-5, O/U>> 6-7

2020-Fresno State

Date	H/A	Opponent	Fres	Opp	S/U	Line	ATS	Total	O/U	Notes
10/24/2020	vs	HAWAII	19	34	L	-3.0	L	64.0	U	"Golden Screwdriver Trophy"
10/31/2020	vs	COLORADO STATE	38	17	W	2.5	W	57.5	U	
11/7/2020	@	Unlv	40	27	W	-11.0	W	57.5	O	
11/14/2020	@	Utah State	35	16	W	-10.5	W	51.5	U	
12/5/2020	@	Nevada	26	37	L	5.5	L	60.0	O	
12/12/2020	vs	New Mexico	39	49	L	-16.5	L	55.5	O	{@ Las Vegas, NV}

Coach: Kalen DeBoer — Season Record >> 197-180, 3-3, ATS>> 3-3, O/U>> 3-3

2019-Fresno State

Date	H/A	Opponent	Fres	Opp	S/U	Line	ATS	Total	O/U	Notes
8/31/2019	@	Usc	23	31	L	14.0	W	50.0	O	
9/7/2019	vs	MINNESOTA	35	38	L	3.0	T	46.0	O	{2 OT}
9/21/2019	vs	SACRAMENTO STATE	34	20	W	-24.5	L	NT	---	
9/28/2019	@	New Mexico State	30	17	W	-20.5	L	62.5	U	
10/12/2019	@	Air Force	24	43	L	2.5	L	49.5	O	
10/19/2019	vs	UNLV	56	27	W	-16.0	W	52.0	O	
10/26/2019	vs	COLORADO STATE	31	41	L	-13.5	L	56.5	O	
11/2/2019	@	Hawaii	41	38	W	2.0	W	68.0	O	"Golden Screwdriver Trophy"
11/9/2019	vs	UTAH STATE	35	37	L	-5.5	L	58.0	O	
11/16/2019	@	San Diego State	7	17	L	2.5	L	43.5	U	"Battle for the Oil Can"
11/23/2019	vs	NEVADA	28	35	L	-13.0	L	51.5	O	
11/30/2019	@	San Jose State	16	17	L	2.5	W	59.5	U	"Valley Rivalry"

Coach: Jeff Tedford — Season Record >> 360-361, 4-8, ATS>> 4-7-1, O/U>> 8-3

2018-Fresno State

Date	H/A	Opponent	Fres	Opp	S/U	Line	ATS	Total	O/U	Notes
9/1/2018	vs	IDAHO	79	13	W	-24.5	W	NT	---	
9/8/2018	@	Minnesota	14	21	L	PK	L	50.0	U	
9/15/2018	@	Ucla	38	14	W	-2.5	W	51.5	O	
9/29/2018	vs	TOLEDO	49	27	W	-10.0	W	62.0	O	
10/6/2018	@	Nevada	21	3	W	-16.0	W	58.5	U	
10/13/2018	vs	WYOMING	27	3	W	-18.0	W	44.0	U	
10/20/2018	@	New Mexico	38	7	W	-14.0	W	52.5	U	
10/27/2018	vs	HAWAII	50	20	W	-24.0	W	60.0	O	
11/3/2018	@	Unlv	48	3	W	-27.0	W	60.0	U	
11/10/2018	@	Boise State	17	24	L	-2.5	L	55.0	U	"Milk Can"
11/17/2018	vs	SAN DIEGO STATE	23	14	W	-10.0	L	42.0	U	"Battle for the Oil Can"
11/24/2018	vs	SAN JOSE STATE	31	13	W	-32.0	L	52.0	U	"Valley Rivalry"
12/1/2018	@	Boise State	19	16	W	PK	W	51.0	U	MWC CHAMPIONSHIP
12/15/2018	vs	Arizona State	31	20	W	-6.0	W	53.5	U	Las Vegas Bowl

Coach: Jeff Tedford — Season Record >> 485-198, 12-2, ATS>> 10-4, O/U>> 3-10, MWC CHAMPIONS

FRESNO STATE BULLDOGS   MOUNTAIN WEST West

STADIUM: Bulldog Stadium {40,727} **Location:** Fresno, CA **COACH:** Jeff Tedford

DATE		Opponent	Fres	Opp	S/U	Line	ATS	Total	O/U	Trends & Angles
9/3/2022	vs	CAL POLY-SLO								8-0 S/U vs Cal Poly-SLO since 1980
9/10/2022	vs	OREGON STATE								6-0 S/U & ATS @ home vs Oregon St. since 1986
9/17/2022	@	Usc								0-4 S/U vs USC since 2005
10/1/2022	@	Connecticut								vs Connecticut - Fresno State leads series 1-0
10/8/2022	@	Boise State								1-14 S/U vs Boise State as Dog since 2002
10/15/2022	vs	SAN JOSE STATE								13-2 S/U @ home vs San Jose State since 1989
10/22/2022	@	New Mexico								5-0 S/U & ATS @ New Mexico since 1993
10/29/2022	vs	SAN DIEGO STATE								4-1 S/U @ home vs San Diego State since 2002
11/5/2022	vs	HAWAII								Game 1-4 O/U @ home vs Hawaii since 2012
11/12/2022	@	Unlv								vs Unlv - Fresno State leads series 17-7
11/19/2022	@	Nevada								5-1 ATS @ Nevada since 2011
11/26/2022	vs	WYOMING								5-1 S/U & ATS @ home vs Wyoming since 1992
12/3/2022	vs									MWC Championship
	vs									BOWL GAME

Pointspread Analysis - Non-Conference
- 0-25 S/U vs Non-Conf. as 15.5 point or more Dog since 1987
- 2-10 S/U vs Non-Conf. as 10.5-15 point Dog since 1994
- 7-0 O/U vs Non-Conf. as 10.5-15 point Dog since 2002
- 7-1 S/U & ATS vs Non-Conf. as 3 point or less favorite since 1985
- 1-9 ATS vs Non-Conf. as 3.5-7 point favorite since 2001
- 6-1 O/U vs Non-Conf. as 3.5-7 point favorite since 2008
- 10-0 S/U vs Non-Conf. as 7.5-10 point favorite since 1985
- 10-1 S/U vs Non-Conf. as 10.5-15 point favorite since 2005
- 39-1 S/U vs Non-Conf. as 15.5 point or more favorite since 1985
- 4-0 S/U @ home vs Oregon State as favorite since 1986
- vs Cal Poly-SLO - Fresno State leads series 33-9-2

Bowl Games
- 3-6 S/U in Bowl Games since 2008
- 3-0 S/U vs ACC in Bowl Games
- 0-3 O/U in Las Vegas Bowl

Dog
- 0-37 S/U as 15.5 point or more Dog since 1987
- 7-1 O/U as 20.5-25 point Dog since 2005
- 0-9 S/U @ home as 10.5 point or more dog since 1994
- 10-0 O/U as 10.5-15 point Dog since 2002
- 2-14 S/U on road as 7.5-10 point Dog since 1988
- 3-12 O/U as 3.5-7 point Dog since 2008

Favorite
- 8-2 S/U & ATS as 3 point or less favorite since 2010
- 13-0 S/U @ home as 7.5-10 point favorite since 1986
- 8-1 S/U on road as 10.5-15 point favorite since 2005
- 13-2 S/U on road as 15.5-20 point favorite since 1985
- 23-3 S/U @ home as 15.5-20 point favorite since 1985
- 25-3-1 S/U as 20.5-25 point favorite since 1987
- 1-7 O/U as 20.5-25 point favorite since 2009
- 2-6 O/U @ home as 25.5-30 point favorite since 2001
- 25-0 S/U @ home as 25.5 point or more favorite since 1986
- 8-1 S/U on road as 25.5-30 point favorite since 1989

- 4-24 S/U vs ranked teams since 2005
- 5-38 S/U on road vs ranked teams all time
- 1-6 S/U vs ranked San Diego State all time
- 0-12 S/U vs #14 - #17 ranked teams all time

Pointspread Analysis - Conference
- 4-0 ATS vs Boise State as Dog since 2014
- 5-2 ATS vs Hawaii since 2015
- 5-2 S/U vs Hawaii as favorite since 2012
- 5-0 ATS vs Hawaii as Dog since 2007
- vs Hawaii - Fresno State leads series 29-24-1
- vs Nevada - Fresno State leads series 30-22-1
- Game 1-3 O/U @ Nevada since 2014
- 8-1 S/U & ATS vs New Mexico since 1995
- vs New Mexico - Fresno State leads series 14-4
- 7-1 S/U & ATS vs New Mexico as favorite since 1995
- vs San Jose State - Fresno State leads series 43-38-3
- Game 0-5 O/U vs San Jose State since 2016
- 14-1 S/U @ home vs San Jose State as favorite since 1985
- vs San Diego State - San Diego State leads series 30-26-4
- Game 1-6 O/U vs San Diego State since 2014
- 1-4 O/U vs UNLV as favorite since 2013
- vs Wyoming - Fresno State leads series 8-5
- 0-3 S/U & ATS vs Air Force as 3 point or less favorite since 1994
- 0-12 S/U vs Boise State as 7 point or more Dog since 2002
- 0-5 S/U & ATS vs Hawaii as 9 point or less favorite since 1995
- 5-0 S/U & ATS vs Hawaii as 12.5-17.5 point favorite since 1993
- 0-4 S/U vs Nevada as 7.5 point or more Dog since 2009
- 4-0 S/U vs Nevada as 19.5 point or more favorite since 2000
- 4-1 S/U & ATS @ Nevada as 7 point or less Dog since 1999
- 7-1 S/U vs New Mexico as 14 point or more favorite since 1988
- 0-5 S/U vs San Jose State as 4 point or more Dog since 1987
- 16-0 S/U vs San Jose State as 9.5 point or more favorite since 1985
- 0-4 S/U vs San Diego State as 7.5 point or more Dog since 1995
- 5-0 S/U vs San Diego St. as 5.5 point or more favorite since 1993
- 6-0-1 S/U vs Utah State as 15.5-25.5 point favorite since 1989
- 0-5 ATS vs Utah State as 14.5-20.5 point favorite since 1991
- 4-0 S/U & ATS vs Wyoming as 9 point or less favorite since 1992

CAL POLY-SLO	19-4 S/U in 1st home game of season since 1999
OREGON STATE	10-3 O/U in 2nd home game of season since 2008
Connecticut	9-3 O/U in 2nd road game of season since 2010
Connecticut	9-1-1 ATS prior to playing Boise State since 2005
New Mexico	3-8 O/U prior to playing San Diego State since 2002
New Mexico	6-1 ATS after San Jose State since 2009

GEORGIA BULLDOGS — SEC East

2021-Georgia		Opponent	UGA	Opp	S/U	Line	ATS	Total	O/U	
9/4/2021	vs	Clemson	10	3	W	3.0	W	51.5	U	Bank of America Stadium
9/11/2021	vs	ALABAMA-BIRMINGHAM	56	7	W	-23.5	W	43.5	O	
9/18/2021	vs	SOUTH CAROLINA	40	13	W	-31.0	L	47.0	O	
9/25/2021	@	Vanderbilt	62	0	W	-37.0	W	54.0	O	
10/2/2021	vs	ARKANSAS	37	0	W	-16.0	W	47.0	U	
10/9/2021	@	Auburn	34	10	W	-14.5	W	45.5	U	"Deep South's Oldest Rivalry"
10/16/2021	vs	KENTUCKY	30	13	W	-21.5	L	44.5	U	
10/30/2021	vs	Florida	34	7	W	-14.0	W	51.0	U	"Okefenokee Oar"
11/6/2021	vs	MISSOURI	43	6	W	-40.0	L	58.5	U	
11/13/2021	@	Tennessee	41	17	W	-19.0	W	56.0	O	
11/20/2021	vs	CHARLESTON SOUTHERN	56	7	W	-53.0	L	59.5	O	
11/27/2021	@	Georgia Tech	45	0	W	-35.5	W	54.5	U	"Clean, old-fashioned Hate"
12/4/2021	vs	Alabama	24	41	L	-6.0	L	48.5	O	SEC Championship Game
12/31/2021	vs	Michigan	34	11	W	-7.5	W	46.5	U	Orange Bowl {National Semifinal}
1/10/2022	vs	Alabama	33	18	W	-3.0	W	53.0	U	CFB Championship Game
Coach: Kirby Smart		Season Record >>	579	153	14-1	ATS>>	10-5	O/U>>	6-9	National Champions

2020-Georgia		Opponent	UGA	Opp	S/U	Line	ATS	Total	O/U	
9/26/2020	@	Arkansas	37	10	W	-27.5	L	53.0	U	
10/3/2020	vs	AUBURN	27	6	W	-7.5	W	44.5	U	"Deep South's Oldest Rivalry"
10/10/2020	vs	TENNESSEE	44	21	W	-12.0	W	63.0	O	
10/17/2020	@	Alabama	24	41	L	5.5	L	56.5	O	
10/31/2020	@	Kentucky	14	3	W	-16.5	L	41.5	U	
11/7/2020	vs	Florida	28	44	L	-2.5	L	54.5	O	"Okefenokee Oar"
11/21/2020	vs	MISSISSIPPI STATE	31	24	W	-26.5	L	44.0	U	
11/28/2020	@	South Carolina	45	16	W	-23.0	W	50.0	U	
12/12/2020	@	Missouri	49	14	W	-14.0	W	54.5	O	
1/1/2021	vs	Cincinnati	24	21	W	-8.0	L	53.0	U	Chick-Fil-A Peach Bowl
Coach: Kirby Smart		Season Record >>	323	200	8-2	ATS>>	4-6	O/U>>	6-4	

2019-Georgia		Opponent	UGA	Opp	S/U	Line	ATS	Total	O/U	
8/31/2019	@	Vanderbilt	30	6	W	-22.5	W	57.0	U	
9/7/2019	vs	MURRAY STATE	63	17	W	-49.0	L	NT	---	
9/14/2019	vs	ARKANSAS STATE	55	0	W	-32.5	W	58.0	U	
9/21/2019	vs	NOTRE DAME	23	17	W	-15.5	L	58.5	U	
10/5/2019	@	Tennessee	43	14	W	-24.0	W	51.0	O	
10/12/2019	vs	SOUTH CAROLINA	17	20	L	-21.0	L	52.5	U	{2 OT}
10/19/2019	vs	KENTUCKY	21	0	W	-24.0	L	45.5	U	
11/2/2019	vs	Florida	24	17	W	-6.0	W	47.5	U	"Okefenokee Oar"
11/9/2019	vs	MISSOURI	27	0	W	-18.5	W	47.5	U	
11/16/2019	@	Auburn	21	14	W	-3.0	W	43.0	U	"Deep South's Oldest Rivalry"
11/23/2019	vs	TEXAS A&M	19	13	W	-12.5	L	43.5	U	
11/30/2019	@	Georgia Tech	52	7	W	-28.5	W	46.0	O	"Clean, old-fashioned Hate"
12/7/2019	vs	Lsu	10	37	L	7.0	L	57.0	U	SEC Championship
1/1/2020	vs	Baylor	26	14	W	-3.5	W	44.0	U	Sugar Bowl
Coach: Kirby Smart		Season Record >>	431	176	12-2	ATS>>	8-6	O/U>>	2-11	

2018-Georgia		Opponent	UGA	Opp	S/U	Line	ATS	Total	O/U	
9/1/2018	vs	AUSTIN PEAY	45	0	W	-46.0	L	NT	---	
9/8/2018	@	South Carolina	41	17	W	-8.0	W	59.0	U	
9/15/2018	vs	MIDDLE TENNESSEE	49	7	W	-33.5	W	54.5	O	
9/22/2018	@	Missouri	43	29	W	-14.5	L	68.0	O	
9/29/2018	vs	TENNESSEE	38	12	W	-29.5	L	55.0	U	
10/6/2018	vs	VANDERBILT	41	13	W	-26.0	W	55.5	U	
10/13/2018	@	Lsu	16	36	L	-6.5	L	50.5	O	
10/27/2018	vs	Florida	36	17	W	-7.0	W	52.5	O	"Okefenokee Oar"
11/3/2018	@	Kentucky	34	17	W	-9.0	W	46.0	O	
11/10/2018	vs	AUBURN	27	10	W	-13.5	L	52.5	U	"Deep South's Oldest Rivalry"
11/17/2018	vs	MASSACHUSETTS	66	27	W	-41.5	L	67.0	O	
11/24/2018	vs	GEORGIA TECH	45	21	W	-17.0	W	59.5	O	"Clean, old-fashioned Hate"
12/1/2018	vs	Alabama	28	35	L	11.0	W	63.0	T	SEC Championship
1/1/2019	vs	Texas	21	28	L	-13.5	L	60.5	U	Sugar Bowl
Coach: Kirby Smart		Season Record >>	530	269	11-3	ATS>>	8-6	O/U>>	7-5-1	

GEORGIA BULLDOGS — SEC East

STADIUM: Sanford Stadium {92,746} | **Location:** Athens, GA | **COACH:** Kirby Smart

DATE		Opponent	UGA	Opp	S/U	Line	ATS	Total	O/U	Trends & Angles
9/3/2022	vs	Oregon {@ Atlanta}								vs Oregon - Georgia leads series 1-0
9/10/2022	vs	SAMFORD								vs Samford - Georgia leads series 2-0
9/17/2022	@	South Carolina								6-1 S/U vs South Carolina since 2015
9/24/2022	vs	KENT STATE								vs Kent State - Georgia leads series 1-0
10/1/2022	@	Missouri								5-0 S/U @ Missouri since 2012
10/8/2022	vs	AUBURN								12-1 S/U vs Auburn as favorite since 2007
10/15/2022	vs	VANDERBILT								25-3 S/U @ home vs Vanderbilt since 1963
10/29/2022	vs	Florida								vs Florida - Georgia leads series 54-44-2
11/5/2022	vs	TENNESSEE								6-1 S/U @ home vs Tennessee since 2008
11/12/2022	@	Mississippi State								4-1 S/U @ Mississippi State since 1982
11/19/2022	@	Kentucky								7-0 S/U @ Kentucky since 2008
11/26/2022	vs	GEORGIA TECH								vs Georgia Tech - Georgia leads series 69-41-5
12/3/2022	vs									SEC Championship
	vs									BOWL GAME

Pointspread Analysis — Non-Conference

- 8-2 S/U & ATS vs Non-Conf. as 3 point or less Dog since 1981
- 1-7 O/U vs Non-Conf. as 3.5-7 point favorite since 2010
- 17-2 S/U vs Non-Conf. as 7.5-10 point favorite since 1986
- 11-3 S/U vs Non-Conf. as 10.5-15 point favorite since 1983
- 47-0 S/U vs Non-Conf. as 15.5 point or more favorite since 1985
- 17-3 S/U vs Georgia Tech since 2001
- 5-1 ATS vs Georgia Tech as Dog since 1991
- 10-0 S/U vs Ga Tech as 13.5 point or more favorite since 1983

Bowl Games
- 10-2 S/U vs Big 10 in Bowl Games since 1989
- 4-0 S/U in Citrus Bowl since 1993
- 5-0 ATS in Citrus Bowl since 1984
- 7-0-1 ATS in Bowl Games since 2014
- 3-1 O/U in Peach Bowl since 1995
- 4-0 S/U & ATS in Bowl Games as 3 point or less Dog since 1981
- 3-0 O/U in Bowl Games as 3 point or less Dog since 1998
- 11-1 S/U in Bowl Games as 7.5-10 point favorite since 1987
- 0-5 O/U in Bowl Games as 3.5-7 point favorite since 2009

Dog
- 1-6 S/U & ATS as 3.5-7 point Dog since 2013
- 0-4 S/U & ATS @ home as 3 point or less Dog since 2000

Favorite
- 18-1 S/U on road as 7.5-10 point favorite since 1989
- 2-8 O/U on road as 7.5-10 point favorite since 2004
- 29-3 S/U as 7.5-10 point favorite since 2000
- 17-0 S/U on road as 10.5-15 point favorite since 1983
- 17-2 S/U @ home as 10.5-15 point favorite since 2008
- 7-0 S/U on road as 15.5-20 point favorite since 2005
- 25-1 S/U @ home as 15.5-20 point favorite since 1983
- 23-0 S/U as 15.5-20 point favorite since 1998
- 70-1 S/U as 20.5 point or more favorite since 1983
- 6-0 S/U & ATS @ home vs ranked Auburn since 2007
- 1-10 ATS prior to playing Florida since 2011
- 7-0 S/U @ home when #1 ranked all time
- 8-0 S/U @ home when #2 ranked all time
- 21-0 S/U when ranked vs Kentucky since 1991 {10-0 on road}
- 17-1 S/U @ home when ranked vs Vanderbilt all time
- 11-0 S/U in final road game of season since 2011
- 10-1 ATS after playing Kentucky since 2011

Pointspread Analysis — Conference

- 23-2 S/U vs Kentucky since 1997 {12 W}
- vs Kentucky - Georgia leads series 61-12-2
- 8-0 S/U vs Missouri as favorite since 2014
- vs Missouri - Georgia leads series 10-1
- 10-0 S/U vs Mississippi State as favorite since 1983
- Game 3-10 O/U @ South Carolina since 1996
- 0-5 S/U & ATS vs South Carolina as Dog since 1988
- vs South Carolina - Georgia leads series 52-19-2
- Game 5-1 O/U @ home vs Tennessee since 2010
- 6-0 S/U @ home vs Tennessee as favorite since 2008
- vs Tennessee - Georgia leads series 26-23-2
- 2-10 S/U vs Tennessee as Dog since 1989
- vs Vanderbilt - Georgia leads series 59-20-2
- 25-3 S/U vs Vanderbilt since 1995
- 5-0 ATS vs Auburn as 10.5 point or more Dog since 1994
- 0-9 S/U & ATS vs Auburn as 8 point or less Dog since 1983
- 1-12 S/U vs Florida as 9.5 point or more Dog since 1990
- 0-5 O/U vs Florida as 6 point or less Dog since 1984
- 5-2 O/U vs Florida as 5.5 point or more favorite since 1992
- 2-5 O/U vs Florida as 3 point or less favorite since 1988
- 20-1 S/U vs Kentucky as 10 point or more favorite since 1983
- 14-1 S/U vs Mississippi as 7 point or more favorite since 1983
- 8-1 S/U vs S. Carolina as 14 point or more favorite since 1983
- 0-5 S/U vs Tennessee as 3.5-10 point Dog since 1989
- 8-0 S/U vs Vanderbilt as 7.5-12 point favorite since 1983
- 11-0 S/U vs Vanderbilt as 21.5 point or more favorite since 1990

SAMFORD	24-1 S/U in 1st home game of season since 1997
SAMFORD	8-2 O/U in 1st home game of season since 2009
SAMFORD	10-1 O/U prior to playing South Carolina since 2010
KENT STATE	9-2 O/U in 2nd home game of season since 2010
Missouri	12-0 S/U prior to playing Auburn since 2010
AUBURN	9-1 S/U prior to playing Vanderbilt since 2010
VANDERBILT	22-3 S/U prior to playing Florida since 1997
VANDERBILT	12-0 S/U after playing Auburn since 2010
Florida	9-2 S/U after playing Vanderbilt since 2010
TENNESSEE	15-0 S/U after playing Florida since 2007
Mississippi State	2-8 ATS prior to playing Kentucky since 2012
Kentucky	10-0 S/U prior to playing Georgia Tech since 2011
GEORGIA TECH	16-2 S/U after playing Kentucky since 2005

Bulldog Nation! History of Georgia Bulldogs Football

Available at: www.stevesfootballbible.com (Blueblood Series)

GEORGIA SOUTHERN EAGLES   SUN BELT East

2021-Ga Southern		Opponent	GSU	Opp	S/U	Line	ATS	Total	O/U	
9/4/2021	vs	GARDNER-WEBB	30	25	W	-28.0	L	48.0	O	
9/11/2021	@	Florida Atlantic	6	38	L	6.5	L	48.5	U	
9/18/2021	@	Arkansas	10	45	L	24.0	L	53.0	O	
9/25/2021	vs	LOUISIANA	20	28	L	14.5	W	54.5	U	
10/2/2021	vs	ARKANSAS STATE	59	33	W	-1.5	W	66.5	O	
10/9/2021	@	Troy	24	27	L	5.5	W	51.0	T	
10/14/2021	@	South Alabama	13	41	L	2.5	L	49.5	O	
10/30/2021	vs	GEORIGA STATE	19	21	L	6.0	W	55.0	U	
11/6/2021	vs	COASTAL CAROLINA	8	28	L	16.0	L	56.5	U	
11/13/2021	@	Texas State	38	30	W	2.0	W	52.0	O	
11/20/2021	vs	BYU	17	34	L	20.0	W	57.5	U	
11/27/2021	@	Appalachian State	3	27	L	24.5	L	55.5	O	"Deeper Than Hate Rivalry"
Coach: Chad Lunsford		Season Record >>	247	377	3-9	ATS>>	7-5	O/U>>	5-6-1	

2020-Ga Southern		Opponent	GSU	Opp	S/U	Line	ATS	Total	O/U	
9/12/2020	vs	CAMPBELL	27	26	W	-34.0	L	58.5	U	
9/26/2020	@	Louisiana	18	20	L	11.5	W	50.0	U	
10/3/2020	@	Louisiana-Monroe	35	30	W	-18.5	L	49.5	O	
10/17/2020	vs	MASSACHUSETTS	41	0	W	-30.0	W	62.0	U	
10/24/2020	@	Coastal Carolina	14	28	L	1.5	L	48.5	U	
10/29/2020	vs	SOUTH ALABAMA	24	17	W	-3.5	W	51.5	U	
11/7/2020	vs	TROY	20	13	W	2.5	W	52.0	U	
11/14/2020	vs	TEXAS STATE	40	38	W	-13.0	L	50.0	O	
11/21/2020	@	Army	27	28	L	3.5	W	38.5	O	
11/28/2020	@	Georgia State	24	30	L	2.5	L	51.5	O	
12/5/2020	vs	FLORIDA ATLANTIC	20	3	W	-2.0	W	41.0	U	
12/12/2020	vs	APPALACHIAN STATE	26	34	L	9.5	W	45.0	O	"Deeper Than Hate Rivalry"
12/23/2020	vs	Louisiana Tech	38	3	W	-7.5	W	47.5	U	New Orleans Bowl
Coach: Chad Lunsford		Season Record >>	354	270	8-5	ATS>>	8-5	O/U>>	5-8	

2019-Ga Southern		Opponent	GSU	Opp	S/U	Line	ATS	Total	O/U	
8/31/2019	@	Lsu	3	55	L	27.0	L	52.5	O	
9/7/2019	vs	MAINE	26	18	W	-9.0	L	NT	---	
9/14/2019	@	Minnesota	32	35	L	17.0	W	45.5	O	
9/28/2019	vs	LOUISIANA-LAFAYETTE	24	37	L	3.0	L	55.0	O	
10/3/2019	@	South Alabama	20	17	W	-10.0	L	44.5	U	{2 OT}
10/19/2019	vs	COASTAL CAROLINA	30	27	W	-7.0	L	43.0	O	{2 OT}
10/26/2019	vs	NEW MEXICO STATE	41	7	W	-14.0	W	54.5	U	
10/31/2019	@	Appalachian State	24	21	W	13.5	W	41.5	O	"Deeper Than Hate Rivalry"
11/9/2019	@	Troy	28	49	L	-2.5	L	57.0	O	
11/16/2019	vs	LOUISIANA-MONROE	51	29	W	-6.0	W	58.0	O	
11/23/2019	@	Arkansas State	33	38	L	PK	L	52.5	O	
11/30/2019	vs	GEORGIA STATE	38	10	W	-7.0	W	56.0	U	
12/21/2019	vs	Liberty	16	23	L	-5.0	L	58.5	U	AutoNation Cure Bowl
Coach: Chad Lunsford		Season Record >>	366	366	7-6	ATS>>	5-8	O/U>>	8-4	

2018-Ga Southern		Opponent	GSU	Opp	S/U	Line	ATS	Total	O/U	
9/1/2018	vs	SOUTH CAROLINA STATE	37	6	W	-27.5	W	NT	---	
9/8/2018	vs	MASSACHUSETTS	34	13	W	-1.5	W	61.0	U	
9/15/2018	@	Clemson	7	38	L	31.5	W	48.5	U	
9/29/2018	vs	ARKANSAS STATE	28	21	W	3.0	W	53.5	U	
10/6/2018	vs	SOUTH ALABAMA	48	13	W	-13.0	W	57.5	U	
10/11/2018	@	Texas State	15	13	W	-17.0	L	51.0	U	
10/20/2018	@	New Mexico State	48	31	W	-10.0	W	52.5	O	
10/25/2018	vs	APPALACHIAN STATE	34	14	W	11.0	W	47.5	O	"Deeper Than Hate Rivalry"
11/3/2018	@	Louisiana-Monroe	25	44	L	-7.0	L	60.5	O	
11/10/2018	vs	TROY	21	35	L	2.5	L	44.5	O	
11/17/2018	@	Coastal Carolina	41	17	W	-7.5	W	53.0	O	
11/24/2018	@	Georgia State	35	14	W	-10.0	W	58.0	U	
12/15/2018	vs	Eastern Michigan	23	21	W	-3.0	L	45.5	U	Camelia Bowl
Coach: Chad Lunsford		Season Record >>	396	280	10-3	ATS>>	9-4	O/U>>	6-6	

GEORGIA SOUTHERN EAGLES — SUN BELT East

STADIUM: Paulson Stadium {25,000} **Location:** Statesboro, GA **COACH:** Clay Helton

DATE		Opponent	GSU	Opp	S/U	Line	ATS	Total	O/U	Trends & Angles
9/3/2022	vs	MORGAN STATE								14-1 S/U in 1st home game of season since 2007
9/10/2022	@	Nebraska								2-12 S/U in 1st road game of season since 2008
9/17/2022	@	Alabama-Birmingham								1st Meeting
9/24/2022	vs	BALL STATE								12-2 S/U in 2nd home game of season since 2008
10/1/2022	@	Coastal Carolina								vs Coastal - Ga Southern leads series 5-3
10/8/2022	@	Georgia State								vs Georgia State - G State leads series 5-3
10/15/2022	vs	JAMES MADISON								7-0 S/U vs James Madison since 1986
10/22/2022	@	Old Dominion								vs Old Dominion - Ga Southern leads series 2-0
11/5/2022	vs	SOUTH ALABAMA								4-0 S/U @ home vs South Alabama since 2015
11/10/2022	@	Louisiana								vs Louisiana - Louisiana leads series 4-1
11/19/2022	vs	MARSHALL								0-4 S/U vs Marshall since 1993
11/26/2022	vs	APPALACHIAN STATE								vs App State - App.State leads series 20-14-1
12/3/2022	vs									Sun Belt Championship
	vs									BOWL GAME

Pointspread Analysis — Non-Conference
- 0-14 S/U vs Non-Conf. as 15.5 or more Dog since 2014

Bowl Games
- 4-1 S/U in Bowl Games

Dog
- 2-18 S/U as 10.5 point or more Dog since 2014
- 12-5-1 O/U as 9.5 point or less Dog since 2017
- 2-10 S/U on road as 9.5 point or less Dog since 2014

Favorite
- 8-0 S/U @ home as 7.5 point or less favorite since 2018
- 29-1 S/U as 10 point or more favorite since 2014
- 2-7 O/U on road as 10 point or more favorite since 2014

Pointspread Analysis — Conference
- vs James Madison - Ga Southern leads series 7-1
- vs Marshall - Marshall leads series 4-2
- 6-2 ATS vs South Alabama since 2014
- vs South Alabama - Georgia Southern leads series 7-1

Nebraska — 1-7 O/U in 1st road game of season since 2014
Louisiana — 2-9 S/U in final road game of season since 2011
MARSHALL — 9-2 S/U prior to playing Appalachian State since 2010
2-7 S/U vs ranked teams all time

Baseball Fans – We have books on Baseball as well

Print Version $39.95 — Every Diamond Does Sparkle... "The Playoffs" — By STEVE FULTON

Print Version $39.95 — Every Diamond Sparkles More... "The World Series" — By STEVE FULTON

These books available at numerous online retailers

GEORGIA STATE PANTHERS   SUN BELT East

2021 - Georgia State		Opponent	State	Opp	S/U	Line	ATS	Total	O/U	
9/4/2021	vs	ARMY	10	43	L	-2.5	L	48.5	O	
9/11/2021	@	North Carolina	17	59	L	25.5	L	66.0	O	
9/18/2021	vs	CHARLOTTE	20	9	W	-4.0	W	63.0	U	
9/25/2021	@	Auburn	24	34	L	27.5	W	57.5	O	
10/2/2021	vs	APPALACHIAN STATE	16	45	L	10.5	L	54.0	O	
10/9/2021	@	Louisiana-Monroe	55	21	W	-15.5	W	49.5	O	
10/23/2021	vs	TEXAS STATE	28	16	W	-10.5	W	58.5	U	
10/30/2021	@	Georgia Southern	21	19	W	-6.0	L	55.0	U	
11/4/2021	@	Louisiana	17	21	L	13.5	W	53.5	U	
11/13/2021	@	Coastal Carolina	42	40	W	12.5	W	53.0	O	
11/20/2021	vs	ARKANSAS STATE	28	20	W	-15.5	L	65.5	U	
11/27/2021	vs	TROY	37	10	W	-6.5	W	49.5	U	
12/25/2021	vs	**Ball State**	51	20	W	-6.5	W	53.0	O	**Camelia Bowl**
Coach: Shawn Elliott		Season Record >>	366	357	8-5	ATS>>	8-5	O/U>>	7-6	

2020 - Georgia State		Opponent	State	Opp	S/U	Line	ATS	Total	O/U	
9/19/2020	vs	LOUISIANA	31	34	L	16.5	W	57.0	O	{OT}
10/3/2020	vs	EAST CAROLINA	49	29	W	1.5	W	70.0	O	
10/15/2020	@	Arkansas State	52	59	L	3.5	L	73.0	O	
10/24/2020	@	Troy	36	34	W	2.5	W	68.5	O	
10/31/2020	vs	COASTAL CAROLINA	0	51	L	4.0	L	60.5	U	
11/7/2020	vs	LOUISIANA-MONROE	52	34	W	-18.5	L	60.0	O	
11/14/2020	@	Appalachian State	13	17	L	18.0	W	63.0	U	
11/21/2020	@	South Alabama	31	14	W	-3.5	W	58.5	U	"Clash of the Claws"
11/28/2020	vs	GEORGIA SOUTHERN	30	24	W	-2.5	W	51.5	O	
12/26/2020	vs	**Western Kentucky**	39	21	W	-3.0	W	49.0	O	**Lending Tree Bowl**
Coach: Shawn Elliott		Season Record >>	333	317	6-4	ATS>>	7-3	O/U>>	7-3	

2019 - Georgia State		Opponent	State	Opp	S/U	Line	ATS	Total	O/U	
8/31/2019	@	Tennessee	38	30	W	24.5	W	58.0	O	
9/7/2019	vs	FURMAN	48	42	W	-6.0	T	NT	---	
9/14/2019	@	Western Michigan	10	57	L	9.0	L	69.5	U	
9/21/2019	@	Texas State	34	37	L	3.0	T	62.5	O	{3 OT}
10/5/2019	vs	ARKANSAS STATE	52	38	W	6.0	W	69.0	O	
10/12/2019	@	Coastal Carolina	31	21	W	3.0	W	63.0	U	
10/19/2019	vs	ARMY	28	21	W	4.0	W	54.0	U	
10/26/2019	vs	TROY	52	33	W	-1.0	W	67.0	O	
11/9/2019	@	Louisiana-Monroe	31	45	L	-2.5	L	76.0	T	
11/16/2019	vs	APPALCHIAN STATE	27	56	L	15.0	L	61.5	O	
11/23/2019	vs	SOUTH ALABAMA	28	15	W	-9.5	W	56.0	U	"Clash of the Claws"
11/30/2019	@	Georgia Southern	10	38	L	7.0	L	56.0	U	
12/31/2019	vs	**Wyoming**	17	38	L	7.0	L	49.0	O	**Arizona Bowl**
Coach: Shawn Elliott		Season Record >>	406	471	7-6	ATS>>	6-5-2	O/U>>	6-5-1	

2018 - Georgia State		Opponent	State	Opp	S/U	Line	ATS	Total	O/U	
8/30/2018	vs	KENNESAW STATE	24	20	W	-2.0	W	NT	---	
9/8/2018	@	NC State	7	41	L	24.5	L	56.0	U	
9/14/2018	@	Memphis	22	59	L	28.5	L	59.0	O	
9/22/2018	vs	WESTERN MICHIGAN	15	34	L	9.0	L	61.0	U	-
9/29/2018	vs	LOUISIANA-MONROE	46	14	W	5.5	W	65.5	U	
10/4/2018	@	Troy	20	37	L	17.0	T	55.5	O	
10/18/2018	@	Arkansas State	35	51	L	13.0	L	56.5	O	
10/27/2018	vs	COASTAL CAROLINA	34	37	L	2.5	L	60.5	O	
11/3/2018	vs	TEXAS STATE	31	40	L	-7.0	L	52.5	O	
11/10/2018	@	Louisiana-Lafayette	22	36	L	13.0	L	70.0	U	
11/17/2018	@	Appalachian State	17	45	L	27.5	L	54.0	O	
11/24/2018	vs	GEORGIA SOUTHERN	14	35	L	10.0	L	58.0	U	
Coach: Shawn Elliott		Season Record >>	287	449	2-10	ATS>>	2-9-1	O/U>>	6-5	

GEORGIA STATE PANTHERS   SUN BELT East

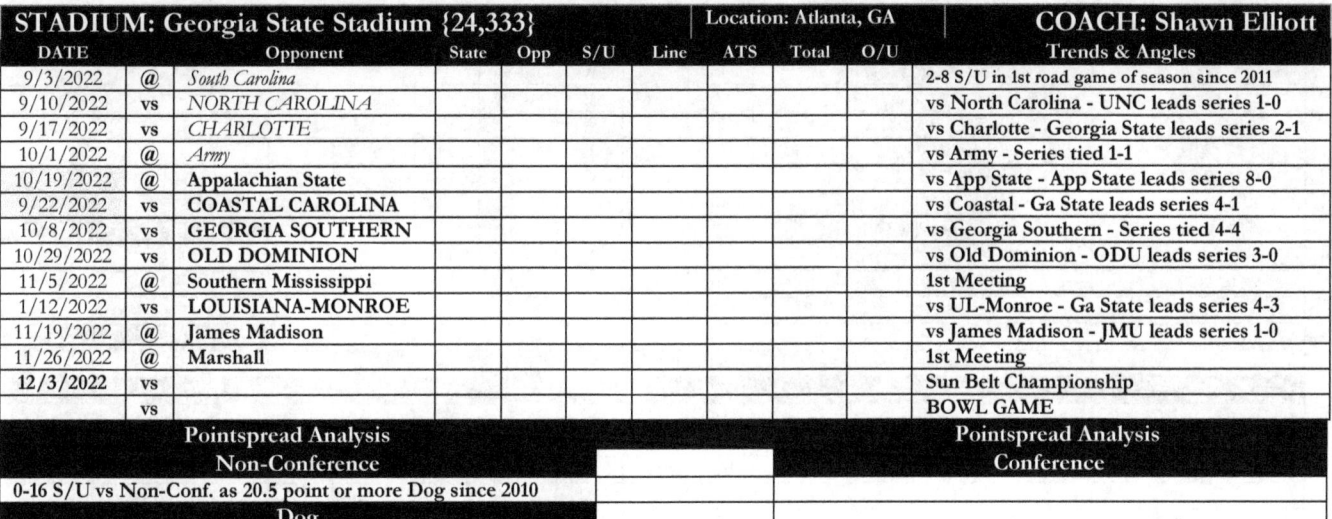

STADIUM: Georgia State Stadium {24,333} **Location:** Atlanta, GA **COACH:** Shawn Elliott

DATE		Opponent	State	Opp	S/U	Line	ATS	Total	O/U	Trends & Angles
9/3/2022	@	South Carolina								2-8 S/U in 1st road game of season since 2011
9/10/2022	vs	NORTH CAROLINA								vs North Carolina - UNC leads series 1-0
9/17/2022	vs	CHARLOTTE								vs Charlotte - Georgia State leads series 2-1
10/1/2022	@	Army								vs Army - Series tied 1-1
10/19/2022	@	Appalachian State								vs App State - App State leads series 8-0
9/22/2022	vs	COASTAL CAROLINA								vs Coastal - Ga State leads series 4-1
10/8/2022	vs	GEORGIA SOUTHERN								vs Georgia Southern - Series tied 4-4
10/29/2022	vs	OLD DOMINION								vs Old Dominion - ODU leads series 3-0
11/5/2022	@	Southern Mississippi								1st Meeting
1/12/2022	vs	LOUISIANA-MONROE								vs UL-Monroe - Ga State leads series 4-3
11/19/2022	@	James Madison								vs James Madison - JMU leads series 1-0
11/26/2022	@	Marshall								1st Meeting
12/3/2022	vs									Sun Belt Championship
	vs									BOWL GAME

Pointspread Analysis — Non-Conference
- 0-16 S/U vs Non-Conf. as 20.5 point or more Dog since 2010

Dog
- 1-19 S/U as 20.5 point or more Dog since 2010
- 2-24 S/U as 10.5-20 point Dog since 2013
- 0-5 S/U & ATS as 7.5-10 point Dog since 2013
- 0-15 S/U as home Dog of 5 pts or more since 2013

Favorite
- 6-2 S/U & ATS as 3 point or less favorite since 2015
- 4-0 S/U on road as 3.5-7 point favorite since 2017

Pointspread Analysis — Conference

CHARLOTTE	3-8 S/U in 2nd home game of season since 2010
Army	2-9 S/U in 2nd road game of season since 2010
Army	2-9 S/U in 2nd road game of season since 2010
	1-9 S/U vs ranked teams all time

This book is a definitive account of College Football Trophy games across all divisions in FBS, FCS, Division 2 and Division 3. Full of historical information and game recaps of some of the memorable and notable games for each trophy game/rivalry. This book is for College Football fans of all ages, being both entertaining and educational, it is a must read if you love college football.

College Football History "Trophy Games"

{8.5" x 11"} {430 pages}

$34.95

These books available at numerous online retailers

GEORGIA TECH YELLOWJACKETS   ACC Coastal

2021-Georgia Tech		Opponent	Tech	Opp	S/U	Line	ATS	Total	O/U	
9/4/2021	vs	NORTHERN ILLINOIS	21	22	L	-19.0	L	57.0	U	
9/11/2021	vs	KENNESAW STATE	45	17	W	-19.5	W	53.5	O	
9/18/2021	@	Clemson	8	14	L	27.0	W	52.5	U	
9/25/2021	vs	NORTH CAROLINA	45	22	W	14.5	W	66.0	O	
10/2/2021	vs	PITTSBURGH	21	52	L	3.0	L	57.5	O	
10/9/2021	@	Duke	31	27	W	-4.5	L	61.0	U	
10/23/2021	@	Virginia	40	48	L	7.0	L	66.0	O	
10/30/2021	vs	VIRGINIA TECH	17	26	L	-3.0	L	55.5	U	"Battle of the Techs"
11/6/2021	@	Miami	30	33	L	10.0	W	62.5	O	
11/13/2021	vs	BOSTON COLLEGE	30	41	L	2.0	L	56.0	O	
11/20/2021	@	Notre Dame	0	55	L	18.5	L	58.0	U	
11/27/2021	vs	GEORGIA	0	45	L	35.5	L	54.5	U	"Clean, old-fashioned Hate"
Coach: Geoff Collins		Season Record >>	288	402	3-9	ATS>>	4-8	O/U>>	6-6	

2020-Georgia Tech		Opponent	Tech	Opp	S/U	Line	ATS	Total	O/U	
9/12/2020	@	Florida State	16	13	W	13.5	W	50.0	U	
9/19/2020	vs	CENTRAL FLORIDA	21	49	L	8.0	L	63.5	O	
9/26/2020	@	Syracuse	20	37	L	-7.0	L	51.5	O	
10/9/2020	vs	LOUISVILLE	46	27	W	4.5	W	63.0	O	
10/17/2020	vs	CLEMSON	7	73	L	27.0	L	63.5	O	
10/24/2020	@	Boston College	27	48	L	3.5	L	57.5	O	
10/31/2020	vs	NOTRE DAME	13	31	L	20.5	W	58.0	U	
11/28/2020	vs	DUKE	56	33	W	2.5	W	57.5	O	
12/5/2020	@	NC State	13	23	L	7.0	L	61.0	U	
12/10/2020	vs	PITTSBURGH	20	34	L	7.0	L	56.0	U	
Coach: Geoff Collins		Season Record >>	239	368	3-7	ATS>>	4-6	O/U>>	6-4	

2019-Georgia Tech		Opponent	Tech	Opp	S/U	Line	ATS	Total	O/U	
8/29/2019	@	Clemson	14	52	L	36.5	L	61.0	O	
9/7/2019	vs	SOUTH FLORIDA	14	10	W	-4.5	L	58.5	U	
9/14/2019	vs	THE CITADEL	24	27	L	-26.5	L	NT	---	{OT}
9/28/2019	@	Temple	3	24	L	9.5	L	48.0	U	
10/5/2019	vs	NORTH CAROLINA	22	38	L	10.0	L	47.0	O	
10/12/2019	@	Duke	23	41	L	17.5	L	47.5	O	
10/19/2019	@	Miami	28	21	W	18.0	W	46.0	O	{OT}
11/2/2019	vs	PITTSBURGH	10	20	L	9.0	L	44.0	U	
11/9/2019	@	Virginia	28	33	L	16.0	W	45.5	O	
11/16/2019	vs	VIRGINIA TECH	0	45	L	6.0	L	51.5	U	"Battle of the Techs"
11/23/2019	vs	NC STATE	28	26	W	2.5	W	46.5	O	
11/30/2019	vs	GEORGIA	7	52	L	28.5	L	46.0	O	"Clean, old-fashioned Hate"
Coach: Geoff Collins		Season Record >>	201	389	3-9	ATS>>	3-9	O/U>>	7-4	

2018-Georgia Tech		Opponent	Tech	Opp	S/U	Line	ATS	Total	O/U	
9/1/2018	vs	ALCORN STATE	41	0	W	-42.0	L	NT	---	
9/8/2018	@	South Florida	38	49	L	-3.0	L	60.0	O	
9/15/2018	@	Pittsburgh	19	24	L	-3.5	L	54.5	U	
9/22/2018	vs	CLEMSON	21	49	L	15.5	L	56.5	O	
9/29/2018	vs	BOWLING GREEN	63	17	W	-28.5	W	65.0	O	
10/5/2018	@	Louisville	66	31	W	-5.5	W	56.0	O	
10/13/2018	vs	DUKE	14	28	L	-1.0	L	55.0	U	
10/25/2018	@	Virginia Tech	49	28	W	3.0	W	58.5	O	"Battle of the Techs"
11/3/2018	@	North Carolina	38	28	W	-3.5	W	65.0	O	
11/10/2018	vs	MIAMI	27	21	W	-1.0	W	50.5	U	
11/17/2018	vs	VIRGINIA	30	27	W	-6.5	L	52.0	O	{OT}
11/24/2018	@	Georgia	21	45	L	17.0	L	59.5	O	"Clean, old-fashioned Hate"
12/26/2018	vs	Minnesota	10	34	L	-5.0	L	57.0	U	Quick Lane Bowl
Coach: Paul Johnson		Season Record >>	437	381	7-6	ATS>>	5-8	O/U>>	8-4	

GEORGIA TECH YELLOWJACKETS   ACC Coastal

STADIUM: Bobby Dodd Stadium @ Historic Grant Field {55,000} | **Location:** Atlanta, GA | **COACH:** Geoff Collins

DATE		Opponent	Tech	Opp	S/U	Line	ATS	Total	O/U	Trends & Angles
9/5/2022	vs	CLEMSON								vs Clemson - Georgia Tech leads series 51-34-2
9/10/2022	vs	WESTERN CAROLINA								vs Western Carolina - G Tech leads series 5-0
9/17/2022	vs	MISSISSIPPI								vs Ole Miss - Series tied 2-2
9/24/2022	@	Central Florida								vs Central Florida - G Tech leads series 3-0
10/1/2022	@	Pittsburgh								1-5 S/U @ Pittsburgh since 1918
10/8/2022	vs	DUKE								vs Duke - Georgia Tech leads series 53-13-1
10/20/2022	vs	VIRGINIA								5-0 S/U @ home vs Virginia since 2010 {4-1 ATS}
10/29/2022	@	Florida State								vs Georgia Tech - FSU leads series 14-11-1
11/5/2022	@	Virginia Tech								3-0 S/U @ Virginia Tech since 2014 {3-0 ATS}
11/12/2022	vs	MIAMI								4-0 ATS vs Miami since 2017
11/19/2022	@	North Carolina								Game 5-0 O/U @ North Carolina since 2010
11/26/2022	@	Georgia								vs Georgia - Georgia leads series 69-41-5
12/5/2020	vs									ACC Championship
	vs									BOWL GAME

Pointspread Analysis — Non-Conference

- 0-8 S/U vs Non-Conf. as 15.5 point or more Dog since 1983
- 3-13 S/U vs Non-Conf. as 10.5-15 point Dog since 1983
- 1-7 O/U vs Non-Conf. as 3 point or less Dog since 1993
- 0-4 S/U vs Non-Conf. as 3 point or less Dog since 2010
- 7-1 S/U vs Non-Conf. as 10.5-15 point favorite since 1993
- 21-3 S/U vs Non-conf. as 15.5 point or more favorite since 1998
- 0-10 S/U vs Georgia as 13.5 point or more Dog since 1983

Bowl Games
- 4-0 S/U in Sugar Bowl
- 2-7 S/U vs SEC in Bowl Games since 1960
- 0-4 S/U in Chick-Fil-A Peach Bowl
- 2-7 O/U in Bowl Games since 2008
- 6-1 O/U in Bowl Games as 3 point or less favorite since 1991

Dog
- 0-13 S/U as 20.5 point or more Dog since 1993
- 2-14 S/U as 15.5-20 point Dog since 1983
- 1-6 S/U @ home as 10.5-15 point Dog since 1992
- 1-5 O/U @ home as 10.5-15 point Dog since 1998
- 1-8 S/U @ home as 7.5-10 point Dog since 1985
- 1-7 O/U @ home as 3.5-7 point Dog since 2009

Favorite
- 5-0 S/U @ home as 3.5-7 point favorite since 2016
- 5-0 S/U & ATS @ home as 7.5-10 point favorite since 2010
- 14-2 S/U @ home as 10.5-15 point favorite since 2005
- 7-2 O/U on road as 10.5-15 point favorite since 2001
- 20-3 S/U as 10.5-15 point favorite since 2005
- 20-1 S/U as 15.5-20 point favorite since 1990
- 8-0 S/U on road as 15.5-25 point favorite since 1984
- 15-1 S/U as 25.5 point or more favorite since 1991

Pointspread Analysis — Conference

- 0-6 ATS vs Duke as favorite since 2014
- 1-7 S/U vs Miami as Dog since 2009
- 3-9 S/U vs Miami since 2009
- vs Miami - Series tied 13-13
- vs North Carolina - Georgia Tech leads series 31-22-3
- 13-2 S/U vs North Carolina as favorite since 1991
- 0-4 S/U & ATS vs Pittsburgh since 2018
- Game 1-4 O/U vs Pittsburgh since 2017
- vs Pittsburgh - Pittsburgh leads series 11-5
- vs Virginia - Series tied 21-21-1
- 4-1 ATS @ home vs Virginia since 2010
- 7-0 ATS @ Virginia Tech since 2006
- Game 1-5 O/U @ Virginia Tech since 2008
- vs Virginia Tech - Virginia Tech leads series 11-7
- 4-1 S/U vs Virginia Tech as Dog since 2014
- 0-5 ATS vs Virginia Tech as favorite since 1990
- 9-3 S/U vs Clemson as 6.5 point or less Dog since 1984
- 10-2 ATS vs Clemson as 6.5 point or less Dog since 1984
- 1-12 S/U vs Clemson as 7.0-15.5 Dog since 1983
- 23-1 S/U vs Duke as 8 point or more favorite since 1984
- 0-13 S/U vs Florida State as 7.5 point or more Dog since 1992
- 1-6 S/U vs North Carolina as 8 point or more Dog since 1983
- 8-0-1 S/U vs UNC as 10 point or more favorite since 1989
- 1-8 S/U vs Virginia as 3.5-7 point Dog since 1988
- 6-0 S/U vs Virginia as 9.5-12 point favorite since 2000

- 2-16 S/U on road vs ranked teams since 2009
- 1-8 S/U on road vs #1 ranked teams all time
- 1-8-1 S/U vs #2 ranked teams all time
- 1-10 S/U vs #3 ranked teams all time {0-5 at home}
- 1-10 S/U vs #4 ranked teams all time
- 0-6 S/U @ ranked North Carolina all time
- 4-0 ATS @ ranked Virginia Tech since 2006

CLEMSON	24-3 S/U in 1st home game of season since 1995
WEST CAROLINA	9-3 S/U in 2nd home game of season since 2011 (8-2 ATS)
Central Florida	7-1 O/U prior to playing Pittsburgh since 2013
DUKE	3-10 O/U prior to playing Virginia since 2007
DUKE	11-2 S/U prior to playing Virginia since 2008
VIRGINIA	3-10 S/U after playing Duke since 2009
Virginia Tech	2-6 O/U prior to playing Miami since 2013
North Carolina	13-3 S/U prior to playing Georgia since 2005

HAWAII RAINBOW WARRIORS   MOUNTAIN WEST West

2021-Hawaii		Opponent	HAW	Opp	S/U	Line	ATS	Total	O/U	
8/28/2021	@	Ucla	10	44	L	17.5	L	66.5	U	
9/4/2021	vs	PORTLAND STATE	49	28	W	-26.0	L	57.0	O	
9/11/2021	@	Oregon State	27	45	L	11.0	L	65.5	O	
9/18/2021	vs	SAN JOSE STATE	13	17	L	7.5	W	62.5	U	
9/25/2021	@	New Mexico State	41	21	W	-16.5	W	62.5	U	
10/2/2021	vs	FRESNO STATE	27	24	W	11.5	W	63.5	U	"Golden Screwdriver Trophy"
10/16/2021	@	Nevada	17	34	L	14.0	L	62.5	U	
10/23/2021	vs	NEW MEXICO STATE	41	34	W	-19.0	L	63.5	O	
10/30/2021	@	Utah State	31	51	L	3.5	L	66.0	O	
11/6/2021	vs	SAN DIEGO STATE	10	17	L	7.0	T	45.0	U	
11/13/2021	@	Unlv	13	27	L	-3.5	L	55.5	U	
11/20/2021	vs	COLORADO STATE	50	45	W	3.0	W	54.0	O	
11/27/2021	@	Wyoming	38	14	W	13.5	W	48.5	O	"Paniolo Trophy"
Coach: Todd Graham		Season Record >>	367	401	6-7	ATS>>	5-7-1	O/U>>	6-7	
2020-Hawaii		Opponent	HAW	Opp	S/U	Line	ATS	Total	O/U	
10/24/2020	@	Fresno State	34	19	W	3.0	W	64.0	U	"Golden Screwdriver Trophy"
10/30/2020	@	Wyoming	7	31	L	-3.0	L	59.5	U	"Paniolo Trophy"
11/7/2020	vs	NEW MEXICO	39	33	W	-13.0	L	66.5	O	
11/14/2020	@	San Diego State	10	34	L	9.5	L	51.0	U	
11/21/2020	vs	BOISE STATE	32	40	L	13.0	W	55.5	O	
11/28/2020	vs	NEVADA	24	21	W	7.0	L	63.0	U	
12/5/2020	vs	SAN JOSE STATE	24	35	L	2.5	L	59.5	U	
12/12/2020	vs	UNLV	38	21	W	-18.5	L	60.0	U	
12/24/2020	vs	Houston	28	14	W	7.0	W	61.0	U	New Mexico Bowl
Coach: Todd Graham		Season Record >>	236	248	5-4	ATS>>	4-5	O/U>>	2-7	
2019-Hawaii		Opponent	HAW	Opp	S/U	Line	ATS	Total	O/U	
8/24/2019	vs	ARIZONA	45	38	W	10.5	W	70.5	O	
9/7/2019	vs	OREGON STATE	31	28	W	-7.0	L	77.0	U	
9/14/2019	@	Washington	20	52	L	21.5	L	59.0	O	
9/21/2019	vs	CENTRAL ARKANSAS	35	16	W	-14.5	W	NT	---	
9/28/2019	@	Nevada	54	3	W	1.5	W	63.0	U	
10/12/2019	@	Boise State	37	59	L	12.5	L	60.0	U	
10/19/2019	vs	AIR FORCE	26	56	L	3.5	L	65.5	O	"Kuter Trophy"
10/26/2019	@	New Mexico	45	31	W	-10.0	W	71.5	O	
11/2/2019	vs	FRESNO STATE	38	41	L	-2.0	L	68.0	O	"Golden Screwdriver Trophy"
11/9/2019	vs	SAN JOSE STATE	42	40	W	-7.5	L	78.5	O	
11/16/2019	@	Unlv	21	7	W	-7.0	W	72.5	U	
11/23/2019	vs	SAN DIEGO STATE	14	11	W	1.5	W	46.5	U	
11/30/2019	vs	ARMY	52	31	W	-2.0	W	55.0	O	
12/7/2019	@	Boise State	10	31	L	14.0	L	65.0	U	MWC CHAMPIONSHIP GAME
12/24/2019	vs	BYU	38	34	W	2.5	W	64.5	O	HAWAI'I BOWL
Coach: Nick Rolovich		Season Record >>	508	478	10-5	ATS>>	8-7	O/U>>	9-5	
2018-Hawaii		Opponent	HAW	Opp	S/U	Line	ATS	Total	O/U	
8/25/2018	@	Colorado State	43	34	W	17.0	W	58.0	O	
9/1/2018	vs	NAVY	59	41	W	13.0	W	61.5	O	
9/8/2018	vs	RICE	43	29	W	-17.0	L	68.5	O	
9/15/2018	@	Army	21	28	L	7.0	T	62.0	U	
9/22/2018	vs	DUQUESNE	42	21	W	-37.5	L	NT	---	
9/29/2018	@	San Jose State	44	41	W	-9.5	L	62.0	O	{5 OT}
10/6/2018	vs	WYOMING	17	13	W	3.0	W	53.0	U	"Paniolo Trophy"
10/13/2018	@	Byu	23	49	L	10.5	L	57.5	O	
10/20/2018	vs	NEVADA	22	40	L	-2.0	L	67.5	O	
10/27/2018	@	Fresno State	20	50	L	24.0	L	60.0	O	"Golden Screwdriver Trophy"
11/3/2018	vs	UTAH STATE	17	56	L	18.0	L	72.0	O	
11/17/2018	vs	UNLV	35	28	W	-7.0	T	72.5	U	
11/24/2018	@	San Diego State	31	30	W	18.5	W	54.0	O	{OT}
12/22/2018	vs	Louisiana Tech	14	31	L	-1.0	L	61.5	U	HAWAI'I BOWL
Coach: Nick Rolovich		Season Record >>	431	491	8-6	ATS>>	4-8-2	O/U>>	8-5	

HAWAII RAINBOW WARRIORS — MOUNTAIN WEST West

STADIUM: Ching Complex {20,000} | **Location:** Honolulu, HI | **COACH:** Todd Graham

DATE		Opponent	Haw	Opp	S/U	Line	ATS	Total	O/U	Trends & Angles
8/27/2022	vs	VANDERBILT								9-1 ATS in 1st home game of season since 2006
9/3/2022	vs	WESTERN KENTUCKY								10-2 O/U in 2nd home game of season since 2009
9/10/2022	@	Michigan								vs Michigan - Michigan leads series 3-0
9/17/2022	vs	DUQUESNE								vs Duquesne - Hawaii leads series 1-0
9/24/2022	@	New Mexico State								vs New Mexico St - Hawaii leads series 10-0
10/8/2022	@	San Diego State								1-9 S/U @ San Diego State since 1990
10/15/2022	vs	NEVADA								Game 0-9 O/U vs Nevada since 2013
10/22/2022	@	Colorado State								2-7 S/U vs Colorado State as Dog since 1995
10/29/2022	vs	WYOMING								vs Wyoming - Wyoming leads series 15-11
11/5/2022	@	Fresno State								vs Fresno State - Fresno leads series 29-24-1
11/12/2022	vs	UTAH STATE								0-6 S/U & ATS vs Utah State since 2011
11/19/2022	vs	UNLV								10-2 S/U @ home vs UNLV since 1981
11/26/2022	@	San Jose State								8-1 S/U @ San Jose State since 1999
12/3/2022	vs									MWC Championship
	vs									BOWL GAME

Pointspread Analysis — Non-Conference
- 0-28 S/U vs Non-Conf. as 15.5 point or more Dog since 1991
- 6-0 O/U vs Non-Conf. as 3 point or less Dog since 2003
- 9-0 S/U vs Non-Conf. as 3.5-7 point favorite since 2002
- 10-1 S/U vs Non-Conf. as 15.5-20 point favorite since 1990
- 2-8-1 ATS vs Non-Conf. as 15.5-20 point favorite since 1990
- 21-1 S/U vs Non-Conf. as 20.5 point or more favorite since 1989
- 9-0 S/U vs New Mexico State as favorite since 2005

Dog
- 0-12 S/U as 30.5 point or more Dog since 1996
- 0-12 S/U as 25.5 point or more Dog since 1996
- 0-14 S/U @ home as 20.5 point or more Dog Since 1991
- 4-16 S/U as 15.5-20 point Dog since 1985
- 9-2 O/U as 15.5-20 point Dog since 2011
- 5-19 S/U as 10.5-15 point Dog since 2000
- 5-16 S/U @ home as 10.5-15 point Dog since 1985
- 1-8 S/U on road as 7.5-10 point Dog since 2009 {2-7 ATS}
- 2-8 O/U on road as 7.5-10 point Dog since 1992
- 2-15 S/U @ home as 7.5-10 point Dog since 1987
- 3-17 S/U as 3.5-7 point Dog since 2012
- 1-15 S/U on road as 3.5-7 point Dog since 2002

Favorite
- 2-21-1 ATS as a favorite since 2015
- 2-7 O/U @ home as 3 point or less favorite since 2007
- 0-7 O/U on road as 3.5-7 point favorite since 2010
- 10-2 S/U @ home as 3.5-7 point favorite since 2002
- 23-2 S/U as 10.5-15 point favorite since 1985
- 15-1 S/U @ home as 15.5-20 point favorite since 1989
- 0-8 ATS @ home as 15.5-20 point favorite since 2006
- 37-1 S/U as 20.5 point or more favorite since 1987
- 4-0 S/U on road as 20.5 point or more favorite since 2006

- 0-10 S/U vs #14 - #17 ranked teams all time
- 1-9 S/U vs #24 - #25 ranked teams all time
- 5-0 S/U on road when ranked since 2007
- 8-0 S/U @ home when ranked since 2007
- 1-20 S/U on road vs ranked teams all time

Pointspread Analysis — Conference
- 6-0 O/U vs Colorado State as Dog since 2012
- 2-5 S/U vs Fresno State as Dog since 2012
- vs Nevada - Nevada leads series 15-11
- 0-6 S/U @ UNLV as Dog since 1997
- 1-6-1 ATS vs UNLV since 2014
- vs Unlv - Hawaii leads series 18-13
- 4-20-2 ATS vs San Diego State since 1985
- 1-8 ATS vs San Diego State as favorite since 1985
- 4-17 S/U vs San Diego since 1990
- vs San Diego State - SDSU leads series 23-11-2
- 2-15 S/U vs San Diego State as Dog since 1986
- vs San Jose State - Hawaii leads series 22-21-1
- vs Utah State - Utah State leads series 11-6
- 0-5 S/U & ATS vs Utah State as Dog since 2013
- Game 6-0 O/U @ home vs Utah State since 2005
- vs Wyoming - Wyoming leads series 15-11
- 3-8 S/U vs Wyoming since 1993
- 1-9 S/U vs Fresno State as 12.5 point or more Dog since 1993
- 5-0 S/U & ATS vs Fresno State as 9 point or less Dog since 1995
- 5-0 S/U vs Fresno State as 4 point or less favorite since 1986
- 1-5 S/U vs Nevada as 7 point or more Dog since 2009
- 4-0 S/U vs Nevada as 10.5 point or more favorite since 2000
- 0-5 S/U vs San Jose State as 4.0-8.5 point Dog since 1998
- 1-4 ATS vs San Jose State as 4.0-8.5 point Dog since 1998
- 10-0 S/U vs San Jose St. as 9.5 point or more favorite since 2001
- 0-6 S/U vs Wyoming as 6.5 point or more Dog since 1987
- 4-0 S/U @ home vs Wyoming as 2 point or more favorite since 1986

Opponent	Trend
New Mexico State	1-12 S/U in 2nd road game of season since 2008
New Mexico State	2-8-1 ATS in 2nd road game of season since 2010
New Mexico State	5-12 S/U prior to playing San Diego State since 1993
San Diego State	1-9 S/U prior to playing Nevada since 2011
NEVADA	0-9 S/U after playing San Diego State since 1997
NEVADA	0-6 S/U prior to playing Colorado State since 1996
Colorado State	3-8 S/U prior to playing Wyoming since 1992
WYOMING	3-9 S/U prior to playing Fresno State since 2008
WYOMING	1-7 ATS prior to playing Fresno State since 2012
UTAH STATE	1-9 ATS after playing Fresno State since 2011
UNLV	10-3 O/U in final home game of season since 2008

HOUSTON COUGARS — AMERICAN West

2021-Houston		Opponent	HOU	Opp	S/U	Line	ATS	Total	O/U	
9/4/2021	vs	Texas Tech	21	38	L	-3.0	L	63.0	U	NRG Stadium
9/11/2021	@	Rice	44	7	W	-7.5	W	50.0	O	"Bayou Bucket Classic"
9/18/2021	vs	GRAMBLING STATE	45	0	W	-41.0	W	52.0	U	
9/25/2021	vs	NAVY	28	20	W	-20.0	L	47.0	O	
10/1/2021	@	Tulsa	45	10	W	3.0	W	54.0	O	"Battle for the Best City"
10/7/2021	@	Tulane	40	22	W	-6.5	W	60.0	O	
10/23/2021	vs	EAST CAROLINA	31	24	W	-13.5	L	56.5	U	
10/30/2021	vs	SMU	44	37	W	6.0	W	62.0	O	
11/6/2021	@	South Florida	54	42	W	-13.5	L	53.0	O	
11/13/2021	@	Temple	37	8	W	-26.0	W	52.5	U	
11/19/2021	vs	MEMPHIS	31	13	W	-10.0	W	59.5	U	
11/27/2021	@	Connecticut	45	17	W	-32.0	L	54.0	O	
12/4/2021	vs	Cincinnati	20	35	L	10.5	L	52.5	O	AAC CHAMPIONSHIP
12/28/2021	vs	Auburn	17	13	W	-2.0	W	49.0	U	Birmingham Bowl
Coach: Dana Holgerson		Season Record >>	502	286	12-2	ATS>>	8-6	O/U>>	8-6	

2020-Houston		Opponent	HOU	Opp	S/U	Line	ATS	Total	O/U	
10/8/2020	vs	TULANE	49	31	W	-7.0	W	58.0	O	
10/16/2020	vs	BYU	26	43	L	5.0	L	62.5	O	
10/24/2020	@	Navy	37	21	W	-15.5	W	57.0	O	
10/31/2020	vs	CENTRAL FLORIDA	21	44	L	3.0	L	81.0	U	
11/7/2020	@	Cincinnati	10	38	L	11.5	L	51.5	U	
11/14/2020	vs	SOUTH FLORIDA	56	21	W	-15.0	W	58.5	O	
12/12/2020	@	Memphis	27	30	L	-4.5	L	63.0	O	
12/24/2020	vs	Hawaii	14	28	L	-7.0	L	61.0	U	New Mexico Bowl
Coach: Dana Holgerson		Season Record >>	240	256	3-5	ATS>>	3-5	O/U>>	4-4	

2019-Houston		Opponent	HOU	Opp	S/U	Line	ATS	Total	O/U	
8/31/2019	@	Oklahoma	31	49	L	22.0	W	79.5	O	
9/7/2019	vs	PRAIRIE VIEW A&M	37	17	W	-37.5	L	NT	---	
9/13/2019	vs	Washington State	24	31	L	8.5	W	74.0	U	NRG Stadium
9/19/2019	@	Tulane	31	38	L	4.5	L	57.5	O	
9/28/2019	@	North Texas	46	25	W	8.0	W	59.0	O	
10/12/2019	vs	CINCINNATI	23	38	L	9.5	L	50.0	O	
10/19/2019	@	Connecticut	24	17	W	-21.5	L	56.0	U	
10/24/2019	vs	SMU	31	34	L	12.0	W	65.0	T	
11/2/2019	@	Central Florida	29	44	L	21.0	L	72.5	O	
11/16/2019	vs	MEMPHIS	27	45	L	9.5	L	71.5	O	
11/23/2019	@	Tulsa	24	14	W	6.5	W	57.0	U	"Battle for the Best City"
11/30/2019	vs	NAVY	41	56	L	9.5	L	56.5	O	
Coach: Dana Holgerson		Season Record >>	368	408	4-8	ATS>>	6-6	O/U>>	7-3-1	

2018-Houston		Opponent	HOU	Opp	S/U	Line	ATS	Total	O/U	
9/1/2018	@	Rice	45	27	W	-26.0	L	56.0	O	"Bayou Bucket Classic"
9/8/2018	vs	ARIZONA	45	18	W	-3.0	W	70.0	U	
9/15/2018	@	Texas Tech	49	63	L	PK	L	69.0	O	
9/22/2018	vs	TEXAS SOUTHERN	70	14	W	-55.0	W	NT	---	
10/4/2018	vs	TULSA	41	26	W	-17.5	L	70.0	U	"Battle for the Best City"
10/13/2018	@	East Carolina	42	20	W	-16.0	W	69.5	U	
10/20/2018	@	Navy	49	36	W	-11.0	W	58.5	O	
10/27/2018	vs	SOUTH FLORIDA	57	36	W	-9.5	W	77.5	O	
11/3/2018	@	Smu	31	45	L	-13.5	L	70.5	O	
11/10/2018	vs	TEMPLE	49	59	L	-3.5	L	69.5	O	
11/15/2018	vs	TULANE	48	17	W	-7.5	W	68.0	U	
11/23/2018	@	Memphis	31	52	L	9.5	L	74.5	O	
12/22/2018	vs	Army	14	70	L	6.5	L	56.0	O	Armed Forces Bowl
Coach: Major Applewhite		Season Record >>	571	483	8-5	ATS>>	6-7	O/U>>	8-4	

HOUSTON COUGARS — AMERICAN West

STADIUM: TDECU Stadium {40,000} **Location:** Houston, TX **COACH:** Dana Holgerson

DATE		Opponent	Hou	Opp	S/U	Line	ATS	Total	O/U	Trends & Angles
9/3/2022	@	Texas-San Antonio								vs Texas-San Antonio - Series tied 1-1
9/10/2022	@	Texas Tech								1-9 S/U vs Texas Tech since 1991
9/17/2022	vs	KANSAS								vs Kansas - Kansas leads series 3-0
9/24/2022	vs	RICE								4-0 ATS @ home vs Rice since 2009
9/29/2022	vs	TULANE								8-1 S/U @ home vs Tulane since 2004
10/7/2022	@	Memphis								Game 4-1 O/U @ Memphis since 2010
10/22/2022	@	Navy								vs Navy - Houston leads series 6-2
10/29/2022	vs	SOUTH FLORIDA								6-0 S/U vs South Florida since 2013
11/5/2022	@	Smu								vs Smu - Houston leads series 22-13-1
11/12/2022	vs	TEMPLE								vs Temple - Houston leads series 7-1
11/19/2022	@	East Carolina								3-12 S/U in final road game of season since 2007
11/26/2022	vs	TULSA								0-5 ATS @ home vs Tulsa since 2010
12/3/2022	vs									AAC Championship
	vs									BOWL GAME

Pointspread Analysis — Non-Conference

- 0-14 S/U vs Non-Conf. as 20.5 point or more Dog since 1993
- 2-14 S/U vs Non-Conf. as 15.5-20 point Dog since 1986
- 8-0 O/U vs Non-Conf. as 3.5-7 point Dog since 2003
- 1-7 O/U vs Non-Conf. as 3.5-7 point favorite since 2008
- 15-2 S/U vs Non-Conf. as 10.5 point or more favorite since 1983
- vs Texas Tech - Houston leads series 18-14-1
- 5-0 S/U @ home vs Rice since 2005
- vs Rice - Houston leads series 32-11
- 6-0 S/U vs Rice since 2011
- 13-0 S/U vs Rice as 10.5 point or more favorite since 1983
- 4-0 S/U vs Texas Tech as 7.5 point or more favorite since 1983
- 0-4 S/U vs Texas Tech as Dog since 1992

Dog

- 0-18 S/U as 20.5 point or more Dog since 1986
- 4-27 S/U as 15.5-20 point Dog since 1983
- 2-16 S/U on road as 15.5-20 point Dog since 1985
- 2-18 S/U on road as 10.5-15 point Dog since 1986
- 5-2 ATS on road as 10.5-15 point Dog since 2005
- 0-6 S/U @ home as 10.5-15 point Dog since 1983
- 8-3 ATS on road as 7.5-10 point Dog since 1995
- 3-10 S/U on road as 3.5-7 point Dog since 1999
- 6-1 S/U & ATS on road as 3 point or less Dog since 1999
- 13-3 O/U as 3.5-7 point Dog since 2005

Favorite

- 2-7 S/U on road as 3.5-7 point favorite since 2008
- 1-9 ATS on road as 3.5-7 point favorite since 2007
- 2-14 O/U as 7.5-10 point favorite since 2013
- 14-1 S/U @ home as 7.5-10 point favorite since 1999
- 16-5 S/U as 10.5-15 point favorite since 2006
- 24-4 S/U as 15.5-20 point favorite since 1984
- 19-0 S/U @ home as 20.5-25 point favorite since 1989
- 10-0 S/U as 25.5-30 point favorite since 1988
- 18-1 S/U @ home as 25.5 point or more favorite since 1988
- 7-0 S/U on road as 25.5 point or more favorite since 1988

Pointspread Analysis — Bowl Games

- 4-1 O/U in Armed Forces Bowl since 2005
- 1-6 S/U in Bowl Games as 3.5-7 point Dog since 1979

Conference

- vs Cincinnati - Houston leads series 15-13
- vs Memphis - Houston leads series 16-14
- 1-6 ATS vs Memphis since 2015
- 1-5 S/U vs Memphis since 2016
- Game 6-1 O/U vs Navy since 2015
- vs South Florida - Houston leads series 6-2
- Game 1-4 O/U vs Temple since 2014
- vs Tulane - Houston leads series 19-7
- 3-10 ATS vs Tulsa as favorite since 1985
- vs Tulsa - Houston leads series 25-19
- 6-0 S/U @ home vs SMU as 16.5 point or more favorite since 1989
- 3-0 S/U vs UCF as 9.5 point or more favorite since 2006
- 10-1 S/U vs Tulane as 12.5 point or more favorite since 1999
- 1-5 S/U & ATS vs Tulsa as 2.5-4.5 point favorite since 1985

Texas-San Antonio	2-6 S/U prior to playing Texas Tech since 1991
KANSAS	15-2 S/U in 1st home game of season since 2005
TULANE	8-1 S/U & ATS after playing Rice since 2007
Memphis	12-3 S/U after playing Tulane since 2006
SOUTH FLORIDA	13-2 S/U prior to playing SMU since 2005
TEMPLE	8-1 S/U prior to playing East Carolina since 2003
TULSA	15-2 S/U in final home game of season since 2005
TULSA	9-2 ATS in final home game of season since 2011

- 30-1 S/U @ home when ranked since 1988
- 10-0 S/U when ranked vs Rice all time
- 4-0 S/U when ranked vs Tulane all time
- 3-33 S/U on road vs ranked teams since 1985
- 10-1 S/U when #6 ranked all time {6-0 @ home}
- 8-1 S/U when ranked vs Memphis all time {5-0 @ home}

ILLINOIS FIGHTING ILLINI — BIG TEN West

2021-Illinois		Opponent	ILL	Opp	S/U	Line	ATS	Total	O/U	
8/28/2021	vs	NEBRASKA	30	22	W	6.5	W	52.0	T	
9/4/2021	vs	TEXAS-SAN ANTONIO	30	37	L	-4.5	L	52.0	O	
9/11/2021	@	Virginia	14	42	L	10.5	L	56.5	U	
9/17/2021	vs	MARYLAND	17	20	L	7.0	W	67.5	U	
9/25/2021	@	Purdue	9	13	L	10.5	W	53.0	U	"Purdue Cannon"
10/2/2021	vs	CHARLOTTE	24	14	W	-10.0	T	53.5	U	
10/9/2021	vs	WISCONSIN	0	24	L	12.5	L	42.0	U	
10/23/2021	@	Penn State	20	18	W	24.5	W	45.5	U	{9 OT}
10/30/2021	vs	RUTGERS	14	20	L	1.5	L	41.5	U	
11/6/2021	@	Minnesota	14	6	W	14.5	W	44.0	U	
11/20/2021	@	Iowa	23	33	L	12.0	W	37.5	O	
11/27/2021	vs	NORTHWESTERN	47	14	W	-7.0	W	44.5	O	"Land of Lincoln Trophy"
Coach: Bret Bielema		Season Record >>	242	263	5-7	ATS>>	7-4-1	O/U>>	3-8-1	

2020-Illinois		Opponent	ILL	Opp	S/U	Line	ATS	Total	O/U	
10/23/2020	@	Wisconsin	7	45	L	20.5	L	51.5	O	
10/31/2020	vs	PURDUE	24	31	L	10.0	L	54.5	O	"Purdue Cannon"
11/7/2020	vs	MINNESOTA	14	41	L	7.5	L	64.5	U	
11/14/2020	@	Rutgers	23	20	W	5.5	W	51.5	U	
11/21/2020	@	Nebraska	41	23	W	16.5	W	62.0	O	
12/5/2020	vs	IOWA	21	35	L	13.5	L	53.0	O	
12/12/2020	@	Northwestern	10	28	L	13.0	L	41.0	U	"Land of Lincoln Trophy"
12/19/2020	@	Penn State	21	56	L	16.0	L	53.5	O	
Coach: Lovie Smith		Season Record >>	161	279	2-6	ATS>>	3-5	O/U>>	5-3	

2019-Illinois		Opponent	ILL	Opp	S/U	Line	ATS	Total	O/U	
8/31/2019	vs	AKRON	42	3	W	-18.0	W	60.0	U	
9/7/2019	@	Connecticut	31	23	W	-21.5	L	59.0	U	
9/14/2019	vs	EASTERN MICHIGAN	31	34	L	-7.5	L	57.0	O	
9/21/2019	vs	NEBRASKA	38	42	L	13.0	W	63.0	O	
10/5/2019	@	Minnesota	17	40	L	14.5	L	57.0	T	
10/12/2019	vs	MICHIGAN	25	42	L	24.5	W	48.5	O	
10/19/2019	vs	WISCONSIN	24	23	W	31.0	W	52.0	U	
10/26/2019	@	Purdue	24	6	W	9.5	W	53.5	U	"Purdue Cannon"
11/2/2019	vs	RUTGERS	38	10	W	-18.5	W	48.5	U	
11/9/2019	@	Michigan State	37	34	W	15.5	W	47.5	O	
11/23/2019	@	Iowa	10	19	L	15.5	W	48.5	U	
11/30/2019	vs	NORTHWESTERN	10	29	L	-6.0	L	39.0	T	"Land of Lincoln Trophy"
12/30/2019	vs	California	20	35	L	6.0	L	48.0	O	Redbox Bowl
Coach: Lovie Smith		Season Record >>	347	340	6-7	ATS>>	8-5	O/U>>	5-6-2	

2018-Illinois		Opponent	ILL	Opp	S/U	Line	ATS	Total	O/U	
9/1/2018	vs	KENT STATE	31	24	W	-18.0	L	57.0	U	
9/8/2018	vs	WESTERN ILLINOIS	34	14	W	-7.0	W	NT	---	
9/15/2018	vs	SOUTH FLORIDA	19	25	L	14.0	W	58.5	U	Soldier Field
9/21/2018	vs	PENN STATE	24	63	L	27.0	L	60.0	O	
10/6/2018	@	Rutgers	38	17	W	-4.5	W	50.5	O	
10/13/2018	vs	PURDUE	7	46	L	10.0	L	64.0	U	"Purdue Cannon"
10/20/2018	@	Wisconsin	20	49	L	24.0	L	53.0	O	
10/27/2018	@	Maryland	33	63	L	16.5	L	53.5	O	
11/3/2018	vs	MINNESOTA	55	31	W	10.0	W	62.0	O	
11/10/2018	@	Nebraska	35	54	L	17.5	L	71.0	O	
11/17/2018	vs	IOWA	0	63	L	15.0	L	59.5	O	
11/24/2018	@	Northwestern	16	24	L	14.5	W	57.5	U	"Land of Lincoln Trophy"
Coach: Lovie Smith		Season Record >>	312	473	4-8	ATS>>	5-7	O/U>>	7-4	

ILLINOIS FIGHTING ILLINI — BIG TEN West

STADIUM: Memorial Stadium {60,670}
Location: Champaign, IL
COACH: Bret Bielema

DATE		Opponent	ILL	Opp	S/U	Line	ATS	Total	O/U	Trends & Angles
8/27/2022	vs	WYOMING								22-2 S/U in 1st home game of season since 1998
9/3/2022	@	Indiana								0-5 S/U & ATS @ Indiana as Dog since 1987
9/10/2022	vs	VIRGINIA								vs Virginia - Illinois leads series 2-1
9/24/2022	vs	CHATTANOOGA								1st Meeting
10/1/2022	@	Wisconsin								0-8 S/U @ Wisconsin since 2004
10/8/2022	vs	IOWA								1-6 S/U @ home vs Iowa since 2004
10/15/2022	vs	MINNESOTA								2-6 S/U & ATS @ home vs Minnesota since 2003
10/29/2022	@	Nebraska								2-9 S/U @ Nebraska since 1892
11/5/2022	vs	MICHIGAN STATE								3-9 ATS vs Michigan State since 2000 (2 W)
11/12/2022	vs	PURDUE								0-5 S/U @ home vs Purdue since 2012
11/19/2022	@	Michigan								3-18-1 S/U @ Michigan since 1968
11/26/2022	@	Northwestern								1-6 S/U vs Northwestern since 2015
12/3/2022	vs									Big Ten Championship
	vs									BOWL GAME

Pointspread Analysis — Non-Conference
- 0-5 S/U vs Non-Conf. as 15.5 point or more Dog since 1986
- 1-17 S/U vs Non-Conf. as 3.5-7 point Dog since 1982
- 2-8 ATS vs Non-Conf. as 3.5-7 point favorite since 2003
- 31-1 S/U vs Non-Conf. as 10.5 point or more favorite since 1991

Bowl Games
- 0-3 S/U vs SEC in Bowl Games

Dog
- 1-20 S/U @ home as 15.5 point or more Dog since 1999
- 1-10 S/U on road as 25.5 point or more Dog since 1997
- 2-19 S/U as 20.5-25 point Dog since 1986
- 3-24-1 S/U as 15.5-20 point Dog since 1986
- 3-9 ATS as 15.5-20 point Dog since 2012
- 10-1 O/U on road as 15.5-20 point Dog since 2009
- 1-18 S/U @ home as 10.5-15 point Dog since 1987
- 1-14 S/U on road as 10.5-15 point Dog since 2008
- 1-25 S/U as 10.5-15 point Dog since 2008
- 6-17-1 O/U as 10.5-15 point Dog since 2009
- 2-12 S/U @ home vs Big Ten as 7.5-10 point Dog since 2000
- 14-6 O/U as 7.5-10 point Dog since 2004
- 3-9 S/U on road as 7.5-10 point Dog since 1993
- 2-10-1 O/U @ home as 3.5-7 point Dog since 2009
- 9-31 S/U as 3.5-7 point Dog since 1996
- 3-13 S/U on road as 3.5-7 point Dog since 1996
- 3-11 S/U @ home vs Big Ten as 3 point or less Dog since 1988 {3-10 ATS}
- 5-18-1 S/U vs Big Ten as 3 point or less Dog since 1986

Favorite
- 0-6 O/U on road as 3 point or less favorite since 2003
- 3-8 ATS @ home as 3.5-7 point favorite since 2003
- 2-6 O/U on road as 3.5-7 point favorite since 2001
- 5-16-2 ATS as 7.5-10 point favorite since 1985
- 26-1 S/U as 10.5-15 point favorite since 1985
- 18-2 S/U as 15.5-20 point favorite since 1985
- 14-0 S/U as 25.5 point or more favorite since 1983

- 2-8 S/U in 1st road game of season since 2012 — Indiana
- 2-11 S/U in 2nd road game of season since 2009 — Wisconsin
- 3-12 O/U after playing Wisconsin since 2005 — IOWA
- 0-11 S/U prior to playing Minnesota since 2010 — IOWA
- 3-10-1 O/U after playing Iowa since 2003 — MINNESOTA
- 0-10 S/U after playing Nebraska since 1986 — MICHIGAN ST.
- 2-12 S/U in final home game of season since 2008 — PURDUE
- 2-21 S/U in final road game of season since 2008 — Northwestern
- 3-26 S/U on road vs ranked teams since 2003
- 4-27 S/U @ home vs ranked teams since 2002
- 0-11 S/U vs #2 ranked teams since 1940

Pointspread Analysis — Conference
- vs Iowa - Illinois leads series 38-36-2
- 0-15 S/U vs Iowa as Dog since 1996
- 1-13 S/U vs Iowa since 2003
- Game 2-5 O/U @ home vs Iowa since 2004
- 3-12 S/U vs Michigan State since 1995 (2 W)
- 2-11 S/U vs Michigan State as Dog since 1986 {3-10 ATS}
- 1-8 S/U @ home vs Michigan State as Dog since 1986 {2-7 ATS}
- 6-14 S/U vs Minnesota since 1996
- 4-10 S/U vs Minnesota as Dog since 1996
- vs Minnesota - Minnesota leads series 40-30-3
- vs Nebraska - Nebraska leads series 13-5-1
- 3-8 S/U vs Nebraska since 1985
- 1-5 S/U @ Nebraska as Dog since 1985
- vs Northwestern - Illinois leads series 55-53-5
- 2-13 S/U vs Northwestern as Dog since 1996
- Game 8-3-1 O/U vs Northwestern since 2010
- vs Penn State - Penn State leads series 20-6
- vs Purdue - Purdue leads series 46-45-6
- 1-9 S/U vs Purdue as Dog since 2003
- 1-7 O/U vs Purdue as Dog since 2005
- vs Purdue - ROAD team 8-2 S/U since 2012
- Game 7-2 O/U @ home vs Purdue since 2002
- 2-14 S/U vs Wisconsin since 2003
- 1-14 S/U vs Wisconsin as Dog since 2003
- vs Wisconsin - Wisconsin leads series 43-37-7
- Game 5-0 O/U @ Wisconsin since 2012
- 7-0 S/U vs Indiana as 9.5 point or more favorite since 1984
- 0-6 O/U vs Indiana as 3.5 point or less favorite since 2001
- 3-0 S/U vs Iowa as 6.5 point or more favorite since 1994
- 3-17-2 S/U vs Michigan as 2.5 point or more favorite since 1986
- 3-0 S/U vs Michigan State as 5.5 point or less favorite since 1985
- 0-5 S/U vs Minnesota as 4.5 point or less Dog since 1996
- 0-5 S/U vs Northwestern as 14.5 point or more Dog since 2005
- 1-4 S/U & ATS vs Northwestern as 5 point or less favorite since 1995
- 11-2 S/U vs Northwestern as 10.5 point or more favorite since 1984
- 1-12 S/U vs Penn State as 9.5 point or more Dog since 1993
- 0-11 S/U vs Purdue as 6 point or more Dog since 1997
- 3-0 S/U & ATS vs Purdue as 3.5 point or less Dog since 1993
- 5-0 S/U vs Purdue as 6.5-8.5 point favorite since 1984
- 9-0 S/U vs Wisconsin as 2.5 point or more favorite since 1983
- 1-15 S/U vs Wisconsin as 7 point or more Dog since 1996
- 2-17 ATS @ home when ranked since 1990
- 5-0 S/U @ home when ranked vs Minnesota all time
- 9-1 S/U when ranked vs Northwestern since 1951 {4-0 @ home}
- 0-9 S/U vs ranked Iowa since 1990

INDIANA HOOSIERS — BIG TEN East

2021-Indiana		Opponent	IND	Opp	S/U	Line	ATS	Total	O/U	
9/4/2021	@	Iowa	6	34	L	3.5	L	45.5	U	
9/11/2021	vs	*IDAHO*	56	14	W	-31.0	W	52.5	O	
9/18/2021	vs	*CINCINNATI*	24	38	L	4.0	L	50.0	O	
9/25/2021	@	Western Kentucky	35	33	W	-9.0	L	63.0	O	
10/2/2021	@	Penn State	0	24	L	12.0	L	54.5	U	
10/16/2021	vs	MICHIGAN STATE	15	20	L	3.5	L	48.5	U	"Old Brass Spittoon"
10/23/2021	vs	OHIO STATE	7	54	L	21.0	L	58.5	O	
10/30/2021	@	Maryland	35	38	L	3.5	W	48.0	O	
11/6/2021	@	Michigan	7	29	L	20.5	L	50.5	U	
11/13/2021	vs	RUTGERS	3	38	L	-6.5	L	42.5	U	
11/20/2021	vs	MINNESOTA	14	35	L	7.5	L	43.0	O	
11/27/2021	@	Purdue	7	44	L	17.5	L	50.5	O	"The Old Oaken Bucket"
Coach: Tom Allen		Season Record >>	209	401	2-10	ATS>>	2-10	O/U>>	7-5	

2020-Indiana		Opponent	IND	Opp	S/U	Line	ATS	Total	O/U	
10/24/2020	vs	PENN STATE	36	35	W	6.5	W	61.5	O	{OT}
10/31/2020	@	Rutgers	37	21	W	-11.5	W	54.0	O	
11/7/2020	vs	MICHIGAN	38	21	W	4.5	W	54.5	O	
11/14/2020	@	Michigan State	24	0	W	-7.5	W	52.5	U	"Old Brass Spittoon"
11/21/2020	@	Ohio State	35	42	L	20.5	W	67.0	O	
11/28/2020	vs	MARYLAND	27	11	W	-12.0	W	64.5	U	
12/5/2020	@	Wisconsin	14	6	W	13.0	W	44.5	U	
1/2/2021	vs	*Mississippi*	20	26	L	-7.5	L	67.5	U	Outback Bowl
Coach: Tom Allen		Season Record >>	231	162	6-2	ATS>>	7-1	O/U>>	4-4	

2019-Indiana		Opponent	IND	Opp	S/U	Line	ATS	Total	O/U	
8/31/2019	vs	*Ball State*	34	24	W	-18.0	L	60.5	U	Lucas Oil Field
9/7/2019	vs	EASTERN ILLINOIS	52	0	W	-35.5	W	NT	---	
9/14/2019	vs	OHIO STATE	10	51	L	17.5	L	60.5	O	
9/21/2019	vs	CONNECTICUT	38	3	W	-26.0	W	56.0	U	
9/28/2019	@	Michigan State	31	40	L	14.0	W	43.0	O	"Old Brass Spittoon"
10/12/2019	vs	RUTGERS	35	0	W	-27.5	W	49.5	U	
10/19/2019	@	Maryland	34	28	W	-6.5	L	59.0	O	
10/26/2019	@	Nebraska	38	31	W	2.5	W	54.5	O	
11/2/2019	vs	NORTHWESTERN	34	3	W	-8.5	W	44.0	U	
11/16/2019	@	Penn State	27	34	L	14.5	W	55.0	O	
11/23/2019	vs	MICHIGAN	14	39	L	10.0	L	54.0	U	
11/30/2019	@	Purdue	44	41	W	-7.0	L	56.5	O	"The Old Oaken Bucket"
1/2/2020	vs	*Tennessee*	22	23	L	3.5	W	56.0	U	Gator Bowl
Coach: Tom Allen		Season Record >>	413	317	8-5	ATS>>	8-5	O/U>>	6-6	

2018-Indiana		Opponent	IND	Opp	S/U	Line	ATS	Total	O/U	
9/1/2018	@	*Florida International*	38	28	W	-13.0	L	55.0	O	
9/8/2018	vs	*VIRGINIA*	20	16	W	-5.0	L	50.0	U	
9/15/2018	vs	*BALL STATE*	38	10	W	-15.0	W	60.0	U	
9/22/2018	vs	MICHIGAN STATE	21	35	L	6.5	L	51.0	O	"Old Brass Spittoon"
9/29/2018	@	Rutgers	24	17	W	-16.5	L	49.0	U	
10/6/2018	@	Ohio State	26	49	L	28.0	W	64.5	O	
10/13/2018	vs	IOWA	16	42	L	3.5	L	52.5	O	
10/20/2018	vs	PENN STATE	28	33	L	14.0	W	57.0	O	
10/26/2018	@	Minnesota	31	38	L	-2.5	L	54.0	O	
11/10/2018	vs	MARYLAND	34	32	W	-1.0	W	55.0	O	
11/17/2018	@	Michigan	20	31	L	28.0	W	53.5	U	
11/24/2018	vs	PURDUE	21	28	L	3.5	L	65.0	U	"The Old Oaken Bucket"
Coach: Tom Allen		Season Record >>	317	359	5-7	ATS>>	5-7	O/U>>	7-5	

INDIANA HOOSIERS — BIG TEN East

STADIUM: Memorial Stadium {52,626} **Location:** Bloomington, IN **COACH:** Tom Allen

DATE		Opponent	IND	Opp	S/U	Line	ATS	Total	O/U	Trends & Angles
9/3/2022	vs	ILLINOIS								5-0 S/U @ home vs Illinois as favorite since 1987
9/10/2022	vs	IDAHO								vs Idaho - Indiana leads series 1-0
9/17/2022	vs	WESTERN KENTUCKY								vs Western KY - Indiana leads series 4-0
9/24/2022	@	Cincinnati								3-0 S/U & ATS vs Cincinnati as favorite since 1994
10/1/2022	vs	Nebraska								1-5 S/U vs Nebraska since 1975
10/8/2022	vs	MICHIGAN								2-19 S/U @ home vs Michigan since 1968
10/15/2022	vs	MARYLAND								vs Maryland - Indiana leads series 7-3
10/22/2022	@	Rutgers								5-1 S/U vs Rutgers since 2016
11/5/2022	vs	PENN STATE								2-11 S/U @ home vs Penn State since 1994
11/12/2022	@	Ohio State								0-15 S/U @ Ohio State since 1989
11/19/2022	@	Michigan State								1-8 S/U @ Michigan State since 2003 {2-7 ATS}
11/26/2022	vs	PURDUE								Game 0-3 O/U @ home vs Purdue since 2014
12/3/2022	vs									Big Ten Championship
	vs									BOWL GAME

Pointspread Analysis — Non-Conference
- 2-15 S/U vs Non-Conf. as 3.5-7 point Dog since 1983
- 37-2 S/U vs Non-conf. as 10.5 point or more favorite since 1986
- vs Cincinnati - Indiana leads series 9-4-1

Bowl Games
- 4-8 S/U in Bowl Games

Dog
- 3-0 ATS @ home as 25.5 point or more Dog since 1994
- 0-50 S/U as 20.5 point or more Dog since 1983
- 1-19 S/U on road as 15.5-20 point Dog since 198420
- 2-12 S/U @ home as 15.5-20 point Dog since 1992
- 1-16 S/U @ home as 10.5-15 point Dog since 1986
- 9-1 O/U @ home as 10.5-15 point Dog since 2005
- 3-21 S/U on road as 10.5-15 point Dog since 1989
- 9-1 O/U as 7.5-10 point Dog since 2008
- 2-12 S/U on road as 7.5-10 point Dog since 1987
- 0-13 S/U @ home as 7.5-10 point Dog since 2000
- 0-8 ATS as 7.5-10 point Dog since 2011
- 0-7 S/U on road as 3.5-7 point Dog since 2012 {1-6 ATS}
- 5-27 S/U @ home as 3.5-7 point Dog since 1983
- 3-12 S/U on road as 3 point or less Dog since 1984

Favorite
- 19-5-1 S/U @ home as 3.5-7 point favorite since 1986
- 8-1 S/U on road as 7.5-10 point favorite since 1986
- 25-3 S/U as 10.5-15 point favorite since 1991
- 20-2 S/U @ home as 10.5-15 point favorite since 1986
- 34-1 S/U as 15.5 point or more favorite since 1987

- 17-2 S/U in 1st home game of season since 2002 — ILLINOIS
- 2-10 ATS in 2nd road game of season since 2010 — Nebraska
- 15-1 ATS prior to playing Michigan since 2000 — Nebraska
- 4-11 S/U after playing Michigan since 2003 — MARYLAND
- 5-11 S/U prior to playing Penn State since 2004 — Rutgers
- 10-2 O/U prior to playing Michigan State since 2008 — Ohio State
- 5-13 S/U prior to playing Michigan State since 2002 — Ohio State
- 10-3 O/U after playing Penn State since 2008 — Ohio State
- 3-15 S/U after playing Penn State since 2002 — Ohio State
- 3-13 ATS after playing Penn State since 2004 — Ohio State
- 2-20 S/U prior to playing Purdue since 1999 — Michigan State
- 6-2 ATS prior to playing Purdue since 2013 — Michigan State
- 4-20 S/U in final road game of season since 1997 — Michigan State
- 2-17 S/U after playing Michigan State since 2001 — PURDUE

Pointspread Analysis — Conference
- Game 6-1 O/U vs Maryland since 2015
- 2-40 S/U vs Michigan since 1968
- vs Michigan - Michigan leads series 60-10
- Game 3-1 O/U @ home vs Michigan since 2010
- 4-20 S/U vs Michigan State since 1994
- vs Michigan State - Michigan State leads series 50-16-2
- Game 10-4 O/U vs Michigan State since 2006
- vs Nebraska - Indiana leads series 10-8-3
- 6-0 ATS @ Ohio State since 2011
- 0-27 S/U vs Ohio State since 1991
- vs Ohio State - Ohio State leads series 78-12-5
- 8-3 ATS vs Ohio State since 2011
- Game 5-0 O/U vs Ohio State since 2017
- vs Penn State - Penn State leads series 23-2
- 0-5 ATS vs Purdue since 2016
- 9-0 S/U vs Purdue as favorite since 1990
- Game 10-3 O/U vs Purdue since 2008
- vs Purdue - Purdue leads series 75-42-6
- 1-3 ATS @ Rutgers since 2014
- vs Rutgers - Indiana leads series 5-3
- 0-7 S/U vs Illinois as 9.5 point or more Dog since 1984
- 0-5 ATS vs Illinois as 9.5 point or more Dog since 1989
- 0-6 S/U & ATS vs Iowa as 6.5 point or less Dog since 1987
- 1-9 S/U vs Iowa as 13.5 point or more Dog since 1983
- 1-25 S/U vs Michigan as 9 point or more Dog since 1983
- 1-16 S/U vs Michigan St. as 8 point or more Dog since 1984
- 0-3 S/U & ATS vs Michigan St. as 3 point or less favorite since 1988
- 0-24 S/U vs Ohio State as 16 point or more Dog since 1983
- 0-8 S/U vs Ohio State as 14 point or less Dog since 1985
- 1-20 S/U vs Penn State as 4.5 point or more Dog since 1993
- 0-13 S/U vs Purdue as 6.5 point or more Dog since 1984

- 13-124-1 S/U on road vs ranked teams all time
- 1-82 S/U vs Top #1 - #7 ranked teams all time
- 0-58 S/U on road vs Top #1 - #7 ranked teams all time
- 2-43 S/U vs ranked Michigan all time
- 1-43 S/U vs ranked Ohio State since 1952
- 1-12 S/U vs ranked Penn State all time
- 0-8 S/U vs ranked Purdue since 1968
- 1-9 S/U on road when ranked vs ranked teams all time

IOWA HAWKEYES — BIG TEN West

2021-Iowa		Opponent	Iowa	Opp	S/U	Line	ATS	Total	O/U	
9/4/2021	vs	INDIANA	34	6	W	-3.5	W	45.5	U	
9/11/2021	@	Iowa State	27	17	W	4.0	W	45.0	U	"Cy-Hawk Trophy"
9/18/2021	vs	KENT STATE	30	7	W	-22.5	W	55.0	U	
9/25/2021	vs	COLORADO STATE	24	14	W	-24.0	L	43.5	U	
10/2/2021	@	Maryland	51	14	W	-3.0	W	47.5	O	
10/9/2021	vs	PENN STATE	23	20	W	-2.5	W	41.0	O	
10/16/2021	vs	PURDUE	7	24	L	-12.0	L	42.5	U	
10/30/2021	@	Wisconsin	7	27	L	3.0	L	36.0	U	"Heartland Trophy"
11/6/2021	@	Northwestern	17	12	W	-11.5	L	40.0	U	
11/13/2021	vs	MINNESOTA	27	22	W	-4.0	W	37.0	O	"Floyd of Rosedale"
11/20/2021	vs	ILLINOIS	33	23	W	-12.0	L	37.5	O	
11/26/2021	@	Nebraska	28	21	W	1.5	W	41.0	O	"Heroes Trophy"
12/4/2021	vs	Michigan	3	42	L	12.0	L	44.0	O	Big Ten Championship
1/1/2022	vs	Kentucky	17	20	L	3.0	T	43.5	U	Citrus Bowl
Coach: Kirk Ferentz		Season Record >>	328	269	10-4	ATS>>	7-6-1	O/U>>	6-8	

2020-Iowa		Opponent	Iowa	Opp	S/U	Line	ATS	Total	O/U	
10/24/2020	@	Purdue	20	24	L	-3.0	L	52.5	U	
10/31/2020	vs	NORTHWESTERN	20	21	L	1.0	T	43.0	U	
11/7/2020	vs	MICHIGAN STATE	49	7	W	-5.5	W	45.5	O	
11/14/2020	@	Minnesota	35	7	W	-3.0	W	58.0	U	"Floyd of Rosedale"
11/21/2020	@	Penn State	41	21	W	-1.0	W	45.5	O	
11/27/2020	vs	NEBRASKA	26	20	W	-12.5	L	53.0	U	"Heroes Trophy"
12/5/2020	@	Illinois	35	21	W	-13.5	W	53.0	O	
12/12/2020	vs	WISCONSIN	28	7	W	1.0	W	39.5	U	"Heartland Trophy"
Coach: Kirk Ferentz		Season Record >>	254	128	6-2	ATS>>	5-2-1	O/U>>	3-5	

2019-Iowa		Opponent	Iowa	Opp	S/U	Line	ATS	Total	O/U	
8/31/2019	vs	MIAMI-OHIO	38	14	W	-24.5	L	47.0	O	
9/7/2019	vs	RUTGERS	30	0	W	-18.0	W	48.0	U	
9/14/2019	@	Iowa State	18	17	W	-1.0	T	42.0	U	"Cy-Hawk Trophy"
9/28/2019	vs	MIDDLE TENNESSEE	48	3	W	-23.5	W	51.0	T	
10/5/2019	@	Michigan	3	10	L	4.0	L	49.0	U	
10/12/2019	vs	PENN STATE	12	17	L	3.5	L	43.5	U	
10/19/2019	vs	PURDUE	26	20	W	-17.5	L	48.0	U	
10/26/2019	@	Northwestern	20	0	W	-8.5	W	36.5	U	
11/9/2019	@	Wisconsin	22	24	L	7.5	W	37.5	O	"Heartland Trophy"
11/16/2019	vs	MINNESOTA	23	19	W	-3.0	W	45.0	U	"Floyd of Rosedale"
11/23/2019	vs	ILLINOIS	19	10	W	-15.5	L	48.5	U	
11/29/2019	@	Nebraska	27	24	W	-3.5	L	46.0	O	"Heroes Trophy"
12/27/2019	vs	Usc	49	24	W	1.5	W	54.5	O	Holiday Bowl
Coach: Kirk Ferentz		Season Record >>	335	182	10-3	ATS>>	6-6-1	O/U>>	4-8-1	

2018-Iowa		Opponent	Iowa	Opp	S/U	Line	ATS	Total	O/U	
9/1/2018	vs	NORTHERN ILLINOIS	33	7	W	-9.5	W	46.5	U	
9/8/2018	vs	IOWA STATE	13	3	W	-3.5	W	47.0	U	"Cy-Hawk Trophy"
9/15/2018	vs	NORTHERN IOWA	38	14	W	-18.0	W	NT	---	
9/22/2018	vs	WISCONSIN	17	28	L	3.0	L	43.5	O	"Heartland Trophy"
10/6/2018	@	Minnesota	48	31	W	-7.0	W	41.5	O	"Floyd of Rosedale"
10/13/2018	@	Indiana	42	16	W	-3.5	W	52.5	O	
10/20/2018	vs	MARYLAND	23	0	W	-9.5	W	44.0	U	
10/27/2018	@	Penn State	24	30	L	5.5	L	52.0	O	
11/3/2018	@	Purdue	36	38	L	2.0	T	50.5	O	
11/10/2018	vs	NORTHWESTERN	10	14	L	-11.5	L	44.0	U	
11/17/2018	@	Illinois	63	0	W	-15.0	W	59.5	O	
11/23/2018	vs	NEBRASKA	31	28	W	-7.5	L	52.0	O	"Heroes Trophy"
1/1/2019	vs	Mississippi State	27	22	W	7.0	W	40.0	O	Outback Bowl
Coach: Kirk Ferentz		Season Record >>	405	231	9-4	ATS>>	8-4-1	O/U>>	8-4	

IOWA HAWKEYES — BIG TEN West

STADIUM: Nile Kinnick Stadium {69,250} **Location:** Iowa City, IA **COACH:** Kirk Ferentz

DATE		Opponent	Iowa	Opp	S/U	Line	ATS	Total	O/U	Trends & Angles
9/3/2022	vs	SOUTH DAKOTA STATE								19-0 S/U prior to playing Iowa State since 2001
9/10/2022	vs	IOWA STATE								6-0 S/U vs Iowa State since 2015 {4-0-2 ATS}
9/17/2022	vs	NEVADA								9-1 S/U after playing Iowa State since 2011
9/24/2022	@	Rutgers								vs Rutgers - Iowa leads series 2-0
10/1/2022	vs	MICHIGAN								4-0 S/U @ home vs Michigan since 2009
10/8/2022	@	Illinois								13-1 S/U vs Illinois since 2003
10/22/2022	@	Ohio State								2-13 S/U vs Ohio State since 1992
10/29/2022	vs	NORTHWESTERN								0-3 S/U @ home vs Northwestern since 2016
11/5/2022	@	Purdue								9-1 S/U @ Purdue as favorite since 1984
11/12/2022	vs	WISCONSIN								1-5 S/U @ home vs Wisconsin since 2010
11/19/2022	@	Minnesota								7-0 S/U vs Minnesota since 2015
11/25/2022	vs	NEBRASKA								7-0 S/U vs Nebraska since 2015
12/3/2022	vs									Big Ten Championship
	vs									BOWL GAME

Pointspread Analysis — Non-Conference
- 0-11 S/U vs Non-Conf. as 7.5 point or more Dog since 1990
- 7-1 S/U vs Non-Conf. as 3 point or less favorite since 1993
- 0-5 O/U vs Non-Conf. as 7.5-10 point favorite since 2003
- 15-3 S/U vs Non-Conf. as 15.5-20 point favorite since 1986
- 32-2 S/U vs Non-Conf. as 20.5 point or more favorite since 1984
- vs Iowa State - Iowa leads series 46-22
- Game 3-14 O/U vs Iowa State since 2004
- 16-2 S/U vs Iowa State as 13.5 point or more favorite since 1984
- 0-7 O/U vs Iowa State as 13.5 point or more favorite since 1998

Dog
- 0-6 S/U as 25.5 point or more Dog since 1998
- 0-6 S/U on road as 20.5-25 point Dog since 1990
- 1-8 S/U as 15.5-20 point Dog since 1993
- 0-8 S/U on road as 10.5-15 point Dog since 1998
- 1-13 S/U as 10.5-15 point Dog since 1996
- 2-10 O/U as 7.5-10 point Dog since 2005
- 1-6 O/U on road as 7.5-10 point Dog since 2005
- 3-10 O/U on road as 3.5-7 point Dog since 2005
- 3-9 S/U on road as 3.5-7 point Dog since 2007
- 3-9 S/U @ home as 3 point or less Dog since 1989

Favorite
- 16-4-2 ATS as a road favorite since 2013
- 16-3 S/U on road as 3 point or less favorite since 1987
- 16-1 S/U as 3.5-7 point favorite since 2013
- 10-2 ATS on road as 3.5-7 point favorite since 2008
- 19-3 S/U @ home as 7.5-10 point favorite since 1989
- 18-2 S/U on road as 10.5-15 point favorite since 1984
- 30-3 S/U @ home as 15.5-20 point favorite since 1983
- 18-0 S/U @ home as 20.5-25 point favorite since 1983
- 27-1 S/U as 25.5 point or more favorite since 1986
- 12-4 ATS as 25.5-30 point favorite since 1990

Bowl Games
- 2-7 S/U & ATS vs PAC-12 in Bowl Games since 1981
- 0-4 S/U & ATS in Rose Bowl since 1982
- 3-0 O/U in Rose Bowl since 1986
- 0-4 O/U in Alamo Bowl since 1993
- 0-10-1 S/U vs #1 ranked teams all time
- 11-0 S/U when ranked vs Illinois since 1990
- 13-1 S/U when ranked vs Iowa State all time {6-0 @ home}
- 0-8 S/U when ranked vs Ohio State since 1995
- 1-19 S/U @ ranked Ohio State since 1950
- 1-10 S/U @ ranked Purdue all time
- 5-0-1 ATS @ home vs ranked Michigan since 1994

Pointspread Analysis — Conference
- vs Illinois - Illinois leads series 39-35-2
- 15-0 S/U vs Illinois as favorite since 1996 {11-4 ATS}
- 0-3 S/U @ Illinois as Dog since 1994
- 5-2 S/U vs Michigan since 2009
- 9-3-1 ATS vs Michigan as Dog since 1993
- 4-1 S/U vs Michigan as favorite since 1984
- vs Michigan - Michigan leads series 43-15-4
- 3-0 S/U @ home vs Michigan as Dog since 2003
- vs Minnesota - Minnesota leads series 62-51-2
- vs Nebraska - Nebraska leads series 28-20-3
- 5-0 S/U vs Nebraska as favorite since 2015
- Game 7-2 O/U vs Nebraska since 2013
- vs Northwestern - Iowa leads series 52-28-3
- 0-6 O/U vs Northwestern as Dog since 2000
- 1-5 ATS vs Northwestern since 2016
- 0-7 S/U @ Ohio State as Dog since 1995
- vs Purdue - Purdue leads series 50-39-3
- 1-5 S/U vs Purdue as Dog since 1998
- 4-1-1 ATS @ Purdue since 2011
- 2-8 S/U vs Wisconsin since 2010
- 13-2-1 S/U vs Wisconsin as favorite since 1983
- vs Wisconsin - Wisconsin leads series 49-44-2
- 1-7 S/U @ home vs Wisconsin as Dog since 1998
- 0-10-1 S/U vs Michigan as 6.0-13.5 point Dog since 1983
- 6-0 S/U vs Northwestern as 21 point or more favorite since 1986
- 0-11 S/U vs Ohio State as 3.0-18.0 point Dog since 1989
- 18-2 S/U vs Purdue as 6.5 point or more favorite since 1983
- 0-4 S/U vs Nebraska as 9.5 point or more Dog since 1999
- 0-3 S/U vs Minnesota as 7 point or more Dog since 1998
- 13-0 S/U vs Minnesota as 2.0-8.5 point favorite since 1986
- 15-1 S/U vs Illinois as 7 point or more favorite since 1985
- 0-8 S/U vs Wisconsin as 7 point or more Dog since 1998
- 8-0 S/U vs Wisconsin as 8.5 point or more favorite since 1985

S. DAKOTA STATE	1-10-1 O/U prior to playing Iowa State since 2006
IOWA STATE	14-0 S/U in 2nd home game of season since 2008
Rutgers	9-1 S/U in 1st road game of season since 2012
MICHIGAN	3-10 O/U prior to playing Illinois since 2004
Illinois	4-13 O/U in 2nd road game of season since 2005
Ohio State	1-9-2 ATS prior to playing Northwestern since 2010
Purdue	9-1 S/U prior to playing Wisconsin since 2008
WISCONSIN	10-1 O/U prior to playing Minnesota since 2011
Minnesota	9-0 S/U in final road game of season since 2013 {8-1 ATS}
NEBRASKA	10-1 S/U after playing Minnesota since 2011

IOWA STATE CYCLONES   BIG TWELVE

2021-Iowa State		Opponent	ISU	Opp	S/U	Line	ATS	Total	O/U	
9/4/2021	vs	NORTHERN IOWA	16	10	W	-28.0	L	50.0	U	
9/11/2021	vs	IOWA	17	27	L	-4.0	L	45.0	U	"Cy-Hawk Trophy"
9/18/2021	@	Unlv	48	3	W	-31.5	W	53.0	U	
9/25/2021	@	Baylor	29	31	L	-7.0	L	46.0	O	
10/2/2021	vs	KANSAS	59	7	W	-34.5	W	57.5	O	
10/16/2021	@	Kansas State	33	20	W	-6.5	W	51.0	O	
10/23/2021	vs	OKLAHOMA STATE	24	21	W	-7.5	L	47.5	U	
10/30/2021	@	West Virginia	31	38	L	-7.5	L	48.5	O	
11/6/2021	vs	TEXAS	30	7	W	-6.0	W	59.5	U	
11/13/2021	@	Texas Tech	38	41	L	-12.5	L	55.5	O	Lose on GW 62 yard field goal
11/20/2021	@	Oklahoma	21	28	L	3.0	L	59.0	U	
11/26/2021	vs	TCU	48	14	W	-16.0	W	61.0	O	
12/29/2021	vs	Clemson	13	20	L	2.0	L	45.0	U	Cheez-it Bowl
Coach: Matt Campbell		Season Record >>	407	267	7-6	ATS>>	5-8	O/U>>	6-7	
2020-Iowa State		Opponent	ISU	Opp	S/U	Line	ATS	Total	O/U	
9/12/2020	vs	LOUISIANA	14	31	L	-11.5	L	56.0	U	
9/26/2020	@	Tcu	37	34	W	-3.0	T	44.0	O	
10/3/2020	vs	OKLAHOMA	37	30	W	7.5	W	62.0	O	
10/10/2020	vs	TEXAS TECH	31	15	W	-10.0	W	63.0	U	
10/24/2020	@	Oklahoma State	21	24	L	2.5	L	54.0	U	
10/31/2020	@	Kansas	52	22	W	-27.5	W	49.5	O	
11/7/2020	vs	BAYLOR	38	31	W	-14.0	L	46.5	O	
11/21/2020	vs	KANSAS STATE	45	0	W	-13.5	W	47.5	U	
11/27/2020	@	Texas	23	20	W	-2.0	W	58.0	U	
12/5/2020	vs	WEST VIRGINIA	42	6	W	-5.5	W	47.5	O	
12/19/2020	vs	Oklahoma	21	27	L	5.5	L	59.5	U	Big 12 Championship
1/2/2021	vs	Oregon	34	17	W	-4.0	W	57.5	U	Fiesta Bowl
Coach: Matt Campbell		Season Record >>	395	257	9-3	ATS>>	7-4-1	O/U>>	5-7	
2019-Iowa State		Opponent	ISU	Opp	S/U	Line	ATS	Total	O/U	
8/31/2019	vs	NORTHERN IOWA	29	26	W	-23.5	L	NT	---	{3 OT}
9/14/2019	vs	IOWA	17	18	L	1.0	T	42.0	U	"Cy-Hawk Trophy"
9/21/2019	vs	LOUISIANA-MONROE	72	20	W	-17.5	W	52.0	O	
9/28/2019	@	Baylor	21	23	L	-2.5	L	55.5	O	
10/5/2019	vs	TCU	49	24	W	-3.5	W	46.5	O	
10/12/2019	@	West Virginia	38	14	W	-10.0	W	55.0	U	
10/19/2019	vs	TEXAS TECH	34	24	W	-7.5	W	57.0	O	
10/26/2019	@	Oklahoma State	27	34	L	-10.5	L	64.0	U	
11/9/2019	@	Oklahoma	41	42	L	14.5	W	70.0	O	
11/16/2019	vs	TEXAS	23	21	W	-7.0	L	64.5	U	
11/23/2019	vs	KANSAS	41	31	W	-26.0	L	58.5	O	
11/30/2019	@	Kansas State	17	27	L	-4.5	L	45.5	U	
12/28/2019	vs	Notre Dame	9	33	L	3.5	L	54.0	U	Camping World Bowl
Coach: Matt Campbell		Season Record >>	418	337	7-6	ATS>>	5-7-1	O/U>>	5-7	
2018-Iowa State		Opponent	ISU	Opp	S/U	Line	ATS	Total	O/U	
9/8/2018	@	Iowa	3	13	L	3.5	L	47.0	U	"Cy-Hawk Trophy"
9/15/2018	vs	OKLAHOMA	27	37	L	18.5	W	54.0	O	
9/22/2018	vs	AKRON	26	13	W	-18.5	L	47.0	U	
9/29/2018	@	Tcu	14	17	L	11.0	W	45.0	U	
10/6/2018	@	Oklahoma State	48	42	W	10.0	W	55.5	O	
10/13/2018	vs	WEST VIRGINIA	30	14	W	4.0	W	55.0	U	
10/27/2018	vs	TEXAS TECH	40	31	W	-4.5	W	59.0	O	
11/3/2018	@	Kansas	27	3	W	-19.0	W	46.5	U	
11/10/2018	vs	BAYLOR	28	14	W	-17.0	L	51.0	U	
11/17/2018	@	Texas	10	24	L	1.5	L	51.0	U	
11/24/2018	vs	KANSAS STATE	42	38	W	-10.5	L	41.0	O	
12/1/2018	vs	DRAKE	27	24	W	-40.5	L	NT	---	
12/28/2018	vs	Washington State	26	28	L	1.5	L	56.0	U	Alamo Bowl
Coach: Matt Campbell		Season Record >>	348	298	8-5	ATS>>	6-7	O/U>>	4-8	

Page | 92

Copyright © 2022 by Steve's Football Bible, LLC

IOWA STATE CYCLONES   BIG TWELVE

STADIUM: Jack Trice Stadium {61,500}   Location: Ames, IA   **COACH:** Matt Campbell

DATE		Opponent	ISU	Opp	S/U	Line	ATS	Total	O/U	Trends & Angles
9/3/2022	vs	SE MISSOURI STATE								1st meeting
9/10/2022	@	Iowa								1-13 S/U vs ranked Iowa all time {0-6 @ Iowa}
9/17/2022	vs	OHIO								5-0 S/U vs Ohio as favorite since 1989
9/24/2022	vs	BAYLOR								vs Baylor - Baylor leads series 11-9
10/1/2022	@	Kansas								17-2-1 S/U vs Kansas as favorite since 1987
10/8/2022	vs	KANSAS STATE								9-3 S/U vs Kansas State as favorite since 1985
10/15/2022	@	Texas								2-8 S/U @ Texas since 1979
10/29/2022	vs	OKLAHOMA								1-27 S/U @ home vs ranked Oklahoma all time
11/5/2022	vs	WEST VIRGINIA								vs West Virginia - West Virginia leads series 6-4
11/12/2022	@	Oklahoma State								1-6 S/U @ Oklahoma State since 2004
11/19/2022	vs	TEXAS TECH								5-1 S/U & ATS vs Texas Tech since 2016
11/26/2022	@	Tcu								1-3 S/U @ TCU since 2014
12/3/2022	vs									BIG XII Championship
	vs									BOWL GAME

Pointspread Analysis		Pointspread Analysis
Non-Conference		**Conference**
1-15 S/U vs Iowa as 13.5-25 point Dog since 1984		1-8 S/U vs Baylor as Dog since 1988
1-11 S/U vs Non-Conf. as 10.5-15 point Dog since 1983		8-3 S/U vs Baylor as favorite since 2000
30-4 S/U vs Non-Conf. as 7.5 point or more favorite since 1985		vs Kansas - Kansas leads series 50-45-6
13-2 S/U vs Non-Conf. as 7.5-10 point favorite since 1985 {10-5 ATS}		11-1 S/U vs Kansas since 2010
0-6 O/U vs ranked Iowa since 2005		Game 2-5 O/U @ home vs Kansas since 2010
vs Iowa - Iowa leads series 46-22		0-9 S/U vs Kansas as Dog since 1984
vs Ohio - Iowa State leads series 7-0		3-11 S/U vs Kansas State since 2008
Bowl Games		vs Kansas State - Iowa State leads series 51-49-4
1-10 O/U in Bowl Games since 2001		4-22 S/U vs Kansas State as Dog since 1983
Dog		Game 3-1 O/U @ home vs Kansas State since 2014
1-18 S/U as 30.5 point or more Dog since 1985		3-49-1 S/U vs Oklahoma since 1962
0-13 S/U on road as 25.5-30 point Dog since 1985		vs Oklahoma - Oklahoma leads series 78-7-2
0-11 S/U @ home as 20.5-25 point Dog since 1984		Game 8-3 O/U vs Oklahoma since 2012
2-12 S/U on road as 20.5-25 point Dog since 1984		4-53-1 S/U vs ranked Oklahoma all time
1-19 S/U on road as 15.5-20 point Dog since 1986		1-24 S/U @ home vs Oklahoma since 1962
4-15-1 ATS on road as 15.5-20 point Dog since 1986		2-8 S/U vs Oklahoma State since 2012
2-14 S/U on road as 10.5-15 point Dog since 2006		Game 4-1 O/U @ home vs Oklahoma State since 2011
0-7 S/U @ home as 10.5-15 point Dog since 2008		vs Oklahoma State - Oklahoma State leads series 33-20-3
2-9 S/U on road as 7.5-10 point Dog since 1997		4-1 S/U vs OK State as favorite since 2000
1-4 S/U @ home as 7.5-10 point Dog since 2008		5-0-1 ATS vs TCU since 2016
1-9 O/U as 3.5-7 point Dog since 2017		vs TCU - TCU leads series 8-5
1-8 S/U @ home as 3 point or less Dog since 2006		vs Texas - Texas leads series 14-5
0-9 S/U as 3 point or less Dog since 2015 {1-6-2 ATS}		Game 0-7 O/U vs Texas since 2015
Favorite		0-4 S/U @ Texas as Dog since 2012
7-0 S/U on road as 7.5-10 point favorite since 1989		vs Texas Tech - Texas Tech leads series 12-8
15-3 S/U @ home as 7.5-10 point favorite since 1992		1-9 S/U vs Kansas as 7 point or more Dog since 1985
11-0 S/U on road as 7.5 point or more favorite since 1988		0-8 S/U vs Oklahoma State as 11-17.5 point Dog since 1983
41-4 S/U as 10.5 point or more favorite since 1986		0-9 S/U vs Kansas State as 15 point or more Dog since 1994
		1-17 S/U vs Oklahoma as 23 point or less Dog since 1983
2-10 O/U in 1st road game of season since 2010	Iowa	15-4 S/U @ home when ranked since 1981
8-0 ATS after playing Iowa since 2013	OHIO	4-16-2 S/U when ranked vs ranked teams all time
4-26 S/U in 2nd road game of season since 1992	Kansas	0-5 S/U when ranked vs Oklahoma State all time
7-2 ATS prior to playing Texas since 2013	KANSAS STATE	0-4-1 S/U when ranked vs Oklahoma all time
0-8 O/U after playing Kansas State since 2010	Texas	0-5 S/U vs ranked Baylor all time
8-2 ATS prior to playing West Virginia since 2012	OKLAHOMA	0-11 S/U vs ranked Kansas State since 1994
11-0 O/U after playing Texas since 2011	OKLAHOMA	4-52-1 S/U vs ranked Oklahoma all time
3-7 S/U prior to playing Oklahoma State since 2012	WEST VIRGINIA	0-11 S/U vs #1 ranked teams all time
11-3 ATS after playing Oklahoma State since 2005	TEXAS TECH	1-8 S/U vs #2 ranked teams all time {0-6 on road}
3-15 S/U & ATS after playing Texas Tech since 1998	Tcu	1-17-1 S/U vs #3 ranked teams all time

Page | 93   Copyright © 2022 by Steve's Football Bible, LLC

JAMES MADISON DUKES   SUN BELT East

2021-James Madison		Opponent	JSU	Opp	S/U	Line	ATS	Total	O/U	
9/4/2021	vs	MOREHEAD STATE	68	10	W	-45.5	W	54.5	O	
9/11/2021	vs	MAINE	55	7	W	-24.0	W	63.5	U	
9/18/2021	@	Weber State	37	24	W	-7.0	W	55.0	O	
10/2/2021	@	New Hampshire	23	21	W	-24.0	L	57.5	U	
10/9/2021	vs	VILLANOVA	27	28	L	-13.0	L	63.0	U	
10/16/2021	@	Richmond	19	3	W	-17.0	L	47.5	U	
10/23/2021	@	Delaware	22	10	W	-17.0	L	48.5	U	
10/30/2021	vs	ELON	45	21	W	-21.5	W	46.0	O	
11/6/2021	vs	CAMPBELL	51	14	W	-27.5	W	52.5	O	
11/13/2021	@	William & Mary	32	22	W	-15.5	L	47.0	O	
11/20/2021	vs	TOWSON	56	10	W	-25.5	W	52.5	O	
12/4/2021	vs	SE LOUISIANA	59	20	W	-14.0	W	70.0	O	FCS 2nd Round Playoff Game
12/10/2021	vs	MONTANA	28	6	W	-8.5	W	49.5	U	FCS Quarterfinal Playoff Game
12/18/2021	@	North Dakota State	14	20	L	4.0	L	48.5	U	FCS Semifinal Playoff Game
Coach: Curt Cignetti		Season Record >>	536	216	12-2	ATS>>	8-6	O/U>>	7-7	

2021-James Madison		Opponent	JSU	Opp	S/U	Line	ATS	Total	O/U	
2/21/2021	vs	MOREHEAD STATE	54	0	W					
3/6/2021	@	Elon	20	17	W					
3/27/2021	@	William & Mary	38	10	W					
4/3/2021	@	Richmond	23	6	W					
4/24/2021	vs	VIRGINIA MILITARY	31	24	W					FCS 1st Round Playoff Game
5/1/2021	vs	NORTH DAKOTA	34	21	W					FCS Quarterfinal Playoff Game
5/8/2021	@	Sam Houston State	35	38	L					FCS Semifinal Playoff Game
Coach: Curt Cignetti		Season Record >>	235	116	6-1					

2019-James Madison		Opponent	JSU	Opp	S/U	Line	ATS	Total	O/U	
8/31/2019	@	West Virginia	13	20	L					
9/7/2019	vs	ST. FRANCIS-PA	44	7	W					
9/14/2019	vs	MORGAN STATE	63	12	W					
9/21/2019	@	Tennessee-Chatt	37	14	W					
9/28/2019	@	Elon	45	10	W					
10/5/2019	@	SUNY-Stony Brook	45	38	W					{OT}
10/12/2019	vs	VILLANOVA	38	24	W					
10/19/2019	@	William & Mary	38	10	W					
10/26/2019	vs	TOWSON	27	10	W					
11/9/2019	vs	NEW HAMPSHIRE	54	16	W					
11/16/2019	vs	RICHMOND	48	6	W					
11/23/2019	@	Rhode Island	55	21	W					
12/7/2019	vs	MONMOUTH	66	21	W					FCS 2nd Round Playoff Game
12/13/2019	vs	NORTHERN IOWA	17	0	W					FCS Quarterfinal Playoff Game
12/21/2019	vs	WEBER STATE	30	14	W					FCS Semifinal Playoff Game
1/11/2020	vs	North Dakota State	20	28	L					FCS Championship Game
Coach: Curt Cignetti		Season Record >>	640	251	14-2					Colonial Athletic Champions

2018-James Madison		Opponent	JSU	Opp	S/U	Line	ATS	Total	O/U	
9/1/2018	@	NC State	13	24	L					
9/8/2018	@	Norfolk State	17	0	W					
9/15/2018	vs	ROBERT MORRIS	73	7	W					
9/22/2018	vs	WILLIAM & MARY	51	0	W					
9/29/2018	@	Richmond	63	10	W					
10/6/2018	vs	ELON	24	27	L					
10/13/2018	@	Villanova	37	0	W					
10/27/2018	vs	SUNY-STONY BROOK	13	10	W					
11/3/2018	@	New Hampshire	24	35	L					
11/10/2018	vs	RHODE ISLAND	48	31	W					
11/17/2018	@	Towson	38	17	W					
11/24/2018	vs	DELAWARE	20	6	W					FCS 1st Round Playoff Game
12/1/2018	@	Colgate	20	23	L					FCS 2nd Round Playoff Game
Coach: Mike Houston		Season Record >>	441	190	9-4					

JAMES MADISON DUKES — SUN BELT East

STADIUM: Bridgeforth Stadium **Location:** Harrisonburg, VA **COACH:** Curt Cignetti

DATE		Opponent	JMU	Opp	S/U	Line	ATS	Total	O/U	Trends & Angles
9/3/2022	vs	*MIDDLE TENNESSEE*								vs Middle Tenn - JMU leads series 1-0
9/10/2022	vs	*NORFOLK STATE*								vs Norfolk State - JMU leads series 2-0
9/24/2022	@	Appalachian State								vs Appalachian - App State leads series 12-4
10/1/2022	vs	TEXAS STATE								1st Meeting
10/8/2022	@	Arkansas State								8-0 S/U in 2nd road game of season since 2014
10/15/2022	@	Georgia Southern								vs Ga Southern - GSU leads series 7-1
10/22/2022	vs	MARSHALL								vs Marshall - Marshall leads series 2-0
11/5/2022	@	*Louisville*								1st Meeting
11/12/2022	@	Old Dominion								vs Old Dominion - ODU leads series 2-0
11/19/2022	vs	GEORGIA STATE								vs Ga State - JMU leads series 1-0
11/26/2022	vs	COASTAL CAROLINA								vs Coastal Carolina - Series tied 1-1
12/3/2022	vs									Sun Belt Championship
	vs									BOWL GAME

Pointspread Analysis — Non-Conference

Trend	Opponent
19-0 S/U in 1st home game of season since 2003	MTSU
11-1 S/U in 2nd home game of season since 2010	NORFOLK STATE
8-0 S/U in final road game of season since 2014	Old Dominion
7-0 S/U in final home game of season since 2014	COASTAL CAROLINA

Pointspread Analysis — Favorite

6-0 S/U as 21.5 point or more favorite in 2021 {5-1 ATS}

Print Version $24.95   Print Version $34.95    Print Version $34.95

These books available at numerous online retailers

KANSAS JAYHAWKS — BIG TWELVE

2021-Kansas		Opponent	KU	Opp	S/U	Line	ATS	Total	O/U	
9/4/2021	vs	SOUTH DAKOTA	17	14	W	-8.5	L	55.5	U	
9/11/2021	@	Coastal Carolina	22	49	L	27.0	T	51.5	O	
9/18/2021	vs	BAYLOR	7	45	L	17.0	L	48.5	U	
9/25/2021	@	Duke	33	52	L	16.5	L	58.5	O	
10/2/2021	@	Iowa State	7	59	L	34.5	L	57.5	O	
10/16/2021	vs	TEXAS TECH	14	41	L	18.5	L	67.5	U	
10/23/2021	vs	OKLAHOMA	23	35	L	38.0	W	66.5	U	
10/30/2021	@	Oklahoma State	3	55	L	29.0	L	54.0	O	
11/6/2021	vs	KANSAS STATE	10	35	L	24.0	L	55.5	U	"Governors Cup"
11/13/2021	@	Texas	57	56	W	31.0	W	61.5	O	{OT}
11/20/2021	@	Tcu	28	31	L	21.0	W	64.0	U	
11/27/2021	vs	WEST VIRGINIA	28	34	L	16.0	W	55.5	O	
Coach: Jordan Leopold		Season Record >>	249	506	2-10	ATS>>	4-7-1	O/U>>	6-6	

2020-Kansas		Opponent	KU	Opp	S/U	Line	ATS	Total	O/U	
9/12/2020	@	Coastal Carolina	23	35	L	-40.0	L	56.0	O	
9/26/2020	@	Baylor	14	47	L	17.5	L	62.0	U	
10/3/2020	vs	OKLAHOMA STATE	7	47	L	21.5	L	53.0	O	
10/17/2020	@	West Virginia	17	38	L	22.5	W	51.5	O	
10/24/2020	@	Kansas State	14	55	L	18.5	L	46.0	O	"Governor's Cup"
10/31/2020	vs	IOWA STATE	22	52	L	27.5	L	49.5	O	
11/7/2020	@	Oklahoma	9	62	L	38.5	L	62.0	O	
11/28/2020	vs	TCU	23	59	L	23.0	L	51.0	O	
12/5/2020	@	Texas Tech	13	16	L	27.0	W	63.0	U	
12/12/2021	vs	TEXAS	31	69	L	7.0	L	53.5	O	
Coach: Les Miles		Season Record >>	173	480	0-10	ATS>>	2-8	O/U>>	8-2	

2019-Kansas		Opponent	KU	Opp	S/U	Line	ATS	Total	O/U	
8/31/2019	vs	INDIANA STATE	24	17	W	-12.0	L	NT	---	
9/7/2019	vs	COASTAL CAROLINA	7	12	L	-7.0	L	54.0	U	
9/13/2019	@	Boston College	48	24	W	19.5	W	51.0	O	
9/21/2019	vs	WEST VIRGINIA	24	29	L	4.5	L	49.5	O	
9/28/2019	@	Tcu	14	51	L	14.5	L	48.0	O	
10/5/2019	vs	OKLAHOMA	20	45	L	31.5	W	67.0	U	
10/19/2019	@	Texas	48	50	L	21.0	W	63.0	O	
10/26/2019	vs	TEXAS TECH	37	34	W	6.0	W	65.5	O	
11/2/2019	vs	KANSAS STATE	10	38	L	4.5	L	54.5	U	"Governor's Cup"
11/16/2019	@	Oklahoma State	13	31	L	17.0	L	69.0	U	
11/23/2019	@	Iowa State	31	41	L	26.0	W	58.5	O	
11/30/2019	vs	BAYLOR	6	61	L	14.0	L	58.5	O	
Coach: Les Miles		Season Record >>	282	433	3-9	ATS>>	5-7	O/U>>	7-4	

2018-Kansas		Opponent	KU	Opp	S/U	Line	ATS	Total	O/U	
9/1/2018	vs	NICHOLLS STATE	23	26	L	-7.5	L	NT	---	{OT}
9/8/2018	@	Central Michigan	31	7	W	3.0	W	48.0	U	
9/15/2018	vs	RUTGERS	55	14	W	PK	W	44.0	O	
9/22/2018	@	Baylor	7	26	L	7.5	L	55.0	U	
9/29/2018	vs	OKLAHOMA STATE	28	48	L	17.0	L	53.5	O	
10/6/2018	@	West Virginia	22	38	L	27.5	W	62.0	U	
10/20/2018	@	Texas Tech	16	48	L	17.5	L	59.0	O	
10/27/2018	vs	TCU	27	26	W	13.5	W	47.0	O	
11/3/2018	vs	IOWA STATE	3	27	L	19.0	L	46.5	U	
11/10/2018	@	Kansas State	17	21	L	8.5	W	46.0	U	"Governor's Cup"
11/17/2018	@	Oklahoma	40	55	L	34.5	W	69.5	O	
11/23/2018	vs	TEXAS	17	24	L	15.0	W	50.0	U	
Coach: David Beaty		Season Record >>	286	360	3-9	ATS>>	7-5	O/U>>	5-6	

Page | 96

Copyright © 2022 by Steve's Football Bible, LLC

KANSAS JAYHAWKS — BIG TWELVE

STADIUM: Kansas Memorial Stadium {50,071} | **Location:** Lawrence, KS | **COACH:** Lance Leipold

DATE		Opponent	KU	Opp	S/U	Line	ATS	Total	O/U	Trends & Angles
9/2/2022	vs	TENNESSEE TECH								2-11 ATS in 1st home game of season since 2008
9/10/2022	@	West Virginia								0-6 S/U @ West Virginia since 1941
9/17/2022	@	Houston								vs Houston - Kansas leads series 3-0
9/24/2022	vs	DUKE								vs Duke - Duke leads series 2-1
10/1/2022	vs	IOWA STATE								vs Iowa State - Kansas leads series 50-45-6
10/8/2022	vs	TCU								4-1 ATS @ home vs TCU since 2012
10/15/2022	@	Oklahoma								0-8 S/U @ Oklahoma since 2000
10/22/2022	@	Baylor								0-17 S/U vs Baylor as Dog since 1988
11/5/2022	vs	OKLAHOMA STATE								0-9 S/U @ home vs Oklahoma State since 1998
11/12/2022	@	Texas Tech								1-10 S/U @ Texas Tech since 1965
11/19/2022	vs	TEXAS								1-8 S/U @ home vs Texas since 1996
11/26/2022	@	Kansas State								1-14 S/U @ Kansas State since 1991
12/3/2022	vs									BIG XII Championship
	vs									BOWL GAME

Pointspread Analysis — Non-Conference
- 0-6 S/U vs Non-Conf. as 20.5 point or more Dog since 1987
- 1-8 S/U vs Non-Conf. as 15.5-25 point Dog since 1984
- 2-10 S/U vs Non-Conf. as 10.5-15 point Dog since 1984
- 9-1 S/U vs Non-Conf. as 3.5-7 point favorite since 1995
- 8-2 ATS vs Non-Conf. as 3.5-7 point favorite since 1995
- 37-4 S/U vs Non-Conf. as 7.5 point or more favorite since 1986

Dog
- 1-78 S/U as 25.5 point or more Dog since 1984
- 4-47 S/U as 20.5-25 point Dog since 1983
- 7-13 O/U as 15.5-20 point Dog since 2010
- 3-38 S/U as 15.5-20 point Dog since 1984
- 0-18 S/U @ home as 15.5-20 point Dog since 1984
- 11-3 O/U @ home as 10.5-15 point Dog since 2001
- 5-32 S/U as 10.5-15 point Dog since 1984
- 0-7 S/U on road as 7.5-10 point Dog since 1991
- 0-7 S/U on road as 3.5-7 point Dog since 2008
- 1-4 S/U on road as 3 point or less Dog since 1993

Favorite
- 0-5 S/U & ATS as 3 point or less favorite since 2007
- 9-1 S/U @ home as 3.5-7 point favorite since 1993
- 8-2 ATS @ home as 3.5-7 point favorite since 1993
- 9-2 S/U on road as 3.5-7 point favorite since 1985
- 8-1 S/U @ home as 7.5-10 point favorite since 1993
- 15-1 S/U @ home as 10.5-15 point favorite since 1986
- 6-0 S/U on road as 10.5-15 point favorite since 1992
- 30-2 S/U as 15.5 point or more favorite since 1985

18-5 S/U in 1st home game of season since 1999	TENN TECH
1-11 S/U in 1st road game of season since 2010	West Virginia
0-13 S/U in 2nd road game of season since 2009	Houston
2-12 ATS in 2nd road game of season since 2008	Houston
2-10 S/U prior to playing Iowa State since 2010	DUKE
12-3 O/U prior to playing Iowa State since 2007	DUKE
0-10 S/U after playing TCU since 2012	Oklahoma
0-12 S/U prior to playing Oklahoma State since 2010	Baylor
0-20 S/U after playing Oklahoma since 1995	Baylor
4-16-1 ATS after playing Oklahoma since 1994	Baylor
1-10 S/U after playing Baylor since 2010	OK STATE
1-17 S/U prior to playing Texas since 1996 {5-13 ATS}	Texas Tech
1-11 S/U after playing Texas Tech since 2009	TEXAS
2-12 S/U in final home game of season since 2008	TEXAS
10-2 ATS after playing Texas since 2004	Kansas State
0-14 S/U in final road game of season since 2008	Kansas State

Pointspread Analysis — Conference
- 3-0 S/U vs Baylor as favorite since 1999
- 0-10 ATS vs Baylor as Dog since 2012
- 9-0 S/U @ home vs Iowa State as favorite since 1984
- vs Kansas State - Kansas leads series 66-47-5
- 3-10 ATS @ Kansas State since 1995
- 0-3 S/U @ Kansas State as favorite since 1986
- 1-12 S/U @ Kansas State as Dog since 1993
- 0-13 S/U vs Kansas State since 2009 {3-10 ATS}
- 0-17 S/U vs Oklahoma since 2000
- vs Oklahoma - Oklahoma leads series 78-27-6
- 0-17 S/U vs Oklahoma as Dog since 2000
- 0-12 S/U vs Oklahoma State since 2010
- vs Oklahoma State - Oklahoma State leads series 39-29-3
- 1-23 S/U vs Oklahoma State as Dog since 1983
- 6-1 S/U vs Oklahoma State as favorite since 1991
- 1-9 S/U vs TCU since 2012
- 1-9 S/U vs TCU as Dog since 2012
- 8-3 ATS vs TCU as Dog since 1983
- vs Tcu - TCU leads series 24-9-4
- Game 1-5 O/U @ home vs Texas since 2008
- vs Texas - Texas leads series 16-4
- 2-16 S/U vs Texas as Dog since 1996
- 2-17 S/U vs Texas since 1996
- vs Texas Tech - Texas Tech leads series 21-1
- 1-13 S/U vs Texas Tech as Dog since 2004
- 0-3 S/U & ATS vs Texas Tech as favorite since 1996
- vs West Virginia - West Virginia leads series 9-1
- 5-1 ATS vs West Virginia since 2016
- 0-5 S/U @ West Virginia as Dog since 2012
- 0-8 S/U vs West Virginia since 2014
- 0-17-1 S/U vs Iowa State as 4.5 point or more Dog since 1983
- 11-1 S/U vs Iowa State as 6-26 point or more favorite since 1984
- 0-19 S/U vs Kansas State as 6 point or more Dog since 1996
- 0-19 S/U vs Oklahoma as 21.5 point or more Dog since 1986

Bowl Games
- 5-1 S/U & ATS in Bowl Games since 1992
- 0-16 S/U @ home vs ranked teams since 2010
- 0-7 S/U @ home when ranked vs ranked teams since 1974
- 9-0 S/U when ranked vs Iowa State all time
- 0-39 S/U vs ranked teams since 2010
- 1-41 S/U on road vs ranked teams since 1995
- 0-12 S/U vs #1 ranked teams since 1960
- 0-9 S/U @ home vs #1 ranked teams all time
- 0-12 S/U vs ranked Oklahoma State all time

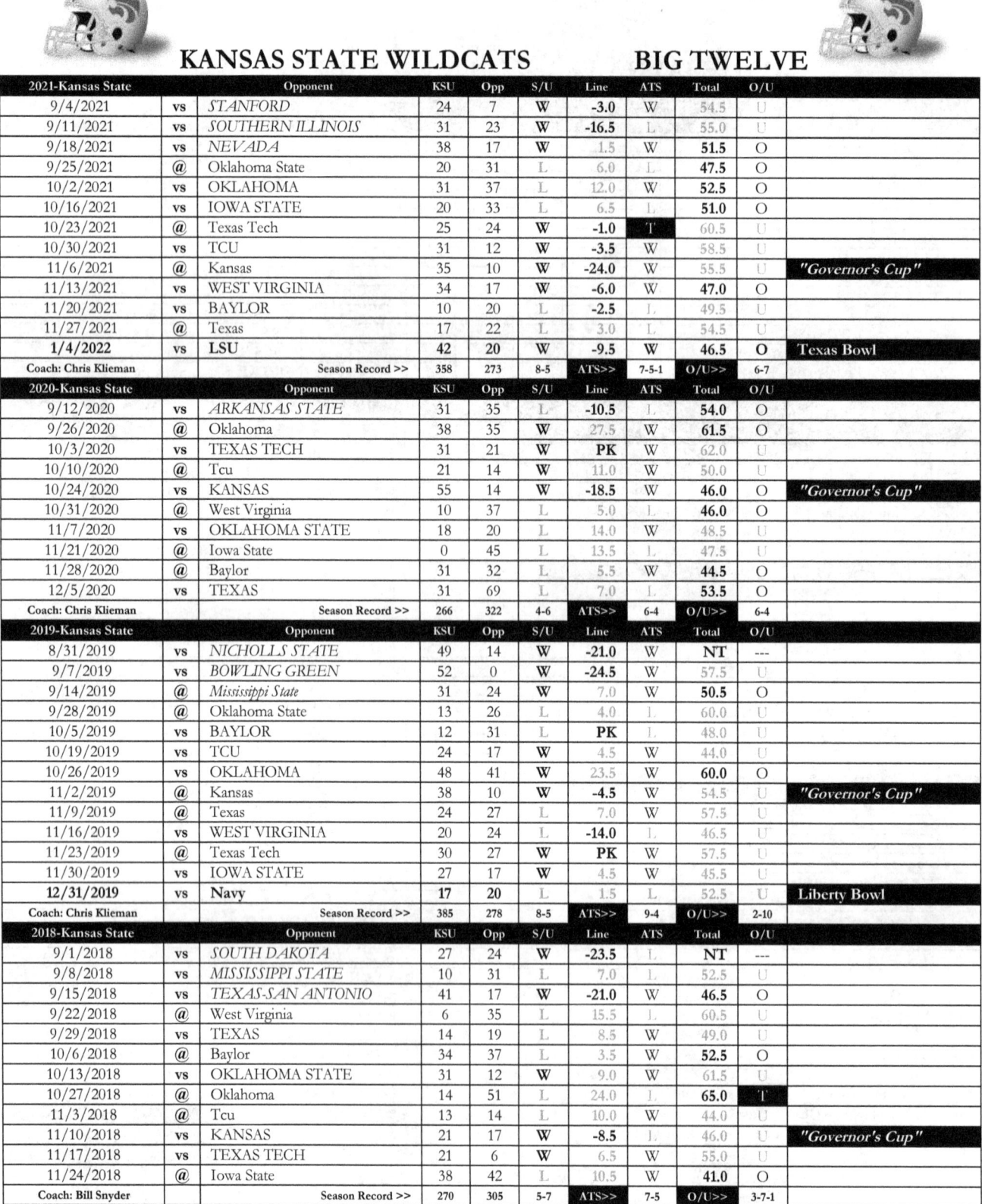

KANSAS STATE WILDCATS — BIG TWELVE

2021-Kansas State		Opponent	KSU	Opp	S/U	Line	ATS	Total	O/U	
9/4/2021	vs	STANFORD	24	7	W	-3.0	W	54.5	U	
9/11/2021	vs	SOUTHERN ILLINOIS	31	23	W	-16.5	L	55.0	U	
9/18/2021	vs	NEVADA	38	17	W	1.5	W	51.5	O	
9/25/2021	@	Oklahoma State	20	31	L	6.0	L	47.5	O	
10/2/2021	vs	OKLAHOMA	31	37	L	12.0	W	52.5	O	
10/16/2021	vs	IOWA STATE	20	33	L	6.5	L	51.0	O	
10/23/2021	@	Texas Tech	25	24	W	-1.0	T	60.5	U	
10/30/2021	vs	TCU	31	12	W	-3.5	W	58.5	U	
11/6/2021	@	Kansas	35	10	W	-24.0	W	55.5	U	"Governor's Cup"
11/13/2021	vs	WEST VIRGINIA	34	17	W	-6.0	W	47.0	O	
11/20/2021	vs	BAYLOR	10	20	L	-2.5	L	49.5	U	
11/27/2021	@	Texas	17	22	L	3.0	L	54.5	U	
1/4/2022	vs	LSU	42	20	W	-9.5	W	46.5	O	Texas Bowl
Coach: Chris Klieman		Season Record >>	358	273	8-5	ATS>>	7-5-1	O/U>>	6-7	

2020-Kansas State		Opponent	KSU	Opp	S/U	Line	ATS	Total	O/U	
9/12/2020	vs	ARKANSAS STATE	31	35	L	-10.5	L	54.0	O	
9/26/2020	@	Oklahoma	38	35	W	27.5	W	61.5	O	
10/3/2020	vs	TEXAS TECH	31	21	W	PK	W	62.0	U	
10/10/2020	@	Tcu	21	14	W	11.0	W	50.0	U	
10/24/2020	vs	KANSAS	55	14	W	-18.5	W	46.0	O	"Governor's Cup"
10/31/2020	@	West Virginia	10	37	L	5.0	L	46.0	O	
11/7/2020	vs	OKLAHOMA STATE	18	20	L	14.0	W	48.5	U	
11/21/2020	@	Iowa State	0	45	L	13.5	L	47.5	O	
11/28/2020	@	Baylor	31	32	L	5.5	W	44.5	O	
12/5/2020	vs	TEXAS	31	69	L	7.0	L	53.5	O	
Coach: Chris Klieman		Season Record >>	266	322	4-6	ATS>>	6-4	O/U>>	6-4	

2019-Kansas State		Opponent	KSU	Opp	S/U	Line	ATS	Total	O/U	
8/31/2019	vs	NICHOLLS STATE	49	14	W	-21.0	W	NT	---	
9/7/2019	vs	BOWLING GREEN	52	0	W	-24.5	W	57.5	U	
9/14/2019	@	Mississippi State	31	24	W	7.0	W	50.5	O	
9/28/2019	@	Oklahoma State	13	26	L	4.0	L	60.0	U	
10/5/2019	vs	BAYLOR	12	31	L	PK	L	48.0	U	
10/19/2019	vs	TCU	24	17	W	4.5	W	44.0	U	
10/26/2019	vs	OKLAHOMA	48	41	W	23.5	W	60.0	O	
11/2/2019	@	Kansas	38	10	W	-4.5	W	54.5	U	"Governor's Cup"
11/9/2019	@	Texas	24	27	L	7.0	W	57.5	U	
11/16/2019	vs	WEST VIRGINIA	20	24	L	-14.0	L	46.5	U	
11/23/2019	@	Texas Tech	30	27	W	PK	W	57.5	U	
11/30/2019	vs	IOWA STATE	27	17	W	4.5	W	45.5	U	
12/31/2019	vs	Navy	17	20	L	1.5	L	52.5	U	Liberty Bowl
Coach: Chris Klieman		Season Record >>	385	278	8-5	ATS>>	9-4	O/U>>	2-10	

2018-Kansas State		Opponent	KSU	Opp	S/U	Line	ATS	Total	O/U	
9/1/2018	vs	SOUTH DAKOTA	27	24	W	-23.5	L	NT	---	
9/8/2018	vs	MISSISSIPPI STATE	10	31	L	7.0	L	52.5	U	
9/15/2018	vs	TEXAS-SAN ANTONIO	41	17	W	-21.0	W	46.5	O	
9/22/2018	@	West Virginia	6	35	L	15.5	L	60.5	U	
9/29/2018	vs	TEXAS	14	19	L	8.5	W	49.0	U	
10/6/2018	@	Baylor	34	37	L	3.5	W	52.5	O	
10/13/2018	vs	OKLAHOMA STATE	31	12	W	9.0	W	61.5	U	
10/27/2018	@	Oklahoma	14	51	L	24.0	L	65.0	T	
11/3/2018	@	Tcu	13	14	L	10.0	L	44.0	U	
11/10/2018	vs	KANSAS	21	17	W	-8.5	L	46.0	U	"Governor's Cup"
11/17/2018	vs	TEXAS TECH	21	6	W	6.5	W	55.0	U	
11/24/2018	@	Iowa State	38	42	L	10.5	W	41.0	O	
Coach: Bill Snyder		Season Record >>	270	305	5-7	ATS>>	7-5	O/U>>	3-7-1	

Page | 98

Copyright © 2022 by Steve's Football Bible, LLC

KANSAS STATE WILDCATS — BIG TWELVE

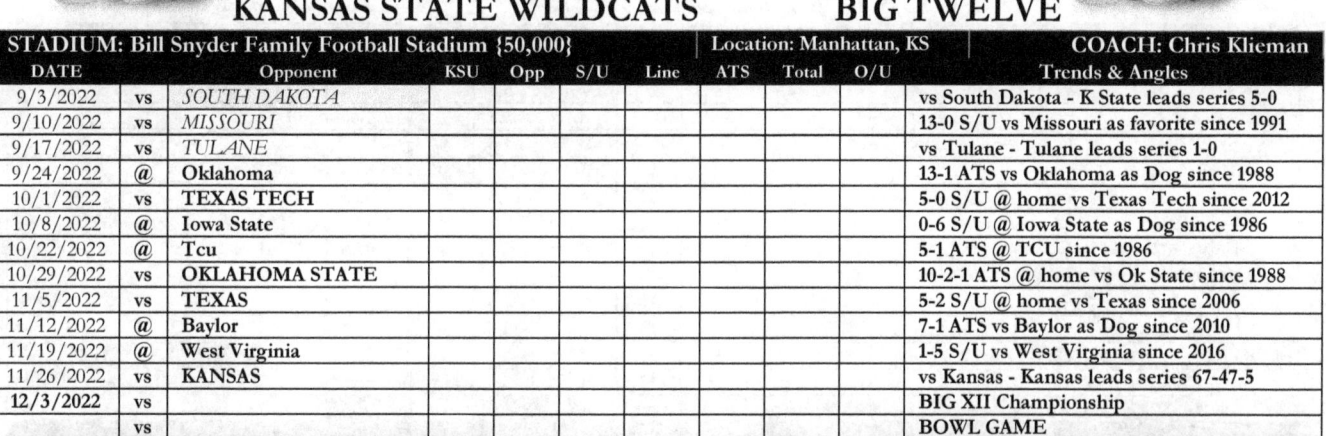

STADIUM: Bill Snyder Family Football Stadium {50,000} | **Location:** Manhattan, KS | **COACH:** Chris Klieman

DATE		Opponent	KSU	Opp	S/U	Line	ATS	Total	O/U	Trends & Angles
9/3/2022	vs	SOUTH DAKOTA								vs South Dakota - K State leads series 5-0
9/10/2022	vs	MISSOURI								13-0 S/U vs Missouri as favorite since 1991
9/17/2022	vs	TULANE								vs Tulane - Tulane leads series 1-0
9/24/2022	@	Oklahoma								13-1 ATS vs Oklahoma as Dog since 1988
10/1/2022	vs	TEXAS TECH								5-0 S/U @ home vs Texas Tech since 2012
10/8/2022	@	Iowa State								0-6 S/U @ Iowa State as Dog since 1986
10/22/2022	@	Tcu								5-1 ATS @ TCU since 1986
10/29/2022	vs	OKLAHOMA STATE								10-2-1 ATS @ home vs Ok State since 1988
11/5/2022	vs	TEXAS								5-2 S/U @ home vs Texas since 2006
11/12/2022	@	Baylor								7-1 ATS vs Baylor as Dog since 2010
11/19/2022	@	West Virginia								1-5 S/U vs West Virginia since 2016
11/26/2022	vs	KANSAS								vs Kansas - Kansas leads series 67-47-5
12/3/2022	vs									BIG XII Championship
	vs									BOWL GAME

Pointspread Analysis — Non-Conference
- 4-21 S/U vs Non-Conf. as 3 point or more Dog since 1982
- 0-5 O/U vs Non-Conf. as 3.5-7 point favorite since 2009
- 9-0 S/U vs Non-Conf. as 7.5-10 point favorite since 1991
- 50-1 S/U vs Non-Conf. as 15.5 point or more favorite since 1992
- 1-5 S/U vs Missouri since 2006
- 3-12 S/U vs Missouri as a Dog since 1984
- vs Missouri - Missouri leads series 59-33-5

Dog
- 2-46 S/U as 20.5 point or more Dog since 1984
- 1-11 S/U @ home as 20.5 point or more Dog since 1984
- 5-1 ATS as 15.5-20 point Dog since 2009
- 0-12-1 S/U @ home as 10.5-15 point Dog since 1984
- 5-21 S/U as 10.5-15 point Dog since 1984
- 1-6 S/U @ home as 7.5-10 point Dog since 2005
- 3-14 S/U on road as 3.5-7 point Dog since 2013
- 13-5-1 ATS as 3 point or less Dog since 1993
- 4-1 S/U & ATS on road as 3 point or less Dog since 2012

Favorite
- 16-3 S/U @ home as 3.5-7 point favorite since 1990
- 7-0 S/U @ home as 7.5-10 point favorite since 2006
- 7-3 S/U @ home as 10.5-15 point favorite since 2011
- 7-0 S/U on road as 15.5-20 point favorite since 1994
- 12-0 S/U @ home as 15.5-20 poinit favorite since 1994
- 5-0 ATS on road as 15.5-20 point favorite since 1995
- 12-0 S/U on road as 20.5 point or more favorite since 1992
- 73-1 S/U as 20.5 point or more favorite since 1992

Bowl Games
- 3-0 S/U in Holiday Bowl
- 0-3 O/U in Cactus Bowl since 2001
- 1-4 S/U & ATS vs Big Ten teams in Bowl Games
- 0-3 S/U & ATS in Bowl Games as 7.5-10 point Dog since 2006
- 0-7 S/U vs ranked teams in Bowl games since 2001 {0-7 ATS}
- 0-8 S/U vs #3 ranked teams all time
- 19-2 S/U @ home when ranked since 2011
- 11-0 S/U when ranked vs Iowa State since 1994
- 11-0 S/U when ranked vs Missouri since 1993
- 5-0 S/U @ home when ranked vs Oklahoma State all time
- 1-13 S/U @ home vs ranked teams since 2013
- 0-19 S/U vs #2 ranked teams all time
- 1-12 S/U vs ranked Oklahoma State all time
- 12-1 S/U when ranked vs Kansas all time {7-0 on road}

Pointspread Analysis — Conference
- vs Baylor - Baylor leads series 10-9
- vs Iowa State - Iowa State leads series 51-49-4
- 3-0 S/U @ home vs Kansas as Dog since 1986
- vs Oklahoma - Oklahoma leads series 77-21-4
- Game 11-2-1 O/U vs Oklahoma since 2005
- 9-3 S/U @ home vs Oklahoma State since 1990
- 13-5 ATS vs Oklahoma State since 1998
- vs Oklahoma State - Oklahoma State leads series 42-26
- 11-3 ATS vs Oklahoma State as Dog since 1988
- vs TCU - Kansas State leads series 8-7
- 3-0 S/U vs TCU as favorite since 1983
- Game 0-6 O/U vs TCU since 2016
- 0-5 S/U vs Texas since 2017
- vs Texas - Texas leads series 12-10
- vs Texas - HOME team 8-2 ATS since 2012
- 6-1 ATS @ home vs Texas since 2006
- 4-1 ATS @ home vs Texas as Dog since 2006
- Game 1-3 O/U @ home vs Texas since 2014
- vs Texas Tech - Kansas State leads series 13-9
- 7-1 O/U vs Texas Tech as Dog since 2005
- 10-1 S/U vs Texas Tech since 2011 {8-2-1 ATS}
- Game 3-7 O/U vs West Virginia since 2012
- vs West Virginia - Series tied 6-6
- 0-4 S/U vs Baylor as 6.5 point or more Dog since 2010
- 8-0 S/U vs Iowa State as 6 point or less favorite since 1991
- 9-0 S/U vs Iowa State as 15 point or more favorite since 1994
- 19-0 S/U vs Kansas as 6 point or more favorite since 1996
- 2-14 S/U vs Oklahoma as 16 point or more Dog since 1983
- 10-0 S/U vs OK State as 3.5 point or more favorite since 1991
- 0-6 S/U vs Oklahoma State as 21 point or more Dog since 1984

SOUTH DAKOTA	30-2 S/U in 1st home game of season since 1990
MISSOURI	15-2 S/U in 2nd home game of season since 2005
Oklahoma	11-4 S/U prior to playing Texas Tech since 2004
Oklahoma	3-9 O/U prior to playing Texas Tech since 2009
Iowa State	12-4 O/U after playing Texas Tech since 2001
Baylor	8-1 S/U prior to playing West Virginia since 2012
KANSAS	9-3 S/U in final home game of season since 2010

Page | 99 — Copyright © 2022 by Steve's Football Bible, LLC

KENTUCKY WILDCATS — SEC East

2021-Kentucky		Opponent	UK	Opp	S/U	Line	ATS	Total	O/U	
9/4/2021	vs	LOUISIANA-MONROE	45	10	W	-31.0	W	54.5	O	
9/11/2021	vs	MISSOURI	35	28	W	-5.5	W	56.5	O	
9/18/2021	vs	CHATTANOOGA	28	23	W	-33.5	L	47.5	O	
9/25/2021	@	South Carolina	16	10	W	-4.5	W	48.5	U	
10/2/2021	vs	FLORIDA	20	13	W	7.5	W	56.0	U	
10/9/2021	vs	LSU	42	21	W	-2.0	W	50.5	U	
10/16/2021	@	Georgia	13	30	L	21.5	W	44.5	U	
10/30/2021	@	Mississippi State	17	31	L	1.0	L	47.0	U	
11/6/2021	vs	TENNESSEE	42	45	L	1.5	L	57.5	O	
11/13/2021	@	Vanderbilt	34	17	W	-21.5	L	52.5	U	
11/20/2021	vs	NEW MEXICO STATE	56	14	W	-36.0	W	60.0	O	
11/27/2021	@	Louisville	52	21	W	3.0	W	58.0	O	"Governor's Cup"
1/1/2022	vs	Iowa	20	17	W	-3.0	T	43.5	U	Citrus Bowl
Coach: Mark Stoops		Season Record >>	420	280	10-3	ATS>>	8-4-1	O/U>>	8-5	

2020-Kentucky		Opponent	UK	Opp	S/U	Line	ATS	Total	O/U	
9/26/2020	@	Auburn	13	29	L	6.5	L	48.0	U	
10/3/2020	vs	MISSISSIPPI	41	42	L	-6.5	L	63.0	O	{OT}
10/10/2020	vs	MISSISSIPPI STATE	24	2	W	-3.0	W	57.5	U	
10/17/2020	@	Tennessee	34	7	W	6.0	W	45.5	U	
10/24/2020	@	Missouri	10	20	L	-3.0	L	47.0	U	
10/31/2020	vs	GEORGIA	3	14	L	16.5	W	41.5	U	
11/14/2020	vs	VANDERBILT	38	35	W	-17.5	L	41.5	O	
11/21/2020	@	Alabama	3	63	L	31.0	L	57.5	O	
11/28/2020	@	Florida	10	34	L	23.5	L	60.5	U	
12/5/2020	vs	SOUTH CAROLINA	41	18	W	-11.5	W	47.5	O	
1/2/2021	vs	NC State	23	21	W	-3.5	L	50.0	U	Gator Bowl
Coach: Mark Stoops		Season Record >>	240	285	5-6	ATS>>	4-7	O/U>>	4-7	

2019-Kentucky		Opponent	UK	Opp	S/U	Line	ATS	Total	O/U	
8/31/2019	vs	TOLEDO	38	24	W	-9.0	W	60.5	O	
9/7/2019	vs	EASTERN MICHIGAN	38	17	W	-15.5	W	52.0	O	
9/14/2019	vs	FLORIDA	21	29	L	9.5	W	46.5	O	
9/21/2019	@	Mississippi State	13	28	L	5.5	L	48.0	U	
9/28/2019	@	South Carolina	7	24	L	3.5	L	54.0	U	
10/12/2019	vs	ARKANSAS	24	20	W	-3.0	W	52.0	U	
10/19/2019	@	Georgia	0	21	L	24.0	W	45.5	U	
10/26/2019	vs	MISSOURI	29	7	W	9.5	W	43.5	U	
11/9/2019	vs	TENNESSEE	13	17	L	PK	L	42.0	U	
11/16/2019	@	Vanderbilt	38	14	W	-9.0	W	43.0	O	
11/23/2019	vs	TENNESSEE-MARTIN	50	7	W	-30.5	W	NT	---	
11/30/2019	vs	LOUISVILLE	45	13	W	-2.5	W	51.5	O	"Governor's Cup"
12/31/2019	vs	Virginia Tech	37	30	W	2.0	W	46.0	O	Belk Bowl
Coach: Mark Stoops		Season Record >>	353	251	8-5	ATS>>	10-3	O/U>>	6-6	

2018-Kentucky		Opponent	UK	Opp	S/U	Line	ATS	Total	O/U	
9/1/2018	vs	CENTRAL MICHIGAN	35	20	W	-17.5	L	49.0	O	
9/8/2018	@	Florida	27	16	W	13.5	W	52.5	U	
9/15/2018	vs	MURRAY STATE	48	10	W	-39.5	L	NT	---	
9/22/2018	vs	MISSISSIPPI STATE	28	7	W	9.5	W	56.0	U	
9/29/2018	vs	SOUTH CAROLINA	24	10	W	-1.0	W	52.0	U	
10/6/2018	@	Texas A&M	14	20	L	4.5	L	48.5	U	{OT}
10/20/2018	vs	VANDERBILT	14	7	W	-10.0	L	45.0	U	
10/27/2018	@	Missouri	15	14	W	7.5	W	54.5	U	
11/3/2018	vs	GEORGIA	17	34	L	9.0	L	46.0	O	
11/10/2018	@	Tennessee	7	24	L	-6.0	L	42.5	U	
11/17/2018	vs	MIDDLE TENNESSEE	34	23	W	-16.5	L	48.0	O	
11/24/2018	@	Louisville	56	10	W	-16.5	W	53.0	O	"Governor's Cup"
1/1/2019	vs	Penn State	27	24	W	4.5	W	47.5	O	Citrus Bowl
Coach: Mark Stoops		Season Record >>	346	219	10-3	ATS>>	6-7	O/U>>	5-7	

KENTUCKY WILDCATS — SEC East

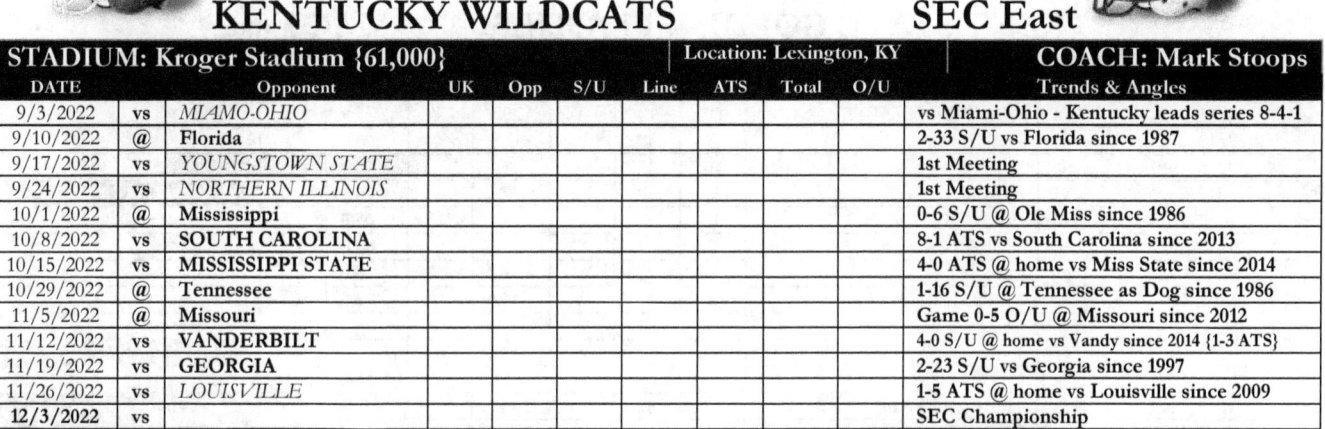

STADIUM: Kroger Stadium {61,000} | **Location:** Lexington, KY | **COACH:** Mark Stoops

DATE		Opponent	UK	Opp	S/U	Line	ATS	Total	O/U	Trends & Angles
9/3/2022	vs	MIAMO-OHIO								vs Miami-Ohio - Kentucky leads series 8-4-1
9/10/2022	@	Florida								2-33 S/U vs Florida since 1987
9/17/2022	vs	YOUNGSTOWN STATE								1st Meeting
9/24/2022	vs	NORTHERN ILLINOIS								1st Meeting
10/1/2022	@	Mississippi								0-6 S/U @ Ole Miss since 1986
10/8/2022	vs	SOUTH CAROLINA								8-1 ATS vs South Carolina since 2013
10/15/2022	vs	MISSISSIPPI STATE								4-0 ATS @ home vs Miss State since 2014
10/29/2022	@	Tennessee								1-16 S/U @ Tennessee as Dog since 1986
11/5/2022	@	Missouri								Game 0-5 O/U @ Missouri since 2012
11/12/2022	vs	VANDERBILT								4-0 S/U @ home vs Vandy since 2014 {1-3 ATS}
11/19/2022	vs	GEORGIA								2-23 S/U vs Georgia since 1997
11/26/2022	vs	LOUISVILLE								1-5 ATS @ home vs Louisville since 2009
12/3/2022	vs									SEC Championship
	vs									BOWL GAME

Pointspread Analysis — Non-Conference

- 8-1-1 O/U vs Non-Conf. as 3.5-7 point favorite since 2000
- 8-0 S/U vs Non-Conf. as 7.5-10 point favorite since 1989
- 54-2 S/U vs Non-Conf. as 10.5 point or more favorite since 1984
- vs Louisville - Kentucky leads series 18-15
- 1-4 S/U @ home vs Louisville since 2011

Bowl Games
- 1-4 O/U in Music City Bowl
- 0-3 O/U vs Clemson in Bowl Games

Dog
- 6-15 ATS as home Dog since 2012
- 0-12 S/U @ home as 20.5 point or more Dog since 1990
- 1-46 S/U as 20.5 point or more Dog since 1990
- 2-25 S/U as 15.5-20 point Dog since 1983
- 4-11 ATS on road as 10.5-15 point Dog since 2010
- 1-19 S/U as 10.5-15 point Dog since 2010
- 0-15 S/U @ home as 10.5-15 point Dog since 1983
- 4-10 S/U @ home as 7.5-10 point Dog since 2000
- 2-9 S/U @ home as 3 point or less Dog since 1998

Favorite
- 17-2 S/U & ATS @ home as 3 point or less favorite since 1983
- 14-2-1 ATS as 3 point or less favorite since 2004
- 2-8 ATS as 3.5-7 point favorite since 2012
- 2-8 ATS @ home as 3.5-7 point favorite since 2008
- 11-3-1 O/U as 3.5-7 point favorite since 2007
- 16-0 S/U as 7.5-10 point favorite since 1989
- 65-3 S/U as 10.5 point or more favorite since 1984

14-2 S/U in 1st home game of season since 2006	MIAMO-OHIO
1-9 ATS prior to playing South Carolina since 2012	Mississippi
4-14 S/U in 2nd road game of season since 2004	Mississippi
0-10 O/U in 2nd road game of season since 2012	Mississippi
2-7 S/U & ATS prior to playing Tennessee since 2013	MISS STATE
11-3 O/U prior to playing Mississippi State since 2007	Tennessee
1-9 O/U prior to playing Vanderbilt since 2012	Missouri
5-17 S/U in final road game of season since 2000	Missouri
1-9 ATS after playing Missouri since 2012	VANDERBILT
3-12 S/U after playing Georgia since 2007	LOUISVILLE
3-12 ATS after playing Georgia since 2007	LOUISVILLE

Pointspread Analysis — Conference

- vs Florida - Florida leads series 53-19
- vs Georgia - Georgia leads series 61-12-2
- 0-5 S/U @ Mississippi as Dog since 1990
- 3-0 S/U @ home vs Mississippi State since 2016
- vs Mississippi - Ole Miss leads series 29-14-1
- 3-10 S/U vs Mississippi State since 2009
- vs Mississippi State - Mississippi State leads series 26-23
- vs Missouri - Kentucky leads series 8-4
- 6-1 S/U vs Missouri since 2015
- 4-0 S/U @ home vs South Carolina since 2014 {4-0 ATS}
- Game 1-6 O/U vs South Carolina since 2015
- 3-1 S/U & ATS vs South Carolina as Dog since 2014
- 7-1 S/U vs South Carolina as favorite since 1992
- 7-1 S/U vs South Carolina since 2014
- vs South Carolina - South Carolina leads series 18-14-1
- 1-17 S/U @ Tennessee since 1986
- 3-34 S/U vs Tennessee since 1985
- 3-12 ATS vs Tennessee since 2007
- vs Tennessee - Tennessee leads series 82-26-9
- 6-0 S/U vs Vanderbilt since 2016
- vs Vanderbilt - Kentucky leads series 48-42-4
- Game 1-4 O/U @ home vs Vanderbilt since 2012
- 0-25 S/U vs Florida as 14 point or more Dog since 1983
- 0-14 S/U vs Georgia as 16 point or more Dog since 1983
- 0-7 S/U vs Georgia as 10-13 point Dog since 1985
- 0-5 S/U & ATS vs Georgia as 6 point or less Dog since 1984
- 0-7 S/U vs Mississippi State as 10 point or more Dog since 1991
- 0-6 S/U vs South Carolina as 12.5 point or more Dog since 2001
- 0-20 S/U vs Tennessee as 9 point or more Dog since 1990
- 1-10 S/U vs Tennessee as 6.5 point or less Dog since 1983
- 6-0 S/U vs Vanderbilt as 3.5 point or less favorite since 1996
- 9-0 S/U vs Vanderbilt as 10 point or more favorite since 1986
- 25-9 S/U @ home when ranked since 1950
- 0-7 S/U when ranked vs #6 #8 #9 ranked teams all time
- 5-64 S/U on road vs ranked teams since 1978
- 2-15 S/U vs #1 ranked teams since 1951
- 1-18 S/U vs ranked Florida all time
- 1-33 S/U vs ranked Georgia since 1967
- 1-16 S/U @ ranked Tennessee all time

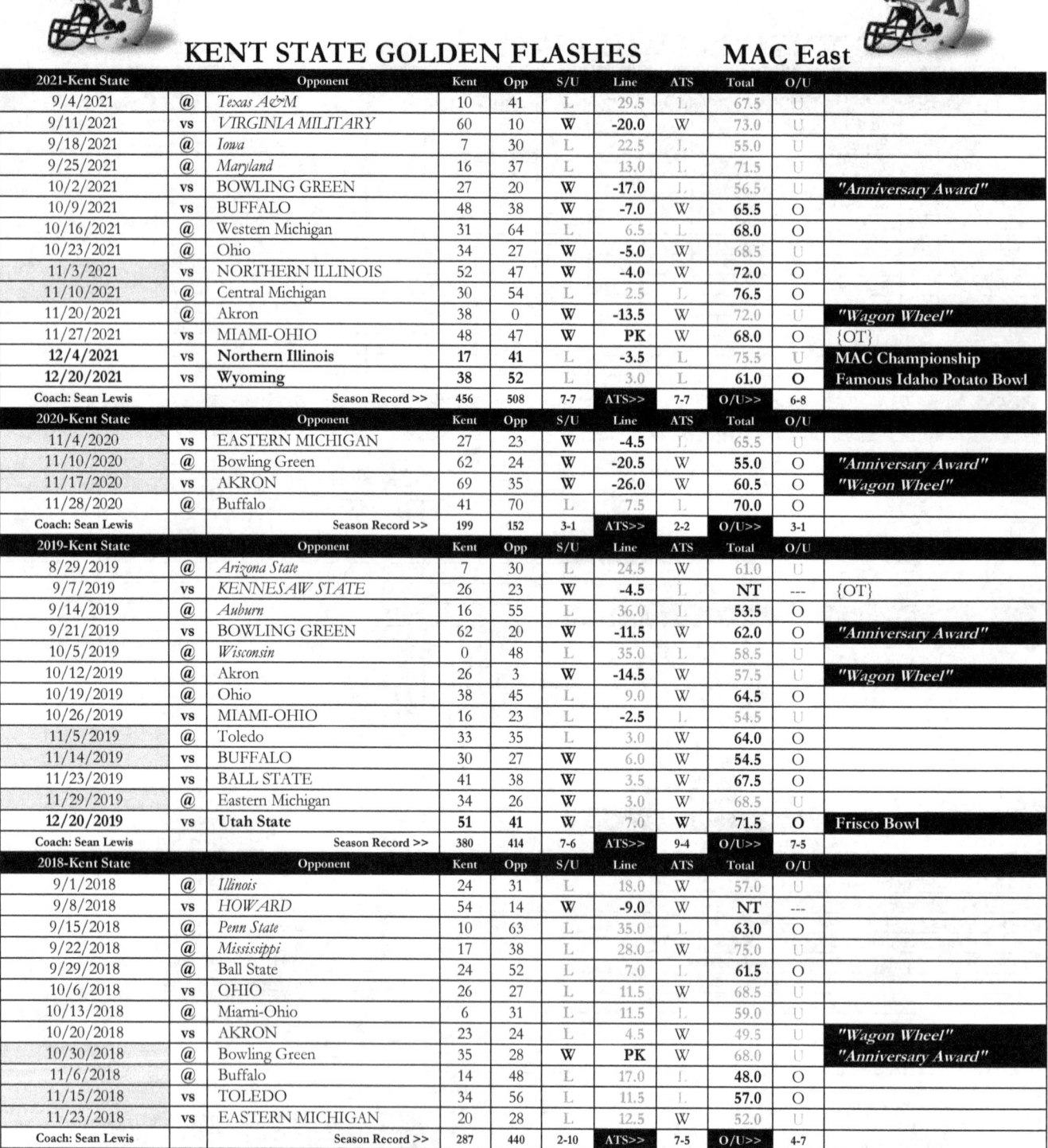

KENT STATE GOLDEN FLASHES   MAC East

2021-Kent State		Opponent	Kent	Opp	S/U	Line	ATS	Total	O/U	
9/4/2021	@	Texas A&M	10	41	L	29.5	L	67.5	U	
9/11/2021	vs	VIRGINIA MILITARY	60	10	W	-20.0	W	73.0	U	
9/18/2021	@	Iowa	7	30	L	22.5	L	55.0	U	
9/25/2021	@	Maryland	16	37	L	13.0	L	71.5	U	
10/2/2021	vs	BOWLING GREEN	27	20	W	-17.0	L	56.5	U	"Anniversary Award"
10/9/2021	vs	BUFFALO	48	38	W	-7.0	W	65.5	O	
10/16/2021	@	Western Michigan	31	64	L	6.5	L	68.0	O	
10/23/2021	@	Ohio	34	27	W	-5.0	W	68.5	U	
11/3/2021	vs	NORTHERN ILLINOIS	52	47	W	-4.0	W	72.0	O	
11/10/2021	@	Central Michigan	30	54	L	2.5	L	76.5	O	
11/20/2021	@	Akron	38	0	W	-13.5	W	72.0	U	"Wagon Wheel"
11/27/2021	vs	MIAMI-OHIO	48	47	W	PK	W	68.0	O	{OT}
12/4/2021	vs	Northern Illinois	17	41	L	-3.5	L	75.5	U	MAC Championship
12/20/2021	vs	Wyoming	38	52	L	3.0	L	61.0	O	Famous Idaho Potato Bowl
Coach: Sean Lewis		Season Record >>	456	508	7-7	ATS>>	7-7	O/U>>	6-8	

2020-Kent State		Opponent	Kent	Opp	S/U	Line	ATS	Total	O/U	
11/4/2020	vs	EASTERN MICHIGAN	27	23	W	-4.5	L	65.5	U	
11/10/2020	@	Bowling Green	62	24	W	-20.5	W	55.0	O	"Anniversary Award"
11/17/2020	vs	AKRON	69	35	W	-26.0	W	60.5	O	"Wagon Wheel"
11/28/2020	@	Buffalo	41	70	L	7.5	L	70.0	O	
Coach: Sean Lewis		Season Record >>	199	152	3-1	ATS>>	2-2	O/U>>	3-1	

2019-Kent State		Opponent	Kent	Opp	S/U	Line	ATS	Total	O/U	
8/29/2019	@	Arizona State	7	30	L	24.5	W	61.0	U	
9/7/2019	vs	KENNESAW STATE	26	23	W	-4.5	L	NT	---	{OT}
9/14/2019	@	Auburn	16	55	L	36.0	L	53.5	O	
9/21/2019	vs	BOWLING GREEN	62	20	W	-11.5	W	62.0	O	"Anniversary Award"
10/5/2019	@	Wisconsin	0	48	L	35.0	L	58.5	U	
10/12/2019	@	Akron	26	3	W	-14.5	W	57.5	U	"Wagon Wheel"
10/19/2019	@	Ohio	38	45	L	9.0	W	64.5	O	
10/26/2019	vs	MIAMI-OHIO	16	23	L	-2.5	L	54.5	U	
11/5/2019	@	Toledo	33	35	L	3.0	W	64.0	O	
11/14/2019	vs	BUFFALO	30	27	W	6.0	W	54.5	O	
11/23/2019	vs	BALL STATE	41	38	W	3.5	W	67.5	O	
11/29/2019	@	Eastern Michigan	34	26	W	3.0	W	68.5	U	
12/20/2019	vs	Utah State	51	41	W	7.0	W	71.5	O	Frisco Bowl
Coach: Sean Lewis		Season Record >>	380	414	7-6	ATS>>	9-4	O/U>>	7-5	

2018-Kent State		Opponent	Kent	Opp	S/U	Line	ATS	Total	O/U	
9/1/2018	@	Illinois	24	31	L	18.0	W	57.0	U	
9/8/2018	vs	HOWARD	54	14	W	-9.0	W	NT	---	
9/15/2018	@	Penn State	10	63	L	35.0	L	63.0	O	
9/22/2018	@	Mississippi	17	38	L	28.0	W	75.0	U	
9/29/2018	@	Ball State	24	52	L	7.0	L	61.5	O	
10/6/2018	vs	OHIO	26	27	L	11.5	W	68.5	U	
10/13/2018	@	Miami-Ohio	6	31	L	11.5	L	59.0	U	
10/20/2018	vs	AKRON	23	24	L	4.5	W	49.5	U	"Wagon Wheel"
10/30/2018	@	Bowling Green	35	28	W	PK	W	68.0	U	"Anniversary Award"
11/6/2018	@	Buffalo	14	48	L	17.0	L	48.0	O	
11/15/2018	vs	TOLEDO	34	56	L	11.5	L	57.0	O	
11/23/2018	vs	EASTERN MICHIGAN	20	28	L	12.5	W	52.0	U	
Coach: Sean Lewis		Season Record >>	287	440	2-10	ATS>>	7-5	O/U>>	4-7	

KENT STATE GOLDEN FLASHES — MAC East

STADIUM: Dix Stadium {25,319} | **Location:** Kent, OH | **COACH:** Sean Lewis

DATE		Opponent	Kent	Opp	S/U	Line	ATS	Total	O/U	Trends & Angles
9/3/2022	@	Washington								1-13 S/U in 1st road game of season since 2008
9/10/2022	@	Oklahoma								0-12 ATS in 2nd road game of season since 2010
9/17/2022	vs	LONG ISLAND U.								1st Meeting
9/24/2022	@	Georgia								vs Georgia - Georgia leads series 1-0
10/1/2022	vs	OHIO								Game 0-7 O/U @ home vs Ohio since 2006
10/8/2022	@	Miami-Ohio								0-3 S/U & ATS @ Miami-Ohio since 2014
10/15/2022	@	Toledo								0-12 S/U @ Toledo since 1979
10/22/2022	vs	AKRON								3-10 S/U after playing Toledo since 1989
11/1/2022	vs	BALL STATE								vs Ball State - Ball State leads series 21-8
11/9/2022	@	Bowling Green								vs Bowling Green - BGU leads series 58-24-6
11/16/2022	vs	EASTERN MICHIGAN								5-0 S/U vs Eastern Mich. as favorite since 2004
11/26/2022	@	Buffalo								vs Buffalo - Buffalo leads series 14-13
12/2/2022	vs									MAC Championship
	vs									BOWL GAME

Pointspread Analysis — Non-Conference
- 0-54 S/U vs Non-Conf. as 15.5 point or more Dog since 1989
- 5-21 S/U vs Non-Conf. as a 15 point or less Dog since 1989
- 1-9 S/U vs Non-Conf. as 10.5-15 point Dog since 1989
- 5-0 S/U vs Non-Conf. as 15.5 point or more favorite since 2010

Bowl Games
- 1-4 S/U in Bowl Games

Dog
- 0-36 S/U on road as 25.5 point or more Dog since 1989
- 1-31 S/U as 20.5-25 point Dog since 1993
- 0-9 S/U @ home as 20.5 point or more Dog since 1994
- 0-27 S/U on road as 15.5-20 point Dog since 1990
- 8-155 S/U as 10.5 point or more Dog since 1989
- 0-12 S/U @ home as 10.5-15 point Dog since 2001
- 0-13 S/U as 10.5-15 point Dog since 2013
- 2-13 S/U @ home as 7.5-10 point Dog since 1992
- 8-1 O/U @ home as 3.5-7 point Dog since 2011
- 1-10 S/U @ home as 3 point or less Dog since 2008

Favorite
- 10-1 S/U as 3.5-7 point favorite since 2011 {8-3 ATS}
- 9-0 S/U @ home as 3.5-7 point favorite since 2011 {7-2 ATS}
- 5-1 ATS @ home as 3.5-7 point favorite since 2011
- 19-2 S/U @ home as 10.5 point or more favorite since 1999

- 2-32 S/U vs ranked teams all time
- 0-3 S/U vs ranked Toledo all time

Pointspread Analysis — Conference
- vs Akron - Akron leads series 35-27-1
- 0-4 S/U @ home vs Eastern Michigan as Dog since 1994
- vs Eastern Michigan - Kent State leads series 18-13
- vs Miami-Ohio - Miami-Ohio leads series 50-18
- Game 1-7 O/U vs Miami-Ohio since 2013
- 1-6 S/U vs Ohio since 2014
- 1-6 S/U @ home vs Ohio as Dog since 1996
- vs Ohio - Ohio leads series 44-27-2
- Game 3-10 O/U vs Ohio since 2008
- 0-7 S/U @ Toledo as Dog since 1990
- 0-9 S/U vs Toledo as Dog since 1992
- vs Toledo - Toledo leads series 27-21
- 2-12 S/U vs Toledo since 1988
- 1-11 S/U vs Ball State as 7 point or more Dog since 1989
- 1-13 S/U vs Bowling Green as 11 point or more Dog since 1991
- 0-10 S/U vs Miami-Ohio as 14 point or more Dog since 1991
- 0-5 S/U vs Ohio as 14 point or more Dog since 1997

Washington	8-3 O/U in 1st road game of season since 2011
Oklahoma	2-29 S/U in 2nd road game of season since 1993
Toledo	1-8 S/U prior to playing Akron since 2013
BALL STATE	10-2 O/U after playing Akron since 2009
Bowling Green	7-1 ATS prior to playing Eastern Michigan since 2005
EASTERN MICH	3-13 S/U prior to playing Buffalo since 2002
EASTERN MICH	12-3 O/U after playing Bowling Green since 2006
EASTERN MICH	7-1 O/U in final home game of season since 2014
Buffalo	2-6 S/U in final road game of season since 2014
Buffalo	2-6 O/U in final road game of season since 2014

Yea Alabama! History of the Alabama Crimson Tide
Paperback $34.95
Hardcover $36.95

Tiger Rag! History of Clemson Tigers Football
Paperback $29.95
Hardcover $34.95

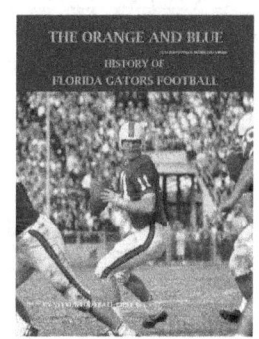

The Orange and Blue! History of the Florida Gators
Paperback $29.95
Hardcover $34.95

College Football Blueblood Series available at: www.stevesfootballbible.com

LIBERTY FLAMES — INDEPENDENT

2021-Liberty		Opponent	Lib	Opp	S/U	Line	ATS	Total	O/U	
9/4/2021	vs	CAMPBELL	48	7	W	-35.5	W	65.0	U	
9/11/2021	@	Troy	21	13	W	-3.0	W	62.5	U	
9/18/2021	vs	OLD DOMINION	45	17	W	-27.5	W	53.0	O	
9/24/2021	@	Syracuse	21	24	L	-6.5	L	54.0	U	
10/2/2021	@	Alabama-Birmingham	36	12	W	2.5	W	49.0	U	
10/9/2021	vs	MIDDLE TENNESSEE	41	13	W	-20.0	W	58.5	U	
10/16/2021	@	Louisiana-Monroe	28	31	L	-32.5	L	57.0	O	
10/23/2021	@	North Texas	35	26	W	-21.0	L	61.0	T	
10/30/2021	vs	MASSACHUSETTS	62	17	W	-35.5	W	56.0	O	
11/6/2021	@	Mississippi	14	27	L	7.5	L	67.0	U	
11/20/2021	vs	LOUISIANA	14	42	L	-4.0	L	53.0	O	
11/27/2021	vs	ARMY	16	31	L	-3.0	L	52.0	U	
12/18/2021	vs	**Eastern Michigan**	56	20	W	-9.5	W	58.0	O	**Lending Tree Bowl**
Coach: Hugh Freeze		Season Record >>	437	280	8-5	ATS>>	7-6	ATS>>	5-7-1	

2020-Liberty		Opponent	Lib	Opp	S/U	Line	ATS	Total	O/U	
9/19/2020	@	Western Kentucky	30	24	W	14.0	W	51.5	O	
9/26/2020	vs	FLORIDA INTERNATIONAL	36	34	W	-7.5	L	60.5	O	
10/3/2020	vs	NORTH ALABAMA	28	7	W	-32.5	L	63.5	U	
10/10/2020	vs	LOUISIANA-MONROE	40	7	W	-17.0	W	63.0	U	
10/17/2020	@	Syracuse	38	21	W	-3.0	W	52.5	O	
10/24/2020	vs	SOUTHERN MISSISSIPPI	56	35	W	-15.0	W	59.5	O	
11/7/2020	@	Virginia Tech	38	35	W	16.5	W	67.5	O	
11/14/2020	vs	WESTERN CAROLINA	58	14	W	-39.0	W	63.0	O	
11/21/2020	@	NC State	14	15	L	4.0	W	66.5	U	
11/27/2020	vs	MASSACHUSETTS	45	0	W	-35.0	W	57.5	U	
12/26/2020	vs	**Coastal Carolina**	37	34	W	6.5	W	60.0	O	**FBC Mortgage Cure Bowl**
Coach: Hugh Freeze		Season Record >>	420	226	10-1	ATS>>	9-2	ATS>>	7-4	

2019-Liberty		Opponent	Lib	Opp	S/U	Line	ATS	Total	O/U	
8/31/2019	vs	SYRACUSE	0	24	L	19.5	L	68.0	U	
9/7/2019	@	Louisiana-Lafayette	14	35	L	14.0	L	65.5	U	
9/14/2019	vs	BUFFALO	35	17	W	6.0	W	55.0	U	
9/21/2019	vs	HAMPTON	62	27	W	NL	---	NT	---	
9/28/2019	vs	NEW MEXICO	17	10	W	-7.0	T	72.0	U	
10/5/2019	@	New Mexico State	20	13	W	-4.0	W	63.5	U	
10/19/2019	vs	MAINE	59	44	W	-14.5	W	NT	---	
10/26/2019	@	Rutgers	34	44	L	-7.5	L	43.5	O	
11/2/2019	@	Massachusetts	63	21	W	-23.5	W	71.0	O	
11/9/2019	@	Byu	24	31	L	17.0	W	62.0	U	
11/23/2019	@	Virginia	27	55	L	16.0	L	58.0	O	
11/30/2019	vs	NEW MEXICO STATE	49	28	W	-14.5	W	68.0	O	
12/21/2019	vs	**Georgia Southern**	23	16	W	5.0	W	58.5	U	**AutoNation Cure Bowl**
Coach: Hugh Freeze		Season Record >>	427	365	8-5	ATS>>	7-4-1	ATS>>	4-7	

2018-Liberty		Opponent	Lib	Opp	S/U	Line	ATS	Total	O/U	
9/1/2018	vs	OLD DOMINION	52	10	W	5.0	W	58.0	O	
9/8/2018	@	Army	14	38	L	7.5	L	59.5	U	
9/22/2018	vs	NORTH TEXAS	7	47	L	11.0	L	67.0	U	
9/29/2018	@	New Mexico	52	43	W	7.0	W	66.0	O	
10/6/2018	@	New Mexico State	41	49	L	-3.5	L	64.0	O	
10/13/2018	vs	TROY	22	16	W	10.0	W	63.0	U	
10/20/2018	vs	IDAHO STATE	48	41	W	NL	---	NT	---	
11/3/2018	@	Massachusetts	59	62	L	1.0	L	67.5	O	{3 OT}
11/10/2018	@	Virginia	24	45	L	23.5	W	59.0	O	
11/17/2018	@	Auburn	0	53	L	28.5	L	64.5	U	
11/24/2018	vs	NEW MEXICO STATE	28	21	W	-5.5	W	72.5	U	
12/1/2018	vs	NORFOLK STATE	52	17	W	-29.5	W	NT	---	
Coach: Turner Gill		Season Record >>	399	442	6-6	ATS>>	6-5	ATS>>	5-5	

Page | 104

LIBERTY FLAMES — INDEPENDENT

STADIUM: Williams Stadium {25,000} **Location:** Lynchburg, VA **COACH:** Hugh Freeze

DATE		Opponent	Lib	Opp	S/U	Line	ATS	Total	O/U	Trends & Angles
9/3/2022	@	Southern Mississippi								vs Southern Miss - Liberty leads series 1-0
9/10/2022	vs	ALABAMA-BIRMINGHAM								vs UAB - Liberty leads series 1-0
9/17/2022	@	Wake Forest								vs Wake Forest - Wake Forest leads series 2-0
9/24/2022	vs	AKRON								vs Akron - Akron leads series 1-0
10/1/2022	@	Old Dominion								vs Old Dominion- Liberty leads series 2-1
10/8/2022	@	Massachusetts								vs Massachusetts - Liberty leads series 3-1
10/15/2022	vs	GARDNER-WEBB								5-0 S/U @ home vs Gardner-Webb since 2008
10/22/2022	vs	BYU								vs BYU - BYU leads series 1-0
11/5/2022	@	Arkansas								1st Meeting
11/12/2022	@	Connecticut								vs Connecticut - UCONN leads series 1-0
11/19/2022	vs	VIRGINIA TECH								vs Virginia Tech - Series tied 1-1
11/26/2022	vs	NEW MEXICO STATE								vs New Mexico State - Liberty leads series 3-1
	vs									BOWL GAME

Pointspread Analysis		Pointspread Analysis
Dog		
2-7 S/U as 11 point or more Dog since 2018	UAB	17-2 S/U in 1st home game of season since 2003
5-2 ATS as 5-10 point Dog since 2018	Connecticut	0-7 S/U in final road game of season since 2015
Favorite	NEW MEXICO ST	13-3 S/U in final home game of season since 2006
14-1 S/U as 14.5 point or more favorite since 2018 {12-3 ATS}		
Non-Conference		
10-1 S/U vs Gardner-Webb since 2007		

Steve's Football Bible also offers the Pro Football Bible, the Pro football handicapper's best friend for the 2022 football season.

To order Go to: www.stevesfootballbible.com

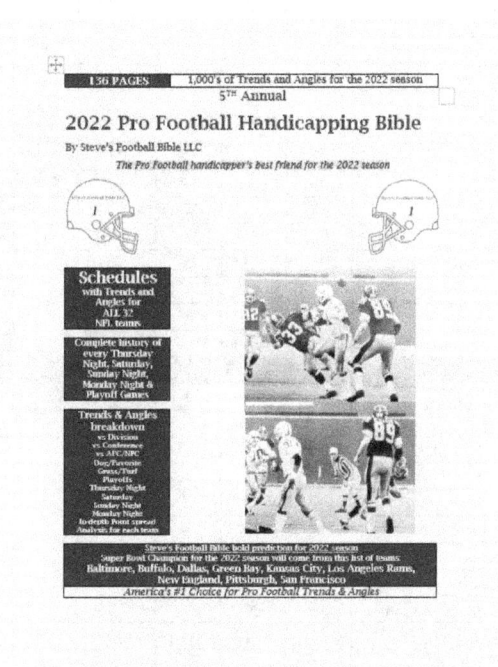

2022 Pro Football Bible $24.95

Page | 105 Copyright © 2022 by Steve's Football Bible, LLC

LOUISIANA RAGIN' CAJUNS — SUN BELT West

2021-Louisiana

Date		Opponent	ULL	Opp	S/U	Line	ATS	Total	O/U	
9/4/2021	@	Texas	18	38	L	8.5	L	58.5	U	
9/11/2021	vs	NICHOLLS STATE	27	24	W	-26.0	L	63.5	U	
9/16/2021	vs	OHIO	49	14	W	-18.5	W	57.0	O	
9/25/2021	@	Georgia Southern	28	20	W	-14.5	L	54.5	U	
10/2/2021	@	South Alabama	20	18	W	-12.0	L	53.0	U	
10/12/2021	vs	APPALACHIAN STATE	41	13	W	4.5	W	57.5	U	
10/21/2021	@	Arkansas State	28	27	W	-18.0	L	70.0	U	
10/30/2021	vs	TEXAS STATE	45	0	W	-21.0	W	58.0	U	
11/4/2021	vs	GEORGIA STATE	21	17	W	-13.5	L	53.5	U	
11/13/2021	@	Troy	35	21	W	-6.5	W	48.0	O	
11/20/2021	@	Liberty	42	14	W	3.0	W	53.0	O	
11/27/2021	vs	LOUISIANA-MONROE	21	16	W	-21.5	L	55.0	U	"Battle of the Bayou"
12/4/2021	vs	Appalachian State	24	16	W	2.0	W	52.0	U	SUN BELT CHAMPIONSHIP
12/18/2021	vs	Marshall	36	21	W	-4.0	W	56.0	O	New Orleans Bowl
Coach: Billy Napier		Season Record >>	435	259	13-1	ATS>>	7-7	O/U>>	4-10	SUN BELT CHAMPIONS

2020-Louisiana

Date		Opponent	ULL	Opp	S/U	Line	ATS	Total	O/U	
9/12/2020	@	Iowa State	31	14	W	11.5	W	56.0	U	
9/19/2020	@	Georgia State	34	31	W	-16.5	L	57.0	O	{OT}
9/26/2020	vs	GEORGIA SOUTHERN	20	18	W	-11.5	L	50.0	U	
10/14/2020	vs	COASTAL CAROLINA	27	30	L	-9.0	L	57.0	T	
10/23/2020	@	Alabama-Birmingham	24	20	W	-2.5	W	50.5	U	
10/31/2020	@	Texas State	44	34	W	-16.5	L	56.5	O	
11/7/2020	vs	ARKANSAS STATE	27	20	W	-14.5	L	68.5	U	
11/14/2020	vs	SOUTH ALABAMA	38	10	W	-14.5	W	53.5	U	
11/28/2020	@	Louisiana-Monroe	70	20	W	-29.0	W	58.0	O	"Battle of the Bayou"
12/4/2020	@	Appalachian State	24	21	W	3.0	W	51.0	U	
12/26/2020	vs	Texas-San Antonio	31	24	W	-13.5	L	55.0	T	First Responder Bowl
Coach: Billy Napier		Season Record >>	370	242	10-1	ATS>>	5-6	O/U>>	3-6-2	

2019-Louisiana

Date		Opponent	ULL	Opp	S/U	Line	ATS	Total	O/U	
8/31/2019	vs	Mississippi State	28	38	L	18.5	W	60.5	O	
9/7/2019	vs	LIBERTY	35	14	W	-14.0	W	65.5	U	
9/14/2019	vs	TEXAS SOUTHERN	77	6	W	-46.5	W	NT	---	
9/21/2019	@	Ohio	45	25	W	3.0	W	68.0	O	
9/28/2019	@	Georgia Southern	37	24	W	-3.0	W	55.0	O	
10/9/2019	vs	APPALACHIAN STATE	7	17	L	-3.0	L	69.0	U	
10/17/2019	@	Arkansas State	37	20	W	6.0	W	68.5	U	
11/2/2019	vs	TEXAS STATE	31	3	W	-23.0	W	55.0	U	
11/7/2019	@	Coastal Carolina	48	7	W	-14.0	W	58.0	U	
11/16/2019	@	South Alabama	37	27	W	-27.5	L	52.5	O	
11/23/2019	vs	TROY	53	3	W	-12.5	W	74.0	U	
11/30/2019	vs	LOUISIANA-MONROE	31	30	W	-20.0	L	71.0	U	"Battle of the Bayou"
12/7/2019	vs	Appalachian State	38	45	L	5.0	L	57.0	O	SUN BELT CHAMPIONSHIP
1/6/2020	vs	Miami-Ohio	27	17	W	-16.0	L	55.0	U	Lending Tree Bowl
Coach: Billy Napier		Season Record >>	531	276	11-3	ATS>>	9-5	O/U>>	5-8	

2018-Louisiana

Date		Opponent	ULL	Opp	S/U	Line	ATS	Total	O/U	
9/1/2018	vs	GRAMBLING STATE	49	17	W	-13.5	W	NT	---	
9/15/2018	@	Mississippi State	10	56	L	33.5	L	63.0	O	
9/22/2018	vs	COASTAL CAROLINA	28	30	L	-3.0	L	63.0	U	
9/29/2018	@	Alabama	14	56	L	49.0	W	69.0	O	
10/6/2018	@	Texas State	42	27	W	-3.5	W	58.5	O	
10/13/2018	vs	NEW MEXICO STATE	66	38	W	-7.0	W	67.5	O	
10/20/2018	@	Appalachian State	17	27	L	25.5	W	67.0	U	
10/27/2018	vs	ARKANSAS STATE	47	43	W	3.0	W	70.0	O	
11/3/2018	@	Troy	16	26	L	7.5	L	64.5	U	
11/10/2018	vs	GEORGIA STATE	36	22	W	-13.0	W	70.0	U	
11/17/2018	vs	SOUTH ALABAMA	48	38	W	-19.5	L	65.5	O	
11/24/2018	@	Louisiana-Monroe	31	28	W	1.5	W	72.0	U	"Battle of the Bayou"
12/1/2018	@	Appalachian State	19	30	L	17.0	W	55.0	U	SUN BELT CHAMPIONSHIP
12/15/2018	vs	Tulane	24	41	L	3.0	L	60.5	O	AutoNation Cure Bowl
Coach: Billy Napier		Season Record >>	447	479	7-7	ATS>>	9-5	O/U>>	7-6	

LOUISIANA RAGIN' CAJUNS — SUN BELT West

STADIUM: Cajun Field {41,264} **Location:** Lafayette, LA **COACH:** Michael DeSormeaux

DATE		Opponent	ULL	Opp	S/U	Line	ATS	Total	O/U	Trends & Angles
9/3/2022	vs	SE LOUISIANA								8-1 S/U vs SE Louisiana since 1966
9/10/2022	vs	EASTERN MICHIGAN								vs Eastern Michigan - Series tied 1-1
9/17/2022	@	Rice								vs Rice - Louisiana leads series 3-2
9/24/2022	@	Louisiana-Monroe								9-0 ATS @ Louisiana-Monroe since 2004
10/1/2022	vs	SOUTH ALABAMA								5-0 S/U @ home vs S. Alabama since 2012
10/12/2022	@	Marshall								vs Marshall - Louisiana leads series 1-0
10/22/2022	vs	ARKANSAS STATE								14-2 S/U vs Ark State as favorite since 1990
10/27/2022	@	Southern Mississippi								0-6 S/U @ Southern Miss since 1994
11/5/2022	vs	TROY								vs Troy - Louisiana leads series 13-9
11/10/2022	@	GEORGIA SOUTHERN								vs Ga Southern - Louisiana leads series 4-1
11/19/2022	@	Florida State								1st Meeting
11/26/2022	@	Texas State								vs Texas State - Louisiana leads series 9-0
12/3/2022	vs									Sun Belt Championship
	vs									BOWL GAME

Pointspread Analysis — Non-Conference

- 1-58 S/U vs Non-Conf. as 20.5 point or more Dog since 1989
- 3-21 S/U vs Non-Conf. as 10.5-20 point Dog since 1988
- 16-1 S/U vs Non-Conf. as 10.5 point or more favorite since 1988
- vs SE Louisiana - Louisiana leads series 19-17-3

Dog
- 0-41 S/U as 25.5 point or more Dog since 1991
- 0-66 S/U on road as 20.5 point or more Dog since 1989
- 3-17 S/U as 15.-20 point Dog since 1988
- 1-11 S/U as 10.5-15 point Dog since 2009
- 1-7 ATS as 10.5-15 point Dog since 2013
- 6-0 S/U @ home as 3.5-7 point Dog since 2009
- 6-21-1 O/U as 3.5-7 point Dog since 2001
- 11-1 ATS as 3 point or less Dog since 2013

Favorite
- 5-0 S/U & ATS on road as 3 point or less favorite since 2012
- 6-0 S/U on road as 3.5-7 point favorite since 2013
- 15-3 S/U as 7.5-10 point favorite since 1995
- 7-0 S/U on road as 7.5-10 point favorite since 1995
- 14-0 S/U as 10.5-15 point favorite since 2017
- 0-11-1 O/U as 10.5-15 point favorite since 2017
- 10-0 S/U on road as 10.5 point or more favorite since 1993
- 15-0 S/U @ home as 20.5 point or more favorite since 1996

Bowl Games
- 5-1 S/U & ATS in New Orleans Bowl
- 0-3 O/U in New Orleans Bowl since 2013
- 1-4 ATS in Bowl Games since 2016
- 7-2 S/U in Bowl Games since 2011

SE LOUISIANA	
E MICHIGAN	
Rice	
UL-Monroe	
UL-Monroe	
Marshall	
Southern Miss	
GA SOUTHERN	

Pointspread Analysis — Conference

- vs Arkansas State - Louisiana leads series 28-21-1
- vs UL-Monroe - Louisiana leads series 32-25
- vs Louisiana-Monroe - ROAD team 18-1 ATS since 2003
- 4-0 S/U & ATS vs UL-Monroe as Dog since 2009
- Game 5-2 O/U @ home vs Troy since 2005
- 8-0 S/U @ Louisiana-Monroe since 2005
- 4-0 S/U @ UL-Monroe as Dog since 2005
- 7-0 ATS @ UL-Monroe as Dog since 1998
- 5-0 S/U & ATS @ UL-Monroe as favorite since 2008
- 6-0 S/U vs South Alabama since 2016
- vs South Alabama - Louisiana leads series 8-2
- 7-0 S/U vs South Alabama as favorite since 2012
- 0-9 S/U vs Southern Miss since 1994
- vs Southern Miss - USM leads series 39-11-1
- 8-0 S/U vs Texas State as favorite since 2013 {7-1 ATS}
- 13-1 S/U in 1st home game of season since 2008
- 8-3-1 O/U in 2nd home game of season since 2007
- 3-28 S/U in 1st road game of season since 1990
- 5-23 S/U in 2nd road game of season since 1994
- 7-1 S/U prior to playing South Alabama since 2014
- 7-1 ATS prior to playing Arkansas State since 2013
- 9-1 S/U after playing Arkansas State since 2012
- 3-10 ATS in final home game of season since 2009
- 2-31 S/U vs ranked teams since 1985
- 8-3 O/U vs ranked teams since 2009
- 12-2 S/U when ranked all time

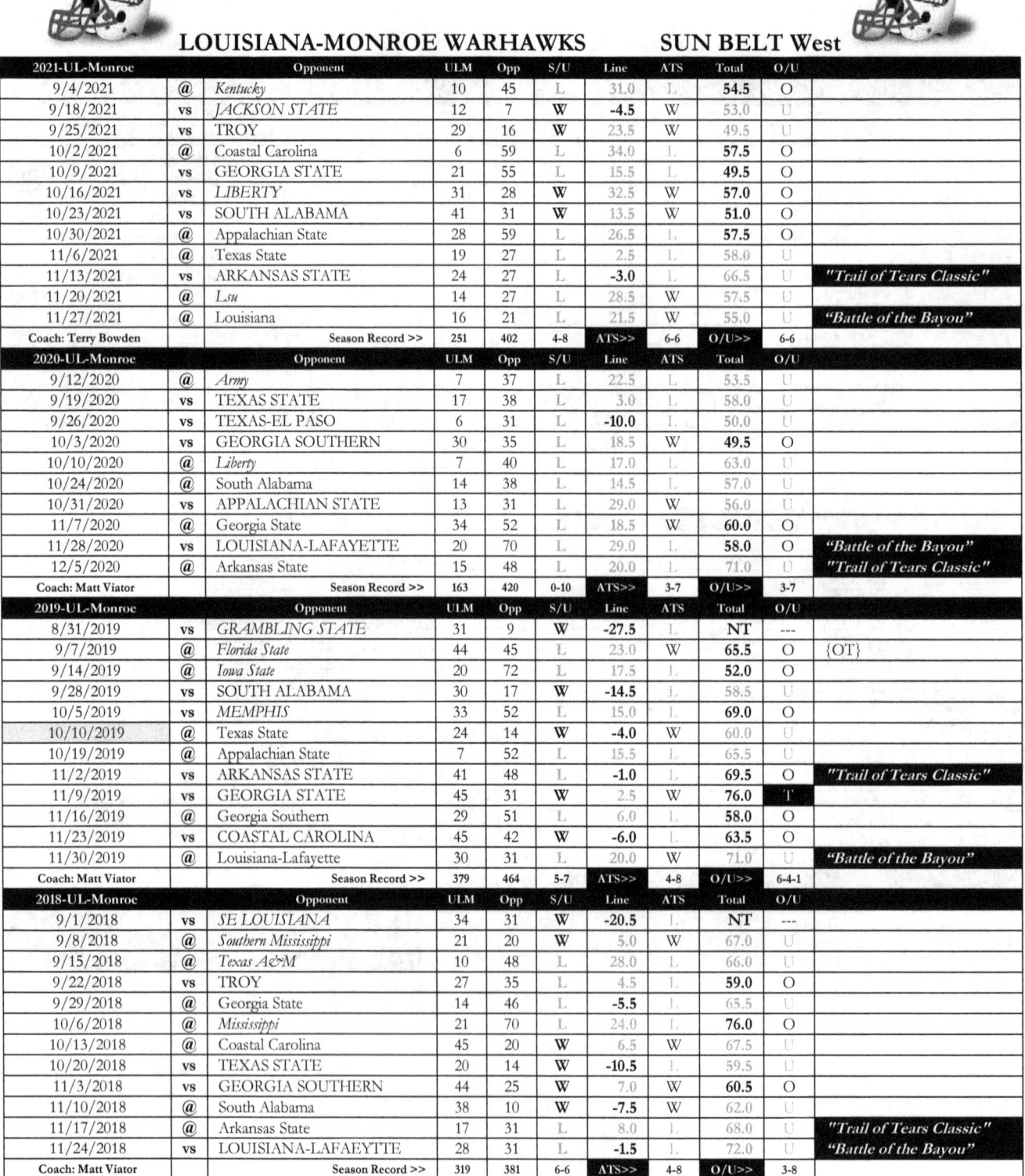

LOUISIANA-MONROE WARHAWKS   SUN BELT West

2021-UL-Monroe		Opponent	ULM	Opp	S/U	Line	ATS	Total	O/U	
9/4/2021	@	Kentucky	10	45	L	31.0	L	54.5	O	
9/18/2021	vs	JACKSON STATE	12	7	W	-4.5	W	53.0	U	
9/25/2021	vs	TROY	29	16	W	23.5	W	49.5	U	
10/2/2021	@	Coastal Carolina	6	59	L	34.0	L	57.5	O	
10/9/2021	vs	GEORGIA STATE	21	55	L	15.5	L	49.5	O	
10/16/2021	vs	LIBERTY	31	28	W	32.5	W	57.0	O	
10/23/2021	vs	SOUTH ALABAMA	41	31	W	13.5	W	51.0	O	
10/30/2021	@	Appalachian State	28	59	L	26.5	L	57.5	O	
11/6/2021	@	Texas State	19	27	L	2.5	L	58.0	U	
11/13/2021	vs	ARKANSAS STATE	24	27	L	-3.0	L	66.5	U	"Trail of Tears Classic"
11/20/2021	@	Lsu	14	27	L	28.5	W	57.5	U	
11/27/2021	@	Louisiana	16	21	L	21.5	W	55.0	U	"Battle of the Bayou"
Coach: Terry Bowden		Season Record >>	251	402	4-8	ATS>>	6-6	O/U>>	6-6	

2020-UL-Monroe		Opponent	ULM	Opp	S/U	Line	ATS	Total	O/U	
9/12/2020	@	Army	7	37	L	22.5	L	53.5	U	
9/19/2020	vs	TEXAS STATE	17	38	L	3.0	L	58.0	U	
9/26/2020	vs	TEXAS-EL PASO	6	31	L	-10.0	L	50.0	U	
10/3/2020	vs	GEORGIA SOUTHERN	30	35	L	18.5	W	49.5	O	
10/10/2020	@	Liberty	7	40	L	17.0	L	63.0	U	
10/24/2020	@	South Alabama	14	38	L	14.5	L	57.0	U	
10/31/2020	vs	APPALACHIAN STATE	13	31	L	29.0	W	56.0	U	
11/7/2020	@	Georgia State	34	52	L	18.5	W	60.0	O	
11/28/2020	vs	LOUISIANA-LAFAYETTE	20	70	L	29.0	L	58.0	O	"Battle of the Bayou"
12/5/2020	@	Arkansas State	15	48	L	20.0	L	71.0	U	"Trail of Tears Classic"
Coach: Matt Viator		Season Record >>	163	420	0-10	ATS>>	3-7	O/U>>	3-7	

2019-UL-Monroe		Opponent	ULM	Opp	S/U	Line	ATS	Total	O/U	
8/31/2019	vs	GRAMBLING STATE	31	9	W	-27.5	L	NT	---	
9/7/2019	@	Florida State	44	45	L	23.0	W	65.5	O	{OT}
9/14/2019	@	Iowa State	20	72	L	17.5	L	52.0	U	
9/28/2019	vs	SOUTH ALABAMA	30	17	W	-14.5	L	58.5	U	
10/5/2019	vs	MEMPHIS	33	52	L	15.0	L	69.0	O	
10/10/2019	@	Texas State	24	14	W	-4.0	W	60.0	U	
10/19/2019	@	Appalachian State	7	52	L	15.5	L	65.5	U	
11/2/2019	vs	ARKANSAS STATE	41	48	L	-1.0	L	69.5	O	"Trail of Tears Classic"
11/9/2019	vs	GEORGIA STATE	45	31	W	2.5	W	76.0	T	
11/16/2019	@	Georgia Southern	29	51	L	6.0	L	58.0	O	
11/23/2019	vs	COASTAL CAROLINA	45	42	W	-6.0	L	63.5	O	
11/30/2019	@	Louisiana-Lafayette	30	31	L	20.0	W	71.0	U	"Battle of the Bayou"
Coach: Matt Viator		Season Record >>	379	464	5-7	ATS>>	4-8	O/U>>	6-4-1	

2018-UL-Monroe		Opponent	ULM	Opp	S/U	Line	ATS	Total	O/U	
9/1/2018	vs	SE LOUISIANA	34	31	W	-20.5	L	NT	---	
9/8/2018	@	Southern Mississippi	21	20	W	5.0	W	67.0	U	
9/15/2018	@	Texas A&M	10	48	L	28.0	L	66.0	U	
9/22/2018	vs	TROY	27	35	L	4.5	L	59.0	O	
9/29/2018	@	Georgia State	14	46	L	-5.5	L	65.5	U	
10/6/2018	@	Mississippi	21	70	L	24.0	L	76.0	O	
10/13/2018	@	Coastal Carolina	45	20	W	6.5	W	67.5	U	
10/20/2018	vs	TEXAS STATE	20	14	W	-10.5	L	59.5	U	
11/3/2018	vs	GEORGIA SOUTHERN	44	25	W	7.0	W	60.5	O	
11/10/2018	@	South Alabama	38	10	W	-7.5	W	62.0	U	
11/17/2018	@	Arkansas State	17	31	L	8.0	L	68.0	U	"Trail of Tears Classic"
11/24/2018	vs	LOUISIANA-LAFAEYTTE	28	31	L	-1.5	L	72.0	U	"Battle of the Bayou"
Coach: Matt Viator		Season Record >>	319	381	6-6	ATS>>	4-8	O/U>>	3-8	

LOUISIANA-MONROE WARHAWKS — SUN BELT West

STADIUM: Malone Stadium {27,617} | **Location:** Monroe, LA | **COACH:** Terry Bowden

DATE		Opponent	ULM	Opp	S/U	Line	ATS	Total	O/U	Trends & Angles
9/3/2022	@	Texas								vs Texas - Texas leads series 1-0
9/10/2022	vs	NICHOLLS STATE								14-1 S/U @ home vs Nicholls State since 1973
9/17/2022	@	Alabama								vs Alabama - Series tied 2-2
9/24/2022	vs	LOUISIANA								vs Louisiana - Louisiana leads series 32-25
10/1/2022	@	Arkansas State								vs Ark State - Ark State leads series 29-14
10/8/2022	vs	COASTAL CAROLINA								vs Coastal Carolina - ULM leads series 3-1
10/15/2022	@	South Alabama								vs South Alabama - ULM leads series 5-3
10/22/2022	@	Army								vs Army - Army leads series 1-0
11/5/2022	vs	TEXAS STATE								vs Texas State - UL-Monroe leads series 12-6
11/12/2022	@	Georgia State								vs Georgia State - ULM leads series 4-3
11/19/2022	@	Troy								vs Troy - Troy leads series 10-8-1
11/26/2022	vs	SOUTHERN MISS								vs Southern Miss - USM leads series 4-2
12/3/2022	vs									Sun Belt Championship
	vs									BOWL GAME

Pointspread Analysis — Non-Conference

- 5-94 S/U vs Non-Conf. as 10.5 point or more Dog since 1994
- 6-0 S/U vs Non-Conf. as 15.5 point or more favorite since 2011
- vs Nicholls State - UL-Monroe leads series 23-3

Dog
- 1-38 S/U as 30.5 point or more Dog since 1994
- 1-22 S/U as 25.5-30 point Dog since 1997
- 3-20 S/U as 20.5-25 point Dog since 1995
- 5-13 ATS as 20.5-25 point Dog since 1997
- 2-21 S/U on road as 15.5-20 point Dog since 1994
- 13-5 O/U as 15.5-20 point Dog since 2002
- 3-18 S/U on road as 10.5-15 point Dog since 1994
- 11-4-1 O/U as 7.5-10 point Dog since 2001
- 1-10 S/U @ home as 3.5-7 point Dog since 2003

Favorite
- 3-0 S/U & ATS on road as 3 point or less favorite since 2004
- 1-8 O/U as 10.5-15 point favorite since 2006
- 10-0 S/U as 15.5 point or more favorite since 2008

- 2-35 S/U vs ranked teams all time

Pointspread Analysis — Conference

- 1-6 S/U & ATS vs Arkansas State as favorite since 1998
- 0-11 S/U vs Arkansas State as 6.5 point or more Dog since 2003
- 0-4 S/U & ATS vs Louisiana as favorite since 2009
- 0-5 O/U vs Louisiana as favorite since 2007
- 0-4 S/U & ATS @ home vs Louisiana as favorite since 2005
- 0-5 S/U @ home vs Louisiana as Dog since 2008 {1-4 ATS}
- Game 0-4 O/U vs Texas State since 2018

Texas	1-27 S/U in 1st road game of season since 1994
NICHOLLS	2-9 O/U in 1st home game of season since 2004
Alabama	2-28 S/U in 2nd road game of season since 1992
Alabama	1-8 S/U prior to playing Louisiana since 2013
LOUISIANA	2-9 ATS in 2nd home game of season since 2011
LOUISIANA	1-6 S/U prior to playing Arkansas State since 2015
Army	0-5 S/U after playing South Alabama since 2017 {1-4 ATS}
Army	2-10 S/U prior to playing Texas State since 1992
Georgia State	1-7 S/U after playing Texas State since 2014
Georgia State	2-12 S/U prior to playing Troy since 2001
Troy	8-3 ATS in final road game of season since 2011
SOUTHERN MISS	3-10 S/U in final home game of season since 2009
SOUTHERN MISS	2-11 ATS in final home game of season since 2009
SOUTHERN MISS	0-7 S/U after playing Troy since 2010

Print Version $29.95

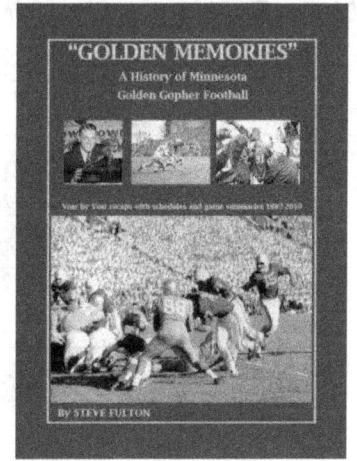

"GOLDEN MEMORIES" — A History of Minnesota Golden Gopher Football — By Steve Fulton

"Golden Gopher Fans" This book is available from Steve's Football Bible LLC

These books available at numerous online retailers

LOUISIANA TECH BULLDOGS   C-USA West

2021-Louisiana Tech		Opponent	Tech	Opp	S/U	Line	ATS	Total	O/U	
9/4/2021	@	Mississippi State	34	35	L	20.5	W	53.0	O	
9/11/2021	vs	SE LOUISIANA	45	42	W	-11.5	L	70.5	O	
9/18/2021	vs	SMU	37	39	L	11.0	W	66.0	O	
9/25/2021	vs	NORTH TEXAS	24	17	W	-9.5	L	65.0	U	
10/2/2021	@	NC State	27	34	L	18.5	W	55.5	O	
10/16/2021	@	Texas-El Paso	3	19	L	-6.5	L	55.5	U	
10/23/2021	vs	TEXAS-SAN ANTONIO	16	45	L	5.5	L	59.5	O	
10/30/2021	@	Old Dominion	20	23	L	-4.0	L	52.5	U	
11/6/2021	@	Alabama-Birmingham	38	52	L	14.0	T	48.5	O	
11/13/2021	vs	CHARLOTTE	42	32	W	-6.5	W	58.0	O	
11/20/2021	vs	SOUTHERN MISSISSIPPI	19	35	L	-15.0	L	47.5	O	"Rivalry in Dixie"
11/27/2021	@	Rice	31	35	L	-4.0	L	52.5	O	
Coach: Skip Holtz		Season Record >>	336	408	3-9	ATS>>	4-7-1	O/U>>	9-3	
2020-Louisiana Tech		Opponent	Tech	Opp	S/U	Line	ATS	Total	O/U	
9/19/2020	@	Southern Mississippi	31	30	W	7.5	W	58.5	O	"Rivalry in Dixie"
9/26/2020	vs	HOUSTON BAPTIST	66	38	W	-24.0	W	73.5	O	
10/3/2020	@	Byu	14	45	L	24.0	L	61.5	U	
10/10/2020	vs	TEXAS-EL PASO	21	17	W	-14.0	L	56.0	U	
10/17/2020	vs	MARSHALL	17	35	L	11.5	L	48.0	O	
10/24/2020	@	Texas-San Antonio	26	27	L	-2.5	L	54.5	U	
10/31/2020	vs	ALABAMA-BIRMINGHAM	37	34	W	13.0	W	47.0	O	{2 OT}
12/3/2020	@	North Texas	42	31	W	-1.0	W	65.0	O	
12/12/2020	@	Tcu	10	52	L	21.5	L	50.5	O	
12/23/2020	vs	Georgia Southern	3	38	L	7.5	L	47.5	U	New Orleans Bowl
Coach: Skip Holtz		Season Record >>	267	347	5-5	ATS>>	4-6	O/U>>	6-4	
2019-Louisiana Tech		Opponent	Tech	Opp	S/U	Line	ATS	Total	O/U	
8/31/2019	@	Texas	10	45	L	19.0	L	55.5	U	
9/7/2019	vs	GRAMBLING STATE	20	14	W	-30.0	L	NT	---	
9/14/2019	@	Bowling Green	35	17	W	-12.5	W	58.5	U	
9/21/2019	vs	FLORIDA INTERNATIONAL	43	31	W	-6.5	W	51.5	O	
9/28/2019	@	Rice	23	20	W	-8.0	L	49.0	U	{OT}
10/12/2019	vs	MASSACHUSETTS	69	21	W	-31.5	W	64.0	O	
10/19/2019	vs	SOUTHERN MISS	45	30	W	2.5	W	58.0	O	"Rivalry in Dixie"
10/26/2019	@	Texas-El Paso	42	21	W	-18.5	W	50.0	L	
11/9/2019	vs	NORTH TEXAS	52	17	W	-5.0	W	71.5	U	
11/16/2019	@	Marshall	10	31	L	6.0	L	54.5	U	
11/23/2019	@	Alabama-Birmingham	14	20	L	6.5	W	44.0	U	
11/30/2019	vs	TEXAS-SAN ANTONIO	41	27	W	-21.0	L	56.0	O	
12/26/2019	vs	Miami	14	0	W	7.0	W	49.5	U	Independence Bowl
Coach: Skip Holtz		Season Record >>	418	294	10-3	ATS>>	8-5	O/U>>	5-7	
2018-Louisiana Tech		Opponent	Tech	Opp	S/U	Line	ATS	Total	O/U	
9/1/2018	@	South Alabama	30	26	W	-10.5	L	53.0	O	
9/8/2018	vs	SOUTHERN	54	17	W	-34.5	W	NT	---	
9/22/2018	@	Lsu	21	38	L	19.5	W	51.0	O	
9/29/2018	@	North Texas	29	27	W	7.0	W	63.0	U	
10/6/2018	vs	ALABAMA-BIRMINGHAM	7	28	L	-6.5	L	55.5	U	
10/13/2018	@	Texas-San Antonio	31	3	W	-13.0	W	45.5	U	
10/20/2018	vs	TEXAS-EL PASO	31	24	W	-23.0	L	50.5	O	
10/27/2018	@	Florida Atlantic	21	13	W	3.5	W	58.5	U	
11/3/2018	@	Mississippi State	3	45	L	23.0	L	48.5	U	
11/10/2018	vs	RICE	28	13	W	-24.0	L	53.0	U	
11/17/2018	@	Southern Mississippi	20	21	L	2.0	W	47.0	U	"Rivalry in Dixie"
11/24/2018	vs	WESTERN KENTUCKY	15	30	L	-10.5	L	49.0	U	
12/22/2018	vs	Hawaii	31	14	W	1.0	W	61.5	U	HAWAI'I BOWL
Coach: Skip Holtz		Season Record >>	321	299	8-5	ATS>>	7-6	O/U>>	3-9	

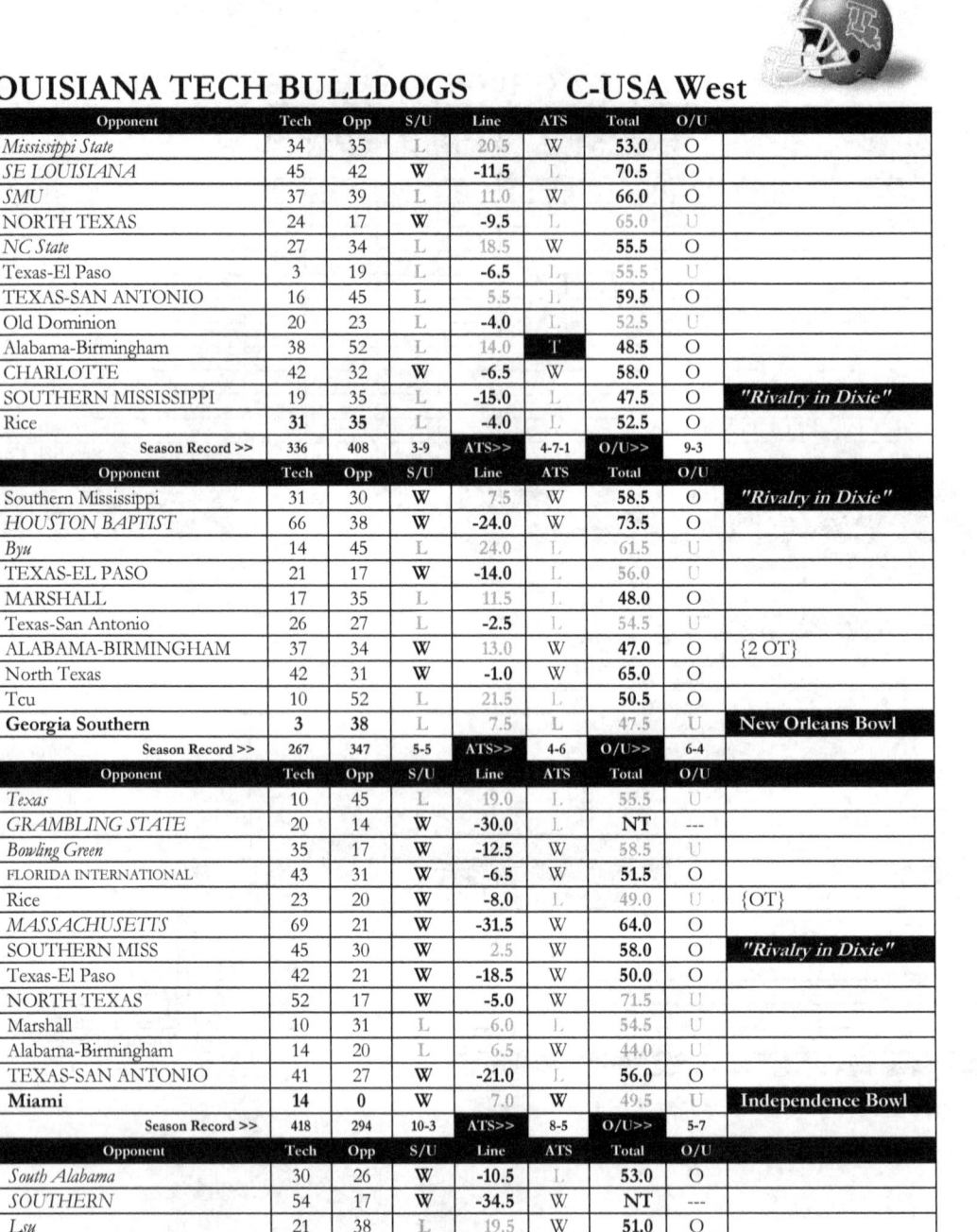

LOUISIANA TECH BULLDOGS — C-USA West

STADIUM: Joe Aillet Stadium {28,562} | **Location:** Ruston, LA | **COACH:** Sonny Cumbie

DATE		Opponent	Tech	Opp	S/U	Line	ATS	Total	O/U	Trends & Angles
9/1/2022	@	Missouri								4-20 S/U in 1st road game of season since 1997
9/10/2022	vs	STEPHEN F. AUSTIN								vs S.F. Austin - LA Tech leads series 4-1
9/17/2022	@	Clemson								0-3 S/U & ATS vs Clemson as Dog since 2001
9/24/2022	@	South Alabama								vs South Alabama - La Tech leads series 2-0
10/8/2022	vs	TEXAS-EL PASO								7-1 S/U @ home vs UTEP since 1940
10/15/2022	@	North Texas								5-0 S/U @ N. Texas since 2006 {5-0 ATS}
10/22/2022	vs	RICE								4-0 S/U @ home vs Rice since 2012
10/29/2022	@	Fla International								vs FIU - La Tech leads series 4-0
11/5/2022	vs	MIDDLE TENNESSEE								4-0 S/U @ home vs MTSU since 1984
11/12/2022	@	Texas-San Antonio								vs UTSA - La Tech leads series 7-3
11/19/2022	@	Charlotte								vs Charlotte - LA Tech leads series 1-0
11/26/2022	vs	ALABAMA-BIRMINGHAM								vs UAB - La Tech leads series 6-4
12/3/2022	vs									C-USA Championship
	vs									BOWL GAME

Non-Conference | Conference

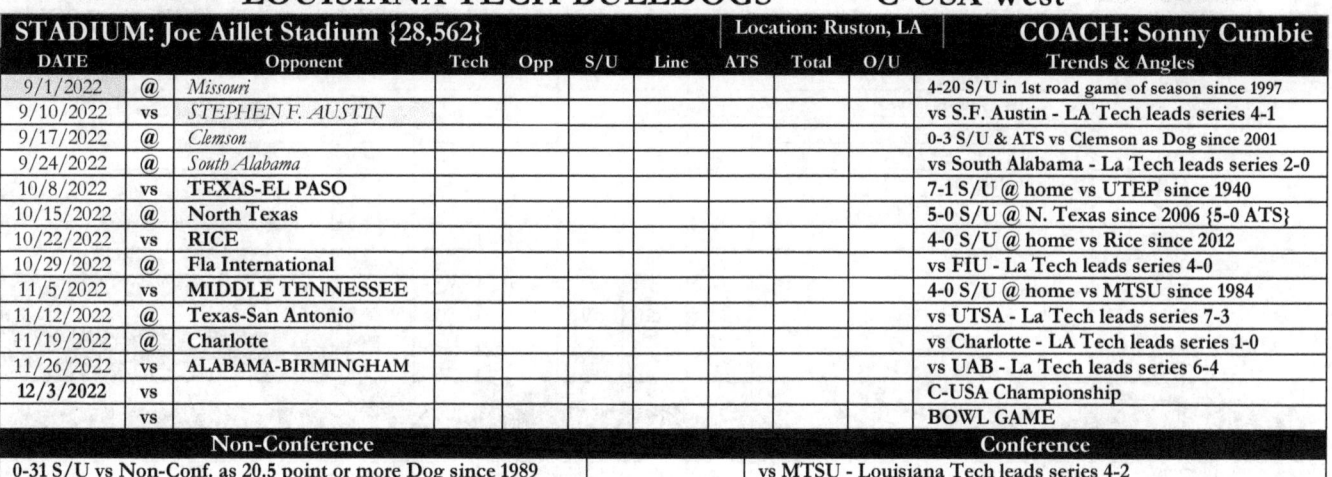

Non-Conference		Conference
0-31 S/U vs Non-Conf. as 20.5 point or more Dog since 1989		vs MTSU - Louisiana Tech leads series 4-2
2-11 S/U vs Non-Conf. as 15.5-20 point Dog since 1990		13-3 S/U vs North Texas since 1983
2-18 S/U vs Non-Conf. as 10.5-15 point Dog since 1993		vs North Texas - Louisiana Tech leads series 13-7
2-12 ATS vs Non-Conf. as 10.5-15 point Dog since 2001		6-0 S/U vs North Texas as favorite since 2005 {5-1 ATS}
4-15 S/U vs Non-Conf. as 3.5-10 point Dog since 1992		Game 4-1 O/U @ North Texas since 2006
4-0 S/U & ATS vs Non-Conf. as 3.5-7 point favorite since 1999		Game 3-1 O/U @ home vs Rice since 2012
4-0 S/U vs Non-Conf. as 15.5-20 point favorite since 1990		7-1 S/U vs Rice as favorite since 2012
8-0 S/U vs Non-Conf. as 25.5 point or more favorite since 2010		vs Rice - Louisiana Tech leads series 9-5

Dog

Dog		
		6-1 S/U vs Rice since 2014
0-21 S/U as 25.5 point or more Dog since 1993		6-1 S/U vs Texas-San Antonio as favorite since 2012
6-1 O/U as 25.5 point or more Dog since 2006		Game 5-2 O/U @ UTEP since 2001
1-23 S/U as 20.5-25 point Dog since 1989		8-1 S/U vs UTEP since 2013
0-7 S/U @ home as 20.5 point or more Dog since 1995		vs Texas-El Paso - Louisiana Tech leads series 14-3-1
0-10 S/U as 15.5-20 point Dog since 2000		10-0 S/U vs UTEP as 12.5 point or more favorite since 2001
1-14 S/U on road as 10.5-15 point Dog since 2005		**Bowl Games**
2-17 S/U as 10.5-15 point Dog since 2005		6-0 S/U in Bowl Games since 2014
9-0 O/U as 10.5-15 point Dog since 2014		
1-15 S/U on road as 7.5-10 point Dog since 1992		2-38 S/U on road vs ranked teams all time
0-7 S/U @ home as 3.5-7 point Dog since 2008		0-25 S/U vs Top 10 ranked teams all time
10-2 ATS on road as 3.5-7 point Dog since 2008	S.F. AUSTIN	16-1 S/U in 1st home game of season since 2004
Favorite	S.F. AUSTIN	2-9 ATS in 1st home game of season since 2010
20-6 S/U as 3.5-7 point favorite since 2003	Clemson	3-14 S/U in 2nd road game of season since 2004
18-8 ATS as 3.5-7 point favorite since 2003	Clemson	8-2 ATS in 2nd road game of season since 2011
8-1 S/U on road as 7.5-10 point favorite since 1990	South Alabama	8-2 O/U prior to playing Texas-El Paso since 2003
13-2 S/U @ home as 10.5-15 point favorite since 1993	South Alabama	9-0 ATS prior to playing North Texas since 2013 {7-2 S/U}
14-0 S/U on road as 15.5 point or more favorite since 1997	RICE	0-5 S/U after playing North Texas since 2017
53-1 S/U as 15.5 point or more favorite since 1990	FIU	8-2 O/U after playing Rice since 2001
9-1 O/U as 15.5-20 point favorite since 2009	Charlotte	0-6 O/U prior to playing UAB since 2014

Garnet and Gold – History of Florida State Seminoles Football
Paperback $29.95
Hardcover $34.95

Wild Blue Yonder! History of Air Force Falcons Football
Paperback $29.95
Hardcover $34.95

College Football Blueblood Series available at: www.stevesfootballbible.com

College Football Patriot Series available at: www.stevesfootballbible.com

LOUISVILLE CARDINALS — ACC Atlantic

2021-Louisville		Opponent	Ville	Opp	S/U	Line	ATS	Total	O/U	
9/6/2021	vs	Mississippi	28	43	L	9.0	L	75.0	U	Mercedes Benz Stadium
9/11/2021	vs	EASTERN KENTUCKY	30	3	W	-30.0	L	62.5	U	
9/17/2021	vs	CENTRAL FLORIDA	42	35	W	7.0	W	67.0	O	
9/25/2021	@	Florida State	31	23	W	1.5	W	61.0	U	
10/2/2021	@	Wake Forest	34	37	L	7.0	W	64.0	O	
10/9/2021	vs	VIRGINIA	33	34	L	-2.5	L	69.5	U	
10/23/2021	vs	BOSTON COLLEGE	28	14	W	-4.0	W	57.5	U	
10/30/2021	@	NC State	13	28	L	6.0	L	57.0	U	
11/6/2021	vs	CLEMSON	24	30	L	3.5	L	46.5	O	
11/13/2021	vs	SYRACUSE	41	3	W	-3.0	W	56.0	U	
11/18/2021	@	Duke	62	22	W	-20.0	W	60.5	O	
11/27/2021	vs	KENTUCKY	21	52	L	-3.0	L	58.0	O	"Governor's Cup"
12/28/2021	vs	Air Force	28	31	L	2.0	L	55.0	O	First Responder Bowl
Coach: Scott Satterfield		Season Record >>	415	355	6-7	ATS>>	6-7	O/U>>	6-7	

2020-Louisville		Opponent	Ville	Opp	S/U	Line	ATS	Total	O/U	
9/12/2020	vs	WESTERN KENTUCKY	35	21	W	-12.5	W	56.5	U	
9/19/2020	vs	MIAMI	34	47	L	2.5	L	66.0	O	
9/26/2020	@	Pittsburgh	20	23	L	3.0	T	54.0	U	
10/9/2020	@	Georgia Tech	27	46	L	-4.5	L	63.0	O	
10/17/2020	@	Notre Dame	7	12	L	17.0	W	62.0	U	
10/24/2020	vs	FLORIDA STATE	48	16	W	-5.0	W	62.0	O	
10/31/2020	vs	VIRGINIA TECH	35	42	L	2.5	L	67.5	O	
11/7/2020	@	Virginia	17	31	L	5.5	L	63.0	O	
11/20/2020	vs	SYRACUSE	30	0	W	-19.5	W	56.0	U	
11/28/2020	@	Boston College	27	34	L	1.0	L	57.0	O	
12/12/2020	vs	WAKE FOREST	45	21	W	2.0	W	61.0	O	
Coach: Scott Satterfield		Season Record >>	325	293	4-7	ATS>>	5-5-1	O/U>>	6-5	

2019-Louisville		Opponent	Ville	Opp	S/U	Line	ATS	Total	O/U	
9/2/2019	vs	NOTRE DAME	17	35	L	19.0	W	54.5	O	
9/7/2019	vs	EASTERN KENTUCKY	42	0	W	-20.0	W	NT	---	
9/14/2019	vs	Western Kentucky	38	21	W	-10.5	W	49.0	O	Nissan Stadium
9/21/2019	@	Florida State	24	35	L	7.0	L	61.0	U	
10/5/2019	vs	BOSTON COLLEGE	41	39	W	-3.5	L	61.0	O	
10/12/2019	@	Wake Forest	62	59	W	7.0	W	65.5	O	
10/19/2019	vs	CLEMSON	10	45	L	25.0	L	62.0	U	
10/26/2019	vs	VIRGINIA	28	21	W	4.0	W	51.0	U	
11/9/2019	@	Miami	27	52	L	6.5	L	49.0	O	
11/16/2019	@	NC State	34	20	W	-4.0	W	52.0	O	
11/23/2019	vs	SYRACUSE	56	34	W	-7.5	W	65.0	O	
11/30/2019	@	Kentucky	13	45	L	2.5	L	51.5	O	"Governor's Cup"
12/30/2019	vs	Mississippi State	38	28	W	4.5	W	63.5	O	Music City Bowl
Coach: Scott Satterfield		Season Record >>	430	434	8-5	ATS>>	8-5	O/U>>	8-4	

2018-Louisville		Opponent	Ville	Opp	S/U	Line	ATS	Total	O/U	
9/1/2018	vs	Alabama	14	51	L	23.5	L	60.0	O	Camping World Stadium
9/8/2018	vs	INDIANA STATE	31	7	W	-42.0	L	NT	---	
9/15/2018	vs	WESTERN KENTUCKY	20	17	W	-23.5	L	53.5	U	
9/22/2018	@	Virginia	3	27	L	5.0	L	51.5	U	
9/29/2018	vs	FLORIDA STATE	24	28	L	5.0	W	46.0	O	
10/5/2018	vs	GEORGIA TECH	31	66	L	5.5	L	56.0	O	
10/13/2018	@	Boston College	20	38	L	12.0	L	56.5	O	
10/27/2018	vs	WAKE FOREST	35	56	L	-2.5	L	67.5	O	
11/3/2018	@	Clemson	16	77	L	38.0	L	61.0	O	
11/9/2018	@	Syracuse	23	54	L	20.5	L	69.0	O	
11/17/2018	vs	NC STATE	10	52	L	16.0	L	65.5	U	
11/24/2018	vs	KENTUCKY	10	56	L	16.5	L	53.0	O	"Governor's Cup"
Coach: Bobby Petrino		Season Record >>	237	529	2-10	ATS>>	1-11	O/U>>	8-3	

LOUISVILLE CARDINALS — ACC Atlantic

STADIUM: Papa John's Cardinal Stadium {61,000} **Location:** Louisville, KY **COACH:** Scott Satterfield

DATE		Opponent	UL	Opp	S/U	Line	ATS	Total	O/U	Trends & Angles
9/3/2022	@	Syracuse								7-1 ATS vs Syracuse since 2014
9/10/2022	@	Central Florida								vs C. Florida - Louisville leads series 2-1
9/16/2022	vs	FLORIDA STATE								vs Florida State - Florida St leads series 17-5
9/24/2022	vs	SOUTH FLORIDA								4-1 S/U @ home vs South Florida since 2004
10/1/2022	@	Boston College								0-4 S/U & ATS @ BC as Dog since 1986
10/8/2022	@	Virginia								0-4 ATS @ Virginia since 2014
10/22/2022	vs	PITTSBURGH								Game 0-4 O/U @ home vs Pitt since 2005
10/29/2022	vs	WAKE FOREST								Game 5-0 O/U vs Wake Forest since 2017
11/5/2022	vs	JAMES MADISON								1st Meeting
11/12/2022	@	Clemson								vs Clemson - Clemson leads series 7-0
11/19/2022	vs	NC STATE								4-1 S/U @ home vs NC State since 1951
11/26/2022	@	Kentucky								vs Kentucky - Kentucky leads series 18-15
12/3/2022	vs									ACC Championship
	vs									BOWL GAME

Pointspread Analysis — Non-Conference

- 1-14 S/U vs Non-Conf. as 15.5 point or more Dog since 1984
- 1-10 S/U vs Non-Conf. as 10.5-15 point Dog since 1992
- 1-8 ATS vs Non-conf. as 3 point or less Dog since 2002
- 1-8 S/U vs Non-conf. as 3 point or less Dog since 2002
- 0-5 S/U vs Non-Conf. as 7.5-10 point favorite since 2004
- 13-4 S/U vs Non-Conf. as 10.5-15 point favorite since 2002
- 38-1 S/U vs Non-conf. as 20.5 point or more favorite since 1990
- vs South Florida - Louisville leads series 6-5
- Game 0-3 O/U @ home vs South Florida since 2008
- 6-2 S/U @ Kentucky as favorite since 1999

Dog

- 5-1 ATS as 30.5 point or more Dog since 1984
- 0-9 S/U @ home as 15.5 point or more Dog since 1984
- 2-33 S/U as 15.5 point or more Dog since 1984
- 1-8 ATS @ home as 15.5-25 point Dog since 1984
- 2-15 S/U on road as 10.5-15 point Dog since 1989
- 1-10 S/U as 7.5-10 point Dog since 1995
- 0-5 S/U & ATS @ home as 7.5-10 point Dog since 1985
- 3-8 S/U & ATS @ home as 3.5-7 point Dog since 2008
- 2-9 S/U & ATS @ home as 3 point or less Dog since 1997

Favorite

- 9-18 O/U as 3.5-7 point favorite since 2001
- 14-4 S/U as 3.5-7 point favorite since 2008
- 3-11 O/U @ home as 3.5-7 point favorite since 2001
- 2-9 O/U as 7.5-10 point favorite since 2001
- 6-1 S/U on road as 7.5-10 point favorite since 1988
- 12-1 S/U on road as 10.5-15 point favorite since 2000
- 1-8 O/U on road as 10.5-15 point favorite since 2005
- 27-7 S/U @ home as 10.5-15 point favorite since 1989
- 14-1 S/U @ home as 15.5-20 point favorite since 1990
- 22-0 S/U as 20.5-25 point favorite since 1990
- 14-0 S/U @ home as 20.5-25 point favorite since 1990
- 1-7 O/U @ home as 20.5-25 point favorite since 2005
- 18-0 S/U on road as 20.5 point or more favorite since 1990
- 1-7 O/U as 25.5-30 point favorite since 2004
- 24-1 S/U as 30.5 point or more favorite since 2000
- 3-13-1 ATS as 30.5 point or more favorite since 2006

Pointspread Analysis — Conference

- vs Boston College - Louisville leads series 8-6
- 0-6 S/U vs Clemson as Dog since 2014
- vs NC State - Louisville leads series 7-4
- 1-6 S/U vs Pittsburgh since 2008
- 0-3 S/U & ATS vs Pittsburgh as Dog since 2008
- 0-3 O/U vs Pittsburgh as Dog since 2008
- vs Syracuse - Louisville leads series 13-7
- 7-0 S/U & ATS vs Syracuse as favorite since 2014
- 10-2 S/U vs Syracuse since 2009
- Game 0-6 O/U vs Virginia since 2016
- vs Virginia - Series tied 5-5
- 3-1 S/U vs Virginia as favorite since 2015
- vs Wake Forest - Louisville leads series 6-3
- 0-5 ATS vs Wake Forest as favorite since 2014
- 6-0 S/U vs Pittsburgh as 3.5 point or more favorite since 1992

Bowl Games

- 0-4 S/U & ATS in Bowl Games as 3 point or less Dog since 2002
- 3-0 S/U & ATS in Bowl Games as 3 point or less favorite since 2001
- 2-5 O/U in Bowl Games since 2013

S. FLORIDA	18-4 S/U in 2nd home game of season since 2000
S. FLORIDA	4-10 ATS in 2nd home game of season since 2007
S. FLORIDA	2-8-1 ATS after playing Florida State since 1991
S. FLORIDA	2-10 ATS prior to playing Boston College since 1990
Virginia	7-2 S/U after playing Boston College since 1998
NC STATE	3-11 ATS in final home game of season since 2008
Kentucky	1-8 ATS after playing NC State since 1994

- 21-7 S/U on road when ranked since 2005
- 44-8 S/U @ home when ranked all time
- 0-7 S/U on road when ranked vs ranked teams all time
- 13-0 S/U when ranked #5 #6 #7 all time
- 4-42 S/U on road vs ranked teams all time
- 0-3 S/U vs #1 ranked teams all time
- 0-5 S/U & ATS vs ranked Clemson all time

Page | 113 Copyright © 2022 by Steve's Football Bible, LLC

LSU TIGERS — SEC West

2021-LSU		Opponent	LSU	Opp	S/U	Line	ATS	Total	O/U	
9/4/2021	@	Ucla	27	38	L	-1.5	L	64.0	O	
9/11/2021	vs	MCNEESE STATE	34	7	W	-39.0	L	66.0	U	
9/18/2021	vs	CENTRAL MICHIGAN	49	21	W	-19.5	W	60.5	O	
9/25/2021	@	Mississippi State	28	25	W	-1.5	W	54.5	U	
10/2/2021	vs	AUBURN	19	24	L	-3.0	L	56.0	U	
10/9/2021	@	Kentucky	21	42	L	2.0	L	50.5	O	
10/16/2021	vs	FLORIDA	49	42	W	12.5	W	61.0	O	
10/23/2021	@	Mississippi	17	31	L	9.5	L	77.5	U	"Magnolia Bowl Trophy"
11/6/2021	@	Alabama	14	20	L	29.0	W	66.5	U	
11/13/2021	vs	ARKANSAS	13	16	L	3.0	T	59.5	U	"The Golden Boot"
11/20/2021	vs	LOUISIANA-MONROE	27	14	W	-28.5	L	57.5	U	
11/27/2021	vs	TEXAS A&M	27	24	W	6.0	W	46.5	O	
1/4/2022	vs	Kansas State	20	42	L	9.5	L	46.5	O	Texas Bowl
Coach: Ed Orgeron		Season Record >>	345	346	6-7	ATS>>	5-7-1	O/U>>	6-7	

2020-LSU		Opponent	LSU	Opp	S/U	Line	ATS	Total	O/U	
9/26/2020	vs	MISSISSIPPI STATE	34	44	L	-14.0	L	57.0	O	
10/3/2020	@	Vanderbilt	41	7	W	-21.0	W	50.0	U	
10/10/2020	@	Missouri	41	45	L	-13.5	L	53.0	O	
10/24/2020	vs	SOUTH CAROLINA	52	24	W	-5.0	W	55.0	O	
10/31/2020	@	Auburn	11	48	L	PK	L	63.5	U	
11/21/2020	@	Arkansas	27	24	W	-1.5	W	65.0	U	"The Golden Boot"
11/28/2020	@	Texas A&M	7	20	L	16.0	W	59.5	U	
12/5/2020	vs	ALABAMA	17	55	L	28.5	L	63.5	O	
12/12/2020	@	Florida	37	34	W	23.0	W	66.0	O	
12/19/2020	vs	MISSISSIPPI	53	48	W	PK	W	74.5	O	"Magnolia Bowl Trophy"
Coach: Ed Orgeron		Season Record >>	320	349	5-5	ATS>>	6-4	O/U>>	6-4	

2019-LSU		Opponent	LSU	Opp	S/U	Line	ATS	Total	O/U	
8/31/2019	vs	GEORGIA SOUTHERN	55	3	W	-27.0	W	52.5	O	
9/7/2019	@	Texas	45	38	W	-7.0	T	57.0	O	
9/14/2019	vs	NORTHWESTERN STATE	65	14	W	-51.5	L	NT	---	
9/21/2019	@	Vanderbilt	66	38	W	-24.0	W	62.5	O	
10/5/2019	vs	UTAH STATE	42	6	W	-27.5	W	72.5	U	
10/12/2019	vs	FLORIDA	42	28	W	-14.0	T	55.0	O	
10/19/2019	@	Mississippi State	36	13	W	-19.0	W	62.5	U	
10/26/2019	vs	AUBURN	23	20	W	-11.5	L	59.5	U	
11/9/2019	@	Alabama	46	41	W	4.5	W	65.0	O	
11/16/2019	@	Mississippi	58	37	W	-21.5	W	67.0	O	"Magnolia Bowl Trophy"
11/23/2019	vs	ARKANSAS	56	20	W	-40.0	L	69.5	O	"The Golden Boot"
11/30/2019	vs	TEXAS A&M	50	7	W	-18.0	W	64.5	U	
12/7/2019	vs	Georgia	37	10	W	-7.0	W	57.0	U	SEC Championship
12/28/2019	vs	Oklahoma	63	28	W	-12.0	W	75.0	O	Chick-Fil-A Peach Bowl (National Semifinal)
1/13/2020	vs	Clemson	42	25	W	-4.0	W	66.5	O	CFB Championship Game
Coach: Ed Orgeron		Season Record >>	726	328	15-0	ATS>>	10-3-2	O/U>>	9-5	SEC Champions/National Champs

2018-LSU		Opponent	LSU	Opp	S/U	Line	ATS	Total	O/U	
9/2/2018	vs	Miami	33	17	W	3.0	W	47.5	O	AT&T Stadium
9/8/2018	vs	SE LOUISIANA	31	0	W	-40.0	L	NT	---	
9/15/2018	@	Auburn	22	21	W	10.0	W	45.0	U	
9/22/2018	vs	LOUISIANA TECH	38	21	W	-19.5	L	51.0	O	
9/29/2018	vs	MISSISSIPPI	45	16	W	-11.5	W	59.0	O	"Magnolia Bowl Trophy"
10/6/2018	@	Florida	19	27	L	-1.5	L	44.5	O	
10/13/2018	vs	GEORGIA	36	16	W	6.5	W	50.5	O	
10/20/2018	vs	MISSISSIPPI STATE	19	3	W	-6.0	W	45.0	U	
11/3/2018	vs	ALABAMA	0	29	L	13.5	L	51.5	U	
11/10/2018	@	Arkansas	24	17	W	-13.0	L	49.5	U	"The Golden Boot"
11/17/2018	vs	RICE	42	10	W	-42.0	L	51.5	O	
11/24/2018	@	Texas A&M	72	74	L	2.5	W	45.5	O	{7 OT}
1/1/2019	vs	Central Florida	40	32	W	-7.0	W	58.5	O	Fiesta Bowl
Coach: Ed Orgeron		Season Record >>	421	283	10-3	ATS>>	7-6	O/U>>	8-4	

LSU TIGERS — SEC West

STADIUM: Tiger Stadium (Death Valley) {102,321} **Location:** Baton Rouge, LA **COACH:** Brian Kelly

DATE		Opponent	LSU	Opp	S/U	Line	ATS	Total	O/U	Trends & Angles
9/4/2022	vs	*Florida State {@ New Orleans}*								0-4 S/U vs Florida State since 1983
9/10/2022	vs	SOUTHERN								25-2 S/U in 1st home game of season since 1995
9/17/2022	vs	MISSISSIPPI STATE								13-2 S/U @ home vs Mississippi State since 1992
9/24/2022	vs	*NEW MEXICO*								12-0 S/U prior to playing Auburn since 2010
10/1/2022	@	Auburn								2-8 S/U @ Auburn as Dog since 1989
10/8/2022	vs	TENNESSEE								5-0 S/U vs Tennessee since 2006
10/15/2022	@	Florida								vs Florida - Florida leads series 33-32-3
10/22/2022	vs	MISSISSIPPI								6-0 S/U @ home vs Mississippi since 2010
11/5/2022	vs	ALABAMA								1-10 S/U vs Alabama as Dog since 2012
11/12/2022	@	Arkansas								0-4 S/U @ Arkansas as Dog since 1998
11/19/2022	vs	*ALABAMA-BIRMINGHAM*								1st Meeting
11/26/2022	@	Texas A&M								11-0 ATS vs Texas A&M since 2011
12/3/2022	vs									SEC Championship
	vs									BOWL GAME

Pointspread Analysis — Non-Conference
- 0-7 S/U vs Non-Conf. as 10.5 point or more Dog since 1990
- 4-0 S/U vs Non-Conf. as 3.5-7 point Dog since 2004
- 11-2 S/U vs Non-Conf. as 3.5-7 point favorite since 1995
- 9-1 O/U vs Non-Conf. as 3.5-7 point favorite since 1997
- 0-4 ATS vs Non-Conf. as 7.5-10 point favorite since 2010
- 12-1 S/U vs Non-Conf. as 10.5-15 point favorite since 1984
- 12-1 S/U vs Non-Conf. as 15.5-20 point favorite since 1985
- 62-1 S/U vs Non-conf. as 20.5 point or more favorite since 1983
- vs Florida State - FSU leads series 7-2

Dog
- 9-1 ATS as 20.5 point or more Dog since 1991
- 2-8 S/U as 20.5 point or more Dog since 1991
- 1-6 S/U as 15.5-20 point Dog since 1990
- 1-16 S/U as 10.5-15 point Dog since 1990
- 4-13 ATS as 10.5-15 point Dog since 1990
- 1-8-1 O/U as 7.5-10 point Dog since 2000
- 2-7 S/U on road as 7.5-10 point Dog since 1994

Favorite
- 2-9 ATS @ home as 3 point or less favorite since 1989
- 2-9 O/U as 3 point or less favorite since 2014
- 2-8 O/U on road as 3 point or less favorite since 2008
- 2-8 ATS @ home as 3 point or less favorite since 1989
- 16-2 S/U on road as 3.5-7 point favorite since 1997
- 13-3 S/U @ home as 3.5-7 point favorite since 1998
- 9-1 S/U @ home as 7.5-10 point favorite since 2003
- 24-4 S/U @ home as 10.5-15 point favorite since 1987
- 14-2 S/U on road as 10.5-15 point favorite since 1984
- 10-0 S/U on road as 15.5-20 point favorite since 1997
- 25-0 S/U as 15.5-20 point favorite since 1997
- 78-1 S/U as 20.5 point or more favorite since 1983

Bowl Games
- 6-1 S/U in Chick-Fil-A Peach Bowl
- 0-4 S/U vs Nebraska in Bowl Games
- 10-2 S/U vs ACC teams in Bowl Games
- 1-4 O/U in Peach Bowl since 1996
- 3-0 S/U & ATS in Sugar Bowl since 2002
- 0-3 O/U in Citrus Bowl since 2010
- 0-3 S/U in Orange Bowl since 1971

Pointspread Analysis — Conference
- vs Alabama - Alabama leads series 55-26-5
- 6-0 S/U vs Alabama as favorite since 2000
- Game 2-8-2 O/U vs Alabama since 2011
- 1-12-1 S/U @ home vs Alabama as Dog since 1983
- vs Arkansas - LSU leads series 42-23-2
- vs Auburn - LSU leads series 31-24-1
- 0-3 ATS @ Florida as favorite since 2012
- vs Mississippi - LSU leads series 64-42-4
- 5-1 S/U & ATS vs Ole Miss since 2016
- 19-3 S/U vs Mississippi State since 2000
- 26-3 S/U vs Mississippi State as favorite since 1985
- Game 1-6 O/U vs Mississippi State since 2015
- vs Mississippi State - LSU leads series 74-38-3
- 6-0 ATS vs Mississippi State as Dog since 1992
- 4-0 ATS vs Tennessee as Dog since 1993
- 9-2 S/U vs Texas A&M since 2011
- 10-1 S/U vs Texas A&M as favorite since 1986
- vs Texas A&M - LSU leads series 35-22-3
- 1-7 S/U vs Texas A&M as Dog since 1991
- 12-1 S/U vs Arkansas as 9.5 point or more favorite since 1996
- 10-1 S/U vs Auburn as 5.5 point or more favorite since 1998
- 10-1 S/U vs Ole Miss as 12 point or more favorite since 1987

MISS STATE	23-1 S/U in 2nd home game of season since 1998
MISS STATE	2-9-1 ATS in 2nd home game of season since 2010
Auburn	3-9 O/U in 1st road game of season since 2010
TENNESSEE	19-1 S/U after playing Auburn since 2002
Florida	18-1 S/U prior to playing Mississippi since 2003
Alabama	1-8 S/U after playing Mississippi since 2012
MISSISSIPPI	12-2 S/U after playing Florida since 2008
MISSISSIPPI	17-3 S/U prior to playing Alabama since 2002
MISSISSIPPI	9-2 ATS prior to playing Alabama since 2011
Arkansas	19-3 S/U after playing Alabama since 2000

- 0-6 S/U when ranked vs #1 Alabama all time
- 19-2 S/U @ home when ranked vs Mississippi State since 1949
- 10-1 ATS when ranked vs Texas A&M since 1986
- 1-21-1 S/U @ home vs ranked Alabama all time
- 1-6 S/U @ home vs ranked Tennessee all time

Geaux Tigers! History of the LSU Tigers Football

Available at: www.stevesfootballbible.com (Blueblood Series)

MARSHALL THUNDERING HERD   Sun Belt East

2021-Marshall		Opponent	Marsh	Opp	S/U	Line	ATS	Total	O/U	
9/4/2021	@	Navy	49	7	W	-3.5	W	45.5	O	
9/11/2021	vs	NORTH CAROLINA CENTRAL	44	10	W	-42.5	L	53.5	O	
9/18/2021	vs	EAST CAROLINA	38	42	L	-10.5	L	58.5	O	
9/23/2021	@	Appalachian State	30	31	L	7.0	W	57.0	O	
10/2/2021	@	Middle Tennessee	28	34	L	-10.5	L	66.0	U	
10/9/2021	vs	OLD DOMINION	20	13	W	-21.0	L	62.0	U	{OT}
10/15/2021	@	North Texas	49	21	W	-11.0	W	66.0	O	
10/30/2021	vs	FLORIDA INTERNATIONAL	38	0	W	-21.5	W	64.0	U	
11/6/2021	@	Florida Atlantic	28	13	W	-1.5	W	58.0	U	
11/13/2021	vs	ALABAMA-BIRMINGHAM	14	21	L	-4.5	L	55.0	U	
11/20/2021	@	Charlotte	48	29	W	-14.5	W	62.5	O	
11/27/2021	vs	WESTERN KENTUCKY	21	53	L	2.0	L	76.0	U	
12/18/2021	vs	Louisiana	21	36	L	4.0	L	56.0	O	New Orleans Bowl
Coach: Charles Huff		Season Record >>	428	310	7-6	ATS>>	6-7	O/U>>	7-6	
2020-Marshall		Opponent	Marsh	Opp	S/U	Line	ATS	Total	O/U	
9/5/2020	@	EASTERN KENTUCKY	59	0	W	-25.5	W	55.0	O	
9/19/2020	vs	APPALACHIAN STATE	17	7	W	6.0	W	59.5	U	
10/10/2020	@	Western Kentucky	38	14	W	-6.5	W	43.0	O	
10/17/2020	@	Louisiana Tech	35	17	W	-11.5	W	48.0	O	
10/24/2020	vs	FLORIDA ATLANTIC	20	9	W	-19.5	L	51.0	U	
11/7/2020	vs	MASSACHUSETTS	51	10	W	-44.0	L	55.5	O	
11/14/2020	vs	MIDDLE TENNESSEE	42	14	W	-23.5	W	55.5	O	
12/5/2020	vs	RICE	0	20	L	-24.5	L	42.5	L	
12/18/2020	vs	ALABAMA-BIRMINGHAM	13	22	L	-4.0	L	44.0	U	C-USA Championship Game
12/25/2020	vs	Buffalo	10	17	L	5.0	L	53.5	U	Camelia Bowl
Coach: Doc Holliday		Season Record >>	285	130	7-3	ATS>>	5-5	O/U>>	5-5	
2019-Marshall		Opponent	Marsh	Opp	S/U	Line	ATS	Total	O/U	
8/31/2019	vs	VIRGINIA MILITARY	56	17	W	-41.0	L	NT	---	
9/6/2019	@	Boise State	7	14	L	14.0	W	57.0	U	
9/14/2019	vs	OHIO	33	31	W	-4.5	L	47.5	O	"Battle for the Bell"
9/28/2019	vs	CINCINNATI	14	52	L	4.0	L	47.5	O	
10/5/2019	@	Middle Tennessee	13	24	L	-4.0	L	53.5	U	
10/12/2019	vs	OLD DOMINION	31	17	W	-16.0	L	46.5	O	
10/19/2019	@	Florida Atlantic	36	31	W	4.0	W	58.0	O	
10/26/2019	vs	WESTERN KENTUCKY	26	23	W	-3.5	L	45.0	O	
11/2/2019	@	Rice	20	7	W	-12.0	W	48.0	U	
11/16/2019	vs	LOUISIANA TECH	31	10	W	-6.0	W	54.5	U	
11/23/2019	@	Charlotte	13	24	L	-7.0	L	55.5	U	
11/30/2019	vs	FLORIDA INTERNATIONAL	30	27	W	-10.0	L	49.5	O	
12/23/2019	vs	Central Florida	25	48	L	15.5	L	59.5	O	Gasparilla Bowl
Coach: Doc Holliday		Season Record >>	335	325	8-5	ATS>>	4-9	O/U>>	7-5	
2018-Marshall		Opponent	Marsh	Opp	S/U	Line	ATS	Total	O/U	
9/1/2018	@	Miami-Ohio	35	28	W	1.5	W	51.5	O	
9/8/2018	vs	EASTERN KENTUCKY	32	16	W	-31.0	L	NT	---	
9/22/2018	vs	NC STATE	20	37	L	5.5	L	57.0	T	
9/29/2018	@	Western Kentucky	20	17	W	-3.5	L	51.5	U	
10/5/2018	vs	MIDDLE TENNESSEE	24	34	L	-3.0	L	50.5	O	
10/13/2018	@	Old Dominion	42	20	W	-3.5	W	57.0	O	
10/20/2018	vs	FLORIDA ATLANTIC	31	7	W	2.5	W	60.0	U	
11/3/2018	@	Southern Mississippi	24	26	L	-2.5	L	45.5	O	
11/10/2018	vs	CHARLOTTE	30	13	W	-12.0	W	41.5	O	
11/17/2018	vs	TEXAS-SAN ANTONIO	23	0	W	-27.5	L	47.0	U	
11/24/2018	@	Florida International	28	25	W	-3.0	T	52.5	O	
12/1/2018	@	Virginia Tech	20	41	L	4.0	L	51.5	O	
12/20/2018	vs	South Florida	38	20	W	-3.0	W	50.0	O	Gasparilla Bowl
Coach: Doc Holliday		Season Record >>	367	284	9-4	ATS>>	5-7-1	O/U>>	8-3-1	

MARSHALL THUNDERING HERD — Sun Belt East

STADIUM: Joan C. Edwards Stadium {38,227} **Location:** Huntington, WV **COACH:** Charles Huff

DATE		Opponent	Herd	Opp	S/U	Line	ATS	Total	O/U	Trends & Angles
9/3/2022	vs	NORFOLK STATE								vs Norfolk State - Marshall leads series 1-0
9/10/2022	@	Notre Dame								6-0 ATS in 1st road game of season since 2016
9/17/2022	@	Bowling Green								vs Bowling Green - BGU leads series 21-8
9/24/2022	@	Troy								vs Troy - Marshall leads series 3-2
10/1/2022	vs	GARDNER-WEBB								vs Gardner-Webb - Marshall leads series 1-0
10/15/2022	vs	LOUISIANA								vs Louisiana - Louisiana leads series 1-0
10/22/2022	@	James Madison								vs James Madison - Marshall leads series 2-0
10/29/2022	vs	COASTAL CAROLINA								1st Meeting
11/5/2022	@	Old Dominion								6-0 S/U vs Old Dominion as favorite since 2014
11/12/2022	vs	APPALACHIAN STATE								vs App State - App State leads series 15-7
11/19/2022	@	Georgia Southern								vs Ga Southern - Marshall leads series 4-2
11/26/2022	vs	GEORGIA STATE								13-4 O/U in final home game of season since 2005
12/3/2022	vs									Sun Belt Championship
	vs									BOWL GAME

Pointspread Analysis — Non-Conference
- 1-28 S/U vs Non-Conf. as 7.5 point or more Dog since 1997
- 8-2 S/U & ATS vs Non-conf. as 3 point or less Dog since 1997
- 2-6 O/U vs Non-Conf. as 3 point or less favorite since 1999
- 12-0 S/U vs Non-Conf. as 20.5 point or more favorite since 2012

Dog
- 1-23 S/U on road as 15.5 point or more Dog since 1997
- 0-6 S/U @ home as 10.5 point or more Dog since 2007
- 11-3 O/U as 20.5 point or more Dog since 2005
- 2-12 S/U as 10.5-15 point Dog since 2002
- 1-12 O/U as 10.5-15 point Dog since 2003
- 1-9 S/U on road as 7.5-10 point Dog since 2000
- 2-7 S/U on road as 3.5-7 point Dog since 2006

Favorite
- 6-1 S/U & ATS @ home as 3 point or less favorite since 1998
- 10-3 S/U on road as 3.5-7 point favorite since 1999
- 10-2 S/U @ home as 3.5-7 point favorite since 2009
- 8-1 S/U @ home as 7.5-10 point favorite since 1997
- 3-9 O/U as 10.5-15 point favorite since 2011
- 12-3 S/U @ home as 10.5-15 point favorite since 1997
- 16-4 S/U on road as 10.5-15 point favorite since 1997
- 16-2 S/U as 15.5-20 point favorite since 1998
- 0-5 O/U on road as 15.5-20 point favorite since 2002
- 10-0 S/U on road as 20.5 point or more favorite since 1997
- 50-2 S/U as 20.5 point or more favorite since 1997

Pointspread Analysis — Conference
- vs Old Dominion - Marshall leads series 6-1
- 5-1 ATS vs Old Dominion as favorite since 2014

Bowl Games
- 12-5 S/U in Bowl Games
- 12-3 ATS in Bowl Games since 1998

- 9-1 S/U @ home when ranked all time
- 1-7 ATS on road vs ranked teams since 2006
- 0-17 S/U vs ranked teams since 2003

Opponent	Trend
NORFOLK STATE	10-0 S/U in 1st home game of season since 2011
Notre Dame	4-18 S/U in 1st road game of season since 2000
Notre Dame	10-3 O/U in 1st road game of season since 2008
Troy	8-0 S/U after playing Bowling Green since 1997
APP STATE	7-0 S/U after playing Old Dominion since 2014 {7-0 ATS}
Ga Southern	5-13 S/U in final road game of season since 2004
Ga Southern	7-2 S/U after playing Appalachian State since 1991

MARYLAND TERRAPINS   BIG TEN East

2021-Maryland		Opponent	MD	Opp	S/U	Line	ATS	Total	O/U	
9/4/2021	vs	WEST VIRGINIA	30	24	W	2.5	W	57.0	U	
9/11/2021	vs	HOWARD	62	0	W	-49.0	W	56.5	U	
9/17/2021	@	Illinois	20	17	W	-7.0	L	67.0	U	
9/25/2021	vs	KENT STATE	37	16	W	-13.0	W	71.5	U	
10/2/2021	vs	IOWA	14	51	L	3.0	L	47.5	O	
10/9/2021	@	Ohio State	17	66	L	22.0	L	71.5	O	
10/23/2021	@	Minnesota	16	34	L	4.0	L	52.0	U	
10/30/2021	vs	INDIANA	38	35	W	-3.5	L	48.0	O	
11/6/2021	vs	PENN STATE	14	31	L	10.0	L	56.0	U	
11/13/2021	@	Michigan State	21	40	L	11.5	L	59.5	O	
11/20/2021	vs	MICHIGAN	18	59	L	16.0	L	58.0	O	
11/27/2021	@	Rutgers	40	14	W	2.0	W	53.0	O	
12/29/2021	vs	Virginia Tech	54	10	W	-4.5	W	56.0	O	Pinstripe Bowl
Coach: Mike Locksley		Season Record >>	381	397	7-6	ATS>>	5-8	O/U>>	7-6	

2020-Maryland		Opponent	MD	Opp	S/U	Line	ATS	Total	O/U	
10/24/2020	@	Northwestern	3	43	L	14.0	L	52.5	U	
10/30/2020	vs	MINNESOTA	45	44	W	17.0	W	60.5	O	{OT}
11/7/2020	@	Penn State	35	19	W	27.0	W	62.5	U	
11/28/2020	@	Indiana	11	27	L	12.0	L	64.5	U	
12/12/2020	vs	RUTGERS	27	27	L	-3.0	L	54.0	U	{OT}
Coach: Mike Locksley		Season Record >>	121	160	2-3	ATS>>	2-3	O/U>>	1-4	

2019-Maryland		Opponent	MD	Opp	S/U	Line	ATS	Total	O/U	
8/31/2019	vs	HOWARD	79	0	W	-32.0	W	NT	---	
9/7/2019	vs	SYRACUSE	63	20	W	-1.0	W	58.5	O	
9/14/2019	@	Temple	17	20	L	-5.5	L	66.0	U	
9/27/2019	vs	PENN STATE	0	59	L	6.5	L	61.0	U	
10/5/2019	@	Rutgers	48	7	W	-14.5	W	55.5	U	
10/12/2019	@	Purdue	14	40	L	-4.5	L	52.0	O	
10/19/2019	vs	INDIANA	28	34	L	6.5	W	59.0	O	
10/26/2019	@	Minnesota	10	52	L	14.5	L	58.5	O	
11/2/2019	vs	MICHIGAN	7	38	L	21.0	L	57.5	U	
11/9/2019	@	Ohio State	14	73	L	42.5	L	64.5	O	
11/23/2019	vs	NEBRASKA	7	54	L	6.5	L	62.5	U	
11/30/2019	@	Michigan State	16	19	L	22.0	W	47.5	U	
Coach: Mike Locksley		Season Record >>	303	416	3-9	ATS>>	5-7	O/U>>	5-6	

2018-Maryland		Opponent	MD	Opp	S/U	Line	ATS	Total	O/U	
9/1/2018	vs	TEXAS	34	29	W	12.0	W	54.5	O	FedEx Field
9/8/2018	@	Bowling Green	45	14	W	-13.5	W	66.0	U	
9/15/2018	vs	TEMPLE	14	35	L	-15.0	L	53.5	U	
9/29/2018	vs	MINNESOTA	42	13	W	PK	W	46.5	O	
10/6/2018	@	Michigan	21	42	L	17.5	L	44.0	O	
10/13/2018	vs	RUTGERS	34	7	W	-24.0	W	50.5	U	
10/20/2018	@	Iowa	0	23	L	9.5	L	44.0	U	
10/27/2018	vs	ILLINOIS	63	33	W	-16.5	W	53.5	O	
11/3/2018	vs	MICHIGAN STATE	3	24	L	3.5	L	42.5	U	
11/10/2018	@	Indiana	32	34	L	1.0	L	55.0	O	
11/17/2018	vs	OHIO STATE	51	52	L	14.0	W	61.5	O	{OT}
11/24/2018	@	Penn State	3	38	L	12.0	L	50.5	U	
Coach: DJ Durkin		Season Record >>	342	344	5-7	ATS>>	6-6	O/U>>	6-6	

MARYLAND TERRAPINS   BIG TEN East

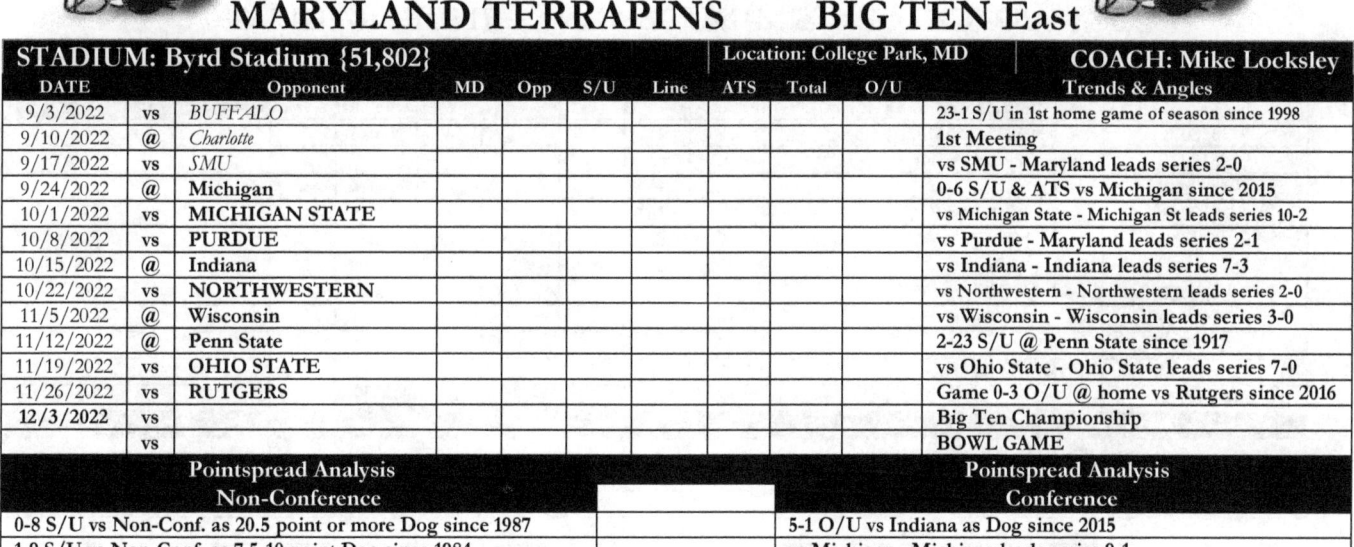

STADIUM: Byrd Stadium {51,802}   **Location:** College Park, MD   **COACH:** Mike Locksley

DATE		Opponent	MD	Opp	S/U	Line	ATS	Total	O/U	Trends & Angles
9/3/2022	vs	BUFFALO								23-1 S/U in 1st home game of season since 1998
9/10/2022	@	Charlotte								1st Meeting
9/17/2022	vs	SMU								vs SMU - Maryland leads series 2-0
9/24/2022	@	Michigan								0-6 S/U & ATS vs Michigan since 2015
10/1/2022	vs	MICHIGAN STATE								vs Michigan State - Michigan St leads series 10-2
10/8/2022	vs	PURDUE								vs Purdue - Maryland leads series 2-1
10/15/2022	@	Indiana								vs Indiana - Indiana leads series 7-3
10/22/2022	vs	NORTHWESTERN								vs Northwestern - Northwestern leads series 2-0
11/5/2022	@	Wisconsin								vs Wisconsin - Wisconsin leads series 3-0
11/12/2022	@	Penn State								2-23 S/U @ Penn State since 1917
11/19/2022	vs	OHIO STATE								vs Ohio State - Ohio State leads series 7-0
11/26/2022	vs	RUTGERS								Game 0-3 O/U @ home vs Rutgers since 2016
12/3/2022										Big Ten Championship
	vs									BOWL GAME

Pointspread Analysis — Non-Conference

- 0-8 S/U vs Non-Conf. as 20.5 point or more Dog since 1987
- 1-9 S/U vs Non-Conf. as 7.5-10 point Dog since 1984
- 12-3 S/U vs Non-Conf. as 10.5-15 point favorite since 1988
- 25-0 S/U vs Non-Conf. as 15.5 point or more favorite since 1983
- 1-14 S/U vs West Virginia as 6.5 point or more Dog since 1988
- 1-6 S/U vs West Virginia as Dog since 2004
- vs West Virginia - WVU leads series 28-23-2

Dog

- 2-23 S/U on road as 20.5 point or more Dog since 1987
- 0-11 S/U @ home as 20.5 point or more Dog since 1991
- 12-5 O/U as 20.5 point or more Dog since 2000
- 4-19 S/U on road as 15.5-20 point Dog since 1986
- 1-4 S/U @ home as 15.5-20 point Dog since 2002
- 3-28 S/U on road as 10.5-15 point Dog since 1987
- 3-14 ATS as 10.5-15 point Dog since 2011
- 1-11 S/U @ home as 7.5-10 point Dog since 1987
- 4-1 O/U @ home as 7.5-10 point Dog since 2000
- 1-10 S/U @ home as 3.5-7 point Dog since 2009

Favorite

- 9-3 O/U as 3 point or less favorite since 2005
- 5-14 ATS as 3 point or less favorite since 1998
- 15-5 S/U on road as 3.5-7 point favorite since 1983
- 16-4 S/U @ home as 10.5-15 point favorite since 1983
- 8-0 S/U on road as 15.5 point or more favorite since 1983
- 31-1 S/U @ home as 15.5 point or more favorite since 1983

Pointspread Analysis — Conference

- 5-1 O/U vs Indiana as Dog since 2015
- vs Michigan - Michigan leads series 9-1
- Game 1-6 O/U vs Michigan State since 2014
- Game 7-0 O/U vs Ohio State since 2014
- vs Penn State - Penn State leads series 40-3-1
- vs Rutgers - Maryland leads series 10-7
- 0-3 S/U vs Wisconsin as Dog since 2014
- 1-11 S/U vs Penn State as 7.5 point or more Dog since 1984

Bowl Games

- 0-3 S/U in Orange Bowl
- 3-0-1 S/U in Gator Bowl

SMU	1-6 S/U prior to playing Michigan since 2014
MICHIGAN STATE	2-6 S/U after playing Michigan since 1990
Wisconsin	3-9 S/U prior to playing Penn State since 1990
OHIO STATE	3-10 S/U after playing Penn State since 1987
RUTGERS	2-12 S/U in final home game of season since 2008
RUTGERS	9-3 O/U in final home game of season since 2010

- 24-8 S/U @ home when ranked since 1976
- 1-16 S/U @ home vs ranked teams since 2011
- 2-36 S/U vs ranked teams since 2011
- 1-22 S/U on road vs ranked teams since 2008
- 0-9 S/U vs ranked Michigan all time
- 0-7 ATS vs ranked Michigan since 1990
- 0-7 S/U vs ranked Ohio State all time
- 0-22-1 S/U vs ranked Penn State all time
- 0-7 ATS vs ranked Penn State since 1991

Print Version $24.95   Print Version $34.95    Print Version $34.95

These books available at numerous online retailers

MASSACHUSETTS MINUTEMEN — INDEPENDENT

2021 - Massachusetts		Opponent	Umass	Opp	S/U	Line	ATS	Total	O/U	
9/4/2021	@	Pittsburgh	7	51	L	38.0	L	56.0	O	
9/11/2021	vs	BOSTON COLLEGE	28	45	L	40.0	W	57.0	O	"Battle of The Bay State"
9/18/2021	vs	EASTERN MICHIGAN	28	42	L	22.0	W	56.5	O	
9/25/2021	@	Coastal Carolina	3	53	L	36.0	L	66.0	U	
10/2/2021	vs	TOLEDO	7	45	L	27.0	L	56.5	U	
10/9/2021	vs	CONNECTICUT	27	13	W	3.0	W	57.0	O	
10/23/2021	@	Florida State	3	59	L	35.0	L	59.0	U	
10/30/2021	@	Liberty	17	62	L	35.5	L	56.0	O	
11/6/2021	vs	RHODE ISLAND	22	35	L	PK	L	55.0	O	
11/13/2021	vs	MAINE	10	35	L	5.5	L	58.5	U	
11/20/2021	@	Army	17	33	L	37.5	W	56.5	U	
11/27/2021	@	New Mexico State	27	44	L	7.0	L	59.0	O	
Coach: Walt Bell		Season Record >>	196	517	1-11	ATS>>	4-8	O/U>>	6-6	

2020 - Massachusetts		Opponent	Umass	Opp	S/U	Line	ATS	Total	O/U	
10/17/2020	@	Georgia Southern	0	41	L	30.0	L	62.0	U	
11/7/2020	@	Marshall	10	51	L	44.0	W	55.5	U	
11/20/2020	@	Florida Atlantic	2	24	L	34.0	W	50.5	U	
11/27/2020	@	Liberty	0	45	L	35.0	L	57.5	U	
Coach: Walt Bell		Season Record >>	12	161	0-4	ATS>>	2-2	O/U>>	0-4	

2019 - Massachusetts		Opponent	Umass	Opp	S/U	Line	ATS	Total	O/U	
8/30/2019	@	Rutgers	21	48	L	16.5	L	54.5	O	
9/7/2019	vs	SOUTHERN ILLINOIS	20	45	L	-5.5	L	NT	---	
9/14/2019	@	Charlotte	17	52	L	21.0	L	66.5	O	
9/21/2019	vs	COASTAL CAROLINA	28	62	L	17.0	L	62.0	O	
9/28/2019	vs	AKRON	37	29	W	9.5	W	60.5	O	
10/5/2019	@	Florida International	0	44	L	28.0	L	70.0	U	
10/12/2019	@	Louisiana Tech	21	69	L	31.5	L	64.0	O	
10/26/2019	vs	CONNECTICUT	35	56	L	9.5	L	62.0	O	Gillette Stadium
11/2/2019	vs	LIBERTY	21	63	L	23.5	L	71.0	O	
11/9/2019	@	Army	7	63	L	34.5	L	61.0	O	
11/16/2019	@	Northwestern	6	45	L	38.0	L	57.5	U	
11/23/2019	vs	BYU	24	56	L	42.0	W	69.0	O	
Coach: Walt Bell		Season Record >>	237	632	1-11	ATS>>	2-10	O/U>>	9-2	

2018 - Massachusetts		Opponent	Umass	Opp	S/U	Line	ATS	Total	O/U	
8/25/2018	vs	DUQUESNE	63	15	W	-21.0	W	68.5	O	
9/1/2018	@	Boston College	21	55	L	20.5	L	62.5	O	"Battle of The Bay State"
9/8/2018	@	Georgia Southern	13	34	L	1.5	L	61.0	U	
9/15/2018	@	Florida International	24	63	L	3.5	L	66.5	O	
9/22/2018	vs	CHARLOTTE	49	31	W	-6.0	W	55.0	O	
9/29/2018	@	Ohio	42	58	L	11.5	L	70.0	O	
10/6/2018	vs	SOUTH FLORIDA	42	58	L	16.0	T	71.0	O	
10/20/2018	vs	COASTAL CAROLINA	13	24	L	-2.0	L	74.0	U	
10/27/2018	@	Connecticut	22	17	W	-3.5	W	62.5	U	
11/3/2018	vs	LIBERTY	62	59	W	-1.0	W	67.5	O	{3 OT}
11/10/2018	vs	BYU	16	35	L	14.0	L	57.5	U	Gillette Stadium
11/17/2018	@	Georgia	27	66	L	41.5	W	67.0	O	
Coach: Mark Whipple		Season Record >>	394	515	4-8	ATS>>	5-6-1	O/U>>	8-4	

MASSACHUSETTS MINUTEMEN — INDEPENDENT

STADIUM: McGuirk Stadium {17,000}   **Location:** Amherst, MA   **COACH:** Don Brown

DATE		Opponent	Mass	Opp	S/U	Line	ATS	Total	O/U	Trends & Angles
9/3/2022	@	Tulane								vs Tulane - Tulane leads series 1-0
9/10/2022	@	Toledo								0-3 S/U @ Toledo since 1983
9/17/2022	vs	SUNY-STONY BROOK								vs Stony Brook - U Mass leads series 3-0
9/24/2022	@	Temple								vs Temple - Temple leads series 2-0
10/1/2022	@	Eastern Michigan								vs Eastern Michigan - U Mass leads series 2-1
10/8/2022	vs	LIBERTY								vs Liberty - Liberty leads series 2-1
10/15/2022	vs	BUFFALO								vs Buffalo - Buffalo leads series 7-6
10/29/2022	vs	NEW MEXICO STATE								vs New Mexico State - NMSU leads series 1-0
11/5/2022	@	Connecticut								vs Connecticut - U Mass leads series 38-35-2
11/12/2022	@	Arkansas State								1st Meeting
11/19/2022	@	Texas A&M								2-12 S/U in final road game of season since 2008
11/26/2022	vs	ARMY								vs Army - Army leads series 4-0
	vs									BOWL GAME

Pointspread Analysis Dog			Pointspread Analysis Conference
0-54 S/U as 15.5 point or more Dog since 2012			vs Toledo - Toledo leads series 5-1
0-18 S/U @ home as 10.5 point or more Dog since 2012			
1-13 S/U as 10.5-15 point Dog since 2011			
Favorite		Tulane	0-10 S/U in 1st road game of season since 2012
3-0 S/U as 15 point or more favorite since 2014		Toledo	0-13 S/U in 2nd road game of season since 2008
		STONY BROOK	1-8 S/U in 1st home game of season since 2012
0-13 S/U vs ranked teams all time		LIBERTY	0-4 O/U prior to playing Buffalo since 2012

Baseball Fans – We have books on Baseball as well

Print Version $39.95   Print Version $39.95

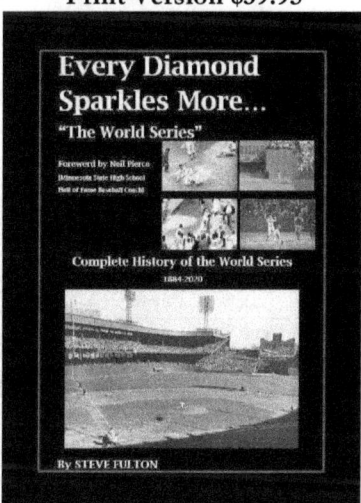

These books available at numerous online retailers

Page | 121   Copyright © 2022 by Steve's Football Bible, LLC

MEMPHIS TIGERS — AMERICAN West

2021-Memphis		Opponent	Mem	Opp	S/U	Line	ATS	Total	O/U	
9/4/2021	vs	NICHOLLS STATE	42	17	W	-22.5	W	69.0	U	
9/11/2021	@	Arkansas State	55	50	W	-5.0	T	64.5	O	"Paint Bucket Bowl"
9/18/2021	vs	MISSISSIPPI STATE	31	29	W	3.5	W	63.0	U	
9/25/2021	vs	TEXAS-SAN ANTONIO	28	31	L	-2.5	L	65.5	U	
10/2/2021	@	Temple	31	34	L	-11.0	L	58.5	O	
10/9/2021	@	Tulsa	29	35	L	3.0	L	60.5	O	
10/14/2021	vs	NAVY	35	17	W	-10.5	W	56.0	U	
10/22/2021	@	Central Florida	7	24	L	-1.5	L	63.0	U	
11/6/2021	vs	SMU	28	25	W	3.0	W	72.0	U	
11/13/2021	vs	EAST CAROLINA	29	30	L	-4.0	L	59.0	T	{OT}
11/19/2021	@	Houston	13	31	L	10.0	L	59.5	U	
11/27/2021	vs	TULANE	33	28	W	-5.0	T	58.0	O	
Coach: Ryan Silverfield		Season Record >>	361	351	6-6	ATS>>	4-6-2	O/U>>	4-7-1	

2020-Memphis		Opponent	Mem	Opp	S/U	Line	ATS	Total	O/U	
9/5/2020	vs	ARKANSAS STATE	37	24	W	-18.5	L	72.5	U	"Paint Bucket Bowl"
10/1/2020	@	Smu	27	30	L	2.0	L	75.0	U	
10/16/2020	vs	CENTRAL FLORIDA	50	49	W	3.0	W	74.0	O	
10/24/2020	vs	TEMPLE	41	29	W	-14.0	L	70.5	U	
10/31/2020	@	Cincinnati	10	49	L	6.5	L	56.5	O	
11/7/2020	vs	SOUTH FLORIDA	34	33	W	-17.5	L	67.0	T	
11/21/2020	vs	STEPHEN F. AUSTIN	56	14	W	-32.5	W	61.5	O	
11/28/2020	@	Navy	10	7	W	-13.0	L	63.5	U	
12/5/2020	@	Tulane	21	35	L	3.5	L	64.0	U	
12/12/2020	vs	HOUSTON	30	27	W	4.5	W	63.0	U	
12/23/2020	vs	Florida Atlantic	25	10	W	-9.5	W	52.5	U	Montgomery Bowl
Coach: Ryan Silverfield		Season Record >>	341	307	8-3	ATS>>	4-7	O/U>>	3-7-1	

2019-Memphis		Opponent	Mem	Opp	S/U	Line	ATS	Total	O/U	
8/31/2019	vs	MISSISSIPPI	15	10	W	-3.5	W	64.5	U	
9/7/2019	vs	SOUTHERN	55	24	W	-41.0	L	NT	---	
9/14/2019	@	South Alabama	42	6	W	-20.5	W	55.0	U	
9/26/2019	vs	NAVY	35	23	W	-10.5	W	53.5	O	
10/5/2019	@	Louisiana-Monroe	52	33	W	-15.0	W	69.0	O	
10/12/2019	@	Temple	28	30	L	-4.0	L	50.0	O	
10/19/2019	vs	TULANE	47	17	W	-2.5	W	60.5	O	
10/26/2019	@	Tulsa	42	41	W	-9.5	L	59.0	O	
11/2/2019	vs	SMU	54	48	W	-5.5	W	72.0	O	
11/16/2019	@	Houston	45	27	W	-9.5	W	71.5	O	
11/23/2019	@	South Florida	49	10	W	-14.5	W	59.5	U	
11/30/2019	vs	CINCINNATI	34	24	W	-13.5	L	59.5	U	
12/7/2019	vs	CINCINNATI	29	24	W	-8.0	L	58.0	U	AAC Championship Game
12/28/2019	vs	Penn State	39	53	L	6.5	L	59.0	O	Cotton Bowl
Coach: Mike Norvell		Season Record >>	566	370	12-2	ATS>>	8-6	O/U>>	8-5	AAC CHAMPIONS

2018-Memphis		Opponent	Mem	Opp	S/U	Line	ATS	Total	O/U	
9/1/2018	vs	MERCER	66	14	W	-30.0	W	NT	---	
9/8/2018	@	Navy	21	22	L	-6.5	L	67.0	U	
9/14/2018	vs	GEORGIA STATE	59	22	W	-28.5	W	59.0	O	
9/22/2018	vs	SOUTH ALABAMA	52	35	W	-32.0	L	66.0	O	
9/28/2018	@	Tulane	24	40	L	-14.5	L	66.0	U	
10/6/2018	vs	CONNECTICUT	55	14	W	-36.0	W	76.0	U	
10/13/2018	vs	CENTRAL FLORIDA	30	31	L	5.5	W	80.5	U	
10/20/2018	@	Missouri	33	65	L	8.5	L	69.5	O	
11/3/2018	@	East Carolina	59	41	W	-10.5	W	66.0	O	
11/10/2018	vs	TULSA	47	21	W	-16.5	W	64.5	O	
11/16/2018	@	Smu	28	18	W	-8.5	W	74.5	U	
11/23/2018	vs	HOUSTON	52	31	W	-9.5	W	74.5	O	
12/1/2018	@	Central Florida	41	56	L	PK	L	65.0	O	AAC Championship
12/22/2018	vs	Wake Forest	34	37	L	-2.0	L	71.5	U	Birmingham Bowl
Coach: Mike Norvell		Season Record >>	601	447	8-6	ATS>>	8-6	O/U>>	7-6	

MEMPHIS TIGERS — AMERICAN West

STADIUM: Liberty Bowl Memorial Stadium {58,318}
Location: Memphis, TN
COACH: Ryan Silverfield

DATE		Opponent	Mem	Opp	S/U	Line	ATS	Total	O/U	Trends & Angles
9/3/2022	@	Mississippi State								0-6 S/U @ Mississippi State since 1995
9/10/2022	@	Navy								vs Navy - Memphis leads series 4-3
9/17/2022	vs	ARKANSAS STATE								12-1-1 S/U vs Arkansas State as favorite since 1990
9/24/2022	vs	NORTH TEXAS								vs North Texas - Memphis leads series 16-4
10/1/2022	vs	TEMPLE								0-7 ATS vs Temple since 2013
10/8/2022	vs	HOUSTON								2-6 S/U vs Houston as Dog since 2006
10/15/2022	@	East Carolina								5-1 S/U vs E. Carolina as favorite since 2003
10/22/2022	@	Tulane								Game 0-7 O/U @ Tulane since 2003
11/5/2022	vs	CENTRAL FLORIDA								1-10 S/U vs C. Florida as Dog since 2006
11/12/2022	vs	TULSA								1-8 ATS @ home vs Tulsa since 1988
11/19/2022	vs	NORTH ALABAMA								1st Meeting
11/26/2022	@	Smu								7-1 S/U & ATS vs SMU since 2014
12/3/2022	vs									AAC Championship
	vs									BOWL GAME

Pointspread Analysis

Non-Conference
- 2-15 S/U vs Non-Conf. as 20.5 point or more Dog since 1986
- 2-13 S/U vs Non-Conf. as 15.5-20 point Dog since 1985
- 2-14 S/U vs Non-Conf. as 10.5-15 point Dog since 1984
- 4-15 S/U vs Non-Conf. as 3 point or less Dog since 1984
- 8-1 S/U vs Non-Conf. as 3.5-7 point favorite since 1990
- 34-1 S/U vs Non-Conf. as 10.5 point or more favorite since 1991
- 1-12 S/U vs Mississippi State since 1994
- 1-6 ATS vs Mississippi State since 2000
- vs Mississippi State - M State leads series 34-11
- 1-11 S/U vs Mississippi State as Dog since 1994
- 1-5 ATS vs Mississippi State as Dog since 2000

Dog
- 1-10 S/U as 25.5 point or more Dog since 1986
- 0-13 S/U on road as 20.5-25 point Dog since 1993
- 0-15 S/U as 20.5-25 point Dog since 1993
- 1-17 S/U on road as 15.5-20 point Dog since 1991
- 0-5 S/U @ home as 15.5-20 point Dog since 1998
- 0-13 S/U @ home as 10.5-15 point Dog since 1989
- 4-18 S/U on road as 10.5-15 point Dog since 1984
- 1-8 O/U as 7.5-10 point Dog since 2008
- 1-13 S/U on road as 7.5-10 point Dog since 1988
- 1-10 S/U on road as 3.5-7 point Dog since 2006
- 2-13 S/U on road as 3 point or less Dog since 1994

Favorite
- 10-4 S/U on road as 3.5-7 point favorite since 1995
- 2-12 ATS @ home as 7.5-10 point favorite since 2003
- 8-1 O/U @ home as 7.5-10 point favorite since 2006
- 19-0 S/U @ home as 10.5-15 point favorite since 1993
- 14-3 ATS @ home as 10.5-15 point favorite since 1994
- 6-14-1 O/U as 10.5-15 point favorite since 2002
- 34-0 S/U @ home as 15.5 point or more favorite since 1991
- 39-1 S/U as 15.5 point or more favorite since 1991

Conference
- 1-12 S/U vs East Carolina as Dog since 1991
- vs Smu - Memphis leads series 10-4
- vs Temple - Temple leads series 4-3
- vs Tulane - Memphis leads series 24-13-1
- 13-2 S/U vs Tulane since 2002
- 5-1-1 ATS vs Tulane as Dog since 1988
- 5-2 S/U @ Tulane since 2003
- 15-1 S/U vs Tulane as 3 point or more favorite since 1985
- vs Tulsa - Memphis leads series 19-12
- 0-5 S/U vs Tulsa as Dog since 2005
- 5-0 S/U @ Tulsa as favorite since 1987

Bowl Games
- 1-5 S/U & ATS in Bowl Game since 2015
- 3-14 S/U in 1st road game of season since 2005 — Mississippi State
- 3-10 ATS in 2nd road game of season since 2009 — Navy
- 20-3 S/U in 2nd home game of season since 1999 — NORTH TEXAS
- 1-10 O/U prior to playing Central Florida since 2007 — Tulane
- 3-13 ATS after playing Tulane since 1998 — CENTRAL FLORIDA

- 9-3 S/U on road when ranked all time
- 3-0 S/U when ranked vs Cincinnati since 2016
- 0-3 O/U when ranked vs Cincinnati since 2016
- 0-16 S/U on road vs ranked teams since 1993
- 1-8 S/U vs ranked Houston all time

Page | 123 — Copyright © 2022 by Steve's Football Bible, LLC

MIAMI HURRICANES — ACC Coastal

2021-MIAMI		Opponent	Miami	Opp	S/U	Line	ATS	Total	O/U	
9/4/2021	vs	Alabama	13	44	L	19.5	L	61.5	U	@ Atlanta, GA
9/11/2021	vs	APPALACHIAN STATE	25	23	W	-7.5	L	54.5	U	
9/18/2021	vs	MICHIGAN STATE	17	38	L	-7.0	L	57.5	U	
9/25/2021	vs	CENTRAL CONNECTICUT	69	0	W	-46.0	W	55.5	O	
9/30/2021	vs	VIRGINIA	28	30	L	-3.5	L	53.5	O	
10/16/2021	@	North Carolina	42	45	L	7.5	W	63.5	O	
10/23/2021	vs	NC STATE	31	30	W	4.0	W	54.5	O	
10/30/2021	@	Pittsburgh	38	34	W	9.5	W	61.0	O	
11/6/2021	vs	GEORGIA TECH	33	30	W	-10.0	L	62.5	O	
11/13/2021	@	Florida State	28	31	L	-2.5	L	61.0	O	
11/20/2021	vs	VIRGINIA TECH	38	26	W	-7.0	W	55.5	O	
11/27/2021	@	Duke	47	10	W	-20.5	W	67.0	U	
Coach: Manny Diaz		Season Record >>	409	341	7-5	ATS>>	6-6	O/U>>	7-5	
2020-MIAMI		Opponent	Miami	Opp	S/U	Line	ATS	Total	O/U	
9/10/2020	vs	ALABAMA-BIRMINGHAM	31	14	W	-14.5	L	54.5	U	
9/19/2020	@	Louisville	47	34	W	-2.5	W	66.0	O	
9/26/2020	vs	FLORIDA STATE	52	10	W	-10.5	W	54.0	O	
10/10/2020	@	Clemson	17	42	L	14.0	L	60.5	U	
10/17/2020	vs	PITTSBURGH	31	19	W	-13.5	L	47.5	O	
10/24/2020	vs	VIRGINIA	19	14	W	-13.5	L	54.5	U	
11/6/2020	@	NC State	44	41	W	-11.0	L	58.0	O	
11/14/2020	@	Virginia Tech	25	24	W	2.0	W	67.5	U	
12/5/2020	@	Duke	48	0	W	-14.0	W	62.5	U	
12/12/2020	vs	NORTH CAROLINA	26	62	L	-3.0	L	72.5	O	
12/29/2020	vs	**Oklahoma State**	34	37	L	1.5	L	63.0	O	**Cheez-it Bowl**
Coach: Manny Diaz		Season Record >>	374	297	8-3	ATS>>	5-6	O/U>>	6-5	
2019-MIAMI		Opponent	Miami	Opp	S/U	Line	ATS	Total	O/U	
8/24/2019	vs	Florida	20	24	L	7.0	W	46.0	U	"Seminole War Canoe Trophy"
9/7/2019	@	North Carolina	25	28	L	-5.0	L	46.0	O	
9/14/2019	vs	BETHUNE-COOKMAN	63	0	W	-40.5	W	NT	---	
9/21/2019	vs	CENTRAL MICHIGAN	17	12	W	-30.5	L	48.5	U	
10/5/2019	vs	VIRGINIA TECH	35	42	L	-14.0	L	45.0	O	
10/11/2019	vs	VIRGINIA	17	9	W	-3.0	W	43.5	U	
10/19/2019	vs	GEORGIA TECH	21	28	L	-18.0	L	46.0	O	{OT}
10/26/2019	@	Pittsburgh	16	12	W	4.5	W	41.5	U	
11/2/2019	@	Florida State	27	10	W	3.0	W	50.5	U	
11/9/2019	vs	LOUISVILLE	52	27	W	-6.5	W	49.0	O	
11/23/2019	@	Florida International	24	30	L	-21.0	L	51.5	O	
11/30/2019	vs	DUKE	17	27	L	-9.0	L	44.0	T	
12/26/2019	vs	**Louisiana Tech**	0	14	L	-7.0	L	49.5	U	**Independence Bowl**
Coach: Manny Diaz		Season Record >>	334	263	6-7	ATS>>	6-7	O/U>>	5-6-1	
2018-MIAMI		Opponent	Miami	Opp	S/U	Line	ATS	Total	O/U	
9/2/2018	vs	Lsu	17	33	L	-3.0	L	47.5	O	AT&T Stadium
9/8/2018	vs	SAVANNAH STATE	77	0	W	-61.5	W	NT	---	
9/15/2018	@	Toledo	49	24	W	-12.0	W	58.5	O	
9/22/2018	vs	FLORIDA INTERNATIONAL	31	17	W	-25.5	L	56.5	U	
9/29/2018	vs	NORTH CAROLINA	47	10	W	-18.5	W	55.0	O	
10/6/2018	vs	FLORIDA STATE	28	27	W	-14.0	L	48.0	O	
10/13/2018	@	Virginia	13	16	L	-7.0	L	46.5	U	
10/27/2018	@	Boston College	14	27	L	-4.0	L	49.0	U	
11/3/2018	vs	DUKE	12	20	L	-8.5	L	50.5	U	
11/10/2018	@	Georgia Tech	21	27	L	1.0	L	50.5	U	
11/17/2018	@	Virginia Tech	38	14	W	-6.5	W	52.5	U	
11/24/2018	vs	PITTSBURGH	24	3	W	-5.0	W	46.5	U	
12/27/2018	vs	**Wisconsin**	3	35	L	-2.5	L	44.0	U	**Pinstripe Bowl**
Coach: Mark Richt		Season Record >>	374	253	7-6	ATS>>	5-8	O/U>>	4-8	

MIAMI HURRICANES — ACC Coastal

STADIUM: Hard Rock Stadium {64,767}
Location: Coral Gables, FL
COACH: Mario Cristobal

DATE		Opponent	Mia	Opp	S/U	Line	ATS	Total	O/U	Trends & Angles
9/3/2022	vs	BETHUNE-COOKMAN								vs Bethune-Cookman - Miami leads series 5-0
9/10/2022	vs	SOUTHERN MISSISSIPPI								9-1 S/U in 2nd home game of season since 2012
9/17/2022	@	Texas A&M								vs Texas A&M - Miami leads series 2-1
9/24/2022	vs	MIDDLE TENNESSEE								vs Middle Tennessee - Miami leads series 2-0
10/8/2022	vs	NORTH CAROLINA								Game 4-0 O/U vs North Carolina since 2018
10/15/2022	@	Virginia Tech								Game 2-8 O/U @ Virginia Tech since 2001
10/22/2022	vs	DUKE								14-3 S/U vs Duke as favorite since 1983
10/29/2022	@	Virginia								1-4 S/U @ Virginia since 2010
11/5/2022	vs	FLORIDA STATE								2-7 ATS vs Florida State as favorite since 2005
11/12/2022	@	Georgia Tech								3-0 S/U @ Georgia Tech as favorite since 2004
11/19/2022	@	Clemson								vs Clemson - Series tied 6-6
11/26/2022	vs	PITTSBURGH								12-1 S/U @ home vs Pittsburgh since 1966
12/3/2022	vs									ACC Championship
	vs									BOWL GAME

Pointspread Analysis — Non-Conference

- 0-8 S/U vs Non-Conf. as 10.5 point or more Dog since 1993
- 1-4 O/U vs Non-Conf. as 3 point or less Dog since 2004
- 8-2 S/U vs Non-Conf. as 3 point or less favorite since 1985
- 0-5 O/U vs Non-Conf. as 7.5-10 point favorite since 2004
- 63-1 S/U vs Non-Conf. as 15.5 point or more favorite since 1984

Dog
- 0-7 S/U as 15.5 point or more Dog since 1995
- 1-9 S/U as 10.5-15 point Dog since 1993
- 9-0 O/U on road as 7.5-10 point Dog since 1996
- 2-7 S/U as 7.5-10 point Dog since 2010
- 4-14 O/U as 3 point or less Dog since 2004

Favorite
- 13-5 S/U & ATS as 3 point or less favorite since 2011
- 7-1 S/U & ATS on road as 3 point or less favorite since 2010
- 3-10 O/U as 3 point or less favorite since 2014
- 11-4 S/U @ home as 3.5-7 point favorite since 2010
- 10-2 S/U on road as 7.5-10 point favorite since 1988
- 1-11 ATS @ home as 7.5-10 point favorite since 1991
- 5-11 ATS as 10.5-15 point favorite since 2010
- 2-9 O/U on road as 10.5-15 point favorite since 2000
- 14-1 S/U @ home as 15.5-20 point favorite since 2005
- 18-1 S/U as 15.5-20 point favorite since 2005
- 14-0 S/U on road as 15.5-20 point favorite since 1985
- 1-8 ATS as 20.5-25 point favorite since 2004
- 34-2 S/U on road as 20.5 point or more favorite since 1984
- 84-0 S/U @ home as 20.5 point or more favorite since 1984
- 0-8 O/U as 25.5-30 point favorite since 2002
- 0-4 ATS on road as 30.5 point or more favorite since 1994

- 23-1 S/U in 1st home game of season since 1998 — BETHUNE-COOK
- 0-13 O/U in 1st home game of season since 2004 — BETHUNE-COOK
- 2-11 O/U prior to playing Virginia Tech since 2008 — NORTH CAROLINA
- 3-8 O/U after playing North Carolina since 2009 — Virginia Tech
- 11-3 S/U prior to playing Virginia since 2008 — DUKE
- 1-9 O/U after playing Duke since 2008 — Virginia
- 11-2 S/U prior to playing Georgia Tech since 2008 — FLORIDA STATE
- 13-3 S/U after playing Florida State since 2006 — Georgia Tech
- 3-8 ATS prior to playing Pittsburgh since 2003 — Clemson
- 4-12 O/U in final road game of season since 2006 — Clemson
- 10-3 S/U & ATS in final road game of season since 2009 — Clemson

Pointspread Analysis — Conference

- vs Duke - Miami leads series 16-3
- vs Florida State - Miami leads series 35-30
- 1-5 S/U vs Florida State as Dog since 2011
- 0-6 O/U vs Florida State as Dog since 2011
- 7-1 S/U vs Georgia Tech as favorite since 2009
- vs Georgia Tech - Series tied 13-13
- vs North Carolina - UNC leads series 14-11
- 22-3 S/U vs Pittsburgh since 1984
- vs Pittsburgh - Miami leads series 29-11-1
- Game 6-19 O/U vs Pittsburgh since 1989
- 10-1 S/U @ home vs Pittsburgh as favorite since 1984
- Game 2-8 O/U @ Pittsburgh since 1995
- Game 1-6 O/U @ Virginia since 2004
- vs Virginia - Miami leads series 11-8
- 3-12 ATS vs Virginia as favorite since 2005
- vs Virginia Tech - Miami leads series 24-15
- Game 5-14 O/U vs Virginia Tech since 2003
- 3-8 O/U vs Virginia Tech as favorite since 2003
- 5-1 S/U & ATS vs Virginia Tech as favorite since 2014
- 9-0 S/U vs Duke as 15.5 point or more favorite since 1983
- 10-1 ATS vs Florida State as 3.0-7.0 Dog since 1983
- 0-8 S/U vs Florida State as 9.5 point or more Dog since 1993
- 6-0 S/U vs North Carolina as 9.0-21 point favorite since 2005
- 7-0 S/U vs Pittsburgh as 9 point or less favorite since 1989
- 9-0 S/U vs Pittsburgh as 19.5 point or more favorite since 1986
- 2-7 S/U vs Virginia Tech as 2 point or more Dog since 1997
- 6-1 S/U vs Virginia Tech as 14 point or more favorite since 1987

Bowl Games
- 0-4 S/U in Fiesta Bowl
- 5-2 S/U in Orange Bowl since 1984
- 1-10 S/U in Bowl Games since 2008
- 2-11 ATS in Bowl Games since 2005
- 3-9 O/U in Bowl Games since 2006
- 0-3 S/U & ATS vs Wisconsin in Bowl Games
- 60-13 S/U @ home when ranked since 2000
- 20-0 S/U @ home when #1 ranked all time
- 28-0 S/U when #1 ranked in regular season since 1991
- 8-0 S/U when ranked vs Florida since 1984 {7-1 ATS}
- 7-0 S/U when ranked @ home vs Pittsburgh since 1984
- 4-17 S/U on road vs ranked teams since 2006
- 0-6 S/U vs ranked Florida State since 2010
- 5-0 S/U vs ranked Pittsburgh since 1989
- 3-10 ATS when ranked vs Virginia Tech since 1995

MIAMI-OHIO REDHAWKS   MAC East

2021-Miami-Ohio		Opponent	M-O	Opp	S/U	Line	ATS	Total	O/U	
9/4/2021	@	Cincinnati	14	49	L	23.5	L	48.5	O	"Victory Bell"
9/11/2021	@	Minnesota	26	31	L	18.0	W	55.0	O	
9/18/2021	vs	LONG ISLAND U	42	7	W	-39.0	L	55.5	U	
9/25/2021	@	Army	10	23	L	8.0	L	48.5	U	
10/2/2021	vs	CENTRAL MICHIGAN	28	17	W	2.5	W	56.5	U	
10/9/2021	@	Eastern Michigan	12	13	L	-2.5	L	58.0	U	
10/16/2021	vs	AKRON	34	21	W	-20.0	L	51.0	U	
10/23/2021	@	Ball State	24	17	W	3.5	W	53.0	U	
11/2/2021	@	Ohio	33	35	L	-7.0	L	54.0	O	"Battle of the Bricks"
11/9/2021	vs	BUFFALO	45	18	W	-7.0	W	58.5	O	
11/16/2021	vs	BOWLING GREEN	34	7	W	-17.0	W	52.0	U	
11/27/2021	@	Kent State	47	48	L	PK	L	68.0	O	
12/23/2021	vs	North Texas	27	14	W	-1.5	W	56.5	U	Frisco Football Classic
Coach: Chuck Martin		Season Record >>	376	300	7-6	ATS>>	6-7	O/U>>	6-7	

2020-Miami-Ohio		Opponent	M-O	Opp	S/U	Line	ATS	Total	O/U	
11/4/2020	vs	BALL STATE	38	31	W	1.0	W	56.5	O	
11/10/2020	@	Buffalo	10	42	L	7.0	L	56.0	U	
11/28/2020	@	Akron	38	7	W	-14.0	W	55.0	U	
Coach: Chuck Martin		Season Record >>	86	80	2-1	ATS>>	2-1	O/U>>	1-2	

2019-Miami-Ohio		Opponent	M-O	Opp	S/U	Line	ATS	Total	O/U	
8/31/2019	@	Iowa	14	38	L	24.5	W	47.0	O	
9/7/2019	vs	TENNESSEE TECH	48	17	W	-37.0	L	NT	---	
9/14/2019	@	Cincinnati	13	35	L	17.5	L	49.5	U	"Victory Bell"
9/21/2019	@	Ohio State	5	76	L	38.5	L	57.0	O	
9/28/2019	vs	BUFFALO	34	20	W	2.5	W	48.5	O	
10/12/2019	@	Western Michigan	16	38	L	12.0	L	57.5	U	
10/19/2019	vs	NORTHERN ILLINOIS	27	24	W	1.5	W	48.0	U	
10/26/2019		Kent State	23	16	W	2.5	W	54.5	U	
11/6/2019	@	Ohio	24	21	W	7.0	W	57.5	U	"Battle of the Bricks"
11/13/2019	vs	BOWLING GREEN	44	3	W	-17.0	W	47.4	U	
11/20/2019	vs	AKRON	20	17	W	-28.5	L	45.0	U	
11/29/2019	@	Ball State	27	41	L	3.0	L	55.5	O	
12/7/2019	vs	Central Michigan	26	21	W	5.5	W	56.5	U	MAC Championship Game
1/6/2020	vs	Louisiana	17	27	L	16.0	W	55.0	U	Lending Tree Bowl
Coach: Chuck Martin		Season Record >>	338	394	8-6	ATS>>	8-6	O/U>>	5-8	MAC Champions

2018-Miami-Ohio		Opponent	M-O	Opp	S/U	Line	ATS	Total	O/U	
9/1/2018	vs	MARSHALL	28	35	L	-1.5	L	51.5	O	
9/8/2018	@	Cincinnati	0	21	L	-1.5	L	45.5	U	"Victory Bell"
9/15/2018	@	Minnesota	3	26	L	13.5	L	46.5	U	
9/22/2018	@	Bowling Green	38	23	W	-6.5	W	54.5	O	
9/29/2018	vs	WESTERN MICHIGAN	39	40	L	2.5	W	52.0	O	
10/6/2018	@	Akron	41	17	W	5.0	W	47.5	O	
10/13/2018	vs	KENT STATE	31	6	W	-11.5	W	59.0	U	
10/20/2018	@	Army	30	31	L	6.5	W	47.0	O	{2 OT}
10/30/2018	@	Buffalo	42	51	L	7.0	L	53.0	O	
11/7/2018	vs	OHIO	30	28	W	4.5	W	59.0	U	"Battle of the Bricks"
11/14/2018	@	Northern Illinois	13	7	W	6.0	W	48.0	U	
11/20/2018	vs	BALL STATE	42	21	W	-14.5	W	55.0	O	
Coach: Chuck Martin		Season Record >>	337	306	6-6	ATS>>	8-4	O/U>>	7-5	

MIAMI-OHIO REDHAWKS — MAC East

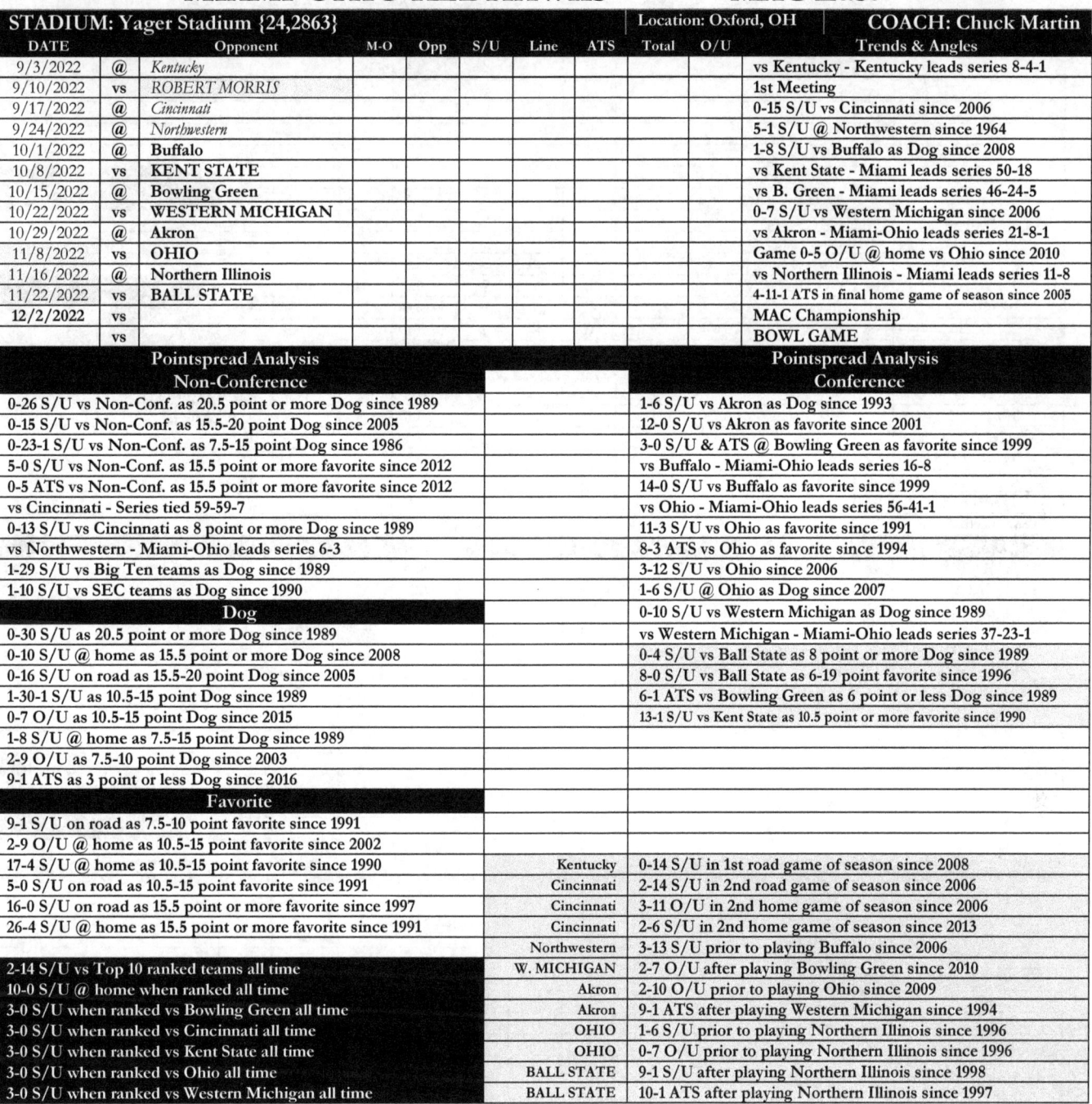

STADIUM: Yager Stadium {24,2863}
Location: Oxford, OH
COACH: Chuck Martin

DATE		Opponent	M-O	Opp	S/U	Line	ATS	Total	O/U	Trends & Angles
9/3/2022	@	Kentucky								vs Kentucky - Kentucky leads series 8-4-1
9/10/2022	vs	ROBERT MORRIS								1st Meeting
9/17/2022	@	Cincinnati								0-15 S/U vs Cincinnati since 2006
9/24/2022	@	Northwestern								5-1 S/U @ Northwestern since 1964
10/1/2022	@	Buffalo								1-8 S/U vs Buffalo as Dog since 2008
10/8/2022	vs	KENT STATE								vs Kent State - Miami leads series 50-18
10/15/2022	@	Bowling Green								vs B. Green - Miami leads series 46-24-5
10/22/2022	vs	WESTERN MICHIGAN								0-7 S/U vs Western Michigan since 2006
10/29/2022	@	Akron								vs Akron - Miami-Ohio leads series 21-8-1
11/8/2022	vs	OHIO								Game 0-5 O/U @ home vs Ohio since 2010
11/16/2022	@	Northern Illinois								vs Northern Illinois - Miami leads series 11-8
11/22/2022	vs	BALL STATE								4-11-1 ATS in final home game of season since 2005
12/2/2022	vs									MAC Championship
	vs									BOWL GAME

Pointspread Analysis — Non-Conference
- 0-26 S/U vs Non-Conf. as 20.5 point or more Dog since 1989
- 0-15 S/U vs Non-Conf. as 15.5-20 point Dog since 2005
- 0-23-1 S/U vs Non-Conf. as 7.5-15 point Dog since 1986
- 5-0 S/U vs Non-Conf. as 15.5 point or more favorite since 2012
- 0-5 ATS vs Non-Conf. as 15.5 point or more favorite since 2012
- vs Cincinnati - Series tied 59-59-7
- 0-13 S/U vs Cincinnati as 8 point or more Dog since 1989
- vs Northwestern - Miami-Ohio leads series 6-3
- 1-29 S/U vs Big Ten teams as Dog since 1989
- 1-10 S/U vs SEC teams as Dog since 1990

Dog
- 0-30 S/U as 20.5 point or more Dog since 1989
- 0-10 S/U @ home as 15.5 point or more Dog since 2008
- 0-16 S/U on road as 15.5-20 point Dog since 2005
- 1-30-1 S/U as 10.5-15 point Dog since 1989
- 0-7 O/U as 10.5-15 point Dog since 2015
- 1-8 S/U @ home as 7.5-15 point Dog since 1989
- 2-9 O/U as 7.5-10 point Dog since 2003
- 9-1 ATS as 3 point or less Dog since 2016

Favorite
- 9-1 S/U on road as 7.5-10 point favorite since 1991
- 2-9 O/U @ home as 10.5-15 point favorite since 2002
- 17-4 S/U @ home as 10.5-15 point favorite since 1990
- 5-0 S/U on road as 10.5-15 point favorite since 1991
- 16-0 S/U on road as 15.5 point or more favorite since 1997
- 26-4 S/U @ home as 15.5 point or more favorite since 1991

- 2-14 S/U vs Top 10 ranked teams all time
- 10-0 S/U @ home when ranked all time
- 3-0 S/U when ranked vs Bowling Green all time
- 3-0 S/U when ranked vs Cincinnati all time
- 3-0 S/U when ranked vs Kent State all time
- 3-0 S/U when ranked vs Ohio all time
- 3-0 S/U when ranked vs Western Michigan all time

Pointspread Analysis — Conference
- 1-6 S/U vs Akron as Dog since 1993
- 12-0 S/U vs Akron as favorite since 2001
- 3-0 S/U & ATS @ Bowling Green as favorite since 1999
- vs Buffalo - Miami-Ohio leads series 16-8
- 14-0 S/U vs Buffalo as favorite since 1999
- vs Ohio - Miami-Ohio leads series 56-41-1
- 11-3 S/U vs Ohio as favorite since 1991
- 8-3 ATS vs Ohio as favorite since 1994
- 3-12 S/U vs Ohio since 2006
- 1-6 S/U @ Ohio as Dog since 2007
- 0-10 S/U vs Western Michigan as Dog since 1989
- vs Western Michigan - Miami-Ohio leads series 37-23-1
- 0-4 S/U vs Ball State as 8 point or more Dog since 1989
- 8-0 S/U vs Ball State as 6-19 point favorite since 1996
- 6-1 ATS vs Bowling Green as 6 point or less Dog since 1989
- 13-1 S/U vs Kent State as 10.5 point or more favorite since 1990

Opponent	Trend
Kentucky	0-14 S/U in 1st road game of season since 2008
Cincinnati	2-14 S/U in 2nd road game of season since 2006
Cincinnati	3-11 O/U in 2nd home game of season since 2006
Cincinnati	2-6 S/U in 2nd home game of season since 2013
Northwestern	3-13 S/U prior to playing Buffalo since 2006
W. MICHIGAN	2-7 O/U after playing Bowling Green since 2010
Akron	2-10 O/U prior to playing Ohio since 2009
Akron	9-1 ATS after playing Western Michigan since 1994
OHIO	1-6 S/U prior to playing Northern Illinois since 1996
OHIO	0-7 O/U prior to playing Northern Illinois since 1996
BALL STATE	9-1 S/U after playing Northern Illinois since 1998
BALL STATE	10-1 ATS after playing Northern Illinois since 1997

MICHIGAN WOLVERINES   BIG TEN East

2021-Michigan		Opponent	UM	Opp	S/U	Line	ATS	Total	O/U	
9/4/2021	vs	WESTERN MICHIGAN	47	14	W	-16.0	W	65.5	U	
9/11/2021	vs	WASHINGTON	31	10	W	-6.5	W	57.5	U	
9/18/2021	vs	NORTHERN ILLINOIS	63	10	W	-27.5	W	55.0	O	
9/25/2021	vs	RUTGERS	20	13	W	-20.5	L	50.0	U	
10/2/2021	@	Wisconsin	38	17	W	1.5	W	43.5	O	
10/9/2021	@	Nebraska	32	29	W	-2.5	W	50.5	O	
10/23/2021	vs	NORTHWESTERN	33	7	W	-23.5	W	51.0	U	"George Jewett Trophy"
10/30/2021	@	Michigan State	33	37	L	-4.0	L	50.5	O	"Paul Bunyan Trophy"
11/6/2021	vs	INDIANA	29	7	W	-20.5	W	50.5	U	
11/13/2021	@	Penn State	21	17	W	-2.5	W	48.0	U	
11/20/2021	@	Maryland	59	18	W	-16.0	W	58.0	O	
11/27/2021	vs	OHIO STATE	42	27	W	6.0	W	63.0	O	"100 Yard War"
12/4/2021	vs	Iowa	42	3	W	-12.0	W	44.0	O	Big Ten Championship
12/31/2021	vs	Georgia	11	34	L	7.5	L	46.5	U	Orange Bowl {National Semifinal}
Coach: Jim Harbaugh		Season Record >>	501	243	12-2	ATS>>	11-3	O/U>>	7-7	Big Ten Champions

2020-Michigan		Opponent	UM	Opp	S/U	Line	ATS	Total	O/U	
10/24/2020	@	Minnesota	49	24	W	-2.5	W	54.5	O	"Little Brown Jug"
10/31/2020	vs	MICHIGAN STATE	24	27	L	-22.0	L	51.5	U	"Paul Bunyan Trophy"
11/7/2020	@	Indiana	21	38	L	-4.5	L	54.5	O	
11/14/2020	vs	WISCONSIN	11	49	L	7.0	L	51.5	O	
11/21/2020	@	Rutgers	48	42	W	-11.5	L	52.0	O	{3 OT}
11/28/2020	vs	PENN STATE	17	27	L	PK	L	56.0	U	
Coach: Jim Harbaugh		Season Record >>	170	207	2-4	ATS>>	1-5	O/U>>	4-2	

2019-Michigan		Opponent	UM	Opp	S/U	Line	ATS	Total	O/U	
8/31/2019	vs	MIDDLE TENNESSEE	40	21	W	-36.5	L	55.0	O	
9/7/2019	vs	ARMY	24	21	W	-22.0	L	47.5	U	{2 OT}
9/21/2019	@	Wisconsin	14	35	L	3.0	L	45.0	O	
9/28/2019	vs	RUTGERS	52	0	W	-27.5	W	49.0	O	
10/5/2019	vs	IOWA	10	3	W	-4.0	W	49.0	U	
10/12/2019	@	Illinois	42	25	W	-24.5	L	48.5	O	
10/19/2019	@	Penn State	21	28	L	7.5	L	46.5	O	
10/26/2019	vs	NOTRE DAME	45	14	W	-1.0	W	46.5	O	
11/2/2019	@	Maryland	38	7	W	-21.0	W	57.5	U	
11/16/2019	vs	MICHIGAN STATE	44	10	W	-14.0	W	43.5	O	"Paul Bunyan Trophy"
11/23/2019	@	Indiana	39	14	W	-10.0	W	54.0	U	
11/30/2019	vs	OHIO STATE	27	56	L	8.5	L	53.0	O	"100 Yard War"
1/1/2020	vs	Alabama	16	35	L	8.0	L	60.0	U	Citrus Bowl
Coach: Jim Harbaugh		Season Record >>	412	269	9-4	ATS>>	7-6	O/U>>	8-5	

2018-Michigan		Opponent	UM	Opp	S/U	Line	ATS	Total	O/U	
9/1/2018	@	Notre Dame	17	24	L	-3.0	L	48.0	U	
9/8/2018	vs	WESTERN MICHIGAN	49	3	W	-28.0	W	55.0	U	
9/15/2018	vs	SMU	45	20	W	-36.0	L	54.0	O	
9/22/2018	vs	NEBRASKA	56	10	W	-17.0	W	50.5	O	
9/29/2018	@	Northwestern	20	17	W	-14.5	L	46.5	U	
10/6/2018	vs	MARYLAND	42	21	W	-17.5	W	44.0	O	
10/13/2018	vs	WISCONSIN	38	13	W	-9.5	W	48.0	O	
10/20/2018	@	Michigan State	21	7	W	-7.0	W	39.0	U	"Paul Bunyan Trophy"
11/3/2018	vs	PENN STATE	42	7	W	-11.0	W	49.5	U	
11/10/2018	@	Rutgers	42	7	W	-37.0	L	44.5	U	
11/17/2018	vs	INDIANA	31	20	W	-28.0	L	53.5	U	
11/24/2018	@	Ohio State	39	62	L	-4.0	L	53.5	O	"100 Yard War"
12/29/2018	vs	Florida	15	41	L	-4.0	L	51.0	O	Chick-Fil-A Peach Bowl
Coach: Jim Harbaugh		Season Record >>	457	252	10-3	ATS>>	6-7	O/U>>	7-6	

MICHIGAN WOLVERINES   BIG TEN East

STADIUM: Michigan Stadium {107,601} | **Location:** Ann Arbor, MI | **COACH:** Jim Harbaugh

DATE		Opponent	Mich	Opp	S/U	Line	ATS	Total	O/U	Trends & Angles
9/3/2022	vs	COLORADO STATE								vs Colorado St - Michigan leads series 1-0
9/10/2022	vs	HAWAII								3-0 S/U vs Hawaii as favorite since 1986
9/17/2022	vs	CONNECTICUT								vs Connecticut - Michigan leads series 2-0
9/24/2022	vs	MARYLAND								vs Maryland - Michigan leads series 9-1
10/1/2022	@	Iowa								vs Iowa - Michigan leads series 43-15-4
10/8/2022	@	Indiana								10-1 S/U @ Indiana as favorite since 1990
10/15/2022	vs	PENN STATE								8-2 S/U @ home vs Penn State since 1998
10/29/2022	vs	MICHIGAN STATE								1-6 ATS @ home vs Michigan State since 2008
11/5/2022	@	Rutgers								7-0 S/U vs Rutgers since 2015
11/12/2022	vs	NEBRASKA								vs Nebraska - Michigan leads series 6-4-1
11/19/2022	vs	ILLINOIS								vs Illinois - Michigan leads series 71-23-2
11/26/2022	@	Ohio State								0-9 S/U @ Ohio State since 2002
12/3/2022	vs									Big Ten Championship
	vs									BOWL GAME

Pointspread Analysis — Non-Conference
- 0-5 S/U vs Non-Conf. as 3.5-7 point Dog since 2012
- 14-2 S/U vs Non-Conf. as 10.5-15 point favorite since 1983
- 52-1 S/U vs Non-Conf. as 15.5 point or more favorite since 1986

Dog
- 0-7 S/U as 7.5-10 Point Dog since 2009
- 1-6 S/U on road as 10.5 point or more Dog since 1996
- 3-17 S/U as 3.5-7 point Dog since 2008 {6-14 ATS}

Favorite
- 10-3 O/U as 3.5-7 point favorite since 2015
- 7-0 S/U @ home as 7.5-10 point favorite since 2007
- 13-1 S/U on road as 10.5-15 point favorite since 1996
- 27-2 S/U @ home as 10.5-15 point favorite since 1995
- 2-12 O/U @ home as 10.5-15 point favorite since 2006
- 21-2 S/U @ home as 15.5-20 point favorite since 1983
- 32-2 S/U as 15.5-20 point favorite since 1983
- 8-1 O/U @ home as 15.5-20 point favorite since 2009
- 12-0 S/U on road as 15.5-20 point favorite since 1992
- 1-5 O/U on road as 15.5-20 point favorite since 2004
- 44-4 S/U as 20.5-25 point favorite since 1983
- 3-9 ATS as 20.5-25 point favorite since 2016
- 62-0-1 S/U as 25.5 point or more favorite since 1983

Bowl Games
- 1-6 S/U & ATS vs USC in Bowl Games since 70
- 4-12 S/U in Rose Bowl since 1969
- 10-4 O/U in Bowl Games since 2005
- 3-9 S/U vs ranked teams in Bowl games since 2004
- 3-1 S/U & ATS vs Florida in Bowl Games since 2003
- 4-0 O/U vs Florida in Bowl Games since 2003
- 1-11 S/U in Bowl Games as 3.5-7 point Dog since 1976
- 5-1 O/U in Citrus Bowl since 1999
- 4-2 S/U in Citrus Bowl since 1999
- 5-1 O/U in Outback Bowl since 1988

- 22-1 S/U @ home when #4 ranked since 1976
- 19-2 S/U on road when #4 ranked since 1971
- 47-6 S/U @ home when ranked since 2009
- 303-61-9 S/U @ home when ranked all time
- 0-8 S/U when ranked vs #1 ranked teams since 1985
- 22-1 S/U when ranked vs Indiana since 1988
- 0-6 S/U when ranked @ Ohio State since 2002

Pointspread Analysis — Conference
- vs Indiana - Michigan leads series 60-10
- 3-0 ATS vs Iowa as Dog since 2005
- 2-12 ATS vs Michigan State since 2008
- vs Michigan State - Michigan leads series 71-38-5
- 0-5 S/U & ATS vs Michigan State as Dog since 2008
- 15-2 S/U vs Northwestern since 1997
- vs Ohio State - Michigan leads series 59-52-6
- Game 6-0 O/U @ home vs Ohio State since 2011
- 2-15 S/U vs Ohio State since 2004
- Game 8-0 O/U vs Ohio State since 2013
- 1-14 S/U vs Ohio State as Dog since 2002
- 7-0 O/U vs Ohio State as Dog since 2013
- 0-5 ATS @ Ohio State as favorite since 1986
- 6-0 S/U @ home vs Penn State as favorite since 2000
- vs Penn State - Michigan leads series 15-10
- Game 6-1 O/U @ Penn State since 2008
- 0-4 S/U vs Penn State as Dog since 2008
- vs Rutgers - Michigan leads series 7-1
- Game 7-1 O/U vs Rutgers since 2014
- 26-0 S/U vs Indiana as 9 point or more favorite since 1983
- 10-0-1 S/U vs Iowa as 6-13.5 point favorite since 1983
- 4-0 S/U vs Iowa as 17-21 point favorite since 1992
- 9-1 S/U vs Michigan State as 13.5 point or more favorite since 1983
- 1-8 S/U vs Ohio State as 7.5 point or more Dog since 1996
- 8-0 S/U vs Penn State as 3.5 point or more favorite since 2000
- 16-1 S/U vs Wisconsin as 3.5 point or more favorite since 1983

COLO STATE	10-3 ATS in 1st home game of season since 2009
COLO STATE	12-1 S/U in 1st home game of season since 2009
HAWAII	13-1 S/U in 2nd home game of season since 2008
MARYLAND	13-2 S/U prior to playing Iowa since 1997
Indiana	9-2 O/U prior to playing Penn State since 2009
Indiana	11-3 O/U in 2nd road game of season since 2008
PENN STATE	13-0 S/U prior to playing Michigan State since 2009
MICH STATE	3-9 ATS after playing Penn State since 2007
Rutgers	7-1 S/U prior to playing Nebraska since 1905
ILLINOIS	8-0 S/U after playing Nebraska since 1905

- 3-21 S/U on road vs ranked teams since 2006
- 0-9 S/U vs #1 ranked teams since 1984
- 0-7 S/U on road vs #1 ranked teams all time

Hail to the Victors! History of Michigan Wolverines Football

Available at: www.stevesfootballbible.com (Blueblood Series)

MICHIGAN STATE SPARTANS — BIG TEN East

2021-Michigan State		Opponent	MSU	Opp	S/U	Line	ATS	Total	O/U	
9/3/2021	@	Northwestern	38	21	W	3.0	W	45.0	O	
9/11/2021	vs	YOUNGSTOWN STATE	42	14	W	-29.0	L	52.0	O	
9/18/2021	@	Miami	38	17	W	7.0	W	57.5	U	
9/25/2021	vs	NEBRASKA	23	20	W	-3.5	L	54.5	U	{OT}
10/2/2021	vs	WESTERN KENTUCKY	48	31	W	-11.0	W	67.0	O	
10/9/2021	@	Rutgers	31	13	W	-4.0	W	49.5	U	
10/16/2021	@	Indiana	20	15	W	-3.5	W	48.5	U	"Old Brass Spittoon"
10/30/2021	vs	MICHIGAN	37	33	W	4.0	W	50.5	O	"Paul Bunyan Trophy"
11/6/2021	@	Purdue	29	40	L	-2.5	L	53.0	O	
11/13/2021	vs	MARYLAND	40	21	W	-11.5	W	59.5	O	
11/20/2021	@	Ohio State	7	56	L	19.0	L	70.5	U	
11/27/2021	vs	PENN STATE	30	27	W	3.5	W	51.5	O	"Land Grant Trophy"
12/30/2021	vs	Pittsburgh	31	21	W	-3.0	W	54.5	U	Chick-Fil-A Peach Bowl
Coach: Mel Tucker		Season Record >>	414	329	11-2	ATS>>	9-4	O/U>>	7-6	

2020-Michigan State		Opponent	MSU	Opp	S/U	Line	ATS	Total	O/U	
10/24/2020	vs	RUTGERS	27	38	L	-9.5	L	45.0	O	
10/31/2020	@	Michigan	27	24	W	22.0	W	51.5	U	"Paul Bunyan Trophy"
11/7/2020	@	Iowa	7	49	L	5.5	L	45.5	O	
11/14/2020	vs	INDIANA	0	24	L	7.5	L	52.5	U	"Old Brass Spittoon"
11/28/2020	vs	NORTHWESTERN	23	20	W	13.5	W	40.0	U	
12/5/2020	vs	OHIO STATE	12	52	L	22.0	L	58.5	O	
12/12/2020	@	Penn State	24	39	L	14.5	L	46.5	O	"Land Grant Trophy"
Coach: Mel Tucker		Season Record >>	120	246	2-5	ATS>>	2-5	O/U>>	4-3	

2019-Michigan State		Opponent	MSU	Opp	S/U	Line	ATS	Total	O/U	
8/30/2019	vs	TULSA	28	7	W	-23.5	L	47.0	U	
9/7/2019	vs	WESTERN MICHIGAN	51	17	W	-15.0	W	46.0	O	
9/14/2019	vs	ARIZONA STATE	7	10	L	-15.5	L	42.0	U	
9/21/2019	@	Northwestern	31	10	W	-7.5	W	35.5	O	
9/28/2019	vs	INDIANA	40	31	W	-14.0	L	43.0	O	"Old Brass Spittoon"
10/5/2019	@	Ohio State	10	34	L	20.0	L	51.0	U	
10/12/2019	@	Wisconsin	0	38	L	8.0	L	40.5	U	
10/26/2019	vs	PENN STATE	7	28	L	4.5	L	42.0	U	"Land Grant Trophy"
11/9/2019	vs	ILLINOIS	34	37	L	-15.5	L	47.5	O	
11/16/2019	@	Michigan	10	44	L	14.0	L	43.5	O	"Paul Bunyan Trophy"
11/23/2019	@	Rutgers	27	0	W	-22.0	W	43.5	U	
11/30/2019	vs	MARYLAND	19	16	W	-22.0	L	47.5	U	
12/27/2019	vs	Wake Forest	27	21	W	-4.0	W	51.5	U	Pinstripe Bowl
Coach: Mark Dantonio		Season Record >>	291	293	7-6	ATS>>	4-9	O/U>>	5-8	

2018-Michigan State		Opponent	MSU	Opp	S/U	Line	ATS	Total	O/U	
8/31/2018	vs	UTAH STATE	38	31	W	-23.5	L	52.0	O	
9/8/2018	@	Arizona State	13	16	L	-4.5	L	54.0	U	
9/22/2018	@	Indiana	35	21	W	-6.5	W	51.0	O	"Old Brass Spittoon"
9/29/2018	vs	CENTRAL MICHIGAN	31	20	W	-28.0	L	45.0	O	
10/6/2018	vs	NORTHWESTERN	19	29	L	-10.0	L	43.5	O	
10/13/2018	@	Penn State	21	17	W	13.5	W	53.5	U	"Land Grant Trophy"
10/20/2018	vs	MICHIGAN	7	21	L	7.0	L	39.0	U	"Paul Bunyan Trophy"
10/27/2018	vs	PURDUE	23	13	W	2.5	W	49.0	U	
11/3/2018	@	Maryland	24	3	W	-3.5	W	42.5	U	
11/10/2018	vs	OHIO STATE	6	26	L	3.5	L	49.5	U	
11/17/2018	@	Nebraska	6	9	L	1.0	L	48.0	U	
11/24/2018	vs	RUTGERS	14	10	W	-24.5	L	37.0	U	
12/31/2018	vs	Oregon	6	7	L	-1.5	L	47.0	U	Redbox Bowl
Coach: Mark Dantonio		Season Record >>	243	223	7-6	ATS>>	4-9	O/U>>	4-9	

Page | 130

MICHIGAN STATE SPARTANS — BIG TEN East

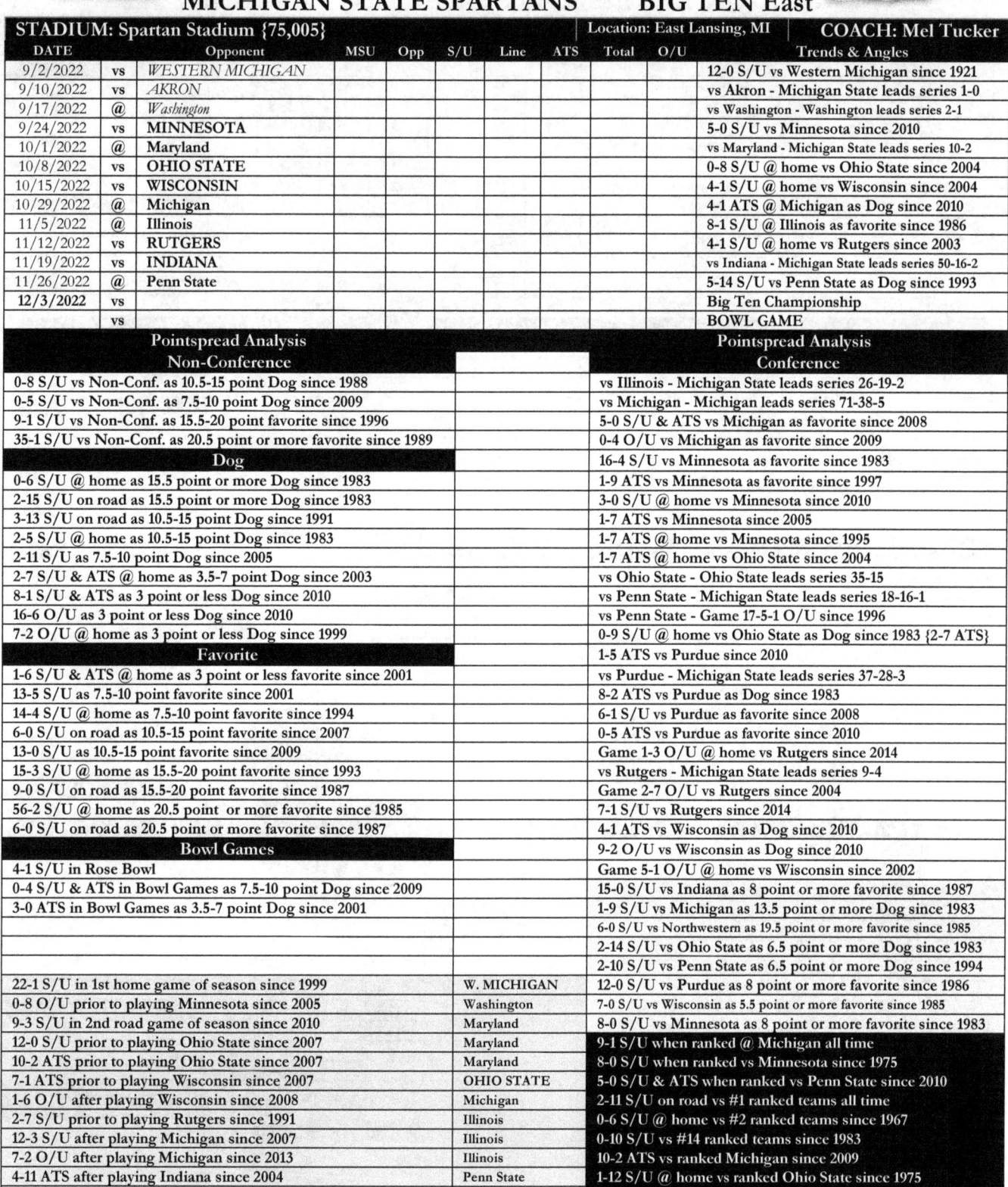

STADIUM: Spartan Stadium {75,005}
Location: East Lansing, MI
COACH: Mel Tucker

DATE		Opponent	MSU	Opp	S/U	Line	ATS	Total	O/U	Trends & Angles
9/2/2022	vs	WESTERN MICHIGAN								12-0 S/U vs Western Michigan since 1921
9/10/2022	vs	AKRON								vs Akron - Michigan State leads series 1-0
9/17/2022	@	Washington								vs Washington - Washington leads series 2-1
9/24/2022	vs	MINNESOTA								5-0 S/U vs Minnesota since 2010
10/1/2022	@	Maryland								vs Maryland - Michigan State leads series 10-2
10/8/2022	vs	OHIO STATE								0-8 S/U @ home vs Ohio State since 2004
10/15/2022	vs	WISCONSIN								4-1 S/U @ home vs Wisconsin since 2004
10/29/2022	@	Michigan								4-1 ATS @ Michigan as Dog since 2010
11/5/2022	@	Illinois								8-1 S/U @ Illinois as favorite since 1986
11/12/2022	vs	RUTGERS								4-1 S/U @ home vs Rutgers since 2003
11/19/2022	vs	INDIANA								vs Indiana - Michigan State leads series 50-16-2
11/26/2022	@	Penn State								5-14 S/U vs Penn State as Dog since 1993
12/3/2022	vs									Big Ten Championship
	vs									BOWL GAME

Pointspread Analysis — Non-Conference

- 0-8 S/U vs Non-Conf. as 10.5-15 point Dog since 1988
- 0-5 S/U vs Non-Conf. as 7.5-10 point Dog since 2009
- 9-1 S/U vs Non-Conf. as 15.5-20 point favorite since 1996
- 35-1 S/U vs Non-Conf. as 20.5 point or more favorite since 1989

Dog
- 0-6 S/U @ home as 15.5 point or more Dog since 1983
- 2-15 S/U on road as 15.5 point or more Dog since 1983
- 3-13 S/U on road as 10.5-15 point Dog since 1991
- 2-5 S/U @ home as 10.5-15 point Dog since 1983
- 2-11 S/U as 7.5-10 point Dog since 2005
- 2-7 S/U & ATS @ home as 3.5-7 point Dog since 2003
- 8-1 S/U & ATS as 3 point or less Dog since 2010
- 16-6 O/U as 3 point or less Dog since 2010
- 7-2 O/U @ home as 3 point or less Dog since 1999

Favorite
- 1-6 S/U & ATS @ home as 3 point or less favorite since 2001
- 13-5 S/U as 7.5-10 point favorite since 2001
- 14-4 S/U @ home as 7.5-10 point favorite since 1994
- 6-0 S/U on road as 10.5-15 point favorite since 2007
- 13-0 S/U as 10.5-15 point favorite since 2009
- 15-3 S/U @ home as 15.5-20 point favorite since 1993
- 9-0 S/U on road as 15.5-20 point favorite since 1987
- 56-2 S/U @ home as 20.5 point or more favorite since 1985
- 6-0 S/U on road as 20.5 point or more favorite since 1987

Bowl Games
- 4-1 S/U in Rose Bowl
- 0-4 S/U & ATS in Bowl Games as 7.5-10 point Dog since 2009
- 3-0 ATS in Bowl Games as 3.5-7 point Dog since 2001

- 22-1 S/U in 1st home game of season since 1999 — W. MICHIGAN
- 0-8 O/U prior to playing Minnesota since 2005 — Washington
- 9-3 S/U in 2nd road game of season since 2010 — Maryland
- 12-0 S/U prior to playing Ohio State since 2007 — Maryland
- 10-2 ATS prior to playing Ohio State since 2007 — Maryland
- 7-1 ATS prior to playing Wisconsin since 2007 — OHIO STATE
- 1-6 O/U after playing Wisconsin since 2008 — Michigan
- 2-7 S/U prior to playing Rutgers since 1991 — Illinois
- 12-3 S/U after playing Michigan since 2007 — Illinois
- 7-2 O/U after playing Michigan since 2013 — Illinois
- 4-11 ATS after playing Indiana since 2004 — Penn State
- 9-4 S/U in final road game of season since 2009 — Penn State
- 9-4 ATS in final road game of season since 2009 — Penn State
- 4-11 O/U after playing Indiana since 2004 — Penn State

Pointspread Analysis — Conference

- vs Illinois - Michigan State leads series 26-19-2
- vs Michigan - Michigan leads series 71-38-5
- 5-0 S/U & ATS vs Michigan as favorite since 2008
- 0-4 O/U vs Michigan as favorite since 2009
- 16-4 S/U vs Minnesota as favorite since 1983
- 1-9 ATS vs Minnesota as favorite since 1997
- 3-0 S/U @ home vs Minnesota since 2010
- 1-7 ATS vs Minnesota since 2005
- 1-7 ATS @ home vs Minnesota since 1995
- 1-7 ATS @ home vs Ohio State since 2004
- vs Ohio State - Ohio State leads series 35-15
- vs Penn State - Michigan State leads series 18-16-1
- vs Penn State - Game 17-5-1 O/U since 1996
- 0-9 S/U @ home vs Ohio State as Dog since 1983 {2-7 ATS}
- 1-5 ATS vs Purdue since 2010
- vs Purdue - Michigan State leads series 37-28-3
- 8-2 ATS vs Purdue as Dog since 1983
- 6-1 S/U vs Purdue as favorite since 2008
- 0-5 ATS vs Purdue as favorite since 2010
- Game 1-3 O/U @ home vs Rutgers since 2014
- vs Rutgers - Michigan State leads series 9-4
- Game 2-7 O/U vs Rutgers since 2004
- 7-1 S/U vs Rutgers since 2014
- 4-1 ATS vs Wisconsin as Dog since 2010
- 9-2 O/U vs Wisconsin as Dog since 2010
- Game 5-1 O/U @ home vs Wisconsin since 2002
- 15-0 S/U vs Indiana as 8 point or more favorite since 1987
- 1-9 S/U vs Michigan as 13.5 point or more Dog since 1983
- 6-0 S/U vs Northwestern as 19.5 point or more favorite since 1985
- 2-14 S/U vs Ohio State as 6.5 point or more Dog since 1983
- 2-10 S/U vs Penn State as 6.5 point or more Dog since 1994
- 12-0 S/U vs Purdue as 8 point or more favorite since 1986
- 7-0 S/U vs Wisconsin as 5.5 point or more favorite since 1985
- 8-0 S/U vs Minnesota as 8 point or more favorite since 1983
- 9-1 S/U when ranked @ Michigan all time
- 8-0 S/U when ranked vs Minnesota since 1975
- 5-0 S/U & ATS when ranked vs Penn State since 2010
- 2-11 S/U on road vs #1 ranked teams all time
- 0-6 S/U @ home vs #2 ranked teams since 1967
- 0-10 S/U vs #14 ranked teams since 1983
- 10-2 ATS vs ranked Michigan since 2009
- 1-12 S/U @ home vs ranked Ohio State since 1975
- 12-1 S/U @ home when #1 ranked all time
- 24-2-1 S/U when #2 ranked all time
- 22-4 S/U when ranked vs Indiana all time

MIDDLE TENNESSEE BLUE RAIDERS   C-USA East

2021-Middle Tennessee		Opponent	MTSU	Opp	S/U	Line	ATS	Total	O/U	
9/4/2021	vs	MONMOUTH	50	15	W	-9.5	W	58.0	O	
9/11/2021	@	Virginia Tech	14	35	L	20.0	L	54.5	U	
9/18/2021	@	Texas-San Antonio	13	27	L	10.5	L	59.5	U	
9/24/2021	@	Charlotte	39	42	L	2.5	L	55.5	O	
10/2/2021	vs	MARSHALL	34	28	W	10.5	W	66.0	U	
10/9/2021	@	Liberty	13	41	L	20.0	L	58.5	U	
10/23/2021	@	Connecticut	44	13	W	-14.5	W	54.0	O	
10/30/2021	vs	SOUTHERN MISS	35	10	W	-12.5	W	47.0	U	
11/6/2021	@	Western Kentucky	21	48	L	17.5	L	67.0	O	100 Miles of Hate Rivalry
11/13/2021	vs	FLORIDA INTERNATIONAL	50	10	W	-10.5	W	54.5	O	
11/20/2021	vs	OLD DOMINION	17	24	L	-3.0	L	48.5	U	
11/27/2021	@	Florida Atlantic	27	17	W	3.5	W	49.0	U	
12/17/2021	vs	Toledo	31	24	W	10.5	W	50.5	O	Bahamas Bowl
Coach: Rick Stockstill		Season Record >>	388	334	7-6	ATS>>	7-6	O/U>>	6-7	

2020-Middle Tennessee		Opponent	MTSU	Opp	S/U	Line	ATS	Total	O/U	
9/5/2020	@	Army	0	42	L	3.5	L	54.0	U	
9/19/2020	vs	TROY	14	47	L	2.5	L	65.0	U	"The Palladium Trophy"
9/26/2020	@	Texas-San Antonio	35	37	L	-16.5	L	58.5	O	
10/3/2020	vs	WESTERN KENTUCKY	17	20	L	7.0	W	51.0	U	100 Miles of Hate Rivalry
10/10/2020	@	Florida International	38	28	W	6.5	W	56.5	O	
10/17/2020	vs	NORTH TEXAS	35	52	L	-3.5	L	70.5	O	
10/24/2020	@	Rice	40	34	W	4.0	W	48.0	O	{OT}
11/14/2020	@	Marshall	14	42	L	23.5	L	55.5	O	
11/21/2020	@	Troy	20	17	W	10.5	W	60.5	U	"The Palladium Trophy"
Coach: Rick Stockstill		Season Record >>	213	319	3-6	ATS>>	4-5	O/U>>	5-4	

2019-Middle Tennessee		Opponent	MTSU	Opp	S/U	Line	ATS	Total	O/U	
8/31/2019	@	Michigan	21	40	L	36.5	W	55.0	O	
9/7/2019	vs	TENNESSEE STATE	45	26	W	-26.5	L	NT	---	
9/14/2019	vs	DUKE	18	41	L	6.5	L	51.0	O	
9/28/2019	@	Iowa	3	48	L	23.5	L	51.0	T	
10/5/2019	vs	MARSHALL	24	13	W	4.0	W	53.5	U	
10/12/2019	@	Florida Atlantic	13	28	L	12.5	L	63.5	U	
10/19/2019	@	North Texas	30	33	L	7.0	W	59.5	O	
10/26/2019	vs	FLORIDA INTERNATIONAL	50	17	W	1.5	W	57.5	O	
11/2/2019	@	Charlotte	20	34	L	-3.5	L	65.5	U	
11/16/2019	vs	RICE	28	31	L	-13.0	L	47.0	O	
11/23/2019	vs	OLD DOMINION	38	17	W	-13.5	W	47.0	O	
11/30/2019	@	Western Kentucky	26	31	L	10.0	W	46.0	O	100 Miles of Hate Rivalry
Coach: Rick Stockstill		Season Record >>	316	359	4-8	ATS>>	6-6	O/U>>	7-3-1	

2018-Middle Tennessee		Opponent	MTSU	Opp	S/U	Line	ATS	Total	O/U	
9/1/2018	@	Vanderbilt	7	35	L	3.0	L	56.5	U	
9/8/2018	vs	TENNESSEE-MARTIN	61	37	W	-19.5	W	NT	---	
9/15/2018	@	Georgia	7	49	L	33.5	L	59.5	U	
9/29/2018	vs	FLORIDA ATLANTIC	25	24	W	2.5	W	62.0	U	
10/6/2018	@	Marshall	34	24	W	3.0	W	50.5	O	
10/13/2018	@	Florida International	21	24	L	1.5	L	60.5	U	
10/20/2018	vs	CHARLOTTE	21	13	W	-15.0	L	50.0	U	
10/27/2018	@	Old Dominion	51	17	W	-4.5	W	62.0	O	
11/3/2018	vs	WESTERN KENTUCKY	29	10	W	-11.5	W	52.5	U	100 Miles of Hate Rivalry
11/10/2018	@	Texas-El Paso	48	32	W	-13.5	W	48.0	O	
11/17/2018	@	Kentucky	23	34	L	16.5	W	48.0	O	
11/24/2018	vs	ALABAMA-BIRMINGHAM	27	3	W	3.0	W	52.0	U	
12/1/2018	vs	ALABAMA-BIRMINGHAM	25	27	L	-1.0	L	44.0	O	C-USA Championship Game
12/15/2018	vs	Appalachian State	13	45	L	6.5	L	49.0	O	New Orleans Bowl
Coach: Rick Stockstill		Season Record >>	392	374	8-6	ATS>>	8-6	O/U>>	6-7	

MIDDLE TENNESSEE BLUE RAIDERS — C-USA East

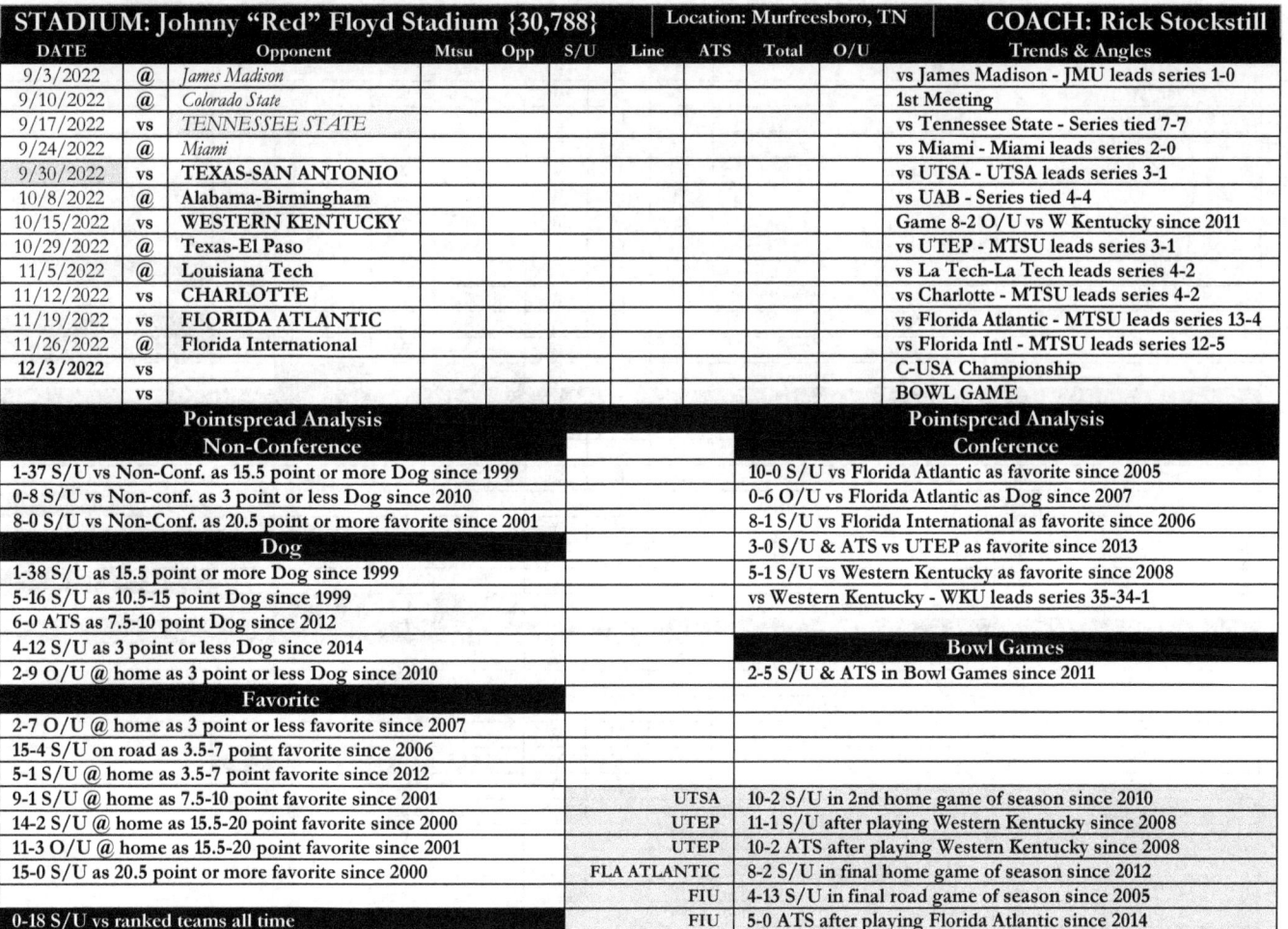

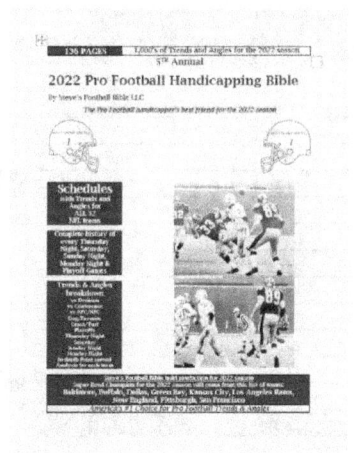

STADIUM: Johnny "Red" Floyd Stadium {30,788} | **Location:** Murfreesboro, TN | **COACH:** Rick Stockstill

DATE		Opponent	Mtsu	Opp	S/U	Line	ATS	Total	O/U	Trends & Angles
9/3/2022	@	James Madison								vs James Madison - JMU leads series 1-0
9/10/2022	@	Colorado State								1st Meeting
9/17/2022	vs	TENNESSEE STATE								vs Tennessee State - Series tied 7-7
9/24/2022	@	Miami								vs Miami - Miami leads series 2-0
9/30/2022	vs	TEXAS-SAN ANTONIO								vs UTSA - UTSA leads series 3-1
10/8/2022	@	Alabama-Birmingham								vs UAB - Series tied 4-4
10/15/2022	vs	WESTERN KENTUCKY								Game 8-2 O/U vs W Kentucky since 2011
10/29/2022	vs	Texas-El Paso								vs UTEP - MTSU leads series 3-1
11/5/2022	@	Louisiana Tech								vs La Tech-La Tech leads series 4-2
11/12/2022	vs	CHARLOTTE								vs Charlotte - MTSU leads series 4-2
11/19/2022	vs	FLORIDA ATLANTIC								vs Florida Atlantic - MTSU leads series 13-4
11/26/2022	@	Florida International								vs Florida Intl - MTSU leads series 12-5
12/3/2022	vs									C-USA Championship
	vs									BOWL GAME

Pointspread Analysis — Non-Conference
- 1-37 S/U vs Non-Conf. as 15.5 point or more Dog since 1999
- 0-8 S/U vs Non-conf. as 3 point or less Dog since 2010
- 8-0 S/U vs Non-Conf. as 20.5 point or more favorite since 2001

Dog
- 1-38 S/U as 15.5 point or more Dog since 1999
- 5-16 S/U as 10.5-15 point Dog since 1999
- 6-0 ATS as 7.5-10 point Dog since 2012
- 4-12 S/U as 3 point or less Dog since 2014
- 2-9 O/U @ home as 3 point or less Dog since 2010

Favorite
- 2-7 O/U @ home as 3 point or less favorite since 2007
- 15-4 S/U on road as 3.5-7 point favorite since 2006
- 5-1 S/U @ home as 3.5-7 point favorite since 2012
- 9-1 S/U @ home as 7.5-10 point favorite since 2001
- 14-2 S/U @ home as 15.5-20 point favorite since 2000
- 11-3 O/U @ home as 15.5-20 point favorite since 2001
- 15-0 S/U as 20.5 point or more favorite since 2000

- 0-18 S/U vs ranked teams all time

Pointspread Analysis — Conference
- 10-0 S/U vs Florida Atlantic as favorite since 2005
- 0-6 O/U vs Florida Atlantic as Dog since 2007
- 8-1 S/U vs Florida International as favorite since 2006
- 3-0 S/U & ATS vs UTEP as favorite since 2013
- 5-1 S/U vs Western Kentucky as favorite since 2008
- vs Western Kentucky - WKU leads series 35-34-1

Bowl Games
- 2-5 S/U & ATS in Bowl Games since 2011

UTSA	10-2 S/U in 2nd home game of season since 2010
UTEP	11-1 S/U after playing Western Kentucky since 2008
UTEP	10-2 ATS after playing Western Kentucky since 2008
FLA ATLANTIC	8-2 S/U in final home game of season since 2012
FIU	4-13 S/U in final road game of season since 2005
FIU	5-0 ATS after playing Florida Atlantic since 2014

2022 Pro Football Bible $24.95   2022 FCS College Football Bible $19.95
www.stevesfootballbible.com

MINNESOTA GOLDEN GOPHERS BIG TEN West

2021-Minnesota		Opponent	MN	Opp	S/U	Line	ATS	Total	O/U	
9/2/2021	vs	OHIO STATE	31	45	L	14.0	T	62.0	O	
9/11/2021	vs	MIAMI-OHIO	31	26	W	-18.0	L	55.0	O	
9/18/2021	@	Colorado	30	0	W	2.0	W	49.0	U	
9/25/2021	vs	BOWLING GREEN	10	14	L	-30.5	L	50.5	U	
10/2/2021	@	Purdue	20	13	W	2.5	W	46.0	U	
10/16/2021	vs	NEBRASKA	30	23	W	4.5	W	49.0	O	
10/23/2021	vs	MARYLAND	34	16	W	-4.0	W	52.0	U	
10/30/2021	@	Northwestern	41	14	W	-7.5	W	43.5	O	
11/6/2021	vs	ILLINOIS	6	14	L	-14.5	L	44.0	U	
11/13/2021	@	Iowa	22	27	L	4.0	L	37.0	U	"Floyd of Rosedale"
11/20/2021	@	Indiana	35	14	W	-7.5	W	43.0	O	
11/27/2021	vs	WISCONSIN	23	13	W	7.0	W	39.0	U	"Paul Bunyan Axe"
12/28/2021	vs	West Virginia	18	6	W	-6.5	W	45.0	U	Guaranteed Rate Bowl
Coach: P.J. Fleck		Season Record >>	331	225	9-4	ATS>>	8-4-1	O/U>>	5-8	

2020-Minnesota		Opponent	MN	Opp	S/U	Line	ATS	Total	O/U	
10/24/2020	vs	MICHIGAN	24	49	L	2.5	L	54.5	O	"Little Brown Jug"
10/30/2020	@	Maryland	44	45	L	-17.0	L	60.5	O	{OT}
11/7/2020	@	Illinois	41	14	W	-7.5	W	64.5	O	
11/13/2020	vs	IOWA	7	35	L	3.0	L	58.0	U	"Floyd of Rosedale"
11/20/2020	vs	PURDUE	34	31	W	2.5	W	62.5	O	
12/12/2020	@	Nebraska	24	17	W	8.5	W	61.5	U	
12/19/2020	@	Wisconsin	17	20	L	10.0	W	47.0	U	"Paul Bunyan Axe"
Coach: P.J. Fleck		Season Record >>	191	211	3-4	ATS>>	4-3	O/U>>	4-3	

2019-Minnesota		Opponent	MN	Opp	S/U	Line	ATS	Total	O/U	
8/30/2019	vs	SOUTH DAKOTA STATE	28	21	W	-14.0	L	NT	---	
9/7/2019	@	Fresno State	38	35	W	-3.0	T	46.0	O	{2 OT}
9/14/2019	vs	GEORGIA SOUTHERN	35	32	W	-17.0	L	45.5	O	
9/28/2019	@	Purdue	38	31	W	1.5	W	56.0	O	
10/5/2019	vs	ILLINOIS	40	17	W	-14.5	W	57.0	T	
10/12/2019	vs	NEBRASKA	34	7	W	-7.5	W	47.5	U	
10/19/2019	@	Rutgers	42	7	W	-28.5	W	46.5	O	
10/26/2019	vs	MARYLAND	52	10	W	-14.5	W	58.5	O	
11/9/2019	vs	PENN STATE	31	26	W	5.5	W	48.5	O	"Governor's Victory Bell"
11/16/2019	@	Iowa	19	23	L	3.0	L	45.0	U	"Floyd of Rosedale"
11/23/2019	@	Northwestern	38	22	W	-15.5	W	41.5	O	
11/30/2019	vs	WISCONSIN	17	38	L	3.0	L	45.0	O	"Paul Bunyan Axe"
1/1/2020	vs	Auburn	31	24	W	7.0	W	53.5	O	Outback Bowl
Coach: P.J. Fleck		Season Record >>	443	293	11-2	ATS>>	8-4-1	O/U>>	9-2-1	

2018-Minnesota		Opponent	MN	Opp	S/U	Line	ATS	Total	O/U	
8/30/2018	vs	NEW MEXICO STATE	48	10	W	-21.5	W	47.5	O	
9/8/2018	vs	FRESNO STATE	21	14	W	PK	W	50.0	U	
9/15/2018	vs	MIAMI-OHIO	26	3	W	-13.5	W	46.5	U	
9/29/2018	@	Maryland	13	42	L	PK	L	46.5	O	
10/6/2018	vs	IOWA	31	48	L	7.0	L	41.5	O	"Floyd of Rosedale"
10/13/2018	@	Ohio State	14	30	L	29.5	W	60.0	U	
10/20/2018	@	Nebraska	28	53	L	5.5	L	55.0	O	
10/26/2019	vs	INDIANA	38	31	W	2.5	W	54.0	O	
11/3/2018	@	Illinois	31	55	L	-10.0	L	62.0	O	
11/10/2018	vs	PURDUE	41	10	W	10.5	W	58.0	U	
11/17/2018	vs	NORTHWESTERN	14	24	L	-3.0	L	48.5	U	
11/24/2018	@	Wisconsin	37	15	W	12.5	W	54.0	U	"Paul Bunyan Axe"
12/26/2018	vs	Georgia Tech	34	10	W	5.0	W	57.0	U	Quick Lane Bowl
Coach: P.J. Fleck		Season Record >>	376	345	7-6	ATS>>	8-5	O/U>>	6-7	

"Golden Memories" History of the Minnesota Golden Gophers

Available at: www.stevesfootballbible.com

MINNESOTA GOLDEN GOPHERS BIG TEN West

STADIUM: TCF Bank Stadium {50,805} | **Location:** Minneapolis, MN | **COACH:** P.J. Fleck

DATE		Opponent	Minn	Opp	S/U	Line	ATS	Total	O/U	Trends & Angles
9/1/2022	vs	NEW MEXICO STATE								vs New Mexico State - Minnesota leads series 2-1
9/10/2022	vs	WESTERN ILLINOIS								vs Western Illinois - Minnesota leads series 1-0
9/17/2022	vs	COLORADO								vs Colorado - Colorado leads series 3-1
9/24/2022	@	Michigan State								9-1 ATS vs Michigan State as Dog since 1997
10/1/2022	vs	PURDUE								6-0 S/U @ home vs Purdue since 2009
10/15/2022	@	Illinois								vs Illinois - Minnesota leads series 40-31-3
10/22/2022	@	Penn State								0-3 S/U @ Penn State since 2005
10/29/2022	vs	RUTGERS								vs Rutgers - Minnesota leads series 2-0
11/5/2022	@	Nebraska								2-9 S/U @ Nebraska since 1967
11/12/2022	vs	NORTHWESTERN								Game 0-4 O/U @ home vs NW since 2012
11/19/2022	vs	IOWA								0-7 S/U vs Iowa since 2015
11/26/2022	@	Wisconsin								1-12 S/U @ Wisconsin since 1996
12/3/2022	vs									Big Ten Championship
	vs									BOWL GAME

Pointspread Analysis — Non-Conference
- 0-10 S/U vs Non-Conf. as 10.5 point or more Dog since 1985
- 7-0 S/U vs Non-Conf. as 3 point or less Dog since 1989
- 5-0 S/U vs Non-Conf. as 3 point or less favorite since 1998
- 7-1 S/U vs Non-Conf. as 7.5-10 point favorite since 2000
- 14-2 S/U vs Non-Conf. as 10.5-15 point favorite since 1994
- 23-4 S/U vs Non-Conf. as 15.5 point or more favorite since 1995

Dog
- 0-15 S/U on road as 25.5 point or more Dog since 1983
- 0-11 S/U @ home as 20.5 point or more Dog since 1983
- 2-15 S/U on road as 20.5-25 point Dog since 1989
- 0-4 O/U @ home as 15.5-20 point Dog since 2011
- 0-18 S/U on road as 15.5-20 point Dog since 1985
- 3-10 ATS on road as 15.5-20 point Dog since 1990
- 1-26 S/U as 15.5-20 point Dog since 1985
- 14-3-2 ATS as 10.5-15 point Dog since 2007
- 3-13 S/U @ home as 10.5-15 point Dog since 1994
- 2-21 S/U on road as 3.5-7 point Dog since 1993
- 7-33 S/U as 3.5-7 point Dog since 1993
- 2-11 S/U @ home as 3.5-7 point Dog since 1992
- 8-1 O/U @ home as 3.5-7 point Dog since 2001

Favorite
- 7-3 S/U @ home as 3 point or less favorite since 1998
- 10-4-1 ATS as 3 point or less favorite since 2006
- 7-2-1 ATS on road as 3 point or less favorite since 1986
- 8-2 S/U on road as 3 point or less favorite since 1986
- 8-2 S/U on road as 3.5-7 point favorite since 1985
- 6-0 S/U as 3.5-7 point favorite since 2015 {5-1 ATS}
- 5-0 S/U @ home as 3.5-7 point favorite since 2011 {5-0 ATS}
- 7-0 O/U on road as 7.5-10 point favorite since 2000
- 2-6 ATS @ home as 7.5-10 point favorite since 2003
- 7-2 S/U on road as 10.5-15 point favorite since 1985
- 19-3 S/U @ home as 10.5-15 point favorite since 1994
- 9-0 S/U @ home as 15.5-20 point favorite since 2002
- 19-3 S/U @ home as 20.5 point or more favorite since 1995

Bowl Games
- 0-4 S/U vs Big 12 in Bowl Games
- 5-0 S/U & ATS in Bowl Games since 2015
- 1-4 O/U in Bowl Games since 2015

- 1-8 S/U @ ranked Nebraska since 1967
- 0-5 S/U @ ranked Illinois all time
- 9-1-1 S/U @ home when ranked vs Northwestern all time

Pointspread Analysis — Conference
- 3-0 S/U & ATS vs Illinois as Dog since 2008
- vs Iowa - Minnesota leads series 63-50-2
- 0-6 ATS vs Iowa since 2016
- 0-5 S/U vs Michigan State as Dog since 2010
- 1-9 S/U @ Michigan State as Dog since 1983
- 6-0 ATS @ Michigan State as Dog since 1995
- vs Nebraska - Minnesota leads series 35-25-2
- vs Northwestern - Minnesota leads series 55-36-5
- Game 2-7-1 O/U vs Northwestern since 2011
- 2-5 S/U vs Penn State since 2005
- 4-1 S/U vs Penn State as favorite since 2000
- 2-8 S/U vs Penn State as Dog since 1993
- 8-0 S/U @ home vs Purdue as favorite since 1987
- Game 12-1 O/U @ home vs Purdue since 1993
- 10-2 S/U vs Purdue as favorite since 1983
- Game 8-2 O/U vs Purdue since 2011
- vs Purdue - Minnesota leads series 41-33-3
- vs Wisconsin - Wisconsin leads series 62-61-8
- 2-16 S/U vs Wisconsin since 2004
- 3-21 S/U vs Wisconsin as Dog since 1995
- 1-7 ATS vs Wisconsin as favorite since 1987
- Game 9-2 O/U @ Wisconsin since 2000
- 5-0 S/U vs Illinois as 4.5 point or less favorite since 1996
- 0-6 S/U vs Nebraska as 19 point or more Dog since 1983
- 0-5 S/U vs Northwestern as 5-10.5 point Dog since 1996
- 7-0-1 S/U vs Northwestern as 10.5 point or more favorite since 1985

WESTERN ILL	10-1 S/U in 2nd home game of season since 2011
Illinois	10-3 O/U in 2nd road game of season since 2008
Illinois	3-13 S/U after playing Purdue since 2005
Illinois	8-2 S/U prior to playing Penn State since 2000
RUTGERS	0-6 S/U after playing Penn State since 2006 {1-5 ATS}
IOWA	3-9 O/U in final home game of season since 2010
Wisconsin	12-3-1 ATS in final road game of season since 2006
Wisconsin	3-8 S/U in final road game of season since 2011

- 2-16 S/U when ranked vs ranked teams since 1962
- 1-13 S/U on road when ranked vs ranked teams since 1942
- 7-1 S/U @ home when ranked vs Iowa all time
- 6-77 S/U on road vs ranked teams since 1970
- 0-12 S/U on road vs #1 ranked teams all time
- 1-8 S/U @ ranked Michigan State all time
- 2-17 S/U vs ranked Wisconsin since 1954

MISSISSIPPI REBELS   SEC West

2021-Mississippi		Opponent	Miss	Opp	S/U	Line	ATS	Total	O/U	
9/6/2021	vs	Louisville	43	24	W	-9.0	W	75.0	U	@ Atlanta, GA
9/11/2021	vs	AUSTIN PEAY	54	17	W	-37.0	T	69.5	O	
9/18/2021	vs	TULANE	61	21	W	-14.0	W	77.0	O	
10/2/2021	@	Alabama	21	42	L	14.5	L	79.5	U	
10/9/2021	vs	ARKANSAS	52	51	W	-4.5	L	66.5	O	
10/16/2021	@	Tennessee	31	26	W	-1.0	W	82.5	U	
10/23/2021	vs	LSU	31	17	W	-9.5	W	77.0	U	"Magnolia Bowl Trophy"
10/30/2021	@	Auburn	20	31	L	3.0	L	67.5	U	
11/6/2021	vs	LIBERTY	27	14	W	-7.5	W	67.0	U	
11/13/2021	vs	TEXAS A&M	29	19	W	-1.0	W	58.5	U	
11/20/2021	vs	VANDERBILT	31	17	W	35.5	L	64.5	U	
11/27/2021	@	Mississippi State	31	21	W	2.0	W	65.5	U	""Egg Bowl" - "Golden Egg Trophy""
1/1/2022	vs	Baylor	7	21	L	-2.0	L	60.0	U	Sugar Bowl
Coach: Lane Kiffin		Season Record >>	438	321	10-3	ATS>>	7-5-1	O/U>>	3-10	

2020-Mississippi		Opponent	Miss	Opp	S/U	Line	ATS	Total	O/U	
9/26/2020	vs	FLORIDA	35	51	L	14.0	L	58.5	O	
10/3/2020	@	Kentucky	42	41	W	6.5	W	63.0	O	{OT}
10/10/2020	vs	ALABAMA	48	63	L	24.0	W	74.0	O	
10/17/2020	@	Arkansas	20	33	L	-1.5	L	75.0	U	
10/24/2020	vs	AUBURN	28	35	L	3.5	L	73.5	U	
10/31/2020	@	Vanderbilt	54	21	W	-17.0	W	63.5	O	
11/14/2020	vs	SOUTH CAROLINA	59	42	W	-12.0	W	73.0	O	
11/28/2020	vs	MISSISSIPPI STATE	31	24	W	-10.0	L	70.5	U	""Egg Bowl" - "Golden Egg Trophy""
12/19/2020	@	Lsu	48	53	L	PK	L	74.5	O	
1/2/2021	vs	Indiana	26	20	W	7.5	W	67.5	U	Outback Bowl
Coach: Lane Kiffin		Season Record >>	391	383	5-5	ATS>>	5-5	O/U>>	6-4	

2019-Mississippi		Opponent	Miss	Opp	S/U	Line	ATS	Total	O/U	
8/31/2019	@	Memphis	10	15	L	3.5	L	64.5	U	
9/7/2019	vs	ARKANSAS	31	17	W	-5.5	W	51.5	U	
9/14/2019	vs	SE LOUISIANA	40	29	W	-30.5	L	NT	---	
9/21/2019	vs	CALIFORNIA	20	28	L	-3.0	L	41.5	O	
9/28/2019	@	Alabama	31	59	L	37.5	L	62.5	O	
10/5/2019	vs	VANDERBILT	31	6	W	-7.0	W	64.5	U	
10/12/2019	@	Missouri	27	38	L	11.5	W	56.5	O	
10/19/2019	vs	TEXAS A&M	17	24	L	6.0	L	55.5	U	
11/2/2019	@	Auburn	14	20	L	17.5	W	53.5	U	
11/9/2019	vs	NEW MEXICO STATE	41	3	W	-29.0	W	65.0	U	
11/16/2019	vs	LSU	37	58	L	21.5	W	67.0	O	"Magnolia Bowl Trophy"
11/28/2019	@	Mississippi State	20	21	L	-2.0	L	59.0	U	""Egg Bowl" - "Golden Egg Trophy""
Coach: Matt Luke		Season Record >>	319	318	4-8	ATS>>	7-5	O/U>>	4-7	

2018-Mississippi		Opponent	Miss	Opp	S/U	Line	ATS	Total	O/U	
9/1/2018	vs	Texas Tech	47	27	W	-2.0	W	71.5	O	NRG Stadium
9/8/2018	vs	SOUTHERN ILLINOIS	76	41	W	-27.5	W	NT	---	
9/15/2018	vs	ALABAMA	7	62	L	22.5	L	71.0	U	
9/22/2018	vs	KENT STATE	38	17	W	-28.0	T	75.0	U	
9/29/2018	@	Lsu	16	45	L	11.5	L	59.0	O	"Magnolia Bowl Trophy"
10/6/2018	vs	LOUISIANA-MONROE	70	21	W	-24.0	W	76.0	O	
10/13/2018	@	Arkansas	37	33	W	-6.5	L	66.5	O	War Memorial Stadium
10/20/2018	vs	AUBURN	16	31	L	5.0	L	63.5	U	
11/3/2018	vs	SOUTH CAROLINA	44	48	L	-2.5	L	69.5	O	
11/10/2018	@	Texas A&M	24	38	L	13.0	L	67.5	U	
11/17/2018	@	Vanderbilt	29	36	L	3.0	L	73.0	U	{OT}
11/22/2018	vs	MISSISSIPPI STATE	3	35	L	12.5	L	61.0	U	""Egg Bowl" - "Golden Egg Trophy""
Coach: Matt Luke		Season Record >>	407	434	5-7	ATS>>	3-9	O/U>>	5-6	PROBATION

MISSISSIPPI REBELS — SEC West

STADIUM: Vaught-Hemingway Stadium {64,038} **Location:** Oxford, MS **COACH:** Lane Kiffin

DATE		Opponent	Miss	Opp	S/U	Line	ATS	Total	O/U	Trends & Angles
9/3/2022	vs	TROY								vs Troy - Ole Miss leads series 1-0
9/10/2022	vs	CENTRAL ARKANSAS								vs Central Arkansas - Ole Miss leads series 1-0
9/17/2022	@	Georgia Tech								vs Georgia Tech - Series tied 2-2
9/24/2022	vs	TULSA								vs Tulsa - Tulsa leads series 3-0
10/1/2022	vs	KENTUCKY								5-0 S/U @ home vs Kentucky as favorite since 1990
10/8/2022	@	Vanderbilt								vs Vanderbilt - Mississippi leads series 54-40-2
10/15/2022	vs	AUBURN								0-9 S/U @ home vs Auburn as Dog since 1994
10/22/2022	@	Lsu								2-11 S/U vs LSU as Dog since 2002
10/29/2022	@	Texas A&M								Game 0-7 O/U vs Texas A&M since 2014
11/12/2022	vs	ALABAMA								vs Alabama - Alabama leads series 57-10-2
11/19/2022	@	Arkansas								1-8 ATS vs Arkansas as favorite since 2013
11/24/2022	vs	MISSISSIPPI STATE								Game 2-8 O/U @ home vs Miss State since 2002
12/3/2022	vs									SEC Championship
	vs									BOWL GAME

Pointspread Analysis — Non-Conference

- 11-2 S/U vs Non-Conf. as 7.5-10 point favorite since 1990
- 7-0 S/U vs Non-Conf. as 10.5-15 point favorite since 1990
- 47-1 S/U vs Non-Conf. as 15.5 point or more favorite since 1990

Dog
- 1-20 S/U as 20.5 point or more Dog since 1994
- 0-11 S/U @ home as 15.5 point or more Dog since 1994
- 0-12 S/U as 15.5-20 point Dog since 2004
- 8-2 ATS as 15.5-20 point Dog since 2006
- 4-20 S/U on road as 10.5-15 point Dog since 1987
- 4-10 O/U on road as 10.5-15 point Dog since 2002
- 1-10 S/U @ home as 10.5-15 point Dog since 1983
- 3-12 S/U on road as 7.5-10 point Dog since 1991
- 2-19 S/U @ home as 3.5-7 point Dog since 1995
- 1-7 O/U @ home as 3 point or less Dog since 2006
- 10-4 S/U on road as 3 point or less Dog since 1988
- 11-4 ATS on road as 3 point or less Dog since 1985
- 0-7 O/U as 3 point or less Dog since 2013

Favorite
- 9-1 O/U @ home as 3 point or less favorite since 2008
- 0-8 O/U on road as 3 point or less favorite since 2007
- 2-8 ATS on road as 3 point or less favorite since 2001
- 11-0 S/U @ home as 3.5-7 point favorite since 2008
- 2-10 O/U as 3.5-7 point favorite since 2013
- 2-7 S/U on road as 3.5-7 point favorite since 2009
- 1-10 ATS on road as 3.5-7 point favorite since 2004
- 5-13 ATS as 10.5-15 point favorite since 1984
- 12-4 ATS as 15.5-20 point favorite since 1990
- 8-0 S/U on road as 15.5 point or more favorite since 1994
- 27-1 S/U @ home as 15.5 point or more favorite since 1990
- 56-2 S/U as 15.5 point or more favorite since 1990

Bowl Games
- 4-0 S/U in Liberty Bowl
- 4-0 S/U & ATS in Independence Bowl since 1986
- 7-3 S/U & ATS vs Big 12 in Bowl Games since 1986
- 3-0 S/U & ATS vs Oklahoma State in Bowl Games since 2004
- 0-3 O/U vs Oklahoma State in Bowl Games since 2004
- 4-0 S/U vs ACC in Bowl Games since 1968
- 12-3 S/U in Bowl Games since 1992
- 12-3 ATS in Bowl Games since 1992
- 6-2 S/U in Sugar Bowl since 1958

Pointspread Analysis — Conference

- vs Arkansas - Arkansas leads series 36-28-1
- 10-3 S/U vs Arkansas as favorite since 1991
- 0-12 S/U vs Auburn as Dog since 2004
- vs Auburn - Auburn leads series 34-10
- vs LSU - LSU leads series 64-42-4
- vs Mississippi State - Mississippi leads series 63-48-6
- Game 4-16 O/U vs Mississippi State since 2002
- 8-1 S/U @ home vs Mississippi State as favorite since 1988
- 1-6 O/U @ home vs Mississippi State as favorite since 1992
- vs Texas A&M - Texas A&M leads series 9-4
- 4-0 S/U vs ranked Texas A&M since 2014
- 5-0 ATS vs ranked Texas A&M since 2013
- 1-3 S/U & ATS @ Vanderbilt as Dog since 2005
- 1-19 S/U vs Alabama as 10 point or more Dog since 1983
- 1-8 S/U vs Alabama as 7 point or less Dog since 1989
- 0-6 S/U vs Arkansas as 4.0-6.0 point Dog since 1985
- 0-5 ATS vs Arkansas as 4.0-6.0 point Dog since 1987
- 0-14 S/U vs Auburn as 10 point or more Dog since 1984
- 1-10 S/U vs LSU as 12 point or more Dog since 1987
- 7-0-1 O/U vs LSU as 12 point or more Dog since 1987
- 2-9 ATS vs Vanderbilt as 12 point or more favorite since 1990

TROY	9-1 S/U in 1st home game of season since 2012
Vanderbilt	3-9 S/U prior to playing Auburn since 2010
Vanderbilt	3-13-2 O/U prior to playing Auburn since 2004
Texas A&M	11-2 S/U prior to playing Alabama since 2009
Arkansas	3-9 S/U prior to playing Mississippi State since 2010
Arkansas	4-14 S/U in final road game of season since 2004

- 22-3 S/U @ home when ranked since 2014
- 0-6 S/U when ranked vs #1 ranked teams all time
- 10-1 S/U @ home when ranked vs Mississippi State all time
- 15-1 S/U when ranked vs Vanderbilt since 1948 {6-0 @ home}
- 0-14 S/U vs #1 ranked teams all time
- 1-9 S/U vs #2 ranked teams all time
- 0-20 S/U vs ranked Auburn all time
- 3-15 S/U @ ranked LSU since 1970
- 5-0 ATS vs ranked Texas A&M since 2013
- 3-26 S/U vs ranked Alabama since 1977

MISSISSIPPI STATE BULLDOGS   SEC West

2021-Mississippi State		Opponent	MSU	Opp	S/U	Line	ATS	Total	O/U	
9/4/2021	vs	LOUISIANA TECH	35	34	W	-20.5	L	53.0	O	
9/11/2021	vs	NC STATE	24	10	W	2.0	W	55.0	U	
9/18/2021	@	Memphis	29	31	L	-3.5	L	63.0	U	
9/25/2021	vs	LSU	25	28	L	1.5	L	54.5	U	
10/2/2021	@	Texas A&M	26	22	W	7.0	W	46.0	O	
10/16/2021	vs	ALABAMA	9	49	L	17.5	L	59.5	U	
10/23/2021	@	Vanderbilt	45	6	W	-20.5	W	53.0	U	
10/30/2021	vs	KENTUCKY	31	17	W	-1.0	W	47.0	O	
11/6/2021	@	Arkansas	28	31	L	4.0	W	54.0	O	
11/13/2021	@	Auburn	43	34	W	6.0	W	51.0	O	
11/20/2021	vs	TENNESSEE STATE	55	10	W	-44.0	W	56.5	O	
11/25/2021	vs	MISSISSIPPI	21	31	L	-2.0	L	65.5	U	"Egg Bowl" - "Golden Egg Trophy"
12/28/2021	vs	Texas Tech	7	34	L	-10.0	L	58.0	U	Liberty Bowl
Coach: Mike Leach		Season Record >>	378	337	7-6	ATS>>	7-6	O/U>>	6-7	

2020-Mississippi State		Opponent	MSU	Opp	S/U	Line	ATS	Total	O/U	
9/26/2020	@	Lsu	44	34	W	14.0	W	57.0	O	
10/3/2020	vs	ARKANSAS	14	21	L	-17.0	L	68.5	U	
10/10/2020	@	Kentucky	2	24	L	3.0	L	57.5	U	
10/17/2020	vs	TEXAS A&M	14	28	L	3.5	L	57.0	U	
10/31/2020	@	Alabama	0	41	L	29.0	L	63.5	U	
11/7/2020	vs	VANDERBILT	24	17	W	-18.5	L	45.0	U	
11/21/2020	@	Georgia	24	31	L	26.5	W	44.0	O	
11/28/2020	@	Mississippi	24	31	L	10.0	W	70.5	U	"Egg Bowl" - "Golden Egg Trophy"
12/12/2020	vs	AUBURN	10	24	L	5.5	L	50.5	U	
12/19/2020	vs	MISSOURI	51	32	W	1.5	W	49.0	O	
12/31/2020	vs	Tulsa	28	26	W	-1.0	W	44.5	O	Armed Forces Bowl
Coach: Mike Leach		Season Record >>	235	309	4-7	ATS>>	5-6	O/U>>	4-7	

2019-Mississippi State		Opponent	MSU	Opp	S/U	Line	ATS	Total	O/U	
8/31/2019	vs	Louisiana-Lafayette	38	28	W	-18.5	L	60.5	O	Mercedes Benz Superdome
9/7/2019	vs	SOUTHERN MISSISSIPPI	35	15	W	-15.5	W	51.0	U	
9/14/2019	vs	KANSAS STATE	24	31	L	-7.0	L	50.5	O	
9/21/2019	vs	KENTUCKY	28	13	W	-5.5	W	48.0	U	
9/28/2019	@	Auburn	23	56	L	8.0	L	60.0	O	
10/12/2019	@	Tennessee	10	20	L	-5.0	L	52.0	U	
10/19/2019	vs	LSU	13	36	L	19.0	L	62.5	U	
10/26/2019	@	Texas A&M	30	49	L	10.5	L	50.0	O	
11/2/2019	@	Arkansas	54	24	W	-7.0	W	59.0	O	
11/16/2019	vs	ALABAMA	7	38	L	19.0	L	61.5	U	
11/23/2019	vs	ABILENE CHRISTIAN	45	7	W	-37.0	W	NT	---	
11/28/2019	vs	MISSISSIPPI	21	20	W	2.0	W	59.0	U	"Egg Bowl" - "Golden Egg Trophy"
12/30/2019	vs	Louisville	28	38	L	-4.5	L	63.5	O	Music City Bowl
Coach: Joe Moorhead		Season Record >>	356	375	6-7	ATS>>	5-8	O/U>>	6-6	

2018-Mississippi State		Opponent	MSU	Opp	S/U	Line	ATS	Total	O/U	
9/1/2018	vs	STEPHEN F. AUSTIN	63	6	W	-48.0	W	NT	---	
9/8/2018	@	Kansas State	31	10	W	-7.0	W	52.5	U	
9/15/2018	vs	LOUISIANA-LAFAYETTE	56	10	W	33.5	W	63.0	O	
9/22/2018	@	Kentucky	7	28	L	-9.5	L	56.0	U	
9/29/2018	vs	FLORIDA	6	13	L	-7.0	L	51.0	U	
10/6/2018	vs	AUBURN	23	9	W	3.0	W	45.0	U	
10/20/2018	@	Lsu	3	19	L	6.0	L	45.0	U	
10/27/2018	vs	TEXAS A&M	28	13	W	-1.0	W	42.5	U	
11/3/2018	vs	LOUISIANA TECH	45	3	W	-23.0	W	48.5	U	
11/10/2018	@	Alabama	0	24	L	21.5	L	51.0	U	
11/17/2018	vs	ARKANSAS	52	6	W	-22.5	W	48.0	O	
11/22/2018	@	Mississippi	35	3	W	-12.5	W	61.0	U	"Egg Bowl" - "Golden Egg Trophy"
1/1/2019	vs	Iowa	22	27	L	-7.0	L	40.0	O	Outback Bowl
Coach: Joe Moorhead		Season Record >>	371	171	8-5	ATS>>	8-5	O/U>>	3-9	

MISSISSIPPI STATE BULLDOGS — SEC West

STADIUM: Davis Wade Stadium @ Scott Field {61,337} | **Location:** Starkville, MS | **COACH:** Mike Leach

DATE		Opponent	MSU	Opp	S/U	Line	ATS	Total	O/U	Trends & Angles
9/3/2022	vs	MEMPHIS								12-1 S/U vs Memphis since 1994
9/10/2022	@	Arizona								1st Meeting
9/17/2022	@	Lsu								vs LSU - LSU leads series 74-38-3
9/24/2022	vs	BOWLING GREEN								vs Bowling Green - M State leads series 1-0
10/1/2022	vs	TEXAS A&M								vs Texas A&M - Mississippi State leads series 8-7
10/8/2022	vs	ARKANSAS								3-14-1 S/U Arkansas as Dog since 1993
10/15/2022	@	Kentucky								2-8 S/U vs Kentucky as Dog since 1984
10/22/2022	@	Alabama								0-14 S/U vs Alabama as Dog since 2008
11/5/2022	vs	AUBURN								6-26 S/U vs Auburn as Dog since 1983
11/12/2022	vs	GEORGIA								0-9 S/U vs Georgia as Dog since 1983
11/19/2022	vs	EAST TENNESSEE STATE								vs East Tennessee State - M State leads series 1-0
11/24/2022	@	Mississippi								vs Mississippi - Ole Miss leads series 63-48-6
12/3/2022	vs									SEC Championship
	vs									BOWL GAME

Pointspread Analysis — Non-Conference

- 0-7 S/U vs Non-Conf. as 10.5 point or more Dog since 1980
- 6-1 S/U & ATS vs Non-Conf. as 3 point or less Dog since 1992
- 18-2 S/U vs Non-Conf. as 10.5-15 point favorite since 1983
- 12-1 S/U vs Non-Conf. as 15.5-20 point favorite since 2010
- 21-1-1 S/U vs Non-Conf. as 25.5 point or more favorite since 1991
- 11-1 S/U vs Memphis as favorite since 1994
- 5-1 ATS vs Memphis as favorite since 2000

Dog
- 0-20 S/U on road as 20.5 point or more Dog since 1987
- 1-24 S/U as 15.5-20 point Dog since 1983
- 0-11 S/U @ home as 10.5-15 point Dog since 2002
- 0-13 S/U as 10.5-15 point Dog since 2007
- 7-1 ATS as 7.5-10 point Dog since 2014
- 4-11 S/U on road as 3.5-7 point Dog since 1998
- 2-14 S/U @ home as 3.5-7 point Dog since 1996
- 2-12 ATS @ home as 3.5-7 point Dog since 2002
- 3-15 O/U as 3 point or less Dog since 2006

Favorite
- 9-3 S/U & ATS as 3 point or less favorite since 2010
- 13-3 S/U @ home as 3.5-7 point favorite since 1997
- 1-6 O/U as 7.5-10 point favorite since 2001
- 6-1 S/U @ home as 7.5-10 point favorite since 1983
- 14-2 S/U @ home as 10.5-15 point favorite since 1992
- 7-0 S/U on road as 10.5-15 point favorite since 1998
- 22-2 S/U as 10.5-15 point favorite since 1992
- 40-6-1 S/U @ home as 15.5 point or more favorite since 1991
- 7-0 S/U on road as 15.5 point or more favorite since 1986

Bowl Games
- 10-4 ATS in Bowl Games since 1999
- 1-5 S/U vs ranked teams in Bowl games since 1980 {1-5 ATS}

- 0-11 S/U vs #4 ranked teams since 1961
- 0-10 S/U on road vs #5 ranked teams all time
- 1-9 S/U @ ranked Mississippi since 1948
- 2-16-1 O/U vs ranked Alabama since 1995

Pointspread Analysis — Conference

- vs Alabama - Alabama leads series 86-17-3
- 6-1 S/U vs Arkansas as favorite since 2012
- vs Arkansas - Arkansas leads series 18-12-1
- 8-0 O/U vs Arkansas as Dog since 2007
- vs Auburn - Auburn leads series 62-30-3
- 3-0 S/U @ home vs Auburn as favorite since 1992
- vs Kentucky - Mississippi State leads series 26-23
- 1-5 S/U vs LSU as favorite since 1992
- 0-6 ATS vs LSU as favorite since 1992
- 3-0 S/U & ATS vs Texas A&M as favorite since 2014
- 0-16 S/U vs Alabama as 16 point or more Dog since 1983
- 0-9 S/U vs Alabama as 6.0-11.0 point Dog since 1985
- 0-11 S/U vs Arkansas as 7 point or more Dog since 1995
- 1-13 S/U vs Auburn as 13.5 point or more Dog since 1983
- 0-7 S/U vs LSU as 7 point or less Dog since 1989
- 0-6 O/U vs LSU as 7 point or less Dog since 1998
- 1-14 S/U vs LSU as 12.5 point or more Dog since 1987
- 8-2 O/U vs LSU as 12.5 point or more Dog since 2004
- 6-2 S/U prior to playing LSU since 2013
- 9-2 S/U in 2nd home game of season since 2011
- 3-11 S/U prior to playing Arkansas since 2008
- 10-3 ATS prior to playing Alabama since 2009
- 7-2 O/U prior to playing Alabama since 2013
- 11-2 S/U prior to playing Alabama since 2009
- 0-12 S/U when ranked vs ranked Alabama since 1974
- 6-1 S/U when ranked vs Kentucky since 1992
- 0-5 S/U when ranked @ LSU since 1992
- 1-7 ATS when ranked vs LSU since 1992
- 14-95-1 S/U on road vs ranked teams since 1958
- 0-5 S/U on road vs #1 ranked teams all time
- 1-10 S/U vs #1 ranked teams all time
- 1-12 S/U vs #2 ranked teams all time
- 0-23 S/U @ ranked Alabama since 1961
- 0-9 S/U vs ranked Georgia since 1967
- 2-19 S/U @ ranked LSU since 1949

Middle column entries:
- Arizona
- BOWLING GREEN
- TEXAS A&M
- Kentucky
- Kentucky
- Kentucky

Page | 139 — Copyright © 2022 by Steve's Football Bible, LLC

MISSOURI TIGERS   SEC East

2021-Missouri		Opponent	Mizzu	Opp	S/U	Line	ATS	Total	O/U	
9/4/2021	vs	CENTRAL MICHIGAN	34	24	W	-14.0	L	59.0	U	
9/11/2021	@	Kentucky	28	35	L	5.5	L	56.5	O	
9/18/2021	vs	SE MISSOURI	59	28	W	-35.0	L	58.5	O	
9/25/2021	@	Boston College	34	41	L	1.0	L	58.0	O	{OT}
10/2/2021	vs	TENNESSEE	24	62	L	-2.0	L	66.5	O	
10/9/2021	vs	NORTH TEXAS	48	35	W	-18.5	L	68.5	O	
10/16/2021	vs	TEXAS A&M	14	35	L	11.5	L	59.0	U	
10/30/2021	@	Vanderbilt	37	28	W	-16.5	L	62.5	O	
11/6/2021	@	Georgia	6	43	L	40.0	W	58.5	U	
11/13/2021	vs	SOUTH CAROLINA	31	28	W	PK	W	56.5	O	
11/20/2021	vs	FLORIDA	24	23	W	9.0	W	69.0	U	{OT}
11/26/2021	@	Arkansas	17	34	L	14.5	L	62.5	U	"Battle Line Trophy"
12/22/2021	vs	Army	22	24	L	7.0	W	54.0	U	Armed Forces Bowl
Coach: Eli Drinkwitz		Season Record >>	378	440	6-7	ATS>>	4-9	O/U>>	7-6	

2020-Missouri		Opponent	Mizzu	Opp	S/U	Line	ATS	Total	O/U	
9/26/2020	vs	ALABAMA	19	38	L	29.0	L	55.5	O	
10/3/2020	@	Tennessee	12	35	L	10.0	L	48.5	U	
10/10/2020	vs	LSU	45	41	W	13.5	W	53.0	O	
10/24/2020	vs	KENTUCKY	20	10	W	3.0	W	47.0	U	
10/31/2020	@	Florida	17	41	L	13.5	L	62.5	U	
11/21/2020	@	South Carolina	17	10	W	-4.5	W	57.5	U	
11/28/2020	vs	VANDERBILT	41	0	W	-14.0	W	51.5	U	
12/5/2020	vs	ARKANSAS	50	48	W	-2.0	T	55.5	O	"Battle Line Trophy"
12/12/2020	vs	GEORGIA	14	49	L	14.0	L	54.5	O	
12/19/2020	@	Mississippi State	32	51	L	-1.5	L	49.0	O	
Coach: Eli Drinkwitz		Season Record >>	267	323	5-5	ATS>>	5-4-1	O/U>>	5-5	

2019-Missouri		Opponent	Mizzu	Opp	S/U	Line	ATS	Total	O/U	
8/31/2019	@	Wyoming	31	37	L	-15.5	L	52.5	O	
9/7/2019	vs	WEST VIRGINIA	38	7	W	-13.5	W	62.5	U	
9/14/2019	vs	SE MISSOURI STATE	50	0	W	-34.0	W	NT	---	
9/21/2019	vs	SOUTH CAROLINA	34	14	W	-9.5	W	60.5	U	
10/5/2019	vs	TROY	42	10	W	-25.5	W	65.5	U	
10/12/2019	vs	MISSISSIPPI	38	27	W	-11.5	L	56.5	U	
10/19/2019	@	Vanderbilt	14	21	L	-21.0	L	55.5	U	
10/26/2019	@	Kentucky	7	29	L	-9.5	L	43.5	U	
11/9/2019	@	Georgia	0	27	L	18.5	L	47.5	U	
11/16/2019	vs	FLORIDA	6	23	L	6.5	L	51.0	U	
11/23/2019	vs	TENNESSEE	20	24	L	-2.0	L	47.5	U	
11/30/2019	@	Arkansas	24	14	W	-14.5	L	52.5	U	"Battle Line Trophy"
Coach: Barry Odom		Season Record >>	304	233	6-6	ATS>>	4-8	O/U>>	2-9	

2018-Missouri		Opponent	Mizzu	Opp	S/U	Line	ATS	Total	O/U	
9/1/2018	vs	TENNESSEE-MARTIN	51	14	W	-34.0	W	NT	---	
9/8/2018	vs	WYOMING	40	13	W	-19.5	W	52.5	O	
9/15/2018	@	Purdue	40	37	W	-5.0	L	67.5	O	
9/22/2018	vs	GEORGIA	29	43	L	14.5	W	68.0	O	
10/6/2018	@	South Carolina	35	37	L	PK	L	63.0	O	
10/13/2018	@	Alabama	10	39	L	28.0	L	72.5	U	
10/20/2018	vs	MEMPHIS	65	33	W	-8.5	W	69.5	O	
10/27/2018	vs	KENTUCKY	14	15	L	-7.5	L	54.5	U	
11/3/2018	@	Florida	38	17	W	5.0	W	58.5	O	
11/10/2018	vs	VANDERBILT	33	28	W	-14.0	L	64.5	O	
11/17/2018	@	Tennessee	50	17	W	-6.0	W	57.0	O	
11/24/2018	vs	ARKANSAS	38	0	W	-24.0	W	59.0	U	"Battle Line Trophy"
12/31/2018	vs	Oklahoma State	33	38	L	-9.5	L	72.5	U	Liberty Bowl
Coach: Barry Odom		Season Record >>	476	331	8-5	ATS>>	7-6	O/U>>	6-6	

MISSOURI TIGERS
SEC East

STADIUM: Faurot Field @ Memorial Stadium {60,168} | **Location:** Columbia, MO | **COACH:** Eli Drinkwitz

DATE		Opponent	Mizz	Opp	S/U	Line	ATS	Total	O/U	Trends & Angles
9/1/2022	vs	LOUISIANA TECH								19-1 S/U in 1st home game of season since 2002
9/10/2022	@	Kansas State								0-13 S/U vs Kansas State as Dog since 1991
9/17/2022	vs	ABILENE CHRISTIAN								1st Meeting
9/24/2022	@	Auburn								vs Auburn - Auburn leads series 2-1
10/1/2022	vs	GEORGIA								vs Georgia - Georgia leads series 10-1
10/8/2022	@	Florida								vs Florida - Missouri leads series 6-5
10/22/2022	vs	VANDERBILT								4-0 S/U @ home vs Vanderbilt since 2014
10/29/2022	@	South Carolina								Game 2-8 O/U vs South Carolina since 2012
11/5/2022	vs	KENTUCKY								vs Kentucky - Kentucky leads series 8-4
11/12/2022	@	Tennessee								vs Tennessee - Series tied 5-5
11/19/2022	vs	NEW MEXICO STATE								1st Meeting
11/25/2022	vs	ARKANSAS								6-0 S/U vs Arkansas as favorite since 2004
12/3/2022	vs									SEC Championship
	vs									BOWL GAME

Pointspread Analysis — Non-Conference
- 0-4 S/U vs Non-Conf. as 15.5 point or more Dog since 1988
- 9-1 S/U vs Non-Conf. as 10.5-15 point favorite since 2006
- 10-2 O/U vs Non-Conf. as 10.5-15 point favorite since 2002
- 38-0 S/U vs Non-Conf. as 15.5 point or more favorite since 1986
- 10-1 S/U vs Kansas State as 7 point or more favorite since 1983

Dog
- 8-2 ATS as 30.5 point or more Dog since 1986
- 5-14 ATS as 20.5-25 point Dog since 1985
- 0-64 S/U as 15.5 point or more Dog since 1983
- 1-37 S/U @ home as 10.5 point or more Dog since 1983
- 4-41 S/U as 10.5-15 point Dog since 1983
- 1-7 S/U on road as 7.5-10 point Dog since 2001
- 6-0 ATS @ home as 7.5-10 point Dog since 1986
- 8-2 S/U & ATS on road as 3.5-7 point Dog since 2010
- 2-10 S/U @ home as 3.5-7 point Dog since 1999

Favorite
- 2-6 O/U @ home as 3 point or less favorite since 2006
- 4-1 S/U & ATS on road as 3 point or less favorite since 2009
- 1-8 O/U @ home as 3.5-7 point favorite since 2005
- 4-1 S/U on road as 7.5-10 point favorite since 2009
- 14-1 S/U @ home as 10.5-15 point favorite since 2009
- 13-2 S/U on road as 10.5-15 point favorite since 1983
- 19-1 S/U as 10.5-15 point favorite since 2009
- 11-4 ATS on road as 10.5-15 point favorite since 1983
- 56-2-1 S/U @ home as 15.5 point or more favorite since 1983
- 2-9 O/U as 20.5-25 point favorite since 2006

Pointspread Analysis — Conference
- vs Arkansas - Missouri leads series 9-4
- 0-8 S/U vs Georgia as Dog since 2014
- vs South Carolina - Missouri series 7-5
- Game 1-7 O/U vs Vanderbilt since 2014
- 7-1 S/U vs Vanderbilt as favorite since 2013
- vs Vanderbilt - Missouri leads series 9-4-1
- Game 0-5 O/U @ home vs Vanderbilt since 2012

Bowl Games
- 0-4 S/U in Bowl Games as 3.5 point or less Dog since 1983
- 7-56 S/U on road vs ranked teams since 1982
- 0-11 S/U @ home vs ranked teams since 2014
- 0-16 S/U vs #1 ranked teams all time
- 0-11 S/U vs ranked Kansas State all time
- 30-7 S/U @ home when ranked since 1998
- 15-2 S/U when ranked vs Kansas State all time
- 1-9 S/U vs ranked Georgia all time
- 0-8 S/U @ home vs #2 ranked teams since 1979
- 2-12 S/U vs #3 ranked teams all time

GEORGIA	1-7 O/U prior to playing Florida since 2014
Florida	8-1 O/U after playing Georgia since 2013
KENTUCKY	0-10 O/U after playing South Carolina since 2012
KENTUCKY	3-7 O/U prior to playing Tennessee since 2012
NEW MEXICO ST	2-6 O/U after playing Tennessee since 2014
ARKANSAS	13-4 S/U in final home game of season since 2005

NAVY MIDSHIPMEN   AMERICAN West

2021-Navy		Opponent	Navy	Opp	S/U	Line	ATS	Total	O/U	
9/4/2021	vs	MARSHALL	7	49	L	3.5	L	45.5	O	
9/11/2021	vs	AIR FORCE	3	23	L	6.0	L	39.5	U	
9/25/2021	@	Houston	20	28	L	20.0	W	47.0	O	
10/2/2021	vs	CENTRAL FLORIDA	34	30	W	15.0	W	53.0	O	
10/9/2021	vs	SMU	24	31	L	13.0	W	57.5	U	"Ganzs Trophy"
10/14/2021	@	Memphis	17	35	L	10.5	L	56.0	U	
10/23/2021	vs	CINCINNATI	20	27	L	29.0	W	49.0	U	
10/29/2021	@	Tulsa	20	17	W	12.0	W	46.0	U	
11/6/2021	@	Notre Dame	6	34	L	21.0	L	47.5	U	"Rip Miller Trophy"
11/20/2021	vs	EAST CAROLINA	35	38	L	3.5	W	46.5	O	
11/27/2021	@	Temple	38	14	W	-13.5	W	41.5	O	
12/11/2021	vs	Army	17	13	W	7.0	W	36.0	U	"Thompson Cup"
Coach: Ken Niumatalolo		Season Record >>	241	339	4-8	ATS>>	8-4	O/U>>	5-7	

2020-Navy		Opponent	Navy	Opp	S/U	Line	ATS	Total	O/U	
9/7/2020	vs	BYU	3	55	L	1.0	L	48.5	O	
9/19/2020	@	Tulane	27	24	W	6.5	W	47.5	O	
9/26/2020	@	Air Force	7	40	L	-6.0	L	47.5	U	
10/3/2020	vs	TEMPLE	31	29	W	4.0	W	51.0	O	
10/17/2020	@	East Carolina	27	23	W	-3.0	W	55.5	U	
10/24/2020	vs	HOUSTON	21	37	L	15.5	L	57.0	O	
10/31/2020	@	Smu	37	51	L	12.5	L	59.0	O	"Ganzs Trophy"
11/28/2020	vs	MEMPHIS	7	10	L	13.0	W	63.5	U	
12/5/2020	vs	TULSA	6	19	L	12.0	L	45.5	U	
12/12/2020	@	Army	0	15	L	7.0	L	35.5	U	"Thompson Cup"
Coach: Ken Niumatalolo		Season Record >>	166	303	3-7	ATS>>	4-6	O/U>>	5-5	

2019-Navy		Opponent	Navy	Opp	S/U	Line	ATS	Total	O/U	
8/31/2019	vs	HOLY CROSS	45	7	W	-24.0	W	NT	---	
9/14/2019	vs	EAST CAROLINA	42	10	W	-7.5	W	54.0	U	
9/26/2019	@	Memphis	23	35	L	10.5	L	53.5	O	
10/5/2019	vs	AIR FORCE	34	25	W	3.0	W	46.5	O	
10/12/2019	@	Tulsa	45	17	W	2.0	W	52.0	O	
10/19/2019	vs	SOUTH FLORIDA	35	3	W	-15.5	W	51.0	U	
10/26/2019	vs	TULANE	41	38	W	-4.5	L	58.5	O	
11/1/2019	@	Connecticut	56	10	W	-26.5	W	54.5	O	
11/16/2019	@	Notre Dame	20	52	L	7.0	L	56.0	O	"Rip Miller Trophy"
11/23/2019	vs	SMU	35	28	W	-3.0	W	69.0	U	"Ganzs Trophy"
11/30/2019	@	Houston	56	41	W	-9.5	W	56.5	O	
12/14/2019	vs	Army	31	7	W	-11.5	W	41.5	U	"Thompson Cup"
12/31/2019	vs	Kansas State	20	17	W	-1.5	W	52.5	U	Liberty Bowl
Coach: Ken Niumatalolo		Season Record >>	483	290	11-2	ATS>>	10-3	O/U>>	7-5	"Commander-in-Chief Trophy"

2018-Navy		Opponent	Navy	Opp	S/U	Line	ATS	Total	O/U	
9/1/2018	@	Hawaii	41	59	L	-13.0	L	61.5	O	
9/8/2018	vs	MEMPHIS	22	21	W	6.5	W	67.0	U	
9/15/2018	vs	LEHIGH	51	21	W	-33.0	L	NT	---	
9/22/2018	@	Smu	30	31	L	-6.0	L	58.0	O	"Ganzs Trophy"
10/6/2018	@	Air Force	7	35	L	-3.0	L	47.0	U	
10/13/2018	vs	TEMPLE	17	24	L	6.5	L	49.0	U	
10/20/2018	vs	HOUSTON	36	49	L	11.0	L	58.5	O	
10/27/2018	vs	Notre Dame	22	44	L	22.5	W	57.0	O	"Rip Miller Trophy"
11/3/2018	@	Cincinnati	0	42	L	13.0	L	48.0	U	
11/10/2018	@	Central Florida	24	35	L	23.5	W	68.0	U	
11/17/2018	vs	TULSA	37	29	W	-5.0	W	51.0	O	
11/24/2018	@	Tulane	28	29	L	6.5	W	53.0	O	
12/8/2018	vs	Army	10	17	L	9.0	W	38.5	U	"Thompson Cup"
Coach: Ken Niumatalolo		Season Record >>	325	436	3-10	ATS>>	6-7	O/U>>	6-6	

NAVY MIDSHIPMEN — AMERICAN West

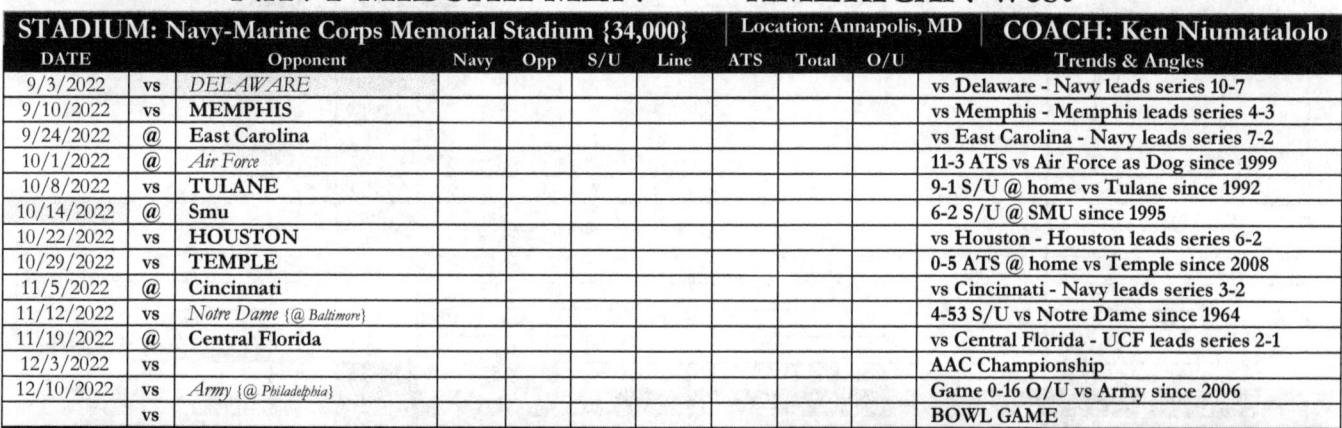

STADIUM: Navy-Marine Corps Memorial Stadium {34,000} | **Location:** Annapolis, MD | **COACH:** Ken Niumatalolo

DATE		Opponent	Navy	Opp	S/U	Line	ATS	Total	O/U	Trends & Angles
9/3/2022	vs	DELAWARE								vs Delaware - Navy leads series 10-7
9/10/2022	vs	MEMPHIS								vs Memphis - Memphis leads series 4-3
9/24/2022	@	East Carolina								vs East Carolina - Navy leads series 7-2
10/1/2022	@	Air Force								11-3 ATS vs Air Force as Dog since 1999
10/8/2022	vs	TULANE								9-1 S/U @ home vs Tulane since 1992
10/14/2022	@	Smu								6-2 S/U @ SMU since 1995
10/22/2022	vs	HOUSTON								vs Houston - Houston leads series 6-2
10/29/2022	vs	TEMPLE								0-5 ATS @ home vs Temple since 2008
11/5/2022	@	Cincinnati								vs Cincinnati - Navy leads series 3-2
11/12/2022	vs	Notre Dame {@ Baltimore}								4-53 S/U vs Notre Dame since 1964
11/19/2022	@	Central Florida								vs Central Florida - UCF leads series 2-1
12/3/2022	vs									AAC Championship
12/10/2022	vs	Army {@ Philadelphia}								Game 0-16 O/U vs Army since 2006
	vs									BOWL GAME

Pointspread Analysis — Non-Conference

- vs Notre Dame - Notre Dame leads series 80-13-1
- 0-29 S/U vs Notre Dame as 13 point or more Dog since 1983
- 9-2 O/U vs Notre Dame as 13 point or more Dog since 2002
- Game 8-3 O/U vs Notre Dame since 2010
- 3-9 O/U vs Air Force as Dog since 2001
- 2-14 S/U vs Air Force as 9.5 point or more Dog since 1984
- vs Air Force - Air Force leads series 31-23
- vs Army - Navy leads series 62-52-7
- 1-8 S/U vs Army as 6.5 point or less Dog since 1984
- 0-13 O/U vs Army as favorite since 2006
- 15-0 S/U vs Army as 6.5 point or more favorite since 1997
- 2-8 S/U vs Army as Dog since 1992

Dog
- 10-0 ATS as 25.5-30 point Dog since 1991
- 0-53 S/U as 20.5 point or more Dog since 1983
- 2-18 S/U as 15.5-20 point Dog since 1996
- 2-14 S/U @ home as 10.5-15 point Dog since 1989
- 13-1-1 ATS as 7.5-10 point Dog since 1999
- 1-10 S/U on road as 3.5-7 point Dog since 2011
- 4-11 O/U @ home as 3.5-7 point Dog since 1999
- 11-1 S/U & ATS on road as 3 point or less Dog since 2004
- 3-9 S/U @ home as 3 point or less Dog since 1993

Favorite
- 9-2 S/U @ home as 3 point or less favorite since 2007
- 8-2 S/U @ home as 3.5-7 point favorite since 2011
- 13-1 S/U @ home as 7.5-10 point favorite since 2003
- 7-0 S/U on road as 7.5-10 point favorite since 2011
- 20-2 S/U as 7.5-10 point favorite since 2003
- 19-3 S/U as 10.5-15 point favorite since 2004
- 15-2 S/U @ home as 10.5-15 point favorite since 2003
- 6-0 S/U on road as 15.5 point or more favorite since 1983
- 24-1 S/U @ home as 15.5 point or more favorite since 1986

Pointspread Analysis — Conference

- 9-3 S/U vs SMU since 2002
- 12-4 ATS vs SMU since 1995
- vs Smu - Navy leads series 13-10
- 2-6 ATS vs Temple as favorite since 2007
- 1-4 S/U vs Temple as Dog since 1988
- vs Temple - Series tied 8-8
- 9-0 S/U @ home vs Tulane as favorite since 1992
- vs Tulane - Series tied 12-12-1

Bowl Games
- 6-0 ATS in Bowl Games since 2013
- 5-0 S/U & ATS in Bowl Games as 3 point or less favorite since 1996
- 4-1 O/U in Bowl Games as 3 point or less favorite since 1996

DELAWARE	11-3 S/U in 1st home game of season since 2008
East Carolina	3-8 O/U prior to playing Air Force since 2011
East Carolina	9-3-1 ATS in 1st road game of season since 2009
TULANE	9-1 O/U prior to playing SMU since 2008
HOUSTON	2-5 O/U prior to playing Temple since 2008
TEMPLE	17-2 S/U in final home game of season since 2003

- 8-2-1 S/U when ranked vs Army since 1963
- 2-9-1 S/U vs ranked Army since 1944
- 5-33 S/U on road vs ranked teams since 1975
- 2-16 S/U @ home vs ranked teams since 1985
- 0-31 S/U on Neutral fields vs ranked teams since 1958
- 0-14 S/U vs #1 ranked teams all time
- 30-1-3 S/U @ home when ranked all time

Navy Blue and Gold – History of Navy Midshipmen Football

Available at: www.stevesfootballbible.com (Patriot Series)

NEBRASKA CORNHUSKERS — BIG TEN West

2021-Nebraska

Date		Opponent	Neb	Opp	S/U	Line	ATS	Total	O/U	
8/28/2021	@	Illinois	22	30	L	-6.5	L	52.0	T	
9/4/2021	vs	FORDHAM	52	7	W	-41.0	W	55.0	O	
9/11/2021	vs	BUFFALO	28	3	W	-13.5	W	54.5	U	
9/18/2021	@	Oklahoma	16	23	L	22.5	W	63.0	U	
9/25/2021	@	Michigan State	20	23	L	3.5	W	54.5	U	{OT}
10/2/2021	vs	NORTHWESTERN	56	7	W	-10.5	W	51.0	O	
10/9/2021	vs	MICHIGAN	29	32	L	2.5	L	50.5	O	
10/16/2021	@	Minnesota	23	30	L	-4.5	L	49.0	O	
10/30/2021	vs	PURDUE	23	28	L	-7.5	L	54.0	U	
11/6/2021	vs	OHIO STATE	17	26	L	14.0	W	67.5	U	
11/20/2021	@	Wisconsin	28	35	L	10.0	W	43.5	O	"Freedom Trophy"
11/26/2021	vs	IOWA	21	28	L	-1.5	L	41.0	O	"Heroes Trophy"
Coach: Scott Frost		Season Record >>	335	272	3-9	ATS>>	7-5	O/U>>	6-5-1	

2020-Nebraska

Date		Opponent	Neb	Opp	S/U	Line	ATS	Total	O/U	
10/24/2020	@	Ohio State	17	52	L	27.5	L	70.5	U	
11/7/2020	@	Northwestern	13	21	L	4.0	L	53.0	U	
11/14/2020	vs	PENN STATE	30	23	W	2.5	W	57.5	U	
11/21/2020	vs	ILLINOIS	23	41	L	-16.5	L	62.0	O	
11/27/2020	@	Iowa	20	26	L	12.5	W	53.0	U	"Heroes Trophy"
12/5/2020	@	Purdue	37	27	W	2.0	W	64.5	U	
12/12/2020	vs	MINNESOTA	17	24	L	-8.5	L	61.5	U	
12/18/2020	@	Rutgers	28	21	W	-6.5	W	51.5	U	
Coach: Scott Frost		Season Record >>	185	235	3-5	ATS>>	4-4	O/U>>	1-7	

2019-Nebraska

Date		Opponent	Neb	Opp	S/U	Line	ATS	Total	O/U	
8/31/2019	vs	SOUTH ALABAMA	35	21	W	-36.0	L	64.5	U	
9/7/2019	@	Colorado	31	34	L	-4.0	L	64.5	O	{OT}
9/14/2019	vs	NORTHERN ILLINOIS	44	8	W	-14.0	W	54.0	U	
9/21/2019	@	Illinois	42	38	W	-13.0	L	62.0	O	
9/28/2019	vs	OHIO STATE	7	48	L	17.0	L	66.0	U	
10/5/2019	vs	NORTHWESTERN	13	10	W	-7.5	L	48.5	U	
10/12/2019	@	Minnesota	7	34	L	7.5	L	47.5	U	
10/26/2019	vs	INDIANA	31	38	L	-2.5	L	54.5	O	
11/2/2019	@	Purdue	27	31	L	-3.5	L	58.0	T	
11/16/2019	vs	WISCONSIN	21	37	L	14.0	L	50.0	O	"Freedom Trophy"
11/23/2019	@	Maryland	54	7	W	-6.5	W	62.5	O	
11/29/2019	vs	IOWA	24	27	L	3.5	W	46.0	O	"Heroes Trophy"
Coach: Scott Frost		Season Record >>	336	333	5-7	ATS>>	3-9	O/U>>	5-6-1	

2018-Nebraska

Date		Opponent	Neb	Opp	S/U	Line	ATS	Total	O/U	
9/8/2018	vs	COLORADO	28	33	L	-3.0	L	63.5	U	
9/15/2018	vs	TROY	19	24	L	-10.5	L	55.5	U	
9/22/2018	@	Michigan	10	56	L	17.0	L	50.5	O	
9/29/2018	vs	PURDUE	28	42	L	3.0	L	57.5	O	
10/6/2018	@	Wisconsin	24	41	L	18.0	W	60.5	O	"Freedom Trophy"
10/13/2018	@	Northwestern	31	34	L	3.5	W	59.5	O	{OT}
10/20/2018	vs	MINNESOTA	53	28	W	-5.5	W	55.0	O	
10/27/2018	vs	BETHUNE-COOKMAN	45	9	W	-46.5	L	NT	---	
11/3/2018	@	Ohio State	31	36	L	17.0	W	75.5	U	
11/10/2018	vs	ILLINOIS	54	35	W	-17.5	W	71.0	O	
11/17/2018	vs	MICHIGAN STATE	9	6	W	-1.0	W	48.0	U	
11/23/2018	@	Iowa	28	31	L	7.5	W	52.0	O	"Heroes Trophy"
Coach: Scott Frost		Season Record >>	360	375	4-8	ATS>>	7-5	O/U>>	7-4	

NEBRASKA CORNHUSKERS — BIG TEN West

STADIUM: Memorial Stadium {85,458} **Location:** Lincoln, NE **COACH:** Scott Frost

DATE		Opponent	Neb	Opp	S/U	Line	ATS	Total	O/U	Trends & Angles
8/27/2022	vs	Northwestern {@ Dublin, IR}								vs Northwestern - Nebraska leads series 9-6
9/3/2022	vs	NORTH DAKOTA								vs North Dakota - Nebraska leads series 1-0
9/10/2022	vs	GEORGIA SOUTHERN								11-3 S/U in 2nd home game of season since 2008
9/17/2022	vs	OKLAHOMA								7-1 S/U @ home vs Oklahoma since 1989 {6-2 ATS}
10/1/2022	vs	INDIANA								vs Indiana - Indiana leads series 10-8-3
10/8/2022	@	Rutgers								vs Rutgers - Nebraska leads series 5-0
10/15/2022	@	Purdue								vs Purdue - Series tied 5-5
10/29/2022	vs	ILLINOIS								vs Illinois - Nebraska leads series 13-5-1
11/5/2022	vs	MINNESOTA								vs Minnesota - Minnesota leads series 35-25-2
11/12/2022	@	Michigan								vs Michigan - Michigan leads series 6-4-1
11/19/2022	vs	WISCONSIN								0-8 S/U vs Wisconsin since 2012
11/25/2022	@	Iowa								0-6 S/U vs Iowa as Dog since 2015
12/3/2022	vs									Big Ten Championship
	vs									BOWL GAME

Pointspread Analysis — Non-Conference
- 2-10 S/U vs Non-Conf. as 7.5 point or more Dog since 1992
- 2-8 S/U vs Non-Conf. as 3.5-7 point Dog since 1986
- 9-0 S/U vs Non-Conf. as 7.5-10 point favorite since 1984
- 9-0 S/U vs Non-Conf. as 15.5-20 point favorite since 1983
- 14-0 S/U vs Non-Conf. as 20.5-25 point favorite since 1998
- 54-0 S/U vs Non-Conf. as 25.5 point or more favorite since 1983
- vs Oklahoma - Oklahoma leads series 46-38-3
- 6-1 S/U @ home vs Oklahoma as favorite since 1989
- 1-9 S/U vs Oklahoma as Dog since 1979

Dog
- 2-27 S/U as 10.5 point or more Dog since 1979
- 2-13 S/U on road as 3.5-7 point Dog since 2003

Favorite
- 6-1 S/U on road as 7.5-10 point favorite since 2006
- 17-4 S/U @ home as 7.5-10 point favorite since 1984
- 20-4 S/U @ home as 10.5-15 point favorite since 1984
- 14-2 S/U on road as 10.5-15 point favorite since 1983
- 16-4 S/U @ home as 15.5-20 point favorite since 1987
- 10-0 S/U on road as 15.5-20 point favorite since 1989
- 2-8 ATS as 15.5-20 point favorite since 2008
- 130-0 S/U @ home as 20.5 point or more favorite since 1983
- 39-3 S/U on road as 20.5 point or more favorite since 1983

- 5-19 S/U on road when ranked vs ranked teams since 1998
- 17-3 S/U @ home when ranked vs ranked teams since 1991
- 170-15 S/U @ home when ranked since 1982
- 13-2 S/U when ranked vs Minnesota since 1967
- 6-0 S/U @ home when ranked vs Oklahoma since 1989
- 0-14 S/U on road vs ranked teams since 2011
- 0-19 S/U vs ranked times since 2016
- 1-12 S/U vs #1 ranked teams all time
- 4-0 S/U @ home vs ranked Oklahoma since 1991
- 1-11 O/U vs ranked Oklahoma since 1987
- 0-7 S/U vs ranked Wisconsin all time

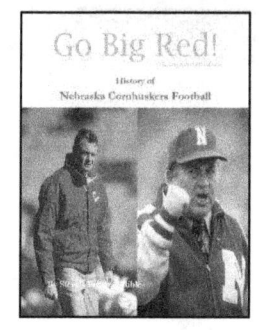

Pointspread Analysis — Conference
- 5-1 S/U @ home vs Illinois as favorite since 1985
- vs Iowa - Nebraska leads series 28-20-3
- 4-0 S/U vs Rutgers as favorite since 2014
- vs Wisconsin - Wisconsin leads series 11-4
- 0-8 S/U vs Wisconsin as Dog since 2011

Bowl Games
- 0-4 S/U vs Florida State in Bowl Games
- 0-3 S/U & ATS in Citrus Bowl
- 3-0 S/U & ATS in Alamo Bowl
- 4-0 S/U vs LSU in Bowl Games
- 3-0 S/U in Sugar Bowl since 1974
- 2-8 S/U in Bowl Games as 7.5 point or more Dog since 1979
- 1-5 S/U in Bowl Games as 3.5-7 point Dog since 1986
- 0-3 O/U in Bowl Games as 3 point or less Dog since 2007

NORTH DAKOTA	7-3 S/U after playing Northwestern since 2011
NORTH DAKOTA	34-2 S/U in 1st home game of season since 1986
MINNESOTA	1-8 O/U after playing Illinois since 2013
MINNESOTA	8-1 ATS after playing Illinois since 2013
Michigan	9-3 S/U after playing Minnesota since 1983
Michigan	1-6-1 O/U prior to playing Wisconsin since 2011
Iowa	1-7 S/U after playing Wisconsin since 2012
Iowa	2-7 ATS after playing Wisconsin since 2011

Go Big Red! History of Nebraska Cornhuskers Football

Available at: www.stevesfootballbible.com (Blueblood Series)

NEVADA WOLFPACK   MOUNTAIN WEST West

2021-Nevada		Opponent	Nev	Opp	S/U	Line	ATS	Total	O/U	
9/4/2021	@	California	22	17	W	2.5	W	52.5	U	
9/11/2021	vs	IDAHO STATE	49	10	W	-35.0	W	56.5	O	
9/18/2021	@	Kansas State	17	38	L	-1.5	L	51.5	O	
10/2/2021	@	Boise State	41	31	W	3.5	W	59.0	O	
10/9/2021	vs	NEW MEXICO STATE	55	28	W	-28.5	L	65.0	O	
10/16/2021	vs	HAWAII	34	17	W	-14.0	W	62.5	U	
10/23/2021	@	Fresno State	32	34	L	3.5	W	64.0	O	
10/30/2021	vs	UNLV	51	20	W	-18.5	W	58.5	O	"Fremont Cannon"
11/6/2021	vs	SAN JOSE STATE	27	24	W	-11.5	L	55.0	U	
11/13/2021	@	San Diego State	21	23	L	2.5	W	45.0	U	
11/20/2021	vs	AIR FORCE	39	41	L	2.0	T	54.0	O	{2 OT}
11/27/2021	@	Colorado State	52	10	W	-3.0	W	58.5	O	
12/27/2021	vs	Western Michigan	24	52	L	6.5	L	57.0	O	Quick Lane Bowl
Coach: Jay Norvell		Season Record >>	464	345	8-5	ATS>>	8-4-1	O/U>>	9-4	

2020-Nevada		Opponent	Nev	Opp	S/U	Line	ATS	Total	O/U	
10/24/2020	vs	WYOMING	37	34	W	3.0	W	53.5	O	{OT}
10/31/2020	@	Unlv	37	19	W	-13.5	W	60.0	U	"Fremont Cannon"
11/6/2020	vs	UTAH STATE	34	9	W	-17.0	W	58.0	U	
11/14/2020	@	New Mexico	27	20	W	-17.5	L	63.0	U	
11/21/2020	vs	SAN DIEGO STATE	26	21	W	1.5	W	46.0	O	
11/28/2020	@	Hawaii	21	24	L	-7.0	L	63.0	U	
12/5/2020	vs	FRESNO STATE	37	26	W	-5.5	W	60.0	O	
12/12/2020	@	San Jose State	20	30	L	-2.5	L	62.0	U	
12/22/2020	vs	Tulane	38	27	W	-1.0	W	56.5	O	Famous Idaho Potato Bowl
Coach: Jay Norvell		Season Record >>	277	210	7-2	ATS>>	6-3	O/U>>	4-5	

2019-Nevada		Opponent	Nev	Opp	S/U	Line	ATS	Total	O/U	
8/30/2019	vs	PURDUE	34	31	W	11.0	W	58.5	O	
9/7/2019	@	Oregon	6	77	L	24.5	L	61.5	O	
9/14/2019	vs	WEBER STATE	19	13	W	-7.0	L	NT	---	
9/21/2019	@	Texas-El Paso	37	21	W	-14.0	W	52.0	O	
9/28/2019	vs	HAWAII	3	54	L	-1.5	L	63.0	U	
10/12/2019	vs	SAN JOSE STATE	41	38	W	-2.5	W	58.5	O	
10/19/2019	@	Utah State	10	36	L	21.5	L	59.0	U	
10/26/2019	@	Wyoming	3	31	L	14.0	L	43.5	U	
11/2/2019	vs	NEW MEXICO	21	10	W	-3.5	W	57.5	U	
11/9/2019	@	San Diego State	17	13	W	17.0	W	34.5	U	
11/23/2019	@	Fresno State	35	28	W	13.0	W	51.5	O	
11/30/2019	vs	UNLV	30	33	L	-6.5	L	52.0	O	"Fremont Cannon"
1/3/2020	vs	Ohio	21	30	L	10.0	W	62.0	U	Famous Idaho Potato Bowl
Coach: Jay Norvell		Season Record >>	277	415	7-6	ATS>>	7-6	O/U>>	6-6	

2018-Nevada		Opponent	Nev	Opp	S/U	Line	ATS	Total	O/U	
8/31/2018	vs	PORTLAND STATE	72	19	W	-28.0	W	NT	---	
9/8/2018	@	Vanderbilt	10	41	L	10.0	L	61.0	U	
9/15/2018	vs	OREGON STATE	37	35	W	-3.5	L	67.5	O	
9/22/2018	@	Toledo	44	63	L	12.0	L	69.0	O	
9/29/2018	@	Air Force	28	25	W	3.5	W	63.0	U	
10/6/2018	vs	FRESNO STATE	3	21	L	16.0	L	58.5	U	
10/13/2018	vs	BOISE STATE	27	31	L	14.0	W	58.0	T	
10/20/2018	@	Hawaii	40	22	W	2.0	W	67.5	U	
10/27/2018	vs	SAN DIEGO STATE	28	24	W	1.0	W	46.0	O	
11/10/2018	vs	COLORADO STATE	49	10	W	-14.0	W	62.0	U	
11/17/2018	@	San Jose State	21	12	W	-14.5	L	58.5	U	
11/24/2018	@	Unlv	29	34	L	-14.0	L	61.0	O	"Fremont Cannon"
12/29/2018	vs	Arkansas State	16	13	W	PK	W	57.0	U	Arizona Bowl
Coach: Jay Norvell		Season Record >>	404	350	8-5	ATS>>	7-6	O/U>>	4-7-1	

NEVADA WOLFPACK — MOUNTAIN WEST West

STADIUM: Mackay Stadium {27,000} **Location:** Reno, NV **COACH:** Ken Wilson

DATE		Opponent	UNR	Opp	S/U	Line	ATS	Total	O/U	Trends & Angles
8/27/2022	@	New Mexico State								6-0 S/U @ NMSU as favorite since 1995
9/3/2022	vs	TEXAS STATE								vs Texas State - Nevada leads series 1-0
9/10/2022	vs	INCARNATE WORD								17-3 S/U in 2nd home game of season since 2002
9/17/2022	@	Iowa								1st Meeting
9/24/2022	@	Air Force								vs Air Force - Air Force leads series 4-2
10/8/2022	vs	COLORADO STATE								vs Colorado State - CSU leads series 12-5
10/15/2022	@	Hawaii								vs Hawaii - Nevada leads series 15-11
10/22/2022	vs	SAN DIEGO STATE								vs San Diego State - SDSU leads series 8-6
10/29/2022	@	San Jose State								16-3 S/U vs San Jose State since 2002
11/12/2022	vs	BOISE STATE								2-15 S/U vs Boise State as Dog since 2001
11/19/2022	vs	FRESNO STATE								vs Fresno State - Fresno leads series 30-22-1
11/26/2022	@	Unlv								7-1 S/U @ UNLV since 2006
12/3/2022	vs									MWC Championship
	vs									BOWL GAME

Pointspread Analysis — Non-Conference
- 0-13 S/U vs Non-Conf. as 20.5 point or more Dog since 2000
- 2-17 S/U vs Non-Conf. as 7.5-20 point Dog since 1996
- Game 7-1 O/U vs New Mexico State since 2005
- vs New Mexico State - Nevada leads series 14-2
- 8-0 S/U @ New Mexico State since 1993

Dog
- 0-27 S/U on road as 20.5 point or more Dog since 2000
- 3-10 S/U on road as 15.5-20 point Dog since 1996
- 3-14 S/U on road as 10.5-15 point Dog since 2000
- 9-3 ATS as 10.5-15 point Dog since 2009
- 1-12 S/U as 7.5-10 point Dog since 2005
- 3-8 S/U on road as 3.5-7 point Dog since 1995
- 8-1 O/U on road as 3.5-7 point Dog since 2001
- 7-0-1 ATS as 3 point or less Dog since 2017

Favorite
- 3-11 O/U as 3.5-7 point favorite since 2013
- 18-0 S/U as 7.5-10 point favorite since 1995
- 9-0 S/U on road as 7.5-10 point favorite since 1995
- 15-1 S/U @ home as 10.5-15 point favorite since 1995
- 10-1 S/U on road as 10.5-15 point favorite since 1995
- 34-3 S/U @ home as 15.5 point or more favorite since 1995
- 9-0 S/U on road as 15.5 point or more favorite since 1995

Bowl Games
- 3-9 S/U in Bowl Games since 2006
- 3-1 ATS in Bowl Games as 3.5-7 point Dog since 1992
- 1-3 ATS in Bowl Games as 3 point or less favorite since 2005

Pointspread Analysis — Conference
- 1-10 S/U vs Colorado State as Dog since 1997
- 6-1 S/U vs Fresno State as favorite since 2009
- 6-2 S/U vs Hawaii as favorite since 2011
- 4-0 ATS vs Hawaii as Dog since 2006
- 7-1 S/U @ UNLV as favorite since 1996
- vs Unlv - Nevada leads series 28-19
- 13-4 S/U vs UNLV since 2005
- 4-0 S/U & ATS vs UNLV as Dog since 2005
- 4-0 ATS vs San Diego State since 2018
- vs San Jose State - Nevada leads series 23-10-2
- Game 0-5 O/U @ San Jose State since 2011
- 9-1 S/U vs San Jose State as favorite since 2008

- 2-12 S/U @ home vs ranked teams all time
- 1-17 S/U on road vs ranked teams all time
- 5-0 S/U @ home when ranked all time

New Mex State	4-22 S/U in 1st road game of season since 1996
Hawaii	6-2 ATS after playing Colorado State since 2005
SAN DIEGO ST	11-3 S/U after playing Hawaii since 2008
FRESNO STATE	10-2-1 ATS in final home game of season since 2009

NEVADA-LAS VEGAS REBELS   MOUNTAIN WEST West

2021-UNLV		Opponent	Unlv	Opp	S/U	Line	ATS	Total	O/U	
9/2/2021	vs	EASTERN WASHINGTON	33	35	L	2.5	W	66.0	O	{2 OT}
9/11/2021	@	Arizona State	10	37	L	34.5	W	56.0	U	
9/18/2021	vs	IOWA STATE	3	48	L	31.5	L	53.0	O	
9/24/2021	@	Fresno State	30	38	L	30.0	W	59.5	O	
10/2/2021	@	Texas-San Antonio	17	24	L	21.5	W	55.5	U	
10/16/2021	vs	UTAH STATE	24	28	L	7.5	W	64.0	U	
10/21/2021	vs	SAN JOSE STATE	20	27	L	6.0	L	44.0	O	
10/30/2021	@	Nevada	20	51	L	18.5	L	58.5	O	"Fremont Cannon"
11/6/2021	@	New Mexico	31	17	W	1.5	W	45.0	O	
11/13/2021	vs	HAWAII	27	13	W	3.5	W	55.5	U	
11/20/2021	vs	SAN DIEGO STATE	20	28	L	11.5	W	41.0	O	
11/27/2021	@	Air Force	14	48	L	18.5	L	49.5	O	
Coach: Tony Sanchez		Season Record >>	249	394	2-10	ATS>>	8-4	O/U>>	8-4	

2020-UNLV		Opponent	Unlv	Opp	S/U	Line	ATS	Total	O/U	
10/24/2020	@	San Diego State	6	34	L	13.5	L	49.5	U	
10/31/2020	vs	NEVADA	19	37	L	13.5	L	60.0	U	"Fremont Cannon"
11/7/2020	vs	FRESNO STATE	27	40	L	11.0	L	57.5	O	
11/14/2020	@	San Jose State	17	34	L	17.0	T	61.5	U	
11/27/2020	vs	WYOMING	14	45	L	17.0	L	52.0	O	
12/12/2020	@	Hawaii	21	38	L	18.5	W	60.0	U	
Coach: Marcus Arroyo		Season Record >>	104	228	0-6	ATS>>	1-4-1	O/U>>	2-4	

2019-UNLV		Opponent	Unlv	Opp	S/U	Line	ATS	Total	O/U	
8/31/2019	vs	SOUTHERN UTAH	56	23	W	-24.0	W	NT	---	
9/7/2019	vs	ARKANSAS STATE	17	43	L	PK	L	64.0	U	
9/14/2019	@	Northwestern	14	30	L	18.5	W	51.5	U	
9/28/2019	@	Wyoming	17	53	L	8.0	L	44.5	O	
10/5/2019	vs	BOISE STATE	13	38	L	24.5	L	57.5	U	
10/12/2019	@	Vanderbilt	34	10	W	15.5	W	57.5	U	
10/19/2019	@	Fresno State	27	56	L	16.0	L	52.0	O	
10/26/2019	vs	SAN DIEGO STATE	17	20	L	11.5	W	44.5	U	
11/2/2019	@	Colorado State	17	37	L	7.0	L	64.0	U	
11/16/2019	vs	HAWAII	7	21	L	7.0	L	72.5	U	
11/23/2019	vs	SAN JOSE STATE	38	35	W	7.0	W	65.0	O	
11/30/2019	@	Nevada	33	30	W	6.5	W	52.0	O	"Fremont Cannon"
Coach: Tony Sanchez		Season Record >>	290	396	4-8	ATS>>	6-6	O/U>>	4-7	

2018-UNLV		Opponent	Unlv	Opp	S/U	Line	ATS	Total	O/U	
9/1/2018	@	Usc	21	43	L	24.5	W	59.0	O	
9/8/2018	vs	TEXAS-EL PASO	52	24	W	-22.0	W	53.5	O	
9/15/2018	vs	PRAIRIE VIEW A&M	46	17	W	-31.0	L	NT	---	
9/22/2018	@	Arkansas State	20	27	L	8.0	W	66.5	U	
10/6/2018	vs	NEW MEXICO	14	50	L	-7.5	L	62.5	O	
10/13/2018	@	Utah State	28	59	L	27.0	L	65.5	O	
10/19/2018	vs	AIR FORCE	35	41	L	9.5	W	54.0	O	
10/27/2018	@	San Jose State	37	50	L	2.5	L	57.0	O	
11/3/2018	vs	FRESNO STATE	3	48	L	27.0	L	60.0	U	
11/10/2018	@	San Diego State	27	24	W	24.0	W	51.5	U	
11/17/2018	@	Hawaii	28	35	L	7.0	T	72.5	U	
11/24/2018	vs	NEVADA	34	29	W	14.0	W	61.0	O	"Fremont Cannon"
Coach: Tony Sanchez		Season Record >>	345	447	4-8	ATS>>	6-5-1	O/U>>	7-4	

NEVADA-LAS VEGAS REBELS   MOUNTAIN WEST West

STADIUM: Allegiant Stadium {65,000} | **Location:** Las Vegas, NV | **COACH:** Marcus Arroyo

DATE		Opponent	Unlv	Opp	S/U	Line	ATS	Total	O/U	Trends & Angles
9/3/2022	vs	IDAHO STATE								vs Idaho State - UNLV leads series 6-2
9/10/2022	@	California								2-20 S/U in 1st road game of season since 2000
9/17/2022	vs	NORTH TEXAS								vs North Texas - UNLV leads series 4-1
9/24/2022	@	Utah State								0-6 S/U vs Utah State as Dog since 1995
10/1/2022	vs	NEW MEXICO								HOME team 4-0 S/U & ATS since 2014
10/8/2022	@	San Jose State			-					1-10-1 S/U @ San Jose State since 1983
10/15/2022	vs	AIR FORCE								5-1 ATS @ home vs Air Force as Dog since 2006
10/22/2022	@	Notre Dame								1st Meeting
11/5/2022	@	San Diego State								1-9 S/U @ San Diego State since 2002 {3-7 ATS}
11/12/2022	vs	FRESNO STATE								vs Fresno State - Fresno leads series 17-7
11/19/2022	@	Hawaii								3-9 S/U vs Hawaii as Dog since 1995
11/26/2022	vs	NEVADA								4-1 O/U @ home vs Nevada as Dog since 2010
12/3/2022	vs									MWC Championship
	vs									BOWL GAME

Pointspread Analysis - Non-Conference

0-14 S/U vs Non-Conf. as 25.5 point or more Dog since 1996	
4-28 S/U vs Non-Conf. as 3.5-20 point Dog since 1985	

Dog

0-25 S/U on road as 25.5 point or more Dog since 1995	
1-14 S/U as 25.5-30 point Dog since 1996	
2-16 S/U as 20.5-25 point Dog since 2008	
0-6 S/U @ home as 20.5-25 point Dog since 1998	
3-37 S/U as 15.5-20 point Dog since 1994	
0-13 S/U on road as 10.5-15 point Dog since 2002	
4-32 S/U as 10.5-15 point Dog since 1985	
12-5 O/U as 10.5-15 point Dog since 2008	
7-0 O/U on road as 3 point or less Dog since 2002	
1-7 S/U @ home as 3 point or less Dog since 1998	

Favorite

0-7-1 ATS as 3 point or less favorite since 2012	
0-5 S/U on road as 3 point or less favorite since 2012	
8-2 O/U as 10.5-15 point favorite since 2002	
3-14 ATS as road favorite since 2003	
10-1 S/U @ home as 15.5 point or more favorite since 1985	

Pointspread Analysis - Conference

- 10-1-1 O/U vs Air Force as Dog since 2006
- vs Hawaii - Hawaii leads series 18-13
- vs Nevada - Nevada leads series 28-19
- 0-4 S/U & ATS vs Nevada as favorite since 2005
- vs New Mexico - UNLV leads series 13-12
- vs San Diego State - San Diego State leads series 21-10
- 3-13 S/U vs San Diego State since 2006
- Game 0-5 O/U @ San Diego State since 2012
- 1-9 S/U @ San Diego State as Dog since 1997
- 0-5 O/U @ San Diego State as Dog since 2012
- vs San Jose State - San Jose State leads series 18-7-1
- 1-8 S/U vs San Jose State as Dog since 1995 {2-6-1 ATS}
- 2-10 S/U vs San Jose State since 1995
- vs Utah State - Utah State leads series 18-7
- 0-6 S/U vs Utah State since 2012

Utah State	2-16 S/U prior to playing New Mexico since 1999
Utah State	6-1 ATS prior to playing New Mexico since 2012
Utah State	2-16 S/U in 2nd road game of season since 2004
NEW MEXICO	8-3 ATS prior to playing San Jose State since 1996
San Jose State	2-7 S/U after playing New Mexico since 2009
San Jose State	0-7 S/U prior to playing Air Force since 2011
AIR FORCE	3-10 S/U after playing San Jose State since 1994
San Diego State	2-9 S/U prior to playing Fresno State since 1985
FRESNO STATE	4-11 S/U prior to playing Hawaii since 2006
Hawaii	2-16 S/U in final road game of season since 2004
Hawaii	11-3 O/U in final road game of season since 2008
Hawaii	5-12-1 ATS in final road game of season since 2004
Hawaii	6-2-1 ATS prior to playing Nevada since 2013
Hawaii	10-4 O/U prior to playing Nevada since 2008
NEVADA	3-10 S/U after playing Hawaii since 2009
NEVADA	3-9 S/U in final home game of season since 2010

0-28 S/U vs ranked teams since 2008	
0-25 S/U @ home vs ranked teams all time	
1-17 S/U on road vs ranked teams since 2004	
0-8 S/U vs #10 #11 #12 #13 ranked teams all time	
0-34 S/U vs #18 - #25 ranked teams all time	

NEW MEXICO LOBOS   MOUNTAIN WEST Mountain

2021-New Mexico		Opponent	UNM	Opp	S/U	Line	ATS	Total	O/U	
9/4/2021	vs	HOUSTON BAPTIST	27	17	W	-25.5	L	66.0	U	
9/11/2021	vs	NEW MEXICO STATE	34	25	W	-19.5	L	56.0	O	"Rio Grande Rivalry"
9/18/2021	@	Texas A&M	0	34	L	30.0	L	50.0	U	
9/25/2021	@	Texas-El Paso	13	20	L	-2.5	L	54.5	U	
10/2/2021	vs	AIR FORCE	10	38	L	11.5	L	45.5	O	
10/9/2021	@	San Diego State	7	31	L	19.5	L	42.5	U	
10/16/2021	vs	COLORADO STATE	7	36	L	13.0	L	45.0	U	
10/23/2021	@	Wyoming	14	3	W	19.5	W	40.5	U	
11/6/2021	vs	UNLV	17	31	L	-1.5	L	45.0	O	
11/13/2021	@	Fresno State	7	34	L	24.0	L	50.5	U	
11/20/2021	@	Boise State	0	37	L	27.5	L	48.0	U	
11/27/2021	vs	UTAH STATE	10	35	L	17.0	L	48.0	U	
Coach: Danny Gonzales		Season Record >>	146	341	3-9	ATS>>	1-11	O/U>>	3-9	
2020-New Mexico		Opponent	UNM	Opp	S/U	Line	ATS	Total	O/U	
10/31/2020	@	San Jose State	21	38	L	13.5	L	56.5	O	
11/7/2020	@	Hawaii	33	39	L	13.0	W	66.5	O	
11/14/2020	vs	NEVADA	20	27	L	17.5	W	63.0	U	
11/21/2020	@	Air Force	0	28	L	8.0	L	55.5	U	
11/26/2020	@	Utah State	27	41	L	-6.5	L	49.0	O	
12/5/2020	vs	WYOMING	17	16	W	15.0	W	51.0	U	
12/12/2020	vs	FRESNO STATE	49	39	W	16.5	W	55.5	O	
Coach: Danny Gonzales		Season Record >>	167	228	2-5	ATS>>	4-3	O/U>>	4-3	
2019-New Mexico		Opponent	UNM	Opp	S/U	Line	ATS	Total	O/U	
8/31/2019	vs	SAM HOUSTON STATE	39	31	W	-6.0	W	NT	---	
9/14/2019	@	Notre Dame	14	66	L	34.5	L	64.0	O	
9/21/2019	vs	NEW MEXICO STATE	55	52	W	-4.0	L	69.0	O	"Rio Grande Rivalry"
9/28/2019	@	Liberty	10	17	L	7.0	T	72.0	U	
10/5/2019	@	San Jose State	21	32	L	7.0	W	69.5	U	
10/12/2019	vs	COLORADO STATE	21	35	L	5.0	L	66.0	U	
10/19/2019	@	Wyoming	10	23	L	17.5	W	49.0	U	
10/26/2019	vs	HAWAII	31	45	L	10.0	L	71.5	O	
11/2/2019	@	Nevada	10	21	L	3.5	L	57.5	U	
11/9/2019	vs	AIR FORCE	9	42	L	26.0	L	57.5	U	
11/16/2019	@	Boise State	22	44	L	24.0	W	56.5	O	
11/30/2019	vs	UTAH STATE	25	38	L	12.0	L	64.0	U	
Coach: Bob Davie		Season Record >>	267	446	2-10	ATS>>	4-7-1	O/U>>	4-7	
2018-New Mexico		Opponent	UNM	Opp	S/U	Line	ATS	Total	O/U	
9/1/2018	vs	INCARNATE WORD	62	30	W	-35.5	L	NT	---	
9/8/2018	@	Wisconsin	14	45	L	35.0	W	58.5	O	
9/15/2018	@	New Mexico State	42	25	W	-3.0	W	59.0	O	"Rio Grande Rivalry"
9/29/2018	vs	LIBERTY	43	52	L	-7.0	L	66.0	O	
10/6/2018	@	Unlv	50	14	W	7.5	W	62.5	O	
10/13/2018	@	Colorado State	18	20	L	-2.5	L	64.0	U	
10/20/2018	vs	FRESNO STATE	7	38	L	14.0	L	52.5	U	
10/27/2018	@	Utah State	19	61	L	19.5	L	64.0	O	
11/3/2018	vs	SAN DIEGO STATE	23	31	L	12.5	W	45.0	O	
11/10/2018	@	Air Force	24	42	L	13.0	L	55.5	O	
11/17/2018	vs	BOISE STATE	14	45	L	22.0	L	61.5	U	
11/27/2018	vs	WYOMING	3	31	L	7.0	L	43.0	U	
Coach: Bob Davie		Season Record >>	319	434	3-9	ATS>>	4-8	O/U>>	7-4	

NEW MEXICO LOBOS — MOUNTAIN WEST Mountain

STADIUM: Dreamstyle Stadium {39,224} | **Location:** Albuquerque, NM | **COACH:** Danny Gonzales

DATE		Opponent	Nmex	Opp	S/U	Line	ATS	Total	O/U	Trends & Angles
9/3/2022	vs	MAINE								1st Meeting
9/10/2022	vs	BOISE STATE								1-10 S/U vs Boise State as Dog since 2000
9/17/2022	vs	TEXAS-EL PASO								Game 1-8-1 O/U vs UTEP since 1998
9/24/2022	@	Lsu								2-13 S/U in 1st road game of season since 2007
10/1/2022	@	Unlv								vs UNLV - UNLV leads series 13-12
10/8/2022	vs	WYOMING								9-3 S/U @ home vs Wyoming since 1993
10/15/2022	@	New Mexico State								Game 7-1 O/U vs New Mexico State since 2013
10/22/2022	vs	FRESNO STATE								1-8 S/U & ATS vs Fresno St as Dog since 1995
11/5/2022	@	Utah State								0-5 S/U & ATS vs Utah State since 2017
11/12/2022	@	Air Force								0-9 S/U @ Air Force as Dog since 2002
11/19/2022	vs	SAN DIEGO STATE								6-1 ATS @ home vs San Diego St. since 2002
11/26/2022	@	Colorado State								0-10 S/U vs Colorado State as Dog since 2010
12/3/2022	vs									MWC Championship
	vs									BOWL GAME

Pointspread Analysis — Non-Conference

- 0-19 S/U vs Non-Conf. as 20.5 point or more Dog since 1985
- 1-9 S/U vs Non-Conf. as 10.5-15 point Dog since 1998
- 12-1 S/U vs Non-Conf. as 15.5 point or more favorite since 1986
- vs New Mexico State - New Mexico leads series 72-33-5
- 1-6 ATS vs New Mexico State since 2014
- 11-2 O/U vs New Mexico State as favorite since 2005
- vs Texas-El Paso - New Mexico leads series 43-32-1

Dog
- 1-40 S/U as 25.5 point or more Dog since 1985
- 0-8 S/U @ home as 25.5 point or more Dog since 1985
- 2-23 S/U as 20.5-25 point Dog since 1984
- 0-14 S/U on road as 20.5-25 point Dog since 1986
- 6-36 S/U as 15.5-20 point Dog since 1985
- 0-15 S/U on road as 10.5-15 point Dog since 2001
- 0-5 O/U on road as 3 point or less Dog since 2010

Favorite
- 0-7 ATS as 7.5-10 point favorite since 2004
- 0-7-1 O/U as 7.5-10 point favorite since 2003
- 3-0 S/U on road as 7.5-10 point favorite since 1997
- 16-2 S/U @ home as 10.5-15 point favorite since 1989
- 5-0 O/U as 10.5-15 point favorite since 2013
- 13-0 S/U @ home as 15.5 point or more favorite since 1986

Pointspread Analysis — Conference

- 6-2 O/U vs Air Force as Dog since 2014
- vs Air Force - Air Force leads series 24-13
- vs Boise State - Boise State leads series 11-1
- vs Colorado State - Colorado State leads series 43-25
- 1-6 S/U vs Colorado State as favorite since 1985
- 0-7 ATS vs Colorado State as favorite since 1985
- 0-8 S/U vs San Diego State since 2009
- vs San Diego State - San Diego State leads series 28-15
- 0-9 S/U @ home vs San Diego State as Dog since 1985
- 7-0 S/U vs San Diego State as favorite since 2001 {6-1 ATS}
- Game 2-6 O/U vs Utah State since 2014
- vs Utah State - Utah State leads series 15-13
- vs Wyoming - Wyoming leads series 38-36
- 7-0 S/U vs Wyoming as favorite since 1985
- 1-11 S/U vs Colorado State as 5-10 point Dog since 1986
- 1-11 S/U vs Fresno State as 5.5 point or more Dog since 1990
- 1-18 S/U vs San Diego State as 5 point or more Dog since 1985
- 2-11 S/U vs Wyoming as 10 point or more Dog since 1987

- 0-24 S/U vs ranked teams since 2004
- 2-35 S/U on road vs ranked teams all time
- 4-28 S/U @ home vs ranked teams all time
- 0-12 S/U vs #4 #5 #6 #7 #8 ranked teams all time
- 0-6 S/U vs #10 #11 #12 ranked teams all time
- 0-13 S/U vs #14 #15 #16 #17 ranked teams all time
- 0-17 S/U vs #19 #20 #21 #22 ranked teams all time

Opponent	Trend
BOISE STATE	4-10 S/U in 2nd home game of season since 2008
BOISE STATE	11-3 O/U in 2nd home game of season since 2008
BOISE STATE	2-12 ATS in 2nd home game of season since 2008
Lsu	1-12 S/U prior to playing UNLV since 2004
Lsu	7-2 O/U prior to playing UNLV since 2009
WYOMING	1-9 S/U after playing UNLV since 2008
FRESNO STATE	0-12 S/U after playing New Mexico State since 2009
Utah State	1-5 O/U after playing Fresno State since 2012
Air Force	1-8 S/U prior to playing San Diego State since 2008
SAN DIEGO ST	3-11 O/U prior to playing Colorado State since 2007
SAN DIEGO ST	2-13 S/U after playing Air Force since 2006
Colorado State	1-15 S/U in final road game of season since 2006

NEW MEXICO STATE AGGIES INDEPENDENT

2021-New Mexico State		Opponent	NNSU	Opp	S/U	Line	ATS	Total	O/U	
8/28/2021	vs	TEXAS-EL PASO	3	30	L	9.5	L	59.0	U	"Brass Spittoon"
9/4/2021	@	San Diego State	10	28	L	31.5	W	50.5	U	
9/11/2021	@	New Mexico	25	34	L	19.5	W	56.0	O	"Rio Grande Rivalry"
9/18/2021	vs	SOUTH CAROLINA STATE	43	35	W	-3.0	W	54.5	O	
9/25/2021	vs	HAWAII	21	41	L	16.5	L	62.5	U	
10/2/2021	vs	San Jose State	31	37	L	25.0	W	51.5	O	
10/9/2021	@	Nevada	28	55	L	28.5	L	65.0	O	
10/23/2021	@	Hawaii	34	41	L	19.0	L	63.5	O	
11/6/2021	vs	UTAH STATE	13	35	L	18.0	L	72.0	U	
11/13/2021	@	Alabama	3	59	L	50.5	L	67.5	U	
11/20/2021	@	Kentucky	14	56	L	36.0	L	60.0	O	
11/27/2021	vs	MASSACHUSETTS	44	27	W	-7.0	W	59.0	O	
Coach: Doug Martin		Season Record >>	269	478	2-10	ATS>>	7-5	O/U>>	7-5	

2019-New Mexico State		Opponent	NNSU	Opp	S/U	Line	ATS	Total	O/U	
8/31/2019	@	Washington State	7	58	L	33.5	L	65.5	U	
9/7/2019	@	Alabama	10	62	L	55.0	W	64.0	O	
9/14/2019	vs	SAN DIEGO STATE	10	31	L	17.0	L	51.0	U	
9/21/2019	@	New Mexico	52	55	L	4.0	W	69.0	O	"Rio Grande Rivalry"
9/28/2019	vs	FRESNO STATE	17	30	L	20.5	L	62.5	U	
10/5/2019	vs	LIBERTY	13	20	L	4.0	L	63.5	U	
10/12/2019	@	Central Michigan	28	42	L	10.5	L	56.5	O	
10/26/2019	@	Georgia Southern	7	41	L	14.0	L	54.5	O	
11/9/2019	@	Mississippi	3	41	L	29.0	L	65.0	U	
11/16/2019	vs	INCARNATE WORD	41	28	W	-7.5	W	NT	---	
11/23/2019	vs	TEXAS-EL PASO	44	35	W	-7.0	W	55.5	O	"Brass Spittoon"
11/30/2019	@	Liberty	28	49	L	14.5	L	68.0	O	
Coach: Doug Martin		Season Record >>	260	492	2-10	ATS>>	5-7	O/U>>	5-6	

2018-New Mexico State		Opponent	NNSU	Opp	S/U	Line	ATS	Total	O/U	
8/25/2018	vs	WYOMING	7	29	L	5.0	L	45.5	U	
8/30/2018	@	Minnesota	10	48	L	21.5	L	47.5	O	
9/8/2018	@	Utah State	13	60	L	21.5	L	62.0	O	
9/15/2018	vs	NEW MEXICO	25	42	L	3.0	L	59.0	O	"Rio Grande Rivalry"
9/22/2018	@	Texas-El Paso	27	20	W	-4.5	W	50.0	U	"Brass Spittoon"
10/6/2018	vs	LIBERTY	49	41	W	3.5	W	64.0	O	
10/13/2018	@	Louisiana-Lafayette	38	66	L	7.0	L	67.5	O	
10/20/2018	vs	GEORGIA SOUTHERN	31	48	L	10.0	L	52.5	O	
10/27/2018	@	Texas State	20	27	L	PK	L	56.0	U	
11/3/2018	vs	ALCORN STATE	52	42	W	-12.5	L	NT	---	
11/17/2018	@	Byu	10	45	L	25.5	L	59.0	U	
11/24/2018	@	Liberty	21	28	L	5.5	L	72.5	U	
Coach: Doug Martin		Season Record >>	303	496	3-9	ATS>>	2-10	O/U>>	6-5	

2017-New Mexico State		Opponent	NNSU	Opp	S/U	Line	ATS	Total	O/U	
8/31/2017	@	Arizona State	31	37	L	25.5	W	68.5	U	
9/9/2017	@	New Mexico	30	28	W	7.5	W	68.5	U	"Rio Grande Rivalry"
9/16/2017	vs	TROY	24	27	L	9.5	W	60.0	U	
9/23/2017	vs	TEXAS-EL PASO	41	14	W	-17.5	W	58.5	U	"Brass Spittoon"
9/30/2017	@	Arkansas	24	42	L	18.5	W	61.0	O	
10/7/2017	@	Appalachian State	31	45	L	12.5	L	55.5	O	
10/14/2017	@	Georgia Southern	35	27	W	-5.0	W	58.0	O	
10/28/2017	vs	ARKANSAS STATE	21	37	L	3.5	L	71.5	U	
11/4/2017	@	Texas State	45	35	W	-9.0	W	56.0	O	
11/18/2017	@	Louisiana-Lafayette	34	47	L	-4.0	L	64.0	O	
11/25/2017	vs	IDAHO	17	10	W	-10.0	L	56.5	U	
12/2/2017	vs	SOUTH ALABAMA	22	17	W	-12.0	L	54.5	U	
12/29/2017	vs	Utah State	26	20	W	5.5	W	64.0	U	Arizona Bowl
Coach: Doug Martin		Season Record >>	381	386	7-6	ATS>>	8-5	O/U>>	5-8	

NEW MEXICO STATE AGGIES INDEPENDENT

STADIUM: Aggie Memorial Stadium {30,343} **Location:** Las Cruces, NM **COACH:** Jerry Kill

DATE		Opponent	Nmsu	Opp	S/U	Line	ATS	Total	O/U	Trends & Angles
8/27/2022	vs	NEVADA								0-6 S/U @ home vs Nevada as Dog since 1995
9/1/2022	@	Minnesota								vs Minnesota - Minnesota leads series 2-1
9/10/2022	@	Texas-El Paso								2-10 S/U @ Texas-El Paso since 1996
9/17/2022	@	Wisconsin								vs Wisconsin - Wisconsin leads series 1-0
9/24/2022	vs	HAWAII								0-9 S/U vs Hawaii as Dog since 2005
10/1/2022	vs	FLORIDA INTERNATIONAL								vs Fla International - NMSU leads series 1-0
10/15/2022	vs	NEW MEXICO								vs New Mexico - UNM leads series 72-33-5
10/22/2022	vs	SAN JOSE STATE								1-9 S/U @ home vs San Jose since 1986 {1-9 ATS}
10/29/2022	@	Massachusetts								vs Massachusetts - NMSU lead series 1-0
11/12/2022	vs	LAMAR								vs Lamar - NMSU leads series 6-4
11/19/2022	@	Missouri								1st Meeting
11/26/2022	@	Liberty								vs Liberty - Liberty leads series 3-1
	vs									BOWL GAME

Pointspread Analysis — Non-Conference
- 7-1 O/U vs Nevada as Dog since 2005
- 11-2 O/U vs New Mexico as Dog since 2005
- vs San Jose State - SJSU leads series 18-3
- vs UTEP - Texas-El Paso leads series 58-38-2
- 0-8 S/U vs Texas-El Paso as Dog since 2009
- 3-1 S/U & ATS vs Texas-El Paso since 2017
- 0-4 O/U vs Texas-El Paso as favorite since 2007
- 1-14 S/U vs San Jose State as 4 point or more Dog since 1985
- 0-6 ATS @ home vs SJSU as 4 point or more Dog since 1985
- 0-12 S/U vs UTEP as 9 point or more Dog since 1989
- 1-12 S/U vs Utah State as 6 point or more Dog since 1986

Dog
- 0-66 S/U as 25.5 point or more Dog since 1985
- 2-36 S/U as 20.5-25 point Dog since 1987
- 10-1 O/U as 20.5-25 point Dog since 2012
- 0-21 S/U @ home as 20.5 point or more Dog since 1986
- 4-18 S/U on road as 15.5-20 point Dog since 1985
- 0-14 S/U @ home as 15.5-20 point Dog since 1988
- 2-25 S/U on road as 10.5-15 point Dog since 1989
- 9-2 O/U as 10.5-15 point Dog since 2012
- 2-12 S/U @ home as 10.5-15 point Dog since 1990
- 2-15 S/U on road as 7.5-10 point Dog since 1985
- 4-13 S/U @ home as 3.5-7 point Dog since 2004
- 2-11 S/U on road as 3.5-7 point Dog since 2002
- 3-10 ATS on road as 3.5-7 point Dog since 2002
- 2-8 S/U & ATS as 3 point or less Dog since 2005

Favorite
- 10-1 S/U @ home as 10.5 point or more favorite since 1999

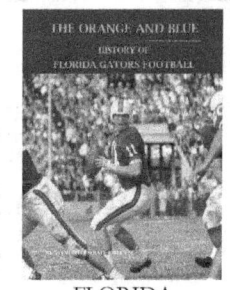

Texas-El Paso
Texas-El Paso
Wisconsin
Wisconsin
Wisconsin
FLA INTER
SAN JOSE STATE
Liberty
Liberty
Liberty

Pointspread Analysis — Bowl Games
- 3-0 S/U in Bowl Games since 1959
- 2-19 S/U in 2nd road game of season since 2000
- 13-1 O/U in 2nd road game of season since 2007
- 6-2 O/U after playing Texas-El Paso since 2013
- 3-13 S/U after playing Texas-El Paso since 2005
- 6-1 ATS after playing Texas-El Paso since 2014
- 0-12 S/U prior to playing New Mexico since 2009
- 2-7 S/U after playing New Mexico since 2012
- 1-10 ATS in final road game of season since 2010
- 8-1 O/U in final road game of season since 2012
- 0-14 S/U in final road game of season since 2007

- 0-7 S/U @ home vs ranked all time
- 1-30 S/U on road vs ranked teams all time
- 2-8 ATS on road vs ranked teams since 2010
- 0-9-1 ATS vs #14 - #18 ranked teams all time
- 5-0 S/U when ranked all time

College Football Blueblood Series available at: www.stevesfootballbible.com

ALABAMA   AUBURN   CLEMSON   FLORIDA   FLORIDA STATE

NORTH CAROLINA TAR HEELS — ACC Coastal

2021-North Carolina		Opponent	UNC	Opp	S/U	Line	ATS	Total	O/U	
9/2/2021	@	Virginia Tech	10	17	L	-4.5	L	63.5	U	
9/11/2021	vs	GEORGIA STATE	59	17	W	-25.5	W	66.0	O	
9/18/2021	vs	VIRGINIA	59	39	W	-7.5	W	66.5	O	"South's Oldest Rivalry"
9/25/2021	@	Georgia Tech	22	45	L	-14.5	L	66.0	O	
10/2/2021	vs	DUKE	38	7	W	-19.5	W	74.0	U	"Victory Bell"
10/9/2021	vs	FLORIDA STATE	25	35	L	-17.5	L	64.0	U	
10/16/2021	vs	MIAMI	45	42	W	-7.5	L	63.5	O	
10/30/2021	@	Notre Dame	34	44	L	3.5	L	62.5	O	
11/6/2021	vs	WAKE FOREST	58	55	W	-2.0	W	78.0	O	
11/11/2021	@	Pittsburgh	23	30	L	6.5	L	72.0	U	{OT}
11/20/2021	vs	WOFFORD	34	14	W	-37.0	L	61.5	U	
11/26/2021	@	NC State	30	34	L	5.0	W	61.5	O	
12/30/2021	vs	South Carolina	21	38	L	-13.0	L	57.5	O	Duke's Mayo Bowl
Coach: Mack Brown		Season Record >>	458	417	6-7	ATS>>	5-8	O/U>>	8-5	

2020-North Carolina		Opponent	UNC	Opp	S/U	Line	ATS	Total	O/U	
9/12/2020	vs	SYRACUSE	31	6	W	-23.0	W	65.5	U	
10/3/2020	@	Boston College	26	22	W	-14.5	L	52.5	U	
10/10/2020	vs	VIRGINIA TECH	56	45	W	-3.0	W	58.5	O	
10/17/2020	@	Florida State	28	31	L	-13.5	L	65.0	U	
10/24/2020	vs	NC STATE	48	21	W	-16.0	W	61.5	O	
10/31/2020	@	Virginia	41	44	L	-8.0	L	61.5	O	"South's Oldest Rivalry"
11/7/2020	@	Duke	56	24	W	-11.0	W	63.0	O	"Victory Bell"
11/14/2020	vs	WAKE FOREST	59	53	W	-13.0	L	70.5	O	
11/27/2020	vs	NOTRE DAME	17	31	L	4.5	L	69.5	U	
12/5/2020	vs	WESTERN CAROLINA	49	9	W	-48.5	L	69.5	U	
12/12/2020	@	Miami	62	26	W	3.0	W	72.5	O	
1/2/2021	vs	Texas A&M	27	41	L	10.0	L	65.5	O	Orange Bowl
Coach: Mack Brown		Season Record >>	500	353	8-4	ATS>>	5-7	O/U>>	7-5	

2019-North Carolina		Opponent	UNC	Opp	S/U	Line	ATS	Total	O/U	
8/31/2019	vs	South Carolina	24	20	W	12.0	W	62.5	U	Bank Of America Stadium
9/7/2019	vs	MIAMI	28	25	W	5.0	W	46.0	O	
9/12/2019	@	Wake Forest	18	24	L	3.0	L	65.0	U	
9/21/2019	vs	APPALACHIAN STATE	31	34	L	-2.0	L	58.0	O	
9/28/2019	vs	CLEMSON	20	21	L	27.5	W	60.0	U	
10/5/2019	@	Georgia Tech	38	22	W	-10.0	W	47.0	O	
10/19/2019	@	Virginia Tech	41	43	L	-4.0	L	57.0	O	{6 OT}
10/26/2019	vs	DUKE	20	17	W	-3.0	T	53.5	U	"Victory Bell"
11/2/2019	vs	VIRGINIA	31	38	L	1.0	L	47.5	O	"South's Oldest Rivalry"
11/14/2019	@	Pittsburgh	27	34	L	4.5	L	48.5	O	{OT}
11/23/2019	vs	MERCER	56	7	W	-38.5	W	NT	---	
11/30/2019	@	NC State	41	10	W	-11.5	W	58.0	U	
12/27/2019	vs	Temple	55	13	W	-6.5	W	56.5	O	Military Bowl
Coach: Mack Brown		Season Record >>	430	308	7-6	ATS>>	7-5-1	O/U>>	7-5	

2018-North Carolina		Opponent	UNC	Opp	S/U	Line	ATS	Total	O/U	
9/1/2018	@	California	17	24	L	7.0	T	58.0	U	
9/8/2018	@	East Carolina	19	41	L	-15.5	L	59.0	O	
9/22/2018	vs	PITTSBURGH	38	35	W	2.5	W	48.0	O	
9/27/2018	@	Miami	10	47	L	18.5	L	55.0	O	
10/13/2018	vs	VIRGINIA TECH	19	22	L	6.5	W	57.5	U	
10/20/2018	@	Syracuse	37	40	L	10.0	W	67.0	O	{2 OT}
10/27/2018	@	Virginia	21	31	L	9.0	L	50.5	O	"South's Oldest Rivalry"
11/3/2018	vs	GEORGIA TECH	28	38	L	3.5	L	65.0	O	
11/10/2018	@	Duke	35	42	L	7.5	W	58.5	O	"Victory Bell"
11/17/2018	vs	WESTERN CAROLINA	49	26	W	-30.5	L	NT	---	
11/24/2018	vs	NC STATE	28	34	L	7.0	W	59.0	O	{OT}
Coach: Larry Fedora		Season Record >>	731	688	2-9	ATS>>	5-5-1	O/U>>	8-2	

NORTH CAROLINA TAR HEELS — ACC Coastal

STADIUM: Kenan Memorial Stadium {50,500} | **Location:** Chapel Hill, NC | **COACH:** Mack Brown

DATE		Opponent	Unc	Opp	S/U	Line	ATS	Total	O/U	Trends & Angles
8/27/2022	vs	FLORIDA A&M								13-2 S/U in 1st home game of season since 2007
9/3/2022	@	Appalachian State								vs Appalachian State - Series tied 1-1
9/10/2022	@	Georgia State								vs Georgia State - UNC leads series 1-0
9/24/2022	vs	NOTRE DAME								0-5 S/U vs Notre Dame as Dog since 2006
10/1/2022	vs	VIRGINIA TECH								2-7 S/U @ home vs Va Tech since 2004
10/8/2022	@	Miami								vs Miami - UNC leads series 14-11
10/15/2022	@	Duke								vs Duke - UNC leads series 62-40-4
10/29/2022	vs	PITTSBURGH								6-0 S/U @ home vs Pittsburgh since 1974
11/5/2022	@	Virginia								1-11 S/U @ Virginia as Dog since 1985
11/12/2022	@	Wake Forest								vs Wake Forest - HOME team 7-0 S/U since 2007
11/19/2022	vs	GEORGIA TECH								vs Georgia Tech - G Tech leads series 31-22-3
11/25/2022	vs	NC STATE								2-5 S/U @ home vs NC State since 2008
12/3/2022	vs									ACC Championship
	vs									BOWL GAME

Pointspread Analysis — Non-Conference
- 1-16 S/U vs Non-Conf. as 10.5 point or more Dog since 1987
- 1-9 S/U vs Non-Conf. as 3.5-7 point Dog since 2003
- 0-7 S/U vs Non-Conf. as 3 point or less Dog since 2003
- 7-2 S/U vs Non-Conf. as 3 point or less favorite sicne 1990
- 2-8-1 O/U vs Non-Conf. as 3.5-7 point favorite since 1998
- 5-0 S/U vs Non-Conf. as 7.5-10 point favorite since 2003
- 6-1 S/U vs Non-Conf. as 15.5-20 point favorite since 2000
- 26-0 S/U vs Non-Conf. as 20.5 point or more favorite since 1987
- vs Notre Dame - Notre Dame leads series 20-2

Dog
- 0-16 S/U on road as 20.5 point or more Dog since 1987
- 1-13 S/U on road as 15.5-20 point Dog since 1989
- 1-7 S/U @ home as 15.5-20 point Dog since 1989
- 3-16 S/U on road as 10.5-15 point Dog since 1984
- 2-7-1 S/U @ home as 10.5-15 point Dog since 1989
- 2-10 S/U as 7.5-10 point Dog since 2004
- 1-7 S/U on road as 7.5-10 point Dog since 2011
- 2-10 S/U @ home as 7.5-10 point Dog since 1985
- 2-11 S/U as 3.5-7 point Dog since 2015
- 4-13 S/U as 3 point or less Dog since 2003

Favorite
- 1-5 O/U on road as 3 point or less favorite since 1996
- 17-4 S/U on road as 3.5-7 point favorite since 1992
- 15-3 S/U as 7.5-10 point favorite since 2001
- 5-1 S/U on road as 7.5-10 point favorite since 2003
- 11-2 S/U as 15.5-20 point favorite since 1998
- 43-0 S/U as 20.5 point or more favorite since 1983

Bowl Games
- 5-2 S/U in Gator Bowl
- 0-3 S/U vs Pacific-12 in Bowl Games
- 0-4 S/U in Bowl Games as 3 point or less Dog since 1994
- 1-4 O/U in Bowl Games as 3.5-7 point favorite since 1993

- 20-3 S/U @ home when ranked since 1996
- 9-1 S/U when ranked vs Duke since 1972 {5-0 @ home}
- 6-0 S/U @ home when ranked vs Georgia Tech all time
- 1-8 S/U vs ranked Virginia Tech all time {0-4 @ home}
- 19-82-2 S/U on road vs ranked teams all time
- 0-11 S/U vs #1 ranked teams all time
- 0-9 S/U vs #2 ranked teams all time
- 0-6 S/U vs #4 ranked teams since 1961
- 0-7 S/U vs #5 ranked teams all time

Pointspread Analysis — Conference
- 5-0 ATS vs Duke as Dog since 1990
- 1-8 S/U vs Georgia Tech as Dog since 2005
- vs NC State - North Carolina leads series 68-37-6
- 12-2 ATS vs NC State as Dog since 1990
- 2-5 S/U & ATS @ home vs NC State as favorite since 2000
- vs Pittsburgh - North Carolina leads series 10-5
- Game 6-2 O/U vs Pittsburgh since 2013
- 6-2 S/U vs Pittsburgh since 2013
- 8-3 ATS vs Pittsburgh since 1998
- 5-2 ATS vs Pittsburgh as Dog since 2000
- 4-0 S/U vs Pittsburgh as favorite since 1998
- vs Virginia - North Carolina leads series 64-57-4
- 1-4 S/U & ATS vs Virginia since 2017
- 8-0 S/U vs Virginia as favorite since 2010
- 1-11 S/U vs Virginia Tech as Dog since 2004
- vs Virginia Tech - Virginia Tech leads series 25-13-6
- 2-7 ATS vs Virginia Tech since 2013
- Game 4-11 O/U vs Virginia Tech since 2007
- 4-14 S/U vs Virginia Tech since 2004
- vs Wake Forest - North Carolina leads series 71-36-2
- 0-3 S/U @ Wake Forest since 2007
- 9-0 S/U vs Duke as 6.5-10 point favorite since 1991
- 11-0 S/U vs Duke as 12.5 point or more favorite since 1983
- 7-0 S/U vs Georgia Tech as 8 point or more favorite since 1983
- 0-8-1 S/U vs Georgia Tech as 10 point or more Dog since 1989
- 6-1 S/U & ATS vs Miami as 7.5 point or less Dog since 2007
- 0-6 S/U vs Miami as 9 point or more Dog since 2005
- 1-5 S/U & ATS vs NC State as 8-11.5 point favorite since 1986
- 0-7 S/U vs Virginia as 8 point or more Dog since 1989
- 8-0 S/U vs Wake Forest as 17 point or more favorite since 1983
- 5-0 S/U & ATS vs Wake Forest as 4.5-9 point favorite since 1985

Miami	7-1-1 ATS after playing Virginia Tech since 2013
Virginia	9-1 S/U after playing Pittsburgh since 1998
Wake Forest	10-3 ATS prior to playing Georgia Tech since 2008
Wake Forest	10-1 ATS in final road game of season since 2011
NC STATE	3-15 O/U after playing Georgia Tech since 2003

NORTH CAROLINA STATE WOLFPACK   ACC Atlantic

2021-NC State		Opponent	NCS	Opp	S/U	Line	ATS	Total	O/U	
9/2/2021	vs	SOUTH FLORIDA	45	0	W	-20.0	W	57.0	U	
9/11/2021	@	Mississippi State	10	24	L	-2.0	L	55.0	U	
9/18/2021	vs	FURMAN	45	7	W	-27.5	W	45.0	O	
9/25/2021	vs	CLEMSON	27	21	W	10.5	W	47.0	O	"Textile Bowl"
10/2/2021	vs	LOUISIANA TECH	34	27	W	-18.5	L	55.5	O	
10/16/2021	@	Boston College	33	7	W	-3.0	W	51.5	U	
10/23/2021	@	Miami	30	31	L	-4.0	L	54.5	O	
10/30/2021	vs	LOUISVILLE	28	13	W	-6.0	W	57.0	U	
11/6/2021	@	Florida State	28	14	W	-3.0	W	55.0	U	
11/13/2021	@	Wake Forest	42	45	L	1.0	L	64.0	O	
11/20/2021	vs	SYRACUSE	41	17	W	-11.0	W	49.5	O	
11/26/2021	vs	NORTH CAROLINA	34	30	W	-5.0	L	61.5	O	
Coach: Dave Doeren		Season Record >>	397	236	9-3	ATS>>	7-5	O/U>>	7-5	

2020-NC State		Opponent	NCS	Opp	S/U	Line	ATS	Total	O/U	
9/19/2020	vs	WAKE FOREST	45	42	W	2.5	W	53.0	O	
9/26/2020	@	Virginia Tech	24	45	L	6.5	L	57.5	O	
10/3/2020	@	Pittsburgh	30	29	W	14.0	W	46.0	O	
10/10/2020	@	Virginia	38	21	W	7.0	W	58.5	O	
10/17/2020	vs	DUKE	31	20	W	-4.5	W	60.0	U	
10/24/2020	@	North Carolina	21	48	L	16.0	L	61.5	O	
11/6/2020	vs	MIAMI	41	44	L	11.0	W	58.0	O	
11/14/2020	vs	FLORIDA STATE	38	22	W	-12.0	W	60.5	U	
11/21/2020	vs	LIBERTY	15	14	W	-4.0	L	66.5	U	
11/28/2020	@	Syracuse	36	29	W	-17.5	L	49.5	O	
12/5/2020	vs	GEORGIA TECH	23	13	W	-7.0	W	61.0	U	
1/2/2021	vs	Kentucky	21	23	L	3.5	W	50.0	U	Gator Bowl
Coach: Dave Doeren		Season Record >>	363	350	8-4	ATS>>	8-4	O/U>>	7-5	

2019-NC State		Opponent	NCS	Opp	S/U	Line	ATS	Total	O/U	
8/31/2019	vs	EAST CAROLINA	34	6	W	-17.5	W	51.5	U	"Victory Barrel"
9/7/2019	vs	WESTERN CAROLINA	41	0	W	-40.5	W	NT	---	
9/14/2019	@	West Virginia	27	44	L	-7.0	L	45.5	O	
9/21/2019	vs	BALL STATE	34	23	W	-19.5	L	58.5	U	
9/28/2019	@	Florida State	13	31	L	7.0	L	62.0	U	
10/10/2019	vs	SYRACUSE	16	10	W	-4.0	W	55.5	U	
10/19/2019	@	Boston College	24	45	L	-4.0	L	54.5	O	
11/2/2019	@	Wake Forest	10	44	L	7.5	L	60.5	U	
11/9/2019	vs	CLEMSON	10	55	L	35.0	L	54.0	O	"Textile Bowl"
11/16/2019	vs	LOUISVILLE	20	34	L	4.0	L	52.0	O	
11/21/2019	@	Georgia Tech	26	28	L	-2.5	L	46.5	O	
11/30/2019	vs	NORTH CAROLINA	10	41	L	11.5	L	58.0	U	
Coach: Dave Doeren		Season Record >>	265	361	4-8	ATS>>	3-9	O/U>>	5-6	

2018-NC State		Opponent	NCS	Opp	S/U	Line	ATS	Total	O/U	
9/1/2018	vs	JAMES MADISON	24	13	W	-14.0	L	NT	---	
9/8/2018	vs	GEORIGA STATE	41	7	W	-24.5	W	56.0	U	
9/22/2018	@	Marshall	37	20	W	-5.5	W	57.0	T	
9/29/2018	vs	VIRGINIA	35	21	W	-6.0	W	52.5	O	
10/6/2018	vs	BOSTON COLLEGE	28	23	W	-6.5	L	60.5	U	
10/20/2018	@	Clemson	7	41	L	18.5	L	58.0	U	"Textile Bowl"
10/27/2018	@	Syracuse	41	51	L	-2.0	L	64.5	O	
11/3/2018	vs	FLORIDA STATE	47	28	W	-9.0	W	52.0	O	
11/8/2018	vs	WAKE FOREST	23	27	L	-19.0	L	66.5	U	
11/17/2018	@	Louisville	52	10	W	-16.0	W	65.5	U	
11/24/2018	@	North Carolina	34	28	W	-7.0	L	59.0	O	{OT}
12/1/2018	vs	EAST CAROLINA	58	3	W	-26.0	W	60.5	O	
12/31/2018	vs	Texas A&M	13	52	L	7.5	L	58.0	O	Gator Bowl
Coach: Dave Doeren		Season Record >>	440	324	9-4	ATS>>	6-7	O/U>>	6-5-1	

NORTH CAROLINA STATE WOLFPACK — ACC Atlantic

STADIUM: Carter-Finley Stadium {57,583} | **Location:** Raleigh, NC | **COACH:** Dave Doeren

DATE		Opponent	NCS	Opp	S/U	Line	ATS	Total	O/U	Trends & Angles
9/3/2022	@	East Carolina								vs East Carolina - NC State leads series 18-13
9/10/2022	vs	CHARLESTON SOUTHERN								12-0 S/U in 1st home game of season since 2010
9/17/2022	vs	TEXAS TECH								4-0 S/U & ATS vs Texas Tech since 1992
9/24/2022	vs	CONNECTICUT								vs Connecticut - NC State leads series 2-0
10/1/2022	@	Clemson								2-15 S/U vs Clemson as Dog since 2000
10/8/2022	vs	FLORIDA STATE								vs Florida State - FSU leads series 27-15
10/15/2022	@	Syracuse								6-1 S/U @ Syracuse since 1974
10/27/2022	vs	VIRGINIA TECH								0-5 S/U & ATS vs Virginia Tech since 2005
11/5/2022	vs	WAKE FOREST								16-2 S/U @ home vs Wake Forest since 1986
11/12/2022	vs	BOSTON COLLEGE								1-8 O/U vs Boston College as favorite since 2011
11/19/2022	@	Louisville								vs Louisville - Louisville leads series 7-4
11/25/2022	@	North Carolina								5-2 S/U & ATS @ N. Carolina as Dog since 2000
12/3/2022	vs									ACC Championship
	vs									BOWL GAME

Pointspread Analysis — Non-Conference
- 1-7 S/U vs Non-Conf. as 7.5-10 point Dog since 1984
- 0-6 S/U vs Non-Conf. as 3.5-7 point Dog since 2008
- 5-1 S/U vs Non-Conf. as 3 point or less favorite since 2010
- 0-4 S/U & ATS vs Non-Conf. as 7.5-10 point favorite since 2006
- 45-0 S/U vs Non-Conf. as 10.5 point or more favorite since 1989
- vs Texas Tech - NC State leads series 4-1

Dog
- 1-8 S/U on road as 20.5 point or more Dog since 1993
- 1-13 S/U on road as 15.5-20 point Dog since 1987
- 1-8 S/U @ home as 10.5-15 point Dog since 1990
- 1-8 S/U @ home as 7.5-10 point Dog since 1996
- 2-13 S/U as 3.5-7 point Dog since 2012
- 4-11 ATS as 3.5-7 point Dog since 2012

Favorite
- 2-10 O/U @ home as 3 point or less favorite since 2000
- 8-0 S/U @ home as 3.5-7 point favorite since 2018
- 2-8 O/U @ home as 3.5-7 point favorite since 2013
- 2-8 O/U as 10.5-15 point favorite since 2012
- 11-2 S/U as 10.5-15 point favorite since 2011
- 48-1 S/U as 15.5 point or more favorite since 1989

Bowl Games
- 6-1 O/U in Bowl Games since 2011
- 10-2 ATS in Bowl Games since 2003
- 5-2 O/U in Bowl Games as 3.5-7 point Dog since 1995
- 3-0 S/U & ATS in Bowl Games as 3.5-7 point favorite since 2005

- 1-6 S/U when ranked @ Clemson since 1967
- 1-15 S/U on road vs ranked teams since 2005
- 1-15 S/U vs #3 ranked teams all time
- 0-5 S/U @ ranked Clemson since 2005
- 0-4 S/U vs ranked Florida State since 2013
- 10-2 ATS vs ranked Florida State since 2001
- 2-9 S/U @ ranked North Carolina all time
- 1-8-1 S/U when ranked vs Top #10 teams all time
- 0-9 S/U vs #5 #6 ranked teams all time

Pointspread Analysis — Conference
- 0-5 S/U vs Boston College as Dog since 2005 {1-4 ATS}
- 4-0 O/U vs Boston College as Dog since 2007
- vs Boston College - Boston College leads series 10-8
- vs Clemson - Clemson leads series 59-29-1
- 14-4 ATS vs Florida State as Dog since 2001
- vs North Carolina - UNC leads series 67-38-6
- 2-12 ATS vs North Carolina as favorite since 1990
- vs Syracuse - NC State leads series 13-2
- 3-0 S/U & ATS vs Syracuse as Dog since 1997
- 3-0 S/U & ATS vs Syracuse as Dog since 1997
- vs Wake Forest - NC State leads series 67-42-6
- 6-1 ATS @ home vs Wake Forest since 2008
- 2-6 S/U & ATS vs Wake Forest as Dog since 1987
- vs Wake Forest - HOME team 13-2 S/U since 2007
- 1-16 S/U vs Clemson as 10 point or more Dog since 1983
- 2-11 S/U vs Florida State as 18 point or more Dog since 1993
- 5-0 S/U & ATS vs UNC as 8.5-11 point Dog since 1986
- 14-1 S/U vs Wake Forest as 9 point or more favorite since 1990

TEXAS TECH	15-0 S/U in 2nd home game of season since 2007
Clemson	5-13 S/U in 2nd road game of season since 2003
FLORIDA STATE	2-8 S/U prior to playing Syracuse since 1998
FLORIDA STATE	1-8 O/U prior to playing Syracuse since 2013
Syracuse	2-10 O/U after playing Florida State since 2010
WAKE FOREST	4-11 S/U prior to playing Boston College since 2006
WAKE FOREST	12-3 O/U prior to playing Boston College since 2006
Louisville	1-12 S/U after playing Boston College since 2007
Louisville	2-8 O/U after playing Boston College since 2010
North Carolina	2-6 O/U after playing Louisville since 2007
North Carolina	5-15 S/U in final road game of season since 2002

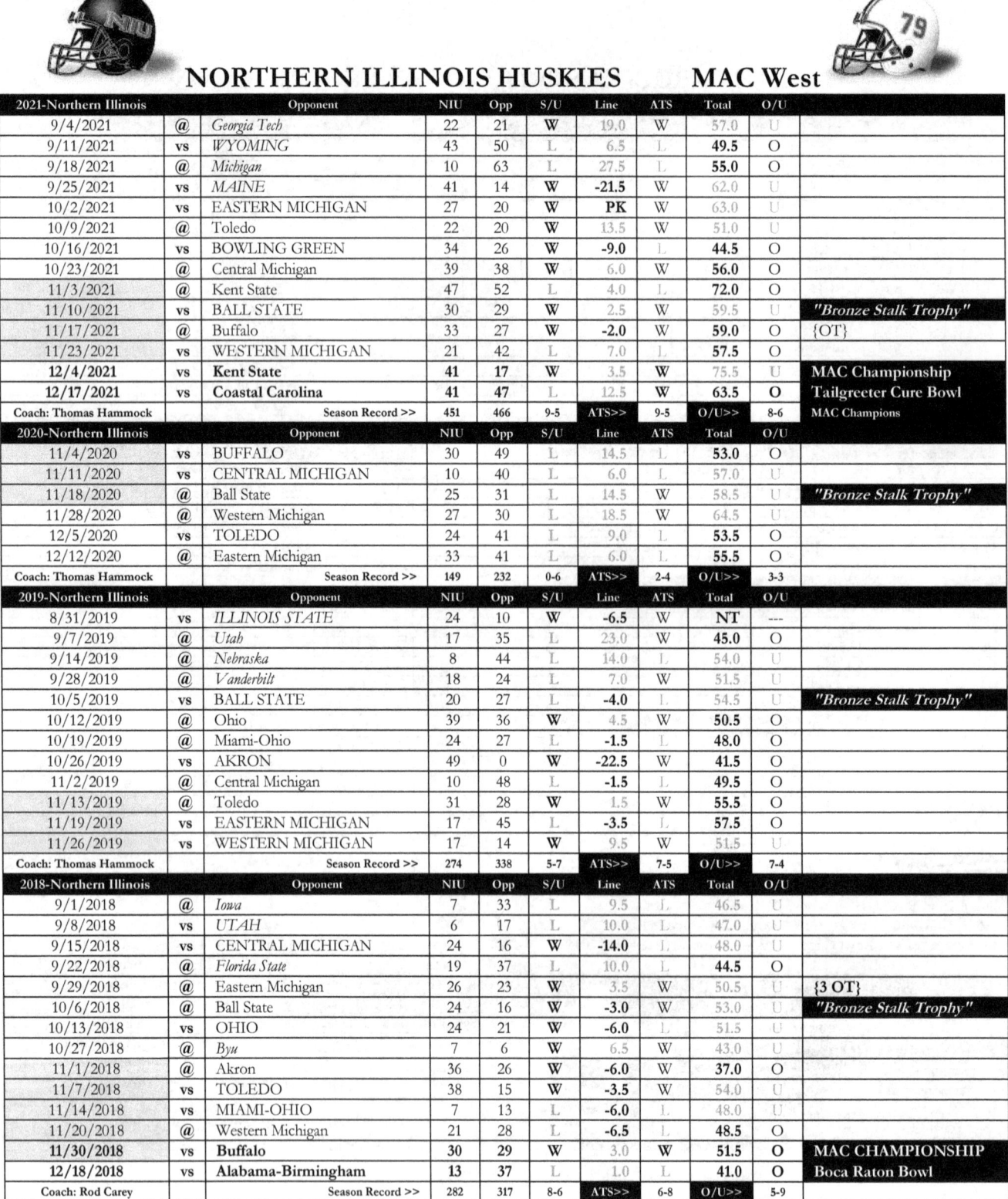

NORTHERN ILLINOIS HUSKIES   MAC West

2021-Northern Illinois		Opponent	NIU	Opp	S/U	Line	ATS	Total	O/U	
9/4/2021	@	Georgia Tech	22	21	W	19.0	W	57.0	U	
9/11/2021	vs	WYOMING	43	50	L	6.5	L	49.5	O	
9/18/2021	@	Michigan	10	63	L	27.5	L	55.0	O	
9/25/2021	vs	MAINE	41	14	W	-21.5	W	62.0	U	
10/2/2021	vs	EASTERN MICHIGAN	27	20	W	PK	W	63.0	U	
10/9/2021	@	Toledo	22	20	W	13.5	W	51.0	U	
10/16/2021	vs	BOWLING GREEN	34	26	W	-9.0	L	44.5	O	
10/23/2021	@	Central Michigan	39	38	W	6.0	W	56.0	O	
11/3/2021	@	Kent State	47	52	L	4.0	L	72.0	O	
11/10/2021	vs	BALL STATE	30	29	W	2.5	W	59.5	U	"Bronze Stalk Trophy"
11/17/2021	@	Buffalo	33	27	W	-2.0	W	59.0	O	{OT}
11/23/2021	vs	WESTERN MICHIGAN	21	42	L	7.0	L	57.5	O	
12/4/2021	vs	**Kent State**	41	17	W	3.5	W	75.5	U	**MAC Championship**
12/17/2021	vs	**Coastal Carolina**	41	47	L	12.5	W	63.5	O	**Tailgreeter Cure Bowl**
Coach: Thomas Hammock		Season Record >>	451	466	9-5	ATS>>	9-5	O/U>>	8-6	MAC Champions
2020-Northern Illinois		Opponent	NIU	Opp	S/U	Line	ATS	Total	O/U	
11/4/2020	vs	BUFFALO	30	49	L	14.5	L	53.0	O	
11/11/2020	vs	CENTRAL MICHIGAN	10	40	L	6.0	L	57.0	U	
11/18/2020	@	Ball State	25	31	L	14.5	W	58.5	U	"Bronze Stalk Trophy"
11/28/2020	@	Western Michigan	27	30	L	18.5	W	64.5	U	
12/5/2020	vs	TOLEDO	24	41	L	9.0	L	53.5	O	
12/12/2020	@	Eastern Michigan	33	41	L	6.0	L	55.5	O	
Coach: Thomas Hammock		Season Record >>	149	232	0-6	ATS>>	2-4	O/U>>	3-3	
2019-Northern Illinois		Opponent	NIU	Opp	S/U	Line	ATS	Total	O/U	
8/31/2019	vs	ILLINOIS STATE	24	10	W	-6.5	W	NT	---	
9/7/2019	@	Utah	17	35	L	23.0	W	45.0	O	
9/14/2019	@	Nebraska	8	44	L	14.0	L	54.0	U	
9/28/2019	@	Vanderbilt	18	24	L	7.0	W	51.5	U	
10/5/2019	vs	BALL STATE	20	27	L	-4.0	L	54.5	U	"Bronze Stalk Trophy"
10/12/2019	@	Ohio	39	36	W	4.5	W	50.5	O	
10/19/2019	@	Miami-Ohio	24	27	L	-1.5	L	48.0	O	
10/26/2019	vs	AKRON	49	0	W	-22.5	W	41.5	O	
11/2/2019	@	Central Michigan	10	48	L	-1.5	L	49.5	O	
11/13/2019	@	Toledo	31	28	W	1.5	W	55.5	O	
11/19/2019	vs	EASTERN MICHIGAN	17	45	L	-3.5	L	57.5	O	
11/26/2019	vs	WESTERN MICHIGAN	17	14	W	9.5	W	51.5	U	
Coach: Thomas Hammock		Season Record >>	274	338	5-7	ATS>>	7-5	O/U>>	7-4	
2018-Northern Illinois		Opponent	NIU	Opp	S/U	Line	ATS	Total	O/U	
9/1/2018	@	Iowa	7	33	L	9.5	L	46.5	U	
9/8/2018	vs	UTAH	6	17	L	10.0	L	47.0	U	
9/15/2018	vs	CENTRAL MICHIGAN	24	16	W	-14.0	L	48.0	U	
9/22/2018	@	Florida State	19	37	L	10.0	L	44.5	O	
9/29/2018	@	Eastern Michigan	26	23	W	3.5	W	50.5	U	{3 OT}
10/6/2018	@	Ball State	24	16	W	-3.0	W	53.0	U	"Bronze Stalk Trophy"
10/13/2018	vs	OHIO	24	21	W	-6.0	L	51.5	U	
10/27/2018	@	Byu	7	6	W	6.5	W	43.0	U	
11/1/2018	@	Akron	36	26	W	-6.0	W	37.0	O	
11/7/2018	vs	TOLEDO	38	15	W	-3.5	W	54.0	U	
11/14/2018	vs	MIAMI-OHIO	7	13	L	-6.0	L	48.0	U	
11/20/2018	@	Western Michigan	21	28	L	-6.5	L	48.5	O	
11/30/2018	vs	**Buffalo**	30	29	W	3.0	W	51.5	O	**MAC CHAMPIONSHIP**
12/18/2018	vs	**Alabama-Birmingham**	13	37	L	1.0	L	41.0	O	**Boca Raton Bowl**
Coach: Rod Carey		Season Record >>	282	317	8-6	ATS>>	6-8	O/U>>	5-9	

NORTHERN ILLINOIS HUSKIES — MAC West

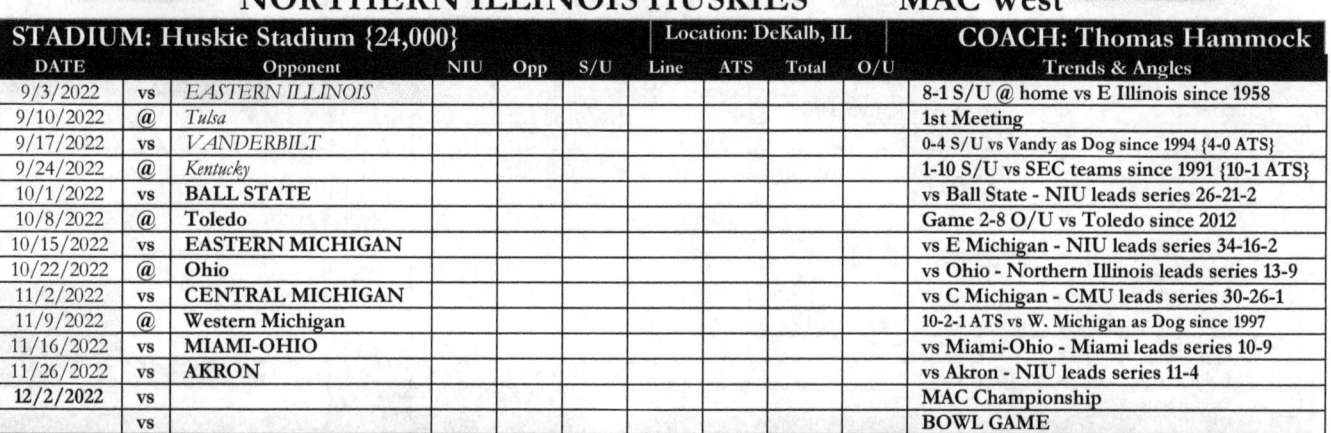

STADIUM: Huskie Stadium {24,000}   **Location:** DeKalb, IL   **COACH:** Thomas Hammock

DATE		Opponent	NIU	Opp	S/U	Line	ATS	Total	O/U	Trends & Angles
9/3/2022	vs	EASTERN ILLINOIS								8-1 S/U @ home vs E Illinois since 1958
9/10/2022	@	Tulsa								1st Meeting
9/17/2022	vs	VANDERBILT								0-4 S/U vs Vandy as Dog since 1994 {4-0 ATS}
9/24/2022	@	Kentucky								1-10 S/U vs SEC teams since 1991 {10-1 ATS}
10/1/2022	vs	BALL STATE								vs Ball State - NIU leads series 26-21-2
10/8/2022	@	Toledo								Game 2-8 O/U vs Toledo since 2012
10/15/2022	vs	EASTERN MICHIGAN								vs E Michigan - NIU leads series 34-16-2
10/22/2022	@	Ohio								vs Ohio - Northern Illinois leads series 13-9
11/2/2022	vs	CENTRAL MICHIGAN								vs C Michigan - CMU leads series 30-26-1
11/9/2022	@	Western Michigan								10-2-1 ATS vs W. Michigan as Dog since 1997
11/16/2022	vs	MIAMI-OHIO								vs Miami-Ohio - Miami leads series 10-9
11/26/2022	vs	AKRON								vs Akron - NIU leads series 11-4
12/2/2022	vs									MAC Championship
	vs									BOWL GAME

Pointspread Analysis

Non-Conference		Conference
1-40 S/U vs Non-Conf. as 15.5 point or more Dog since 1989		6-0 S/U vs Akron as favorite since 2009
1-13 S/U vs Non-Conf. as 7.5-10 point Dog since 1991		2-5 S/U vs Ball State as Dog since 1997 {6-1 ATS}
12-3 S/U vs Non-conf. as 3.5-7 point favorite since 1989		16-2 S/U vs Ball State as favorite since 1997
15-1 S/U vs Non-Conf. as 10.5 point or more favorite since 1993		1-5 S/U vs Central Michigan as favorite since 2014 {0-6 ATS}
vs Vanderbilt - Vanderbilt leads series 4-0		10-1 S/U vs Eastern Michigan as favorite since 2008
vs Eastern Illinois - NIU leads series 27-10-1		1-3 S/U vs Ohio as Dog since 1997

Dog

17-7-1 ATS as road Dog since 2010		1-5 ATS vs Ohio as favorite since 2003
1-51 S/U as 15.5 point or more Dog since 1989		0-4 O/U vs Ohio as favorite since 2011
1-10 O/U as 15.5-20 point Dog since 2004		vs Toledo - Toledo leads series 32-17
12-3 ATS as 15.5-20 point Dog since 1994		1-8 O/U vs Toledo as favorite since 2004
0-13 S/U @ home as 10.5 point or more Dog since 1995		9-4 S/U vs Western Michigan since 2009
2-7 O/U @ home as 3.5-7 point Dog since 2001		vs Western Michigan - WMU leads series 27-20
9-2 ATS on road as 3.5-7 point Dog since 2010		0-5 S/U vs W. Michigan as 8.5 point or more Dog since 1997
		5-0 ATS vs W. Michigan as 8.5 point or more Dog since 1997

Favorite

14-2 S/U @ home as 7.5-10 point favorite since 1989		
7-1 S/U on road as 7.5-10 point favorite since 1989		
7-0 S/U on road as 10.5-15 point favorite since 2005	VANDERBILT	2-12 O/U in 2nd home game of season since 2006
12-1 S/U @ home as 10.5-15 point favorite since 2008	BALL STATE	12-2 S/U prior to playing Toledo since 2010
17-1 S/U as 10.5-15 point favorite since 2008	Toledo	9-2 S/U after playing Ball State since 2010
7-0 S/U as 15.5-20 point favorite since 2011	Toledo	10-2 S/U prior to playing Eastern Michigan since 2009
8-0 S/U on road as 15.5-20 point favorite since 2003	E. MICHIGAN	16-1 S/U after playing Toledo since 2003
19-0 S/U @ home as 20.5 point or more favorite since 2006	E. MICHIGAN	7-3 ATS after playing Toledo since 2010
8-0 S/U on road as 20.5 point or more favorite since 2002	E. MICHIGAN	0-6 O/U prior to playing Ohio since 2003

Bowl Games

	C. MICHIGAN	1-7 ATS after playing Ohio since 1997
0-7 S/U in Bowl Games since 2013 {1-6 ATS}	C. MICHIGAN	9-2 S/U & ATS prior to playing Western Michigan since 2010
0-4 S/U in Bowl Games as 10.5-15 point Dog since 2006 {1-3 ATS}	W. Michigan	9-2 S/U in final road game of season since 2010
0-3 S/U & ATS in Bowl Games as 3.5-7 point Dog since 2010	W. Michigan	15-2 ATS in final road game of season since 2004
5-0 O/U in Bowl Games since 2014	W. Michigan	9-3 S/U after playing Central Michigan since 2008
	MIAMI-OHIO	9-2 ATS prior to playing Akron since 1990
2-22 S/U on road vs ranked teams all time	AKRON	5-0 S/U after playing Miami-Ohio since 2008
0-13 S/U vs Top 10 ranked teams all time	AKRON	2-6 O/U after playing Miami-Ohio since 2008
4-0 S/U & ATS on road when ranked since 2012	AKRON	4-14 O/U in final home game of season since 2004
8-0 S/U @ home when ranked all time	AKRON	1-9-1 ATS in final home game of season since 2011

NORTH TEXAS MEAN GREEN   C-USA West

2021-North Texas		Opponent	UNT	Opp	S/U	Line	ATS	Total	O/U	
9/4/2021	vs	NORTHWESTERN STATE	44	14	W	-20.0	W	65.5	U	
9/11/2021	@	Smu	12	35	L	22.5	L	76.0	U	"Safeway Bowl"
9/18/2021	vs	ALABAMA-BIRMINGHAM	6	40	L	12.5	L	58.0	U	
9/25/2021	@	Louisiana Tech	17	24	L	9.5	W	65.0	U	
10/9/2021	@	Missouri	35	48	L	18.5	W	68.5	O	
10/15/2021	vs	MARSHALL	21	49	L	11.0	L	66.0	O	
10/23/2021	vs	LIBERTY	26	35	L	21.0	W	61.0	T	
10/30/2021	@	Rice	30	24	W	1.0	W	55.0	U	{OT}
11/6/2021	@	Southern Miss	38	14	W	-5.0	W	49.0	O	
11/13/2021	vs	TEXAS-EL PASO	20	17	W	-1.0	W	55.0	U	
11/20/2021	@	Florida International	49	7	W	-10.0	W	57.0	U	
11/27/2021	vs	TEXAS-SAN ANTONIO	45	23	W	8.5	W	59.5	O	
12/23/2021	vs	Miami-Ohio	14	27	L	1.5	L	56.5	U	Frisco Football Classic
Coach: Seth Littrell		Season Record >>	357	357	6-7	ATS>>	9-4	O/U>>	4-8-1	
2020-North Texas		Opponent	UNT	Opp	S/U	Line	ATS	Total	O/U	
9/5/2020	vs	HOUSTON BAPTIST	57	31	W	-23.5	W	73.0	O	
9/19/2020	vs	SMU	35	65	L	14.5	L	71.0	O	"Safeway Bowl"
10/3/2020	vs	SOUTHERN MISSISSIPPI	31	41	L	-1.5	L	75.0	U	
10/10/2020	vs	CHARLOTTE	21	49	L	3.0	L	66.5	O	
10/17/2020	@	Middle Tennessee	52	35	W	3.5	W	70.5	O	
11/21/2020	vs	RICE	27	17	W	-1.0	W	65.0	U	
11/28/2020	@	Texas-San Antonio	17	49	L	1.5	L	67.0	U	
12/3/2020	vs	LOUISIANA TECH	31	42	L	1.0	L	65.0	O	
12/11/2020	vs	TEXAS-EL PASO	45	43	W	-9.5	L	66.0	O	
12/21/2020	vs	Appalachian State	28	56	L	22.5	L	68.0	O	Myrtle Beach Bowl
Coach: Seth Littrell		Season Record >>	344	428	4-6	ATS>>	3-7	O/U>>	7-3	
2019-North Texas		Opponent	UNT	Opp	S/U	Line	ATS	Total	O/U	
8/31/2019	vs	ABILENE CHRISTIAN	51	31	W	-22.5	L	NT	---	
9/7/2019	@	Smu	27	49	L	3.5	L	73.0	O	"Safeway Bowl"
9/14/2019	@	California	17	23	L	14.5	W	50.5	U	
9/21/2019	vs	TEXAS-SAN ANTONIO	45	3	W	-17.0	W	55.5	U	
9/28/2019	vs	HOUSTON	25	46	L	-8.0	L	59.0	O	
10/12/2019	@	Southern Miss	27	45	L	3.0	L	59.0	O	
10/19/2019	vs	MIDDLE TENNESSEE	33	30	W	-7.0	L	59.5	O	
10/26/2019	@	Charlotte	38	39	L	-4.0	L	64.0	O	
11/2/2019	vs	TEXAS-EL PASO	52	26	W	-23.0	W	59.0	O	
11/9/2019	@	Louisiana Tech	17	52	L	5.0	L	71.5	U	
11/23/2019	@	Rice	14	20	L	-6.5	L	55.5	U	
11/30/2019	vs	ALABAMA-BIRMINGHAM	21	26	L	3.0	L	49.5	U	
Coach: Seth Littrell		Season Record >>	367	390	4-8	ATS>>	3-9	O/U>>	6-5	
2018-North Texas		Opponent	UNT	Opp	S/U	Line	ATS	Total	O/U	
9/1/2018	vs	SMU	46	23	W	-3.5	W	71.5	U	"Safeway Bowl"
9/8/2018	vs	INCARNATE WORD	58	16	W	-43.0	L	NT	---	
9/15/2018	@	Arkansas	44	17	W	5.5	W	63.0	U	
9/22/2018	@	Liberty	47	7	W	-11.0	W	67.0	U	
9/29/2018	vs	LOUISIANA TECH	27	29	L	-7.0	L	63.0	U	
10/6/2018	@	Texas-El Paso	27	24	W	-25.5	L	53.0	U	
10/13/2018	vs	SOUTHERN MISSISSIPPI	30	7	W	-7.0	W	53.0	U	
10/20/2018	@	Alabama-Birmingham	21	29	L	1.5	L	53.5	U	
10/27/2018	vs	RICE	41	17	W	-29.0	L	58.5	T	
11/10/2018	@	Old Dominion	31	34	L	-14.5	L	66.0	U	
11/17/2018	vs	FLORIDA ATLANTIC	41	38	W	-4.0	W	63.5	O	
11/24/2018	@	Texas-San Antonio	24	21	W	-24.5	L	51.5	U	
12/15/2018	vs	Utah State	13	52	L	7.0	L	67.5	U	New Mexico Bowl
Coach: Seth Littrell		Season Record >>	450	314	9-4	ATS>>	4-9	O/U>>	1-11	

NORTH TEXAS MEAN GREEN — C-USA West

STADIUM: Apogee Stadium {30,850} | **Location:** Denton, TX | **COACH:** Seth Littrell

DATE		Opponent	UNT	Opp	S/U	Line	ATS	Total	O/U	Trends & Angles
8/27/2022	@	Texas-El Paso								0-3 ATS @ Texas-El Paso since 2014
9/3/2022	vs	SMU								5-2 S/U @ home vs SMU since 1977
9/10/2022	vs	TEXAS SOUTHERN								vs Texas South - N Texas leads series 1-0
9/17/2022	@	Unlv								vs UNLV - UNLV leads series 4-1
9/24/2022	@	Memphis								vs Memphis - Memphis leads series 16-4
10/1/2022	vs	FLORIDA ATLANTIC								3-0 S/U vs FAU as favorite since 2011
10/15/2022	vs	LOUISIANA TECH								vs La Tech - La Tech leads series 13-7
10/22/2022	@	Texas-San Antonio								0-4 ATS @ Texas-San Antonio since 2014
10/29/2022	@	Western Kentucky								0-4 S/U vs WKU since 2011
11/5/2022	vs	FLA INTERNATIONAL								vs Fla International - FIU leads series 5-4
11/12/2022	@	Alabama-Birmingham								vs Alabama-Birm - UAB leads series 5-1
11/26/2022	vs	RICE								4-1 S/U vs Rice as favorite since 2013
12/3/2022	vs									C-USA Championship
	vs									BOWL GAME

Pointspread Analysis — Non-Conference
- 1-42 S/U vs Non-Conf. as 20.5 or more Dog since 1995
- 2-21 S/U vs Non-Conf. as 10.5-20 point Dog since 1995
- 3-13 S/U vs Non-Conf. as 3.5-7 point Dog since 1997
- 11-1 S/U vs Non-Conf. as 10.5 point or more favorite since 2003
- vs Smu - SMU leads series 34-6-1
- 0-7 S/U vs SMU as Dog since 2007 {1-6 ATS}

Dog
- 1-25 S/U as 30.5 point or more Dog since 1995
- 6-0 ATS as 30.5 point or more Dog since 2011
- 1-34 S/U as 20.5-30 point Dog since 1995
- 3-20 S/U as 15.5-20 point Dog since 1995
- 0-15 S/U @ home as 15.5 point or more Dog since 1995
- 0-8 S/U on road as 10.5-15 point Dog since 2011
- 4-14 S/U on road as 3.5-7 point Dog since 2005
- 3-11 ATS as 3.5-7 point Dog since 2012
- 3-12 O/U @ home as 3.5-7 point Dog since 2005
- 1-5 S/U on road as 3 point or less Dog since 2009 {1-5 ATS}

Favorite
- 0-5 ATS @ home as 7.5-10 point Favorite since 2013
- 6-1 S/U on road as 7.5-15 point favorite since 2002
- 8-0 S/U @ home as 10.5-15 point favorite since 2001
- 17-0 S/U @ home as 15.5 point or more favorite since 2002

- 2-45 S/U vs ranked teams all time
- 0-24 S/U vs Top 10 ranked teams all time
- 0-43 S/U on road vs ranked teams all time

Pointspread Analysis — Conference
- 0-4 S/U & ATS vs Fla International as Dog since 2008
- 0-6 S/U vs Louisiana Tech as Dog since 2005
- 5-1 S/U vs Rice since 2016
- vs Rice - North Texas leads series 7-5
- vs Texas-El Paso - North Texas leads series 19-8-3
- Game 1-6 O/U vs Texas-San Antonio since 2015
- vs Texas-San Antonio - North Texas leads series 5-4
- vs Western Kentucky - Series tied 4-4

Bowl Games
- 1-4 S/U in New Orleans Bowl since 2001
- 2-9 S/U in Bowl Games since 1948
- 0-3 S/U in Bowl Games as 10.5-15 point Dog since 2001
- 0-4 S/U & ATS in Bowl Games as 3.5-7 point Dog since 2003

UTEP	2-10 S/U in 1st road game of season since 2010
TX SOUTHERN	4-13 ATS in 2nd home game of season since 2005
UNLV	2-20 S/U in 2nd road game of season since 2000
FAU	2-8 O/U prior to playing Louisiana Tech since 2005
LA TECH	7-2 S/U prior to playing Texas-San Antonio since 2013
LA TECH	8-1 ATS prior to playing Texas-San Antonio since 2013
LA TECH	2-10 S/U after playing Florida Atlantic since 2004
LA TECH	0-12 ATS after playing Florida Atlantic since 2004
LA TECH	7-2 O/U after playing Florida Atlantic since 2007
WKU	1-6 ATS prior to playing Florida International since 2006
FIU	1-5 S/U prior to playing UAB since 1995
FIU	0-4 O/U prior to playing UAB since 2017

NORTHWESTERN WILDCATS   BIG TEN West

2021-Northwestern		Opponent	NW	Opp	S/U	Line	ATS	Total	O/U	
9/4/2021	vs	MICHIGAN STATE	21	38	L	-3.0	L	45.0	O	
9/11/2021	vs	*INDIANA STATE*	24	6	W	-28.5	L	46.0	U	
9/18/2021	@	*Duke*	23	30	L	-2.0	L	49.5	O	
9/25/2021	vs	*OHIO*	35	6	W	-13.5	W	47.5	U	
10/2/2021	@	Nebraska	7	56	L	10.5	L	51.0	O	
10/16/2021	vs	RUTGERS	21	7	W	2.5	W	45.0	U	
10/23/2021	@	Michigan	7	33	L	23.5	L	51.0	U	*"George Jewett Trophy"*
10/30/2021	vs	MINNESOTA	14	41	L	7.5	L	43.5	O	
11/6/2021	vs	IOWA	12	17	L	11.5	L	40.0	U	
11/13/2021	@	Wisconsin	7	35	L	25.5	L	42.0	T	
11/20/2021	vs	PURDUE	14	32	L	11.0	L	47.5	U	
11/27/2021	@	Illinois	14	47	L	7.0	L	44.5	O	*"Land of Lincoln Trophy"*
Coach: Pat Fitzgerald		Season Record >>	199	348	3-9	ATS>>	3-9	O/U>>	5-6-1	

2020-Northwestern		Opponent	NW	Opp	S/U	Line	ATS	Total	O/U	
10/24/2020	vs	MARYLAND	43	3	W	-14.0	W	52.5	U	
10/31/2020	@	Iowa	21	20	W	-1.0	T	43.0	U	
11/7/2020	vs	NEBRASKA	21	13	W	-4.0	W	53.0	U	
11/14/2020	@	Purdue	27	20	W	-3.5	W	48.5	U	
11/21/2020	vs	WISCONSIN	17	7	W	7.0	W	43.0	U	
11/28/2020	@	Michigan State	20	23	L	-13.5	L	40.0	O	
12/12/2020	vs	ILLINOIS	28	10	W	-13.0	W	41.0	U	*"Land of Lincoln Trophy"*
12/19/2020	vs	Ohio State	10	22	L	16.5	W	57.5	U	Big Ten Championship
1/1/2021	vs	Auburn	35	19	W	-3.5	W	45.0	O	Citrus Bowl
Coach: Pat Fitzgerald		Season Record >>	222	137	7-2	ATS>>	7-1-1	O/U>>	2-7	

2019-Northwestern		Opponent	NW	Opp	S/U	Line	ATS	Total	O/U	
8/31/2019	@	*Stanford*	7	17	L	6.5	L	47.0	U	
9/14/2019	vs	*UNLV*	30	14	W	-18.5	L	51.5	U	
9/21/2019	vs	MICHIGAN STATE	10	31	L	7.5	L	35.5	O	
9/28/2019	@	Wisconsin	15	24	L	23.5	W	46.0	U	
10/5/2019	@	Nebraska	10	13	L	7.5	W	48.5	U	
10/19/2019	vs	OHIO STATE	3	52	L	27.0	L	50.0	U	
10/26/2019	vs	IOWA	0	20	L	8.5	L	36.5	U	
11/2/2019	@	Indiana	3	34	L	8.5	L	44.0	U	
11/9/2019	vs	PURDUE	22	24	L	PK	L	39.0	O	
11/16/2019	vs	*MASSACHUSETTS*	45	6	W	-38.0	W	57.5	U	
11/23/2019	vs	MINNESOTA	22	38	L	15.5	L	41.5	O	
11/30/2019	@	Illinois	29	10	W	6.0	W	39.0	T	*"Land of Lincoln Trophy"*
Coach: Pat Fitzgerald		Season Record >>	196	283	3-9	ATS>>	4-8	O/U>>	4-7-1	

2018-Northwestern		Opponent	NW	Opp	S/U	Line	ATS	Total	O/U	
8/30/2018	@	Purdue	31	27	W	PK	W	51.0	O	
9/8/2018	@	*Duke*	7	21	L	-2.5	L	47.5	U	
9/15/2018	vs	*AKRON*	34	39	L	-21.0	L	46.5	O	
9/29/2018	vs	MICHIGAN	17	20	L	14.5	W	46.5	U	
10/6/2018	@	Michigan State	29	19	W	10.0	W	43.5	O	
10/13/2018	vs	NEBRASKA	34	31	W	-3.5	L	59.5	O	{OT}
10/20/2018	@	Rutgers	18	15	W	-20.0	L	49.0	U	
10/27/2018	vs	WISCONSIN	31	17	W	5.0	W	50.5	U	
11/3/2018	vs	*NOTRE DAME*	21	31	L	10.0	T	49.5	O	
11/10/2018	@	Iowa	14	10	W	11.5	W	44.0	U	
11/17/2018	@	Minnesota	24	14	W	3.0	W	48.5	U	
11/24/2018	vs	ILLINOIS	24	16	W	-14.5	L	57.5	U	*"Land of Lincoln Trophy"*
12/1/2018	vs	Ohio State	24	45	L	16.5	L	63.0	O	BIG TEN Championship
12/31/2018	vs	Utah	31	20	W	6.5	W	44.5	O	Holiday Bowl
Coach: Pat Fitzgerald		Season Record >>	339	325	9-5	ATS>>	7-6-1	O/U>>	7-7	

NORTHWESTERN WILDCATS — BIG TEN West

STADIUM: Ryan Field {47,130} **Location:** Evanston, IL **COACH:** Pat Fitzgerald

DATE		Opponent	NW	Opp	S/U	Line	ATS	Total	O/U	Trends & Angles
8/27/2022	vs	Nebraska {@ Dublin, IR}								vs Nebraska - Nebraska leads series 9-6
9/10/2022	vs	DUKE								11-4 S/U in 1st home game of season since 2007
9/17/2022	vs	SOUTHERN ILLINOIS								vs Southern Ill. - Northwestern leads series 1-0
9/24/2022	vs	MIAMI-OHIO								vs Miami-Ohio - Miami leads series 6-3
10/1/2022	@	Penn State								2-7 S/U @ Penn State since 1994 {3-6 ATS}
10/8/2022	vs	WISCONSIN								12-1 ATS @ home vs Wisconsin since 1988
10/22/2022	@	Maryland								vs Maryland - Northwestern leads series 2-0
10/29/2022	@	Iowa								vs Iowa - Iowa leads series 52-28-3
11/5/2022	vs	OHIO STATE								1-17 S/U @ home vs Ohio State since 1961
11/12/2022	@	Minnesota								vs Minnesota - Minnesota leads series 55-36-5
11/19/2022	@	Purdue								5-0 S/U & ATS @ Purdue since 2009
11/26/2022	vs	ILLINOIS								11-1 S/U vs Illinois as favorite since 2000
12/3/2022	vs									Big Ten Championship
	vs									BOWL GAME

Pointspread Analysis — Non-Conference

- 0-7-1 S/U vs Non-Conf as 10.5-15 point favorite since 1988
- 17-0 S/U vs Non-Conf. as 15.5 point or more favorite since 2009
- 3-0 S/U vs Duke as Dog since 1999
- 5-0 ATS vs Duke as Dog since 1989
- vs Duke - Duke leads series 11-10
- 7-2 S/U vs Duke as 4.0 point or more favorite since 1996

Dog
- 2-21 S/U on road as 25.5 point or more Dog since 1983
- 0-7 S/U @ home as 25.5 or more Dog since 1988
- 0-19 S/U on road as 20.5-25 point Dog since 1984
- 1-8 S/U @ home as 20.5-25 point Dog since 1984
- 6-0 ATS on road as 15.5-20 point Dog since 2006
- 0-10 S/U @ home as 15.5-20 point Dog since 1987
- 3-23-1 S/U @ home as 10.5-15 point Dog since 1983
- 2-8 S/U @ home as 3.5-7 point Dog since 2010 {3-7 ATS}
- 11-3 ATS as 3 point or less Dog since 2006

Favorite
- 2-6 O/U @ home as 3 point or less favorite since 2004
- 13-2 S/U @ home as 3.5-7 point favorite since 2002
- 1-8-1 O/U @ home as 3.5-7 point favorite since 2012
- 14-2 S/U on road as 3.5-7 point favorite since 1996
- 7-1 S/U @ home vs Big Ten as 10.5-15 point Favorite since 2004
- 26-0 S/U @ home as 15.5 point or more favorite since 1996
- 5-0 S/U vs Big Ten as 15.5 point or more favorite since 2011

Bowl Games
- 0-5 S/U in Bowl Games as 7.5-10 point Dog since 1997

- 11-2 S/U when ranked @ home since 2013
- 7-0 S/U @ home when ranked vs Illinois since 1940
- 7-0 S/U when ranked vs Minnesota since 1959
- 0-6 S/U when ranked vs Ohio State since 1970
- 0-18 S/U vs #1 ranked teams since 1938
- 0-7 S/U on road vs #2 ranked teams all time
- 0-8 S/U vs #3 ranked teams all time
- 0-15 S/U vs #4 ranked teams since 1948
- 0-4 S/U @ ranked Penn State all time
- 0-6 S/U @ ranked Purdue all time

Pointspread Analysis — Conference

- vs Illinois - Illinois leads series 55-54-5
- 0-7-1 S/U vs Minnesota as 10.5 point or more Dog since 1985
- 1-33 S/U vs Ohio State since 1972
- vs Ohio State - Ohio State leads series 64-14-1
- 1-23 S/U vs Ohio State as Dog since 1984
- vs Purdue - Purdue leads series 52-33-1
- 1-8 O/U vs Purdue as Dog since 2002
- 7-1 S/U vs Purdue as favorite since 1995
- 6-2 S/U vs Purdue since 2014
- Game 2-7 O/U @ home vs Purdue since 2002
- 6-1 S/U @ home vs Wisconsin since 2003
- vs Wisconsin - Wisconsin leads series 61-37-5
- Game 1-7-1 O/U vs Wisconsin since 2013
- 4-0 S/U & ATS vs Illinois as 5 point or less Dog since 1995
- 0-6 S/U vs Iowa as 21 point or more Dog since 1985
- 1-6 S/U & ATS vs Iowa as 6 point or less Dog since 1993
- 0-11 S/U vs Michigan as 17.5 point or more Dog since 1983
- 0-6 S/U vs Michigan as 8.5-16.5 point Dog since 1998
- 6-1 S/U vs Minnesota as 5 point or more favorite since 1996
- 1-6 ATS vs Minnesota as 5 point or more favorite since 1996
- 0-8 S/U vs Penn State as 14.5 point or more Dog since 1993
- 1-7 S/U vs Purdue as 13 point or more Dog since 1983
- 0-8 S/U vs Wisconsin as 16.5 point or more Dog since 1984
- 6-0 S/U & ATS vs Wisconsin as 7-10 point Dog since 1987

DUKE	4-9 O/U in 1st home game of season since 2007
Penn State	9-3 S/U in 1st road game of season since 2010
Penn State	7-3-1 ATS in 1st road game of season since 2011
Maryland	3-10 O/U after playing Wisconsin since 2003
Maryland	3-11-1 ATS prior to playing Iowa since 2007
Maryland	2-11 S/U prior to playing Iowa since 2009
Maryland	2-9 S/U in 2nd road game of season since 2011
OHIO STATE	8-2 ATS after playing Iowa since 2012
Purdue	3-11-1 O/U prior to playing Illinois since 2007
Purdue	10-4 S/U in final road game of season since 2008

NOTRE DAME FIGHTING IRISH   INDEPENDENT

2021-Notre Dame		Opponent	ND	Opp	S/U	Line	ATS	Total	O/U	
9/5/2021	@	Florida State	41	38	W	-7.0	L	53.5	O	
9/11/2021	vs	TOLEDO	32	29	W	-16.5	L	55.5	O	
9/18/2021	vs	PURDUE	27	13	W	-7.5	W	58.0	U	"Shillelagh Trophy"
9/25/2021	vs	Wisconsin	41	13	W	6.0	W	43.5	O	Soldiers Field
10/2/2021	vs	CINCINNATI	13	24	L	2.5	L	50.0	U	
10/9/2021	@	Virginia Tech	32	29	W	1.0	W	47.0	O	
10/23/2021	vs	USC	31	16	W	-8.0	W	59.5	U	"Jeweled Shillelagh"
10/30/2021	vs	NORTH CAROLINA	44	34	W	-3.5	W	62.5	O	
11/6/2021	vs	NAVY	34	6	W	-21.0	W	47.5	U	"Rip Miller Trophy"
11/13/2021	@	Virginia	28	3	W	-9.0	W	61.5	U	
11/20/2021	vs	GEORGIA TECH	55	0	W	-18.5	W	58.0	U	
11/27/2021	@	Stanford	45	14	W	-21.0	W	51.5	O	"Legends Trophy"
1/1/2022	vs	Oklahoma State	35	37	L	1.0	L	48.5	O	Fiesta Bowl
Coach: Brian Kelly		Season Record >>	458	256	11-2	ATS>>	9-4	O/U>>	7-6	
2020-Notre Dame		Opponent	ND	Opp	S/U	Line	ATS	Total	O/U	
9/12/2020	vs	DUKE	27	13	W	-21.5	L	51.5	U	
9/19/2020	vs	SOUTH FLORIDA	52	0	W	-23.0	W	49.5	O	
10/10/2020	vs	FLORIDA STATE	42	26	W	-21.0	L	54.0	O	
10/17/2020	vs	LOUISVILLE	12	7	W	-17.0	L	62.0	U	
10/24/2020	@	Pittsburgh	45	3	W	-10.0	W	43.5	O	
10/31/2020	@	Georgia Tech	31	13	W	-20.5	L	58.0	U	
11/7/2020	vs	CLEMSON	47	40	W	4.5	W	50.5	O	{2 OT}
11/14/2020	@	Boston College	45	31	W	-13.0	W	52.0	O	"Holy War"
11/27/2020	@	North Carolina	31	17	W	-4.5	W	69.5	U	
12/5/2020	vs	SYRACUSE	45	21	W	-35.0	L	51.0	O	
12/19/2020	vs	Clemson	13	34	L	11.0	L	58.0	U	ACC CHAMPIONSHIP GAME
1/1/2021	vs	Alabama	14	31	L	18.0	W	65.5	U	Rose Bowl {CFP Semifinal}
Coach: Brian Kelly		Season Record >>	404	236	10-2	ATS>>	6-6	O/U>>	6-6	
2019-Notre Dame		Opponent	ND	Opp	S/U	Line	ATS	Total	O/U	
9/2/2019	@	Louisville	35	17	W	-19.0	L	54.5	U	
9/14/2019	vs	NEW MEXICO	66	14	W	-34.5	W	64.0	O	
9/21/2019	@	Georgia	17	23	L	15.5	W	58.5	U	
9/28/2019	vs	VIRGINIA	35	20	W	-11.0	W	46.5	O	
10/5/2019	vs	BOWLING GREEN	52	0	W	-46.0	W	64.5	U	
10/12/2019	vs	USC	30	27	W	-10.5	L	59.0	U	"Jeweled Shillelagh"
10/26/2019	@	Michigan	14	45	L	1.0	L	46.5	O	
11/2/2019	vs	VIRGINIA TECH	21	20	W	-17.5	L	58.0	U	
11/9/2019	@	Duke	37	7	W	-7.0	W	49.5	U	
11/16/2019	vs	NAVY	52	20	W	-7.0	W	56.0	O	"Rip Miller Trophy"
11/23/2019	vs	BOSTON COLLEGE	40	7	W	-21.0	W	65.5	U	"Holy War"
11/30/2019	@	Stanford	45	24	W	-17.5	W	45.5	O	"Legends Trophy"
12/28/2019	vs	Iowa State	33	9	W	-3.5	W	54.0	U	Camping World Bowl
Coach: Brian Kelly		Season Record >>	477	233	11-2	ATS>>	9-4	O/U>>	5-8	
2018-Notre Dame		Opponent	ND	Opp	S/U	Line	ATS	Total	O/U	
9/1/2018	vs	MICHIGAN	24	17	W	3.0	W	48.0	U	
9/8/2018	vs	BALL STATE	24	16	W	-34.0	L	60.5	U	
9/15/2018	vs	VANDERBILT	22	17	W	-13.5	L	51.5	U	
9/22/2018	@	Wake Forest	56	27	W	-6.0	W	59.5	O	
9/29/2018	vs	STANFORD	38	17	W	-5.0	W	54.0	O	"Legends Trophy"
10/6/2018	@	Virginia Tech	45	23	W	-6.5	W	55.0	O	
10/13/2018	vs	PITTSBURGH	19	14	W	-21.0	L	55.5	U	
10/27/2018	vs	Navy	44	22	W	-22.5	L	57.0	O	"Rip Miller Trophy"
11/3/2018	@	Northwestern	31	21	W	-10.0	T	49.5	O	
11/10/2018	vs	Syracuse	42	13	W	-17.0	W	51.0	O	Yankee Stadium
11/17/2018	vs	FLORIDA STATE	36	3	W	-10.0	W	64.5	U	
11/24/2018	@	Usc	24	17	W	-14.0	L	54.0	U	"Jeweled Shillelagh"
12/29/2018	vs	Clemson	3	30	L	10.0	L	58.0	U	Cotton Bowl (National Semi-Final)
Coach: Brian Kelly		Season Record >>	408	237	12-1	ATS>>	6-6-1	O/U>>	6-7	

NOTRE DAME FIGHTING IRISH   INDEPENDENT

STADIUM: Notre Dame Stadium {77,622} | **Location:** South Bend, IN | **COACH:** Marcus Freeman

DATE		Opponent	ND	Opp	S/U	Line	ATS	Total	O/U	Trends & Angles
9/3/2022	@	Ohio State								0-4 S/U & ATS vs Ohio State as Dog since 1995
9/10/2022	vs	MARSHALL								12-1 S/U in 1st home game of season since 2008
9/17/2022	vs	CALIFORNIA								vs California - Notre Dame leads series 4-0
9/24/2022	@	North Carolina								vs North Carolina - Notre Dame leads series 20-2
10/8/2022	vs	Byu {@ Las Vegas}								vs BYU - Notre Dame leads series 6-2
10/15/2022	vs	STANFORD								10-2 S/U @ home vs Stanford since 1994
10/22/2022	vs	UNLV								1st Meeting
10/29/2022	@	Syracuse								4-0 S/U vs Syracuse since 2014
11/5/2022	vs	CLEMSON								vs Clemson - Clemson leads series 4-2
11/12/2022	vs	Navy {@ Baltimore}								vs Navy - Notre Dame leads series 80-13-1
11/19/2022	vs	BOSTON COLLEGE								7-0 S/U vs Boston College as favorite since 2009
11/26/2022	@	Usc								5-0 S/U @ home vs USC since 2013
	vs									BOWL GAME

Pointspread Analysis — Dog
- 2-10 S/U on road as 10.5-20 point Dog since 1985
- 1-6 S/U @ home as 10.5-20 point Dog since 2000
- 3-19 S/U as 10.5-20 point Dog since 1985
- 2-11 S/U on road as 7.5-10 point Dog since 1998
- 6-1 O/U as 7.5-10 point Dog since 2008
- 8-0 O/U as 3.5-7 point Dog since 2013

Favorite
- 12-1 S/U as 3.5-7 point favorite since 2017 {11-2 ATS}
- 3-12 O/U as 7.5-10 point favorite since 2009
- 11-2 S/U @ home as 7.5-10 point favorite since 2003
- 17-0 S/U on road as 10.5-15 point favorite since 1997
- 22-0 S/U as 10.5-15 point favorite since 2011
- 17-2 S/U @ home as 15.5-20 point favorite since 1995
- 11-1 S/U on road as 15.5-20 point favorite since 1991
- 7-3 O/U @ home as 15.5-20 point favorite since 2012
- 41-2 S/U as 20.5-25 point favorite since 1984
- 14-0 S/U on road as 20.5-25 point favorite since 1986
- 37-1 S/U as 25.5 point or more favorite since 1983
- 3-9 O/U as 25.5 point or more favorite since 2005

Bowl Games
- 0-5 S/U & ATS in Fiesta Bowl since 1995
- 5-2 S/U in Cotton Bowl since 1971
- 0-6 S/U & ATS in Bowl Games as 3.5-7 point Dog since 1995
- 3-0 S/U & ATS in Bowl Games as 3 point or less favorite since 1989

Pointspread Analysis — Non-Conference
- vs Boston College - Notre Dame leads series 16-9
- 0-4 S/U vs Boston College as Dog since 2001
- vs Ohio State - Ohio State leads series 4-2
- vs Stanford - Notre Dame leads series 22-13
- Game 2-8 O/U @ home vs Stanford since 2000
- vs Syracuse - Notre Dame leads series 5-3
- vs USC - Notre Dame leads series 50-37-5
- 4-0 S/U vs USC since 2017
- 1-11 S/U vs USC as Dog since 1998
- 11-1 S/U vs Boston College as 11 point or more favorite since 1987
- 29-0 S/U vs Navy as 13 point or more favorite since 1983
- 17-2 S/U vs Stanford as 5 point or more favorite since 1988
- 0-3 S/U & ATS vs Stanford as 3 point or less favorite since 1997
- 6-0-1 S/U vs USC as 4.5 point or less Dog since 1984 {7-0 ATS}
- 9-1 S/U vs USC as 7.5 point or less favorite since 1986
- 0-11 S/U vs USC as 6.5 point or more Dog since 1998

Opponent	Trend
Ohio State	10-3 O/U in 1st road game of season since 2009
CALIFORNIA	3-9 O/U in 2nd home game of season since 2010
CALIFORNIA	10-1 S/U prior to playing North Carolina since 1962
North Carolina	10-3 S/U in 2nd road game of season since 2009
Byu	1-9 O/U prior to playing Stanford since 2011
CLEMSON	4-11 O/U prior to playing Navy since 2006
BOSTON COLL	4-13 O/U in final home game of season since 2005
BOSTON COLL	9-2 S/U prior to playing USC since 2010
BOSTON COLL	10-2 ATS prior to playing USC since 2009
Usc	5-0 ATS after playing Boston College since 2012

- 52-5 S/U @ home when ranked since 2011
- 1-8 S/U when ranked vs #4 ranked teams since 1991
- 38-1 S/U when ranked vs Navy since 1964
- 15-0 S/U when ranked vs North Carolina all time
- 0-4 S/U & ATS when ranked vs Ohio State all time
- 8-0 S/U @ home when ranked vs Stanford since 1994

- 1-7 S/U on road vs #4 ranked teams since 1957
- 0-5 S/U & ATS vs #5 ranked teams since 2001
- 0-5 S/U vs #6 ranked teams since 1994
- 1-9 S/U vs ranked USC since 2002
- 0-5 S/U @ ranked USC since 2002

Page | 165 *Copyright © 2022 by Steve's Football Bible, LLC*

OHIO BOBCATS — MAC East

2021-Ohio		Opponent	Ohio	Opp	S/U	Line	ATS	Total	O/U	
9/4/2021	vs	SYRACUSE	9	29	L	-2.0	L	55.5	U	
9/11/2021	vs	DUQUESNE	26	28	L	-28.5	L	46.5	O	
9/17/2021	@	Louisiana	14	49	L	18.5	L	57.0	O	
9/25/2021	@	Northwestern	6	35	L	13.5	L	47.5	U	
10/2/2021	@	Akron	34	17	W	-9.5	W	55.0	U	
10/9/2021	vs	CENTRAL MICHIGAN	27	30	L	5.0	W	57.5	U	
10/16/2021	@	Buffalo	26	27	L	7.5	W	54.5	U	
10/23/2021	vs	KENT STATE	27	34	L	5.0	L	68.5	U	
11/2/2021	vs	MIAMI-OHIO	35	33	W	7.0	W	54.0	O	"Battle of the Bricks"
11/9/2021	@	Eastern Michigan	34	26	W	6.0	W	62.0	U	
11/16/2021	vs	TOLEDO	23	35	L	7.5	L	57.0	O	
11/26/2021	@	Bowling Green	10	21	L	-6.0	L	48.5	U	
Coach: Frank Solich		Season Record >>	271	364	3-9	ATS>>	5-7	O/U>>	4-8	

2020-Ohio		Opponent	Ohio	Opp	S/U	Line	ATS	Total	O/U	
11/4/2020	@	Central Michigan	27	30	L	-3.0	L	54.5	O	
11/10/2020	vs	AKRON	24	10	W	-27.0	L	58.0	U	
11/28/2020	vs	BOWLING GREEN	52	10	W	-22.5	W	55.0	O	
Coach: Frank Solich		Season Record >>	103	50	2-1	ATS>>	1-2	O/U>>	2-1	

2019-Ohio		Opponent	Ohio	Opp	S/U	Line	ATS	Total	O/U	
8/31/2019	vs	RHODE ISLAND	41	20	W	-25.0	L	NT	---	
9/7/2019	@	Pittsburgh	10	20	L	4.0	L	54.5	U	
9/14/2019	@	Marshall	31	33	L	4.5	W	47.5	O	"Battle for the Bell"
9/21/2019	vs	LOUISIANA-LAFAYETTE	25	45	L	-3.0	L	68.0	O	
10/5/2019	@	Buffalo	21	20	W	-3.0	L	51.5	U	{OT}
10/12/2019	vs	NORTHERN ILLINOIS	36	39	L	-4.5	L	50.5	O	
10/19/2019	vs	KENT STATE	45	38	W	-9.0	L	64.5	O	
10/26/2019	@	Ball State	34	21	W	2.0	W	59.5	U	
1/6/2019	vs	MIAMI-OHIO	21	24	L	-7.0	L	57.5	U	"Battle of the Bricks"
11/12/2019	vs	WESTERN MICHIGAN	34	37	L	-1.5	L	63.5	O	{OT}
11/19/2019	@	Bowling Green	66	24	W	-21.0	W	55.5	O	
11/26/2019	@	Akron	52	3	W	-27.5	W	52.5	O	
1/3/2020	vs	Nevada	30	21	W	-10.0	L	62.0	U	Famous Idaho Potato Bowl
Coach: Frank Solich		Season Record >>	446	345	7-6	ATS>>	4-9	O/U>>	7-5	

2018-Ohio		Opponent	Ohio	Opp	S/U	Line	ATS	Total	O/U	
9/1/2018	vs	HOWARD	38	32	W	-31.0	L	NT	---	
9/15/2018	@	Virginia	31	45	L	5.5	L	53.5	O	
9/22/2018	@	Cincinnati	30	34	L	7.0	W	54.5	O	
9/29/2018	vs	MASSACHUSETTS	58	42	W	-11.5	W	70.0	O	
10/6/2018	@	Kent State	27	26	W	-11.5	L	68.5	U	
10/13/2018	@	Northern Illinois	21	24	L	6.0	W	51.5	U	
10/20/2018	vs	BOWLING GREEN	49	14	W	-16.5	W	66.5	U	
10/25/2018	vs	BALL STATE	52	14	W	-10.0	W	65.5	O	
11/1/2018	@	Western Michigan	59	14	W	-3.0	W	65.0	O	
11/17/2018	@	Miami-Ohio	28	30	L	-4.5	L	59.0	U	"Battle of the Bricks"
11/14/2018	vs	BUFFALO	52	17	W	-2.5	W	65.0	O	
11/23/2018	vs	AKRON	49	28	W	-23.5	L	56.5	O	
12/19/2018	vs	San Diego State	27	0	W	-2.0	W	47.5	U	Frisco Bowl
Coach: Frank Solich		Season Record >>	521	320	9-4	ATS>>	8-5	O/U>>	7-5	

OHIO BOBCATS — MAC East

STADIUM: Peden Stadium {27,000} **Location:** Athens, OH **COACH:** Tom Albin

DATE		Opponent	Ohio	Opp	S/U	Line	ATS	Total	O/U	Trends & Angles
9/3/2022	vs	FLORIDA ATLANTIC								10-2 S/U in 1st home game of season since 2010
9/10/2022	@	Penn State								vs Penn State - Penn State leads series 5-1
9/17/2022	@	Iowa State								0-5 S/U vs Iowa State as Dog since 1989
9/24/2022	vs	FORDHAM								9-2 S/U in 2nd home game of season since 2011
10/1/2022	@	Kent State								vs Kent State - Ohio leads series 44-27-2
10/8/2022	vs	AKRON								7-0 S/U @ home vs Akron as favorite since 2006
10/15/2022	@	Western Michigan								1-3 S/U @ Western Michigan since 2000
10/22/2022	vs	NORTHERN ILLINOIS								vs Northern Illinois - NIU leads series 13-9
11/1/2022	vs	BUFFALO								vs Buffalo - HOME team 10-1 S/U since 2010
11/8/2022	@	Miami-Ohio								3-11-1 S/U vs Miami-Ohio as Dog since 1989
11/15/2022	@	Ball State								1-8 S/U vs Ball State as Dog since 1989
11/22/2022	vs	BOWLING GREEN								vs Bowling Green - BGU leads series 41-30-2
12/2/2022	vs									MAC Championship
	vs									BOWL GAME

Pointspread Analysis — Non-Conference
- 4-46 S/U vs Non-Conf. as 10.5 point or more Dog since 1989
- 11-0 S/U vs Non-Conf. as 3.5-15 point favorite since 2010
- 10-2 S/U vs Non-Conf. as 15.5 point or more favorite since 2010

Dog
- 3-22-1 S/U @ home as 7.5 point or more Dog since 1989
- 1-33 S/U on road as 20.5 point or more Dog since 1989
- 2-24-1 S/U as 15.5-20 point Dog since 1989
- 6-30 S/U as 10.5-15 point Dog since 1989
- 0-9-1 O/U as 10.5-15 point Dog since 2005
- 3-19 S/U as 7.5-10 point Dog since 1989
- 1-13 S/U on road as 3.5-7 point Dog since 2008
- 1-11 O/U as 3 point or less Dog since 2011

Favorite
- 13-3 S/U on road as 3 point or less favorite since 2004
- 9-2 O/U @ home as 3 point or less favorite since 2003
- 8-3 S/U & ATS @ home as 3.5-7 point favorite since 2006
- 16-4 S/U as 7.5-10 point favorite since 2000 {5-1 road}
- 13-3 S/U @ home as 10.5-15 point favorite since 1997
- 15-3 S/U as 15.5-20 point favorite since 1997
- 21-1 S/U as 20.5 point or more favorite since 1997

Bowl Games
- 4-8 S/U in Bowl Games

- 3-17 S/U in 2nd road game of season since 2001 — Iowa State
- 1-5 O/U prior to playing Western Michigan since 2006 — AKRON
- 6-0 S/U prior to playing Northern Illinois since 2009 — Western Michigan
- 6-2-1 O/U prior to playing Buffalo since 2012 — N. ILLINOIS
- 2-11-1 ATS prior to playing Buffalo since 2007 — N. ILLINOIS
- 2-7 O/U after playing Buffalo since 2011 — Miami-Ohio
- 0-9 ATS after playing Buffalo since 2011 — Miami-Ohio
- 1-8 ATS prior to playing Bowling Green since 2013 — Ball State
- 2-8-1 ATS in final road game of season since 2010 — Ball State
- 1-9-1 O/U in final road game of season since 2010 — Ball State
- 7-2 S/U & ATS after playing Ball State since 1996 — BOWL GREEN
- 12-4 S/U in final home game of season since 2006 — BOWL GREEN

Pointspread Analysis — Conference
- 3-0 S/U @ home vs Akron as Dog since 1993
- vs Akron - Ohio leads series 24-12-1
- vs Ball State - Ball State leads series 16-10
- 5-1 S/U vs Ball State as favorite since 1999
- 3-13 S/U vs Bowling Green as Dog since 1991
- vs Buffalo - Ohio leads series 16-11
- 10-1 S/U @ home vs Buffalo as favorite since 1999
- 0-4 O/U @ Kent State as favorite since 2008
- 6-1 S/U @ Kent State as favorite since 1996
- vs Miami-Ohio - Miami-Ohio leads series 56-41-1
- 5-1 ATS vs Northern Illinois as Dog since 2003
- 0-4 O/U vs Northern Illinois as Dog since 2011
- 3-1 S/U vs Northern Illinois as favorite since 1997
- Game 7-1 O/U vs Western Michigan since 2003
- 1-12 S/U vs Western Michigan as Dog since 1989
- 1-5 S/U vs Western Michigan since 2008
- vs Western Michigan - WMU leads series 34-29-1
- 3-0 S/U @ Western Michigan as favorite since 1996
- 8-1 S/U vs Akron as 11 point or more favorite since 1997
- 8-0 S/U vs Bowling Green as 9 point or more favorite since 1997
- 6-0 S/U vs Miami-Ohio as 3 point or less favorite since 2006
- 2-10 S/U vs Miami-Ohio as 6 point or more Dog since 1991
- 1-9 S/U vs Toledo as 6.5 point or more Dog since 1989
- 6-2 ATS vs Toledo as 6.5 point or more Dog since 1991

0-26 S/U vs ranked teams all time

OHIO STATE BUCKEYES   BIG TEN East

2021-Ohio State		Opponent	OSU	Opp	S/U	Line	ATS	Total	O/U	
9/2/2021	@	Minnesota	45	31	W	-14.0	T	62.0	O	
9/11/2021	vs	OREGON	28	35	L	-15.0	L	65.0	U	
9/18/2021	vs	TULSA	41	20	W	-24.5	L	60.5	O	
9/25/2021	vs	AKRON	59	7	W	-48.0	W	66.5	U	
10/2/2021	@	Rutgers	52	13	W	-15.0	W	58.0	O	
10/9/2021	vs	MARYLAND	66	17	W	-22.0	W	71.5	O	
10/23/2021	@	Indiana	54	7	W	-21.0	W	58.5	O	
10/30/2021	vs	PENN STATE	33	24	W	-19.0	L	60.5	U	
11/6/2021	@	Nebraska	26	17	W	-14.0	L	67.5	U	
11/13/2021	vs	PURDUE	59	31	W	-19.0	W	65.5	O	
11/20/2021	vs	MICHIGAN STATE	56	7	W	-19.0	W	70.5	U	
11/27/2021	@	Michigan	27	42	L	-6.0	L	63.0	O	*"100 Yard War"*
1/1/2022	vs	Utah	48	45	W	-4.0	L	64.5	O	Rose Bowl
Coach: Ryan Day		Season Record >>	594	296	11-2	ATS>>	6-6-1	O/U>>	8-5	
2020-Ohio State		Opponent	OSU	Opp	S/U	Line	ATS	Total	O/U	
10/24/2020	vs	NEBRASKA	52	17	W	-27.5	W	70.5	U	
10/31/2020	@	Penn State	38	23	W	-10.0	W	63.0	U	
11/7/2020	vs	RUTGERS	49	27	W	-37.5	L	63.0	O	
11/21/2020	vs	INDIANA	42	35	W	-20.5	L	67.0	O	
12/5/2020	@	Michigan State	52	12	W	-22.0	W	58.5	O	
12/19/2020	vs	Northwestern	22	10	W	-16.5	L	57.5	U	Big Ten Championship
1/1/2021	vs	Clemson	49	28	W	7.5	W	69.0	O	Sugar Bowl {National Semifinal}
1/11/2021	vs	Alabama	24	52	L	9.5	L	75.5	O	CFB Championship Game
Coach: Ryan Day		Season Record >>	328	204	7-1	ATS>>	4-4	O/U>>	5-3	Big Ten Champions
2019-Ohio State		Opponent	OSU	Opp	S/U	Line	ATS	Total	O/U	
8/31/2019	vs	FLORIDA ATLANTIC	45	21	W	-27.5	L	65.5	O	
9/7/2019	vs	CINCINNATI	42	0	W	-14.5	W	52.5	U	
9/14/2019	@	Indiana	51	10	W	-17.5	W	60.5	O	
9/21/2019	vs	MIAMI-OHIO	76	5	W	-38.5	W	57.0	O	
9/28/2019	@	Nebraska	48	7	W	-17.0	W	66.0	U	
10/5/2019	vs	MICHIGAN STATE	34	10	W	-20.0	W	51.0	U	
10/18/2019	@	Northwestern	52	3	W	-27.0	W	52.0	U	
10/26/2019	vs	WISCONSIN	38	7	W	-14.5	W	47.5	U	
11/9/2019	vs	MARYLAND	73	14	W	-42.5	W	64.5	O	
11/16/2019	@	Rutgers	56	21	W	-52.0	L	62.5	O	
11/23/2019	vs	PENN STATE	28	17	W	-19.5	L	58.0	U	
11/30/2019	@	Michigan	56	27	W	-8.5	W	53.0	O	*"100 Yard War"*
12/7/2019	vs	Wisconsin	34	21	W	-16.5	L	58.0	U	Big Ten Championship
12/28/2019	vs	Clemson	23	29	L	2.5	L	62.0	U	Fiesta Bowl (National Semi-Final)
Coach: Ryan Day		Season Record >>	656	192	13-1	ATS>>	9-5	O/U>>	7-7	Big Ten Champions
2018-Ohio State		Opponent	OSU	Opp	S/U	Line	ATS	Total	O/U	
9/1/2018	vs	OREGON STATE	77	31	W	-40.0	W	63.0	O	
9/8/2018	vs	RUTGERS	52	3	W	-35.0	W	59.0	U	
9/15/2018	vs	Tcu	40	28	W	-12.5	L	58.5	O	AT&T Stadium
9/22/2018	vs	TULANE	49	6	W	-38.0	W	67.5	U	
9/29/2018	@	Penn State	27	26	W	-3.5	L	69.5	U	
10/6/2018	vs	INDIANA	49	26	W	-28.0	L	64.5	O	
10/13/2018	vs	MINNESOTA	30	14	W	-29.5	L	60.0	U	
10/20/2018	@	Purdue	20	49	L	-12.0	L	66.0	O	
11/3/2018	vs	NEBRASKA	36	31	W	-17.0	L	75.5	U	
11/10/2018	@	Michigan State	26	6	W	-3.5	W	49.5	U	
11/17/2018	@	Maryland	52	51	W	-14.0	L	61.5	O	{OT}
11/24/2018	vs	MICHIGAN	62	39	W	4.0	W	53.5	O	*"100 Yard War"*
12/1/2018	vs	Northwestern	45	24	W	-16.5	W	63.0	O	Big Ten Championship
1/1/2019	vs	Washington	28	23	W	-5.5	L	55.0	U	Rose Bowl
Coach: Urban Meyer		Season Record >>	593	357	13-1	ATS>>	6-8	O/U>>	7-7	Big Ten Champions

OHIO STATE BUCKEYES — BIG TEN East

STADIUM: Ohio Stadium {102,082} **Location:** Columbus, OH **COACH:** Ryan Day

DATE		Opponent	OSU	Opp	S/U	Line	ATS	Total	O/U	Trends & Angles
9/3/2022	vs	NOTRE DAME								4-0 S/U & ATS vs Notre Dame as favorite s/1995
9/10/2022	vs	ARKANSAS STATE								11-0 S/U in 2nd home game of season since 2010
9/17/2022	vs	TOLEDO								vs Toledo - Ohio State leads series 3-0
9/24/2022	vs	WISCONSIN								8-0 S/U vs Wisconsin since 2011
10/1/2022	vs	RUTGERS								vs Rutgers - Ohio State leads series 8-0 {6-2 ATS}
10/8/2022	@	Michigan State								9-0 S/U @ Michigan State as favorite since 1984
10/22/2022	vs	IOWA								7-0 S/U @ home vs Iowa as favorite since 1995
10/29/2022	@	Penn State								6-1 S/U @ Penn State since 2007
11/5/2022	@	Northwestern								vs Northwestern - Ohio State leads series 63-14-1
11/12/2022	vs	INDIANA								vs Indiana - Ohio State leads series 78-12-4
11/19/2022	@	Maryland								vs Maryland - Ohio State leads series 6-0
11/26/2022	vs	MICHIGAN								14-3 S/U vs Michigan as favorite since 2002
12/3/2022	vs									Big Ten Championship
	vs									BOWL GAME

Pointspread Analysis — Non-Conference
- 9-1 S/U vs Non-Conf. as 7.5-10 point favorite since 1984
- 19-3 S/U vs Non-Conf. as 10.5-15 point favorite since 1981
- 71-0 S/U vs Non-Conf. as 15.5 point or more favorite since 1983

Dog
- 14-4 ATS as a Dog since 2009
- 1-7 S/U on road as 10.5 point or more Dog since 1988
- 7-1 ATS as 7.5-10 point Dog since 1992
- 7-0 S/U as 3.5-7 point Dog since 2009
- 8-0 ATS as 3.5-7 point Dog since 2009
- 1-8 O/U on road as 3 point or less Dog since 1993
- 0-8 O/U as 3 point or less Dog since 2004
- 1-6 S/U @ home as 3 point or less Dog since 1986

Favorite
- 7-0 S/U on road as 3 point or less favorite since 2004
- 6-0-1 ATS on road as 3 point or less favorite since 2004
- 13-2 S/U @ home as 3.5-7 point favorite since 2001
- 10-2 S/U on road as 3.5-7 point favorite since 2005
- 9-3 ATS on road as 3.5-7 point favorite since 2005
- 9-1 S/U on road as 7.5-10 point favorite since 2000
- 6-1 O/U on road as 7.5-10 point favorite since 2003
- 14-1 S/U @ home as 7.5-10 point favorite since 1983
- 25-3 S/U on road as 10.5-15 point favorite since 1985
- 46-2 S/U @ home as 15.5-20 point favorite since 1985
- 43-1 S/U as 15.5-20 point favorite since 1997
- 12-2 S/U on road as 15.5-20 point favorite since 1986
- 138-2 S/U as 20.5 point or more favorite since 1983
- 33-1 S/U on road as 20.5 point or more favorite since 1983
- 102-1 S/U @ home as 20.5 point or more favorite since 1983

Bowl Games
- 1-4 S/U vs Clemson in Bowl Games
- 1-7 O/U in Rose Bowl since 1975
- 0-3 S/U & ATS in Citrus Bowl since 1993
- 4-10 S/U vs SEC teams in Bowl Games {3-11 ATS}
- 0-4 S/U & ATS in Outback Bowl
- 4-0 S/U in Sugar Bowl since 1999
- 6-2 ATS in Fiesta Bowl since 1984
- 5-1 S/U & ATS in Bowl Games as 3.5-7 point Dog since 2004
- 1-6 S/U & ATS in Bowl Games as 3 point or less Dog since 1978
- 0-5 ATS in Bowl Games as 10.5-15 point favorite since 1976

- 41-4 S/U on road when ranked since 2012
- 10-1 S/U on road when ranked vs ranked teams since 2010
- 48-2 S/U @ home when #1 ranked all time

Pointspread Analysis — Conference
- 28-0 S/U vs Indiana as favorite since 1989
- 0-6 ATS @ home vs Indiana as favorite since 2011
- 7-0 O/U vs Maryland as favorite since 2014
- vs Michigan - Michigan leads series 59-52-6
- vs Michigan State - Ohio State leads series 34-15
- vs Nebraska - Ohio State leads series 9-1
- 22-1 S/U vs Northwestern as favorite since 1984
- vs Penn State - Ohio State leads series 23-14
- 1-4 S/U vs Penn State as Dog since 1994
- Game 0-3 O/U @ Penn State since 2016
- 4-0 S/U & ATS vs Wisconsin as Dog since 2000
- 9-2 ATS vs Wisconsin since 2007
- 5-0 S/U & ATS @ home vs Wisconsin since 2007
- 12-1 S/U vs Iowa as 3.5 point or more favorite since 1989
- 8-1 S/U vs Michigan as 3-8.5 point favorite since 1984
- 13-2 S/U vs Michigan State as 6.5 point or more favorite since 1983
- 13-1 S/U vs Penn State as 7 point or more favorite since 1996
- 1-11-1 O/U vs Wisconsin as 9 point or less favorite since 1984
- 9-1 S/U vs Wisconsin as 10 point or more favorite since 1988

- 74-4 S/U @ home when ranked since 2010
- 8-0 S/U @ home when ranked vs Michigan since 2002
- 26-1 S/U when ranked vs Northwestern since 1972
- 4-0 S/U when ranked vs Notre Dame all time
- 7-0 S/U vs ranked Wisconsin since 2011

Opponent	Trend
NOTRE DAME	40-3 S/U in 1st home game of season since 1979
ARKANSAS STATE	4-12 O/U in 2nd home game of season since 2006
RUTGERS	12-1 S/U prior to playing Michigan State since 2006
Michigan State	10-0 S/U in 1st road game of season since 2012
Michigan State	8-1-1 ATS in 1st road game of season since 2012
IOWA	28-1 S/U prior to playing Penn State since 1993
IOWA	9-3 O/U prior to playing Penn State since 2010
IOWA	6-1 S/U after playing Michigan State since 2012
Penn State	9-1 S/U in 2nd road game of season since 2012
Penn State	9-2 O/U in 2nd road game of season since 2011
Northwestern	14-0 S/U prior to playing Indiana since 2005
Northwestern	25-2 S/U after playing Penn State since 1994
Maryland	2-10 ATS after playing Indiana since 2010
Maryland	2-9 O/U prior to playing Michigan since 2010
Maryland	1-7 ATS prior to playing Michigan since 2013
Maryland	15-2 S/U in final road game of season since 2005
Michigan	2-7 ATS in final home game of season since 2013

OKLAHOMA SOONERS   BIG TWELVE

2021-Oklahoma		Opponent	OU	Opp	S/U	Line	ATS	Total	O/U	
9/4/2021	vs	TULANE	40	35	W	-31.0	L	66.5	O	
9/11/2021	vs	WESTERN CAROLINA	76	0	W	-55.5	W	66.0	O	
9/18/2021	vs	NEBRASKA	23	16	W	-22.5	L	63.0	U	
9/25/2021	vs	WEST VIRGINIA	16	13	W	-17.5	L	57.0	U	
10/2/2021	@	Kansas State	37	31	W	-12.0	L	52.5	O	
10/9/2021	vs	Texas	55	48	W	-4.0	W	65.5	O	"Red River Rivalry - Golden Hat"
10/16/2021	vs	TCU	52	31	W	-12.5	W	64.5	O	
10/23/2021	@	Kansas	35	23	W	-38.0	L	66.5	U	
10/30/2021	vs	TEXAS TECH	52	21	W	-19.5	W	67.0	O	
11/13/2021	@	Baylor	14	27	L	-4.0	L	63.5	U	
11/20/2021	vs	IOWA STATE	28	21	W	-3.0	W	59.0	U	
11/27/2021	@	Oklahoma State	33	37	L	4.5	W	51.0	O	"The Bedlam Series" (Bedlam Bell)
12/29/2021	vs	Oregon	47	32	W	-7.0	W	64.5	O	Alamo Bowl
Coach: Lincoln Riley		Season Record >>	508	335	11-2	ATS>>	7-6	O/U>>	8-5	

2020-Oklahoma		Opponent	OU	Opp	S/U	Line	ATS	Total	O/U	
9/12/2020	vs	MISSOURI STATE	48	0	W	-49.5	L	73.0	U	
9/26/2020	vs	KANSAS STATE	35	38	L	-27.5	L	61.5	O	
10/3/2020	@	Iowa State	30	37	L	-7.5	L	62.0	O	
10/10/2020	vs	Texas	53	45	W	-3.0	W	74.0	O	"Red River Rivalry - Golden Hat"
10/24/2020	@	Tcu	33	14	W	-6.5	W	58.5	U	
10/31/2020	@	Texas Tech	62	28	W	-17.0	W	65.0	O	
11/7/2020	vs	KANSAS	62	9	W	-38.5	W	62.0	O	
11/21/2020	vs	OKLAHOMA STATE	41	13	W	-6.5	W	60.5	U	"The Bedlam Series" (Bedlam Bell)
12/5/2020	vs	BAYLOR	27	14	W	-23.5	L	60.5	U	
12/19/2020	vs	Iowa State	27	21	W	-5.5	W	59.5	U	Big 12 Championship
12/30/2020	vs	Florida	55	20	W	-8.5	W	65.0	O	Cotton Bowl
Coach: Lincoln Riley		Season Record >>	473	239	9-2	ATS>>	7-4	O/U>>	6-5	Big 12 Champions

2019-Oklahoma		Opponent	OU	Opp	S/U	Line	ATS	Total	O/U	
8/31/2019	vs	HOUSTON	49	31	W	-22.0	L	79.5	O	
9/7/2019	vs	SOUTH DAKOTA	70	14	W	-45.5	W	NT	---	
9/14/2019	@	Ucla	48	14	W	-23.0	W	72.0	U	
9/28/2019	vs	TEXAS TECH	55	16	W	-27.0	W	69.0	O	
10/5/2019	@	Kansas	45	20	W	-31.5	L	67.0	U	
10/12/2019	vs	Texas	34	27	W	-10.5	L	77.5	U	"Red River Rivalry - Golden Hat"
10/19/2019	vs	WEST VIRGINIA	52	14	W	-32.0	L	63.5	O	
10/26/2019	@	Kansas State	41	48	L	-23.5	L	60.0	O	
11/9/2019	vs	IOWA STATE	42	41	W	-14.5	L	70.0	O	
11/16/2019	@	Baylor	34	31	W	-10.5	L	68.5	U	
11/23/2019	vs	TCU	28	24	W	-18.5	L	64.5	U	
11/30/2019	@	Oklahoma State	34	16	W	-14.0	W	68.0	U	"The Bedlam Series" (Bedlam Bell)
12/7/2019	vs	Baylor	30	23	W	-9.0	L	66.0	U	Big 12 Championship
12/28/2019	vs	Lsu	28	63	L	12.0	L	75.0	O	Chick-Fil-A Peach Bowl (National Semifinal)
Coach: Lincoln Riley		Season Record >>	590	382	12-2	ATS>>	5-9	O/U>>	6-7	Big 12 Champions

2018-Oklahoma		Opponent	OU	Opp	S/U	Line	ATS	Total	O/U	Heisman Trophy: Kyler Murray
9/1/2018	vs	FLORIDA ATLANTIC	63	14	W	-19.0	W	68.0	O	
9/8/2018	vs	UCLA	49	21	W	-31.0	L	65.5	O	
9/15/2018	@	Iowa State	37	27	W	-18.5	L	54.0	O	
9/22/2018	vs	ARMY	28	21	W	-28.5	L	60.5	U	{OT}
9/29/2018	vs	BAYLOR	66	33	W	-21.0	W	68.0	O	
10/6/2018	vs	Texas	45	48	L	-7.0	L	60.0	O	"Red River Rivalry - Golden Hat"
10/20/2018	@	Tcu	52	27	W	-7.5	W	61.5	O	
10/27/2018	vs	KANSAS STATE	51	14	W	-24.0	W	65.0	T	
11/3/2018	@	Texas Tech	51	46	W	-14.0	L	78.5	O	
11/10/2018	vs	OKLAHOMA STATE	48	47	W	-21.5	L	80.0	O	"The Bedlam Series" (Bedlam Bell)
11/17/2018	vs	KANSAS	55	40	W	-34.5	L	69.5	O	
11/24/2018	@	West Virginia	59	56	W	-3.0	T	87.0	O	
12/1/2018	vs	Texas	39	27	W	-9.5	W	79.5	U	Big 12 Championship
12/29/2018	vs	Alabama	34	45	L	15.0	W	80.5	U	Orange Bowl {National Semifinal}
Coach: Lincoln Riley		Season Record >>	677	466	12-2	ATS>>	6-7-1	O/U>>	11-3	Big 12 Champions

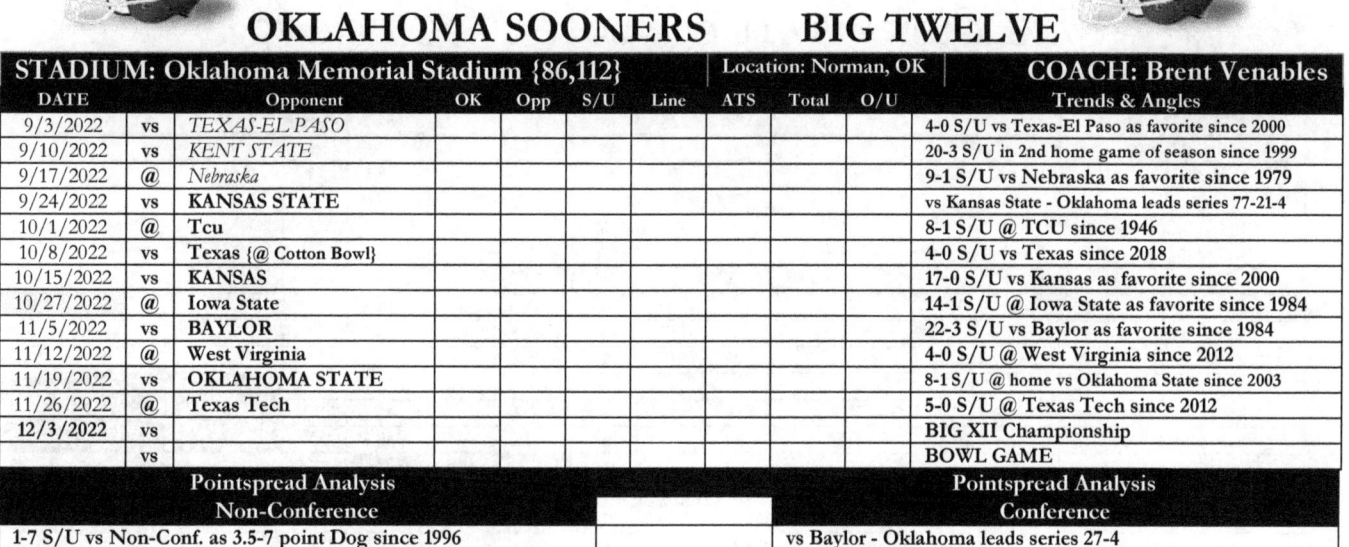

OKLAHOMA SOONERS — BIG TWELVE

STADIUM: Oklahoma Memorial Stadium {86,112}   **Location:** Norman, OK   **COACH:** Brent Venables

DATE		Opponent	OK	Opp	S/U	Line	ATS	Total	O/U	Trends & Angles
9/3/2022	vs	TEXAS-EL PASO								4-0 S/U vs Texas-El Paso as favorite since 2000
9/10/2022	vs	KENT STATE								20-3 S/U in 2nd home game of season since 1999
9/17/2022	@	Nebraska								9-1 S/U vs Nebraska as favorite since 1979
9/24/2022	vs	KANSAS STATE								vs Kansas State - Oklahoma leads series 77-21-4
10/1/2022	@	Tcu								8-1 S/U @ TCU since 1946
10/8/2022	vs	Texas {@ Cotton Bowl}								4-0 S/U vs Texas since 2018
10/15/2022	vs	KANSAS								17-0 S/U vs Kansas as favorite since 2000
10/27/2022	@	Iowa State								14-1 S/U @ Iowa State as favorite since 1984
11/5/2022	vs	BAYLOR								22-3 S/U vs Baylor as favorite since 1984
11/12/2022	@	West Virginia								4-0 S/U @ West Virginia since 2012
11/19/2022	vs	OKLAHOMA STATE								8-1 S/U @ home vs Oklahoma State since 2003
11/26/2022	@	Texas Tech								5-0 S/U @ Texas Tech since 2012
12/3/2022	vs									BIG XII Championship
	vs									BOWL GAME

Pointspread Analysis — Non-Conference
- 1-7 S/U vs Non-Conf. as 3.5-7 point Dog since 1996
- 2-7 ATS vs Non-Conf. as 7.5-10 point favorite since 1989
- 12-0 S/U vs Non-Conf. as 15.5-20 point favorite since 1984
- 58-1 S/U vs Non-Conf. as 20.5 point or more favorite since 1986
- vs Texas-El Paso - Oklahoma leads series 4-0
- 1-8 O/U vs Nebraska as favorite since 1984
- 0-9 S/U vs Nebraska as 6.5 point or more Dog since 1983
- 4-1 S/U & ATS vs Nebraska as 5.5 point or less Dog since 1987

Dog
- 13-4 ATS as a road Dog since 1999
- 0-7 S/U on road as 10.5-20 point Dog since 1989
- 5-0 ATS as 7.5-10 point Dog since 1998
- 6-21-1 S/U as 3.5-7 point Dog since 1983
- 6-0 S/U & ATS on road as 3 point or less Dog since 1994

Favorite
- 10-1 S/U as 3 point or less favorite since 1999
- 11-2 S/U @ home as 3.5-7 point favorite since 1998
- 8-2 S/U & ATS on road as 3.5-7 point favorite since 2011
- 6-0 S/U @ home as 7.5-10 point favorite since 1997
- 13-1 S/U as 7.5-10 point favorite since 2009
- 12-1 S/U on road as 10.5-15 point favorite since 2004
- 12-3 O/U on road as 10.5-15 point favorite since 2002
- 20-1 S/U @ home as 10.5-15 point favorite since 1999
- 28-2 S/U @ home as 15.5-20 point favorite since 1984
- 16-1 S/U on road as 15.5-20 point favorite since 1983
- 17-0 S/U @ home as 20.5-25 point favorite since 2010
- 17-1 S/U on road as 20.5-25 point favorite since 1985
- 24-0 S/U on road as 25.5 point or more favorite since 1984
- 73-4 S/U @ home as 25.5 point or more favorite since 1983

Bowl Games
- 3-0 S/U in Sun Bowl
- 12-7 S/U in Orange Bowl since 1954
- 3-0 O/U in Fiesta Bowl since 2007
- 7-0 S/U vs Big Ten in Bowl Games
- 6-2 S/U in Sugar Bowl
- 0-3 S/U & ATS vs Clemson in Bowl Games
- 0-3 O/U vs Clemson in Bowl Games
- 1-4 S/U & ATS in Bowl Games as 3 point or less Dog since 1994
- 0-5 O/U in Bowl Games as 3 point or less favorite since 1988
- 0-9 O/U in Bowl Games as 3.5-7 point favorite since 1986
- 38-0 S/U @ home when #1 ranked all time
- 17-0 S/U @ home when #2 ranked since 1984
- 16-1 S/U @ home when #5 ranked all time

	TEXAS-EL PASO
	Nebraska
	KANSAS STATE
	KANSAS STATE
	Tcu
	Tcu
	Tcu
	KANSAS
	Iowa State
	Iowa State
	Iowa State
	BAYLOR
	West Virginia
	West Virginia
	OK STATE
	Texas Tech

Pointspread Analysis — Conference
- vs Baylor - Oklahoma leads series 27-4
- vs Iowa State - Oklahoma leads series 78-7-2
- vs Kansas - Oklahoma leads series 79-27-6
- 16-3 S/U vs Oklahoma State since 2003
- vs Oklahoma State - Oklahoma leads series 91-18-7
- vs TCU - Oklahoma leads series 17-5
- vs Texas - Texas leads series 65-50-5
- 0-3 S/U vs Texas as Dog since 2005
- 2-5 ATS @ Texas Tech since 2007
- Game 10-1 O/U vs Texas Tech since 2011
- 10-0 S/U vs Texas Tech since 2012
- vs Texas Tech - Oklahoma leads series 23-6
- 9-0 S/U vs West Virginia since 2012
- Game 4-0 O/U @ West Virginia since 2012
- Game 8-2 O/U vs West Virginia since 2008
- vs West Virginia - Oklahoma leads series 11-2
- 5-1-1 ATS vs West Virginia since 2014
- 17-1 S/U vs Iowa State as 23 point or less favorite since 1983
- 19-0 S/U vs Kansas as 16.5 point or more favorite since 1986
- 13-2 S/U vs Kansas State as 16 point or more favorite since 1983
- 17-0 S/U vs Oklahoma State as 14 point or less favorite since 1983
- 11-0 S/U vs TCU as 6-19 point favorite since 1998
- 0-6 ATS vs Texas as 12-17.5 point favorite since 1988
- 14-1 S/U vs Texas Tech as 13.5 point or more favorite since 1994
- 24-1 S/U in 1st home game of season since 1997
- 10-2 S/U in 1st road game of season since 2010
- 10-1 O/U prior to playing TCU since 2008
- 10-2 S/U prior to playing TCU since 1998
- 7-3 O/U in 2nd road game of season since 2012
- 11-0 S/U in 2nd road game of season since 2011
- 10-1 S/U after playing Kansas State since 2011
- 22-1 S/U after playing Texas since 1999
- 13-4 ATS prior to playing Baylor since 2005
- 13-4 O/U after playing Kansas since 2000
- 12-0 S/U prior to playing Baylor since 2010
- 9-0 S/U prior to playing West Virginia since 2012
- 9-2 S/U after playing Baylor since 2010
- 12-0 S/U prior to playing Oklahoma State since 2010
- 19-1 S/U in final home game of season since 2002
- 9-1 S/U in final road game of season since 2012
- 1-8 S/U vs #1 ranked teams since 1994
- 8-1 S/U @ home vs ranked Oklahoma State since 1972
- 11-1 S/U @ home when ranked vs Baylor all time

OKLAHOMA STATE COWBOYS   BIG TWELVE

2021-Oklahoma State		Opponent	OSU	Opp	S/U	Line	ATS	Total	O/U	
9/4/2021	vs	MISSOURI STATE	23	16	W	-32.0	L	51.0	U	
9/11/2021	vs	TULSA	28	23	W	-10.5	L	51.0	T	
9/18/2021	@	Boise State	21	20	W	3.5	W	57.5	U	
9/25/2021	vs	KANSAS STATE	31	20	W	-6.0	W	47.5	O	
10/2/2021	vs	BAYLOR	24	14	W	-3.5	W	48.0	U	
10/16/2021	@	Texas	32	24	W	3.5	W	64.0	U	
10/23/2021	@	Iowa State	21	24	L	7.5	L	47.5	U	
10/30/2021	vs	KANSAS	55	3	W	-29.0	W	54.0	O	
11/6/2021	@	West Virginia	24	3	W	-3.5	W	48.5	U	
11/13/2021	vs	TCU	63	17	W	-11.5	W	53.5	O	
11/20/2021	@	Texas Tech	23	0	W	-10.0	W	55.5	U	
11/27/2021	vs	OKLAHOMA	37	33	W	-4.5	L	51.0	O	"The Bedlam Series" (Bedlam Bell)
12/4/2021	vs	Baylor	16	21	L	-7.0	L	45.0	U	BIG XII CHAMPIONSHIP
1/1/2022	vs	Notre Dame	37	35	W	-1.0	W	48.5	O	Fiesta Bowl
Coach: Mike Gundy		Season Record >>	435	253	12-2	ATS>>	10-4	O/U>>	5-8-1	

2020-Oklahoma State		Opponent	OSU	Opp	S/U	Line	ATS	Total	O/U	
9/19/2020	vs	TULSA	16	7	W	-23.0	L	66.0	U	
9/26/2020	vs	WEST VIRGINIA	27	13	W	-6.5	W	49.0	U	
10/3/2020	@	Kansas	47	7	W	-21.5	W	53.0	U	
10/24/2020	vs	IOWA STATE	24	21	W	-2.5	W	54.0	U	
10/31/2020	vs	TEXAS	34	41	L	-3.5	L	58.0	O	{OT}
11/7/2020	@	Kansas State	20	18	W	-14.0	L	48.5	U	
11/21/2020	@	Oklahoma	13	41	L	6.5	L	60.5	U	"The Bedlam Series" (Bedlam Bell)
11/28/2020	vs	TEXAS TECH	50	44	W	-12.0	L	57.0	O	
12/5/2020	@	Tcu	22	29	L	-2.5	L	53.0	U	
12/12/2020	@	Baylor	42	3	W	-6.0	W	49.5	U	
12/29/2020	vs	Miami	37	34	W	-1.5	W	63.0	O	Cheez-it Bowl
Coach: Mike Gundy		Season Record >>	332	258	8-3	ATS>>	5-6	O/U>>	4-7	

2019-Oklahoma State		Opponent	OSU	Opp	S/U	Line	ATS	Total	O/U	
8/30/2019	@	Oregon State	52	36	W	-13.0	W	72.5	O	
9/7/2019	vs	MCNEESE STATE	56	14	W	-42.0	T	NT	---	
9/14/2019	@	Tulsa	40	21	W	-13.5	W	64.5	U	
9/21/2019	@	Texas	30	36	L	7.0	W	72.5	U	
9/28/2019	vs	KANSAS STATE	26	13	W	-4.0	W	60.0	U	
10/5/2019	@	Texas Tech	35	45	L	-9.5	L	62.5	O	
10/19/2019	vs	BAYLOR	27	45	L	-5.5	L	68.5	O	
10/26/2019	@	Iowa State	34	27	W	10.5	W	64.0	U	
11/2/2019	vs	TCU	34	27	W	-1.5	W	59.0	O	
11/16/2019	vs	KANSAS	31	13	W	-17.0	W	69.0	U	
11/23/2019	@	West Virginia	20	13	W	-6.5	W	56.5	U	
11/30/2019	vs	OKLAHOMA	16	34	L	14.0	L	68.0	U	"The Bedlam Series" (Bedlam Bell)
12/27/2019	vs	Texas A&M	21	24	L	5.0	W	55.5	U	Texas Bowl
Coach: Mike Gundy		Season Record >>	422	348	8-5	ATS>>	9-3-1	O/U>>	4-8	

2018-Oklahoma State		Opponent	OSU	Opp	S/U	Line	ATS	Total	O/U	
9/1/2018	vs	MISSOURI STATE	58	17	W	-44.0	L	NT	---	
9/8/2018	vs	SOUTH ALABAMA	55	13	W	-30.5	W	64.0	O	
9/15/2018	vs	BOISE STATE	44	21	W	2.0	W	66.5	U	
9/22/2018	vs	TEXAS TECH	17	41	L	-14.5	L	74.5	U	
9/29/2018	@	Kansas	48	28	W	-17.0	W	53.5	O	
10/6/2018	vs	IOWA STATE	42	48	L	-10.0	L	55.5	O	
10/13/2018	@	Kansas State	12	31	L	-9.0	L	61.5	U	
10/27/2018	vs	TEXAS	38	35	W	1.0	W	59.5	O	
11/3/2018	@	Baylor	31	35	L	-6.5	L	68.5	U	
11/10/2018	@	Oklahoma	47	48	L	21.5	W	80.0	O	"The Bedlam Series" (Bedlam Bell)
11/17/2018	vs	WEST VIRGINIA	45	41	W	6.0	W	73.5	O	
11/24/2018	@	Tcu	24	31	L	-5.5	L	54.0	O	
12/31/2018	vs	Missouri	38	33	W	9.5	W	72.5	U	Liberty Bowl
Coach: Mike Gundy		Season Record >>	499	422	7-6	ATS>>	7-6	O/U>>	7-5	

OKLAHOMA STATE COWBOYS   BIG TWELVE

STADIUM: Boone-Pickens Stadium {56,790} | **Location:** Stillwater, OK | **COACH:** Mike Gundy

DATE		Opponent	OSU	Opp	S/U	Line	ATS	Total	O/U	Trends & Angles
9/3/2022	vs	CENTRAL MICHIGAN								vs Central Michigan - Series tied 1-1
9/10/2022	vs	ARIZONA STATE								vs Arizona State - ASU leads series 2-1
9/17/2022	vs	ARKANSAS-PINE BLUFF								1st Meeting
10/1/2022	@	Baylor								0-4 S/U @ Baylor as Dog since 1994
10/8/2022	vs	TEXAS TECH								8-1 S/U @ home vs Texas Tech since 2003
10/15/2022	@	Tcu								1-5 S/U @ Tcu since 1990
10/22/2022	vs	TEXAS								2-9 S/U @ home vs Texas since 1999
10/29/2022	@	Kansas State								3-11 ATS vs Kansas State as favorite since 1988
11/5/2022	@	Kansas								23-1 S/U vs Kansas as favorite since 1983
11/12/2022	vs	IOWA STATE								vs Iowa State - Ok State leads series 33-20-3
11/19/2022	@	Oklahoma								vs Oklahoma - Oklahoma leads series 91-18-7
11/26/2022	vs	West Virginia								7-0 S/U & ATS vs West Virginia since 2015
12/3/2022	vs									BIG XII Championship
	vs									BOWL GAME

Pointspread Analysis — Non-Conference

- 1-9 S/U vs Non-Conf as 7.5 point or more Dog since 1990
- 10-1 S/U vs Non-Conf. as 3.5-7 point favorite since 1987
- 12-0 S/U vs Non-Conf. as 10.5-15 point favorite since 2000
- 37-2 S/U vs Non-Conf. as 15.5 point or more favorite since 1985

Dog
- 1-20 S/U as 25.5 point or more Dog since 1986
- 8-0 ATS as 25.5 point or more Dog since 1995
- 1-13 S/U as 20.5-25 point Dog since 1983
- 2-13 S/U as 15.5-20 point Dog since 1990
- 5-1 O/U as 15.5-20 point Dog since 2001
- 4-25-1 S/U as 10.5-15 point Dog since 1985
- 4-11 ATS on road as 10.5-15 point Dog since 1999
- 0-11 S/U on road as 7.5-10 point Dog since 1984 {1-10 ATS}
- 2-9 S/U @ home as 7.5-10 point Dog since 1983
- 6-1 O/U on road as 3 point or less Dog since 2002

Favorite
- 8-1 O/U @ home as 3 point or less favorite since 2006
- 12-2 S/U @ home as 3.5-7 point favorite since 2009
- 16-3 S/U on road as 3.5-7 point favorite since 1995
- 7-17 O/U as 3.5-7 point favorite since 2010
- 14-0 S/U on road as 10.5-15 point favorite since 1983
- 11-4-1 O/U as 10.5-15 point favorite since 2013
- 18-2 S/U @ home as 10.5-15 point favorite since 1986
- 22-5 S/U as 15.5-20 point favorite since 1985
- 9-0 S/U on road as 20.5-25 point favorite since 1984
- 13-0 S/U @ home as 20.5-25 point favorite since 1984
- 31-0 S/U @ home as 25.5 point or more favorite since 1984

Bowl Games
- 0-3 S/U & ATS vs Mississippi in Bowl Games
- 0-3 O/U vs Mississippi in Bowl Games
- 0-3 S/U in Cotton Bowl since 2004
- 13-2 S/U as a favorite in Bowl Games since 1976
- 12-3 ATS as a favorite in Bowl Games since 1976
- 2-8 S/U as a Dog in Bowl Games since 1981
- 3-7 ATS as a Dog in Bowl Games since 1981
- 6-1 S/U & ATS in Bowl Games as 3 point or less favorite since 1984
- 4-0 S/U in Bowl Games as 3.5-7 point favorite since 2007
- 3-0 S/U & ATS in Bowl Games as 7.5-20 point favorite since 1976

- 0-11 S/U vs #1 ranked teams all time
- 0-16 S/U vs #2 ranked teams all time

Pointspread Analysis — Conference

- vs Baylor - Oklahoma State leads series 22-19
- 1-4 S/U & ATS vs Iowa State as Dog since 2000
- vs Kansas - Oklahoma State leads series 40-29-3
- 20-3-1 ATS vs Kansas as favorite since 1983
- vs Kansas State - Oklahoma State leads series 42-26
- 2-10 S/U vs Kansas State as Dog since 1991
- vs TCU - Oklahoma State leads series 17-13-2
- vs Texas - Texas leads series 25-10
- 6-1 S/U vs Texas as favorite since 2010
- 2-15 S/U vs Texas as Dog since 1998
- Game 11-1 O/U @ home vs Texas since 1997
- 11-2 S/U vs Texas Tech since 2009
- vs Texas Tech - Texas Tech leads series 24-22-3
- 1-7 S/U @ Texas Tech as Dog since 1996
- 11-2 S/U vs Texas Tech as favorite since 1999
- vs West Virginia - Oklahoma State leads series 9-4
- 14-0 S/U vs Baylor as 7 point or more favorite since 1997
- 0-10 S/U vs Baylor as 9.5 point or more Dog since 1989
- 8-0 S/U vs Iowa State as 11-17.5 point favorite since 1983
- 0-10 S/U vs Kansas State as 3.5 point or more Dog since 1991
- 6-0 S/U vs Kansas State as 21 point or more favorite since 1984
- 0-17 S/U vs Oklahoma as 14 point or less Dog since 1983
- 26-0 S/U in 1st home game of season since 1996 — CENTRAL MICH
- 10-4-1 O/U in 2nd home game of season since 2006 — ARIZONA STATE
- 8-3 O/U prior to playing Texas Tech since 2010 — Baylor
- 11-2 S/U prior to playing Texas Tech since 2008 — Baylor
- 22-3 ATS prior to playing Texas Tech since 1997 — Baylor
- 10-0 S/U prior to playing TCU since 2012 — TEXAS TECH
- 13-3 S/U prior to playing Texas since 2006 — Tcu
- 11-3 ATS prior to playing Texas since 2008 — Tcu
- 2-12 O/U in 2nd road game of season since 2008 — Tcu
- 11-3 S/U in 2nd road game of season since 2008 — Tcu
- 10-3 S/U after playing Texas since 2008 — Kansas State
- 9-3 S/U after playing Kansas State since 2010 — Kansas
- 7-1 S/U @ home when ranked vs Iowa State all time
- 12-1 S/U when ranked vs Kansas State all time {7-0 on road}
- 3-18 S/U when ranked vs Oklahoma since 1972
- 5-0 S/U vs ranked Iowa State all time
- 6-55 S/U vs ranked Oklahoma all time
- 20-100-1 S/U on road vs ranked teams all time

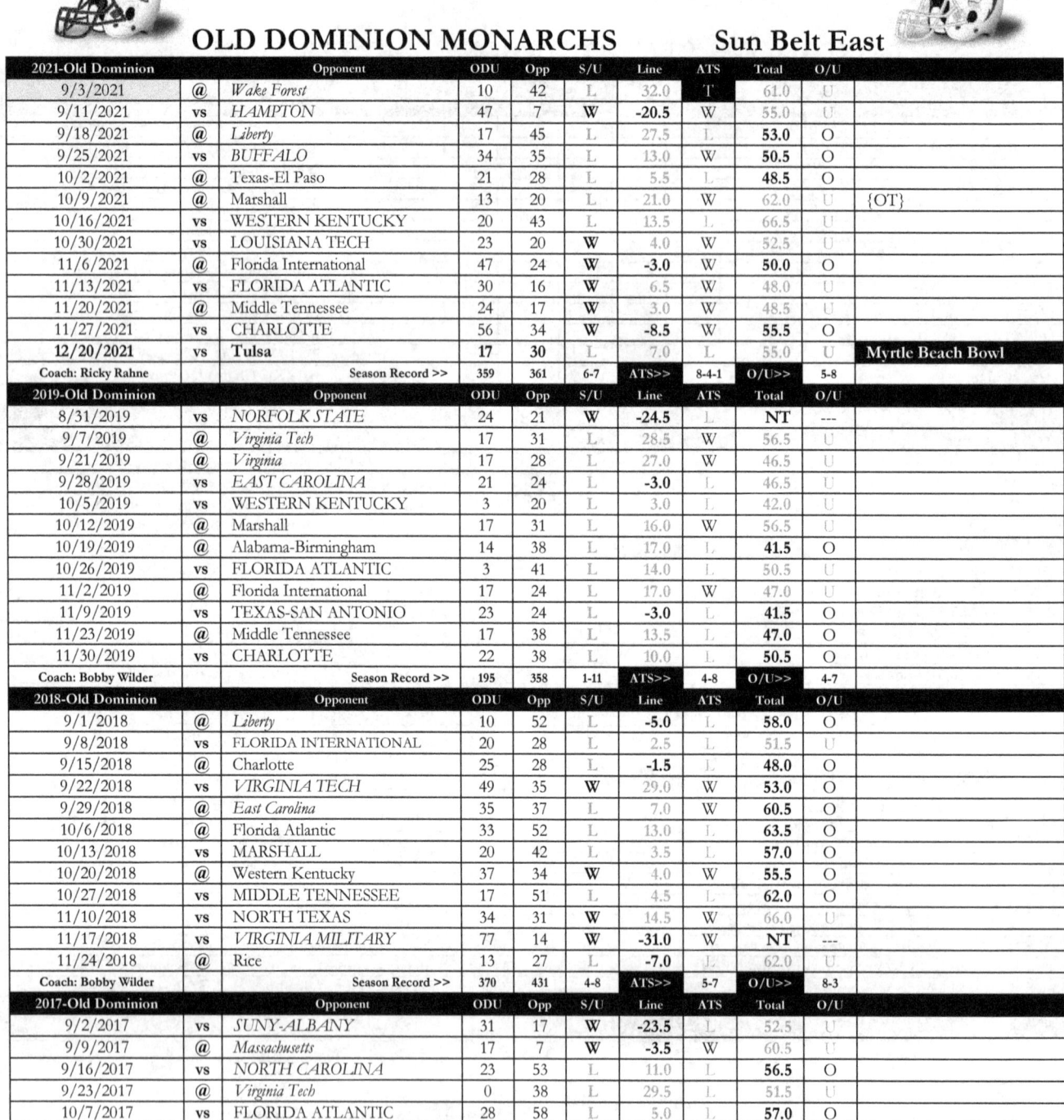

OLD DOMINION MONARCHS — Sun Belt East

2021-Old Dominion		Opponent	ODU	Opp	S/U	Line	ATS	Total	O/U	
9/3/2021	@	Wake Forest	10	42	L	32.0	T	61.0	U	
9/11/2021	vs	HAMPTON	47	7	W	-20.5	W	55.0	U	
9/18/2021	@	Liberty	17	45	L	27.5	L	53.0	O	
9/25/2021	vs	BUFFALO	34	35	L	13.0	W	50.5	O	
10/2/2021	@	Texas-El Paso	21	28	L	5.5	L	48.5	O	
10/9/2021	@	Marshall	13	20	L	21.0	W	62.0	U	{OT}
10/16/2021	vs	WESTERN KENTUCKY	20	43	L	13.5	L	66.5	U	
10/30/2021	vs	LOUISIANA TECH	23	20	W	4.0	W	52.5	U	
11/6/2021	@	Florida International	47	24	W	-3.0	W	50.0	O	
11/13/2021	vs	FLORIDA ATLANTIC	30	16	W	6.5	W	48.0	U	
11/20/2021	@	Middle Tennessee	24	17	W	3.0	W	48.5	U	
11/27/2021	vs	CHARLOTTE	56	34	W	-8.5	W	55.5	O	
12/20/2021	vs	Tulsa	17	30	L	7.0	L	55.0	U	Myrtle Beach Bowl
Coach: Ricky Rahne		Season Record >>	359	361	6-7	ATS>>	8-4-1	O/U>>	5-8	

2019-Old Dominion		Opponent	ODU	Opp	S/U	Line	ATS	Total	O/U	
8/31/2019	vs	NORFOLK STATE	24	21	W	-24.5	L	NT	---	
9/7/2019	@	Virginia Tech	17	31	L	28.5	W	56.5	U	
9/21/2019	@	Virginia	17	28	L	27.0	W	46.5	U	
9/28/2019	vs	EAST CAROLINA	21	24	L	-3.0	L	46.5	U	
10/5/2019	vs	WESTERN KENTUCKY	3	20	L	3.0	L	42.0	U	
10/12/2019	@	Marshall	17	31	L	16.0	W	56.5	U	
10/19/2019	@	Alabama-Birmingham	14	38	L	17.0	L	41.5	O	
10/26/2019	vs	FLORIDA ATLANTIC	3	41	L	14.0	L	50.5	U	
11/2/2019	@	Florida International	17	24	L	17.0	W	47.0	U	
11/9/2019	vs	TEXAS-SAN ANTONIO	23	24	L	-3.0	L	41.5	O	
11/23/2019	@	Middle Tennessee	17	38	L	13.5	L	47.0	U	
11/30/2019	vs	CHARLOTTE	22	38	L	10.0	L	50.5	O	
Coach: Bobby Wilder		Season Record >>	195	358	1-11	ATS>>	4-8	O/U>>	4-7	

2018-Old Dominion		Opponent	ODU	Opp	S/U	Line	ATS	Total	O/U	
9/1/2018	@	Liberty	10	52	L	-5.0	L	58.0	O	
9/8/2018	vs	FLORIDA INTERNATIONAL	20	28	L	2.5	L	51.5	U	
9/15/2018	@	Charlotte	25	28	L	-1.5	L	48.0	O	
9/22/2018	vs	VIRGINIA TECH	49	35	W	29.0	W	53.0	O	
9/29/2018	@	East Carolina	35	37	L	7.0	W	60.5	O	
10/6/2018	@	Florida Atlantic	33	52	L	13.0	L	63.5	O	
10/13/2018	vs	MARSHALL	20	42	L	3.5	L	57.0	O	
10/20/2018	@	Western Kentucky	37	34	W	4.0	W	55.5	O	
10/27/2018	vs	MIDDLE TENNESSEE	17	51	L	4.5	L	62.0	O	
11/10/2018	vs	NORTH TEXAS	34	31	W	14.5	W	66.0	U	
11/17/2018	vs	VIRGINIA MILITARY	77	14	W	-31.0	W	NT	---	
11/24/2018	@	Rice	13	27	L	-7.0	L	62.0	U	
Coach: Bobby Wilder		Season Record >>	370	431	4-8	ATS>>	5-7	O/U>>	8-3	

2017-Old Dominion		Opponent	ODU	Opp	S/U	Line	ATS	Total	O/U	
9/2/2017	vs	SUNY-ALBANY	31	17	W	-23.5	L	52.5	U	
9/9/2017	@	Massachusetts	17	7	W	-3.5	W	60.5	U	
9/16/2017	vs	NORTH CAROLINA	23	53	L	11.0	L	56.5	O	
9/23/2017	@	Virginia Tech	0	38	L	29.5	L	51.5	U	
10/7/2017	vs	FLORIDA ATLANTIC	28	58	L	5.0	L	57.0	O	
10/14/2017	@	Marshall	3	35	L	12.5	L	48.5	U	
10/20/2017	vs	WESTERN KENTUCKY	31	35	L	6.5	W	50.0	O	
10/28/2017	@	North Texas	38	45	L	12.0	W	60.0	O	
11/4/2017	vs	CHARLOTTE	6	0	W	-9.5	L	50.0	U	
11/11/2017	@	Florida International	37	30	W	10.5	W	48.0	O	
11/18/2017	vs	RICE	24	21	W	-7.0	L	51.5	U	
11/25/2017	@	Middle Tennessee	10	41	L	14.0	L	48.5	O	
Coach: Bobby Wilder		Season Record >>	248	380	5-7	ATS>>	4-8	O/U>>	6-6	

OLD DOMINION MONARCHS — Sun Belt East

STADIUM: Foreman Field {22,480}
Location: Norfolk, VA
COACH: Ricky Rahne

DATE		Opponent	ODU	Opp	S/U	Line	ATS	Total	O/U	Trends & Angles
9/3/2022	vs	VIRGINIA TECH								vs Virginia Tech - VPI leads series 2-1
9/10/2022	@	East Carolina								vs East Carolina - ECU leads series 6-3-1
9/17/2022	@	Virginia								vs Virginia - UVA leads series 1-0
9/24/2022	vs	ARKANSAS STATE								1st Meeting
10/1/2022	vs	LIBERTY								vs Liberty - Liberty leads series 2-1
10/15/2022	@	Coastal Carolina								vs Coastal Carolina - ODU leads series 1-0
10/22/2022	vs	GEORGIA SOUTHERN								vs Ga Southern - Ga Southern leads series 2-0
10/29/2022	@	Georgia State								vs Georgia State - ODU leads series 3-0
11/5/2022	vs	MARSHALL								vs Marshall - Marshall leads series 6-1
11/12/2022	vs	JAMES MADISON								vs James Madison - ODU leads series 2-0
11/19/2022	@	Appalachian State								vs App State - App State leads series 1-0
11/26/2022	@	South Alabama								1st Meeting
12/3/2022	vs									C-USA Championship
	vs									BOWL GAME

Pointspread Analysis — Non-Conference
- 1-14 S/U vs Non-conf. as 3.0 point or more Dog since 2014
- 11-3 S/U vs Non-Conf. as 3.0 point or more favorite since 2014

Dog
- 1-21 S/U as 15.5 point or more Dog since 2013
- 1-26 S/U on road as 10.5 or more Dog since 2013

Favorite
- 2-7 ATS as 3.0-10 point favorite since 2017
- 11-0 S/U as 10.5 point favorite since 2013
- 17-3 S/U @ home as 3 point or more favorite since 2014

Pointspread Analysis — Conference

VIRGINIA TECH — 9-1 S/U in 1st home game of season since 2011
JAMES MADISON — 10-2 S/U in final home game of season since 2009

This book is for football fans of all ages. It is both educational and entertaining as you can read nostalgically about former great College teams and players, as well as some of the great Bowl Games from the past. This book covers all the Bowl Games of the 20th Century (1902-1999), so you can read about your football heroes, past and present.

College Football History "Bowl Games of the 20th Century"

8.5" x 11" {596 pages}

$39.95

These books available at numerous online retailers

OREGON DUCKS   PACIFIC-12 North

2021-Oregon		Opponent	ORE	Opp	S/U	Line	ATS	Total	O/U	
9/4/2021	vs	FRESNO STATE	31	24	W	-18.0	L	62.0	U	
9/11/2021	@	Ohio State	35	28	W	15.0	W	65.0	U	
9/18/2021	vs	SUNY-STONY BROOK	48	7	W	-42.0	L	54.0	O	
9/25/2021	vs	ARIZONA	41	19	W	-30.0	L	59.0	O	
10/2/2021	@	Stanford	24	31	L	-8.5	L	57.5	U	{2 OT}
10/15/2021	vs	CALIFORNIA	24	17	W	-13.5	L	53.5	U	
10/23/2021	@	Ucla	34	31	W	PK	W	62.5	O	
10/30/2021	@	Colorado	52	29	W	-24.5	L	49.5	O	
11/6/2021	@	Washington	26	16	W	-7.0	W	48.5	U	
11/13/2021	vs	WASHINGTON STATE	38	24	W	-13.5	W	58.5	O	
11/20/2021	@	Utah	7	38	L	3.0	L	58.5	U	
11/27/2021	vs	OREGON STATE	38	29	W	-7.0	W	61.5	O	"Civil War" (Platypus Trophy)
12/4/2021	vs	Utah	10	38	L	3.0	L	48.0	U	PAC-12 CHAMPIONSHIP GAME
12/29/2021	vs	Oklahoma	32	47	L	7.0	L	64.5	O	Alamo Bowl
Coach: Mario Cristobal		Season Record >>	440	378	10-4	ATS>>	5-9	O/U>>	7-7	

2020-Oregon		Opponent	ORE	Opp	S/U	Line	ATS	Total	O/U	
11/7/2020	vs	STANFORD	35	14	W	-12.5	W	49.0	T	
11/14/2020	@	Washington State	43	29	W	-10.0	W	58.5	O	
11/20/2020	vs	UCLA	38	35	W	-18.0	L	62.0	O	
11/27/2020	@	Oregon State	38	41	L	-13.0	L	64.5	O	"Civil War" (Platypus Trophy)
12/5/2020	@	California	17	21	L	-8.0	L	59.0	U	
12/18/2020	@	Usc	31	24	W	3.0	W	65.5	U	PAC-12 Championship
1/2/2021	vs	Iowa State	17	34	L	4.0	L	57.5	U	Fiesta Bowl
Coach: Mario Cristobal		Season Record >>	219	198	4-3	ATS>>	3-4	O/U>>	3-3-1	PAC-12 Champions

2019-Oregon		Opponent	ORE	Opp	S/U	Line	ATS	Total	O/U	
8/31/2019	vs	Auburn	21	27	L	3.5	L	55.5	U	AT&T Stadium
9/7/2019	vs	MONTANA	77	6	W	-24.5	W	61.5	O	
9/14/2019	vs	NEVADA	35	3	W	-38.0	L	NT	---	
9/21/2019	@	Stanford	21	6	W	-12.5	W	55.5	U	
10/5/2019	vs	CALIFORNIA	17	7	W	-21.5	L	46.5	U	
10/12/2019	vs	COLORADO	45	3	W	-22.5	W	62.0	U	
10/19/2019	@	Washington	35	31	W	-2.5	W	48.5	O	
10/26/2019	vs	WASHINGTON STATE	37	35	W	-19.5	L	67.5	O	
11/2/2019	@	Usc	56	24	W	-3.5	W	60.0	O	
11/16/2019	vs	ARIZONA	34	6	W	-27.0	W	68.5	U	
11/23/2019	@	Arizona State	28	31	L	-13.5	L	55.0	O	
11/30/2019	vs	OREGON STATE	24	10	W	-20.5	L	65.0	U	"Civil War" (Platypus Trophy)
12/6/2019	vs	Utah	37	15	W	6.5	W	45.0	O	PAC-12 Championship
1/1/2020	vs	Wisconsin	28	27	W	3.0	W	52.5	O	Rose Bowl
Coach: Mario Cristobal		Season Record >>	495	231	12-2	ATS>>	8-6	O/U>>	7-6	PAC-12 Champions

2018-Oregon		Opponent	ORE	Opp	S/U	Line	ATS	Total	O/U	
9/1/2018	vs	BOWLING GREEN	58	24	W	-34.0	T	70.0	O	
9/8/2018	vs	PORTLAND STATE	62	14	W	-49.5	L	NT	---	
9/15/2018	vs	SAN JOSE STATE	35	22	W	-42.5	L	69.5	U	
9/22/2018	vs	STANFORD	31	38	L	3.0	L	59.0	O	{OT}
9/29/2018	@	California	42	24	W	-2.0	W	57.5	O	
10/13/2018	vs	WASHINGTON	30	27	W	3.5	W	58.0	U	{OT}
10/20/2018	@	Washington State	20	34	L	3.0	L	69.5	U	
10/27/2018	@	Arizona	15	44	L	-7.5	L	66.0	U	
11/3/2018	vs	UCLA	42	21	W	-11.0	W	59.0	O	
11/10/2018	@	Utah	25	32	L	6.0	L	51.0	O	
11/17/2018	vs	ARIZONA STATE	31	29	W	-3.5	L	66.0	U	
11/24/2018	@	Oregon State	55	15	W	-17.5	W	70.0	T	"Civil War" (Platypus Trophy)
12/31/2018	vs	Michigan State	7	6	W	1.5	W	47.0	U	Redbox Bowl
Coach: Mario Cristobal		Season Record >>	453	330	9-4	ATS>>	5-7-1	O/U>>	5-6-1	

- 45-4 S/U @ home when ranked since 2012
- 9-1 S/U on road when #2 ranked since 2012
- 8-0 S/U when ranked vs California since 2010
- 13-0 S/U & ATS when ranked vs Washington since 2005
- 0-11 S/U vs #1 ranked teams all time
- 0-5 S/U on road vs #2 ranked teams all time
- 0-6 S/U on road vs #5 ranked teams all time
- 1-8 S/U @ ranked California all time

OREGON DUCKS   PACIFIC-12 North

STADIUM: Autzen Stadium {54,000}   **Location:** Eugene, OR   **COACH:** Dan Lanning

DATE		Opponent	Ore	Opp	S/U	Line	ATS	Total	O/U	Trends & Angles
9/3/2022	vs	*Georgia {@ Atlanta}*								vs Georgia - Georgia leads series 1-0
9/10/2022	vs	*EASTERN WASHINGTON*								vs Eastern Wash - Oregon leads series 1-0
9/17/2022	vs	BYU								vs BYU - Series tied 3-3
9/24/2022	@	Washington State								2-8 ATS vs Wash State as favorite since 2010
10/1/2022	vs	STANFORD								7-1 S/U @ home vs Stanford as favorite since 2002
10/8/2022	@	Arizona								vs Arizona - Oregon leads series 28-17
10/22/2022	vs	ULCA								7-0 S/U @ home vs UCLA since 2006
10/29/2022	@	California								7-2 S/U @ California as favorite since 1995
11/5/2022	@	Colorado								7-1 S/U vs Colorado as favorite since 2011 {6-2 ATS}
11/12/2022	vs	WASHINGTON								8-1 S/U & ATS @ home vs Washington since 2004
11/19/2022	vs	UTAH								4-0 S/U @ home vs Utah as favorite since 1997
11/25/2022	@	Oregon State								6-2 ATS @ Oregon State since 2006
12/2/2022	vs									PAC-12 Championship
	vs									BOWL GAME

Pointspread Analysis — Non-Conference
- 0-6 S/U vs Non-Conf. as 15.5 point or more Dog since 1983
- 1-8 O/U vs Non-Conf. as 3 point or less Dog since 1990
- 10-1 S/U vs Non-conf. as 10.5-15 point favorite since 1999
- 42-1 S/U vs Non-Conf. as 15.5 point or more favorite since 1985

Dog
- 2-8 S/U as 20.5 point or more Dog since 1983
- 2-11 S/U as 15.5-20 point Dog since 1984
- 2-9 S/U as 10.5-15 point Dog since 1987
- 3-12 S/U on road as 3.5-7 point Dog since 1996
- 11-4-1 ATS on road as 3 point or less Dog since 1999

Favorite
- 16-2 S/U @ home as 3 point or less favorite since 1985
- 15-3 ATS @ home as 3 point or less favorite since 1985
- 20-2 S/U on road as 3.5-7 point favorite since 1993
- 12-3 O/U on road as 3.5-7 point favorite since 2000
- 6-0 S/U @ home as 7.5-10 point favorite since 2003
- 9-3 S/U on road as 7.5-10 point favorite since 2000
- 13-5 S/U on road as 10.5-15 point favorite since 1992
- 10-1-1 O/U @ home as 10.5-15 point favorite since 2007
- 25-4 S/U @ home as 15.5-20 point favorite since 1985
- 8-1 S/U on road as 15.5-20 point favorite since 2007
- 11-0 S/U on road as 20.5 point or more favorite since 1990
- 52-1 S/U @ home as 20.5 point or more favorite since 1990

Bowl Games
- 1-6 O/U in Bowl Games as 3 point or less Dog since 1999
- 1-4 S/U & ATS in Bowl Games as 3.5-7 point favorite since 1998
- 3-0 S/U in Bowl Games as 10.5-15 point favorite since 1989

Pointspread Analysis — Conference
- 1-7 O/U vs Arizona as favorite since 2012
- 11-1 S/U @ home vs California as favorite since 1989 {8-4 ATS}
- vs California - Series tied 41-41-2
- vs Colorado - Oregon leads series 14-9
- Game 14-4-2 O/U vs Oregon State since 2002
- vs Oregon State - Oregon leads series 67-49-9
- 12-2 S/U vs Oregon State since 2008
- Game 8-1 O/U @ home vs Oregon State since 2005
- Game 6-1-1 O/U @ home vs Stanford since 2006
- vs Stanford - Stanford leads series 50-34-1
- Game 8-1 O/U @ home vs Oregon State since 2005
- 9-1 S/U vs UCLA since 2008
- 0-4 S/U @ home vs UCLA as Dog since 1983
- vs Ucla - UCLA leads series 40-31
- 8-0 S/U vs UCLA as favorite since 2008
- vs Utah - Oregon leads series 23-12
- 5-1 S/U @ home vs Utah since 1997
- 15-2 S/U & ATS vs Washington since 2004
- vs Washington - Washington leads series 59-48-6
- 16-1 S/U vs Washington as favorite since 1988
- Game 4-1 O/U @ home vs Washington since 2010
- vs Washington State - Oregon leads series 52-40-7
- 2-10 ATS vs Washington State since 2010
- Game 5-2 O/U @ home vs Wazzu since 2009
- 9-0 S/U vs California as 13 point or more favorite since 2000
- 19-2-1 S/U vs Oregon State as 9.5 point or more favorite since 1983
- 1-6 S/U vs Stanford as 5.5 point or more Dog since 1986
- 1-8 S/U vs Washington as 10 point or more Dog since 1983
- 10-0 S/U vs Wash. State as 16 point or more favorite since 1999

17-0 S/U in 1st home game of season since 2005	EASTERN WASH	10-1-1 O/U in 1st home game of season since 2009
11-1 S/U prior to playing Washington State since 2009	BYU	26-0 S/U in 2nd home game of season since 1996
1-7 ATS prior to playing Arizona since 2010	STANFORD	10-2 S/U prior to playing Arizona since 2007
12-2 S/U after playing Stanford since 2008	Arizona	17-5 S/U in 2nd road game of season since 2000
1-9 ATS prior to playing UCLA since 2006	Arizona	16-6 ATS in 2nd road game of season since 2000
11-5 ATS prior to playing California since 2006	UCLA	9-1 S/U after playing Arizona since 2008
13-2 O/U prior to playing California since 2007	UCLA	14-4 S/U prior to playing California since 2004
	California	11-1-1 O/U after playing UCLA since 2002
11-2 S/U prior to playing Washington since 2007	Colorado	16-2 S/U after playing California since 2005
	Colorado	9-1-1 ATS prior to playing Washington since 2010
	WASHINGTON	3-7 ATS prior to playing Utah since 2001
14-4 O/U in final home game of season since 2004	UTAH	12-2 S/U in final home game of season since 2008
	Oregon State	1-7 O/U after playing Utah since 2008

OREGON STATE BEAVERS   PACIFIC-12 North

2021-Oregon State		Opponent	State	Opp	S/U	Line	ATS	Total	O/U	
9/4/2021	@	Purdue	21	30	L	7.0	L	67.0	U	
9/11/2021	vs	HAWAII	45	27	W	-11.0	W	65.5	O	
9/18/2021	vs	IDAHO	42	0	W	-28.5	W	63.5	U	
9/25/2021	@	Usc	45	27	W	10.0	W	63.5	O	
10/2/2021	vs	WASHINGTON	27	24	W	-2.5	W	58.0	U	
10/9/2021	@	Washington State	24	31	L	-4.5	L	59.0	U	
10/23/2021	vs	UTAH	42	34	W	3.0	W	57.0	O	
10/30/2021	@	California	25	39	L	-2.5	L	56.5	O	
11/6/2021	@	Colorado	34	37	L	-11.5	L	55.5	O	
11/13/2021	vs	STANFORD	35	14	W	-13.0	W	56.0	U	
11/20/2021	vs	ARIZONA STATE	24	10	W	3.0	W	59.0	U	
11/27/2021	@	Oregon	29	38	L	7.0	L	61.5	O	"Civil War" (Platypus Trophy)
12/18/2021	vs	**Utah State**	**13**	**24**	L	**-6.0**	L	69.0	U	Los Angeles Bowl
Coach: Jonathan Smith		Season Record >>	406	335	7-6	ATS>>	7-6	O/U>>	6-7	

2020-Oregon State		Opponent	State	Opp	S/U	Line	ATS	Total	O/U	
11/7/2020	vs	WASHINGTON STATE	28	38	L	-3.5	L	64.0	O	
11/14/2020	@	Washington	21	27	L	13.5	W	51.0	U	
11/21/2020	vs	CALIFORNIA	31	27	W	1.0	W	46.5	O	
11/27/2020	vs	OREGON	41	38	W	13.0	W	64.5	O	"Civil War" (Platypus Trophy)
12/5/2020	@	Utah	24	30	L	13.5	W	51.0	O	
12/12/2020	vs	STANFORD	24	27	L	2.0	L	55.5	U	
12/19/2020	vs	ARIZONA STATE	33	46	L	7.5	L	54.5	O	
Coach: Jonathan Smith		Season Record >>	202	233	2-5	ATS>>	4-3	O/U>>	5-2	

2019-Oregon State		Opponent	State	Opp	S/U	Line	ATS	Total	O/U	
8/30/2019	vs	OKLAHOMA STATE	36	52	L	13.0	L	72.5	O	
9/7/2019	@	Hawaii	28	31	L	7.0	W	77.0	U	
9/14/2019	vs	CAL POLY-SLO	45	7	W	-16.5	W	NT	---	
9/28/2019	vs	STANFORD	28	31	L	3.0	T	55.5	O	
10/5/2019	@	Ucla	48	31	W	4.5	W	63.5	O	
10/12/2019	vs	UTAH	7	52	L	15.0	L	59.5	O	
10/19/2019	@	California	21	17	W	11.0	W	51.0	U	
11/2/2019	@	Arizona	56	38	W	5.0	W	71.5	O	
11/9/2019	vs	WASHINGTON	7	19	L	10.5	L	64.5	U	
11/16/2019	vs	ARIZONA STATE	35	34	W	1.5	W	56.5	O	
11/23/2019	vs	Washington State	53	54	L	10.5	W	77.5	O	
11/30/2019	@	Oregon	10	24	L	20.5	W	65.0	U	"Civil War" (Platypus Trophy)
Coach: Jonathan Smith		Season Record >>	374	390	5-7	ATS>>	8-3-1	O/U>>	6-5	

2018-Oregon State		Opponent	State	Opp	S/U	Line	ATS	Total	O/U	
9/1/2018	@	Ohio State	31	77	L	40.0	L	63.0	O	
9/8/2018	vs	SOUTHERN UTAH	48	25	W	-13.0	W	NT	---	
9/15/2018	@	Nevada	35	37	L	3.5	W	67.5	O	
9/22/2018	vs	ARIZONA	14	35	L	4.0	L	73.5	U	
9/29/2018	@	Arizona State	24	52	L	22.0	L	64.5	O	
10/6/2018	vs	WASHINGTON STATE	37	56	L	18.5	L	64.5	O	
10/20/2018	vs	CALIFORNIA	7	49	L	8.5	L	58.5	U	
10/27/2018	@	Colorado	41	34	W	24.5	W	60.0	O	{OT}
11/3/2018	vs	USC	21	38	L	15.0	L	65.5	U	
11/10/2018	@	Stanford	17	48	L	24.0	L	60.5	O	
11/17/2018	@	Washington	23	42	L	32.5	W	58.5	O	
11/23/2018	vs	OREGON	15	55	L	17.5	L	70.0	T	"Civil War" (Platypus Trophy)
Coach: Jonathan Smith		Season Record >>	313	548	2-10	ATS>>	4-8	O/U>>	7-3-1	

OREGON STATE BEAVERS — PACIFIC-12 North

STADIUM: Reser Stadium {43,363} **Location:** Corvallis, OR **COACH:** Jonathan Smith

DATE		Opponent	OSU	Opp	S/U	Line	ATS	Total	O/U	Trends & Angles
9/3/2022	vs	BOISE STATE								0-4 S/U vs Boise State as Dog since 2004
9/10/2022	@	FRESNO STATE								vs Fresno State - Fresno leads series 8-5
9/17/2022	vs	MONTANA STATE {@ Portland}								2-8 O/U prior to playing USC since 2006
9/24/2022	vs	USC								5-1 ATS @ home vs USC as Dog since 2000
10/1/2022	@	Utah								2-8 S/U vs Utah as Dog since 1992
10/8/2022	@	Stanford								0-6 S/U @ Stanford since 2008 {1-5 ATS}
10/15/2022	vs	WASHINGTON STATE								0-8 S/U vs Wash State since 2014 {2-6 ATS}
10/22/2022	vs	COLORADO								1-4 S/U vs Colorado as Dog since 1983
11/5/2022	@	Washington								0-6 S/U @ Washington since 2010
11/12/2022	vs	CALIFORNIA								8-1 S/U vs California as favorite since 1999
11/19/2022	@	Arizona State								1-15 S/U @ Arizona State as Dog since 1983
11/25/2022	vs	OREGON								vs Oregon - Oregon leads series 67-49-9
12/2/2022	vs									PAC-12 Championship
	vs									BOWL GAME

Pointspread Analysis — Non-Conference
- 1-14 S/U vs Non-conf. as 15.5 point or more Dog since 1984
- 1-10 S/U vs Non-Conf. as 10.5-15 point Dog since 1986
- 14-3 S/U vs Non-Conf. as 3.5-7 point favorite since 1994
- 17-2 S/U vs Non-Conf. as 15.5 point or more favorite since 1994
- 3-0 S/U vs Boise State as favorite since 2003

Dog
- 1-11 S/U as 30.5 point or more Dog since 1985
- 9-3 ATS as 30.5 point or more Dog since 1985
- 0-13 S/U as 25.5-30 point Dog since 1983
- 1-23 S/U on road as 20.5-25 point Dog since 1983
- 2-11 S/U @ home as 20.5-25 point Dog since 1983
- 1-17 S/U @ home as 15.5-20 point Dog since 1985
- 2-26 S/U on road as 15.5-20 point Dog since 1983
- 2-35 S/U on road as 10.5-15 point Dog since 1984
- 3-14 S/U @ home as 10.5-15 point Dog since 1992
- 8-3 O/U @ home as 10.5-15 point Dog since 2006
- 1-6 S/U as 7.5-10 point Dog since 2015
- 5-14 S/U on road as 7.5-10 point Dog since 1995
- 3-11 S/U @ home as 3.5-7 point Dog since 1994
- 2-12 S/U as 3.5-7 point Dog since 2012
- 45-208-4 S/U as 3.5 point or more Dog since 1983
- 10-2 S/U on road as 3 point or less Dog since 1999
- 11-1 ATS on road as 3 point or less Dog since 1999
- 5-0 O/U on road as 3 point or less Dog since 2010

Favorite
- 5-13 ATS as 3 point or less favorite since 2006
- 2-6-1 O/U on road as 3 point or less favorite since 2002
- 18-5 S/U @ home as 3.5-7 point favorite since 1994
- 0-8 ATS on road as 3.5-7 point favorite since 2000
- 9-2 S/U as 7.5-10 point favorite since 2004
- 15-1 S/U @ home as 10.5-15 point favorite since 1993
- 12-0 S/U as 15.5-20 point favorite since 1994
- 1-6 ATS @ home as 20.5 point favorite since 2013

Bowl Games
- 5-1 S/U in Bowl Games as 3.5-7 point favorite since 2001

- 6-76 S/U on road vs ranked teams since 1970
- 1-10 S/U @ home vs ranked teams since 2012
- 0-11 S/U vs #3 ranked teams all time
- 0-4 S/U @ home vs ranked California all time
- 0-11 S/U vs ranked Stanford since 1969
- 0-9 S/U @ ranked Washington since 1955

Pointspread Analysis — Conference
- 5-0 S/U vs Arizona State as favorite since 2003
- vs California - California leads series 39-35
- vs Stanford - Stanford leads series 59-26-3
- 1-11 S/U vs Stanford since 2010 {3-8-1 ATS}
- 0-10 S/U @ Stanford as Dog since 1990
- vs USC - USC leads series 63-12-4
- Game 1-5 O/U vs USC since 2010
- 5-2 ATS @ home vs USC since 2000
- vs Utah - Oregon State leads series 12-11-1
- 1-5 S/U vs Utah since 2014
- 1-5 S/U @ Utah since 1992 {4-2 ATS}
- vs Washington - Washington leads series 66-35-4
- 1-11 S/U @ Washington as Dog since 1987
- 1-9 S/U vs Washington since 2012
- 6-1 S/U & ATS vs Washington as favorite since 2004
- vs Washington State - Washington State leads series 56-47-3
- 1-8 S/U @ home vs Washington State as Dog since 1983
- Game 8-1 O/U vs Washington State since 2013
- 1-5 ATS @ home vs Washington State since 2010
- 1-15 S/U vs Arizona State as 9 point or more Dog since 1983
- 2-19 S/U vs Oregon as 9.5 point or more Dog since 1985
- 0-15 S/U vs Stanford as 10 point or more Dog since 1985
- 5-0 S/U vs Stanford as 9.5 point or more favorite since 2003
- 1-18 S/U vs USC as 12 point or more Dog since 1983
- 0-16 S/U vs Washington as 10 point or more Dog since 1986
- 0-19 S/U vs Washington State as 7.5 point or more Dog since 1983
- 3-0 S/U & ATS @ Wazzu as 3 point or less Dog since 2013

BOISE STATE	3-9 ATS in 1st home game of season since 2010
BOISE STATE	16-4 S/U in 1st home game of season since 2002
Utah	10-4 ATS prior to playing Stanford since 2007
Stanford	12-2 O/U prior to playing Washington State since 2007
WASH STATE	3-12 S/U after playing Stanford since 2007
WASH STATE	1-5 O/U prior to playing Colorado since 2014
Washington	2-10 S/U prior to playing California since 2010
CALIFORNIA	2-7 S/U after playing Washington since 2013
Arizona State	9-2 O/U in final road game of season since 2011
Arizona State	0-13 S/U in final road game of season since 2009

- 0-7 S/U on road when ranked vs ranked teams since 1968
- 0-8 S/U when ranked vs ranked teams since 2009
- 4-0 S/U when ranked vs Washington State since 1962
- 0-4 S/U when ranked vs Washington since 2000
- 0-4 S/U when ranked @ Washington since 1940
- 0-11 S/U vs #4 ranked teams all time

PENN STATE NITTANY LIONS — BIG TEN East

2021-Penn State		Opponent	State	Opp	S/U	Line	ATS	Total	O/U	
9/4/2021	@	Wisconsin	16	10	W	5.0	W	48.5	U	
9/11/2021	vs	BALL STATE	44	13	W	-22.5	W	58.0	U	
9/18/2021	vs	AUBURN	28	20	W	-4.0	W	52.0	U	
9/25/2021	vs	VILLANOVA	38	17	W	-28.5	L	53.0	O	
10/2/2021	vs	INDIANA	24	0	W	-12.0	W	54.5	U	
10/9/2021	@	Iowa	20	23	L	2.5	L	41.0	O	
10/23/2021	vs	ILLINOIS	18	20	L	-24.5	L	45.5	U	{9 OT}
10/30/2021	@	Ohio State	24	33	L	19.0	W	60.5	U	
11/6/2021	@	Maryland	31	14	W	-10.0	W	56.0	U	
11/13/2021	vs	MICHIGAN	17	21	L	2.5	L	48.0	U	
11/20/2021	vs	RUTGERS	28	0	W	-14.0	W	45.0	U	
11/27/2021	@	Michigan State	27	30	L	-3.5	L	51.5	O	"Land Grant Trophy"
1/1/2022	vs	Arkansas	10	24	L	3.5	L	51.5	U	Outback Bowl
Coach: James Franklin		Season Record >>	325	225	7-6	ATS>>	7-6	O/U>>	3-10	

2020-Penn State		Opponent	State	Opp	S/U	Line	ATS	Total	O/U	
10/24/2020	@	Indiana	35	36	L	-6.5	L	61.5	O	{OT}
10/31/2020	vs	OHIO STATE	23	38	L	10.0	L	63.0	U	
11/7/2020	vs	MARYLAND	19	35	L	-27.0	L	62.5	U	
11/14/2020	@	Nebraska	23	30	L	-2.5	L	57.5	U	
11/21/2020	vs	IOWA	21	41	L	1.0	L	45.5	O	
11/28/2020	@	Michigan	27	17	W	PK	W	56.0	U	
12/5/2020	@	Rutgers	23	7	W	-13.0	W	51.5	U	
12/12/2020	vs	MICHIGAN STATE	39	24	W	-14.5	W	46.5	O	"Land Grant Trophy"
12/19/2020	vs	ILLINOIS	56	21	W	-16.0	W	53.5	O	
Coach: James Franklin		Season Record >>	266	249	4-5	ATS>>	4-5	O/U>>	4-5	

2019-Penn State		Opponent	State	Opp	S/U	Line	ATS	Total	O/U	
8/31/2019	vs	IDAHO	79	7	W	-41.5	W	NT	---	
9/7/2019	vs	BUFFALO	45	13	W	-31.5	W	55.0	O	
9/14/2019	vs	PITTSBURGH	17	10	W	-17.0	L	53.0	U	
9/27/2019	@	Maryland	59	0	W	-6.5	W	61.0	U	
10/5/2019	vs	PURDUE	35	7	W	-28.5	L	55.0	U	
10/12/2019	@	Iowa	17	12	W	-3.5	L	43.5	U	
10/19/2019	vs	MICHIGAN	28	21	W	-7.5	L	46.5	O	
10/26/2019	@	Michigan State	28	7	W	-4.5	W	42.0	U	"Land Grant Trophy"
11/9/2019	@	Minnesota	26	31	L	-5.5	L	48.5	O	"Governor's Victory Bell"
11/16/2019	vs	INDIANA	34	27	W	-14.5	L	55.0	O	
11/23/2019	@	Ohio State	17	28	L	19.5	W	58.0	U	
11/30/2019	vs	RUTGERS	27	6	W	-39.0	L	50.5	U	
12/28/2019	vs	Memphis	53	39	W	-6.5	W	59.0	O	Cotton Bowl
Coach: James Franklin		Season Record >>	465	208	11-2	ATS>>	7-6	O/U>>	5-7	

2018-Penn State		Opponent	State	Opp	S/U	Line	ATS	Total	O/U	
9/1/2018	vs	APPALACHIAN STATE	45	38	W	-24.0	L	54.0	O	{OT}
9/8/2018	@	Pittsburgh	51	6	W	-7.0	W	50.0	O	
9/15/2018	vs	KENT STATE	63	10	W	-35.0	W	63.0	O	
9/22/2018	@	Illinois	63	24	W	-27.0	W	60.0	O	
9/29/2018	vs	OHIO STATE	26	27	L	3.5	W	69.5	U	
10/13/2018	vs	MICHIGAN STATE	17	21	L	-13.5	L	53.5	U	"Land Grant Trophy"
10/19/2019	@	Indiana	33	28	W	-14.0	L	57.0	O	
10/27/2018	vs	IOWA	30	24	W	-5.5	W	52.0	U	
11/3/2018	@	Michigan	7	42	L	11.0	L	49.5	U	
11/10/2018	vs	WISCONSIN	22	10	W	-7.5	W	54.0	U	
11/17/2018	@	Rutgers	20	7	W	-28.0	L	51.5	U	
11/24/2018	vs	MARYLAND	38	3	W	-12.0	W	50.5	U	
1/1/2019	vs	Kentucky	24	27	L	-4.5	L	47.5	O	Citrus Bowl
Coach: James Franklin		Season Record >>	439	267	9-4	ATS>>	7-6	O/U>>	7-6	

PENN STATE NITTANY LIONS — BIG TEN East

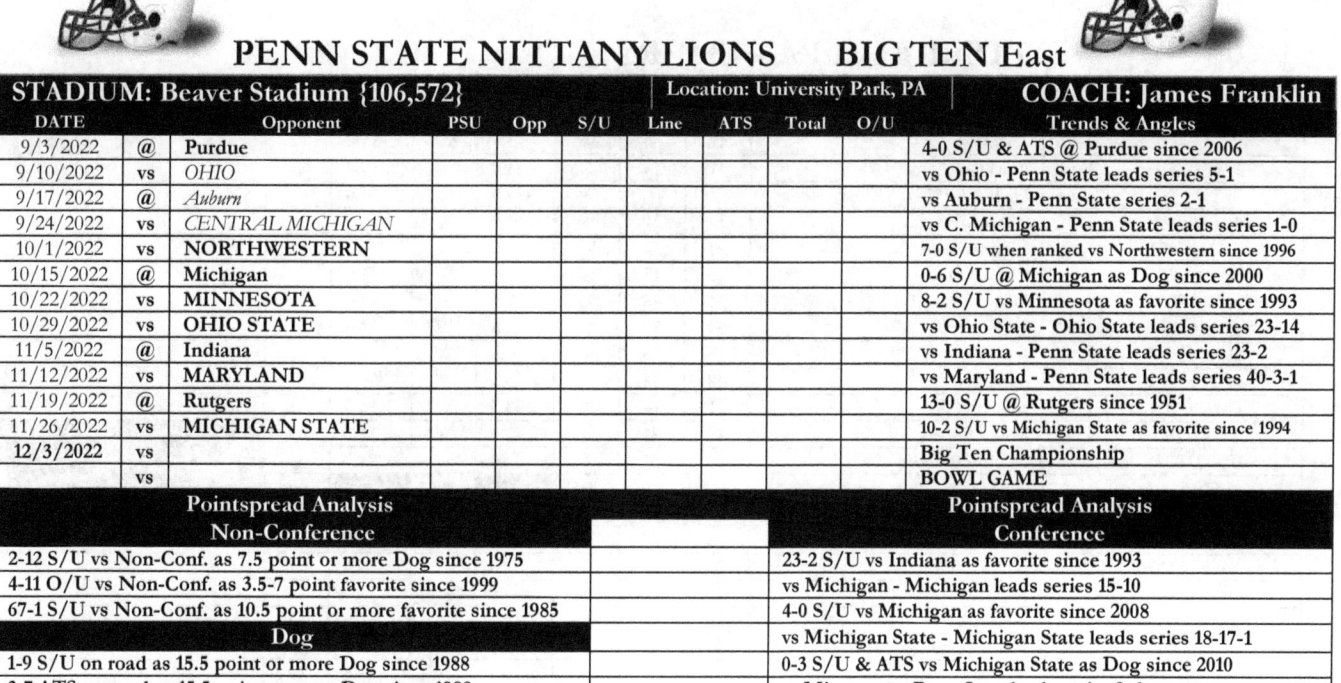

STADIUM: Beaver Stadium {106,572}   **Location:** University Park, PA   **COACH:** James Franklin

DATE		Opponent	PSU	Opp	S/U	Line	ATS	Total	O/U	Trends & Angles
9/3/2022	@	Purdue								4-0 S/U & ATS @ Purdue since 2006
9/10/2022	vs	OHIO								vs Ohio - Penn State leads series 5-1
9/17/2022	@	Auburn								vs Auburn - Penn State series 2-1
9/24/2022	vs	CENTRAL MICHIGAN								vs C. Michigan - Penn State leads series 1-0
10/1/2022	vs	NORTHWESTERN								7-0 S/U when ranked vs Northwestern since 1996
10/15/2022	@	Michigan								0-6 S/U @ Michigan as Dog since 2000
10/22/2022	vs	MINNESOTA								8-2 S/U vs Minnesota as favorite since 1993
10/29/2022	vs	OHIO STATE								vs Ohio State - Ohio State leads series 23-14
11/5/2022	@	Indiana								vs Indiana - Penn State leads series 23-2
11/12/2022	vs	MARYLAND								vs Maryland - Penn State leads series 40-3-1
11/19/2022	@	Rutgers								13-0 S/U @ Rutgers since 1951
11/26/2022	vs	MICHIGAN STATE								10-2 S/U vs Michigan State as favorite since 1994
12/3/2022	vs									Big Ten Championship
	vs									BOWL GAME

Pointspread Analysis — Non-Conference

- 2-12 S/U vs Non-Conf. as 7.5 point or more Dog since 1975
- 4-11 O/U vs Non-Conf. as 3.5-7 point favorite since 1999
- 67-1 S/U vs Non-Conf. as 10.5 point or more favorite since 1985

Dog
- 1-9 S/U on road as 15.5 point or more Dog since 1988
- 3-7 ATS on road as 15.5 point or more Dog since 1988
- 0-4 S/U @ home as 10.5-15 point Dog since 2001
- 1-10 S/U on road as 10.5-15 point Dog since 1988
- 0-11 S/U on road as 7.5-10 point Dog since 1991
- 2-10 S/U on road as 3.5-7 point Dog since 2000

Favorite
- 3-9 O/U @ home as 3.5-7 point favorite since 2011
- 5-1 O/U on road as 7.5-10 point favorite since 2007
- 11-3 S/U on road as 7.5-10 point favorite since 1983
- 44-0 S/U on road as 10.5 point or more favorite since 1983
- 33-4 S/U @ home as 10.5-15 point favorite since 1985
- 33-2 S/U @ home as 15.5-20 point favorite since 1984
- 64-2 S/U @ home as 20.5 point or more favorite since 1986

Bowl Games
- 7-0 S/U & ATS in Fiesta Bowl
- 3-0 S/U in Liberty Bowl
- 3-0 O/U in Rose Bowl since 1995
- 3-0 S/U & ATS vs Tennessee in Bowl Games
- 0-3 S/U vs Florida in Bowl Games
- 4-1 S/U in Orange Bowl
- 2-8 S/U in Bowl Games as 3.5-7 point Dog since 1976
- 6-0 S/U in Bowl Games as 3 point or less favorite since 1979
- 4-0-2 ATS in Bowl Games as 3 point or less favorite since 1979
- 3-0 S/U in Bowl Games as 7.5-10 point favorite since 1977

- 4-0 S/U @ home when ranked vs Northwestern all time
- 0-13 S/U when ranked vs Top #5 ranked Ohio State all time
- 10-0 S/U when ranked vs Purdue all time
- 17-1 S/U when ranked vs Rutgers all time {6-0 on road}
- 0-5 S/U & ATS vs ranked Michigan State since 2010
- 0-5 S/U @ ranked Michigan since 1998

Pointspread Analysis — Conference

- 23-2 S/U vs Indiana as favorite since 1993
- vs Michigan - Michigan leads series 15-10
- 4-0 S/U vs Michigan as favorite since 2008
- vs Michigan State - Michigan State leads series 18-17-1
- 0-3 S/U & ATS vs Michigan State as Dog since 2010
- vs Minnesota - Penn State leads series 9-6
- 4-1 S/U vs Ohio State as favorite since 1994
- 9-0 S/U vs Purdue since 2005
- vs Purdue - Penn State leads series 15-3-1
- 14-0 S/U vs Purdue as favorite since 1995
- 15-0 S/U vs Rutgers since 1989
- Game 0-8 O/U vs Rutgers since 2014
- vs Rutgers - Penn State leads series 30-2
- 20-1 S/U vs Rutgers as favorite since 1983
- 13-1-1 S/U vs Maryland as 5.5 point or more favorite since 1984
- 0-8 S/U vs Michigan as 3.5 point or more Dog since 2000
- 8-0 S/U vs Northwestern as 14.5 point or more favorite since 1993
- 5-0 ATS vs Northwestern as 14.5 point or more favorite since 1998
- 1-13 S/U vs Ohio State as 7 point or more Dog since 1996
- 1-6 S/U vs Ohio State as 4.5 point or less Dog since 1993

OHIO	18-2 S/U in 1st home game of season since 2002
CENTRAL MICH	15-3 S/U in 2nd home game of season since 2004
MINNESOTA	9-4-1 ATS prior to playing Ohio State since 2008
MINNESOTA	11-4 S/U prior to playing Ohio State since 2007
MARYLAND	9-4 S/U after playing Indiana since 2008
MARYLAND	10-3 ATS after playing Indiana since 2008
MARYLAND	9-3 S/U prior to playing Rutgers since 1992
MARYLAND	11-3 ATS prior to playing Rutgers since 1990
Rutgers	0-7 O/U after playing Maryland since 1993
MICH STATE	5-1 O/U after playing Rutgers since 2014
MICH STATE	12-2 S/U after playing Rutgers since 1988

- 46-9 S/U @ home when ranked since 2008
- 7-0 S/U @ home when #1 ranked all time
- 4-27 S/U on road vs ranked teams since 2002
- 2-9 S/U on road vs #1 ranked teams all time

Page | 181   Copyright © 2022 by Steve's Football Bible, LLC

PITTSBURGH PANTHERS — ACC Coastal

2021-Pittsburgh		Opponent	Pitt	Opp	S/U	Line	ATS	Total	O/U	
9/4/2021	vs	MASSACHUSETTS	51	7	W	-38.0	W	56.0	O	
9/11/2021	@	Tennessee	41	34	W	-3.5	W	56.0	O	
9/18/2021	vs	WESTERN MICHIGAN	41	44	L	-14.0	L	59.0	O	
9/25/2021	vs	NEW HAMPSHIRE	77	7	W	-29.0	W	51.0	O	
10/2/2021	@	Georgia Tech	52	21	W	-3.0	W	57.5	O	
10/16/2021	@	Virginia Tech	28	7	W	-6.0	W	56.0	U	
10/23/2021	vs	CLEMSON	27	17	W	-3.5	W	47.0	U	
10/30/2021	vs	MIAMI	34	38	L	-9.5	L	61.0	O	
11/6/2021	@	Duke	54	29	W	-21.5	W	64.5	O	
11/11/2021	vs	NORTH CAROLINA	30	23	W	-6.5	W	72.0	O	
11/20/2021	vs	VIRGINIA	48	38	W	-13.0	L	69.0	O	
11/27/2021	@	Syracuse	31	14	W	-11.5	W	58.5	U	
12/4/2021	vs	**Wake Forest**	45	21	W	-3.5	W	74.0	U	ACC CHAMPIONSHIP GAME
12/30/2021	vs	**Michigan State**	21	31	L	3.0	L	54.5	U	Chick-Fil-A Peach Bowl
Coach: Pat Narduzzi		Season Record >>	580	331	11-3	ATS>>	10-4	O/U>>	9-5	ACC CHAMPIONS

2020-Pittsburgh		Opponent	Pitt	Opp	S/U	Line	ATS	Total	O/U	
9/12/2020	vs	AUSTIN PEAY	55	0	W	-29.0	W	48.5	O	
9/19/2020	vs	SYRACUSE	21	10	W	-21.0	L	49.0	U	
9/26/2020	vs	LOUISVILLE	23	20	W	-3.0	T	54.0	U	
10/3/2020	vs	NC STATE	29	30	L	-14.0	L	46.0	O	
10/10/2020	@	Boston College	30	31	L	-6.0	L	42.0	O	{OT}
10/17/2020	@	Miami	19	31	L	13.5	W	47.5	O	
10/24/2020	vs	NOTRE DAME	3	45	L	10.0	L	43.5	O	
11/7/2020	@	Florida State	41	17	W	-1.5	W	52.5	O	
11/21/2020	vs	VIRGINIA TECH	47	14	W	6.0	W	52.0	O	
11/28/2020	@	Clemson	17	52	L	23.5	L	58.5	O	
12/10/2020	@	Georgia Tech	34	20	W	-7.0	W	54.0	U	
Coach: Pat Narduzzi		Season Record >>	319	270	6-5	ATS>>	5-5-1	O/U>>	8-3	

2019-Pittsburgh		Opponent	Pitt	Opp	S/U	Line	ATS	Total	O/U	
8/31/2019	vs	VIRGINIA	14	30	L	2.5	L	45.5	U	
9/7/2019	vs	OHIO	20	10	W	-4.0	W	54.5	U	
9/14/2019	@	Penn State	10	17	L	17.0	W	53.0	U	
9/21/2019	vs	CENTRAL FLORIDA	35	34	W	10.0	W	60.5	O	
9/28/2019	vs	DELAWARE	17	14	W	-27.0	L	NT	---	
10/5/2019	@	Duke	33	30	W	3.5	W	47.0	O	
10/18/2019	@	Syracuse	27	20	W	-3.5	W	53.5	U	
10/26/2019	vs	MIAMI	12	16	L	-4.5	L	41.5	U	
11/2/2019	@	Georgia Tech	20	10	W	-9.0	W	44.0	U	
11/14/2019	vs	NORTH CAROLINA	34	27	W	-4.5	W	48.5	O	{OT}
11/23/2019	@	Virginia Tech	0	28	L	4.0	L	43.5	U	
11/30/2019	vs	BOSTON COLLEGE	19	26	L	-8.5	L	51.5	U	
12/26/2019	vs	**Eastern Michigan**	34	30	W	-12.5	L	51.0	O	Quick Lane Bowl
Coach: Pat Narduzzi		Season Record >>	275	292	8-5	ATS>>	7-6	O/U>>	4-8	

2018-Pittsburgh		Opponent	Pitt	Opp	S/U	Line	ATS	Total	O/U	
9/1/2018	vs	SUNY-ALBANY	33	7	W	-25.5	W	NT	---	
9/8/2018	vs	PENN STATE	6	51	L	7.0	L	50.0	O	
9/15/2018	vs	GEORGIA TECH	24	19	W	3.5	W	54.5	U	
9/22/2018	@	North Carolina	35	38	L	-2.5	L	48.0	O	
9/29/2018	@	Central Florida	15	45	L	13.0	L	65.5	U	
10/6/2018	vs	SYRACUSE	44	37	W	3.0	W	58.5	O	{OT}
10/13/2018	@	Notre Dame	14	19	L	21.0	W	55.5	U	
10/27/2018	vs	DUKE	54	45	W	3.0	W	45.5	O	
11/2/2018	@	Virginia	23	13	W	7.0	W	45.5	U	
11/10/2018	vs	VIRGINIA TECH	52	22	W	-3.0	W	54.0	O	
11/17/2018	@	Wake Forest	34	13	W	-5.0	W	62.5	U	
11/24/2018	@	Miami	3	24	L	5.0	L	46.5	U	
12/1/2018	vs	**Clemson**	10	42	L	27.5	L	53.0	U	ACC CHAMPIONSHIP
12/31/2018	vs	**Stanford**	13	14	L	3.0	W	52.5	U	Sun Bowl
Coach: Pat Narduzzi		Season Record >>	360	389	7-7	ATS>>	9-5	O/U>>	5-8	

PITTSBURGH PANTHERS — ACC Coastal

STADIUM: Heinz Field {68,400}   **Location:** Pittsburgh, PA   **COACH:** Pat Narduzzi

DATE		Opponent	Pitt	Opp	S/U	Line	ATS	Total	O/U	Trends & Angles
9/3/2022	vs	WEST VIRGINIA								0-4 S/U & ATS vs West Va as favorite since 2002
9/10/2022	vs	TENNESSEE								vs Tennessee - Pitt leads series 3-0
9/17/2022	@	Western Michigan								vs Western Michigan - WMU leads series 1-0
9/24/2022	vs	RHODE ISLAND								1st Meeting
10/1/2022	vs	GEORGIA TECH								vs Georgia Tech - Pittsburgh leads series 11-5
10/8/2022	vs	VIRGINIA TECH								9-0 ATS @ home vs Virginia Tech since 1997
10/22/2022	@	Louisville								2-7 S/U vs Louisville as Dog since 1990
10/29/2022	@	North Carolina								0-4 S/U vs North Carolina as Dog since 1998
11/5/2022	vs	SYRACUSE								9-0 S/U @ home vs Syracuse since 2003
11/12/2022	@	Virginia								3-0 ATS @ Virginia since 2014
11/19/2022	vs	DUKE								vs Duke - Pittsburgh leads series 16-9
11/26/2022	@	Miami								vs Miami - Miami leads series 29-11-1
12/3/2022	vs									ACC Championship
	vs									BOWL GAME

Pointspread Analysis — Non-Conference
- 1-15 S/U vs Non-conf. as 15.5 point or more Dog since 1992
- 2-10 S/U vs Non-Conf. as 7.5-15 point Dog since 1993
- 0-8 S/U vs Non-Conf. as 3 point or less Dog since 2003
- 31-2 S/U vs Non-Conf. as 15.5 point or more favorite since 1990
- 1-9 S/U vs West Virginia as 3.5-23 point Dog since 1983
- 5-0 ATS vs West Virginia as 3 point or less Dog since 1985
- 0-6 S/U & ATS vs W. Virginia as 3.5 point or less favorite since 1984
- vs West Virginia - Pittsburgh leads series 61-40-3

Dog
- 1-12 S/U as 25.5 or more Dog since 1993
- 4-1 ATS as 25.5 point or more Dog since 1997
- 1-12 S/U as 20.5-25 point Dog since 1990
- 0-9 S/U on road as 15.5-20 point Dog since 1990
- 1-12 S/U @ home as 15.5 point or more Dog since 1986
- 2-12 S/U as 10.5-15 point Dog since 2005
- 1-6 O/U on road as 10.5-15 Dog since 2007
- 2-7 S/U on road as 7.5-10 point Dog since 1994
- 2-7 O/U on road as 7.5-10 point Dog since 1993
- 4-20 S/U on road as 3.5-7 point Dog since 1988
- 5-16 S/U @ home as 3.5-7 point Dog since 1985

Favorite
- 6-1 S/U on road as 3 point or less favorite since 2010
- 7-1 S/U & ATS on road as 3.5-7 point favorite since 2014
- 10-3 S/U as 7.5-10 point favorite since 2009
- 16-6 S/U @ home as 10.5-15 point favorite since 1983
- 10-2 S/U on road as 10.5-15 point favorite since 1992
- 8-0 S/U on road as 15.5 point or more favorite since 1983
- 18-1 S/U @ home as 15.5-20 point favorite since 1983
- 9-1 S/U as 20.5-25 point favorite since 2001
- 19-0 S/U @ home as 25.5 point or more favorite since 1989

Bowl Games
- 5-1 S/U & ATS vs SEC teams in Bowl Games
- 3-10 ATS in Bowl Games since 2003
- 0-4 S/U & ATS vs AAC teams in Bowl Games
- 3-1 S/U & ATS in Bowl Games as 3.5-7 point Dog since 1975
- 1-5 S/U in Bowl Games as 3 point or less Dog since 1984
- 1-5 S/U & ATS in Bowl Games as 3.5-7 point favorite since 1978

Pointspread Analysis — Conference
- 3-0 S/U & ATS vs Louisville as favorite since 2008
- 0-3 O/U vs Louisville as favorite since 2008
- vs North Carolina - UNC leads series 10-5
- vs Syracuse - Pittsburgh leads series 42-32-3
- 15-2 S/U vs Syracuse since 2005
- 2-17-1 S/U vs Syracuse as Dog since 1984
- 16-0 S/U vs Syracuse as favorite since 1989
- vs Virginia - Pittsburgh leads series 9-4
- 5-0 S/U vs Virginia as favorite since 2006
- vs Virginia Tech - Virginia Tech leads series 11-10
- 13-2 ATS vs Virginia Tech since 1999
- 6-1 S/U @ home vs Virginia Tech since 2001
- 0-9 S/U vs Miami as 19.5 point or more Dog since 1986
- 0-7 S/U & ATS vs Miami as 9 point or less Dog since 1989
- 0-14 S/U vs Syracuse as 3.5 point or more Dog since 1984

TENNESSEE	5-13 ATS in 2nd home game of season since 2003
Louisville	4-10 S/U in 2nd road game of season since 2009
DUKE	8-1 ATS after playing Virginia since 2006
Miami	2-13 O/U in final road game of season since 2007
Miami	9-2-1 ATS in final road game of season since 2010

- 12-0-1 S/U when #2 ranked all time
- 5-0 S/U when ranked vs Louisville all time
- 0-5 S/U when ranked vs Miami since 1989
- 12-1-1 S/U when ranked vs Syracuse since 1976
- 0-4-1 S/U when ranked vs West Virginia since 1988
- 6-43-1 S/U on road vs ranked teams since 1984
- 0-12-1 S/U vs #1 ranked teams all time
- 1-11 S/U on road vs #2 ranked teams all time
- 0-8 S/U @ ranked Miami since 1984
- 0-7 S/U vs ranked Syracuse since 1991

PURDUE BOILERMAKERS   BIG TEN West

2021-Purdue		Opponent	Purd	Opp	S/U	Line	ATS	Total	O/U	
9/4/2021	vs	OREGON STATE	30	21	W	-7.0	W	67.0	U	
9/11/2021	@	Connecticut	49	0	W	-35.5	W	56.5	U	
9/18/2021	@	Notre Dame	13	27	L	7.5	L	58.0	U	
9/25/2021	vs	ILLINOIS	13	9	W	-10.5	L	53.0	U	"Purdue Cannon"
10/2/2021	vs	MINNESOTA	13	20	L	-2.5	L	46.0	U	
10/16/2021	@	Iowa	24	7	W	12.0	W	42.5	U	
10/23/2021	vs	WISCONSIN	13	30	L	3.5	L	41.0	O	
10/30/2021	@	Nebraska	28	23	W	7.5	W	54.0	U	
11/6/2021	vs	MICHIGAN STATE	40	29	W	2.5	W	53.0	O	
11/13/2021	@	Ohio State	31	59	L	19.0	L	65.5	O	
11/20/2021	@	Northwestern	32	14	W	-11.0	W	47.5	U	at Wrigley Field
11/27/2021	vs	INDIANA	44	7	W	-17.5	W	50.5	O	"Old Oaken Bucket"
12/30/2021	vs	Tennessee {OT}	48	45	W	8.0	W	66.5	O	Music City Bowl
Coach: Jeff Brohm		Season Record >>	378	291	9-4	ATS>>	8-5	O/U>>	5-8	

2020-Purdue		Opponent	Purd	Opp	S/U	Line	ATS	Total	O/U	
10/24/2020	vs	IOWA	24	20	W	3.0	W	52.5	U	
10/31/2020	@	Illinois	31	24	W	-10.0	L	54.5	O	"Purdue Cannon"
11/14/2020	vs	NORTHWESTERN	20	27	L	3.5	L	48.5	U	
11/20/2020	@	Minnesota	31	34	L	-2.5	L	62.5	O	
11/28/2020	vs	RUTGERS	30	37	L	-12.0	L	61.0	O	
12/5/2020	vs	NEBRASKA	27	37	L	-2.0	L	64.5	U	
Coach: Jeff Brohm		Season Record >>	163	179	2-4	ATS>>	1-5	O/U>>	3-3	

2019-Purdue		Opponent	Purd	Opp	S/U	Line	ATS	Total	O/U	
8/30/2019	@	Nevada	31	34	L	-11.0	L	58.5	O	
9/7/2019	vs	VANDERBILT	42	24	W	-7.0	W	55.5	O	
9/14/2019	vs	TCU	13	34	L	3.5	L	52.5	U	
9/28/2019	vs	MINNESOTA	31	38	L	-1.5	L	56.0	O	
10/5/2019	@	Penn State	7	35	L	28.5	W	55.0	U	
10/12/2019	vs	MARYLAND	40	14	W	4.5	W	52.0	O	
10/19/2019	@	Iowa	20	26	L	17.5	W	48.0	U	
10/26/2019	vs	ILLINOIS	6	24	L	-9.5	L	53.5	U	"Purdue Cannon"
11/2/2019	vs	NEBRASKA	31	27	W	3.5	W	58.0	T	
11/9/2019	@	Northwestern	24	22	W	PK	W	39.0	O	
11/23/2019	@	Wisconsin	24	45	L	24.5	W	48.5	O	
11/30/2019	vs	INDIANA	41	44	L	7.0	W	56.5	O	"Old Oaken Bucket"
Coach: Jeff Brohm		Season Record >>	310	367	4-8	ATS>>	8-4	O/U>>	7-4-1	

2018-Purdue		Opponent	Purd	Opp	S/U	Line	ATS	Total	O/U	
8/30/2018	vs	NORTHWESTERN	27	31	L	PK	L	51.0	O	
9/8/2018	vs	EASTERN MICHIGAN	19	20	L	-15.0	L	50.0	U	
9/15/2018	vs	MISSOURI	37	40	L	5.0	W	67.5	O	
9/22/2018	vs	BOSTON COLLEGE	30	13	W	6.5	W	62.5	U	
9/29/2018	@	Nebraska	42	28	W	-3.0	W	57.5	O	
10/13/2018	@	Illinois	46	7	W	-10.0	W	64.0	U	"Purdue Cannon"
10/20/2018	vs	OHIO STATE	49	20	W	12.0	W	66.0	O	
10/27/2018	@	Michigan State	13	23	L	-2.5	L	49.0	U	
11/3/2018	vs	IOWA	38	36	W	-2.0	T	50.5	O	
11/10/2018	@	Minnesota	10	41	L	-10.5	L	58.0	U	
11/17/2018	vs	WISCONSIN	44	47	L	-3.5	L	56.0	O	{2 OT}
11/24/2018	@	Indiana	28	21	W	-3.5	W	65.0	U	"Old Oaken Bucket"
12/28/2018	vs	Auburn	14	63	L	3.5	L	58.0	O	Music City Bowl
Coach: Jeff Brohm		Season Record >>	397	390	6-7	ATS>>	6-6-1	O/U>>	7-6	

PURDUE BOILERMAKERS   BIG TEN West

STADIUM: Ross-Ade Stadium {57,326}			Location: West Lafayette, IN					COACH: Jeff Brohm
DATE		Opponent	Pur	Opp	S/U	Line	ATS	Total	O/U	Trends & Angles
9/3/2022	vs	PENN STATE								vs Penn State - Penn State leads series 15-3-1
9/10/2022	vs	INDIANA STATE								vs Indiana State - Purdue leads series 5-0
9/17/2022	@	Syracuse								vs Syracuse - Purdue leads series 1-0
9/24/2022	vs	FLORIDA ATLANTIC								1-11 O/U prior to playing Minnesota since 2010
10/1/2022	@	Minnesota								0-7 S/U @ Minnesota as Dog since 1987
10/8/2022	@	Maryland								vs Maryland - Maryland leads series 2-1
10/15/2022	vs	NEBRASKA								vs Nebraska - Series tied 5-5
10/22/2022	@	Wisconsin								0-15 S/U vs Wisconsin since 2004 {3-12 ATS}
11/5/2022	vs	IOWA								1-9 S/U @ home vs Iowa as Dog since 1984
11/12/2022	@	Illinois								9-1 S/U vs Illinois as favorite since 2003
11/19/2022	vs	NORTHWESTERN								vs Northwestern - Purdue leads series 52-33-1
11/26/2022	@	Indiana								0-6 S/U @ Indiana as Dog since 1991
12/3/2022	vs									Big Ten Championship
	vs									BOWL GAME

Pointspread Analysis Non-Conference	Pointspread Analysis Conference
0-13 S/U vs Non-Conf. as 20.5 point or more Dog since 1986	vs Illinois - Purdue leads series 46-45-6
3-17 S/U vs Non-Conf. as 7.5-15 point Dog since 1983	1-7 O/U vs Illinois as favorite since 2005
2-13 S/U vs Non-Conf. as 3.5-7 point Dog since 1986	4-0 O/U @ Illinois as Dog since 2006
4-0 O/U vs Non-Conf. as 3 point or less Dog since 2002	vs Indiana - Purdue leads series 51-32-1
0-9 ATS vs Non-Conf. as 7.5-10 point favorite since 1987	0-6 S/U vs Indiana as Dog since 2001
28-0 S/U vs Non-Conf. as 15.5 point or more favorite since 1989	5-1 S/U vs Iowa as favorite since 1998
Dog	vs Iowa - Purdue leads series 50-39-3
7-23 ATS as a home Dog since 2012	0-4 O/U @ Minnesota as Dog since 2005
17-4 ATS as a road Dog since 2014	vs Minnesota - Minnesota leads series 41-33-3
0-45 S/U as 20.5 point or more Dog since 1983	1-7 S/U vs Northwestern as Dog since 1995
10-0 ATS as 20.5-25 point Dog since 2013	0-14 S/U vs Penn State as Dog since 1995
0-11 S/U on road as 15.5-20 point Dog since 1995	0-8 S/U @ Wisconsin since 2005
8-2 ATS on road as 15.5-20 point Dog since 2006	vs Wisconsin - Wisconsin leads series 51-29-8
1-10 S/U @ home as 15.5-20 point Dog since 1986	1-19-1 S/U vs Wisconsin as Dog since 1983
0-15 S/U as 15.5-20 point Dog since 2006	3-0 S/U @ Wisconsin as favorite since 1988
1-7 S/U @ home as 10.5-15 point Dog since 2010	12-0 S/U vs Indiana as 7.5 point or more favorite since 1984
2-6 ATS @ home as 10.5-15 point Dog since 2010	2-17 S/U vs Iowa as 6.5 point or more Dog since 1983
2-15 S/U as 10.5-15 point Dog since 2010	8-0 S/U vs Minnesota as 3.0-6.0 point favorite since 1983
1-17-1 S/U on road as 10.5-15 point Dog since 1993	4-0 S/U vs Minnesota as 13 point or more favorite since 1984
3-13 S/U @ home as 3.5-7 point Dog since 2012	7-1 S/U vs Northwestern as 13 point or more favorite since 1983
2-6 S/U & ATS @ home as 3 point or less Dog since 2006	
2-9 S/U on road as 3 point or less Dog since 1985	
Favorite	
11-4-1 O/U @ home as 3 point or less favorite since 2000	
5-0 S/U on road as 3.5-7 point favorite since 2002	
2-14 ATS as 7.5-10 point favorite since 2000	PENN STATE — 17-1 S/U in 1st home game of season since 2004
8-2 S/U on road as 10.5-15 point favorite since 1997	INDIANA STATE — 1-8 S/U in 2nd home game of season since 2013
14-4 S/U @ home as 10.5-15 point favorite since 2003	FLA ATLANTIC — 2-8 S/U prior to playing Minnesota since 2011
42-0 S/U as 15.5 point or more favorite since 1983	Minnesota — 9-3 ATS in 2nd road game of season since 2010
Bowl Games	Minnesota — 3-11 S/U in 2nd road game of season since 2008
6-0 O/U in Bowl Games since 2007	Maryland — 1-10 S/U after playing Minnesota since 2010
	Maryland — 1-7 S/U prior to playing Nebraska since 2013
5-73-1 S/U on road vs ranked teams since 1974	NEBRASKA — 3-8 S/U prior to playing Wisconsin since 2010
12-2 ATS on road vs ranked teams since 2012	Illinois — 4-13 S/U prior to playing Northwestern since 2001
0-10 S/U vs ranked Penn State all time	NORTHWESTERN — 3-11 S/U prior to playing Indiana since 2007
0-9 S/U vs ranked Wisconsin since 2004 {2-7 ATS}	NORTHWESTERN — 3-10 S/U in final home game of season since 2009
8-0 S/U when ranked vs Indiana since 1968	NORTHWESTERN — 13-2 O/U in final home game of season since 2007
10-1 S/U @ home when ranked vs Iowa all time	Indiana — 3-11 S/U after playing Northwestern since 2005
12-1 S/U when ranked vs Northwestern since 1958 {7-0 @ home}	Indiana — 11-3 ATS in final road game of season since 2009

RICE OWLS — C-USA West

2021-Rice		Opponent	Rice	Opp	S/U	Line	ATS	Total	O/U	
9/4/2021	@	Arkansas	17	38	L	19.5	L	50.0	O	
9/11/2021	vs	HOUSTON	7	44	L	7.5	L	50.0	O	"Bayou Bucket Classic"
9/18/2021	@	Texas	0	58	L	26.0	L	52.0	U	
9/25/2021	vs	TEXAS SOUTHERN	48	34	W	-36.5	L	53.5	O	
10/2/2021	vs	SOUTHERN MISS	24	19	W	-1.5	W	44.5	U	
10/16/2021	@	Texas-San Antonio	0	45	L	17.0	L	53.0	U	
10/23/2021	@	Alabama-Birmingham	30	24	W	24.0	W	44.5	O	
10/30/2021	vs	NORTH TEXAS	24	30	L	-1.0	L	55.0	U	{OT}
11/6/2021	@	Charlotte	24	31	L	6.5	L	51.5	O	{OT}
11/13/2021	vs	WESTERN KENTUCKY	21	42	L	19.0	L	61.0	O	
11/20/2021	@	Texas-El Paso	28	38	L	9.0	L	47.0	O	
11/27/2021	vs	LOUISIANA TECH	35	31	W	4.0	W	52.5	O	
Coach: Mike Bloomgren		Season Record >>	258	434	4-8	ATS>>	3-9	O/U>>	8-4	

2020-Rice		Opponent	Rice	Opp	S/U	Line	ATS	Total	O/U	
10/24/2020	vs	MIDDLE TENNESSEE	34	40	L	-4.0	L	48.0	O	{2 OT}
10/31/2020	@	Southern Mississippi	30	6	W	-1.5	W	58.5	U	
11/21/2020	@	North Texas	17	27	L	1.0	L	65.0	U	
12/5/2020	@	Marshall	20	0	W	24.5	W	42.5	U	
12/12/2020	vs	ALABAMA-BIRMINGHAM	16	21	L	7.0	W	42.0	U	
Coach: Mike Bloomgren		Season Record >>	117	94	2-3	ATS>>	3-2	O/U>>	1-4	

2019-Rice		Opponent	Rice	Opp	S/U	Line	ATS	Total	O/U	
8/30/2019	@	Army	7	14	L	23.0	W	47.5	U	
9/7/2019	vs	WAKE FOREST	21	41	L	19.5	L	58.5	O	
9/14/2019	vs	Texas	13	48	L	32.0	L	57.0	O	NRG Stadium
9/21/2019	vs	BAYLOR	13	21	L	27.0	W	57.5	U	
9/28/2019	vs	LOUISIANA TECH	20	23	L	8.0	W	49.0	U	{OT}
10/5/2019	@	Alabama-Birmingham	20	35	L	10.0	L	43.5	O	
10/19/2019	@	Texas-San Antonio	27	31	L	-5.5	L	42.0	O	
10/26/2019	vs	SOUTHERN MISS	6	20	L	10.0	L	51.5	U	
11/2/2019	vs	MARSHALL	7	20	L	12.0	L	48.0	U	
11/16/2019	@	Middle Tennessee	31	28	W	13.0	W	47.0	O	
11/23/2019	vs	NORTH TEXAS	20	14	W	6.5	W	55.5	U	
11/30/2019	@	Texas-El Paso	30	16	W	-6.5	W	43.5	O	
Coach: Mike Bloomgren		Season Record >>	215	311	3-9	ATS>>	6-6	O/U>>	6-6	

2018-Rice		Opponent	Rice	Opp	S/U	Line	ATS	Total	O/U	
8/25/2018	vs	PRAIRIE VIEW A&M	31	28	W	-22.0	L	58.5	O	
9/1/2018	vs	HOUSTON	27	45	L	26.0	W	56.0	O	"Bayou Bucket Classic"
9/8/2018	@	Hawaii	29	43	L	17.0	W	68.5	O	
9/22/2018	@	Southern Mississippi	22	40	L	13.5	L	54.5	O	
9/29/2018	@	Wake Forest	24	56	L	27.5	L	66.0	O	
10/6/2018	vs	TEXAS-SAN ANTONIO	3	20	L	-1.0	L	50.0	U	
10/13/2018	vs	ALABAMA-BIRMINGHAM	0	42	L	16.5	L	52.0	U	
10/20/2018	@	Florida International	17	36	L	23.0	W	53.5	U	
10/27/2018	@	North Texas	17	41	L	29.0	W	58.5	U	
11/3/2018	vs	TEXAS-EL PASO	26	34	L	2.5	L	44.5	O	
11/10/2018	@	Louisiana Tech	13	28	L	24.0	W	53.0	U	
11/17/2018	@	Lsu	10	42	L	42.0	W	51.5	O	
11/24/2018	vs	OLD DOMINION	27	13	W	7.0	W	62.0	U	
Coach: Mike Bloomgren		Season Record >>	246	468	2-11	ATS>>	7-6	O/U>>	7-6	

RICE OWLS C-USA West

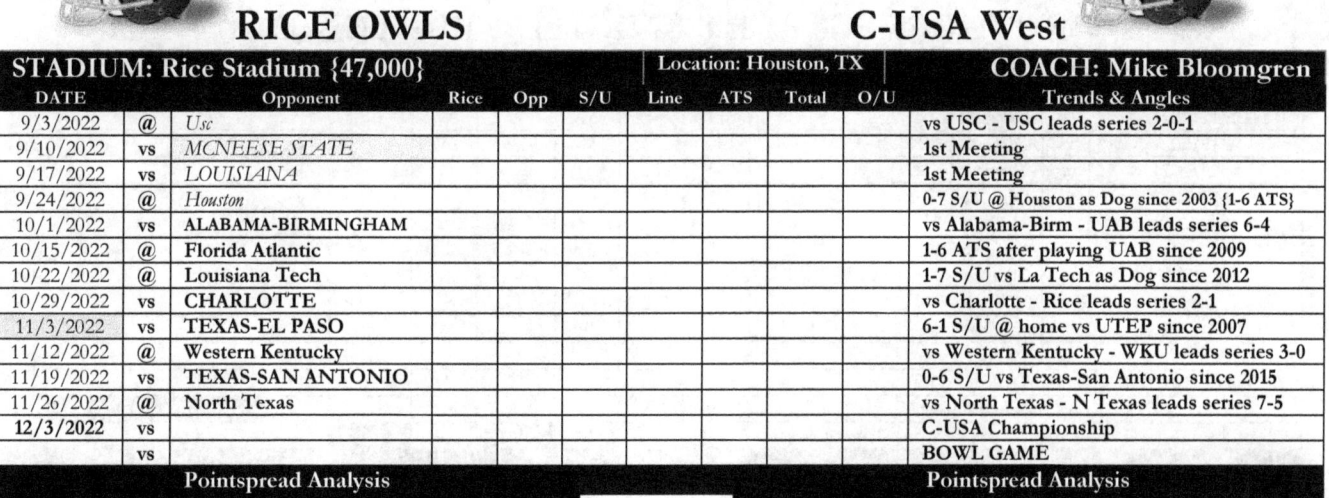

STADIUM: Rice Stadium {47,000} | Location: Houston, TX | **COACH:** Mike Bloomgren

DATE		Opponent	Rice	Opp	S/U	Line	ATS	Total	O/U	Trends & Angles
9/3/2022	@	*Usc*								vs USC - USC leads series 2-0-1
9/10/2022	vs	MCNEESE STATE								1st Meeting
9/17/2022	vs	LOUISIANA								1st Meeting
9/24/2022	@	*Houston*								0-7 S/U @ Houston as Dog since 2003 {1-6 ATS}
10/1/2022	vs	ALABAMA-BIRMINGHAM								vs Alabama-Birm - UAB leads series 6-4
10/15/2022	@	Florida Atlantic								1-6 ATS after playing UAB since 2009
10/22/2022	@	Louisiana Tech								1-7 S/U vs La Tech as Dog since 2012
10/29/2022	vs	CHARLOTTE								vs Charlotte - Rice leads series 2-1
11/3/2022	vs	TEXAS-EL PASO								6-1 S/U @ home vs UTEP since 2007
11/12/2022	@	Western Kentucky								vs Western Kentucky - WKU leads series 3-0
11/19/2022	vs	TEXAS-SAN ANTONIO								0-6 S/U vs Texas-San Antonio since 2015
11/26/2022	@	North Texas								vs North Texas - N Texas leads series 7-5
12/3/2022	vs									C-USA Championship
	vs									BOWL GAME

Pointspread Analysis Non-Conference		Pointspread Analysis Conference
0-41 S/U vs Non-Conf. as 15.5 point or more Dog since 1983		vs Louisiana Tech - Louisiana Tech leads series 9-5
4-23-1 S/U vs Non-Conf. as 3.0-15 point Dog since 1983		4-1 O/U vs North Texas as favorite since 2008
4-0 S/U & ATS vs Non-Conf. as 3 point or less favorite since 2008		vs Texas-El Paso - Rice leads series 15-9
10-1 S/U vs Non-Conf. as 7.5 point or more favorite since 1990		8-1 ATS @ home vs Texas-El Paso since 2003
0-13 S/U vs Houston as 10.5 point or more Dog since 1983		6-0 S/U @ home vs Texas-El Paso as favorite since 2001
Dog		14-4 ATS vs Texas-El Paso since 2003
0-48 S/U as 25.5 point or more Dog since 1983		Game 2-7 O/U vs Texas-San Antonio since 2012
3-24 S/U on road as 20.5-25 point Dog since 1983		vs Texas-San Antonio - UTSA leads series 6-3
0-8 S/U @ home as 20.5-25 point Dog since 1983		0-4 S/U vs Texas-San Antonio as Dog since 2015
0-31 S/U as 15.5-20 point Dog since 1990		Game 0-4 O/U @ home vs UTSA since 2012
0-21 S/U on road as 15.5-20 point Dog since 1992		0-4 S/U vs UTEP as 9.5 point or more Dog since 2000
0-16 S/U @ home as 15.5-20 point Dog since 1983		5-2 S/U & ATS vs UTEP as 9 point or less Dog since 2006
0-15 S/U @ home as 10.5-15 point Dog since 1987		**Bowl Games**
0-7 ATS @ home as 10.5-15 point Dog since 2011		3-0 S/U & ATS in Bowl Games as 3 point or less favorite since 2008
8-2 ATS on road as 10.5-15 point Dog since 2003		
2-13 S/U on road as 7.5-10 point Dog since 1990		
0-8 ATS on road as 7.5-10 point Dog since 2007		
13-5 O/U as 7.5-10 point Dog since 2007		
1-6 O/U @ home as 3.5-7 point Dog since 2009		
Favorite	Houston	1-23 S/U in 2nd road game of season since 1998
7-2 S/U & ATS @ home as 3 point or less favorite since 2008	Houston	3-15 ATS in 2nd road game of season since 2004
14-2 S/U & ATS as 3 point or less favorite since 2008	UTSA	9-1 ATS prior to playing North Texas since 2010
5-0 S/U @ home as 7.5-10 point favorite since 2002	Fla Atlantic	8-3-1 ATS prior to playing Louisiana Tech since 2002
1-5 O/U @ home as 7.5-10 point favorite since 2002	CHARLOTTE	1-6-1 ATS after playing Louisiana Tech since 2005
13-1 S/U @ home as 10.5-15 point favorite since 1993	W. Kentucky	1-7 S/U after playing Texas-El Paso since 2011
0-3 S/U & ATS on road as 10.5-15 point favorite since 1996	W. Kentucky	1-5 S/U prior to playing Texas-San Antonio since 2015
14-0 S/U as 20.5 point or more favorite since 1997	W. Kentucky	5-1 O/U prior to playing Texas-San Antonio since 2015
	UTSA	14-3 ATS in final home game of season since 2008
1-71 S/U on road vs ranked teams since 1971	UTSA	3-10 O/U in final home game of season since 2009
3-31 S/U @ home vs ranked teams since 1975	UTSA	12-2 S/U in final home game of season since 2008
0-10 S/U vs ranked Houston all time	North Texas	13-3 O/U in final road game of season since 2006

RUTGERS SCARLET KNIGHTS BIG TEN East

2021-Rutgers		Opponent	Rutg	Opp	S/U	Line	ATS	Total	O/U	
9/4/2021	vs	TEMPLE	61	14	W	-14.0	W	53.0	O	
9/11/2021	@	Syracuse	17	7	W	-2.5	W	51.0	U	
9/18/2021	vs	DELAWARE	45	13	W	-20.5	W	45.0	O	
9/25/2021	@	Michigan	13	20	L	20.5	W	50.0	U	
10/2/2021	vs	OHIO STATE	13	52	L	15.0	L	58.0	O	
10/9/2021	vs	MICHIGAN STATE	13	31	L	4.0	L	49.5	U	
10/16/2021	@	Northwestern	7	21	L	-2.5	L	45.0	U	
10/30/2021	@	Illinois	20	14	W	-1.5	W	41.5	U	
11/6/2021	vs	WISCONSIN	3	52	L	13.0	L	38.0	O	
11/13/2021	@	Indiana	38	3	W	6.5	W	42.5	U	
11/20/2021	@	Penn State	0	28	L	14.0	L	45.0	U	
11/27/2021	vs	MARYLAND	16	40	L	-2.0	L	53.0	O	
12/31/2021	vs	Wake Forest	10	38	L	17.0	L	62.5	U	Gator Bowl
Coach: Greg Schiano		Season Record >>	256	333	5-8	ATS>>	6-7	O/U>>	5-8	

2020-Rutgers		Opponent	Rutg	Opp	S/U	Line	ATS	Total	O/U	
10/24/2020	@	Michigan State	38	27	W	9.5	W	45.0	O	
10/31/2020	vs	INDIANA	21	37	L	11.5	L	54.0	O	
11/7/2020	@	Ohio State	27	49	L	37.5	W	63.0	O	
11/14/2020	vs	ILLINOIS	20	23	L	-5.5	L	51.5	U	
11/21/2020	vs	MICHIGAN	42	48	L	11.5	W	52.0	O	{3 OT}
11/28/2020	@	Purdue	37	30	W	12.0	W	61.0	O	
12/5/2020	vs	PENN STATE	7	23	L	13.0	L	51.5	U	
12/12/2020	@	Maryland	27	24	W	3.0	W	54.0	U	{OT}
12/19/2020	vs	NEBRASKA	21	28	L	6.5	L	51.5	U	
Coach: Greg Schiano		Season Record >>	240	289	3-6	ATS>>	5-4	O/U>>	5-4	

2019-Rutgers		Opponent	Rutg	Opp	S/U	Line	ATS	Total	O/U	
8/30/2019	vs	MASSACHUSETTS	48	21	W	-16.5	W	54.5	O	
9/7/2019	@	Iowa	0	30	L	18.0	L	48.0	U	
9/21/2019	vs	BOSTON COLLEGE	16	30	L	7.5	L	57.5	U	
9/28/2019	@	Michigan	0	52	L	27.5	L	49.0	O	
10/5/2019	vs	MARYLAND	7	48	L	14.5	L	55.5	U	
10/12/2019	@	Indiana	0	35	L	27.5	L	49.5	U	
10/19/2019	vs	MINNESOTA	7	42	L	28.5	L	46.5	O	
10/26/2019	vs	LIBERTY	44	34	W	7.5	W	43.5	O	
11/2/2019	@	Illinois	10	38	L	18.5	L	48.5	U	
11/16/2019	vs	OHIO STATE	21	56	L	52.0	W	62.5	O	
11/23/2019	vs	MICHIGAN STATE	0	27	L	22.0	L	43.5	U	
11/30/2019	@	Penn State	6	27	L	39.0	W	50.5	U	
Coach: Chris Ash		Season Record >>	159	440	2-10	ATS>>	4-8	O/U>>	5-7	

2018-Rutgers		Opponent	Rutg	Opp	S/U	Line	ATS	Total	O/U	
9/1/2018	vs	TEXAS STATE	35	7	W	-16.5	W	48.0	U	
9/8/2018	@	Ohio State	3	52	L	35.0	L	59.0	U	
9/15/2018	@	Kansas	14	55	L	PK	L	44.0	O	
9/22/2018	vs	BUFFALO	13	42	L	6.0	L	52.0	O	
9/29/2018	vs	INDIANA	17	24	L	16.5	W	49.0	U	
10/6/2018	vs	ILLINOIS	17	38	L	4.5	L	50.5	O	
10/13/2018	@	Maryland	7	34	L	24.0	L	50.5	U	
10/20/2018	vs	NORTHWESTERN	15	18	L	20.0	W	49.0	U	
11/3/2018	@	Wisconsin	17	31	L	28.5	W	50.5	U	
11/10/2018	vs	MICHIGAN	7	42	L	37.0	W	44.5	O	
11/17/2018	vs	PENN STATE	7	20	L	28.0	W	51.5	U	
11/24/2018	@	Michigan State	10	14	L	24.5	W	37.0	U	
Coach: Chris Ash		Season Record >>	162	377	1-11	ATS>>	7-5	O/U>>	4-8	

RUTGERS SCARLET KNIGHTS   BIG TEN East

STADIUM: High Point Solutions Stadium {52,454} | **Location:** Piscataway, NJ | **COACH:** Greg Schiano

DATE		Opponent	Rut	Opp	S/U	Line	ATS	Total	O/U	Trends & Angles
9/3/2022	@	Boston College								0-14-1 S/U vs Boston College as Dog since 1990
9/10/2022	vs	WAGNER								10-2 S/U in 1st home game of season since 2010
9/17/2022	@	Temple								5-0 S/U vs Temple since 2003
9/24/2022	vs	IOWA								vs Iowa - Iowa leads series 2-0
10/1/2022	@	Ohio State								vs Ohio State - Ohio State leads series 8-0
10/8/2022	vs	NEBRASKA								vs Nebraska - Nebraska leads series 5-0
10/22/2022	vs	INDIANA								vs Indiana - Indiana leads series 5-3
10/29/2022	@	Minnesota								vs Minnesota - Minnesota leads series 2-0
11/5/2022	vs	MICHIGAN								vs Michigan - Michigan leads series 7-1
11/12/2022	@	Michigan State								1-4 S/U @ Michigan State as Dog since 2003
11/19/2022	vs	PENN STATE								1-20 S/U vs Penn State as Dog since 1983
11/26/2022	@	Maryland								vs Maryland - Maryland leads series 10-7
12/3/2022	vs									Big Ten Championship
	vs									BOWL GAME

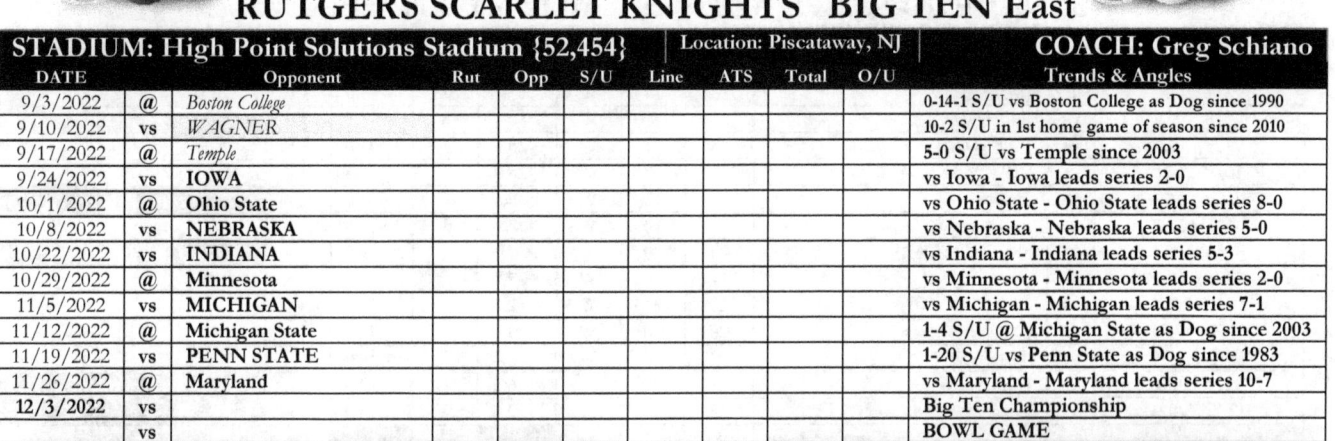

Pointspread Analysis — Non-Conference
- 2-32-1 S/U vs Non-Conf. as 10.5 point or more Dog since 1983
- 8-1 ATS vs Non-Conf. as 7.5-10 point Dog since 1989
- 7-3 S/U vs Non-Conf. as 3.5-7 point Dog since 2002
- 6-0 S/U & ATS vs Non-Conf. as 3 point or less favorite since 2009
- 47-3-1 S/U vs Non-Conf. as 7.5 point or more favorite since 1984
- vs Boston College - Boston College leads series 20-6-1
- 0-8 S/U vs Boston College as 14.5 point or more Dog since 1984
- 0-13-1 S/U vs Boston College since 1992
- vs Temple - Rutgers leads series 21-16
- 9-0 S/U vs Temple as favorite since 1991
- 0-7 S/U vs Temple as 6 point or more Dog since 1985
- Game 2-5 O/U vs Temple since 2001

Dog
- 1-22 S/U as 30.5 point or more Dog since 1993
- 0-24 S/U on road as 25.5 point or more Dog since 1993
- 1-18 S/U on road as 20.5-25 point Dog since 1983
- 0-9 S/U @ home as 20.5-25 point or more Dog since 1996
- 0-46 S/U as 20.5 point or more Dog since 2000
- 0-24 S/U on road as 15.5-20 point Dog since 1988
- 1-12 S/U @ home as 15.5-20 point Dog since 1983
- 1-36 S/U as 15.5-20 point Dog since 1998
- 0-22 S/U @ home as 10.5-15 point Dog since 1983
- 1-19-1 S/U on road as 10.5-15 point Dog since 1991
- 16-4 ATS as 7.5-10 point Dog since 1998
- 12-1 ATS on road as 7.5-10 point Dog since 1998
- 0-7 S/U @ home as 3.5-7 point Dog since 2011 {1-6 ATS}
- 6-0 S/U & ATS on road as 3.5-7 point Dog since 2006
- 1-11 O/U as 3 point or less Dog since 2008

- 1-38-1 S/U vs Top #10 ranked teams all time
- 1-39-1 S/U on road vs ranked teams since 1989
- 0-16 S/U @ home vs ranked teams since 2009
- 0-23 S/U vs #10 #11 #12 #13 #14 ranked teams all time
- 0-8 S/U vs ranked Ohio State all time
- 1-16 S/U vs ranked Penn State all time

Pointspread Analysis — Conference
- vs Michigan State - Michigan State leads series 9-4
- vs Penn State - Penn State leads series 30-2
- 1-37-1 S/U vs Top #10 ranked teams all time
- 1-38-1 S/U on road vs ranked teams since 1989
- 0-15 S/U @ home vs ranked teams since 2009
- 0-5 S/U vs ranked Michigan all time
- 0-7 S/U vs ranked Ohio State all time
- 1-16 S/U vs ranked Penn State all time

Bowl Games
- 7-3 ATS in Bowl Games

Favorite
- 7-2 S/U & ATS on road as 3 point or less favorite since 2009
- 1-7 ATS @ home as 3 point or less favorite since 2005
- 7-1 O/U @ home as 3 point or less favorite since 2005
- 6-1 O/U on road as 3.5-7 point favorite since 2003
- 4-0 S/U & ATS as 7.5-10 point favorite since 2011
- 21-1 S/U as 10.5-15 point favorite since 1991
- 1-9 O/U as 15.5-20 point favorite since 2007
- 7-0-1 S/U on road as 15.5-20 point favorite since 1986
- 17-0 S/U as 20.5 point or more favorite since 1984

NEBRASKA	1-7 S/U prior to playing Indiana since 2014
Minnesota	0-8 S/U after playing Indiana since 2014 {1-7 ATS}
Maryland	1-9 O/U in final road game of season since 2012
Maryland	0-5 O/U after playing Penn State since 2014
Maryland	3-8 ATS after playing Penn State since 1990

SAN DIEGO STATE AZTECS   MOUNTAIN WEST West

2021-San Diego State		Opponent	SDSU	Opp	S/U	Line	ATS	Total	O/U	
9/4/2021	vs	NEW MEXICO STATE	28	10	W	-31.5	L	50.5	U	
9/11/2021	@	Arizona	38	14	W	1.5	W	46.0	O	
9/18/2021	vs	UTAH	33	31	W	8.0	W	42.5	O	{3 OT}
9/25/2021	vs	TOWSON	48	21	W	-23.5	W	41.0	O	
10/9/2021	vs	NEW MEXICO	31	7	W	-28.5	L	42.5	U	
10/16/2021	@	San Jose State	19	13	W	-9.5	L	41.5	U	"El Camino Real Rivalry"
10/23/2021	@	Air Force	20	14	W	3.0	W	39.0	U	
10/30/2021	vs	FRESNO STATE	20	30	L	2.5	L	49.0	O	"Battle for the Oil Can"
11/6/2021	@	Hawaii	17	10	W	-7.0	T	45.0	U	
11/13/2021	vs	NEVADA	23	21	W	-2.5	L	45.0	U	
11/20/2021	@	Unlv	28	20	W	-11.5	L	41.0	O	
11/27/2021	vs	BOISE STATE	27	16	W	3.0	W	44.0	U	
12/4/2021	vs	Utah State	13	46	L	-6.5	L	49.5	O	MWC Championship
12/21/2021	vs	Texas-San Antonio	38	24	W	-2.5	W	48.0	O	Frisco Bowl
Coach: Brady Hoke		Season Record >>	383	277	12-2	ATS>>	6-7-1	O/U>>	7-7	
2020-San Diego State		Opponent	SDSU	Opp	S/U	Line	ATS	Total	O/U	
10/24/2020	vs	UNLV	34	6	W	-13.5	W	49.5	U	
10/31/2020	@	Utah State	38	7	W	-8.5	W	40.5	O	
11/6/2020	vs	SAN JOSE STATE	17	28	L	-10.0	L	50.0	U	"El Camino Real Rivalry"
11/14/2020	vs	HAWAII	34	10	W	-9.5	W	51.0	U	
11/21/2020	@	Nevada	21	26	L	-1.5	L	46.0	O	
11/27/2020	@	Colorado	10	20	L	6.0	L	51.5	U	
12/5/2020	vs	COLORADO STATE	29	17	W	-8.0	W	45.5	O	
12/12/2020	@	Byu	14	28	L	16.5	W	47.5	U	
Coach: Brady Hoke		Season Record >>	197	142	4-4	ATS>>	5-3	O/U>>	3-5	
2019-San Diego State		Opponent	SDSU	Opp	S/U	Line	ATS	Total	O/U	
8/31/2019	vs	WEBER STATE	6	0	W	-13.5	L	NT	---	
9/7/2019	@	Ucla	23	14	W	7.5	W	45.0	U	
9/14/2019	@	New Mexico State	31	10	W	-17.0	W	51.0	O	
9/21/2019	vs	UTAH STATE	17	23	L	4.0	L	53.0	U	
10/5/2019	@	Colorado State	24	10	W	-6.5	W	48.0	U	
10/12/2019	vs	WYOMING	26	22	W	-3.5	W	38.0	O	
10/19/2019	@	San Jose State	27	17	W	-7.5	W	45.5	U	"El Camino Real Rivalry"
10/26/2019	@	Unlv	20	17	W	-11.5	L	44.5	U	
11/9/2019	vs	NEVADA	13	17	L	-17.0	L	34.5	U	
11/16/2019	vs	FRESNO STATE	17	7	W	-2.5	W	43.5	U	"Battle for the Oil Can"
11/23/2019	@	Hawaii	11	14	L	-1.5	L	46.5	U	
11/30/2019	vs	BYU	13	3	W	4.0	W	38.5	U	
12/21/2019	vs	Central Michigan	48	11	W	-4.0	W	40.5	O	New Mexico Bowl
Coach: Rocky Long		Season Record >>	276	165	10-3	ATS>>	8-5	O/U>>	2-10	
2018-San Diego State		Opponent	SDSU	Opp	S/U	Line	ATS	Total	O/U	
8/31/2018	@	Stanford	10	31	L	13.5	L	49.5	U	
9/8/2018	vs	SACRAMENTO STATE	28	14	W	-25.0	L	NT	---	
9/15/2018	vs	ARIZONA STATE	28	21	W	5.0	W	47.5	O	
9/22/2018	vs	EASTERN MICHIGAN	23	20	W	-11.0	L	48.0	U	
10/6/2018	@	Boise State	19	13	W	14.0	W	51.0	U	
10/13/2018	vs	AIR FORCE	21	17	W	-11.0	L	42.5	U	
10/20/2018	vs	SAN JOSE STATE	16	13	W	-25.5	L	45.5	U	"El Camino Real Rivalry"
10/27/2018	@	Nevada	24	28	L	-1.0	L	46.0	O	
11/3/2018	@	New Mexico	31	23	W	-12.5	L	45.0	U	
11/10/2018	vs	UNLV	24	27	L	-24.0	L	51.5	U	
11/17/2018	@	Fresno State	14	23	L	10.0	W	42.0	U	"Battle for the Oil Can"
11/24/2018	vs	HAWAII	30	31	L	-18.5	L	54.0	O	{OT}
12/19/2018	vs	Ohio	0	27	L	2.0	L	47.5	U	Frisco Bowl
Coach: Rocky Long		Season Record >>	268	288	7-6	ATS>>	3-10	O/U>>	4-8	

SAN DIEGO STATE AZTECS   MOUNTAIN WEST West

STADIUM: Dignity Health Sports Park {27,000} **Location:** San Diego, CA **COACH:** Brady Hoke

DATE		Opponent	Sdsu	Opp	S/U	Line	ATS	Total	O/U	Trends & Angles
9/3/2022	vs	ARIZONA								vs Arizona - Arizona leads series 10-6
9/10/2022	vs	IDAHO STATE								vs Idaho State - SDSU leads series 1-0
9/17/2022	@	Utah								1-5 S/U & ATS vs Utah as Dog since 2006
9/24/2022	vs	TOLEDO								7-0 S/U prior to playing Boise State since 2011
10/1/2022	@	Boise State								6-0 ATS vs Boise State as Dog since 2011
10/8/2022	vs	HAWAII								15-2 S/U vs Hawaii as favorite since 1986
10/22/2022	@	Nevada								vs Nevada - San Diego State leads series 8-6
10/29/2022	@	Fresno State								0-6 S/U vs Fresno State as Dog since 2002
11/5/2022	vs	UNLV								9-1 S/U @ home vs UNLV since 2002
11/12/2022	vs	SAN JOSE STATE								11-2 S/U @ home vs San Jose State since 1968
11/19/2022	@	New Mexico								8-0 S/U vs New Mexico as favorite since 2009
11/26/2022	vs	AIR FORCE								5-0 S/U vs Air Force as favorite since 2012
12/3/2022	vs									MWC Championship
	vs									BOWL GAME

Pointspread Analysis — Non-Conference
- 3-44 S/U vs Non-Conf. as 7.5 point or more Dog since 1985
- 10-0 S/U vs Non-Conf. as 20.5 point or more favorite since 2010
- 0-5 S/U vs Utah as 14.5 point or more Dog since 2001
- vs Utah - Utah leads series 17-13-1
- 1-5 S/U @ Utah since 1999
- 1-3 S/U vs Arizona as Dog since 1997

Dog
- 4-0-1 ATS @ home as a Dog since 2013
- 0-22 S/U as 20.5 point or more Dog since 1988
- 1-7 O/U as 20.5-25 point Dog since 1990
- 2-15 S/U on road as 15.5-20 point Dog since 1984
- 6-0 ATS as 15.5-20 point Dog since 2009
- 0-7 S/U @ home as 15.5-20 point Dog since 1989
- 3-27 S/U on road as 10.5-15 point Dog since 1985
- 3-10 S/U @ home as 10.5-15 point Dog since 1986
- 2-12 S/U @ home as 7.5-10 point Dog since 1988
- 8-3-1 ATS as 3.5-7 point Dog since 2011
- 6-15 O/U as 3 point or less Dog since 1999
- 2-6 O/U @ home as 3 point or less Dog since 1999

Favorite
- 1-8 S/U & ATS on road as 3 point or less favorite since 1992
- 8-1 S/U on road as 3.5-7 point favorite since 2012
- 11-1 S/U @ home as 7.5-10 point favorite since 2001
- 22-4 S/U @ home as 10.5-15 point favorite since 1985
- 13-0 S/U on road as 10.5-15 point favorite since 1985
- 13-4 S/U @ home as 15.5-20 point favorite since 1991
- 5-2 ATS @ home as 15.5-20 point favorite since 2015
- 33-2 S/U as 20.5 point or more favorite since 1985
- 28-1 S/U @ home as 20.5 point or more favorite since 1987

Bowl Games
- 1-3 O/U in Bowl Games as 3 point or less favorite since 1991
- 1-4 ATS in Bowl Games as 3.5-7 point favorite since 2011

- 3-37 S/U on road vs ranked teams all time
- 1-23 S/U vs Top #10 ranked teams all time
- 1-15 O/U on road vs ranked teams since 1997
- 1-23 S/U vs Top #10 ranked teams all time
- 0-4 S/U vs ranked Utah since 2004
- 0-4 ATS vs ranked Utah since 2004

Pointspread Analysis — Conference
- vs Fresno State - SDSU leads series 30-26-4
- 7-1 S/U vs Fresno State as favorite since 1995
- vs Hawaii - San Diego State leads series 23-11-2
- 11-2-2 ATS vs Hawaii as favorite since 1992
- 8-1 ATS vs Hawaii as Dog since 1985
- 8-2 S/U vs Nevada as favorite since 1995
- 0-7 S/U vs New Mexico as Dog since 2001 {1-6 ATS}
- vs San Jose State - San Diego State leads series 23-20-2
- 8-1 S/U vs San Jose State since 2013
- Game 1-7 O/U vs San Jose State since 2014
- vs UNLV - San Diego State leads series 21-10
- 13-3 S/U vs UNLV since 2006
- Game 1-5 O/U vs UNLV since 2016
- Game 0-5 O/U @ home vs UNLV since 2012
- 4-0 ATS vs UNLV as Dog since 2003
- 9-0 ATS vs Air Force as 7 point or less Dog since 1991
- 18-1 S/U vs New Mexico as 5 point or more favorite since 1985
- 1-11 ATS vs New Mexico as 5 point or more favorite since 1993
- 11-1 S/U vs San Jose State as 5 point or more favorite since 1995
- 9-3 ATS vs San Jose State as 5 point or more favorite since 1995
- 13-1 S/U vs UNLV as 7-18 point favorite since 1997

ARIZONA	12-1 S/U in 1st home game of season since 2009
ARIZONA	0-6-1 O/U in 1st home game of season since 2012
Utah	4-12 O/U in 1st road game of season since 2006
IDAHO STATE	11-4 S/U in 2nd home game of season since 2007
TOLEDO	1-6 O/U prior to playing Boise State since 2011
HAWAII	10-0 S/U prior to playing Nevada since 2012
Fresno State	3-7 O/U after playing Nevada since 2004
UNLV	10-0 S/U prior to playing San Jose State since 2012
UNLV	7-2 S/U after playing Fresno State since 2012
SAN JOSE STATE	0-8 O/U after playing UNLV since 2012
New Mexico	5-1 ATS prior to playing Air Force since 2013
AIR FORCE	10-2 S/U in final home game of season since 2010

Page | 191

Copyright © 2022 by Steve's Football Bible, LLC

SAN JOSE STATE SPARTANS   MOUNTAIN WEST West

2021-San Jose State		Opponent	SJSU	Opp	S/U	Line	ATS	Total	O/U	
8/28/2021	vs	SOUTHERN UTAH	45	14	W	-28.0	W	57.5	O	
9/4/2021	@	Usc	7	30	L	13.5	L	61.0	U	
9/18/2021	@	Hawaii	17	13	W	-7.5	L	62.5	U	
9/25/2021	@	Western Michigan	3	23	L	2.5	L	61.5	U	
10/2/2021	vs	NEW MEXICO STATE	37	31	W	-25.0	L	51.5	O	
10/9/2021	@	Colorado State	14	32	L	3.5	L	44.0	O	
10/16/2021	vs	SAN DIEGO STATE	13	19	L	9.5	W	41.5	U	"El Camino Real Rivalry"
10/21/2021	@	Unlv	27	20	W	-6.0	W	44.0	O	
10/30/2021	vs	WYOMING	27	21	W	-3.0	W	40.5	O	
11/6/2021	@	Nevada	24	27	L	11.5	W	55.0	O	
11/13/2021	vs	UTAH STATE	17	48	L	-3.5	L	58.0	O	
11/27/2021	vs	FRESNO STATE	9	40	L	7.0	L	52.5	U	"Valley Rivalry"
Coach: Brent Brennan		Season Record >>	240	318	5-7	ATS>>	5-7	O/U>>	6-6	

2020-San Jose State		Opponent	SJSU	Opp	S/U	Line	ATS	Total	O/U	
10/24/2020	vs	AIR FORCE	17	6	W	7.5	W	64.5	U	
10/31/2020	vs	NEW MEXICO	38	21	W	-13.5	W	56.5	O	
11/6/2020	@	San Diego State	28	17	W	10.0	W	50.0	U	"El Camino Real Rivalry"
11/14/2020	vs	UNLV	34	17	W	-17.0	T	61.5	U	
12/5/2020	vs	HAWAII	35	24	W	-2.5	W	59.5	U	
12/11/2020	vs	NEVADA	30	20	W	2.5	W	62.0	U	
12/19/2020	vs	Boise State	34	20	W	6.5	W	59.5	U	MWC CHAMPIONSHIP
12/31/2020	vs	Ball State	13	34	L	-7.5	L	66.0	U	Arizona Bowl
Coach: Brent Brennan		Season Record >>	229	159	7-1	ATS>>	6-1-1	O/U>>	1-7	MWC CHAMPIONS

2019-San Jose State		Opponent	SJSU	Opp	S/U	Line	ATS	Total	O/U	
8/29/2019	vs	NORTHERN COLORADO	35	18	W	-17.0	T	NT	---	
9/7/2019	vs	TULSA	16	34	L	6.5	L	53.5	U	
9/21/2019	@	Arkansas	31	24	W	20.5	W	61.0	U	
9/28/2019	@	Air Force	24	41	L	19.0	W	58.0	O	
10/5/2019	vs	NEW MEXICO	32	21	W	-7.0	L	69.5	U	
10/12/2019	@	Nevada	38	41	L	2.5	L	58.5	O	
10/19/2019	vs	SAN DIEGO STATE	17	27	L	7.5	L	45.5	U	"El Camino Real Rivalry"
10/26/2019	@	Army	34	29	W	9.5	W	54.0	O	
11/2/2019	vs	BOISE STATE	42	52	L	16.5	W	61.0	O	
11/9/2019	@	Hawaii	40	42	L	7.5	W	78.5	O	
11/23/2019	@	Unlv	35	38	L	-7.0	L	65.0	O	
11/30/2019	vs	FRESNO STATE	17	16	W	-2.5	L	59.5	U	"Valley Rivalry"
Coach: Brent Brennan		Season Record >>	361	383	5-7	ATS>>	5-6-1	O/U>>	6-5	

2018-San Jose State		Opponent	SJSU	Opp	S/U	Line	ATS	Total	O/U	
8/30/2018	vs	CALIFORNIA-DAVIS	38	44	L	-3.5	L	NT	---	
9/8/2018	@	Washington State	0	31	L	30.0	L	62.5	U	
9/15/2018	@	Oregon	22	35	L	42.5	W	69.5	U	
9/29/2018	vs	HAWAII	41	44	L	9.5	W	62.0	O	{5 OT}
10/6/2018	vs	COLORADO STATE	30	42	L	3.0	L	59.5	O	
10/13/2018	vs	ARMY	3	52	L	17.0	L	49.5	O	
10/20/2018	@	San Diego State	13	16	L	25.5	W	45.5	U	"El Camino Real Rivalry"
10/27/2018	vs	UNLV	50	37	W	-2.5	W	57.0	O	
11/3/2018	@	Wyoming	9	24	L	17.0	W	39.0	U	
11/10/2018	@	Utah State	24	62	L	31.0	L	63.5	O	
11/17/2018	vs	NEVADA	12	21	L	14.5	W	58.5	U	
11/24/2018	@	Fresno State	13	31	L	32.0	W	52.0	U	"Valley Rivalry"
Coach: Brent Brennan		Season Record >>	255	439	1-11	ATS>>	7-5	O/U>>	5-6	

SAN JOSE STATE SPARTANS   MOUNTAIN WEST West

STADIUM: Spartan Stadium {30,456}						Location: San Jose, CA				COACH: Brent Brennan
DATE		Opponent	Sjsu	Opp	S/U	Line	ATS	Total	O/U	Trends & Angles
9/3/2022	vs	PORTLAND STATE								vs Portland State - SJSU leads series 1-0
9/10/2022	@	Auburn								vs Auburn - Auburn leads series 2-0
9/24/2022	vs	WESTERN MICHIGAN								vs Western Michigan - WMU leads series 1-0
10/1/2022	@	Wyoming								vs Wyoming - Wyoming leads series 8-4
10/8/2022	vs	UNLV								vs UNLV - San Jose State leads series 17-8-1
10/15/2022	@	Fresno State								0-13 S/U @ Fresno State as Dog since 1985
10/22/2022	@	New Mexico State								vs NMSU - San Jose State leads series 18-3
10/29/2022	vs	NEVADA								vs Nevada - Nevada leads series 23-10-2
11/5/2022	vs	COLORADO STATE								vs Colorado State - CSU leads series 7-4
11/12/2022	@	San Diego State								vs San Diego State - SDSU leads series 23-20-2
11/19/2022	@	Utah State								0-6 ATS vs Utah State since 2012
11/26/2022	vs	HAWAII								vs Hawaii - Hawaii leads series 22-21-1
12/3/2022	vs									MWC Championship
	vs									BOWL GAME

Pointspread Analysis Non-Conference
- 2-38 S/U vs Non-Conf. as 20.5 point or more Dog since 1985
- 0-12 S/U vs Non-Conf. as 15.5-20 point Dog since 2001
- 1-5 S/U & ATS vs Non-Conf. as 7.5-10 point Dog since 2008
- 15-1 S/U vs New Mexico State as 4 point or more favorite since 1985

Dog
- 0-42 S/U as 25.5 point or more Dog since 1989
- 0-9 S/U @ home as 20.5 point or more Dog since 1996
- 2-57 S/U on road as 20.5 point or more Dog since 1985
- 1-25 S/U as 15.5-20 point Dog since 2001
- 0-18 S/U on road as 15.5-20 point Dog since 2001
- 0-9 S/U @ home as 10.5-15 point Dog since 2004
- 0-19 S/U on road as 10.5-15 point Dog since 1998
- 2-9 S/U on road as 7.5-10 point Dog since 1999
- 4-15 S/U as 7.5-10 point Dog since 2008
- 1-8 S/U & ATS as 3.5-7 point Dog since 2014

Favorite
- 20-5 ATS as a road favorite since 1998
- 6-1 S/U & ATS on road as 3 point or less favorite since 2000
- 11-3 S/U on road as 3.5-7 point favorite since 1987
- 6-1 O/U @ home as 3.5-7 point favorite since 2009
- 7-1 S/U on road as 7.5-10 point favorite since 1986
- 8-1 S/U @ home as 7.5-10 point favorite since 2001
- 12-2 S/U @ home as 10.5-15 point favorite since 1986
- 14-0 S/U on road as 10.5 point or more favorite since 1986
- 10-1 S/U @ home as 15.5-20 point favorite since 1987
- 0-4 ATS on road as 15.5-20 point favorite since 1987
- 15-0 S/U as 20.5 point or more favorite since 1986

Bowl Games
- 4-1 S/U & ATS in Bowl Games since 1990

- 0-36 S/U on road vs ranked teams since 1981
- 1-11 S/U @ home vs ranked teams since 2001
- 1-15 S/U vs Top #10 ranked teams all time
- 5-35 S/U vs #10 - #19 ranked teams all time
- 0-17 S/U vs #20 - #25 ranked teams all time
- 0-3 S/U vs ranked Wyoming all time

Pointspread Analysis Conference
- 0-3 S/U @ home vs Colorado State as Dog since 1997
- 3-21 S/U vs Fresno State as Dog since 1985
- 6-1 S/U vs Fresno State as favorite since 1987
- vs Fresno State - Fresno State leads series 43-38-3
- 0-3 S/U & ATS @ home vs Hawaii as favorite since 1999
- 8-1 S/U vs UNLV as favorite since 1995 {6-2-1 ATS}
- Game 7-1 O/U vs Utah State since 2010
- 0-9 S/U vs Utah State since 2009
- 1-9 S/U vs Utah State as Dog since 1985
- 9-2 S/U vs Utah State as favorite since 1986
- vs Utah State - San Jose State leads series 20-19-1
- 4-0 ATS @ Wyoming since 1992
- 0-16 S/U vs Fresno State as 9.5 point or more Dog since 1985
- 0-9 S/U vs Hawaii as 9.5 point or more Dog since 2001
- 0-12 S/U vs Nevada as 6 point or more Dog since 1994
- 1-11 S/U vs San Diego State as 5 point or more Dog since 1995

PORTLAND STATE	2-7 O/U in 1st home game of season since 2009
PORTLAND STATE	8-1-1 ATS in 1st home game of season since 2012
Auburn	2-17 S/U in 1st road game of season since 2003
Wyoming	3-18 S/U in 2nd road game of season since 2001
UNLV	1-12 S/U prior to playing Fresno State since 2007
New Mexico State	3-10 S/U prior to playing Nevada since 2007
New Mexico State	3-9 ATS prior to playing Nevada since 2008
New Mexico State	4-10 O/U prior to playing Nevada since 2006
New Mexico State	0-6 S/U after playing Fresno State since 2007
NEVADA	4-1 S/U prior to playing Colorado State since 2011
COLORADO STATE	4-15 S/U after playing Nevada since 2001
COLORADO STATE	3-10 O/U after playing Nevada since 2008
Utah State	1-12 S/U prior to playing Hawaii since 2008
HAWAII	2-11 O/U after playing Utah State since 2005

SOUTH ALABAMA JAGUARS   SUN BELT West

2021-South Alabama		Opponent	USA	Opp	S/U	Line	ATS	Total	O/U	
9/4/2021	vs	SOUTHERN MISS	31	7	W	-2.0	W	57.0	U	
9/11/2021	@	Bowling Green	22	19	W	-14.0	L	47.5	U	
9/18/2021	vs	ALCORN STATE	28	21	W	-21.0	L	44.0	O	
10/2/2021	vs	LOUISIANA	18	20	L	12.0	W	53.0	U	
10/9/2021	@	Texas State	31	33	L	-4.0	L	52.0	O	{4 OT}
10/14/2021	vs	GEORGIA SOUTHERN	41	13	W	-2.5	W	49.5	O	
10/23/2021	@	Louisiana-Monroe	31	41	L	-13.5	L	51.0	O	
10/30/2021	vs	ARKANSAS STATE	31	13	W	-9.0	L	67.0	U	
11/6/2021	@	Troy	24	31	L	3.5	L	47.5	O	"The Championship Belt"
11/13/2021	@	Appalachian State	7	31	L	21.5	L	51.5	U	
11/20/2021	@	Tennessee	14	60	L	28.5	L	61.5	O	
11/26/2021	vs	COASTAL CAROLINA	21	27	L	14.5	W	55.5	U	{OT}
Coach: Steve Campbell		Season Record >>	299	316	5-7	ATS>>	5-7	O/U>>	6-6	
2020-South Alabama		Opponent	USA	Opp	S/U	Line	ATS	Total	O/U	
9/3/2020	@	Southern Mississippi	32	21	W	13.5	W	54.5	U	
9/12/2020	vs	TULANE	24	27	L	10.5	W	52.0	U	
9/24/2020	vs	ALABAMA-BIRMINGHAM	10	42	L	7.0	L	47.5	O	
10/17/2020	vs	TEXAS STATE	30	20	W	-3.0	W	58.0	U	
10/24/2020	vs	LOUISIANA-MONROE	38	14	W	-14.5	W	57.0	U	
10/29/2020	@	Georgia Southern	17	24	L	3.5	L	51.5	U	
11/7/2020	@	Coastal Carolina	6	23	L	17.0	T	57.0	U	
11/14/2020	@	Louisiana	10	38	L	14.5	L	53.5	U	
11/21/2020	vs	GEORGIA STATE	14	31	L	3.5	L	58.5	U	"Clash of the Claws"
11/28/2020	@	Arkansas State	38	31	W	7.0	W	63.5	O	
12/5/2020	vs	TROY	0	29	L	4.0	L	54.0	U	"The Championship Belt"
Coach: Steve Campbell		Season Record >>	219	300	4-7	ATS>>	5-5-1	O/U>>	2-9	
2019-South Alabama		Opponent	USA	Opp	S/U	Line	ATS	Total	O/U	
8/31/2019	@	Nebraska	21	35	L	36.0	W	64.5	U	
9/7/2019	vs	JACKSON STATE	37	14	W	-25.5	L	NT	---	
9/14/2019	vs	MEMPHIS	6	42	L	20.5	L	55.0	U	
9/21/2019	@	Alabama-Birmingham	3	35	L	12.0	L	48.0	U	
9/28/2019	@	Louisiana-Monroe	17	30	L	14.5	W	58.5	U	
10/3/2019	vs	GEORGIA SOUTHERN	17	20	L	10.0	W	44.5	U	{2 OT}
10/16/2019	@	Troy	13	37	L	17.0	L	54.5	U	"The Championship Belt"
10/26/2019	vs	APPALACHIAN STATE	3	30	L	26.5	L	51.0	U	
11/9/2019	@	Texas State	28	30	L	7.0	W	41.5	O	
11/16/2019	vs	LOUISIANA-LAFAYETTE	27	37	L	27.5	W	52.5	O	
11/23/2019	@	Georgia State	15	28	L	9.5	L	56.0	U	
11/30/2019	vs	ARKANSAS STATE	34	30	W	10.0	W	53.0	O	
Coach: Steve Campbell		Season Record >>	221	368	2-10	ATS>>	6-6	O/U>>	3-8	
2018-South Alabama		Opponent	USA	Opp	S/U	Line	ATS	Total	O/U	
9/1/2018	vs	LOUISIANA TECH	26	30	L	10.5	W	53.0	O	
9/8/2018	@	Oklahoma State	13	55	L	30.5	L	64.0	O	
9/15/2018	vs	TEXAS STATE	41	31	W	-9.5	W	49.0	O	
9/22/2018	@	Memphis	35	52	L	32.0	W	66.0	O	
9/29/2018	@	Appalachian State	7	52	L	25.0	L	56.5	O	
10/6/2018	@	Georgia Southern	13	48	L	12.0	L	57.5	O	
10/13/2018	vs	ALABAMA STATE	45	7	W	-27.0	W	NT	---	
10/23/2018	vs	TROY	17	38	L	11.5	L	52.0	O	"The Championship Belt"
11/3/2018	@	Arkansas State	14	38	L	14.0	L	61.5	U	
11/10/2018	vs	LOUISIANA-MONROE	10	38	L	7.5	L	62.0	U	
11/17/2018	@	Louisiana-Lafayette	38	48	L	19.5	W	65.5	O	
11/24/2018	vs	COASTAL CAROLINA	31	28	W	1.0	W	58.5	O	
Coach: Steve Campbell		Season Record >>	290	465	3-9	ATS>>	6-6	O/U>>	9-2	

SOUTH ALABAMA JAGUARS   SUN BELT West

STADIUM: Ladd Peebles Stadium {40,000} **Location:** Mobile, AL **COACH:** Kane Wommack

DATE		Opponent	USA	Opp	S/U	Line	ATS	Total	O/U	Trends & Angles
9/3/2022	vs	NICHOLLS STATE								vs Nicholls - South Alabama leads series 3-0
9/10/2022	@	Central Michigan								1st Meeting
9/17/2022	@	Ucla								1st Meeting
9/24/2022	vs	LOUISIANA TECH								vs Louisiana Tech - LA Tech leads series 2-0
10/1/2022	@	Louisiana								0-7 S/U vs Louisiana as Dog since 2012
10/15/2022	vs	LOUISIANA-MONROE								vs UL-Monroe - UL-Monroe leads series 5-3
10/20/2022	vs	TROY								0-4 S/U @ home vs Troy as Dog since 2012
10/29/2022	@	Arkansas State								1-4 S/U @ Arkansas State as Dog since 2012
11/5/2022	@	Georgia Southern								0-6 S/U vs Ga South as Dog since 2014 {1-5 ATS}
11/12/2022	vs	TEXAS STATE								vs Texas State - HOME team 7-0 S/U since 2013
11/19/2022	@	Southern Mississippi								vs Southern Miss - USA leads series 2-0
11/26/2022	vs	OLD DOMINION								1st Meeting
12/3/2022	vs									Sun Belt Championship
	vs									BOWL GAME

Pointspread Analysis — Non-Conference

- 1-12 S/U vs Non-Conf. as 20.5 point or more Dog since 2011
- 2-10 S/U vs Non-Conf. as 7.5-15 point Dog since 2011

Dog

- 1-19 S/U as 20.5 point or more Dog since 2011
- 6-2-1 ATS as 15.5-20 point Dog since 2013
- 2-16 S/U as 10.5-15 point Dog since 2014
- 1-8 S/U as 7.5-10 point Dog since 2011
- 3-15 S/U as 7 point or less Dog since 2013
- 4-12-1 ATS as 7 point or less Dog since 2014

Favorite

- 13-0 S/U @ home as 7.5 point or more favorite since 2014

- 1-6 S/U vs Ranked teams all time

Pointspread Analysis — Conference

- vs Arkansas State - Arkansas State leads series 6-4
- vs Georgia Southern - Georgia Southern leads series 7-1
- vs Louisiana - Louisiana leads series 8-2
- vs Texas State - Texas State leads series 4-3
- vs Troy - Troy leads Series 7-3

NICHOLLS	3-7 ATS in 1st home game of season since 2012
LA TECH	3-7 O/U prior to playing Louisiana since 2012
Arkansas State	2-6 O/U prior to playing Georgia Southern since 2014
Arkansas State	1-6 ATS after playing Troy since 2014
Ga Southern	1-7 ATS after playing Arkansas State since 2012
Ga Southern	0-6 S/U prior to playing Texas State since 2014 {1-5 ATS}
Southern Miss	2-9 S/U in final road game of season since 2011
Southern Miss	4-0 ATS after playing Texas State since 2018

This book is for football fans of all ages. It is both educational and entertaining as you can read nostalgically about former great College teams and players, as well as some of the great Bowl Games from the past. This book covers all the Bowl Games of the 21st Century (2000-2010), so you can read about your football heroes, past and present.

College Football History "Bowl Games of the 21st Century" Part I {2000-2010}

$28.95

SOUTH CAROLINA GAMECOCKS   SEC East

2021-South Carolina		Opponent	USC	Opp	S/U	Line	ATS	Total	O/U	
9/4/2021	vs	EASTERN ILLINOIS	46	0	W	-30.5	W	55.5	U	
9/11/2021	@	East Carolina	20	17	W	-2.5	W	56.5	U	
9/18/2021	@	Georgia	13	40	L	31.0	W	47.0	O	
9/25/2021	vs	KENTUCKY	10	16	L	4.5	L	48.5	U	
10/2/2021	vs	TROY	23	14	W	-6.5	W	43.0	U	
10/9/2021	@	Tennessee	20	45	L	10.5	L	56.5	O	
10/16/2021	vs	VANDERBILT	21	20	W	-19.0	L	50.0	U	
10/23/2021	@	Texas A&M	14	44	L	19.0	L	46.0	U	
11/6/2021	vs	FLORIDA	40	17	W	20.5	W	52.0	O	
11/13/2021	@	Missouri	28	31	L	PK	L	56.5	O	
11/20/2021	vs	AUBURN	21	17	W	7.0	W	45.5	U	
11/27/2021	vs	CLEMSON	0	30	L	11.0	L	43.0	U	"Palmetto Bowl"
12/30/2021	vs	North Carolina	38	21	W	13.0	W	57.5	O	Duke's Mayo Bowl
Coach: Shane Beamer		Season Record >>	294	312	7-6	ATS>>	7-6	O/U>>	6-7	

2020-South Carolina		Opponent	USC	Opp	S/U	Line	ATS	Total	O/U	
9/26/2020	vs	TENNESSEE	27	31	L	4.0	T	44.5	O	
10/3/2020	@	Florida	24	38	L	15.0	W	56.5	O	
10/10/2020	@	Vanderbilt	41	7	W	-14.0	W	41.5	O	
10/17/2020	vs	AUBURN	30	22	W	3.0	W	51.5	O	
10/24/2020	@	Lsu	24	52	L	5.0	L	55.0	O	
11/7/2020	vs	TEXAS A&M	3	48	L	9.0	L	58.0	U	
11/14/2020	@	Mississippi	42	59	L	12.0	L	73.0	O	
11/21/2020	vs	MISSOURI	10	17	L	4.5	L	57.5	U	
11/28/2020	vs	GEORGIA	16	45	L	23.0	L	50.0	O	
12/5/2020	@	Kentucky	18	41	L	11.5	L	47.5	O	
Coach: Will Muschamp		Season Record >>	235	360	2-8	ATS>>	3-6-1	O/U>>	8-2	

2019-South Carolina		Opponent	USC	Opp	S/U	Line	ATS	Total	O/U	
8/31/2019	vs	North Carolina	20	24	L	-12.0	L	62.5	U	Bank Of America Stadium
9/7/2019	vs	CHARLESTON SOUTHERN	72	10	W	-36.0	W	NT	---	
9/14/2019	vs	ALABAMA	23	47	L	26.0	W	59.5	O	
9/21/2019	@	Missouri	14	34	L	9.5	L	60.5	U	
9/28/2019	vs	KENTUCKY	24	7	W	-3.5	W	54.0	U	
10/12/2019	@	Georgia	20	17	W	21.0	W	52.5	U	{2 OT}
10/19/2019	vs	FLORIDA	27	38	L	3.5	L	45.0	O	
10/26/2019	@	Tennessee	21	41	L	-4.0	L	47.0	O	
11/2/2019	vs	VANDERBILT	24	7	W	-15.5	W	51.5	U	
11/9/2019	vs	APPALACHIAN STATE	15	20	L	-6.5	L	51.0	L	
11/16/2019	@	Texas A&M	6	30	L	10.5	L	47.0	U	
11/30/2019	vs	CLEMSON	3	38	L	27.0	L	50.5	U	"Palmetto Bowl"
Coach: Will Muschamp		Season Record >>	269	313	4-8	ATS>>	5-7	O/U>>	3-8	

2018-South Carolina		Opponent	USC	Opp	S/U	Line	ATS	Total	O/U	
9/1/2018	vs	COASTAL CAROLINA	49	15	W	-31.0	W	55.5	O	
9/8/2018	vs	GEORGIA	17	41	L	8.0	L	54.0	O	
9/22/2018	@	Vanderbilt	37	14	W	-1.5	W	54.5	U	
9/29/2018	@	Kentucky	10	24	L	1.0	L	52.0	U	
10/6/2018	vs	MISSOURI	37	35	W	PK	W	63.0	O	
10/13/2018	vs	TEXAS A&M	23	26	L	2.5	L	50.0	U	
10/27/2018	vs	TENNESSEE	27	24	W	-10.5	L	53.0	U	
11/3/2018	@	Mississippi	48	44	W	2.5	W	69.5	O	
11/10/2018	@	Florida	31	35	L	6.5	W	54.0	O	
11/17/2018	vs	TENNESSEE-CHATTANOOGA	49	9	W	-30.5	W	NT	---	
11/24/2018	@	Clemson	35	56	L	25.5	W	58.5	O	"Palmetto Bowl"
12/1/2018	vs	AKRON	28	3	W	-28.5	L	56.5	U	
12/29/2018	vs	Virginia	0	28	L	-3.5	L	54.0	U	Belk Bowl
Coach: Will Muschamp		Season Record >>	391	354	7-6	ATS>>	7-6	O/U>>	6-6	

SOUTH CAROLINA GAMECOCKS — SEC East

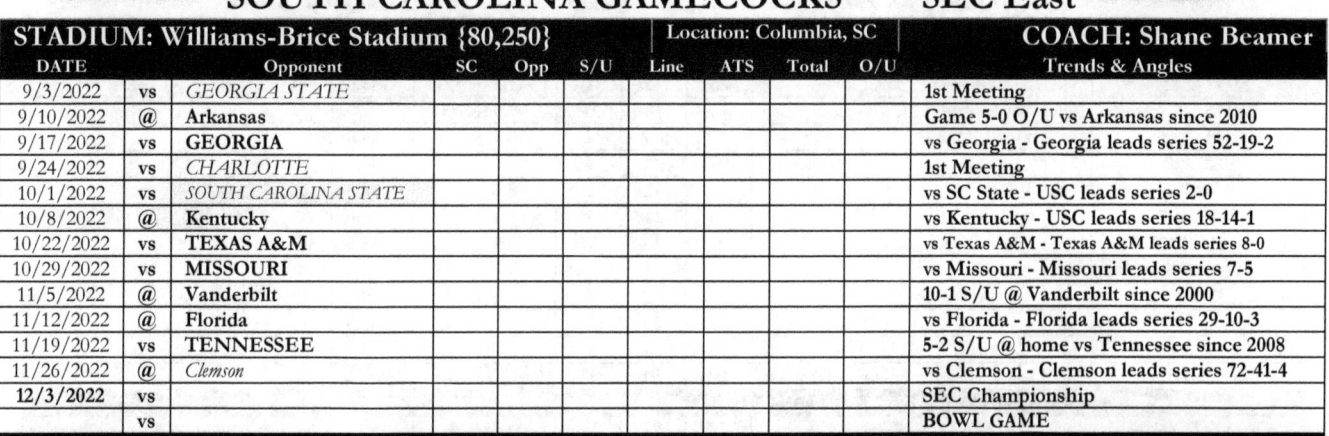

STADIUM: Williams-Brice Stadium {80,250} | **Location:** Columbia, SC | **COACH:** Shane Beamer

DATE		Opponent	SC	Opp	S/U	Line	ATS	Total	O/U	Trends & Angles
9/3/2022	vs	GEORGIA STATE								1st Meeting
9/10/2022	@	Arkansas								Game 5-0 O/U vs Arkansas since 2010
9/17/2022	vs	GEORGIA								vs Georgia - Georgia leads series 52-19-2
9/24/2022	vs	CHARLOTTE								1st Meeting
10/1/2022	vs	SOUTH CAROLINA STATE								vs SC State - USC leads series 2-0
10/8/2022	@	Kentucky								vs Kentucky - USC leads series 18-14-1
10/22/2022	vs	TEXAS A&M								vs Texas A&M - Texas A&M leads series 8-0
10/29/2022	vs	MISSOURI								vs Missouri - Missouri leads series 7-5
11/5/2022	@	Vanderbilt								10-1 S/U @ Vanderbilt since 2000
11/12/2022	@	Florida								vs Florida - Florida leads series 29-10-3
11/19/2022	vs	TENNESSEE								5-2 S/U @ home vs Tennessee since 2008
11/26/2022	@	Clemson								vs Clemson - Clemson leads series 72-41-4
12/3/2022	vs									SEC Championship
	vs									BOWL GAME

Pointspread Analysis — Non-Conference
- 2-15 S/U vs Non-Conf. as 10.5 point or more Dog since 1983
- 0-5 O/U vs Non-Conf. as 3.5-7 point Dog since 2009
- 8-2 S/U vs Non-Conf. as 3 point or less favorite since 1990
- 55-2-1 S/U vs Non-Conf. as 10.5 point or more favorite since 1984
- 1-13 S/U vs Clemson as 7.5 point or more Dog since 1983
- 5-0 S/U vs Clemson as favorite since 1987
- 10-0 S/U vs East Carolina as 9 point or more favorite since 1984

Dog
- 1-41 S/U as 15.5 point or more Dog since 1986
- 1-7 S/U @ home as 10.5-15 point Dog since 1993
- 1-15 S/U on road as 10.5-15 point Dog since 1998
- 0-10 S/U on road as 7.5-10 point Dog since 1998
- 2-13-1 S/U @ home as 7.5-10 point Dog since 1983
- 1-6 O/U on road as 3 point or less Dog since 2013

Favorite
- 10-0 S/U as 3 point or less favorite since 2011
- 1-12 O/U as 3 point or less favorite since 2010
- 9-0 S/U on road as 3 point or less favorite since 1997
- 9-3 S/U on road as 3.5-7 point favorite since 2004
- 5-0 S/U @ home as 7.5-10 point favorite since 2000
- 0-8 ATS as 7.5-10 point favorite since 2001
- 0-4 O/U on road as 7.5-10 point favorite since 2001
- 20-3 S/U @ home as 10.5-15 point favorite since 1997
- 58-2 S/U as 15.5 point or favorite since 1984
- 12-3 O/U as 20.5 point or more favorite since 2009

Bowl Games
- 6-2 S/U & ATS in Bowl Games since 2013
- 1-5 ATS in Bowl Games as 3.5-7 point favorite since 1987
- 29-5 S/U @ home when ranked since 2009
- 4-0 S/U & ATS when ranked vs Clemson since 2010
- 0-7 O/U when ranked vs Clemson since 2000
- 0-13 S/U on road vs ranked teams since 2014
- 0-14 S/U vs #2 ranked teams all time
- 0-4 S/U vs Arkansas all time
- 2-21 S/U vs ranked Florida all time
- 3-15 S/U vs ranked Tennessee all time

Pointspread Analysis — Conference
- 5-0 O/U vs Arkansas as favorite since 2004
- vs Arkansas - Arkansas leads series 13-10
- 3-0 S/U vs Florida as favorite since 2011
- 5-0 S/U vs Georgia as favorite since 1988
- 1-3 S/U & ATS vs Kentucky as favorite since 2014
- vs Tennessee - Tennessee leads series 28-10-2
- 0-5 ATS vs Tennessee as favorite since 2012
- 1-6 S/U @ home vs Tennessee as Dog since 1994
- Game 1-5 O/U vs Texas A&M since 2016
- 23-3 S/U vs Vanderbilt as favorite since 1993
- vs Vanderbilt - South Carolina leads series 27-4
- 3-0 S/U @ Vanderbilt as Dog since 1992
- 13-0 S/U vs Vanderbilt since 2009
- Game 2-5 O/U @ Vanderbilt since 2008
- 0-6 S/U & ATS vs Arkansas as 5 point or more Dog since 1998
- 1-20 S/U vs Florida as 7 point or more Dog since 1992
- 1-8 S/U vs Georgia as 14 point or more Dog since 1983
- 1-11 S/U vs Georgia as 5.5-8.5 point Dog since 1985
- 5-0 S/U vs Kentucky as 13 point or more favorite since 2001
- 0-8 S/U vs Tennessee as 15.5 point or more Dog since 1993
- 1-8 S/U vs Tennessee as 7.5 point or less Dog since 1994
- 7-0 S/U vs Vanderbilt as 6.5 point or less favorite since 1993
- 12-1 S/U vs Vanderbilt as 12 point or more favorite since 1995

Arkansas	15-4 S/U prior to playing Georgia since 2003
GEORGIA	11-5 S/U in 2nd home game of season since 2006
CHARLOTTE	7-2-1 O/U after playing Georgia since 2012
CHARLOTTE	10-4 S/U after playing Georgia since 2008
S. C. STATE	2-9 O/U prior to playing Kentucky since 2011
TEXAS A&M	3-10 O/U after playing Kentucky since 2007
Florida	7-2 O/U prior to playing Tennessee since 2012
TENNESSEE	10-1 O/U after playing Florida since 2008
TENNESSEE	9-4 S/U after playing Florida since 2009

SOUTHERN CALIFORNIA TROJANS   PACIFIC-12 South

2021-Southern California		Opponent	USC	Opp	S/U	Line	ATS	Total	O/U	
9/4/2021	vs	SAN JOSE STATE	30	7	W	-13.5	W	61.0	U	
9/11/2021	vs	STANFORD	28	42	L	-17.5	L	53.5	O	
9/18/2021	@	Washington State	45	14	W	-7.0	W	61.0	U	
9/25/2021	vs	OREGON STATE	27	45	L	-10.0	L	63.5	O	
10/2/2021	@	Colorado	37	14	W	-9.0	W	50.5	O	
10/9/2021	vs	UTAH	26	42	L	-3.0	L	53.5	O	
10/23/2021	@	Notre Dame	16	31	L	8.0	L	59.5	U	"Jeweled Shillelagh"
10/30/2021	vs	ARIZONA	41	34	W	-21.5	L	55.5	O	
11/6/2021	@	Arizona State	16	31	L	9.5	L	61.0	U	
11/20/2021	vs	UCLA	33	62	L	4.5	L	69.5	O	"Victory Bell"
11/27/2021	vs	BYU	31	35	L	8.5	W	65.5	O	
12/4/2021	@	California	14	24	L	4.5	L	57.0	U	
Coach: Clay Helton		Season Record >>	344	381	4-8	ATS>>	4-8	O/U>>	7-5	

2020-Southern California		Opponent	USC	Opp	S/U	Line	ATS	Total	O/U	
11/7/2020	vs	ARIZONA STATE	28	27	W	-11.5	L	57.5	U	
11/14/2020	@	Arizona	34	30	W	-14.5	L	67.0	U	
11/21/2020	@	Utah	33	17	W	-2.5	W	58.5	U	
12/6/2020	vs	WASHINGTON STATE	38	13	W	-11.0	W	68.0	U	
12/12/2020	@	Ucla	43	38	W	-3.5	W	65.0	O	"Victory Bell"
12/18/2020	vs	OREGON	24	31	L	-3.0	L	65.5	U	PAC-12 Championship
Coach: Clay Helton		Season Record >>	200	156	5-1	ATS>>	3-3	O/U>>	1-5	

2019-Southern California		Opponent	USC	Opp	S/U	Line	ATS	Total	O/U	
8/31/2019	vs	FRESNO STATE	31	23	W	-14.0	L	50.0	O	
9/7/2019	vs	STANFORD	45	20	W	-3.0	W	43.0	O	
9/14/2019	@	Byu	27	30	L	-4.5	L	57.5	U	{OT}
9/20/2019	vs	UTAH	30	23	W	3.5	W	53.0	T	
9/28/2019	@	Washington	14	28	L	11.0	L	60.5	U	
10/12/2019	@	Notre Dame	27	30	L	10.5	W	59.0	U	"Jeweled Shillelagh"
10/19/2019	vs	ARIZONA	41	14	W	-10.0	W	69.0	U	
10/25/2019	@	Colorado	35	31	W	-10.5	L	64.5	O	
11/2/2019	vs	OREGON	24	56	L	3.5	L	60.0	O	
11/9/2019	@	Arizona State	31	26	W	-4.5	W	54.0	O	
11/16/2019	@	California	41	17	W	-4.0	W	48.5	O	
11/23/2019	vs	UCLA	52	35	W	-13.0	W	66.5	O	"Victory Bell"
12/27/2019	vs	Iowa	24	49	L	-1.5	L	54.5	O	Holiday Bowl
Coach: Clay Helton		Season Record >>	422	382	8-5	ATS>>	7-6	O/U>>	8-4-1	

2018-Southern California		Opponent	USC	Opp	S/U	Line	ATS	Total	O/U	
9/1/2018	vs	UNLV	43	21	W	-24.5	L	59.0	O	
9/8/2018	@	Stanford	3	17	L	4.5	L	54.5	U	
9/15/2018	@	Texas	14	37	L	3.5	L	47.5	O	
9/21/2018	vs	WASHINGTON STATE	39	36	W	-4.5	L	50.5	O	
9/29/2018	@	Arizona	24	20	W	-3.0	W	61.5	U	
10/13/2018	vs	COLORADO	31	20	W	-7.0	W	57.5	U	
10/20/2018	@	Utah	28	41	L	6.5	L	48.0	O	
10/27/2018	vs	ARIZONA STATE	35	38	L	-3.0	L	52.0	O	
11/3/2018	@	Oregon State	38	21	W	-15.0	W	65.5	U	
11/10/2018	vs	CALIFORNIA	14	15	L	-4.0	L	45.5	U	
11/17/2018	@	Ucla	27	34	L	-2.5	L	54.5	O	"Victory Bell"
11/24/2018	vs	NOTRE DAME	17	24	L	14.0	W	54.0	U	"Jeweled Shillelagh"
Coach: Clay Helton		Season Record >>	313	324	5-7	ATS>>	4-8	O/U>>	6-6	

SOUTHERN CALIFORNIA TROJANS — PACIFIC-12 South

STADIUM: Los Angeles Memorial Coliseum {78,500}
Location: Los Angeles, CA
COACH: Lincoln Riley

DATE		Opponent	USC	Opp	S/U	Line	ATS	Total	O/U	Trends & Angles
9/3/2022	vs	RICE								vs Rice - USC leads series 2-0-1
9/10/2022	@	Stanford								Game 0-4 O/U @ Stanford since 2012
9/17/2022	vs	FRESNO STATE								vs Fresno State - USC leads series 4-1
9/24/2022	@	Oregon State								Game 0-3 O/U @ Oregon State since 2008
10/1/2022	vs	ARIZONA STATE								vs Arizona State - USC leads series 25-13
10/8/2022	vs	WASHINGTON STATE								12-2 S/U vs Washington State since 2003
10/15/2022	@	Utah								1-4 ATS @ Utah since 2012
10/29/2022	@	Arizona								vs Arizona - USC leads series 37-8
11/5/2022	vs	CALIFORNIA								15-1 S/U vs California as favorite since 2004
11/12/2022	vs	COLORADO								vs Colorado - USC leads series 15-0
11/19/2022	@	Ucla								Game 4-0 O/U vs UCLA since 2018
11/26/2022	vs	NOTRE DAME								vs Notre Dame - Notre Dame leads series 50-37-5
12/3/2022	vs									PAC-12 Championship
	vs									BOWL GAME

Pointspread Analysis — Non-Conference
- 1-6-1 O/U vs Non-Conf. as 3 point or less Dog since 1990
- 13-1 S/U vs Non-Conf. as 7.5-10 point favorite since 1993
- 11-0 S/U vs Non-Conf. as 10.5-15 point favorite since 1990
- 12-2 S/U vs Non-Conf. as 15.5-20 point favorite since 1993
- 29-1 S/U vs Non-Conf. as 20.5 point or more favorite since 1983
- 1-10 S/U Notre Dame as 7.5 point or less Dog since 1986
- 11-1 S/U vs Notre Dame as favorite since 1998

Dog
- 3-15 ATS as a Dog since 2015
- 1-11 S/U & ATS as 3.5-7 point Dog since 2014
- 1-5 S/U & ATS on road as 3 point or less Dog since 2002
- 1-6 S/U @ home as 3 point or less Dog since 1983

Favorite
- 21-5 S/U as 3.5-7 point favorite since 2013
- 10-2 S/U @ home as 3.5-7 point favorite since 2013
- 3-8 O/U as 7.5-10 point favorite since 2011
- 8-1 S/U on road as 7.5-10 point favorite since 1998
- 19-2 S/U @ home as 10.5-15 point favorite since 2002
- 11-0 S/U on road as 10.5-15 point favorite since 2008
- 26-2 S/U as 10.5-15 point favorite since 2008
- 3-12 O/U on road as 10.5-15 point favorite since 2005
- 15-2 S/U on road as 15.5-20 point favorite since 1988
- 16-3 S/U @ home as 15.5-20 point favorite since 1998
- 6-21-1 O/U as 15.5-20 point favorite since 2004
- 51-2 S/U @ home as 20.5 point or more favorite since 1983
- 21-1 S/U on road as 20.5 point or more favorite since 1983
- 4-12 O/U as 25.5 point or more favorite since 2006

Bowl Games
- 25-9 S/U in Rose Bowl
- 7-0 S/U vs Big Ten in Rose Bowl since 1990 {6-1 ATS}
- 8-3 S/U vs Big Ten in Bowl Games since 1996
- 6-1 S/U & ATS vs Michigan in bowl Games since 1970
- 0-3 S/U & ATS in Sun Bowl
- 1-4 ATS in Bowl Games as 7.5-10 point favorite since 1980

- 1-12 S/U on road vs ranked teams since 2014
- 0-6 S/U vs ranked Notre Dame since 2012
- 69-6-2 S/U when #1 ranked all time
- 32-2 S/U on road when #1 ranked all time
- 16-0 S/U @ home when #1 ranked since 2004
- 22-0 S/U when #4 ranked since 1976 {9-0 on road}
- 18-0 S/U @ home when #4 ranked since 1967

Pointspread Analysis — Conference
- 5-1 O/U vs Arizona State as Dog since 1996
- 1-6 S/U vs Arizona State as Dog since 1983
- vs California - USC leads series 71-32-5
- 3-13 O/U vs California as favorite since 2004
- 1-4 S/U @ Stanford since 2010
- vs Stanford - USC leads series 64-34-3
- vs Ucla - USC leads series 51-33-7
- 1-3 S/U @ Utah since 2014
- vs Utah - USC leads series 13-7
- vs Washington State - USC Leads series 62-10-4
- Game 1-5 O/U @ home vs Washington State since 2005
- 11-1 S/U vs Arizona as 6.5 point or less favorite since 1984
- 9-0 S/U vs Arizona as 14 point or more favorite since 2003
- 1-6 O/U vs Arizona as 14 point or more favorite since 2006
- 13-1 S/U vs Arizona State as 9 point or more favorite since 1988
- 9-0 S/U vs CAL as 16 point or more favorite since 1986
- 18-1 S/U vs Oregon State as 12 point or more favorite since 1983
- 15-1 S/U vs Stanford as 10.5 point or more favorite since 1983
- 2-7 ATS vs UCLA as 5 point or less favorite since 1990
- 10-0 S/U vs UCLA as 13 point or more favorite since 2003
- 1-6 O/U vs UCLA as 13 point or more favorite since 2007
- 9-0 S/U vs Washington State as 7.5-9.5 point favorite since 1983
- 8-0 S/U vs Wash. State as 16.5 point or more favorite since 1987

RICE	23-1 S/U in 1st home game of season since 1998
RICE	17-2 S/U prior to playing Stanford since 2002
Stanford	3-10 ATS in 1st road game of season since 2009
Stanford	0-10 O/U in 1st road game of season since 2012
FRESNO STATE	18-2 S/U in 2nd home game of season since 2002
FRESNO STATE	9-2 ATS in 2nd home game of season since 2011
FRESNO STATE	15-4 S/U after playing Stanford since 2002
Oregon State	2-7 S/U in 2nd road game of season since 2013
Oregon State	2-8 ATS in 2nd road game of season since 2012
Oregon State	10-2 O/U prior to playing Arizona State since 2009
Oregon State	2-10 ATS prior to playing Arizona State since 2009
ARIZONA STATE	12-4 S/U prior to playing Washington State since 2000
ARIZONA STATE	1-7 ATS prior to playing Washington State since 2009
Utah	15-2 S/U after playing Washington State since 1999
Utah	3-8 O/U after playing Washington State since 2006
Utah	2-7 O/U prior to playing Washington State since 2008
Arizona	15-3 S/U prior to playing California since 2003
CALIFORNIA	8-1 S/U prior to playing Colorado since 2012
CALIFORNIA	3-9 O/U prior to playing Colorado since 2000
CALIFORNIA	3-12-1 O/U after playing Arizona since 2005
Ucla	2-10 ATS after playing Colorado since 2000
NOTRE DAME	4-10-1 O/U in final home game of season since 2007
NOTRE DAME	9-3 ATS after playing UCLA since 1996

SOUTH FLORIDA BULLS   AMERICAN East

2021-South Florida		Opponent	USF	Opp	S/U	Line	ATS	Total	O/U	
9/2/2021	@	NC State	0	45	L	20.0	L	57.0	U	
9/11/2021	vs	FLORIDA	20	42	L	29.0	W	56.5	O	
9/18/2021	vs	FLORIDA A&M	38	17	W	-22.5	L	49.0	O	
9/25/2021	@	Byu	27	35	L	23.0	W	54.5	O	
10/2/2021	@	Smu	17	41	L	21.5	L	68.5	U	
10/16/2021	vs	TULSA	31	32	L	7.0	W	55.5	O	
10/23/2021	vs	TEMPLE	34	14	W	-1.5	W	55.0	U	
10/28/2021	@	East Carolina	14	29	L	9.5	L	55.5	U	
11/6/2021	vs	HOUSTON	42	54	L	13.5	W	53.0	O	
11/12/2021	vs	CINCINNATI	28	38	L	24.0	W	58.5	O	
11/20/2021	@	Tulane	14	45	L	5.5	L	59.5	U	
11/26/2021	@	Central Florida	13	17	L	17.0	W	62.0	U	"War on I-4 Trophy"
Coach: Jeff Scott		Season Record >>	278	409	2-10	ATS>>	7-5	O/U>>	6-6	
2020-South Florida		Opponent	USF	Opp	S/U	Line	ATS	Total	O/U	
9/12/2020	vs	THE CITADEL	27	6	W	-17.5	W	53.5	U	
9/19/2020	@	Notre Dame	0	52	L	23.0	L	49.5	O	
10/3/2020	@	Cincinnati	7	28	L	22.5	W	45.5	U	
10/10/2020	vs	EAST CAROLINA	24	44	L	-5.0	L	58.0	O	
10/17/2020	@	Temple	37	39	L	10.5	W	54.0	O	
10/23/2020	vs	TULSA	13	42	L	12.5	L	52.0	O	
11/7/2020	@	Memphis	33	34	L	17.5	W	67.0	T	
11/14/2020	@	Houston	21	56	L	15.0	L	58.5	O	
11/27/2020	vs	CENTRAL FLORIDA	46	58	L	25.0	W	70.5	O	"War on I-4 Trophy"
Coach: Jeff Scott		Season Record >>	208	359	1-8	ATS>>	5-4	O/U>>	6-2-1	
2019-South Florida		Opponent	USF	Opp	S/U	Line	ATS	Total	O/U	
8/30/2019	vs	WISCONSIN	0	49	L	10.5	L	58.5	U	
9/7/2019	@	Georgia Tech	10	14	L	4.5	W	58.5	U	
9/14/2019	vs	SOUTH CAROLINA STATE	55	16	W	-26.0	W	NT	---	
9/28/2019	vs	SMU	21	48	L	7.0	L	62.0	O	
10/5/2019	@	Connecticut	48	22	W	-11.0	W	48.0	O	
10/12/2019	vs	BYU	27	23	W	4.5	W	49.5	O	
10/19/2019	@	Navy	3	35	L	15.5	L	51.0	U	
10/26/2019	@	East Carolina	45	20	W	-1.5	W	51.0	O	
11/7/2019	vs	TEMPLE	7	17	L	PK	L	50.5	U	
11/16/2019	vs	CINCINNATI	17	20	L	13.0	W	46.5	U	
11/23/2019	vs	MEMPHIS	10	49	L	14.5	L	59.5	O	
11/29/2019	@	Central Florida	7	34	L	24.0	L	61.5	U	"War on I-4 Trophy"
Coach: Charlie Strong		Season Record >>	250	347	4-8	ATS>>	6-6	O/U>>	5-6	
2018-South Florida		Opponent	USF	Opp	S/U	Line	ATS	Total	O/U	
9/1/2018	vs	ELON	34	14	W	-27.0	L	NT	---	
9/8/2018	vs	GEORGIA TECH	49	38	W	3.0	W	60.0	O	
9/15/2018	@	Illinois	25	19	W	-14.0	L	58.5	U	Soldier Field
9/22/2018	vs	EAST CAROLINA	20	13	W	-19.5	L	68.5	U	
10/6/2018	@	Massachusetts	58	42	W	-16.0	T	71.0	O	
10/12/2018	@	Tulsa	25	24	W	-10.0	L	60.5	U	
10/20/2018	vs	CONNECTICUT	38	30	W	-33.5	L	67.5	O	
10/27/2018	@	Houston	36	57	L	9.5	L	77.5	O	
11/3/2018	vs	TULANE	15	41	L	-5.5	L	61.5	U	
11/10/2018	@	Cincinnati	23	35	L	16.0	W	52.5	O	
11/17/2018	@	Temple	17	27	L	14.0	W	62.5	U	
11/23/2018	vs	CENTRAL FLORIDA	10	38	L	15.5	L	69.5	U	"War on I-4 Trophy"
12/20/2018	vs	Marshall	20	38	L	2.0	L	50.0	O	Gasparilla Bowl
Coach: Charlie Strong		Season Record >>	370	416	7-6	ATS>>	3-9-1	O/U>>	6-6	

SOUTH FLORIDA BULLS   AMERICAN East

STADIUM: Raymond James Stadium {65,618} **Location:** Tampa, FL **COACH:** Jeff Scott

DATE		Opponent	USF	Opp	S/U	Line	ATS	Total	O/U	Trends & Angles
9/3/2022	vs	BYU								vs BYU - Series tied 1-1
9/10/2022	vs	HOWARD								1st Meeting
9/17/2022	@	Florida								vs Florida - Florida leads series 2-0
9/24/2022	@	Louisville								0-6 O/U vs Louisville as Dog since 2004
10/1/2022	vs	EAST CAROLINA								vs East Carolina - USF leads series 9-3
10/8/2022	@	Cincinnati								0-4 S/U @ Cincinnati as Dog since 2012
10/15/2022	vs	TULANE								vs Tulane - Tulane leads series 2-1
10/29/2022	@	Houston								vs Houston - Houston leads series 6-2
11/5/2022	@	Temple								0-4 S/U @ Temple since 2012
11/12/2022	vs	SMU								1-5 ATS vs SMU since 2013
11/19/2022	@	Tulsa								vs Tulsa - South Florida leads series 3-2
11/26/2022	vs	CENTRAL FLORIDA								0-7 S/U vs Central Fla as Dog since 2013
12/3/2022	vs									AAC Championship
	vs									BOWL GAME

Pointspread Analysis — Non-Conference

- 1-10 S/U vs non-Conf. as 15.5 point or more Dog since 2001
- 1-7 S/U vs Non-Conf. as 3.5-7 point Dog since 2005
- 7-1 S/U vs Non-Conf. as 7 point or less favorite since 2002
- 30-2 S/U vs Non-Conf. as 10.5 point or more favorite since 2001

Dog
- 12-4 ATS as 20.5 point or more Dog since 2001
- 7-3 ATS as 15.5-20 point Dog since 2012
- 0-5 O/U @ home as 15.5-20 point Dog since 2005
- 1-10 S/U as 15.5-20 point Dog since 2006
- 0-12 S/U as 10.5-15 point Dog since 2012
- 1-8 S/U @ home as 3.5-7 point Dog since 2009
- 1-9 S/U on road as 3.5-7 point Dog since 2008
- 5-11 O/U as 3.5-7 point Dog since 2012
- 4-10-1 ATS as 3.5-7 point Dog since 2012
- 10-1 O/U as 3 point or less Dog since 2003

Favorite
- 6-0 S/U & ATS as 3 point or less favorite since 2014
- 0-4 S/U @ home as 7.5-10 point favorite since 2012
- 0-7 ATS @ home as 7.5-10 point favorite since 2008
- 0-11 ATS as 7.5-10 point favorite since 2008
- 19-0 S/U on road as 10.5 point or more favorite since 2002
- 37-3 S/U @ home as 10.5 point or more favorite since 2001

Bowl Games
- 5-0 O/U in Bowl Games since 2010
- 3-0 S/U in Birmingham Bowl since 2006

Pointspread Analysis — Conference

- vs Central Florida - UCF leads series 7-6
- 6-0 S/U vs Central Florida as favorite since 2005
- vs Cincinnati - Cincinnati leads series 12-7
- 7-1 S/U vs East Carolina as favorite since 2003
- Game 1-5 O/U vs SMU since 2013
- vs SMU - Series tied 3-3
- 3-0 S/U vs SMU as favorite since 2014
- vs Temple - Temple leads series 5-3
- 3-0 S/U vs Tulsa as favorite since 2014

- 9-1 S/U @ home when ranked since 2011
- 4-12 ATS on road when ranked since 2007
- 0-9 S/U on road vs ranked teams since 2012
- 9-1 ATS on road vs ranked teams since 2011
- 2-13 S/U @ home vs ranked teams since 2009
- 0-5 S/U vs ranked Cincinnati since 2009

Florida	1-8 O/U in 1st road game of season since 2013
BYU	22-3 S/U in 1st home game of season since 1997
Louisville	7-1 O/U in 2nd road game of season since 2014

Print Version $24.95   Print Version $34.95   Print Version $34.95

These books available at numerous online retailers

SOUTHERN METHODIST MUSTANGS — AMERICAN West

2021-SMU		Opponent	SMU	Opp	S/U	Line	ATS	Total	O/U	
9/4/2021	vs	ABILENE CHRISTIAN	56	9	W	-32.0	W	66.0	U	
9/11/2021	vs	NORTH TEXAS	35	12	W	-2.5	W	76.0	U	"Safeway Bowl"
9/18/2021	@	Louisiana Tech	39	37	W	-11.0	L	66.0	O	
9/25/2021	@	Tcu	42	34	W	9.5	W	66.0	O	"Iron Skillet"
10/2/2021	vs	SOUTH FLORIDA	41	17	W	-21.5	W	68.5	U	
10/9/2021	@	Navy	31	24	W	-13.0	L	57.5	U	"Ganzs Trophy"
10/21/2021	vs	TULANE	55	26	W	-14.0	W	70.5	O	
10/30/2021	@	Houston	37	44	L	-1.0	L	62.0	O	
11/6/2021	@	Memphis	25	28	L	-3.0	L	72.0	U	
11/13/2021	vs	CENTRAL FLORIDA	55	28	W	-7.0	W	61.5	O	
11/20/2021	@	Cincinnati	14	48	L	9.5	L	65.0	U	
11/27/2021	vs	TULSA	31	34	L	-6.0	L	62.5	O	
Coach: Sonny Dykes		Season Record >>	461	341	8-4	ATS>>	6-6	O/U>>	6-6	

2020-SMU		Opponent	SMU	Opp	S/U	Line	ATS	Total	O/U	
9/5/2020	@	Texas State	31	24	W	-24.0	L	70.0	U	
9/19/2020	@	North Texas	65	35	W	-14.5	W	71.0	O	"Safeway Bowl"
9/26/2020	vs	STEPHEN F. AUSTIN	50	7	W	-38.0	W	63.5	U	
10/1/2020	vs	MEMPHIS	30	27	W	-2.0	W	75.0	U	
10/16/2020	@	Tulane	37	34	W	-6.5	L	64.5	O	{OT}
10/24/2020	vs	CINCINNATI	13	42	L	1.0	L	57.5	U	
10/31/2020	vs	NAVY	51	37	W	-12.5	W	59.0	O	"Ganzs Trophy"
11/7/2020	@	Temple	47	23	W	-17.0	W	63.5	O	
11/14/2020	@	Tulsa	24	28	L	-2.0	L	63.5	U	
11/28/2020	@	East Carolina	38	52	L	-12.5	L	72.0	O	
Coach: Sonny Dykes		Season Record >>	386	309	7-3	ATS>>	5-5	O/U>>	5-5	

2019-SMU		Opponent	SMU	Opp	S/U	Line	ATS	Total	O/U	
8/31/2019	@	Arkansas State	37	30	W	2.5	W	56.0	O	
9/7/2019	vs	NORTH TEXAS	49	27	W	-3.5	W	73.0	O	"Safeway Bowl"
9/14/2019	vs	TEXAS STATE	47	17	W	-17.5	W	62.5	O	
9/21/2019	@	Tcu	41	38	W	7.5	W	54.0	O	"Iron Skillet"
9/28/2019	@	South Florida	48	21	W	-7.0	W	62.0	O	
10/5/2019	vs	TULSA	43	37	W	-12.0	L	63.0	O	{3 OT}
10/19/2019	vs	TEMPLE	45	21	W	-9.5	W	60.0	O	
10/24/2019	@	Houston	34	31	W	-12.0	L	65.0	T	
11/2/2019	@	Memphis	48	54	L	5.5	L	72.0	O	
11/9/2019	vs	EAST CAROLINA	59	51	W	-22.5	L	74.0	O	
11/23/2019	@	Navy	28	35	L	3.0	L	69.0	U	"Ganzs Trophy"
11/30/2019	vs	TULANE	37	20	W	-3.0	W	72.0	U	
12/21/2019	@	Florida Atlantic	28	52	L	-7.0	L	63.5	O	Boca Raton Bowl
Coach: Sonny Dykes		Season Record >>	544	434	10-3	ATS>>	7-6	O/U>>	10-2-1	

2018-SMU		Opponent	SMU	Opp	S/U	Line	ATS	Total	O/U	
9/1/2018	vs	NORTH TEXAS	23	46	L	3.5	L	71.5	U	"Safeway Bowl"
9/7/2018	@	Tcu	12	42	L	23.5	L	59.0	U	"Iron Skillet"
9/15/2018	@	Michigan	20	45	L	36.0	W	54.0	O	
9/22/2018	vs	NAVY	31	30	W	6.0	W	58.0	O	"Ganzs Trophy"
9/29/2018	vs	HOUSTON BAPTIST	63	27	W	-43.5	L	NT	---	
10/6/2018	@	Central Florida	20	48	L	25.0	L	74.0	O	
10/20/2018	@	Tulane	27	23	W	7.0	W	55.5	U	
10/27/2018	vs	CINCINNATI	20	26	L	9.5	W	49.5	U	{OT}
11/3/2018	vs	HOUSTON	45	31	W	13.5	W	70.5	O	
11/10/2018	@	Connecticut	62	50	W	-18.0	W	65.5	O	
11/16/2018	vs	MEMPHIS	18	28	L	8.5	L	74.5	U	
11/24/2018	@	Tulsa	24	27	L	-2.5	L	53.5	U	
Coach: Sonny Dykes		Season Record >>	365	423	5-7	ATS>>	6-6	O/U>>	5-7	

SOUTHERN METHODIST MUSTANGS — AMERICAN West

STADIUM: Gerald R. Ford Stadium {32,000} | **Location:** Dallas, TX | **COACH:** Rhett Lashlee

DATE		Opponent	SMU	Opp	S/U	Line	ATS	Total	O/U	Trends & Angles
9/3/2022	@	North Texas								vs North Texas - SMU leads series 34-6-1
9/10/2022	vs	LAMAR								1st Meeting
9/17/2022	@	Maryland								vs Maryland - Maryland leads series 2-0
9/24/2022	vs	TCU								1-9 S/U @ home vs TCU since 2000
10/1/2022	@	Central Florida								vs Central Florida - UCF leads series 8-2
10/14/2022	vs	NAVY								vs Navy - Navy leads series 13-10
10/22/2022	vs	CINCINNATI								0-5 S/U vs Cincinnati as Dog since 2013
10/29/2022	@	Tulsa								0-5 S/U @ Tulsa since 2011
11/5/2022	vs	HOUSTON								vs Houston - Houston leads series 22-13-1
11/12/2022	@	South Florida								vs South Florida - Series tied 3-3
11/17/2022	@	Tulane								7-0 S/U vs Tulane since 2015
11/26/2022	vs	MEMPHIS								vs Memphis - Memphis leads series 10-4
12/5/2020	vs									AAC Championship
	vs									BOWL GAME

Pointspread Analysis — Non-Conference
- 0-28 S/U vs Non-Conf. as 15.5 point or more Dog since 1994
- 1-6 O/U vs Non-Conf. as 10.5-15 point Dog since 2002
- 2-6 S/U vs Non-Conf. as 7.5-10 point Dog since 1998
- 1-8 S/U vs Non-Conf. as 3.5-7 point Dog since 1998
- 1-5 S/U & ATS vs Non-conf. as 3 point or less Dog since 2003
- 6-22 S/U vs TCU as Dog since 1984
- 6-1 S/U vs TCU as favorite since 1983
- 4-17 S/U vs TCU since 1999
- vs Tcu - TCU leads series 51-41-7

Dog
- 0-34 S/U as 25.5 point or more Dog since 1989
- 1-7 ATS as 25.5-30 point Dog since 1991
- 1-16 S/U on road as 20.5-25 point Dog since 1994
- 1-12 S/U @ home as 20.5-25 point Dog since 1995
- 1-21 S/U on road as 15.5-20 point Dog since 1990
- 1-7 S/U @ home as 15.5-20 point Dog since 1989
- 1-6 S/U as 10.5-15 point Dog since 2015
- 1-7 O/U @ home as 10.5-15 point Dog since 2008
- 1-10 S/U @ home as 10.5-15 point Dog since 2007
- 12-3 ATS @ home as 10.5-15 point Dog since 2002
- 2-21 S/U as 7.5-10 point Dog since 1998
- 4-12 O/U as 7.5-10 point Dog since 2002
- 5-16 ATS as 7.5-10 point Dog since 1999
- 19-4 O/U as 3.5-7 point Dog since 2005
- 2-15 S/U & ATS as 3 point or less Dog since 2000
- 4-11 O/U as 3 point or less Dog since 2003

Favorite
- 1-7 O/U as 3 point or less favorite since 2017
- 5-0 S/U on road as 3.5-7 point favorite since 2013
- 6-1 S/U @ home as 3.5-7 point favorite since 2009
- 5-0 S/U on road as 7.5-10 point favorite since 1985
- 15-1 S/U @ home as 10.5-15 point favorite since 2000
- 19-0 S/U @ home as 15.5 point or more favorite since 1997

Pointspread Analysis — Conference
- 0-8 S/U vs Central Florida as Dog since 2007
- 0-6 S/U & ATS vs Memphis as Dog since 2014
- 1-10 S/U vs Navy as Dog since 1996
- vs Tulane - SMU leads series 15-13
- 7-1 O/U vs Tulane as favorite since 2011
- Game 7-2 O/U vs Tulane since 2011
- vs Tulsa - SMU leads series 15-13
- 9-3 S/U vs Tulsa as favorite since 1997
- 2-6 O/U vs Tulsa as favorite since 2001
- 0-7 ATS vs Tulsa as favorite since 2002
- 1-7 S/U vs Houston as 19.5 point or more Dog since 1989
- 9-0 ATS vs Tulsa as 5.5 point or more Dog since 2004

Bowl Games
- 3-0 S/U in Hawaii Bowl since 1984
- 1-5 O/U in Bowl Games since 2009
- 0-4 S/U & ATS in Bowl Games as 3.5-7 point favorite since 1983

North Texas	5-20 S/U in 1st road game of season since 1997
NAVY	2-7 S/U after playing Central Florida since 2007
Tulsa	6-1 O/U prior to playing Houston since 2014
Tulsa	3-11 S/U prior to playing Houston since 2007
Tulane	7-2-1 O/U prior to playing Memphis since 2012

- 2-34 S/U on road vs ranked teams since 1989
- 5-21-1 S/U @ home vs ranked teams since 1986
- 6-56-1 S/U vs ranked teams since 1986
- 26-5-1 S/U @ home when ranked since 1979
- 3-0 S/U when ranked vs North Texas all time
- 6-0 S/U when ranked vs TCU since 1979

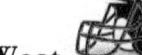

SOUTHERN MISS GOLDEN EAGLES Sun Belt West

2021-Southern Miss		Opponent	USM	Opp	S/U	Line	ATS	Total	O/U	
9/4/2021	@	South Alabama	7	31	L	2.0	L	57.0	U	
9/11/2021	vs	GRAMBLING STATE	37	0	W	-23.5	W	48.0	U	
9/18/2021	vs	TROY	9	21	L	11.0	L	49.5	U	
9/25/2021	@	Alabama	14	63	L	45.5	L	57.5	O	
10/2/2021	@	Rice	19	24	L	1.5	L	44.5	U	
10/9/2021	vs	TEXAS-EL PASO	13	26	L	1.0	L	46.5	U	
10/16/2021	vs	ALABAMA-BRIMINGHAM	0	34	L	17.5	L	43.5	U	
10/30/2021	@	Middle Tennessee	10	35	L	12.5	L	47.0	U	
11/6/2021	vs	NORTH TEXAS	14	38	L	5.0	L	49.0	O	
11/13/2021	@	Texas-San Antonio	17	27	L	32.5	W	54.0	U	
11/20/2021	@	Louisiana Tech	35	19	W	15.0	W	47.5	O	"Rivalry in Dixie"
11/27/2021	vs	FLORIDA INTERNATIONAL	37	17	W	-15.0	W	45.5	O	
Coach: Will Hall		Season Record >>	212	335	3-9	ATS>>	4-8	O/U>>	4-8	
2020-Southern Miss		Opponent	USM	Opp	S/U	Line	ATS	Total	O/U	
9/3/2020	vs	SOUTH ALABAMA	21	32	L	-13.5	L	54.5	U	
9/19/2020	vs	LOUISIANA TECH	30	31	L	-7.5	L	58.5	O	"Rivalry in Dixie"
9/26/2020	vs	TULANE	24	66	L	3.5	L	54.5	O	"Battle for the Bell"
10/3/2020	@	North Texas	41	31	W	1.5	W	75.0	U	
10/24/2020	@	Liberty	35	56	L	15.0	L	59.5	O	
10/31/2020	vs	RICE	6	30	L	1.5	L	58.5	U	
11/7/2020	vs	NORTH ALABAMA	24	13	W	-15.5	L	51.0	U	
11/14/2020	@	Western Kentucky	7	10	L	8.0	W	45.0	U	
11/21/2020	vs	TEXAS-SAN ANTONIO	20	23	L	9.0	W	53.5	U	
12/10/2020	vs	FLORIDA ATLANTIC	45	31	W	9.0	W	43.0	O	
Coach: Jay Hopson		Season Record >>	253	323	3-7	ATS>>	4-6	O/U>>	4-6	
2019-Southern Miss		Opponent	USM	Opp	S/U	Line	ATS	Total	O/U	
8/31/2019	vs	ALCORN STATE	38	10	W	-24.5	W	NT	---	
9/7/2019	@	Mississippi State	15	35	L	15.5	L	51.0	U	
9/14/2019	@	Troy	47	42	W	3.0	W	49.0	O	
9/21/2019	@	Alabama	7	49	L	38.0	L	63.0	U	
9/28/2019	vs	TEXAS-EL PASO	31	13	W	-26.0	L	49.5	U	
10/12/2019	vs	NORTH TEXAS	45	27	W	-3.0	W	59.0	O	
10/19/2019	@	Louisiana Tech	30	45	L	-2.5	L	58.0	O	"Rivalry in Dixie"
10/26/2019	@	Rice	20	6	W	-10.0	W	51.5	U	
11/9/2019	vs	ALABAMA-BIRMINGHAM	37	2	W	-7.5	W	50.0	U	
11/16/2019	@	Texas-San Antonio	36	17	W	-17.0	W	55.5	U	
11/23/2019	vs	WESTERN KENTUCKY	10	28	L	-3.5	L	51.0	U	
11/30/2019	@	Florida Atlantic	17	34	L	9.0	L	58.5	U	
1/4/2020	vs	Tulane	13	30	L	7.5	L	57.5	U	Armed Forces Bowl
Coach: Jay Hopson		Season Record >>	346	338	7-6	ATS>>	6-7	O/U>>	3-9	
2018-Southern Miss		Opponent	USM	Opp	S/U	Line	ATS	Total	O/U	
9/1/2018	vs	JACKSON STATE	55	7	W	-33.0	W	NT	---	
9/8/2018	vs	LOUISIANA-MONROE	20	21	L	-5.0	L	67.0	U	
9/22/2018	vs	RICE	40	22	W	-13.5	W	54.5	O	
9/29/2018	@	Auburn	13	24	L	27.0	W	50.0	U	
10/13/2018	@	North Texas	7	30	L	7.0	L	53.0	U	
10/20/2018	vs	TEXAS-SAN ANTONIO	27	17	W	-16.0	L	43.5	O	
10/27/2018	@	Charlotte	17	20	L	-6.5	L	45.0	U	
11/3/2018	vs	MARSHALL	26	24	W	2.5	W	45.5	O	
11/10/2018	@	Alabama-Birmingham	23	26	L	13.5	W	45.0	O	{OT}
11/17/2018	vs	LOUISIANA TECH	21	20	W	-2.0	L	47.0	U	"Rivalry in Dixie"
11/24/2018	@	Texas-El Paso	39	7	W	-14.0	W	45.0	O	
Coach: Jay Hopson		Season Record >>	634	556	6-5	ATS>>	6-5	O/U>>	5-5	

SOUTHERN MISS GOLDEN EAGLES Sun Belt West

STADIUM: M.M Roberts Stadium {36,000}			Location: Hattiesburg, MS					COACH: Will Hall
DATE		Opponent	USM	Opp	S/U	Line	ATS	Total	O/U	Trends & Angles
9/3/2022	vs	LIBERTY								vs Liberty - Liberty leads series 1-0
9/10/2022	@	Miami								1st Meeting
9/17/2022	vs	NORTHWESTERN STATE								vs Northwestern State - USM leads series 8-2
9/24/2022	@	Tulane								3-0 S/U @ Tulane since 2004
10/8/2022	@	Troy								8-2 S/U vs Troy since 1936
10/15/2022	vs	ARKANSAS STATE								6-0 S/U vs Arkansas State since 1978
10/22/2022	@	Texas State								vs Texas State - Series tied 1-1
10/29/2022	vs	LOUISIANA								9-0 S/U s Louisiana since 1994
11/5/2022	vs	GEORGIA STATE								8-2 S/U after playing Louisiana since 1988
11/12/2022	@	Coastal Carolina								1st Meeting
11/19/2022	vs	SOUTH ALABAMA								vs South Alabama - USA lead series 2-0
11/25/2022	@	Louisiana-Monroe								vs UL-Monroe - Series tied 1-1
12/3/2022	vs									Sun Belt Championship
	vs									BOWL GAME

Pointspread Analysis — Non-Conference

- 1-35 S/U vs Non-Conf. as 15.5 point or more Dog since 1985
- 2-19 S/U vs Non-Conf. as 10.5-15 point Dog since 1992
- 1-13 S/U vs Non-Conf. as 7.5-10 point Dog since 1983
- 9-2 S/U vs Non-Conf. as 3.5-7 point favorite since 1995
- 15-1 S/U vs Non-Conf. as 10.5 point or more favorite since 1985
- 15-2 S/U vs Tulane as 7 point or more favorite since 1983

Dog

- 0-7 S/U @ home as 15.5 point or more Dog since 1987
- 1-38 S/U on road as 15.5 point or more Dog since 1985
- 4-11 ATS as 25.5 point or more Dog since 1988
- 11-2 O/U on road as 10.5-15 point Dog since 2005
- 9-30 S/U as 10.5-15 point Dog since 1983
- 1-6 S/U @ home as 7.5-10 point Dog since 2003
- 1-10 O/U on road as 7.5-10 point Dog since 1998
- 3-20 S/U as 3.5-7 point Dog since 2001
- 12-4 O/U as 3.5-7 point Dog since 2006

- 4-32 S/U on road vs ranked teams since 1992
- 1-11 S/U @ home vs ranked teams since 1987

- 0-8 O/U in 1st home game of season since 2010
- 6-1 S/U prior to playing Troy since 1935
- 1-5-1 S/U after playing Troy since 1938
- 11-3 ATS in final home game of season since 2008

LIBERTY	
Tulane	
ARKANSAS STATE	
SOUTH ALABAMA	

Pointspread Analysis — Conference

- vs Arkansas State - USM leads series 9-2
- 9-0 S/U vs Louisiana as favorite since 1994
- 7-0 ATS vs Louisiana as favorite since 1996
- vs Louisiana - USM leads series 39-11-1
- vs Troy - Southern Miss leads series 8-3

Bowl Games

- 4-1 S/U in New Orleans Bowl
- 0-5 S/U in Bowl Games as 7.5-15 point Dog since 2002
- 6-1 S/U in Bowl Games as 3.5-10 point favorite since 1999
- 1-6 O/U in Bowl Games as 3.5-10 point favorite since 1999
- 0-3 O/U in Liberty Bowl since 1997
- 0-3 S/U in Citrus Bowl since 1957

Favorite

- 16-5 S/U as 3 point or less favorite since 2003
- 14-1 S/U @ home as 3 point or less favorite since 1988
- 14-6-1 ATS as 3 point or less favorite since 2003
- 1-5 O/U @ home as 3 point or less favorite since 2007
- 9-3 S/U on road as 3.5-7 point favorite since 2003
- 2-7 ATS @ home as 7.5-10 point favorite since 2010
- 11-3 O/U @ home as 7.5-10 point favorite since 2008
- 11-2 S/U on road as 7.5-10 point favorite since 1997
- 12-1 S/U on road as 10.5-15 point favorite since 1996
- 10-2 ATS on road as 10.5-15 point favorite since 1997
- 21-4 S/U @ home as 10.5-15 point favorite since 1994
- 18-3 S/U @ home as 15.5-20 point favorite since 1984
- 2-9 ATS as 15.5-20 point favorite since 2005
- 23-1 S/U @ home as 20.5 point or more favorite since 1991

GEORGIA    LSU    MICHIGAN    NEBRASKA

College Football Blueblood Series available at: www.stevesfootballbible.com

STANFORD CARDINAL   PACIFIC-12 North

2021-Stanford		Opponent	Stan	Opp	S/U	Line	ATS	Total	O/U	
9/4/2021	vs	Kansas State {@ Arlington}	7	24	L	3.0	L	54.5	U	
9/11/2021	@	Usc	42	28	W	17.5	W	53.5	O	
9/18/2021	@	Vanderbilt	41	23	W	-12.0	W	49.0	O	
9/25/2021	vs	UCLA	24	35	L	4.0	L	60.5	U	
10/2/2021	vs	OREGON	31	24	W	8.5	W	57.5	U	{2 OT}
10/8/2021	@	Arizona State	10	28	L	13.5	L	53.5	U	
10/16/2021	@	Washington State	31	34	L	1.5	L	53.0	O	
10/30/2021	vs	WASHINGTON	13	20	L	-2.5	L	46.0	U	
11/5/2021	vs	UTAH	7	52	L	11.0	L	51.5	O	
11/13/2021	@	Oregon State	14	35	L	13.0	L	56.0	U	
11/20/2021	vs	CALIFORNIA	11	41	L	2.5	L	45.5	O	"Big Game" (Stanford Axe)
11/27/2021	vs	NOTRE DAME	14	45	L	21.0	L	53.5	O	"Legends Trophy"
Coach: David Shaw		Season Record >>	245	389	3-9	ATS>>	3-9	O/U>>	6-6	

2020-Stanford		Opponent	Stan	Opp	S/U	Line	ATS	Total	O/U	
11/7/2020	@	Oregon	14	35	L	12.5	L	49.0	T	
11/14/2020	vs	COLORADO	32	35	L	-10.0	L	55.5	O	
11/28/2020	@	California	24	23	W	-2.0	L	51.0	U	"Big Game" (Stanford Axe)
12/5/2020	@	Washington	31	26	W	12.0	W	49.5	O	
12/12/2020	@	Oregon State	27	24	W	-2.0	W	55.5	U	
12/19/2020	@	Ucla	48	47	W	7.0	W	61.0	O	{2 OT}
Coach: David Shaw		Season Record >>	176	190	4-2	ATS>>	3-3	O/U>>	3-2-1	

2019-Stanford		Opponent	Stan	Opp	S/U	Line	ATS	Total	O/U	
8/31/2019	vs	NORTHWESTERN	17	7	W	-6.5	W	47.0	U	
9/7/2019	@	Usc	20	45	L	3.0	L	43.0	O	
9/14/2019	@	Central Florida	27	45	L	9.5	L	59.0	O	
9/21/2019	vs	OREGON	6	21	L	12.5	L	55.5	U	
9/28/2019	@	Oregon State	31	28	W	-3.0	T	55.5	O	
10/12/2019	vs	WASHINGTON	23	13	W	12.5	W	52.0	U	
10/17/2019	vs	UCLA	16	34	L	-4.0	L	48.5	O	
10/26/2019	vs	ARIZONA	41	31	W	-3.0	W	54.0	O	
11/9/2019	@	Colorado	13	16	L	-4.0	L	56.5	U	
11/16/2019	@	Washington State	22	49	L	11.0	L	66.0	O	
11/23/2019	vs	CALIFORNIA	20	24	L	1.0	L	41.5	O	"Big Game" (Stanford Axe)
11/30/2019	vs	NOTRE DAME	24	45	L	17.5	L	45.5	O	"Legends Trophy"
Coach: David Shaw		Season Record >>	260	358	4-8	ATS>>	3-8-1	O/U>>	8-4	

2018-Stanford		Opponent	Stan	Opp	S/U	Line	ATS	Total	O/U	
9/1/2018	vs	SAN DIEGO STATE	31	10	W	-13.5	W	49.5	U	
9/8/2018	vs	USC	17	3	W	-4.5	W	54.5	U	
9/15/2018	vs	CALIFORNIA-DAVIS	30	10	W	-30.5	L	NT	---	
9/22/2018	@	Oregon	38	31	W	-3.0	W	59.0	O	{OT}
9/29/2018	@	Notre Dame	17	38	L	5.0	L	54.0	O	"Legends Trophy"
10/6/2018	vs	UTAH	21	40	L	-4.0	L	45.0	O	
10/18/2018	@	Arizona State	20	13	W	-2.5	W	57.5	U	
10/27/2018	vs	WASHINGTON STATE	38	41	L	-2.5	L	55.0	O	
11/3/2018	@	Washington	23	27	L	9.5	W	44.0	O	
11/10/2018	vs	OREGON STATE	48	17	W	-24.0	W	60.5	O	
11/24/2018	@	Ucla	49	42	W	-7.0	T	60.5	O	
12/1/2018	@	California	23	13	W	-3.0	W	46.0	U	"Big Game" (Stanford Axe)
12/31/2018	vs	Pittsburgh	14	13	W	-3.0	L	52.5	U	Sun Bowl
Coach: David Shaw		Season Record >>	369	298	9-4	ATS>>	7-5-1	O/U>>	7-5	

STANFORD CARDINAL — PACIFIC-12 North

STADIUM: Stanford Stadium {50,424} | **Location:** Palo Alto, CA | **COACH:** David Shaw

DATE		Opponent	Stan	Opp	S/U	Line	ATS	Total	O/U	Trends & Angles
9/3/2022	vs	*COLGATE*								13-1 S/U in 1st home game of season since 2008
9/10/2022	vs	USC								vs USC - USC leads series 64-34-3
9/24/2022	@	Washington								vs Washington - Series tied 44-44-4
10/1/2022	@	Oregon								vs Oregon - Stanford leads series 50-34-1
10/8/2022	vs	OREGON STATE								11-0 S/U @ home vs OSU as favorite since 1990
10/15/2022	@	*Notre Dame*								vs Notre Dame - Notre Dame leads series 22-13
10/22/2022	vs	ARIZONA STATE								vs Arizona State - ASU leads series 18-15
10/29/2022	@	Ucla								6-0 S/U @ Ucla since 2010
11/5/2022	vs	WASHINGTON STATE								0-5 S/U vs Washington State since 2016
11/12/2022	@	Utah								vs Utah - Utah leads series 6-4
11/19/2022	@	California								1-8 S/U vs California as Dog since 2002
11/26/2022	vs	*BYU*								vs BYU - Stanford leads series 2-0
12/3/2022	vs									PAC-12 Championship
	vs									BOWL GAME

Pointspread Analysis — Non-Conference

- 3-12 S/U vs Non-Conf. as 10.5 point or more Dog since 1983
- 0-6 S/U vs Non-Conf. as 7.5-10 point Dog since 1999
- 0-7 S/U vs Non-Conf. as 3.5-7 point Dog since 2003
- 10-2 S/U vs Non-Conf. as 3.5-7 point favorite since 1999
- 6-0 S/U vs Non-Conf. as 10.5-15 point favorite since 2003
- 7-0 S/U & ATS vs Non-Conf. as 15.5-20 point favorite since 2001
- 15-0 S/U vs Non-Conf. as 20.5 point or more favorite since 1992
- 0-9 S/U vs Notre Dame as 5-11.5 point Dog since 1991
- 7-2 S/U vs Notre Dame as favorite since 1999 {2-7 ATS}
- 2-13 S/U vs Notre Dame as 7.5 point or more Dog since 1988

Dog
- 2-6 O/U as 20.5 point or more Dog since 2006
- 1-14 S/U as 20.5 point or more Dog since 1989
- 0-5 S/U @ home as 15.5-20 point Dog since 2002
- 5-0 O/U @ home as 15.5-20 point Dog since 2002
- 4-14 S/U as 15.5-20 point Dog since 1983
- 4-15 S/U on road as 10.5-15 point Dog since 2000
- 2-9-1 O/U @ home as 10.5-15 point Dog since 2000
- 1-10 S/U on road as 7.5-10 point Dog since 2002
- 3-13 S/U as 7.5-10 point Dog since 2002
- 13-4 O/U as 3.5-7 point Dog since 2009

Favorite
- 11-2 S/U on road as 3 point or less favorite since 2012
- 9-3 ATS @ home as 3.5-7 point favorite since 2011
- 10-2 S/U @ home as 3.5-7 point favorite since 2011
- 2-10 O/U on road as 3.5-7 point favorite since 2010
- 0-5 O/U on road as 7.5-10 point favorite since 2013
- 0-5 ATS on road as 7.5-10 point favorite since 2013
- 15-0 S/U as 10.5-15 point favorite since 2003
- 13-2 ATS as 10.5-15 point favorite since 2003
- 5-0 S/U on road as 10.5-15 point favorite since 1997
- 10-1 S/U on road as 15.5 point or more favorite since 1986
- 11-0 S/U @ home as 15.5-20 point favorite since 2002
- 29-0 S/U as 20.5 point or more favorite since 1990

Bowl Games
- 8-2 ATS in Bowl Games since 2009
- 4-1 S/U in Sun Bowl
- 5-0 ATS in Bowl Games as 3.5-15 point Dog since 1996
- 3-0 S/U & ATS in Bowl Games as 3.5-7 point favorite since 2011
- 42-6 S/U @ home when ranked since 2010
- 11-0 S/U when ranked vs Oregon State since 1969
- 8-0 S/U when ranked vs UCLA since 2001 {7-1 ATS}
- 10-2 ATS vs ranked USC since 2007

Pointspread Analysis — Conference

- vs California - Stanford leads series 60-46-9
- 10-0 S/U vs California as favorite since 2010
- 4-0 S/U @ Oregon as favorite since 1986
- 2-9 S/U vs Oregon State as Dog since 1998
- vs Oregon State - Stanford leads series 59-26-3
- 11-0 S/U vs Oregon State as favorite since 1990
- 10-1 S/U vs UCLA as favorite since 2009
- vs Ucla - UCLA leads series 47-43-3
- 12-2 S/U vs Ucla since 2009
- 10-3-1 ATS vs Ucla since 2009
- 9-3 ATS vs USC as Dog since 2004
- 7-2 S/U vs Washington as favorite since 2004
- vs Washington State - Stanford leads sereies 40-30-1
- 0-6 ATS vs Washington State since 2015
- Game 3-8 O/U @ Washington State since 2000
- 2-6 O/U vs Washington State as Dog since 2002
- 0-3 S/U @ home vs Washington State as Dog since 2002
- 0-9 S/U vs Arizona State as 11 point or more Dog since 1983
- 9-2 S/U vs Arizona State as 2 point or more favorite since 1988
- 0-5 S/U vs UCLA as 14 point or more Dog since 1987
- 9-1-1 ATS @ UCLA as 5.5 point or more Dog since 1984
- 2-13 S/U vs USC as 13.5 point or more Dog since 1983
- 2-14 S/U vs Washington as 7 point or more Dog since 1983
- 10-0 S/U vs Wash. State as 8 point or more favorite since 1986

COLGATE	9-1 S/U & ATS prior to playing USC since 2011
USC	12-2 S/U in 2nd home game of season since 2007 {11-3 ATS}
USC	11-3 S/U prior to playing Washington since 2008
Washington	13-2 S/U prior to playing Oregon since 2004
Oregon	2-8 ATS after playing Washington since 2012
Oregon	12-4 S/U prior to playing Oregon State since 2006 {15-3 ATS}
OREGON STATE	8-3 S/U prior to playing Notre Dame since 2010
Notre Dame	7-2 O/U prior to playing Arizona State since 2007
ARIZONA STATE	12-2 S/U prior to playing UCLA since 2008
ARIZONA STATE	3-12 O/U prior to playing UCLA since 2006
ARIZONA STATE	2-10 O/U after playing Notre Dame since 2000
Ucla	5-2 S/U after playing Arizona State since 2009
WASH STATE	0-7 ATS prior to playing Utah since 1989
Utah	11-5-1 ATS prior to playing California since 2003
Utah	7-3 S/U after playing Washington State since 2010
California	5-1 S/U after playing Utah since 1996
California	9-4 S/U & ATS in final road game of season since 2009
BYU	10-2 S/U after playing California since 2009
BYU	9-3 S/U in final home game of season since 2009

SYRACUSE ORANGEMEN — ACC Atlantic

2021-Syracuse		Opponent	Cuse	Opp	S/U	Line	ATS	Total	O/U	
9/4/2021	@	Ohio	29	9	W	2.0	W	55.5	U	
9/11/2021	vs	RUTGERS	7	17	L	2.5	L	51.0	U	
9/18/2021	vs	SUNY-ALBANY	62	24	W	-21.0	W	41.0	O	
9/24/2021	vs	LIBERTY	24	21	W	6.5	W	54.0	U	
10/2/2021	@	Florida State	30	33	L	5.5	W	50.0	O	
10/9/2021	vs	WAKE FOREST	37	40	L	5.5	W	58.5	O	{OT}
10/15/2021	vs	CLEMSON	14	17	L	13.0	W	44.0	U	
10/23/2021	@	Virginia Tech	41	36	W	3.5	W	45.5	O	
10/30/2021	vs	BOSTON COLLEGE	21	6	W	-6.5	W	51.5	U	
11/13/2021	@	Louisville	3	41	L	3.0	L	56.0	U	
11/20/2021	@	NC State	17	41	L	11.0	L	49.5	O	
11/27/2021	vs	PITTSBURGH	14	31	L	11.5	L	58.5	U	
Coach: Dino Babers		Season Record >>	299	316	5-7	ATS>>	8-4	O/U>>	5-7	

2020-Syracuse		Opponent	Cuse	Opp	S/U	Line	ATS	Total	O/U	
9/12/2020	@	North Carolina	6	31	L	23.0	L	65.5	U	
9/19/2020	@	Pittsburgh	10	21	L	21.0	W	49.0	U	
9/26/2020	vs	GEORGIA TECH	37	20	W	7.0	W	51.5	O	
10/10/2020	vs	DUKE	24	38	L	2.5	L	51.5	O	
10/17/2020	vs	LIBERTY	21	38	L	3.0	L	52.5	O	
10/24/2020	@	Clemson	21	47	L	46.5	W	64.5	O	
10/31/2020	vs	WAKE FOREST	14	38	L	14.0	L	59.5	U	
11/7/2020	vs	BOSTON COLLEGE	13	16	L	15.0	W	53.5	U	
11/20/2020	@	Louisville	0	30	L	19.5	L	56.0	U	
11/28/2020	vs	NC STATE	29	36	L	17.5	W	49.5	O	
12/5/2020	@	Notre Dame	21	45	L	35.0	W	51.0	O	
Coach: Dino Babers		Season Record >>	196	360	1-10	ATS>>	6-5	O/U>>	6-5	

2019-Syracuse		Opponent	Cuse	Opp	S/U	Line	ATS	Total	O/U	
8/31/2019	@	Liberty	24	0	W	-19.5	W	68.0	U	
9/7/2019	@	Maryland	20	63	L	1.0	L	58.5	O	
9/14/2019	vs	CLEMSON	6	41	L	28.0	L	64.5	U	
9/21/2019	vs	WESTERN MICHIGAN	52	33	W	-3.5	W	66.5	O	
9/28/2019	vs	HOLY CROSS	41	3	W	-41.5	L	NT	---	
10/10/2019	@	NC State	10	16	L	4.0	L	55.5	U	
10/18/2019	vs	PITTSBURGH	20	27	L	3.5	L	53.5	O	
10/26/2019	@	Florida State	17	35	L	12.0	L	59.5	U	
11/2/2019	vs	BOSTON COLLEGE	27	58	L	-3.0	L	59.0	O	
11/16/2019	@	Duke	49	6	W	9.0	W	49.0	O	
11/23/2019	@	Louisville	34	56	L	7.5	L	65.0	O	
11/30/2019	vs	WAKE FOREST	39	30	W	6.5	W	66.5	O	{OT}
Coach: Dino Babers		Season Record >>	339	368	5-7	ATS>>	4-8	O/U>>	6-5	

2018-Syracuse		Opponent	Cuse	Opp	S/U	Line	ATS	Total	O/U	
9/1/2018	@	Western Michigan	55	42	W	-5.0	W	66.0	O	
9/8/2018	vs	WAGNER	62	10	W	-45.0	W	NT	---	
9/15/2018	vs	FLORIDA STATE	30	7	W	3.0	W	69.5	U	
9/22/2018	vs	CONNECTICUT	51	21	W	-30.5	L	75.5	U	
9/29/2018	@	Clemson	23	27	L	24.5	W	64.5	U	
10/6/2018	@	Pittsburgh	37	44	L	-3.0	L	58.5	O	{OT}
10/20/2018	vs	NORTH CAROLINA	40	37	W	-10.0	L	67.0	O	{2 OT}
10/27/2018	vs	NC STATE	51	41	W	2.0	W	64.5	O	
11/3/2018	@	Wake Forest	41	24	W	-6.5	W	77.5	U	
11/9/2018	vs	LOUISVILLE	54	23	W	-20.5	W	69.0	O	
11/17/2018	vs	Notre Dame	3	36	L	10.0	L	64.5	U	Yankee Stadium
11/24/2018	@	Boston College	42	21	W	6.0	W	60.5	O	
12/28/2018	vs	West Virginia	34	18	W	-3.0	W	67.0	U	Camping World Bowl
Coach: Dino Babers		Season Record >>	523	351	10-3	ATS>>	9-4	O/U>>	6-6	

SYRACUSE ORANGEMEN — ACC Atlantic

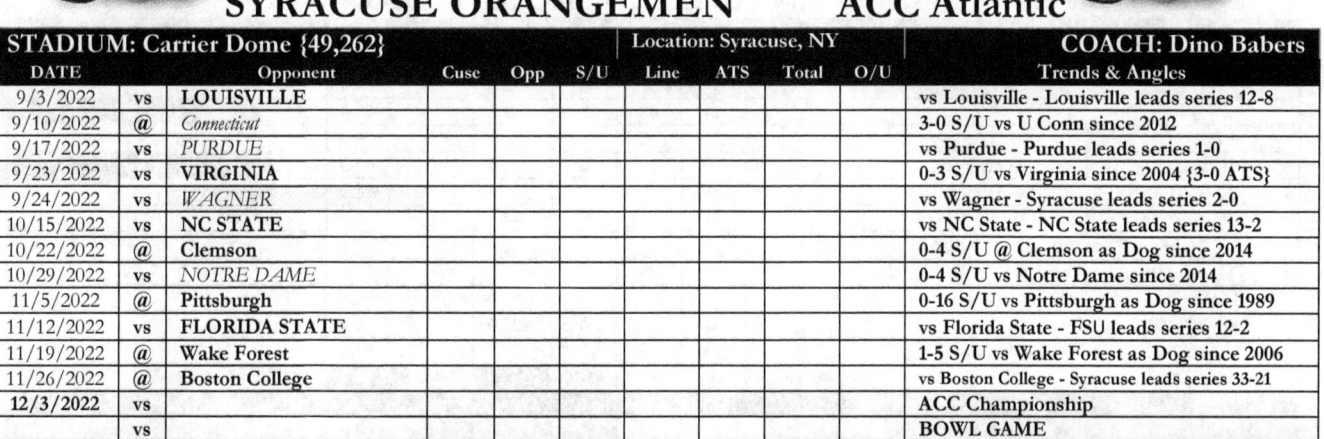

STADIUM: Carrier Dome {49,262}
Location: Syracuse, NY
COACH: Dino Babers

DATE		Opponent	Cuse	Opp	S/U	Line	ATS	Total	O/U	Trends & Angles
9/3/2022	vs	LOUISVILLE								vs Louisville - Louisville leads series 12-8
9/10/2022	@	Connecticut								3-0 S/U vs U Conn since 2012
9/17/2022	vs	PURDUE								vs Purdue - Purdue leads series 1-0
9/23/2022	vs	VIRGINIA								0-3 S/U vs Virginia since 2004 {3-0 ATS}
9/24/2022	vs	WAGNER								vs Wagner - Syracuse leads series 2-0
10/15/2022	vs	NC STATE								vs NC State - NC State leads series 13-2
10/22/2022	@	Clemson								0-4 S/U @ Clemson as Dog since 2014
10/29/2022	vs	NOTRE DAME								0-4 S/U vs Notre Dame since 2014
11/5/2022	@	Pittsburgh								0-16 S/U vs Pittsburgh as Dog since 1989
11/12/2022	vs	FLORIDA STATE								vs Florida State - FSU leads series 12-2
11/19/2022	@	Wake Forest								1-5 S/U vs Wake Forest as Dog since 2006
11/26/2022	@	Boston College								vs Boston College - Syracuse leads series 33-21
12/3/2022	vs									ACC Championship
	vs									BOWL GAME

Pointspread Analysis — Non-Conference

- 2-25 S/U vs Non-Conf. as 10.5 point or more Dog since 1983
- 6-2 ATS vs Non-Conf. as 7.5-10 point Dog since 1991
- 12-4 ATS vs Non-Conf. as 3.5-7 point Dog since 1987
- 10-2 ATS vs Non-Conf. as 3.5-7 point favorite since 1995
- 14-3 S/U vs Non-Conf. as 10.5-15 point favorite since 1984
- 27-1 S/U vs Non-Conf. as 15.5 point or more favorite since 1987
- 1-5 S/U & ATS vs Connecticut as Dog since 2005
- vs Connecticut - U Conn leads series 6-5
- vs Notre Dame - Notre Dame leads series 6-3

Dog
- 1-14 S/U as 25.5 point or more Dog since 2004
- 9-3 O/U as 25.5 point or more Dog since 2006
- 8-2 ATS as 20.5-25 point Dog since 2012
- 0-13 S/U on road as 20.5-25 point Dog since 1983
- 1-11 S/U on road as 15.5-20 point Dog since 2003
- 0-8 S/U @ home as 15.5-20 point Dog since 2004
- 7-2 O/U as 15.5-20 point Dog since 2011
- 2-6 O/U @ home as 15.5-20 point Dog since 2004
- 1-14 S/U on road as 10.5-15 point Dog since 2005
- 0-13 S/U as 10.5-15 point Dog since 2013
- 1-10 S/U as 7.5-10 point Dog since 2011
- 2-8 S/U on road as 7.5-10 point Dog since 2002
- 1-8 S/U @ home as 7.5-10 point Dog since 1994
- 3-9 S/U @ home as 3.5-7 point Dog since 2006

Favorite
- 1-8-2 ATS as 3 point or less favorite since 2011
- 5-12-1 O/U as 3 point or less favorite since 2005
- 10-0 S/U & ATS as 3.5-7 point favorite since 2011
- 2-8 O/U on road as 3.5-7 point favorite since 1996
- 8-2 S/U @ home as 7.5-10 point favorite since 1994
- 10-2 S/U on road as 7.5-10 point favorite since 1985
- 9-0 S/U @ home as 10.5-15 point favorite since 1992
- 9-0 S/U as 10.5-15 point favorite since 1998
- 13-2 S/U on road as 10.5-15 point favorite since 1984
- 20-2 S/U as 15.5-20 point favorite since 1988
- 8-0 S/U on road as 15.5 point or more favorite since 1991
- 17-1 S/U as 20.5-25 point favorite since 1991
- 18-0 S/U @ home as 25.5 point or more favorite since 1987
- 23-1 S/U as 25.5 point or more favorite since 1987

Pointspread Analysis — Conference

- 13-4 S/U vs Boston College as favorite since 1985
- 5-0 S/U & ATS @ Boston College as favorite since 1988
- vs Clemson - Clemson leads series 8-2
- 0-7 S/U & ATS vs Louisville as Dog since 2014
- 0-4 S/U vs NC State as favorite since 1997 {1-3 ATS}
- vs Pittsburgh - Pittsburgh leads series 42-23-2
- 17-2-1 S/U vs Pittsburgh as favorite since 1984
- 5-0 S/U vs Virginia Tech as favorite since 1987
- vs Virginia Tech - Syracuse leads series 11-8
- vs VPI - HOME team 12-3 S/U since 1988
- Game 0-4 O/U @ Wake Forest since 2006
- 5-0 S/U & ATS vs Wake Forest as favorite since 2011
- vs Wake Forest - Syracuse leads series 6-5
- 0-11 S/U vs Florida State as 5 point or more Dog since 1989
- 0-8 S/U vs Pittsburgh as 10 point or more Dog since 1983
- 14-0 S/U vs Pittsburgh as 3.5 point or more favorite since 1984

Bowl Games
- 0-3 S/U in Orange Bowl
- 4-0 S/U & ATS in Bowl Games as 3 point or less favorite since 1989

Schedule trends (opponent column)
Opponent	Trend
LOUISVILLE	9-4 O/U in 1st home game of season since 2007
LOUISVILLE	7-2 S/U in 1st home game of season since 2013
Clemson	1-7 O/U after playing NC State since 2014
NOTRE DAME	2-6 S/U after playing Clemson since 2014
NOTRE DAME	0-11 S/U prior to playing Pittsburgh since 2011
Pittsburgh	2-5 S/U prior to playing Florida State since 2014
Pittsburgh	0-7 O/U prior to playing Florida State since 2013
Pittsburgh	1-4 S/U after playing Notre Dame since 2005
Pittsburgh	1-4 O/U after playing Notre Dame since 2005
FLORIDA STATE	8-1 O/U prior to playing Wake Forest since 2013
Wake Forest	3-9 ATS after playing Florida State since 1989
Wake Forest	2-9 S/U prior to playing Boston College since 2003
Boston College	2-7 O/U after playing Wake Forest since 2006
Boston College	1-8 S/U in final road game of season since 2013

- 0-5 S/U @ home vs #1 ranked teams since 1992
- 1-13 S/U vs #2 ranked teams all time {0-6 on road}
- 7-0 S/U @ home when ranked since 1998
- 4-0 S/U when ranked vs Boston College since 1995
- 7-0 S/U when ranked vs Pittsburgh since 1991
- 5-0 S/U @ home when ranked vs Pittsburgh since 1968

TEXAS CHRISTIAN HORNED FROGS   BIG TWELVE

2021-Texas Christian		Opponent	TCU	Opp	S/U	Line	ATS	Total	O/U	
9/4/2021	vs	DUQUESNE	45	3	W	-42.0	T	54.0	U	
9/11/2021	vs	CALIFORNIA	34	32	W	-12.0	L	46.0	O	
9/25/2021	vs	SMU	34	42	L	-9.5	L	66.0	O	"Iron Skillet"
10/2/2021	vs	TEXAS	27	32	L	3.5	L	65.0	U	
10/9/2021	@	Texas Tech	52	31	W	-2.5	W	60.0	O	"Saddle Trophy"
10/16/2021	@	Oklahoma	31	52	L	12.5	L	64.5	O	
10/23/2021	vs	WEST VIRGNIA	17	29	L	-4.5	L	58.0	U	
10/30/2021	@	Kansas State	12	31	L	3.5	L	58.5	U	
11/6/2021	vs	BAYLOR	30	28	W	7.5	W	57.5	O	
11/13/2021	@	Oklahoma State	17	63	L	11.5	L	53.5	O	
11/20/2021	vs	KANSAS	31	28	W	-21.0	L	64.0	U	
11/27/2021	@	Iowa State	14	48	L	16.0	L	61.0	O	
Coach: Gary Patterson		Season Record >>	344	419	5-7	ATS>>	2-9-1	O/U>>	7-5	

2020-Texas Christian		Opponent	TCU	Opp	S/U	Line	ATS	Total	O/U	
9/26/2020	vs	IOWA STATE	34	37	L	3.0	T	44.0	O	
10/3/2020	@	Texas	33	31	W	10.5	W	61.5	O	
10/10/2020	vs	KANSAS STATE	14	21	L	-11.0	L	50.0	U	
10/24/2020	vs	OKLAHOMA	14	33	L	6.5	L	58.5	U	
10/31/2020	@	Baylor	33	23	W	-2.5	W	47.5	O	
11/7/2020	vs	TEXAS TECH	34	18	W	-9.5	W	60.0	U	"Saddle Trophy"
11/14/2020	@	West Virginia	6	24	L	3.0	L	44.0	U	
11/28/2020	@	Kansas	59	23	W	-23.0	W	51.0	O	
12/5/2020	vs	OKLAHOMA STATE	29	22	W	2.5	W	53.0	U	
12/12/2020	vs	LOUISIANA TECH	52	10	W	-21.5	L	50.5	O	
Coach: Gary Patterson		Season Record >>	308	242	6-4	ATS>>	6-3-1	O/U>>	4-6	

2019-Texas Christian		Opponent	TCU	Opp	S/U	Line	ATS	Total	O/U	
8/31/2019	vs	ARKANSAS-PINE BLUFF	39	7	W	-53.5	L	NT	---	
9/14/2019	@	Purdue	34	13	W	-3.5	W	52.5	L	
9/21/2019	vs	SMU	38	41	L	-7.5	L	54.0	O	"Iron Skillet"
9/28/2019	vs	KANSAS	51	14	W	-14.5	W	48.0	O	
10/5/2019	@	Iowa State	24	49	L	3.5	L	46.5	O	
10/19/2019	@	Kansas State	17	24	L	-4.5	L	44.0	U	
10/26/2019	vs	TEXAS	37	27	W	-1.0	W	56.5	O	
11/2/2019	@	Oklahoma State	27	34	L	1.5	L	59.0	O	
11/9/2019	vs	BAYLOR	23	29	L	2.0	L	48.5	O	{3 OT}
11/16/2019	@	Texas Tech	33	31	W	-3.5	W	53.5	O	"Saddle Trophy"
11/23/2019	@	Oklahoma	24	28	L	18.5	W	64.5	U	
11/30/2019	vs	WEST VIRGINIA	17	20	L	-14.0	L	44.0	U	
Coach: Gary Patterson		Season Record >>	364	317	5-7	ATS>>	4-8	O/U>>	7-4	

2018-Texas Christian		Opponent	TCU	Opp	S/U	Line	ATS	Total	O/U	
9/1/2018	vs	SOUTHERN U	55	7	W	-50.0	L	NT	---	
9/8/2018	@	Smu	42	12	W	-23.5	W	59.0	U	"Iron Skillet"
9/15/2018	vs	Ohio State	28	40	L	12.5	W	58.5	O	
9/22/2018	@	Texas	16	31	L	-2.5	L	50.0	U	
9/29/2018	vs	IOWA STATE	17	14	W	-11.0	L	45.0	U	
10/11/2018	vs	TEXAS TECH	14	17	L	-7.0	L	57.5	U	"Saddle Trophy"
10/20/2018	vs	OKLAHOMA	27	52	L	7.5	L	61.5	O	
10/27/2018	@	Kansas	26	27	L	-13.5	L	47.0	O	
11/3/2018	vs	KANSAS STATE	14	13	W	-10.0	L	44.0	U	
11/10/2018	@	West Virginia	10	47	L	12.0	L	56.0	O	
11/17/2018	@	Baylor	16	9	W	1.0	W	50.0	U	
11/24/2018	vs	OKLAHOMA STATE	31	24	W	5.5	W	54.0	O	
12/26/2018	vs	California	10	7	W	-2.5	W	38.0	U	Cheez-it Bowl
Coach: Gary Patterson		Season Record >>	306	300	7-6	ATS>>	5-8	O/U>>	5-7	

TEXAS CHRISTIAN HORNED FROGS — BIG TWELVE

STADIUM: Amon Carter Stadium {45,000} — **Location:** Fort Worth, TX — **COACH:** Sonny Dykes

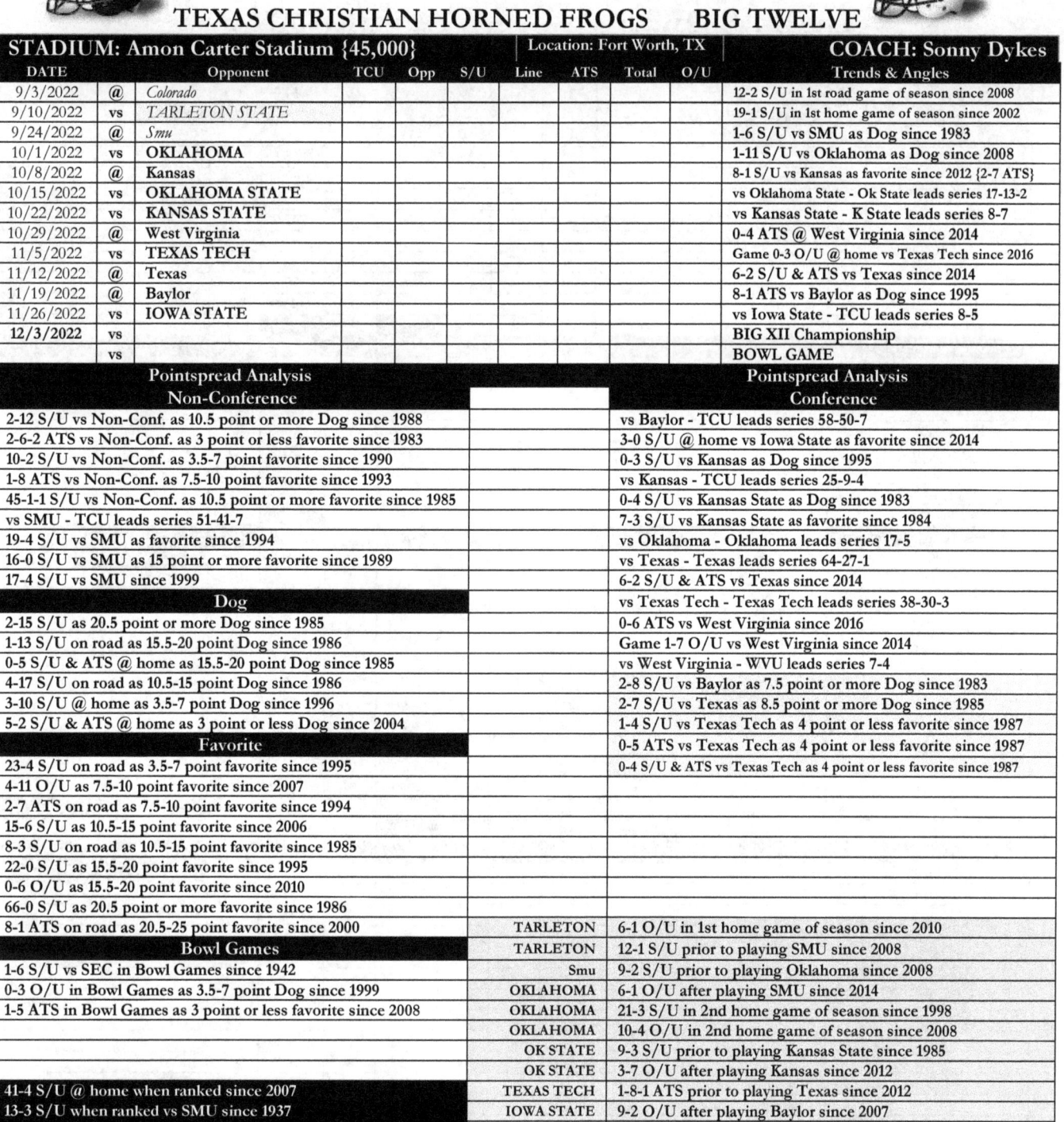

DATE		Opponent	TCU	Opp	S/U	Line	ATS	Total	O/U	Trends & Angles
9/3/2022	@	Colorado								12-2 S/U in 1st road game of season since 2008
9/10/2022	vs	TARLETON STATE								19-1 S/U in 1st home game of season since 2002
9/24/2022	@	Smu								1-6 S/U vs SMU as Dog since 1983
10/1/2022	vs	OKLAHOMA								1-11 S/U vs Oklahoma as Dog since 2008
10/8/2022	@	Kansas								8-1 S/U vs Kansas as favorite since 2012 {2-7 ATS}
10/15/2022	vs	OKLAHOMA STATE								vs Oklahoma State - Ok State leads series 17-13-2
10/22/2022	vs	KANSAS STATE								vs Kansas State - K State leads series 8-7
10/29/2022	@	West Virginia								0-4 ATS @ West Virginia since 2014
11/5/2022	vs	TEXAS TECH								Game 0-3 O/U @ home vs Texas Tech since 2016
11/12/2022	@	Texas								6-2 S/U & ATS vs Texas since 2014
11/19/2022	@	Baylor								8-1 ATS vs Baylor as Dog since 1995
11/26/2022	vs	IOWA STATE								vs Iowa State - TCU leads series 8-5
12/3/2022	vs									BIG XII Championship
	vs									BOWL GAME

Pointspread Analysis — Non-Conference
- 2-12 S/U vs Non-Conf. as 10.5 point or more Dog since 1988
- 2-6-2 ATS vs Non-Conf. as 3 point or less favorite since 1983
- 10-2 S/U vs Non-Conf. as 3.5-7 point favorite since 1990
- 1-8 ATS vs Non-Conf. as 7.5-10 point favorite since 1993
- 45-1-1 S/U vs Non-Conf. as 10.5 point or more favorite since 1985
- vs SMU - TCU leads series 51-41-7
- 19-4 S/U vs SMU as favorite since 1994
- 16-0 S/U vs SMU as 15 point or more favorite since 1989
- 17-4 S/U vs SMU since 1999

Dog
- 2-15 S/U as 20.5 point or more Dog since 1985
- 1-13 S/U on road as 15.5-20 point Dog since 1986
- 0-5 S/U & ATS @ home as 15.5-20 point Dog since 1985
- 4-17 S/U on road as 10.5-15 point Dog since 1986
- 3-10 S/U @ home as 3.5-7 point Dog since 1996
- 5-2 S/U & ATS @ home as 3 point or less Dog since 2004

Favorite
- 23-4 S/U on road as 3.5-7 point favorite since 1995
- 4-11 O/U as 7.5-10 point favorite since 2007
- 2-7 ATS on road as 7.5-10 point favorite since 1994
- 15-6 S/U as 10.5-15 point favorite since 2006
- 8-3 S/U on road as 10.5-15 point favorite since 1985
- 22-0 S/U as 15.5-20 point favorite since 1995
- 0-6 O/U as 15.5-20 point favorite since 2010
- 66-5 S/U as 20.5 point or more favorite since 1986
- 8-1 ATS on road as 20.5-25 point favorite since 2000

Bowl Games
- 1-6 S/U vs SEC in Bowl Games since 1942
- 0-3 O/U in Bowl Games as 3.5-7 point Dog since 1999
- 1-5 ATS in Bowl Games as 3 point or less favorite since 2008

- 41-4 S/U @ home when ranked since 2007
- 13-3 S/U when ranked vs SMU since 1937
- 1-9 ATS when ranked vs SMU since 2003
- 2-13 S/U vs ranked Oklahoma since 1946
- 0-6 S/U vs ranked SMU since 1979
- 2-11 S/U @ ranked Texas since 1963

Pointspread Analysis — Conference
- vs Baylor - TCU leads series 58-50-7
- 3-0 S/U @ home vs Iowa State as favorite since 2014
- 0-3 S/U vs Kansas as Dog since 1995
- vs Kansas - TCU leads series 25-9-4
- 0-4 S/U vs Kansas State as Dog since 1983
- 7-3 S/U vs Kansas State as favorite since 1984
- vs Oklahoma - Oklahoma leads series 17-5
- vs Texas - Texas leads series 64-27-1
- 6-2 S/U & ATS vs Texas since 2014
- vs Texas Tech - Texas Tech leads series 38-30-3
- 0-6 ATS vs West Virginia since 2016
- Game 1-7 O/U vs West Virginia since 2014
- vs West Virginia - WVU leads series 7-4
- 2-8 S/U vs Baylor as 7.5 point or more Dog since 1983
- 2-7 S/U vs Texas as 8.5 point or more Dog since 1985
- 1-4 S/U vs Texas Tech as 4 point or less favorite since 1987
- 0-5 ATS vs Texas Tech as 4 point or less favorite since 1987
- 0-4 S/U & ATS vs Texas Tech as 4 point or less favorite since 1987

Opponent	Trend
TARLETON	6-1 O/U in 1st home game of season since 2010
TARLETON	12-1 S/U prior to playing SMU since 2008
Smu	9-2 S/U prior to playing Oklahoma since 2008
OKLAHOMA	6-1 O/U after playing SMU since 2014
OKLAHOMA	21-3 S/U in 2nd home game of season since 1998
OKLAHOMA	10-4 O/U in 2nd home game of season since 2008
OK STATE	9-3 S/U prior to playing Kansas State since 1985
OK STATE	3-7 O/U after playing Kansas since 2012
TEXAS TECH	1-8-1 ATS prior to playing Texas since 2012
IOWA STATE	9-2 O/U after playing Baylor since 2007
Baylor	4-11 S/U after playing Texas since 1992
Baylor	2-12 ATS after playing Texas since 1993
Baylor	12-5 S/U in final road game of season since 2005
Baylor	12-1 ATS in final road game of season since 2009

Page | 211 — Copyright © 2022 by Steve's Football Bible, LLC

TEMPLE OWLS — AMERICAN East

2021-Temple		Opponent	Temp	Opp	S/U	Line	ATS	Total	O/U	
9/4/2021	@	Rutgers	14	61	L	14.0	L	53.0	O	
9/11/2021	@	Akron	45	24	W	-6.5	W	51.0	O	
9/18/2021	vs	BOSTON COLLEGE	3	28	L	15.0	L	55.5	U	
9/25/2021	vs	WAGNER	41	7	W	-35.5	L	53.0	U	
10/2/2021	vs	MEMPHIS	34	31	W	11.0	W	58.5	O	
10/8/2021	@	Cincinnati	3	52	L	30.0	L	52.5	O	
10/23/2021	@	South Florida	14	34	L	1.5	L	55.0	U	
10/30/2021	vs	CENTRAL FLORIDA	7	49	L	12.0	L	42.0	O	
11/4/2021	@	East Carolina	3	45	L	15.5	L	52.0	U	
11/13/2021	vs	HOUSTON	8	37	L	26.0	L	52.5	U	
11/20/2021	@	Tulsa	10	44	L	22.0	L	50.5	O	
11/27/2021	vs	NAVY	14	38	L	13.5	L	41.5	O	
Coach: Rod Carey		Season Record >>	196	450	3-9	ATS>>	2-10	O/U>>	7-5	

2020-Temple		Opponent	Temp	Opp	S/U	Line	ATS	Total	O/U	
10/10/2020	@	Navy	29	31	L	-4.0	L	51.0	O	
10/17/2020	vs	SOUTH FLORIDA	39	37	W	-10.5	L	54.0	O	
10/24/2020	@	Memphis	29	41	L	14.0	W	70.5	U	
10/31/2020	@	Tulane	3	38	L	7.0	L	56.0	U	
11/7/2020	vs	SMU	23	47	L	17.0	L	63.5	O	
11/14/2020	@	Central Florida	13	38	L	29.0	W	71.5	U	
11/21/2020	vs	EAST CAROLINA	3	28	L	7.0	L	53.0	U	
Coach: Rod Carey		Season Record >>	139	260	1-6	ATS>>	2-5	O/U>>	3-4	

2019-Temple		Opponent	Temp	Opp	S/U	Line	ATS	Total	O/U	
8/31/2019	vs	BUCKNELL	56	12	W	-39.0	W	NT	---	"The Old Shoes Trophy"
9/14/2019	vs	MARYLAND	20	17	W	5.5	W	66.0	U	
9/21/2019	@	Buffalo	22	38	L	-14.0	L	51.0	O	
9/28/2019	vs	GEORGIA TECH	24	3	W	-9.5	W	48.0	U	
10/3/2019	@	East Carolina	27	17	W	-12.5	L	46.5	U	
10/12/2019	vs	MEMPHIS	30	28	W	4.0	W	50.0	O	
10/19/2019	@	Smu	21	45	L	9.5	L	60.0	O	
10/26/2019	vs	CENTRAL FLORIDA	21	63	L	10.5	L	61.0	O	
11/7/2019	@	South Florida	17	7	W	PK	W	50.5	U	
11/16/2019	vs	TULANE	29	21	W	6.5	W	52.5	U	
11/23/2019	@	Cincinnati	13	15	L	8.5	W	45.5	U	
11/30/2019	vs	CONNECTICUT	49	17	W	-27.0	W	48.0	O	
12/27/2019	vs	North Carolina	13	55	L	6.5	L	56.5	O	Military Bowl
Coach: Rod Carey		Season Record >>	342	338	8-5	ATS>>	8-5	O/U>>	6-6	

2018-Temple		Opponent	Temp	Opp	S/U	Line	ATS	Total	O/U	
9/1/2018	vs	VILLANOVA	17	19	L	-15.0	L	NT	---	"Mayor's Cup"
9/8/2018	vs	BUFFALO	26	36	L	-4.0	L	52.0	O	
9/15/2018	@	Maryland	35	14	W	15.0	W	55.5	U	
9/20/2018	vs	TULSA	31	17	W	-6.0	W	54.0	U	
9/29/2018	@	Boston College	35	45	L	11.5	W	54.0	O	
10/6/2018	vs	EAST CAROLINA	49	6	W	-10.5	W	52.0	O	
10/13/2018	@	Navy	24	17	W	-6.5	W	49.0	U	
10/20/2018	vs	CINCINNATI	24	17	W	-2.5	W	47.0	U	{OT}
11/1/2018	@	Central Florida	40	52	L	10.0	L	60.0	O	
11/10/2018	@	Houston	59	49	W	3.5	W	69.5	O	
11/17/2018	vs	SOUTH FLORIDA	27	17	W	-14.0	L	62.5	U	
11/24/2018	@	Connecticut	57	7	W	-31.0	W	69.0	U	
12/27/2018	vs	Duke	27	56	L	-3.5	L	56.5	O	Independence Bowl
Coach: Geoff Collins		Season Record >>	451	352	8-5	ATS>>	8-5	O/U>>	6-6	

TEMPLE OWLS — AMERICAN East

STADIUM: Lincoln Financial Field {69,176} | **Location:** Philadelphia, PA | **COACH:** Stan Drayton

DATE		Opponent	Tem	Opp	S/U	Line	ATS	Total	O/U	Trends & Angles
9/2/2022	@	Duke								vs Duke - Duke leads series 1-0
9/10/2022	vs	LAFAYETTE								vs Lafayette - Temple leads series 8-4-1
9/17/2022	vs	RUTGERS								0-9 S/U vs Rutgers as Dog since 1991
9/24/2022	vs	MASSACHUSETTS								vs Massachusetts - Temple leads series 2-0
10/1/2022	@	Memphis								7-0 ATS vs Memphis as Dog since 2013
10/13/2022	@	Central Florida								vs Central Florida - UCF leads series 7-2
10/21/2022	vs	TULSA								3-1 S/U vs Tulsa since 2014
10/29/2022	@	Navy								vs Navy - Temple leads series 9-7
11/5/2022	vs	SOUTH FLORIDA								vs South Florida - Temple leads series 5-3
11/12/2022	@	Houston								1-7 S/U vs Houston as Dog since 1987
11/19/2022	vs	CINCINNATI								1-7 S/U vs Cincinnati as Dog since 2002
11/26/2022	vs	EAST CAROLINA								vs East Carolina - Temple leads series 10-9
12/3/2022	vs									AAC Championship
	vs									BOWL GAME

Pointspread Analysis — Non-Conference

- 0-46 S/U vs Non-Conf. as 15.5 point or more Dog since 1983
- 2-8 S/U vs Non-Conf. as 7.5-10 point Dog since 1985
- 15-4 S/U vs Non-Conf. as 10.5 point or more favorite since 1987
- 7-0 S/U vs Rutgers as 6 point or more favorite since 1985

Dog
- 1-32 S/U as 30.5 point or more Dog since 1989
- 11-4 O/U as 30.5 point or more Dog since 2002
- 0-30 S/U as 25.5-30 point Dog since 1989
- 1-7 O/U as 25.5-30 point Dog since 2007
- 0-23 S/U @ home as 20.5 point or more Dog since 1989
- 0-30 S/U as 20.5-25 point Dog since 1987
- 7-2 ATS as 20.5-25 point Dog since 2003
- 2-33 S/U as 15.5-20 point Dog since 1983
- 1-10 S/U @ home as 10.5-15 point Dog since 2002
- 3-13 S/U on road as 10.5-15 point Dog since 2000
- 14-3-1 ATS on road as 10.5-15 point Dog since 1998
- 3-17 S/U on road as 7.5-10 point Dog since 1985
- 2-11 S/U @ home as 7.5-10 point Dog since 1995
- 14-3-1 ATS @ home as 3.5-7 point Dog since 2005
- 0-7 O/U as 3 point or less Dog since 2010
- 1-6-1 ATS @ home as 3 point or less Dog since 1985
- 1-8 S/U @ home as 3 point or less Dog since 1985

Favorite
- 15-5 S/U as 3.5-7 point favorite since 2008
- 14-5-1 ATS as 3.5-7 point favorite since 2008
- 0-5 O/U on road as 7.5-10 point favorite since 2002
- 5-1 S/U on road as 7.5-10 point favorite since 1993
- 16-3 S/U @ home as 10.5-15 point favorite since 1999
- 23-1 S/U as 15.5 point or more favorite since 1986

Pointspread Analysis — Conference

- 1-7 S/U vs Central Florida as Dog since 2013
- vs Cincinnati - Temple leads series 13-9-1
- 5-0 S/U vs Cincinnati as favorite since 1984
- 5-0 S/U vs East Carolina as favorite since 1990
- 4-1 ATS vs East Carolina as favorite since 1990
- vs Memphis - Temple leads series 4-3
- 4-1 S/U vs Navy as favorite since 1988
- 0-5 S/U vs Navy as 12.5 point or more Dog since 1997
- vs Tulsa - Series tied 3-3
- 3-0 S/U vs Tulsa as favorite since 2014

Bowl Games
- 3-6 S/U in Bowl games

EAST CAROLINA	9-4 S/U after playing Cincinnati since 1984
CINCINNATI	10-3 ATS prior to playing East Carolina since 1988
SOUTH FLORIDA	7-1 O/U after playing Navy since 2007

- 4-63-1 S/U on road vs ranked teams all time
- 5-45 S/U @ home vs ranked teams all time
- 0-40 S/U vs Top #1 - #9 ranked teams all time
- 0-10 S/U vs #11 #12 ranked teams all time

ARMY  — AIR FORCE  — NAVY

College Football Patriot Series available at: www.stevesfootballbible.com

TENNESSEE VOLUNTEERS   SEC East

2021-Tennessee		Opponent	Tenn	Opp	S/U	Line	ATS	Total	O/U	
9/4/2021	vs	BOWLING GREEN	38	6	W	-37.0	L	60.5	U	
9/11/2021	vs	PITTSBURGH	34	41	L	3.5	L	56.0	O	
9/18/2021	vs	TENNESSEE TECH	56	0	W	-38.0	W	52.5	O	
9/25/2021	@	Florida	14	38	L	19.0	L	64.5	U	
10/2/2021	@	Missouri	62	24	W	2.0	W	66.5	O	
10/9/2021	vs	SOUTH CAROLINA	45	20	W	-10.5	W	56.5	O	
10/16/2021	vs	MISSISSIPPI	26	31	L	1.0	L	82.5	U	
10/23/2021	@	Alabama	24	52	L	24.5	L	68.0	O	Third Saturday in October Rivalry
11/6/2021	@	Kentucky	45	42	W	-1.5	W	57.5	O	
11/13/2021	vs	GEORGIA	17	41	L	19.0	L	56.0	O	
11/20/2021	vs	SOUTH ALABAMA	60	14	W	-28.5	W	61.5	O	
11/27/2021	vs	VANDERBILT	45	21	W	-33.0	L	64.5	O	
12/30/2021	vs	**Purdue {OT}**	45	48	L	-8.0	L	66.5	O	Music City Bowl
Coach: Josh Heupel		Season Record >>	511	378	7-6	ATS>>	5-8	O/U>>	10-3	
2020-Tennessee		Opponent	Tenn	Opp	S/U	Line	ATS	Total	O/U	
9/26/2020	@	South Carolina	31	27	W	-4.0	T	44.5	O	
10/3/2020	vs	MISSOURI	35	12	W	-10.0	W	48.5	U	
10/10/2020	@	Georgia	21	44	L	12.0	L	43.5	O	
10/17/2020	vs	KENTUCKY	7	34	L	-6.0	L	45.5	U	
10/24/2020	vs	ALABAMA	17	48	L	22.0	L	66.5	U	Third Saturday in October Rivalry
11/7/2020	@	Arkansas	13	24	L	-2.5	L	54.5	U	
11/21/2020	@	Auburn	17	30	L	10.0	L	51.0	U	
12/5/2020	vs	FLORIDA	19	31	L	18.5	W	63.0	U	
12/12/2020	@	Vanderbilt	42	17	W	-15.0	W	51.0	O	
12/19/2020	vs	TEXAS A&M	13	34	L	13.5	L	50.0	U	
Coach: Jeremy Pruitt		Season Record >>	215	301	3-7	ATS>>	3-6-1	O/U>>	3-7	
2019-Tennessee		Opponent	Tenn	Opp	S/U	Line	ATS	Total	O/U	
8/31/2019	vs	GEORGIA STATE	30	38	L	-24.5	L	58.0	O	
9/7/2019	vs	BYU	26	29	L	-3.5	L	52.5	O	{2 OT}
9/14/2019	vs	TENNESSEE-CHATT	45	0	W	-30.0	W	NT	---	
9/21/2019	@	Florida	3	34	L	14.0	L	48.5	U	
10/5/2019	vs	GEORGIA	14	43	L	24.0	L	51.0	O	
10/12/2019	vs	MISSISSIPPI STATE	20	10	W	5.0	W	52.0	U	
10/19/2019	@	Alabama	13	35	L	34.5	W	62.5	U	Third Saturday in October Rivalry
10/26/2019	vs	SOUTH CAROLINA	41	21	W	4.0	W	47.0	O	
11/2/2019	vs	ALABAMA-BIRMINGHAM	30	7	W	-13.5	W	49.0	U	
11/9/2019	@	Kentucky	17	13	W	PK	W	42.0	U	
11/23/2019	@	Missouri	24	20	W	2.0	W	47.5	U	
11/30/2019	vs	VANDERBILT	28	10	W	-23.5	L	48.0	U	
1/2/2020	vs	**Indiana**	23	22	W	-3.5	L	56.0	U	Gator Bowl
Coach: Jeremy Pruitt		Season Record >>	314	282	8-5	ATS>>	7-6	O/U>>	4-8	
2018-Tennessee		Opponent	Tenn	Opp	S/U	Line	ATS	Total	O/U	
9/1/2018	vs	West Virginia	14	40	L	10.0	L	59.5	U	Bank of America Stadium
9/8/2018	vs	EAST TENNESSEE STATE	59	3	W	-37.5	W	NT	---	
9/15/2018	vs	TEXAS-EL PASO	24	0	W	-34.0	L	51.5	U	
9/22/2018	vs	FLORIDA	21	47	L	3.5	L	45.5	O	
9/29/2018	@	Georgia	12	38	L	27.5	W	55.0	U	
10/13/2018	@	Auburn	30	24	W	14.5	W	47.0	O	
10/20/2018	vs	ALABAMA	21	58	L	28.5	L	57.5	O	Third Saturday in October Rivalry
10/27/2018	@	South Carolina	24	27	L	10.5	W	53.0	U	
11/3/2018	vs	CHARLOTTE	14	3	W	-21.5	L	45.0	U	
11/10/2018	vs	KENTUCKY	24	7	W	6.0	W	42.5	U	
11/17/2018	vs	MISSOURI	17	50	L	6.0	L	57.0	O	
11/24/2018	@	Vanderbilt	13	38	L	3.0	L	51.5	U	
Coach: Jeremy Pruitt		Season Record >>	273	335	5-7	ATS>>	5-7	O/U>>	4-7	

TENNESSEE VOLUNTEERS — SEC East

STADIUM: Neyland Stadium {102,455}
Location: Knoxville, TN
COACH: Josh Heupel

DATE		Opponent	Tenn	Opp	S/U	Line	ATS	Total	O/U	Trends & Angles
9/1/2022	vs	BALL STATE								26-1 S/U in 1st home game of season since 1995
9/10/2022	@	Pittsburgh								vs Pittsburgh - Pitt leads series 3-0
9/17/2022	vs	AKRON								vs Akron - Tennessee leads series 2-0
9/24/2022	vs	FLORIDA								vs Florida - Florida leads series 31-20
10/8/2022	vs	LSU								0-4 ATS vs LSU as favorite since 1993
10/15/2022	@	Alabama								0-21-1 S/U vs Alabama as Dog since 1983
10/22/2022	vs	TENNESSEE-MARTIN								vs UT-Martin - Tennessee leads series 1-0
10/29/2022	vs	KENTUCKY								33-3 S/U vs Kentucky as favorite since 1983
11/5/2022	@	Georgia								1-11 S/U vs Georgia as Dog since 2008
11/12/2022	vs	MISSOURI								vs Missouri - Series tied 5-5
11/19/2022	@	South Carolina								vs S. Carolina - Tennessee leads series 28-10-2
11/26/2022	@	Vanderbilt								16-3 S/U @ Vandy since 1984
12/3/2022	vs									SEC Championship
	vs									BOWL GAME

Pointspread Analysis — Non-Conference
- 11-3 S/U vs Non-Conf. as 7.5-10 point favorite since 1989
- 10-4 ATS vs Non-Conf. as 7.5-10 point favorite since 1989
- 13-2 S/U vs Non-Conf. as 10.5-15 point favorite since 1983
- 20-0 S/U vs Non-Conf. as 15.5-20 point favorite since 1986
- 18-1 S/U vs Non-Conf. as 20.5-25 point favorite since 1986
- 36-2 S/U vs Non-Conf. as 25.5 point or more favorite since 1986

Dog
- 0-12 S/U as 20.5 point or more Dog since 2009
- 0-7 S/U @ home as 15.5-20 point Dog since 2010
- 0-6 S/U on road as 15.5-20 point Dog since 2010
- 6-2 ATS on road as 15.5-20 point Dog since 1989
- 1-11 S/U on road as 10.5-15 point Dog since 2008
- 0-6 S/U @ home as 10.5-15 point Dog since 1986
- 1-7 S/U @ home as 7.5-10 point Dog since 1984
- 0-7 S/U on road as 7.5-10 point Dog since 1985
- 1-9 S/U on road as 3.5-7 point Dog since 2005
- 3-9 S/U @ home as 3.5-7 point Dog since 1994

Favorite
- 1-6 S/U & ATS as 3 point or less favorite since 2013
- 6-1 O/U on road as 3 point or less favorite since 2003
- 11-4 S/U on road as 3 point or less favorite since 1988
- 10-2 S/U on road as 3.5-7 point favorite since 1995
- 13-0 S/U @ home as 7.5-10 point favorite since 1989
- 0-6 O/U @ home as 7.5-10 point favorite since 2000
- 6-1 S/U on road as 7.5-10 point favorite since 2001
- 10-1 S/U @ home as 10.5-15 point favorite since 2006
- 11-1 S/U on road as 10.5-15 point favorite since 1994
- 14-2 S/U as 10.5-15 point favorite since 2006
- 131-5-1 S/U as 15.5 point or more favorite since 1983
- 32-0 S/U @ home as 15.5-20 point favorite since 1986
- 11-0 S/U on road as 15.5-20 point favorite since 1983
- 25-1 S/U @ home as 20.5-25 point favorite since 1993
- 46-1 S/U @ home as 25.5 point or more favorite since 1986

- 0-5 S/U when ranked vs #1 ranked teams since 1979
- 7-1 ATS when ranked @ Alabama since 1993
- 1-7 ATS when ranked vs Georgia since 2000
- 23-1 S/U when ranked vs Kentucky since 1967
- 8-1 S/U @ home when ranked vs LSU all time
- 38-1 S/U when ranked vs Vanderbilt all time {22-0 @ home}
- 3-33 S/U on road vs ranked teams since 2006
- 0-13 S/U vs #1 ranked teams since 1990
- 0-7 S/U on road vs #1 ranked teams all time
- 0-5 S/U vs ranked LSU since 2006

Pointspread Analysis — Conference
- 10-2 S/U vs Alabama as favorite since 1995
- vs Alabama - Alabama leads series 58-37-8
- 4-21 S/U vs Florida as Dog since 1984
- vs Georgia - Georgia leads series 26-23-2
- 10-2 S/U vs Georgia as favorite since 1989
- vs Kentucky - Tennessee leads series 82-26-9
- 0-5 S/U vs LSU as Dog since 2006
- 11-0 S/U vs South Carolina as favorite since 1993
- vs Vanderbilt - Tennessee leads series 78-32-5
- 2-8 ATS vs Vanderbilt since 2012
- Game 1-6 O/U @ Vanderbilt since 2006
- 0-6 ATS vs Florida as 3.5 point or less favorite since 1993 {1-5 S/U}
- 24-0 S/U vs Vanderbilt as 12 point or more favorite since 1985

Bowl Games
- 3-0 S/U in Liberty Bowl
- 0-3 S/U & ATS vs Penn State in Bowl Games
- 0-3 S/U vs ACC teams in Bowl Games since 2002
- 1-4 S/U in Peach Bowl {0-5 ATS}
- 3-0 S/U in Sugar Bowl since 1971
- 0-3 S/U in Orange Bowl since 1947
- 6-1 O/U in Bowl Games since 2009
- 3-0 O/U in Bowl Games as 3 point or less Dog since 1990
- 4-1 S/U in Bowl Games as 7.5-10 point favorite since 1994
- 5-0 O/U in Bowl Games as 7.5-10 point favorite since 1994

BALL STATE	11-2 S/U in 1st game of season since 2009
Pittsburgh	2-13 S/U in 1st road game of season since 2007
AKRON	3-16 ATS in 2nd home game of season since 2003
LSU	10-3 S/U after playing Florida since 2009
Alabama	2-13 S/U in 2nd road game of season since 2007
Georgia	7-1 S/U prior to playing Missouri since 2014
KENTUCKY	3-7 ATS prior to playing Georgia since 2012
MISSOURI	2-12 S/U prior to playing South Carolina since 2007
MISSOURI	7-2 O/U prior to playing South Carolina since 2012
South Carolina	1-9 ATS after playing Missouri since 2012
South Carolina	10-3 O/U prior to playing Vanderbilt since 2009
Vanderbilt	10-3 S/U after playing South Carolina since 2009

TEXAS LONGHORNS — BIG TWELVE

2021-Texas		Opponent	Texas	Opp	S/U	Line	ATS	Total	O/U	
9/4/2021	vs	LOUISIANA	38	18	W	-8.5	W	58.5	U	
9/11/2021	@	Arkansas	21	40	L	-6.0	L	56.5	O	
9/18/2021	vs	RICE	58	0	W	-26.0	W	52.0	O	
9/25/2021	vs	TEXAS TECH	70	35	W	-9.0	W	63.0	O	"Chancellor's Spurs"
10/2/2021	@	Tcu	32	27	W	-3.5	W	65.0	U	
10/9/2021	vs	Oklahoma	48	55	L	4.0	L	65.5	O	"Red River Rivalry - Golden Hat"
10/16/2021	vs	OKLAHOMA STATE	24	32	L	-3.5	L	61.0	U	
10/30/2021	@	Baylor	24	31	L	2.0	L	61.5	U	
11/6/2021	@	Iowa State	7	30	L	6.0	L	59.5	U	
11/13/2021	vs	KANSAS	56	57	L	-31.0	L	61.5	O	{OT}
11/20/2021	@	West Virginia	23	31	L	2.0	L	56.5	U	
11/27/2021	vs	KANSAS STATE	22	17	W	-3.0	W	54.5	U	
Coach: Steve Sarkisian		Season Record >>	423	373	5-7	ATS>>	5-7	O/U>>	5-7	

2020-Texas		Opponent	Texas	Opp	S/U	Line	ATS	Total	O/U	
9/12/2020	vs	TEXAS-EL PASO	59	3	W	-49.5	W	57.5	O	
9/26/2020	@	Texas Tech	63	56	W	-17.5	L	71.0	O	"Chancellor's Spurs"
10/3/2020	vs	TCU	31	33	L	-10.5	L	61.5	O	
10/10/2020	vs	Oklahoma	45	53	L	3.0	L	74.0	O	"Red River Rivalry - Golden Hat"
10/24/2020	vs	BAYLOR	27	16	W	-10.5	W	61.0	U	
10/31/2020	@	Oklahoma State	41	34	W	3.5	W	58.0	O	{OT}
11/7/2020	vs	WEST VIRGINIA	17	13	W	-6.0	L	55.5	U	
11/28/2020	vs	IOWA STATE	20	23	L	2.0	L	58.0	U	
12/5/2020	@	Kansas State	69	31	W	-7.0	W	53.5	O	
12/12/2020	@	Kansas	69	31	W	-7.0	W	53.5	O	
12/29/2020	vs	Colorado	55	23	W	-9.0	W	67.0	O	Alamo Bowl
Coach: Tom Herman		Season Record >>	496	316	8-3	ATS>>	6-5	O/U>>	8-3	

2019-Texas		Opponent	Texas	Opp	S/U	Line	ATS	Total	O/U	
8/31/2019	vs	LOUISIANA TECH	45	10	W	-19.0	W	55.5	U	
9/7/2019	vs	LSU	38	45	L	7.0	T	57.0	O	
9/14/2019	@	Rice	48	13	W	-32.0	W	57.0	O	
9/21/2019	vs	OKLAHOMA STATE	36	30	W	-7.0	L	72.5	U	
10/5/2019	@	West Virginia	42	31	W	-10.5	W	62.0	O	
10/12/2019	vs	Oklahoma	27	34	L	10.5	W	77.5	U	"Red River Rivalry - Golden Hat"
10/19/2019	vs	KANSAS	50	48	W	-21.0	L	63.0	O	
10/26/2019	@	Tcu	27	37	L	1.0	L	56.5	O	
11/9/2019	vs	KANSAS STATE	27	24	W	-7.0	L	57.5	U	
11/16/2019	@	Iowa State	21	23	L	7.0	W	64.5	U	
11/23/2019	@	Baylor	10	24	L	4.0	L	57.5	U	
11/30/2019	vs	TEXAS TECH	49	24	W	-8.0	W	65.0	O	"Chancellor's Spurs"
12/31/2019	vs	Utah	38	10	W	7.0	W	56.0	U	Alamo Bowl
Coach: Tom Herman		Season Record >>	458	353	8-5	ATS>>	7-4-1	O/U>>	6-7	

2018-Texas		Opponent	Texas	Opp	S/U	Line	ATS	Total	O/U	
9/1/2018	@	Maryland	29	34	L	-12.0	L	54.5	O	FedEx Field
9/8/2018	vs	TULSA	28	21	W	-21.5	L	59.5	U	
9/15/2018	vs	USC	37	14	W	-3.5	W	47.5	O	
9/22/2018	vs	TCU	31	16	W	2.5	W	50.0	O	
9/29/2018	@	Kansas State	19	14	W	-8.5	L	49.0	U	
10/6/2018	vs	Oklahoma	48	45	W	7.0	W	60.0	O	"Red River Rivalry - Golden Hat"
10/13/2018	vs	BAYLOR	23	17	W	-13.0	L	58.5	U	
10/27/2018	@	Oklahoma State	35	38	L	-1.0	L	59.5	O	
11/3/2018	vs	WEST VIRGINIA	41	42	L	1.0	T	58.0	O	
11/10/2018	@	Texas Tech	41	34	W	-2.0	W	62.0	O	"Chancellor's Spurs"
11/17/2018	vs	IOWA STATE	24	10	W	-1.5	W	51.0	U	
11/24/2018	@	Kansas	24	17	W	-15.0	L	50.0	U	
12/1/2018	vs	Oklahoma	27	39	L	9.5	L	79.5	U	Big 12 Championship
1/1/2019	vs	Georgia	28	21	W	13.5	W	60.5	U	Sugar Bowl
Coach: Tom Herman		Season Record >>	435	362	10-4	ATS>>	6-7-1	O/U>>	6-8	

TEXAS LONGHORNS — BIG TWELVE

STADIUM: Darrell K. Royal Texas Memorial Stadium {100,119} | **Location:** Austin, TX | **COACH:** Steve Sarkisian

DATE		Opponent	TEX	Opp	S/U	Line	ATS	Total	O/U	Trends & Angles
9/3/2022	vs	LOUISIANA-MONROE								vs UL-Monroe - Texas leads series 1-0
9/10/2022	vs	ALABAMA								vs Alabama - Texas leads series 7-1-1
9/17/2022	vs	TEXAS-SAN ANTONIO								1st Meeting
9/24/2022	@	Texas Tech								6-0 S/U @ Texas Tech since 2010 {5-1 ATS}
10/1/2022	vs	WEST VIRGINIA								vs West Virginia - West Va leads series 6-5
10/8/2022	vs	Oklahoma								vs Oklahoma - Texas leads series 65-50-5
10/15/2022	vs	IOWA STATE								vs Iowa State - Texas leads series 14-5
10/22/2022	@	Oklahoma State								vs Oklahoma State - Texas leads series 25-10
11/5/2022	@	Kansas State								vs Kansas State - Texas leads series 12-10
11/12/2022	vs	TCU								vs TCU - Texas leads series 64-27-1
11/19/2022	@	Kansas								17-2 S/U vs Kansas as favorite since 1996
11/26/2022	vs	BAYLOR								16-1 S/U vs Baylor as favorite since 1998
12/3/2022	vs									BIG XII Championship
	vs									BOWL GAME

Pointspread Analysis — Non-Conference
- 1-5 S/U vs Non-Conf. as 10.5-20 point Dog since 1987
- 7-2 O/U vs Non-Conf. as 3.5-7 point Dog since 1996
- 7-2 S/U & ATS vs Non-Conf. as 3 point or less Dog since 1982
- 3-11 ATS vs Non-Conf. as 7.5-10 point favorite since 1984
- 8-2 S/U vs Non-Conf. as 10.5-15 point favorite since 1987
- 34-0 S/U vs Non-Conf. as 20.5 point or more favorite since 1988

Dog
- 8-1 ATS as 15.5-20 point Dog since 1988
- 4-17 S/U as 10.5-15 point Dog since 1987
- 1-10 S/U on road as 10.5-15 point Dog since 1987
- 0-7 S/U as 7.5-10 point Dog since 2014
- 1-10 O/U as 7.5-10 point Dog since 1999
- 1-8 S/U @ home as 3 point or less Dog since 2010
- 1-7-1 ATS @ home as 3 point or less Dog since 2010

Favorite
- 14-1 S/U @ home as 3.5-7 point favorite since 2000
- 17-3 S/U as 3.5-7 point favorite since 2011 {13-6 ATS}
- 2-6 ATS @ home as 7.5-10 point favorite since 2010
- 8-2 S/U on road as 7.5-10 point favorite since 1999
- 15-2 S/U as 10.5-15 point favorite since 2008
- 14-1 S/U on road as 10.5-15 point favorite since 2000
- 17-2 S/U @ home as 15.5-20 point favorite since 1991
- 11-1 S/U on road as 15.5-20 point favorite since 1983
- 9-1 S/U on road as 20.5-25 point favorite since 1991
- 15-1 S/U @ home as 20.5-25 point favorite since 1985
- 67-1 S/U as 25.5 point or more favorite since 1983
- 1-4 O/U on road as 25.5 point or more favorite since 2007

Bowl Games
- 4-1-1 S/U vs Alabama in Bowl Games
- 0-3 S/U & ATS in Bowl Games as 7.5-15 point Dog since 1991
- 1-5 ATS in Bowl Games as 7.5-10 point favorite since 1984

- 8-0 S/U @ home when #1 ranked since 1965
- 19-1 S/U on road when #2 ranked all time
- 19-0 S/U @ home when ranked vs Baylor since 1953

Pointspread Analysis — Conference
- vs Baylor - Texas leads series 78-28-5
- 0-6 O/U vs Baylor as Dog since 2013
- 13-2 S/U vs Iowa State as favorite since 1998
- vs Kansas - Texas leads series 17-4
- 1-6 S/U vs Oklahoma State as Dog since 2010 {2-5 ATS}
- 15-2 S/U vs Oklahoma State as favorite since 1998
- 16-3 S/U vs Texas Tech since 2003
- vs Texas Tech - Texas leads series 54-17
- Game 2-5 O/U @ Texas Tech since 2008
- 16-0 S/U vs Baylor as 10 point or more favorite since 1983
- 0-4-1 ATS vs Oklahoma as 3 point or less favorite since 1984
- 6-1 S/U vs Oklahoma as 3.5-14 point favorite since 1983
- 6-0 ATS vs Oklahoma as 12-17.5 point Dog since 1988
- 7-2 S/U vs TCU as 8.5 point or more favorite since 1985
- 14-0 S/U vs Texas Tech as 10 point or more favorite since 1983

UL-MONROE	21-1 S/U in 1st home game of season since 2000
UTSA	4-10 O/U prior to playing Texas Tech since 2008
Texas Tech	8-2 S/U prior to playing West Virginia since 2012
Kansas State	13-2 S/U prior to playing TCU since 1992
WEST VIRGINIA	4-9 ATS prior to playing Oklahoma since 2009
WEST VIRGINIA	1-8 O/U after playing Texas Tech since 2011
IOWA STATE	3-10 O/U after playing Oklahoma since 2009
TCU	1-8 O/U prior to playing Kansas since 2013
Kansas	1-8 O/U in final road game of season since 2013

- 1-7 S/U vs #2 ranked teams since 1972
- 0-5 ATS vs ranked Kansas State since 2003
- 7-2 ATS vs ranked Oklahoma since 2013
- 1-6 S/U vs ranked Oklahoma State since 2010

TEXAS A&M AGGIES — SEC West

2021-Texas A&M		Opponent	A&M	Opp	S/U	Line	ATS	Total	O/U	
9/4/2021	vs	KENT STATE	41	10	W	-29.5	W	67.5	U	
9/11/2021	@	Colorado	10	7	W	-17.5	L	50.0	U	
9/18/2021	vs	NEW MEXICO	34	0	W	-30.0	W	50.0	U	
9/25/2021	vs	Arkansas	10	20	L	-4.0	L	47.0	U	"Southwest Classic"
10/2/2021	vs	MISSISSIPPI STATE	22	26	L	-7.0	L	46.0	O	
10/9/2021	vs	ALABAMA	41	38	W	19.0	W	50.5	O	
10/16/2021	@	Missouri	35	14	W	-11.5	W	59.0	U	
10/23/2021	vs	SOUTH CAROLINA	44	14	W	-19.0	W	46.0	O	
11/6/2021	vs	AUBURN	20	3	W	-4.0	W	49.0	U	
11/13/2021	@	Mississippi	19	29	L	1.0	L	58.5	U	
11/20/2021	vs	PRAIRIE VIEW A&M	52	3	W	-41.0	W	51.0	O	
11/27/2021	@	Lsu	24	27	L	-6.0	L	46.5	O	
Coach: Jimbo Fisher		Season Record >>	352	191	8-4	ATS>>	7-5	O/U>>	5-7	

2020-Texas A&M		Opponent	A&M	Opp	S/U	Line	ATS	Total	O/U	
9/26/2020	vs	VANDERBILT	17	12	W	-31.0	L	45.5	U	
10/3/2020	@	Alabama	24	52	L	18.0	L	54.0	O	
10/10/2020	vs	FLORIDA	41	38	W	5.5	W	60.0	O	
10/17/2020	@	Mississippi State	28	14	W	-3.5	W	57.0	U	
10/31/2020	vs	ARKANSAS	42	31	W	-14.5	L	54.5	O	"Southwest Classic"
11/7/2020	@	South Carolina	48	3	W	-9.0	W	58.0	U	
11/28/2020	vs	LSU	20	7	W	-16.0	L	59.5	U	
12/5/2020	@	Auburn	31	20	W	-5.0	W	49.0	O	
12/19/2020	@	Tennessee	34	13	W	-13.5	W	50.0	U	
1/2/2021	vs	North Carolina	41	27	W	-10.0	W	65.5	O	Orange Bowl
Coach: Jimbo Fisher		Season Record >>	326	217	9-1	ATS>>	6-4	O/U>>	5-5	

2019-Texas A&M		Opponent	A&M	Opp	S/U	Line	ATS	Total	O/U	
8/29/2019	vs	TEXAS STATE	41	7	W	-33.5	W	57.0	U	
9/7/2019	@	Clemson	10	24	L	16.0	W	62.5	O	
9/14/2019	vs	LAMAR	62	3	W	-45.0	W	NT	---	
9/21/2019	vs	AUBURN	20	28	L	-4.0	L	48.0	T	
9/28/2019	vs	Arkansas	31	27	W	-23.0	L	60.0	O	"Southwest Classic"
10/12/2019	vs	ALABAMA	28	47	L	17.0	L	61.0	O	
10/19/2019	@	Mississippi	24	17	W	-6.0	W	55.5	U	
10/26/2019	vs	MISSISSIPPI STATE	49	30	W	-10.5	W	50.0	O	
11/2/2019	vs	TEXAS-SAN ANTONIO	45	14	W	-38.0	L	53.0	O	
11/16/2019	vs	SOUTH CAROLINA	30	6	W	-10.5	W	47.0	U	
11/23/2019	@	Georgia	13	19	L	12.5	W	43.5	U	
11/30/2019	@	Lsu	7	50	L	18.0	L	64.5	U	
12/27/2019	vs	Oklahoma State	24	21	W	-5.0	L	55.5	U	Texas Bowl
Coach: Jimbo Fisher		Season Record >>	384	293	8-5	ATS>>	7-6	O/U>>	3-8-1	

2018-Texas A&M		Opponent	A&M	Opp	S/U	Line	ATS	Total	O/U	
9/1/2018	vs	NORTHWESTERN STATE	59	7	W	-46.5	W	NT	---	
9/8/2018	vs	CLEMSON	26	28	L	12.0	W	52.5	O	
9/15/2018	vs	LOUISIANA-MONROE	48	10	W	-28.0	W	66.0	U	
9/22/2018	@	Alabama	23	45	L	23.5	W	58.5	O	
9/29/2018	vs	Arkansas	24	17	W	-20.0	L	54.0	U	"Southwest Classic"
10/6/2018	vs	KENTUCKY	20	14	W	-4.5	W	48.5	U	{OT}
10/13/2018	@	South Carolina	26	23	W	-2.5	W	50.0	U	
10/27/2018	@	Mississippi State	13	28	L	1.0	L	42.5	U	
11/3/2018	@	Auburn	24	28	L	3.5	L	47.5	O	
11/10/2018	vs	MISSISSIPPI	38	24	W	-13.0	W	67.5	U	
11/17/2018	vs	ALABAMA-BIRMINGHAM	41	20	W	-17.0	W	46.5	O	
11/24/2018	vs	LSU	74	72	W	-2.5	L	45.5	O	{7 OT}
12/31/2018	vs	NC State	52	13	W	-7.5	W	58.0	O	Gator Bowl
Coach: Jimbo Fisher		Season Record >>	468	329	9-4	ATS>>	9-4	O/U>>	6-6	

TEXAS A&M AGGIES — SEC West

STADIUM: Kyle Field {102,733}
Location: College Station, TX
COACH: Jimbo Fisher

DATE		Opponent	A&M	Opp	S/U	Line	ATS	Total	O/U	Trends & Angles
9/3/2022	vs	SAM HOUSTON STATE								vs Sam Houston - Texas A&M leads series 12-0
9/10/2022	vs	APPALACHIAN STATE								17-2 S/U in 2nd home game of season since 2003
9/17/2022	vs	MIAMI								vs Miami - Miami leads series 2-1
9/24/2022	vs	Arkansas {@ Arlington, TX}								9-1 S/U vs Arkansas as favorite since 2012
10/1/2022	@	Mississippi State								vs Mississippi State - M State leads series 8-7
10/8/2022	@	Alabama								1-8 S/U vs Alabama as Dog since 2013
10/22/2022	@	South Carolina								vs South Carolina - Texas A&M leads series 8-0
10/29/2022	vs	MISSISSIPPI								0-5 O/U vs Mississippi as favorite since 2014
11/5/2022	vs	FLORIDA								vs Florida - Texas A&M leads series 3-2
11/12/2022	@	Auburn								vs Auburn - Texas A&M leads series 7-5
11/19/2022	vs	MASSACHUSETTS								10-2 S/U prior to playing LSU since 1990
11/26/2022	vs	LSU								vs LSU - LSU leads series 35-22-3
12/3/2022	vs									SEC Championship
	vs									BOWL GAME

Pointspread Analysis — Non-Conference
- 0-7 S/U vs Non-Conf. as 7.5-15 point Dog since 1994
- 2-8 S/U vs Non-Conf. as 3.5-7 point Dog since 1992
- 1-7 S/U & ATS vs Non-Conf. as 3 point or less Dog since 2000
- 3-11 ATS vs Non-Conf. as 3.5-7 point favorite since 1983
- 7-0 S/U vs Non-Conf. as 7.5-10 point favorite since 1992
- 13-0 S/U vs Non-Conf. as 10.5-15 point favorite since 1987
- 12-1 ATS vs Non-Conf. as 10.5-15 point favorite since 1987
- 12-2 S/U & ATS vs Non-conf. as 15.5-20 point favorite since 1986
- 47-1 S/U vs Non-Conf. as 20.5 point or more favorite since 1990
- 12-3 ATS vs Non-Conference since 2018

Dog
- 4-1 ATS @ home as 20.5 point or more Dog since 2005
- 0-5 S/U @ home as 20.5 point or more Dog since 2005
- 0-7 S/U on road as 15.5-20 point Dog since 2001
- 3-11 S/U on road as 10.5-15 point Dog since 1999
- 0-4 S/U @ home as 10.5-15 point Dog since 2001
- 8-1 O/U as 7.5-10 point Dog since 1994
- 2-10 S/U as 7.5-10 point Dog since 1983
- 1-7 S/U @ home as 3.5-7 point Dog since 2008
- 2-9 S/U on road as 3.5-7 point Dog since 2000
- 3-16 S/U as 3.5-7 point Dog since 2007
- 2-9 ATS as 3 point or less Dog since 2009
- 3-10 O/U @ home as 3 point or less Dog since 1999
- 1-7 S/U @ home as 3 point or less Dog since 2006

Favorite
- 5-0 S/U as 3 point or less favorite since 2015
- 4-0 S/U & ATS on road as 3 point or less favorite since 2010
- 3-10-2 O/U @ home as 3.5-7 point favorite since 2007
- 6-1 S/U on road as 3.5-7 point favorite since 2012 {5-2 ATS}
- 12-2 S/U as 7.5-10 point favorite since 2003
- 1-7 ATS @ home as 7.5-10 point favorite since 1998
- 11-5 O/U as 10.5-15 point favorite since 2009
- 21-3 S/U @ home as 10.5-15 point favorite since 1990
- 20-1 S/U on road as 10.5-15 point favorite since 1987
- 12-2 S/U on road as 15.5-20 point favorite since 1983
- 1-9 ATS on road as 15.5-20 point favorite since 1990
- 33-1 S/U @ home as 15.5-20 point favorite since 1984
- 8-1 O/U @ home as 15.5-20 point favorite since 2009
- 18-1-1 S/U @ home as 20.5-25 point favorite since 1986
- 8-2 S/U on road as 20.5-25 point favorite since 1985
- 57-0 S/U as 25.5 point or more favorite since 1986

Pointspread Analysis — Conference
- vs Alabama - Alabama leads series 11-3
- vs Arkansas - Arkansas leads series 42-33-3
- 0-4 S/U & ATS vs Arkansas as Dog since 1984
- 7-1 S/U vs LSU as favorite since 1991
- 1-10 S/U & ATS vs LSU as Dog since 1987
- vs Mississippi - Texas A&M leads series 9-4
- 0-3 S/U & ATS vs Mississippi State as Dog since 2014
- 7-0 S/U vs South Carolina as favorite since 2015
- 11-0 S/U vs Arkansas as 5 point or more favorite since 1987

Bowl Games
- 1-6 S/U in Cotton Bowl since 1992
- 0-4 S/U vs PAC-12 teams in Bowl Games
- 6-1 S/U vs Big 12 teams in Bowl Games
- 5-2 ATS vs Big 12 teams in Bowl Games
- 0-3 S/U & ATS in Alamo Bowl since 1999
- 1-4 S/U in Bowl Games as 7.5-20 point Dog since 1994
- 4-1 ATS in Bowl Games as 7.5-20 point Dog since 1994
- 2-7 S/U in Bowl Games as 3.5-7 point Dog since 1992

SAM HOUSTON	32-2 S/U in 1st home game of season since 1988
APP STATE	10-3 O/U in 2nd home game of season since 2006
MIAMI	8-2 S/U prior to playing Arkansas since 2012
Arkansas	9-1 S/U prior to playing Mississippi State since 2012
Arkansas	1-8 O/U prior to playing Mississippi State since 2013
Mississippi State	3-9 ATS after playing Arkansas since 2010
Mississippi State	8-3 S/U after playing Arkansas since 2011
Alabama	1-7-1 ATS after playing Mississippi State since 2013
Alabama	13-0 S/U in 2nd road game of season since 2009
South Carolina	8-1 O/U prior to playing Mississippi since 2012
South Carolina	10-1 S/U after playing Alabama since 1985
South Carolina	1-8 O/U after playing Alabama since 2013
FLORIDA	3-7 ATS prior to playing Auburn since 2012

- 12-0 S/U @ home when #5 ranked all time
- 0-7 S/U when ranked vs Alabama since 2013
- 0-5 ATS when ranked vs Mississippi since 2013
- 3-16 S/U vs #1 ranked teams all time
- 2-10 S/U vs #2 ranked teams all time
- 0-7 ATS vs ranked LSU since 2011

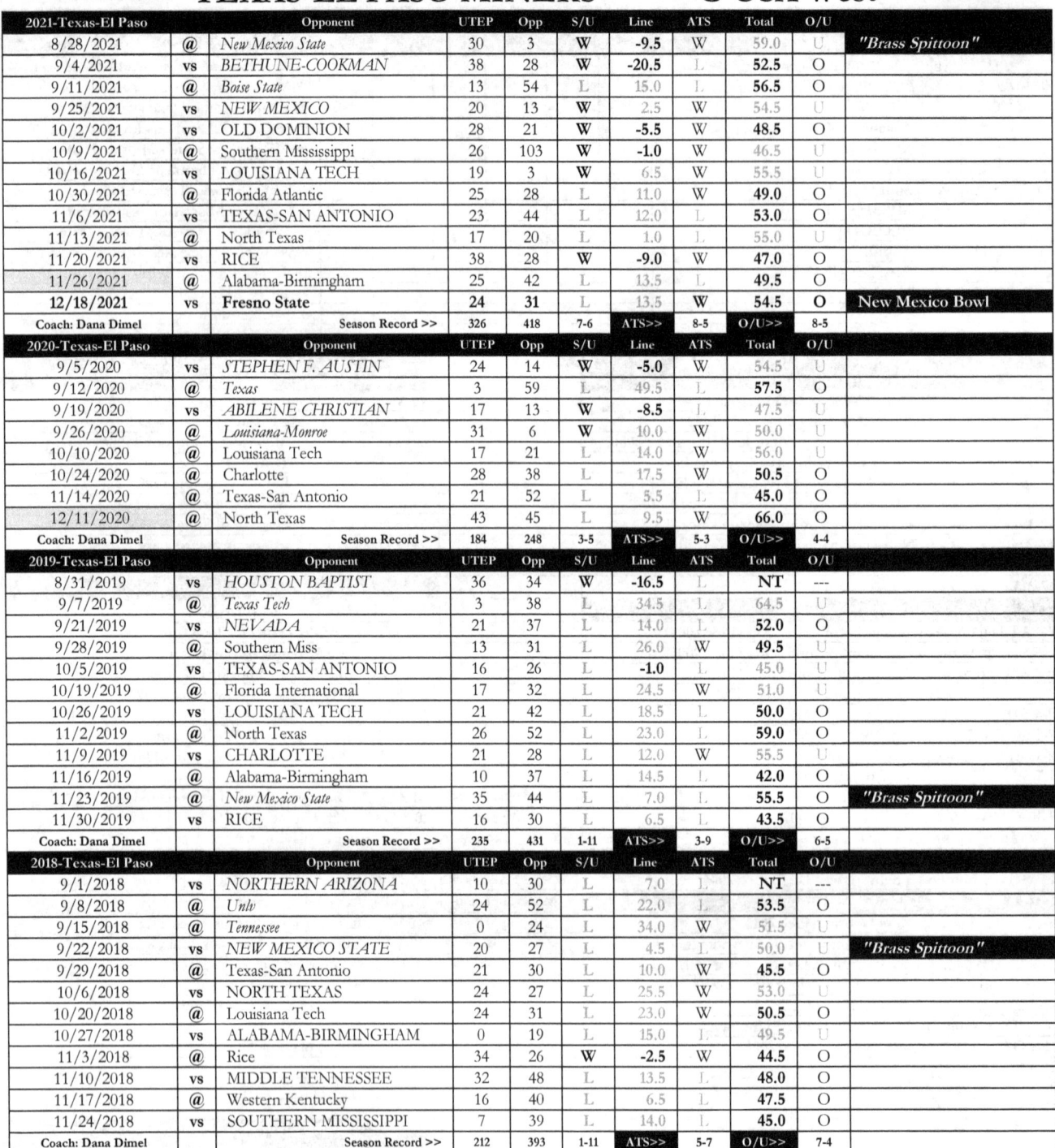

TEXAS-EL PASO MINERS   C-USA West

2021-Texas-El Paso		Opponent	UTEP	Opp	S/U	Line	ATS	Total	O/U	
8/28/2021	@	New Mexico State	30	3	W	-9.5	W	59.0	U	"Brass Spittoon"
9/4/2021	vs	BETHUNE-COOKMAN	38	28	W	-20.5	L	52.5	O	
9/11/2021	@	Boise State	13	54	L	15.0	L	56.5	O	
9/25/2021	vs	NEW MEXICO	20	13	W	2.5	W	54.5	U	
10/2/2021	vs	OLD DOMINION	28	21	W	-5.5	W	48.5	O	
10/9/2021	@	Southern Mississippi	26	103	W	-1.0	W	46.5	U	
10/16/2021	vs	LOUISIANA TECH	19	3	W	6.5	W	55.5	U	
10/30/2021	@	Florida Atlantic	25	28	L	11.0	W	49.0	O	
11/6/2021	vs	TEXAS-SAN ANTONIO	23	44	L	12.0	L	53.0	O	
11/13/2021	@	North Texas	17	20	L	1.0	L	55.0	U	
11/20/2021	vs	RICE	38	28	W	-9.0	W	47.0	O	
11/26/2021	@	Alabama-Birmingham	25	42	L	13.5	L	49.5	O	
12/18/2021	vs	Fresno State	24	31	L	13.5	W	54.5	O	New Mexico Bowl
Coach: Dana Dimel		Season Record >>	326	418	7-6	ATS>>	8-5	O/U>>	8-5	
2020-Texas-El Paso		Opponent	UTEP	Opp	S/U	Line	ATS	Total	O/U	
9/5/2020	vs	STEPHEN F. AUSTIN	24	14	W	-5.0	L	54.5	U	
9/12/2020	@	Texas	3	59	L	49.5	L	57.5	O	
9/19/2020	vs	ABILENE CHRISTIAN	17	13	W	-8.5	L	47.5	U	
9/26/2020	@	Louisiana-Monroe	31	6	W	10.0	W	50.0	U	
10/10/2020	@	Louisiana Tech	17	21	L	14.0	W	56.0	U	
10/24/2020	@	Charlotte	28	38	L	17.5	W	50.5	O	
11/14/2020	@	Texas-San Antonio	21	52	L	5.5	L	45.0	O	
12/11/2020	@	North Texas	43	45	L	9.5	W	66.0	O	
Coach: Dana Dimel		Season Record >>	184	248	3-5	ATS>>	5-3	O/U>>	4-4	
2019-Texas-El Paso		Opponent	UTEP	Opp	S/U	Line	ATS	Total	O/U	
8/31/2019	vs	HOUSTON BAPTIST	36	34	W	-16.5	L	NT	---	
9/7/2019	@	Texas Tech	3	38	L	34.5	L	64.5	U	
9/21/2019	vs	NEVADA	21	37	L	14.0	L	52.0	O	
9/28/2019	@	Southern Miss	13	31	L	26.0	W	49.5	U	
10/5/2019	vs	TEXAS-SAN ANTONIO	16	26	L	-1.0	L	45.0	U	
10/19/2019	@	Florida International	17	32	L	24.5	W	51.0	U	
10/26/2019	vs	LOUISIANA TECH	21	42	L	18.5	L	50.0	O	
11/2/2019	@	North Texas	26	52	L	23.0	L	59.0	O	
11/9/2019	vs	CHARLOTTE	21	28	L	12.0	W	55.5	U	
11/16/2019	@	Alabama-Birmingham	10	37	L	14.5	L	42.0	O	
11/23/2019	@	New Mexico State	35	44	L	7.0	L	55.5	O	"Brass Spittoon"
11/30/2019	vs	RICE	16	30	L	6.5	L	43.5	O	
Coach: Dana Dimel		Season Record >>	235	431	1-11	ATS>>	3-9	O/U>>	6-5	
2018-Texas-El Paso		Opponent	UTEP	Opp	S/U	Line	ATS	Total	O/U	
9/1/2018	vs	NORTHERN ARIZONA	10	30	L	7.0	L	NT	---	
9/8/2018	@	Unlv	24	52	L	22.0	L	53.5	O	
9/15/2018	@	Tennessee	0	24	L	34.0	W	51.5	U	
9/22/2018	vs	NEW MEXICO STATE	20	27	L	4.5	L	50.0	U	"Brass Spittoon"
9/29/2018	@	Texas-San Antonio	21	30	L	10.0	W	45.5	O	
10/6/2018	vs	NORTH TEXAS	24	27	L	25.5	W	53.0	U	
10/20/2018	@	Louisiana Tech	24	31	L	23.0	W	50.5	O	
10/27/2018	vs	ALABAMA-BIRMINGHAM	0	19	L	15.0	L	49.5	U	
11/3/2018	@	Rice	34	26	W	-2.5	W	44.5	O	
11/10/2018	vs	MIDDLE TENNESSEE	32	48	L	13.5	L	48.0	O	
11/17/2018	@	Western Kentucky	16	40	L	6.5	L	47.5	O	
11/24/2018	vs	SOUTHERN MISSISSIPPI	7	39	L	14.0	L	45.0	O	
Coach: Dana Dimel		Season Record >>	212	393	1-11	ATS>>	5-7	O/U>>	7-4	

TEXAS-EL PASO MINERS — C-USA West

STADIUM: Sun Bowl Stadium {51,500} **Location:** El Paso, TX **COACH:** Dana Dimel

DATE		Opponent	Utep	Opp	S/U	Line	ATS	Total	O/U	Trends & Angles
8/27/2022	vs	NORTH TEXAS								vs North Texas - N Texas leads series 19-8-3
9/3/2022	@	Oklahoma								0-4 S/U vs Oklahoma as Dog since 2000
9/10/2022	vs	NEW MEXICO STATE								vs NMSU - UTEP leads series 58-38-2
9/17/2022	@	New Mexico								vs New Mexico - UNM leads series 43-32-3
9/23/2022	vs	BOISE STATE								0-6 S/U vs Boise State as Dog since 2000
10/1/2022	@	Charlotte								vs Charlotte - Charlotte leads series 2-0
10/8/2022	@	Louisiana Tech								1-8 S/U vs La Tech as Dog since 2013
10/22/2022	vs	FLORIDA ATLANTIC								vs Florida Atlantic - FAU leads series 2-1
10/29/2022	vs	MIDDLE TENNESSEE								0-3 S/U vs Middle Tenn. as Dog since 2013
11/3/2022	@	Rice								0-6 S/U @ Rice as Dog since 2001
11/19/2022	vs	FLORIDA INTL.								vs Florida Intl. - FIU leads series 3-1
11/26/2022	@	Texas-San Antonio								vs UTSA - ROAD team 8-1 ATS 2013
12/3/2022	vs									C-USA Championship
	vs									BOWL GAME

Pointspread Analysis — Non-Conference
- 0-45 S/U vs Non-Conf. as 15.5 point or more Dog since 1986
- 14-1 S/U vs Non-Conf. as 10.5 point or more favorite since 1989
- 1-4 O/U vs New Mexico State as Dog since 2007
- 14-1 S/U vs NMSU as 7.5 point or more favorite since 1987
- 0-4 S/U vs New Mexico as 13.5 point or more Dog since 1993
- 5-1 S/U @ home vs New Mexico as favorite since 1987
- Game 1-8-1 O/U vs New Mexico since 1998

Dog
- 0-19 S/U as 30.5 point or more Dog since 1985
- 0-71 S/U as 20.5 point or more Dog since 1985
- 0-13 S/U @ home as 20.5 point or more Dog since 1985
- 0-8 S/U @ home as 15.5-20 point Dog since 2002
- 1-22 S/U on road as 15.5-20 point Dog since 1987
- 3-19 S/U on road as 10.5-15 point Dog since 1998
- 18-5 O/U as 10.5-15 point Dog since 2009
- 2-10 O/U as 7.5-10 point Dog since 2009
- 1-6-1 S/U @ home as 7.5-10 point Dog since 1987
- 1-11 S/U on road as 3.5-7 point Dog since 2001
- 5-2 O/U @ home as 3 point or less Dog since 2003
- 1-4 S/U & ATS @ home as 3 point or less Dog since 2007

Favorite
- 16-3 S/U @ home as 3.5-7 point favorite since 1988
- 8-0 S/U on road as 10.5 point or more favorite since 1988
- 1-7 O/U @ home as 10.5-15 point favorite since 2005
- 15-0 S/U as 15.5 point or more favorite since 1987

Pointspread Analysis — Conference
- vs Louisiana Tech - Louisiana Tech leads series 14-3-1
- vs Rice - Rice leads series 15-9
- 0-5 ATS @ Rice as Dog since 2003
- vs Texas-San Antonio - UTSA leads series 7-2

Bowl Games
- 0-6 S/U & ATS in Bowl Games since 1988
- 5-1 S/U in Sun Bowl since 1950

Opponent	Trend
Oklahoma	1-15 S/U prior to playing New Mexico State since 2002
Oklahoma	0-7 S/U after playing UTSA since 2015
Oklahoma	1-5 O/U after playing UTSA since 2016
New Mexico	2-8 S/U after New Mexico State since 2011
New Mexico	1-9 S/U in 2nd road game of season since 2012
Charlotte	2-7 S/U prior to playing Louisiana Tech since 2013
	1-6 ATS after playing Rice since 2013
FIU	0-6 S/U prior to playing UTSA since 2016
FIU	2-28 S/U in final road game of season since 1992
UTSA	3-15-1 ATS in final road game of season since 2003
UTSA	
MTSU	0-6 S/U prior to playing Rice since 2015

- 1-37 S/U on road vs ranked teams all time
- 2-23 S/U @ home vs ranked teams all time

TEXAS-SAN ANTONIO ROADRUNNERS   C-USA West

2021-UTSA		Opponent	UTSA	Opp	S/U	Line	ATS	Total	O/U	
9/4/2021	@	Illinois	37	30	W	4.5	W	52.0	O	
9/11/2021	vs	LAMAR	54	0	W	-39.0	W	65.0	U	
9/18/2021	vs	MIDDLE TENNESSEE	27	13	W	-10.5	W	59.5	U	
9/25/2021	@	Memphis	31	28	W	2.5	W	65.5	U	
10/2/2021	vs	UNLV	24	17	W	-21.5	L	55.5	U	
10/9/2021	@	Western Kentucky	52	46	W	3.5	W	71.0	O	
10/16/2021	vs	RICE	45	0	W	-17.0	W	53.0	U	
10/23/2021	@	Louisiana Tech	45	16	W	-5.5	W	59.5	O	
11/6/2021	@	Texas-El Paso	44	23	W	-12.0	W	53.0	O	
11/13/2021	vs	SOUTHERN MISS	27	17	W	-32.5	L	54.0	U	
11/20/2021	vs	ALABAMA-BIRMINGHAM	34	31	W	-3.5	L	53.5	O	
11/27/2021	@	North Texas	23	45	L	-8.5	L	59.5	O	
12/4/2021	vs	Western Kentucky	49	41	W	3.5	W	74.5	O	C-USA CHAMPIONSHIP
12/21/2021	vs	San Diego State	24	38	L	2.5	L	48.0	O	Frisco Bowl
Coach: Jeff Traylor		Season Record >>	516	345	12-2	ATS>>	9-5	O/U>>	8-6	C-USA CHAMPIONS

2020-UTSA		Opponent	UTSA	Opp	S/U	Line	ATS	Total	O/U	
9/12/2020	@	Texas State	51	48	W	6.5	W	56.0	O	{OT}
9/19/2020	vs	STEPHEN F. AUSTIN	24	10	W	-16.0	L	54.5	U	
9/25/2020	vs	MIDDLE TENNESSEE	37	35	W	16.5	W	58.5	O	
10/3/2020	@	Alabama-Birmingham	13	21	L	21.5	W	55.0	U	
10/10/2020	@	Byu	20	27	L	34.0	W	63.0	U	
10/17/2020	vs	ARMY	16	28	L	7.5	L	49.0	U	
10/24/2020	vs	LOUISIANA TECH	27	26	W	2.5	W	54.5	U	
10/31/2020	@	Florida Atlantic	3	24	L	4.5	L	47.0	U	
11/14/2020	vs	TEXAS-EL PASO	52	21	W	-5.5	W	45.0	O	
11/21/2020	@	Southern Mississippi	23	20	W	-9.0	L	53.5	U	
11/28/2020	vs	NORTH TEXAS	49	17	W	-1.5	W	67.0	O	
12/19/2020	vs	Louisiana	24	31	L	13.5	W	55.0	T	First Responder Bowl
Coach: Frank Wilson		Season Record >>	339	308	7-5	ATS>>	8-4	O/U>>	3-8-1	

2019-UTSA		Opponent	UTSA	Opp	S/U	Line	ATS	Total	O/U	
8/31/2019	vs	INCARNATE WORD	35	7	W	-7.0	W	NT	---	
9/7/2019	@	Baylor	14	63	L	25.0	L	58.0	O	
9/14/2019	vs	ARMY	13	31	L	14.5	L	49.0	U	
9/21/2019	@	North Texas	3	45	L	17.0	L	55.5	U	
10/5/2019	@	Texas-El Paso	26	16	W	1.0	W	45.0	U	
10/12/2019	vs	ALABAMA-BIRMINGHAM	14	33	L	12.5	L	47.0	T	
10/19/2019	vs	RICE	31	27	W	5.5	W	42.0	O	
11/2/2019	@	Texas A&M	14	45	L	38.0	W	53.0	O	
11/9/2019	@	Old Dominion	24	23	W	3.0	W	41.5	O	
11/16/2019	vs	SOUTHERN MISS	17	36	L	17.0	L	55.5	U	
11/23/2019	vs	FLORIDA ATLANTIC	26	40	L	21.5	W	57.0	O	
11/30/2019	@	Louisiana Tech	27	41	L	21.0	W	56.0	O	
Coach: Frank Wilson		Season Record >>	244	407	4-8	ATS>>	7-5	O/U>>	6-4-1	

2018-UTSA		Opponent	UTSA	Opp	S/U	Line	ATS	Total	O/U	
9/1/2018	@	Arizona State	7	49	L	17.5	L	52.0	O	
9/8/2018	vs	BAYLOR	20	37	L	17.0	T	55.0	O	
9/15/2018	@	Kansas State	17	41	L	21.0	L	46.5	O	
9/22/2018	vs	TEXAS STATE	25	21	W	-7.0	L	49.0	U	
9/29/2018	vs	TEXAS-EL PASO	30	21	W	-10.0	L	45.5	O	
10/6/2018	@	Rice	20	3	W	1.0	W	50.0	U	
10/13/2018	vs	LOUISIANA TECH	3	31	L	13.0	L	45.5	U	
10/20/2018	@	Southern Mississippi	17	27	L	16.0	W	43.5	O	
11/3/2018	@	Alabama-Birmingham	3	52	L	21.5	L	42.0	O	
11/10/2018	vs	FLORIDA INTERNATIONAL	7	45	L	10.5	L	47.0	O	
11/17/2018	@	Marshall	0	23	L	27.5	W	47.0	U	
11/24/2018	vs	NORTH TEXAS	21	24	L	24.5	W	51.5	U	
Coach: Frank Wilson		Season Record >>	170	374	3-9	ATS>>	4-7-1	O/U>>	7-5	

TEXAS-SAN ANTONIO ROADRUNNERS   C-USA West

STADIUM: AlamoDome {64,000}   **Location:** San Antonio, TX   **COACH:** Jeff Traylor

DATE		Opponent	Utsa	Opp	S/U	Line	ATS	Total	O/U	Trends & Angles
9/3/2022	vs	HOUSTON								vs Houston - Series tied 1-1
9/10/2022	@	Army								vs Army - Army leads series 1-0
9/17/2022	@	Texas								1st Meeting
9/24/2022	vs	TEXAS SOUTHERN								2-7 S/U in 2nd home game of season since 2013
9/30/2022	@	Middle Tennessee								vs MTSU - UTSA leads series 3-1
10/8/2022	vs	WESTERN KENTUCKY								vs Western Kentucky - Series tied 1-1
10/14/2022	@	Florida International								1-8 ATS prior to playing N. Texas since 2013
10/22/2022	vs	NORTH TEXAS								vs North Texas - N Texas leads series 5-4
11/5/2022	@	Alabama-Birmingham								vs Alabama-Birm. - UAB leads series 4-2
11/12/2022	vs	LOUISIANA TECH								vs La Tech - La Tech leads series 7-3
11/19/2022	@	Rice								vs Rice - UTSA leads series 6-3
11/26/2022	vs	TEXAS-EL PASO								vs Texas-El Paso - UTSA leads series 7-2
12/3/2022	vs									C-USA Championship
	vs									BOWL GAME

Pointspread Analysis — Non-Conference
- 6-24 S/U vs Non-Conf. as Dog since 2012
- 8-0 S/U vs Non-Conf as 3.5 point or more favorite since 2012

Dog
- 0-19 S/U as 20.5 point or more Dog since 2012
- 4-20 S/U @ home as Dog since 2012
- 5-2 O/U on road as 10.5 point or more Dog since 2014
- 0-5 S/U on road as 7.5-10 point Dog since 2014
- 1-9 O/U as 7.5-10 point Dog since 2013
- 10-2 S/U as 3 point or less Dog since 2018 {10-2 ATS}

Favorite
- 1-4 ATS as 3 point or less favorite since 2016
- 0-5 O/U as 3 point or less favorite since 2016
- 5-0 S/U as 3.5-7 point favorite since 2018
- 7-2 S/U as 7.5-10 point favorite since 2012
- 0-7 ATS as 7.5-10 point favorite since 2013
- 7-0 S/U @ home as 10.5 point or more favorite since 2017

Pointspread Analysis — Conference
- 1-6 S/U vs Louisiana Tech as Dog since 2012
- 1-4 O/U vs Rice as Dog since 2012
- 4-0 S/U vs Rice as favorite since 2015

UAB	7-2 S/U prior to playing Louisiana Tech since 2013
FIU	2-6 S/U prior to playing North Texas since 2014
Rice	1-5 ATS prior to playing Texas-El Paso since 2016
Rice	1-5 O/U prior to playing Texas-El Paso since 2016
Rice	2-5 O/U after playing Louisiana Tech since 2013

This book takes a comprehensive look at College Football's most memorable plays and memorable moments throughout the years. You will read about games most people have never heard of but have played an important role in shaping College Football as we know it today. It is a must read for fans of College Football. Games include all divisions of College Football (FBS, FCS, Division II and Division III). It is truly a walk down memory lane for fans who enjoy the rich traditions and history of college football.

College Football History "Memorable Plays and Memorable Moments" {8.5" x 11"} {156 pages}

This book is available from Steve's Football Bible LLC
These books available at numerous online retailers

TEXAS STATE BOBCATS   SUN BELT West

2021-Texas State		Opponent	State	Opp	S/U	Line	ATS	Total	O/U	
9/4/2021	vs	BAYLOR	20	29	L	13.5	W	53.0	U	
9/11/2021	@	Florida International	23	17	W	2.0	W	54.5	U	{OT}
9/18/2021	vs	INCARNATE WORD	34	42	L	-10.5	L	68.5	O	
9/25/2021	@	Eastern Michigan	21	59	L	7.5	L	62.5	O	
10/9/2021	vs	SOUTH ALABAMA	33	31	W	4.0	W	52.0	O	{4 OT}
10/16/2021	vs	TROY	28	31	L	7.0	W	48.5	O	
10/23/2021	@	Georgia State	16	28	L	10.5	L	58.5	U	
10/30/2021	@	Louisiana	0	45	L	21.0	L	58.0	U	
11/6/2021	vs	LOUISIANA-MONROE	27	19	W	-2.5	W	58.0	U	
11/13/2021	vs	GEORGIA SOUTHERN	30	38	L	-2.0	L	52.0	O	
11/20/2021	@	Coastal Carolina	21	35	L	24.5	W	60.5	U	
11/27/2021	@	Arkansas State	24	22	W	2.0	W	62.0	U	
Coach: Jake Spavital		Season Record >>	277	396	4-8	ATS>>	7-5	O/U>>	5-7	

2020-Texas State		Opponent	State	Opp	S/U	Line	ATS	Total	O/U	
9/5/2020	vs	SMU	24	31	L	24.0	W	70.0	U	
9/12/2020	vs	TEXAS-SAN ANTONIO	48	51	L	-6.5	L	56.0	O	{OT}
9/19/2020	@	Louisiana-Monroe	38	17	W	-3.0	W	58.0	U	
9/26/2020	@	Boston College	21	24	L	20.5	W	56.5	U	
10/10/2020	@	Troy	17	37	L	7.0	L	59.5	U	
10/17/2020	@	South Alabama	20	30	L	3.0	L	58.0	U	
10/24/2020	@	Byu	14	52	L	30.0	L	61.5	O	
10/31/2020	vs	LOUISIANA	34	44	L	16.5	W	56.5	O	
11/7/2020	vs	APPALACHIAN STATE	17	38	L	21.5	W	59.0	U	
11/14/2020	@	Georgia Southern	38	40	L	13.0	W	50.0	O	
11/21/2020	vs	ARKANSAS STATE	47	45	W	4.5	W	69.0	O	
11/28/2020	vs	COASTAL CAROLINA	14	49	L	16.5	L	59.0	O	
Coach: Everett Withers		Season Record >>	332	458	2-10	ATS>>	7-5	O/U>>	6-6	

2019-Texas State		Opponent	State	Opp	S/U	Line	ATS	Total	O/U	
8/29/2019	@	Texas A&M	7	41	L	33.5	L	57.0	U	
9/7/2019	vs	WYOMING	14	23	L	7.0	L	47.5	U	
9/14/2019	@	Smu	17	47	L	17.5	L	62.5	O	
9/21/2019	vs	GEORGIA STATE	37	34	W	-3.0	T	62.5	O	{3 OT}
9/28/2019	vs	NICHOLLS STATE	24	3	W	NL	---	NT	---	"Battle for the Paddle"
10/10/2019	vs	LOUISIANA-MONROE	14	24	L	4.0	L	60.0	U	
10/26/2019	@	Arkansas State	14	38	L	11.0	L	60.5	U	
11/2/2019	@	Louisiana-Lafayette	3	31	L	23.0	L	55.0	U	
11/9/2019	vs	SOUTH ALABAMA	30	28	W	-7.0	L	41.5	O	
11/16/2019	vs	TROY	27	63	L	7.0	L	64.5	O	
11/23/2019	@	Appalachian State	13	35	L	28.0	W	50.0	U	
11/30/2019	@	Coastal Carolina	21	24	L	7.0	W	52.0	U	
Coach: Everett Withers		Season Record >>	221	391	3-9	ATS>>	2-8-1	O/U>>	4-7	

2018-Texas State		Opponent	State	Opp	S/U	Line	ATS	Total	O/U	
9/1/2018	@	Rutgers	7	35	L	16.5	L	48.0	U	
9/8/2018	vs	TEXAS SOUTHERN	36	20	W	-31.5	L	NT	---	
9/15/2018	@	South Alabama	31	41	L	9.5	L	49.0	O	
9/22/2018	@	Texas-San Antonio	21	25	L	7.0	W	49.0	U	
10/6/2018	vs	LOUISIANA-LAFAYETTE	27	42	L	3.5	L	58.5	O	
10/13/2018	vs	GEORGIA SOUTHERN	13	15	L	17.0	W	51.0	U	
10/20/2018	@	Louisiana-Monroe	14	20	L	10.5	L	59.5	U	
10/27/2018	vs	NEW MEXICO STATE	27	20	W	PK	W	56.0	U	
11/3/2018	@	Georgia State	40	31	W	7.0	W	52.5	O	
11/10/2018	vs	APPALACHIAN STATE	7	38	L	19.0	L	45.5	U	
11/17/2018	@	Troy	7	12	L	22.0	W	47.5	U	
11/24/2018	vs	ARKANSAS STATE	7	33	L	13.0	L	48.5	U	
Coach: Everett Withers		Season Record >>	237	332	3-9	ATS>>	6-6	O/U>>	3-8	

TEXAS STATE BOBCATS   SUN BELT West

STADIUM: Jim Wacker Field at Bobcat Stadium {30,008}   **Location:** Mc Allen, TX   **COACH:** Jake Spavital

DATE		Opponent	State	Opp	S/U	Line	ATS	Total	O/U	Trends & Angles
9/3/2022	@	Nevada								vs Nevada - Nevada leads series 1-0
9/10/2022	vs	FLA INTERNATIONAL								vs Fla Inter - Texas State leads series 1-0
9/17/2022	@	Baylor								vs Baylor - Baylor leads series 8-0
9/24/2022	vs	HOUSTON BAPTIST								vs Houston Bapt - Texas State leads series 1-0
10/1/2022	@	James Madison								1st Meeting
10/8/2022	vs	APPALACHIAN STATE								vs App State - App State leads series 6-0
10/15/2022	@	Troy								0-7 S/U @ Troy since 1996
10/22/2022	vs	SOUTHERN MISS								vs Southern Miss - Series tied 1-1
11/5/2022	@	Louisiana-Monroe								vs UL-Monroe - ULM leads series 12-6
11/12/2022	@	South Alabama								vs South Ala - Texas State leads series 4-3
11/19/2022	vs	ARKANSAS STATE								vs Arkansas State - Ark State leads series 6-3
11/26/2022	vs	LOUISIANA								vs Louisiana - Louisiana leads series 9-0
12/3/2022	vs									Sun Belt Championship
	vs									BOWL GAME

Pointspread Analysis Non-Conference		Pointspread Analysis Conference
2-17 S/U vs Non-Conf. as 15.5 point or more Dog since 2012		0-5 O/U vs Appalachian State as Dog since 2016
7-1 S/U vs Non-Conf. as 10.5 point or more favorite since 2013		0-8 S/U vs Louisiana as Dog since 2013
Dog		0-10 S/U vs Troy since 1998
0-24 S/U as 20.5 point or more Dog since 2012		vs Troy - Troy leads series 11-1
3-16 O/U as 20.5 point more Dog since 2016		0-7 S/U vs Troy as Dog since 2013
1-12 S/U as 15.5-20 point Dog since 2012		
0-10 S/U as 10.5-15 point Dog since 2013		
0-3 S/U & ATS @ home as 7.5-10 point Dog since 2014		
1-8 S/U on road as 3.5-7 point Dog since 2012	FLA INTER	21-5 S/U in 1st home game of season since 1996
2-8 S/U @ home as 3.5-7 point Dog since 2016	Baylor	1-12 S/U in 2nd road game of season since 2009
6-1 S/U & ATS as 3 point or less Dog since 2013	SOUTHERN MISS	1-8 S/U prior to playing UL-Monroe since 2013
Favorite	SOUTHERN MISS	0-5 S/U after playing Troy since 2015
2-5 S/U @ home as 3 point or less favorite since 2012	South Alabama	1-7 ATS prior to playing Louisiana-Monroe since 2013
1-5-1 ATS @ home as 3 point or less favorite since 2012	South Alabama	0-8 S/U prior to playing Arkansas State since 2014
11-4 S/U @ home as 6 point or more favorite since 2012	South Alabama	2-10 S/U in final road game of season since 2010
3-0 S/U & ATS on road as 6 point or more favorite since 2013	ARKANSAS STATE	0-5 S/U after playing South Alabama since 2015

Steve's Football Bible also offers the FCS Football Bible, the FCS football handicapper's best friend for the 2022 football season. To order Go to: www.stevesfootballbible.com

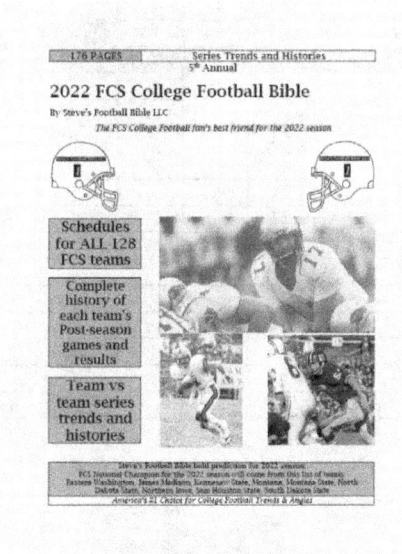

2022 FCS Football Bible $19.95

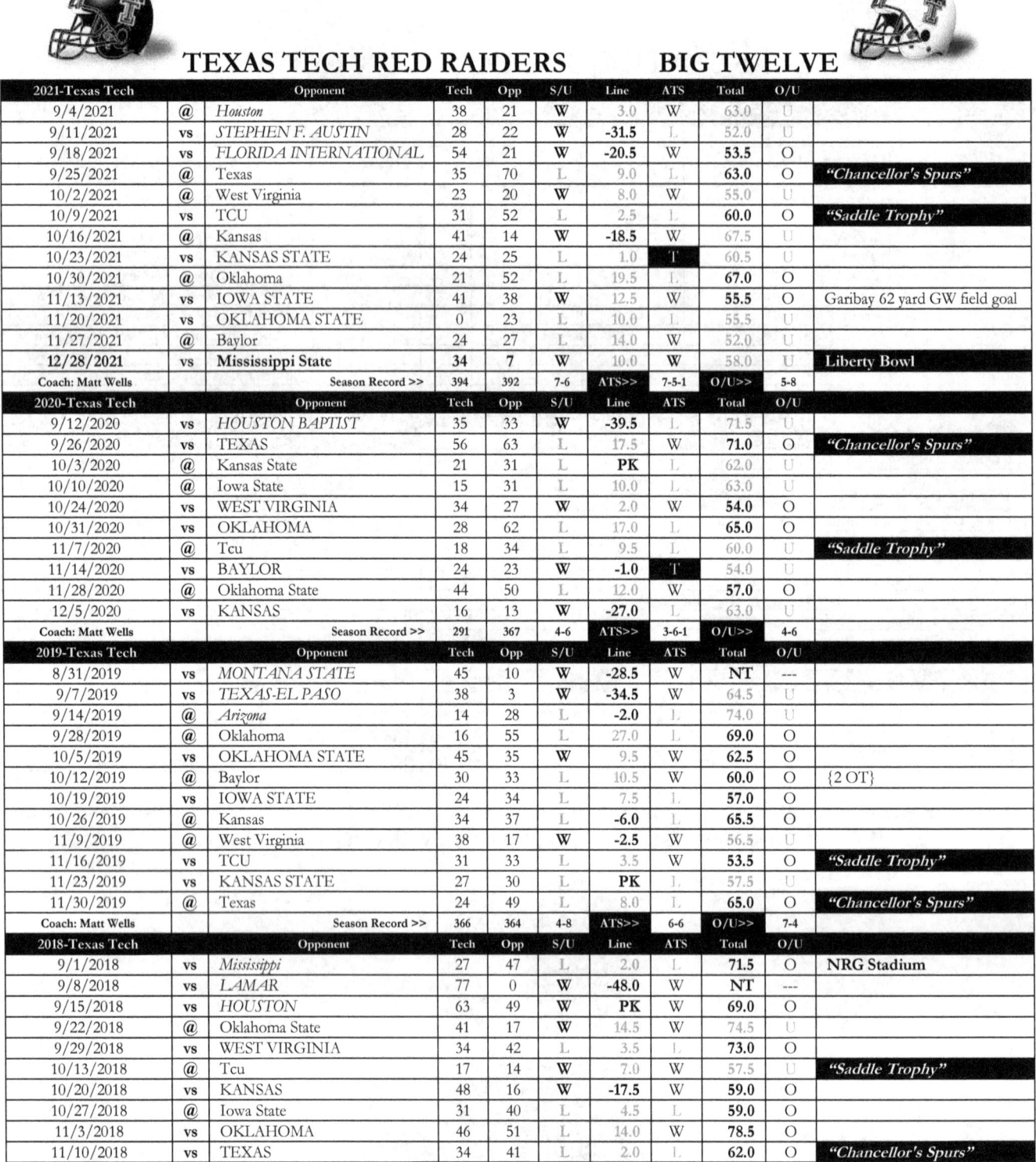

TEXAS TECH RED RAIDERS — BIG TWELVE

2021-Texas Tech		Opponent	Tech	Opp	S/U	Line	ATS	Total	O/U	
9/4/2021	@	Houston	38	21	W	3.0	W	63.0	U	
9/11/2021	vs	STEPHEN F. AUSTIN	28	22	W	-31.5	L	52.0	U	
9/18/2021	vs	FLORIDA INTERNATIONAL	54	21	W	-20.5	W	53.5	O	
9/25/2021	@	Texas	35	70	L	9.0	L	63.0	O	"Chancellor's Spurs"
10/2/2021	@	West Virginia	23	20	W	8.0	W	55.0	U	
10/9/2021	vs	TCU	31	52	L	2.5	L	60.0	O	"Saddle Trophy"
10/16/2021	@	Kansas	41	14	W	-18.5	W	67.5	U	
10/23/2021	vs	KANSAS STATE	24	25	L	1.0	T	60.5	U	
10/30/2021	@	Oklahoma	21	52	L	19.5	L	67.0	O	
11/13/2021	vs	IOWA STATE	41	38	W	12.5	W	55.5	O	Garibay 62 yard GW field goal
11/20/2021	vs	OKLAHOMA STATE	0	23	L	10.0	L	55.5	U	
11/27/2021	@	Baylor	24	27	L	14.0	W	52.0	U	
12/28/2021	vs	Mississippi State	34	7	W	10.0	W	58.0	U	Liberty Bowl
Coach: Matt Wells		Season Record >>	394	392	7-6	ATS>>	7-5-1	O/U>>	5-8	

2020-Texas Tech		Opponent	Tech	Opp	S/U	Line	ATS	Total	O/U	
9/12/2020	vs	HOUSTON BAPTIST	35	33	W	-39.5	L	71.5	U	
9/26/2020	vs	TEXAS	56	63	L	17.5	W	71.0	O	"Chancellor's Spurs"
10/3/2020	@	Kansas State	21	31	L	PK	L	62.0	U	
10/10/2020	@	Iowa State	15	31	L	10.0	L	63.0	U	
10/24/2020	vs	WEST VIRGINIA	34	27	W	2.0	W	54.0	O	
10/31/2020	vs	OKLAHOMA	28	62	L	17.0	L	65.0	O	
11/7/2020	@	Tcu	18	34	L	9.5	L	60.0	U	"Saddle Trophy"
11/14/2020	vs	BAYLOR	24	23	W	-1.0	T	54.0	U	
11/28/2020	@	Oklahoma State	44	50	L	12.0	W	57.0	O	
12/5/2020	vs	KANSAS	16	13	W	-27.0	L	63.0	U	
Coach: Matt Wells		Season Record >>	291	367	4-6	ATS>>	3-6-1	O/U>>	4-6	

2019-Texas Tech		Opponent	Tech	Opp	S/U	Line	ATS	Total	O/U	
8/31/2019	vs	MONTANA STATE	45	10	W	-28.5	W	NT	---	
9/7/2019	vs	TEXAS-EL PASO	38	3	W	-34.5	W	64.5	U	
9/14/2019	@	Arizona	14	28	L	-2.0	L	74.0	U	
9/28/2019	@	Oklahoma	16	55	L	27.0	L	69.0	O	
10/5/2019	vs	OKLAHOMA STATE	45	35	W	9.5	W	62.5	O	
10/12/2019	@	Baylor	30	33	L	10.5	W	60.0	O	{2 OT}
10/19/2019	vs	IOWA STATE	24	34	L	7.5	L	57.0	O	
10/26/2019	@	Kansas	34	37	L	-6.0	L	65.5	O	
11/9/2019	@	West Virginia	38	17	W	-2.5	W	56.5	U	
11/16/2019	vs	TCU	31	33	L	3.5	W	53.5	O	"Saddle Trophy"
11/23/2019	vs	KANSAS STATE	27	30	L	PK	L	57.5	U	
11/30/2019	@	Texas	24	49	L	8.0	L	65.0	O	"Chancellor's Spurs"
Coach: Matt Wells		Season Record >>	366	364	4-8	ATS>>	6-6	O/U>>	7-4	

2018-Texas Tech		Opponent	Tech	Opp	S/U	Line	ATS	Total	O/U	
9/1/2018	vs	Mississippi	27	47	L	2.0	L	71.5	O	NRG Stadium
9/8/2018	vs	LAMAR	77	0	W	-48.0	W	NT	---	
9/15/2018	vs	HOUSTON	63	49	W	PK	W	69.0	O	
9/22/2018	@	Oklahoma State	41	17	W	14.5	W	74.5	U	
9/29/2018	vs	WEST VIRGINIA	34	42	L	3.5	L	73.0	O	
10/13/2018	@	Tcu	17	14	W	7.0	W	57.5	U	"Saddle Trophy"
10/20/2018	vs	KANSAS	48	16	W	-17.5	W	59.0	O	
10/27/2018	@	Iowa State	31	40	L	4.5	L	59.0	O	
11/3/2018	vs	OKLAHOMA	46	51	L	14.0	W	78.5	O	
11/10/2018	vs	TEXAS	34	41	L	2.0	L	62.0	O	"Chancellor's Spurs"
11/17/2018	@	Kansas State	6	21	L	-6.5	L	55.0	U	
11/24/2018	vs	Baylor	24	35	L	-6.5	L	63.5	U	AT&T Stadium
Coach: Kliff Kingsbury		Season Record >>	448	373	5-7	ATS>>	6-6	O/U>>	7-4	

TEXAS TECH RED RAIDERS — BIG TWELVE

STADIUM: Jones AT&T Stadium {60,454} | **Location:** Lubbock, TX | **COACH:** Joey McGuire

DATE		Opponent	Tech	Opp	S/U	Line	ATS	Total	O/U	Trends & Angles
9/3/2022	vs	MURRAY STATE								22-0 S/U in 1st home game of season since 2000
9/10/2022	vs	HOUSTON								9-1 S/U vs Houston since 1991 {8-2 ATS}
9/17/2022	@	NC State								0-4 S/U vs NC State since 1992 {0-4 ATS}
9/24/2022	vs	TEXAS								3-17 S/U vs Texas as Dog since 1999
10/1/2022	@	Kansas State								1-5 S/U @ Kansas State as Dog since 1996
10/8/2022	@	Oklahoma State								2-11 S/U vs Oklahoma State as Dog since 1999
10/22/2022	vs	WEST VIRGINIA								1-3 S/U @ home vs West Virginia since 2014
10/29/2022	vs	BAYLOR								vs Baylor - Baylor leads series 40-38-1
11/5/2022	@	Tcu								5-2 S/U & ATS @ TCU as Dog since 1988
11/12/2022	vs	KANSAS								13-1 S/U vs Kansas as favorite since 2004
11/19/2022	@	Iowa State								vs Iowa State - Texas Tech leads series 12-8
11/26/2022	vs	OKLAHOMA								0-10 S/U vs Oklahoma as Dog since 2012
12/3/2022	vs									BIG XII Championship
	vs									BOWL GAME

Pointspread Analysis — Non-Conference

- 0-5 S/U vs Non-Conf. as 15.5 point or more Dog since 1986
- 1-7 S/U vs Non-Conf. as 3.5-7 point Dog since 1986
- 0-10 S/U & ATS vs Non-Conf. as 3 point or less favorite since 1992
- 7-0-1 O/U vs Non-Conf. as 3.5-7 point favorite since 2002
- 63-3 S/U vs Non-Conf. as 7.5 point or more favorite since 1985
- 6-0-1 S/U vs Houston as favorite since 1986
- 0-3 S/U @ home vs Houston as Dog since 1984
- vs NC State - Texas Tech leads series 4-1

Dog

- 2-19 S/U as 20.5 point or more Dog since 1983
- 8-3 ATS on road as 20.5 point or more Dog since 1994
- 6-1 O/U as 20.5 point or more Dog since 2001
- 0-16 S/U on road as 15.5-20 point Dog since 1983
- 1-23 S/U as 15.5-20 point Dog since 1983
- 7-0 ATS @ home as 10.5-15 point Dog since 1999
- 3-14 S/U on road as 10.5-15 point Dog since 1985
- 0-7 S/U @ home as 3.5-7 point Dog since 2012
- 3-20 S/U on road as 3.5-7 point Dog since 1998
- 4-18 ATS on road as 3.5-7 point Dog since 1999
- 11-2 S/U on road as 3 point or less Dog since 1996
- 12-2 ATS on road as 3 point or less Dog since 1993
- 2-7-1 S/U & ATS as 3 point or less Dog since 2015

Favorite

- 1-5 S/U & ATS @ home as 3 point or less favorite since 2002
- 13-5-2 O/U as 3.5-7 point favorite since 2007
- 10-0 S/U @ home as 7.5-10 point favorite since 1985
- 7-2-1 ATS @ home as 7.5-10 point favorite since 1985
- 8-1 S/U on road as 7.5-10 point favorite since 1984
- 5-0 S/U & ATS on road as 10.5-15 point favorite since 1993
- 23-4 S/U @ home as 10.5-15 point favorite since 1985
- 23-0 S/U as 15.5-20 point favorite since 1983
- 18-4 ATS as 15.5-20 point favorite since 1987
- 32-1 S/U @ home as 20.5 point or more favorite since 2000
- 12-1 S/U on road as 20.5 point or more favorite since 1989

Bowl Games

- 0-4 S/U in Cotton Bowl
- 1-7 S/U in Sun Bowl
- 1-5 S/U vs SEC in Bowl Games since 1986
- 7-2-1 O/U in Bowl Games since 2006
- 3-8 ATS in Bowl Games since 2006
- 0-4 S/U in Bowl Games as 3.5-7 point Dog since 1986
- 0-3 S/U & ATS in Bowl Games as 3 point or less favorite since 2000
- 3-0 S/U in Bowl Games as 7.5-10 point favorite since 2006

Pointspread Analysis — Conference

- 7-1 O/U vs Baylor as Dog since 2011
- 18-1 S/U vs Baylor as favorite since 1992
- vs Kansas - Texas Tech leads series 21-2
- 3-0 S/U & ATS vs Kansas as Dog since 1996
- 7-1 O/U vs Kansas State as favorite since 2005
- 1-4 S/U & ATS vs Kansas State as favorite since 2011
- vs Kansas State - K State leads series 13-9
- vs Oklahoma - Oklahoma leads series 23-6
- vs Oklahoma State - Series tied 23-23-3
- vs TCU - Texas Tech leads series 38-30-3
- vs Texas - Texas leads series 54-17
- vs West Virginia - West Virginia leads series 6-5
- 3-0 S/U & ATS vs West Virginia since 2019
- 1-14 S/U vs Oklahoma as 13.5 point or more Dog since 1994
- 5-0-1 S/U vs TCU as 6 point or more favorite since 1983
- 5-1 ATS vs TCU as 6 point or more favorite since 1985
- 0-14 S/U vs Texas as 10 point or more Dog since 1983

MURRAY STATE	10-4-1 ATS in 1st game of season since 2005
MURRAY STATE	18-1 S/U in 1st game of season since 2003
HOUSTON	16-3 S/U in 2nd home game of season since 2003
NC State	11-4 ATS in 1st road game of season since 2007
NC State	14-4 S/U in 1st road game of season since 2004
WEST VIRGINIA	3-14 S/U prior to playing Baylor since 2005
BAYLOR	7-2-1 ATS prior to playing TCU since 2012
BAYLOR	8-3 S/U prior to playing TCU since 2006
Tcu	7-2 ATS prior to playing Kansas since 2013
KANSAS	8-1 O/U prior to playing Iowa State since 2013
Iowa State	2-9 S/U after playing Kansas since 2009
Iowa State	8-2 O/U after playing Kansas since 2011
Iowa State	2-7 O/U prior to playing Oklahoma since 2013
Iowa State	1-7-1 ATS prior to playing Oklahoma since 2013

- 1-19 S/U vs ranked teams since 2014
- 7-68 S/U on road vs ranked teams since 1977
- 0-13 S/U @ home vs ranked teams since 2013
- 0-13 S/U vs #2 ranked teams all time
- 1-9 S/U vs ranked Texas since 2003
- 11-0 O/U on road when ranked since 2008
- 0-11 ATS @ home when ranked since 2008

TOLEDO ROCKETS — MAC West

2021-Toledo		Opponent	Tol	Opp	S/U	Line	ATS	Total	O/U	
9/4/2021	vs	NORFOLK STATE	49	10	W	-39.5	L	56.0	O	
9/11/2021	@	Notre Dame	29	32	L	16.5	W	55.5	O	
9/18/2021	vs	COLORADO STATE	6	22	L	-14.5	L	58.5	U	
9/25/2021	@	Ball State	22	12	W	-4.5	W	56.5	U	
10/2/2021	@	Massachusetts	45	7	W	-27.0	W	56.5	U	
10/9/2021	vs	NORTHERN ILLINOIS	20	22	L	-13.5	L	51.0	U	
10/16/2021	@	Central Michigan	23	26	L	-5.0	L	53.0	U	{OT}
10/23/2021	vs	WESTERN MICHIGAN	34	15	W	1.5	W	54.5	U	
11/2/2021	vs	EASTERN MICHIGAN	49	52	L	-9.0	L	54.5	O	
11/10/2021	@	Bowling Green	49	17	W	-10.5	W	50.0	O	"Battle of I-75 Trophy"
11/16/2021	@	Ohio	35	23	W	-7.5	W	57.0	O	
11/27/2021	vs	AKRON	49	14	W	-28.5	W	57.5	O	
12/17/2021	vs	Middle Tennessee	24	31	L	-10.5	L	50.5	O	Bahamas Bowl
Coach: Jason Candle		Season Record >>	434	283	7-6	ATS>>	7-6	O/U>>	7-6	

2020-Toledo		Opponent	Tol	Opp	S/U	Line	ATS	Total	O/U	
11/4/2020	vs	BOWLING GREEN	38	3	W	-24.0	W	62.0	U	"Battle of I-75 Trophy"
11/11/2020	@	Western Michigan	38	41	L	1.0	L	58.5	O	
11/18/2020	@	Eastern Michigan	45	28	W	-6.5	W	62.5	O	
11/28/2020	vs	BALL STATE	24	27	L	-9.5	L	67.0	U	
12/5/2020	@	Northern Illinois	41	24	W	-9.0	W	53.5	O	
12/12/2020	vs	CENTRAL MICHIGAN	24	23	W	-10.0	L	55.0	U	
Coach: Jason Candle		Season Record >>	210	146	4-2	ATS>>	3-3	O/U>>	3-3	

2019-Toledo		Opponent	Tol	Opp	S/U	Line	ATS	Total	O/U	
8/31/2019	@	Kentucky	24	38	L	9.0	L	60.5	O	
9/14/2019	vs	MURRAY STATE	45	0	W	-36.0	W	NT	---	
9/21/2019	@	Colorado State	41	35	W	-6.0	T	67.0	O	
9/28/2019	vs	BYU	28	21	W	1.5	W	62.5	U	
10/5/2019	vs	WESTERN MICHIGAN	31	24	W	-1.5	W	73.5	U	
10/12/2019	@	Bowling Green	7	20	L	-27.0	L	65.0	U	"Battle of I-75 Strophy"
10/19/2019	@	Ball State	14	52	L	3.0	L	58.0	O	
10/26/2019	vs	EASTERN MICHIGAN	37	34	W	-2.5	W	53.5	O	{OT}
11/5/2019	vs	KENT STATE	35	33	W	-3.0	L	64.0	O	
11/13/2019	vs	NORTHERN ILLINOIS	28	31	L	-1.5	L	55.5	O	
11/20/2019	@	Buffalo	30	49	L	10.0	L	54.0	O	
11/29/2019	@	Central Michigan	7	49	L	14.5	L	63.5	U	
Coach: Jason Candle		Season Record >>	327	386	6-6	ATS>>	4-7-1	O/U>>	7-4	

2018-Toledo		Opponent	Tol	Opp	S/U	Line	ATS	Total	O/U	
9/1/2018	vs	VIRGINIA MILITARY	66	3	W	-48.5	W	NT	---	
9/15/2018	vs	MIAMI-FL	24	49	L	12.0	L	58.5	O	
9/22/2018	vs	NEVADA	63	44	W	-12.0	W	69.0	O	
9/29/2018	@	Fresno State	27	49	L	10.0	L	62.0	O	
10/6/2018	vs	BOWLING GREEN	52	36	W	-23.0	L	71.0	O	"Battle of I-75 Trophy"
10/13/2018	@	Eastern Michigan	26	28	L	-2.0	L	63.0	U	
10/20/2018	vs	BUFFALO	17	31	L	-3.0	L	62.5	U	
10/25/2018	@	Western Michigan	51	24	W	4.0	W	68.0	O	
10/31/2018	vs	BALL STATE	45	13	W	-20.0	W	63.5	U	
11/7/2018	@	Northern Illinois	15	38	L	3.5	L	54.0	U	
11/15/2018	@	Kent State	56	34	W	-11.5	W	57.0	O	
11/23/2018	vs	CENTRAL MICHIGAN	51	13	W	-18.5	W	57.5	O	
12/21/2018	vs	Florida International	18	49	L	-7.0	L	57.5	O	Bahamas Bowl
Coach: Jason Candle		Season Record >>	511	411	7-6	ATS>>	6-7	O/U>>	8-4	

TOLEDO ROCKETS — MAC West

STADIUM: Glass Bowl {26,038} **Location:** Toledo, OH **COACH:** Jason Candle

DATE		Opponent	Tol	Opp	S/U	Line	ATS	Total	O/U	Trends & Angles
9/3/2022	vs	LONG ISLAND U								vs Long Island - Long Island leads series 2-0
9/10/2022	vs	MASSACHUSETTS								vs UMASS - Toledo leads series 5-1
9/17/2022	@	Ohio State								0-3 S/U vs Ohio State as Dog since 1998
9/24/2022	@	San Diego State								9-3 S/U prior to playing C. Michigan since 2010
10/1/2022	vs	CENTRAL MICHIGAN								20-4 S/U vs C. Michigan as favorite since 1993
10/8/2022	@	Northern Illinois								0-5 S/U vs Northern Illinois as Dog since 2010
10/15/2022	vs	KENT STATE								vs Kent State - Toledo leads series 27-21
10/22/2022	@	Buffalo								vs Buffalo - Toledo leads series 7-5
10/29/2022	@	Eastern Michigan								vs E. Michigan - Toledo leads series 36-13
11/8/2022	vs	BALL STATE								vs Ball State - Toledo leads series 25-21-1
11/15/2022	vs	BOWLING GREEN								11-1 S/U vs B. Green as favorite since 2002
11/25/2022	@	Western Michigan								10-3 ATS vs W. Michigan as Dog since 1989
12/2/2022	vs									MAC Championship
	vs									BOWL GAME

Pointspread Analysis — Non-Conference
- 1-9 S/U vs Non-Conf. as 20.5 point or more Dog since 1989
- 1-6 O/U vs Non-Conf. as 20.5 point or more Dog since 2007
- 1-7 S/U & ATS vs Non-Conf. as 10.5-15 point Dog since 1993
- 3-7 S/U vs Non-Conf. as 3 point or less Dog since 1996
- 8-3 S/U vs Non-Conf. as 3.5-7 point favorite since 1990
- 9-1 S/U vs Non-Conf. as 7.15-15 point favorite since 1990
- 6-2 ATS vs Non-Conf. as 10.5-15 point favorite since 1992
- 9-0 S/U vs Non-Conf. as 20.5 point or more favorite since 2001

Dog
- 1-10 S/U as 20.5 point or more Dog since 1989
- 1-7 O/U as 20.5 point or more Dog since 1999
- 0-6 S/U as 15.5-20 point Dog since 2008
- 2-5 O/U as 15.5-20 point Dog since 2008
- 2-12 S/U as 10.5-15 point Dog since 1993
- 8-3 ATS as 3.5-7 point Dog since 2009

Favorite
- 9-3 O/U @ home as 3 point or less favorite since 2002
- 0-5 O/U as 3 point or less favorite since 2012
- 14-2 S/U on road as 3.5-7 point favorite since 1990
- 8-2 S/U & ATS as 7.5-10 point favorite since 2015
- 10-2 S/U on road as 7.5-10 point favorite since 1993
- 15-3 S/U @ home as 10.5-15 point favorite since 2001
- 21-4 S/U as 10.5-15 point favorite since 2010
- 10-0 S/U on road as 10.5-15 point favorite since 2010
- 5-0 S/U on road as 15.5-20 point favorite since 1994
- 17-1 S/U @ home as 15.5-20 point favorite since 1990
- 6-1 S/U on road as 20.5 point or more favorite since 2002
- 32-0 S/U @ home as 20.5 point or more favorite since 1995
- 11-1 O/U @ home as 20.5 point or more favorite since 2005

Pointspread Analysis — Conference
- 0-6 S/U vs Ball State as Dog since 1993
- vs Bowling Green - Toledo leads series 42-40-4
- 0-5 O/U vs Bowling Green as Dog since 2007
- vs Central Michigan - Toledo leads series 27-20
- 0-6 S/U vs Central Michigan as Dog since 1992 {1-5 ATS}
- 18-2 S/U vs Eastern Michigan as favorite since 2000
- 11-1 S/U vs Kent State as favorite since 1989
- vs Northern Illinois - Toledo leads series 32-17
- 1-8 O/U vs Northern Illinois as Dog since 2004
- vs Western Michigan - Toledo leads series 45-31
- 10-1 S/U vs Ball State as 14 point or more favorite since 1998
- 12-1 S/U vs Bowling Green as 6.5 point or more favorite since 1990
- 16-0 S/U vs C. Michigan as 8 point or more favorite since 1995
- 15-0 S/U vs E. Michigan as 13 point or more favorite since 1992
- 7-0 S/U vs W. Michigan as 11.5 point or more favorite since 2001

Bowl Games
- 0-5 S/U in Bowl Games as 3.0-15 point Dog since 1997
- 1-15 S/U on road vs ranked teams all time
- 1-7 S/U vs Top #10 ranked teams all time
- 0-3 S/U vs ranked Ohio State all time
- 11-2 S/U on road when ranked all time

LONG ISLAND U	11-0 S/U in 1st home game of season since 2011
LONG ISLAND U	11-3 ATS in 1st home game of season since 2008
C. MICHIGAN	14-3 S/U prior to playing Northern Illinois since 2005
Eastern Michigan	9-2 ATS prior to playing Ball State since 2010
BALL STATE	8-2 S/U after playing Eastern Michigan since 2011
Western Michigan	11-3 S/U after playing Bowling Green since 1997

TROY TROJANS   SUN BELT West

2021-Troy		Opponent	Troy	Opp	S/U	Line	ATS	Total	O/U	
9/4/2021	vs	SOUTHERN	55	3	W	-25.0	W	54.0	O	
9/11/2021	vs	LIBERTY	13	21	L	3.0	L	62.5	U	
9/18/2021	@	Southern Miss	21	9	W	-11.0	W	49.5	U	
9/25/2021	@	Louisiana-Monroe	16	29	L	-23.5	L	49.5	U	
10/2/2021	@	South Carolina	14	23	L	6.5	L	43.0	U	
10/9/2021	vs	GEORGIA SOUTHERN	27	24	W	-5.5	L	51.0	T	
10/16/2021	@	Texas State	31	28	W	-7.5	L	48.5	O	
10/28/2021	@	Coastal Carolina	28	35	L	17.0	W	50.0	O	
11/6/2021	vs	SOUTH ALABAMA	31	24	W	-3.5	W	47.5	O	"The Championship Belt"
11/13/2021	vs	LOUISIANA	21	35	L	6.5	L	48.0	O	
11/20/2021	vs	APPALACHIAN STATE	7	45	L	9.5	L	51.5	O	
11/27/2021	@	Georgia State	10	37	L	6.5	L	49.5	U	
Coach: Chip Lindsey		Season Record >>	274	313	5-7	ATS>>	4-8	O/U>>	6-5-1	

2020-Troy		Opponent	Troy	Opp	S/U	Line	ATS	Total	O/U	
9/19/2020	@	Middle Tennessee	47	14	W	-2.5	W	65.0	U	"The Palladium Trophy"
9/26/2020	@	Byu	7	48	L	14.0	L	56.5	U	
10/10/2020	vs	TEXAS STATE	37	17	W	-7.0	W	59.5	U	
10/17/2020	vs	EASTERN KENTUCKY	31	29	W	-28.5	L	60.0	T	
10/24/2020	vs	GEORGIA STATE	34	36	L	-2.5	L	68.5	O	
10/31/2020	@	Arkansas State	38	10	W	3.5	W	70.0	U	
11/7/2020	@	Georgia Southern	13	20	L	-2.5	L	52.0	U	
11/21/2020	vs	MIDDLE TENNESSEE	17	20	L	-10.5	L	60.5	U	
11/28/2020	@	Appalachian State	10	47	L	14.0	L	50.5	O	
12/5/2020	@	South Alabama	29	0	W	-4.0	W	54.0	U	"The Championship Belt"
12/12/2020	vs	COASTAL CAROLINA	38	42	L	11.5	W	53.0	O	
Coach: Chip Lindsey		Season Record >>	301	283	5-6	ATS>>	5-6	O/U>>	3-7-1	

2019-Troy		Opponent	Troy	Opp	S/U	Line	ATS	Total	O/U	
8/31/2019	vs	CAMPBELL	43	14	W	-36.5	L	NT	---	
9/14/2019	vs	SOUTHERN MISS	42	47	L	-3.0	L	49.0	O	
9/21/2019	@	Akron	35	7	W	-18.5	W	57.0	U	
9/28/2019	vs	ARKANSAS STATE	43	50	L	-7.0	L	59.5	O	
10/5/2019	@	Missouri	10	42	L	25.5	L	65.5	U	
10/16/2019	vs	SOUTH ALABAMA	17	13	W	-17.0	W	54.5	U	"The Championship Belt"
10/26/2019	@	Georgia State	33	52	L	1.0	L	67.0	O	
11/2/2019	@	Coastal Carolina	35	36	L	PK	L	60.0	O	
11/9/2019	vs	GEORGIA SOUTHERN	49	28	W	2.5	W	57.0	O	
11/16/2019	@	Texas State	63	27	W	-7.0	W	64.5	O	
11/23/2019	@	Louisiana-Lafayette	3	53	L	12.5	L	74.0	U	
11/30/2019	vs	APPALACHIAN STATE	13	48	L	11.0	L	64.0	U	
Coach: Neal Brown		Season Record >>	386	417	5-7	ATS>>	4-8	O/U>>	6-5	

2018-Troy		Opponent	Troy	Opp	S/U	Line	ATS	Total	O/U	
9/1/2018	vs	BOISE STATE	20	56	L	9.0	L	48.0	O	
9/8/2018	vs	FLORIDA A&M	59	7	W	-35.0	W	NT	---	
9/15/2018	@	Nebraska	24	19	W	10.5	W	55.5	U	
9/22/2018	@	Louisiana-Monroe	35	27	W	-4.5	W	59.0	O	
9/29/2018	vs	COASTAL CAROLINA	45	21	W	-13.5	W	57.0	O	
10/4/2018	vs	GEORGIA STATE	37	20	W	-17.0	T	55.5	O	
10/13/2018	@	Liberty	16	22	L	-10.0	L	63.0	U	
10/23/2018	@	South Alabama	38	17	W	-11.5	W	52.0	O	"The Championship Belt"
11/3/2018	vs	LOUISIANA-LAFAYETTE	26	16	W	-7.5	W	64.5	U	
11/10/2018	@	Georgia Southern	35	21	W	-2.5	W	44.5	O	
11/17/2018	vs	TEXAS STATE	12	7	W	-22.0	L	47.5	U	
11/24/2018	@	Appalachian State	10	21	L	11.5	W	45.5	U	
12/22/2018	vs	Buffalo	42	32	W	2.5	W	51.5	O	Dollar General Bowl
Coach: Neal Brown		Season Record >>	399	286	10-3	ATS>>	9-3-1	O/U>>	7-5	

TROY TROJANS — SUN BELT West

STADIUM: Veterans Memorial Stadium {30,402} **Location:** Troy, AL **COACH:** Jon Sumrall

DATE		Opponent	Troy	Opp	S/U	Line	ATS	Total	O/U	Trends & Angles
9/3/2022	@	Mississippi								vs Mississippi - Ole Miss leads series 1-0
9/10/2022	vs	ALABAMA A&M								vs Alabama A&M - Troy leads series 1-0
9/17/2022	@	Appalachian State								vs App State - App State leads series 7-3
9/24/2022	vs	MARSHALL								vs Marshall - Marshall leads series 3-2
10/1/2022	@	Western Kentucky								6-1 S/U @ Western Kentucky since 1991
10/8/2022	vs	SOUTHERN MISS								vs Southern Miss - USM leads series 8-3
10/15/2022	vs	TEXAS STATE								vs Texas State - Troy leads series 11-1
10/20/2022	@	South Alabama								vs South Alabama - Troy leads series 7-3
11/5/2022	@	Louisiana								1-6 S/U vs Louisiana as Dog since 2005
11/12/2022	vs	ARMY								1st Meeting
11/19/2022	vs	LOUISIANA-MONROE								vs UL-Monroe - Troy leads series 10-8-1
11/26/2022	@	Arkansas State								vs Ark State - Ark State leads series 11-7
12/5/2020	vs									Sun Belt Championship
	vs									BOWL GAME

Pointspread Analysis — Non-Conference

- 2-34 S/U vs Non-Conf. as 15.5 point or more Dog since 2001
- 8-1 O/U vs Non-Conf. as 15.5-20 point Dog since 2002
- 2-9 S/U vs Non-Conf. as 10.5-15 point Dog since 2004
- 5-0 O/U vs Non-Conf. as 3.5-7 point favorite since 2010
- 12-0 S/U vs Non-Conf. as 15.5 point or more favorite since 2008
- vs Western Kentucky - Troy leads series 9-2-1

Dog

- 0-17 S/U as 25.5 point or more Dog since 2001
- 1-13 S/U as 20.5-25 point Dog since 2001
- 0-10 S/U as 15.5-20 point Dog since 2002
- 9-1 O/U as 15.5-20 point Dog since 2002
- 2-17 S/U as 10.5-15 point Dog since 2004
- 6-0 O/U as 7.5-10 point Dog since 2007
- 0-3 S/U & ATS @ home as 3.5-7 point Dog since 2005
- 1-7 O/U on road as 3.5-7 point Dog since 2005

Favorite

- 11-4 S/U @ home as 3.5-7 point favorite since 2001
- 9-2-1 O/U @ home as 3.5-7 point favorite since 2012
- 6-1 S/U on road as 7.5-10 point favorite since 2007
- 3-9-1 ATS @ home as 7.5-10 point favorite since 2002
- 15-2 S/U @ home as 10.5-15 point favorite since 2003
- 13-3 S/U as 15.5-20 point favorite since 2007
- 1-7 O/U @ home as 15.5-20 point favorite since 2011
- 17-0 S/U as 20.5 point or more favorite since 2004

Bowl Games

- 8-0 O/U in Bowl Games

Pointspread Analysis — Conference

- 1-3 S/U vs Arkansas State as Dog since 2011
- 4-1 O/U vs Arkansas State as Dog since 2009
- 1-5 O/U vs Arkansas State as favorite since 2007
- vs Louisiana - Louisiana leads series 13-9
- 4-1 O/U vs Louisiana as Dog since 2013
- 6-1 S/U vs Louisiana as favorite since 2004
- 7-0 S/U vs Texas State as favorite since 2013

ALABAMA A&M	0-5 ATS prior to playing Appalachian State since 2016
TEXAS STATE	2-7 S/U prior to playing South Alabama since 2013
ARMY	1-6 S/U after playing Louisiana since 2010
UL-MONROE	5-1 S/U prior to playing Arkansas State since 2012 {5-1 ATS}
Arkansas State	3-10 O/U after playing Louisiana-Monroe since 2001

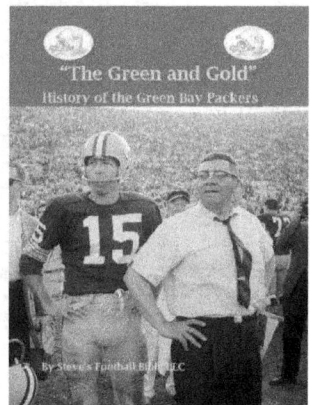

- 1-22 S/U on road vs ranked teams all time
- 0-8 S/U vs Top #10 ranked teams all time

GREEN BAY — MINNESOTA — PITTSBURGH

NFL Football Series available at: www.stevesfootballbible.com

TULANE GREEN WAVE   AMERICAN West

2021-Tulane		Opponent	Wave	Opp	S/U	Line	ATS	Total	O/U	
9/4/2021	@	Oklahoma	35	40	L	31.0	W	66.5	O	
9/11/2021	vs	MORGAN STATE	69	20	W	-47.5	W	55.0	O	
9/18/2021	@	Mississippi	21	61	L	14.0	L	77.0	O	
9/25/2021	vs	ALABAMA-BIRMINGHAM	21	28	L	-2.5	L	54.5	U	
10/2/2021	@	East Carolina	29	52	L	-3.0	L	65.0	O	
10/7/2021	vs	HOUSTON	22	40	L	6.5	L	60.0	O	
10/21/2021	@	Smu	26	55	L	14.0	L	70.5	O	
10/30/2021	vs	CINCINNATI	12	31	L	28.0	W	61.5	U	
11/6/2021	@	Central Florida	10	14	L	13.5	W	57.0	U	
11/13/2021	vs	TULSA	13	20	L	3.0	L	55.5	U	{OT}
11/20/2021	vs	SOUTH FLORIDA	45	14	W	-5.5	W	59.5	U	
11/27/2021	@	Memphis	28	33	L	5.0	T	58.0	O	
Coach: Willie Fritz		Season Record >>	331	408	2-10	ATS>>	5-6-1	O/U>>	7-5	
2020-Tulane		Opponent	Wave	Opp	S/U	Line	ATS	Total	O/U	
9/12/2020	@	South Alabama	27	24	W	-10.5	L	52.0	U	
9/19/2020	vs	NAVY	24	27	L	-6.5	L	47.5	O	
9/26/2020	@	Southern Mississippi	66	24	W	-3.5	W	54.5	O	"Battle for the Bell"
10/8/2020	@	Houston	31	49	L	7.0	L	58.0	O	
10/16/2020	vs	SMU	34	37	L	6.5	W	64.5	O	{OT}
10/24/2020	@	Central Florida	34	51	L	21.5	W	71.0	O	
10/31/2020	vs	TEMPLE	38	3	W	-7.0	W	56.0	U	
11/7/2020	@	East Carolina	38	21	W	-3.5	W	63.5	U	
11/14/2020	vs	ARMY	38	12	W	-3.0	W	46.5	O	
11/19/2020	@	Tulsa	24	30	L	4.5	L	56.5	U	{2 OT}
12/5/2020	vs	MEMPHIS	35	21	W	-3.5	W	64.0	U	
12/22/2020	vs	Nevada	27	38	L	1.0	L	56.5	O	Famous Idaho Potato Bowl
Coach: Willie Fritz		Season Record >>	416	337	6-6	ATS>>	7-5	O/U>>	7-5	
2019-Tulane		Opponent	Wave	Opp	S/U	Line	ATS	Total	O/U	
8/29/2019	vs	FLORIDA INTERNATIONAL	42	14	W	-3.0	W	58.5	U	
9/7/2019	@	Auburn	6	24	L	16.0	L	51.0	U	
9/14/2019	vs	MISSOURI STATE	58	6	W	-32.0	W	NT	---	
9/19/2019	vs	HOUSTON	38	31	W	-4.5	W	57.5	O	
10/5/2019	@	Army	42	33	W	-2.5	W	42.5	O	
10/12/2019	vs	CONNECTICUT	49	7	W	-33.5	W	57.5	U	
10/19/2019	@	Memphis	17	47	L	2.5	L	60.5	O	
10/26/2019	@	Navy	38	41	L	4.5	L	58.5	O	
11/2/2019	vs	TULSA	38	26	W	-9.5	W	59.0	O	
11/16/2019	@	Temple	21	29	L	-6.5	L	52.5	U	
11/23/2019	vs	CENTRAL FLORIDA	31	34	L	7.0	W	74.0	U	
11/30/2019	@	Smu	20	37	L	3.0	L	72.0	U	
1/4/2020	vs	Southern Mississippi	30	13	W	-7.5	W	57.5	U	Armed Forces Bowl
Coach: Willie Fritz		Season Record >>	430	342	7-6	ATS>>	8-5	O/U>>	5-7	
2018-Tulane		Opponent	Wave	Opp	S/U	Line	ATS	Total	O/U	
8/30/2018	vs	WAKE FOREST	17	23	L	7.0	W	55.5	U	{OT}
9/8/2018	vs	NICHOLLS STATE	42	17	W	-15.5	W	NT	---	
9/15/2018	@	Alabama-Birmingham	24	31	L	-3.5	L	57.0	U	
9/22/2018	@	Ohio State	6	49	L	38.0	L	67.5	U	
9/28/2018	vs	MEMPHIS	40	24	W	14.5	W	66.0	U	
10/6/2018	@	Cincinnati	21	37	L	7.0	L	48.0	U	
10/20/2018	vs	SMU	23	27	L	-7.0	L	55.5	U	
10/27/2018	@	Tulsa	24	17	W	-1.5	W	48.5	U	
11/3/2018	@	South Florida	41	15	W	5.5	W	61.5	U	
11/10/2018	vs	EAST CAROLINA	24	18	W	-10.5	L	54.0	U	
11/15/2018	@	Houston	17	48	L	7.5	L	68.0	U	
11/24/2018	vs	NAVY	29	28	W	-6.5	L	53.0	O	
12/15/2018	vs	Louisiana-Lafayette	41	24	W	-3.0	W	60.5	O	AutoNation Cure Bowl
Coach: Willie Fritz		Season Record >>	349	358	7-6	ATS>>	6-7	O/U>>	3-9	

TULANE GREEN WAVE   AMERICAN West

STADIUM: Yulman Stadium {30,000}							Location: New Orleans, LA		COACH: Willie Fritz
DATE		Opponent	Wave	Opp	S/U	Line	ATS	Total	O/U	Trends & Angles
9/3/2022	vs	MASSACHUSETTS								vs Massachusetts - Tulane leads series 1-0
9/10/2022	vs	ALCORN STATE								1st Meeting
9/17/2022	@	Kansas State								vs Kansas State - Tulane leads series 1-0
9/24/2022	vs	SOUTHERN MISSISSIPPI								vs Southern Miss - USM leads series 23-9
9/29/2022	@	Houston								vs Houston - Houston leads series 19-7
10/8/2022	vs	EAST CAROLINA								5-1 S/U vs E. Carolina as favorite since 2003
10/15/2022	@	South Florida								vs South Florida - Tulane leads series 2-1
10/22/2022	vs	MEMPHIS								vs Memphis - Memphis leads series 24-13-1
11/5/2022	@	Tulsa								1-7 S/U & ATS @ Tulsa since 2006
11/12/2022	vs	CENTRAL FLORIDA								vs Central Florida - UCF leads series 9-2
11/17/2022	vs	SMU								1-9 S/U vs SMU as Dog since 2009
11/26/2022	@	Cincinnati								vs Cincinnati -Tulane leads series 11-7
12/3/2022	vs									AAC Championship
	vs									BOWL GAME

Pointspread Analysis — Non-Conference

- 0-35 S/U vs Non-Conf. as 20.5 point or more Dog since 1986
- 2-21 S/U vs Non-Conf. as 15.5-20 point Dog since 1984
- 4-22 S/U vs Non-Conf. as 10.5-15 point Dog since 1985
- 0-12 S/U vs Non-Conf. as 7.5-10 point Dog since 1990
- 1-10 S/U vs Non-Conf. as 3.5-7 point Dog since 1990
- 8-2 S/U vs Non-Conf. as 3.5-7 point favorite since 1987
- 12-2 S/U vs Non-Conf. as 15.5 point or more favorite since 1988

Dog

- 0-52 S/U as 20.5 point or more Dog since 1986
- 4-10 ATS as 30.5 point or more Dog since 1991
- 5-0 ATS as 25.5-30 point Dog since 2011
- 1-7 O/U as 25.5-30 point Dog since 2008
- 2-5 ATS on road as 20.5-25 point Dog since 2001
- 2-5 O/U as 20.5-25 point Dog since 2005
- 2-19 S/U on road as 15.5-20 point Dog since 1995
- 2-9 S/U @ home as 15.5-20 point Dog since 1985
- 2-19 S/U @ home as 10.5-15 point Dog since 1984
- 2-9-1 O/U @ home as 10.5-15 point Dog since 2001
- 2-15 S/U on road as 10.5-15 point Dog since 2006
- 2-18 S/U on road as 7.5-10 point Dog since 1990
- 3-16 S/U @ home as 3.5-7 point Dog since 2003
- 3-18 S/U on road as 3.5-7 point Dog since 1990
- 4-11 ATS on road as 3 point or less Dog since 1983
- 5-1 O/U on road as 3 point or less Dog since 2012

Favorite

- 10-2 S/U as 3 point or less favorite since 2014 {9-3 ATS}
- 23-5 S/U @ home as 3.5-7 point favorite since 1987
- 1-6 O/U on road as 3.5-7 point favorite since 2000
- 7-0 S/U as 7.5-10 point favorite since 1997
- 6-1 S/U @ home as 10.5-15 point favorite since 1997
- 8-2 S/U @ home as 15.5-20 point favorite since 1990
- 5-0 S/U on road as 15.5-20 point favorite since 1998
- 11-0 S/U as 20.5 point or more favorite since 1988

Pointspread Analysis — Conference

- 1-11 S/U vs East Carolina as Dog since 1991
- 3-15 S/U vs Houston as Dog since 1999
- 1-5-1 ATS vs Memphis as favorite since 1988
- 2-18 S/U vs Memphis as Dog since 1985
- 6-2 S/U vs SMU as favorite since 1990
- vs SMU - SMU leads series 15-13
- 7-1 O/U vs SMU as Dog since 2011
- 0-3 S/U vs Temple as Dog since 2014
- vs Tulsa - Tulsa leads series 13-5
- 1-13 S/U vs Tulsa as Dog since 2005
- 4-13 ATS vs Tulsa since 2005
- 0-9 S/U vs Central Florida as 5.5 point or more Dog since 2001
- 1-10 S/U vs Houston as 12.5 point or more Dog since 1999

Bowl Games

- 6-9 S/U in Bowl Games

- 7-0 S/U @ home when ranked since 1974
- 1-60 S/U vs ranked teams since 1984
- 0-35 S/U on road vs ranked teams since 1984
- 1-25 S/U @ home vs ranked teams since 1985
- 0-15 S/U vs #2 ranked teams all time
- 0-18-1 S/U vs #3 - #5 ranked teams all time
- 0-4 S/U vs ranked Houston all time

Houston	2-10 O/U prior to playing East Carolina since 2002
Houston	8-1 O/U in 2nd road game of season since 2013
Houston	4-11 S/U in 2nd road game of season since 2007
EAST CAROLINA	3-10 S/U after playing Houston since 2007
South Florida	2-5 O/U after playing East Carolina since 2012
Tulsa	1-14 S/U after playing Memphis since 1999
Cincinnati	1-7 S/U after playing SMU since 2010
Cincinnati	1-16 S/U in final road game of season since 2005

TULSA GOLDEN HURRICANE   AMERICAN West

2021-Tulsa		Opponent	Tulsa	Opp	S/U	Line	ATS	Total	O/U	
9/2/2021	vs	CALIFORNIA-DAVIS	17	19	L	-22.0	L	54.0	U	
9/11/2021	@	Oklahoma State	23	28	L	10.5	W	51.0	T	
9/18/2021	@	Ohio State	20	41	L	24.5	W	60.5	O	
9/25/2021	vs	ARKANSAS STATE	41	34	W	-14.5	L	64.5	O	
10/1/2021	vs	HOUSTON	10	45	L	-3.0	L	54.0	O	
10/9/2021	vs	MEMPHIS	35	29	W	-3.0	W	60.5	O	
10/16/2021	@	South Florida	32	31	W	-7.0	L	55.5	U	
10/29/2021	vs	NAVY	17	20	L	-12.0	L	46.0	U	
11/6/2021	@	Cincinnati	20	28	L	22.5	W	56.0	U	
11/13/2021	@	Tulane	20	13	W	-3.0	W	55.5	U	{OT}
11/20/2021	vs	TEMPLE	44	10	W	-22.0	W	50.5	O	
11/27/2021	@	Smu	34	31	W	6.0	W	62.5	O	
12/21/2021	vs	Old Dominion	30	17	W	-7.0	W	55.0	U	Myrtle Beach Bowl
Coach: Philip Montgomery		Season Record >>	343	346	7-6	ATS>>	8-5	O/U>>	7-5-1	

2020-Tulsa		Opponent	Tulsa	Opp	S/U	Line	ATS	Total	O/U	
9/19/2020	@	Oklahoma State	7	16	L	23.0	W	66.0	U	
10/3/2020	@	Central Florida	34	26	W	20.0	W	70.0	U	
10/23/2020	@	South Florida	42	13	W	-12.5	W	52.0	O	
10/30/2020	vs	EAST CAROLINA	34	30	W	-17.0	L	59.5	O	
11/14/2020	vs	SMU	28	24	W	2.0	W	63.5	U	
11/21/2020	vs	TULANE	30	24	W	-4.5	W	56.5	U	{2 OT}
12/5/2020	@	Navy	19	6	W	-12.0	W	45.5	U	
12/19/2020	@	Cincinnati	24	27	L	14.0	W	44.5	O	AAC CHAMPIONSHIP
12/31/2020	vs	Mississippi State	26	28	L	1.0	L	44.5	O	Armed Forces Bowl
Coach: Philip Montgomery		Season Record >>	244	194	6-3	ATS>>	7-2	O/U>>	4-5	

2019-Tulsa		Opponent	Tulsa	Opp	S/U	Line	ATS	Total	O/U	
8/30/2019	@	Michigan State	7	28	L	23.5	W	47.0	U	
9/7/2019	@	San Jose State	34	16	W	-6.5	W	53.5	U	
9/14/2019	vs	OKLAHOMA STATE	21	40	L	13.5	L	64.5	U	
9/21/2019	vs	WYOMING	24	21	W	-6.0	L	46.0	U	
10/5/2019	@	Smu	37	43	L	12.0	W	63.0	O	{3 OT}
10/12/2019	vs	NAVY	17	45	L	-2.0	L	52.0	O	
10/19/2019	@	Cincinnati	13	24	L	15.5	W	47.0	U	
10/26/2019	vs	MEMPHIS	41	42	L	9.5	W	59.0	O	
11/2/2019	@	Tulane	26	38	L	9.5	L	59.0	O	
11/8/2019	vs	CENTRAL FLORIDA	34	31	W	16.0	W	68.5	U	
11/23/2019	vs	HOUSTON	14	24	L	-6.5	L	57.0	U	"Battle for the Best City"
11/30/2019	@	East Carolina	49	24	W	-7.0	W	64.0	O	
Coach: Philip Montgomery		Season Record >>	317	376	4-8	ATS>>	7-5	O/U>>	5-7	

2018-Tulsa		Opponent	Tulsa	Opp	S/U	Line	ATS	Total	O/U	
9/1/2018	vs	CENTRAL ARKANSAS	38	27	W	-12.0	L	NT	---	
9/8/2018	@	Texas	21	28	L	21.5	W	59.5	U	
9/15/2018	vs	ARKANSAS STATE	20	29	L	-1.5	L	71.5	U	
9/20/2018	@	Temple	17	31	L	6.0	L	54.0	U	
10/4/2018	@	Houston	26	41	L	17.5	W	70.0	U	"Battle for the Best City"
10/12/2018	vs	SOUTH FLORIDA	24	25	L	10.0	W	60.5	U	
10/20/2018	@	Arkansas	0	23	L	7.5	L	53.0	U	
10/27/2018	vs	TULANE	17	24	L	1.5	L	48.5	U	
11/3/2018	vs	CONNECTICUT	49	14	W	-19.0	W	60.0	O	
11/10/2018	@	Memphis	21	47	L	16.5	L	64.5	O	
11/17/2018	@	Navy	29	37	L	5.0	L	51.0	O	
11/24/2018	vs	SMU	27	24	W	2.5	W	53.5	U	
Coach: Philip Montgomery		Season Record >>	289	350	3-9	ATS>>	5-7	O/U>>	3-8	

TULSA GOLDEN HURRICANE   AMERICAN West

STADIUM: Chapman Stadium {30,000} **Location:** Tulsa, OK **COACH:** Philip Montgomery

DATE		Opponent	Tuls	Opp	S/U	Line	ATS	Total	O/U	Trends & Angles
9/3/2022	@	Wyoming								3-0 ATS vs Wyoming as Dog since 1994
9/10/2022	vs	NORTHERN ILLINOIS								13-3 S/U in 1st home game of season since 2006
9/17/2022	vs	JACKSONVILLE STATE								1st Meeting
9/24/2022	@	Mississippi								vs Ole Miss - Tulsa leads series 3-0
10/1/2022	vs	CINCINNATI								0-6 S/U vs Cincinnati as Dog since 1995
10/8/2022	@	Navy								0-4 S/U vs Navy as Dog since 2015
10/21/2022	@	Temple								vs Temple - Series tied 3-3
10/29/2022	vs	SMU								vs SMU - SMU leads series 15-13
11/5/2022	vs	TULANE								13-1 S/U & ATS vs Tulane as favorite since 2005
11/10/2022	@	Memphis								vs Memphis - Memphis leads series 19-12
10/18/2022	vs	SOUTH FLORIDA								vs South Florida - USF leads series 3-2
11/26/2022	@	Houston								1-5 S/U vs Houston as Dog since 2011
12/3/2022	vs									AAC Championship
	vs									BOWL GAME

Pointspread Analysis — Non-Conference
- 2-39 S/U vs Non-Conf as 15.5 point or more Dog since 1985
- 2-12 S/U vs Non-Conf. as 10.5-15 point Dog since 1985
- 1-8 S/U & ATS vs Non-Conf. as 3 point or less favorite since 1993
- 2-8 ATS vs Non-Conf. as 3.5-7 point favorite since 1985
- 17-1 S/U vs Non-Conf. as 7.5 point or more favorite since 1985
- 3-1 ATS vs Wyoming since 1994
- vs Wyoming - Series tied 3-3

Dog
- 0-44 S/U as 20.5 point or more Dog since 1985
- 1-61 S/U on road as 15.5 point or more Dog since 1984
- 4-0 O/U @ home as 20.5-25 point Dog since 2002
- 1-8 S/U @ home as 10.5-15 point Dog since 1999
- 2-17 S/U on road as 10.5-15 point Dog since 1994
- 2-10 S/U @ home as 7.5-10 point Dog since 2001
- 2-12 S/U on road as 7.5-10 point Dog since 1998
- 2-11 S/U @ home as 3.5-7 point Dog since 1987
- 2-10-1 ATS @ home as 3.5-7 point Dog since 1987
- 5-0 O/U @ home as 3.5-7 point Dog since 2002
- 2-8 O/U on road as 3 point or less Dog since 1993

Favorite
- 3-7 S/U & ATS as 3 point or less favorite since 2013
- 8-2 S/U @ home as 3.5-7 point favorite since 2010
- 8-2 S/U as 7.5-10 point favorite since 2003
- 6-1 S/U on road as 7.5-10 point favorite since 1987
- 9-1 S/U @ home as 10.5-15 point favorite since 2007
- 6-1 O/U @ home as 10.5-15 point favorite since 2008
- 11-0 S/U on road as 10.5-15 point favorite since 2005
- 8-0 S/U on road as 15.5 or more favorite since 1991
- 32-2 S/U @ home as 15.5 point or more favorite since 1986

Bowl Games
- 0-3 S/U in Independence Bowl
- 6-2 ATS in Bowl Games since 2008
- 3-7 O/U in Bowl Games since 2005

Pointspread Analysis — Conference
- vs Cincinnati - Series tied 17-17-2
- 0-5 S/U vs East Carolina as Dog since 1994
- 11-2 ATS vs Houston as Dog since 1985
- vs Houston - Houston leads series 25-19
- 5-0 S/U vs Memphis as favorite since 2005
- vs Navy - Navy leads series 7-2
- 0-3 S/U vs South Florida as Dog since 2014
- 3-9 S/U vs SMU as Dog since 1997
- 2-6 O/U vs SMU as Dog since 2001
- 2-9 ATS vs SMU as favorite since 2004
- 6-1 S/U @ home vs SMU as favorite since 2003
- 13-1 S/U & ATS vs Tulane as favorite since 2005

- 7-0 S/U @ home when ranked since 1945
- 0-7 S/U when ranked vs ranked teams all time
- 12-0 ATS vs ranked teams since 2017
- 2-44 S/U on road vs ranked teams since 1977
- 1-11 S/U @ home vs ranked teams since 2007
- 0-11 S/U vs #4 #5 #6 ranked teams all time
- 0-3 S/U @ ranked Houston all time

Wyoming	1-11 S/U in 1st road game of season since 2010
SMU	2-11 S/U prior to playing Tulane since 2008
Memphis	12-2 S/U after playing Tulane since 2007
Houston	8-1 ATS in final road game of season since 2013

UCLA BRUINS — PACIFIC-12 South

2021-UCLA		Opponent	UCLA	Opp	S/U	Line	ATS	Total	O/U	
8/28/2021	vs	HAWAII	44	10	W	-17.5	W	66.5	U	
9/4/2021	vs	LSU	38	27	W	1.5	W	64.0	O	
9/18/2021	vs	FRESNO STATE	37	40	L	-11.0	L	64.5	O	
9/25/2021	@	Stanford	35	24	W	-4.0	W	60.5	U	
10/2/2021	vs	ARIZONA STATE	23	42	L	-3.0	L	56.5	O	
10/9/2021	@	Arizona	34	16	W	-16.0	W	61.5	U	
10/16/2021	@	Washington	24	17	W	2.0	W	55.0	U	
10/23/2021	vs	OREGON	31	34	L	PK	L	62.5	O	
10/30/2021	@	Utah	24	44	L	6.5	L	60.0	U	
11/13/2021	vs	COLORADO	44	20	W	-18.0	W	57.0	U	
11/20/2021	@	Usc	62	33	W	-4.5	W	65.5	O	"Victory Bell"
11/27/2021	vs	CALIFORNIA	42	14	W	-6.0	W	58.5	U	
Coach: Chip Kelly		Season Record >>	438	321	8-4	ATS>>	8-4	O/U>>	7-5	

2020-UCLA		Opponent	UCLA	Opp	S/U	Line	ATS	Total	O/U	
11/7/2020	@	Colorado	42	48	L	-7.0	L	56.0	O	
11/13/2020	vs	CALIFORNIA	34	10	W	3.0	W	58.0	U	
11/20/2020	@	Oregon	35	38	L	18.0	W	62.0	O	
11/28/2020	vs	ARIZONA	27	10	W	-7.5	W	70.5	U	
12/5/2020	@	Arizona State	25	18	W	2.5	W	57.5	U	
12/12/2020	vs	USC	38	43	L	3.0	L	65.0	O	"Victory Bell"
12/19/2020	vs	STANFORD	47	48	L	-7.0	L	61.0	O	{2 OT}
Coach: Chip Kelly		Season Record >>	248	215	3-4	ATS>>	4-3	O/U>>	4-3	

2019-UCLA		Opponent	UCLA	Opp	S/U	Line	ATS	Total	O/U	
8/31/2019	@	Cincinnati	14	24	L	2.5	L	55.5	U	
9/7/2019	vs	SAN DIEGO STATE	14	23	L	-7.5	L	45.0	U	
9/14/2019	vs	OKLAHOMA	14	48	L	23.0	L	72.0	U	
9/21/2019	@	Washington State	67	63	W	18.0	W	59.5	O	
9/28/2019	@	Arizona	17	20	L	3.0	T	68.0	U	
10/5/2019	vs	OREGON STATE	31	48	L	-4.5	L	63.5	O	
10/17/2019	@	Stanford	34	16	W	4.0	W	48.5	O	
10/26/2019	vs	ARIZONA STATE	42	32	W	3.0	W	56.0	O	
11/2/2019	vs	COLORADO	31	14	W	-6.5	W	64.5	U	
11/16/2019	@	Utah	3	49	L	20.5	L	51.5	O	
11/23/2019	@	Usc	35	52	L	13.0	L	66.5	O	"Victory Bell"
11/30/2019	vs	CALIFORNIA	18	28	L	-1.0	L	51.0	U	
Coach: Chip Kelly		Season Record >>	320	417	4-8	ATS>>	4-7-1	O/U>>	6-6	

2018-UCLA		Opponent	UCLA	Opp	S/U	Line	ATS	Total	O/U	
9/1/2018	vs	CINCINNATI	17	26	L	-14.5	L	62.5	U	
9/8/2018	@	Oklahoma	21	49	L	31.0	W	65.5	O	
9/15/2018	vs	FRESNO STATE	14	38	L	2.5	L	51.5	O	
9/28/2018	@	Colorado	16	38	L	10.0	L	56.5	U	
10/6/2018	vs	WASHINGTON	24	31	L	21.5	W	53.5	U	
10/13/2018	@	California	37	7	W	6.5	W	53.5	U	
10/20/2018	vs	ARIZONA	31	30	W	-10.0	L	57.0	O	
10/26/2018	vs	UTAH	10	41	L	11.0	L	54.0	U	
11/3/2018	@	Oregon	21	42	L	11.0	L	59.0	O	
11/10/2018	@	Arizona State	28	31	L	11.5	W	64.5	U	
11/17/2018	vs	USC	34	27	W	2.5	W	54.5	O	"Victory Bell"
11/24/2018	vs	STANFORD	42	49	L	7.0	T	60.5	O	
Coach: Chip Kelly		Season Record >>	295	409	3-9	ATS>>	5-6-1	O/U>>	7-5	

- 15-1 S/U @ home when #4 ranked all time
- 10-0 S/U @ home when #5 ranked all time
- 8-0-1 S/U @ home when ranked vs Arizona all time
- 7-1 S/U & ATS when ranked vs Arizona since 1993
- 26-3 S/U when ranked vs California since 1952
- 0-5 S/U when ranked vs Oregon since 2000
- 0-9 ATS when ranked vs Oregon since 1988
- 0-7 ATS @ home when ranked vs Stanford since 1984
- 9-0 S/U when ranked vs Washington since 1987
- 14-1-1 S/U @ home when ranked vs Washington all time
- 0-6 S/U vs ranked Oregon since 2009
- 2-10 ATS vs ranked Oregon since 1995
- 0-8 S/U vs ranked Stanford since 2001 {1-7 ATS}
- 1-10 O/U vs ranked USC since 2006

UCLA BRUINS — PACIFIC-12 South

STADIUM: Rose Bowl Stadium {92,542} | **Location:** Westwood, CA | **COACH:** Chip Kelly

DATE		Opponent	Ucla	Opp	S/U	Line	ATS	Total	O/U	Trends & Angles
9/3/2022	vs	BOWLING GREEN								14-3 S/U in 1st home game of season since 2005
9/10/2022	vs	ALABAMA STATE								1st Meeting
9/17/2022	vs	SOUTH ALABAMA								3-9 ATS prior to playing Colorado since 1984
9/24/2022	@	Colorado								8-1 S/U vs Colorado as favorite since 2011
10/1/2022	vs	WASHINGTON								8-1 S/U @ home vs Washington since 1997
10/8/2022	vs	UTAH								0-4 ATS @ home vs Utah since 2012
10/22/2022	@	Oregon								0-7 S/U vs Oregon as Dog since 2008
10/29/2022	vs	STANFORD								0-6 S/U @ home vs Stanford since 2010 {1-4-1 ATS}
11/5/2022	@	Arizona State								vs Arizona State - UCLA leads series 23-14-1
11/12/2022	vs	ARIZONA								vs Arizona - UCLA leads series 27-17-2
11/19/2022	vs	USC								vs USC - USC leads series 51-33-7
11/25/2022	@	California								0-8 ATS @ California as favorite since 1988
12/2/2022	vs									PAC-12 Championship
	vs									BOWL GAME

Pointspread Analysis

Non-Conference
- 9-3 S/U vs Non-Conf. as 7.5-10 point favorite since 1991
- 13-3 S/U vs Non-Conf. as 10.5-15 point favorite since 1985
- 8-1 S/U vs Non-Conf. as 15.5-20 point favorite since 1987
- 9-1 S/U vs Non-Conf. as 20.5-25 point favorite since 1988
- 10-0 S/U vs Non-Conf. as 25.5 point or more favorite since 1987

Dog
- 0-11 S/U as 20.5 point or more since 2003
- 2-13 S/U as 15.5-20 point Dog since 1983
- 3-11 O/U as 10.5-15 point Dog since 2003
- 1-12 S/U on road as 10.5-15 point Dog since 1994
- 0-14 S/U on road as 7.5-10 point Dog since 1990
- 2-6 S/U as 3.5-7 point Dog since 2015
- 2-5 S/U & ATS @ home as 3 point or less Dog since 2012

Favorite
- 0-6 S/U & ATS on road as 3 point or less favorite since 2006
- 22-4 S/U @ home as 3.5-7 point favorite since 1996
- 10-2 S/U on road as 3.5-7 point favorite since 2005
- 6-13 O/U on road as 3.5-7 point favorite since 1995
- 4-11 O/U @ home as 3.5-7 point favorite since 2009
- 13-3 S/U @ home as 7.5-10 point favorite since 1995
- 1-5 ATS @ home as 7.5-10 point favorite since 2012
- 1-7 ATS on road as 7.5-10 point favorite since 1997
- 14-2 S/U on road as 10.5-15 point favorite since 1983
- 11-0 S/U on road as 15.5-20 point favorite since 1986
- 9-0 S/U @ home as 15.5-20 point favorite since 1989
- 1-7 O/U @ home as 15.5-20 point favorite since 1991
- 0-4 ATS on road as 20.5-25 point favorite since 1988
- 7-1 S/U on road as 20.5 point or more favorite since 1987
- 31-1 S/U @ home as 20.5 point or more favorite since 1985

Bowl Games
- 0-3 S/U vs Wisconsin in Bowl Games
- 0-3 S/U & ATS in Foster Farms Bowl
- 3-1 S/U in Sun Bowl
- 0-3 O/U in Las Vegas Bowl
- 0-3 S/U & O/U in Bowl Games as 3.5-7 point Dog since 2000
- 4-0 O/U in Bowl Games as 3.5-7 point favorite since 1995
- 0-4 O/U in Bowl Games as 10.5-15 point favorite since 1986

- 4-11 ATS prior to playing Arizona since 2007
- 1-8-1 ATS in final home game of season since 2012

Conference
- 11-0 S/U @ home vs Arizona as favorite since 1991 {9-2 ATS}
- 0-3 S/U @ home vs Arizona as Dog since 1999
- vs California - UCLA leads series 57-34-1
- 0-7 O/U vs California as favorite since 2013
- vs Colorado - UCLA leads series 12-5
- 0-3 S/U vs Colorado as Dog since 2003
- 0-3 O/U vs Colorado as Dog since 2003
- 2-5 ATS vs Colorado as favorite since 2013
- vs Stanford - UCLA leads series 47-43-3
- 2-12 S/U vs Stanford since 2009
- 3-10-1 ATS vs Stanford since 2009
- 1-10 S/U vs Stanford as Dog since 2009 {2-8-1 ATS}
- 2-7 O/U vs Stanford as favorite since 2002
- 8-3 S/U @ home vs Stanford as favorite since 1988
- 0-3 S/U @ home vs Utah since 2014
- 0-5 S/U & ATS vs Utah as Dog since 2011
- 0-5 S/U & ATS vs Utah since 2016
- vs Utah - UCLA leads series 11-8
- 6-0 S/U @ home vs Washington as favorite since 1997
- vs Washington - UCLA leads series 41-32-2
- 5-2 O/U vs Washington as Dog since 2000
- 1-3 S/U vs Washington as Dog since 2010
- 11-0 S/U vs Arizona as 9.5 point or more favorite since 1987
- 6-0-1 O/U vs Arizona as 4.5 point or less favorite since 1983
- 10-0 S/U vs Arizona as 9.5 point or more favorite since 1987
- 1-5 S/U vs Arizona State as 7 point or more Dog since 2004
- 10-0 S/U vs California as 14 point or more favorite since 1985
- 3-13-1 ATS vs California as 13 point or less favorite since 1983
- 5-0 S/U vs Stanford as 14 point or more favorite since 1987
- 0-10 S/U vs USC as 13 point or more Dog since 2003
- 1-6 O/U vs USC as 13 point or more Dog since 2007
- 6-2 S/U & ATS vs USC as 1.5-5 point Dog since 1993
- 8-0 S/U vs Washington as 6 point or more favorite since 1987

Opponent	Trend
BOWLING GREEN	2-6 ATS in 1st home game of season since 2014
Colorado	6-1 ATS prior to playing Washington since 2009
WASHINGTON	7-2 O/U prior to playing Utah since 2011
UTAH	1-6 S/U & ATS prior to playing Oregon since 2009
Oregon	9-3 S/U in 2nd road game of season since 2010
STANFORD	11-3 S/U prior to playing Arizona State since 2008
Arizona State	8-3 S/U prior to playing Arizona since 2010
Arizona State	2-7 S/U after playing Stanford since 2009
ARIZONA	4-12 O/U after playing Arizona State since 2006
USC	4-12 O/U in final home game of season since 2006

Page | 237

Copyright © 2022 by Steve's Football Bible, LLC

UTAH UTES — PACIFIC-12 South

2021-Utah

Date		Opponent	Utah	Opp	S/U	Line	ATS	Total	O/U	
9/2/2021	vs	WEBER STATE	40	17	W	-29.0	L	49.0	O	
9/11/2021	@	Byu	17	26	L	-7.0	L	50.5	U	"Holy War" (Beehive Boot)
9/18/2021	@	San Diego State	31	33	L	-8.0	L	42.5	O	{3 OT}
9/25/2021	vs	WASHINGTON STATE	24	13	W	-15.0	L	53.5	U	
10/9/2021	@	Usc	42	26	W	3.0	W	53.5	O	
10/16/2021	vs	ARIZONA STATE	35	21	W	1.0	W	52.0	O	
10/23/2021	@	Oregon State	34	42	L	-3.0	L	57.0	O	
10/30/2021	vs	UCLA	44	24	W	-6.5	W	60.0	O	
11/5/2021	@	Stanford	52	7	W	-11.0	W	51.5	O	
11/13/2021	@	Arizona	38	29	W	-23.5	L	54.5	O	
11/20/2021	vs	OREGON	38	7	W	-3.0	W	58.5	U	
11/26/2021	vs	COLORADO	28	13	W	-24.5	L	52.5	U	"Rumble in the Rockies"
12/4/2021	vs	Oregon	38	10	W	-3.0	W	58.0	U	PAC-12 Championship Game
1/1/2022	vs	Ohio State	45	48	L	4.0	W	64.5	O	Rose Bowl
Coach: Kyle Whittingham		Season Record >>	506	316	10-4	ATS>>	7-7	O/U>>	9-5	PAC-12 CHAMPIONS

2020-Utah

Date		Opponent	Utah	Opp	S/U	Line	ATS	Total	O/U	
11/21/2020	vs	USC	17	33	L	2.5	L	58.5	U	
11/29/2020	@	Washington	21	24	L	9.5	W	47.0	U	
12/5/2020	vs	OREGON STATE	30	24	W	-13.5	L	51.0	O	
12/12/2020	@	Colorado	38	21	W	-2.5	W	49.0	O	"Rumble in the Rockies"
12/19/2020	vs	WASHINGTON STATE	45	28	W	-12.0	W	54.5	O	
Coach: Kyle Whittingham		Season Record >>	151	130	3-2	ATS>>	3-2	O/U>>	3-2	

2019-Utah

Date		Opponent	Utah	Opp	S/U	Line	ATS	Total	O/U	
8/29/2019	@	Byu	30	12	W	-5.5	W	49.0	U	"Holy War" (Beehive Boot)
9/7/2019	vs	NORTHERN ILLINOIS	35	17	W	-23.0	L	45.0	O	
9/14/2019	vs	IDAHO STATE	31	0	W	-37.0	L	NT	---	
9/20/2019	@	Usc	23	30	L	-3.5	L	53.0	T	
9/28/2019	vs	WASHINGTON STATE	38	13	W	-5.5	W	56.5	U	
10/12/2019	@	Oregon State	52	7	W	-15.0	W	59.5	U	
10/19/2019	vs	ARIZONA STATE	21	3	W	-14.5	W	46.0	U	
10/26/2019	vs	CALIFORNIA	35	0	W	-21.0	W	36.5	U	
11/2/2019	@	Washington	33	28	W	-3.0	W	48.0	O	
11/16/2019	vs	UCLA	49	3	W	-20.5	W	51.5	O	
11/23/2019	@	Arizona	35	7	W	-23.5	W	56.5	U	
11/30/2019	vs	COLORADO	45	15	W	-28.0	W	50.0	O	"Rumble in the Rockies"
12/6/2019	vs	Oregon	15	37	L	-6.5	L	45.0	O	PAC-12 Championship
12/31/2019	vs	Texas	10	38	L	-7.0	L	56.0	U	Alamo Bowl
Coach: Kyle Whittingham		Season Record >>	452	210	11-3	ATS>>	9-5	O/U>>	5-7-1	

2018-Utah

Date		Opponent	Utah	Opp	S/U	Line	ATS	Total	O/U	
8/30/2018	vs	WEBER STATE	41	10	W	-29.0	W	NT	---	
9/8/2018	@	Northern Illinois	17	6	W	-10.0	W	47.0	U	
9/15/2018	vs	WASHINGTON	7	21	L	4.0	L	46.0	U	
9/29/2018	@	Washington State	24	28	L	-1.5	L	50.0	O	
10/6/2018	@	Stanford	40	21	W	4.0	W	45.0	O	
10/13/2018	vs	ARIZONA	42	10	W	-13.5	W	52.5	U	
10/20/2018	vs	USC	41	28	W	-6.5	W	48.0	O	
10/27/2018	@	Ucla	41	10	W	-11.0	W	54.0	U	
11/3/2018	@	Arizona State	20	38	L	-7.5	L	54.0	O	
11/10/2018	vs	OREGON	32	25	W	-6.0	W	51.0	O	
11/17/2018	@	Colorado	30	7	W	-7.0	W	45.5	U	"Rumble in the Rockies"
11/24/2018	vs	BYU	35	27	W	-10.5	L	44.5	O	"Holy War" (Beehive Boot)
12/1/2018	vs	Washington	3	10	L	4.5	L	46.0	U	PAC-12 Championship
12/31/2018	vs	Northwestern	20	31	L	-6.5	L	44.5	O	Holiday Bowl
Coach: Kyle Whittingham		Season Record >>	393	272	9-5	ATS>>	8-6	O/U>>	7-6	

UTAH UTES — PACIFIC-12 South

STADIUM: Rice-Eccles Stadium {45,807} | **Location:** Salt Lake City, UT | **COACH:** Kyle Whittingham

DATE		Opponent	Utah	Opp	S/U	Line	ATS	Total	O/U	Trends & Angles
9/3/2022	@	Florida								vs Florida - Florida leads series 1-0
9/10/2022	vs	SOUTHERN UTAH								vs Southern Utah - Utah leads series 1-0
9/17/2022	vs	SAN DIEGO STATE								5-1 S/U & ATS vs San Diego State since 2005
9/24/2022	@	Arizona State								vs Arizona State - ASU leads series 21-10
10/1/2022	vs	OREGON STATE								8-2 S/U vs Oregon State as favorite since 1992
10/8/2022	@	Ucla								4-1 ATS vs UCLA as Dog since 2007
10/15/2022	vs	USC								vs USC - USC leads series 13-7
10/29/2022	@	Washington State								0-3 ATS @ Washington State since 2011
11/5/2022	vs	ARIZONA								vs Arizona - Utah leads series 25-19-2
11/12/2022	vs	STANFORD								5-0-1 ATS vs Stanford since 1996
11/19/2022	@	Oregon								1-4 S/U @ Oregon as Dog since 1997
11/26/2022	@	Colorado								9-0 S/U vs Colorado as favorite since 2012
12/2/2022	vs									PAC-12 Championship
	vs									BOWL GAME

Pointspread Analysis — Non-Conference

- 5-12 S/U vs Non-Conf. as 10.5-15 point Dog since 1985
- 8-1 ATS vs Non-Conf. as 7.5-10 point Dog since 1993
- 5-0 S/U & ATS on road vs Non-Conf. as 3.5-7 point Dog since 2011
- 8-1 S/U & ATS vs Non-Conf. as 3 point or less Dog since 1994
- 11-0 S/U vs Non-Conf. as 3 point or less favorite since 2003
- 9-1-1 ATS vs Non-Conf. as 3 point or less favorite since 2003
- 9-4 S/U vs Non-Conf. as 3.5-7 point favorite since 2007
- 1-9 O/U vs Non-Conf. as 3.5-7 point favorite since 2010
- 8-2 S/U on road vs Non-Conf. as 7.5-10 point favorite since 1998
- 15-0 S/U @ home vs Non-Conf. as 10.5-15 point favorite since 1994
- 12-2 ATS @ home vs Non-Conf. as 10.5-15 point favorite since 1994
- 8-0 S/U @ home vs Non-Conf. as 15.5-20 point favorite since 1998
- 37-0 S/U vs Non-Conf. as 20.5 point or more favorite since 1985
- vs BYU - Utah leads series 59-32-4
- 5-1 S/U & ATS vs San Diego State as favorite since 2006
- 5-0 S/U vs San Diego State as 14.5 point or more favorite since 2001

Dog
- 0-17 S/U as 15.5 point or more Dog since 1985
- 8-0 ATS as 10.5-15 point Dog since 2002
- 15-4 ATS as 7.5-10 point Dog since 1992
- 7-18 O/U on road as 3.5-7 point Dog since 1997
- 2-14 S/U @ home as 3.5-7 point Dog since 1986
- 6-1-1 ATS @ home as 3 point or less Dog since 1996
- 1-5 O/U @ home as 3 point or less Dog since 2003

Favorite
- 9-4 S/U on road as 3.5-7 point favorite since 2007
- 9-1 S/U @ home as 3.5-7 point favorite since 2008
- 10-3 S/U on road as 7.5-10 point favorite since 1998
- 3-13 ATS on road as 7.5-10 point favorite since 1994
- 13-3 S/U as 7.5-10 point favorite since 2007
- 13-1 S/U on road as 10.5-15 point favorite since 1998
- 6-0 S/U @ home as 10.5-15 point favorite since 2018
- 11-0 S/U as 15.5-20 point favorite since 2003
- 0-5 O/U as 15.5-20 point favorite since 2009
- 4-0 S/U & ATS on road as 15.5-20 point favorite since 2004
- 9-0 S/U on road as 20.5 point or more favorite since 2004
- 7-2 O/U on road as 20.5 point or more favorite since 2004
- 52-3 S/U @ home as 15.5 point or more favorite since 1985

Pointspread Analysis — Conference

- 0-8 S/U vs Arizona State as Dog since 1985
- vs Colorado - Series tied 33-33-3
- Game 7-2 O/U vs Oregon since 2009
- 4-0 O/U vs Oregon as Dog since 2009
- vs Oregon State - Oregon State leads series 12-11-1
- vs UCLA - UCLA leads series 11-8
- 5-0 S/U & ATS vs UCLA as favorite since 2011
- vs Washington State - Utah leads series 10-9
- Game 3-0 O/U @ Washington State since 2011
- 0-5 O/U vs Arizona as 5 point or less favorite since 2000
- 6-0 S/U vs Arizona as 7.5 point or more favorite since 2004
- 0-4 S/U & ATS vs Arizona as 4.5 point or less favorite since 2000

Bowl Games
- 14-4 S/U in Bowl Games since 1999
- 12-5 ATS in Bowl Games since 2001
- 4-1 S/U in Las Vegas Bowl since 1999
- 1-4 O/U in Las Vegas Bowl since 1999
- 8-1 S/U in Bowl Games as 3.5-10 point favorite since 1999

Florida	7-2 S/U in 1st road game of season since 2013 {8-1 ATS}
SOUTHERN UTAH	13-1 S/U in 1st home game of season since 2008
SAN DIEGO STATE	13-2 S/U in 2nd home game of season since 2007
OREGON STATE	2-7 S/U after playing Arizona State since 2010
OREGON STATE	7-2 O/U after playing Arizona State since 2010
USC	6-1 ATS after playing UCLA since 2013
Washington State	1-9 O/U after playing USC since 2012
Washington State	10-2 S/U & ATS prior to playing Arizona since 2002
ARIZONA	2-6 S/U prior to playing Stanford since 1989
STANFORD	10-2 S/U after playing Arizona since 2002
STANFORD	3-9 ATS in final home game of season since 2010
STANFORD	3-10 O/U in final home game of season since 2009
Colorado	9-3 O/U in final road game of season since 2010
Colorado	9-2 S/U after playing Oregon since 1997 {8-3 ATS}

- 4-0 S/U & ATS when ranked vs San Diego State since 2004
- 8-40 S/U on road vs ranked teams all time
- 9-0 ATS on road vs ranked teams since 2013
- 0-5 S/U @ ranked Arizona State all time

UTAH STATE AGGIES   MOUNTAIN WEST West

2021-Utah State		Opponent	USU	Opp	S/U	Line	ATS	Total	O/U	
9/4/2021	@	Washington State	26	23	W	17.0	W	66.0	U	
9/11/2021	vs	NORTH DAKOTA	48	24	W	-6.5	W	52.5	O	
9/18/2021	@	Air Force	49	45	W	9.0	W	53.5	O	
9/25/2021	vs	BOISE STATE	3	27	L	9.5	L	69.5	U	
10/1/2021	vs	BYU	20	34	L	7.5	L	65.5	U	"The Old Wagon Wheel"
10/16/2021	@	Unlv	28	24	W	-7.5	L	64.0	U	
10/22/2021	vs	COLORADO STATE	26	24	W	3.0	W	58.5	U	
10/30/2021	vs	HAWAII	51	31	W	-3.5	W	66.0	O	
11/6/2021	@	New Mexico State	35	13	W	-18.0	W	72.0	U	
11/13/2021	@	San Jose State	48	17	W	3.5	W	58.0	O	
11/20/2021	vs	WYOMING	17	44	L	-5.5	L	52.0	O	"Bridger's Battle"
11/26/2021	@	New Mexico	35	10	W	-17.0	W	48.0	U	
12/4/2021	vs	**San Diego State**	46	13	W	6.5	W	49.5	O	MWC Championship
12/18/2021	vs	**Oregon State**	24	13	W	6.0	W	69.0	U	Los Angeles Bowl
Coach: Blake Andersen		Season Record >>	456	342	11-3	ATS>>	10-4	O/U>>	6-8	MWC Champions
2020-Utah State		Opponent	USU	Opp	S/U	Line	ATS	Total	O/U	
10/24/2020	@	Boise State	13	42	L	17.0	L	51.0	O	
10/31/2020	vs	SAN DIEGO STATE	7	38	L	8.5	L	40.5	O	
11/6/2020	@	Nevada	9	34	L	17.0	L	58.0	U	
11/14/2020	vs	FRESNO STATE	16	35	L	10.5	L	51.5	U	
11/26/2020	vs	NEW MEXICO	41	27	W	6.5	W	49.0	O	
12/3/2020	vs	AIR FORCE	7	35	L	13.5	L	52.5	U	
Coach: Gary Andersen		Season Record >>	93	211	1-5	ATS>>	1-5	O/U>>	3-3	
2019-Utah State		Opponent	USU	Opp	S/U	Line	ATS	Total	O/U	
8/30/2019	@	Wake Forest	35	38	L	5.0	W	60.0	O	
9/7/2019	vs	SUNY-STONY BROOK	62	7	W	-29.0	W	NT	---	
9/21/2019	@	San Diego State	23	17	W	-4.0	W	53.0	U	
9/28/2019	vs	COLORADO STATE	34	24	W	-24.0	L	69.0	O	
10/5/2019	@	Lsu	6	42	L	27.5	L	72.5	U	
10/19/2019	vs	NEVADA	36	10	W	-21.5	W	59.0	U	
10/26/2019	@	Air Force	7	31	L	3.5	L	60.0	U	
11/2/2019	vs	BYU	14	42	L	-3.0	L	52.0	O	"The Old Wagon Wheel"
11/9/2019	@	Fresno State	37	35	W	5.5	W	58.0	O	
11/16/2019	vs	WYOMING	26	21	W	-5.0	T	51.5	U	"Bridger's Battle"
11/23/2019	vs	BOISE STATE	21	56	L	4.0	L	54.5	O	
11/30/2019	@	New Mexico	38	25	W	-12.0	W	64.0	U	
12/20/2019	vs	**Kent State**	41	51	L	-7.0	L	71.5	O	Frisco Bowl
Coach: Gary Andersen		Season Record >>	380	399	7-6	ATS>>	6-6-1	O/U>>	5-6-1	
2018-Utah State		Opponent	USU	Opp	S/U	Line	ATS	Total	O/U	
8/31/2018	@	Michigan State	31	38	L	23.5	W	52.0	O	
9/8/2018	vs	NEW MEXICO STATE	60	13	W	-31.0	W	62.0	O	
9/13/2018	vs	TENNESSEE TECH	73	12	W	-44.5	W	NT	---	
9/22/2018	vs	AIR FORCE	42	32	W	-9.5	W	59.5	O	
10/5/2018	@	Byu	45	20	W	-1.0	W	55.0	O	"The Old Wagon Wheel"
10/13/2018	vs	UNLV	59	28	W	-27.0	W	65.5	O	
10/20/2018	@	Wyoming	24	16	W	-14.0	L	49.5	U	"Bridger's Battle"
10/27/2018	vs	NEW MEXICO	61	19	W	-19.5	W	64.0	O	
11/3/2018	@	Hawaii	56	17	W	-18.0	W	72.0	O	
11/10/2018	vs	SAN JOSE STATE	62	24	W	-31.0	W	63.5	O	
11/17/2018	@	Colorado State	29	24	W	-30.0	L	66.0	U	
11/24/2018	@	Boise State	24	33	L	2.0	L	64.0	U	
12/15/2018	vs	**North Texas**	52	13	W	-7.0	W	67.5	U	New Mexico Bowl
Coach: Matt Wells		Season Record >>	618	289	11-2	ATS>>	10-3	O/U>>	8-4	

UTAH STATE AGGIES — MOUNTAIN WEST West

STADIUM: Romney Stadium {25,100}
Location: Logan, UT
COACH: Blake Andersen

DATE		Opponent	USU	Opp	S/U	Line	ATS	Total	O/U	Trends & Angles
8/27/2022	vs	CONNECTICUT								vs Connecticut - Utah State leads series 1-0
9/3/2022	@	Alabama								vs Alabama - Alabama leads series 2-0
9/10/2022	vs	WEBER STATE								8-0 S/U vs Weber State since 1979
9/24/2022	vs	UNLV								6-0 S/U vs UNLV as favorite since 1995
9/30/2022	@	Byu								3-22 S/U vs BYU as Dog since 1985
10/8/2022	vs	AIR FORCE								vs Air Force - Air Force leads series 6-4
10/15/2022	@	Colorado State								1-5 S/U vs Colorado State as Dog since 1994
10/22/2022	@	Wyoming								0-5 S/U vs Wyoming as Dog since 2003 {1-4 ATS}
11/5/2022	vs	NEW MEXICO								vs New Mexico - Utah State leads series 15-13
11/12/2022	@	Hawaii								5-0 S/U & ATS vs Hawaii as favorite since 2013
11/19/2022	vs	SAN JOSE STATE								9-1 S/U vs San Jose State as favorite since 1985
11/26/2022	@	Boise State								1-17 S/U vs Boise State as Dog since 1998
12/3/2022	vs									MWC Championship
	vs									BOWL GAME

Pointspread Analysis — Non-Conference
- 1-11 S/U vs Non-Conf. as 25.5-30 point Dog since 1986
- 7-1 ATS vs Non-Conf. as 20.5-25 point Dog since 2005
- 0-8 S/U on road vs Non-Conf. as 10.5-15 point Dog since 1996
- 8-2 ATS on road vs Non-Conf. as 10.5-15 point Dog since 1986
- 1-18 S/U vs BYU as 13.5 point or more Dog since 1985
- vs BYU - BYU leads series 50-37-3
- 1-14 S/U vs ranked BYU all time
- vs Weber State - Utah State leads series 14-1

Dog
- 0-22 S/U as 30.5 point or more Dog since 1985
- 0-33 S/U on road as 25.5 point or more Dog since 1986
- 1-28-1 S/U as 20.5-25 point Dog since 1985
- 2-21 S/U on road as 15.5-20 point Dog since 1985
- 0-9 S/U @ home as 15.5-20 point Dog since 1987
- 1-15 S/U on road as 10.5-15 point Dog since 1993
- 1-6 O/U on road as 10.5-15 point Dog since 2006
- 1-8 S/U @ home as 10.5-15 point Dog since 1996
- 1-9 S/U as 7.5-10 point Dog since 1994
- 2-9 S/U on road as 7.5-10 point Dog since 1985
- 4-12 S/U on road as 3.5-7 point Dog since 2002
- 1-6 S/U & ATS @ home as 3 point or less Dog since 2003
- 7-2 O/U @ home as 3 point or less Dog since 2002

Favorite
- 46-1 S/U @ home as 7.5 point or more favorite since 1995
- 8-0 S/U @ home as 7.5-10 point favorite since 1995
- 6-0 S/U on road as 7.5-10 point favorite since 1987
- 13-0 S/U as 10.5-15 point favorite since 2011
- 6-1 O/U @ home as 10.5-15 point favorite since 2011
- 11-1 S/U @ home as 10.5-15 point favorite since 1993
- 29-0 S/U @ home as 15.5 point or more favorite since 1990

Pointspread Analysis — Conference
- 4-0 O/U vs Air Force as favorite since 2013
- vs Boise State - Boise State leads series 21-5
- vs Colorado State - CSU leads series 39-36-2
- 1-6 S/U vs Fresno State as Dog since 2007
- vs Nevada - Nevada leads series 19-7
- 5-1 ATS vs UNLV as Dog since 1985
- 2-9 S/U vs San Jose State as Dog since 1986
- 6-1 S/U vs Wyoming as favorite since 2011 {4-2-1 ATS}
- Game 6-2 O/U @ home vs Wyoming since 2001
- vs Wyoming - Utah State leads series 40-27-4
- 3-10 S/U @ home vs MWC teams as 3.5-7 point Dog since 1991

Bowl Games
- 1-3 S/U & ATS in Famous Idaho Potato Bowl since 1997
- 1-3 O/U Famous Idaho Potato Bowl since 1997
- 1-7 O/U in Bowl Games since 2011

Alabama	1-23 S/U in 1st road game of season since 1998
CONNECTICUT	12-1 S/U in 1st home game of season since 2009
Byu	6-21 S/U in 2nd road game of season since 1995
Byu	1-8 O/U after playing UNLV since 2006
Hawaii	7-2 O/U after playing New Mexico since 2002
Boise State	2-7 ATS in final road game of season since 2013

- 2-55 S/U on road vs ranked teams all time
- 2-14 S/U @ home vs ranked teams all time
- 0-25 S/U vs Top #10 ranked teams all time
- 0-17 S/U vs #11 - #17 ranked teams all time

VANDERBILT COMMODORES   SEC East

2021-Vanderbilt		Opponent	Vandy	Opp	S/U	Line	ATS	Total	O/U	
9/4/2021	vs	EAST TENNESEE ST.	3	23	L	-21.0	L	45.0	U	
9/11/2021	@	Colorado State	24	21	W	6.5	W	52.0	U	
9/18/2021	vs	STANFORD	23	41	L	12.5	L	49.0	O	
9/25/2021	vs	GEORGIA	0	62	L	37.0	L	54.0	O	
10/2/2021	vs	CONNECTICUT	30	28	W	-14.5	L	51.0	O	
10/9/2021	@	Florida	0	42	L	39.0	L	59.5	U	
10/16/2021	@	South Carolina	20	21	L	19.0	W	50.0	U	
10/23/2021	vs	MISSISSIPPI STATE	6	45	L	20.5	L	53.0	U	
10/30/2021	vs	MISSOURI	28	37	L	16.5	W	62.5	O	
11/13/2021	vs	KENTUCKY	17	34	L	21.5	W	52.5	U	
11/20/2021	@	Mississippi	17	31	L	35.5	W	64.5	U	
11/27/2021	@	Tennessee	21	45	L	33.0	W	64.5	O	
Coach: Clark Lea		Season Record >>	189	430	2-10	ATS>>	6-6	O/U>>	5-7	

2020-Vanderbilt		Opponent	Vandy	Opp	S/U	Line	ATS	Total	O/U	
9/26/2020	@	Texas A&M	12	17	L	31.0	W	45.5	U	
10/3/2020	vs	LSU	7	41	L	21.0	L	50.0	U	
10/10/2020	vs	SOUTH CAROLINA	7	41	L	14.0	L	41.5	O	
10/31/2020	vs	MISSISSIPPI	21	54	L	17.0	L	63.5	O	
11/7/2020	@	Mississippi State	17	24	L	18.5	W	45.0	U	
11/14/2020	@	Kentucky	35	38	L	17.5	W	41.5	O	
11/21/2020	vs	FLORIDA	17	38	L	31.0	W	68.0	U	
11/28/2020	@	Missouri	0	41	L	14.0	L	51.5	U	
12/12/2020	vs	TENNESSEE	17	42	L	15.0	L	51.0	O	
Coach: Derek Mason		Season Record >>	133	336	0-9	ATS>>	4-5	O/U>>	4-5	

2019-Vanderbilt		Opponent	Vandy	Opp	S/U	Line	ATS	Total	O/U	
8/31/2019	vs	GEORGIA	6	30	L	22.5	L	57.0	U	
9/7/2019	@	Purdue	24	42	L	7.0	L	55.5	O	
9/21/2019	vs	LSU	38	66	L	24.0	L	62.5	O	
9/28/2019	vs	NORTHERN ILLINOIS	24	18	W	-7.0	L	51.5	U	
10/5/2019	@	Mississippi	6	31	L	7.0	L	64.5	U	
10/12/2019	vs	UNLV	10	34	L	-15.5	L	57.5	U	
10/19/2019	vs	MISSOURI	21	14	W	21.0	W	55.5	U	
11/2/2019	@	South Carolina	7	24	L	15.5	L	51.5	U	
11/9/2019	@	Florida	0	56	L	27.0	L	49.5	O	
11/16/2019	vs	KENTUCKY	14	38	L	9.0	L	43.0	O	
11/23/2019	vs	EAST TENNESSEE STATE	38	0	W	-20.5	W	NT	---	
11/30/2019	@	Tennessee	10	28	L	23.5	W	48.0	U	
Coach: Derek Mason		Season Record >>	198	381	3-9	ATS>>	3-9	O/U>>	4-7	

2018-Vanderbilt		Opponent	Vandy	Opp	S/U	Line	ATS	Total	O/U	
9/1/2018	vs	MIDDLE TENNESSEE	35	7	W	-3.0	W	56.5	U	
9/8/2018	vs	NEVADA	41	10	W	-10.0	W	60.0	U	
9/15/2018	@	Notre Dame	17	22	L	13.5	W	51.5	U	
9/22/2018	vs	SOUTH CAROLINA	14	37	L	1.5	L	54.5	U	
9/29/2018	vs	TENNESSEE STATE	31	27	W	-28.5	L	NT	---	
10/6/2018	@	Georgia	13	41	L	26.0	L	55.5	U	
10/13/2018	vs	FLORIDA	27	37	L	10.0	T	52.0	O	
10/20/2018	@	Kentucky	7	14	L	10.0	W	45.0	U	
10/27/2018	@	Arkansas	45	31	W	PK	W	53.0	O	
11/10/2018	@	Missouri	28	33	L	14.0	W	64.5	U	
11/17/2018	vs	MISSISSIPPI	36	29	W	-3.0	W	73.0	U	{OT}
11/24/2018	vs	TENNESSEE	38	13	W	-3.0	W	51.5	U	
12/27/2018	vs	Baylor	38	45	L	-4.5	L	56.5	O	Texas Bowl
Coach: Derek Mason		Season Record >>	370	346	6-7	ATS>>	8-4-1	O/U>>	3-9	

VANDERBILT COMMODORES   SEC East

STADIUM: Vanderbilt Stadium {40,550} **Location:** Nashville, TN **COACH:** Clark Lea

DATE		Opponent	Vand	Opp	S/U	Line	ATS	Total	O/U	Trends & Angles
8/27/2022	@	*Hawaii*								3-13-1 O/U in 1st road game of season since 2005
9/3/2022	vs	*ELON*								vs Elon - Vanderbilt leads series 1-0
9/10/2022	vs	*WAKE FOREST*								3-0 S/U vs Wake Forest since 2011
9/17/2022	@	*Northern Illinois*								vs Northern Ill - Vanderbilt leads series 4-0
9/24/2022	@	Alabama								0-22 S/U vs Alabama as Dog since 1985
10/8/2022	vs	MISSISSIPPI								Vs Ole Miss - Ole Miss leads series 54-40-2
10/15/2022	@	Georgia								3-15 S/U @ Georgia as Dog since 1984
10/22/2022	@	Missouri								1-7 S/U vs Missouri as Dog since 2013
11/5/2022	vs	SOUTH CAROLINA								0-12 S/U vs USC as Dog since 2009
11/12/2022	@	Kentucky								0-9 S/U vs Kentucky as Dog since 2009
11/19/2022	vs	FLORIDA								0-16 S/U @ home vs Florida as Dog since 1988
11/26/2022	vs	TENNESSEE								vs Tennessee - UT leads series 78-32-5
12/3/2022	vs									SEC Championship
	vs									BOWL GAME

Pointspread Analysis — Non-Conference
- 0-9 S/U vs Non-Conf. as 10.5-15 point Dog since 1986
- 1-6 S/U @ home vs Non-Conf. as 3.5-7 point favorite since 1998
- 0-7 ATS @ home vs Non-Conf. as 3.5-7 point favorite since 1998
- 4-0 S/U vs Northern Illinois as favorite since 1994 {0-4 ATS}
- vs Wake Forest - Vanderbilt leads series 10-6

Dog
- 2-13-1 O/U on road as 20.5-25 point Dog since 1999
- 1-69 S/U as 20.5 point or more Dog since 1986
- 0-28 S/U as 15.5-20 point Dog since 2000
- 0-27 S/U @ home as 10.5-15 point Dog since 1983
- 16-5 ATS on road as 10.5-15 point Dog since 2005
- 2-18 S/U @ home as 7.5-10 point Dog since 1989
- 2-11 S/U on road as 7.5-10 point Dog since 1983
- 1-10 S/U @ home as 3 point or less Dog since 1984
- 1-9-1 ATS @ home as 3 point or less Dog since 1984

Favorite
- 8-1 S/U & ATS as 3 point or less favorite since 2012
- 4-0 S/U on road as 3.5-7 point favorite since 1993
- 1-9 ATS @ home as 3.5-7 point favorite since 1998
- 5-0 S/U on road as 10.5 point or more favorite since 1992
- 20-2 S/U as 15.5 point or more favorite since 1989

Bowl Games
- 5-0 O/U in Bowl Games since 2011
- 0-24 S/U vs ranked Florida since 1989
- 1-9 S/U @ home vs ranked Georgia since 1997
- 1-15 S/U vs ranked Mississippi since 1948 {0-6 on road}
- 1-38 S/U vs ranked Tennessee all time {0-21 on road}
- 2-6 ATS prior to playing Mississippi since 2014
- 9-1-1 ATS prior to playing Kentucky since 2011
- 6-2 ATS after playing Missouri since 2013
- 1-6 S/U prior to playing Georgia since 2013
- 0-21 S/U in 6th game of season since 2001 {4-17 ATS}
- 2-8 O/U after playing Florida since 2012

Pointspread Analysis — Conference
- vs Florida - Florida leads series 43-10-2
- 1-30 S/U vs Florida as Dog since 1989
- vs Georgia - Georgia leads series 59-20-2
- vs Kentucky - Kentucky leads series 48-42-4
- 3-0 S/U @ home vs Mississippi as favorite since 2005
- vs Missouri - Mizzu leads series 9-4-1
- 1-6 O/U vs Missouri as Dog since 2014
- vs South Carolina - South Carolina leads series 27-4
- 0-4 ATS vs South Carolina as favorite since 1992
- 0-11 S/U vs Georgia as 21.5 point or more Dog since 1990
- 1-11 S/U vs Georgia as 12 point or less Dog since 1983
- 0-8 S/U vs Kentucky as 10 point or more Dog since 1986
- 0-6 S/U vs Kentucky as 3.5 point or less Dog since 1996 {1-5 ATS}
- 11-1 ATS vs Kentucky as 5-13 point Dog since 1985
- 9-2 ATS vs Mississippi as 12 point or more Dog since 1990
- 1-13 S/U vs South Carolina as 12 point or more Dog since 1995
- 0-7 S/U vs South Carolina as 6.5 point or less Dog since 1993
- 0-24 S/U vs Tennessee as 12 point or more Dog since 1985

Alabama	2-8-1 S/U on road when ranked all time
SOUTH CAROLINA	3-119-1 S/U on road vs ranked teams all time
SOUTH CAROLINA	7-51 S/U @ home vs ranked teams since 1992
MISSISSIPPI	5-115 S/U vs Top #10 ranked teams all time
MISSISSIPPI	0-31 S/U vs ranked Alabama since 1971
	0-26 S/U vs ranked Florida since 1989
	1-18 S/U @ ranked Georgia all time
	1-16 S/U vs ranked Mississippi since 1948 {0-7 on road}
TENNESSEE	1-38 S/U vs ranked Tennessee all time {0-21 on road}

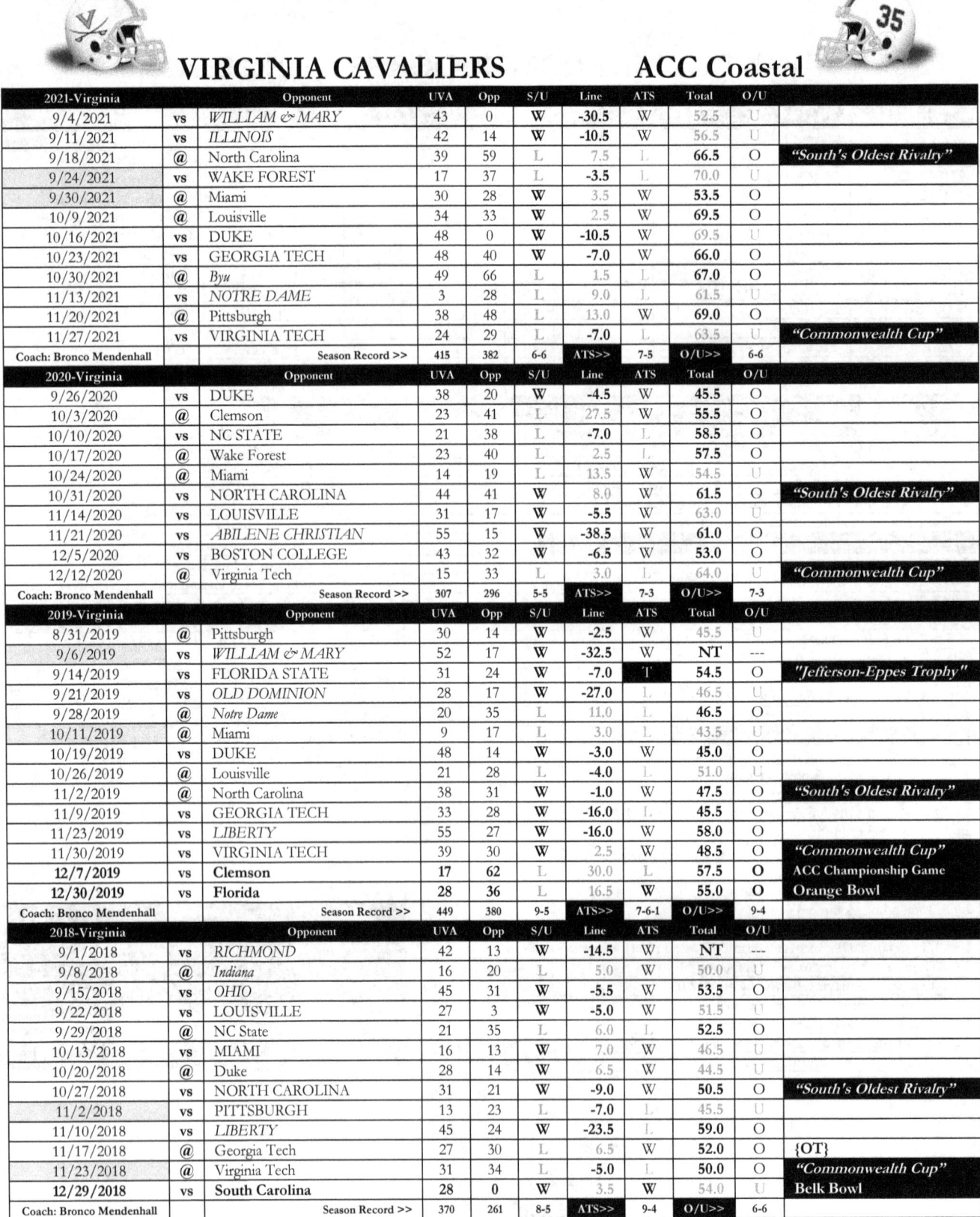

VIRGINIA CAVALIERS — ACC Coastal

2021-Virginia		Opponent	UVA	Opp	S/U	Line	ATS	Total	O/U	
9/4/2021	vs	WILLIAM & MARY	43	0	W	-30.5	W	52.5	U	
9/11/2021	vs	ILLINOIS	42	14	W	-10.5	W	56.5	U	
9/18/2021	@	North Carolina	39	59	L	7.5	L	66.5	O	"South's Oldest Rivalry"
9/24/2021	vs	WAKE FOREST	17	37	L	-3.5	L	70.0	U	
9/30/2021	@	Miami	30	28	W	3.5	W	53.5	O	
10/9/2021	@	Louisville	34	33	W	2.5	W	69.5	O	
10/16/2021	vs	DUKE	48	0	W	-10.5	W	69.5	U	
10/23/2021	vs	GEORGIA TECH	48	40	W	-7.0	W	66.0	O	
10/30/2021	@	Byu	49	66	L	1.5	L	67.0	O	
11/13/2021	vs	NOTRE DAME	3	28	L	9.0	L	61.5	U	
11/20/2021	@	Pittsburgh	38	48	L	13.0	L	69.0	O	
11/27/2021	vs	VIRGINIA TECH	24	29	L	-7.0	L	63.5	U	"Commonwealth Cup"
Coach: Bronco Mendenhall		Season Record >>	415	382	6-6	ATS>>	7-5	O/U>>	6-6	

2020-Virginia		Opponent	UVA	Opp	S/U	Line	ATS	Total	O/U	
9/26/2020	vs	DUKE	38	20	W	-4.5	W	45.5	O	
10/3/2020	@	Clemson	23	41	L	27.5	W	55.5	O	
10/10/2020	vs	NC STATE	21	38	L	-7.0	L	58.5	O	
10/17/2020	@	Wake Forest	23	40	L	2.5	L	57.5	O	
10/24/2020	@	Miami	14	19	L	13.5	W	54.5	U	
10/31/2020	vs	NORTH CAROLINA	44	41	W	8.0	W	61.5	O	"South's Oldest Rivalry"
11/14/2020	vs	LOUISVILLE	31	17	W	-5.5	W	63.0	U	
11/21/2020	vs	ABILENE CHRISTIAN	55	15	W	-38.5	W	61.0	O	
12/5/2020	vs	BOSTON COLLEGE	43	32	W	-6.5	W	53.0	O	
12/12/2020	@	Virginia Tech	15	33	L	3.0	L	64.0	U	"Commonwealth Cup"
Coach: Bronco Mendenhall		Season Record >>	307	296	5-5	ATS>>	7-3	O/U>>	7-3	

2019-Virginia		Opponent	UVA	Opp	S/U	Line	ATS	Total	O/U	
8/31/2019	@	Pittsburgh	30	14	W	-2.5	W	45.5	U	
9/6/2019	vs	WILLIAM & MARY	52	17	W	-32.5	W	NT	---	
9/14/2019	vs	FLORIDA STATE	31	24	W	-7.0	T	54.5	O	"Jefferson-Eppes Trophy"
9/21/2019	vs	OLD DOMINION	28	17	W	-27.0	L	46.5	U	
9/28/2019	@	Notre Dame	20	35	L	11.0	L	46.5	O	
10/11/2019	@	Miami	9	17	L	3.0	L	43.5	U	
10/19/2019	vs	DUKE	48	14	W	-3.0	W	45.0	O	
10/26/2019	@	Louisville	21	28	L	-4.0	L	51.0	U	
11/2/2019	@	North Carolina	38	31	W	-1.0	W	47.5	O	"South's Oldest Rivalry"
11/9/2019	vs	GEORGIA TECH	33	28	W	-16.0	L	45.5	O	
11/23/2019	vs	LIBERTY	55	27	W	-16.0	W	58.0	O	
11/30/2019	vs	VIRGINIA TECH	39	30	W	2.5	W	48.5	O	"Commonwealth Cup"
12/7/2019	vs	Clemson	17	62	L	30.0	L	57.5	O	ACC Championship Game
12/30/2019	vs	Florida	28	36	L	16.5	W	55.0	O	Orange Bowl
Coach: Bronco Mendenhall		Season Record >>	449	380	9-5	ATS>>	7-6-1	O/U>>	9-4	

2018-Virginia		Opponent	UVA	Opp	S/U	Line	ATS	Total	O/U	
9/1/2018	vs	RICHMOND	42	13	W	-14.5	W	NT	---	
9/8/2018	@	Indiana	16	20	L	5.0	W	50.0	U	
9/15/2018	vs	OHIO	45	31	W	-5.5	W	53.5	O	
9/22/2018	vs	LOUISVILLE	27	3	W	-5.0	W	51.5	U	
9/29/2018	@	NC State	21	35	L	6.0	L	52.5	O	
10/13/2018	vs	MIAMI	16	13	W	7.0	W	46.5	O	
10/20/2018	@	Duke	28	14	W	6.5	W	44.5	U	
10/27/2018	vs	NORTH CAROLINA	31	21	W	-9.0	W	50.5	O	"South's Oldest Rivalry"
11/2/2018	vs	PITTSBURGH	13	23	L	-7.0	L	45.5	U	
11/10/2018	vs	LIBERTY	45	24	W	-23.5	L	59.0	O	
11/17/2018	@	Georgia Tech	27	30	L	6.5	W	52.0	O	{OT}
11/23/2018	@	Virginia Tech	31	34	L	-5.0	L	50.0	O	"Commonwealth Cup"
12/29/2018	vs	South Carolina	28	0	W	3.5	W	54.0	U	Belk Bowl
Coach: Bronco Mendenhall		Season Record >>	370	261	8-5	ATS>>	9-4	O/U>>	6-6	

VIRGINIA CAVALIERS — ACC Coastal

STADIUM: Scott Stadium {61,500} **Location:** Charlottesville, VA **COACH:** Tony Elliott

DATE		Opponent	UVA	Opp	S/U	Line	ATS	Total	O/U	Trends & Angles
9/3/2022	vs	RICHMOND								12-1 S/U @ home vs Richmond since 1945
9/10/2022	@	Illinois								vs Illinois - Illinois leads series 2-1
9/17/2022	vs	OLD DOMINION								vs Old Dominion - Virginia leads series 1-0
9/23/2022	@	Syracuse								3-0 S/U vs Syracuse as favorite since 2004
10/1/2022	@	Duke								vs Duke - Virginia leads series 40-33
10/8/2022	vs	LOUISVILLE								vs Louisville - Series tied 5-5
10/20/2022	@	Georgia Tech								0-5 S/U @ Georgia Tech as Dog since 2010
10/29/2022	vs	MIAMI								vs Miami - Miami leads series 11-8
11/5/2022	vs	NORTH CAROLINA								1-7 S/U vs UNC as Dog since 2010 {2-6 ATS}
11/12/2022	vs	PITTSBURGH								0-5 S/U vs Pittsburgh as Dog since 2006
11/19/2022	vs	COASTAL CAROLINA								1-8 ATS after playing Pittsburgh since 2006
11/26/2022	@	Virginia Tech								0-11 S/U @ Va Tech since 2000 {3-7-1 ATS}
12/3/2022	vs									ACC Championship
	vs									BOWL GAME

Pointspread Analysis — Non-Conference

- 0-7 S/U vs Non-Conf. as 15.5-20 point Dog since 1987
- 1-7 S/U vs Non-Conf. as 10.5-15 point Dog since 1987
- 4-1 ATS vs Non-Conf. as 10.5-15 point Dog since 2009
- 7-0 O/U vs Non-Conf. as 10.5-15 point Dog since 2008
- 10-2 ATS vs Non-Conf. as 3.5-7 point Dog since 2001
- 1-6 S/U vs Non-Conf. as 3 point or less Dog since 1988
- 9-1 O/U vs Non-Conf. as 3.5-7 point favorite since 1995
- 1-6 ATS vs Non-Conf. as 7.5-10 point favorite since 2000
- 7-2 S/U vs Non-Conf. as 7.5-10 point favorite since 1991
- 31-0 S/U vs Non-Conf. as 15.5 point or more favorite since 1990
- vs Richmond - Virginia leads series 28-3-3

Dog

- 0-16 S/U as 20.5 point or more Dog since 1987
- 1-15 S/U on road as 15.5-20 point Dog since 1983
- 0-4 S/U @ home as 15.5-20 point Dog since 1997
- 3-9 S/U @ home as 10.5-15 point Dog since 1984
- 1-11 S/U as 10.5-15 point Dog since 2013
- 0-11 S/U on road as 7.5-10 point Dog since 2000
- 1-11 S/U on road as 3.5-7 point Dog since 2008
- 4-13 O/U @ home as 3.5-7 point Dog since 2008

Favorite

- 4-0 S/U & ATS as 3 point or less favorite since 2017
- 20-5 S/U @ home as 7.5-10 point favorite since 1984
- 6-0 S/U on road as 7.5-10 point favorite since 1997
- 1-6 O/U as 7.5-10 point favorite since 2006
- 11-1 S/U @ home as 10.5-15 point favorite since 1995
- 19-0 S/U on road as 10.5 point or more favorite since 1985
- 15-0 S/U on road as 15.5 point or more favorite since 1990
- 32-1 S/U @ home as 20.5 point or more favorite since 1990

Bowl Games

- 11-2-1 O/U in Bowl Games since 1995
- 5-1 O/U vs SEC in Bowl Games since 1995
- 0-3 S/U & ATS in Bowl Games as 3 point or less Dog since 1990

Pointspread Analysis — Conference

- 3-0 S/U & ATS vs Duke as Dog since 2015
- vs Georgia Tech - Series tied 21-21-1
- 1-3 S/U vs Louisville as Dog since 2015
- 12-3 ATS vs Miami as Dog since 2005
- vs North Carolina - UNC leads series 64-57-4
- 9-1 S/U & ATS vs North Carolina as favorite since 1998
- vs Pittsburgh - PITT leads series 9-4
- vs Virginia Tech - Virginia Tech leads series 60-38-5
- 1-17 S/U vs Virginia Tech since 2004
- 1-18 S/U vs Virginia Tech as Dog since 1999
- 5-1 O/U vs Virginia Tech as favorite since 1995
- vs Wake Forest - Virginia leads series 34-17
- 0-5 S/U & ATS vs Wake Forest since 2008
- 17-1 S/U vs Duke as 9.5 point or more favorite since 1985
- 0-6 S/U vs Georgia Tech as 9.5-12 point Dog since 1991
- 15-0 S/U vs Wake Forest as 4.5 point or more favorite since 1984

Illinois	3-13 S/U in 1st road game of season since 2006
Duke	9-1 ATS prior to playing Louisville since 1988
LOUISVILLE	2-7 S/U after playing Duke since 2012
Georgia Tech	7-1 O/U after playing Louisville since 2014
MIAMI	1-12 S/U after playing Georgia Tech since 2008
MIAMI	3-10 ATS after playing Georgia Tech since 2008
MIAMI	10-4 O/U prior to playing North Carolina since 2008
N. CAROLINA	5-11 S/U after playing Miami since 2006
N. CAROLINA	6-1 O/U prior to playing Pittsburgh since 2007
PITTSBURGH	3-8 S/U after playing North Carolina since 2011
Virginia Tech	3-19 S/U in final road game of season since 2000
Virginia Tech	8-1 O/U in final road game of season since 2013

- 4-13 ATS on road when ranked since 1999
- 0-4 S/U when ranked in Bowl games since 1998
- 6-0 S/U when ranked vs Duke since 1995
- 5-0 S/U & ATS @ home when ranked vs North Carolina all time
- 2-26 S/U on road vs ranked teams since 2001
- 0-23 S/U vs Top #5 ranked teams
- 1-12 S/U vs ranked Virginia Tech since 1999

VIRGINIA TECH HOKIES   ACC Coastal

2021-Virginia Tech		Opponent	VPI	Opp	S/U	Line	ATS	Total	O/U	
9/2/2021	vs	NORTH CAROLINA	17	10	W	4.5	W	63.5	U	
9/11/2021	vs	MIDDLE TENNESSEE	35	14	W	-20.0	W	54.5	U	
9/18/2021	@	West Virginia	21	27	L	2.0	L	50.0	U	"Black Diamond Trophy"
9/25/2021	vs	RICHMOND	21	10	W	-28.5	L	50.0	U	
10/9/2021	vs	NOTRE DAME	29	32	L	-1.0	L	47.0	O	
10/16/2021	vs	PITTSBURGH	7	28	L	6.0	L	56.0	U	
10/23/2021	vs	SYRACUSE	36	41	L	-3.5	L	45.5	O	
10/30/2021	@	Georgia Tech	26	17	W	3.0	W	55.5	O	"Battle of the Techs"
11/5/2021	@	Boston College	3	17	L	-1.0	L	51.0	U	
11/13/2021	vs	DUKE	48	17	W	-13.5	W	50.5	O	
11/20/2021	@	Miami	26	38	L	7.0	L	55.5	O	
11/27/2021	@	Virginia	29	24	W	7.0	W	63.5	U	"Commonwealth Cup"
12/29/2021	vs	**Maryland**	10	54	L	4.5	L	56.0	O	Pinstripe Bowl
Coach: Justin Fuente		Season Record >>	308	329	6-7	ATS>>	5-8	O/U>>	5-8	
2020-Virginia Tech		Opponent	VPI	Opp	S/U	Line	ATS	Total	O/U	
9/26/2020	vs	NC STATE	45	24	W	-6.5	W	57.5	O	
10/3/2020	@	Duke	38	31	W	-10.5	L	54.0	O	
10/10/2020	@	North Carolina	45	56	L	3.0	L	58.5	O	
10/17/2020	vs	BOSTON COLLEGE	40	14	W	-13.5	W	61.5	U	
10/24/2020	@	Wake Forest	16	23	L	-10.5	L	69.0	U	
10/31/2020	@	Louisville	42	35	W	-2.5	W	67.5	O	
11/7/2020	vs	LIBERTY	35	38	L	-16.5	L	67.5	O	
11/14/2020	vs	MIAMI	24	25	L	-2.0	L	67.5	O	
11/21/2020	@	Pittsburgh	14	47	L	-6.0	L	52.0	O	
12/5/2020	vs	CLEMSON	10	45	L	23.0	L	66.5	U	
12/12/2020	vs	VIRGINIA	33	15	W	-3.0	W	64.0	U	"Commonwealth Cup"
Coach: Justin Fuente		Season Record >>	342	353	5-6	ATS>>	4-7	O/U>>	6-5	
2019-Virginia Tech		Opponent	VPI	Opp	S/U	Line	ATS	Total	O/U	
8/31/2019	@	Boston College	28	35	L	-4.0	L	58.0	O	
9/7/2019	vs	OLD DOMINION	31	17	W	-28.5	L	56.5	U	
9/14/2019	vs	FURMAN	24	17	W	-23.5	L	NT	---	
9/27/2019	vs	DUKE	10	45	L	-2.5	L	51.5	O	
10/5/2019	@	Miami	42	35	W	14.0	W	45.0	U	
10/12/2019	vs	RHODE ISLAND	34	17	W	-26.5	L	NT	---	
10/19/2019	vs	NORTH CAROLINA	43	41	W	4.0	W	57.0	O	{6 OT}
11/2/2019	@	Notre Dame	20	21	L	17.5	W	58.0	U	
11/9/2019	vs	WAKE FOREST	36	17	W	2.5	W	60.0	U	
11/16/2019	@	Georgia Tech	45	0	W	-6.0	W	51.5	U	"Battle of the Techs"
11/23/2019	vs	PITTSBURGH	28	0	W	-4.0	W	43.5	U	
11/29/2019	@	Virginia	30	39	L	-2.5	L	48.5	O	"Commonwealth Cup"
12/31/2019	vs	**Kentucky**	30	37	L	-2.0	L	46.0	O	Belk Bowl
Coach: Justin Fuente		Season Record >>	401	321	8-5	ATS>>	6-7	O/U>>	6-5	
2018-Virginia Tech		Opponent	VPI	Opp	S/U	Line	ATS	Total	O/U	
9/3/2018	@	Florida State	24	3	W	7.5	W	54.0	U	
9/8/2018	vs	WILLIAM & MARY	62	17	W	-42.0	W	NT	---	
9/22/2018	@	Old Dominion	35	49	L	-29.0	L	53.0	O	
9/29/2018	@	Duke	31	14	W	6.5	W	52.5	U	
10/6/2018	vs	NOTRE DAME	23	45	L	6.5	L	55.0	O	
10/13/2018	@	North Carolina	22	19	W	-6.5	L	57.5	U	
10/25/2018	vs	GEORGIA TECH	28	49	L	-3.0	L	58.5	O	"Battle of the Techs"
11/3/2018	vs	BOSTON COLLEGE	21	31	L	2.0	L	57.0	U	
11/10/2018	@	Pittsburgh	22	52	L	3.0	L	54.0	O	
11/17/2018	vs	MIAMI	14	38	L	6.5	L	52.5	U	
11/23/2018	vs	VIRGINIA	34	31	W	5.0	W	50.0	O	"Commonwealth Cup"
12/1/2018	vs	MARSHALL	41	20	W	-4.0	W	51.5	O	
12/31/2018	vs	**Cincinnati**	31	35	L	5.5	W	48.5	O	Military Bowl
Coach: Justin Fuente		Season Record >>	388	403	6-7	ATS>>	6-7	O/U>>	7-5	

VIRGINIA TECH HOKIES — ACC Coastal

STADIUM: Lane Stadium {65,632} **Location:** Blacksburg, VA **COACH:** Brent Pry

DATE		Opponent	VPI	Opp	S/U	Line	ATS	Total	O/U	Trends & Angles
9/2/2022	@	Old Dominion								vs Old Dominion - Virginia leads series 2-1
9/10/2022	vs	BOSTON COLLEGE								vs Boston College - VPI leads series 19-11
9/17/2022	vs	WOFFORD								23-3 S/U in 2nd home game of season since 1996
9/24/2022	vs	WEST VIRGINIA								6-1 ATS vs West Virginia as Dog since 1986
10/1/2022	vs	NORTH CAROLINA								vs North Carolina - VPI leads series 24-14-6
10/8/2022	@	Pittsburgh								vs Pittsburgh - VPI leads series 11-10
10/15/2022	vs	MIAMI								vs Miami - Miami leads series 24-15
10/27/2022	@	NC State								9-1 O/U after playing Miami since 2011
11/5/2022	vs	GEORGIA TECH								2-9 ATS vs Georgia Tech as favorite since 2006
11/12/2022	@	Duke								6-0 S/U @ Duke as favorite since 2005
11/19/2022	@	Liberty								vs Liberty - Liberty leads series 1-0
11/26/2022	vs	VIRGINIA								18-1 S/U vs Virginia as favorite since 1999
12/3/2022	vs									ACC Championship
	vs									BOWL GAME

Pointspread Analysis — Non-Conference

- 2-11 S/U vs Non-Conf. as 3.5-7 point Dog since 1987
- 14-3 S/U vs Non-Conf. as 3.5-7 point favorite since 1994
- 8-2 S/U vs Non-Conf. as 15.5-20 point favorite since 2003
- 43-1 S/U vs Non-Conf. as 20.5-30 point favorite since 1987
- 5-0 S/U vs W. Virginia as 2-5 point favorite since 1995
- 4-0 S/U vs W. Virginia as 15 point or more favorite since 1994
- vs West Virginia - WVU leads series 29-23-1

Dog
- 0-9 S/U as 20.5 point or more Dog since 1987
- 5-2 ATS as 20.5 point or more Dog since 1988
- 1-14 S/U as 15.5-20 point Dog since 1985
- 0-10 S/U @ home as 10.5 point or more Dog since 1987
- 7-0 O/U as 10.5-15 point Dog since 2007
- 2-6 S/U as 7.5-10 point Dog since 1989
- 2-5 ATS as 7.5-10 point Dog since 1991

Favorite
- 7-3 O/U as 3 point or less favorite since 2017
- 2-8 S/U & ATS as 3 point or less favorite since 2017
- 21-5 S/U on road as 3.5-7 point since 1994
- 18-8 ATS on road as 3.5-7 point favorite since 1994
- 4-13 ATS as 7.5-10 point favorite since 2006
- 7-2 S/U on road as 7.5-10 point favorite since 1984
- 0-4 ATS on road as 7.5-10 point favorite since 2008
- 3-12 ATS as 10.5-15 point favorite since 2010
- 9-3 S/U on road as 10.5-15 point favorite since 2005
- 13-3 S/U @ home as 15.5-20 point favorite since 2003
- 8-1 S/U on road as 15.5-20 point favorite since 1997
- 1-5 ATS on road as 15.5-20 point favorite since 2001
- 14-2 S/U on road as 20.5 point or more favorite since 1996
- 44-0 S/U @ home as 20.5-30 point favorite since 1985
- 33-1 S/U as 20.5-25 point favorite since 1987
- 23-1 S/U as 25.5-30 point favorite since 1985

Bowl Games
- 0-3 S/U in Sugar Bowl since 2000
- 3-0 S/U in Peach Bowl since 1986
- 0-3 S/U in Orange Bowl since 2008
- 0-11 S/U in Bowl Games as 3.5-20 point Dog since 1981
- 1-10 ATS in Bowl Games as 3.5-20 point Dog since 1981
- 4-1 S/U & ATS in Bowl Games as 3 point or less Dog since 1986
- 7-1-1 ATS when ranked vs Virginia since 2004
- 2-13 S/U @ home vs ranked teams since 2010
- 0-9 S/U vs #1 ranked teams all time

Pointspread Analysis — Conference

- vs Duke - VPI leads series 18-10
- vs Georgia Tech - VPI leads series 11-7
- 4-0 S/U vs Georgia Tech as Dog since 2007
- 5-0 ATS vs Georgia Tech as Dog since 1990
- 0-4 O/U vs Georgia Tech as Dog since 2007
- 1-4 S/U vs Georgia Tech as favorite since 2014
- 1-5 S/U & ATS vs Miami as Dog since 2014
- 2-9 O/U vs Miami as Dog since 2014
- 5-2 S/U @ home vs Miami as favorite since 1997
- 4-0 S/U & ATS vs NC State as favorite since 2005
- 11-1 S/U vs North Carolina as favorite since 2004
- 2-11 ATS vs Pittsburgh as favorite since 1999
- 0-5 S/U vs Syracuse as Dog since 1987 {1-4 ATS}
- vs Virginia - Virginia Tech leads series 60-38-5
- 10-1 S/U @ Virginia as favorite since 1983
- 15-1 S/U vs Duke as 7.5 point or more favorite since 1983
- 13-1 S/U vs Boston College as 6.5 point or more favorite since 1997
- 1-7 S/U vs Miami as 14 point or more Dog since 1987
- 6-0 S/U @ home vs PITT as 14 point or more favorite since 1994
- 9-2 ATS vs Virginia as 4 point or more Dog since 1985

Old Dominion	11-3 S/U in 1st road game of season since 2008
Old Dominion	1-8 S/U prior to playing Boston College since 2012
Old Dominion	1-7 ATS prior to playing Boston College since 2013
BOSTON COLLEGE	24-2 S/U in 1st home game of season since 1996
WOFFORD	3-10-1 O/U in 2nd home game of season since 2006
WOFFORD	10-2 S/U after playing Boston College since 2010
WEST VIRGINIA	13-3 S/U prior to playing North Carolina since 2004
Pittsburgh	1-8 O/U after playing North Carolina since 2013
Pittsburgh	13-4 S/U after playing North Carolina since 2004
MIAMI	2-9 O/U after playing Pittsburgh since 2003
NC State	2-7 ATS after playing Miami since 2013
NC State	1-8-1 O/U prior to playing Georgia Tech since 2010
Duke	8-3 S/U after playing Georgia Tech since 2010
Liberty	2-8 S/U & ATS after playing Duke since 2012
Liberty	9-2 S/U in final road game of season since 2009
VIRGINIA	16-2 S/U in final home game of season since 2004

- 7-23 O/U @ home when ranked since 2008
- 8-1 S/U when ranked vs Duke all time {5-0 on road}
- 0-6 ATS when ranked @ Pittsburgh all time

WAKE FOREST DEMON DEACONS ACC Atlantic

2021-Wake Forest		Opponent	Wake	Opp	S/U	Line	ATS	Total	O/U	
9/3/2021	vs	OLD DOMINION	42	10	W	-32.0	T	61.0	U	
9/11/2021	vs	NORFOLK STATE	41	16	W	-43.0	L	58.0	U	
9/18/2021	vs	FLORIDA STATE	35	14	W	-4.5	W	62.5	U	
9/24/2021	@	Virginia	37	17	W	3.5	W	70.0	U	
10/2/2021	vs	LOUISVILLE	37	34	W	-7.0	L	64.0	O	
10/9/2021	@	Syracuse	40	37	W	-5.5	L	58.5	O	{OT}
10/23/2021	@	Army	70	56	W	-3.0	W	54.0	O	
10/30/2021	vs	DUKE	45	7	W	-16.0	W	76.0	U	
11/6/2021	@	North Carolina	55	58	L	2.0	L	78.0	O	
11/13/2021	vs	NC STATE	45	42	W	-1.0	W	64.0	O	
11/20/2021	@	Clemson	27	48	L	3.5	L	57.0	O	
11/27/2021	@	Boston College	41	10	W	-5.0	W	64.0	O	
12/4/2021	vs	Pittsburgh	21	45	L	3.5	L	74.0	O	ACC Championship Game
12/31/2021	vs	Rutgers	38	10	W	-17.0	W	62.5	U	Gator Bowl
Coach: Dave Clawson		Season Record >>	574	404	11-3	ATS>>	7-6-1	O/U>>	6-8	

2020-Wake Forest		Opponent	Wake	Opp	S/U	Line	ATS	Total	O/U	
9/12/2020	vs	CLEMSON	13	37	L	34.0	W	59.0	U	
9/19/2020	@	NC State	42	45	L	-2.5	L	53.0	O	
10/2/2020	vs	CAMPBELL	66	14	W	-34.0	W	69.0	O	
10/17/2020	vs	VIRGINIA	40	23	W	-2.5	W	57.5	O	
10/24/2020	vs	VIRGINIA TECH	23	16	W	10.5	W	69.0	U	
10/31/2020	@	Syracuse	38	14	W	-14.0	W	59.5	U	
11/14/2020	@	North Carolina	53	59	L	13.0	W	70.5	O	
12/12/2020	@	Louisville	21	45	L	-2.0	L	61.0	O	
12/30/2020	vs	Wisconsin	28	42	L	10.5	L	51.5	O	Duke's Mayo Bowl
Coach: Dave Clawson		Season Record >>	324	295	4-5	ATS>>	6-3	O/U>>	6-3	

2019-Wake Forest		Opponent	Wake	Opp	S/U	Line	ATS	Total	O/U	
8/30/2019	vs	UTAH STATE	38	35	W	-5.0	L	60.0	O	
9/7/2019	@	Rice	41	21	W	-19.5	W	58.5	O	
9/12/2019	vs	NORTH CAROLINA	24	18	W	-3.0	W	65.0	U	
9/21/2019	vs	ELON	49	7	W	-30.0	W	NT	---	
9/28/2019	@	Boston College	27	24	W	-5.0	L	69.5	U	
10/12/2019	vs	LOUISVILLE	59	62	L	-7.0	L	65.5	O	
10/19/2019	vs	FLORIDA STATE	22	20	W	3.0	W	69.0	U	
11/2/2019	vs	NC STATE	44	10	W	-7.5	W	60.5	U	
11/9/2019	@	Virginia Tech	17	36	L	-2.5	L	60.0	U	
11/16/2019	@	Clemson	3	52	L	34.5	L	59.0	U	
11/23/2019	vs	DUKE	39	27	W	-6.0	W	50.0	O	
11/30/2019	@	Syracuse	30	39	L	-6.5	L	66.5	O	{OT}
12/27/2019	vs	Michigan State	21	27	L	4.0	L	51.5	U	Pinstripe Bowl
Coach: Dave Clawson		Season Record >>	414	378	8-5	ATS>>	6-7	O/U>>	5-7	

2018-Wake Forest		Opponent	Wake	Opp	S/U	Line	ATS	Total	O/U	
8/30/2018	@	Tulane	23	17	W	-7.0	L	55.5	U	{OT}
9/8/2018	vs	TOWSON	51	20	W	-34.0	L	NT	---	
9/13/2018	vs	BOSTON COLLEGE	34	41	L	6.5	L	57.5	O	
9/22/2018	vs	NOTRE DAME	27	56	L	6.0	L	59.5	O	
9/29/2018	vs	RICE	56	24	W	-27.5	W	66.0	O	
10/6/2018	vs	CLEMSON	3	63	L	20.5	L	61.0	O	
10/20/2018	@	Florida State	17	38	L	10.5	L	57.5	O	
10/27/2018	@	Louisville	56	35	W	2.5	W	67.5	O	
11/3/2018	vs	SYRACUSE	24	41	L	6.5	L	77.5	O	
11/8/2018	@	NC State	27	23	W	19.0	W	66.5	U	
11/17/2018	vs	PITTSBURGH	13	34	L	5.0	L	62.5	U	
11/24/2018	@	Duke	59	7	W	9.5	W	60.5	O	
12/22/2018	vs	Memphis	37	34	W	2.0	W	71.5	U	Birmingham Bowl
Coach: Dave Clawson		Season Record >>	427	433	7-6	ATS>>	5-7	O/U>>	6-6	

WAKE FOREST DEMON DEACONS ACC Atlantic

STADIUM: BB&T Field {31,500}   Location: Winston-Salem, NC   **COACH:** Dave Clawson

DATE		Opponent	Wake	Opp	S/U	Line	ATS	Total	O/U	Trends & Angles
9/1/2022	vs	VIRGINIA MILITARY								3-0 S/U vs VMI since 1942
9/10/2022	@	Vanderbilt								vs Vanderbilt - Vanderbilt leads series 10-6
9/17/2022	vs	LIBERTY								vs Liberty - Wake Forest leads series 2-0
9/24/2022	vs	CLEMSON								0-7 S/U @ home vs Clemson as Dog since 2006
10/1/2022	@	Florida State								1-7 S/U vs Florida State as Dog since 2012
10/8/2022	vs	ARMY								8-1 S/U vs Army as favorite since 1992
10/22/2022	vs	BOSTON COLLEGE								vs Boston College - BC leads series 14-12-2
10/29/2022	@	Louisville								vs Louisville - Louisville leads series 6-3
11/5/2022	@	NC State								vs NC State - NC State leads series 67-42-6
11/12/2022	vs	NORTH CAROLINA								vs North Carolina - UNC leads series 69-37-2
11/19/2022	vs	SYRACUSE								5-1 S/U vs Syracuse as favorite since 2006
11/26/2022	@	Duke								5-0 S/U @ Duke as favorite since 2001
12/3/2022	vs									ACC Championship
	vs									BOWL GAME

Pointspread Analysis — Non-Conference
- 5-1 ATS vs Non-Conf. as 15.5-20 point Dog since 1985
- 6-1 ATS vs Non-Conf. as 7.5-10 point Dog since 1995
- 11-0 S/U vs Non-Conf. as 3.5-7 point favorite since 1991
- 1-6 S/U vs Vanderbilt as Dog since 1993

Dog
- 0-26 S/U as 25.5 point or more Dog since 1983
- 1-24 S/U as 20.5-25 point Dog since 1989
- 0-14 S/U @ home as 20.5 point or more Dog since 1990
- 1-36 S/U on road as 20.5 point or more Dog since 1983
- 7-1 ATS as 20.5-25 point Dog since 2013
- 2-7 O/U as 20.5-25 point Dog since 2012
- 2-17 S/U on road as 15.5-20 point Dog since 1983
- 3-8 ATS on road as 15.5-20 point Dog since 2003
- 1-10 S/U @ home as 15.5-20 point Dog since 1983
- 0-9 S/U on road as 10.5-15 point Dog since 2004
- 4-18 S/U @ home as 10.5-15 point Dog since 1993
- 1-9 O/U @ home as 10.5-15 point Dog since 2002
- 8-2 ATS on road as 10.5-15 point Dog since 2003
- 8-2 O/U on road as 10.5-15 point Dog since 2003
- 3-7 O/U @ home as 3.5-7 point Dog since 2013
- 0-8 S/U @ home as 3.5-7 point Dog since 2013
- 0-7-1 ATS @ home as 3.5-7 point Dog since 2013
- 2-14 S/U as 3.5-7 point Dog since 2013

Favorite
- 13-1 S/U @ home as 3.5-7 point favorite since 2007
- 9-4-1 ATS @ home as 3.5-7 point favorite since 2007
- 11-1 S/U on road as 7.5 point or more favorite since 1984
- 30-1 S/U @ home as 7.5 point or more favorite since 1989

Bowl Games
- 9-4 S/U & ATS in Bowl Games since 1992

- 2-46 S/U on road vs ranked teams since 1980
- 0-9 S/U vs #1 ranked teams all time
- 0-25 S/U vs #5 - #9 ranked teams all time
- 0-28 S/U vs ranked Clemson since 1948
- 1-12 S/U @ ranked Florida State all time
- 0-7 S/U vs ranked North Carolina since 1980

Pointspread Analysis — Conference
- 0-3 S/U @ home vs Boston College as Dog since 2010
- vs Clemson - Clemson leads series 69-17-1
- vs Duke - Duke leads series 58-41-2
- vs Florida State - FSU leads series 30-8-1
- 0-6 O/U vs Florida State as Dog since 2014
- 5-0 ATS vs Louisville as Dog since 2014
- 1-6 S/U & ATS @ home vs North Carolina as Dog since 1986
- 6-0 S/U & ATS @ home vs NC State as favorite since 1987
- vs Syracuse - Syracuse leads series 6-5
- 0-5 S/U & ATS vs Syracuse as Dog since 2011
- Game 3-0 O/U vs Virginia as favorite since 2002
- 0-19 S/U vs Clemson as 16 point or more Dog since 1983
- 11-4 ATS vs Clemson as 16 point or more Dog since 1990
- 0-3 S/U & ATS vs Duke as 13 point or more Dog since 1989
- 0-21 S/U vs Florida State as 10.5 point or more Dog since 1992
- 0-8 S/U vs North Carolina as 17 point or more Dog since 1983
- 0-5 S/U & ATS vs North Carolina as 4.5-9 point Dog since 1986
- 1-14 S/U vs NC State as 9 point or more Dog since 1990
- 9-2 ATS vs NC State as 7 point or less Dog since 1984
- 0-15 S/U vs Virginia as 4.5 point or more Dog since 1984
- 12-1 S/U vs Duke as 6 point or more favorite since 1984

VMI	11-1 S/U in 1st home game of season since 2010
LIBERTY	14-4 S/U in 2nd home game of season since 2004
LIBERTY	8-1-1 ATS prior to playing Clemson since 2011
LIBERTY	2-9 O/U prior to playing Clemson since 2010
Florida State	3-11 O/U in 2nd road game of season since 2008
Florida State	2-6 S/U & ATS after playing Clemson since 2014
ARMY	1-7 O/U after playing Florida State since 2013
ARMY	1-5 O/U prior to playing Boston College since 2012
Louisville	0-6 S/U after playing Boston College since 2012
UNC	2-8 O/U after playing NC State since 2012
SYRACUSE	4-9 S/U & ATS in final home game of season since 2009
Duke	2-5 O/U after playing Syracuse since 2014

WASHINGTON HUSKIES   PACIFIC-12 North

2021-Washington		Opponent	UW	Opp	S/U	Line	ATS	Total	O/U	
9/4/2021	vs	MONTANA	7	13	L	-22.5	L	54.0	U	
9/11/2021	@	Michigan	10	31	L	6.5	L	47.5	U	
9/18/2021	vs	ARKANSAS STATE	52	3	W	-17.5	W	58.5	U	
9/25/2021	vs	CALIFORNIA	31	24	W	-7.5	L	47.5	O	{OT}
10/2/2021	@	Oregon State	24	27	L	2.5	L	58.0	U	
10/16/2021	vs	UCLA	17	24	L	-2.0	L	55.0	U	
10/22/2021	@	Arizona	21	16	W	-17.0	L	45.5	U	
10/30/2021	@	Stanford	20	13	W	2.5	W	46.0	U	
11/6/2021	vs	OREGON	16	26	L	7.0	L	48.5	U	
11/13/2021	vs	ARIZONA STATE	30	35	L	6.0	W	45.5	O	
11/20/2021	@	Colorado	17	20	L	-6.5	L	43.0	U	
11/27/2021	vs	WASHINGTON STATE	13	40	L	2.0	L	45.5	O	"Apple Cup"
Coach: Jimmy Lake		Season Record >>	258	272	4-8	ATS>>	3-9	O/U>>	3-9	
2020-Washington		Opponent	UW	Opp	S/U	Line	ATS	Total	O/U	
11/14/2020	vs	OREGON STATE	27	21	W	-13.5	L	51.0	U	
11/21/2020	vs	ARIZONA	44	27	W	-12.5	W	53.5	O	
11/28/2020	vs	UTAH	24	21	W	-9.5	L	47.0	U	
12/5/2020	vs	STANFORD	26	31	L	-12.0	L	49.5	O	
Coach: Jimmy Lake		Season Record >>	121	100	3-1	ATS>>	1-3	O/U>>	2-2	
2019-Washington		Opponent	UW	Opp	S/U	Line	ATS	Total	O/U	
8/31/2019	vs	EASTERN WASHINGTON	47	14	W	-24.5	W	NT	---	
9/7/2019	vs	CALIFORNIA	19	20	L	-13.5	L	43.0	U	
9/14/2019	vs	HAWAII	52	20	W	-21.5	W	59.0	O	
9/21/2019	@	Byu	45	19	W	-6.5	W	51.0	O	
9/28/2019	vs	USC	28	14	W	-11.0	W	60.5	U	
10/5/2019	@	Stanford	13	23	L	-12.5	L	52.0	U	
10/12/2019	@	Arizona	51	27	W	-6.0	W	62.0	O	
10/19/2019	vs	OREGON	31	35	L	2.5	L	48.5	O	
11/2/2019	vs	UTAH	28	33	L	3.0	L	48.0	O	
11/8/2019	@	Oregon State	19	7	W	-10.5	W	64.5	U	
11/23/2019	@	Colorado	14	20	L	-14.0	L	53.0	U	
11/29/2019	vs	WASHINGTON STATE	31	13	W	-7.0	W	65.0	U	"Apple Cup"
12/21/2019	vs	Boise State	38	7	W	-4.0	W	48.0	U	Las Vegas Bowl
Coach: Chris Peterson		Season Record >>	416	252	8-5	ATS>>	8-5	O/U>>	5-7	
2018-Washington		Opponent	UW	Opp	S/U	Line	ATS	Total	O/U	
9/1/2018	vs	Auburn	16	21	L	1.5	L	50.5	U	Mercedes Benz Stadium
9/8/2018	vs	NORTH DAKOTA	45	3	W	-46.0	L	NT	---	
9/15/2018	@	Utah	21	7	W	-4.0	W	46.0	U	
9/22/2018	vs	ARIZONA STATE	27	20	W	-18.5	L	53.0	U	
9/29/2018	vs	BYU	35	7	W	-19.0	W	47.5	U	
10/6/2018	@	Ucla	31	24	W	-21.5	L	53.5	O	
10/13/2018	@	Oregon	27	30	L	-3.5	L	58.0	U	
10/20/2018	vs	COLORADO	27	13	W	-17.0	L	50.5	U	
10/27/2018	@	California	10	12	L	-11.5	L	45.5	U	
11/3/2018	vs	STANFORD	27	23	W	-9.5	L	44.0	O	
11/17/2018	vs	OREGON STATE	42	23	W	-32.5	L	58.5	O	
11/23/2018	@	Washington State	28	15	W	3.0	W	49.5	U	"Apple Cup"
11/30/2018	vs	Utah	10	3	W	-4.5	W	46.0	U	PACIFIC 12 Championship
1/1/2019	vs	Ohio State	23	28	L	5.5	W	55.0	U	Rose Bowl
Coach: Chris Peterson		Season Record >>	369	229	10-4	ATS>>	5-9	O/U>>	3-10	PACIFIC 12 Champions

Page | 250   Copyright © 2022 by Steve's Football Bible, LLC

WASHINGTON HUSKIES — PACIFIC-12 North

STADIUM: Husky Stadium {70,083} **Location:** Seattle, WA **COACH:** Kalen DeBoer

DATE		Opponent	Wash	Opp	S/U	Line	ATS	Total	O/U	Trends & Angles
9/3/2022	vs	KENT STATE								11-1 S/U in 1st home game of season since 2010
9/10/2022	vs	PORTLAND STATE								vs Portland State - Washington leads series 2-0
9/17/2022	vs	MICHIGAN STATE								vs Michigan State - Washington leads series 2-1
9/24/2022	vs	STANFORD								vs Stanford - Series tied 44-44-4
10/1/2022	@	Ucla								0-6 S/U @ UCLA as Dog since 1997
10/8/2022	@	Arizona State								0-10 S/U vs ASU as Dog since 2002 {1-9 ATS}
10/15/2022	vs	ARIZONA								7-0 S/U vs Arizona as favorite since 2011
10/22/2022	@	California								0-5 O/U vs California as Dog since 2009
11/5/2022	vs	OREGON STATE								vs Oregon St - Washington leads series 67-35-4
11/12/2022	@	Oregon								vs Oregon - Washington leads series 59-48-6
11/19/2022	vs	COLORADO								7-2 S/U vs Colorado as favorite since 1985
11/26/2022	@	Washington State								7-2 ATS vs Washington State as Dog since 1988
12/2/2022	vs									PAC-12 Championship
	vs									BOWL GAME

Pointspread Analysis — Non-Conference
- 0-6 S/U vs Non-Conf. as 15.5 point or more Dog since 2001
- 1-10 S/U vs Non-Conf. as 10.5-15 point Dog since 1996
- 0-6 S/U vs Non-Conf. as 7.5-10 point Dog since 1981
- 14-3 S/U vs Non-Conf. as 3.5-7 point favorite since 1983
- 13-0 S/U vs Non-Conf. as 7.5-15 point favorite since 1984
- 9-1 S/U vs Non-Conf. as 15.5-20 point favorite since 1983
- 2-7 ATS vs Non-Conf. as 15.5-20 point favorite since 1983
- 36-1 S/U vs Non-Conf. as 20.5 point or more favorite since 1984

Dog
- 0-15 S/U as 20.5 point or more Dog since 2001
- 0-5 ATS as 20.5-25 point Dog since 2008
- 1-7 S/U on road as 15.5-20 point Dog since 2004
- 1-12 S/U on road as 10.5-15 point Dog since 2004
- 0-7 S/U @ home as 10.5-15 point Dog since 1988
- 0-6 O/U as 10.5-15 point Dog since 2010
- 4-11 ATS as 10.5-15 point Dog since 2006
- 0-6 S/U @ home as 7.5-10 point Dog since 2004
- 4-17 S/U as 7.5-10 point Dog since 1981
- 0-6 S/U as 3.5-7 point Dog since 2014
- 2-6 S/U & ATS on road as 3 point or less Dog since 1997
- 3-8 O/U @ home as 3 point or less Dog since 2001

Favorite
- 4-13 ATS as 3 point or less favorite since 2002
- 12-5 S/U on road as 3.5-7 point favorite since 1995
- 8-0 S/U & ATS @ home as 3.5-7 point favorite since 2011
- 12-3 S/U & ATS vs PAC-12 as 3.5-7 point favorite since 2010
- 14-3 S/U @ home as 7.5-10 point favorite since 1984
- 21-3 S/U @ home as 10.5-15 point favorite since 1992
- 10-2 S/U on road as 15.5-20 point favorite since 1983
- 24-3 S/U @ home as 15.5-20 point favorite since 1983
- 4-13 ATS @ home as 15.5-20 point favorite since 1997
- 10-0 S/U on road as 20.5 point or more favorite since 1984
- 50-2 S/U @ home as 20.5 point or more favorite since 1986

Bowl Games
- 3-0 ATS in Holiday Bowl since 1999
- 0-3 S/U in Sun Bowl since 1986
- 0-3 S/U vs Alabama in Bowl Games
- 3-0 ATS in Bowl Games as 10.5-15 point Dog since 1978
- 0-3 S/U in Bowl Games as 7.5-10 point Dog since 1981
- 0-4 S/U in Bowl Games as 3.5-7 point Dog since 1996
- 3-1 O/U in Bowl Games as 3.5-7 point Dog since 1996
- 0-3 S/U & ATS in Bowl Games as 3 point or less Dog since 1983
- 3-0 O/U in Bowl Games as 3 point or less favorite since 1989

Pointspread Analysis — Conference
- vs Arizona - Washington leads series 24-11-1
- 0-4 S/U @ Arizona as Dog since 2008
- vs Arizona State - ASU leads series 21-16
- vs California - Washington leads series 53-41-4
- 3-0 S/U & ATS @ California as Dog since 2010
- 19-3 S/U vs California as favorite since 1984
- vs Colorado - Washington leads series 12-8-1
- 3-0 S/U & ATS vs Colorado as Dog since 1999
- vs Oregon - Washington leads series 59-48-6
- 1-6 S/U & ATS vs Oregon State as Dog since 2004
- 2-7 S/U vs Stanford as Dog since 2004
- vs UCLA - UCLA leads series 41-32-2
- vs Washington State - Washington leads series 74-33-6
- 7-1 S/U vs Washington State since 2013
- 6-1 ATS vs Washington State since 2014
- 8-1 S/U vs Arizona as 9 point or more favorite since 1990
- 6-1 S/U vs Arizona State as 15 point or more favorite since 1991
- 8-1 S/U vs Oregon as 10 point or more favorite since 1983
- 16-0 S/U vs Oregon State as 10 point or more favorite since 1986
- 13-3 S/U vs Stanford as 7 point or more favorite since 1983
- 0-8 S/U vs UCLA as 6 point or more Dog since 1987
- 5-0 S/U vs Wash. State as 16 point or more favorite since 1986
- 7-0 S/U vs Wash. State as 7.5-13 point favorite since 1993
- 10-1 S/U in 2nd home game of season since 2011
- 10-4 O/U in 2nd home game of season since 2008
- 9-2 S/U prior to playing Stanford since 2011
- 3-10 O/U in 1st road game of season since 2008
- 7-1 S/U after playing Arizona State since 2010
- 4-9 S/U prior to playing Oregon State since 2008
- 9-1 S/U prior to playing Oregon since 2011
- 9-1 ATS prior to playing Oregon since 2011
- 8-2 S/U after playing Oregon State since 2011
- 2-8 S/U after playing Oregon since 2011
- 1-7 ATS after playing Oregon since 2013
- 7-2 S/U prior to playing Washington State since 2012
- 11-2 S/U in final home game of season since 2009
- 12-5-1 O/U in final road game of season since 2003
- 2-7 S/U after playing Colorado since 2000
- 5-26 S/U on road vs ranked teams since 2004
- 0-13 S/U vs ranked Oregon since 2005 {0-7 on road}
- 0-13 ATS vs ranked Oregon since 2005 {0-7 on road}
- 1-12 S/U @ ranked UCLA since 1953
- 42-5 S/U @ home when ranked since 2000

Opponent column indicators: PORTLAND STATE, PORTLAND STATE, MICHIGAN STATE, Ucla, ARIZONA, California, OREGON STATE, OREGON STATE, Oregon, COLORADO, COLORADO, COLORADO, Washington State, Washington State

WASHINGTON STATE COUGARS   PACIFIC-12 North

2021-Washington State		Opponent	Wazzu	Opp	S/U	Line	ATS	Total	O/U	
9/4/2021	vs	UTAH STATE	23	26	L	-17.0	L	66.0	U	
9/11/2021	vs	PORTLAND STATE	44	24	W	-31.0	L	66.0	O	
9/18/2021	vs	USC	14	45	L	7.0	L	61.0	U	
9/25/2021	@	Utah	13	24	L	15.0	W	53.5	U	
10/2/2021	@	California	21	6	W	7.5	W	52.5	U	
10/9/2021	vs	OREGON STATE	31	24	W	4.5	W	59.0	U	
10/16/2021	vs	STANFORD	34	31	W	-1.5	W	53.0	O	
10/23/2021	vs	BYU	19	21	L	3.5	W	56.5	U	
10/30/2021	@	Arizona State	34	21	W	16.5	W	55.0	T	
11/13/2021	@	Oregon	24	38	L	13.5	L	58.5	O	
11/19/2021	vs	ARIZONA	44	18	W	-14.5	W	52.0	O	
11/27/2021	@	Washington	40	13	W	-2.0	W	45.5	O	"Apple Cup"
12/31/2021	vs	**Central Michigan**	21	24	L	-5.5	L	55.5	U	Sun Bowl
Coach: Nick Rolovich		Season Record >>	362	315	7-6	ATS>>	8-5	O/U>>	5-7-1	

2020-Washington State		Opponent	Wazzu	Opp	S/U	Line	ATS	Total	O/U	
11/7/2020	@	Oregon State	38	28	W	3.5	W	64.0	O	
11/14/2020	vs	OREGON	29	43	L	10.0	L	58.5	O	
12/6/2020	@	Usc	13	38	L	11.0	L	68.0	U	
12/19/2020	@	Utah	28	45	L	12.0	L	54.5	O	
Coach: Nick Rolovich		Season Record >>	108	154	1-3	ATS>>	1-3	O/U>>	3-1	

2019-Washington State		Opponent	Wazzu	Opp	S/U	Line	ATS	Total	O/U	
8/31/2019	vs	NEW MEXICO STATE	58	7	W	-33.5	W	65.5	U	
9/7/2019	vs	NORTHERN COLORADO	59	17	W	-43.0	L	NT	---	
9/13/2019	@	Houston	31	24	W	-8.5	L	74.0	U	NRG Stadium
9/21/2019	vs	UCLA	63	67	L	-18.0	L	59.5	O	
9/28/2019	@	Utah	13	38	L	5.5	L	56.5	U	
10/12/2019	@	Arizona State	34	38	L	-1.5	L	60.5	O	
10/19/2019	vs	COLORADO	41	10	W	-13.0	W	68.5	U	
10/26/2019	@	Oregon	35	37	L	19.5	W	67.5	O	
11/9/2019	@	California	20	33	L	-8.5	L	52.0	O	
11/16/2019	vs	STANFORD	49	22	W	-11.0	W	66.0	O	
11/23/2019	vs	OREGON STATE	54	53	W	-10.5	L	77.5	O	
11/29/2019	@	Washington	13	31	L	7.0	L	65.0	U	"Apple Cup"
12/27/2019	vs	**Air Force**	21	31	L	2.5	L	71.5	U	Cheez-it Bowl
Coach: Mike Leach		Season Record >>	491	408	6-7	ATS>>	4-9	O/U>>	6-6	

2018-Washington State		Opponent	Wazzu	Opp	S/U	Line	ATS	Total	O/U	
9/1/2018	@	Wyoming	41	19	W	-3.0	W	44.0	O	
9/8/2018	vs	SAN JOSE STATE	31	0	W	-30.0	W	62.5	U	
9/15/2018	vs	EASTERN WASHINGTON	59	24	W	-20.0	W	NT	---	
9/21/2018	@	Usc	36	39	L	4.5	W	50.5	O	
9/29/2018	vs	UTAH	28	24	W	1.5	W	50.0	O	
10/6/2018	@	Oregon State	56	37	W	-18.5	W	64.5	O	
10/20/2018	vs	OREGON	34	20	W	-3.0	W	69.5	U	
10/27/2018	@	Stanford	41	38	W	2.5	W	55.0	O	
11/3/2018	vs	CALIFORNIA	19	13	W	-7.0	L	51.0	U	
11/10/2018	@	Colorado	31	7	W	-5.5	W	59.5	U	
11/17/2018	vs	ARIZONA	69	28	W	-10.5	W	63.5	O	
11/23/2018	vs	WASHINGTON	15	28	L	-3.0	L	49.5	U	"Apple Cup"
12/28/2018	vs	**Iowa State**	28	26	W	-1.5	W	56.0	U	Alamo Bowl
Coach: Mike Leach		Season Record >>	488	303	11-2	ATS>>	11-2	O/U>>	6-6	

WASHINGTON STATE COUGARS PACIFIC-12 North

STADIUM: Martin Stadium {32,952} | **Location:** Pullman, WA | **COACH:** Jake Dickert

DATE		Opponent	WSU	Opp	S/U	Line	ATS	Total	O/U	Trends & Angles
9/3/2022	vs	IDAHO								21-1 @ home vs Idaho since 1967
9/10/2022	@	Wisconsin								vs Wisconsin - Wisconsin leads series 2-0
9/17/2022	vs	COLORADO STATE								vs Colorado State - CSU leads series 1-0
9/24/2022	vs	OREGON								8-2 ATS vs Oregon as Dog since 2010
10/1/2022	vs	CALIFORNIA								9-1 S/U @ home vs CAL as favorite since 1983
10/8/2022	@	Usc								vs USC - USC leads series 62-10-4
10/15/2022	@	Oregon State								vs Oregon State - WAZZU leads series 55-47-3
10/29/2022	vs	UTAH								vs Utah - Series tied 9-9
11/5/2022	@	Stanford								vs Stanford - Stanford leads series 40-30-1
11/12/2022	vs	ARIZONA STATE								vs Arizona State - ASU leads series 27-15-2
11/19/2022	@	Arizona								8-1 S/U vs Arizona as favorite since 1997
11/26/2022	vs	WASHINGTON								2-7 ATS vs Washington as favorite since 1988
12/2/2022	vs									PAC-12 Championship
	vs									BOWL GAME

Pointspread Analysis — Non-Conference
- 0-16 S/U vs Non-Conf. as 10.5 point or more Dog since 1983
- 10-2 ATS vs Non-Conf. as 3.5-7 point Dog since 1988
- 10-2 S/U vs Non-Conf. as 7.5-10 point favorite since 1996
- 0-5-1 ATS vs Non-Conf. as 7.5-10 point favorite since 2010
- 8-1 S/U vs Non-Conf. as 10.5-15 point favorite since 1995
- vs Idaho - Washington State leads series 72-19-3

Dog
- 0-21 S/U as 25.5 point or more Dog since 1991
- 5-0 ATS as 30.5 point or more Dog since 2010
- 0-13 S/U @ home as 20.5 point or more Dog since 1990
- 1-26 S/U on road as 20.5 point or more Dog since 1987
- 0-7 O/U as 20.5-25 point Dog since 2010
- 0-5 S/U @ home as 15.5-20 point Dog since 1986
- 3-11 S/U on road as 15.5-20 point Dog since 1990
- 8-1 ATS as 15.5-20 point Dog since 2012
- 4-9 O/U on road as 10.5-15 point Dog since 2007
- 7-28 S/U on road as 10.5-15 point Dog since 1983
- 0-13 S/U @ home as 7.5-10 point Dog since 1989
- 4-17 S/U on road as 7.5-10 point Dog since 1984
- 4-15 ATS on road as 7.5-10 point Dog since 1984
- 2-7 S/U @ home as 3.5-7 point Dog since 2010
- 11-3 O/U on road as 3.5-7 point Dog since 2001
- 11-4 O/U as 3 point or less Dog since 2002

Favorite
- 11-3 S/U & ATS on road as 3 point or less favorite since 2001
- 1-7 ATS as 3.5-7 point favorite since 2003
- 12-4 S/U @ home as 7.5-10 point favorite since 1985
- 10-1 S/U on road as 7.5-10 point favorite since 1996
- 7-0 S/U on road as 10.5-15 point favorite since 1990
- 17-1 S/U @ home as 10.5-15 point favorite since 2001
- 33-6 S/U @ home as 15.5 point or more favorite since 1992

Bowl Games
- 0-3 S/U in Rose Bowl since 1931
- 0-3 O/U in Bowl Games as 3.5-7 point Dog since 1988

COLORADO ST.	
COLORADO ST.	
Usc	
Oregon State	
Oregon State	
UTAH	
Stanford	
ARIZONA STATE	
Arizona	
Arizona	
WASHINGTON	

Pointspread Analysis — Conference
- 2-13 S/U vs Arizona State as Dog since 1997
- 5-1 S/U @ home vs Arizona State as favorite since 1992
- 1-9 S/U vs California as Dog since 2005
- vs California - California leads series 48-29-5
- vs Oregon - Oregon leads series 52-40-7
- 12-3 O/U vs Oregon as Dog since 2003
- 2-5 O/U vs Stanford as favorite since 2002
- 3-0 S/U @ Stanford as favorite since 2002
- 0-6 S/U vs Washington as Dog since 2013
- vs Washington - Washington leads series 74-33-6
- 0-7 S/U vs Arizona as 13 point or more Dog since 1993
- 0-10 S/U vs Oregon as 16 point or more Dog since 1999
- 18-0 S/U vs Oregon State as 7.5 point or more favorite since 1984
- 0-10 S/U vs Stanford as 8 point or more Dog since 1986
- 0-8 S/U vs USC as 16.5 point or more Dog since 1987
- 0-9 S/U vs USC as 7.5-9.5 point Dog since 1983
- 0-5 S/U vs Washington as 16 point or more Dog since 1986
- 0-6 S/U vs Washington as 9.5-13 point Dog since 1993
- 8-0 S/U in 2nd home game of season since 2013
- 8-0 ATS prior to playing Oregon since 2014
- 8-3-1 ATS in 2nd road game of season since 2010
- 7-2 O/U after playing USC since 2007
- 6-0 ATS after playing USC since 2010
- 9-3 ATS prior to playing Stanford since 2009
- 2-8 S/U after playing Utah since 1985
- 3-9 ATS after playing Stanford since 2009
- 2-9 S/U in final road game of season since 2011
- 3-8 ATS in final road game of season since 2011
- 3-9 S/U after playing Arizona since 2004
- 32-6 S/U @ home when ranked since 1997
- 5-0 S/U @ home when ranked vs California all time
- 0-5 S/U on road when ranked vs USC all time
- 0-7 S/U & ATS when ranked vs Washington since 2001
- 4-26 S/U on road vs ranked teams since 2003
- 5-21 S/U @ home vs ranked teams since 2004
- 0-11 S/U vs ranked Arizona all time
- 2-19 S/U @ ranked USC all time

WESTERN KENTUCKY HILLTOPPERS — C-USA East

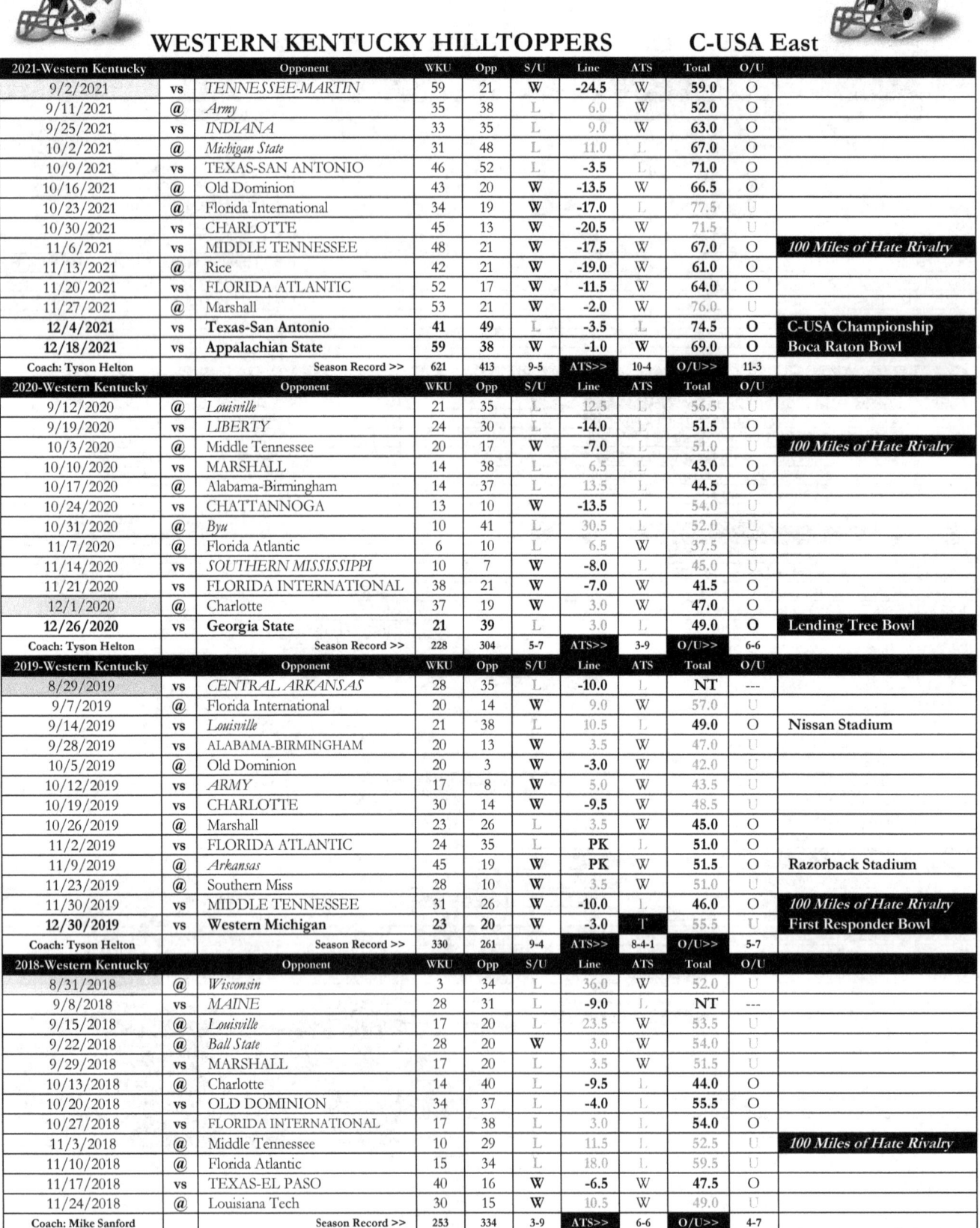

2021-Western Kentucky		Opponent	WKU	Opp	S/U	Line	ATS	Total	O/U	
9/2/2021	vs	TENNESSEE-MARTIN	59	21	W	-24.5	W	59.0	O	
9/11/2021	@	Army	35	38	L	6.0	W	52.0	O	
9/25/2021	vs	INDIANA	33	35	L	9.0	W	63.0	O	
10/2/2021	@	Michigan State	31	48	L	11.0	L	67.0	O	
10/9/2021	vs	TEXAS-SAN ANTONIO	46	52	L	-3.5	L	71.0	O	
10/16/2021	@	Old Dominion	43	20	W	-13.5	W	66.5	O	
10/23/2021	@	Florida International	34	19	W	-17.0	L	77.5	U	
10/30/2021	vs	CHARLOTTE	45	13	W	-20.5	W	71.5	U	
11/6/2021	vs	MIDDLE TENNESSEE	48	21	W	-17.5	W	67.0	O	100 Miles of Hate Rivalry
11/13/2021	@	Rice	42	21	W	-19.0	W	61.0	O	
11/20/2021	vs	FLORIDA ATLANTIC	52	17	W	-11.5	W	64.0	O	
11/27/2021	@	Marshall	53	21	W	-2.0	W	76.0	U	
12/4/2021	vs	Texas-San Antonio	41	49	L	-3.5	L	74.5	O	C-USA Championship
12/18/2021	vs	Appalachian State	59	38	W	-1.0	W	69.0	O	Boca Raton Bowl
Coach: Tyson Helton		Season Record >>	621	413	9-5	ATS>>	10-4	O/U>>	11-3	

2020-Western Kentucky		Opponent	WKU	Opp	S/U	Line	ATS	Total	O/U	
9/12/2020	@	Louisville	21	35	L	12.5	L	56.5	U	
9/19/2020	vs	LIBERTY	24	30	L	-14.0	L	51.5	O	
10/3/2020	@	Middle Tennessee	20	17	W	-7.0	L	51.0	U	100 Miles of Hate Rivalry
10/10/2020	vs	MARSHALL	14	38	L	6.5	L	43.0	O	
10/17/2020	@	Alabama-Birmingham	14	37	L	13.5	L	44.5	O	
10/24/2020	vs	CHATTANNOGA	13	10	W	-13.5	L	54.0	U	
10/31/2020	@	Byu	10	41	L	30.5	L	52.0	U	
11/7/2020	@	Florida Atlantic	6	10	L	6.5	W	37.5	U	
11/14/2020	vs	SOUTHERN MISSISSIPPI	10	7	W	-8.0	L	45.0	U	
11/21/2020	vs	FLORIDA INTERNATIONAL	38	21	W	-7.0	W	41.5	O	
12/1/2020	@	Charlotte	37	19	W	3.0	W	47.0	O	
12/26/2020	vs	Georgia State	21	39	L	3.0	L	49.0	O	Lending Tree Bowl
Coach: Tyson Helton		Season Record >>	228	304	5-7	ATS>>	3-9	O/U>>	6-6	

2019-Western Kentucky		Opponent	WKU	Opp	S/U	Line	ATS	Total	O/U	
8/29/2019	vs	CENTRAL ARKANSAS	28	35	L	-10.0	L	NT	---	
9/7/2019	@	Florida International	20	14	W	9.0	W	57.0	U	
9/14/2019	vs	Louisville	21	38	L	10.5	L	49.0	O	Nissan Stadium
9/28/2019	vs	ALABAMA-BIRMINGHAM	20	13	W	3.5	W	47.0	U	
10/5/2019	@	Old Dominion	20	3	W	-3.0	W	42.0	U	
10/12/2019	vs	ARMY	17	8	W	5.0	W	43.5	U	
10/19/2019	vs	CHARLOTTE	30	14	W	-9.5	W	48.5	U	
10/26/2019	@	Marshall	23	26	L	3.5	W	45.0	O	
11/2/2019	vs	FLORIDA ATLANTIC	24	35	L	PK	L	51.0	O	
11/9/2019	@	Arkansas	45	19	W	PK	W	51.5	O	Razorback Stadium
11/23/2019	@	Southern Miss	28	10	W	3.5	W	51.0	U	
11/30/2019	vs	MIDDLE TENNESSEE	31	26	W	-10.0	L	46.0	O	100 Miles of Hate Rivalry
12/30/2019	vs	Western Michigan	23	20	W	-3.0	T	55.5	U	First Responder Bowl
Coach: Tyson Helton		Season Record >>	330	261	9-4	ATS>>	8-4-1	O/U>>	5-7	

2018-Western Kentucky		Opponent	WKU	Opp	S/U	Line	ATS	Total	O/U	
8/31/2018	@	Wisconsin	3	34	L	36.0	W	52.0	U	
9/8/2018	vs	MAINE	28	31	L	-9.0	L	NT	---	
9/15/2018	@	Louisville	17	20	L	23.5	W	53.5	U	
9/22/2018	@	Ball State	28	20	W	3.0	W	54.0	U	
9/29/2018	vs	MARSHALL	17	20	L	3.5	W	51.5	U	
10/13/2018	@	Charlotte	14	40	L	-9.5	L	44.0	O	
10/20/2018	vs	OLD DOMINION	34	37	L	-4.0	L	55.5	O	
10/27/2018	vs	FLORIDA INTERNATIONAL	17	38	L	3.0	L	54.0	O	
11/3/2018	@	Middle Tennessee	10	29	L	11.5	L	52.5	U	100 Miles of Hate Rivalry
11/10/2018	@	Florida Atlantic	15	34	L	18.0	L	59.5	U	
11/17/2018	vs	TEXAS-EL PASO	40	16	W	-6.5	W	47.5	O	
11/24/2018	@	Louisiana Tech	30	15	W	10.5	W	49.0	U	
Coach: Mike Sanford		Season Record >>	253	334	3-9	ATS>>	6-6	O/U>>	4-7	

WESTERN KENTUCKY HILLTOPPERS — C-USA East

STADIUM: L.T. Smith Stadium {22,113} | **Location:** Bowling Green, KY | **COACH:** Tyson Helton

DATE		Opponent	WKU	Opp	S/U	Line	ATS	Total	O/U	Trends & Angles
8/27/2022	vs	AUSTIN PEAY								5-0 S/U vs Austin Peay since 1996
9/3/2022	@	Hawaii								3-18 S/U in 1st road game of season since 2001
9/17/2022	@	Indiana								0-4 S/U vs Indiana as Dog since 2010
9/24/2022	vs	FLA INTERNATIONAL								vs Fla International - WKU leads series 8-6
10/1/2022	vs	TROY								vs Troy - Troy leads series 9-2-1
10/8/2022	@	Texas-San Antonio								vs UTSA - Series tied 1-1
10/15/2022	@	Middle Tennessee								vs Middle Tenn. - WKU leads series 35-34-1
10/21/2022	vs	ALABAMA-BIRM.								vs UAB - Series tied 4-4
10/29/2022	vs	NORTH TEXAS								4-0 S/U vs North Texas as favorite since 2011
11/5/2022	@	Charlotte								vs Charlotte - WKU leads series 4-1
11/12/2022	vs	RICE								11-0 S/U in final home game of season since 2011
11/19/2022	@	Auburn								vs Auburn - Auburn leads series 2-0
11/26/2022	@	Florida Atlantic								vs Florida Atlantic - FAU leads series 9-4
12/3/2022	vs									C-USA Championship
	vs									BOWL GAME

Pointspread Analysis — Non-Conference
- 0-26 S/U vs Non-Conf. as 10.5 point or more Dog since 2005
- 8-0 S/U vs Non-Conf. as 15.5 point or more favorite since 2012
- vs Austin Peay - WKU leads series 34-6-1

Dog
- 1-24 S/U as 15.5 point or more Dog since 2008
- 0-9 S/U @ home as 7.5 point or more Dog since 2008
- 7-1 ATS as 3.5-7 point Dog since 2018
- 4-1 ATS @ home as 3 point or less Dog since 2010

Favorite
- 9-4 O/U as 3 point or less favorite since 2010
- 8-1 S/U @ home as 10.5-15 point favorite since 2012
- 7-1 O/U @ home as 10.5-15 point favorite since 2014
- 11-0 S/U as 15.5-20 point favorite since 2013
- 13-0 S/U as 20.5 point or more favorite since 2012

Pointspread Analysis — Conference
- 1-6 S/U vs Florida Atlantic as Dog since 2008
- 1-5 S/U vs Middle Tennessee as Dog since 2008

Bowl Games
- 7-2 S/U in Bowl Games

Indiana	2-7 ATS in 2nd road game of season since 2013
UAB	5-1 O/U after playing Middle Tennessee since 2015
RICE	10-3 ATS in final home game of season since 2009
Auburn	8-2 O/U prior to playing Florida Atlantic since 2011
Fla Atlantic	10-1 ATS in final road game of season since 2011

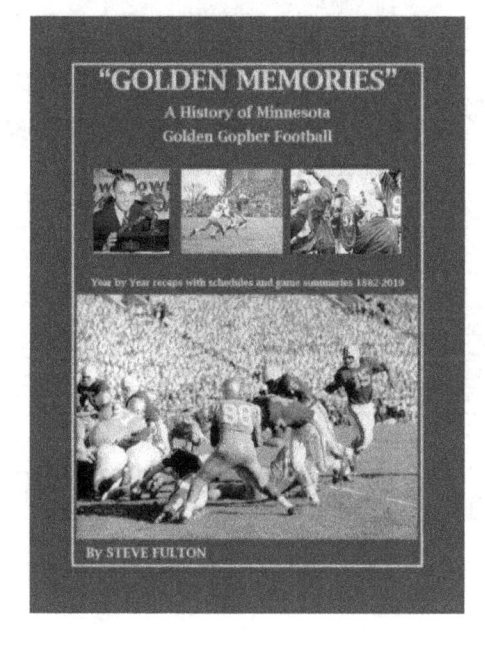

"Golden Memories" is a comprehensive historical look at every year of the University of Minnesota Football teams. From the glory years of the 1930's and 1940's through the 2021 season, it is truly a walk down memory lane for fans who enjoy the rich traditions and history of college football. A must read for all Golden Gopher football fans as well as all College Football fans.

"Golden Memories" – History of Minnesota Gophers Football

8.5" x 11" {288 pages} {Paperback} **$29.95**

Order at: www.stevesfootballbible.com

These books available at numerous online retailers

WESTERN MICHIGAN BRONCOS   MAC West

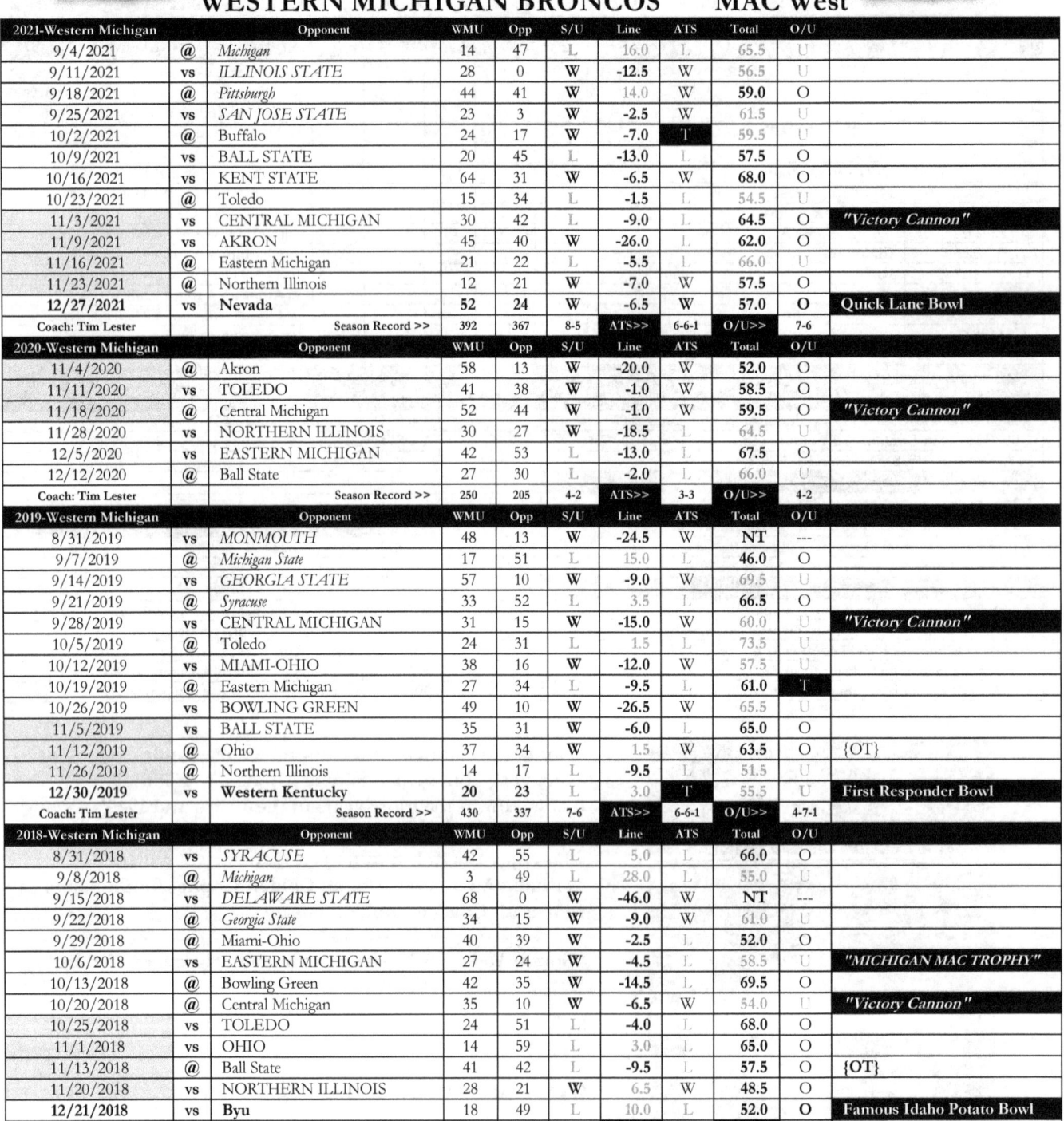

2021-Western Michigan		Opponent	WMU	Opp	S/U	Line	ATS	Total	O/U	
9/4/2021	@	Michigan	14	47	L	16.0	L	65.5	U	
9/11/2021	vs	ILLINOIS STATE	28	0	W	-12.5	W	56.5	U	
9/18/2021	@	Pittsburgh	44	41	W	14.0	W	59.0	O	
9/25/2021	vs	SAN JOSE STATE	23	3	W	-2.5	W	61.5	U	
10/2/2021	@	Buffalo	24	17	W	-7.0	T	59.5	U	
10/9/2021	vs	BALL STATE	20	45	L	-13.0	L	57.5	O	
10/16/2021	vs	KENT STATE	64	31	W	-6.5	W	68.0	O	
10/23/2021	@	Toledo	15	34	L	-1.5	L	54.5	U	
11/3/2021	vs	CENTRAL MICHIGAN	30	42	L	-9.0	L	64.5	O	"Victory Cannon"
11/9/2021	vs	AKRON	45	40	W	-26.0	L	62.0	O	
11/16/2021	@	Eastern Michigan	21	22	L	-5.5	L	66.0	U	
11/23/2021	@	Northern Illinois	12	21	W	-7.0	W	57.5	O	
12/27/2021	vs	Nevada	52	24	W	-6.5	W	57.0	O	Quick Lane Bowl
Coach: Tim Lester		Season Record >>	392	367	8-5	ATS>>	6-6-1	O/U>>	7-6	

2020-Western Michigan		Opponent	WMU	Opp	S/U	Line	ATS	Total	O/U	
11/4/2020	@	Akron	58	13	W	-20.0	W	52.0	O	
11/11/2020	vs	TOLEDO	41	38	W	-1.0	W	58.5	O	
11/18/2020	@	Central Michigan	52	44	W	-1.0	W	59.5	O	"Victory Cannon"
11/28/2020	vs	NORTHERN ILLINOIS	30	27	W	-18.5	L	64.5	U	
12/5/2020	vs	EASTERN MICHIGAN	42	53	L	-13.0	L	67.5	O	
12/12/2020	@	Ball State	27	30	L	-2.0	L	66.0	U	
Coach: Tim Lester		Season Record >>	250	205	4-2	ATS>>	3-3	O/U>>	4-2	

2019-Western Michigan		Opponent	WMU	Opp	S/U	Line	ATS	Total	O/U	
8/31/2019	vs	MONMOUTH	48	13	W	-24.5	W	NT	---	
9/7/2019	@	Michigan State	17	51	L	15.0	L	46.0	O	
9/14/2019	vs	GEORGIA STATE	57	10	W	-9.0	W	69.5	U	
9/21/2019	@	Syracuse	33	52	L	3.5	L	66.5	O	
9/28/2019	vs	CENTRAL MICHIGAN	31	15	W	-15.0	W	60.0	U	"Victory Cannon"
10/5/2019	@	Toledo	24	31	L	1.5	L	73.5	U	
10/12/2019	vs	MIAMI-OHIO	38	16	W	-12.0	W	57.5	U	
10/19/2019	@	Eastern Michigan	27	34	L	-9.5	L	61.0	T	
10/26/2019	vs	BOWLING GREEN	49	10	W	-26.5	W	65.5	U	
11/5/2019	vs	BALL STATE	35	31	W	-6.0	L	65.0	O	
11/12/2019	@	Ohio	37	34	W	1.5	W	63.5	O	{OT}
11/26/2019	@	Northern Illinois	14	17	L	-9.5	L	51.5	U	
12/30/2019	vs	Western Kentucky	20	23	L	3.0	T	55.5	U	First Responder Bowl
Coach: Tim Lester		Season Record >>	430	337	7-6	ATS>>	6-6-1	O/U>>	4-7-1	

2018-Western Michigan		Opponent	WMU	Opp	S/U	Line	ATS	Total	O/U	
8/31/2018	vs	SYRACUSE	42	55	L	5.0	L	66.0	O	
9/8/2018	@	Michigan	3	49	L	28.0	L	55.0	U	
9/15/2018	vs	DELAWARE STATE	68	0	W	-46.0	W	NT	---	
9/22/2018	@	Georgia State	34	15	W	-9.0	W	61.0	U	
9/29/2018	@	Miami-Ohio	40	39	W	-2.5	L	52.0	O	
10/6/2018	vs	EASTERN MICHIGAN	27	24	W	-4.5	L	58.5	U	"MICHIGAN MAC TROPHY"
10/13/2018	@	Bowling Green	42	35	W	-14.5	L	69.5	O	
10/20/2018	@	Central Michigan	35	10	W	-6.5	W	54.0	U	"Victory Cannon"
10/25/2018	vs	TOLEDO	24	51	L	-4.0	L	68.0	O	
11/1/2018	vs	OHIO	14	59	L	3.0	L	65.0	O	
11/13/2018	@	Ball State	41	42	L	-9.5	L	57.5	O	{OT}
11/20/2018	vs	NORTHERN ILLINOIS	28	21	W	6.5	W	48.5	O	
12/21/2018	vs	Byu	18	49	L	10.0	L	52.0	O	Famous Idaho Potato Bowl
Coach: Tim Lester		Season Record >>	416	449	7-6	ATS>>	4-9	O/U>>	8-4	

WESTERN MICHIGAN BRONCOS   MAC West

STADIUM: Waldo Stadium {30,200} **Location:** Kalamazoo, MI **COACH:** Tim Lester

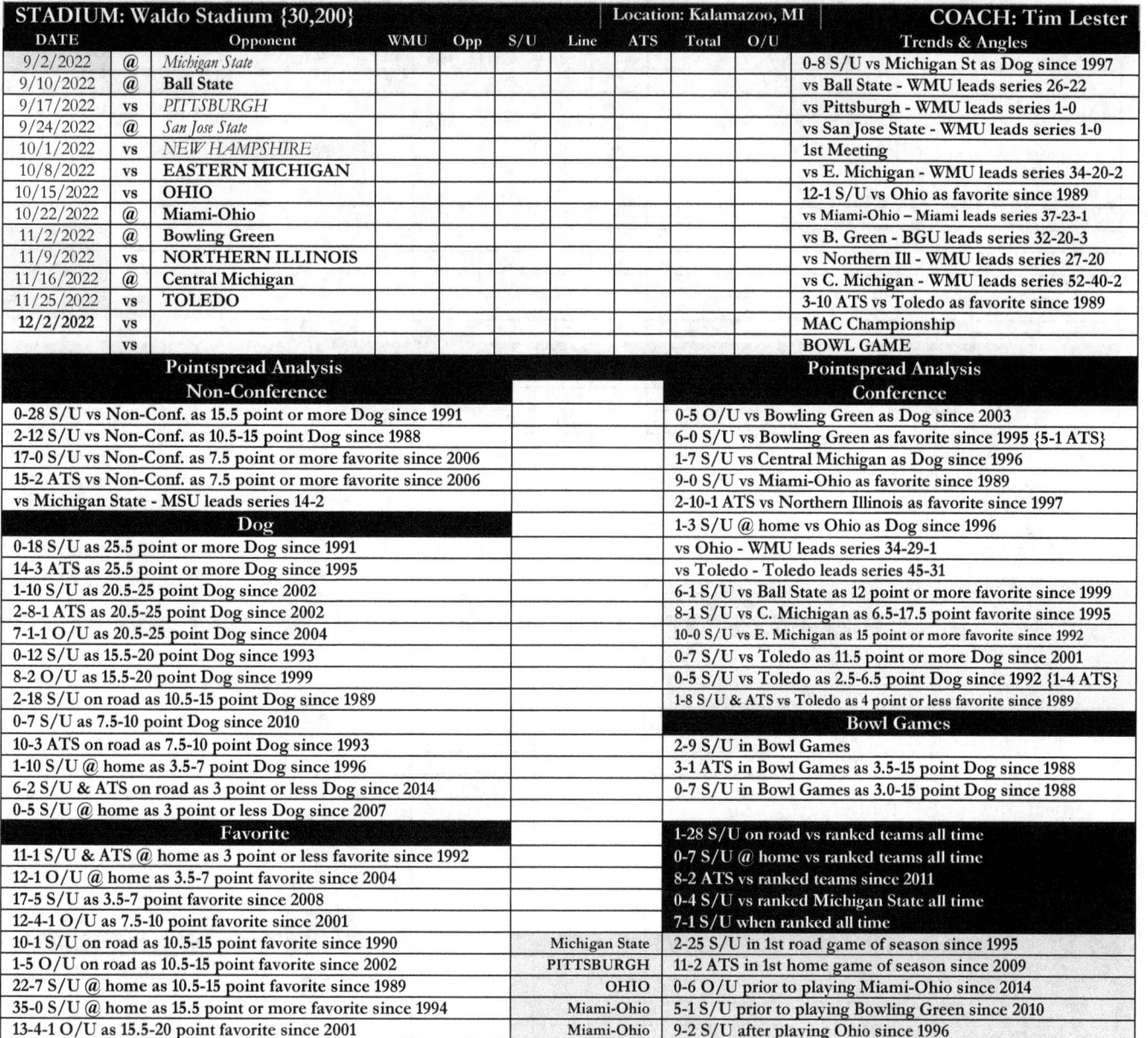

DATE		Opponent	WMU	Opp	S/U	Line	ATS	Total	O/U	Trends & Angles
9/2/2022	@	Michigan State								0-8 S/U vs Michigan St as Dog since 1997
9/10/2022	@	Ball State								vs Ball State - WMU leads series 26-22
9/17/2022	vs	PITTSBURGH								vs Pittsburgh - WMU leads series 1-0
9/24/2022	@	San Jose State								vs San Jose State - WMU leads series 1-0
10/1/2022	vs	NEW HAMPSHIRE								1st Meeting
10/8/2022	vs	EASTERN MICHIGAN								vs E. Michigan - WMU leads series 34-20-2
10/15/2022	vs	OHIO								12-1 S/U vs Ohio as favorite since 1989
10/22/2022	@	Miami-Ohio								vs Miami-Ohio – Miami leads series 37-23-1
11/2/2022	@	Bowling Green								vs B. Green - BGU leads series 32-20-3
11/9/2022	vs	NORTHERN ILLINOIS								vs Northern Ill - WMU leads series 27-20
11/16/2022	vs	Central Michigan								vs C. Michigan - WMU leads series 52-40-2
11/25/2022	vs	TOLEDO								3-10 ATS vs Toledo as favorite since 1989
12/2/2022	vs									MAC Championship
	vs									BOWL GAME

Pointspread Analysis — Non-Conference
- 0-28 S/U vs Non-Conf. as 15.5 point or more Dog since 1991
- 2-12 S/U vs Non-Conf. as 10.5-15 point Dog since 1988
- 17-0 S/U vs Non-Conf. as 7.5 point or more favorite since 2006
- 15-2 ATS vs Non-Conf. as 7.5 point or more favorite since 2006
- vs Michigan State - MSU leads series 14-2

Dog
- 0-18 S/U as 25.5 point or more Dog since 1991
- 14-3 ATS as 25.5 point or more Dog since 1995
- 1-10 S/U as 20.5-25 point Dog since 2002
- 2-8-1 ATS as 20.5-25 point Dog since 2002
- 7-1-1 O/U as 20.5-25 point Dog since 2004
- 0-12 S/U as 15.5-20 point Dog since 1993
- 8-2 O/U as 15.5-20 point Dog since 1999
- 2-18 S/U on road as 10.5-15 point Dog since 1989
- 0-7 S/U as 7.5-10 point Dog since 2010
- 10-3 ATS on road as 7.5-10 point Dog since 1993
- 1-10 S/U @ home as 3.5-7 point Dog since 1996
- 6-2 S/U & ATS on road as 3 point or less Dog since 2014
- 0-5 S/U @ home as 3 point or less Dog since 2007

Favorite
- 11-1 S/U & ATS @ home as 3 point or less favorite since 1992
- 12-1 O/U @ home as 3.5-7 point favorite since 2004
- 17-5 S/U as 3.5-7 point favorite since 2008
- 12-4-1 O/U as 7.5-10 point favorite since 2001
- 10-1 S/U on road as 10.5-15 point favorite since 1990
- 1-5 O/U on road as 10.5-15 point favorite since 2002
- 22-7 S/U @ home as 10.5-15 point favorite since 1989
- 35-0 S/U @ home as 15.5 point or more favorite since 1994
- 13-4-1 O/U as 15.5-20 point favorite since 2001
- 7-1 S/U on road as 15.5 point or more favorite since 1998

Pointspread Analysis — Conference
- 0-5 O/U vs Bowling Green as Dog since 2003
- 6-0 S/U vs Bowling Green as favorite since 1995 {5-1 ATS}
- 1-7 S/U vs Central Michigan as Dog since 1996
- 9-0 S/U vs Miami-Ohio as favorite since 1989
- 2-10-1 ATS vs Northern Illinois as favorite since 1997
- 1-3 S/U @ home vs Ohio as Dog since 1996
- vs Ohio - WMU leads series 34-29-1
- vs Toledo - Toledo leads series 45-31
- 6-1 S/U vs Ball State as 12 point or more favorite since 1999
- 8-1 S/U vs C. Michigan as 6.5-17.5 point favorite since 1995
- 10-0 S/U vs E. Michigan as 15 point or more favorite since 1992
- 0-7 S/U vs Toledo as 11.5 point or more Dog since 2001
- 0-5 S/U vs Toledo as 2.5-6.5 point Dog since 1992 {1-4 ATS}
- 1-8 S/U & ATS vs Toledo as 4 point or less favorite since 1989

Bowl Games
- 2-9 S/U in Bowl Games
- 3-1 ATS in Bowl Games as 3.5-15 point Dog since 1988
- 0-7 S/U in Bowl Games as 3.0-15 point Dog since 1988

- 1-28 S/U on road vs ranked teams all time
- 0-7 S/U @ home vs ranked teams all time
- 8-2 ATS vs ranked teams since 2011
- 0-4 S/U vs ranked Michigan State all time
- 7-1 S/U when ranked all time

Michigan State	2-25 S/U in 1st road game of season since 1995
PITTSBURGH	11-2 ATS in 1st home game of season since 2009
OHIO	0-6 O/U prior to playing Miami-Ohio since 2014
Miami-Ohio	5-1 S/U prior to playing Bowling Green since 2010
Miami-Ohio	9-2 S/U after playing Ohio since 1996
Central Michigan	13-1 ATS prior to playing Toledo since 1995
Central Michigan	4-9 O/U in final road game of season since 2009

Page | 257

Copyright © 2022 by Steve's Football Bible, LLC

WEST VIRGINIA MOUNTAINEERS   BIG TWELVE

2021-West Virginia		Opponent	Wva	Opp	S/U	Line	ATS	Total	O/U	
9/4/2021	@	Maryland	24	30	L	-2.5	L	57.0	U	
9/11/2021	vs	LONG ISLAND U	66	0	W	-49.5	W	56.0	O	
9/18/2021	vs	VIRGINIA TECH	27	21	W	-2.0	W	50.0	U	"Black Diamond Trophy"
9/25/2021	@	Oklahoma	13	16	L	17.5	W	57.0	U	
10/2/2021	vs	TEXAS TECH	20	23	L	-8.0	L	55.0	U	
10/9/2021	@	Baylor	20	45	L	1.5	L	45.5	O	
10/23/2021	@	Tcu	29	17	W	4.5	W	58.0	U	
10/30/2021	vs	IOWA STATE	38	31	W	7.5	W	48.5	O	
11/6/2021	vs	OKLAHOMA STATE	3	24	L	3.5	L	48.5	U	
11/13/2021	@	Kansas State	17	34	L	6.0	L	47.0	O	
11/20/2021	vs	TEXAS	31	23	W	-2.0	W	56.5	U	
11/27/2021	@	Kansas	34	28	W	-16.0	L	55.5	O	
12/28/2021	vs	Minnesota	6	18	L	6.5	L	45.0	U	Guaranteed Rate Bowl
Coach: Neal Brown		Season Record >>	328	310	6-7	ATS>>	6-7	O/U>>	5-8	
2020-West Virginia		Opponent	Wva	Opp	S/U	Line	ATS	Total	O/U	
9/12/2020	vs	EASTERN KENTUCKY	56	10	W	-44.5	W	57.5	O	
9/26/2020	@	Oklahoma State	13	27	L	6.5	L	49.0	U	
10/3/2020	vs	BAYLOR	27	21	W	1.0	W	54.0	U	{2 OT}
10/17/2020	vs	KANSAS	38	17	W	-22.5	L	51.5	O	
10/24/2020	@	Texas Tech	27	34	L	-2.0	L	54.0	O	
10/31/2020	vs	KANSAS STATE	37	10	W	-5.0	W	46.0	O	
11/7/2020	@	Texas	13	17	L	6.0	L	55.5	U	
11/14/2020	vs	TCU	24	6	W	-3.0	W	44.0	U	
12/5/2020	@	Iowa State	6	42	L	5.5	L	47.5	O	
12/31/2020	vs	Army	24	21	W	-9.0	L	41.0	O	Liberty Bowl
Coach: Neal Brown		Season Record >>	265	205	6-4	ATS>>	5-5	O/U>>	6-4	
2019-West Virginia		Opponent	Wva	Opp	S/U	Line	ATS	Total	O/U	
8/31/2019	vs	JAMES MADISON	20	13	W	-7.0	T	NT	---	
9/7/2019	@	Missouri	7	38	L	13.5	L	62.5	U	
9/14/2019	vs	NC STATE	44	27	W	7.0	W	45.5	O	
9/21/2019	@	Kansas	29	24	W	-4.5	W	49.5	O	
10/5/2019	vs	TEXAS	31	42	L	10.5	L	62.0	O	
10/12/2019	vs	IOWA STATE	14	38	L	10.0	L	55.0	U	
10/19/2019	@	Oklahoma	14	52	L	32.0	L	63.5	O	
10/31/2019	@	Baylor	14	17	L	17.5	W	56.5	U	
11/9/2019	vs	TEXAS TECH	17	38	L	2.5	L	56.5	U	
11/16/2019	@	Kansas State	24	20	W	14.0	W	46.5	U	
11/23/2019	vs	OKLAHOMA STATE	13	20	L	6.5	L	56.5	U	
11/29/2019	@	Tcu	20	17	W	14.0	W	44.0	U	
Coach: Neal Brown		Season Record >>	247	346	5-7	ATS>>	5-6-1	O/U>>	4-7	
2018-West Virginia		Opponent	Wva	Opp	S/U	Line	ATS	Total	O/U	
9/1/2018	vs	Tennessee	40	14	W	-10.0	W	59.5	U	Bank of America Stadium
9/8/2018	vs	YOUNGSTOWN STATE	52	17	W	-30.5	W	NT	---	
9/22/2018	vs	KANSAS STATE	35	6	W	-15.5	W	60.5	U	
9/29/2018	@	Texas Tech	42	34	W	-3.5	W	73.0	O	
10/6/2018	vs	KANSAS	38	22	W	-27.5	L	62.0	U	
10/13/2018	@	Iowa State	14	30	L	-4.0	L	55.0	U	
10/25/2018	vs	BAYLOR	58	14	W	-15.0	W	67.0	O	
11/3/2018	@	Texas	42	41	W	-1.0	T	58.0	O	
11/10/2018	vs	TCU	47	10	W	-12.0	W	56.0	O	
11/17/2018	@	Oklahoma State	41	45	L	-6.0	L	73.5	O	
11/23/2018	vs	OKLAHOMA	56	59	L	3.0	T	87.0	O	
12/28/2018	vs	Syracuse	18	34	L	3.0	L	67.0	U	Camping World Bowl
Coach: Dana Holgerson		Season Record >>	730	672	8-4	ATS>>	6-4-1	O/U>>	6-5	

WEST VIRGINIA MOUNTAINEERS   BIG TWELVE

STADIUM: Milan Pusker Stadium {60,000} | **Location:** Morgantown, WV | **COACH:** Neal Brown

DATE		Opponent	WVU	Opp	S/U	Line	ATS	Total	O/U	Trends & Angles
9/3/2022	@	*Pittsburgh*								4-0 S/U & ATS vs Pittsburgh as Dog since 2002
9/10/2022	vs	KANSAS								5-0 S/U @ home vs Kansas as favorite since 2012
9/17/2022	vs	*TOWSON*								vs Towson - West Virginia leads series 1-0
9/24/2022	@	*Virginia Tech*								1-7-1 ATS vs Va Tech as favorite since 1986
10/1/2022	@	Texas								vs Texas - West Virginia leads series 6-5
10/13/2022	vs	BAYLOR								vs Baylor - West Virginia leads series 6-4
10/22/2022	@	Texas Tech								vs Texas Tech - West Virginia leads series 6-5
10/29/2022	vs	TCU								vs TCU - West Virginia leads series 7-4
11/5/2022	@	Iowa State								vs Iowa State - West Virginia leads series 6-4
11/12/2022	vs	OKLAHOMA								0-9 S/U vs Oklahoma as Dog since 2012
11/19/2022	vs	KANSAS STATE								1-6 O/U vs Kansas State as favorite since 2012
11/26/2022	@	Oklahoma State								vs Oklahoma State - Ok State leads series 9-4
12/3/2022	vs									BIG XII Championship
	vs									BOWL GAME

Pointspread Analysis — Non-Conference
- 0-15 S/U vs Non-Conf. as 15.5 point or more Dog since 1986
- 1-11 S/U vs Non-Conf. as 10.5-15 point Dog since 1987
- 7-0 S/U vs Non-Conf. as 7.5-10 point favorite since 2009
- 6-0 S/U & ATS vs Pittsburgh as 3.5 point or less Dog since 1984
- 9-1 S/U vs Pittsburgh as 3.5-23 point favorite since 1983
- 0-3 S/U vs Pittsburgh as 3 point or less favorite since 1991
- 0-5 ATS vs Pittsburgh as 3 point or less favorite since 1985
- 2-8 S/U vs Virginia Tech as 2 point or more Dog since 1994

Dog
- 0-12 S/U as 20.5 point or more Dog since 1986
- 0-13 S/U on road as 15.5 point or more Dog since 1987
- 3-14 S/U on road as 10.5-15 point Dog since 1987
- 3-8 S/U @ home as 7.5-10 point Dog since 1987
- 3-15 S/U as 3.5-7 point Dog since 2013
- 6-15 ATS as 3.5-7 point Dog since 2009
- 1-7 S/U @ home as 3.5-7 point Dog since 2011
- 5-2 S/U & ATS on road as 3 point or less Dog since 2005

Favorite
- 4-15 O/U as 3 point or less favorite since 2010
- 6-2 S/U on road as 3 point or less favorite since 2012
- 5-2-1 ATS on road as 3 point or less favorite since 2012
- 2-7 O/U on road as 3 point or less favorite since 2012
- 6-0 S/U @ home as 3.5-7 point favorite since 2016 {4-1-1 ATS}
- 7-1 S/U on road as 7.5-10 point favorite since 1989
- 6-1 ATS on road as 7.5-10 point favorite since 1989
- 14-3 S/U as 7.5-10 point favorite since 2000
- 7-2 S/U @ home as 7.5-10 point favorite since 2000
- 12-1 S/U on road as 10.5-15 point favorite since 1986
- 12-2 S/U @ home as 10.5-15 point favorite since 1998
- 30-2 S/U @ home as 15.5-20 point favorite since 1983
- 20-1 S/U on road as 15.5 point or more favorite since 1988
- 22-1 S/U @ home as 20.5-25 point favorite since 1983
- 2-6 O/U @ home as 20.5-25 point favorite since 2007
- 30-1 S/U @ home as 25.5 point or more favorite since 1984

Pointspread Analysis — Conference
- 4-0 S/U vs Baylor as favorite since 2012
- vs Kansas - West Virginia leads series 10-1
- vs Kansas State - Series tied 6-6
- vs Oklahoma - Oklahoma leads series 11-2
- 6-1 O/U vs Oklahoma as Dog since 2014
- 0-3 S/U & ATS vs Oklahoma State as favorite since 2015
- 5-2 S/U vs Texas Tech as favorite since 2014

Bowl Games
- 1-6 S/U in Gator Bowl
- 0-7 ATS in Gator Bowl
- 1-11 ATS in Bowl Games since 2008
- 0-3 S/U vs Florida State in Bowl Games
- 2-8 S/U in Bowl Games as 3.5-7 point Dog since 1989
- 1-5 S/U & ATS in Bowl Games as 3 point or less Dog since 1982
- 0-5 ATS in Bowl Games as 3 point or less favorite since 1995
- 0-3 S/U & ATS in Bowl Games as 3.5-7 point favorite since 2002

KANSAS	18-0 S/U in 1st home game of season since 2004
Virginia Tech	8-2 S/U prior to playing Texas since 2012
Virginia Tech	2-10 S/U in 2nd road game of season since 2010
BAYLOR	1-7 O/U prior to playing Texas Tech since 2014
BAYLOR	17-1 S/U in 2nd home game of season since 2004
TCU	7-1 S/U after playing Texas Tech since 2014
Iowa State	2-7 ATS after playing TCU since 2012
KANSAS STATE	3-12 O/U in final home game of season since 2007

- 0-9 S/U vs #1 ranked teams all time
- 0-9 S/U vs #2 ranked teams all time
- 0-9 S/U vs #5 ranked teams all time
- 0-8 S/U vs ranked Oklahoma since 2013
- 4-0 S/U when ranked vs Baylor all time
- 0-4 ATS when ranked @ Virginia Tech since 1988

WISCONSIN BADGERS   BIG TEN West

2021-Wisconsin		Opponent	UW	Opp	S/U	Line	ATS	Total	O/U	
9/4/2021	vs	PENN STATE	10	16	L	-5.0	L	48.5	U	
9/11/2021	vs	EASTERN MICHIGAN	34	7	W	-26.0	W	52.0	U	
9/25/2021	vs	Notre Dame	13	41	L	-6.0	L	43.5	O	Soldiers Field
10/2/2021	vs	MICHIGAN	17	38	L	-1.5	L	43.5	O	
10/9/2021	@	Illinois	24	0	W	-12.5	W	42.0	U	
10/16/2021	vs	ARMY	20	14	W	-14.0	L	37.0	U	
10/23/2021	@	Purdue	30	13	W	-3.5	W	41.0	O	
10/30/2021	vs	IOWA	27	7	W	-3.0	W	36.0	U	"Heartland Trophy"
11/6/2021	@	Rutgers	52	3	W	-13.0	W	38.0	O	
11/13/2021	vs	NORTHWESTERN	35	7	W	-25.5	W	42.0	T	
11/20/2021	vs	NEBRASKA	35	28	W	-10.0	L	43.5	O	"Freedom Trophy"
11/27/2021	@	Minnesota	13	23	L	-7.0	L	39.0	U	"Paul Bunyan Axe"
12/30/2021	vs	Arizona State	20	13	W	-8.5	L	42.5	U	Las Vegas Bowl
Coach: Paul Chryst		Season Record >>	330	210	9-4	ATS>>	6-7	O/U>>	5-7-1	
2020-Wisconsin		Opponent	UW	Opp	S/U	Line	ATS	Total	O/U	
10/23/2020	vs	ILLINOIS	45	7	W	-20.5	W	51.5	O	
11/14/2020	@	Michigan	49	11	W	-7.0	W	51.5	O	
11/21/2020	@	Northwestern	7	17	L	-7.0	L	43.0	U	
12/5/2020	vs	INDIANA	6	14	L	-13.0	L	44.5	U	
12/12/2020	@	Iowa	7	28	L	-1.0	L	39.5	U	"Heartland Trophy"
12/19/2020	vs	MINNESOTA	20	17	W	-10.0	L	47.0	U	"Paul Bunyan Axe"
12/30/2020	vs	Wake Forest	42	28	W	-10.5	W	51.5	O	Duke's Mayo Bowl
Coach: Paul Chryst		Season Record >>	176	122	4-3	ATS>>	3-4	O/U>>	3-4	
2019-Wisconsin		Opponent	UW	Opp	S/U	Line	ATS	Total	O/U	
8/31/2019	@	South Florida	49	0	W	-10.5	W	58.5	U	
9/7/2019	vs	CENTRAL MICHIGAN	61	0	W	-35.0	W	54.0	O	
9/21/2019	vs	MICHIGAN	35	14	W	-3.0	W	45.0	O	
9/28/2019	vs	NORTHWESTERN	24	15	W	-23.5	L	46.0	U	
10/5/2019	vs	KENT STATE	48	0	W	-35.0	W	58.5	U	
10/12/2019	vs	MICHIGAN STATE	38	0	W	-8.0	W	40.5	U	
10/19/2019	@	Illinois	23	24	L	-31.0	L	52.0	U	
10/26/2019	@	Ohio State	7	38	L	14.5	L	47.5	U	
11/9/2019	vs	IOWA	24	22	W	-7.5	L	37.5	O	"Heartland Trophy"
11/16/2019	@	Nebraska	37	21	W	-14.0	W	50.0	O	"Freedom Trophy"
11/23/2019	vs	PURDUE	45	24	W	-24.5	L	48.5	O	
11/30/2019	@	Minnesota	38	17	W	-3.0	W	45.0	O	"Paul Bunyan Axe"
12/7/2019	vs	Ohio State	21	34	L	16.5	W	58.0	U	Big Ten Championship
1/1/2020	vs	Oregon	27	28	L	-3.0	L	52.5	O	Rose Bowl
Coach: Paul Chryst		Season Record >>	477	237	10-4	ATS>>	8-6	O/U>>	7-7	
2018-Wisconsin		Opponent	UW	Opp	S/U	Line	ATS	Total	O/U	
8/31/2018	vs	WESTERN KENTUCKY	34	3	W	-36.0	L	52.0	U	
9/8/2018	vs	NEW MEXICO	45	14	W	-35.0	L	58.5	U	
9/15/2018	vs	BYU	21	24	L	-23.5	L	51.5	U	
9/22/2018	@	Iowa	28	17	W	-3.0	W	43.5	O	"Heartland Trophy"
10/6/2018	vs	NEBRASKA	41	24	W	-18.0	L	60.5	O	"Freedom Trophy"
10/13/2018	@	Michigan	13	38	L	9.5	L	48.0	O	
10/20/2018	vs	ILLINOIS	49	20	W	-24.0	W	53.0	O	
10/27/2018	@	Northwestern	17	31	L	-5.0	L	50.5	U	
11/3/2018	vs	RUTGERS	31	17	W	-28.5	L	50.5	U	
11/10/2018	@	Penn State	10	22	L	7.5	L	54.0	U	
11/17/2018	@	Purdue	47	44	W	3.5	W	56.0	O	{2 OT}
11/24/2018	vs	MINNESOTA	15	37	L	-12.5	L	54.0	U	"Paul Bunyan Axe"
12/27/2018	vs	Miami	35	3	W	2.5	W	44.0	U	Pinstripe Bowl
Coach: Paul Chryst		Season Record >>	386	294	8-5	ATS>>	4-9	O/U>>	5-8	

WISCONSIN BADGERS — BIG TEN West

STADIUM: Camp Randall Stadium {80,321} | **Location:** Madison, WI | **COACH:** Paul Chryst

DATE		Opponent	UW	Opp	S/U	Line	ATS	Total	O/U	Trends & Angles
9/3/2022	vs	*ILLINOIS STATE*								25-1 S/U in 1st home game of season since 1996
9/10/2022	vs	*WASHINGTON STATE*								vs Wash State - Wisconsin leads series 2-0
9/17/2022	vs	*NEW MEXICO STATE*								vs New Mexico St - Wisconsin leads series 1-0
9/24/2022	@	Ohio State								vs Ohio State - Ohio State leads series 61-18-5
10/1/2022	vs	ILLINOIS								14-1 S/U vs Illinois as favorite since 2003
10/8/2022	@	Northwestern								vs Northwestern - UW leads series 61-37-5
10/15/2022	@	Michigan State								1-9 S/U vs Michigan State as Dog since 1985
10/22/2022	vs	PURDUE								15-0 S/U vs Purdue as favorite since 1996
11/5/2022	vs	MARYLAND								3-0 S/U vs Maryland as favorite since 2014
11/12/2022	@	Iowa								2-12 S/U vs Iowa as Dog since 1985
11/19/2022	@	Nebraska								8-0 S/U vs Nebraska as favorite since 2011
11/26/2022	vs	MINNESOTA								21-3 S/U vs Minnesota as favorite since 1995
12/3/2022	vs									Big Ten Championship
	vs									BOWL GAME

Pointspread Analysis — Non-Conference

- 10-3 S/U vs Non-Conf. as 3.5-7 point favorite since 1989
- 2-6 O/U vs Non-Conf. as 3.5-7 point favorite since 2002
- 13-0 S/U vs Non-conf. as 7.5-10 point favorite since 1990
- 17-1 S/U vs Non-Conf. as 10.5-15 point favorite since 1985
- 7-0 S/U vs Non-Conf. as 15.5-20 point favorite since 1991
- 11-2 S/U vs Non-Conf. as 20.5-25 point favorite since 1994
- 33-1 S/U vs Non-Conf. as 25.5 or more favorite since 1994

Dog
- 0-20 S/U as 20.5 point or more Dog since 1986
- 0-18 S/U on road as 15.5 point or more Dog since 1986
- 1-7 O/U on road as 10.5-15 point Dog since 2001
- 0-7 S/U on road as 10.5-15 point Dog since 2002
- 14-6-1 ATS as 10.5-15 point Dog since 1986
- 0-8 S/U on road as 7.5-10 point Dog since 1985
- 2-11-1 S/U @ home as 3.5-7 point Dog since 1983

Favorite
- 9-2 S/U on road as 3 point or less favorite since 2003
- 9-3 O/U on road as 3 point or less favorite since 2001
- 1-6 O/U @ home as 3.5-7 point favorite since 2006
- 17-7 S/U on road as 3.5-7 point favorite since 1996
- 14-7 ATS on road as 3.5-7 point favorite since 1998
- 26-0 S/U @ home as 7.5-10 point favorite since 1983
- 3-8 O/U as 7.5-10 point favorite since 2013
- 1-9 ATS as 7.5-10 point favorite since 2014
- 16-3 S/U @ home as 10.5-15 point favorite since 2002
- 15-0 S/U on road as 10.5-15 point favorite since 2004
- 12-3-1 ATS as 10.5-15 point favorite since 2012
- 10-0 S/U on road as 15.5-25 point favorite since 1983
- 11-0 S/U @ home as 15.5-20 point favorite since 2004
- 25-4 S/U @ home as 20.5-25 point favorite since 1984
- 16-6 O/U as 20.5-25 point favorite since 2005
- 7-2 S/U on road as 25.5 point or more favorite since 1996
- 36-0 S/U @ home as 25.5 point or more favorite since 1994

Bowl Games
- 3-0 S/U vs UCLA in Bowl Games
- 3-0 S/U & ATS vs Miami in Bowl Games
- 1-3 S/U in Outback Bowl
- 7-1 S/U in Bowl Games since 2015
- 0-4 S/U in Rose Bowl since 2011
- 0-5 ATS in Rose Bowl since 2000
- 8-3 S/U vs PAC-12 in Bowl Games since 1994
- 0-5 O/U in Bowl Games as 3 point or less Dog since 2003
- 4-0 S/U in Bowl Games as 7.5-10 point favorite since 1995

Pointspread Analysis — Conference

- vs Illinois - Wisconsin leads series 43-37-7
- 1-10 S/U vs Illinois as Dog since 1983
- vs Iowa - Wisconsin leads series 49-44-2
- 7-1 S/U @ Iowa as favorite since 1998
- vs Michigan State - Michigan State leads series 31-23
- 9-2 O/U vs Michigan State as favorite since 2001
- vs Minnesota - Wisconsin leads series 62-61-8
- vs Nebraska - Wisconsin leads series 11-4
- 0-4 S/U & ATS vs Ohio State as favorite since 2000
- vs Purdue - Wisconsin leads series 51-29-8
- 11-0-1 S/U @ home vs Purdue as favorite since 1994
- 0-3 S/U @ home vs Purdue as Dog since 1988
- 8-0 S/U vs Northwestern as 16.5 point or more favorite since 1984
- 1-10 S/U vs Ohio State as 10 point or more Dog since 1988
- 67-9 S/U @ home when ranked since 2006
- 13-1 S/U when ranked vs Illinois since 1962 {6-0 @ home}
- 13-1 S/U when ranked vs Minnesota since 1998
- 9-0 S/U @ home when ranked vs Minnesota since 1954
- 9-0 S/U when ranked vs Purdue since 2004 {7-2 ATS}
- 9-1-1 S/U @ home when ranked vs Purdue all time
- 0-7 S/U when ranked vs Ohio State since 2011
- 1-10-1 S/U when ranked @ Ohio State all time
- 24-90-3 S/U on road vs ranked teams all time
- 0-10 S/U on road vs #1 ranked teams all time
- 0-10 S/U vs #2 ranked teams since 1960
- 1-5 S/U @ ranked Michigan State since 1956

Opponent	Trend
WASH STATE	17-1 S/U in 2nd home game of season since 2004
ILLINOIS	13-1 S/U prior to playing Northwestern since 2004
Northwestern	9-2 S/U after playing Illinois since 2011
Northwestern	9-3 ATS after playing Illinois since 2008
Michigan State	12-1 S/U after playing Northwestern since 2004
Michigan State	11-3 O/U after playing Northwestern since 2003
Michigan State	13-3 ATS after playing Northwestern since 1999
MARYLAND	13-2 S/U after playing Purdue since 2004
Nebraska	14-0 S/U after playing Iowa since 2005
Nebraska	13-3 S/U prior to playing Minnesota since 2006
Nebraska	14-3 S/U in final road game of season since 2005
MINNESOTA	7-2 S/U after playing Nebraska since 2011

WYOMING COWBOYS MOUNTAIN WEST Mountain

2021-Wyoming		Opponent	WYO	Opp	S/U	Line	ATS	Total	O/U	
9/4/2021	vs	MONTANA STATE	19	16	W	-19.0	L	45.0	U	
9/11/2021	@	Northern Illinois	50	43	W	-6.5	W	49.5	O	
9/18/2021	vs	BALL STATE	45	12	W	-6.5	W	53.5	O	
9/25/2021	@	Connecticut	24	22	W	-21.5	L	53.5	U	
10/9/2021	@	Air Force	14	24	L	5.5	L	46.5	U	
10/16/2021	vs	FRESNO STATE	0	17	L	3.0	L	53.5	U	
10/23/2021	vs	NEW MEXICO	3	14	L	-19.5	L	40.5	U	
10/30/2021	@	San Jose State	21	27	L	3.0	L	40.5	O	
11/6/2021	vs	COLORADO STATE	31	17	W	3.0	W	41.5	O	"Bronze Boot"
11/12/2021	@	Boise State	13	23	L	13.5	W	48.5	U	
11/20/2021	@	Utah State	44	17	W	5.5	W	52.0	O	"Bridger's Battle"
11/27/2021	vs	HAWAII	14	38	L	-13.5	L	48.5	O	"Paniolo Trophy"
12/21/2021	vs	**Kent State**	52	38	W	-3.0	W	61.0	O	Famous Idaho Potato Bowl
Coach: Craig Bohl		Season Record >>	330	308	7-6	ATS>>	6-7	O/U>>	7-6	

2020-Wyoming		Opponent	WYO	Opp	S/U	Line	ATS	Total	O/U	
10/24/2020	@	Nevada	34	37	L	-3.0	L	53.5	O	{OT}
10/30/2020	vs	HAWAII	38	7	W	3.0	W	59.5	U	
11/6/2020	@	Colorado State	24	34	L	-3.5	L	63.0	U	"Bronze Boot"
11/27/2020	@	Unlv	45	14	W	-17.0	W	52.0	O	
12/5/2020	@	New Mexico	16	17	L	-15.0	L	51.0	U	
12/12/2020	vs	BOISE STATE	9	17	L	9.5	W	47.0	U	
Coach: Craig Bohl		Season Record >>	166	126	2-4	ATS>>	3-3	O/U>>	2-4	

2019-Wyoming		Opponent	WYO	Opp	S/U	Line	ATS	Total	O/U	
8/31/2019	vs	MISSOURI	37	31	W	15.5	W	52.5	O	
9/7/2019	@	Texas State	23	14	W	-7.0	W	47.5	U	
9/14/2019	vs	IDAHO	21	16	W	-27.0	L	NT	---	
9/21/2019	@	Tulsa	21	24	L	6.0	W	46.0	U	
9/28/2019	vs	UNLV	53	17	W	-8.0	W	44.5	O	
10/12/2019	@	San Diego State	22	26	L	3.5	L	38.0	O	
10/19/2019	vs	NEW MEXICO	23	10	W	-17.5	L	49.0	U	
10/26/2019	vs	NEVADA	31	3	W	-14.0	W	43.5	U	
11/9/2019	@	Boise State	17	20	L	16.5	W	48.0	U	
11/16/2019	@	Utah State	21	26	L	5.0	T	51.5	U	"Bridger's Battle"
11/23/2019	vs	COLORADO STATE	17	7	W	-4.0	W	51.0	U	"Bronze Boot"
11/30/2019	@	Air Force	6	20	L	13.0	L	41.5	U	
12/31/2019	vs	**Georgia State**	38	17	W	-7.0	W	49.0	O	Arizona Bowl
Coach: Craig Bohl		Season Record >>	330	231	8-5	ATS>>	8-4-1	O/U>>	4-8	

2018-Wyoming		Opponent	WYO	Opp	S/U	Line	ATS	Total	O/U	
8/25/2018	@	New Mexico State	29	7	W	-5.0	W	45.5	U	
9/1/2018	vs	WASHINGTON STATE	19	41	L	3.0	L	44.0	O	
9/8/2018	@	Missouri	13	40	L	19.5	L	52.5	O	
9/15/2018	vs	WOFFORD	17	14	W	-14.0	L	NT	---	
9/29/2018	vs	BOISE STATE	14	34	L	16.0	L	46.0	O	
10/6/2018	@	Hawaii	13	17	L	-3.0	L	52.0	U	"Paniolo Trophy"
10/13/2018	@	Fresno State	3	27	L	18.0	L	44.0	U	
10/20/2018	vs	UTAH STATE	16	24	L	14.0	W	49.5	U	"Bridger's Battle"
10/27/2018	@	Colorado State	34	21	W	-3.0	W	47.5	O	"Bronze Boot"
11/3/2018	vs	SAN JOSE STATE	24	9	W	-17.0	L	39.0	U	
11/17/2018	vs	AIR FORCE	35	27	W	-2.5	W	43.0	O	
11/24/2018	@	New Mexico	31	3	W	-7.0	W	43.0	U	
Coach: Craig Bohl		Season Record >>	248	264	6-6	ATS>>	5-7	O/U>>	5-6	

WYOMING COWBOYS   MOUNTAIN WEST Mountain

STADIUM: War Memorial Stadium {29,181} | **Location:** Laramie, WY | **COACH:** Craig Bohl

DATE		Opponent	WYO	Opp	S/U	Line	ATS	Total	O/U	Trends & Angles
8/27/2022	@	Illinois								4-16 S/U in 1st road game of season since 2002
9/3/2022	vs	TULSA								vs Tulsa - Series tied 3-3
9/10/2022	vs	NORTHERN COLORADO								8-0 S/U vs Northern Colorado since 1937
9/17/2022	vs	AIR FORCE								vs Air Force - Air Force leads series 29-26-3
9/24/2022	@	Byu								0-9 S/U @ BYU as Dog since 1989
10/1/2022	vs	SAN JOSE STATE								vs San Jose State - WYO leads series 7-5
10/8/2022	@	New Mexico								vs New Mexico - Wyoming leads series 38-36
10/22/2022	vs	UTAH STATE								5-0 S/U vs Utah St as favorite since 2003 {4-1 ATS}
10/29/2022	@	Hawaii								1-4 S/U & ATS @ Hawaii as Dog since 1986
11/12/2022	@	Colorado State								3-1 S/U @ Colorado St as favorite since 1996
11/19/2022	vs	BOISE STATE								vs Boise State - Boise State leads series 15-1
11/26/2022	@	Fresno State								vs Fresno State - Fresno leads series 8-5
12/3/2022	vs									MWC Championship
	vs									BOWL GAME

Pointspread Analysis — Non-Conference
- 1-11 S/U vs Non-Conf. as 15.5-20 point Dog since 1976
- 1-20 S/U vs Non-Conf. as 10.5-15 point Dog since 1985
- 20-1 S/U vs Non-Conf. as 15.5 point or more favorite since 1988
- vs Northern Colorado - Wyoming leads series 18-5-3
- 0-14 S/U vs BYU as 8 point or more Dog since 1985

Dog
- 5-0 ATS as 30.5 point or more Dog since 2011
- 0-13 S/U as 30.5 point or more Dog since 1994
- 3-9 O/U as 30.5 point or more Dog since 1997
- 1-9 S/U as 25.5-30 point Dog since 1982
- 0-16 S/U as 20.5-25 point Dog since 1991
- 0-6 O/U as 20.5-25 point Dog since 2010
- 0-6 O/U on road as 20.5-25 point Dog since 2003
- 1-7 ATS as 20.5-25 point Dog since 2008
- 0-8 S/U @ home as 20.5 point or more Dog since 2001
- 2-13 S/U on road as 15.5-20 point Dog since 1998
- 2-24 S/U on road as 10.5-15 point Dog since 1985
- 1-7 S/U @ home as 7.5-10 point Dog since 2001
- 1-9 S/U on road as 7.5-10 point Dog since 2001

Favorite
- 9-1 S/U @ home as 3.5-7 point favorite since 2008
- 9-1 S/U as 3.5-7 point favorite since 2016
- 6-0 O/U as 7.5-10 point favorite since 2006
- 8-1 S/U @ home as 7.5-10 point favorite since 1995
- 23-4-1 S/U @ home as 10.5-15 point favorite since 1986
- 2-10 ATS as 10.5-15 point favorite since 2006
- 15-2 S/U @ home as 15.5-20 point favorite since 1987
- 17-1 S/U as 20.5 point or more favorite since 1988

Bowl Games
- 3-0 S/U in Sun Bowl
- 6-1 ATS in Bowl Games since 2004
- 0-4 S/U in Bowl Games as 3.5-7 point Dog since 1987

Pointspread Analysis — Conference
- 1-10 O/U vs Air Force as Dog since 2007
- 12-3 ATS vs Air Force as Dog since 2001
- 1-15 S/U vs Boise State as Dog since 2002
- vs Colorado State - CSU leads series 59-49-5
- 8-3 S/U vs Hawaii since 1993 {7-4 ATS}
- 1-8 S/U vs New Mexico as Dog since 1985
- vs Utah State - Utah State leads series 40-27-4
- 1-6 S/U vs Utah State as Dog since 2011 {2-4-1 ATS}
- 1-8 S/U vs Air Force as 3-11 point Dog since 1985
- 8-1 ATS vs Air Force as 11 point or more Dog since 2001
- 5-0 ATS vs Colorado State as 11 point or more Dog since 1994
- 5-0 O/U vs Colorado State as 11 point or more Dog since 1994
- 11-2 S/U vs New Mexico as 10 point or more favorite since 1987

- 4-26 S/U @ home vs ranked teams since 1974
- 3-39 S/U on road vs ranked teams all time
- 2-22 S/U vs ranked teams since 2004
- 0-29 S/U vs Top #10 ranked teams all time
- 0-7-1 ATS on road when ranked since 1988
- 14-2 S/U @ home when ranked all time
- 0-4 S/U when ranked vs ranked teams since 1988

TULSA	16-3 S/U in 1st home game of season since 2003
N. COLORADO	7-3 ATS prior to playing Air Force since 2011
N. COLORADO	3-7 S/U prior to playing Air Force since 2011
Byu	2-10 O/U after playing Air Force since 2008
New Mexico	6-1 ATS prior to playing Utah State since 2014
UTAH STATE	3-8 S/U after playing New Mexico since 2007
UTAH STATE	3-12 ATS prior to playing Hawaii since 1988
Hawaii	3-12 S/U prior to playing Colorado State since 2007
BOISE STATE	0-6 S/U prior to playing Fresno State since 1997
Fresno State	2-7 S/U & ATS in final road game of season since 2013

Books available from Steve's Football Bible LLC

Print Version $29.95 — College Football History "Glorious Games of the Past" — A historical look at some of college football's greatest and most memorable games — A celebration of 150 years of college football — By Steve Fulton

Print Version $34.95 — College Football History "Trophy Games" — The most complete historical look at college football's trophy games — FBS, FCS, DIVISION II AND DIVISION III — A CELEBRATION OF 150 YEARS OF COLLEGE FOOTBALL — BY STEVE FULTON

Print Version $34.95 — COLLEGE FOOTBALL HISTORY "RIVALRY GAMES" — AN IN DEPTH LOOK AT SOME OF COLLEGE FOOTBALL'S BIGGEST AND MOST HISTORIC RIVALRY GAMES — FBS, FCS, DIVISION II AND DIVISION III — A CELEBRATION OF 150 YEARS OF COLLEGE FOOTBALL — BY STEVE FULTON

Print Version $29.95 — COLLEGE FOOTBALL HISTORY "MEMORABLE PLAYS" AND "MEMORABLE MOMENTS" — A LOOK AT SOME OF COLLEGE FOOTBALLS MOST MEMORABLE PLAYS AND MOMENTS — A CELEBRATION OF 150 YEARS OF COLLEGE FOOTBALL — BY STEVE FULTON

These books available at numerous online retailers

Books available from Steve's Football Bible LLC

Print Version $39.95 — College Football "Bowl Games of the 20th Century" (1902-1999) BY STEVE FULTON

Print Version $28.95 — College Football "Bowl Games of the 21st Century" Part II (2011-2020) BY STEVE FULTON

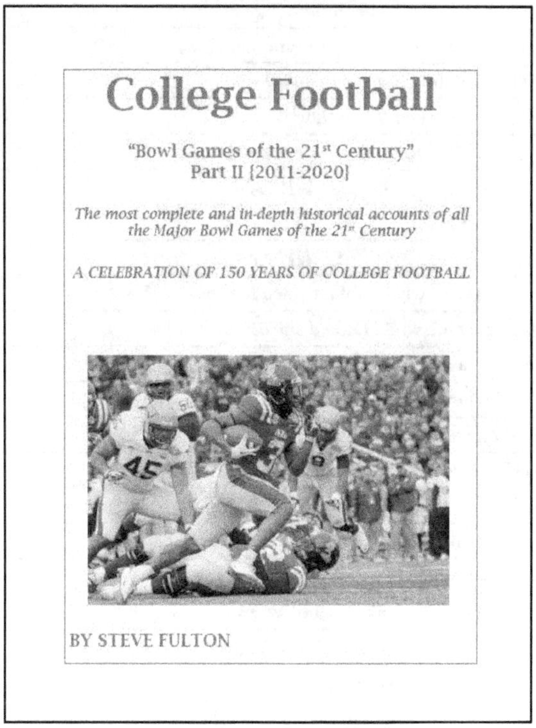

Print Version $29.95 — "GOLDEN MEMORIES" A History of Minnesota Golden Gopher Football — Year by Year recaps with schedules and game summaries 1882-2019 — By STEVE FULTON

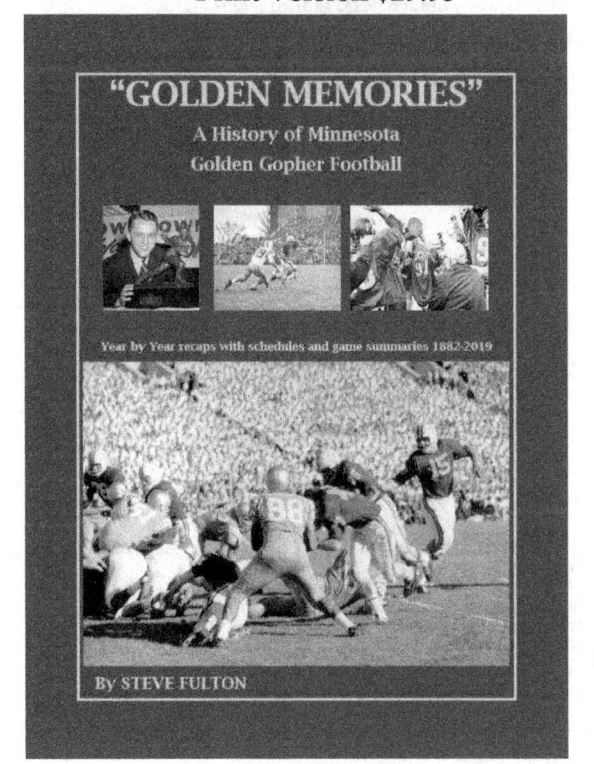

Print Version $19.95 — 2022 FCS College Football Bible, 5th Annual, 176 PAGES, Series Trends and Histories. By Steve's Football Bible LLC. The FCS College Football fan's best friend for the 2022 season
- Schedules for ALL 128 FCS teams
- Complete history of each team's Post-season games and results
- Team vs team series trends and histories

Steve's Football Bible bold prediction for 2022 season: FCS National Champion for the 2022 season will come from this list of teams: Eastern Washington, James Madison, Kennesaw State, Montana, Montana State, North Dakota State, Northern Iowa, Sam Houston State, South Dakota State. America's #1 Choice for College Football Trends & Angles

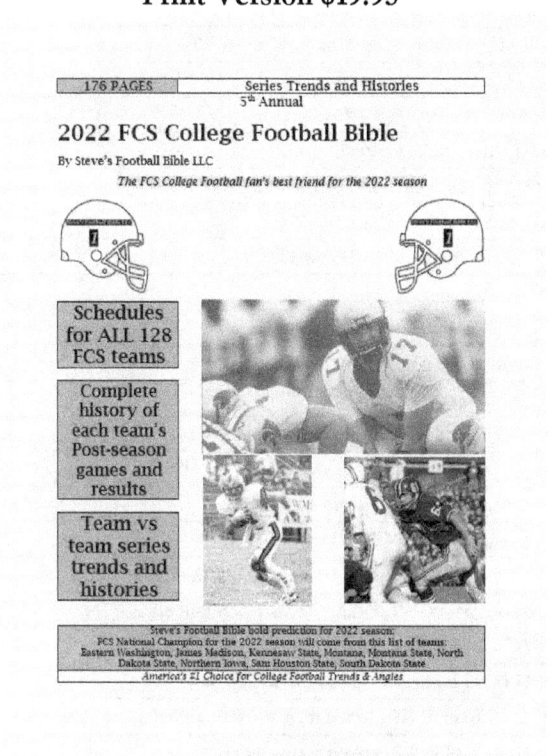

These books available at numerous online retailers

Team records vs Ranked teams

TEAM records {when ranked}	
AIR FORCE	0-5 O/U vs #17 ranked teams when ranked since 2001
5-1 S/U when ranked #10 all time	5-0 S/U vs #18 ranked teams when ranked since 2006
4-0 S/U vs when ranked #13 all time	6-1 S/U vs #20 ranked teams when ranked all time
5-0 S/U when ranked #20 since 1969	14-0 S/U vs Arkansas when ranked since 2008
4-0 S/U when ranked #7 all time	21-1-1 S/U @ LSU when ranked since 1965
7-1 S/U vs Colorado State when ranked {4-0 on road}	2-8-2 O/U vs LSU when ranked since 2011
AKRON	10-1 S/U vs LSU when ranked since 2012
NEVER RANKED	11-1 S/U vs Miami when ranked all time
	24-0 S/U @ home vs Mississippi State when ranked since 1961
ALABAMA	2-17-1 O/U vs Mississippi State when ranked since 1995
47-7 S/U on road when ranked since 2008	44-3 S/U vs Mississippi State when ranked since 1961
61-1 S/U @ home when ranked since 2013	21-2 S/U vs Mississippi when ranked since 1989
86-10 S/U when ranked #1 since 2009	16-0 S/U vs Tennessee when ranked since 2002
42-10 S/U when ranked #1 vs ranked teams since 1978	8-1 S/U vs Texas A&M when ranked since 2013
12-0 S/U on road when ranked #2 since 1992	31-0 S/U vs Vanderbilt when ranked since 1971
11-0 S/U at Neutral sites when ranked #2 since 1979	18-0 S/U @ home vs Vanderbilt when ranked since 1960
7-1 S/U on road when ranked #2 vs ranked teams all time	**ALABAMA-BIRMINGHAM**
35-0 S/U when ranked #2 vs unranked teams since 1986	NEVER RANKED
23-0 S/U @ home when ranked #3 since 1964	**APPALACHIAN STATE**
5-0 S/U @ home vs ranked teams when ranked #3 all time	7-3 S/U when ranked all time
21-1 S/U on road when ranked #4 all time	**ARIZONA**
28-1 S/U @ home when ranked #4 all time	1-8 S/U on road when ranked vs ranked teams since 1999
12-1 S/U @ home when ranked #5 since 1961	10-1 S/U on road when ranked vs ranked teams since 1998
8-0 S/U on road when ranked #6 since 1981	26-5 S/U @ home when ranked vs unranked teams since 1993
18-2 S/U when ranked #6 since 1971	0-3 S/U when ranked vs #3 ranked teams all time
16-0-1 S/U @ home when ranked #7 since 1945	4-1 S/U when ranked #7 all time
10-1 S/U @ home when ranked #8 all time	0-4 ATS when ranked #7 since 1993
17-3-1 S/U when ranked #9 all time	0-3 S/U on road when #13 ranked all time
9-2 S/U when ranked #10 since 1977	5-0 S/U @ home when #14 ranked since 1986
3-17 O/U when ranked #11 since 1983	11-2 S/U when #15 ranked all time
8-1 S/U when ranked #12 since 1981	11-2 S/U when #17 ranked all time {7-0 @ home}
15-2 S/U when ranked #13 since 1985 {5-0 on road}	0-5 S/U when ranked vs #17 #18 ranked teams all time
12-1 S/U when ranked #14 all time	0-4 ATS when #18 ranked all time
12-2 S/U @ home when ranked #15 all time	5-0 ATS when ranked #21 since 1992
8-1 S/U @ home when ranked #16 since 1983	1-5 ATS when ranked #22 since 1992
1-5 ATS when ranked #18 since 1983	4-0 O/U when ranked #23 all time
5-0 S/U @ home when ranked #20 since 1985	4-0 S/U vs Arizona State when ranked since 1993
10-1-1 S/U when ranked #20 since 1976	1-9 ATS vs California when ranked all time {0-4 @ home}
0-4 S/U when ranked #22 since 1998	0-4 S/U when ranked vs Oregon since 2000
3-0 S/U when ranked #24 all time	3-0 S/U vs San Diego State when ranked all time
10-2 S/U vs #1 ranked teams when ranked since 1977	0-8 ATS vs UCLA when ranked since 1993
0-4 S/U on road vs #2 ranked teams when ranked all time	0-5 S/U & ATS when ranked vs ranked UCLA since 1993
2-10 S/U vs #2 ranked teams when ranked all time	1-8 S/U vs USC when ranked all time
7-1 S/U vs #3 ranked teams when ranked since 2008	0-6 S/U when ranked vs ranked USC all time
4-0 S/U on road vs #5 ranked teams when ranked since 1971	4-0 S/U vs Washington when ranked since 1992
1-5 S/U on road vs #6 ranked teams when ranked all time	11-0 S/U vs Washington State when ranked all time
8-1-1 S/U vs #10 ranked teams when ranked since 1977	**ARIZONA STATE**
5-0 S/U vs #12 ranked teams when ranked all time	13-2 S/U @ home when ranked since 2011
11-1 S/U vs #14 ranked teams when ranked all time	6-0 S/U when #4 ranked since 1996
6-0 ATS vs #14 ranked teams when ranked since 1989	3-0 S/U when #5 ranked all time
5-1 S/U vs #16 ranked teams when ranked since 1975	7-1 S/U when #9 ranked all time {4-0 @ home}

Team records when ranked

8-0 S/U when #10 ranked all time	21-0-2 S/U when #1 ranked all time
10-0-1 S/U when ranked #11 since 1973	13-1-1 S/U when #2 ranked all time
0-6 S/U when ranked #12 since 1977	8-1-1 S/U when #3 ranked all time {4-0 on road}
10-2 S/U @ home when ranked #13 all time	6-1 S/U when #5 ranked all time
0-6 ATS when ranked #15 since 2004	1-4 S/U when #19 ranked all time
6-2 S/U when ranked #17 all time	7-0 S/U when ranked vs #15 - #19 ranked teams all time
6-0 S/U @ home when #18 ranked since 1981	3-0 S/U when ranked vs Villanova all time
8-1 S/U when #19 ranked all time	**AUBURN**
8-0 S/U @ home when #20 ranked since 1981	5-18 S/U on road when ranked vs ranked teams since 2007
5-0 S/U @ home when #21 ranked since 2003	46-6 S/U @ home when ranked since 2009
4-0 S/U @ home when ranked #23 all time	18-5 S/U @ home when ranked vs ranked teams since 2004
0-3 S/U vs #7 ranked teams when ranked all time	0-5 S/U in Bowl Games vs ranked teams since 2014 {-14 ATS}
3-1 S/U vs Colorado when ranked all time	7-1 S/U @ home when #2 ranked all time
4-0 S/U @ home vs Oregon State when ranked since 1982	5-1-1 S/U on road when #2 ranked since 1957
0-3 S/U vs ranked Oregon team when ranked all time	10-1-2 S/U @ home when #3 ranked all time
7-2 S/U vs Utah when ranked since 1974	16-1-3 S/U When #3 ranked since 1983 {4-0-1 on road}
5-0 S/U vs Washington State when ranked since 2004	11-0-2 S/U when #3 ranked vs ranked team all time
ARKANSAS	12-0 S/U @ home when #4 ranked all time
11-2 O/U on road when ranked since 2007	11-1 S/U @ home when #5 ranked since 1983
22-5 S/U @ home when ranked since 2007	10-2 S/U @ home when #6 ranked since 1988
6-1 S/U @ home when #2 ranked since 1965	5-2 S/U on road when #7 ranked since 1983
3-0 S/U on road when ranked #2 all time	14-1 S/U @ home when #8 ranked all time
4-0 S/U @ home when ranked #3 all time	12-2 S/U @ home when #9 ranked all time
1-4 S/U @ home when ranked #4 since 1970	13-0 S/U @ home when #10 ranked all time
6-0 S/U @ home when ranked #6 all time	9-1 S/U @ home when #11 ranked since 1969
4-0 S/U on road when #7 ranked since 1962	16-1 S/U when #12 ranked since 1970 {6-1 on road}
7-2 S/U on road when #8 ranked all time	5-0 S/U when #12 ranked vs ranked teams since 1972
8-2 S/U @ home when #8 ranked since 1977	6-0 S/U @ home when #14 ranked since 1955
10-0 S/U @ home when #9 ranked since 1970	*2-7 O/U when #16 ranked since 2005*
6-0 S/U on road when #11 ranked all time	3-7 S/U when #16 ranked vs ranked teams all time
6-1 S/U on road when #13 ranked all time	*1-9 ATS when #17 ranked since 2000*
8-2 S/U @ home when #13 ranked since 1959	5-1 S/U @ home when #18 ranked since 1984
9-0 S/U @ home when #14 ranked since 1976	0-4 S/U on road when #19 ranked all time
9-1 S/U @ home when #15 ranked all time	7-0 S/U @ home when #19 ranked since 1980
10-1 S/U @ home when #17 ranked all time	8-2 S/U @ home when #20 ranked all time
8-2 S/U @ home when ranked #18 all time	0-3 S/U when #20 ranked vs ranked team all time
5-0 S/U when ranked #19 since 1959	*6-1 O/U when #21 ranked since 1995*
8-1 S/U @ home when ranked #20 all time	6-0 S/U when #22 ranked all time
0-5 O/U when #22 ranked all time	3-0 S/U on road when #24 ranked all time
0-6 S/U when ranked vs #1 ranked teams since 1969	*1-7 ATS when #25 ranked all time*
0-7 S/U when ranked vs #3 ranked teams all time	*0-6 O/U when #25 ranked since 1998*
5-0 S/U when ranked vs #14 ranked teams all time	12-5 S/U when ranked vs ranked Alabama since 1983
1-8 S/U when ranked vs Alabama all time	6-0 S/U @ home when ranked vs Arkansas since 2010
4-0 S/U when ranked vs Mississippi State since 1999	0-6 S/U when ranked @ Georgia since 2007
4-1 S/U when ranked vs Mississippi since 2006	*2-5 O/U when ranked vs Mississippi State since 2006*
4-0 S/U @ home when ranked vs Mississippi since 1998	20-0 S/U when ranked vs Mississippi all time
4-0 S/U when ranked vs South Carolina all time	**BALL STATE**
ARKANSAS STATE	5-2 S/U when ranked all time
NEVER RANKED	**BAYLOR**
ARMY	31-4 S/U @ home when ranked since 2011
13-1 S/U @ home when ranked since 1956	3-0 S/U when #2 ranked all time

Page | 267   Copyright © 2022 by Steve's Football Bible, LLC

Team records when ranked

4-0 S/U @ home when #5 ranked all time	6-0 S/U when #14 #15 ranked all time
5-0 S/U on road when #10 ranked all time	0-5-1 S/U @ home when #17 ranked all time
7-0 S/U when #11 ranked since 1980	5-1 S/U when #18 ranked since 1976
3-0 S/U on road when #12 ranked all time	7-1 S/U when ranked #19 since 1983
1-4 ATS when #13 ranked since 1986	5-0 S/U @ home when #25 ranked all time
3-1 S/U & ATS when #14 ranked all time	*7-0 O/U when #25 ranked since 1999*
4-0 S/U on road when #16 ranked since 1956	0-4 S/U & ATS when ranked vs #5 ranked teams all time
6-0 S/U when #17 ranked since 1985 {4-0 @ home}	3-0 S/U when ranked vs #9 ranked teams all time
8-0 S/U when #19 ranked since 1948	1-4 S/U when ranked vs Florida State all time
3-1 S/U when #21 ranked all time	**BOWLING GREEN**
4-0 S/U when #23 ranked all time	5-0 S/U @ home when ranked all time
0-4 S/U when ranked vs #7 ranked teams all time	**BYU**
0-4 S/U on road when ranked vs #5 ranked teams since 1976	2-8 S/U on road when ranked vs ranked teams since 1991
0-5 S/U when ranked vs #19 ranked teams all time	30-4 S/U @ home when ranked since 2001
5-0 S/U when ranked vs Iowa State all time	4-0 S/U @ home when #4 ranked all time
5-0 S/U when ranked vs Kansas all time	4-0 S/U when ranked #5 all time
6-0 S/U when ranked vs Texas Tech since 2011	*0-4 ATS when ranked #7 since 1984*
5-1 O/U when ranked vs Texas Tech since 2011	*1-6 ATS when #9 ranked since 1985*
0-6 O/U when ranked vs Texas since 2013	7-1 S/U When #10 ranked all time
BOISE STATE	10-1 S/U when ranked #11 all-time {7-0 @ home}
54-4 S/U @ home when ranked all time	5-1 S/U when #12 ranked all time
7-1 S/U when #3 ranked all time	6-0 S/U @ home when #13 ranked all time
0-5 O/U when #3 ranked since 2010	11-1 S/U when #15 ranked all time {6-0 @ home}
4-0 S/U when #4 ranked all time	4-0 S/U on road when #16 ranked all time
6-1 S/U when #5 ranked all time	10-1 S/U when #17 ranked since 1977 {3-0 on road}
9-0 S/U when #6 ranked all time	10-2 S/U when #18 ranked all time
4-0 S/U when #8 ranked all time	0-6 S/U when #19 ranked vs ranked teams all time
3-0 S/U when #11 ranked all time	5-1 S/U @ home when #20 ranked all time
6-0 S/U when #15 ranked all time	10-1 S/U when #21 ranked all time {6-0 @ home}
5-0 S/U when #16 ranked all time	*0-5 O/U when #22 ranked all time*
0-5 O/U when #16 ranked all time	6-0-1 S/U when #23 ranked all time
4-1 S/U when #18 ranked all time	5-0 S/U when #24 ranked since 1996
8-1 S/U when #21 ranked all time	5-0 S/U @ home when #25 ranked since 1994
6-0 S/U @ home when #22 ranked all time	0-3 S/U & ATS when ranked vs #7 ranked teams all time
6-0 S/U when #23 ranked all time	14-1 S/U when ranked vs Utah State all time {5-0 on road}
6-1 S/U when #24 ranked all time	4-0 S/U @home when ranked vs Wyoming all time
5-0 S/U when #25 ranked all time	**BUFFALO**
5-0 O/U when #25 ranked all time	1-1 S/U when ranked all time
0-6 S/U on road when ranked vs ranked teams all time	**CALIFORNIA**
5-0 S/U when ranked vs Colorado State all time	2-10 S/U on road when ranked since 2007
0-4 O/U when ranked vs Fresno State since 2012	22-6 S/U @ home when ranked since 2004
8-1 S/U when ranked vs Nevada all time {3-0 @ home}	13-3 S/U when ranked vs Non-Conference since 2005
0-4 ATS when ranked vs Nevada since 2009	5-1 S/U when #2 ranked all time {3-0 on road}
4-0 S/U when ranked vs New Mexico all time	6-0-1 S/U @ home when #4 ranked since 1948
8-1 S/U when ranked vs Utah State all time {5-0 @ home}	9-1 S/U when #5 ranked all time {5-0 @ home - 4-0 on road}
BOSTON COLLEGE	3-0 S/U @ home when #6 ranked all time
13-2 S/U @ home when ranked since 2005	*0-5 O/U when #7 ranked since 1991*
4-1 S/U when #4 ranked all time	5-0 S/U @ home when #8 ranked all time
4-0 S/U when ranked #5 #6 #7 all time	0-3 S/U on road when #9 ranked since 1951
4-0 S/U when #10 ranked all time	5-0 S/U @ home when #9 ranked all time
1-4 S/U when #13 ranked all time	9-1 S/U when #10 ranked all time {5-0 @ home}

Team records when ranked

5-0 S/U when #12 ranked since 2004	0-4 S/U & ATS on road when #18 ranked since 1992
4-1 S/U @ home when ranked #17 all time	5-0-1 S/U @ home when ranked #18 all time
4-1 S/U @ home when ranked #19 all time	4-11 ATS when #19 ranked since 1986
3-0 S/U @ home when ranked #21 ranked all time	6-0 S/U when #21 ranked all time
1-4 S/U when ranked #23 all time	2-6 ATS when #22 ranked since 1990
1-4 O/U when ranked #23 all time	4-0 S/U @ home when #23 ranked all time
0-6 ATS when #24 ranked all time	4-0 S/U on road when #24 ranked all time
0-3 S/U when ranked vs #1 ranked team all time	5-0 S/U when ranked vs #16 ranked teams all time
0-5 S/U when ranked vs #7 ranked team all time	3-0 S/U when ranked vs #17 ranked teams all time
8-1 S/U @ home when ranked vs Oregon all time	1-4 S/U on road when ranked vs #20 ranked teams all time
5-0 S/U when ranked @ Oregon State all time	0-4 S/U when ranked vs #24 ranked teams all time
0-5 S/U when ranked @ USC since 1952	3-0 S/U when ranked vs #25 ranked teams all time
0-7 S/U when ranked @ ranked USC since 1938	11-0 S/U when ranked vs Boston College since 2011
4-0 S/U when ranked vs unranked USC all time	4-0 S/U when ranked vs Louisville all time
10-2-2 S/U when ranked vs unranked Washington all time	12-2 S/U when ranked vs NC State since 1997 {5-0 @ home}
0-3 S/U when ranked vs ranked Washington since 1991	2-7 O/U when ranked vs Syracuse all time
CENTRAL FLORIDA	28-0 S/U when ranked vs Wake Forest since 1948 {12-0 on road}
37-5 S/U when ranked all time	**COASTAL CAROLINA**
5-1 S/U when ranked vs ranked teams all time	15-3 S/U when ranked all time
13-2 S/U on road when ranked all time	**COLORADO**
3-0 S/U when ranked #10 all time	0-6 S/U on road when ranked vs ranked teams since 1996
0-3 O/U when ranked #10 all time	23-5 S/U @ home when ranked since 1996
4-0 S/U when ranked #17 all time	5-0 S/U @ home when #2 ranked all time
CENTRAL MICHIGAN	5-1 S/U when #4 ranked all time {2-0 on road}
CHARLOTTE	1-6 ATS when #5 ranked since 1990
NEVER RANKED	5-0 S/U @ home when #6 ranked all time
CINCINNATI	10-2 S/U when #7 ranked since 1993
26-2 S/U @ home when ranked since 2008	6-0 S/U @ home when #8 ranked since 1967
7-0 S/U when #5 ranked all time	0-3 S/U on road when #8 ranked since 1970
CLEMSON	7-0 S/U @ home when #9 ranked since 1972
27-3 S/U on road when ranked since 2015	5-0 S/U on road when #9 ranked since 1990
46-1 S/U @ home when ranked since 2014	7-0 S/U @ home when #10 ranked all time
19-3 S/U when ranked #1 all time	9-1 S/U @ home when #12 ranked all time
22-3 S/U when ranked #2 all-time {10-0 @ home}	4-0 S/U on road when #12 ranked all time
23-5 S/U when ranked #3 all-time {8-0 on road}	4-0 S/U @ home when #14 ranked all time
6-0 ATS on road when #3 ranked since 2013	4-0 S/U on road when #15 ranked all time
16-0 S/U when #4 ranked all time	7-1 S/U @ home when #16 ranked all time
10-1 ATS when #4 ranked since 2016	0-3 S/U on road when #17 ranked since 1973
10-1 S/U when #5 ranked all time {4-0 on road}	5-0 S/U @ home when #19 ranked all time
4-0 S/U @ home when #7 ranked since 1989	8-1 S/U when #20 ranked all time {4-0 on road}
9-0 S/U @ home when #8 ranked all time	4-1 S/U @ home when #21 ranked all time
6-0 ATS when #8 ranked 1991	1-4 O/U when #21 ranked since 2002
5-0 S/U @ home when #9 ranked all time	4-0 S/U when #25 ranked all time
5-0 S/U @ home when #10 ranked all time	0-4 S/U on road when ranked vs #2 ranked teams all time
11-1 S/U when #12 ranked since 1959	0-4 ATS when ranked vs #2 ranked teams since 1995
1-5 ATS when #13 ranked since 1991	0-3 S/U when ranked vs #6 ranked teams since 1972
6-1 S/U & ATS when #14 ranked since 1989	0-3 S/U when ranked vs #8 ranked teams since 1991
13-2-1 S/U when #15 ranked since 1977	0-4 ATS when ranked vs #8 ranked teams all time
10-3 ATS when #15 ranked since 1988	0-4 O/U when ranked vs #9 ranked teams since 1991
0-4 S/U & ATS when #16 ranked since 2007	5-0 S/U when ranked vs #10 ranked teams all time
7-0 S/U @ home when ranked #17 all time	3-0 S/U when ranked vs #12 ranked teams all time

Team records when ranked

4-0 S/U when ranked vs #22 ranked teams all time	9-2 S/U @ home when #11 ranked all time
5-0 S/U when ranked vs Air Force all time	*11-1-1 ATS when #11 ranked since 2004*
3-0 S/U when ranked vs Arizona all time	*1-5 ATS when #12 ranked since 2002*
0-3 S/U when ranked vs USC all time	*1-11 ATS when #13 ranked since 1986*
0-3 O/U when ranked vs USC all time	10-2 S/U @ home when #14 ranked since 1970
COLORADO STATE	5-0 S/U @ home when #15 ranked all time
0-3 O/U when ranked vs Air Force all time	5-0 S/U when #16 ranked since 2004
4-0 S/U when ranked vs New Mexico all time	*1-6 ATS when #17 ranked since 2003*
CONNECTICUT	5-0 S/U @ home when #18 ranked since 1987
0-3 S/U & ATS on road when ranked all time	*9-0 ATS when #18 ranked since 1983*
DUKE	0-5 S/U on road when #19 ranked since 1980
6-0 S/U & ATS on road when ranked since 2010	10-0 S/U @ home when #19 ranked since 1959
1-8 S/U @ home when ranked since 1994	*1-6 ATS when #19 ranked since 2004*
1-7 ATS @ home when ranked since 2007	6-0 S/U @ home when #20 ranked since 1988
5-0-1 S/U @ home when #4 ranked all time	*6-1 ATS when #20 ranked since 1992*
3-0 S/U @ home when ranked #7 all time	4-0 S/U @ home when #22 ranked since 2011
6-0-1 S/U when #10 ranked all time	7-0 S/U when #23 ranked all time
8-2 S/U when #11 ranked all time	*0-5 ATS when #23 ranked since 2002*
9-2-1 S/U when #13 ranked all time	*0-4 O/U when #25 ranked since 2003*
0-3 S/U when #14 ranked all time	0-3 S/U on road when ranked vs #1 ranked team all time
6-1 S/U when #15 ranked all time {3-0 @ home}	0-5 S/U on road when ranked vs #3 ranked team all time
0-4 S/U & ATS when #16 ranked since 1958	10-0 S/U when ranked vs #4 ranked team since 1990
4-0 S/U on road when #20 ranked all time	*9-0-1 ATS when ranked vs #4 ranked team since 1990*
3-0 S/U on road when #25 ranked all time	0-4 S/U on road when ranked vs #5 ranked teams all time
0-4 S/U when ranked vs #1 ranked teams all time	5-2 S/U & ATS when ranked vs #8 ranked teams since 1995
0-4 S/U when ranked @ Georgia Tech since 1947	*7-1 O/U when ranked vs #8 ranked teams since 1990*
0-3 S/U @ home when ranked vs North Carolina since 1957	*1-5 O/U when ranked vs #10 ranked teams since 1987*
6-0 S/U when ranked vs Virginia all time	3-0 S/U @ home when ranked vs #11 ranked team since 1976
13-1 S/U when ranked vs Wake Forest all time {6-0 on road}	0-4 S/U & ATS when ranked vs #12 ranked teams since 2003
EAST CAROLINA	1-7 S/U & ATS when ranked vs #14 ranked teams since 1992
0-5 ATS on road when ranked since 2008	*0-4 O/U when ranked vs #15 ranked teams since 1994*
0-4 ATS @ home when ranked since 2007	5-1 S/U & ATS when ranked vs #21 ranked teams all time
3-0 S/U when #16 ranked all time	6-1 S/U when ranked vs #23 ranked teams all time
EASTERN MICHIGAN	3-0 S/U when ranked vs #25 ranked teams all time
NEVER RANKED	31-2 S/U when ranked vs Kentucky since 1980 {16-1 on road}
FLORIDA	22-2 S/U when ranked vs South Carolina all time
13-0 S/U @ home when #1 ranked since 1996	26-0 S/U when ranked vs Vanderbilt since 1989
12-1 S/U when #1 ranked since 2009	**FLORIDA ATLANTIC**
6-1 S/U @ home when #2 ranked all time	NEVER RANKED
7-1 S/U on road when #3 ranked all time	**FLORIDA INTERNATIONAL**
14-2 S/U @ home when #3 ranked since 1995	NEVER RANKED
5-1 S/U on road when #4 ranked since 2001	**FLORIDA STATE**
13-2 S/U @ home when #4 ranked since 1992	19-3 S/U on road when ranked since 2012
17-0 S/U @ home when ranked #5 all time	25-0 S/U @ home when #1 ranked since 1993
8-0 ATS when #5 ranked since 2006	*1-8 ATS when #1 ranked since 2014*
14-2 S/U @ home when #6 ranked all time	13-0 S/U @ home when #2 ranked all time
8-1 S/U @ home when #7 ranked all time	*8-2 O/U when #2 ranked since 2013*
15-1 S/U when #8 ranked since 1993 {8-0 @ home}	18-0 S/U @ home when #3 ranked all time
8-0 S/U @ home when #9 ranked since 1983	8-0 S/U @ home when #4 ranked since 1987
4-11 O/U when #10 ranked since 2000	*0-6 ATS on road when #4 ranked since 1994*
14-1 S/U @ home when #10 ranked all time	28-3 S/U when #5 ranked all time {11-1 on road}

Team records when ranked

24-3 S/U when #6 ranked since 1985 {13-1 @ home}	12-1 S/U when #10 ranked since 2002 {5-0 on road}
8-0-1 S/U @ home when #7 ranked all time	9-1 S/U @ home when #11 ranked since 1971
17-0 S/U when #8 ranked all time	7-0 S/U @ home when #12 ranked since 1999
1-6 ATS when #9 ranked since 2004	11-1 S/U @ home when #13 ranked all time
6-0 O/U when #10 ranked since 2006	10-0 S/U when #13 ranked since 2011
8-1 S/U @ home when #11 ranked all time	10-0 S/U on road when #14 ranked all time
5-1 S/U on road when #12 ranked all time	*0-5 O/U on road when #15 ranked since 1983*
9-0 S/U when #13 ranked since 1978	8-0 S/U @ home when #15 ranked all time
8-2 S/U when #14 ranked all time	6-0 S/U @ home when #18 ranked since 1985
0-4 O/U when #14 ranked since 2002	6-0 S/U @ home when ranked #20 all time
4-0-1 S/U @ home when #15 ranked all time	5-0 S/U when #21 ranked since 1997
2-7 ATS when #16 ranked since 1989	6-0 S/U when #24 ranked all time
4-0 S/U @ home when #17 ranked all time	*5-1 ATS when ranked vs #2 ranked teams since 1984*
0-3 S/U on road when #20 ranked since 1986	0-3 S/U & ATS when ranked vs #5 ranked teams since 1999
3-0 S/U & ATS when #22 ranked all time	2-6 S/U when ranked vs #8 ranked teams since 1982
0-5 S/U when ranked vs #1 ranked teams since 1999	*6-1 O/U when ranked vs #8 ranked teams since 1987*
0-5 O/U when ranked vs #1 ranked teams since 1999	*0-4 O/U when ranked vs #17 ranked teams since 1987*
1-7 S/U when ranked vs #3 ranked teams since 1995	*4-0 ATS when ranked vs #20 ranked teams since 1999*
1-5 S/U when ranked vs #5 ranked teams all time	4-0 S/U when ranked vs #22 ranked teams since 2002
0-5 O/U when ranked vs #7 ranked teams all time	*0-5 O/U when ranked vs #22 ranked teams since 2002*
5-0 S/U @ home when ranked vs #10 ranked teams since 1991	*1-6 O/U when ranked vs #24 ranked teams all time*
6-0 S/U when ranked vs #11 ranked teams since 1989	21-0 S/U when ranked vs Kentucky since 1991 {10-0 on road}
0-3 S/U when ranked vs #12 ranked teams all time	9-0 S/U when ranked vs Mississippi State since 1967 {6-0 @ home}
4-0 O/U when ranked vs #12 ranked teams since 1985	5-0 S/U when ranked @ Missouri all time
6-0 S/U when ranked vs #15 ranked teams all time	*2-9 O/U when ranked @ South Carolina since 1998*
3-0 S/U when ranked vs #16 ranked teams all time	*2-6 ATS when ranked @ home vs Tennessee since 2004*
6-1 S/U when ranked vs #19 ranked teams all time {3-0 @ home}	17-1 S/U @ home when ranked vs Vanderbilt all time
4-0 S/U & ATS when ranked vs #25 ranked all time	**GEORGIA SOUTHERN**
8-1 S/U when ranked vs Boston College all time	NEVER RANKED
3-10 O/U when ranked vs Florida since 2000	**GEORGIA STATE**
5-0 S/U @ home when ranked vs Georgia Tech all time	NEVER RANKED
6-0 S/U when ranked vs Miami since 2010	**GEORGIA TECH**
2-11 O/U when ranked vs Miami since 2002	10-2 S/U when #2 ranked all time
2-11 ATS when ranked vs NC State since 2001	12-1-2 S/U when #3 ranked all time {9-0-1 @ home}
9-0 S/U when ranked vs Syracuse all time	9-2 S/U when ranked #4 all time
12-1 S/U when ranked @ home vs Wake Forest all time	14-2 S/U when #6 ranked all time
FRESNO STATE	6-1 S/U @ home when #8 ranked all time
5-1 S/U @ home when ranked since 2013	4-0-1 S/U on road when #8 ranked all time
GEORGIA	10-3 S/U when ranked #9 all time
28-1 S/U @ home when ranked since 2017	4-0-1 S/U on road when #11 ranked all time
7-0 S/U @ home when #1 ranked all time	7-1-1 S/U when #11 ranked since 1951
8-0 S/U @ home when #2 ranked all time	*0-4 ATS when #14 ranked since 2008*
6-1 S/U on road when #3 ranked since 1982	0-4 S/U when #15 ranked all time
10-1 S/U @ home when #4 ranked all time	*1-6 ATS when #15 ranked since 2000*
1-9-1 O/U when #4 ranked since 1983	11-2 S/U when #16 ranked all time
13-0 S/U @ home when #5 ranked all time	4-0 S/U on road when #17 ranked since 1991
11-0 S/U @ home when #6 ranked all time	6-0 S/U when #18 ranked since 1984
20-2 S/U when ranked #6 since 1971	3-0 S/U @ home when #19 ranked all time
11-1 S/U when #7 ranked since 2005 {4-0 on road}	0-3 S/U on road when #19 ranked since 1960
2-7 ATS when #8 ranked since 2004	0-4 S/U & ATS when #20 ranked since 2008
14-2 S/U when #9 ranked since 1966 {5-0 on road}	3-0 S/U @ home when #23 ranked all time

Team records when ranked

0-3 S/U when ranked vs #3 ranked teams all time	5-0 S/U @ home when ranked vs Minnesota all time
5-1 S/U when ranked vs #9 ranked teams all time {3-0 @ home}	9-1 S/U when ranked vs Northwestern since 1951 {4-0 @ home}
0-5 O/U when ranked vs #19 ranked teams since 2000	4-1 S/U @ home when ranked vs Purdue all time
11-1 S/U when ranked @ home vs Clemson all time	4-0 S/U when ranked vs Wisconsin since 1963
1-5 S/U when ranked vs Florida State since 1992	**INDIANA**
1-7 O/U when ranked vs Georgia since 2000	3-11 S/U on road when ranked since 1987
HAWAII	8-0-1 S/U @ home when ranked since 1987
5-0 S/U on road when ranked since 2007	5-1 S/U when ranked #6 #7 #8 all time
8-0 S/U @ home when ranked since 2007	0-4 S/U when #19 ranked since 1950
4-0 S/U when ranked #16 ranked all time	2-11 S/U on road when ranked vs ranked teams all time
0-4 ATS when ranked #16 ranked all time	4-0 S/U when ranked vs Purdue since 1942
HOUSTON	**IOWA**
30-1 S/U @ home when ranked since 1988	8-16 S/U when ranked vs ranked teams since 1994
10-1 S/U when #6 ranked all time {6-0 @ home}	5-0 S/U @ home when #1 ranked all time
5-1 S/U when #11 ranked since 1978	6-1 S/U when #2 ranked all time {3-0 on road}
0-3 S/U on road when #12 ranked all time	4-0-1 S/U on road when #3 ranked all time
5-0 S/U @ home when #12 ranked all time	3-0 S/U @ home when #3 ranked all time
4-0 S/U @ home when #13 ranked all time	4-0 S/U when #6 ranked since 2002
4-0 S/U on road when #14 ranked since 1973	0-4 S/U on road when #8 ranked since 1986
10-1 S/U @ home when #14 ranked since 1989	*0-4 ATS when #8 ranked since 1997*
5-1 S/U when ranked #16 all time	5-0 S/U @ home when #9 ranked since 1991
10-1 S/U when #17 ranked all time {5-0 @ home}	1-6 S/U on road when #9 ranked since 1954
7-1 S/U @ home when #18 ranked all time	6-0 S/U @ home when #10 ranked all time
12-1 S/U when ranked #19 all-time {7-0 on road}	8-1 S/U when #11 ranked all time {4-0 on road}
3-0 O/U when #21 ranked since 2011	5-0 S/U @ home when #12 ranked all time
3-0 S/U when #24 ranked all time	7-0 S/U @ home when #15 ranked all time
3-0 S/U when ranked vs #20 ranked teams all time	6-0 S/U @ home when #16 ranked since 1997
8-1 S/U when ranked vs Memphis all time {5-0 @ home}	5-1 S/U @ home when #17 ranked since 1997
10-0 S/U when ranked vs Rice all time	6-0 S/U on road when #17 ranked all time
4-0 S/U when ranked vs SMU since 1979	8-2 S/U when #17 ranked since 1991
4-0 S/U when ranked vs Tulane all time	*9-3-2 ATS when #19 ranked since 1997*
3-0 S/U @ home when ranked vs Tulsa all time	12-1 S/U @ home when #19 ranked since 1960
ILLINOIS	*5-1 ATS when #20 ranked since 1996*
2-17 ATS @ home when ranked since 1990	*0-4 O/U when #21 ranked since 1996*
3-0 S/U on road when #4 ranked all time	4-0 S/U @ home when #22 ranked all time
7-2 S/U when #5 ranked all time	3-0 S/U on road when #23 ranked all time
9-1 S/U when #8 ranked all time {4-0 on road}	0-4 S/U when ranked vs #6 ranked teams since 1957
3-0 S/U when #9 ranked all time	1-5 S/U when ranked vs #8 ranked teams since 1985
4-1 S/U on road when #11 ranked all time	*0-4 O/U when ranked vs #8 ranked teams since 2002*
0-4 S/U when #17 ranked all time	5-0 S/U when ranked vs #9 ranked teams all time
5-0 S/U when #19 ranked since 1983	11-0 S/U when ranked vs Illinois since 1990
4-0 S/U @ home when #20 ranked all time	13-1 S/U when ranked vs Iowa State all time {6-0 @ home}
4-0 S/U when #21 ranked all time	*0-6 O/U when ranked vs Iowa State since 2005*
0-3 S/U on road when #22 ranked since 2000	4-1 S/U when ranked vs Michigan since 2002
4-0 O/U when #22 ranked since 2000	*9-4 ATS when ranked vs Michigan since 1983*
3-0 S/U when #24 ranked all time	0-8 S/U when ranked vs Ohio State since 1995
0-3 S/U when #25 ranked all time	2-10 S/U when ranked @ Ohio State all time
3-0 S/U when ranked vs #20 ranked teams all time	8-1-1 S/U @ home when ranked vs Wisconsin all time

Team records when ranked

	13-1 S/U when ranked vs Kansas all time {7-0 on road}
	5-0 S/U @ home when ranked vs Oklahoma State all time
	5-1 O/U when ranked vs Oklahoma State since 2003
IOWA STATE	4-1 S/U when ranked @ Oklahoma all time
4-13-1 S/U on road when ranked since 1978	6-1 S/U when ranked vs Texas Tech all time {4-0 @ home}
3-8 ATS on road when ranked since 2002	*7-1 ATS when ranked vs Texas all time {4-0 on road}*
15-4 S/U @ home when ranked since 1981	**Kent State**
4-16-2 S/U when ranked vs ranked teams all time	0-2 S/U when ranked vs ranked teams all time
0-5 S/U when ranked vs Oklahoma State all time	**Kentucky**
0-4-1 S/U when ranked vs Oklahoma all time	25-9 S/U @ home when ranked since 1950
Kansas	3-0 S/U when #4 ranked all time
12-2 S/U @ home when ranked since 1996	3-0 S/U @ home when #6 ranked all time
4-0 S/U when #7 ranked since 1960	6-0 S/U when #7 ranked since 1951
4-0-1 S/U when #9 ranked all time	3-0 S/U when #10 ranked all time
0-3 S/U on road when #18 ranked all time	5-0 S/U @ home when #13 ranked since 1949
4-0 S/U @ home when #19 ranked since 1952	7-1 S/U when #14 ranked all time {3-0 on road}
3-0 S/U on road when #24 ranked all time	*0-3 O/U when #14 ranked since 2007*
3-0 S/U when #25 ranked all time	4-0-1 S/U when #17 ranked since 1977
0-4 S/U when ranked vs #3 ranked teams all time	1-4 S/U when ranked vs #11 ranked teams all time
0-4 S/U when ranked vs #6 ranked teams all time	0-7 S/U when ranked vs #6 #8 #9 ranked teams all time
0-7 S/U @ home when ranked vs ranked teams since 1974	6-1 S/U when ranked vs Vanderbilt all time
9-0 S/U when ranked vs Iowa State all time	**Liberty**
5-1 S/U when ranked vs Kansas State all time	3-1 S/U when ranked all time
6-1 S/U when ranked vs Oklahoma State all time {3-0 @ home}	**UL-Lafayette**
Kansas State	12-2 S/U when ranked all time
19-2 S/U @ home when ranked since 2011	**UL-Monroe**
5-0 O/U when #2 ranked all time	NEVER RANKED
4-0 S/U @ home when #4 ranked all time	**Louisiana Tech**
4-0 S/U & ATS on road when #4 ranked all time	*5-1 O/U when ranked all time*
3-0 S/U @ home when #5 ranked all time	*1-5 ATS when ranked all time*
5-1 S/U when #6 ranked all time	**LSU**
0-4 O/U when #6 ranked since 1999	55-10 S/U @ home when ranked since 2010
7-0 S/U @ home when #7 ranked since 2000	15-1 S/U @ home when #1 ranked all time
5-0 S/U & ATS @ home when #9 ranked all time	10-2 S/U on road when #1 ranked all time
4-0 S/U @ home when #11 ranked all time	7-0 S/U @ home when #2 ranked all time
3-0 S/U on road when #12 ranked since 2001	13-1 S/U when #2 ranked since 2004
3-0 S/U on road when #14 ranked all time	9-0 S/U @ home when #3 ranked all time
4-0 S/U when #15 ranked since 1994	1-3 S/U @ home when #4 ranked since 2005
5-0 S/U when #19 ranked since 1995	12-2-1 S/U @ home when #5 ranked all time
10-2 S/U when #20 ranked since 1993 {3-1 on road}	13-3 S/U @ home when #6 ranked all time
6-0 S/U when #21 ranked all time	6-1 S/U on road when #7 ranked all time
3-0 S/U @ home when #25 ranked all time	10-0 S/U when #7 ranked since 1998
0-4 S/U when ranked vs #2 ranked teams all time	*6-1 O/U when #8 ranked since 2006*
0-3 S/U when ranked vs #3 ranked teams all time	24-2 S/U @ home when #9 ranked all time
0-3 S/U when ranked vs #5 ranked teams all time	15-1 S/U @ home when #10 ranked all time
0-3 O/U when ranked vs #5 ranked teams all time	6-0 S/U when #11 ranked team since 2009
0-8 S/U when ranked vs #7 #8 #9 ranked teams all time	*1-7 ATS @ home when #11 ranked since 1988*
0-7 ATS when ranked vs #7 #8 #9 ranked teams all time	12-2 S/U @ home when #12 ranked since 1978
3-0 S/U when ranked vs #25 ranked teams all time	14-1 S/U @ home when #13 ranked all time
11-0 S/U when ranked vs Iowa State since 1994	15-1 S/U when #13 ranked since 1988

Team records when ranked

8-2 O/U when #13 ranked since 2003	4-0 S/U when #16 ranked all time
10-1 S/U @ home when #14 ranked since 1971	5-1 S/U when #18 ranked all time
0-5 O/U when #14 ranked since 2006	4-0 S/U when #19 ranked since 2013
1-7-1 ATS when #15 ranked since 2008	0-3 ATS when #21 ranked all time
2-9 O/U when #15 ranked since 1985	0-3 O/U when #21 ranked all time
5-1 S/U on road when #16 ranked since 1978	3-0 S/U @ home when #22 ranked all time
12-2 S/U when #17 ranked since 1979 {9-1 @ home}	5-0 S/U when #23 ranked all time
5-1 S/U on road when #18 ranked all time	5-1 S/U when #24 ranked all time
14-1 S/U when #19 ranked since 1946 {10-0 @ home}	5-1 S/U when #25 ranked all time
6-1 S/U @ home when #20 ranked all time	4-1 S/U when ranked vs Pittsburgh all time
5-0 S/U when #21 ranked since 2001	1-4 ATS When ranked vs Syracuse all time
0-7 S/U when ranked vs #1 ranked teams since 2008	**Marshall**
0-5-1 O/U when ranked vs #1 ranked teams since 2009	12-2 S/U @ home when ranked all time
0-6 S/U when ranked vs #1 Alabama all time	**Maryland**
0-5 S/U when ranked on road vs #3 ranked teams all time	24-8 S/U @ home when ranked since 1976
6-0 S/U @ home when ranked vs #7 ranked teams all time	0-6 O/U @ home when ranked since 2001
4-0 S/U when ranked vs #8 ranked teams all time	0-4 S/U on road when ranked since 2006
6-1 S/U @ home when ranked vs #9 ranked teams all time	4-0 S/U @ home when #1 ranked all time
1-5 S/U @ home when ranked vs #12 ranked teams all time	12-0 S/U @ home when #2 ranked all time
0-5 ATS @ home when ranked vs #12 ranked teams since 1983	7-2 S/U when #3 ranked all time
7-2 S/U when ranked vs #14 ranked teams all time	3-0 S/U @ home when #4 ranked all time
3-0 S/U on road when ranked vs #15 ranked teams all time	6-1 S/U when #5 ranked all time {4-0 @ home}
6-1 S/U when ranked vs #16 ranked teams since 1970	3-0 S/U @ home when #6 ranked since 1976
3-0 S/U @ home when ranked vs #17 ranked teams all time	3-0 S/U when #9 ranked all time
5-0 S/U when ranked vs #18 ranked teams all time	5-1 S/U on road when #10 ranked all time
5-0 O/U when ranked vs #18 ranked teams all time	4-0 S/U when #12 ranked all time
4-0 S/U @ home when ranked vs #19 ranked teams all time	6-0 S/U @ home when #15 ranked all time
3-0 ATS when ranked vs #20 ranked teams since 1985	3-0 S/U on road when #16 ranked all time
3-0 S/U @ home when ranked vs #22 ranked teams all time	4-0 S/U when #19 ranked since 1982
3-0 S/U & ATS when ranked vs #25 ranked teams all time	5-0 S/U when #20 ranked since 1975
0-3 O/U when ranked vs #25 ranked teams all time	0-3 S/U when #21 ranked all time
1-8 S/U when ranked vs Alabama since 2012	0-3 O/U when #22 ranked all time
1-7-2 O/U when ranked vs Alabama since 2011	0-3 S/U when ranked vs #14 ranked teams all time
5-0 ATS when ranked vs Georgia since 2009	0-8 S/U when ranked vs #4 - #9 ranked teams all time
9-3 O/U when ranked vs Georgia since 1987	0-4 S/U when ranked vs Penn State all time
19-2 S/U @ home when ranked vs Mississippi State since 1949	**Massachusetts**
22-3 S/U when ranked vs Mississippi State since 1985	NEVER RANKED
5-0 S/U @ home when ranked vs Mississippi since 2010	**Memphis**
5-0 S/U when ranked vs Tennessee since 2006	9-3 S/U on road when ranked all time
10-1 ATS when ranked vs Texas A&M since 1986	6-2 O/U @ home when ranked all time
Louisville	4-1 S/U when #25 ranked all time
21-8 S/U on road when ranked since 2005	3-1 S/U when ranked vs SMU since 2017
44-9 S/U @ home when ranked all time	**Miami**
0-8 S/U on road when ranked vs ranked teams all time	60-13 S/U @ home when ranked since 2000
1-6 ATS on road when ranked vs ranked teams all time	20-0 S/U @ home when #1 ranked all time
13-0 S/U when ranked #5 #6 #7 all time	14-0 S/U on road when #1 ranked since 1991
6-1 S/U when #8 ranked all time	28-0 S/U when #1 ranked in regular season since 1991
0-6 ATS when #8 ranked since 2004	24-0 S/U @ home when #2 ranked all time
3-0 S/U when #10 ranked all time	16-1 S/U @ home when #3 ranked all time
5-0 S/U when #12 ranked all time	11-1 S/U on road when #3 ranked all time

Team records when ranked

5-0 S/U @ home when #4 ranked since 1985	180-80-6 S/U on road when ranked all time
12-0 S/U when #5 ranked all time	14-1 S/U @ home when #1 ranked all time
7-0 S/U @ home when #7 ranked all time	11-2-1 S/U @ home when #2 ranked since 1947
0-7 O/U when #7 ranked since 2000	0-4 S/U on road when #3 ranked since 1999
4-0 S/U on road when #8 ranked since 1983	*1-6 ATS when #3 ranked since 2000*
5-1 S/U @ home when #8 ranked all time	22-1 S/U @ home when #4 ranked since 1976
0-4 ATS when #8 ranked since 1999	19-2 S/U on road when #4 ranked since 1971
9-3 S/U @ home when #9 ranked since 1956	10-2 S/U when #5 ranked since 1986
7-0 S/U on road when #10 ranked all time	10-1 S/U on road when #5 ranked since 1970
7-1 S/U @ home when #10 ranked all time	11-0 S/U @ home when #6 ranked since 1983
0-4 ATS when #10 ranked since 2005	0-3 S/U on road when #7 ranked since 1995
1-5 O/U when #10 ranked since 2003	11-1 S/U @ home when #8 ranked since 1970
6-0 S/U on road when #11 ranked all time	5-0 S/U when #10 ranked since 1995
4-0 S/U on road when #13 ranked since 1981	9-1 S/U @ home when #11 ranked since 1972
8-1 S/U when #14 ranked since 1984 {4-0 S/U & ATS on road}	*5-12 O/U when #11 ranked since 1989*
7-0 S/U @ home when #14 ranked all time	*0-4 ATS @ home when ranked #11 since 1995*
5-0 S/U @ home when #17 ranked all time	*5-1 O/U when #12 ranked since 2004*
3-0 S/U on road when #18 ranked all time	*7-1 ATS when #13 ranked since 2002*
3-0 S/U @ home when #19 ranked all time	*3-10 O/U when #14 ranked since 1997*
4-0 S/U when #20 ranked all time	11-0 S/U @ home when #14 ranked since 1982
5-1 S/U when #23 ranked all time	11-0 S/U when #15 ranked since 1998
0-4 ATS when #24 ranked since 2009	7-1 S/U when #16 ranked since 1981
7-0 S/U when #25 ranked all time {6-1 ATS}	7-1 S/U when #17 ranked since 2011
4-0 S/U & ATS @ home when ranked vs #1 ranked team all time	*6-2 O/U when #19 ranked since 2013*
0-3 S/U on road when ranked vs #2 ranked teams all time	14-0 S/U @ home when #19 ranked since 1960
6-0 O/U when ranked vs #2 ranked teams since 1990	*6-1 O/U when #19 ranked since 2013*
3-0 S/U @ home when ranked vs #8 ranked teams all time	7-1 S/U on road when #19 ranked since 1982
0-6 O/U when ranked vs #8 ranked teams all time	11-1 S/U when #20 ranked all time
4-0 S/U when ranked vs #9 ranked teams since 1991	5-1 S/U when #22 ranked all time
5-0 S/U when ranked vs #13 ranked teams all time	*0-6 O/U when #22 ranked all time*
4-0 ATS when ranked vs #13 ranked teams since 1993	3-0 S/U @ home when #23 ranked all time
1-4 S/U @ home when ranked vs #14 ranked teams all time	5-0 S/U when #25 ranked all time
0-5 O/U when ranked vs #14 ranked teams since 1989	0-6 S/U on road when ranked vs #1 ranked teams all time
6-0 S/U when ranked vs #20 ranked teams all time	0-8 S/U when ranked vs #1 ranked teams since 1985
3-9 O/U when ranked vs Florida State since 2002	*6-1 O/U when ranked vs #1 ranked teams since 1988*
2-6 ATS when ranked vs Florida State since 2005	1-6 S/U @ home when ranked vs #2 ranked teams all time
4-0 S/U when ranked vs Georgia Tech since 2009	2-6 S/U when ranked vs #2 ranked teams since 1998
8-0 S/U when ranked @ home vs Pittsburgh since 1984	*6-0 O/U when ranked vs #2 ranked teams since 2006*
2-8 O/U when ranked vs Pittsburgh since 1997	1-8-2 S/U when ranked vs #3 ranked teams since 1951
4-10 ATS when ranked vs Virginia Tech since 1995	0-4 S/U in Bowl games when ranked vs #3 ranked teams all time
1-7 O/U when ranked vs Virginia Tech since 2003	3-0 S/U @ home when ranked vs #4 ranked teams all time
## Miami-Ohio	0-3-1 S/U on road when ranked vs #4 ranked teams since 1945
10-0 S/U @ home when ranked all time	*0-4 ATS when ranked vs #8 ranked teams since 2002*
4-0 S/U when #15 ranked all time	5-0-1 S/U @ home when ranked vs #10 ranked teams all time
7-0 S/U when #16 ranked all time	*7-1 O/U when ranked vs #11 ranked teams since 1993*
3-0 S/U when #17 ranked all time	4-0 S/U @ home when ranked vs #14 ranked teams since 1977
3-0 S/U when ranked vs Cincinnati all time	6-0 S/U @ home when ranked vs #15 ranked teams all time
## Michigan	*3-7 O/U when ranked vs #15 ranked teams since 1985*
47-6 S/U @ home when ranked since 2009	*0-4 ATS when ranked vs #16 ranked teams since 1984*
303-61-9 S/U @ home when ranked all time	6-1 S/U @ home when ranked vs #17 ranked teams all time

Team records when ranked

4-0 O/U when ranked vs #19 ranked teams since 1995	2-5 O/U when ranked vs Michigan since 2010
10-0 S/U when ranked vs Illinois since 2000	8-0 S/U when ranked vs Minnesota since 1975
1-5 O/U when ranked vs Illinois since 2004	0-4 ATS when ranked vs Minnesota since 2010
22-1 S/U when ranked vs Indiana since 1988	0-4 S/U & ATS @ home when ranked vs Ohio State since 2008
2-6-1 ATS when ranked vs Indiana since 2009	5-0 S/U & ATS when ranked vs Penn State since 2010
0-3 S/U when ranked @ Iowa since 2003	4-0 S/U when ranked vs Western Michigan all time
0-5-1 ATS when ranked @ Iowa since 1994	5-1 O/U when ranked vs Wisconsin since 2003
8-0 S/U & ATS when ranked vs Maryland all time	**Middle Tennessee**
2-10 ATS when ranked vs Michigan State since 2009	NEVER RANKED
0-6 S/U when ranked @ Ohio State since 2002	**Minnesota**
10-1 O/U when ranked vs Ohio State since 2003	5-1 S/U @ home when #1 ranked all time
5-0 S/U @ home when ranked vs Penn State since 1998	4-0 S/U @ home when #2 ranked all time
Michigan State	4-0 S/U when #6 ranked since 1957
12-1 S/U @ home when #1 ranked all time	4-0 S/U @ home when #10 ranked all time
10-2 S/U on road when #1 ranked all time	6-1 S/U when #14 ranked all time {3-0 on road}
24-2-1 S/U when #2 ranked all time	3-0 S/U @ home when #18 ranked all time
13-1-1 S/U when #4 ranked all time	0-4 S/U on road when #19 ranked all time
0-4-1 ATS when #5 ranked since 1999	2-5 S/U when #20 ranked all time
4-0 S/U @ home when #6 ranked all time	2-16 S/U when ranked vs ranked teams since 1962
0-3 S/U on road when #6 ranked since 1961	1-13 S/U on road when ranked vs ranked teams since 1942
6-1 O/U when #7 ranked since 2011	0-4 S/U when ranked vs #20 ranked teams since 1957
11-1 S/U when #8 ranked since 1957 {3-0 on road}	0-4 S/U when ranked vs #6 ranked teams all time
5-0 S/U on road when #10 ranked all time	7-1 S/U @ home when ranked vs Iowa all time
4-0 S/U @ home when #11 ranked since 2010	9-1-1 S/U @ home when ranked vs Northwestern all time
12-1 S/U when #12 ranked all time {8-0 @ home}	7-2 S/U when ranked vs Purdue all time
10-1 S/U when #13 ranked since 1960 {6-0 @ home}	1-7 S/U when ranked vs Wisconsin since 1961 {0-2 on road}
0-4 O/U when #13 ranked since 2012	**Mississippi**
5-1 S/U & ATS when #18 ranked since 2002	4-20-1 O/U on road when ranked since 2002
6-0 S/U @ home when #19 ranked all time	22-3 S/U @ home when ranked since 2014
0-5 ATS @ home when #20 ranked since 1997	5-1 S/U when #1 ranked all time
1-4 S/U @ home when #20 ranked since 1997	10-1-2 S/U when #2 ranked all time
4-0 S/U when #21 ranked since 2012	7-0 S/U @ home when #3 ranked all time
5-1 O/U when #21 ranked all time	0-5 O/U when #3 ranked since 2014
0-6 ATS when #22 ranked since 1993	7-0 S/U @ home when #5 ranked all time
4-0 S/U @ home when #23 ranked all time	5-0 S/U on road when #5 ranked since 1959
5-1 ATS when #23 ranked all time	7-1 S/U when #6 ranked since 1958 {2-0 @ home}
4-0 S/U @ home when #25 ranked since 1997	13-2-1 S/U when #7 ranked since 1954
3-1 ATS @ home when #25 ranked since 1997	6-0 S/U @ home when #9 ranked all time
6-1 S/U when ranked vs #4 ranked teams all time	3-0 S/U @ home when #11 ranked all time
7-1 S/U when ranked vs #6 ranked teams all time {3-0 on road}	5-0 S/U @ home when #13 ranked all time
0-5 S/U when ranked vs #8 ranked teams since 1960	8-0 S/U when #14 ranked since 1952
0-3 S/U when ranked vs #15 ranked teams since 2005	5-0 S/U on road when #15 ranked since 1955
3-0 O/U when ranked vs #15 ranked teams since 2005	7-0 S/U when #17 ranked since 1976
3-0 S/U when ranked vs Eastern Michigan all time	5-0 ATS when #17 ranked since 1990
4-0 S/U when ranked vs Illinois since 1999	9-1 S/U when #18 ranked since 1952 {3-0 on road}
5-0 ATS when ranked vs Illinois since 1990	3-0 S/U on road when #19 ranked since 1957
22-4 S/U when ranked vs Indiana all time	0-3 O/U when #21 ranked since 2002
7-2 ATS when ranked vs Indiana since 2003	0-6 S/U when ranked vs #1 ranked teams all time
1-3 O/U when ranked vs Maryland since 2014	1-3 S/U when ranked vs Arkansas since 2014
9-1 S/U when ranked @ Michigan all time	0-4 ATS when ranked vs Arkansas since 2014

Team records when ranked

0-4 S/U @ home when ranked vs Auburn since 1972		8-1 S/U when #25 ranked all time
6-1 S/U @ home when ranked vs Kentucky all time		0-6 S/U when ranked vs #1 ranked teams all time
10-1 S/U @ home when ranked vs Mississippi State all time		0-5 S/U when ranked vs #6 ranked teams all time
8-1 ATS when ranked vs Mississippi State since 1990		3-0 S/U @ home when ranked vs #14 ranked teams all time
15-1 S/U when ranked vs Vanderbilt since 1948 {6-0 @ home}		3-0 S/U when ranked vs #22 ranked teams all time
Mississippi State		3-0 S/U when ranked vs #25 ranked teams all time
0-3 ATS when #8 ranked all time		15-2 S/U when ranked vs Kansas State all time
5-1 S/U when #11 ranked all time		**NAVY**
0-4 S/U when #13 ranked since 1986		30-1-3 S/U @ home when ranked all time
0-5 ATS when #13 ranked since 1986		4-0 S/U when #5 ranked since 1955
3-0 S/U & ATS when #15 ranked since 1999		4-0 S/U when #8 ranked all time
0-3 O/U when #15 ranked since 1999		3-0-1 S/U when #9 ranked since 1955
0-3 S/U on road when #15 ranked since 1945		5-0 S/U when #10 ranked since 1954
0-5 ATS when #17 ranked since 2001		6-0-1 S/U when #12 ranked all time
0-5 O/U when #17 ranked since 2001		3-0 S/U when #19 ranked all time
4-0 S/U when #19 ranked since 1992		4-0 S/U when #21 ranked all time
1-5 O/U @ home when #23 ranked since 1999		3-0 S/U when #24 ranked all time
3-0 S/U @ home when #24 ranked all time		0-3 S/U when ranked #25 all time
0-4 S/U when ranked vs #1 ranked teams all time		0-5 S/U when ranked vs #1 ranked teams all time
0-3 S/U when ranked vs #3 ranked teams all time		8-2-1 S/U when ranked vs Army since 1963
0-3 S/U when ranked vs #5 ranked teams all time		**Nebraska**
0-3 S/U when ranked vs #8 ranked teams all time		5-19 S/U on road when ranked vs ranked teams since 1998
0-3 S/U & ATS when ranked vs #11 ranked teams since 1999		17-3 S/U @ home when ranked vs ranked teams since 1991
0-4 S/U when ranked vs #14 ranked teams all time		170-15 S/U @ home when ranked since 1982
0-3 O/U when ranked vs #14 ranked teams since 1991		19-4-1 S/U on road when #1 ranked all time
0-3 S/U when ranked vs #18 ranked teams since 1976		23-2 S/U @ home when #1 ranked all time
0-12 S/U when ranked vs ranked Alabama since 1974		9-0 S/U on road when #2 ranked vs unranked teams since 1979
4-1 S/U when ranked vs Arkansas since 2014		23-0 S/U @ home when #2 ranked since 1979
6-1 S/U when ranked vs Kentucky since 1992		7-0 S/U @ home when #2 ranked vs ranked teams all time
1-5 O/U when ranked vs Kentucky since 1999		12-1 S/U @ home when #3 ranked since 1982
0-5 S/U when ranked @ LSU since 1992		26-2 S/U when #4 ranked since 1982
0-4 S/U when ranked vs ranked LSU since 2011		10-1 S/U on road when #4 ranked since 1975
1-7 ATS when ranked vs LSU since 1992		15-0 S/U @ home when #4 ranked since 1984
3-9 O/U when ranked vs Mississippi since 1992		14-0 S/U on road when #5 ranked all time
Missouri		14-2 S/U @ home when #5 ranked since 1976
6-2 S/U on road when ranked since 2013		10-0 S/U on road when #6 ranked all time
30-7 S/U @ home when ranked since 1998		17-0 S/U @ home when #6 ranked since 1975
1-9 O/U @ home when ranked since 2013		13-3 S/U on road when #7 ranked since 1982
4-0 S/U when ranked #6 since 2007		11-1 S/U @ home when #7 ranked all time
5-1 S/U when #8 ranked all time		18-0 S/U @ home when #8 ranked all time
6-0 S/U on road when #9 ranked since 1965		*1-5 ATS on road when #8 ranked since 1992*
0-3-1 S/U on road when #10 ranked since 1961		*7-2 ATS @ home when #8 ranked since 1984*
9-2 S/U when #12 ranked all time {3-0 on road}		11-2 S/U @ home when #9 ranked since 1986
3-0 S/U @ home when #13 ranked since 1981		*0-5 O/U @ home when #9 ranked since 1999*
1-4 S/U on road when #14 ranked since 1972		10-2 S/U @ home when #10 ranked all time
11-2 S/U when #16 ranked all time		11-0 S/U @ home when #11 ranked all time
5-0 S/U @ home when #17 ranked since 1978		*0-4 O/U when #12 ranked since 1992*
1-8 S/U when #19 ranked since 1981		4-0 S/U @ home when #12 ranked since 1977
8-1 S/U when #20 ranked all time		8-2 S/U when #13 ranked all time {2-0 on road}
4-1 S/U when #24 ranked since 2010		4-0 S/U & ATS on road when #14 ranked all time

Team records when ranked

8-1 S/U @ home when #14 ranked all time	7-0 S/U when #14 ranked since 1980
6-1 S/U @ home when #16 ranked all time	6-0-1 S/U @ home when #15 ranked since 1946
4-0-1 O/U when #16 ranked since 2010	7-0 S/U when #16 ranked since 1972
6-1 S/U when #17 ranked all time {3-0 @ home}	5-1 S/U on road when #19 ranked since 1947
8-1 S/U @ home when #18 ranked all time	3-0 S/U when #21 ranked all time
0-4-1 ATS when #18 ranked since 2003	0-4 S/U when ranked vs #1 ranked teams all time
3-0 S/U @ home when #19 ranked all time	0-4 S/U when ranked vs #2 ranked teams all time
2-7 O/U when #19 ranked since 2003	0-3 S/U when ranked vs #13 ranked teams all time
9-0 S/U @ home when #22 ranked all time	10-1 S/U when ranked vs Duke since 1972 {5-0 @ home}
0-4 ATS when #23 ranked all time	6-0 S/U @ home when ranked vs Georgia Tech all time
7-0 O/U when #25 ranked all time	9-2 S/U @ home when ranked vs NC State all time
1-9 S/U when ranked vs #1 ranked teams all time	1-5 S/U when ranked @ Virginia since 1983
5-0 ATS when ranked vs #2 ranked teams since 1994	4-0 S/U when ranked @ Wake Forest all time
0-3 S/U on road when ranked vs #3 ranked teams since 1973	## NC State
1-5 S/U when ranked vs #4 ranked teams all time	4-12 S/U on road when ranked since 2002
1-4 S/U on road when ranked vs #7 ranked teams all time	5-0 S/U when ranked #4 - #9 all time
0-5 S/U when ranked vs #10 ranked teams since 2006	0-4 S/U when #10 ranked since 1957
0-5 O/U when ranked vs #10 ranked teams since 2006	6-0-1 S/U when #13 ranked all time
7-1 S/U when ranked vs #12 ranked teams all time	5-1 S/U @ home when #16 ranked all time
5-1 S/U when ranked vs #13 ranked teams all time {3-0 @ home}	4-0 S/U @ home when #17 ranked all time
3-0-1 S/U when ranked vs #15 ranked teams all time	4-0 S/U on road when #19 ranked since 1979
0-3 S/U on road when ranked vs #18 ranked teams all time	4-1 S/U @ home when #19 ranked all time
5-0 S/U @ home when ranked vs #19 ranked teams all time	0-3 S/U & ATS on road when #20 ranked since 1998
0-4 ATS when ranked vs #19 ranked teams since 1988	*1-6 ATS when #21 ranked all time*
4-0 ATS when ranked vs #24 ranked teams all time	*2-7 ATS when #22 ranked all time*
4-0 S/U when ranked vs Illinois all time	5-0 S/U @ home when #24 ranked all time
5-0 S/U when ranked vs Indiana since 1975	6-1 S/U when #25 ranked all time
13-2 S/U when ranked vs Minnesota since 1967	0-8-1 S/U when ranked vs Top #10 teams all time
6-0 S/U @ home when ranked vs Oklahoma since 1989	*1-6 ATS when ranked vs Top #10 teams since 1992*
3-0 S/U @ home when ranked vs Wisconsin all time	1-6 S/U when ranked @ Clemson since 1967
## Nevada	1-4 S/U when ranked vs Florida State since 1992
5-0 S/U @ home when ranked all time	9-4 S/U when ranked vs Wake Forest all time
7-2 S/U on road when ranked all time	## North Texas
## UNLV	1-1 S/U when ranked all time
NEVER RANKED	## Northern Illinois
## New Mexico	4-0 S/U & ATS on road when ranked since 2012
0-1 S/U when ranked all time	8-0 S/U @ home when ranked all time
## New Mexico State	3-0 S/U & ATS when #20 ranked all time
5-0 S/U when ranked all time	4-0 S/U when #23 ranked all time
## North Carolina	*0-3 O/U when #24 ranked all time*
4-13 ATS on road when ranked since 2001	## Northwestern
4-10 O/U on road when ranked since 1997	11-2 S/U when ranked @ home since 2013
23-4 S/U @ home when ranked since 1996	5-1 S/U when #2 ranked all time
4-0 S/U when #4 ranked all time	4-0 S/U when #7 ranked since 1940
5-1 S/U @ home when #5 ranked all time	7-0 S/U @ home when #10 ranked all time
7-0 S/U @ home when #8 ranked since 1983	0-3 S/U on road when #13 ranked since 1949
4-0 S/U when #9 ranked since 1981	3-0 S/U on road when #18 ranked all time
6-1 S/U when #11 ranked since 1981 {3-0 @ home}	1-4 S/U on road when #20 ranked all time
4-1 S/U on road when #13 ranked all time	*5-0 ATS when #22 ranked all time*
3-0 S/U @ home when #13 ranked since 1993	5-0 S/U & ATS when #23 ranked all time

Team records when ranked

0-3 S/U when ranked vs #1 ranked teams since 1938	0-4-1 S/U on road when ranked vs #1 ranked teams all time
0-4 S/U when ranked vs #4 ranked teams all time	3-0 S/U @ home when ranked vs #2 ranked teams all time
0-3 S/U when ranked vs #9 ranked teams all time	*5-1 ATS when ranked vs #3 ranked teams since 1989*
7-0 S/U @ home when ranked vs Illinois since 1940	1-8 S/U when ranked vs #4 ranked teams since 1991
7-0 S/U when ranked vs Minnesota since 1959	*1-9 ATS when ranked vs #4 ranked teams since 1990*
5-1 ATS when ranked vs Minnesota since 1995	*0-6 O/U when ranked vs #4 ranked teams since 2001*
0-6 S/U when ranked vs Ohio State since 1970	1-5 S/U on road when ranked vs #6 ranked teams since 1958
1-4 ATS when ranked vs Ohio State since 2001	*4-0 O/U when ranked vs #6 ranked teams since 1994*
Notre Dame	5-0 S/U @ home when ranked vs #7 ranked teams all time
52-5 S/U @ home when ranked since 2011	0-3 S/U on road when ranked vs #7 ranked teams since 1989
9-1 S/U on road when #1 ranked since 1988	4-1 S/U when ranked vs #8 ranked teams since 1941
16-5-1 S/U on road when #1 ranked vs ranked teams all time	7-0 S/U when ranked vs #9 ranked teams since 1979
13-3-1 S/U @ home when #1 ranked vs ranked teams all time	4-0 S/U @ home when ranked vs #10 ranked teams all time
14-2-2 S/U on road when #2 ranked all time	*4-0 O/U when ranked vs #11 ranked teams since 2002*
19-3-1 S/U @ home when #2 ranked all time	4-0 S/U & ATS when ranked vs #14 ranked teams since 2014
11-2 S/U on road when #3 ranked since 1965	*0-4 O/U when ranked vs #14 ranked teams since 2014*
8-0-1 S/U @ home when #3 ranked all time	3-0 S/U on road when ranked vs #15 ranked teams all time
14-4 S/U on road when #4 ranked all time	6-0 S/U @ home when ranked vs #17 ranked teams all time
8-2 S/U on road when #5 ranked since 1977	*1-4 O/U when ranked vs #18 ranked teams since 1990*
17-3 S/U @ home when #5 ranked since 1968	3-0 S/U on road when ranked vs #18 ranked teams all time
5-1 O/U on road when #6 ranked since 2002	3-1 S/U on road when ranked vs #19 ranked teams all time
11-0 S/U @ home when #6 ranked since 1974	*2-5 ATS when ranked vs Boston College since 2002*
17-1 S/U @ home when #7 ranked since 1941	38-1 S/U when ranked vs Navy since 1964
11-3-1 S/U on road when #8 ranked all time	15-0 S/U when ranked vs North Carolina all time
13-1 S/U @ home when #8 ranked since 1988	0-4 S/U & ATS when ranked vs Ohio State all time
16-2 S/U on road when #9 ranked since 1969	8-0 S/U @ home when ranked vs Stanford since 1994
13-3 S/U @ home when #9 ranked since 1987	*1-5 O/U @ home when ranked vs Stanford since 2000*
8-3 ATS @ home when #9 ranked since 2002	4-0 S/U when ranked vs Syracuse all time
2-9 ATS on road when #9 ranked since 1994	6-0 S/U when ranked vs USC since 2012
5-2 O/U on road when #9 ranked since 2002	**Ohio U**
16-1 S/U @ home when #10 ranked all time	4-2 S/U when ranked all time
9-0 S/U @ home when #11 ranked since 1977	**Ohio State**
7-0 S/U on road when #11 ranked since 1977	41-4 S/U on road when ranked since 2012
9-1 S/U on road when #12 ranked all time	74-4 S/U @ home when ranked since 2010
8-0 S/U @ home when #12 ranked since 1968	10-1 S/U on road when ranked vs ranked teams since 2010
2-7 S/U on road when #13 ranked since 1976	16-1 S/U on road when #1 ranked since 1975
1-5 ATS on road when #13 ranked since 1983	*10-4 ATS on road when #1 ranked since 1998*
5-1 S/U @ home when #13 ranked since 1972	48-2 S/U @ home when #1 ranked all time
1-4 S/U on road when #14 ranked all time	*2-8 ATS @ home when #1 ranked since 2006*
7-1 S/U @ home when #14 ranked since 1976	*2-12 ATS when #2 ranked since 2016*
7-0 S/U @ home when #15 ranked all time	*3-9 ATS on road when #2 ranked since 1993*
3-8 O/U when #16 ranked since 1987	21-5 S/U on road when #2 ranked all time
0-3 S/U on road when #18 ranked since 1982	27-4 S/U @ home when #2 ranked since 1968
8-1 S/U when #19 ranked all time {4-0 on road}	*3-7-1 ATS on road when #3 ranked since 1983*
6-0 S/U when #20 ranked all time	12-2-1 S/U on road when #3 ranked since 1961
4-0 ATS when #20 ranked since 2000	19-3 S/U @ home when #3 ranked since 1961
6-0 S/U when #21 ranked all time	21-0 S/U when #4 ranked since 2006
1-5 ATS when #22 ranked since 2010	*16-4-1 ATS when #4 ranked since 2006*
0-4 O/U when #23 ranked since 2001	18-3 S/U on road when #4 ranked since 1964
1-5 S/U when #24 ranked since 1999 {0-6 ATS}	26-2 S/U @ home when #4 ranked since 1954

Team records when ranked

2-6 O/U on road when #5 ranked since 1993	5-0 S/U @ home when ranked vs #25 ranked teams all time
21-1 S/U @ home when #5 ranked since 1960	5-0 S/U when ranked vs #25 ranked teams since 1995
14-1 S/U when #6 ranked since 2009	23-0 S/U when ranked vs Indiana since 1991 {12-0 @ home}
1-8 ATS on road when #6 ranked since 1983	*0-5 ATS @ home when ranked vs Indiana since 2013*
12-0 S/U @ home when #6 ranked since 2002	*2-5 O/U @ home when ranked vs Indiana since 2006*
8-1 O/U @ home when #6 ranked since 2005	12-1 S/U when ranked vs Iowa since 1995
7-2 ATS on road when #7 ranked since 1985	20-1 S/U @ home when ranked vs Iowa since 1950
9-0 S/U @ home when #7 ranked since 1993	7-0 S/U when ranked vs Maryland all time
15-0 S/U on road when #8 ranked since 1960	*7-0 O/U when ranked vs Maryland all time*
13-2 S/U @ home when #8 ranked since 1979	12-1 S/U when ranked @ Michigan State since 1975
15-0 S/U when #9 ranked since 2004	14-1 S/U when ranked vs Michigan since 2005 {7-1 on road}
19-0-1 S/U on road when #9 ranked all time	8-0 S/U @ home when ranked vs Michigan since 2002
20-2 S/U @ home when #9 ranked all time {10 straight W}	26-1 S/U when ranked vs Northwestern since 1972
5-0 O/U on road when #10 ranked since 1983	14-1 S/U when ranked @ Northwestern since 1961
17-2 S/U @ home when #10 ranked all time	4-0 S/U when ranked vs Notre Dame all time
5-1 O/U @ home when #10 ranked since 2008	7-0 S/U & ATS when ranked vs Rutgers all time
8-0 S/U when #11 ranked since 1993	3-0 S/U when ranked vs Toledo all time
12-0 S/U @ home when #11 ranked since 1955	*4-17-1 O/U when ranked vs Wisconsin since 1992*
8-0 S/U when #12 ranked since 2005	7-0 S/U when ranked vs Wisconsin since 2012
6-0 S/U @ home when #13 ranked since 1999	**Oklahoma**
5-1 S/U on road when #13 ranked since 1971	43-5 S/U @ home when ranked since 2015
13-0 S/U when #14 ranked since 1979	35-5 S/U on road when ranked since 2012
5-0 ATS on road when #14 ranked since 1983	30-3 S/U when #1 ranked all time
3-0 S/U on road when #15 ranked all time	38-0 S/U @ home when #1 ranked all time
9-0 S/U when #16 ranked since 1979 {all home}	5-0 S/U on road when #2 ranked since 2002
0-7 O/U when #17 ranked since 1990	*0-6 ATS on road when #2 ranked since 2001*
1-5 S/U on road when #18 ranked all time	16-0 S/U @ home when #2 ranked since 1984
7-1 S/U @ home when #18 ranked since 1949	*0-6 ATS on road when #3 ranked since 2010*
5-1 ATS @ home when #18 ranked since 1991	34-4 S/U @ home when #3 ranked all time
4-0 S/U on road when #19 ranked all time	18-1 S/U on road when #4 ranked since 1952
6-1 S/U @ home when #20 ranked all time	24-2 S/U @ home when #4 ranked all time
7-0 S/U @ home when #22 ranked all time	16-2 S/U when #5 ranked since 1985
0-4 S/U & ATS when #25 ranked all time	16-1 S/U @ home when #5 ranked all time
4-0 O/U when #25 ranked all time	22-2 S/U @ home when #6 ranked all time
0-3 S/U on road when ranked vs #1 ranked teams all time	14-2 S/U when #6 ranked all time
4-1 S/U @ home when ranked vs #2 ranked teams all time	11-1 S/U when #7 ranked all time
3-7 ATS when ranked vs #2 ranked teams since 1999	14-1 S/U @ home when #7 ranked all time
2-7 S/U when ranked vs #3 ranked teams since 1977	*1-6-1 O/U @ home when #7 ranked since 2005*
1-4 S/U @ home when ranked vs #5 ranked teams all time	13-1-2 S/U on road when #8 ranked all time
1-5 O/U when ranked vs #5 ranked teams since 1986	10-1 S/U @ home when #8 ranked all time
0-7-1 S/U when ranked vs #6 ranked teams since 1964	6-0 S/U on road when #9 ranked all time
3-0 S/U @ home when ranked vs #9 ranked teams since 1961	6-0 S/U when #9 ranked since 2007
4-0 S/U on road when ranked vs #11 ranked teams since 1975	11-2 S/U when #10 ranked since 2000
5-1 S/U @ home when ranked vs #12 ranked teams all time	17-2 S/U when #10 ranked all time
3-0 S/U on road when ranked vs #13 ranked teams all time	5-1 S/U @ home when #11 ranked all time
3-0 S/U @ home when ranked vs #14 ranked teams all time	*1-9 O/U when #12 ranked since 2009*
5-1 S/U when ranked vs #17 ranked teams all time	5-1 S/U on road when #12 ranked all time
12-2 S/U when ranked vs #20 ranked teams all time	6-1 S/U @ home when #12 ranked all time
5-0 S/U when ranked vs #21 ranked teams since 1997	*10-0 O/U when #14 ranked since 2010*
6-0 S/U when ranked vs #24 ranked teams all time	5-0 S/U on road when #14 ranked since 1995

Team records when ranked

5-1 S/U @ home when #15 ranked all time	0-4 ATS when #5 ranked since 1985
5-1 S/U on road when #16 ranked since 1948	3-1 O/U when #5 ranked since 1985
8-2 S/U @ home when #16 ranked all time	3-0 S/U on road when #6 ranked all time
16-0 S/U when #17 ranked all time	3-1 ATS when #7 ranked since 2008
5-0 ATS when #17 ranked since 2006	3-0 S/U @ home when #8 ranked all time
5-0 O/U when #17 ranked since 2006	8-1 S/U when #9 ranked since 1984
10-2 S/U when #18 ranked all time {4-1 on road}	2-7 ATS when #10 ranked since 1984
13-0 S/U when #19 ranked since 1992 {5-0 on road}	1-6 O/U on road when #11 ranked all time
8-0 S/U @ home when #19 ranked all time	9-0 S/U when #12 ranked since 2009
7-1 ATS when #19 ranked since 2010	7-0-1 ATS when #12 ranked since 2010
7-0 S/U @ home when #20 ranked all time	7-0 S/U on road when #12 ranked since 1988
3-0 S/U @ home when #21 ranked all time	4-0 S/U on road when #13 ranked since 1988
5-0 O/U when #22 ranked all time	3-0 S/U @ home when #14 ranked all time
0-5 S/U when ranked vs #1 ranked teams since 2005	1-5 O/U when #15 ranked since 2013
1-8 O/U when ranked vs #1 ranked teams since 1984	8-0 S/U when #16 ranked all time
4-0 S/U @ home when ranked vs #2 ranked teams all time	7-0 S/U on road when #17 ranked all time
0-4 S/U on road when ranked vs #3 ranked teams all time	5-1 S/U & ATS when #18 ranked since 1988
4-0 O/U when ranked vs #4 ranked teams since 1986	5-2 O/U when #19 ranked since 1997
1-5 S/U when ranked vs #7 ranked teams all time	4-0 S/U @ home when #19 ranked since 1987
6-0 S/U when ranked vs #8 ranked teams all time	3-0 S/U on road when #20 ranked since 1977
5-1 S/U on road when ranked vs #10 ranked teams since 1973	8-1 S/U when #21 ranked since 2013
6-0 S/U @ home when ranked vs #11 ranked teams all time	6-1 S/U @ home when #21 ranked since 2008
11-1 S/U when ranked vs #11 ranked teams since 2000	5-0 S/U on road when #22 ranked all time
8-1 S/U when ranked vs #12 ranked teams since 1949	5-0 S/U when #24 ranked since 2003
3-0 S/U @ home when ranked vs #13 ranked teams all time	7-1 ATS when #25 ranked all time
6-1 S/U when ranked vs #14 ranked teams all time	0-3 S/U when ranked vs #1 ranked teams all time
4-0 S/U @ home when ranked vs #16 ranked teams all time	0-5 S/U when ranked vs #2 ranked teams all time
8-1 S/U when ranked vs #17 ranked teams all time	0-5 S/U when ranked vs #9 ranked teams all time
3-0 O/U when ranked vs #22 ranked teams since 2004	0-3 S/U when ranked vs #14 ranked teams since 2010
4-0 S/U when ranked vs #23 ranked teams all time	0-3 S/U when ranked vs #16 ranked teams all time
4-0 S/U when ranked vs #24 ranked teams all time	3-0 S/U when ranked vs #22 ranked teams all time
0-3 S/U on road when ranked vs #25 ranked teams all time	3-0 S/U when ranked vs #24 ranked teams all time
11-1 S/U @ home when ranked vs Baylor all time	9-2 S/U when ranked vs Baylor since 2003
53-3-1 S/U when ranked vs Iowa State all time {27-1 on road}	8-2 ATS when ranked vs Baylor since 2004
21-4 S/U @ home when ranked vs Kansas State all time	12-1 S/U when ranked vs Kansas State all time {7-0 on road}
16-0 S/U when ranked vs Kansas since 2000	13-0 S/U when ranked vs Kansas all time
27-2 S/U @ home when ranked vs Kansas all time	3-18 S/U when ranked vs Oklahoma since 1972
1-14 O/U when ranked vs Nebraska since 1984	11-2 S/U when ranked vs Texas Tech since 2009
0-4 S/U when ranked @ Nebraska since 1991	6-1 S/U @ home when ranked vs Texas Tech since 2003
27-3 S/U @ home when ranked vs Oklahoma State all time	6-1 S/U when ranked vs Texas since 2010
20-2 S/U when ranked vs Texas Tech all time	1-6 O/U when ranked vs Texas since 2010
9-1 O/U when ranked vs Texas Tech since 2011	**Old Dominion**
2-7 ATS when ranked vs Texas since 2013	NEVER RANKED
4-0 S/U when ranked vs Texas-El Paso all time	**Oregon**
9-0 S/U when ranked vs West Virginia since 2012	45-4 S/U @ home when ranked since 2012
6-1 O/U when ranked vs West Virginia since 2014	6-1 S/U when #1 ranked all time {3-0 on road}
Oklahoma State	0-8 O/U when #2 ranked since 2013
18-5 S/U on road when ranked since 2015	9-1 S/U on road when #2 ranked since 2012
4-0 S/U when #3 ranked since 2011	9-1 S/U on road when #2 ranked since 2012
4-0 S/U when #3 ranked since 2011	

Team records when ranked

7-1 S/U @ home when #2 ranked since 2012	0-8 S/U when ranked vs ranked teams since 2009
0-4 O/U on road when #2 ranked since 2013	4-0 S/U when ranked vs Washington State since 1962
7-1 S/U when #3 ranked since 2012	3-0 S/U @ home vs Washington State all time
8-2 S/U when #4 ranked all time	0-4 S/U when ranked vs Washington since 2000
5-0 S/U @ home when #5 ranked since 2007	0-4 S/U when ranked @ Washington since 1940
5-1 S/U on road when #6 ranked since 2001	**Penn State**
6-1 S/U when #6 ranked since 2011	41-7 S/U @ home when ranked since 2008
7-0 S/U @ home when #7 ranked since 2001	7-0 S/U @ home when #1 ranked all time
0-7 ATS @ home when #7 ranked since 2001	33-3 S/U when #2 ranked all time {12-1 on road} {4-0 in Bowls}
7-1 ATS on road when #7 ranked since 2001	22-3 S/U when #3 ranked all time {7-0 @ home}
4-0 S/U when #8 ranked all time	8-1 S/U @ home when #4 ranked all time
8-0 S/U @ home when #9 ranked all time	6-1 S/U @ home when #5 ranked since 1986
10-2 S/U when #9 ranked since 2000	6-1 S/U on road when #5 ranked since 1973
4-0 S/U & ATS when #4 ranked since 2005	11-0 S/U on road when #6 ranked since 1972
9-3 O/U when #11 ranked since 1998	13-5 ATS when #6 ranked since 1986
6-0 S/U @ home when #12 ranked since 1995	0-4 S/U on road when #7 ranked since 1974
0-4-1 ATS @ home when #12 ranked since 1998	7-1 S/U @ home when #7 ranked since 1995
5-0 S/U on road when #13 ranked all time	9-1 S/U @ home when #8 ranked since 1982
8-1 S/U when #13 ranked since 2001	13-3 S/U on road when #9 ranked all time
6-1 ATS when #13 ranked since 2002	12-2 S/U @ home when #9 ranked since 1971
7-2 S/U when #18 ranked all time	33-4 S/U when #10 ranked all time {23-1 @ home}
6-1 S/U & ATS when #20 ranked since 1995	5-0 S/U on road when #12 ranked since 2005
4-0 S/U @ home when #22 ranked all time	15-2-1 S/U when #13 ranked all time {6-0 @ home}
5-0 S/U @ home when #24 ranked since 2006	14-3 S/U when #14 ranked all time {5-1 @ home}
3-0 S/U & ATS when ranked vs #3 ranked teams since 2002	9-0 ATS when #15 ranked snice 1996
1-4 O/U when ranked vs #5 ranked teams all time	7-0 S/U @ home when #15 ranked since 1993
0-4 O/U when ranked vs #6 ranked teams all time	7-0 S/U @ home when #16 ranked all time
3-1 S/U & ATS when ranked vs #12 ranked teams all time	10-1 S/U when #16 ranked since 1987
4-0 S/U & ATS when ranked vs #17 ranked teams since 2001	6-0 S/U when #17 ranked since 1993
4-0-1 O/U when ranked vs #18 ranked teams all time	6-1 S/U @ home when #18 ranked all time
3-0 S/U & ATS when ranked vs #22 ranked teams all time	9-0 S/U @ home when #19 ranked since 1984
1-6 O/U when ranked vs Arizona since 2012	11-1 S/U when #19 ranked since 1985
8-0 S/U when ranked vs California since 2010	5-0 S/U @ home when #20 ranked since 1987
7-0 S/U when ranked vs Colorado since 2002	3-0 S/U @ home when #21 ranked since 1990
6-1 ATS when ranked vs Colorado since 2002	0-7 O/U when #22 ranked all time
9-0 S/U when ranked vs Oregon State since 2008	1-6 ATS when #24 ranked since 2002
6-0 S/U @ home when ranked vs UCLA all time	0-4 S/U & ATS when ranked vs #1 ranked teams since 1998
7-0 S/U when ranked vs UCLA since 2009	2-7 S/U when ranked vs #2 ranked teams all time
3-0 S/U & ATS when ranked vs Utah State all time	0-6 S/U when ranked vs #3 ranked teams all time
10-1 S/U when ranked vs Washington State since 2007	0-4 ATS when ranked vs #3 ranked teams since 1986
2-7 ATS when ranked vs Washington State since 2010	1-9 S/U when ranked vs #4 ranked teams since 1959
13-0 S/U & ATS when ranked vs Washington since 2005	0-4 S/U when ranked vs #5 ranked teams since 1995 {1-3 ATS}
Oregon State	0-3 S/U on road when ranked vs #6 ranked teams since 1979
7-1 O/U on road when ranked since 2009	4-0 ATS when ranked vs #8 ranked teams all time
3-0 S/U @ home when #13 ranked all time	5-0 S/U when ranked vs #10 ranked teams all time
3-0 S/U when #14 ranked all time	7-1 S/U when ranked vs #12 ranked teams since 1972
4-1 S/U @ home when #15 ranked all time	0-4 S/U on road when ranked vs #13 ranked teams since 1987
4-0 S/U when #18 ranked since 1962	1-4 O/U when ranked vs #13 ranked teams since 1989
0-4 S/U when #24 ranked since 2009	6-0 O/U when ranked vs #16 ranked teams since 1996
0-7 S/U on road when ranked vs ranked teams since 1968	5-0 S/U when ranked vs #17 ranked teams since 1969

Team records when ranked

3-0 S/U when ranked vs #19 ranked teams all time	4-0 S/U when #24 ranked all time
1-3 ATS when ranked vs #22 ranked teams all time	3-0 S/U when #25 ranked all time
14-1 S/U when ranked vs Indiana all time	0-6 S/U when ranked vs #4 ranked teams since 1945
23-0-1 S/U when ranked vs Maryland all time	0-3 S/U when ranked vs #11 ranked teams since 1980
9-3 O/U when ranked vs Michigan State since 1996	0-3 S/U & ATS when ranked vs #13 ranked teams since 2003
1-5 S/U when ranked @ Michigan since 1998	0-4 S/U & ATS when ranked vs #21 ranked teams all time
7-0 S/U when ranked vs Northwestern since 1996	10-2-1 S/U when ranked vs Illinois all time
4-0 S/U @ home when ranked vs Northwestern all time	8-0 S/U when ranked vs Indiana since 1968
0-13 S/U when ranked vs Top #5 ranked Ohio State all time	10-1 S/U @ home when ranked vs Iowa all time
10-0 S/U when ranked vs Purdue all time	*4-0 O/U when ranked vs Minnesota since 1999*
6-2 ATS when ranked vs Purdue since 1997	12-1 S/U when ranked vs Northwestern since 1958 {7-0 @ home}
17-1 S/U when ranked vs Rutgers all time {6-0 on road}	3-0 S/U when ranked @ Wisconsin since 1980
Pittsburgh	**Rice**
3-0 S/U on road when #1 ranked all time	RICE was last ranked in 1961
12-0-1 S/U when #2 ranked all time	3-0 S/U when #14 ranked all time
12-2 S/U when #3 ranked all time	0-5 S/U when #15 ranked since 1950
5-1 S/U when #5 ranked all time	7-0 S/U when #16 ranked all time
5-0 S/U @ home when #6 ranked all time	0-3 S/U when #17 ranked all time
0-3 S/U on road when #7 ranked since 1956	3-0 S/U when #19 ranked all time
4-1 S/U on road when #8 ranked all time	3-0 S/U when #20 ranked all time
5-0 S/U @ home when #9 ranked all time	1-6 S/U when ranked vs Top #5 ranked teams all time
5-1 S/U @ home when #10 ranked all time	7-0 S/U when ranked vs #10 - #17 ranked teams all time
6-0 S/U when #11 ranked since 1978	**Rutgers**
5-0 S/U when #12 ranked since 1977	5-0 S/U when #15 ranked all time
3-0 S/U @ home when #13 ranked all time	*0-3 O/U when #22 ranked all time*
0-5 S/U when #15 ranked since 1978	**San Diego State**
0-4 S/U & ATS when #16 ranked since 1983	4-0 S/U when #18 ranked all time
4-0 S/U on road when #19 ranked all time	**San Jose State**
1-6 S/U on road when #20 ranked all time	1-2 S/U when ranked all time
0-3 ATS when #22 ranked all time	**South Alabama**
1-3 S/U @ home when #23 ranked since 1991	NEVER RANKED
3-0 S/U on road when #23 ranked all time	**South Carolina**
0-6 S/U when ranked vs #1 ranked teams all time	29-5 S/U @ home when ranked since 2009
1-12 S/U when ranked vs Top #4 ranked teams all time	8-0 S/U when #12 ranked since 2011
5-0 S/U when ranked vs Louisville all time	7-0 S/U @ home when #12 ranked all time
0-5 S/U when ranked vs Miami since 1989	7-0 S/U when #14 ranked since 2002
1-4 O/U when ranked vs Miami since 1989	4-0 S/U on road when #14 ranked since 1987
12-1-1 S/U when ranked vs Syracuse since 1976	5-0 S/U @ home when #16 ranked all time
0-4-1 S/U when ranked vs West Virginia since 1988	9-1 S/U when #17 ranked since 1980
Purdue	3-0 S/U on road when #18 ranked since 2000
0-6 S/U on road when #10 ranked all time	*1-4 ATS when #21 ranked all time*
0-3 S/U when #11 ranked since 1999	4-1 S/U @ home when #24 ranked all time
3-0 S/U @ home when #13 ranked all time	1-4 S/U & ATS when #25 ranked all time
5-1 S/U @ home when #14 ranked all time	0-4 S/U when ranked vs #2 ranked teams all time
5-1 S/U on road when #15 ranked all time	0-4 S/U when ranked vs #3 ranked teams all time
1-6 O/U when #17 ranked since 1997	0-4 S/U when ranked vs #4 ranked teams all time
3-0 S/U @ home when #18 ranked since 1978	3-0 S/U when ranked vs #6 ranked teams all time
3-0 S/U on road when #19 ranked all time	0-4 S/U when ranked vs #9 ranked teams all time
6-1 S/U when #20 ranked all time {3-0 on road}	4-0 S/U & ATS when ranked vs Clemson since 2010
3-0 S/U when #21 ranked all time	*0-7 O/U when ranked vs Clemson since 2000*

Team records when ranked

5-1 S/U when ranked vs ranked Clemson all time	1-5 S/U on road when ranked vs #11 ranked teams since 1977
5-1 S/U @ home when ranked vs Georgia all time	3-0 S/U @ home when ranked vs #11 ranked teams since 1953
6-0 O/U when ranked vs Kentucky since 2007	5-0 S/U when ranked vs #13 ranked teams all time
0-3 O/U when ranked vs Missouri since 2012	10-0 S/U when ranked vs #14 ranked teams all time
6-0 S/U when ranked vs Vanderbilt since 2009	4-0 S/U when ranked vs #15 ranked teams since 1972
## USC	0-5-1 S/U on road when ranked vs #17 ranked teams all time
11-1 S/U @ home when ranked since 2016	*1-6 ATS when ranked vs #17 ranked teams since 1987*
69-6-2 S/U when #1 ranked all time	3-0-1 S/U @ home when ranked vs #18 ranked teams all time
32-2 S/U on road when #1 ranked all time	*1-3 O/U when ranked vs #19 ranked since 1989*
16-0 S/U @ home when #1 ranked since 2004	*0-5 O/U when ranked vs #21 ranked teams all time*
0-4 ATS when #2 ranked since 2006	3-0 S/U & ATS when ranked vs #24 ranked teams all time
1-6 ATS on road when #3 ranked since 2003	*0-3 O/U when ranked vs #24 ranked teams all time*
15-1-1 S/U @ home when #3 ranked since 1962	*4-0 O/U when ranked vs #25 ranked teams since 2002*
22-0 S/U when #4 ranked since 1976 {9-0 on road}	8-1 S/U @ home when ranked vs Arizona State since 1995
18-0 S/U @ home when #4 ranked since 1967	*1-7 ATS when ranked vs Arizona since 2005*
0-4 ATS on road when #5 ranked since 1995	10-2 S/U when ranked @ Arizona since 1980
15-2 S/U @ home when #5 ranked all time	*1-7 O/U when ranked @ Arizona since 1989*
8-1 O/U when #6 ranked since 2002	8-0 S/U when ranked vs California since 2004
9-0 S/U on road when #6 ranked since 1974	*0-8 O/U when ranked vs California since 2004*
11-1-1 S/U @ home when #6 ranked since 1966	5-0 S/U @ home when ranked vs California since 2002
16-0-1 S/U @ home when #7 ranked all time	8-0 S/U when ranked vs Colorado all time
6-0 S/U when #7 ranked since 2002	*3-0 ATS @ home when ranked vs Colorado all time*
10-1 S/U on road when #8 ranked all time	9-1 S/U when ranked vs Notre Dame since 2002
12-1-2 S/U @ home when #8 ranked all time	0-3 S/U when ranked @ Oregon State since 2006
13-2-1 S/U @ home when #9 ranked since 1955	*0-5 ATS when ranked @ Oregon State since 2000*
4-0 O/U on road when #10 ranked since 1989	*2-9 O/U when ranked vs UCLA since 2006*
0-4 O/U @ home when #11 ranked since 1995	*4-10 ATS when ranked @ UCLA since 1984*
6-1 S/U @ home when #11 ranked since 1959	19-2 S/U @ home when ranked vs Washington State all time
9-0 S/U when #12 ranked since 1984	*0-5 O/U @ home when ranked vs Washington State since 2005*
6-0 S/U @ home when #12 ranked since 1982	## South Florida
2-9 O/U when #13 ranked since 1992	9-1 S/U @ home when ranked since 2011
12-1 S/U @ home when #13 ranked all time	*4-12 ATS on road when ranked since 2007*
4-1 S/U @ home when #14 ranked since 1945	4-0 S/U when #18 ranked all time
11-3 S/U @ home when #16 ranked all time	4-0 S/U when #19 ranked all time
2-7 ATS when #20 ranked since 2010	5-0 S/U when #23 ranked all time
6-1 S/U @ home when #20 ranked since 1984	## SMU
6-2 S/U & ATS when #21 ranked since 1995	26-5-1 S/U @ home when ranked since 1979
0-3 S/U @ home when #23 ranked since 1997	3-0-1 S/U when #2 ranked all time
0-6 ATS when #24 ranked since 2010	5-1-2 S/U when #3 ranked all time
0-3 ATS when #25 ranked all time	5-0 S/U on road when #6 ranked since 1981
0-3 O/U when #25 ranked all time	5-1-1 S/U when #8 ranked all time
0-5 S/U when ranked vs #1 ranked teams since 1988	5-0 S/U when #10 ranked since 1981
7-0 S/U & ATS when ranked vs #3 ranked teams since 1973	4-0 S/U on road when #10 ranked all time
7-0 S/U when ranked in Bowl games vs #3 ranked teams all time	4-0 S/U when #13 ranked since 1981
3-0 S/U on road when ranked vs #4 ranked teams since 1972	0-3 S/U when ranked vs #2 ranked teams all time
10-0 S/U when ranked vs #6 ranked teams all time	5-2 S/U when ranked vs Houston since 1981
7-0 ATS when ranked vs #6 ranked teams since 1985	3-0 S/U when ranked vs North Texas all time
1-4 S/U on road when ranked vs #7 ranked teams since 1952	6-0 S/U when ranked vs TCU since 1979
1-4 S/U @ home when ranked vs #7 ranked teams all time	## Southern Miss
0-4 S/U on road when ranked vs #10 ranked teams all time	0-3 S/U on road when #20 ranked all time

Team records when ranked

5-0 S/U when #25 ranked since 1999	0-6 O/U when #18 ranked since 1988
6-0 S/U when #14 - #17 ranked all time	5-0 S/U when #19 ranked all time
1-9 ATS when ranked since 2000	3-1 S/U when #21 ranked all time
## Stanford	5-0 S/U when #22 ranked since 1997
42-6 S/U @ home when ranked since 2010	7-0 S/U when #24 ranked all time
4-0 S/U @ home when #4 ranked all time	0-3 S/U when ranked vs #1 ranked teams all time
4-0 ATS when #4 ranked since 2011	3-0 S/U @ home when ranked vs Army all time
3-0 S/U @ home when #5 ranked all time	4-0 S/U when ranked vs Boston College since 1995
6-0 S/U @ home when #6 ranked all time	7-0 S/U when ranked vs Pittsburgh since 1991
5-0 ATS when #6 ranked since 2011	## TCU
7-1 S/U @ home when #7 ranked all time	41-4 S/U @ home when ranked since 2007
5-1 ATS @ home when #7 ranked since 2010	5-0 S/U when #2 ranked all time
6-0 S/U when #8 ranked since 2012	7-0 S/U when #3 ranked since 2010
0-5 O/U when #8 ranked since 2013	14-1 S/U when ranked #4 since 2009 {8-0 @ home}
4-0 S/U & ATS when #10 ranked since 2010	4-1 S/U when #5 ranked all time
5-0 S/U when #12 ranked since 1970	5-1 S/U when #6 ranked since 2009
8-1 S/U when #13 ranked since 1980	5-1 S/U when #7 ranked since 1955
1-7 O/U when #13 ranked since 1993	7-0 S/U when #8 ranked all time
11-1 S/U @ home when #13 ranked all time	0-5 S/U on road when #9 ranked all time
4-0 O/U when #14 ranked since 2017	4-1 S/U on road when #10 ranked all time
5-1 S/U @ home when #15 ranked since 1980	0-3 S/U on road when #11 ranked all time
5-1 ATS when #15 ranked since 2012	4-0 S/U @ home when #11 ranked all time
6-0 S/U when #16 ranked since 2001	6-1 S/U when #12 ranked all time {3-0 on road}
5-1-1 S/U @ home when #16 ranked all time	6-0 S/U when #13 ranked since 1959
1-5 S/U on road when #17 ranked all time	7-1 S/U when #14 ranked all time {3-0 @ home}
5-1 S/U @ home when #19 ranked since 1972	11-1 S/U when ranked #16 all-time {6-0 on road}
6-0 S/U when #20 ranked since 1993	0-4 S/U on road when #17 ranked since 1956
5-0 S/U @ home when #21 ranked all time	6-0 S/U when #18 ranked since 1958
5-0 S/U & ATS when #25 ranked since 2009	4-0 S/U @ home when #18 ranked all time
0-3 S/U when ranked vs #3 ranked teams all time	7-1 S/U @ home when #20 ranked all time
3-0 S/U @ home when ranked vs #4 ranked teams all time	3-0 S/U on road when #20 ranked since 1958
4-0 ATS when ranked vs #7 ranked teams all time	6-1 S/U when #25 ranked all time
0-3 S/U when ranked vs #14 ranked teams all time	3-0 S/U on road when ranked vs #6 ranked teams all time
3-0 S/U when ranked vs #15 ranked teams all time	3-0 S/U when ranked vs Kansas State all time
4-0 S/U When ranked vs #20 ranked teams all time	4-0 S/U when ranked vs Kansas since 2012
6-0 S/U when ranked vs California since 2010	0-4 S/U when ranked @ Oklahoma all time
0-3 S/U when ranked @ Notre Dame since 2012	13-3 S/U when ranked vs SMU since 1937
11-0 S/U when ranked vs Oregon State since 1969	*1-9 ATS when ranked vs SMU since 2003*
8-0 S/U when ranked vs UCLA since 2001	5-1 S/U when ranked vs Texas Tech since 1984 {3-0 @ home}
7-1 ATS when ranked vs UCLA since 2001	3-0 S/U when ranked vs West Virginia all time
5-1 S/U @ home when ranked vs USC since 1992	*0-3 O/U when ranked vs West Virginia all time*
## Syracuse	## Temple
5-18 ATS on road when ranked since 1993	2-5 S/U on road when ranked all time
7-0 S/U @ home when ranked since 1998	## Tennessee
5-0 S/U when #1 ranked all time	*11-2 O/U on road when ranked since 2007*
6-0-1 S/U when #6 ranked all time	16-1 S/U when #1 ranked all time {10-0 @ home}
0-3 S/U on road when #9 ranked all time	9-1 S/U @ home when #2 ranked all time
7-1 S/U when #12 ranked all time	0-4 S/U when #2 ranked @ neutral sites since 1940
10-2 S/U when #17 ranked since 1956	7-1 S/U @ home when #3 ranked all time
5-0 S/U @ home when #18 ranked all time	*3-8 ATS when #3 ranked since 1990*

Team records when ranked

8-2 S/U @ home when #4 ranked since 1950	8-1 S/U @ home when ranked vs LSU all time
11-0 S/U @ home when #5 ranked all time	6-1 S/U when ranked @ South Carolina since 1996
11-1 S/U @ home when #6 ranked all time	38-1 S/U when ranked vs Vanderbilt all time {22-0 @ home}
0-5 ATS when #6 ranked since 2000	## Texas
5-1 O/U when #6 ranked since 1999	*5-12 ATS on road when ranked since 2012*
20-1 S/U when #7 ranked since 1965 {10-1 on road}	*16-4 O/U on road when ranked since 2011*
13-0-1 S/U @ home when #7 ranked all time	8-0 S/U @ home when #1 ranked since 1965
12-3 S/U when #8 ranked since 1992	19-1 S/U on road when #2 ranked all time
4-0 O/U when #8 ranked since 2002	*5-1-1 O/U on road when #2 ranked since 2005*
16-4 S/U when #9 ranked since 1971	24-2 S/U @ home when #2 ranked since 1962
9-1 S/U @ home when #10 ranked since 1985	*1-5 ATS @ home when #2 ranked since 2006*
14-2 S/U when #11 ranked since 1989	8-0 S/U when #3 ranked since 2006
16-2-1 S/U @ home when #11 ranked all time	11-1 S/U on road when #3 ranked since 1959
7-1 S/U on road when #11 ranked since 1971	18-1 S/U @ home when #3 ranked all time
12-0 S/U when #12 ranked since 1960	17-2-1 S/U when #4 ranked since 1963
9-0 S/U @ home when #12 ranked all time	13-0-1 S/U @ home when #4 ranked since 1962
2-8 ATS when #13 ranked since 1987	*0-4 O/U @ home when #4 ranked since 2002*
8-2 S/U when #14 ranked since 1987	7-0 S/U when #5 ranked since 2006
7-0 S/U @ home when #14 ranked since 1970	*2-9 O/U when #5 ranked since 2003*
6-1 ATS when #14 ranked since 1991	7-0 S/U on road when #5 ranked since 2001
0-4-1 ATS on road when #15 ranked since 1987	*2-6 ATS on road when #5 ranked since 2000*
8-2 ATS when #17 ranked since 1987	9-0 S/U @ home when #5 ranked since 1990
6-1 S/U @ home when #18 ranked since 1949	9-1 S/U when #6 ranked since 2003
10-0 S/U @ home when #19 ranked all time	15-3 S/U @ home when #6 ranked all time
8-0 S/U when #19 ranked since 1985	32-4 S/U when #7 ranked all time {10-2 on road}
5-0 S/U @ home when #20 ranked all time	16-1 S/U when #8 ranked since 1975
6-0 S/U when #25 ranked all time	9-0 S/U on road when #8 ranked since 1968
0-5 S/U when ranked vs #1 ranked teams since 1979	9-0 S/U @ home when #9 ranked since 1972
0-4 ATS when ranked vs #1 ranked teams since 1990	11-0 S/U when #10 ranked since 1972
3-0 S/U & ATS when ranked vs #2 ranked teams since 1998	9-0 S/U @ home when #10 ranked since 1952
1-7-2 S/U when ranked vs #3 ranked teams since 1952	9-2 S/U on road when #11 ranked all time
1-4 S/U on road when ranked vs #4 ranked teams all time	7-0 S/U @ home when #12 ranked all time
4-1 ATS when ranked vs #5 ranked teams since 1990	1-4 S/U & ATS on road when #13 ranked since 1991
1-5 S/U when ranked vs #6 ranked teams since 1975	*4-0 O/U on road when #13 ranked since 1995*
0-6 S/U when ranked vs #8 ranked teams since 1957	12-1 S/U @ home when #13 ranked since 1957
3-0 S/U @ home when ranked vs #9 ranked teams all time	*5-1 ATS @ home when #13 ranked since 1990*
0-3 S/U on road when ranked vs #10 ranked teams all time	5-0 S/U on road when #14 ranked all time
4-0 O/U when ranked vs #10 ranked teams since 1989	9-0 S/U @ home when #14 ranked all time
3-0 S/U when ranked vs #15 ranked teams all time	10-1 S/U @ home when #15 ranked all time
0-3 O/U when ranked vs #15 ranked teams all time	4-0 S/U on road when #17 ranked all time
3-0 S/U when ranked vs #16 ranked teams all time	*0-4 O/U when #18 ranked since 1999*
4-0 S/U when ranked vs #17 ranked teams all time	*6-1 ATS when #19 ranked since 2000*
3-0 S/U when ranked vs #22 ranked teams all time	4-0 S/U on road when #19 ranked since 2000
0-3 O/U when ranked vs #22 ranked teams all time	6-1 S/U @ home when #19 ranked all time
3-0 S/U when ranked vs #23 ranked teams all time	6-1 S/U when #20 ranked since 1994
3-0 S/U when ranked vs #25 ranked teams all time	1-6 S/U when #22 ranked since 2010
7-1 ATS when ranked @ Alabama since 1993	*0-6 ATS @ home when #22 ranked all time*
1-7 ATS when ranked vs Georgia since 2000	1-4 S/U & ATS when #23 ranked since 2012
5-0 O/U when ranked vs Georgia since 2003	*8-1 O/U when #23 ranked since 1998*
23-1 S/U when ranked vs Kentucky since 1967	3-0 S/U & ATS on road when #25 ranked all time

Team records when ranked

1-7 S/U when ranked vs #2 ranked teams since 1972	6-0 S/U when #23 ranked since 2004
4-0 S/U @ home when #3 ranked all time	5-0 S/U on road when #23 ranked all time
1-5-2 S/U when ranked vs #3 ranked Oklahoma all time	*5-2 O/U when #23 ranked since 2002*
3-0 S/U on road when ranked vs #5 ranked teams all time	8-3 S/U when #24 ranked all time
0-7 S/U when ranked vs #6 ranked teams since 1988	0-4 S/U & ATS on road when #25 ranked all time
0-3 S/U on road when ranked vs #6 ranked teams all time	1-7 S/U when ranked vs #1 ranked teams all time
3-0 S/U @ home when ranked vs #7 ranked teams all time	*4-0 ATS when ranked vs #2 ranked teams since 1998*
0-4 S/U & ATS when ranked vs #8 ranked since 1988	*0-5 O/U when ranked vs #5 ranked teams since 1992*
3-0 S/U on road when ranked vs #12 ranked teams all time	0-4 S/U when ranked vs #6 ranked teams since 1953 {0-3 ATS}
4-0 S/U @ home when ranked vs #13 ranked teams all time	*0-3 O/U when ranked vs #6 ranked teams since 1987*
7-0 S/U when ranked vs #14 ranked teams all time	0-3 S/U & ATS when ranked vs #7 ranked teams since 2002
0-4 S/U & ATS when ranked vs #15 ranked teams since 1985	*0-3 O/U when ranked vs #7 ranked teams since 2002*
4-0 S/U when ranked vs #16 ranked teams since 1994	0-3 S/U & ATS when ranked vs #12 ranked teams all time
4-0 S/U when ranked vs #17 ranked teams all time	1-4 S/U when ranked vs #15 ranked all time
4-0 O/U when ranked vs #19 ranked teams since 1996	5-1 S/U when ranked vs #16 ranked all time
4-1 S/U when ranked vs Alabama all time	1-4 S/U on road when ranked vs #17 ranked all time
19-0 S/U @ home when ranked vs Baylor since 1953	1-4 S/U when ranked vs #18 ranked all time
9-3 S/U when ranked vs Iowa State all time {4-1 on road}	3-0 S/U @ home when ranked vs #20 ranked all time
1-6 ATS when ranked vs Kansas State all time	0-4 S/U on road when ranked vs #20 ranked teams all time
9-0 S/U when ranked vs Kansas all time	0-7 S/U when ranked vs Alabama since 2013
1-4 S/U when ranked vs Oklahoma State since 2013	6-1 S/U when ranked vs Arkansas since 2013
0-5 ATS when ranked vs Oklahoma State since 2013	1-5 S/U when ranked vs LSU since 2011 {0-6 ATS}
8-0 O/U when ranked @ Oklahoma State since 2001	0-4 S/U when ranked vs Mississippi since 2014
21-4 S/U when ranked vs TCU since 1962	*0-5 ATS when ranked vs Mississippi since 2013*
9-1 S/U when ranked vs Texas Tech since 2003	1-3 S/U & ATS when ranked @ Mississippi State since 2014
Texas A&M	5-0 S/U when ranked vs South Carolina all time
4-1 S/U when #1 ranked all time	**Texas-El Paso**
5-1 S/U @ home when #2 ranked all time	2-2 S/U when ranked all time
4-0 S/U @ home when #3 ranked all time	**Texas-San Antonio**
7-0 S/U on road when #4 ranked all time	4-2 S/U when ranked all time
12-0 S/U @ home when #5 ranked all time	**Texas State**
3-7 ATS when #6 ranked since 1994	NEVER RANKED
10-1 S/U @ home when #7 ranked all time	**Texas Tech**
10-1 S/U @ home when #8 ranked since 1974	*11-0 O/U on road when ranked since 2008*
2-8 ATS when #9 ranked since 1994	*0-11 ATS @ home when ranked since 2008*
8-2-1 S/U on road when #9 ranked all time	*4-0 O/U @ home when ranked since 2013*
9-1 S/U @ home when #9 ranked all time	4-0 S/U when ranked #7 since 2008
17-2 S/U when #10 ranked all time {6-0 on road}	4-0 S/U when ranked #11 since 1973
7-1 S/U @ home when #11 ranked all time	6-0 S/U when #12 ranked since 1973
3-1 S/U on road when #12 ranked all time	0-3 S/U & ATS when #15 ranked since 2006
8-0 S/U @ home when #13 ranked since 1986	3-0 S/U when #16 ranked since 2005
5-2 S/U on road when #14 ranked since 1941	4-0-1 S/U @ home when #17 ranked all time
2-8-1 ATS when #15 ranked since 1987	5-1 S/U when #18 ranked since 1940
9-2 S/U when #17 ranked since 1997	3-0 S/U on road when #19 ranked all time
5-1 S/U @ home when #17 ranked since 1977	0-3 S/U when #22 ranked since 1998
0-6 O/U on road when #17 ranked since 1997	*3-0 O/U when #23 ranked since 1995*
4-0 S/U on road when #18 ranked since 1995	*0-4 ATS when #24 ranked since 1995*
4-0 S/U @ home when #18 ranked all time	*0-4 ATS when #25 ranked since 2012*
1-5 ATS when #20 ranked since 1997	*3-0 O/U when ranked vs #4 ranked teams all time*
5-1 O/U when #22 ranked since 2012	0-5 S/U when ranked vs #13 ranked teams since 1970

Team records when ranked

3-0 S/U @ home when ranked vs Baylor all time	0-3 S/U & ATS @ home when #19 ranked since 1990
4-0 O/U when ranked vs Kansas State all time	3-0 S/U & ATS @ home when #23 ranked all time
4-0 S/U when ranked vs Kansas all time	*4-1 O/U when #24 ranked since 1995*
0-3 S/U when ranked @ Oklahoma all time	*6-1 O/U when #25 ranked since 1993*
0-4 ATS when ranked vs Oklahoma all time	0-3 S/U & ATS when ranked vs #1 ranked teams since 1984
5-1 S/U when ranked vs TCU since 1973	0-3 S/U @ home when ranked vs #1 ranked teams all time
Toledo	2-8 S/U when ranked vs #2 ranked teams all time
11-2 S/U on road when ranked all time	0-3 S/U on road when ranked vs #4 ranked teams all time
4-0 S/U when #14 ranked all time	0-5 S/U when ranked vs #5 ranked teams all time
4-0 S/U when #15 ranked all time	0-3 S/U & ATS when ranked vs #7 ranked teams since 2001
3-0 S/U when #19 ranked all time	*4-0 ATS when ranked vs #8 ranked teams since 1978*
0-3 S/U & ATS when ranked vs Ball State all time	4-0 S/U @ home when ranked vs #9 ranked teams all time
3-0 S/U when ranked vs Kent State all time	4-0 S/U when ranked vs #10 ranked teams since 1986
Troy	5-0 S/U @ home when ranked vs #10 ranked teams all time
0-1 S/U when ranked all time	5-0 ATS when ranked vs #10 ranked teams since 1986
Tulane	0-3 S/U on road when ranked vs #13 ranked teams all time
7-0 S/U @ home when ranked since 1974	3-0 S/U @ home when ranked vs #13 ranked teams all time
0-5 S/U when ranked vs Top #3 ranked teams all time	1-4 S/U when ranked vs #14 ranked teams since 1947
4-1 S/U when #14 ranked all time	3-0 S/U & ATS when ranked vs #21 ranked teams all time
4-0 S/U when #19 ranked since 1948	3-0 S/U & ATS when ranked vs #23 ranked teams since 1998
3-0 S/U when #20 ranked all time	4-1 S/U when ranked @ Arizona State all time
Tulsa	*7-0 O/U when ranked vs Arizona State since 1995*
7-0 S/U @ home when ranked since 1945	8-0-1 S/U @ home when ranked vs Arizona all time
0-7 S/U when ranked vs ranked teams all time	7-1 S/U & ATS when ranked vs Arizona since 1993
UCLA	*6-1-1 O/U when ranked vs Arizona since 1993*
7-0 S/U when #2 ranked since 1988	26-3 S/U when ranked vs California since 1952
0-6 ATS when #2 ranked since 1988	6-1 S/U when ranked vs Colorado all time {3-0 on road}
5-0 S/U @ home when #3 ranked since 1954	0-5 S/U when ranked vs Oregon since 2000
15-3 S/U when #3 ranked since 1954	*0-9 ATS when ranked vs Oregon since 1988*
15-1 S/U @ home when #4 ranked all time	1-5 S/U when ranked vs Stanford since 2012
5-0 O/U when #4 ranked since 1986	*0-7 ATS @ home when ranked vs Stanford since 1984*
10-0 S/U @ home when #5 ranked all time	9-0 S/U when ranked vs Washington since 1987
1-6 ATS when #6 ranked since 1988	14-1-1 S/U @ home when ranked vs Washington all time
9-1 S/U on road when #7 ranked all time	*8-2 ATS when ranked vs Washington since 1986*
5-1 S/U @ home when #7 ranked all time	**Utah**
1-5 S/U on road when #8 ranked since 1972	4-0 S/U when #7 ranked all time
1-5 ATS when #8 ranked since 1984	*3-1 O/U when #7 ranked all time*
5-1 S/U @ home when #9 ranked since 1969	4-0 S/U when #8 ranked all time
5-1 S/U @ home when #10 ranked all time	4-0 S/U when #9 ranked since 2008
6-0 S/U @ home when #11 ranked since 1982	*6-0-1 O/U when #10 ranked all time*
10-1 S/U on road when #12 ranked since 1978	8-0 S/U when #13 ranked all time {6-2 ATS}
9-0 S/U @ home when #13 ranked since 1985	*6-2 O/U when ranked #13 all time*
8-2 S/U on road when #14 ranked all time	7-0 S/U when #14 ranked all time {6-1 ATS}
4-0 O/U when #14 ranked since 2005	7-0 S/U when #19 ranked all time
5-1 S/U on road when #15 ranked since 1960	4-0 S/U on road when #20 ranked all time
6-1 S/U when #15 ranked since 1983	8-0 S/U when #23 ranked since 2008
8-1 S/U @ home when #16 ranked since 1973	*0-5 O/U when #23 ranked since 2010*
6-1 S/U @ home when #17 ranked since 1985	6-0 S/U when #24 ranked since 2009
1-6 ATS when #18 ranked since 1994	3-0 S/U when ranked vs #20 ranked teams all time
4-0-1 S/U on road when #19 ranked since 1956	*4-1 O/U when ranked vs #4 ranked teams all time*

Team records when ranked

4-0 S/U & ATS when ranked vs San Diego State since 2004	0-4 O/U when #18 ranked since 2000
Utah State	7-0 S/U when #20 ranked since 1995
3-0 S/U @ home when ranked all time	*2-5 ATS @ home when #20 ranked all time*
Vanderbilt	8-1 S/U when #21 ranked all time {3-0 @ home}
2-8-1 S/U on road when ranked all time	8-2 S/U when #23 ranked all time {3-0 @ home}
0-3 S/U when #13 ranked all time	*7-2 ATS when #23 ranked since 1997*
Virginia	4-1 S/U when #24 ranked all time
4-13 ATS on road when ranked since 1999	*1-4 O/U when #24 ranked all time*
3-8-1 O/U @ home when ranked since 2004	0-3 S/U when ranked vs #1 ranked teams all time
0-4 S/U when ranked in Bowl games since 1998	0-3 S/U & ATS when ranked vs #2 ranked teams since 2007
6-1 S/U when #11 ranked all time {3-0 on road}	0-4 S/U when ranked vs #3 ranked teams all time
3-0 S/U @ home when #12 ranked all time	0-3 S/U & ATS when ranked vs #6 ranked teams all time
0-4 ATS when #12 ranked since 1996	*0-3 O/U when ranked vs #9 ranked teams since 2004*
1-4 S/U & ATS when #13 ranked since 1994	*0-3 O/U when ranked vs #13 ranked teams since 1995*
8-1 S/U when #16 ranked since 1994	6-0 S/U & ATS when ranked vs #16 ranked teams since 1999
0-3 S/U on road when #17 ranked all time	*0-4 O/U when ranked vs #19 ranked teams since 2002*
0-4 S/U & ATS when #18 ranked since 2004	3-0 S/U when ranked vs #22 ranked teams all time
4-0 O/U when #18 ranked since 2004	*3-7 ATS @ home when ranked vs Boston College since 1995*
4-0 S/U when #19 ranked since 1995	8-1 S/U when ranked vs Duke all time {5-0 on road}
4-0 S/U @ home when #20 ranked since 1991	*0-5 O/U when ranked vs Duke since 2010*
7-0 S/U when #21 ranked all time	5-1 S/U when ranked vs Miami since 2006
0-3 O/U when #23 ranked since 1999	8-2 S/U when ranked vs North Carolina all time {4-1 on road}
1-4 S/U & ATS when #24 ranked since 1999	*3-7 O/U when ranked vs North Carolina all time*
1-5 O/U when #24 ranked since 1996	*2-7 ATS when ranked vs Pittsburgh since 1999*
0-3 S/U & ATS when ranked vs #17 ranked teams all time	*0-6 ATS when ranked @ Pittsburgh since all time*
3-0 O/U when ranked vs #20 ranked teams all time	14-2 S/U when ranked vs Virginia since 1996 {6-0 @ home}
1-5 S/U when ranked vs #6 ranked teams all time	*7-1-1 ATS when ranked vs Virginia since 2004*
6-0 S/U when ranked vs Duke since 1995	**Wake Forest**
5-0 S/U & ATS @ home when ranked vs North Carolina all time	0-3 S/U when #15 ranked all time
Virginia Tech	4-0 S/U when #20 ranked all time
7-23 O/U @ home when ranked since 2008	**Washington**
0-5 ATS when #2 ranked since 1999	*3-9 O/U on road when ranked since 2017*
3-0 S/U @ home when #2 ranked all time	42-5 S/U @ home when ranked since 2000
0-4 O/U when #3 ranked since 2005	10-0 S/U @ home when #1 ranked all time
4-1 S/U on road when #3 ranked all time	7-1 S/U when #2 ranked since 1991
7-1 S/U when #4 ranked all time	8-0 S/U when #8 ranked since 1984 {3-0 on road}
7-0 S/U when #6 ranked all time	6-0 S/U on road when #4 ranked all time
9-1 S/U & ATS when #8 ranked all time	*5-0 O/U on road when #4 ranked since 1991*
6-1 S/U @ home when #9 ranked all time	6-1 S/U @ home when #6 ranked all time
0-4 ATS when #9 ranked since 2007	14-2 S/U when #7 ranked all time
5-0 S/U & ATS when #10 ranked since 2000	*7-2-1 ATS when #7 ranked since 1986*
10-2 S/U when #11 ranked all time	8-0-1 S/U @ home when #8 ranked all time
5-0 S/U when #13 ranked since 2010	9-0 S/U @ home when ranked #9 all time
3-0 S/U & ATS on road when #14 ranked since 2007	*1-5 ATS when #9 ranked since 2000*
5-0 S/U @ home when #15 ranked all time	6-0-2 S/U @ home when #10 ranked all time
4-1 S/U when #15 ranked since 2009	9-1 S/U when #10 ranked since 1990
13-1 S/U when #16 ranked all time {5-0 on road}	5-0 S/U @ home when #11 ranked since 2001
0-5 S/U & ATS when #17 ranked since 2008	7-1 S/U @ home when #12 ranked since 1986
6-1 S/U @ home when #17 ranked all time	1-5 S/U on road when #12 ranked since 1990
2-8 ATS when #18 ranked since 1996	*0-5 ATS on road when #12 ranked since 1993*

Team records when ranked

5-0 S/U @ home when #13 ranked since 1987	5-0 S/U when #16 ranked since 1997
9-1 S/U on road when #13 ranked all time	4-0 S/U @ home when #17 ranked since 1951
8-1 O/U when #13 ranked since 1990	5-0-1 S/U when #18 ranked all time
6-1 S/U when #14 ranked all time	3-0 S/U on road when #19 ranked all time
3-1 ATS when #14 ranked since 1983	1-4 S/U on road when #20 ranked all time
6-0 S/U @ home when #15 ranked since 1996	0-6 ATS when #20 ranked since 1988
0-4 S/U on road when #15 ranked since 1978	5-0 O/U when #21 ranked all time
9-2 S/U @ home when #16 ranked all time	5-0 S/U when #22 ranked all time
13-1-1 S/U @ home when #17 ranked all time	3-0 S/U when #24 ranked since 1994
6-0 S/U @ home when #18 ranked since 1981	0-4 O/U when #24 ranked all time
4-0 S/U @ home when #19 ranked since 1977	5-1 S/U @ home when #25 ranked all time
5-1 S/U on road when #20 ranked all time	0-3 S/U when ranked vs #11 ranked teams all time
0-3 S/U & ATS when #20 ranked since 1995	3-0 S/U @ home when ranked vs Arizona State all time
3-0 O/U when #20 ranked since 1995	4-0 O/U when ranked vs Arizona since 2006
5-0 ATS when #21 ranked since 1990	5-0 S/U @ home when ranked vs California all time
3-0 O/U when #21 ranked since 1997	4-0 S/U & ATS when ranked vs Oregon since 2002
1-3 S/U on road when #22 ranked since 1999	5-0 S/U when ranked vs Stanford since 1997
7-0 S/U @ home when #22 ranked all time	0-5 S/U on road when ranked vs USC all time
0-5-1 ATS @ home when #22 ranked since 1994	0-7 S/U & ATS when ranked vs Washington since 2001
5-2 S/U when #25 ranked since 1994	**Western Kentucky**
0-3 S/U when ranked vs #1 ranked teams since 1972	1-0 S/U when ranked all time
0-3 S/U & ATS when ranked vs #2 ranked teams since 2003	**Western Michigan**
3-0 O/U when ranked vs #10 ranked teams since 1986	7-1 S/U when ranked all time
4-1 S/U when ranked vs #15 ranked teams all time	**West Virginia**
4-0 S/U when ranked vs #18 ranked teams all time	4-0 O/U when #3 ranked since 2006
3-0 O/U @ home when ranked vs #20 ranked teams all time	7-0 S/U when #4 ranked since 1988
0-3 S/U on road when ranked vs #20 ranked teams all time	4-0 S/U @ home when #5 ranked all time
0-3 O/U when ranked vs #20 ranked teams since 1992	0-3 ATS on road when #5 ranked since 2007
9-1 S/U @ home when ranked vs Arizona all time	0-4 O/U when #5 ranked since 2007
7-1 O/U when ranked vs Arizona since 1996	3-0 S/U @ home when #6 ranked all time
5-0 S/U when ranked vs Arizona since 2000	4-1 S/U @ home when #7 ranked since 1983
17-3 S/U when ranked vs California since 1959	4-0 S/U @ home when #8 ranked since 1955
5-0 S/U when ranked vs Colorado since 2000	6-0 S/U when #9 ranked since 1993
0-5 O/U when ranked vs Colorado since 2000	8-2 S/U when #11 ranked since 1975
19-1 S/U when ranked vs Oregon State since 1950 {9-0 @ home}	7-2 ATS when #11 ranked since 1988
0-6 S/U & ATS when ranked vs ranked Oregon since 1995	6-1 O/U when #11 ranked since 1998
9-1 S/U @ home when ranked vs Stanford since 1981	7-1 S/U when #12 ranked since 2004 {3-0 on road}
2-7 S/U when ranked @ UCLA since 1981	4-0 S/U when #13 ranked since 2004
0-5 ATS when ranked @ UCLA since 1997	5-0 O/U when #13 ranked since 2002
5-0 O/U when ranked vs UCLA since 2000	6-0 S/U @ home when #14 ranked all time
Washington State	6-1 S/U when #15 ranked all time
32-6 S/U @ home when ranked since 1997	12-1 S/U when #16 ranked all time {5-0 on road}
3-0 S/U & ATS @ home when #8 ranked all time	4-0 O/U when #16 ranked since 2004
3-0 O/U @ home when #8 ranked all time	0-6 O/U when #17 ranked since 1989
0-3 O/U when #10 ranked since 2002	5-1 S/U @ home when #17 ranked all time
1-4 ATS when #10 ranked since 1997	7-0 S/U when #19 ranked since 1989
4-0 S/U & ATS when #11 ranked all time	0-4 S/U when #24 ranked since 2008
3-0 S/U & ATS when #13 ranked since 1997	0-6 ATS when #24 ranked since 1994
3-0 S/U @ home when #15 ranked since 1997	4-0 S/U @ home when #25 ranked since 1993
1-4 S/U on road when #15 ranked since 1942	0-3 S/U when ranked vs #2 ranked teams all time

Team records when ranked

0-4 O/U when ranked vs #4 ranked teams all time	0-3 S/U on road when ranked vs #1 ranked team all time
0-3 S/U when ranked vs #5 ranked teams all time	0-4 S/U & ATS when ranked vs #3 ranked teams since 2011
0-3 S/U when ranked vs #9 ranked teams since 1975	0-3 S/U when ranked vs #4 ranked teams since 1995
5-0 S/U when ranked vs #19 ranked teams all time	0-3 O/U when ranked vs #4 ranked teams since 1995
0-3 ATS when ranked vs #21 ranked teams all time	2-9 S/U when ranked vs #8 ranked teams all time
4-0 S/U when ranked vs #25 ranked teams since 2007	1-3 S/U when ranked vs #9 ranked teams since 1995
4-0 S/U when ranked vs Baylor all time	5-0 S/U when ranked vs #11 ranked teams since 1999
0-3 S/U when ranked vs Oklahoma since 2015	3-0 S/U on road when ranked vs #13 ranked teams all time
4-0 O/U when ranked vs Oklahoma since 2008	4-0 O/U when ranked vs #13 ranked teams since 1995
0-3 S/U & ATS when ranked vs Oklahoma State since 2016	3-0 S/U when ranked vs #14 ranked teams all time
4-0 ATS when ranked vs TCU since 2014	3-0 S/U when ranked vs #22 ranked teams all time
0-3 S/U when ranked @ Virginia Tech since 1996	3-0 S/U when ranked vs #25 ranked teams all time
0-4 ATS when ranked @ Virginia Tech since 1988	13-1 S/U when ranked vs Illinois since 1962 {6-0 @ home}
Wisconsin	9-2 S/U when ranked vs Iowa since 2006 {6-1 on road}
67-9 S/U @ home when ranked since 2006	2-6 ATS when ranked vs Michigan State since 2004
1-4 S/U when #2 ranked all time	13-1 S/U when ranked vs Minnesota since 1998
5-0 S/U @ home when #4 ranked since 2000	9-0 S/U @ home when ranked vs Minnesota since 1954
9-0 S/U @ home when #5 ranked all time	6-0 S/U when ranked vs Nebraska since 2014
7-0 S/U when #5 ranked since 2010	1-6 S/U when ranked @ Northwestern since 2003
6-1 S/U @ home when #6 ranked all time	1-7 ATS when ranked @ Northwestern since 1995
7-2 O/U when #6 ranked since 2010	0-7 S/U when ranked vs Ohio State since 2011
7-0 S/U when #7 ranked since 2007	1-10-1 S/U when ranked @ Ohio State all time
4-0 S/U on road when #7 ranked all time	9-0 S/U when ranked vs Purdue since 2004 {7-2 ATS}
9-1 S/U @ home when #8 ranked all time	9-1-1 S/U @ home when ranked vs Purdue all time
1-4 S/U on road when #8 ranked since 1963	**Wyoming**
10-0 S/U @ home when #9 ranked since 1951	0-7-1 ATS on road when ranked since 1988
2-7 ATS when #9 ranked since 2004	14-2 S/U @ home when ranked all time
8-2 S/U when #10 ranked since 1999	3-0 S/U when #12 ranked all time
5-0 S/U @ home when #10 ranked since 1954	4-1 S/U when #16 ranked all time
10-3 ATS when #10 ranked since 1993	4-0 S/U when #18 ranked all time
8-2 S/U when #11 ranked since 1999 {6-0 @ home}	0-4 S/U when ranked vs ranked teams since 1988
5-1 S/U @ home when #12 ranked since 1959	3-0 S/U when ranked vs San Jose State all time
0-5 ATS when #12 ranked since 2006	
2-8 ATS when #14 ranked since 2003	
5-1 S/U when #15 ranked since 2004	
5-1 O/U when #15 ranked since 2004	
11-1 S/U when #16 ranked since 1953 {6-0 @ home}	
8-1 O/U when #16 ranked since 1993	
7-1 S/U @ home when #17 ranked all time	
0-3 ATS on road when #17 ranked all time	
6-2 S/U @ home when #18 ranked all time	
5-0 S/U @ home when #20 ranked since 2004	
0-4 O/U on road when #20 ranked since 1999	
7-1 S/U when #21 ranked since 2003	
1-8 O/U when #21 ranked since 1993	
6-0 S/U when #22 ranked since 2002	
7-1 ATS when #23 ranked since 2003	
6-1 S/U when #24 ranked since 2005	
2-9 ATS when #24 ranked since 1995	
5-2 S/U when #25 ranked all time	

Team records vs ranked teams

Air Force
0-12 S/U on road vs ranked teams since 2004
13-5 ATS on road vs ranked teams since 1996
0-12 S/U vs #3 - #5 ranked teams all time
1-10 S/U vs #11 - #14 ranked teams all time
0-4 S/U vs ranked Colorado all time

Akron
1-20 S/U vs ranked teams since 1999 {0-18 on road}
2-8 O/U vs ranked teams since 2009

Alabama
121-84-5 S/U @ home vs ranked teams all time
55-47-3 S/U on road vs ranked teams all time
10-3 S/U vs #1 ranked teams since 1977
7-1 S/U vs #3 ranked teams since 2008
2-14 S/U vs #2 ranked teams all time {0-5 on road}
1-6 O/U vs #5 ranked teams since 1987
1-5 S/U on road vs #6 ranked teams all time
1-5 S/U on road vs #7 ranked teams all time
6-1 ATS vs #8 ranked teams since 1987
4-0 S/U & ATS vs #9 ranked teams since 2008
2-7 S/U vs #11 ranked teams since 2001 {1-8 ATS}
6-1 ATS vs #12 ranked teams since 1984
5-0 ATS vs #13 ranked teams since 1992
6-0 S/U & ATS vs #14 ranked teams since 1999
4-0 S/U on road vs #14 ranked teams since 1974
6-1 S/U vs #16 ranked teams since 1975
5-0 S/U @ home vs #16 ranked teams all time
0-7 O/U vs #17 ranked teams since 2001
5-0 S/U vs #18 ranked teams since 2006
5-1 S/U vs #19 ranked teams since 1946
6-0 S/U & ATS vs #20 ranked teams since 1990
3-0 S/U on road vs #20 ranked teams since 1958
4-1 ATS vs #21 ranked teams since 1995
1-4 ATS vs #22 ranked teams since 2003
0-3 ATS vs #25 ranked teams since 2000
0-3 O/U vs #25 ranked teams since 2000
8-1 S/U vs ranked Arkansas all time
1-9 O/U @ home vs ranked Auburn since 1988
8-1 S/U vs ranked LSU since 2012
1-7-2 O/U vs ranked LSU since 2011
16-2 S/U vs ranked Mississippi State since 1944
7-0 S/U vs ranked Texas A&M since 2013

Alabama-Birmingham
1-18 S/U on road vs ranked teams since 1997

Appalachian State
2-13 S/U vs ranked teams all time

Arizona
1-6 ATS on road vs ranked teams since 2015
6-1 O/U on road vs ranked teams since 2015
0-5 S/U on road vs #1 ranked teams since 1984

5-31 S/U on road vs ranked teams since 1999
2-20-1 S/U on road vs #3 - #9 ranked teams since 1970
0-4 S/U on road vs #10 ranked teams all time
4-0 ATS vs #11 ranked teams since 1989
0-3 S/U on road vs #13 ranked teams since 1987
1-4 S/U vs #14 ranked teams all time
0-7 S/U vs #16 ranked teams all time
0-4 S/U on road vs #17 ranked teams all time
0-4 S/U on road vs #18 ranked teams since 1981
1-4 S/U vs #19 ranked teams all time
4-0 S/U & ATS on road vs #20 ranked teams since 1994
4-1 ATS vs #22 ranked teams all time
0-3 S/U vs #24 ranked teams all time
5-1 O/U vs #25 ranked teams since 2003
4-0 S/U @ home vs ranked Arizona State since 1982
0-3 S/U vs ranked Colorado all time
1-6 O/U vs ranked Oregon since 2012
0-4 S/U & ATS vs ranked UCLA since 2012
0-7-1 S/U @ ranked UCLA all time
7-1 ATS vs ranked USC since 2005
1-9 S/U @ ranked Washington all time

Arizona State
8-31 S/U on road vs ranked teams since 1998
0-6 S/U vs ranked teams in Bowl Games since 1997
5-1 S/U vs ranked Non-Conference teams since 2011
0-7 S/U vs #2 ranked teams all time
1-5 S/U vs #5 ranked teams all time
3-18 S/U vs #7 - #9 ranked teams all time {1-10 on road}
0-6 S/U vs #11 ranked teams since 1990
0-6 S/U vs #13 ranked teams since 1992 {1-5 ATS}
1-5 S/U vs #14 ranked teams all time
5-1 ATS vs #16 ranked teams since 1992
4-0 O/U vs #16 ranked teams since 2004
0-7 S/U vs #17 ranked teams all time
4-0 S/U @ home vs #20 ranked teams all time
1-6 S/U vs #21 ranked teams all time
0-6 ATS vs #21 ranked teams since 1994
4-1 ATS vs #23 ranked teams all time
7-0 O/U vs ranked UCLA since 1995
1-4 S/U @ home vs ranked UCLA all time
1-7 S/U @ ranked USC since 1995
0-3 S/U @ ranked Washington State all time

Arkansas
3-22 S/U vs ranked teams since 2016
4-23 S/U vs #1 ranked teams all time {12 straight L}
1-12 S/U vs #3 ranked teams all time
0-6 S/U vs #4 ranked teams since 1994
0-3 S/U on road vs #5 ranked teams all time
1-5 S/U on road vs #6 ranked teams all time
1-4 S/U @ home vs #6 ranked teams all time

Team records vs ranked teams

1-6 S/U vs #7 ranked teams since 2004	4-0 S/U vs #24 ranked teams all time
0-4 S/U on road vs #7 ranked teams all time	3-0 S/U & ATS vs #25 ranked teams all time
1-11 S/U vs #8 ranked teams since 1949	0-5 S/U @ ranked Alabama since 2012
5-1 ATS vs #11 ranked teams since 1985	0-5 S/U @ Georgia since 2007
0-5 S/U on road vs #12 ranked teams all time	0-3 S/U @ ranked Mississippi State since 1992
5-0 S/U @ home vs #15 ranked teams all time	4-0 S/U @ ranked Mississippi since 1972
1-8 S/U vs #16 ranked teams all time	**Ball State**
0-6 S/U on road vs #17 ranked teams all time	3-13 S/U vs ranked teams since 2005
3-0 S/U @ home vs #18 ranked teams all time	**BAYLOR**
1-4 S/U @ home vs #19 ranked teams all time	2-47-1 S/U on road vs ranked teams since 1992 {11 L}
0-3 S/U on road vs #20 ranked teams since 1940	5-17 S/U vs ranked teams since 2016
0-5-1 S/U vs #21 ranked teams all time	1-10 S/U vs #1 ranked teams since 1955
0-5 ATS vs #21 ranked teams since 1993	0-7 S/U vs #2 ranked teams since 1957
4-0 O/U vs #21 ranked teams since 2005	0-5 S/U @ home vs #3 ranked teams all time
0-15 S/U vs ranked Alabama since 2005	1-5 S/U @ home vs #4 ranked teams all time
0-5 S/U @ ranked Auburn since 2010 {1-4 ATS}	0-5 S/U on road vs #6 ranked teams all time
0-7 S/U vs ranked Auburn since 2013 {1-6 ATS}	0-8 S/U on road vs #7 ranked teams all time
9-2 ATS vs LSU since 2007	1-9 S/U vs #8 ranked teams all time
5-0 O/U vs South Carolina since 2007	0-8 S/U on road vs #10 ranked teams since 1967
1-6 S/U vs ranked Texas A&M since 2013	0-7 S/U vs #11 ranked teams since 1957
Arkansas State	1-5 S/U vs #12 ranked teams since 1992
1-23 S/U vs ranked teams since 1994	0-11 S/U vs #13 ranked teams since 1952
ARMY	*1-5 ATS vs #13 ranked teams since 1983*
0-49 S/U vs ranked teams since 1973	0-5 S/U on road vs #14 ranked teams since 1981
0-34 S/U on road vs ranked teams since 1963	0-6 S/U vs #15 ranked teams since 1959
1-7 O/U vs ranked teams since 2014	0-3 S/U & ATS @ home vs #16 ranked teams since 2005
0-4 S/U vs #5 ranked teams since 1980	0-4 S/U on road vs #18 ranked teams since 1946
0-4 S/U vs #6 ranked teams since 1954	1-11 S/U vs #19 ranked teams since 1945
0-6 S/U vs #7 ranked teams since 1960	0-3 S/U vs #21 ranked teams all time
0-6 S/U vs #8 ranked teams since 1957	1-5 S/U vs #22 ranked teams all time {0-3 on road}
0-5 S/U vs #14 ranked teams all time	0-3 S/U @ ranked Texas Tech all time
0-4 S/U vs #15 ranked teams since 1969	0-19 S/U @ ranked Texas since 1953
0-3 ATS vs #19 ranked teams all time	1-14 S/U vs ranked Texas since 1990
0-4 S/U vs #20 ranked teams since 1970	0-4 S/U vs ranked West Virginia all time
AUBURN	**Boise State**
14-7-1 ATS @ home vs ranked teams since 2013	5-14 S/U on road vs ranked teams since 1996
0-7 S/U vs ranked teams in Bowl Games since 2014	*2-11 O/U vs ranked teams since 2014*
0-7 S/U on road vs #1 ranked teams since 1996	**Boston College**
1-6 S/U @ home vs #2 ranked teams since 2009	*6-17 O/U on road vs ranked teams since 2005*
0-12 S/U vs #3 ranked teams all time	1-34 S/U vs ranked teams last 32 {0-16 on road}
1-7 ATS vs #3 ranked teams since 1972	2-6 S/U vs ranked teams in Bowl games all time
1-7 S/U on road vs #5 ranked teams all time	0-4 S/U vs #1 ranked teams since 2001
0-4 S/U @ home vs #8 ranked teams since 1982	*0-3 O/U vs #3 ranked teams since 2001*
1-11 O/U vs #10 ranked teams since 2000	0-9 S/U vs #2 ranked teams all time
1-4 S/U on road vs #12 ranked teams all time	0-6 S/U vs #3 ranked teams all time
3-0 S/U @ home vs #15 ranked teams since 1953	0-4 S/U @ home vs #4 ranked teams since 1968
6-1-1 O/U vs #17 ranked teams since 1995	*4-1 ATS vs #4 ranked teams since 2000*
3-0 S/U @ home vs #18 ranked teams since 1977	0-15 S/U vs #5 & #6 ranked teams all time
1-5 O/U vs #19 ranked teams since 1983	0-3 S/U on road vs #7 ranked teams all time
1-7 S/U vs #20 ranked teams since 1973	1-5 S/U @ home vs #8 ranked teams all time

Team records vs ranked teams

3-0 ATS on road vs #9 ranked teams since 1984	1-5-1 S/U on road vs #16 ranked teams all time
0-3 S/U @ home vs #10 ranked teams since 1974	1-4 S/U vs #17 ranked teams all time
0-4 S/U vs #11 ranked teams since 1995	*4-0 ATS vs #18 ranked teams since 1992*
0-4 S/U @ home vs #15 ranked teams all time {0-3 ATS}	0-3 S/U @ home vs #19 ranked teams since 1970
0-8-1 S/U vs #16 ranked teams all time	0-4 S/U on road vs #20 ranked teams since 1984
1-6 S/U @ home vs #17 ranked teams since 1985	*4-1 O/U vs #21 ranked teams all time*
1-8 S/U vs #17 ranked teams since 1990	1-4 S/U vs #22 ranked teams all time
0-4 S/U on road vs #22 ranked teams all time	*9-1 ATS vs ranked Arizona all time*
0-7 S/U vs #23 ranked teams all time	1-8 S/U vs ranked Oregon since 2010
0-11 S/U vs ranked Clemson since 2011	0-4 S/U & ATS @ home vs ranked Stanford since 1992
1-8 S/U vs Florida State all time {0-3 @ home}	0-7 S/U vs ranked Stanford since 2010
0-5 S/U vs ranked Syracuse since 1995	*4-0 ATS @ home vs ranked UCLA since 1988*
7-2 ATS @ Virginia Tech since 1995	0-8 S/U vs ranked USC since 2004
Bowling Green	0-5 S/U @ ranked USC since 2002
0-10 S/U vs teams ranked in Top Ten all time	*0-8 O/U vs ranked USC since 2004*
0-3 S/U vs ranked teams in Bowl games all time	0-3 S/U @ ranked Washington State all time
0-3 S/U vs #24 ranked teams all time	2-9 S/U @ ranked Washington since 1960
0-3 S/U vs #25 ranked teams snice 2009	**Central Florida**
0-3 S/U vs ranked Miami-Ohio all time	1-20 S/U on road vs ranked teams all time
BYU	**Central Michigan**
10-3 ATS on road vs ranked teams since 2010	1-13 S/U vs ranked teams all time
2-11 O/U on road vs ranked teams since 2010	**Charlotte**
4-21 S/U on road vs ranked teams since 1998	0-3 S/U & ATS vs ranked teams all time {3-0 O/U}
2-9-1 S/U vs ranked teams in Bowl games since 1985	**Cincinnati**
0-13 S/U vs #10 - #13 ranked teams all time	6-17 S/U vs ranked teams since 2010
1-9 O/U vs #14 ranked teams since 1979	3-32 S/U vs Top 10 ranked teams all time
5-0 S/U vs #19 ranked teams since 1980	1-18 S/U on road vs Top 10 ranked teams all time
1-4 ATS vs #20 ranked teams all time	0-12 S/U vs #10 - #13 ranked teams all time
0-8 S/U vs #21 - #22 ranked teams all time	*3-0 ATS vs #12 ranked teams all time*
0-4 O/U vs #21 ranked teams since 2002	4-17 S/U vs #16 - #18 ranked teams all time
0-6 O/U vs #23 #24 ranked teams all time	4-0 S/U vs #21 ranked teams since 2004
4-0 O/U vs #25 ranked teams all time	6-0 ATS vs #21 ranked teams since 1995
Buffalo	0-3 S/U & ATS vs #25 ranked teams all time
1-14 S/U vs ranked teams all time	**Clemson**
California	24-7 S/U vs ranked teams since 2015
0-10 O/U on road vs ranked teams since 2015	2-6 S/U vs #1 ranked teams all time
1-18 S/U on road vs ranked teams since 2010	*5-1 ATS vs #1 ranked teams since 1995*
4-0 O/U vs ranked teams in Bowl games since 1992	2-5 S/U vs #2 ranked teams all time
0-11 S/U vs #1 ranked teams all time	5-1 S/U & ATS vs #3 ranked teams since 2003
0-9 S/U vs #2 ranked teams all time	0-6 S/U on road vs #4 ranked teams all time
1-11-1 S/U vs #3 ranked teams since 1954	1-5 S/U @ home vs #5 ranked teams all time
1-16 S/U vs #4 ranked teams since 1946 {0-8 on road}	0-3 S/U on road vs #6 ranked teams all time
0-6 ATS vs #4 ranked teams since 1996	0-3 S/U on road vs #7 ranked teams all time
0-22-1 S/U vs #5 & #6 ranked teams all time	*4-0 O/U vs #8 ranked teams since 2001*
1-9 S/U vs #7 ranked teams all time	0-4 S/U @ home vs #9 ranked teams all time
1-6 S/U vs #8 ranked teams all time {0-4 on road}	3-0 S/U & ATS vs #11 ranked teams since 2004
0-9 S/U vs #9 ranked teams all time	0-3 S/U on road vs #13 ranked teams all time
0-9 S/U vs #10 ranked teams since 1978	0-3 S/U @ home vs #14 ranked teams since 1980
4-0 ATS @ home vs #13 ranked teams since 1993	1-5 S/U & ATS vs #14 ranked teams since 1990
0-3 S/U & ATS on road vs #15 ranked teams since 2005	1-5 S/U on road vs #15 ranked teams all time

Team records vs ranked teams

5-1 ATS vs #17 ranked teams since 1989	0-8 S/U vs ranked USC all time
1-5 O/U vs #17 ranked teams since 1989	0-4 S/U & O/U vs ranked Washington since 2000
4-1 S/U @ home vs #18 ranked teams all time	## Colorado State
1-6 S/U on road vs #20 ranked teams all time	*6-0 ATS on road vs ranked teams since 2012*
6-0 ATS vs #22 ranked teams all time	0-23 S/U vs ranked teams since 2004
0-4 S/U & ATS on road vs #24 ranked teams all time	0-26 S/U on road vs ranked teams all time
0-4 S/U & ATS vs #24 ranked teams since 2008	0-3 S/U vs #1 ranked teams all time
5-0 S/U vs #25 ranked teams all time	0-8 S/U vs #8 - #9 ranked teams all time
2-10 S/U @ Florida State since 1993	0-5 S/U vs #13 ranked teams all time
11-3 O/U vs Florida State since 2000	*0-3 ATS vs #13 ranked teams since 1990*
1-11 S/U @ Georgia Tech all time	0-9 S/U vs #15 - #18 ranked teams all time
6-1 S/U @ home vs NC State since 1967	*4-0 ATS vs #19 ranked teams since 1990*
0-4 S/U & ATS vs South Carolina since 2010	0-8 S/U vs #20 ranked teams all time
0-7 O/U vs South Carolina since 2000	*1-3 ATS vs #20 ranked teams since 1994*
## Coastal Carolina	0-6 S/U vs #24 - #25 ranked teams all time
2-1 S/U vs ranked teams all time	## Connecticut
## Colorado	*2-8 O/U @ home vs ranked teams since 2005*
4-37 S/U vs ranked teams since 2009	1-22 S/U on road vs ranked teams all time
1-33 S/U on road vs ranked teams since 2002	0-4 S/U vs ranked Central Florida all time
1-10 S/U vs #1 ranked all time	0-5 S/U vs West Virginia all time
1-17 S/U vs #2 ranked teams all time	## DUKE
1-7 ATS vs #2 ranked teams since 2002	*1-6 O/U @ home vs ranked teams since 2015*
1-8 S/U on road vs #3 ranked teams all time	3-29 S/U @ home vs ranked teams since 1996
3-0 ATS @ home vs #3 ranked teams since 1995	2-61 S/U on road vs ranked teams since 1972
1-7 S/U vs #4 ranked teams since 1970	0-12 S/U vs #1 ranked teams all time
0-6 S/U @ home vs #5 ranked teams since 1978	0-6 S/U vs #2 ranked teams all time
0-7 S/U vs #6 ranked teams since 1972	0-4 S/U on road vs #4 ranked teams all time
1-6 S/U on road vs #7 ranked teams all time	0-5 S/U vs #5 ranked teams since 1958
1-5 S/U @ home vs #7 ranked teams all time	0-8 S/U @ home vs #6 ranked teams since 1948
1-4 O/U vs #7 ranked teams since 1995	0-3 S/U on road vs #7 ranked teams since 1972
0-5-1 S/U vs #8 ranked teams all time	*0-3 O/U vs #7 ranked teams since 2005*
0-5 ATS vs #8 ranked teams since 1990	0-4 S/U vs #8 ranked teams all time
1-10-1 S/U @ home vs #9 ranked teams all time	*0-4 ATS vs #9 ranked teams since 1994*
0-6 S/U vs #9 ranked teams since 2000	0-6 S/U vs #11 ranked teams since 1981
1-5 O/U @ home vs #9 ranked teams since 1991	*0-5 ATS vs #11 ranked teams since 1988*
0-4 ATS @ home vs #9 ranked teams since 2000	0-10-1 S/U vs #12 ranked teams since 1953
5-1 O/U vs #10 ranked teams since 1989	1-9 S/U vs #13 ranked teams since 1947 {0-5 on road}
0-7 S/U vs #11 ranked teams since 1977	*6-2 ATS vs #13 ranked teams since 1991*
0-5 O/U vs #11 ranked teams since 1996	0-6 S/U vs #14 ranked teams since 1959
0-4 S/U vs #14 ranked teams all time	0-3 S/U @ home vs #16 ranked teams all time
0-5 S/U vs #15 ranked teams since 2007	0-4 S/U vs #17 ranked teams since 1980
0-5 S/U on road vs #15 ranked teams all time	*0-3 ATS vs #17 ranked teams since 1986*
1-7 S/U vs #16 ranked teams since 1976	0-6 S/U vs #18 ranked teams all time
1-5 S/U vs #17 ranked teams since 1982	0-7 S/U vs #19 ranked teams all time
4-0 S/U @ home vs #22 ranked teams all time	*4-0 ATS vs #19 ranked teams since 1990*
6-1 O/U vs #25 ranked teams all time	0-4 S/U vs #21 ranked teams all time
0-6 S/U & ATS vs ranked Oregon since 2011	0-6 S/U vs #23 ranked teams all time
0-3 S/U @ home vs ranked UCLA all time	1-6 S/U @ home vs ranked North Carolina since 1947
4-0 ATS vs ranked UCLA since 2002	1-8 S/U vs ranked Virginia Tech all time {0-5 @ home}
4-0 O/U vs ranked UCLA since 2002	*0-5 O/U vs ranked Virginia Tech since 2010*

Team records vs ranked teams

0-6 S/U vs ranked Virginia since 1995	0-4 S/U vs #4 ranked teams since 2003
East Carolina	1-7 S/U on road vs #5 ranked teams all time
4-40 S/U on road vs ranked teams all time	*1-4 O/U on road vs #5 ranked since 1990*
2-27 S/U vs Top 10 ranked teams all time	5-1 S/U vs #7 ranked teams all time
8-2 O/U vs ranked teams since 2017	*0-5 O/U vs #7 ranked since 1989*
0-5 S/U vs #10 ranked teams all time	3-1 S/U s #9 ranked since 1992 {4-0 ATS}
0-4 S/U vs #13 ranked teams all time	5-0 S/U @ home vs #10 ranked teams since 1991
0-6 S/U vs #19 ranked teams all time	6-0 O/U @ home vs #10 ranked since 1989
0-3 ATS vs #19 ranked teams since 1994	6-1 S/U vs #11 ranked since 1989
0-3 S/U vs ranked Cincinnati since 2019	0-7 S/U on road vs #12 ranked teams all time
Eastern Michigan	6-0 O/U vs #12 ranked since 1983
0-16 vs ranked teams all time	0-3 S/U on road vs #14 ranked teams all time
5-1 O/U on road vs ranked teams since 2013	6-0 S/U vs #15 ranked teams since 1988
Florida	4-0 S/U vs #16 ranked since 1992
0-4 S/U on road vs #1 ranked team all time	3-0 S/U on road vs #16 ranked since 1982
1-6 S/U @ home vs #2 ranked team all time	*5-0 ATS vs #17 ranked since 1989*
0-7 S/U on road vs #3 ranked team since 1964	4-1 S/U & ATS vs #25 ranked teams all time
10-0 S/U vs #4 ranked since 1990	0-5 S/U vs ranked Clemson since 2015
9-0-1 ATS vs #4 ranked teams since 1990	15-3 O/U vs ranked Clemson since 1988
0-6 S/U on road vs #5 ranked since 1963	5-1 S/U vs ranked Georgia Tech since 1992
1-4 O/U on road vs #6 ranked teams since 1987	6-2 ATS vs ranked Miami since 2005
9-3 ATS vs #8 ranked teams since 1974	3-8 O/U vs ranked Miami since 2002
8-1 O/U vs #8 ranked since 1990	4-1 S/U & ATS vs NC State since 1992
5-1 ATS vs #10 ranked team since 1987	**Fresno State**
1-7 O/U vs #10 ranked since 1987	4-24 S/U vs ranked teams since 2005
5-1 O/U vs #11 ranked since 1998	4-39 S/U on road vs ranked teams all time
0-4 S/U & ATS vs #12 ranked teams since 2003	0-5 S/U vs #1 ranked teams all time
1-7 S/U & ATS vs #14 ranked teams since 1992	*3-0 ATS vs #1 ranked teams since 2003*
0-4 ATS vs #15 ranked teams since 2001	1-5 S/U vs #10 ranked teams all time
0-5 O/U vs #15 ranked since 1994	*4-0 ATS vs #13 ranked teams all time*
0-3 S/U on road vs #17 ranked teams since 1969	0-12 S/U vs #14 - #17 ranked teams all time
5-1 S/U & ATS vs #21 ranked teams all time	1-3 S/U vs #21 ranked teams all time
0-4 S/U & ATS vs #22 ranked teams since 2010	*3-0 ATS vs #23 ranked since 2001*
5-0 S/U vs #23 ranked since 2005	2-9 S/U vs ranked Boise State all time
4-0 S/U vs #25 ranked teams all time	*0-4 O/U @ ranked Boise State since 2010*
7-3 S/U vs ranked teams in Bowl games since 2006	0-6 S/U vs ranked San Diego State all time
8-2 O/U vs ranked teams in Bowl games since 2006	**Georgia**
0-4 S/U vs ranked Florida State since 2013	0-6 S/U vs #1 ranked teams since 1996
Florida Atlantic	*5-1 O/U vs #2 ranked since 1990*
0-24 S/U vs ranked teams all time	0-6 S/U @ home vs #3 ranked since 1952
Florida International	1-9 S/U vs #4 ranked teams all time
0-10 S/U vs ranked teams all time	1-5 S/U vs #5 ranked since 1970
Florida State	*3-0 O/U vs #5 ranked since 2006*
0-8 S/U on road vs ranked teams since 2017	*9-4 O/U vs #6 ranked since 1991*
0-6 S/U vs #1 ranked teams since 1999	*7-3 O/U vs #8 ranked since 1987*
0-6 O/U vs #1 ranked since 1999	0-4-1 S/U on road vs #9 ranked teams all time
1-5-1 S/U on road vs #2 ranked teams all time	*5-1 ATS vs #9 ranked since 1993*
0-4 S/U vs #3 ranked teams since 2015	0-6 S/U on road vs #10 ranked teams all time
5-1 O/U vs #3 ranked since 2006	0-3 S/U & ATS @ home vs #12 ranked teams all time

Team records vs ranked teams

4-0 O/U vs #12 ranked teams since 2004	0-3 S/U & ATS vs #5 ranked teams all time
0-3 S/U on road vs #14 ranked teams all time	0-4 S/U vs #13 ranked teams all time
0-4 O/U vs #17 ranked teams since 1987	0-10 S/U vs #14 - #17 ranked teams all time
5-0 ATS vs #20 ranked teams since 1995	1-9 S/U vs #24 - #25 ranked teams all time
4-0 S/U vs #22 ranked teams since 2002	0-3 S/U vs ranked Michigan all time
0-5 O/U vs #22 ranked teams since 2002	## Houston
1-6 O/U vs #24 ranked teams since 2001	*7-3 ATS on road vs ranked teams since 2008*
5-18 S/U vs ranked Alabama since 1947	*2-6 O/U on road vs ranked teams since 2012*
6-0 S/U & ATS @ home vs ranked Auburn since 2007	3-34 S/U on road vs ranked teams since 1985
4-20 S/U vs ranked Florida since 1990	0-3 S/U vs #1 ranked teams all time
1-5 S/U @ ranked South Carolina all time	0-4 S/U vs #2 ranked teams all time
1-3 S/U @ home vs ranked Tennessee since 2004	*4-0 ATS vs #3 ranked teams since 1984*
## Georgia Southern	0-6 S/U vs #4 ranked teams since 1992
2-7 S/U vs ranked teams all time	0-5 S/U vs #8 ranked teams all time
## Georgia State	0-3 S/U vs #9 ranked teams since 1958
1-9 S/U vs ranked teams all time	0-10-1 S/U vs #13 ranked teams all time
## Georgia Tech	1-8 S/U vs #14 ranked teams all time {0-4 on road}
2-16 S/U on road vs ranked teams since 2009	0-4 S/U vs #15 ranked teams since 1987
1-8 S/U on road vs #1 ranked teams all time	0-3 S/U on road vs #15 ranked teams since 1974
1-8-1 S/U vs #2 ranked teams all time	0-3 S/U on road vs #16 ranked teams all time
1-10 S/U vs #3 ranked teams all time {0-5 at home}	1-3 S/U vs #19 ranked teams since 1982
1-11 S/U vs #4 ranked teams all time	0-4 S/U on road vs #20 ranked teams since 1980
0-7 S/U @ home vs #5 ranked teams since 1971	0-3 S/U & ATS vs #22 ranked teams all time
1-4 S/U @ home vs #6 ranked teams since 1959	2-5 S/U vs ranked SMU all time
0-6 S/U on road vs #7 ranked teams all time	## Illinois
1-5 S/U @ home vs #7 ranked teams since 1971	2-26 S/U vs ranked teams since 2011
0-5 S/U on road vs #8 ranked teams since 1970	3-27 S/U on road vs ranked teams since 2003
1-7 S/U vs #10 ranked teams since 1968	4-28 S/U @ home vs ranked teams since 2002
1-5 S/U @ home vs #10 ranked teams all time	1-9 S/U vs #1 ranked teams since 1966
1-4 S/U on road vs #11 ranked teams all time	0-11 S/U vs #2 ranked teams since 1940
1-4 S/U on road vs #12 ranked teams since 1948	0-7-1 S/U vs #3 ranked teams since 1971
0-4 O/U vs #13 ranked teams since 2007	1-10-1 S/U vs #4 ranked teams since 1964
0-3 S/U on road vs #13 ranked teams all time	*5-0 ATS vs #5 ranked teams since 1985*
0-7 S/U @ home vs #14 ranked teams all time	1-7 S/U vs #6 ranked teams since 1985
0-6 S/U vs #14 ranked teams since 1993	*2-6 ATS vs #6 ranked since 1985*
1-10 S/U vs #15 ranked teams since 1960	2-8 S/U vs #7 ranked teams all time
8-1 S/U @ home vs #17 ranked teams since 1955	1-9-1 S/U vs #8 ranked teams since 1959
8-1 ATS vs #17 ranked teams since 1986	0-9-1 S/U on road vs #8 ranked teams since 1952
0-5 O/U vs #19 ranked teams since 2000	1-4 S/U on road vs #9 ranked all time
0-4 S/U on road vs #20 ranked teams since 1988	0-10 S/U vs #10 ranked teams since 1954
1-4 S/U vs #25 ranked teams all time	2-10-1 S/U vs #11 ranked teams all time
4-0 S/U @ home vs ranked Duke since 1947	0-6 S/U on road vs #11 ranked teams all time
2-13 S/U vs ranked Florida State all time {0-5 @ FSU}	0-7 S/U vs #12 ranked teams all time
0-4 S/U vs ranked Miami since 2009	1-8 S/U on road vs #13 ranked teams all time
0-6 S/U @ ranked North Carolina all time	0-6 S/U vs #13 ranked teams since 1995
4-0 ATS @ ranked Virginia Tech since 2006	0-5 S/U @ home vs #13 ranked teams since 1969
## Hawaii	0-7-1 S/U vs #14 ranked teams all time
1-20 S/U on road vs ranked teams all time	0-10 S/U vs #15 ranked teams since 1971
0-4 S/U vs #1 ranked teams all time	*5-0 ATS vs #15 ranked teams since 1993*

Team records vs ranked teams

0-4 S/U vs #17 ranked teams since 2001	1-6 S/U vs ranked Nebraska all time
0-5 ATS vs #17 ranked teams since 1995	1-44 S/U vs ranked Ohio State since 1952
0-7 S/U vs #18 ranked teams all time	*7-3 ATS vs ranked Ohio State since 2012*
0-7 S/U vs #19 ranked teams since 1990	1-13 S/U vs ranked Penn State all time
4-0 S/U @ home vs #20 ranked teams all time	*4-0 O/U @ home vs ranked Penn State since 2002*
6-1 ATS vs #20 ranked teams since 1988	0-8 S/U vs ranked Purdue since 1968
1-4 S/U vs #22 ranked teams all time	*0-3 O/U vs ranked Purdue since 1999*
0-5 S/U vs #23 ranked teams all time {1-4 ATS}	**Iowa**
4-1 O/U vs #23 ranked teams all time	*9-4 O/U on road vs ranked teams since 2009*
0-10 S/U vs ranked Iowa since 1990	0-10-1 S/U vs #1 ranked teams all time
3-33-1 S/U vs ranked Michigan since 1968	3-14 S/U vs #2 ranked teams all time {0-6 on road}
1-5 O/U vs ranked Michigan since 2004	0-6 S/U on road vs #3 ranked teams all time
0-4 S/U vs ranked Michigan State since 1999	2-10 S/U vs #4 ranked teams all time
0-5 ATS vs ranked Michigan State since 1990	*0-4 O/U vs #5 ranked teams since 2003*
1-7 S/U @ ranked Northwestern since 1940	1-7 S/U @ home vs #5 ranked teams all time
1-4 S/U @ home vs ranked Purdue since 1967	0-8 S/U on road vs #6 ranked teams since 1957
4-16 S/U vs ranked Wisconsin since 1952	1-11 S/U vs #7 ranked teams since 1955 {0-4 on road}
4-0 O/U @ ranked Wisconsin since 2006	1-11 S/U vs #8 ranked teams since 1978 {0-6 @ home}
Indiana	*0-5 O/U on road vs #8 ranked teams since 1985*
2-28 S/U on road vs ranked teams since 2005	4-0 S/U & ATS vs #9 ranked teams since 2003
14-125-1 S/U on road vs ranked teams all time	1-3 S/U on road vs #9 ranked teams since 1963
1-81 S/U vs Top #1 - #7 ranked teams all time	0-4 S/U @ home vs #10 ranked teams since 1976
0-58 S/U on road vs Top #1 - #7 ranked teams all time	3-0 S/U & ATS vs #12 ranked teams since 2000
3-22 S/U @ home vs ranked teams since 2006	4-1 S/U @ home vs #13 ranked teams all time
10-2 O/U @ home vs ranked teams last 12	3-14 S/U vs #14 ranked teams all time
0-16 S/U vs #1 ranked teams all time	0-5 S/U on road vs #16 ranked teams all time
0-15 S/U vs #2 ranked teams all time	1-6 S/U on road vs #17 ranked teams all time
1-9 S/U vs #3 ranked teams all time	*4-1 O/U vs #17 ranked teams since 1998*
0-32 S/U vs #4 #5 #6 ranked teams all time	1-6 S/U vs #18 ranked teams since 1999
0-11 S/U vs #7 ranked teams since 1953	*0-5 O/U vs #19 ranked teams since 2005*
1-8 S/U vs #8 ranked teams since 1976	*1-3 O/U vs #22 ranked teams all time*
0-11 S/U vs #10 ranked teams all time	3-0 S/U vs ranked Illinois since 1990
0-5 ATS vs #10 ranked teams since 1991	3-0 S/U @ home vs ranked Michigan since 2003
0-10 S/U vs #12 ranked teams since 1950	*5-0-1 ATS @ home vs ranked Michigan since 1994*
1-11 S/U vs #13 ranked teams all time	1-7 S/U @ ranked Minnesota all time
1-9 S/U vs #15 ranked teams since 1948	1-19 S/U @ ranked Ohio State since 1950
0-7 S/U vs #16 ranked teams since 1957	1-10 S/U @ ranked Purdue all time
1-5 ATS vs #16 ranked teams since 1984	1-6 S/U @ home vs ranked Wisconsin since 2006
1-11 S/U vs #17 ranked teams since 1969	**Iowa State**
2-11 S/U vs #18 ranked teams since 1957	0-11 S/U vs #1 ranked teams all time
0-7 S/U vs #19 ranked teams since 1978	1-8 S/U vs #2 ranked teams all time {0-6 on road}
5-1 O/U vs #22 ranked teams since 1993	1-17-1 S/U vs #3 ranked teams all time
6-0 ATS vs #23 ranked teams since 1995	*2-7 ATS vs #3 ranked teams since 1984*
0-7 S/U vs #24 & #25 teams all time	1-12 S/U vs #4 ranked teams all time
1-6 ATS vs #24 & #25 teams all time	*0-5 ATS on road vs #4 ranked teams since 1993*
4-22 S/U vs ranked Michigan State all time	0-9-1 S/U vs #5 ranked teams all time
1-4 ATS @ ranked Michigan State since 2003	0-6 S/U on road vs #6 ranked teams all time
3-43 S/U vs ranked Michigan all time	0-6 S/U on road vs #7 ranked teams since 1979
6-1-1 ATS vs ranked Michigan since 2009	*4-0 ATS on road vs #7 ranked teams since 1994*

Team records vs ranked teams

1-5 S/U @ home vs #9 ranked teams all time	0-7 S/U vs #12 ranked teams all time
4-0 ATS vs #9 ranked teams since 1995	*0-3 ATS vs #12 ranked teams since 1984*
0-11 S/U vs #10 ranked teams all time	0-8 S/U vs #13 ranked teams since 1971
0-5 ATS vs #10 ranked teams since 1995	*3-0 ATS vs #13 ranked teams since 1999*
0-17 S/U vs #11 #12 ranked teams all time	0-10 S/U vs #14 ranked teams all time
1-8 S/U vs #13 ranked teams all time	*4-0 O/U vs #14 ranked teams since 2002*
1-18 S/U vs #14 #15 ranked teams all time	0-11 S/U vs #16 ranked teams since 1972
1-10 S/U vs #16 ranked teams all time	1-5 S/U vs #17 ranked teams since 1974
0-8 S/U vs #17 ranked teams all time	0-5 S/U on road vs #18 ranked teams all time
0-4 ATS vs #17 ranked teams since 2002	*4-0 O/U vs #18 ranked teams since 1999*
1-9 S/U vs #19 ranked teams all time	*0-3 S/U & ATS vs #19 ranked teams since 1994*
0-6 S/U vs #21 ranked teams all time	0-7 S/U vs #20 #21 ranked teams all time
3-0 ATS on road vs #22 ranked teams since 2007	0-4 S/U vs #25 ranked teams since 1998
0-3 S/U & ATS vs #23 ranked teams all time	*0-4 S/U & ATS vs ranked Baylor since 2013*
0-5 S/U vs ranked Baylor all time	1-12 S/U & ATS vs ranked Kansas State all time
3-0 ATS vs ranked Baylor since 2014	0-6 S/U @ ranked Kansas State all time
4-1 O/U vs ranked Baylor all time	2-30 S/U vs ranked Oklahoma since 1978
1-13 S/U vs ranked Iowa all time {0-6 S/U @ Iowa}	0-13 S/U vs ranked Oklahoma State all time
0-6 O/U vs ranked Iowa since 2005	*1-10-1 ATS vs ranked Oklahoma State all time*
0-9 S/U vs ranked Kansas all time	0-4 S/U vs ranked TCU since 2012
0-11 S/U vs ranked Kansas State since 1994	0-8 S/U vs ranked Texas all time {2-6 ATS}
4-53-1 S/U vs ranked Oklahoma all time	**Kansas State**
1-27 S/U @ home vs ranked Oklahoma all time	1-14 S/U @ home vs ranked teams since 2013
8-3 O/U vs ranked Oklahoma since 2012	0-7 S/U vs ranked teams in Bowl games since 2001 {0-7 ATS}
1-7 S/U @ ranked Oklahoma State all time	1-9 S/U vs #1 ranked teams all time
3-9 S/U vs ranked Texas all time {1-4 @ home}	0-19 S/U vs #2 ranked teams all time
Kansas	*4-0 ATS vs #2 ranked teams since 2001*
0-42 S/U vs ranked teams since 2010	1-8 S/U vs #3 ranked teams all time
1-41 S/U on road vs ranked teams since 1995	0-5 S/U on road vs #4 ranked teams all time {0-3 ATS}
0-19 S/U @ home vs ranked teams since 2010	1-7 S/U vs #5 ranked teams all time
0-12 S/U vs #1 ranked teams since 1960	2-17 S/U vs #6 ranked teams all time
0-9 S/U @ home vs #1 ranked teams all time	1-13 S/U vs #7 ranked teams all time
0-7 S/U & ATS vs #2 ranked teams since 1985	*1-7 ATS vs #7 ranked teams since 1984*
4-0 O/U vs #2 ranked teams since 2001	*5-1 O/U vs #7 ranked teams since 1999*
0-14-1 S/U vs #3 ranked teams all time	1-11 S/U vs #8 ranked teams all time
1-9 S/U vs #4 ranked teams all time	*0-6 ATS vs #8 ranked teams since 1990*
0-5 ATS vs #4 ranked teams since 1986	0-13 S/U vs #9 ranked teams all time
1-6 S/U @ home vs #5 ranked teams all time	1-7 S/U vs #10 ranked teams all time
0-3 S/U on road vs #5 ranked teams all time	0-4 S/U vs #12 ranked teams all time
0-17 S/U vs #6 ranked teams since 1952	1-8 S/U vs #13 ranked teams all time
4-1 O/U vs #6 ranked teams since 2008	*4-0 ATS vs #15 ranked teams since 1999*
0-7 S/U vs #7 ranked teams all time	0-4-1 S/U vs #16 ranked teams all time
0-4 ATS vs #7 ranked teams since 1992	1-6 S/U vs #18 ranked teams all time
4-0 O/U vs #7 ranked teams since 1992	1-6 S/U vs #19 ranked teams all time
2-9 S/U vs #8 ranked teams all time	0-7 S/U vs #20 ranked teams all time
0-10 S/U vs #9 ranked teams since 1973	0-3 S/U vs #22 ranked teams all time
1-6 S/U vs #10 ranked teams all time	*3-0 O/U vs #22 ranked teams all time*
0-5 S/U on road vs #11 ranked teams all time	*6-0 ATS vs #25 ranked teams since 1994*
0-3 ATS on road vs #11 ranked teams since 1997	0-4 S/U vs ranked Baylor since 2013

Team records vs ranked teams

1-5 S/U vs ranked Kansas all time	**UL-Monroe**
1-12 S/U vs ranked Oklahoma State all time	2-35 S/U vs ranked teams all time
4-1 O/U vs ranked Oklahoma State since 2013	**Louisiana Tech**
0-3 S/U vs ranked TCU all time	2-38 S/U on road vs ranked teams all time
5-0 ATS vs ranked Texas since 2003	0-25 S/U vs Top 10 ranked teams all time
4-0 O/U vs ranked Texas Tech all time	**LSU**
Kent State	0-8 S/U vs #1 ranked teams since 2008
2-32 S/U vs ranked teams all time	0-4 S/U on road vs #1 ranked teams all time
0-3 S/U vs ranked Toledo all time	*1-5-1 O/U vs #1 ranked teams since 2009*
Kentucky	5-1 S/U vs #3 ranked teams since 2011
5-64 S/U on road vs ranked teams since 1978	0-10 S/U on road vs #3 ranked teams all time
2-15 S/U vs #1 ranked teams since 1951	*1-4 ATS on road vs #3 ranked teams since 1995*
0-6 S/U vs #2 ranked teams all time	*5-0-1 ATS vs #7 ranked teams since 2001*
0-9 S/U vs #3 ranked teams all time	*7-2 O/U vs #9 ranked teams since 2003*
0-4 ATS vs #3 ranked teams since 1999	1-7 S/U @ home vs #12 ranked teams all time
1-10 S/U vs #4 ranked teams all time	*0-5 ATS @ home vs #12 ranked teams since 1983*
0-21 S/U vs #5 #6 ranked teams all time	*0-5 O/U on road vs #12 ranked teams since 1999*
1-6 ATS vs #6 ranked teams since 1987	*4-0 ATS on road vs #14 ranked teams since 1996*
4-0 O/U @ home vs #6 ranked teams since 1990	*1-6 O/U vs #15 ranked teams since 1987*
0-15 S/U vs #7 ranked teams since 1972	*4-0 ATS @ home vs #17 ranked since 1999*
0-4 ATS @ home vs #7 ranked teams since 1993	6-0 S/U vs #18 ranked teams since 1988
0-8 S/U vs #8 ranked teams since 1970	*4-0 O/U vs #18 ranked teams since 2007*
0-7 S/U on road vs #9 ranked teams all time	3-0 S/U & ATS vs #25 ranked teams since 2001
0-3 ATS on road vs #9 ranked teams since 1994	*0-3 O/U vs #25 ranked teams since 2001*
1-4 ATS vs #11 ranked teams since 1989	1-21-1 S/U @ home vs ranked Alabama all time
0-9 S/U vs #12 ranked teams since 1970	*2-9 ATS @ home vs ranked Alabama since 1992*
4-0 ATS vs #12 ranked teams since 1987	*2-8-2 O/U vs ranked Alabama since 2005*
1-9 S/U vs #13 ranked teams since 1976	5-0 S/U @ home vs ranked Mississippi State since 1992
0-8 S/U on road vs #14 ranked teams since 1959	5-0 S/U vs ranked Mississippi State since 2000
0-4 ATS on road vs #14 ranked teams since 1999	*8-0 ATS vs ranked Mississippi State since 1992*
0-8 S/U vs #16 ranked teams since 1978	1-6 S/U @ home vs ranked Tennessee all time
3-0 ATS on road vs #17 ranked teams since 1996	5-1 S/U vs ranked Texas A&M since 2011 {6-0 ATS}
1-6 S/U vs #18 ranked teams all time	**Louisville**
4-1 ATS vs #19 ranked teams since 1976	4-42 S/U on road vs ranked teams all time
0-4 S/U vs #24 ranked teams all time	0-3 S/U vs #1 ranked teams all time
5-1 ATS vs #25 ranked teams all time	0-3 S/U on road vs #2 ranked teams all time
1-18 S/U @ ranked Florida all time	*3-0 O/U vs #2 ranked teams since 2014*
1-33 S/U vs ranked Georgia since 1967	*3-1 O/U vs #3 ranked teams since 2004*
1-6 S/U vs ranked Mississippi State since 1992	*4-0 ATS vs #4 ranked teams all time*
1-5 O/U vs ranked Mississippi State since 1999	0-5 S/U vs #6 ranked teams all time
6-0 O/U vs ranked South Carolina since 2007	1-6 S/U vs #9 ranked teams all time
1-16 S/U @ ranked Tennessee all time	0-4 S/U & ATS vs #11 ranked teams all time
1-23 S/U vs ranked Tennessee since 1967	*3-0 ATS vs #15 ranked teams all time*
Liberty	0-4 S/U @ home vs #17 ranked teams all time
1-2 S/U vs ranked teams all time	1-4 S/U on road vs #19 ranked teams all time
Louisiana	1-7 S/U vs #24 ranked teams all time
2-31 S/U vs ranked teams since 1985	0-5 S/U & ATS vs ranked Clemson all time
8-3 O/U vs ranked teams since 2009	2-9 S/U vs ranked Florida State all time

Team records vs ranked teams

0-4 S/U vs ranked Pittsburgh all time	0-6 S/U vs #10 ranked teams since 1967
Marshall	0-3 S/U vs #11 ranked teams all time
1-7 ATS on road vs ranked teams since 2006	1-4 S/U vs #14 ranked teams all time
5-1 O/U on road vs ranked teams since 2009	1-5 S/U vs #16 ranked teams all time
0-18 S/U vs ranked teams since 2003	0-3 S/U vs #19 ranked teams all time
Maryland	0-3 S/U vs ranked Central Florida all time
1-16 S/U @ home vs ranked teams since 2011	1-8 S/U vs ranked Houston all time
2-35 S/U vs ranked teams since 2011	**Miami**
1-22 S/U on road vs ranked teams since 2008	4-17 S/U on road vs ranked teams since 2006
0-4 S/U vs #1 ranked teams since 1956	*4-13 O/U @ home vs ranked teams since 2009*
0-7 S/U vs #2 ranked teams since 1957	6-0 S/U @ home vs #1 ranked teams since 1981
1-7 S/U vs #3 ranked teams all time	*4-0 ATS @ home vs #1 ranked team since 1986*
0-5 ATS vs #3 ranked teams since 1983	1-6 S/U on road vs #1 ranked teams all time
0-7 S/U vs #4 ranked teams all time	0-6 S/U on road vs #2 ranked teams all time
0-7 S/U on road vs #5 ranked teams all time	*6-1 O/U vs #2 ranked teams since 1990*
1-5 ATS vs #5 ranked teams since 2002	1-6 S/U on road vs #4 ranked teams all time
1-10 S/U vs #6 ranked teams all time	1-6 S/U vs #5 ranked teams since 1973 {0-3 @ home}
0-5 ATS vs #6 ranked teams since 1990	1-5 S/U on road vs #6 ranked teams all time
0-13 S/U vs #9 ranked teams all time	*4-0 O/U vs #6 ranked teams since 2002*
4-0 ATS vs #9 ranked teams since 1998	0-3 S/U @ home vs #7 ranked teams all time
1-8 S/U vs #10 ranked teams all time	*2-5-1 ATS vs #8 ranked teams since 1986*
0-9 S/U vs #12 ranked teams all time	*0-8 O/U vs #8 ranked teams since 1986*
1-6 ATS vs #12 ranked teams since 1985	3-0 S/U @ home vs #9 ranked teams since 1980
0-5 S/U on road vs #13 ranked teams all time	0-6 S/U vs #10 ranked teams since 2004 {1-5 ATS}
0-4 S/U on road vs #14 ranked teams all time	*4-1 ATS vs #12 ranked teams since 1983*
1-6 S/U on road vs #15 ranked teams since 1959	6-0 S/U & ATS vs #13 ranked teams since 1983
1-5 ATS on road vs #15 ranked teams since 1991	1-6 S/U @ home vs #14 ranked teams all time
0-5 S/U vs #16 ranked teams all time	*0-6 O/U vs #14 ranked teams since 1989*
1-6 S/U on road vs #17 ranked teams all time	*3-0 O/U vs #15 ranked teams since 1988*
1-4 S/U on road vs #19 ranked teams since 1998	1-3 S/U on road vs #17 ranked teams all time
0-4 S/U & ATS @ home vs #20 ranked teams since 2000	4-0 S/U on road vs #18 ranked teams since 1980
0-7 S/U vs #22 ranked teams all time	4-1 S/U @ home vs #20 ranked teams since 1986
4-0 O/U vs #23 ranked teams since 2005	0-5 S/U & ATS vs #21 ranked teams since 1996
5-1 ATS vs #23 ranked teams since 2003	1-4 S/U vs #24 ranked teams all time
0-9 S/U vs ranked Michigan all time	*1-4 O/U vs #24 ranked teams all time*
0-7 ATS vs ranked Michigan since 1990	0-6 S/U vs ranked Florida State since 2010
0-7 S/U vs ranked Ohio State all time	*2-11 O/U vs ranked Florida State since 2002*
7-0 O/U vs ranked Ohio State all time	0-3 S/U @ ranked Georgia Tech all time
0-22-1 S/U vs ranked Penn State all time	5-0 S/U vs ranked Pittsburgh since 1989
0-7 ATS vs ranked Penn State since 1991	*1-4 O/U vs ranked Pittsburgh since 1989*
Massachusetts	1-5 S/U vs ranked Virginia Tech since 2006
0-14 S/U vs ranked teams all time	**Miami-Ohio**
Memphis	2-14 S/U vs Top 10 ranked teams all time
0-16 S/U on road vs ranked teams since 1993	0-3 S/U vs #17 ranked teams all time
0-3 S/U vs #5 ranked teams all time	**Michigan**
0-3 S/U on road vs #6 ranked teams all time	*6-14 ATS on road vs ranked teams since 2009*
4-0 ATS vs #6 ranked teams since 1984	3-21 S/U on road vs ranked teams since 2006
0-5 S/U vs #7 ranked teams since 1987	*14-4 O/U @ home vs ranked teams since 2010*
0-6 S/U vs #8 #9 ranked teams all time	3-9 S/U vs ranked teams in Bowl games since 2004

Team records vs ranked teams

0-9 S/U vs #1 ranked teams since 1984	0-4 S/U on road vs #9 ranked teams since 1987
0-7 S/U on road vs #1 ranked teams all time	*4-1 O/U vs #10 ranked teams since 1993*
6-1 O/U vs #1 ranked teams since 1988	4-1 S/U @ home vs #10 ranked all time
1-8 S/U @ home vs #2 ranked teams all time	0-3 S/U on road vs #11 ranked teams all time
5-0 O/U vs #2 ranked teams since 2006	1-5 S/U @ home vs #12 ranked teams since 1982
1-9-1 S/U vs #3 ranked teams since 1957	0-10 S/U vs #14 ranked teams since 1983
4-0 O/U vs #3 ranked teams since 1994	0-4 S/U on road vs #14 ranked teams all time
4-0 S/U @ home vs #4 ranked teams all time	0-5 S/U vs #15 ranked teams since 2002
3-0 S/U @ home vs #5 ranked teams since 1975	*5-0 O/U vs #15 ranked teams since 2002*
3-0 O/U vs #6 ranked teams since 1999	0-4 S/U vs #16 ranked teams since 2000
0-6 S/U vs #7 ranked teams since 1994	0-5 S/U on road vs #16 ranked teams since 1982
2-6 S/U & ATS vs #8 ranked teams since 2007	*0-4 O/U vs #16 ranked teams since 2000*
6-2 ATS vs #9 ranked teams since 1993	1-5-1 S/U vs #17 ranked teams since 1956
0-3 S/U on road vs #10 ranked teams all time	4-1 S/U & ATS vs #18 ranked teams since 1984
4-0 S/U @ home vs #10 ranked teams since 1962	4-0 S/U @ home vs #19 ranked teams since 1975
8-1 O/U vs #11 ranked teams since 1993	*3-0 ATS vs #22 ranked teams since 2007*
5-0 S/U @ home vs #14 ranked teams since 1977	*3-0 ATS vs #23 ranked teams since 2001*
6-1 S/U @ home vs #15 ranked teams all time	*0-3 O/U vs #23 ranked teams since 2001*
0-4 O/U on road vs #15 ranked teams since 1985	*0-4 O/U vs #24 ranked teams all time*
1-5 S/U vs #16 ranked teams since 1983	*10-2 ATS vs ranked Michigan since 2009*
0-5 ATS vs #16 ranked teams since 1984	1-12 S/U @ home vs ranked Ohio State since 1975
7-1 S/U @ home vs #17 ranked teams all time	*1-6 O/U vs ranked Ohio State since 2015*
9-1-1 S/U vs #17 ranked teams since 1985	1-6 S/U @ ranked Penn State since 1994
0-3 S/U @ home vs #19 ranked teams all time	*10-3 O/U vs ranked Penn State since 1996*
4-0 O/U vs #19 ranked teams since 1995	*6-2 ATS vs ranked Wisconsin since 2004*
4-1 S/U @ home vs #20 ranked teams all time	**Middle Tennessee**
1-5 ATS vs #20 ranked teams since 1986	0-19 S/U vs ranked teams all time
0-3 S/U on road vs #22 ranked teams all time	**Minnesota**
1-3 ATS on road vs #23 ranked teams all time	6-77 S/U on road vs ranked teams since 1970
3-0 S/U & ATS vs #25 ranked teams all time	11-49 S/U @ home vs ranked teams since 1983
7-0 S/U vs ranked Illinois since 1989	*8-3-1 ATS @ home vs ranked teams since 2013*
2-9 S/U @ home vs ranked Michigan State all time	0-12 S/U on road vs #1 ranked teams all time
1-6 S/U & ATS vs ranked Michigan State since 2010	0-8 S/U @ home vs #2 ranked teams all time
2-5 O/U vs ranked Michigan State since 2010	*4-1 ATS vs #2 ranked teams since 1985*
0-7 S/U @ ranked Ohio State since 2002	0-8 S/U on road vs #3 ranked teams since 1948
1-14 S/U vs ranked Ohio State since 2005	0-11 S/U vs #3 ranked teams since 1962
8-0 O/U vs ranked Ohio State since 2013	0-9 S/U vs #4 ranked teams since 1944
5-1 S/U @ home vs ranked Penn State since 1998	0-8 S/U on road vs #5 ranked teams since 1957
Michigan State	0-8 S/U vs #5 ranked teams since 1967
2-11 S/U on road vs #1 ranked teams all time	0-4 S/U @ home vs #6 ranked teams since 1970
0-6 S/U @ home vs #2 ranked teams since 1967	0-5-1 S/U vs #7 ranked teams since 1963
1-9 S/U vs #3 ranked teams since 1960	0-13-1 S/U vs #8 ranked teams since 1951
4-1 S/U vs #4 ranked teams since 1997	*4-1 ATS vs #8 ranked teams since 1998*
1-6 S/U on road vs #4 ranked teams since 1971	1-7 S/U vs #9 ranked teams since 1959
1-5 S/U @ home vs #5 ranked teams since 1973	2-8-1 S/U vs #10 ranked teams all time
2-6 S/U @ home vs #6 ranked teams since 1967	0-3 S/U on road vs #11 ranked teams since 1979
3-0 S/U @ home vs #7 ranked teams since 1995	2-7 S/U vs #12 ranked teams since 1945
1-4 S/U on road vs #7 ranked teams since 1994	0-5 S/U vs #13 ranked teams since 1997
1-7 S/U @ home vs #8 ranked teams all time	0-5 S/U vs #14 ranked teams since 1988

Team records vs ranked teams

0-6 S/U vs #15 ranked teams since 1996	3-15 S/U @ ranked LSU since 1970
0-5 S/U on road vs #15 ranked teams since 1943	*0-4 O/U vs ranked Mississippi State since 2014*
0-7 S/U vs #16 ranked teams since 1978 {0-4 on road}	4-0 S/U vs ranked Texas A&M since 2014
0-6 S/U vs #17 ranked teams since 1954	*5-0 ATS vs ranked Texas A&M since 2013*
1-6 S/U vs #18 ranked teams since 1987	**Mississippi State**
0-4 S/U on road vs #18 ranked teams since 1978	14-95-1 S/U on road vs ranked teams since 1958
0-8 S/U vs #19 ranked teams since 1991	0-5 S/U on road vs #1 ranked teams all time
1-6 S/U vs #20 ranked teams since 1957	1-10 S/U vs #1 ranked teams all time
4-0-1 ATS vs #21 ranked teams since 2005	1-12 S/U vs #2 ranked teams all time
1-5 S/U vs #22 ranked teams all time	1-9-1 S/U vs #3 ranked teams all time
0-5 S/U @ ranked Illinois all time	0-6 S/U on road vs #3 ranked teams all time
1-8 S/U @ ranked Michigan State all time	0-11 S/U vs #4 ranked teams since 1961
4-0 ATS vs ranked Michigan State since 2010	0-10 S/U on road vs #5 ranked teams all time
4-0 ATS @ ranked Michigan State since 1997	0-12 S/U vs #5 ranked teams since 1971
1-8 S/U @ ranked Nebraska since 1967	1-5 S/U on road vs #6 ranked teams all time
0-4 S/U vs ranked Northwestern since 1959	*5-1 O/U vs #6 ranked teams since 1991*
1-5 S/U vs ranked Penn State all time	0-6 S/U on road vs #7 ranked teams all time
4-0 O/U vs ranked Purdue since 1999	0-7 S/U on road vs #9 ranked teams all time
2-17 S/U vs ranked Wisconsin since 1954	0-7 S/U @ home vs #10 ranked teams all time
5-0 O/U @ ranked Wisconsin since 2004	*1-4 ATS vs #10 ranked teams since 1988*
Mississippi	1-10 S/U vs #11 ranked teams since 1969
0-5 S/U on road vs ranked teams since 2018	2-7 S/U vs #12 ranked teams since 1960
0-14 S/U vs #1 ranked teams all time	0-6 S/U on road vs #13 ranked teams all time
1-9 S/U vs #2 ranked teams all time	1-8 S/U vs #14 ranked teams since 1955
1-7 S/U vs #3 ranked teams since 1995	*0-5 O/U vs #14 ranked teams since 1991*
0-5 S/U vs #5 ranked teams since 1982	1-8 S/U on road vs #16 ranked teams all time
0-5 S/U on road vs #6 ranked teams all time	0-5 S/U @ home vs #18 ranked teams all time
0-5 O/U vs #6 ranked teams since 2002	*0-5 ATS vs #18 ranked teams since 1996*
1-6 S/U vs #7 ranked teams since 1971	1-9 S/U vs #19 ranked teams all time
1-7 S/U on road vs #8 ranked teams all time	*0-4 ATS vs #19 ranked teams since 1988*
0-8 S/U on road vs #9 ranked teams all time	1-5 S/U vs #20 ranked teams since 1971
0-6 S/U vs #9 ranked teams since 1975	1-4 S/U & ATS vs #25 ranked teams since 2005
4-0 ATS on road vs #10 ranked teams since 1991	1-5 S/U vs ranked teams in Bowl games since 1980 {1-5 ATS}
1-6 S/U vs #11 ranked teams since 1981	0-23 S/U @ ranked Alabama since 1961
1-3 S/U @ home vs #13 ranked teams since 1987	*2-16-1 O/U vs ranked Alabama since 1995*
0-4 S/U @ home vs #14 ranked teams all time	0-5-1 S/U vs ranked Arkansas since 1995
0-7 S/U on road vs #15 ranked teams all time	*0-5 O/U @ home vs ranked Auburn since 2006*
1-4 S/U on road vs #16 ranked teams all time	0-9 S/U vs ranked Georgia since 1967
4-0 ATS vs #16 ranked teams since 1992	2-14 S/U vs ranked LSU since 2000
0-4 S/U vs #17 ranked teams since 1972	2-19 S/U @ ranked LSU since 1949
1-9 S/U vs #18 ranked teams since 1984	*0-5 O/U vs ranked LSU since 2015*
1-4 S/U vs #19 ranked teams all time	1-9 S/U @ ranked Mississippi since 1948
1-6 O/U vs #21 ranked teams since 1999	*1-8 ATS vs ranked Mississippi since 1990*
0-3 O/U vs #22 ranked teams since 1997	3-0 S/U & ATS @ home vs ranked Texas A&M since 2014
3-26 S/U vs ranked Alabama since 1977	**Missouri**
0-20 S/U vs ranked Auburn all time	7-56 S/U on road vs ranked teams since 1982
0-5 S/U vs ranked Arkansas since 2006	0-11 S/U @ home vs ranked teams since 2014
0-4 S/U @ ranked Arkansas since 1998	0-16 S/U vs #1 ranked teams all time
5-0 O/U @ home vs ranked Auburn since 2004	0-8 S/U @ home vs #2 ranked teams since 1979

Page | 303

Copyright © 2022 by Steve's Football Bible, LLC

Team records vs ranked teams

5-1 ATS & O/U vs #2 ranked teams since 1998	0-10 S/U vs #23 #24 #25 ranked teams all time
2-12 S/U vs #3 ranked teams all time	0-3 S/U & ATS vs ranked Air Force since 1985
1-4 ATS vs #3 ranked teams since 1989	2-9-1 S/U vs ranked Army since 1944
0-4 S/U on road vs #4 ranked teams all time	1-41 S/U vs ranked Notre Dame since 1964
0-4 S/U @ home vs #4 ranked teams since 1977	*9-3 O/U vs ranked Notre Dame since 2002*
1-4 ATS vs #4 ranked team since 1986	## Nebraska
0-5 S/U @ home vs #5 ranked teams since 1955	0-14 S/U on road vs ranked teams since 2011
0-12 S/U vs #6 ranked teams all time	0-19 S/U vs ranked times since 2016
1-12 S/U vs #7 ranked teams since 1977	1-12 S/U vs #1 ranked teams all time
0-9 S/U @ home vs #7 ranked teams since 1977	0-4 S/U on road vs #1 ranked teams all time
0-4 S/U @ home vs #8 ranked teams all time	*1-4 ATS vs #1 ranked teams since 1982*
0-4 S/U on road vs #9 ranked teams since 1991	2-6 S/U on road vs #2 ranked teams all time
0-7 S/U vs #9 ranked teams since 1983	*6-0 ATS vs #2 ranked teams since 1994*
1-9 S/U vs #11 ranked teams all time	0-5-1 S/U on road vs #3 ranked teams all time
0-5 S/U vs #12 ranked teams since 1975	1-4 S/U @ home vs #3 ranked teams all time
5-1 S/U on road vs #13 ranked teams all time	1-5 S/U @ home vs #4 ranked teams all time
0-5 S/U on road vs #14 ranked teams all time	1-5 S/U on road vs #4 ranked teams all time
3-0 S/U @ home vs #14 ranked teams since 1975	*0-4 ATS vs #4 ranked teams since 1991*
1-4 S/U on road vs #15 ranked teams all time	*4-1 O/U vs #6 ranked teams since 2000*
1-6 S/U vs #17 ranked teams all time	1-7 S/U on road vs #8 ranked teams all time
0-3 S/U & ATS vs #18 ranked teams since 1997	0-5 S/U vs #10 ranked teams since 2007
0-3 O/U vs #19 ranked teams since 2003	*0-5 O/U vs #10 ranked teams since 2006*
1-5 S/U vs #20 ranked teams since 1991	3-0 S/U @ home vs #10 ranked teams since 1973
0-4 O/U vs #21 ranked teams since 2004	0-3 S/U vs #13 ranked teams since 2002
3-0 S/U vs #22 ranked teams since 2007	*4-1 ATS vs #13 ranked teams since 1992*
3-1 S/U vs #25 ranked teams since 2007	7-1 S/U vs #12 ranked teams since 1973
1-9 S/U vs ranked Georgia all time	0-3 S/U on road vs #14 ranked teams all time
0-11 S/U vs ranked Kansas State all time	0-6 S/U vs #16 ranked teams since 2000
0-3 O/U vs ranked South Carolina since 2012	0-3 S/U on road vs #18 ranked teams all time
## NAVY	5-0 S/U @ home or neutral field vs #18 ranked teams all time
5-33 S/U on road vs ranked teams since 1975	5-1 S/U @ home vs #19 ranked teams all time
2-16 S/U @ home vs ranked teams since 1985	1-5 S/U on road vs #19 ranked teams all time
0-31 S/U on Neutral fields vs ranked teams since 1958	7-2 S/U vs #20 ranked teams since 1970
0-14 S/U vs #1 ranked teams all time	4-0 S/U vs #23 ranked teams all time
2-11 S/U vs #2 ranked teams since 1946	*5-0 ATS vs #24 ranked teams since all time*
0-3 S/U on road vs #2 ranked teams all time	0-9 S/U vs ranked Ohio State all time
0-4 S/U vs #3 ranked teams since 1969	4-0 S/U @ home vs Oklahoma since 1991
0-7 S/U vs #5 ranked teams since 1958	*1-11 O/U vs ranked Oklahoma since 1987*
1-5 S/U vs #6 ranked teams all time	0-7 S/U vs ranked Wisconsin all time
0-8 S/U vs #7 ranked teams since 1948	*5-1 O/U vs Wisconsin all time*
1-8 S/U vs #8 ranked teams since 1944	## Nevada
0-6 S/U vs #9 ranked teams since 1962	1-17 S/U on road vs ranked teams all time
4-0 ATS vs #9 ranked teams since 1986	2-12 S/U @ home vs ranked teams all time
0-7 S/U vs #10 ranked teams since 1967	*0-3 O/U vs #12 ranked teams all time*
0-6 S/U vs #11 ranked teams all time	0-3 S/U vs #12 ranked teams all time
0-8 S/U vs #12 ranked teams all time	0-3 S/U & ATS vs #18 ranked teams all time
0-5 S/U vs #13 ranked teams since 1951	*0-3 O/U vs #18 ranked teams all time*
0-3 S/U vs #19 ranked teams since 1983	0-3 S/U vs #22 ranked teams all time
0-4 S/U vs #20 ranked teams since 1989	0-3 S/U vs #25 ranked teams all time

Team records vs ranked teams

1-8 S/U vs ranked Boise State all time	2-5 ATS on road vs #24 ranked teams all time
UNLV	1-6 O/U vs #25 ranked teams since 1997
0-25 S/U vs ranked teams since 2008	3-0 S/U @ ranked Duke since 1957
0-23 S/U @ home vs ranked teams all time	4-0 ATS @ home vs Georgia Tech all time
1-16 S/U on road vs ranked teams since 2004	0-15 S/U vs ranked Notre Dame all time
0-8 S/U vs #10 #11 #12 #13 ranked teams all time	2-8 S/U vs ranked Virginia Tech all time {1-4 @ home}
0-3 O/U vs #24 ranked teams all time	2-5 O/U vs ranked Virginia Tech since 2007
0-32 S/U vs #18 - #25 ranked teams all time	1-3 ATS @ home vs ranked Virginia Tech since 2006
New Mexico	0-5 S/U & ATS @ ranked Virginia all time
0-24 S/U vs ranked teams since 2004	**NC State**
2-35 S/U on road vs ranked teams all time	1-15 S/U on road vs ranked teams since 2005
4-28 S/U @ home vs ranked teams all time	3-9 S/U @ home vs ranked teams aince 2013
0-12 S/U vs #4 #5 #6 #7 #8 ranked teams all time	0-4 S/U vs #1 ranked teams all time
4-0 ATS vs #9 ranked teams since 1985	1-5 S/U on road vs #2 ranked teams all time
0-6 S/U vs #10 #11 #12 ranked teams all time	0-7 S/U on road vs #3 ranked teams all time
0-13 S/U vs #14 #15 #16 #17 ranked teams all time	1-15 S/U vs #3 ranked teams all time
0-8 ATS vs #14 #15 #16 #17 ranked teams since 1988	0-5-1 S/U vs #4 ranked teams all time
0-17 S/U vs #19 #20 #21 #22 ranked teams all time	0-9 S/U vs #5 #6 ranked teams all time
0-5 S/U vs ranked Boise State all time	0-3 S/U & ATS vs #7 ranked teams since 2004
0-4 S/U vs ranked Colorado State all time	0-3 S/U on road vs #9 ranked teams all time
New Mexico State	0-3 S/U on road vs #11 ranked teams all time
0-7 S/U @ home vs ranked all time	1-4 S/U vs #12 ranked teams all time
1-30 S/U on road vs ranked teams all time	1-6 S/U vs #14 ranked teams all time
2-8 ATS on road vs ranked teams since 2010	0-4 S/U vs #16 ranked teams since 1953
0-9-1 ATS vs #14 - #18 ranked teams all time	5-1 ATS @ home vs #16 ranked teams since 1986
3-0 ATS vs #22 ranked teams all time	1-4 S/U @ home vs #18 ranked teams since 1951
North Carolina	0-6 S/U vs #19 ranked teams since 1979
19-82-2 S/U on road vs ranked teams all time	0-3 ATS on road vs #19 ranked teams since 1987
3-11 S/U @ home vs ranked teams since 2010	0-7 S/U vs #20 ranked teams all time
0-11 S/U vs #1 ranked teams all time	3-0 ATS vs #22 ranked teams all time
1-4 ATS vs #1 ranked teams since 1987	3-1 ATS vs #23 ranked teams all time
0-9 S/U vs #2 ranked teams all time	0-4 O/U vs #23 ranked teams all time
1-6 S/U vs #3 ranked teams all time	2-7 ATS vs #24 ranked teams all time
3-0 ATS vs #3 ranked teams since 1994	0-3 S/U & ATS vs #25 ranked teams since 1997
0-6 S/U vs #4 ranked teams since 1961	0-5 S/U @ ranked Clemson since 2005
0-3 ATS vs #4 ranked teams since 1988	5-1 ATS @ ranked Clemson since 1994
0-8 S/U vs #5 ranked teams all time	0-4 S/U vs ranked Florida State since 2013
0-7 S/U on road vs #6 ranked teams all time	10-2 ATS vs ranked Florida State since 2001
5-1 ATS vs #6 ranked teams since 1995	2-9 S/U @ ranked North Carolina all time
0-4 S/U vs #8 ranked teams since 1992	0-6 ATS vs ranked North Carolina since 1993
2-11-1 S/U vs #11 ranked teams all time	**North Texas**
1-6 S/U vs #12 ranked teams since 1952	2-45 S/U vs ranked teams all time
2-9 S/U vs #16 ranked teams all time	0-24 S/U vs Top 10 ranked teams all time
1-8 S/U vs #17 ranked teams all time {0-4 @ home}	0-43 S/U on road vs ranked teams all time
5-0 ATS @ home vs #19 ranked teams since 1984	6-0 ATS vs ranked teams since 2011
0-4 S/U on road vs #20 ranked teams all time	0-3 S/U vs ranked SMU all time
0-4 S/U vs #21 ranked teams all time	**Northern Illinois**
3-0 S/U & ATS vs #23 ranked teams since 2005	2-22 S/U on road vs ranked teams all time
1-7 S/U vs #24 ranked teams since 1996	9-3 ATS on road vs ranked teams since 2000

Team records vs ranked teams

5-12 O/U vs ranked teams since 2002	**Notre Dame**
0-13 S/U vs Top 10 ranked teams all time	3-11 S/U on road vs ranked teams since 2013
3-0 ATS vs #20 ranked teams since 2000	1-7-1 S/U on road vs #1 ranked teams all time
Northwestern	*12-5 ATS vs #1 ranked teams since 1970*
7-22 S/U @ home vs ranked teams since 2005	1-4 S/U @ home vs #2 ranked teams since 1956
0-18 S/U vs #1 ranked teams since 1938	*4-0 ATS on road vs #2 ranked teams since 1988*
0-7 S/U vs #2 ranked teams since 1966	4-1 S/U vs #3 ranked teams since 1989
0-7 S/U on road vs #2 ranked teams all time	0-4-1 S/U @ home vs #3 ranked teams since 1958
0-8 S/U vs #3 ranked teams all time	*6-0-1 ATS vs #3 ranked teams since 1986*
0-15 S/U vs #4 ranked teams since 1948	1-7 S/U on road vs #4 ranked teams since 1957
1-6-1 S/U on road vs #5 ranked teams all time	*2-10 ATS vs #4 ranked teams since 1985*
1-6 S/U vs #6 ranked teams since 1997	*0-7 O/U vs #4 ranked teams since 2001*
1-5 S/U on road vs #6 ranked teams since 1977	0-5 S/U & ATS vs #5 ranked teams since 2001
1-4 S/U @ home vs #8 ranked teams since 1958	0-5 S/U vs #6 ranked teams since 1994
2-8 S/U on road vs #8 ranked teams all time	7-2 S/U @ home vs #7 ranked teams all time
1-14 S/U vs #9 ranked teams since 1939	*4-1 O/U @ home vs #7 ranked teams since 1989*
0-8 S/U @ home vs #9 ranked teams since 1954	*4-0 ATS vs #8 ranked teams since 2004*
1-5 ATS vs #9 ranked teams since 1997	9-3 S/U vs #9 ranked teams since 1979
1-7 S/U vs #10 ranked teams since 1974	6-0 S/U @ home vs #10 ranked teams all time
0-6 S/U on road vs #10 ranked teams all time	10-2 S/U vs #10 ranked teams since 1944
0-7 S/U on road vs #11 ranked teams since 1944	*4-0 O/U vs #11 ranked teams since 2002*
1-5 S/U vs #13 ranked teams all time	0-4 S/U on road vs #13 ranked teams all time
0-3 S/U on road vs #14 ranked teams all time	4-0 S/U & ATS @ home vs #14 ranked teams since 2014
0-5 S/U vs #15 ranked teams all time	*0-4 O/U @ home vs #14 ranked teams since 2014*
1-7 S/U on road vs #16 ranked teams all time	4-1 S/U on road vs #15 ranked teams all time
0-3-1 S/U on road vs #17 ranked teams all time	*1-7 O/U vs #15 ranked teams since 1995*
1-4 ATS vs #17 ranked teams since 1996	*0-4 ATS vs #17 ranked teams since 1997*
2-8 S/U vs #18 ranked teams since 1954	*0-4 O/U @ home vs #17 ranked teams since 1985*
4-0 O/U vs #18 ranked teams since 2000	0-4 S/U vs #20 ranked teams since 1981
0-5 S/U on road vs #19 ranked teams all time	3-0 S/U vs #21 ranked teams all time
0-7 S/U vs #19 ranked teams since 1983	*0-3 O/U vs #21 ranked teams all time*
1-5-1 ATS vs #19 ranked teams since 1983	4-1 S/U vs #23 ranked teams all time
2-6-1 O/U vs #20 ranked teams since 2002	*5-0 O/U vs #23 ranked teams all time*
6-1 ATS vs #22 ranked teams all time	*0-5 O/U vs #25 ranked teams since 2000*
0-4 S/U vs #25 ranked teams all time	0-4 S/U & ATS vs ranked Ohio State all time
2-8 S/U @ home vs ranked Illinois all time	1-9 S/U vs ranked USC since 2002
4-1 ATS vs ranked Illinois since 1990	0-5 S/U @ ranked USC since 2002
2-12-1 S/U vs ranked Minnesota since 1940	**Ohio U**
1-9-1 S/U @ ranked Minnesota all time	0-26 S/U vs ranked teams all time
1-27 S/U vs ranked Ohio State since 1972	*1-7 O/U vs ranked teams since 2005*
1-16 S/U @ home vs ranked Ohio State since 1961	0-3 S/U vs ranked Miami-Ohio all time
5-0 O/U @ home vs ranked Ohio State since 2004	0-3 S/U vs ranked Penn State all time
0-4 S/U @ ranked Penn State all time	**Ohio State**
0-5 ATS vs ranked Penn State since 1998	9-1 S/U on road vs ranked teams since 2012
0-6 S/U @ ranked Purdue all time	*17-5-1 ATS on road vs ranked teams since 2005*
1-11 S/U vs ranked Purdue since 1958	15-2 S/U @ home vs ranked teams since 2009
6-1 S/U @ home vs ranked Wisconsin since 2003	0-5 S/U on road vs #1 ranked teams all time
12-3 ATS vs ranked Wisconsin since 1999	5-1-1 S/U @ home vs #4 ranked teams all time

Team records vs ranked teams

1-5 S/U @ home vs #5 ranked teams all time	9-1 S/U vs #17 ranked teams all time
5-0 S/U @ home vs #7 ranked teams since 1975	0-6-1 S/U vs #18 ranked teams since 1982
6-0 S/U & ATS vs #7 ranked teams since 1988	*1-5 ATS vs #18 ranked teams since 1995*
0-3-1 S/U @ home vs #8 ranked teams all time	7-1 S/U vs #19 ranked teams since 1990
8-1 S/U vs #9 ranked teams since 1961	5-0 S/U vs #21 ranked teams all time
3-0 S/U @ home vs #10 ranked teams since 2002	*2-5 ATS vs #22 ranked teams all time*
5-0 S/U on road vs #11 ranked teams since 1975 {4-0 ATS}	3-0 S/U on road vs #23 ranked teams all time
7-1 S/U & ATS vs #11 ranked teams since 1997	4-0 S/U vs #24 ranked teams all time
4-0 ATS vs #12 ranked teams since 2002	0-3 S/U & ATS on road vs #25 ranked teams all time
8-1-1 S/U vs #13 ranked teams since 1942	4-0-1 S/U vs ranked Iowa State all time
3-0 S/U on road vs #13 ranked teams all time	1-4 S/U @ home vs ranked Kansas State all time
4-0 S/U @ home vs #14 ranked teams all time	0-6 S/U @ ranked Nebraska since 1989
3-0 O/U vs #16 ranked teams since 1992	*0-4 O/U vs ranked Nebraska since 2000*
3-0 S/U & ATS vs #17 ranked teams since 2002	8-1 S/U @ home vs ranked Oklahoma State since 1972
4-0 S/U on road vs #20 ranked teams since 1996	*7-0 ATS vs ranked Oklahoma State since 2013*
5-0 S/U vs #21 ranked teams since 1997	3-0 S/U vs ranked Texas Tech all time
3-0 S/U on road vs #21 ranked teams all time	3-0 S/U vs ranked West Virginia since 2015
6-1 S/U & ATS vs #24 ranked teams all time	*4-0 O/U vs ranked West Virginia since 2008*
5-0 S/U & ATS vs #25 ranked teams since 1995	**Oklahoma State**
8-0 S/U vs ranked Iowa since 1995	20-100-1 S/U on road vs ranked teams all time
4-0 S/U & ATS @ ranked Michigan State since 2008	0-11 S/U vs #1 ranked teams all time
6-0 S/U @ home vs ranked Michigan since 2002	0-16 S/U vs #2 ranked teams all time
10-2 O/U vs ranked Michigan since 2003	2-7 S/U on road vs #3 ranked teams all time
5-0 S/U vs ranked Northwestern since 1970	2-15 S/U vs #4 ranked teams all time
4-0 S/U & ATS vs ranked Notre Dame all time	3-7 S/U vs #5 ranked teams all time
2-11 O/U vs ranked Penn State since 1998	*5-0 O/U vs #5 ranked teams since 2007*
4-0 S/U @ ranked Penn State since 2007	1-12 S/U vs #6 ranked teams all time {0-10 on road}
7-1-1 S/U @ home vs ranked Wisconsin all time	0-4 S/U on road vs #7 ranked teams since 1973
7-0 S/U vs ranked Wisconsin since 2011	1-5 S/U @ home vs #7 ranked teams all time
Oklahoma	0-4 S/U @ home vs #8 ranked teams since 1988
10-3 S/U on road vs ranked teams since 2015	0-7 S/U vs #9 ranked teams all time
9-3-1 ATS on road vs ranked teams since 2015	1-6 S/U on road vs #10 ranked teams all time
1-5 S/U @ home vs #1 ranked teams all time	0-4 S/U @ home vs #11 ranked teams since 1981
1-8 S/U vs #1 ranked teams since 1994	0-3 S/U on road vs #11 ranked teams since 1970
1-8 O/U vs #1 ranked teams since 1984	2-9 S/U vs #12 ranked teams all time
4-0 S/U @ home vs #2 ranked teams since 1975	*0-4 O/U vs #13 ranked teams since 2005*
0-4 S/U on road vs #3 ranked teams since 1970	0-6 S/U vs #14 ranked teams since 1991
4-0 O/U vs #4 ranked teams since 1986	*4-0 O/U vs #14 ranked teams since 2007*
1-5 O/U vs #5 ranked teams since 2001	0-7 S/U vs #16 ranked teams since 1978
1-6-1 S/U vs #7 ranked teams all time	*0-6 ATS vs #16 ranked teams since 1989*
7-0 S/U vs #8 ranked teams all time	0-5 S/U on road vs #16 ranked teams all time
3-0 S/U @ home vs #9 ranked teams all time	0-4 S/U on road vs #17 ranked teams all time
1-4 S/U on road vs #9 ranked teams since 1965	4-0 S/U @ home vs #17 ranked teams since 1972
5-1 S/U on road vs #10 ranked teams since 1973	2-6 S/U vs #18 ranked teams all time
12-1 S/U vs #11 ranked teams since 2000	0-4 S/U on road vs #19 ranked teams all time
7-0 S/U @ home vs #11 ranked teams all time	0-4 S/U on road vs #20 ranked teams all time
4-0 S/U on road vs #12 ranked teams since 1954	*3-0 ATS vs #20 ranked teams since 1993*
7-1 S/U vs #13 ranked teams all time	*5-0-1 ATS vs #24 ranked teams all time*
0-3 S/U on road vs #16 ranked teams all time	0-5 S/U vs ranked Baylor since 2014

Team records vs ranked teams

5-0 S/U vs ranked Iowa State all time	4-11 O/U @ home vs ranked teams since 2010
0-5 S/U @ ranked Kansas State all time	1-7 S/U vs #1 ranked teams since 1968
1-6 S/U vs ranked Kansas all time	0-11 S/U vs #3 ranked teams all time
5-1 O/U vs ranked Kansas State since 2003	*4-0 ATS on road vs #3 ranked teams since 1986*
1-7 ATS vs ranked Kansas State since 1998	0-11 S/U vs #4 ranked teams all time
0-3 S/U @ ranked Kansas all time	0-4 S/U on road vs #5 ranked teams all time
6-55 S/U vs ranked Oklahoma all time	1-12 S/U vs #6 ranked teams all time
5-0 ATS vs ranked Texas since 2013	*5-0 ATS on road vs #6 ranked teams since 1984*
8-0 O/U @ home vs ranked Texas since 2001	0-7 S/U on road vs #7 ranked teams all time
3-0 S/U & ATS vs ranked West Virginia since 2016	0-3 S/U on road vs #8 ranked teams all time
Old Dominion	1-4 S/U on road vs #9 ranked teams all time
1-2 S/U vs ranked teams all time	0-4 S/U on road vs #11 ranked teams all time
Oregon	0-6 S/U vs #12 ranked teams since 1973
0-11 S/U vs #1 ranked teams all time	0-4 S/U on road vs #13 ranked teams since 1953
0-5 S/U on road vs #2 ranked teams all time	1-10 S/U vs #14 ranked teams all time {0-3 @ home}
1-5 S/U on road vs #3 ranked teams all time	1-6 S/U vs #15 ranked teams since 1969
4-0 ATS vs #3 ranked teams since 1991	0-11 S/U vs #16 ranked teams all time
0-3 S/U on road vs #4 ranked teams all time	0-6 S/U vs #17 ranked teams since 1948
0-6 S/U on road vs #5 ranked teams all time	*0-4 O/U vs #18 ranked teams since 2002*
2-8 S/U vs #5 ranked teams all time	1-7 S/U vs #19 ranked teams since 1970
1-5 S/U on road vs #6 ranked teams all time	0-5 S/U vs #21 ranked teams since 1997
0-6 O/U vs #6 ranked teams since 2000	0-4 S/U @ ranked Arizona State since 1982
1-6 S/U on road vs #9 ranked teams all time	*6-1 ATS vs ranked Arizona State since 1996*
1-4 S/U on road vs #13 ranked teams all time	0-4 S/U @ home vs ranked California all time
0-3 S/U on road vs #14 ranked teams all time	2-11 S/U vs ranked Oregon since 2001 {1-4 @ home}
0-6 ATS vs #14 ranked teams since 1983	0-11 S/U vs ranked Stanford since 1969
0-4-1 S/U @ home vs #15 ranked teams all time	*1-5 ATS vs ranked Stanford since 2010*
0-3 ATS @ home vs #15 ranked teams since 1986	3-0 S/U @ home vs ranked USC since 2006
4-1 S/U vs #16 ranked teams since 1987	*5-0 ATS @ home vs ranked USC since 2000*
4-1 ATS vs #16 ranked teams since 1987	0-5 S/U vs ranked Utah all time
4-0 S/U vs #17 ranked teams since 2001	0-9 S/U @ ranked Washington since 1955
4-0 ATS vs #17 ranked teams since 2001	1-18 S/U vs ranked Washington since 1959
5-0-1 O/U vs #18 ranked teams since 2009	**Penn State**
5-1 S/U vs #19 ranked teams since 1955	4-27 S/U on road vs ranked teams since 2002
0-4 S/U vs #20 ranked teams since 1992	*7-16-1 ATS on road vs ranked teams since 2006*
0-4 ATS vs #20 ranked teams since 1992	*12-6 O/U on road vs ranked teams since 2010*
4-0 S/U @ home vs #23 ranked teams since 1998	2-9 S/U on road vs #1 ranked teams all time
4-0 ATS @ home vs #23 ranked teams since 1998	0-5 S/U & ATS vs #1 ranked teams since 1998
4-1 ATS vs #24 ranked teams all time	*0-5 O/U on road vs #1 ranked teams since 1998*
0-3 S/U @ ranked Arizona since 1990	0-5 S/U on road vs #3 ranked teams all time
1-8 S/U @ ranked California all time	0-6 S/U & ATS vs #3 ranked teams since 1986
3-0 S/U vs ranked Oregon State since 2008	0-9 S/U on road vs #4 ranked teams all time
4-0 S/U vs ranked UCLA since 2000	0-6 S/U vs #4 ranked teams since 2002 {1-5 ATS}
8-0 ATS vs ranked UCLA since 1988	0-5 S/U on road vs #6 ranked teams since 1979
0-4 S/U & ATS vs ranked Washington State since 2002	3-0 S/U @ home vs #7 ranked teams since 1987
Oregon State	*6-0 ATS vs #8 ranked teams since 1982*
6-76 S/U on road vs ranked teams since 1970	*3-0 O/U vs #8 ranked teams since 1999*
2-22 S/U vs ranked teams since 2012	*3-1 O/U vs #9 ranked teams since 1984*
1-10 S/U @ home vs ranked teams since 2012	3-0 S/U on road vs #10 ranked teams all time

Team records vs ranked teams

0-3 S/U @ home vs #10 ranked teams since 2004	3-7 S/U vs #24 ranked teams all time
6-1 ATS vs #12 ranked teams since 1975	1-5 S/U vs ranked Duke since 1938
0-4 S/U on road vs #13 ranked teams since 1987	1-4 S/U vs ranked Louisville all time {0-4-1 ATS}
1-4 O/U vs #13 ranked teams since 1989	0-8 S/U @ ranked Miami since 1984
5-1 O/U vs #14 ranked teams since 1988	2-15 S/U vs ranked Miami since 1984
0-3 S/U on road vs #15 ranked teams since 1999	*2-8 O/U vs ranked Miami since 1997*
7-0 O/U vs #16 ranked teams since 1996	0-7 S/U vs ranked Syracuse since 1991
3-0 S/U @ home vs #17 ranked teams all time	*7-2 ATS vs ranked Virginia Tech since 1999*
4-0 S/U & ATS @ home vs #18 ranked teams since 1999	**Purdue**
0-4 S/U on road vs #18 ranked teams since 2003	5-73-1 S/U on road vs ranked teams since 1974
7-1-1 ATS vs #19 ranked teams since 1989	*12-2 ATS on road vs ranked teams since 2012*
0-3 S/U on road vs #20 ranked teams all time	*2-9 O/U on road vs ranked teams since 2012*
0-4 O/U vs #20 ranked teams since 1997	6-20 S/U @ home vs ranked teams since 2004
5-1 S/U vs #22 rankled teams since 2000	0-3 S/U vs #1 ranked Ohio State all time
3-0 S/U vs ranked Maryland all time	0-7 S/U @ home vs #3 ranked teams since 1970
0-5 S/U & ATS vs ranked Michigan State since 2010	1-8 S/U on road vs #3 ranked teams all time
3-11 S/U vs ranked Michigan since 1997	*4-0-1 ATS vs #3 ranked teams since 1986*
0-5 S/U @ ranked Michigan since 1998	0-5 S/U @ home vs #4 ranked teams all time
3-0 S/U & ATS vs ranked Northwestern since 1996	0-8 S/U on road vs #4 ranked teams since 1953
1-11 S/U vs ranked Ohio State since 2009	*0-4 O/U vs #4 ranked teams since 2001*
Pittsburgh	1-5 S/U vs #5 ranked teams all time
6-43-1 S/U on road vs ranked teams since 1984	0-8 S/U on road vs #6 ranked teams all time
0-12-1 S/U vs #1 ranked teams all time	1-10 S/U vs #6 ranked teams since 1970
1-11 S/U on road vs #2 ranked teams all time	*0-4 ATS @ home vs #6 ranked teams since 1997*
0-6 S/U @ home vs #3 ranked teams since 1945	1-6 S/U @ home vs #7 ranked teams all time
5-1 ATS vs #3 ranked teams since 1990	0-3 S/U on road vs #7 ranked teams since 1978
1-11 S/U vs #4 ranked teams all time	0-7 S/U vs #8 ranked teams since 1987
0-4 S/U vs #5 ranked teams since 2005	0-6 S/U on road vs #8 ranked teams all time
0-7 S/U vs #6 ranked teams since 1965	0-5 S/U on road vs #9 ranked teams all time
0-5 S/U vs #7 ranked teams since 1972	0-6-1 S/U on road vs #10 ranked teams all time
0-5 S/U on road vs #7 ranked teams since 1957	0-14 S/U vs #11 ranked teams since 1977
0-9-1 S/U @ home vs #8 ranked teams all time	0-8 S/U @ home vs #11 ranked teams all time
0-11 S/U vs #8 ranked teams since 1954	0-3 S/U on road vs #12 ranked teams since 1987
1-5 ATS vs #8 ranked teams since 1987	0-8 S/U vs #13 ranked teams since 1983
0-4-1 S/U vs #9 ranked teams since 1977	1-6 S/U vs #14 ranked teams all time
0-3-1 S/U on road vs #9 ranked teams since 1958	*4-0 ATS vs #14 ranked teams since 2003*
2-8 S/U vs #10 ranked teams all time	*0-3 O/U vs #16 ranked teams since 1997*
1-9 S/U @ home vs #11 ranked teams since 1940	1-5 S/U vs #16 ranked teams since 1980
0-6 S/U vs #11 ranked teams since 1988	0-3 S/U vs #18 ranked teams since 2008
1-4 S/U on road vs #12 ranked teams since 1946	0-4 S/U on road vs #19 ranked teams all time
1-6 S/U vs #13 ranked teams all time	0-3 S/U @ home vs #20 ranked teams all time
3-0 S/U @ home vs #14 ranked teams since 1958	1-8 S/U vs #20 ranked teams since 1950
0-3 S/U on road vs #17 ranked teams all time	1-7 S/U vs #21 ranked teams all time
1-4 S/U vs #18 ranked teams since 1988	0-3 S/U on road vs #24 ranked teams all time
1-5 S/U @ home vs #19 ranked teams all time	1-6 S/U vs #25 ranked teams all time
1-6 S/U vs #19 ranked teams since 1994	*3-0 ATS on road vs #25 ranked teams all time*
0-6-1 S/U on road vs #20 ranked teams all time	0-4-1 S/U @ ranked Illinois all time
1-8-1 S/U vs #20 ranked teams since 1946	0-4 S/U vs ranked Indiana since 1942
0-5 S/U vs #22 ranked teams all time {1-4 ATS}	2-7 S/U vs ranked Minnesota since 1936

Team records vs ranked teams

0-3 S/U & O/U vs ranked Nebraska since 2013	0-12-1 S/U vs #20 #21 #22 #23 ranked teams all time
3-1 ATS vs ranked Northwestern since 1996	*3-0 ATS vs ranked Boston College all time*
0-10 S/U vs ranked Penn State all time	0-5 S/U vs ranked Michigan all time
1-4 ATS vs ranked Penn State since 2008	*4-1 O/U vs ranked Michigan all time*
0-4 ATS @ home vs ranked Penn State since 1997	0-8 S/U vs ranked Ohio State all time
0-9 S/U vs ranked Wisconsin since 2004 {2-7 ATS}	*2-6 ATS vs ranked Ohio State all time*
1-9-1 S/U @ ranked Wisconsin all time	1-16 S/U vs ranked Penn State all time
Rice	**San Diego State**
1-71 S/U on road vs ranked teams since 1971	3-37 S/U on road vs ranked teams all time
3-31 S/U @ home vs ranked teams since 1975	1-23 S/U vs Top #10 ranked teams all time
0-4-1 S/U vs #1 ranked teams all time	*1-15 O/U on road vs ranked teams since 1997*
0-11 S/U vs #2 ranked teams all time	*12-3-1 O/U @ home vs ranked teams since 2000*
0-6 S/U on road vs #3 ranked teams all time	1-23 S/U vs Top #10 ranked teams all time
0-10 S/U vs #3 ranked teams since 1947	*0-3 ATS vs #7 ranked teams since 1985*
0-5 S/U on road vs #4 ranked teams all time	0-4 S/U vs #10 #11 ranked teams all time
0-6 S/U vs #4 ranked teams since 1962	0-3 S/U on road vs #12 ranked teams all time
0-6 S/U vs #5 ranked teams since 1980	0-4 S/U vs #17 ranked teams since 1999
0-5 S/U vs #6 ranked teams all time	*4-0 ATS vs #17 ranked teams since 1999*
0-7 S/U on road vs #7 ranked teams all time	*0-3 O/U vs #17 ranked teams since 2002*
0-11 S/U vs #7 ranked teams since 1950	0-7 S/U vs #21 ranked teams all time {1-6 ATS}
1-8 S/U vs #8 ranked teams all time	0-4 S/U vs #25 ranked teams since 1995
0-5 S/U vs #9 ranked teams since 1955	0-4 S/U vs ranked Utah since 2004
0-12 S/U vs #10 ranked teams since 1951	*0-4 ATS vs ranked Utah since 2004*
0-5 S/U vs #11 ranked teams since 1978	**San Jose State**
1-6 S/U vs #12 ranked teams since 1959	0-36 S/U on road vs ranked teams since 1981
0-5 S/U vs #13 ranked team since 1974	1-11 S/U @ home vs ranked teams since 2001
0-9 S/U vs #14 ranked teams all time	1-15 S/U vs Top #10 ranked teams all time
0-6-1 S/U vs #15 ranked teams since 1956	5-35 S/U vs #10 - #19 ranked teams all time
0-7-1 S/U vs #16 ranked teams since 1971	*1-3 O/U vs #21 ranked teams all time*
0-6-1 S/U vs #17 ranked teams since 1971	0-17 S/U vs #20 - #25 ranked teams all time
0-9 S/U vs #18 ranked teams since 1972	*4-1 ATS vs ranked Fresno State since 1986*
0-6 S/U vs #19 ranked teams all time	0-3 S/U vs ranked Wyoming all time
0-5 S/U on road vs #20 ranked teams all time	**South Alabama**
0-3 O/U vs #21 ranked teams since 1997	1-6 S/U vs Ranked teams all time
0-10 S/U vs ranked Houston all time	**South Carolina**
Rutgers	0-13 S/U on road vs ranked teams since 2014
1-38-1 S/U vs Top #10 ranked teams all time	1-6 S/U vs #1 ranked teams all time {0-3 on road}
1-39-1 S/U on road vs ranked teams since 1989	*4-0 ATS vs #1 ranked teams since 1996*
0-16 S/U @ home vs ranked teams since 2009	0-14 S/U vs #2 ranked teams all time
0-4 S/U vs #1 ranked teams all time	*11-1 ATS vs #2 ranked teams since 1987*
0-27-1 S/U vs #3 - #9 ranked teams all time	2-12 S/U vs #3 ranked teams all time {0-7 @ home}
5-0 ATS vs #3 ranked teams since 1985	*2-5 ATS vs #3 ranked teams since 1995*
0-4 ATS vs #9 ranked teams all time	1-11 S/U vs #4 ranked teams all time {0-7 on road}
0-23 S/U vs #10 #11 #12 #13 #14 ranked teams all time	0-3 S/U on road vs #6 ranked teams all time
0-4 ATS vs #10 ranked teams since 1996	*4-0 ATS vs #6 ranked teams since 1996*
0-3 ATS vs #13 ranked teams since 1994	0-9 S/U vs #7 ranked teams all time
4-1 ATS vs #15 ranked teams since 1988	0-7 S/U on road vs #8 ranked teams since 1958
0-6 S/U vs #16 ranked teams all time	*4-0 O/U vs #8 ranked teams since 2003*
3-1 S/U vs #17 ranked teams all time	0-12 S/U vs #9 ranked teams all time

Team records vs ranked teams

2-5 O/U vs #9 ranked teams since 1997	0-7 O/U vs #21 ranked teams all time
3-0 ATS on road vs #9 ranked teams since 2001	0-3 S/U & ATS on road vs #21 ranked teams all time
2-7 S/U @ home vs #12 ranked teams since 1976	5-1 S/U on road vs #25 ranked teams all time
2-7 S/U vs #12 ranked teams since 1989	5-0-1 O/U vs #25 ranked teams since 1999
0-4 S/U & ATS vs #13 ranked teams since 1983	8-1 S/U vs ranked Arizona all time {3-0 S/U & ATS @ home}
1-5 S/U on road vs #14 ranked teams all time	3-0 S/U vs ranked Arizona State since 2004
1-9-1 S/U vs #14 ranked teams since 1948	5-0 S/U vs ranked California since 2004
4-0-1 ATS vs #15 ranked teams since 1992	5-0 S/U @ home vs ranked California since 1952
0-5 S/U vs #17 ranked teams since 2007	0-5 O/U vs ranked California since 2004
0-5 ATS vs #17 ranked teams since 2007	3-0 S/U vs ranked Colorado since 2002
5-0 S/U vs #18 ranked teams since 1970 {3-0 ATS}	0-3 O/U vs ranked Colorado since 2002
0-3 O/U vs #18 ranked teams since 2001	0-6 S/U vs ranked Notre Dame since 2012
1-10 S/U vs #20 ranked teams all time {0-6 @ home}	1-5 S/U @ ranked Stanford since 1992
1-4 ATS vs #21 ranked teams all time	4-0 S/U @ home vs ranked Washington State all time
0-4 S/U vs ranked Arkansas all time	## South Florida
0-4 ATS vs ranked Arkansas all time	0-9 S/U on road vs ranked teams since 2012
0-6 S/U vs ranked Clemson since 2014	9-1 ATS on road vs ranked teams since 2011
2-21 S/U vs ranked Florida all time	2-13 S/U @ home vs ranked teams since 2009
3-15 S/U vs ranked Tennessee all time	0-8 S/U vs #12 #13 #14 #15 ranked teams all time
0-5 S/U vs ranked Texas A&M all time	0-6 S/U vs #19 ranked teams all time
## USC	0-3 S/U vs ranked Central Florida all time
1-12 S/U on road vs ranked teams since 2014	0-5 S/U vs ranked Cincinnati since 2009
2-12 ATS on road vs ranked teams since 2014	4-1 ATS vs ranked Cincinnati since 2009
7-2 S/U @ home vs ranked teams since 2015	## SMU
0-6 S/U vs #1 ranked teams since 1988	2-34 S/U on road vs ranked teams since 1989
4-0 O/U vs #2 ranked teams since 1993	5-21-1 S/U @ home vs ranked teams since 1986
8-1 ATS vs #3 ranked teams since 1973	10-3 ATS @ home vs ranked teams since 2003
11-3 S/U vs #3 ranked teams all time	6-56-1 S/U vs ranked teams since 1986
7-2 S/U vs #4 ranked teams since 1963	0-9 S/U vs #1 ranked teams all time
2-8 O/U vs #5 ranked teams since 1987	0-6-1 S/U @ home vs #2 ranked teams all time
10-0 S/U vs #6 ranked teams since 1955	0-7-1 S/U on road vs #3 ranked teams all time
7-0 ATS vs #6 ranked teams since 1985	0-6 S/U vs #4 ranked teams since 1966
3-17 S/U vs #7 ranked teams since 1950	3-0 O/U vs #4 ranked teams since 1985
4-0-1 S/U @ home vs #8 ranked teams since 1962	0-4 S/U on road vs #5 ranked teams since 1962
5-2 S/U vs #9 ranked teams since 1979	0-3 S/U @ home vs #6 ranked teams all time
1-6 S/U on road vs #10 ranked teams all time	0-3 S/U on road vs #6 ranked teams all time
0-6 ATS on road vs #10 ranked teams since 1987	0-7 S/U on road vs #7 ranked teams all time
1-6 S/U on road vs #11 ranked teams since 1977	0-4 S/U vs #8 ranked teams all time
1-4 S/U on road vs #12 ranked teams since 1957	0-4 S/U on road vs #9 ranked teams all time
5-1 S/U @ home vs #13 ranked teams since 1968	0-5 S/U on road vs #10 ranked teams all time
6-2 ATS vs #13 ranked teams since 1992	0-3 S/U @ home vs #10 ranked teams all time
10-2 S/U vs #14 ranked teams all time	0-8 S/U on road vs #11 ranked teams since 1951
0-6-1 S/U on road vs #17 ranked teams all time	1-12 S/U vs #11 ranked teams since 1955
0-6 ATS on road vs #17 ranked teams since 1987	0-8 S/U vs #12 ranked teams all time
3-0 S/U @ home vs #17 ranked teams all time	1-5 S/U on road vs #13 ranked teams all time
3-0 S/U & ATS vs #18 ranked teams since 1988	1-7 S/U vs #13 ranked teams since 1969
1-5 O/U vs #19 ranked teams since 1986	0-7-1 S/U vs #14 ranked teams all time
6-2 S/U vs #19 ranked teams since 1971	0-4 S/U vs #15 ranked teams since 1973
5-1 S/U vs #20 ranked teams since 1979	3-0 ATS vs #15 ranked teams since 2012

Team records vs ranked teams

0-3 O/U vs #15 ranked teams since 2012	*5-1 ATS vs #11 ranked teams since 1992*
0-4 S/U on road vs #17 ranked teams all time	*0-5-1 O/U vs #12 ranked teams since 1995*
0-8-1 S/U vs #18 ranked teams all time	5-0 O/U vs #13 ranked teams since 1990
0-3 ATS on road vs #18 ranked teams since 1985	1-7 S/U vs #14 ranked teams all time
1-5 S/U @ home vs #19 ranked teams since 1952	0-5 S/U vs #16 ranked teams since 1977
3-0 ATS vs #19 ranked teams since 1985	4-1 S/U @ home vs #17 ranked teams all time
0-5 S/U @ home vs #20 ranked teams since 1954	0-4 S/U on road vs #17 ranked teams since 1989
1-8 S/U vs #20 ranked teams since 1954	0-4 S/U on road vs #18 ranked teams since 1981
3-0 ATS vs #20 ranked teams since 1989	4-0 S/U vs #19 ranked teams since 1974 {3-0 ATS since 1983}
4-1 ATS vs #22 ranked teams since 1991	3-0 S/U vs #20 ranked teams since 2011
4-13 S/U vs #21 #22 #23 #24 #25 ranked teams all time	*3-0-1 ATS vs #20 ranked teams since 2006*
0-3 S/U vs ranked Central Florida all time	4-0 S/U vs #22 ranked teams since 1989
0-4 S/U @ ranked Houston since 1979	*5-0 ATS vs #22 ranked teams all time*
9-1 ATS vs ranked TCU since 2003	1-4 S/U vs #23 ranked teams all time
Southern Miss	1-4 S/U & ATS vs #25 ranked teams all time
4-32 S/U on road vs ranked teams since 1992	*0-4 O/U vs #25 ranked teams since 2000*
1-11 S/U @ home vs ranked teams since 1987	5-1 S/U vs ranked UCLA since 2012
0-9 S/U vs #1 #2 #3 ranked teams all time	*13-5 ATS vs ranked UCLA since 1984 {7-0 @ UCLA}*
0-7 S/U vs #4 ranked teams since 1971	*10-2 ATS vs ranked USC since 2007*
0-6 S/U vs #5 ranked teams all time	0-5 S/U vs ranked Washington State since 1997
0-4 ATS vs #5 ranked teams since 1989	0-9 S/U @ ranked Washington since 1981
0-6 S/U vs #8 #9 ranked teams all time	**Syracuse**
0-4 S/U vs #14 ranked teams all time	3-30 S/U on road vs ranked teams since 2001
0-4 S/U vs #15 ranked teams since 2003	6-20 S/U @ home vs ranked teams since 2002
0-3 S/U @ home vs #17 ranked teams all time	0-5 S/U @ home vs #1 ranked teams since 1992
0-3 S/U vs #19 ranked teams all time	0-7 S/U on road vs #1 ranked teams all time
0-3 S/U vs #20 ranked teams since 1985	1-13 S/U vs #2 ranked teams all time {0-6 on road}
3-0 ATS vs #20 ranked teams since 1985	0-4 S/U vs #3 ranked teams all time
0-4 S/U vs #21 #22 ranked teams all time	0-4 S/U & ATS vs #4 ranked teams since 1988
0-4 S/U vs #24 #25 ranked teams all time	*3-0 ATS vs #5 ranked teams since 2001*
Stanford	0-7-1 S/U vs #6 ranked teams since 1985
20-7 S/U @ home vs ranked teams since 2009	1-8 S/U vs #7 ranked teams all time
0-3 S/U @ home vs #1 ranked teams all time	1-7 S/U vs #8 ranked teams all time {0-3 on road}
5-0 ATS vs #1 ranked teams since 1989	1-5 S/U vs #9 ranked teams all time
4-0 ATS vs #2 ranked teams since 1998	0-3 S/U on road vs #10 ranked teams all time
3-0 S/U vs #2 ranked teams since 2007	2-7 S/U @ home vs #10 ranked teams all time
0-3 O/U vs #2 ranked teams since 2007	*4-0 ATS @ home vs #10 ranked teams since 1987*
1-6 S/U vs #3 ranked teams all time	0-4 S/U on road vs #12 ranked teams all time
3-11 S/U vs #4 ranked teams since 1974	1-5 S/U @ home vs #13 ranked teams all time
1-9 S/U on road vs #5 ranked teams all time	0-3 S/U on road vs #14 ranked teams all time
3-0 O/U on road vs #5 ranked teams since 1988	0-3 S/U on road vs #15 ranked teams all time
0-4 S/U @ home vs #6 ranked teams since 2003	0-3 S/U on road vs #16 ranked teams all time
8-2 ATS vs #6 ranked teams since 1988	3-1 S/U on road vs #18 ranked teams all time
5-0 O/U vs #6 ranked teams since 2005	4-1 S/U vs #18 ranked teams since 1978
0-3 S/U on road vs #7 ranked teams since 1981	1-4 S/U vs #19 ranked teams all time
5-0 ATS vs #7 ranked teams since 1992	0-6 S/U on road vs #25 ranked teams all time
0-8 S/U on road vs #8 ranked teams all time	*3-0 ATS @ home vs #25 ranked teams since 2005*
0-12 S/U vs #8 ranked teams since 1966	0-3 S/U vs Cincinnati all time
0-7 S/U vs #10 ranked teams all time	0-4 S/U @ ranked Clemson all time

Team records vs ranked teams

1-3 O/U @ ranked Clemson all time	1-11 S/U vs #22 #23 #24 #25 ranked teams all time
0-9 S/U vs ranked Florida State all time	0-3 S/U vs ranked Central Florida all time
4-1 ATS vs ranked Louisville all time	**Tennessee**
3-0 O/U vs ranked Louisville since 2007	3-33 S/U on road vs ranked teams since 2006
0-4 S/U vs ranked Notre Dame all time	0-13 S/U vs #1 ranked teams since 1990
1-3 O/U vs ranked Notre Dame all time	1-7 ATS vs #1 ranked teams since 2011
1-11-1 S/U vs ranked Pittsburgh since 1976	6-1 O/U vs #1 ranked teams since 2012
1-8 S/U @ ranked Pittsburgh all time	0-7 S/U on road vs #1 ranked teams all time
TCU	0-5 S/U vs #2 ranked teams since 2008
1-6 S/U vs #1 ranked teams all time	1-14-2 S/U vs #3 ranked teams since 1959
0-7 S/U vs #2 ranked teams since 1968	0-5-1 S/U @ home vs #3 ranked teams since 1962
0-8-2 S/U vs #3 ranked teams all time	1-8 S/U on road vs #4 ranked teams all time
0-8 S/U on road vs #4 ranked teams all time	2-8 S/U @ home vs #4 ranked teams all time
0-5 S/U @ home vs #5 ranked teams all time	0-5 S/U vs #5 ranked teams since 2005
1-6 S/U on road vs #7 ranked teams all time	5-2 ATS vs #5 ranked teams since 1990
0-3 S/U on road vs #8 ranked teams since 1974	0-4 S/U @ home vs #6 ranked teams since 2000
0-5 S/U @ home vs #9 ranked teams all time	0-12 S/U vs #8 ranked teams since 1957
0-14 S/U vs #10 ranked teams all time	5-2 O/U vs #9 ranked teams since 1990
0-9 S/U vs #11 ranked teams all time	0-6 S/U on road vs #10 ranked teams all time
0-7 S/U vs #12 ranked teams since 1973	1-5 S/U & ATS vs #10 ranked teams since 1989
0-5 ATS vs #12 ranked teams since 1991	1-5 ATS vs #11 ranked teams since 1997
1-8 S/U vs #13 ranked teams since 1957	4-0 S/U @ home vs #12 ranked teams since 2001
1-4 ATS vs #13 ranked teams since 1985	0-3 S/U on road vs #12 ranked teams since 2007
2-8 S/U vs #14 ranked teams all time	4-0 ATS vs #12 ranked teams since 2010
3-0 S/U vs #15 ranked teams since 2014	0-4 S/U vs #13 ranked teams since 1994
2-6 S/U vs #17 ranked teams all time	4-0 S/U @ home vs #15 ranked teams all time
2-13 S/U vs #18 ranked teams all time	0-5 O/U vs #15 ranked teams since 1985
1-7 S/U @ home vs #20 ranked teams since 1947	3-0 S/U & ATS vs #16 ranked teams since 1983
4-0 S/U vs #23 ranked teams since 1998	0-4 S/U vs #17 ranked teams since 2010
2-6 S/U @ ranked Baylor all time	0-4 S/U on road vs #19 ranked teams all time
5-1 ATS vs ranked Baylor since 2013	1-4 S/U vs #20 ranked teams since 1976
2-13 S/U vs ranked Oklahoma since 1946	6-0 S/U vs #22 #23 ranked teams all time
0-6 S/U vs ranked SMU since 1979	0-3 O/U vs #22 ranked teams all time
2-11 S/U @ ranked Texas since 1963	3-0 S/U vs #25 ranked teams all time
3-23 S/U vs ranked Texas since 1962	0-15 S/U vs ranked Alabama since 2005
0-4 ATS vs ranked West Virginia since 2014	1-13 S/U vs ranked Florida since 2005
Temple	0-5 S/U vs ranked LSU since 2006
4-63-1 S/U on road vs ranked teams all time	3-0 ATS @ ranked South Carolina since 2000
5-45 S/U @ home vs ranked teams all time	**Texas**
0-40 S/U vs Top #1 - #9 ranked teams all time	1-10 O/U on road vs ranked teams since 2013
0-10 S/U vs #11 #12 ranked teams all time	4-1 O/U vs #1 ranked teams since 2003
1-7 S/U vs #14 ranked teams all time	1-7 S/U vs #2 ranked teams since 1972
0-4 S/U vs #15 ranked teams all time	0-3 S/U & ATS vs #3 ranked teams since 1999
0-4 S/U vs #16 ranked teams since 1994	4-0 S/U @ home vs #3 ranked teams all time
0-17-1 S/U vs #17 #18 #19 ranked teams all time	0-3 S/U @ home vs #4 ranked teams since 1982
1-3 ATS vs #17 ranked teams since 1999	4-1 ATS on road vs #4 ranked teams sice 1984
0-3 O/U vs #20 ranked teams since 2010	1-3 S/U on road vs #6 ranked teams all time
2-5 S/U vs #21 ranked teams all time	1-6 S/U vs #8 ranked teams since 1988
0-4 O/U vs #21 ranked teams since 2003	0-4 S/U vs #9 ranked teams since 1992

Team records vs ranked teams

1-4 S/U on road vs #9 ranked teams all time	1-5 ATS vs #18 ranked teams since 1988
0-3 S/U on road vs #10 ranked teams since 1979	0-4 S/U on road vs #19 ranked teams since 1951
1-4 O/U vs #10 ranked teams since 2013	3-0 S/U @ home vs #19 ranked teams since 1985
0-4 S/U vs #11 ranked teams since 2014	0-9 S/U on road vs #20 ranked teams all time
0-4 S/U on road vs #11 ranked teams since 1980	0-4 ATS on road vs #20 ranked teams since 1985
5-1-1 ATS vs #12 ranked teams since 2013	5-0 O/U vs #20 ranked teams since 1997
1-7 O/U vs #12 ranked teams since 2010	0-4 S/U & ATS vs #24 ranked teams all time
4-0 S/U on road vs #12 ranked teams all time	1-8 S/U vs ranked Alabama since 2013
3-0 S/U & ATS vs #14 ranked teams since 1995	1-5 S/U & ATS vs ranked Arkansas since 1988
6-1 S/U @ home vs #14 ranked teams all time	4-0-1 O/U vs ranked Auburn since 1986
0-6 O/U vs #14 ranked teams since 1984	0-7 ATS vs ranked LSU since 2011
0-3 S/U on road vs #15 ranked teams since 1987	**Texas-El Paso**
5-2 S/U vs #16 ranked teams since 1992	1-37 S/U on road vs ranked teams all time
0-5 O/U vs #16 ranked teams since 1995	10-2-1 O/U on road vs ranked teams since 2000
0-4 O/U vs #17 ranked teams since 2002	2-23 S/U @ home vs ranked teams all time
5-1 S/U @ home vs #17 ranked teams all time	0-8 S/U vs #2 - #6 ranked teams all time
6-0 O/U vs #19 ranked teams since 1987	0-5 S/U vs #10 - #11 ranked teams all time {0-3 ATS}
3-0 S/U vs #21 ranked teams since 2001	0-7 S/U vs #13 ranked teams all time
4-1 O/U vs #21 ranked teams since 1992	0-17 S/U vs #15 - #19 ranked teams all time
3-0 S/U & ATS vs #22 ranked teams all time	0-12 S/U vs #20 - #25 ranked teams all time
1-5 O/U vs #24 ranked teams since 2000	7-2 ATS vs #21 - #25 ranked teams all time
0-6 O/U vs ranked Baylor since 2013	0-4 S/U vs ranked Oklahoma all time {0-3 ATS on road}
1-3 S/U vs ranked Kansas State since 2011	**Texas-San Antonio**
0-5 ATS vs ranked Kansas State since 2003	0-2 S/U vs ranked teams all time
1-5 O/U vs ranked Kansas State since 2002	**Texas State**
7-2 ATS vs ranked Oklahoma since 2013	0-9 S/U vs ranked teams all time
1-6 S/U vs ranked Oklahoma State since 2010	**Texas Tech**
1-6 O/U vs ranked Oklahoma State since 2010	1-19 S/U vs ranked teams since 2014
Texas A&M	7-68 S/U on road vs ranked teams since 1977
3-16 S/U vs #1 ranked teams all time	0-13 S/U @ home vs ranked teams since 2013
2-10 S/U vs #2 ranked teams all time	1-7 S/U vs #1 ranked teams all time
6-1 ATS vs #2 ranked teams since 1998	0-13 S/U vs #2 ranked teams all time
1-6 S/U vs #3 ranked teams all time	0-4 O/U vs #2 ranked teams since 2004
0-5 S/U on road vs #4 ranked teams all time	0-7 S/U on road vs #4 ranked teams all time
1-8 S/U vs #4 ranked teams since 1959	7-1 O/U vs #4 ranked teams since 2002
0-6 S/U on road vs #5 ranked teams all time	0-5 S/U on road vs #5 ranked teams all time {0-3 ATS}
0-7 O/U vs #5 ranked teams since 1992	0-7 S/U vs #6 ranked teams since 1975
0-4 S/U & ATS @ home vs #6 ranked teams since 1987	0-9 S/U vs #7 ranked teams all time
0-5 ATS vs #6 ranked teams since 1987	3-0 ATS & O/U vs #7 ranked teams since 2003
0-6 S/U vs #7 ranked teams since 2002	0-5 S/U on road vs #9 ranked teams all time
0-4 S/U on road vs #10 ranked teams all time	0-8 S/U vs #9 ranked teams since 1976
0-5 S/U on road vs #12 ranked teams since 1980	0-6 S/U vs #10 ranked teams all time
1-6 S/U @ home vs #12 ranked teams all time	1-5 S/U vs #11 ranked teams all time
0-4 ATS on road vs #12 ranked teams since 1990	1-5 S/U vs #12 ranked teams all time
5-1 S/U vs #13 ranked teams since 1984	0-12 S/U vs #13 ranked teams all time
0-3 S/U on road vs #14 ranked teams since 1978	1-4 S/U vs #14 ranked teams all time
1-6 S/U on road vs #17 ranked teams since 1959	1-5 S/U vs #15 ranked teams since 1992
0-5 S/U on road vs #18 ranked teams all time	1-4 S/U on road vs #15 ranked teams all time
0-6 S/U vs #18 ranked teams since 1988	1-6 S/U vs #16 ranked teams all time

Team records vs ranked teams

0-6 S/U vs #17 ranked teams since 2009 {1-5 ATS}	0-4 S/U vs #18 ranked teams since 1976
0-5 S/U @ home vs #17 ranked teams since 1986	0-3 S/U & ATS vs #19 ranked teams since 1985
2-8 S/U on road vs #17 ranked teams all time	0-4 S/U vs #20 ranked teams since 1960
5-0 O/U vs #17 ranked teams since 2011	0-10 S/U vs #22 - #25 ranked teams all time
1-5 S/U vs #18 ranked teams since 1990	0-3 S/U vs ranked East Carolina all time
5-1 ATS vs #19 ranked teams since 1989	0-4 S/U vs ranked Houston all time
0-4 S/U & ATS vs #20 ranked teams since 2000	*0-3 ATS vs ranked Houston since 2009*
1-7 S/U vs #21 ranked teams all time {0-4 on road}	## Tulsa
1-5-1 ATS vs #21 ranked teams since 1995	*12-0 ATS vs ranked teams since 2017*
0-3 S/U & ATS vs #23 ranked teams since 2006	2-44 S/U on road vs ranked teams since 1977
5-2 ATS vs #24 ranked teams since 2001	1-11 S/U @ home vs ranked teams since 2007
1-3 S/U & ATS vs #25 ranked teams all time	0-5 S/U vs #1 ranked teams all time
0-6 S/U vs ranked Baylor since 2011	*0-3 ATS vs #1 ranked teams since 1987*
5-1 O/U vs ranked Baylor since 2011	0-4 S/U vs #2 ranked teams all time
0-5 S/U vs ranked Houston since 1979 {0-3 on road}	0-5 S/U vs #3 ranked teams all time
0-4 S/U @ ranked Kansas State all time	0-11 S/U vs #4 #5 #6 ranked teams all time
2-10 S/U vs ranked Oklahoma State since 2009	0-4 S/U vs #7 ranked teams since 1992
1-8 S/U @ home vs ranked Oklahoma all time	0-5 S/U vs #8 #9 ranked teams all time
9-1 O/U vs ranked Oklahoma since 2011	0-3 S/U vs #10 ranked teams since 1984
0-3 S/U vs ranked TCU since 2014	1-4 S/U vs #11 ranked teams since 1968
0-3 S/U @ ranked TCU all time	1-4 S/U on road vs #11 ranked teams all time
1-9 S/U vs ranked Texas since 2003	0-3 S/U vs #12 ranked teams since 1986
## Toledo	0-6 S/U vs #13 ranked teams since 1979
1-15 S/U on road vs ranked teams all time	0-3 S/U vs #14 ranked teams all time
1-7 S/U vs Top #10 ranked teams all time	0-3 S/U vs #16 ranked teams since 1971
0-7 S/U vs #11 - #16 ranked teams all time	3-0 S/U vs #17 ranked teams all time
0-3 S/U vs Ohio State all time	0-7 S/U vs #18 ranked teams all time
## Troy	0-3 S/U @ ranked Houston all time
1-22 S/U on road vs ranked teams all time	## UCLA
0-8 S/U vs Top #10 ranked teams all time	3-13 S/U vs ranked teams since 2016
## Tulane	0-5 S/U & ATS on road vs #1 ranked teams all time
1-60 S/U vs ranked teams since 1984	0-7 S/U vs #1 ranked teams since 1983
0-35 S/U on road vs ranked teams since 1984	*4-1 O/U vs #1 ranked teams since 1986*
4-16 ATS on road vs ranked teams since 1999	0-4 S/U on road vs #2 ranked teams since 1994
1-25 S/U @ home vs ranked teams since 1985	*3-0 ATS vs #3 ranked teams since 1997*
0-6 S/U vs #1 ranked teams all time	0-4 S/U @ home vs #4 ranked teams all time
0-15 S/U vs #2 ranked teams all time	0-5 S/U on road vs #4 ranked teams since 1964
0-18-1 S/U vs #3 - #5 ranked teams all time	1-10 S/U vs #5 ranked teams since 1947 {0-5 on road}
0-5 S/U vs #6 ranked teams since 1964	0-5 S/U @ home vs #7 ranked teams since 2001
1-7 S/U vs #7 ranked teams all time	1-4 S/U on road vs #7 ranked teams all time
1-7 S/U vs #8 ranked teams all time	*9-2 O/U vs #7 ranked teams since 1984*
0-8 S/U vs #10 ranked teams since 1950	0-6 S/U vs #8 ranked teams since 1993
0-6 S/U vs #11 ranked teams all time	0-4 S/U @ home vs #8 ranked teams all time
0-4 S/U vs #12 ranked teams since 1951	0-5 S/U on road vs #8 ranked teams since 2004
0-5 S/U on road vs #13 ranked teams all time	*8-1 ATS vs #8 ranked teams since 1978*
0-5 S/U vs #14 ranked teams since 1973	6-1 S/U @ home vs #9 ranked teams all time
0-3 S/U & ATS vs #15 ranked teams since 1984	8-2 S/U @ home vs #10 ranked teams all time
0-5 S/U on road vs #16 ranked teams all time	*9-2 ATS vs #10 ranked teams since 1986*
0-6 S/U vs #16 ranked teams since 1984	0-3 S/U on road vs #10 ranked teams since 2006

Team records vs ranked teams

5-1 S/U on road vs #11 ranked teams since 1951		**Utah State**
5-0 O/U vs #11 ranked teams since 1995		2-54 S/U on road vs ranked teams all time
0-4 S/U vs #12 ranked teams since 2003		2-14 S/U @ home vs ranked teams all time
0-5 S/U on road vs #12 ranked teams all time		0-25 S/U vs Top #10 ranked teams all time
0-4 S/U & ATS vs #13 ranked teams since 1999		0-17 S/U vs #11 - #17 ranked teams all time
0-4 S/U on road vs #13 ranked teams all time		*3-0 O/U vs #18 ranked teams since 2008*
2-8-1 S/U vs #14 ranked teams all time		0-5 S/U vs #20 ranked teams all time
1-4-1 S/U on road vs #15 ranked teams all time		0-3 S/U vs #22 ranked teams all time
5-0 O/U vs #15 ranked teams since 1992		*3-0 ATS vs #24 ranked teams since 2013*
4-0 S/U @ home vs #21 ranked teams all time		*0-4 O/U vs #24 ranked teams since 2013*
7-0 ATS vs #21 ranked teams all time		0-6 S/U @ ranked Boise State all time
1-4 S/U vs #22 ranked teams all time		1-13 S/U vs ranked BYU all time
6-1 S/U vs #23 ranked teams since 1995		**Vanderbilt**
5-1 ATS vs #24 ranked teams all time		3-119-1 S/U on road vs ranked teams all time
4-1 S/U & ATS @ home vs ranked Arizona since 1993		7-51 S/U @ home vs ranked teams since 1992
6-0 ATS vs ranked Arizona since 1998		*4-1 ATS vs #3 ranked teams since 1994*
4-0 ATS vs ranked California since 2005		*0-5 ATS vs #5 ranked teams since 2002*
0-6 S/U vs ranked Oregon since 2009		*5-0 O/U vs #5 ranked teams since 2002*
2-10 ATS vs ranked Oregon since 1995		*5-1 ATS vs #8 ranked teams since 1983*
0-8 S/U vs ranked Stanford since 2001 {1-7 ATS}		5-115 S/U vs Top #10 ranked teams all time
1-10 O/U vs ranked USC since 2006		0-11 S/U vs #11 ranked teams all time
1-6 O/U @ home vs ranked USC since 2004		*4-0 ATS on road vs #11 ranked teams since 1994*
10-4 ATS @ home vs ranked USC since 1984		*0-3 O/U on road vs #11 ranked teams since 2009*
5-0 ATS @ home vs ranked Washington since 1997 {4-1 S/U}		0-6 S/U vs #12 ranked teams since 1972
5-0 O/U vs ranked Washington since 2000		*0-3 O/U vs #12 ranked teams since 2002*
	Utah	0-12 S/U on road vs #13 ranked teams all time
8-40 S/U on road vs ranked teams all time		*7-0 ATS vs #13 ranked teams since 1997*
9-0 ATS on road vs ranked teams since 2013		*3-0 O/U vs #13 ranked teams since 2005*
1-4 S/U vs #4 ranked teams all time (Reg season)		1-13 S/U vs #14 ranked teams all time {0-7 on road}
4-1 O/U vs #4 ranked teams since 2009		1-6-1 S/U vs #15 ranked teams all time
0-3 O/U vs #8 ranked teams since 1996		0-5 S/U on road vs #17 ranked teams all time
0-4 S/U vs #9 ranked teams all time		*4-0 ATS vs #17 ranked teams since 1987*
1-5 S/U vs #10 ranked teams all time {1-3 ATS}		0-8-1 S/U on road vs #18 ranked teams all time
0-4 O/U vs #10 ranked teams since 2010		1-4 S/U @ home vs #18 ranked teams since 1977
0-5 S/U on road vs #11 ranked teams all time		1-10 S/U vs #19 ranked teams all time {0-6 on road}
4-0 O/U vs #13 ranked teams since 2012		*0-3 ATS @ home vs #19 ranked teams since 2001*
1-5 S/U on road vs #14 ranked teams since 1958		*1-5 O/U vs #19 ranked teams since 2001*
3-0 ATS vs #14 ranked teams since 2002		1-7 S/U vs #20 ranked teams since 1947
0-3 S/U on road vs #15 ranked teams all time		0-11 S/U vs #21 #22 #23 ranked teams all time
1-5 S/U @ home vs #15 ranked teams all time		*0-3 ATS vs #21 ranked teams since 1997*
2-8 S/U vs #16 #17 #18 ranked teams all time		*0-4 O/U vs #23 ranked teams since 2002*
3-1 S/U @ home vs #20 ranked teams all time		*4-0 ATS @ home vs #24 ranked teams since 1991*
0-3 S/U on road vs #20 ranked teams all time		*1-4 O/U vs #24 ranked teams since 1995*
0-3 O/U vs #23 ranked teams since 2007		0-31 S/U vs ranked Alabama since 1971
1-4 S/U vs ranked Arizona all time		*5-1 ATS @ ranked Alabama since 1992*
0-5 S/U @ ranked Arizona State all time		0-26 S/U vs ranked Florida since 1989
2-7 S/U vs ranked Arizona State since 1975		1-18 S/U @ ranked Georgia all time
4-0 ATS @ ranked Oregon since 1994		1-6 S/U vs ranked Kentucky all time
3-1 ATS vs ranked USC all time		*0-4 O/U vs ranked Mississippi since 2009*

Team records vs ranked teams

0-6 S/U vs ranked South Carolina since 2009	3-0 ATS vs #12 ranked teams since 2007
3-0 ATS vs ranked South Carolina since 2012	0-3 O/U vs #12 ranked teams since 2007
1-38 S/U vs ranked Tennessee all time {0-21 on road}	0-3 S/U @ home vs #13 ranked teams all time
Virginia	0-3 O/U vs #13 ranked teams since 1995
2-26 S/U on road vs ranked teams since 2001	1-3 O/U vs #14 ranked teams since 2002
6-1 O/U on road vs ranked teams since 2017	6-1 S/U vs #16 ranked teams since 1999
0-5 S/U vs #1 ranked teams all time	7-0 ATS vs #16 ranked teams since 1999
0-4 S/U vs #2 ranked teams since 2008	5-1-1 O/U vs #16 ranked teams since 1998
0-9 S/U vs #3 #4 ranked teams all time	4-0 ATS vs #18 ranked teams since 1986
0-5 S/U on road vs #5 ranked teams all time	3-0 S/U & ATS on road vs #19 ranked teams all time
0-23 S/U vs Top #5 ranked teams	0-5 O/U vs #19 ranked teams since 2002
3-0 ATS vs #5 ranked teams since 2002	3-0 S/U @ home vs #20 ranked teams all time
0-3 O/U vs #5 ranked teams since 2002	5-1 ATS vs #20 ranked teams since 1995
1-10 S/U vs #6 ranked teams all time {0-4 on road}	4-1 O/U vs #20 ranked teams since 1996
0-5 S/U vs #8 ranked teams all time	5-0 S/U vs #22 ranked teams all time
1-5 S/U vs #9 ranked teams all time	0-3 O/U vs #24 ranked teams since 2008
0-12 S/U vs #10 #11 ranked teams all time	0-3 O/U @ home vs ranked Boston College since 2005
4-0 S/U & ATS vs #12 ranked teams since 1984	10-4 ATS vs ranked Miami since 1995
1-5 S/U vs #13 ranked teams all time	1-7 O/U vs ranked Miami since 2003
0-5 S/U vs #14 ranked teams since 1995	3-0 ATS vs ranked NC State since 1986
1-4 O/U vs #14 ranked teams since 1995	4-0 S/U & ATS vs ranked Virginia since 1999
0-3 S/U on road vs #15 ranked teams all time	3-0 S/U vs ranked West Virginia since 1998
1-6 S/U vs #16 ranked teams all time {1-4 ATS}	8-1 ATS vs ranked West Virginia since 1983
1-8 S/U vs #17 ranked teams all time	**Wake Forest**
1-6 ATS vs #17 ranked teams since 1992	2-46 S/U on road vs ranked teams since 1980
7-0 ATS vs #18 ranked teams since 1989	7-1 ATS on road vs ranked teams since 2015
1-6 S/U on road vs #19 ranked teams all time	1-9 O/U on road vs ranked teams since 2013
2-11 S/U vs #19 ranked teams all time	3-11 S/U @ home vs ranked teams since 2011
4-1 O/U vs #19 ranked teams since 1996	0-9 S/U vs #1 ranked teams all time
5-0 O/U vs #20 ranked teams since 1991	0-6 S/U vs #2 ranked teams all time
0-4 O/U vs #22 ranked teams since 2002	0-9 S/U vs #3 ranked teams all time
0-3 S/U on road vs #24 ranked teams all time	0-4 ATS vs #3 ranked teams since 2005
1-4 S/U & ATS vs #25 ranked teams all time	0-6 S/U vs #4 ranked teams since 1983
0-6 S/U vs ranked Duke all time	6-0 ATS vs #5 ranked teams since 1997
6-1 S/U & ATS @ home vs ranked North Carolina since 1983	0-25 S/U vs #5 - #9 ranked teams all time
1-12 S/U vs ranked Virginia Tech since 1999	0-12 S/U vs #10 #11 ranked teams all time
1-8-1 ATS vs ranked Virginia Tech since 2002	0-3 S/U vs #12 ranked teams since 1982
Virginia Tech	1-5-1 S/U vs #13 ranked teams all time {0-3 on road}
10-4 S/U on road vs ranked teams since 2010	0-4 S/U on road vs #14 ranked teams since 1980
11-3 ATS on road vs ranked teams since 2010	5-0 ATS vs #14 ranked teams since 1992
2-13 S/U @ home vs ranked teams since 2010	2-9 S/U vs #15 ranked teams all time
0-4 S/U & ATS vs ranked teams in Bowl games since 2011	0-7 S/U on road vs #16 ranked teams since 1958
0-9 S/U vs #1 ranked teams all time	4-1 ATS vs #16 ranked teams since 1983
1-7 S/U vs #2 ranked teams all time {0-5 on road}	0-9 S/U vs #17 #18 ranked teams all time
0-8 S/U vs #3 ranked teams all time	0-11 S/U vs #19 ranked teams since 1958 {0-6 @ home}
1-5 S/U vs #5 ranked teams all time	1-5 S/U vs #20 ranked teams all time {0-2 @ home}
0-4 S/U vs #6 ranked teams all time	0-3 ATS vs #20 ranked teams since 1994
1-10 S/U vs #7 ranked teams all time {0-6 on road}	0-28 S/U vs ranked Clemson since 1948
0-3 O/U vs #9 ranked teams since 2004	1-12 S/U vs ranked Duke all time {0-7 @ home}

Team records vs ranked teams

0-5 S/U vs ranked Florida State since 2012	5-21 S/U @ home vs ranked teams since 2004
1-12 S/U @ ranked Florida State all time	1-7 S/U vs #1 ranked teams all time
0-7 S/U vs ranked North Carolina since 1980	0-8 S/U vs #2 ranked teams all time
0-4 S/U @ home vs ranked North Carolina all time	*4-0 ATS vs #2 ranked teams since 1995*
Washington	0-14 S/U vs #3 & #4 ranked teams all time
5-26 S/U on road vs ranked teams since 2004	*3-0 ATS vs #3 ranked teams since 2003*
0-10 S/U vs #1 ranked teams since 1967	0-7 S/U on road vs #5 ranked teams all time
0-6 S/U on road vs #1 ranked teams since 1939	1-5 S/U vs #6 ranked teams since 1969
0-4 S/U vs #2 ranked teams since 2003	0-16 S/U vs #7 & #8 ranked teams all time
1-5 O/U vs #2 ranked teams since 1988	*0-3 O/U vs #8 ranked teams since 2003*
1-4 O/U vs #3 ranked teams since 1998	0-3 S/U vs #10 ranked teams since 1990
1-5 S/U on road vs #5 ranked teams all time	0-11-1 S/U vs #11 ranked teams all time
4-1 O/U vs #5 ranked teams since 1994	1-13 S/U vs #12 ranked teams all time {0-8 on road}
0-5 S/U on road vs #6 ranked teams all time	1-6 S/U vs #13 ranked teams all time
0-5 S/U vs #6 ranked teams since 1966	0-5 S/U on road vs #14 ranked teams since 1959
3-1 S/U & ATS vs #7 ranked teams since 2012	*4-0 O/U vs #15 ranked teams since 2003*
1-5 S/U on road vs #9 ranked teams all time	0-6 S/U on road vs #16 ranked teams all time
3-0 O/U on road vs #9 ranked teams since 1991	0-3 S/U @ home vs #17 ranked teams since 1986
0-5 S/U on road vs #10 ranked teams all time	1-5 S/U on road vs #17 ranked teams all time
3-0 O/U @ home vs #10 ranked teams since 1986	*3-0 ATS vs #17 ranked teams since 2003*
0-4 S/U on road vs #11 ranked teams since 1970	*6-2 ATS vs #18 ranked teams since 1994*
3-0 O/U on road vs #11 ranked teams since 1996	0-8 S/U vs #19 ranked teams all time
0-4 S/U on road vs #12 ranked teams all time	0-3 S/U & ATS vs #20 ranked teams since 2004
0-4 S/U vs #13 ranked teams since 2002	*3-0 O/U on road vs #20 ranked teams since 1997*
1-4 O/U @ home vs #13 ranked teams since 1985	0-5 S/U vs #22 ranked teams all time
4-0-1 O/U vs #15 ranked teams since 1992	*4-1 O/U vs #23 ranked teams all time*
4-0 ATS @ home vs #15 ranked teams since 1989	0-5 S/U vs ranked Arizona State since 2004
0-5 S/U @ home vs #16 ranked teams since 1977	*6-1 O/U vs ranked Arizona State since 1997*
1-5 O/U vs #17 ranked teams since 1994	0-11 S/U vs ranked Arizona all time
0-7 S/U on road vs #20 ranked teams all time	0-3 S/U @ ranked Oregon State all time
4-0 S/U @ home vs #20 ranked teams since 1992	*0-3 O/U vs ranked Oregon State since 2000*
4-0 ATS vs #20 ranked teams since 2007	*7-2 ATS vs ranked Oregon since 2010*
3-0 O/U vs #22 ranked teams all time	*7-1 ATS @ home vs ranked Oregon since 2002*
0-3-1 O/U vs #23 ranked teams since 2002	3-0 S/U vs ranked Stanford since 2016
4-0 S/U vs #25 ranked teams since 1997	*4-0 ATS vs ranked Stanford since 2015*
0-4 S/U vs ranked Arizona since 1992	2-19 S/U @ ranked USC all time
0-3 S/U & ATS vs ranked Arizona State since 2002	0-3 S/U & ATS vs ranked Washington since 2016
6-1 O/U vs ranked California since 1992	**Western Kentucky**
4-0 S/U @ home vs ranked Oregon State all time	0-3 S/U vs #1 ranked teams all time
5-0 S/U vs ranked Oregon State since 1960	**Western Michigan**
0-13 S/U vs ranked Oregon since 2005 {0-7 on road}	1-28 S/U on road vs ranked teams all time
0-13 ATS vs ranked Oregon since 2005 {0-7 on road}	0-7 S/U @ home vs ranked teams all time
7-1 ATS @ home vs ranked Stanford since 1992	*8-2 ATS vs ranked teams since 2011*
0-9 S/U vs ranked UCLA since 1987	0-4 S/U vs ranked Michigan State all time
1-12 S/U @ ranked UCLA since 1953	**West Virginia**
2-8 ATS vs ranked UCLA since 1986	0-9 S/U vs #1 ranked teams all time
7-0 S/U & ATS vs ranked Washington State since 2001	*4-1 O/U vs #1 ranked teams since 1989*
Washington State	0-9 S/U vs #2 ranked teams all time
4-26 S/U on road vs ranked teams since 2003	*3-0 O/U vs #2 ranked teams since 2011*

Team records vs ranked teams

0-6 S/U on road vs #3 ranked teams all time	4-0 O/U vs #11 ranked teams since 2011
1-5 S/U @ home vs #3 ranked teams all time	5-0 O/U vs #13 ranked teams since 1995
0-3 S/U on road vs #4 ranked teams all time	3-0 S/U on road vs #13 ranked teams all time
1-5 O/U vs #4 ranked teams since 1984	5-1 S/U & ATS vs #14 ranked teams since 1998
0-9 S/U vs #5 ranked teams all time	0-3 S/U & ATS vs #15 ranked teams since 1983
0-6 S/U vs #6 ranked teams all time	0-4 S/U on road vs #16 ranked teams all time
0-3 S/U vs #7 ranked teams all time	0-5 S/U @ home vs #17 ranked teams since 1983
1-4 S/U & ATS vs #8 ranked teams all time	1-7 S/U vs #20 ranked teams since 1969
0-8-1 S/U vs #10 ranked teams all time	4-1 S/U & ATS vs #21 ranked teams all time
3-1 S/U & ATS vs #11 ranked teams since 1993	3-0 O/U vs #22 ranked teams since 2005
0-6 S/U @ home vs #12 ranked teams all time	5-0 S/U vs #25 ranked teams since 1993
1-6 S/U vs #15 ranked teams since 2005	0-4 S/U vs ranked Illinois since 1963
0-4 S/U on road vs #16 ranked teams since 1989	1-8-1 S/U @ ranked Iowa all time
6-0 S/U vs #19 ranked teams since 1982	1-5 S/U @ ranked Michigan State since 1956
5-0 S/U @ home vs #19 ranked teams since 1982	7-1 O/U vs ranked Michigan State since 1993
1-4 S/U vs #20 ranked teams since 1978	7-1 S/U vs ranked Minnesota since 1961
1-4 S/U vs #21 ranked teams since 2002 {0-5 ATS}	4-1 ATS vs ranked Nebraska since 2011
4-0 S/U vs #25 ranked teams since 2007	4-1 O/U vs ranked Nebraska since 2011
4-1 O/U vs #25 ranked teams since 2001	0-7 S/U vs ranked Ohio State since 2012
0-8 S/U vs ranked Oklahoma since 2013	0-3 S/U @ home vs ranked Purdue since 1980
6-1 O/U vs ranked Oklahoma since 2014	**Wyoming**
1-5-1 ATS vs ranked Oklahoma since 2014	4-26 S/U @ home vs ranked teams since 1974
1-6 S/U & ATS vs ranked Oklahoma State all time	3-39 S/U on road vs ranked teams all time
4-0-1 S/U vs ranked Pittsburgh since 1988	2-22 S/U vs ranked teams since 2004
5-1 ATS vs ranked Pittsburgh since 1987	0-29 S/U vs Top #10 ranked teams all time
0-3 S/U vs ranked TCU all time	0-5 S/U vs #12 ranked teams all time
0-3 O/U vs ranked TCU all time	0-5 S/U on road vs #14 ranked teams all time
3-0 O/U vs ranked Texas Tech all time	0-10 S/U vs #16 #17 #18 ranked teams since 1960
1-4 S/U & ATS @ ranked Virginia Tech all time	0-4 S/U vs #19 ranked teams all time
Wisconsin	1-4 S/U vs Boise State all time
24-90-3 S/U on road vs ranked teams all time	0-9 S/U vs BYU since 1983 {0-4 on road}
0-10 S/U on road vs #1 ranked teams all time	0-3 ATS @ BYU since 1985
3-0 ATS @ home vs #1 ranked teams since 1985	
0-10 S/U vs #2 ranked teams since 1960	
1-7-1 S/U vs #3 ranked teams since 1989	
0-8 S/U on road vs #4 ranked teams all time	
2-8 S/U @ home vs #4 ranked teams all time	
0-4 O/U vs #4 ranked teams since 1995	
1-5 S/U on road vs #5 ranked teams all time	
0-4 S/U vs #6 ranked teams since 2006	
1-6 S/U on road vs #6 ranked teams all time	
1-5 S/U @ home vs #6 ranked teams all time	
0-4 S/U on road vs #7 ranked teams since 1959	
2-14 S/U vs #8 ranked teams all time	
1-8 S/U on road vs #9 ranked teams all time	
2-10 S/U vs #9 ranked teams since 1960	
2-10 S/U vs #10 ranked teams since 1946	
4-0 S/U vs #11 ranked teams since 2011	

CPSIA information can be obtained
at www.ICGtesting.com
Printed in the USA
LVHW011130310822
727159LV00007B/96